HANDBOOK OF ARTIFICIAL INTELLIGENCE IN EDUCATION

ELGAR HANDBOOKS IN EDUCATION

Elgar Handbooks in Education present a comprehensive analysis of the latest scholarly research in education. Edited by prominent experts, each *Handbook* features a wide range of chapters covering the latest international developments in the field. Often widely cited, individual chapters offer an overview of the current state of research in education, whilst also creating a forum for challenging current perceptions, and offering new perspectives of how research may develop in the future. *Handbooks* in the series often take an interdisciplinary approach, assessing the relationship between education and research areas as diverse as technology studies, social policy, public policy and environmental studies. These *Handbooks* will form a vital reference point for all researchers and students of education, creating a comprehensive and overarching guide to the field.

Titles in the series include:

Research Handbook on University Rankings
Theory, Methodology, Influence and Impact
Edited by Ellen Hazelkorn and Georgiana Mihut

Research Handbook on Academic Careers and Managing Academics
Edited by Cláudia S. Sarrico, Maria J. Rosa and Teresa Carvalho

Handbook of Digital Higher Education
Edited by Rhona Sharpe, Sue Bennett and Tünde Varga-Atkins

Handbook of Civic Engagement and Education
Edited by Richard Desjardins and Susan Wiksten

Handbook of Artificial Intelligence in Education
Edited by Benedict du Boulay, Antonija Mitrovic and Kalina Yacef

Handbook of Artificial Intelligence in Education

Edited by

Benedict du Boulay

Emeritus Professor of Artificial Intelligence, University of Sussex, UK

Antonija Mitrovic

Professor, Department of Computer Science and Software Engineering, University of Canterbury, New Zealand

Kalina Yacef

Associate Professor of Computer Science, University of Sydney, Australia

ELGAR HANDBOOKS IN EDUCATION

 Edward Elgar
PUBLISHING

Cheltenham, UK · Northampton, MA, USA

Published by
Edward Elgar Publishing Limited
The Lypiatts
15 Lansdown Road
Cheltenham
Glos GL50 2JA
UK

Edward Elgar Publishing, Inc.
William Pratt House
9 Dewey Court
Northampton
Massachusetts 01060
USA

A catalogue record for this book
is available from the British Library

Library of Congress Control Number: 2023931651

This book is available electronically in the **Elgar**online
Sociology, Social Policy and Education subject collection
http://dx.doi.org/10.4337/9781800375413

ISBN 978 1 80037 540 6 (cased)
ISBN 978 1 80037 541 3 (eBook)

Printed and bound by CPI Group (UK) Ltd, Croydon, CR0 4YY

Contents

List of figures   viii
List of tables   xii
List of contributors   xiii
Foreword   xvi

PART I   SCENE SETTING

1   Introduction to the *Handbook of Artificial Intelligence in Education*   2
     Benedict du Boulay, Antonija Mitrovic and Kalina Yacef

2   The history of artificial intelligence in education – the first quarter century   10
     Gordon McCalla

PART II   THEORIES UNDERPINNING AIED

3   The role and function of theories in AIED   31
     Stellan Ohlsson

4   Theories of metacognition and pedagogy applied to AIED systems   45
     Roger Azevedo and Megan Wiedbusch

5   Theories of affect, meta-affect, and affective pedagogy   68
     Ivon Arroyo, Kaśka Porayska-Pomsta and Kasia Muldner

6   Scrutable AIED   101
     Judy Kay, Bob Kummerfeld, Cristina Conati, Kaśka Porayska-Pomsta
     and Ken Holstein

PART III   THE ARCHITECTURE AND DESIGN OF AIED SYSTEMS

7   Domain modeling for AIED systems with connections to modeling student
     knowledge: a review   127
     Vincent Aleven, Jonathan Rowe, Yun Huang and Antonija Mitrovic

8   Student modeling in open-ended learning environments   170
     Cristina Conati and Sébastien Lallé

9   Six instructional approaches supported in AIED systems   184
     Vincent Aleven, Manolis Mavrikis, Bruce M. McLaren, Huy A. Nguyen,
     Jennifer K. Olsen and Nikol Rummel

10   Theory-driven design of AIED systems for enhanced interaction and
      problem-solving   229
      Susanne P. Lajoie and Shan Li

11   Deeper learning through interactions with students in natural language   250
      Vasile Rus, Andrew M. Olney and Arthur C. Graesser

12   Authoring tools to build AIED systems   273
      Stephen Blessing, Stephen B. Gilbert and Steven Ritter

PART IV   ANALYTICS

13   Continuous student modeling for programming in the classroom:
      challenges, methods, and evaluation   287
      *Ye Mao, Samiha Marwan, Preya Shabrina, Yang Shi, Thomas W. Price,
      Min Chi and Tiffany Barnes*

14   Human–AI co-orchestration: the role of artificial intelligence in orchestration   309
      Ken Holstein and Jennifer K. Olsen

15   Using learning analytics to support teachers   322
      *Stanislav Pozdniakov, Roberto Martinez-Maldonado, Shaveen Singh,
      Hassan Khosravi and Dragan Gašević*

16   Predictive modeling of student success   350
      Christopher Brooks, Vitomir Kovanović and Quan Nguyen

17   Social analytics to support engagement with learning communities   370
      Carolyn Rosé, Meredith Riggs and Nicole Barbaro

PART V   AIED SYSTEMS IN USE

18   Intelligent systems for psychomotor learning: a systematic review and two
      cases of study   390
      Alberto Casas-Ortiz, Jon Echeverria and Olga C. Santos

19   Artificial intelligence techniques for supporting face-to-face and online
      collaborative learning   422
      Roberto Martinez-Maldonado, Anouschka van Leeuwen and Zachari Swiecki

20   Digital learning games in artificial intelligence in education (AIED): a review   440
      Bruce M. McLaren and Huy A. Nguyen

21   Artificial intelligence-based assessment in education   485
      Ying Fang, Rod D. Roscoe and Danielle S. McNamara

22   Evaluations with AIEd systems   505
      Kurt VanLehn

23   Large-scale commercialization of AI in school-based environments   524
      Steven Ritter and Kenneth R. Koedinger

24   Small-scale commercialisation: the golden triangle of AI EdTech   537
      Rosemary Luckin and Mutlu Cukurova

25   Critical perspectives on AI in education: political economy, discrimination,
      commercialization, governance and ethics   553
      Ben Williamson, Rebecca Eynon, Jeremy Knox and Huw Davies

26   The ethics of AI in education   571
      Kaśka Porayska-Pomsta, Wayne Holmes and Selena Nemorin

PART VI   THE FUTURE

27   The great challenges and opportunities of the next 20 years   606

      1. AIED and equity   606
          Maria Mercedes T. Rodrigo

      2. Engaging learners in the age of information overload   608
          Julita Vassileva

      3. Pedagogical agents for all: designing virtual characters for inclusion
          and diversity in STEM   611
          H. Chad Lane

      4. Intelligent textbooks   614
          Peter Brusilovsky and Sergey Sosnovsky

      5. AI-empowered open-ended learning environments in STEM domains   619
          Gautam Biswas

      6. Ubiquitous-AIED: pervasive AI learning technologies   624
          James C. Lester

      7. Culture, ontology and learner modeling   627
          Riichiro Mizoguchi

      8. Crowdsourcing paves the way for personalized learning   630
          Ethan Prihar and Neil Heffernan

      9. AIED in developing countries: breaking seven WEIRD assumptions in
          the global learning XPRIZE field study   633
          Jack Mostow

      10. The future of learning assessment   637
          Claude Frasson

      11. Intelligent mentoring systems: tapping into AI to deliver the next
          generation of digital learning   640
          Vania Dimitrova

Index   650

Figures

F.1   One byte of computer memory ca. 1969   xvii
4.1   Screenshot of MetaTutor's main interface   52
5.1   Learning companions in the MathSpring tutoring system empathize with the
       student, acknowledging and mirroring their frustration after the student has
       reported it (addressing emotion, left and middle) and then training growth
       mindset (addressing motivation, right)   82
6.1   Placing scrutability within the landscape of related terms in the AI, human–
       computer interaction and FATE literature   103
6.2   Key interfaces and architecture of a scrutable learning system   105
6.3   Example of an OLM that provides scrutability of the main classes of raw data
       that have been used to determine the value of each knowledge component   111
6.4   Screenshot of adaptive CSP where the learner can study the answer to the
       question "Why am I delivered this hint?"   112
6.5   Screenshot of adaptive CSP where the learner can study the answer to the
       question "Why am I predicted to be low learning?"   113
6.6   Illustrative benchmark questions mapped to the elements in Figure 6.2   114
6.7   Benchmark questions for use by designers of AIED systems to define the level
       of scrutability and control, and to drive design and evaluation   115
7.1   Model tracing in action   134
7.2   The basic structure of Andes' BN-based domain and student model   139
7.3   Steps for creating a domain model to detect the skill of designing controlled
       experiments using supervised learning   143
8.1   Sample concept map in Betty's Brain   172
8.2   The CCK simulation (PhET Interactive Simulations)   172
8.3   Unity-CT   173
8.4   Overview of FUMA   177
10.1   BioWorld interface   234
10.2   Screenshot of MetaTutor's interface with Mary the Monitor   235
10.3   The interfaces of the location-based AR app   238
10.4   Crystal Island EcoJourneys: AI interface designs to promote collaboration 240
10.5   The interface of HOWARD dashboard   242
13.1   A pseudocode Squiral solution (left), a solution sample in iSnap (middle), and
       the Squiral problem output (right)   289
13.2   Student Lime's solution (a) without using the Feedback System and (b) using
       the Feedback System   299
13.3   Incorrect solution initially implemented by student Cyan   300
13.4   Solution submitted by student Indigo   301
13.5   Correct solution initially implemented by student Azure   301

15.1 Teachers' sensemaking and decision-making processes of learning analytics use. There is no hierarchy among the types of learning analytics 327

15.2 ZoomSense question-driven interface to support teachers during real-time monitoring of breakout rooms in Zoom 330

15.3 LearnerFlow interface showing the five panels acting as interrogation entry points 333

15.4 Exploring Stressed Modules: (4a) Tracing flow for a selected module, (4b) Tracing inward flow and (4c) Tracing outward flow 334

15.5 The manual filter builder panel used in Course Insights 337

15.6 An overview of how drill-down recommendations are produced 338

15.7 An overview of the filter recommendation interface 339

15.8 An example visualisation demonstrating the assessment result of the filtered students against the entire class 340

15.9 An example visualisation demonstrating the engagement pattern of the filtered students against the entire class 340

15.10 Comparing learning process maps of two recommended cohorts. The process map on the left represents the cohort with a low final exam score. The process map on the right represents the cohort with a high final exam score 341

17.1 Comparison of number of COVID cases over time in the United States with activity levels per week during the same period of time for HighCOVID vs LowCOVID students 380

17.2 Difference in frequency of mentor notes mentioning COVID terms (indicated in red) vs no COVID terms (indicated in green) for students in the LowCOVID group (HighCOVID = no) vs the HighCOVID group (HIghCOVID = yes) in comparison to frequency of COVID cases across the United States 381

17.3 Final structural equation modeling (SEM) results for impact of social support on course units (CUs) earned. Only significant effects shown 383

18.1 Filtering process applied. For the 2021 analysis (SR-chapter), the workflow at the left corresponds to the filtering process applied to papers identified in our systematic review carried out in March 2021 and the workflow in the middle corresponds to the filtering process applied to papers identified in the two previous systematic reviews (SR-2018 and SR-2019) that were also reviewed in this chapter. The queries were run again in January 2023 (just before the publication of the handbook) to cover the period 2021–2023. The workflow of the right shows this filtering process, which resulted in three relevant papers (Hamadani et al., 2022., Vannaprathip et al., 2022, and Yilmaz et al., 2022) whose analysis is left as exercise for the reader to apply the teachings of this chapter 394

18.2 Framework SMDD (Sensing-Modelling-Designing-Delivering) and interaction between the phases involved in the development of AIED psychomotor systems 403

18.3 Five first blocks in American Kenpo Karate's Blocking Set I. This is the set of movements that can be learned using KSAS. From the start position, the learner has to perform an upward block, then an inward block, then an extended outward block, followed by an outward downward block, and finally, a rear elbow block. The photograms shown are performed by the first author (ACO) of this chapter 410

18.4   The architecture of KSAS following the SMDD framework. The application
       starts by giving initial indications to the user (Delivering feedback).
       Following those indications, the learner executes the requested movements,
       which are captured using the inertial and positional sensors of the Android
       device (Sensing movement). The movements are modeled using the EWMA
       algorithm (Modeling movement) and analyzed to design the feedback using an
       LSTM neural network (Designing feedback). The feedback is then delivered
       to the learner using the display, the speakers and the vibrator of the device
       (Delivering feedback). Depending on how was the performance of the
       movements, the application can give new indications to the learner. When the
       training session finishes, the application generates a report of the session using
       the feedback generated for each movement (Delivering feedback). This report
       is available to the learner and can be voluntarily shared with the instructor   411
18.5   Movements of *kihon kumite* currently detected by KUMITRON. Kamae is
       the initial posture, and both participants start in this position. The attacker
       performs sequentially the Gedan Barai (a circular downward block) attacks,
       followed by Oi Tsuki (a horizontal punch with the same leg forwarded). The
       defender executes the movements of Soto Uke (an outward block) and Gyaku
       Tsuki (a horizontal punch with the opposite leg forwarded). The photograms
       shown are performed by the second author (JE) of this chapter   413
18.6   The architecture of the KUMITRON system following the SMDD framework.
       The movements executed by the learners are captured by collecting information
       from the Arduino-based sensors and the video capture device (Sensing
       movement). Subsequently, the movements are modeled using computer vision
       techniques like OpenCV and OpenPose (Modelling movement), and the
       information captured from the Arduino-based sensors is modeled as a diagram
       of directional vectors. Data mining techniques are used to design the feedback
       by integrating the modeled information from the camera and the Arduino-
       based sensors (Designing feedback). Finally, auditory feedback is delivered to
       the learners in the form of verbal instructions, and visual feedback is delivered
       using a display (Delivering feedback)   413
19.1   Overview of types of support in pre-active, inter-active, and post-active phases
       of collaborative learning   424
20.1   In MathSpring, students use math to grow plants representing progress and
       effort in the game (a). Plants might bloom and give peppers, or wither if
       students show disengagement. (b) shows an example of an AI-driven learning
       companion in MathSpring, used to encourage students' effort   447
20.2   Policy World screenshots of the agents involved in the policy debate: (a) the
       player, (b) the lobbyist, (c) the senator, and (d) the tutor   448
20.3   The main game map on the top left allows students to see the 24 mini-games
       of Decimal Point (a), an example mini-game on the top right in which the
       student "whacks" moles in the order of smallest to largest decimal number (b),
       while the recommender dashboard for the control version of the game (c), the
       enjoyment-oriented version of the game (d) and the learning-oriented version
       of the game (e) are shown left to right at the bottom   452

20.4 The figure at the top (a) is an example of a student solving a Physics Playground problem by drawing a lever with a weight on one side of the lever to hit the balloon. At the bottom (b) is the My Backpack view, which provides estimates of student progress, physics skill, and concept understanding   455

20.5 The locations on Crystal Island where the student can visit to solve the infectious disease mystery (a). The student interacts with AI-infused NPCs, such as the camp nurse and patients (b). A diagnosis worksheet scaffolds students learning; they can record their findings in the worksheet (c)   459

20.6 An active dialog in TLCTS. Trainees learn how to use language and act culturally appropriate when interviewing Iraqi civilians   461

20.7 A child listening to TurtleTalk's questions and then commanding the turtle NPC to act through voice command   462

20.8 A level of Refraction. The goal of the game is to use the elements on the right to split lasers into fractional pieces and redirect them to satisfy the target spaceships. All spaceships must be satisfied at the same time to win   466

20.9 This is a screenshot of the intrinsic version of the Zombie Division game. The player's avatar is in the foreground and chooses weapons from the top of the screen to attack zombies as they appear. The goal is to choose weapons that are equal divisors of the zombies, which have numbers on their chests. The "magical book of times tables" is shown in the upper right. The hearts indicate the health of the player, the skull on the bottom right shows how many zombies are yet to appear in this level   467

20.10 Students playing with the Intelligent Science Station (norilla.org)   473

21.1 AI-based assessment (AIBA) framework   486

22.1 A regression discontinuity. There were only five students above the pre-test threshold and thus in the no-treatment condition. Two of them had identical pre- and post-test scores, so they show as one point in the plot above   515

22.2 G-power's graph of the power of a specific statistical test and acceptance level   517

24.1 The Educate Golden Triangle   539

24.2 Significant components accounting for most of the variance in the questionnaire data   542

24.3 The Golden Triangle Framework for multi-stakeholder collaboration in AI for education   545

26.1 'Strawman' framework for the ethics of AIED   589

27.1 Adaptive navigation support and content recommendation in an adaptive textbook developed with InterBook   615

27.2 Interface of the Math-Bridge system: an adaptively assembled textbook with links between different learning objects displayed in the right-hand panel   617

27.3 Social comparison and external content recommendation in ReadingMirror   618

27.4 Quiz interface in the Betty's Brain system   620

27.5 Computational Modeling Interface in the SPICE environment   621

27.6 Causal paths discovered with statistically significant direct effects   623

27.7 A problem in the ASSISTments Tutor with a text-based explanation   631

Tables

5.1	Layout of the chapter	69
7.1	Domain model functions	130
7.2	Strengths and weaknesses of AIED domain modeling paradigms	155
13.1	Data-driven DDFD features derived for the Squiral assignment	290
13.2	Incorrect feedback types, occurrence count, and percentage of causing an impact	297
17.1	Summary of COVID impact groups by hashtags and mean average course units (CUs) earned per group	379
17.2	Summary of COVID impact groups by topic-model analysis and mean average course units (CUs) earned per group and mean average online activity (weeks per group)	382
18.1	Details of the three systematic reviews considered in the chapter: SR-2018 (Santos, 2019), SR-2019 (Neagu et al., 2020), and SR-chapter (this chapter)	393
18.2	The psychomotor AIED systems identified in the papers reviewed indicating the AI techniques used, Mager's components of the educational objective, and Simpson's psychomotor categories. This table also includes the systems KSAS and KUMITRON presented in the chapter as case studies	396
18.3	Analysis of the motion information flow in the systems obtained in the review. When used, AI techniques are mentioned. In addition, this table also includes the systems KSAS and KUMITRON presented in the chapter as case studies	405
19.1	Summary of techniques for supporting collaborative learning	432
20.1	Summary of AIED digital learning games	444
24.1	Unimodal classification of debate tutors' performance based on only the audio variables	543
24.2	Multimodal classification of debate tutors' performance, based on the experience, survey, and two of the strong predictive audio variables	544
26.1	Main types of AI bias, their potential sources and related harms	576
26.2	Key considerations and questions for AIED designers and users	591

Contributors

Vincent Aleven, HCI Institute, Carnegie Mellon University, United States

Ivon Arroyo, University of Massachusetts Amherst, United States

Roger Azevedo, University of Central Florida, United States

Nicole Barbaro, Western Governors University, United States

Tiffany Barnes, North Carolina State University, United States

Gautam Biswas, Vanderbilt University, United States

Stephen Blessing, University of Tampa, United States

Christopher Brooks, University of Michigan, United States

Peter Brusilovsky, University of Pittsburgh, United States

Alberto Casas-Ortiz, Universidad Nacional de Educación a Distancia (UNED), Spain

Min Chi, North Carolina State University, United States

Cristina Conati, University of British Columbia, Canada

Mutlu Cukurova, University College London, United Kingdom

Huw Davies, University of Edinburgh, United Kingdom

Vania Dimitrova, University of Leeds, United Kingdom

Benedict du Boulay, University of Sussex, United Kingdom

Jon Echeverria, Universidad Nacional de Educación a Distancia (UNED), Spain

Rebecca Eynon, University of Oxford, United Kingdom

Ying Fang, Central China Normal University, China

Claude Frasson, University of Montreal, Canada

Dragan Gašević, Monash University, Australia

Stephen B. Gilbert, Iowa State University, United States

Arthur C. Graesser, University of Memphis, United States

Neil Heffernan, Worcester Polytechnic Institute, United States

Wayne Holmes, University College London and International Research Centre of Artificial Intelligence, United Kingdom

Ken Holstein, Carnegie Mellon University, United States

Yun Huang, Carnegie Mellon University, United States

Judy Kay, The University of Sydney, Australia

Hassan Khosravi, University of Queensland, Australia

Jeremy Knox, University of Edinburgh, United Kingdom

Kenneth R. Koedinger, Carnegie Mellon University, United States

Vitomir Kovanović, The University of South Australia, Australia

Bob Kummerfeld, The University of Sydney, Australia

Susanne P. Lajoie, McGill University, Canada

Sébastien Lallé, Sorbonne University, France

H. Chad Lane, University of Illinois, Urbana-Champaign, United States

James C. Lester, North Carolina State University, United States

Shan Li, Lehigh University, United States

Rosemary Luckin, UCL Knowledge Lab, United Kingdom

Ye Mao, SAS Institute, United States

Roberto Martinez-Maldonado, Monash University, Australia

Samiha Marwan, University of Virginia, United States

Manolis Mavrikis, University College London, United Kingdom

Gordon McCalla, University of Saskatchewan, Canada

Bruce M. McLaren, Carnegie Mellon University, United States

Danielle S. McNamara, Arizona State University, United States

Antonija Mitrovic, Intelligent Computer Tutoring Group, University of Canterbury, Christchurch, New Zealand

Riichiro Mizoguchi, Japan Advanced Institute of Science and Technology, Japan

Jack Mostow, Carnegie Mellon University, United States

Kasia Muldner, Carleton University, Canada

Selena Nemorin, Oxford University, Department of Education, Kellogg College, United Kingdom

Huy A. Nguyen, Carnegie Mellon University, United States

Quan Nguyen, University of British Columbia, Canada

Stellan Ohlsson, University of Illinois at Chicago, United States

Andrew M. Olney, University of Memphis, United States

Jennifer K. Olsen, University of San Diego, United States

Kaśka Porayska-Pomsta, University College London, United Kingdom

Stanislav Pozdniakov, Monash University, Australia

Thomas W. Price, North Carolina State University, United States

Ethan Prihar, Worcester Polytechnic Institute, United States

Meredith Riggs, Cycorp, United States

Steven Ritter, Carnegie Learning, Inc., United States

Maria Mercedes T. Rodrigo, Ateneo de Manila University, Philippines

Rod D. Roscoe, Arizona State University, United States

Carolyn Rosé, Carnegie Mellon University, United States

Jonathan Rowe, North Carolina State University, United States

Nikol Rummel, Ruhr Universität Bochum, Germany

Vasile Rus, University of Memphis, United States

Olga C. Santos, Universidad Nacional de Educación a Distancia (UNED), Spain

Preya Shabrina, North Carolina State University, United States

Yang Shi, North Carolina State University, United States

Shaveen Singh, Monash University, Australia

Sergey Sosnovsky, Utrecht University, Netherlands

Zachari Swiecki, Monash University, Australia

Anouschka van Leeuwen, Universiteit Utrecht, Netherlands

Kurt VanLehn, Arizona State University, United States

Julita Vassileva, University of Saskatchewan, Canada

Megan Wiedbusch, University of Central Florida, United States

Ben Williamson, University of Edinburgh, United Kingdom

Kalina Yacef, The University of Sydney, Australia

Foreword

This handbook is really a celebration of an effort that began about half a century ago, as Gord McCalla's chapter details so well, when Patrick Suppes (1966) employed one of the earliest efforts at personal computing to foster learning. Indeed, as a student at Stanford from 1967 to 1971, I recall seeing Suppes's work develop, partly using the first workstations with screen displays, which were beginning to displace teletype-style printers. As is evident in this handbook, we have come a long way. To get a sense of how far, consider the piece of hardware shown in Figure F.1. It is one byte of processor memory from the first computer used to foster learning at the Learning Research and Development Center in the late 60s. A ballpen is alongside it to give a sense of scale; multiple separate transistors were needed to capture each bit. In contrast, I just purchased a single chip to provide my laptop with one trillion bytes, on a board less than an inch wide and less than three inches long. The actual chip containing the trillion bytes would not cover even the two transistors needed in the 60s to provide one bit!

What this volume makes clear is that there has been similar growth on the conceptual and software side. Just over fifty years ago, we envisioned learning as presenting displays to people and then proceeding differentially, depending on how they chose among a few possible responses to those displays. Today, there are intelligent tutors that listen to and speak to the learner. Instead of preprogramming each possible reaction to each possible student action, we now model both expertise and student knowledge using neural networks, Bayesian networks, and other formulations. Instead of being focused solely on student performance and a model of expertise, we also attend to the level of student engagement and even to emotions that might reflect learning impasses, frustrations, or sudden learning breakthroughs. This handbook documents that progress very well.

The various chapters also support the belief that the field is well positioned to deal with a major change in the task of education. While there always have been new things to learn, we live now in a time when both needed knowledge and the division of labor between people and machines are changing exponentially (Azhar, 2021). Many learning requirements will themselves be changing quickly, too. The traditional instructional design approach of investing in a substantial cognitive task analysis of domain expertise and then building an intelligent learning environment to teach the extracted knowledge now needs to be supplemented, or possibly replaced, by a system that can respond dynamically to changes in what should be learned. Much of what we currently do in building instructional systems rests on an underlying assumption that expertise comes after 10,000 hours of experience. For many learning tasks today, though, the knowledge to be taught may not have existed in its current form for enough time for anyone to have 10,000 hours of experience.

I realized this a while ago when Marty Nahemow and I were designing an intelligent tutor to teach technicians to repair computer chip-making machines (Lesgold and Nahemow, 2001). We did the usual task analysis, but a few weeks later, Marty, a manufacturing physicist for most of his career, came to me and pointed out some inexpert bits of knowledge we had extracted from Intel's best experts. The expert model we ended up with no longer reflected completely the expertise extracted from the experts we interviewed; it was enhanced by

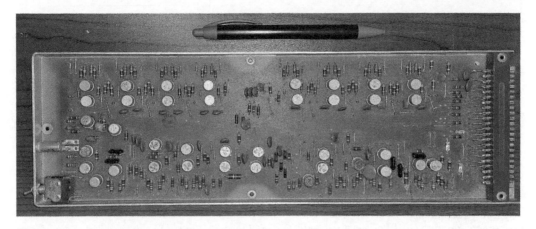

Figure F.1   One byte of computer memory ca. 1969

Marty's deep understanding of the physics involved in what the chipmaking machines did, combined with a lot of experience with related processes. More recently, in helping a friend develop improved training for power grid operators, it became apparent that expertise in that space is continually shifting as climate change and emergent cyberattack potential change the domain significantly. Ten years ago, we did not turn off parts of the grid to prevent forest fires, nor did we need to keep modeling how cyberattacks would evolve.

I am enthusiastic not only about how this handbook has captured where we are today in using intelligent systems to foster learning but also about how a foundation is being laid for a new level of dynamism. Just as some of the chapters in this volume reveal a level of dynamic capability to understand the emotional and cognitive state of the learner, I expect that evolving tools, including transformer technology now seen in natural language processing, will allow a new dynamism in the knowledge to be taught as well. Partly, this will be because what must be known to do valuable activity in the world will keep changing quickly and, partly, it will be because the division of labor between people and machines also will be evolving quickly.

Where half a century ago computational tools were used to teach people to make a specific response to a specific situation, future intelligent learning environments will need to allow learning both of new domains for collaborative human (and machine) activity and of new approaches to organizing collective and machine-mediated intelligent efforts. Giacomelli (2020, 2022), among others, has been developing some approaches to teaching teams of well-educated professionals to function effectively as distributed autonomous organizations. Perhaps the biggest challenge for those who will build upon the work captured in this handbook will be to build intelligent learning environments to help youth and displaced workers acquire the foundation competence that will allow them to participate in the learning and performance that people like him envision.

This handbook presents a broad and substantial picture of artificial intelligence and education as it has evolved so far. It thus provides the foundation for a next generation of tools that will dynamically assess both the competences required for new collective intelligent human activity and the range of experiences needed to support the learning of those competences. Just as computer hardware has expanded in capability by many orders of magnitude, we can expect Wright's Law (Wright, 1936) to apply as well to the future of artificial intelligence in education. The best is yet to come.

Alan Lesgold
University of Pittsburgh

REFERENCES

Azhar, A. (2021). *The exponential age: How accelerating technology is transforming business, politics and society*. Diversion Books.

Giacomelli, Gianni. (2022). The future of Design Thinking: designing "superminds." Downloaded February 15, 2022, from www.linkedin.com/pulse/future-design-thinking-designing-superminds-gianni-giacomelli/.

Giacomelli, Gianni. (2020). *Augmented collective intelligence: Human-AI networks in a virtual future of work*. Downloaded February 14, 2022, from www.supermind.design.

Lesgold, A., & Nahemow, M. (2001). Tools to assist learning by doing: Achieving and assessing efficient technology for learning. In S. M. Carver & D. Klahr (eds), *Cognition and Instruction: Twenty-Five Years of Progress*, 307–346. Lawrence Erlbaum Associates Publishers.

Suppes, P. (1966). The uses of computers in education. *Scientific American*, *215*(3), 206–223.

Wright, T. P. (1936). Factors affecting the cost of airplanes. *Journal of the Aeronautical Sciences*, *3*(4), 122–128.

PART I

SCENE SETTING

1. Introduction to the *Handbook of Artificial Intelligence in Education*

Benedict du Boulay, Antonija Mitrovic and Kalina Yacef

HOW THIS HANDBOOK CAME TO BE

Benedict du Boulay

On 22 November 2019, I was approached out of the blue by Daniel Mather from Edward Elgar Publishing, who asked whether I was interested in being the editor of a *Handbook of Artificial Intelligence and Education*. I certainly was interested since, like Tanja below, I had been harbouring thoughts about writing a book on that topic. I did my due diligence by contacting editors of other handbooks from these publishers and received good reports about working with them. I also contacted Sally Fincher and Anthony Robins who had just published a handbook (Fincher & Robins, 2019) in which I had a chapter, for advice about how to manage such a large project. They made a number of very useful points amongst which was "don't do it alone" – excellent advice indeed. I'm sure I could never have finished the project without the help and guidance of Tanja and Kalina. The three of us drafted an initial outline of the handbook under the slightly different title of "Artificial Intelligence *in* Education" (AIED), created an initial spreadsheet for planning purposes that was soon superseded by events and said yes to Daniel Mather.

Rather than putting out an open call for chapters, we decided from the start what topics we wanted to cover and then invited the best person we could think of to write on that topic. Most of our invitees agreed to be authors but we did have a small number of refusals. As the handbook developed, we realised that there were topics that we had missed, and a small number of extra chapters were commissioned. We also wanted a final chapter that looked to future trends. So we adopted the same process of inviting distinguished authors who were not already chapter authors to write on whatever future issue they chose, bearing in mind what was already in the handbook.

A consequence of this way of working has been that authors with USA affiliations predominate along with others from the richer "western" powers. This imbalance is slightly offset in Chapter 27 where issues around access and equity are discussed. We did a bit better on gender balance with just under half our invitations going to female researchers.

My first exposure to AI and to AI in Education was as a PhD student in the Department of AI in Edinburgh in the 1970s under the supervision of Professor Jim Howe. In the end, I worked on a project involving exploration of the affordances of the programming language LOGO for teachers of mathematics rather than directly on an AI topic. One of my colleagues in the LOGO project was Tim O'Shea (1979) (now Professor) who was finishing his PhD on a "Self-improving Quadratic Tutor", later published in the first journal collection of papers as well as in the first book collection in the field of AIED (Sleeman & Brown, 1982). This system sparked my imagination in AIED in that not only could it teach how to solve quadratic equations, but it could also automatically run experiments to check plausible changes to its teaching strategy to see whether it could be more effective.

Antonija (Tanja) Mitrovic

On 1 January 2020, Ben emailed me to ask whether I would like to join him in editing a handbook on AIED, and I immediately (and enthusiastically) said yes! I had been thinking about writing a book for many years, but frankly it was a scary thought. On the other hand, editing a book like the one Ben had in mind was very exciting. Now, two and a half years later, I can say that it was a great pleasure to work with Ben, Kalina and many of our wonderful colleagues who contributed to the handbook.

I remember the first time I heard about Intelligent Tutoring Systems: in 1990, when I worked on my MSc project at the University of Calgary, on an ML topic supervised by Prof. Ian Witten. One lecture in the AI course (taught by Professor Brian Gaines) was devoted to ITSs. I was hooked immediately. Combining AI with teaching just looked perfect for my PhD project! On my return to Yugoslavia, I started working on my PhD in 1991. It took me three years (during the war) to develop a new student modelling approach, combining model tracing with reconstructive modelling. The only literature I had access to was Etienne Wegner's book on AI and tutoring systems (Wenger, 1987), and a few papers by Bev Woolf, Julita Vassileva and Alessandro Micarelli who kindly answered my letters. My home country was under an embargo by the UN and it was not possible to get any books or papers. There was no one in the country working on AIED, and I did my whole PhD without any advice.

While I was working on this handbook, the same thought occurred to me over and over – how lovely the handbook will be for new AIED researchers! I know that many of the chapter authors also had the same thought. AIED is so much bigger now than 30 years ago. The abundance of papers on AIED topics is good to see, but could overwhelm new PhD students. I sincerely hope that the handbook will inspire and support a new generation of AIED researchers!

Kalina Yacef

It has been an immense pleasure to work with Ben and Tanja on this big enterprise, along with all the many AIED colleagues who contributed to this handbook. When Ben invited me to join him and Tanja as co-editor for a handbook on AIED, I felt honoured and excited at the prospect of working with them on this ambitious – and daunting – project. A handbook on AIED! I recall many years ago, at AIED 2003 in Sydney, sharing thoughts with colleagues about how great it would be to have such a handbook for teaching a course on AIED and to support current and new researchers in the field!

Seeing the collective force of the AIED community working to create this handbook was a remarkable experience and a testimony to the collegiality in the field (especially given the difficult context of a world pandemic). I should mention that our fortnightly meetings with Ben and Tanja were a breath of fresh air and provided a little window to the outside world throughout the COVID lockdowns and border closures!

When I started my PhD in the late nineties, I discovered the world of intelligent tutoring systems, and quickly realised that the domain I was working on (air traffic control training) did not fit into the traditional, well-defined domains of AIED systems at the time. This led me to the concept of intelligent teaching assistant systems, and later on to mine student interaction data to inform teachers and support their sense and decision making. I immediately found the field of AIED fascinating because it is a truly interdisciplinary field which focuses on one of the most critical ground pillars of society, education, and leverages exciting AI advances as well as the wealth of theories about how humans learn, think, communicate, socialise, collaborate and so on. The possibilities and research opportunities seem endless. I agree with Tanja; as the handbook was taking shape, I also took measure of how big the field had grown, and I hope this handbook will be a good roadmap for new and established AIED researchers!

WHY A HANDBOOK ON AIED NOW?

AIED has recently come into much sharper focus because of the impressive achievements of artificial intelligence in general, the much greater public awareness of the subject (both positive and negative) and the effects of COVID on educational practice. The field of AIED initially grew out of computer use in education, going under various titles such as Computer-Assisted Learning (CAL) or Computer-Assisted Instruction (CAI). One of the AIED earliest papers was entitled "AI in CAI: An Artificial-Intelligence Approach to Computer-Assisted Instruction" (Carbonell, 1970). In 1970, there were no personal computers and no internet, and CAI systems were run on large computers with links to the individual terminals (see Chapter 2). At present, there are conferences and journals focusing specifically on AIED as well as a host of education and educational technology conferences and periodicals that include AIED as a sub-topic. Now is a good time to take stock of where the field is.

For many years, AIED research has focused on developing systems that help the student, by providing adaptive feedback and guidance. There have been numerous innovative AIED systems developed to teach various cognitive skills. Other research focused on how to interact with the student, including animated pedagogical agents, simulations and tutorial dialogues. There has also been a lot of attention paid to collaborative learning. In addition to systems that help individual students learn, nowadays there is a lot of work in the AIED community on classroom orchestration, with the goal of supporting the teacher in helping students. There is also research on the institutional level, with the goal of improving curricula and improving student success. It was our intention to cover various types of research in AIED, both "old" and "new", with the final chapter looking at future trends.

In addition to looking beyond learner-focused systems to teacher-focused and administrator-focused systems involving learner analytics and educational data mining, we also wanted to explore the context within which AIED operates. So the latter chapters in Part V look at the commercialisation of AIED systems, the ethics of such systems and, crucially, current criticisms of such systems in terms of biases and corporate exploitation among other issues.

The structure of the handbook therefore represents our sense of the scope of AIED. We apologise if we have omitted some aspect of AIED that you feel should have been included and indeed, for including some aspect that you should have been excluded.

The handbook is organised into six parts, with introductions for each of them as follows.

PART I: SCENE SETTING

Part I is the shortest part; in addition to the current chapter, Chapter 1, Chapter 2 by Gordon McCalla provides an excellent summary of the AIED history. Our recommendation for new researchers is to start with Chapter 2: studying the history of AIED helps to understand how the discipline developed, and why certain types of research exist today.

PART II: THEORIES UNDERPINNING AIED

Part II consists of four chapters that describe various theories that underpin work in AIED. It starts with cognitive and knowledge theories, moves to the metacognitive, then to affect and meta-affect and finally to the concept of scrutability for accountable, transparent, explainable, ethical systems.

Part II starts with Stellan Ohlsson's Chapter 3 which explores the role of theory in the development of AIED systems and then goes on to describe three areas of theory: psychological theories, instructional design theories and formal theories around artificial intelligence. The section on psychological theories includes various theories of learning, with particular focus on learning complex skills and learning from discourse.

In Chapter 4, Roger Azevedo and Megan Wiedbusch explain why metacognition is relevant to AIED systems, theories of metacognition and how the construct of metacognition has influenced the area of AIED systems. This is followed by a description of six systems that have helped develop learners' metacognitive capabilities, including the Help-Seeking Tutor, AutoTutor, MetaTutor, Betty's Brain, iStart and SimStudent. The chapter concludes with pointers to future research in both tracking and developing metacognitive capability.

Chapter 5 on affect by Ivon Arroyo, Kaśka Porayska-Pomsta and Kasia Muldner neatly lays out the structure of the chapter in Table 5.1. The chapter starts with different kinds of emotional theory, distinguishes emotion from other affective categorisations, looks at the neuroscience of emotions in education, and finally at AIED research involving emotion. It then moves on to the issue of motivation, exploring motivational theories, such as Expectancy-Value Theory, as well as AIED work involving motivation. The final part of the chapter examines the issues of emotion and motivation regulation and their applications in AIED.

The final chapter in this part, Chapter 6 by Judy Kay, Bob Kummerfeld, Cristina Conati, Kaśka Porayska-Pomsta and Ken Holstein, looks at Scrutable AIED, that is, "capable of being understood by careful study or investigation". In some ways this chapter can be seen as a theory of effective interaction with AIED systems. The topics explored include fair, accountable, transparent, explainable, ethical (FATE) systems, the architecture of learning systems for scrutability and control and how different elements within AIED contribute to scrutability. This is followed by some examples of scrutiny interfaces, some benchmark questions, user-centred definition of scrutability and control and the distinctive nature of scrutability in AIED. The chapter concludes with a research agenda for the future.

PART III: THE ARCHITECTURE AND DESIGN OF AIED SYSTEMS

Part III consists of six chapters that cover important and foundational aspects of the architecture and design of AIED systems. It starts with the three pillars for the purpose of adaptation and personalised learning: domain modelling, student modelling, and instructional mechanisms. Then it moves to the interaction layer, exploring theory-driven design and natural language interactions, and finishes with the authoring tools for building AIED systems.

In Chapter 7 of Part III, Vincent Aleven, Jonathan Rowe, Yun Huang and Antonija Mitrovic present a comprehensive overview of the major approaches used for domain modelling in AIED systems, their purposes and the central role they play in providing adaptive systems. They highlight the varied forms of knowledge representations and explain how rich an adaptation can be achieved through having a domain model, linking it to student modelling and instruction. This chapter is a good starting point for anyone starting in the field and wanting to understand the mechanism of adaptive and individualised instruction.

In Chapter 8 of Part III, Cristina Conati and Sébastien Lallé tackle student modelling in the challenging context of Open-Ended Learning Environments, for which a domain model is not as well defined, cannot be used for driving adaptation and feedback in the traditional way and must be of a more exploratory nature. They discuss how to build student models that include metacognitive factors such as self-explanation and self-regulatory processes, and review knowledge-based and data-driven approaches used for student modelling.

Then in Chapter 9, Vincent Aleven, Manolis Mavrikis, Bruce M. McLaren, Huy Anh Nguyen, Jennifer K. Olsen and Nikol Rummel review the AIED implementations of six adaptive instructional, or pedagogical, approaches commonly used in AIED systems with proven effectiveness in helping students learn: learning from problem-solving practice, learning from examples, exploratory learning, collaborative learning, game-based learning and learning by teaching. These are explained through the lens of two common conceptual frameworks widely used in AIED, namely assistance and adaptivity, the authors discuss how these approaches are effectively implemented in AIED systems.

In Chapter 10, Susanne P. Lajoie and Shan Li explain the importance of and the challenges in creating effective AI learning and teaching interfaces and argue that their design needs to be driven by theories and models of the cognitive, metacognitive, affective, motivational and behavioural components of learning.

Chapter 11 on natural language interaction by Vasile Rus, Andrew Olney and Arthur Graesser presents the exciting history of conversational AIED systems, explaining how natural language can contribute to deeper, conceptual learning and more effective and satisfying learning experiences. They discuss their effectiveness and challenges and review the opportunities afforded by recent advances in AI and machine learning to scale up their development and deployment.

Part III concludes with Chapter 12 by Stephen Blessing, Stephen B. Gilbert and Steven Ritter, dedicated to authoring tools for building AIED systems. They review tools across several types of tutoring types (model-tracing, constraint-based, agent-based and dialog-based tutors) and discuss the huge – and still unsolved – challenges for creating them. They make us think at a higher level about the knowledge structures involved in an AIED system, and about how to create consistent models between the student and the system: the student "sees" the surface representation and the tutor "sees" the deep structure. They offer some potential solutions and avenues for research.

PART IV: ANALYTICS

Part IV consists of five chapters that cover data-driven methods and analytics in AIED systems.

Chapter 13 of Part IV, by Ye Mao, Samiha Marwan, Preya Shabrina, Yang Shi, Thomas Price, Min Chi and Tiffany Barnes, looks into data-driven, automated approaches for creating student models in "continuous" domains, where problem-solving steps are not discrete, often involve multiple skills and where the notion of correctness is not straightforward to assess. The authors focus here on the Computer Programming domain, explaining fully data-driven skill discovery techniques, including feature-based and machine learning methods, and prediction modelling (temporal modelling and semi-supervised learning when the data size is small). Their chapter also covers the important aspect of evaluating data-driven feedback and concludes with some guidelines on the design choices for student models in continuous domains.

The next two chapters (Chapters 14 and 15) are focused on supporting teachers. Chapter 14, by Ken Holstein and Jennifer K. Olsen, addresses human–AI co-orchestration in a broader sense of learning environments, such as classrooms, and where the AI supports teachers, in a human-in-the-loop and co-agency approach. Chapter 15, by Stanislav Pozdniakov, Roberto Martinez-Maldonado, Shaveen Singh, Hassan Khosravi and Dragan Gasevic, reviews the three types of teacher-facing learning analytics, namely descriptive, predictive and prescriptive analytics, and the role each play in sense-making, decision-making and pedagogical actions.

Chapter 16, by Christopher Brooks, Vitomir Kovanović and Quan Nguyen, covers the research into predictive modelling of student success using various kinds of data about students: general student information data, behavioural interactions within the learning management systems, application-level behavioural traces and non-learning academic data. They discuss the big challenges for translating research into educational practice, in particular the replication, reproduction, and generalisation of predictive modelling and the explainability, fairness and bias in the models.

Finally, Chapter 17 of Part IV, by Carolyn Rosé, Meredith Riggs and Nicole Barbaro, is devoted to social analytics and underpinning theories for fostering positive learning experience in large-scale online communities (Massive Open Online Courses). The authors draw on their considerable experience and provide avenues for further research.

PART V: AIED SYSTEMS IN USE

Part V explores issues around the kinds of learning supported through AIED, methodological issues around assessment and evaluation of systems, the commercialisation of AIED as well as the ethics and biases of the field overall.

The first three chapters look at supporting three specific *kinds of learning*, namely psychomotor learning, online collaborative learning and learning through games. Chapter 18 by Albert Casas-Ortiz, Jon Echeverria and Olga C. Santos provides a systematic review of the area of AIED and psychomotor learning, such as for learners with motor difficulties or, at the other end of the spectrum, those in training to be surgeons. As this is still an emerging field of study, they are able to refer to all of the available studies. In contrast, Chapter 19, by Roberto Martinez-Maldonado, Anouschka van Leeuwen and Zachari Swiecki, covers the much more explored area of online collaborative learning. They explain how AI analytics can be used to assist in group formation, feedback to learners, adaptive scripting for collaboration, group awareness tools, teacher awareness tools and summative assessment. Chapter 20 by Bruce M. McLaren and Huy A. Nguyen argues that the immersive nature of games and the consequent experience of "flow" helps counteract some of the more distancing aspects of formal education. They enumerate the roles of AI as supporting dynamic adaptation of the game during play, providing decision support tools to learners during play, creating non-player characters within the game, and using learner analytics both to understand the learners and improve the games.

The next two chapters are *methodological* and cover assessment and evaluation. Chapter 21 by Ying Fang, Rod D. Roscoe and Danielle S. McNamara explores AI-based assessment (AIBA) via the goals of the assessment, the target constructs which are used to form the assessment, the data sources that act as proxies for those constructs, the computational methods deployed to analyse that data, and visibility, i.e., whether the assessment is known to the learner or not. Chapter 22 by Kurt VanLehn maps out methods for designing evaluations of AIED projects. It covers evaluations of assessment systems, instructional systems and systems that instructors and developers use. The central section on evaluation of instructional systems covers common variables, outcome variables and moderators, single condition studies, comparing multiple versions of a system, comparisons to baseline instruction, and determining how many student participants are needed.

The next two chapters cover the *commercialisation* of AIED systems. Chapter 23 by Steven Ritter and Kenneth R. Koedinger explores the commercialisation of AI in school-based environments. They argue for the value of different kinds of personalisation such as adjusting progress through the curriculum and choice of activities within the curriculum or curricular content. However, they make the important point that in most schools progress through the curriculum is mandated to take place in age-related segments and that this can be at odds with individually optimised progress. The authors also deal with the commercialisation of assessment systems and systems to support teachers. Chapter 24 by Rosemary Luckin and Mutlu Cukurova covers small-scale commercialisation, in particular the need to educate small-scale education technology companies about educational research so that they can better design, test and evaluate their projects. They provide a case study of how they helped a company that "provides programmes and competitions to participating secondary-level schools in some of the most deprived communities in the UK and in other parts of the world" to use AI to "identify two categories of the decision-making process involved in the process of interviewing and selecting young people to run the after-school debate clubs".

The final two chapters of Part V look at AIED in *social and ethical* terms. Chapter 25 by Ben Williamson, Rebecca Eynon, Jeremy Knox and Huw Davies offers a critical perspective on AIED in terms of its "political economy, discrimination, commercialisation, governance and ethics". In contrast to the two preceding chapters, Chapter 25 delineates how far "the field of AIED has been shaped by the wider political and economic environment". They also investigate biases in AI that lead to "algorithmic discrimination", as well as the problematic reasons for big tech companies to enter the field of educational technology. Chapter 26 by Kaśka Porayska-Pomsta, Wayne Holmes and Selena Nemorin also explores the issue of bias in AIED systems through an ethical lens. They tabulate various types of bias as well as develop an ethical approach to design and development of AIED systems that would help to mitigate these issues. As part of their analysis, the authors focus on the issue of equity in terms of learner accessibility and system pedagogy.

PART VI: THE FUTURE

Part VI of the handbook is designed to provide some sense of where the field of AIED is heading. Authors were approached with the following open-ended brief:

We are planning a final chapter in the handbook made up of short sections of around 1500 words from distinguished researchers in the field, such as yourself. We hope that you might be interested in writing such a section. Each short section can be either an opinion piece about the future of AIED or a descriptive piece on an AIED topic that does not already have a chapter to itself, e.g., leveraging broader AI innovations for education, intelligent textbooks, pedagogical agents, cross-cultural social and pedagogic issues.

We ended up with 11 short sections covering a range of topics.

1. AIED and equity – Maria Mercedes T. Rodrigo
2. Engaging learners in the age of information overload – Julita Vassileva
3. Pedagogical agents for all: Designing virtual characters for inclusion and diversity in STEM – H. Chad Lane
4. Intelligent textbooks – Peter Brusilovsky and Sergey Sosnovsky
5. AI-empowered open-ended learning environments in STEM domains – Gautam Biswas
6. Ubiquitous-AIED: Pervasive AI learning technologies – James C. Lester
7. Culture, ontology and learner modelling – Richiiro Mizoguchi
8. Crowdsourcing paves the way for personalized learning – Ethan Prihar and Neil Heffernan
9. AIED in developing countries: Breaking seven WEIRD assumptions in the global learning XPRIZE field study – Jack Mostow
10. The future of learning assessment – Claude Frasson
11. Intelligent mentoring systems: Tapping into AI to deliver the next generation of digital learning – Vania Dimitrova

ACKNOWLEDGEMENTS

We thank the authors and co-authors for all their hard work, Professor Alan Lesgold for writing the Foreword, Daniel Mather of Edward Elgar Publishing for his unswerving positive help and encouragement throughout, and the various teams at Edward Elgar Publishing who have created this book from the files that we sent them.

REFERENCES

Carbonell, J. R. (1970). AI in CAI: An Artificial-Intelligence Approach to Computer-Assisted Instruction. *IEEE Transactions On Man-Machine Systems, MMS-11*(4), 190–202.

Fincher, S. & Robins, A. (2019). *The Cambridge Handbook of Computing Education Research.* Cambridge University Press.

O'Shea, T. (1979). A Self-Improving Quadratic Tutor. *International Journal of Man-Machine Studies, 11*(1), 97–124.

Sleeman, D. & Brown, J. S. (1982). *Intelligent Tutoring Systems.* Academic Press.

Wenger, E. (1987). *Artificial Intelligence and Tutoring Systems: Computational and Cognitive Approaches to the Communication of Knowledge.* Morgan Kaufmann.

2. The history of artificial intelligence in education – the first quarter century
Gordon McCalla

INTRODUCTION

Artificial intelligence in education (AIED) is an interdisciplinary field, with roots in computer science, cognitive science, education and other areas of social science. It is an applied area as well, with the goal of creating software that helps people to learn better. In the early days, researchers who began to explore what we now call AIED were often attracted to the field for other reasons beyond this immediate application goal. Artificial intelligence researchers saw the "education domain" as an interesting microworld whose "forcing functions" would lead to better and more generalizable computational models than other domains such as robotics or expert systems, since issues such as learning, forgetting and change are central to education (Brown 1990). Cognitive scientists, then emerging from the dominating shadow of behaviourist psychology, saw education as a perfect domain to demonstrate the value of cognitive modelling in explaining psychological phenomena. Education researchers saw the potential of learning technology to provide new kinds of computational precision to their studies of human learning and teaching, and perhaps to provide new kinds of learning environments.

Over time, ideas from these multi-disciplinary perspectives would weave together into a coherent applied field of study that drew aggressively from a large (and ever growing) number of advanced computational techniques to build a wide variety of systems to help learners in authentic learning contexts. Moreover, the design of these systems would draw from the best ideas explored by the social sciences, and they would be evaluated using tried and tested social science techniques for human subject evaluation. In essence, the "AI" in AIED became a placeholder for advanced computing technology (not just AI), and "ED" became a placeholder for state-of-the-art social science perspectives and techniques (not just formal EDucation).[1] In this chapter, I will show how AIED became its own field. But first I want to look back at some "pre-history".

BEFORE THE BEGINNING

Long before computers, Pressey (1926) designed special-purpose machines that would present multiple-choice questions to students who would have to answer them correctly before moving onto the next question. Later, Skinner (1954) drew on Pressey's work, conceptualizing learning in terms of his behaviourist theories of learning. Soon, Skinner (1958) was advocating for "teaching machines" that presented "frames" with questions posed to students who could answer them and get automatically graded before moving on to the next frame. What is interesting about these early approaches is that they recognized the possibility of supporting learning through automation, and that one-on-one learning should be paced according to the needs of individual learners. This perspective aligns well with AIED's individualized, adaptive learning approach. Skinner's embedding of his approach to automating teaching in behaviourist psychology also foreshadowed how AIED often also draws from psychological theory, albeit usually cognitive psychology with its emphasis on modelling.

Pressey's and Skinner's approaches could readily be adapted to computers, and by the 1960s, the area of "computer-assisted instruction" (CAI) had already emerged (Suppes 1966). CAI systems were teaching systems consisting of a database of frames containing material to be presented to the student, along with a set of questions based on the material. The CAI system would "branch" the student to another appropriate frame, either a remedial lesson or natural follow-up material, depending on the student's answers. CAI thus also focused on adapting to individual students' needs, again much like the personalized approaches favoured in AIED.

By the 1970s, two canonical CAI platforms, PLATO (Rahmlow et al. 1980) and TICCIT (Merrill et al. 1980), had been developed and made available to course designers. Each of these platforms was actually an evolving series of authoring environments that embedded a basic CAI control structure along with the ability for course designers to use text, graphics and animation. A wide variety of courses were developed by a diverse user community. But the downside of the CAI approach was that every student outcome had to be explicitly anticipated and system responses had to be built in by the course designer for each possible response. The branching structure could get very complex, especially if the system were to try to track and respond to cascading student misconceptions. By the end of the decade, the CAI community began to discuss the notion of "generative CAI" (Chambers and Sprecher 1980), where the CAI system could actually generate its own questions and answers, for example generating new mathematical expressions for mathematics students to evaluate. Generative CAI echoes to a small degree the desire of pioneering AIED researchers for a teaching system to "know" its subject.

Finally, it should be noted that in addition to CAI systems that "taught", Suppes (1966) also discussed the longer-term prospects for systems that could provide an "opportunity for discussion between learner and computer". In fact it actually wasn't too many years later that one system with this exact goal was designed and became what is now generally deemed to be the first AIED system. That system was called SCHOLAR.

IN THE BEGINNING: THE FIRST ERA OF AIED RESEARCH, 1970–1982

By 1970, as CAI was entering its golden era, the area of artificial intelligence (AI) was also beginning to come into its own as the avant-garde of computer science. Various sub-disciplines had emerged within AI, such as knowledge representation and reasoning, natural language understanding, problem solving and search and machine learning, among others. It wasn't surprising therefore that researchers interested in supporting human learning would look to AI as a source of ideas, models and techniques. A system to support human learning would ideally know its subject, be able to reason and solve problems about the subject, have good models of how people learn and how that learning can go wrong, be able to communicate with a learner in the learner's own terms, and so on. What was needed was "intelligent" CAI systems, or ICAI.

The SCHOLAR system (Carbonell 1970) is generally recognized to be the first learning support system to seriously attempt to incorporate AI ideas, becoming therefore the first ICAI system and thus the marker of the beginning of the first era of AIED research. SCHOLAR was an inquiry-based system that engaged students[2] in Socratic dialogue about South American geography. Unlike CAI systems, SCHOLAR actually "knew" its subject to a degree, with knowledge about South American geography embedded in a semantic network that allowed it not only to retrieve facts but to make inferences using the reasoning mechanisms built into the semantic network. SCHOLAR also had rudimentary natural language understanding capabilities and its inquiry paradigm lessened the need for it to be totally accurate in its understanding of the student. This is still a key aspect in many successful applied AI systems – finding a context in which the limitations of the system are not perceived by the user of the system as failure.

SCHOLAR stimulated a growing body of research in the 1970s, drawing researchers not only from AI but also from education and cognitive science. The WHY system (Stevens and Collins 1977) was a direct follow-up to SCHOLAR that captured Socratic tutoring strategies as production rules. Collins and Stevens (1981) continued to explore the implications of such pedagogical strategies, leading to a theory of inquiry teaching. The SOPHIE electronic troubleshooting environment (Brown et al. 1975, 1982) allowed students to build simulated electronic circuits and the system would "coach" the student about "bugs" diagnosed in their circuit design. Brown and Burton (1979) continued to explore both coaching and diagnosis in the WEST system. WEST was a coaching system built on top of an educational game, "How the West was Won". Students had to create and solve arithmetic equations to compute their move, and WEST would coach students as to strategies that would improve their progress through the game. Wumpus (Goldstein 1982) was a system that advised students as to the strategies they should follow when playing the adventure game "Hunt the Wumpus" by tracking the evolution of their strategies in a "genetic graph" and suggesting generalizations, specializations or analogies to strategies already used. Ramani and Newell (1973) explored the automatic generation of problems for students to solve, using linguistic and generalization strategies that could reason from a domain-specific semantic network. The BIP-II system (Westcourt et al. 1977) for teaching the BASIC programming language used a "curriculum information network" to determine what to teach next. Sleeman's (1983) LMS represented the rules for solving linear algebra problems as production rules, including both correct rules and "mal-rules", thus allowing the system to recognize and react to a student's own problem-solving steps (and missteps). Genesereth (1982) explored the need to recognize the plans of users of the MACSYMA symbolic algebra system in order to be able to advise them on how to use it better. Rich et al. (1979) also focused on capturing programmer plans as a key element of the "programmer's apprentice", conceived as a system to help programmers at all stages of software design and implementation. Soloway et al.'s (1981) MENO-II system (to help novices learn the programming language Pascal) kept a task-specific library of plans, bugs and explanations for the bugs consisting of common misconceptions that could cause the bugs. Student programs would be matched to the library, with both bugs and underlying misconceptions being pointed out to the students. Some researchers were interested in how the teaching system itself could learn. For example, O'Shea (1979) built a system for teaching students the rules for solving quadratic equations that could reflect on how well the teaching strategies (expressed as production rules) met various educational objectives and could then update the rules accordingly. Another system that itself was able to learn supported students as they learned about symbolic integration (Kimball 1982).

This first era of AIED research resulted in a number of emerging areas of focus. A goal of much of the research was to support students as they actually solved problems, mostly in STEM domains, such as programming, mathematics, science and engineering. The researchers had to solve two main challenges: diagnosing student problem-solving strategies (both correct and buggy) and devising pedagogical approaches to help the student overcome any issues diagnosed. A typical pedagogical approach was that the system should interact as a "guide on the side" rather than taking charge as a formal teacher, that is, that the system should be reactive and adaptive to individual students (and in fact the word "tutor" was used in exactly this sense at that time). Most researchers actually built complete systems to be used by students, but highly targeted at a specific topic, a domain limitation that was crucial for achieving success. A system would usually be tested with students in small-scale studies, but there was very little in the way of empirical evaluation of systems with carefully conducted statistical studies in the modern sense. There were few or no replicated studies by other researchers.

By the late 1970s, there was a growing body of papers that cross referenced each other, and an emerging community of researchers who began to consider the application goal of "intelligent support for learning" as important in and of itself. Several papers had appeared that began to consider student modelling as its own issue, including John Self's (1974) seminal paper and Brown and VanLehn's (1980) formal theory of diagnosis in problem-solving domains called "repair theory". Various representation schemes for subject knowledge were starting to be explored, including production rules and semantic networks. There was explicit work on particular pedagogical strategies such as coaching and inquiry-based learning. Near the end of the decade, Sleeman and Brown guest-edited a special issue of the International Journal of Man-Machine Studies[3] (Volume 11, Issue 1, January 1979) devoted to papers on "intelligent tutoring systems", later expanded into an influential edited book (Sleeman and Brown 1982).

In the 1970s, there was a parallel development in learning support environments, spearheaded by Papert (1980), which did not involve adapting traditional teaching and learning approaches, but instead took a "constructivist" approach. Papert and his team developed a new programming language, Logo, to be used by children. Logo was an easy-to-use language that allowed children to write programs to direct a so-called "turtle" (a small wheeled robot or virtual version) that could draw lines in its wake (on paper or on screen). Children were encouraged to develop programs to explore goals that they found interesting, including drawing pictures but also exploring mathematical and computational ideas and replicating physics experiments, and so on. In fact, while simple to use, the Logo language is powerful and can represent much of geometry and many other mathematical and physics ideas (see Abelson and diSessa 1986). The Logo work stimulated much research worldwide looking into how programming could be used to help students learn, for example learning mathematics with Logo (Howe et al. 1982) or learning history using PROLOG (Ennals 1982). Learning environments such as Scratch in widespread use today are direct descendants of the Logo approach.

EMERGING AS A DISCIPLINE: THE SECOND ERA OF AIED RESEARCH, 1982–1995

The edited collection of important, early papers by Sleeman and Brown (1982) became a bible for an emerging field, marking the start of a second era of AIED research, if not quite yet under that name. In fact, the term "intelligent tutoring system" (ITS) taken from the title of the book became, briefly, the most commonly used term for systems meant to support learners in responsive, one-on-one interactive sessions, before AIED took over.[4] The goal was to achieve the effectiveness of human one-on-one tutoring, which could lead to 2-sigma gains in learning outcomes (Bloom 1984).

The Standard Intelligent Tutoring System Architecture

Early in the second era, a fairly standard intelligent tutoring system architecture emerged, in which an ITS consisted of various modules, typically the domain knowledge component, the student modelling component, the pedagogical component, the communication component and the control component. Some ITS architectures also included a system learning component. In the limit, building an ITS is clearly an "AI complete" problem, but researchers had reason to believe that the educational application had natural constraints that would make it tractable. The knowledge representation problem was limited since only knowledge of the subject domain being tutored needed to be represented and that was often knowledge that was already well codified (especially in STEM domains). The student modelling component could also take advantage of the limited domain and not have to understand ("diagnose") the student beyond his or her subject knowledge (or bugs). The pedagogical component could draw on human tutoring strategies and existing curricula, and did not have to be fully sophisticated as long as the system provided a coherent ordering of domain topics and could be adaptive to the needs of individual students. In many domains, the communication component could take advantage of specialized terminology in the domain to avoid the need to interact with the student in natural language. So, the educational application was constrained enough to make the task of building a tutor tractable, but also interesting enough to provide many challenges to (and opportunities for) the AI techniques of the day. Not all researchers were committed to the standard ITS architecture, but it is a useful lens through which to view AIED research in the second era. Interestingly, the ITS architecture still implicitly or explicitly underlies many AIED systems. It is, for example, at the heart of an influential modern adaptive learning system architecture, the Generalized Intelligent Framework for Tutoring (GIFT) (Sottilare et al. 2017), which is widely used in military training (and other) applications.

Cognitive and Constraint-Based Tutoring Approaches

A highly influential research effort in the second era was dedicated to what became known as the "cognitive tutoring" paradigm, developed under the direction of John Anderson at Carnegie Mellon University. A series of tutoring systems were built in STEM domains, including a LISP tutor (Anderson and Reiser 1985), a geometry tutor (Anderson et al. 1985) and an algebra tutor (Koedinger et al. 1997), each of which drew on Anderson's (1983) ACT* cognitive theory in their design. The goal of these systems was "skill acquisition": to tutor students to actually learn how to solve problems in their domain, for example to learn to program in LISP or to solve algebra problems. Each of the cognitive tutoring systems represented the domain knowledge as production rules that replicated the problem-solving strategies of humans, both correct and buggy. The student modelling component would "trace" students as they solved problems, inferring the production rules whose firing would match their behaviour. When no match was found, students would be interrupted, given hints about what their misconception might be, and not allowed to go on until their behaviour once again matched a correct rule. Such "model tracing" effectively implemented a pedagogical strategy in which a student was constrained at the finest grain size to stay within the rules (the model). This "immediate feedback" strategy was justified by the well-documented importance of correcting student errors quickly, but it could often be perceived to be rigid and even dictatorial.

The cognitive tutoring paradigm has left an indelible mark on AIED. Perhaps the most impressive aspect is that the paradigm is still going strong after 40 years. Many new tutoring systems have been developed over the years and many deep issues have been explored in learning, teaching/tutoring, modelling, system building, evaluation and deployment in real-world situations. In fact, there was a deep commitment made to integrating cognitive tutoring systems into the school system and learning the lessons of such real-world deployment (Koedinger et al. 1997). A number of critical issues arose. One of these was how to integrate a cognitive tutor into a broader technical and social environment. This involved making the system robust and easy to use, training both teachers and students and even providing the teachers with the ability to tune the system to their own needs. The large amount of research into building and deploying cognitive tutors also reflected back into the ACT* theory itself, with Anderson formulating a revised theory to ACT* called ACT-R that came to underpin cognitive tutors in the mid-1990s (Anderson 1993). The cognitive tutoring paradigm shows the value of committing to an approach and following where it leads over the long term, not only in producing a vast amount of research but also in leading to major real-world impact. For a summary of the formative years of cognitive tutoring research, see Anderson et al. (1995).

Many researchers responded to perceived issues with the cognitive tutoring paradigm, particularly the model tracing student modelling approach that led to its "rigid" immediate feedback pedagogy. Ohlsson (1992), for example, tackled the need in the cognitive tutors to represent every possible student bug as mal rules in the tutor's knowledge base. Ohlsson proposed that the rules for correct behaviour be encoded, instead, as constraints. Constraint violations indicated bugs. This meant that the system designer did not need to anticipate all of the ways students could go wrong. Moreover, the student would be much freer to explore without being totally controlled by the system. Of course, the system designer did have to figure out what the student had done wrong when a constraint violation was detected (i.e. what bug they had!) if the system were to help the student to understand their mistake. One particularly long-term commitment to exploring the constraint-based tutoring approach has been led by Tanja Mitrovic. Starting just after the end of the second era Mitrovic (1998) and her team have investigated all aspects of the constraint-based approach, including exploring each component of the ITS architecture, building complete systems, and doing real-world deployment (see Mitrovic and Ohlsson 2016; Chapter 7 by Aleven et al.).

Diagnosis and Student Modelling

Sharing the goals of the constraint-based approach, many other research projects in the second era also targeted the issue of doing flexible diagnosis. Not least of these was the cognitive tutoring group itself, which generalized the fine-grained diagnosis of model tracing to "knowledge tracing" (Corbett and Anderson 1995) where the probability that a student knows any particular rule is kept and continuously updated using Bayesian inference at each opportunity the learner has to apply the rule (and does or doesn't). This allows the tutor to track how well a student has mastered a subject over the many problems they work on. Also, like constraint-based approaches, it alleviates the need to keep an explicit bug library. Students were informed of their progress with a "skill meter" displaying how well they knew the various rules (perhaps the first feature that could be considered "open learner modelling"). The

PROUST system (Johnson and Soloway 1984) was an outgrowth of the MENO-II system that incorporated a much more flexible and less task-specific plan recognition process. In their SCENT programming advisor, Greer and McCalla (1994) represented possible strategies to solve a programming task in granularity hierarchies (related to semantic networks) that allowed the strategy underlying a student's program to be recognized at least at a coarse grain size, even if the student's solution was too distorted for fine-grained recognition. Elsom-Cook (1988) developed bounded student modelling, an approach to diagnosis that recognized student behaviour within a range of possible outcomes that would slowly narrow as more information about the student became available, but at any stage could still be used to guide the student's "discovery process". Weber's (1996) ELM system for tutoring novice programmers kept a growing "episodic" case base, tracking individual learner behaviour that could, over time, allow increasingly refined personalized diagnosis. Kay (1994a) explored the advantages and hazards in using stereotypes as part of a user (including student) modelling system.

Throughout the 1980s, the student modelling component had usually been crafted to a particular domain or set of pedagogical goals. By late in the second era, though, as AI itself began to explore probabilistic methods, AIED researchers began also to experiment with probability, and particularly with Bayesian belief networks, as a principled way of managing uncertainty and change in the student modelling component. Villano's (1992) paper was among the first to raise the issue, followed quickly by a burst of papers in the following year, including Sime (1993), Martin and VanLehn (1993) and Petrushin and Sinitsa (1993). An extensive summary of the state of the probabilistic art in student (and user) modelling near the end of the second era can be found in Jameson (1995). There was also a foray into using fuzzy reasoning (Hawkes et al. 1990) but without much follow-up by others.

The central role of personalization and adaptivity, and thus student modelling, in the AIED systems of the second era resulted in a number of good surveys and collections focused on the subject. Recommended among these are VanLehn's (1988) survey paper and an entire edited collection about student modelling (Greer and McCalla 1994). A very readable paper from this edited collection is an overview of the state of the student modelling art in the late second era by Holt et al. (1994). In another chapter of the same book, Self (1994) provides a masterful analysis of student modelling, unified by a formal perspective. More controversial was Self's (1990) influential "intractable student modelling" paper. Often cited as arguing that student modelling was intractable, the paper actually discussed how to *overcome* difficult student modelling problems.

To this day adaptivity to individual learner differences remains a critical, perhaps defining attribute of AIED. To be sure, learner models now incorporate many more characteristics beyond the largely content-based models of the first quarter century, including affective, motivational and metacognitive attributes (as illustrated by many chapters in this handbook).

Domain Knowledge

In the second era, work was also undertaken on the domain knowledge component. One track of this research was developing qualitative and causal models such as those investigated by White and Frederiksen (1990). The STEAMER system (Hollan et al. 1984) helped naval personnel learn the intricacies of steam boiler plants on ships. At its core, STEAMER's knowledge base consisted of a simulation of a steam boiler that a learner could interact with through a sophisticated graphical interface. The simulation allowed the system to readily represent causal aspects of the steam boiler. STEAMER eventually became part of the formal certification process for naval steam engineers, one of the first directly practical spinoffs of AIED research.

In a similar vein, the Sherlock system (Gott and Lesgold 2000) supported US air force technicians in learning how to use a complex diagnostic device deployed to troubleshoot problems with F-15 jet aircraft. Sherlock's key knowledge component feature was a simulation of the device, but the knowledge component also had declarative descriptions of the function of the device components and coaching rules drawing from a deep cognitive task analysis that provided insight into how technicians made the transition from novice to expert. Learners would solve preset troubleshooting tasks by interacting with the simulation through a visualization of the device control panel, with Sherlock providing personalized feedback and ordering tasks (using its learner and competency models) to help them become experts. The system was remarkably effective, allowing technicians to gain expertise in hours that normally would take years to attain.

Another long-term project was Clancey's (1982a) GUIDON, which transcended the first and second eras. Clancey reasoned that the knowledge base of an expert system could be re-purposed to fuel a system to tutor this expertise. The first system he developed was GUIDON, whose knowledge base consisted of the rules of the MYCIN medical diagnosis expert system. GUIDON's student model was an "overlay" on this knowledge base indicating the degree of belief the system had about the student's knowledge of each rule (observed through the student's behaviour). This could be reasoned about by a separate rule-based pedagogical component that would determine whether or not to proactively intervene to help the student (Clancey 1982b). Clancey found, though, that the MYCIN rules weren't organized in a way that reflected how human doctors reasoned when performing a diagnosis, so he developed NEOMYCIN that separated the medical knowledge (the productions in the MYCIN knowledge base) from the diagnostic strategies, represented as "metarules" that could be reasoned about by the pedagogical component. A series of increasingly sophisticated systems ensued to broaden functionality, drawing on (and contributing to) many mainstream AI ideas (Clancey 1986). Chapter 7 by Aleven et al. in this handbook provides a modern review of domain modelling for AIED systems.

Pedagogical Strategies

The pedagogical component of an ITS is also critical. As Sleeman (1987a) observed, even very good diagnosis is not enough without appropriate remediation strategies. Some researchers explicitly carried out studies into how human teaching strategies could be used to inform intelligent tutoring systems (Goodyear 1991). We have already encountered various pedagogical strategies, including strategies such as the explicit branching through content frames of the CAI systems, immediate feedback in the cognitive tutors, exploration-based learning with coaching in STEAMER and Sherlock and rule-based intervention strategies in the GUIDON-style tutors. In contrast, Peachey and McCalla (1986) did not build a big system but explored a specific issue in pedagogy: how AI-based planning techniques could be deployed to greatly improve upon the explicit CAI branching model, allowing the tutoring system to automatically re-compute a content plan as diagnosed student behaviour changed the student model without the need to anticipate explicitly all possible subsequent steps. This work kicked off the AIED sub-discipline of "instructional planning" (now called "pedagogical planning"). Macmillan and Sleeman (1987) explored how instructional plans could be improved over time by feeding the pedagogical outcomes of previous plans into the future planning process. Vassileva (1990) developed a tutoring system architecture where domain knowledge is localized so completely that the planning system can still work even if deployed in a new domain. Wasson (Brecht et al. 1989) explored the distinction between content planning (what the student should learn) and delivery planning (how the content is presented). Brusilovsky (1992) looked at methodologies for both knowledge and task sequencing. The CIRCSIM-Tutor (Freedman and Evens 1996) used a dialogue planning system to engage cardiophysiology students in tutorial dialogue as a basic pedagogical approach. del Soldato and du Boulay (1995) explored not only how to plan content but also how to plan tactics to motivate a student, one of the first examples of AIED exploring "affective" dimensions, not just content, an area that would boom in subsequent eras of AIED research (see Chapter 5 by Arroyo et al.). Chapter 9 by Aleven et al. in this handbook explores six "instructional approaches" that are currently being used by AIED systems.

Authoring Environments and Frameworks

For ITS architectures that were to be used in many experiments over time, a natural goal was to develop a shell or an authoring environment to shorten the design–implementation–evaluation–redesign cycle. Several such authoring environments were developed, each of which was tailored to a specific ITS architecture, such as Sleeman's (1987b) PIXIE environment, Vivet's (1989) shell for knowledge-based tutors, Anderson and Pelletier's (1991) development system for model-tracing tutors, Gecsei and Frasson's (1994) SAFARI environment to support industrial training or Ikeda and Mizoguchi's (1994) FITS system. Kay's (1994b) um-toolkit was more widely applicable but was focused on only the user modelling component of an ITS (or other adaptive system). Murray's (1999) survey a few years later is the definitive source of information on authoring environments in the early years of AIED. Chapter 12 by Blessing et al. in this handbook is a modern survey of authoring environments for AIED systems.

As the many bespoke intelligent tutoring system architectures exploded onto the scene in the 1980s, there was also a desire for some sort of framework or formalism that would allow better cross-system comparison. Just about every researcher, it seems, tried their hand at writing issue-oriented papers or surveys that tried to help organize the field, with varying degrees of insight. Here are just a few of the more influential of such papers: Sleeman (1987a), Rickel (1989), Nwana (1990), Shute and Regian (1990), Winkels and Breuker (1992), Brusilovsky (1995) and the most influential of all, Wenger's (1987) *tour-de-force* book providing a deep analysis of the whole field. There were many workshops and invited talks at conferences with the same goal. From 1988 through 1993, there was even a NATO-sponsored program on "advanced educational technology" that funded some 25 international research workshops and scientific institutes. The NATO program was a key building block for AIED, forging deep and recurring interactions among many AIED researchers, particularly those in Europe and North America. The program also generated a large number of books, since each workshop spun off an edited collection (published by Springer) of papers by workshop participants. The book based on the first workshop was edited by Scanlon and O'Shea (1992), while that for the final workshop was edited by Liao (1996). One of the most influential events in the NATO program was a scientific institute that brought social scientists and computer scientists together for two weeks of deep interaction – see Jones and Winne (1992). Perhaps the most ambitious idea for unifying the field was, unsurprisingly, proposed by Self (1992), who suggested in a well-argued paper that a new field should be defined, analogous to computational linguistics, called "computational mathetics" (mathetics meaning "pertaining to learning"), which he provisionally defined to be "the study of learning, and how it may be promoted, using the techniques, concepts and methodologies of computer science and artificial intelligence". There was no follow-up to computational mathetics, but subsequent eras of AIED research have seen no shortage of papers providing theoretical perspectives on the field (including chapters in this handbook, for example Chapter 3 by Ohlsson and Chapter 25 by Williamson et al., taking a sociopolitico-economic perspective on issues in AIED).

Expanding the Range of AIED Domains

The focus in the second era was typically on "hard science" domains at the high school or university level, but there were other domains. We've already seen in Sherlock and STEAMER that workplace skills were also targeted, as was medicine in the GUIDON and CIRCSIM systems. Lajoie et al. (1995) focused on biology (with medical implications) in their Bio-World system. Acker et al. (1991) built an explanation-based tutor for botany. Gecsei and Frasson (1994) were interested in industrial training. Language learning was a focus for some, such as Bull et al. (1993), Tasso et al. (1992) and Goodfellow and Laurillard (1994). There was even an entire NATO-sponsored workshop on "foreign language learning" (Swartz and Yazdani 1992). Ashley and Aleven (1991) ventured into what we would now call the "ill-defined" domain of teaching legal argumentation. These atypical domains often required new kinds of techniques, drawing, for example, on natural language understanding and generation (for language learning and also useful in medicine and botany) and case-based reasoning techniques for legal argument. In subsequent eras of AIED research, such ill-defined domains became much more common (see, for example, Chapter 13 by Ye Mao et al. on supporting learning in open-ended domains).

The ITS paradigm was often accused of being essentially "instructivist", with too much tutor control. Some ITS systems definitely fit this bill. However, there were also many other projects that were much more "constructivist" in philosophy. As we've already seen, systems like SOPHIE, STEAMER and Sherlock emphasized a pedagogy where students would be able to much more freely explore their environment as they solved problems. There were many "discovery" environments often inspired by the microworld approach first developed in the Logo project. For example, Vivet (1996) developed "micro-robots' to motivate students to explore geometric concepts. Balacheff and Sutherland's (1993) mathematical discovery environment, *cabri-géometre*, came with a tool kit that allowed students to "play" with geometric ideas. White's (1993) Thinkertools provided a series of increasingly sophisticated microworlds through which students could progress as they explored physics concepts. The SMISLE project of de Jong et al. (1994) created simulation-based learning environments in which students could immerse themselves, aided by instructional support tools. Shute and Glaser's (1990) Smithtown inquiry environment allowed students a lot of freedom to create hypotheses about microeconomic principles and explore their implications while at the same time providing ITS-style feedback. An influential edited collection (Lajoie and Derry 1993a) contains chapters discussing a range of instructivist vs constructivist systems from the second era, organized as to whether the system uses or doesn't use student modelling. Lajoie and Derry's (1993b) introductory chapter is a thoughtful discussion of student modelling and pedagogical approaches, which argues that whichever approach is used, modellers and non-modellers should learn from each other.

As the second era progressed, ideas from situated learning (Lave and Wenger 1991), with its emphasis on the social context of learning, began to filter into AIED. The most committed situated learning advocates rejected almost the entire AIED agenda, arguing that knowledge was as much in the environment as in the mind and that representation-oriented approaches were fundamentally misguided. Much heated discussion ensued, with some situated learning advocates leaving AIED. Even so, many learning technology researchers began to take on situated ideas and explore much more avidly the social context of learning. For example, Schank et al. (1994) developed systems based on "goal-based scenarios" that allowed learners to be immersed in realistic situations in which they learned as a by-product of achieving their goals. Work such as this foreshadowed later work on "serious" games for learning (see Chapter 20 by McLaren and Nguyen on AIED for game-based learning) and an increasing interest in professional learning.

Another pedagogical philosophy that began to be explored was "cognitive apprenticeship" (Collins et al. 1989). In AIED, this took the form of creating "scaffolding" to support the student as they began to learn, and then fading this scaffolding as they gained expertise. Student modelling could be an important part of doing this. Conati and VanLehn (1996), for example, were able to show how their student modelling system could be used to tailor the scaffolding and fading provided to students as they explored physics concepts. The instructivist orientation of many intelligent tutoring systems was also contrasted by research that explicitly re-oriented the system to work in a collaborative mode. Verdejo (1996), for example, looked at how technology could mediate collaboration in a distance learning context. Often AIED work on collaboration in this era took the form of creating an artificial agent to work as a collaborator. Chan and Baskin (1988) introduced the idea of including an artificial "learning companion" in addition to the tutor and the student. Dillenbourg and Self (1992) created an artificial co-learner with whom the actual learner could have a conversation, implemented in a microworld where learners could explore the implications of various decisions about electoral seat distribution. Dillenbourg continued to develop collaborative learning environments populated by artificial agents in systems like MEMOLAB (Dillenbourg et al. 1994), which had roles for many different kinds of agents taking on various roles (expert, tutor, learning companion, etc.). VanLehn et al. (1994) discussed various ways in which simulated agents (and simulation more generally) could play an important part in AIED going forward, a good prediction given the subsequent explosion of work on simulated pedagogical agents (see, for example, Chapter 27.3 by Lane) and the more recent growing interest in AIED in using simulation as part of system design and testing.

Another area of AIED research in the second era was reflection and metacognition (Collins and Brown 1988). One reflective activity is "self-explanation", which had been shown by Chi et al. (1989) in human subject experiments to improve the problem-solving skills of students learning physics. VanLehn et al. (1992) created a rule-based computational model called Cascade that could replicate the self-explanation effect. Computation, of course, also allows the building of tools to support learning at a metacognitive level. Chan's (1991) Integration-Kid system supported the metacognitive approach of reciprocal learning (aka "learning by teaching"), where the role of the student was to teach the system rather than the other way around. Nichols (1994) built a reciprocal learning system with a proof-of-concept trial carried out in the domain of qualitative economics. His paper provides a good summary of AIED work and perspectives on learning by teaching late in the second era. Another metacognitive track was open learner modelling, now a major stream of AIED research. Cumming and Self (1991) were among the first to discuss opening the learner model so that the learner could interact with it and reflect on what they knew by seeing what the system thought they knew. Judy Kay would operationalize this idea much more fully over the coming years in her exploration of "scrutable" learner models, starting with papers such as Cook and Kay (1994) and including a chapter in this handbook (Chapter 6 by Kay et al.). Chapter 4 by Azevedo and Wiedbusch is a full discussion of current issues in metacognition.

Some AIED researchers were interested in building advisory systems, rather than fully fledged ITSs, providing help and advice only. Eurohelp (Breuker et al. 1987), for example, was an architecture for building systems that would help users as they went about their tasks "looking over their shoulders and interrupting when appropriate". The SCENT programming advisor (McCalla et al. 1986) would help university students learning LISP to discover the strategy errors in the programs they were writing. Sharples et al. (1989) developed a Writer's Assistant to help professional writers with the process of writing. Such advising systems have continued to attract the attention of AIED researchers (see Chapter 27.11 by Dimitrova, for example), often in the context of workplace and/or lifelong learning.

Evaluation and Deployment

When an AIED system was deployed with actual students, the first goal was normally to look for learning gains, seeking the elusive 2-sigma effect. But even as full ITSs with significant capabilities were created and control group studies were carried out, it was usually the case that students using the ITS (the treatment group) didn't statistically outperform those learning in some other way (the control group). Quite frequently, students in the treatment group would learn faster, sometimes much faster as in the Sherlock system, but other measures of success were elusive. Towards the end of the second era, therefore, it was not surprising that AIED researchers began to reflect on the evaluation problem. Evaluation is very difficult in AIED, since it requires evaluating an adaptive system, whose knowledge base and student model are always changing, deployed in a noisy educational setting where the very goal is to stimulate ongoing change in students. So, it was apropos that after more than two decades of AIED research, a special issue of the AIED journal (volume 4, 1993) was devoted to evaluation, with papers discussing quantitative and qualitative, as well as formal and informal evaluation methodologies.[5] Evaluation was to become an ever more central issue in AIED going forward (see Chapter 22 by VanLehn).

Many early systems were content with demonstrating a proof of concept, with deployment only a distant long-term objective. When wider deployment was attempted, it often revealed that the AIED system design had failed to take into account personal, social, organizational and cultural factors that were critical in supporting learners in the real world. Starting with STEAMER (Hollan et al. 1984), however, successful real-world deployment began to happen, and soon other systems followed suit, with cognitive tutors being deployed in schools (Koedinger et al. 1997) and Sherlock being used by the military (Gott and Lesgold 2000). This led not only to much better insight into the real issues facing an AIED system if it were to be successfully deployed, but also to the possibility of commercial spinoffs of AIED research. Such commercialization is now booming, on both the small scale (see Chapter 24 by Luckin and Cukurova) and large scale (see Chapter 23 by Ritter and Koedinger).

AIED – THE FIRST 25 YEARS: TAKING STOCK

The first AIED era was marked by the pioneering explorations of an ambitious and disparate set of paradigm-breaking computer scientists and social scientists investigating how computational ideas could transform teaching and learning. The second AIED era was fundamentally about the coming together of AIED as a discipline, culminating in shared paradigms and the emergence of subdisciplines such as student modelling, instructional planning, and so on. The international AIED society was established with its own AIED journal and its own AIED conference.[6] There were also significant conferences organized outside of the society's purview, including the ITS conference spearheaded by Claude Frasson and Gilles Gauthier, the Learning Sciences conference, first established in lieu of the 1991 AIED conference by Roger Schank, and regional conferences such as the International Conference on Computers in Education (ICCE) coordinated by Asia-Pacific AIED researchers. All of these are still going strong.

Another 25 years of AIED research have now passed. Many issues have been explored and systems built. New sub-disciplines have arisen such as the related areas of educational data mining (EDM) and learning analytics and knowledge (LAK; see Chapter 15 by Pozdniakov et al.). AIED is no longer the only game in town. The Learning Sciences quickly took on a different focus from AIED, and soon came to be considered as a separate discipline by many in both the Learning Sciences and AIED.[7] Other communities emerged more or less independently of AIED. The computer-supported collaborative learning (CSCL) area, for example, spun off from the HCI-based computer-supported cooperative work community during the second era of AIED research with the first CSCL conference in 1995,[8] right at the end of the second era. Massive open online courses (MOOCs) later exploded onto the scene without much reference to AIED, and the corresponding learning at scale (L@S) subdiscipline is now its own very active community.

This "diaspora" has had its advantages in allowing focused exploration of various perspectives, but the opportunities for researchers with diverse perspectives to interact and learn from one another has been diminished. So, it is heartening that recently there has been a recognition by AIED and other advanced learning technology communities that there is much to be gained by trying to re-establish deeper and broader links. The formation of the International Alliance to Advance Learning in the Digital Era (ISSLDE) in 2016 was a commitment by many of these communities to work together to learn from each other and to have a stronger impact on the world (https://alliancelss.com/). Following up on this, the 2018 "Festival of Learning" in London was designed as a multi-conference with the goal of bringing the AIED, Learning Sciences and L@S conferences together.

Looking back to the early years of a research discipline can provide interesting perspectives on the "modern" research landscape. So, I would like to conclude this chapter with some lessons for AIED today, drawn from the first quarter century of AIED research.

- Those who don't know history may be doomed to repeat it. As I have tried to show throughout this chapter, many (most?) current AIED ideas can trace their roots back to the first and second eras of AIED research. There are many papers from these early eras that can still provide valuable insight today.
- The old can be new again. Machine learning was incorporated into some AIED systems in the early eras, but without much immediate follow-up during the first quarter century. But the subsequent machine-learning revolution in AI and the availability of vast amounts of online data about learners and the learning process led to machine learning becoming widely practical and useful in AIED. So, maybe other neglected early ideas could become "great again". Is it time to revisit the genetic graph or computational mathetics or bounded student modelling or other abandoned early ideas?

- It is useful to stick to a paradigm and to continue to develop it. The cognitive tutoring paradigm started in the early years of AIED and is still going strong, having explored a vast number of issues, built a large number of systems and spun off many successful commercial applications. The issues AIED is investigating are hard and complex, and it can take decades to explore the implications of an approach. The constraint-based tutoring framework (Mitrovic and Ohlsson 2016) and the ASSISTments platform (Heffernan and Heffernan 2014) are two subsequent examples of how long-term commitment to a paradigm can yield major rewards and insights.
- The flip side is that the field as a whole should welcome a diversity of approaches. As this chapter has shown, such diversity can yield all sorts of new and interesting techniques, pedagogical frameworks and ideas.
- AIED should not, narrowly, *only* be AI and education. To be sure, during the first quarter century AIED drew liberally from AI and cognitive science and education but it also incorporated ideas from other computer science areas (simulation, software engineering, programming languages, distributed systems ...) and other social science disciplines (anthropology, sociology ...). Since the mid-1990s, mutually reinforcing changes in technology and society have proceeded at an ever-quicker pace and, for the most part, AIED has continued to track the rapidly changing research frontier across a wide range of computer science and social science disciplines. More change is ahead so this must continue.
- Influence can go both ways. In the early years, AIED didn't just adapt ideas from other disciplines, but actually also had influence on these other disciplines. In the 1980s and 1990s, major AI conferences featured "education applications" in their calls for papers and many had at least one AIED paper session; similarly, for cognitive science and education research. It is not so clear that AIED is quite so influential any more. This seems especially true in the case of AI. Yet, there are opportunities for AIED to influence AI again, since, as in the early days, the education application still has the right "forcing functions" for AI. For example, AIED could be a home for "model-based" AI research as it was in the early days. In an AIED system, there have to be explanations comprehensible to learners and opportunities for learners to reflect on what has been learned (or not learned), which require both a higher-level symbolic representational perspective than that provided by neural networks and a careful design of the interaction protocols to satisfy pedagogical goals.
- It is important to give new ideas time to mature. Not every paper needs to fully validate its hypotheses the first time out. There are many examples of such papers in the first quarter century. Self's (1974) very early student modelling ideas opened the way to the development of the student modelling sub-area, which, in turn, was one of the "founding partners" in the emergence of the user modelling, adaptation and personalization (UMAP) research area. Peachey and McCalla's (1986) simple demonstration of how AI-based planning could be used in a tutoring context led to the subarea of pedagogical planning. Chan and Baskin's (1988) speculations on "studying with the Prince" eventually grew into the pedagogical agents area. We need to welcome into AIED new and different ideas, even if at first they are not quite fully baked.

Looking back, it is remarkable how dynamic AIED was during its first quarter century, both in its ambitions and in its eclectic range of perspectives, ideas, techniques and people. AIED really was *the* exciting place to be for researchers wanting to explore cutting-edge issues in learning technology, whatever their background. I hope that this chapter will play its own small role in encouraging researchers from every advanced learning technology community today to more fully engage with one another by reconnecting to a shared and illustrious past.

ACKNOWLEDGEMENTS

I would like to thank Benedict du Boulay, Tanja Mitrovic and Kalina Yacef for inviting me to write this chapter. My gratitude also goes to Tak-Wai Chan, Peter Goodyear, Monique Grandbastien, Lewis Johnson, Alan Lesgold, Tim O'Shea, Mike Sharples, Kurt VanLehn, Etienne Wenger-Trayner and Phil Winne for providing interesting insights into the early years of AIED. Finally, I'd like to thank the reviewers of an earlier version of this chapter for helping to make this version better. Of course, this chapter ultimately is my own take on events. Hopefully, I have been true to the spirit, energy and ambitions of the pioneers of the first quarter century of AIED research, even though space limitations have meant that I have had to leave out so many worthy contributors and contributions.

NOTES

1. See Chapter 3 by Ohlsson for a current perspective on the "tight intertwining" of AIED with education, psychology and AI.
2. A learner was usually referred to as a "student" throughout much of the first quarter century of AIED research, but as time wore on and AIED began to move into non-traditional learning domains, "learner" came to be seen as a more general term.
3. IJMMS, a human–computer interaction journal that was often favoured by AIED researchers of the first era, has since changed its name to Human–Computer Studies.
4. The term "artificial intelligence and education" also began to be used early in the second era, initially attached to conferences in 1983 and 1985 hosted by Masoud Yazdani in Exeter, UK (see Lawler and Yazdani 1987). Gradually, "*in*" replaced "*and*", and "artificial intelligence in education" became the increasingly common term for the field.
5. Mark and Greer's (1993) paper from this issue has been particularly influential.
6. For an insider's look at the formative years of these scholarly structures, see Self (2016).
7. See Pea (2016) and Lee (2017) for insight into the history of the Learning Sciences.
8. The CSCL community later joined the International Society for the Learning Sciences.

REFERENCES

Abelson, H. and diSessa, A. (1986). *Turtle Geometry: The Computer as a Medium for Exploring Mathematics*. MIT Press.
Acker, L., Lester, J., Souther, A. and Porter, B. (1991). Generating coherent explanations to answer students' questions. In H. Burns, J.W. Parlett, and C.L. Redfield (eds.), *Intelligent Tutoring Systems: Evolutions in Design*. Lawrence Erlbaum, 151–176.
Anderson, J.R. (1983). *The Architecture of Cognition*. Harvard University Press.
Anderson, J.R. (1993). *Rules of the Mind*. Lawrence Erlbaum.
Anderson, J.R., Boyle, C.F. and Yost, G. (1985). The geometry tutor. *Proceedings of the 9th International Joint Conference on Artificial Intelligence*, Los Angeles, 1–7.
Anderson, J.R., Corbett, A.T., Koedinger, K. and Pelletier, R. (1995). Cognitive tutors: Lessons learned. *The Journal of Learning Sciences*, 4, 167–207.

Anderson, J.R. and Pelletier, R. (1991). A development system for model-tracing tutors. In *Proceedings 1st International Conference of the Learning Sciences*, Evanston, IL, 1–8.

Anderson, J.R. and Reiser, B.J. (1985). The LISP tutor. *Byte*, *10*(4), 159–175.

Ashley, K.D. and Aleven, V. (1991). Toward an intelligent tutoring system for teaching law students to argue with cases. In *Proceedings 3rd International Conference on Artificial Intelligence and Law*, 42–52.

Balacheff, N. and Sutherland, R. (1993). Epistemological domain of validity of microworlds: the case of logo and cabri-géometre. In *Proceedings IFIP TC3/WG3, 3rd Working Conference on Lessons from Learning*, 137–150.

Bloom, B.S. (1984). The 2 sigma problem: The search for methods of group instruction as effective as one-to-one tutoring. *Educational Researcher*, *13*(6), 4–16.

Brecht (Wasson), B., McCalla, G.I., Greer, J.E. and Jones, M.L. (1989). Planning the Content of Instruction. In *Proceedings of 4th International Conference on Artificial Intelligence in Education*, Amsterdam, 32–41.

Breuker, J., Winkels, R. and Sandberg, J. (1987). A shell for intelligent help systems. In *Proceedings of 10th International Joint Conference on Artificial Intelligence (Vol. 1)*, Milan, 167–173.

Brown, J.S. (1990). Toward a new epistemology for learning. In Frasson and Gauthier (1990), 266–282.

Brown, J.S., Burton, R.R. and Bell A. (1975). SOPHIE: A step toward a reactive learning environment. *International Journal of Man-Machine Studies*, *7*, 675–696.

Brown, J.S., Burton, R.R. and de Kleer, J. (1982). Pedagogical, natural language, and knowledge engineering techniques in SOPHIE I, II, and III. In Sleeman and Brown, 227–282.

Brown, J.S. and VanLehn, K. (1980). Repair theory: A generative theory of bugs in procedural skills. *Cognitive Science Journal*, *4*(4), 379–426.

Brusilovsky, P.L. (1992). A framework for intelligent knowledge sequencing and task sequencing. In *Proceedings of 2nd International Conference on Intelligent Tutoring Systems*, Montréal, 499–506.

Brusilovsky, P.L. (1995). Intelligent learning environments for programming: The case for integration and adaptation. In *Proceedings of International Conference on Artificial Intelligence in Education*, Washington, DC, 1–8.

Bull, S., Pain, H.G. and Brna, P. (1993). Collaboration and reflection in the construction of a student model for intelligent computer assisted language learning. In *Proceedings of 7th International PEG Conference*, Edinburgh.

Burton, R.R. and Brown, J.S. (1979). An investigation of computer coaching for informal learning activities. *International Journal of Man-Machine Studies*, *11*(1), 5–24. Also in Sleeman and Brown (1982).

Carbonell, J. R. (1970). AI in CAI: An artificial-intelligence approach to computer-assisted instruction. *IEEE Transactions on Man-Machine Systems*, *11*(4), 190–202.

Chambers, J.A. and Sprecher, J.W. (1980). Computer assisted instruction: Current trends and critical issues. *Communications of the ACM*, *23*(6), 332–342.

Chan, T.-W. (1991). Integration-Kid: A learning companion system. In *Proceedings of 12th International Joint Conference on Artificial Intelligence (Vol. 2)*, Sydney, Australia, 1094–1099.

Chan, T.-W. and Baskin, A.B. (1988). Studying with the prince: The computer as a learning companion. *Proceedings of 1st International Conference on Intelligent Tutoring Systems*, Montréal, 194–200.

Chi, M.T., Bassok, M., Lewis, M.W., Reimann, P. and Glaser, R. (1989). Self-explanations: how students study and use examples in learning to solve problems. *Cognitive Science Journal*, *13*, 259–294.

Clancey, W.J. (1982a). GUIDON. In Barr and Feigenbaum (eds.), *The Handbook of Artificial Intelligence*. Kauffmann, 267–278.

Clancey, W.J. (1982b). Tutoring rules for guiding a case method dialogue. In Sleeman and Brown (1982), 201–225.

Clancey, W.J. (1986). From GUIDON to NEOMYCIN and HERACLES in twenty short lessons. *AI Magazine*, *7*(3), 40–60.

Collins, A. and Brown, J.S. (1988). The computer as a tool for learning through reflection. In A.M. Lesgold and H. Mandl (eds.), *Learning Issues for Intelligent Tutoring Systems*. Springer, 1–18.

Collins, A., Brown, J.S. and Newman, S.E. (1989). Cognitive apprenticeship: Teaching the craft of reading, writing and mathematics. In L.B. Resnick (ed.), *Knowing, Learning, and Instruction: Essays in Honor of Robert Glaser*. Erlbaum.

Collins, A.M. and Stevens, A.L. (1981). A cognitive theory of interactive teaching. Bolt Beranek and Newman Technical Report, Cambridge, MA, 55 p.

Conati, C. and VanLehn, K. (1996). Probabilistic plan recognition for cognitive apprenticeship. In *Proceedings of 18th Annual Conference of the Cognitive Science Society*, 403–408.

Cook, R. and Kay, J. (1994). The justified user model: a viewable, explained user model. In *Proceedings of 4th International Conference on User Modeling*, Hyannis, MA, 145–150.

Corbett, A.T. and Anderson, J.R. (1995). Knowledge tracing: Modeling the acquisition of procedural knowledge. *User Modeling and User-Adapted Interaction Journal*, *4*, 253–278.

Costa, E. (ed.) (1992). *New Directions for Intelligent Tutoring Systems*. NATO Workshop, Springer.

Cumming, G.D. and Self, J.A. (1991). Learner modelling in collaborative intelligent educational systems. In Goodyear (1991), 85–104.

de Jong, T., van Joolingen, W., Scott, D., de Hoog, R., Lapied, L. and Valent, R. (1994). SMISLE: System for multimedia integrated simulation learning environments. In T. de Jong and L. Sarti, L. (eds.), *Design and Production of Multimedia and Simulation-Based Learning Material*, Springer, 133–165.

del Soldato, T. and du Boulay, B. (1995). Implementation of motivational tactics in tutoring systems. *Journal of Artificial Intelligence in Education*, *6*, 337–378.

Dillenbourg, P. and Self, J.A. (1992). People power: A human-computer collaborative learning system. In *Proceedings of 2nd International Conference on Intelligent Tutoring Systems*, Montréal, 651–660.

Dillenbourg, P., Hilario, M., Mendelsohn, P., Schneider, D. and Borcic, B. (1994). Intelligent learning environments. In *Proceedings of 2nd NRP23 Symposium on Artificial Intelligence and Robotics*, 57–74.

Elsom-Cook, M.T. (1988). Guided discovery tutoring and bounded user modelling. In Self, J.A. (ed.), *Artificial Intelligence and Human Learning*. Chapman and Hall.

Ennals, R. (1982). History teaching and artificial intelligence. *Teaching History*, *33*, 3–5.

Frasson, C. and Gauthier, G. (eds.) (1990). *Intelligent Tutoring Systems: At the Crossroads of Artificial Intelligence and Education*. Ablex.

Freedman, R. and Evens, M.W. (1996). Generating and revising hierarchical multi-turn text plans in an ITS. In *Proceedings of 3rd International Conference on Intelligent Tutoring Systems*, Montréal, 632–640.

Gecsei, J. and Frasson, C. (1994). SAFARI: an environment for creating tutoring systems in industrial training. In *Proceedings EdMedia94 Conference*, Vancouver.

Genesereth, M.R. (1982). The role of plans in intelligent teaching systems. In Sleeman and Brown (1982), 137–155.

Goldstein, I. (1982). The Genetic Graph: A representation for the evolution of procedural knowledge. In Sleeman and Brown (1982), 51–77.

Goodfellow, R. and Laurillard, D. (1994). Modeling learning processes in lexical CALL, *CALICO Journal*, 19–46.

Goodyear, P. (ed.) (1991). *Teaching Knowledge and Intelligent Tutoring*. Ablex.

Gott, S. and Lesgold, A.M. (2000). Competence in the workplace: how cognitive performance models and situated instruction can accelerate skill acquisition. In R. Glaser (ed.), *Advances in Educational Psychology. Educational Design and Cognitive Science* (Vol. 5). Lawrence Erlbaum, 239–327.

Greer, J.E. and McCalla, G.I. (eds.) (1994). *Student Modelling: The Key to Individualized Knowledge-Based Instruction*. NATO Workshop, Springer.

Hawkes, L.W., Derry, S.J. and Rundensteiner, E.A. (1990). Individualized tutoring using an intelligent fuzzy temporal relational database. *International Journal of Man-Machine Studies*, *33*, 409–429.

Heffernan, N.T. and Heffernan, C.L. (2014). The ASSISTments ecosystem: Building a platform that brings scientists and teachers together for minimally invasive research on human learning and teaching. *International Journal of Artificial Intelligence in Education*, *24*(4), 470–497.

Hollan, J.D., Hutchins, E.L. and Weitzman, L. (1984). STEAMER: An interactive inspectable simulation based training system. *AI Magazine*, Summer, 15–27.

Holt, P., Dubs, S., Jones, M. and Greer, J.E. (1994). The state of student modelling. In Greer and McCalla (1994), 3–35.

Howe, J.A.M., Ross, P.M., Johnson, K.R., Plane, F. and Inglis, R. (1982). Teaching mathematics through programming in the classroom. *Computers and Education*, *6*(1), 85–91.

Ikeda, M. and Mizoguchi, R. (1994). FITS: A framework for ITS – A computational model of tutoring. *Journal of Artificial Intelligence in Education*, 5(3), 319–348.

Jameson, A. (1995). Numerical uncertainty management in user and student modeling: An overview of systems and issues. *User Modeling and User-Adapted Interaction Journal*, 5(3), 193–251.

Johnson, W.L. and Soloway, E. (1984). Intention-based diagnosis of programming errors. In *Proceedings National Conference on Artificial Intelligence (AAAI-84)*, Austin, TX, 162–168.

Jones, M. and Winne, P.H. (eds.). (1992). *Adaptive Learning Environments: Foundations and Frontiers*. NATO Research Institute, Springer.

Kay, J. (1994a). Lies, damned lies and stereotypes: pragmatic approximations of users. In *Proceedings of 4th International Conference on User Modeling*, Hyannis, MA, 73–78.

Kay, J. (1994b). The um toolkit for cooperative user modelling. *User Modeling and User-Adapted Interaction*, 4(3), 149–196.

Kimball, R. (1982). A self-improving tutor for symbolic integration. In Sleeman and Brown (1982), 283–308.

Koedinger, K.R., Anderson, J.R., Hadley, W.H. and Mark, M.A. (1997). Intelligent tutoring goes to school in the big city. *International Journal of Artificial Intelligence in Education*, 8, 30–43.

Lajoie, S.P and Derry, S.J. (eds.) (1993a). *Computers as Cognitive Tools*. Erlbaum.

Lajoie, S.P. and Derry, S.J. (1993b). A middle camp for (un)intelligent instructional computing: an introduction. In Lajoie and Derry (1993a), 9–20.

Lajoie, S.P., Greer, J.E., Munsie, S., Wilkie, T.V., Guerrera, C. and Aleong, P. (1995). Establishing an argumentation environment to foster scientific reasoning with Bio-World. In *Proceedings of International Conference on Computers in Education*, Singapore, 89–96.

Lave, J. and Wenger, E. (1991). *Situated Learning: Legitimate Peripheral Participation*. Cambridge University Press.

Lawler, R. and Yazdani, M. (1987) (eds.). *Artificial Intelligence and Education: Learning Environments and Tutoring Systems* (Vol. 1). Intellect Books.

Lee, V. (2017). A short history of the learning sciences. In R.E. West (ed.), *Foundations of Learning and Instructional Design Technology*. Pressbooks.

Liao, T.T. (ed.) (1996). *Advanced Educational Technology: Research Issues and Future Potential*. NATO Workshop, Springer.

Macmillan, S.A. and Sleeman, D.H. (1987). An architecture for a self-improving instructional planner for intelligent tutoring systems. *Computational Intelligence Journal*, 3(1), 17–27.

Mark, M.A. and Greer, J.E. (1993). Evaluation methodologies for intelligent tutoring systems. *Journal of Artificial Intelligence in Education*, 4(3/4), 129–153.

Martin, J. D. and VanLehn, K. (1993). OLAE: progress toward a multi-activity, Bayesian student modeler. In *Proceedings of 6th International Conference on Artificial Intelligence in Education*, Edinburgh, 410–417.

McCalla, G.I., Bunt, R.B. and Harms, J.J. (1986). The design of the SCENT automated advisor. *Computational Intelligence*, 2(1), 76–92.

McCalla, G.I. and Greer, J.E. (1994). Granularity-based reasoning and belief revision in student models. In Greer and McCalla (1994), 9–62.

Merrill, M.D., Schneider, E.W. and Fletcher, K.A. (1980). *Instructional Design Library (Vol 40): TICCIT*. Educational Technology Publications.

Mitrovic, A. (1998). A knowledge-based teaching system for SQL. In *Proceedings of ED-MEDIA*, 1027–1032.

Mitrovic, A. and Ohlsson, S. (2016). Implementing CBM: SQL-Tutor after fifteen years. *International Journal of Artificial Intelligence in Education*, 26(1), 150–159.

Murray, T. (1999). Authoring intelligent tutoring systems: An analysis of the state of the art. *International Journal of Artificial Intelligence in Education*, 10, 98–129.

Nichols, D.M. (1994). Issues in designing learning by teaching systems. In *Proceedings of East-West International Conference on Computer Technologies in Education (EW-ED'94)*, Crimea, Ukraine, 176–181.

Nwana, H.S. (1990). Intelligent tutoring systems: an overview. *Artificial Intelligence Review, 4*, 251–277.

Ohlsson, S. (1992). Constraint-based student modeling. *Journal of Artificial Intelligence in Education*, *3*(4), 429–447.

O'Shea, T. (1979). A self-improving quadratic tutor, *International Journal of Man-Machine Studies*, *11*(1), 97–124.

Papert, S. (1980). *Mindstorms*. Basic Books.

Pea, R. (2016). The prehistory of the learning sciences. In M.A. Evans, M.J. Packer, and R.K Sawyer (eds.), *Reflections on the Learning Sciences*. Cambridge University Press.

Peachey, D. and McCalla, G.I. (1986). Using planning techniques in intelligent tutoring systems. *International Journal of Man-Machine Studies*, *24*(1), 77–98.

Petrushin, V.A. and K.M. Sinitsa (1993). Using probabilistic reasoning techniques for learner modeling. In *Proceedings of 6th International Conference on Artificial Intelligence in Education*, Edinburgh, 418–425.

Pressey, S.L. (1926). A simple apparatus which gives tests and scores and teaches. *School and Society*, *23*, 373–376.

Rahmlow, H. F., Fratini, R. C., and Ghesquiere, J. R. (1980). *PLATO: Instructional Design Library* (Vol 30). Educational Technology Publications.

Ramani, S. and Newell, A. (1973). *On the Generation of Problems*. Technical Report, Carnegie Mellon University.

Rich, C., Shrobe, H.E. and Waters, R.C. (1979). Overview of the Programmer's Apprentice. In *Proceedings of 6th International Joint Conference on Artificial Intelligence (Vol. 2)*, Tokyo, 827–828.

Rickel, J.W. (1989). Intelligent computer-aided instruction: A survey organized around system components. *IEEE Transactions on Systems, Man, and Cybernetics*, *19*(1), 40–57.

Scanlon, E. and T. O'Shea, T. (eds.) (1992). *New Directions in Educational Technology*. NATO Workshop, Springer.

Schank, R.C., Fano, A., Bell, B., and Jona, M. (1994). The design of goal-based scenarios. *Journal of the Learning Sciences*, *3*(4), 305–345.

Self, J.A. (1974). Student models in computer-aided instruction. *International Journal of Man-Machine Studies*, *6*(2), 261–276.

Self, J.A. (1990). Bypassing the intractable problem of student modeling. In Frasson and Gauthier (1990), 107–123.

Self, J.A. (1992). Computational Mathetics: the missing link in intelligent tutoring systems research? In Costa (1992), 38–56.

Self, J.A. (1994). Formal approaches to student modelling. In Greer and McCalla (1994), 295–352.

Self, J.A. (2016). The birth of IJAIED. *International Journal of Artificial Intelligence in Education*, *26*(1), 4–12.

Sharples, M., Goodlet, J., and Pymberton, L. (1989). Developing a writer's assistant. *Computers and Writing*, 22–37.

Shute, V.J. and Glaser, R. (1990). A large-scale evaluation of an intelligent discovery world: Smithtown. *Interactive Learning Environments Journal*, *1*(1), 51–77.

Shute, V.J. and Regian, J.W. (1990). Rose garden promises of intelligent tutoring systems: Blossom or thorn? In *Space Operations, Automation and Robotics Conference*, Albuquerque, NM, 431–438.

Sime, J.-A. (1993). Modelling a learner's multiple models with Bayesian belief networks. In *Proceedings of 6th International Conference on Artificial Intelligence in Education*, Edinburgh, 426–432.

Skinner, B.F. (1954). The science of learning and the art of teaching. *Harvard Educational Review*, *24*, 86–97.

Skinner, B.F. (1958) Teaching machines. *Science*, 128, 969–977.

Sleeman, D. (1983). Inferring student models for intelligent computer-aided instruction. In R.S. Michalski, J.G. Carbonell and T.M. Mitchell (eds.), *Machine Learning* (Vol. 1). Tioga Press.

Sleeman, D.H. (1987a). Some challenges for intelligent tutoring systems. In *Proceedings of 10th International Joint Conference on Artificial Intelligence*, Milan, 1166–1168.

Sleeman, D. (1987b). PIXIE: A shell for developing intelligent tutoring systems. In R.W. Lawler and M. Yazdani, M. (eds.), *Artificial Intelligence and Education: Learning Environments and Tutoring Systems*. Intellect Books, 239–265.

Sleeman, D. and Brown, J.S. (eds.) (1982). *Intelligent Tutoring Systems*. Academic Press.

Soloway, E.M, Woolf, B., Rubin, E. and Barth, P. (1981). MENO-II: An intelligent tutoring system for novice programmers. In *Proceedings of 7th International Joint Conference on Artificial Intelligence*, Vancouver, 975–977.

Sottilare, R.A., Brawner, K.W., Sinatra, A.M., and Johnston, J.H. (2017). An updated concept for a Generalized Intelligent Framework for Tutoring (GIFT). *GIFTtutoring.org*, 1–19.

Stevens, A. and Collins, A. (1977). The goal structure of a Socratic tutor. In *Proceedings National ACM Annual Conference*, Seattle.

Suppes, P. (1966). The uses of computers in education. *Scientific American*, *25*, 206–221.

Swartz, M.L. and Yazdani, M. (eds.) (1992). *Intelligent Tutoring Systems for Foreign Language Learning: The Bridge to International Communication*. NATO Workshop, Springer.

Tasso, C., Fum, D., and Giangrandi, P. (1992). The use of explanation-based learning for modelling student behavior in foreign language tutoring. In Swartz and Yazdani (1992), 151–170.

VanLehn, K. (1988). Student modeling. In M. Polson and J. Richardson (eds.), *Foundations of Intelligent Tutoring Systems*. Lawrence Erlbaum, 55–78.

VanLehn, K., Jones, R.M. and Chi, M.T. (1992). A model of the self-explanation effect. *Journal of the Learning Sciences*, *2*(1), 1–59.

VanLehn, K., Ohlsson, S., and Nason, R. (1994). Applications of simulated students: An exploration. *Journal of Artificial Intelligence in Education*, *5*, 135–175.

Vassileva, J. (1990). An architecture and methodology for creating a domain-independent, plan-based intelligent tutoring system. *Educational and Training Technology International*, *27*(4), 386–397.

Verdejo, M.F. (1996). Interaction and collaboration in distance learning through computer mediated technologies. In Liao (1996), 77–88.

Villano, M. (1992). Probabilistic student models: Bayesian belief networks and knowledge space theory. In *Proceedings of 2nd International Conference on Intelligent Tutoring Systems*, Montréal, 491–498.

Vivet, M. (1989). Knowledge based tutors: towards the design of a shell. *International Journal of Educational Research (IJER)*, *12*(8), 839–850.

Vivet, M. (1996). Micro-robots as a source of motivation for geometry. In *Intelligent Learning Environments: The Case of Geometry*. Springer, 231–245.

Weber, G. (1996). Episodic learner modeling. *Cognitive Science Journal*, *20*(2), 195–236.

Wenger, E. (1987). *Artificial Intelligence and Tutoring Systems: Computational and Cognitive Approaches to the Communication of Knowledge*. Morgan Kaufmann.

Westcourt, K., Beard, M. and Gould, L. (1977). Knowledge-based adaptive curriculum sequencing for CAI: Application of a network representation. In *Proceedings of National ACM Conference*, Seattle, 234–240.

White, B. (1993). Thinkertools: Casual models, conceptual change, and science education. *Cognition and Instruction Journal*, *10*, 1, 1–100.

White, B.Y. and Frederiksen, J.R. (1990). Causal model progressions as a foundation for intelligent learning environments, *Artificial Intelligence Journal*, *42*, 99–157.

Winkels, R. and Breuker, J. (1992). What's in an ITS? A functional decomposition. In Costa (1992), 57–68.

PART II

THEORIES UNDERPINNING AIED

3. The role and function of theories in AIED

Stellan Ohlsson

THEORY VERSUS PRACTICE

Society-wide practices, institutions, and technologies require a rational basis for decisions. When has a pandemic slowed down enough to justify the repeal of lockdown restrictions on social life? Is solar power a workable alternative to coal-fired power plants? Can college admissions be used as a tool to combat ethnic inequalities in economic opportunity? Decisions that are inconsistent with the relevant mechanisms and processes are likely to have negative or even disastrous consequences for human affairs. Society responds by creating educational institutions to ensure that the next generation of decision makers possess the relevant knowledge.

Implementing this solution is not straightforward, because education is itself one of the society-wide practices that require rational, grounded decisions. What should be taught? How should it be taught? People have known that some ways of teaching are more effective than others from as far back as there are written records. Nevertheless, the basis of effective instruction has not yet been systematized into a body of explicit, well-defined knowledge, comparable to what is available in, for example, accounting, agriculture, architecture, business, engineering, and medicine. One reason is that the systematic, scientific study of cognitive functions like memory, thinking, and language has emerged only recently.[1]

In addition, educational researchers have had to work with tools that were too coarse-grained for the job of explaining and predicting instructional outcomes. Concepts like "subject matter unit", "explanation", "learning goal", and "comprehension" refer to processes that unfold over hours, days, months, or even years. On the other hand, the time it takes to create a new link in long-term memory – presumably a basic cognitive process in learning – is only a few seconds. To derive the former from the latter through informal reasoning is a complex task. The invention of computers and higher-order programming languages made it possible to bridge this gap in a rigorous way (Anderson, 2002).

At the beginning of personal, distributed computing, a small number of visionaries combined a commitment to education with a deep understanding of the new information technologies (Sleeman & Brown, 1982). They saw that the computer enabled educational research to investigate knowledge, and hence learning, at a much finer grain size than with paper-based information technologies. For example, in the hands of cognitive scientists like John Seely Brown and Kurt VanLehn, the hopelessly blunt concept of an "arithmetic error" was analyzed into a hundred different types of errors for subtraction, each of which requires its own pedagogy to overcome. This analysis would have been too cumbersome to support the derivation of arithmetic instruction in the absence of computers (Brown & VanLehn, 1980).

When cognitive psychologists, educators, and Artificial Intelligence (AI) researchers began to interact in the 1970s, they found themselves building a new intellectual community. Its members shared the goal of increasing the effectiveness of instruction by harnessing the power of the computer. They developed personal contacts, founded peer-reviewed journals, created a learned society, and organized an annual conference.[2] The work carried out by its members has a unique flavor and deserves its own label. Although nobody has taken a vote, researchers informally converged on "Artificial Intelligence in Education", with its snappy acronym, "AIED". Given the importance of effective instruction for society, the emergence of AIED as a separate field of research and development was a revolutionary event.

The purpose of this chapter is not to review the field of AIED. A traditional review would duplicate the review sections in the individual chapters. For a more detailed history of educational research, see McCalla, Part I, Chapter 2. The purpose instead is to distinguish three types of theory – psychological process theories, professional expertise for instructional design, and formal disciplines like programming and artificial intelligence (AI) – and to exemplify the role and function of each type in AIED research.

PSYCHOLOGICAL THEORIES

Scientists strive to express the knowledge gained from basic research in abstract, tightly interrelated, and empirically validated principles. A small set of related principles is referred to as a "theory".[3] In practical contexts, a theory serves as a tool for making decisions that exhibit higher levels of precision, predictability, and reliability than is possible with informal reasoning. For example, the laws of mechanics can be used to calculate what acceleration is required to launch a rocket into orbit around the Earth. But there is no single theory that can be used to derive the answer to every question that arises in designing a space shuttle or any other type of artifact. A scientific discipline therefore tends to appear as a loosely structured collection of *theories of limited scope*. Each such theory is relevant for some phenomena but not others. For example, the mechanical principles that apply to rocketry do not resolve problems regarding light and heat, which find their explanations in the principles of optics and thermodynamics, respectively.

Cognitive psychology exhibits a similarly quilted appearance. We do not yet have a universal and widely adopted theory of human cognition that can be applied to every issue that arises in designing effective instruction. Some cognitive psychologists have tried to envision such a theory (e.g., Anderson, 2019; Kieras, 2016; Laird, 2019; Taatgen & Anderson, 2010). Their proposals have so far been incomplete. Instead, there are pockets of theory that pertain to particular aspects of human cognition. For example, there are limited-scope theories of working memory, long-term memory, decision making, problem solving, visual imagery, language comprehension, and so on. A theory of any one of these cognitive processes or functions might have the potential to guide the design of instruction.

Basic psychological research has primarily turned to theories of *learning*, specifically for guidance about effective instruction. By a theory of learning, we mean here a set of principles that refer to the cognitive processes by which a learner's knowledge changes in the course of deliberate attempts to acquire more, or more accurate, knowledge. If we knew how knowledge changes in the course of learning, it should be possible to determine the most effective instruction for any given subject matter.

Basic research on learning has a long and rich history, and there have been many attempts to describe the relevant change processes. In some cases, the derivation of the instructional implications from a psychological principle is straightforward; in others, it is quite complicated. In the following section, the transition from principles of learning to prescriptions for instruction is illustrated using historical examples.

Historical Theories

One of the oldest theories, perhaps *the* oldest theory of learning, is that new knowledge is constructed by creating *associations*. Two pieces of previously acquired knowledge – two concepts, say, or two skills – are linked to each other in memory, thus creating a new knowledge structure that is more complex than either of its parts. For this principle to be operational, the theoretician has to specify when, under which circumstances, a new associative link is formed. In the first half of the twentieth century, Guthrie (1952) and others proposed *contiguity* as the crucial condition for learning. The contiguity hypothesis can be re-stated in contemporary terms:

> *The Contiguity Hypothesis: The longer two knowledge items (concepts, skills, etc.) reside together in working memory, the higher the probability of them being linked by an association.*

The instructional implications of the contiguity hypothesis are straightforward: provide the learner with presentations (examples, explanations, definitions, etc.) of the two items, A and B, so that he or she becomes aware of both at the same time. This hypothesis is plausible but limited. How much of the subject matter in, for example, a high-school science course can be broken down into pairwise associations?

One response to this objection is to enrich the description of the student's prior knowledge, and the processes by which it changes. In the past century, multiple principles have been considered. Two concepts that share some features (F1, …) but which differ with respect to other features (G1, …) can trigger the creation of a third concept that is defined solely in terms of the shared features (abstraction, generalization, schema extraction). This is probably the second oldest principle of learning. It implies that all learning moves towards knowledge of higher and higher abstraction levels. But consider a biology student who is studying the human double loop circulatory system. The facts of the double loop are not more abstract than whatever misconception about the circulatory system the student acquired before systematic instruction in the topic. The double loop model is richer, more complicated, and more correct, not more abstract, than a typical student misconception.

A different strand of thought has focused on the *temporal sequence* in which knowledge is constructed. If two knowledge items repeatedly occur in the same sequence in the learner's experience, then a new link is created between the two, such that the probability of the second concept occurring after the first is higher than when the sequence varies. In theories of this sort, the first concept is usually thought of as a *stimulus* (perception) and the second as a *response* (action). Once again, the instructional implications of this learning mechanism are simple: the instructor should arrange the subject matter presentation in such a way that the response repeatedly occurs in the presence of the stimulus.

Finally, another influential strand of thought has focused on the *needs* of the learner: A connection is more likely to be formed if it is followed by some rewarding experience (positive reinforcement), and less likely when followed by punishment (negative reinforcement).

In summary, multiple theoretical principles about learning have been investigated during the twentieth century, including association, generalization, discrimination, temporal sequence and reinforcement (Ohlsson, 2011, Chapters 6–7; Hilgard & Bower, 1956; Skinner,

1938; Thorndike, 1932). These principles are no longer considered sufficient to explain all of human learning, but they have not been shown to be false. On the contrary, each of these hypotheses is supported by a body of experimental results. The limitations of these historical mechanisms do not lie in the specification of the mechanisms themselves, but in the shallow and simplistic knowledge representation they were built on.

Learning theories do not prescribe how to teach, tutor, or instruct. But no complicated reasoning is needed to derive their instructional implications. If the theory says that contiguity is the key factor in learning from instruction, then arrange the subject matter units in such a way that the learner attends to them in the desired sequence. Alternatively, if learning is claimed to be driven by discrimination (Langley, 1987; Restle, 1955a, 1955b), the instructor should provide a set of similar experiences, some with negative outcomes and some with positive outcomes. No complicated procedures are needed. The description of learning and the prescription for instruction are so closely related that they risk being confused. This is no longer true when the simplistic representations of the subject matter in the historical theories are replaced by more complex knowledge representations (Aleven et al., Part III, Chapter 7).

Learning Complex Cognitive Skills

Contemporary studies of skill acquisition focus on complex skills. A key feature of complex skills is that the target behavior consists of a sequence of actions rather than a single action. Examples include *making c*offee and *proving a geometry theorem*. In complex skills, successful learning must resolve the order of the component actions. The first formal, computational theory of complex skill acquisition was published by Anzai and Simon (1979). The following two decades saw an explosive expansion of theoretical work on complex learning. Multiple principles of skill learning through practice were proposed and tested. They were built on different hypotheses about the underlying knowledge representation and the cognitive change mechanisms (Ohlsson, 2008). Examples of learning mechanisms include analogy, error correction, worked example and shortcut detection:

1. Analogy – a novel and unfamiliar task is solved by setting up a match to a familiar, already-mastered task (Gentner, 2010).

   Instructional implication: present the learner with a relevant analogy or verify that the learner already has a relevant analogy and then prompt its retrieval from long-term memory.
2. Error correction – an incorrect or incomplete skill representation is revised by applying it in a more constrained manner, to satisfy constraints on correctness in the relevant domain (Ohlsson, 1996, 2011).

   Instructional implication: the student should rehearse the relevant constraints.
3. Worked examples – the instructor supplies one or more examples of a desired problem solution (VanLehn & Jones, 1993).

   Instructional implication: the learner should identify and explain the successive steps
4. Shortcut detection – the learner compares different solutions to the same problem type to eliminate redundant steps (Neches, 1987).

   Instructional implication: the learner should be encouraged to find shortcuts.

Each of these change mechanisms has been validated against empirical data from human learners in laboratory studies. However, unlike the case of the historical principles, the instructional implications of these and other complex learning mechanisms are not obvious or easy to derive.

Learning from Discourse

When the target subject matter consists of skills, the main instructional mode of operation is to prescribe practice. But in many learning situations, the target subject matter is descriptive (declarative) in character. History and geography come to mind. In those cases, the dominant form of instruction is not to prescribe practice but to read expository texts or engage in some other discourse-oriented task. This puts language at the center of learning. There are two main forms of instruction that rely on language: learning by reading a text and learning from a tutor.

To learn from a text, the learner must understand it, but also encode his or her understanding into long-term memory. Specifically, the subject matter needs to be encoded in such a way that it will be retained until needed (Graesser et al., 1997). Mechanisms for learning by reading have had less impact on AIED research than learning by solving problems (but see Ritter et al. (2020) for an AIED system that teaches skills, habits, and strategies for avoiding infection during a pandemic and grounds those skills in declarative knowledge of how a virus pandemic operates).

It is widely believed that one-on-one tutoring is the most effective form of instruction. Multiple empirical studies have verified gains of up to 2 sigma (Bloom, 1984; Cohen et al., 1982), that is, the mean of the score distribution "moves" two standard deviations from pre-test to post-test. Because this outcome is impressive when compared with the learning gains typically obtained in other learning scenarios (VanLehn, 2011), researchers are interested in the cognitive processes that are active during one-on-one tutoring.

How does tutoring work? Why is one-on-one tutoring so effective? The goal of research on tutoring is to simulate the key features of human tutors during tutor–student interactions (Ohlsson, 1986; Chi et al., 2001; VanLehn et al, 2003; Lu et al., 2007; Di Eugenio et al, 2009; VanLehn, 2011). Patterns that recur in such interactions are called *tutoring strategies*. Researchers have tried to identify successful strategies and make them explicit. If an AI system is programmed to simulate a tutor's behavior, the system should be able to reproduce the superior learning outcomes obtained by human tutors. But tutors are not always able to make their strategies explicit. One method for identifying tutoring strategies is to analyze video recordings of tutoring sessions with students and human tutors (Di Eugenio et al., 2022).

The leading hypothesis in tutoring research is that tutoring is effective because the tutor can adapt instruction to individual differences among learners (VanLehn et al., 2003, 2007). Small differences in how knowledge is acquired, represented, or revised can have significant effects on the effectiveness of the underlying learning mechanisms. Putting AI behind the computer screen, as it were, enables an instructional system to mimic the moment-by-moment flexibility of a human tutor.

At the time of writing, there are multiple ITSs, operating on different principles of learning. For example, the widely known ACT-R theory (Anderson, 1993, 2019; Anderson et al., 1995) assumes that knowledge consists of sets of condition–action rules, and that the major changes in the learner's knowledge during skill practice is the transformation of knowledge from declarative form into procedural form. Learning in ACT-R also requires revision of the values of several quantitative parameters that are hypothesized to characterize the human cognitive system (Stamper & Koedinger, 2018). Another family of ITSs characterizes learning as a process of incorporating domain-specific constraints into the learner's representation of the target skill (Ohlsson, 1992, 1996, 2015; Ohlsson & Mitrovic, 2006, 2007). Neither of these approaches analyzes the behavior of the tutor. In contrast, the iList system (Di Eugenio et al., 2022; Fossati et al., 2009, 2015) is based on detailed analyses of what tutors and students say to each other during tutoring.

Summary

Cognitive psychology in general, and the psychology of learning in particular, strives to be a science in the same sense as the natural sciences. It seeks fundamental laws of cognition. Findings from laboratory experiments and other types of empirical observations are encapsulated in theoretical principles that describe the processes by which knowledge changes during learning. There are multiple proposals in the psychological research literature as to how those processes should be described. As is the case in the natural sciences, basic theories do not by themselves prescribe how to design effective applications. The instructional implications of theories of learning have to be derived from those principles. This is sometimes easy, sometimes not. There is no complete or widely adopted theory of learning, and each theory has its own set of implications. One reason is that not all proposed learning theories are false. Some of them are instructional incomplete, a lesser misdemeanor. If a theory is false or incomplete, we cannot expect its prescriptions to be correct or effective.

Cognitive psychology provides researchers with a range of theories about other cognitive processes and structures which may or may not be involved in the generation of new knowledge. A prominent example is Sweller's idea that too much information makes it difficult for a learner to learn (Chandler & Sweller, 1991; Sweller et al., 1998). The derivation of instructional prescriptions from psychological theories that do not specifically reference learning is difficult. For example, a severely constrained working memory might have multiple instructional implications, but it is not transparent what they are. There are multiple hypotheses in the literature about the nature of the capacity limitation on working memory, each with its own set of instructional implications.

INSTRUCTIONAL DESIGN THEORIES

Some physicists believe that a "theory of everything" is within their reach. They mean by this a single equation that connects all the fundamental forces of physics. Scientists in other fields estimate that this level of synthesis and integration will only be reached in the distant future, if ever. While awaiting the arrival of this blessed state of affairs, a scientific discipline will appear as a quilt, a patchwork of *theories of limited scope*. Each theory supports rational decisions with respect to some phenomena but not others. Medicine provides ready-at-hand examples: virus infections are understood at the level of physiology but movement disorders like Parkinson's disease are not.

Prescriptions for rational action cannot be derived from yet-to-be-discovered laws and theories, so they must have some other source. In areas that lack a general, basic theory, knowledge does not always grow piecemeal by testing predictions of a current theory in laboratory experiments, in the manner described by philosophers of science. Instead, knowledge might grow via the accumulation of personal, professionally relevant experience. In their daily practice, instructors encounter diverse types of information, including at least the following:

(a) case studies; (b) participant observer reports; (c) heuristics ("rules of thumb"); (d) paradigmatic instances; (e) informal reasoning; (f) outcomes of trial-and-error actions; and so on.

In this chapter, I refer to the accumulation of these types of information as *experiential knowledge*. Fields of activity in which practitioners operate on the basis of experiential rather than theoretical knowledge are often referred to as "professions", not "sciences", and the practitioners call themselves "professionals", not "scientists." Accounting, agriculture, architecture, business, engineering, law, and medicine share these features. There is a patchwork of theories of small scope, some of which are potentially useful in understanding how to design effective instruction. The practitioners in this field refer to themselves as "educators", "instructional designers", "teachers", "tutors", or "textbook authors", rather than psychologists.[4] Their self-appointed task is to design instructional artifacts (curricula, lesson plans, videos, tests, textbooks, webinars, etc.) that result in effective learning. Expertise in instructional design is not primarily encoded in explicit, formally codified, and experimentally verified theories but in informally held classroom practices.

Society endorses the view that there are two types of knowledge by accrediting professional schools that are separate from university departments. For example, institutes of technology and schools of engineering are typically separate from departments of chemistry and physics. Similarly, medical schools are typically integrated into university hospitals rather than biology departments, and business management is typically taught in a different building than economics.

One of the founders of cognitive science, Herbert A. Simon, once proposed that we refer to the professions as *sciences of the artificial* (Simon, 1970). His rationale was that the decision-making processes of professionals result in artifacts of various kinds: buildings, bridges, therapies, investment strategies, lesson plans, and so on. Those artifacts are supposed to function in a certain way, but in the absence of a basic and general theory, their behavior cannot be predicted ahead of time. We have to create the envisioned artifact – a library building, let's say – and subject it to empirical tests, an activity that looks very similar to basic research. However, the goal of a scientist is to understand natural systems as he or she finds them, whereas the goal of a professional is to study artifacts. This fundamental difference has so far prevented Simon's proposal from attracting widespread support.

How does the distinction between science and profession affect AIED? If there are two types of theories about instruction, how do their differences relate to the goal of harnessing the power of the computer to increase the effectiveness of instruction?

One radical difference between scientific theories and design principles is that they operate at different *grain sizes* (levels of analysis). The basic building blocks of psychological theories are primitive cognitive processes such as retrieving a knowledge element from long-term memory. Those processes have a duration measured in seconds, or even fractions of a second. Instructional design principles, on the other hand, typically conceptualize learning and instruction in terms of processes that are measured in hours, days, months, semesters, or even longer time periods (life-long learning). This provides instructional design principles with a high degree of face validity (Smith & Ragan, 1999).

What are some examples of instructional design principles that AIED researchers might incorporate into their systems? The most basic questions pertain to *scope* and *sequence*. What is the goal of the instruction? How much knowledge can a learner acquire in a given instructional situation? Closely related to scope is *sequence*. Once the subject matter units have been specified, there is a question of the order in which they should be taught and learned

(Ohlsson, 2007). If the target subject matter includes concepts A and B, in which order are they to be taught? First A, then B, or the opposite? Historical answers to this question include *complexity*, *abstraction*, and *prerequisite*. A widely adopted principle is to teach simple concepts before more complex ones. Another is to introduce the subject matter in terms of concrete concepts and skills, and gradually increase the level of abstraction. Finally, if knowing A is a prerequisite for knowing B, then it may seem obvious that one needs to teach A before B.[5] These sequencing principles – simple to complex, concrete to abstract, and prerequisites first – are informal, even vague, but nevertheless useful.

When the design of instruction moved from paper-based to digital technologies, these traditional principles became less important. Indeed, one of the advantages of the computer medium is precisely that the sequence of subject matter units need no longer be fixed. On the contrary, an AI-based instructional system can design a system to dynamically compute the next instructional topic. This is fairly common in AIED systems, but the connection to the traditional sequencing principles is obscured by differences in terminology and other factors.

Sequencing is only one type of design issue. Perhaps the most influential instructional design theory is the elaboration theory developed by Reigeluth and co-workers (Reigeluth et al., 1980, 1983; Wilson et al., 1993; Wilson & Cole, 1992). A central principle of this theory is that knowledge grows through elaboration. Knowledge of a topic – the human circulatory system, say – starts out simple and concise, but lacking in detail. In the course of learning, components of the initial, crude, and simplified knowledge representation are revised and expanded by the addition of new concepts and components, each of which can be elaborated further.

Another influential design principle claims that the growth of knowledge is stimulated if the learner has to resolve *cognitive conflicts*, states of mind in which the learner simultaneously considers two or more mutually exclusive concepts or ideas. For example, the Earth cannot be both flat and round. The driving force of cognitive conflicts has been advocated by such otherwise diverse thinkers as Jean Piaget (1985) in developmental psychology, Thomas Kuhn (1970) in the philosophy of science, and Leon Festinger (1957) in social psychology. The main instructional implication of this principle is straightforward: present the learner with a relevant conflict and ask him or her to resolve it. A widespread application of this principle is the *refutational text* (Sinatra & Broughton, 2011). A refutational text has two main parts: an explicit statement of a misconception and a correct description. The learner's task is to understand the differences and learn which one is correct.

A third example of an instructional design principle is the concept of *feedback*. There is general agreement that learners need information about how their academic performance, problem solutions, and so on compare to their learning goals (Bandura, 1977). However, there are many issues with respect to the details of feedback. It is widely assumed that positive feedback is more impactful than negative feedback; that feedback is more useful when it is immediate rather than delayed; and that feedback should be specific rather than general or vague. These three principles can readily be incorporated into ITSs and other instructional systems and artifacts.

There have been several attempts to formulate far-reaching principles that characterize the entire enterprise of education. Examples include at least the following three: (a) *Apprenticeship*. The idea behind this concept is that learning – even academic learning – should be designed to mimic the salient features of the training of novices in particular skills (Collins et al., 1991). (b) *Spiral curricula* (Bruner, 1966). The learner should return to a particular subject matter multiple times during an instructional program, each time adding concepts, facts, and skills, so that the learner's knowledge base becomes richer over time. (c) *The structure of the subject matter.* Calculus is not like history. Deriving the implications of instructional design theories at this level of generality is a challenge.

FORMAL THEORIES: ARTIFICIAL INTELLIGENCE

The goal of AIED research and development is to harness the power of AI in the service of instruction. This raises multiple practical, conceptual, and pedagogical issues. For the purpose of this chapter, a central question is what kind of theory is embodied in an AI system? The formal character of computer programming invites an analogy with the role of mathematics in the natural sciences. The conceptual rationale for the algorithms in an AI system corresponds to the substantive natural science theory, whereas the code of the AI system corresponds to the mathematical statement of the natural science theory.

In the first few decades of AI research, AI and cognitive psychology were indeed seen as related in this manner. A chess-playing computer program, for example, would be discussed as a theoretical contribution to research on the psychology of problem solving, and observations of the behavior of human chess players were a source of inspiration for those who strove to create a program that could play as well as the best human players (Newell & Simon, 1972). Similarly, a question-answering system was seen as an embodiment of a psychological theory of retrieval from long-term memory (Collins & Loftus, 1975; Quillian, 1968). In short, the role and function of AI in the study of learning was to be analogous to the role and function of mathematics in the natural sciences.

There are both historical and conceptual reasons why this concept of the role and function of AI no longer dominates. Over time, the mutual sharing of concepts and techniques between psychology and AI faded. AI researchers discovered that they could build systems quicker, and, in some cases, achieve higher system performance by inventing algorithms that have little resemblance to anything going on in human cognition. The first chess-playing computer to beat a world-class human player used the speed of its hardware to explore a very large set of possible moves, way beyond what a human player can do. Also, the emergence of the internet and Big Data has posed problems and solutions that do not bear any simple relation to what people do when they exercise their cognitive capabilities. The inductive algorithms used in these systems are so strongly bottom-up that AI researchers sometimes have difficulty interpreting what knowledge their systems have acquired in a particular application (Adadi & Berrada, 2018). The successes of such systems are awe-inspiring: face recognition across a database of, say, one billion faces would be one example, and a self-driving car would be another. Whether awe-inspiring or not, the purely inductive approach to learning that underpins such successes has no prospect of evolving into a theory of human learning.

If the role of AI is not to contribute formal theories of human learning, how should we think about its role in AIED? There are multiple contributions of AI to the design and implementation of instructional systems, but those contributions take various shapes. In this respect, the role and function of AI in AIED is similar to the role of, say, statistics or calculus in other types of research. There is no single role for mathematical theories in science. Mathematics provides tools that enable researchers to carry out analyses that otherwise could not be undertaken. (Imagine Big Data without statistics.)

Artificial Intelligence as a Tool Kit

The body of well-understood AI techniques enables the development and implementation of AI-based instructional artifacts. The individual chapters in this Handbook provide multiple examples of the tool kit perspective. A particularly salient example is *natural language processing*. Researchers can create this capability by studying, modeling, and implementing the processes by which humans use language (Graesser et al., 1997). But this is not the only path. In the tool kit perspective, an AI system can make use of any algorithm that results in the desired capability. It does not matter, from the tool kit point of view, how the grammar of sentences and other aspects of language use are achieved.

A second example of the tool kit perspective in AIED research is *pattern matching*. Consider a computational problem that at one time had an important role to play in the development of AI and its application to psychology: pattern matching. Many of the early AI systems represented knowledge in terms of so-called *condition-action rules*. Such rules are processed by computing the best match between a situation and a set of rules (Klahr et al., 1987; Newell & Simon, 1972; Anderson, 1993). An early solution to this problem was the RETE pattern matcher (Forgy, 1982), used in many early rule-based systems to decide whether a rule condition matched a given situation. Crucially, the complexity of the RETE algorithm, that is, how much work the algorithm has to do to decide on a given match, does not increase exponentially with the complexity of the patterns involved (this would have prevented its application to any but the simplest problems). In the first decades of AI, the rule representation and the associated pattern matching algorithms were interpreted as theoretical constructs, that is, they were conceptualized as substantive hypotheses. However, it does not matter exactly how the pattern matching process operates, as long as it correctly sorts rules into those that match a particular situation and those that do not. The pattern matcher is a tool, not a hypothesis. The tool kit perspective applies to a wide range of computational problems that arise in the design and implementation of AI-based instructional artifacts.

Intelligent Tutoring Systems

One-on-one tutoring is an effective form of instruction probably because it engages tutors and students in a close interaction with respect to the problem or task that the learner aims to master. An Intelligent Tutoring System or ITS (Sleeman & Brown, 1982) is a program running on a personal computer that serves as a platform (in the computer science sense). The instructor poses problems and offers verbal feedback on the student's solution. The feedback arrives quickly, and its content is certain to be relevant to the subject matter. An ITS needs enough computational power behind the screen to support multiple capabilities: generating an instructional presentation, using standard representations; encoding a course-relevant dialogue; interpreting the learner's answers and behaviors; inferring the systems' knowledge base; and so on. Given the concept of such a system, the task for the system builder is to use the information in psychological learning theories and successful instructional designs to program the components of the system. AI is what makes the realization of this vision possible.

CONCLUSION

The unique contribution of AIED to educational research is the integration of three strands of work, each grounded in a different type of theory.

Cognitive psychology models itself on basic research in the natural sciences. The goal is to hypothesize abstract principles and verify their truth in experimental studies. As is the case in other sciences, there is as yet no single "cognitive theory of everything" that explains all learning phenomena. Instead, there is a quilt of local theories, each with a limited scope. Principles about the cognitive mechanism behind learning-by-practicing offer in-depth explanations of the well-documented, negatively accelerated shape of practice curves. But those principles do not also explain the role of discourse in tutoring, or why one-on-one tutoring is so effective. Theories of tutoring, on the other hand, tend to be silent about the shape of learning curves.

Psychological theories tend to be formulated at a very fine-grained level of analysis. Some theories postulate basic cognitive processes with a duration of less than one second. There is no standard procedure for deriving the instructional implications of psychological theories of learning. Researchers and teachers have to rely on intuition and informal reasoning. When the theoretical principles are simple, deriving their implications for practice tends to require no more than common sense. However, when a principle is complicated, the gap between common sense concepts like "attention", "error", "understanding", "misconception", on the one hand, and the fine-grained processes postulated in psychological theories (*post a goal*, *create a link*, *retrieve a chunk from long-term memory*, etc.) is so wide that the only workable way to derive the instructional implications is to simulate the postulated cognitive processes, and observe how or what the simulation model learns. When this is the case, AI serves as a tool for bridging the gap between the different levels of analysis (Anderson, 2002).

The field of instructional design models itself on the role and function of design in other fields. The instructional designer, like designers in other professions, operates at a level of analysis that is directly relevant in practice. Scope and sequence remain key concepts in instructional design because they directly address the very first questions that have to be answered in designing instruction: what is to be taught, and how is it to be taught? Instructional designs are grounded in ideas and concepts that seem useful to the designer, regardless of their grounding in controlled studies. For example, the idea that adding a visual illustration to a text improves learning is widely embraced in educational practice: No recent textbook lacks pictures or graphs. This design principle has been around for at least one hundred years. To the best of the present author's knowledge, there is no convincing body of empirical studies that support it. But the idea has too much face validity to be discarded.

Like designers in other fields, instructional designers operate on the basis of personal knowledge. Their foundations are laid during their professional training. The knowledge base includes multiple sources of information, from explicit teachings ("do no harm") to rules of thumb, and so on. Unlike psychological hypotheses, the components of professional expertise in education do not require the derivation of instructional implications. Expertise based on personal experience is already at the level of analysis that applies directly to design problems. A second difference is that psychological theories are declarative in character – they assert what is the case, or what someone thinks in the case – whereas design principles are prescriptive. They do not describe how learning works. Instead, they prescribe how to teach in order to reach some pedagogical goal, such as a certain level of academic achievement, a 2-sigma improvement in learning outcomes, a low error rate, or a deeper understanding of the subject matter.

Artificial intelligence can be seen as a theory of intelligence. However, the current state of AI does not support this view. AI researchers do not strive for good fit to human behavioral data. A more fruitful view is that the body of well-understood algorithms and advanced programming languages constitutes a tool kit that AIED researchers can draw upon when designing, implementing, and evaluating AI-based instructional systems, in particular, when creating ITSs. The ITS concept is the unique contribution of AIED, and it requires that researchers intertwine psychological theorizing with instructional designs, and use AI to implement those designs.

NOTES

1. The historical reasons why the natural sciences matured before the human ones is a fascinating question which cannot be addressed here.
2. Co-Chair with Jeffrey Bonar of *The Third International Conference on Artificial Intelligence and Education*. The Conference was held at the University of Pittsburgh, 8–10 May 1987, Pittsburgh, Pennsylvania, USA.
3. In some contexts, the word "theoretical" is used in a pejorative sense to mean "speculative" or "useless". But three centuries of experience with the application of natural science to human affairs has confirmed the ability of good theories to guide action
4. Recently, the terminology has began to shift, so that some educational researchers now refer to their profession as "the learning sciences". Whether this signals a change in the substance of educational research remains to be seen.
5. Strangely, empirical tests of this proposition do not always support it.

REFERENCES

Adadi, A., & Berrada, M. (2018). Peeking inside the black box: a survey on explainable artificial intelligence (XAI). *IEEE Access*, *6*, 52138–52160.

Anderson, J. R. (1993). *Rules of the mind*. Hillsdale, NJ: Erlbaum.

Anderson, J. R. (2002). Spanning seven orders of magnitude: A challenge for cognitive modeling. *Cognitive Science*, *26*, 85–112.

Anderson, J. R. (2019). Cognitive architectures including ACT-R. *Cognitive Studies: Bulletin of the Japanese Cognitive Science Society*, *26*(3), 295–296.

Anderson, J. R., Corbett, A. T., Koedinger, K. R., & Pelletier, R. (1995). Cognitive tutors: Lessons learned. *The Journal of the Learning Sciences*, *4*(2), 167–207.

Anzai, Y., & Simon, H. A. (1979). The theory of learning by doing. *Psychological Review*, *86*, 124–140.

Bandura, A. (1977). Self-efficacy: Toward a unifying theory of behavioral change. *Psychological Review*, *84*, 191–215.

Bloom, B. S. (1984). The 2 sigma problem: The search for methods of group instruction as effective as one-to-one tutoring. *Educational Researcher*, *13*, 4–16.

Brown, J. S., & VanLehn, K. (1980). Repair theory: A generative theory of bugs in procedural skills. *Cognitive Science*, *4*(4), 379–426.

Bruner, J. S. (1966). *The process of education*. Boston, MA: Harvard University Press.

Chandler, P., & Sweller, J. (1991). Cognitive load theory and the format of instruction. *Cognition and Instruction*, *8*, 293–332.

Chi, M. T. H., Siler, S. A., Jeong, H., Yamauchi, T., & Hausmann, R. G. (2001). Learning from human tutoring. *Cognitive Science*, *25*, 471–533.

Cohen, P. A., Kulik, J. A., & Kulik, C.-L. C. (1982). Educational outcomes of tutoring: A meta-analysis of findings. *American Educational Research Journal*, *19*, 237–248.

Collins, A., Brown, J. S., & Holum, A. (1991). Cognitive apprenticeship: Making thinking visible. *American Educator*, *15*(3), 6–11.

Collins, A. M., & Loftus, E. F. (1975). A spreading-activation theory of semantic processing. *Psychological Review*, *82*(6), 407–428.

Di Eugenio, B., Fossati, D., Ohlsson, S., & Cosejo, D. G. (2022). *Intelligent support for computer science: Pedagogy enhanced by Artificial Intelligence.* Boca Raton, FL: CRC Press/Taylor & Francis.

Festinger, L. (1957). *A theory of cognitive dissonance.* Stanford, CA: Stanford University Press.

Forgy, C. L. (1982). Rete: A fast algorithm for the many pattern/many object pattern match problem. *Artificial Intelligence, 19,* 17–37.

Fossati, D., Di Eugenio, B., Brown, C., Ohlsson, S., Cosejo, D., & Chen, L. (2009). Supporting Computer Science curriculum: Exploring and learning linked lists with iList. *IEEE Transactions on Learning Technologies, 2,* 107–120.

Fossati, D., Di Eugenio, B., Ohlsson, S., Brown, C., and Chen, L. (2015). Data driven automatic feedback generation in the iList intelligent tutoring system. *Technology, Instruction, Cognition and Learning, 10*(1), 5–26.

Gentner, D. (2010). Bootstrapping the mind: Analogical processes and symbol systems. *Cognitive Science, 34*(5), 752–775.

Graesser, A. C., Millis, K. K., & Zwaan, R. A. (1997). Discourse comprehension. *Annual Review of Psychology, 48,* 163–189.

Guthrie, E. R. (1952, rev. ed.). *The psychology of learning.* New York: The Ronald Press Company.

Hilgard, E. R., & Bower, G. (1956). *Theories of learning.* New York: Appleton-Century-Crofts.

Kieras, D. E. (2016). A summary of the EPIC Cognitive Architecture. *The Oxford Handbook of Cognitive Science, 1,* 24.

Kieras, D. E., & Meyer, D. E. (1997). An overview of the EPIC architecture for cognition and performance with application to human-computer interaction. *Human–Computer Interaction, 12*(4), 391–438.

Klahr, D., Langley, P., & Neches, R. (Eds.). (1987). *Production system models of learning and development.* Cambridge, MA: MIT Press.

Kuhn, T. S. (1970). *The structure of scientific revolutions* (2nd ed.). Chicago, IL: University of Chicago Press.

Langley, P. (1987). A general theory of discrimination learning. In D. Klahr, P. Langley & R. Neches (Eds.), *Production system models of learning and development* (99–161). Cambridge, MA: MIT Press.

Laird, J. E. (2019). *The Soar cognitive architecture.* Boston, MA: MIT Press.

Lu, X., Di Eugenio, B., Kershaw, T., Ohlsson, S., & Corrigan-Halpern, A. (2007). Expert vs. non-expert tutoring: Dialogue moves, interaction patterns and multi-utterance turns. *Lecture Notes in Computer Science, 4394,* 456–467.

Neches, R. (1987). Learning through incremental refinement of procedures. In D. Klahr, P. Langley & R. Neches (Eds.), *Production system models of learning and development* (163–219). Cambridge, MA: MIT Press.

Newell, A., & Simon, H. A. (1972). *Human problem solving.* Englewood Cliffs, NJ: Prentice-Hall.

Ohlsson, S. (1986). Some principles of intelligent tutoring. *Instructional Science, 14,* 293–326.

Ohlsson, S. (1992). Constraint-based student modeling. *Journal of Artificial Intelligence and Education, 3,* 429–447.

Ohlsson, S. (1996). Learning from performance errors. *Psychological Review, 103,* 241–262.

Ohlsson, S. (2007). The effects of order: A constraint-based explanation. In F. E. Ritter, J. Nerb, E. Lehtinen & T. M. O'Shea (Eds.), *In order to learn: How the sequence of topics influences learning* (151–165). New York: Oxford University Press.

Ohlsson, S. (2008). Computational models of skill acquisition. In R. Sun (Ed.), *The Cambridge handbook of computational psychology* (359–395). Cambridge, UK: Cambridge University Press.

Ohlsson, S. (2011). *Deep learning: How the mind overrides experience.* Cambridge, MA: Cambridge University Press.

Ohlsson, S. (2015). Constraint-based modeling: from cognitive theory to computer tutoring – and back again. *International Journal of Artificial Intelligence in Education, 26*(1), 457–473.

Ohlsson, S. & Mitrovic, A. (2006). Constraint-based knowledge representation for individualized instruction. *Computer Science and Information Systems, 3,* 1–22.

Ohlsson, S., Di Eugenio, B., Chow, B., Fossati, D., Lu, X., & Kershaw, T. C. (2007). Beyond the *code-and-count* analysis of tutoring dialogues. In R. Luckin, K. R. Koedinger, & J. Greer (Eds.), *Artificial intelligence in education: Building technology rich learning contexts that work* (349–356). Amsterdam, The Netherlands: IOS Press.

Ohlsson, S., & Mitrovic, A. (2007). Cognitive fidelity and computational efficiency of knowledge representations for intelligent tutoring systems. *Technology, Instruction, Cognition and Learning, 5*, 101–132.

Piaget, J. (1985). *The equilibration of cognitive structures: The central problem of intellectual development* (transl. T. Brown and K. J. Thampy). Chicago, IL: University of Chicago Press.

Quillian, M. R. (1968). Semantic memory. In M. Minski (Ed.), *Semantic information processing* (227–271). Cambridge, MA: MIT Press.

Reigeluth, C. M., Merrill, M. D., Wilson, B. G., & Spiller, R. T. (1980). The elaboration theory of instruction: A model for sequencing and synthesizing instruction. *Instructional Science, 9*(3), 195–219.

Reigeluth, C. M., & Stein, F. S. (1983). The Elaboration Theory of instruction. In C. M. Reigeluth (Ed.), *Instructional-design theories and models: An overview of their current status* (335–381). Hillsdale, NJ: Erlbaum.

Restle, F. (1955a). A theory of discrimination learning. *Psychological Review, 62*(1), 11–19.

Restle, F. (1955b). Axioms of a theory of discrimination learning. *Psychometrika, 20*(3), 201–208.

Ritter, F., Clase, A., Harvill, S., Yeh, M., Joseph, R., Oury, J.J., Oury, J. D., Glanz, E., Fenstermacher, A., Brener, M., & James, J. (2020). *Skills to obstruct pandemics: How to protect yourself and your community from Covid-19 and similar infections.* Mechanicsburg, PA: Sunbury Press.

Simon, H. A. (1970). *The sciences of the artificial.* Cambridge, MA: MIT Press.

Sinatra, G. M., & Broughton, S. H. (2011). Bridging comprehension and conceptual change in science education: The promise of refutational text. *Reading Research Quarterly, 46*(4), 374–393.

Skinner, B.F. (1938). *The behavior of organisms: An experimental analysis.* New York: Appleton-Century-Crofts.

Sleeman, D., & Brown, J. S. (Eds.). (1982). *Intelligent tutoring systems.* London, UK: Academic Press.

Smith, P. L., & Ragan, T. J. (1999). *Instructional design.* New York: Macmillan Publishing Company.

Stamper, J., & Koedinger, K. (2018, June). An instructional factors analysis of an online logical fallacy tutoring system. In *International Conference on Artificial Intelligence in Education* (pp. 86–97).

Sweller, J., Van Merrienboer, J. J., & Paas, F. G. (1998). Cognitive architecture and instructional design. *Educational Psychology Review, 10*(3), 251–296.

Taatgen, N., & Anderson, J. R. (2010). The past, present, and future of cognitive architectures. *Topics in Cognitive Science, 2*(4), 693–704.

Thorndike, E. L. (1932). *The fundamentals of learning.* New York: Teachers College.

VanLehn, K. (2011). The relative effectiveness of human tutoring, intelligent tutoring systems, and other tutoring systems. *Educational Psychologist, 46*(4), 197–221.

VanLehn, K., Graesser, A. C., Jackson, G. T., Jordan, P., Olney, A., & Rosé, C. P. (2007). When are tutorial dialogues more effective than reading? *Cognitive Science, 31*(1), 3–62.

VanLehn, K., & Jones, R. (1993). Learning by explaining examples to oneself: A computational model. In S. Chipman & A. L. Meyrowitz (Eds.), *Foundations of knowledge acquisition: Cognitive models of complex learning* (25–82). Boston, MA: Kluwer.

VanLehn, K., Siler, S., Murray, C., Yamauchi, T., & Baggett, W. B. (2003). Why do only some events cause learning during human tutoring? *Cognition and Instruction, 21*(3), 209–249.

Wilson, B., & Cole, P. (1992). A critical review of Elaboration Theory. *Educational Technology Research and Development, 40*(3), 63–79.

Wilson, B. G., Jonassen, D. H., & Cole, P. (1993). Cognitive approaches to instructional design. In G. M. Piskurich (Ed.), *The ASTD handbook of instructional technology* (21.1–21.22). New York: McGraw-Hill.

4. Theories of metacognition and pedagogy applied to AIED systems

Roger Azevedo and Megan Wiedbusch

INTRODUCTION

The field of Artificial Intelligence in Education (AIED) has spanned several decades and gone through several major transformations (du Boulay & Luckin, 2016; Conati, 2016; Roll & Wylie, 2016; Self, 2016; VanLehn, 2016a; Woolf, 2009), including the design, implementation, and testing of several families of AIED systems that have made significant contributions to the field (Azevedo et al., 2022; Chapter 27.5 by Biswas, this volume; Koedinger & Aleven, 2016; Graesser et al., 2018; Sottilare et al., 2018; VanLehn, 2016b). AIED systems are technology-based learning and training environments that range from augmented reality, virtual reality (VR), and serious games to tangible computing, intelligent tutoring systems (ITSs), simulations, hypermedia, and multimedia. A recent focus in the field has been on designing AIED systems based on metacognition[1] (Azevedo & Aleven, 2013), using these systems as both research and learning tools designed to detect, measure, track, model, foster, and support students' metacognition (Azevedo et al., 2018). Metacognition plays a critical role in fostering and enhancing learning, reasoning, problem solving, and performance across students of all ages, domains (e.g., medicine, STEM, and military training), training contexts and tasks (e.g., algebra, human circulatory system, and thermodynamics), and AIED systems (Ariel et al., 2009; Pintrich, 2002; Veenman, 2015; Winne, 2017; Winne & Azevedo, 2022; Zimmerman & Moylan, 2009). As such, recent advances in studying metacognition and self-regulated learning (SRL) have been the result of measuring and quantifying processes as temporally unfolding events during real-time learning, reasoning, and problem solving (Schunk & Greene, 2018; Winne, 2019). For example, new methods for detecting, tracking, collecting, and analyzing metacognitive judgments such as log-files, screen recordings, think-alouds, and eye tracking as dynamically propertied events (e.g., frequency of use, duration, time-dependent patterns of use, and dynamics that include feedback mechanisms) offer novel ways for examining and understanding the role of these processes across learning contexts, age groups, domains, tasks, and learning activities while engaging with AIED systems (Azevedo et al., 2018, 2019, 2022).

In this chapter, we first provide a brief overview of metacognition and its relevance to AIED systems. Next, we examine how the construction of metacognition has influenced these systems and how metacognition has contributed to the current theory, research, and design of this topic. We then provide two examples of metacognition pedagogy applied to future systems and conclude with several challenges for future work in the area of metacognition and AIED.

WHAT IS METACOGNITION AND WHY IS IT RELEVANT TO AIED SYSTEMS?

Metacognition is thinking about the contents and processes of one's cognition (Bjork et al., 2013; Dunlosky & Tauber, 2011; Koriat, 2015; Tarricone, 2011; Winne, 2018). At a basic level (Nelson, 1990), metacognition involves the dynamic and accurate monitoring (i.e., meta-level) and regulation (i.e., object-level) during any learning activity such as reading, writing, thinking, reasoning, and problem solving within an AIED system. Metacognition occurs across the timeline of cognitive events. It may precede a task when a learner forecasts whether knowledge and skills are available to successfully tackle an assignment. It also occurs simultaneously with thinking, as a learner monitors their progress and considers whether switching to a different strategy would be more successful (Winne, 2018). Additionally, metacognition can occur when a learner retrospectively considers (i.e., reflects) properties of prior learning events, such as evaluating how effective, efficient, easy, and risky their learning strategies were after using an AIED system (Winne & Azevedo, 2022). What differentiates metacognition from cognition is not operations or cognitive processes, but topics which a learner thinks about (Winne, 2018).

Metacognition is usually divided into three types of knowledge. *Declarative knowledge* includes beliefs about oneself, others, tasks, strategies, topics, knowledge, and so on. For example, a student might have the metacognitive belief that "scanning the multimedia content in this ITS usually helps me understand the structure of the instructional material." *Procedural knowledge* lists steps for performing cognitive work by enacting both domain-specific (e.g., balancing chemical equations) and general (e.g., how to inspect diagrams) strategies. This type of knowledge can be algorithmic or heuristic in the sense of probably, but not certainly, achieving a particular product (Winne & Azevedo, 2022). Procedural knowledge is key in allowing the learner to modify their working cognitive architecture and make adaptive modifications as informed by their metacognitive monitoring. For example, while monitoring their understanding, a learner realizes they do not comprehend the physics problem after trying to reread the word problem and, therefore, selects a different strategy (e.g., revisiting class notes) to enhance their comprehension of the problem. However, if they are still unsuccessful in comprehending the problem, an AIED system can offer several additional metacognitive strategies (e.g., highlight the key variable in the problem, represent the problem diagrammatically). Lastly, *conditional knowledge* identifies circumstances in which a proposition is valid or a procedure is appropriate for approaching a goal. For example, if rereading does not work when I am trying to comprehend science texts and diagrams, then I should engage in help-seeking behavior with the ITS. Conditional knowledge plays a key role relative to procedural knowledge such that it forms production rules with which to enact procedural knowledge.

In terms of AIED systems, we emphasize the use of Winne and Hadwin's information processing theory of SRL (Winne & Hadwin, 1998, 2008; Winne 2018), which states that learning occurs through a series of four cyclical phases. According to this theory, metacognitive monitoring and regulation act as the hubs of SRL. These processes are captured as events that unfold over time and across several phases. Specifically, the four phases involve: (1) understanding the task; (2) setting goals and making plans to accomplish goals; (3) using learning strategies planned out in (2); and (4) making adaptations to (2)–(3). The model explains that these four phases are cyclical in nature but not necessarily sequential such that learners can engage in these phases in any order or even simultaneously. These phases can be mapped onto the learning and instructional activities with which learners typically engage while learning with AIED systems, regardless of tasks, topic, or domain.

In terms of AIED systems, this model is appropriate because metacognition is viewed as a series of events (e.g., planning → cognitive strategy A → metacognitive monitoring process C → cognitive strategy F → metacognitive monitoring process W → ...) that occur during learning. For example, the model posits that there is a set of cognitive conditions (e.g., prior knowledge) impacting how learners progress through all four phases. Learners' prior knowledge can influence their ability to understand the task, set meaningful goals and plans, use sophisticated learning strategies, and make adaptations to engage in metacognitive monitoring and regulation during learning. Within AIED systems, a major emphasis of this model posits that multimodal data (e.g., concurrent think-alouds or eye movements) of metacognitive and other self-regulatory processes are key in detecting, tracking, modeling, supporting, and fostering metacognition prior to, during, and following learning with an AIED system. A major challenge of this model to the design, testing, and implementation of AIED systems includes *when*, *what*, and *how* to best optimize the scaffolding of metacognitive knowledge and skills across individuals, AIED systems, tasks, topics, and domains. However, as we illustrate in a separate section, other models, theories, and frameworks of metacognition have been used to model metacognition across several AIED systems in attempts to address this challenge.

HOW THE CONSTRUCT OF METACOGNITION INFLUENCED THE AREA OF AIED SYSTEMS

Contemporary metacognitive research has contributed to the theory and literature in the area of AIED systems by simultaneously raising and addressing several conceptual and theoretical issues regarding the nature and role of metacognition and self-regulation (Azevedo, 2020; Dunlosky & Rawson, 2019; Efklides et al., 2018; Koriat, 2015; Winne, 2018). Although researchers are becoming more knowledgeable about metacognition, there is still a need for them to clearly articulate the theoretical framework, model, or theory being used in their studies involving AIED systems. Most studies adhere (either implicitly or explicitly) fairly generally or abstractly to a specific model of metacognition. Such is the case with the MetaTutor ITS of Azevedo and colleagues (2018, 2022) for teaching about the human circulatory system and SRL, utilizing Winne's (2018) information processing model to inform some aspects of ITS features and production rules. Research using this and other models of metacognition (e.g., Griffin, Mielicki, & Willey, 2019; Hacker & Bol, 2019) has contributed to our understanding of how individual differences, internal and external conditions (e.g., prior knowledge and study time), calibration, internal standards, evaluations, feedback mechanisms, adaptivity, and so forth conceptualize metacognition with AIED systems. However, despite adherence, most research does not make explicit assumptions about which specific underlying mechanisms, processes, and other aspects of metacognition are being measured and tested using such a model, and in specific AIED systems. Instead, they generally point to metacognition as a potential influence for which cognitive strategies are employed by learners without directly measuring metacognition. We argue that it is imperative that AIED researchers not only choose a specific model of metacognition for the design of systems, but also generate hypotheses and make assumptions regarding the role, timing, duration, and quality of specific metacognitive processes, mechanisms, and constructs used during learning, reasoning, and problem solving with AIED systems.

In general, most research using AIED systems has focused on cognitive strategies and implemented experimental designs that foster learning across domains and topics, measuring learning gains by using pretests–posttests based on experimental comparisons of different scaffolding methods, human and computerized tutor interventions, and so forth (e.g., Aleven & Koedinger, 2002; Chi et al., 2001; Taub & Azevedo, 2020). This research has implied metacognitive processes may have been wholly or partially responsible for both short-term and long-term learning gains (e.g., Sonnenberg & Bannert, 2019). In comparison, the majority of metacognition research has focused on self-report measures embedded in AIED systems and, in some cases, made inferences about metacognitive judgments, processes and evaluations without collecting process data while students used AIED systems. Although these measures have greatly contributed to our understanding of metacognitive processes in AIED systems, limitations driven by ignoring process data have come to light and been increasingly debated in recent years (e.g., Azevedo, 2020; Hadwin, 2021; Winne, 2019). In other words, non-process-oriented metacognitive measures, typically administered only prior to and after learning has occurred, fail to capture the temporal fluctuations of one's metacognition that would occur *during* learning. Furthermore, the metacognitive self-reports embedded within the AIED systems are still dependent on how effectively and accurately a learner can verbalize and reflect on their cognitive processes, which can be disruptive to their learning (Penttinen et al., 2013; Winne & Jamieson-Noel, 2002).

New advances in computing and engineering sciences, modeling and simulation, statistics, data mining, machine learning, and artificial intelligence (AI) have led to novel interdisciplinary methods, techniques, and sensors that reveal critical patterns of metacognitive and self-regulatory processes (e.g., inferring cognitive processes through eye-tracking data). These methods utilize various types of multimodal data (e.g., utterances, conversational turns, log-files, eye tracking, and screen recordings of human–machine interactions). These data types significantly enhance our current understanding of the sequential and temporal nature of these processes, how they contribute to learning with AIED systems, contemporary models, theories, and frameworks of metacognition and SRL, and develop teaching and training regimens designed to foster and support metacognition (Azevedo & Gasevic, 2019; Winne, 2018).

These new methods have significantly augmented and contributed to current conceptual models and theories of metacognition and SRL by delineating micro-level processes (e.g., specific metacognitive processes such as judgments-of-learning (JOLs), feelings-of-knowing (FOKs), content evaluations, or monitoring progress toward goals) as the expansion of macro-level processes (e.g., monitoring), and by generating testable hypotheses based on types of process data used and the results (Winne, 2018). For example, Greene and colleagues (Greene & Azevedo, 2009; Greene et al., 2015) elaborate on a detailed coding scheme that explains over a dozen metacognitive processes captured, coded, and analyzed using concurrent think-aloud protocols from hundreds of students using AIED systems to learn, problem solve, understand, and reason across domains.

The research area of metacognition and AIED systems has fundamentally changed how both researchers and educators think about metacognition and has led to the design and development of AIED systems that act as both research (e.g., to collect rich traces of temporally unfolding metacognitive processes, using a variety of cutting-edge and innovative techniques) and learning tools (e.g., to support and foster metacognition during task performance; see Azevedo et al., 2022). We expect greater strides in this area given the accelerating advances in computing sciences and AI, making it possible for students' metacognitive processes, judgments, evaluations, and reflections to be interpreted by artificial agents in real time (Johnson & Lester, 2016). This work could make human–machine interactions seamless by providing instructional resources in immersive virtual environments capable of accelerating the acquisition, development, internalization, use, and transfer of declarative, procedural, and conditional metacognitive knowledge and skills.

HOW HAS METACOGNITIVE RESEARCH BEEN APPLIED TO THE DESIGN OF AIED SYSTEMS?

Research on metacognition as a temporally unfolding process has led to designing and developing several AIED systems for various students, domains, tasks, and outcomes (e.g., Aleven et al., 2016; Arroyo et al., 2014; Azevedo et al., 2022; Azevedo & Aleven, 2013; Azevedo & Lajoie, 1998; Feyzi-Behnagh et al., 2014; Lajoie, 2020; Lajoie & Azevedo, 2006; Matsuda et al., 2020; McCarthy et al., 2018; Porayska-Pomsta, 2016; Suleman et al., 2016; Winne, 2020). In general, research using trace data methods has revealed that students, in general, do not engage in effective metacognitive monitoring and lack the regulatory processes (e.g., Azevedo et al., 2019). For example, extensive research on MetaTutor (Azevedo et al., 2019, 2022; Harley et al., 2018; Taub & Azevedo, 2019) revealed that students typically lack the metacognitive and regulatory skills needed to dynamically monitor and regulate their cognitive processes during learning. However, as is the case with MetaTutor, including pedagogical agents is effective for prompting and scaffolding students to monitor and regulate during learning with AIED. Artificial agents (e.g., pedagogical agents, virtual humans, and avatars) increase metacognitive awareness and provide students with opportunities to practice metacognitive and regulatory processes while receiving real-time individualized, adaptive feedback from embedded agents (Biswas et al., 2018; Kim & Baylor, 2016; Wiedbusch & Azevedo, 2020).

BRIEF AND SELECT REVIEW OF EXISTING AIED SYSTEMS SUPPORTING METACOGNITION

The *International Journal of Artificial Intelligence in Education* (IJAIED) serves as the official journal for the AIED Society, a group of interdisciplinary scholars that began in 1997 and which has hosted over twenty international conferences. Within just the past five years of empirical publications in the journal, we found more than 75 unique systems spanning multiple system types (e.g., ITSs, computer-based learning environments, intelligent games, and MOOC courses) with underlying features and built-in mechanisms associated with metacognition. Due to space limitations, we will only cover a subset of these AIED systems in this section, taking a closer look at six of these AIED systems and how they each detect, model, track, foster, and/or support metacognition in their learners.

Help-Seeking Tutor

Historically based on the Cognitive Tutors (Anderson et al., 1995), the Help Tutor teaches learners effective help-seeking behaviors by providing feedback on their behaviors and, specifically, errors in help-seeking (Roll et al., 2007). For example, the environment would stress the recommended next steps for the user in coordination with the recommendation of the domain-level cognitive tutor (e.g., a Geometry tutor). Although this did help lessen the number of help-seeking errors during a learning session, there was no improved performance, domain knowledge acquisition, or knowledge about ideal help-seeking behaviors (Roll et al., 2007).

In response to this finding, Roll and colleagues (2007) developed the Help-Seeking Support Environment (HSSE) that included a collection of tutors designed to help develop effective help-seeking behaviors in learners. Within this environment, there is the Updated Help Tutor, which provides information about the principles and benefits of different scaffolding. For example, instead of just telling a learner to "slow down," it explains that "hurrying through these steps may lead to later errors." Additionally, with the Self-Assessment Tutor, learners practice evaluating their skills instead of their responses to traditional questions. Finally, there was also declarative instruction about help-seeking behavior with the framing of learning this knowledge as an additional goal to learning the content knowledge. Unfortunately, although this environment improved learners' help-seeking declarative knowledge, there was no improvement in content knowledge or help-seeking behaviors (Roll et al., 2007). In a follow-up data mining study of the log trace data, students with a medium level of skill benefited from hints, especially at the next opportunity to apply the same skill (Roll et al., 2014). Aleven and colleagues (2016), in a review of help-seeking tutors, proposed a few potential explanations for this finding, such as the wording of help and hints, timing of feedback, individual learner differences, and motivation, among others, but continued to advocate for the support of metacognition and self-regulation support in ITSs despite their findings.

AutoTutor

AutoTutor (Graesser et al., 2017) is an ITS that uses natural language to hold conversations with learners and has been used across multiple domains (e.g., physics, critical thinking, algebra), and has birthed over a dozen additional systems (i.e., AutoMentor, AutoTutor-3D, AutoTutor-Affect-Sensitive, AutoTutor-Lite, DeepTutor, GnuTutor, GuruTutor, HURA-Adviser, iDRIVE, MetaTutor, Operation-ARIES, Adult Literacy Tutor (CSAL), Source, Evidence, Explanation, and Knowledge web tutor (SEEK) and Electronic Tutor; see Nye et al., 2014). AutoTutor's pedagogical approach has three major design principles for a tutor, based on the instructional strategies of both expert and no-expert tutors: (1) help learners construct explanations; (2) ask reasoning and collaborative questions; and (3) solve problems that require deep reasoning (Graesser et al., 1995; Nye et al., 2014).

Given the extensive history of AutoTutor and its family of projects (including MetaTutor), there have been many features and mechanisms implemented and tested to improve learner performance, with varying degrees of success. For example, following the second design principle (ask reasoning and collaborative questions), one attempt was made to have learners generate questions for the tutor to answer, which has been shown to improve metacognitive skills (Rosenshine et al., 1996). However, AutoTutor was unable to answer all student questions, so this strategy proved unfruitful and frustrating for learners to use (Graesser, 2009). Other attempts were more effective, such as eliciting prior knowledge through metacognitive question checks after short lecture explanations of content (D'Mello et al., 2010). Additionally, the SEEK web tutor required content evaluations to help in the scientific inquiry process through spoken hints, rating questionnaires, and journaling practices (Graesser et al., 2007).

MetaTutor

MetaTutor is a hypermedia-based ITS for teaching about the human circulatory system and is designed to target specific cognitive and metacognitive self-regulatory processes in learners (Azevedo et al., 2019, 2022). Based on Winne and Hadwin's (2008) and Winne's (2018) model of SRL, the system fires event-based and time-based production rules to prompt learners to use various cognitive and metacognitive strategies during their learning session, and then provides feedback on their strategy use, with embedded assessment through multiple pedagogical agents. These mechanisms were also made available to students throughout the session to self-initiate in an SRL palette and throughout the environment (e.g., a timer and progress bar).

Extensive research (Azevedo et al., 2013, 2018, 2019, 2022; Bouchet et al., 2016; Cloude et al., 2018; Dever & Azevedo, 2020; Harley et al., 2018; Taub et al., 2014; Taub & Azevedo, 2019) has shown that the culmination of both content and SRL processes through adaptive human scaffolding enhances learning (see Azevedo & Witherspoon, 2009, for empirical reviews). As such, MetaTutor was designed to train students on cognitive and metacognitive SRL processes as well as content through four major phases. During the first phase, the system *modeled key SRL processes* by providing video clips of human tutors modeling and explaining proper and improper use of SRL processes with biology-related content. This help provided learners with metacognitive conditional knowledge. The second phase required learners to complete a *discrimination task* by identifying proper and improper use of SRL processes. This allowed learners to practice recognizing SRL in other learners and adapt their models of SRL from the previous phase through feedback provided by the system. Next, they completed a *detection task* by stopping video clips of other learners engaging in SRL processes and indicating which process they detected. This step allowed for more reflection and model adaptation. Finally, in the fourth phase, learners used MetaTutor themselves to learn as much as they could about the human circulatory system.

The learning environment set an overall goal for learners (i.e., "*Your task is to learn all you can about the circulatory system. Make sure you know about its components, how they work together , and how they support the healthy functioning of the human body*") but asked the learner to generate subgoals. Learners were presented with a navigation bar along the left-hand side of the environment with a list of topics and subtopics. When a link was chosen from this bar, text and static and dynamic representations of the content were presented in the center of the environment. Directly below this content, learners were able to communicate with MetaTutor using a dialog box. Here students were prompted by various pedagogical agents that resided in the top right-hand corner of the interface (see Figure 4.1).

MetaTutor had four pedagogical agents, each representing a component of SRL: (1) Gavin guided learners through the environment and administered self-report questionnaires; (2) Sam prompted summarizing; (3) Mary helped learners monitor their understanding of content relative to their sub-goals; and (4) Pam prompted learners to activate their prior knowledge by writing out what they already knew about a topic or subtopic. In addition to scaffolding learners' SRL processes, all agents provided feedback on their strategy use. For example, Mary

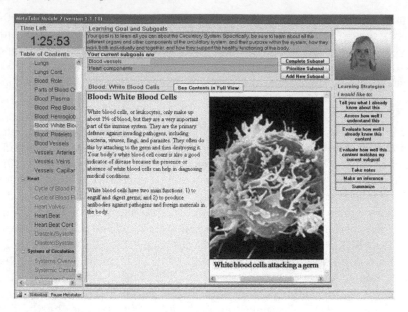

Figure 4.1   Screenshot of MetaTutor's main interface

provided feedback about learners' accuracy in their evaluation of how well they felt they understood the content and Sam provided feedback on the quality of learner summaries based on length and keywords. There were nine unique SRL processes that agents could scaffold, four of which were metacognitive processes (i.e., monitoring progress toward goals, JOL, FOK, and content evaluations). Additionally, learners had cognitive strategies (i.e., coordinating informational sources, inference making, summarizing, taking notes, and rereading) they could choose from, allowing them to examine metacognitive regulation mechanisms during learning.

During the final phase of MetaTutor, after setting subgoals, learners were allowed to freely learn by reading and inspecting multimedia content, completing quizzes and self-reports (administered through production rules), indicating use of various cognitive and metacognitive strategies through the SRL palette, and responding to pedagogical agent prompts. After 60 minutes, learners took a post-test and completed a final set of self-report measures to assess their perceptions of several motivational and affective processes, and the utility of the pedagogical agents in supporting metacognition.

Various studies with MetaTutor have shown that learners tend to have little prior knowledge about SRL processes (Azevedo et al., 2011) and struggle to learn a lot about the circulatory system in a two-hour session (Azevedo et al., 2008, 2009, 2016; Taub & Azevedo, 2019). However, cognitive strategy was influenced by the presence of pedagogical agents and their feedback such that students with low prior knowledge without scaffolding took a greater quantity of notes, similar to the note taking when scaffolded, compared with their counterparts with high prior knowledge (Trevors et al., 2014). Additionally, these notes had fewer instances of repetitive content, suggesting agents helped increase more effective strategy choices and metacognitive regulation. Duffy and Azevedo (2015) showed that learners who received scaffolding and feedback also deployed more SRL strategies and reviewed relevant material, suggesting higher metacognitive regulation and monitoring. Azevedo and colleagues (2016) found similar results in that learners with adaptive scaffolding learned more than those who did not receive prompts or feedbacks. Furthermore, these learners spent proportionally less time reading content (compared with other cognitive and metacognitive activities), took more quizzes and performed better on quizzes, checked notes more often, and expanded on their summaries more often.

MetaTutor has also been shown to have lower reported levels of negative emotions during studying compared with typical emotions toward studying, which could positively impact academic achievement as learners can focus more on the content and task and less on emotion regulation (Harley et al., 2018). Taub and colleagues (2019) examined levels of expressed emotions during different cognitive and metacognitive processes, finding that they varied based on processes and were associated with the accuracy of those processes. For example, expressions of surprise were negatively correlated with accuracy on feelings-of-knowing metacognitive judgments and frustration was positively correlated with note accuracy. These findings might suggest that emotions can play a significant role in how accurate one's cognitive and metacognitive performance can be and should be considered in the design of ITSs.

Betty's Brain

Betty's Brain (Biswas et al., 2016; Leelawong & Biswas, 2008) is an open-ended learning environment (OELE) that has learners research and construct models of various science phenomena to teach a virtual agent, Betty, about complex science topics (e.g., ecology). Learners can ask Betty questions (self-testing), set tasks and subtasks, have her take quizzes to evaluate her learning (goal evaluations), provide feedback about her performance (metacognitive reflection and monitoring), and provide explanations about her answers (adapting models). A mentor agent also provided learners with strategy suggestions when prompted (strategy selection). The underlying learning-by-teaching paradigm (Bargh & Schul, 1980; Benwar & Deci, 1984; Biswas et al., 2005) behind Betty's Brain engages learners through teaching and, specifically, collaborating socially with both Betty and the mentor agent. The interactions between the agents and the learner stimulate metacognitive strategy use such as finding causal links in informational text, rereading text to adapt and correct previous links and models, and asking probing questions and checking explanations. Learners who received feedback on these processes exhibited more effective learning (Biswas et al., 2016).

After a decade of research, Biswas and colleagues (2016) demonstrated that the focus on metacognition using the learning-by-teaching paradigm of Betty's Brain helped students become effective and independent science learners by providing a social framework that engages students and helps them learn. However, students also face difficulties when going about the complex tasks of learning, constructing, and analyzing their learned science models. Biswas and colleagues (2016) have developed approaches for identifying and supporting students who have difficulties in the environment, and we are actively working toward adding more adaptive scaffolding functionality to support student learning.

iSTART

The Interactive Strategy Training for Active Reading and Thinking (iSTART) environment is a web-based tutoring program used for teaching middle-school and college-level reading strategies through animated agents (McNamara et al., 2007). The underlying principle of iSTART stems from the Self-Explanation Reading Training (SERT; McNamara, 2004) intervention that suggests that self-explanation in conjunction with comprehension monitoring, inference making, and elaboration provides deeper conceptual understanding (Magliano et al., 2005; McNamara, 2004; O'Reilly et al., 2004). iSTART divides reading instruction into three phases – introduction, demonstration, and practice – to provide learners with access to various reading strategies, with feedback from agents. Metacognition within reading entails comprehension monitoring and active strategy selection and evaluation (McNamara et al., 2007). iSTART addresses these components by explicitly teaching students metacognitive reading strategies and their conditional application in addition to providing a constructivist modeling–scaffolding–fading paradigm. Within this paradigm, learners take on various perspectives including (i) the observer (vicariously watching two agents model reading strategies), (ii) the critic (evaluating and providing feedback on an agent's self-explanation), and finally, (iii) the producer (providing their own actively generated self-explanations). Throughout the session, learners are encouraged to apply explicitly taught strategies, including monitoring, paraphrasing, predicting, and inferencing.

iSTART has evolved into iSTART-ME (Motivationally Enhanced), which was designed to increase learner motivation and engagement within the iSTART environment. This has been done by allotting more agency and personalization to learners through co-construction, coached practice, and game-based practice (Jackson et al., 2011; McNamara et al., 2009). Results from this new environment found that, despite decreases in self-explanation during practice, post-training self-explanation and performance were comparable to iSTART, with increased motivation and enjoyment leading to longer practice and engagement but also overconfidence in their metacognitive judgments of learning and feelings-of-knowing (Jackson & McNamara, 2013).

SimStudent

SimStudent (Matsuda et al., 2020) was designed to be implemented in various cognitive tutor and AIED systems across domains (e.g., algebra and programming) as a computational model of human learning. The model, when applied as a teachable agent, "learns" cognitive skills through positive and negative examples provided by learners, as well as feedback on performed steps. For example, within the Artificial Peer Learning environment using SimStudent (APLUS), learners estimate how correct a step was for solving an algebra linear equation. When negative feedback is provided, SimStudent attempts the step again, if possible; however, when the feedback is positive, SimStudent continues on to the next step (Matsuda et al., 2020). Initial implementations of this model found no conditional differences on post-test performance (controlling for pretest scores), but there was an aptitude–treatment interaction such that low-prior-knowledge learners found more benefit teaching SimStudent than did high-prior-knowledge learners (Matsuda et al., 2011). Closer evaluation of the learner–system interaction showed that learners who taught SimStudent incorrectly were unaware they had made any errors, leading to the development of a teacher-agent to provide scaffolding (Matsuda et al., 2014).

In response to this lack of learner metacognitive knowledge about their own performance, five types of scaffolding were introduced to provide support: (1) selecting the next problem to teach; (2) selecting when to quiz; (3) reviewing resources; (4) reminding to provide SimStudent feedback; and (5) demonstrating the next steps to teach SimStudent (Matsuda et al., 2020). This metacognitive help is administered both when requested by the learner through a pop-up menu for the teacher-agent and proactively when the underlying model of the system detects help is needed through model-tracing (Anderson et al., 1990; e.g., when a learner's behavior cannot be predicted when compared with a metacognitive model the system will provide help).

In sum, we have provided a brief overview of several major AIED systems that focus on several different dimensions of metacognition using different theoretical models, and have emphasized different instructional methods to detect, model, track, support, and foster metacognition across different ages groups, task, domains, and learning contexts.

TWO EXAMPLES OF METACOGNITION PEDAGOGY APPLIED TO FUTURE AIED SYSTEMS

We envision a new generation of AIED systems that include a solid pedagogy and take advantage of the new affordances provided by emerging technologies. Here we describe two specific examples of where we see these systems being effectively used to support metacognition and provide new insights into the conceptualization and theory surrounding metacognition. The first scenario involves the use of natural language processing (NLP) using natural conversations between the learner and the AIED system, where metacognition is expressed naturally and we can get the system machine to meta-reason.

Because metacognition is primarily a set of covert processes, it has been notoriously difficult to capture without explicit prompting or making assumptions about one's internal models through behavior analysis and trace data (Winne, 2019). Think-aloud methodologies and other verbalizations of the learning process provide access to the temporally unfolding metacognitive monitoring and regulation of cognitive processes while learning with AIED systems, and, therefore, provide accurate real-time measurements of various cognitive and metacognitive processes (Azevedo & Gasevic, 2019). Unfortunately, coding and analyzing transcriptions of verbalizations is extremely time consuming, resource intensive, and occurs after a learning session. Therefore, automatic detection of metacognition should be studied to help develop specialized algorithms and semantic models using NLP. Various aspects of different metacognitive processes could be semantically modeled for key phrases. For example, a learner might express a content evaluation through statements of certainty or uncertainty about the relevance of a piece of information. Crucial phrases could be collected and then generalized to other contexts, using similar techniques of cognitive and affective detection systems (e.g., AES Systems, E-rater [Burstein et al., 2013], Project Essay Grader [p. 2003]). Other metacognitive processes could also be captured, such as choosing strategies by looking for comparison words between options, or goal monitoring by looking for references to previously stated or predefined goal phrases.

While automatic detection of metacognition is a non-trivial task, there is also a strong need for our systems to meta-reason and "learn" as well. That is, as we move away from well-structured problems, there is a need for more approximate solutions that are rationalized using limited resources and information in much the same way as many humans are thought to do (e.g., using decision trees, simplified heuristic rules or cost–reward analysis). Some work has begun in this area; however, current meta-learning agents have focused on task transfers across similar task types and are biased toward simpler statistical models (Kumar et al., 2020). For example, memory-augmented neural networks have been trained to generalize compositionality (i.e., how new words behave grammatically or within a composition) in new meta sequence-to-sequence learning (Lake, 2019). This technique trains on small episodic datasets (compared to the typical large single dataset), which allows for the training of compositional skills that can in turn be applied to new compositional problems. Meta sequence-to-sequence learning creates higher-level abstractions of compositional rules and "memories," which can then be stored and applied to entirely new sequences. But how far can we push these types of techniques? What kinds of rules and heuristics can we begin to teach our AIED systems and how different can transfer tasks be? The field should begin to develop intelligent agents that can meta-reason and make inductive and deductive reasoning decisions outside of hard-coded production rules. We should aim for meta-reasoning agents that do not require massive amounts of data or examples to learn very specific tasks. Instead, we should attempt to create models that have generative and highly adaptable working models that can be generalized across contexts. In other words, instead of considering domain-specific problem sets and approaches, we should design and model AIED systems using generalized metacognitive skills and abilities (e.g., general monitoring, evaluation, and reflection).

The second example of future AIED systems involves the externalization and increased visibility of internal standards and visualization of metacognitive processes captured through multimodal data within immersive VR systems, extended reality (XR), and open-learner models (OLMs; Bull, 2020) that can be negotiated and manipulated by stakeholders such as students and teachers. The future workforce is one that is interdisciplinary and collaborative, a shift we are already seeing today. Science-based collaborative inquiry learning is already being explored to provide learners with the opportunity to practice and learn interdisciplinary problem-solving skills while being provided with various adaptive scaffolds (Saleh et al., 2020). However, more work can push what this collaboration looks like when AI pedagogical agents are introduced in a larger capacity than just as tutors or teachers.

Imagine a collaborative VR environment that allows for multiple humans and agents to meet and work together on large-scale societal problems (e.g., solving pandemics) in a world in which they have full control over running simulations and developing models. Not only are these agents intelligent and able to reason and learn from their human teammates, but so too can the environment by providing real-time data about how the team is operating, which strategies are proving most fruitful, and which are causing the most negative outcomes through the use of OLMs. This environment could help monitor and direct the team toward information it believes to be most useful given the current problem and discussions. For example, imagine that a human learning scientist poses a question about doctors' and patients' emotions when discussing cancer treatments, and the environment automatically provides data of high-intensity emotions to provide a space for creating examples. The scientist may be concerned about what work has previously been done on doctor empathy or how various doctor–patient dynamics and interactions could impact patient health outcomes. As the discussion continues, an intelligent virtual human embodying content evaluation sifts through archived literature to provide a small literature search and synthesis on the topic at hand. Using this new, targeted information, the scientist can then begin to generate a list of more targeted questions to pose back to the environment to track and collaborate on toward a new conceptual understanding of this particular space. We can imagine how conceptual diagrams or maps could be drawn by the scientist and then populated by the environment based on the previous work it has retrieved.

Beyond research, though, training the future workforce could be done entirely through problem solving and project-based virtual environments that allow for the development of team and soft skills (e.g., empathy and emotion regulation skills) in conjunction with the technical expertise required of various positions. Environments such as this could develop complex and challenging problems while intelligent agents provide developmentally appropriate metacognitive scaffolding that is individualized and adaptable; all the while, learners are developing new skills and approaches to challenges as are the system and agents. As the system is used throughout longer and longer sessions, underlying architectures and models are being adapted and modified based on interactions with learners as well as trace and multimodal data collected from the learners.

OPEN CHALLENGES FOR FUTURE WORK ON METACOGNITION, PEDAGOGY, AND AIED SYSTEMS

Despite numerous contributions provided by the currently available AIED systems, future work in the area of metacognition and AIED systems needs to address several outstanding issues. Below, we raise several series of questions as a way to generate new discussions within this field about the direction and challenges we should take on, given the current state of AIED systems. We begin by addressing the systems themselves and the driving features and theoretical considerations that inform instructional and system design. We then raise a second series of questions about the role of metacognition within AIED systems. This then leads onto a third set of questions about the current state of metacognitive pedagogy. We end this section by asking about how best to introduce dynamical considerations in AIED systems such as the temporal unfolding of (meta)cognitive processes.

Instructional and Design Considerations

We begin by considering the future of metacognitive processing-fostering AIED systems by raising unanswered or incompletely explored design considerations. First, *who* and *what* does the modeling of metacognitive processes (e.g., the learner and/or the AIED system, and how these processes are represented or articulated) while using an AIED system? For example, what are the components of the learning context (e.g., human agents, artificial agents, nature, characteristics and interdependence of the personal, physical, embodied, and virtual space(s))? We have seen some work begin on these types of questions regarding agentic characteristics, but only some associated with small, positive effects on learning (Heidig & Clarebout, 2011; Schroeder et al., 2013, 2017). Furthermore, these processes have not been connected back to metacognitive processing and could greatly benefit from social interaction theory (e.g., Van Kleef's Emotions as Social Information Model [2009], or the supra-personal theoretical framework of Shea et al. [2014]).

Second, what are the learning goal(s) of these systems? Furthermore, what are the provisions of a challenging learning goal(s)? Are they self- or other-generated and how much time should be allocated to completing the learning goal(s)? While many systems have domain-specific or knowledge mastery goals in mind, we posit a more general approach to these systems, that is, teaching students how to apply metacognitive strategies and processes not just within context-specific learning, but also for transfer and application to other domains (Chapter 7 by Aleven et al., this volume; Chapter 3 by Ohlsson, this volume). Furthermore, learning gains related to the development of metacognitive skills will be observed if we extend our experiments to more than a few hours of practice with AIED systems, integrate our systems with curriculum goals and objectives, and provide time-adaptive scaffolding to learners. Otherwise, we will continue to struggle to show the benefits of metacognitive AIED systems in enhancing student learning and academic performance.

Third, what are the dynamic interactions between the student(s) and other external/in-system regulating agents while considering various features of the interaction (e.g., pedagogical agents' role(s), levels of interaction, types and timing of scaffolding and feedback, and embodiment of modeling–scaffolding–fading metaphor behaviors)? This question opens up an entire discipline and discussion around dynamical systems theory to help capture the nuance and complexity of human–computer interactions that AIED systems need to support. We fully believe that the future of these systems must behave and adapt in real time in order to provide the most effective support.

Finally, fourth, what is the role of assessment in enhancing performance, learning, understanding, and problem solving with AIED systems? That is, how can we better design our systems to capture more than just knowledge acquisition but also the *process* of learning. We would like to see some systems that push the use of assessment outside of creating learner models' current knowledge states to also include measurements and metrics of their metacognitive awareness or affective states. Perhaps we should consider how receptive a learner is toward an embedded pedagogical agent and if that agreeableness indicates something about their ability to continue with a learning session or if saturation is starting to set in. We believe a more holistic approach to learner models outside of assessment should be considered when developing AIED systems so that assessment serves not to just tell us how successful one is in interacting with a system, but rather *how* someone is learning and will continue to learn.

The role of metacognition in future AIED systems

There are other more specific issues, open questions, and challenges related to metacognition and AIED systems. Our chapter has already highlighted the current state of metacognition in AIED systems, but we believe that this role is not supported nearly enough and the field should continue to push and question what a truly metacognitively aware system looks like. Below, we raise a series of curated questions that provide ample opportunity for the AIED communities to push current systems for the future support and fostering of metacognition.

First, should an AIED system offer opportunities for learning about metacognition while fostering complex processes through explicit and implicit methods? Second, will the AIED system provide opportunities for students to practice and receive feedback about these metacognitive processes? Third, what are students' individual differences (e.g., prior knowledge, personality traits, emotion regulation skills, self-efficacy, interest, task value, and goal orientations) that may influence their ability to accurately monitor and self-regulate, and how do their fluctuations/changes over time impact learning? Fourth, how should AIED systems be designed to account for temporal fluctuations and accuracy in students' metacognitive monitoring, judgments, evaluations, and reflection? Fifth, how do we design AIED systems capable of both (1) training students to acquire, internalize, integrate, retrieve, apply, and transfer declarative, procedural, and conditional metacognitive knowledge and skills; and (2) tracking (1) development and using AI-based methods to modify the system based on an individual student's emerging metacognitive competencies? Sixth, how can we use emerging AIED systems (e.g., augmented reality, mixed reality, or extended reality) to enhance students' understanding, acquisition, internalization, sharing, usage, and transfer of monitoring and regulatory knowledge and skills to other tasks and domains? Lastly, how do we design AIED systems to teach teachers and instructors to develop their own self-regulatory skills (Mudrick et al., 2018) while they learn about students' multimodal multichannel self-regulatory skills that can be used to design dashboards that provide them with real-time trace data to facilitate instructional decision making (Wiedbusch et al., 2021)?

These are only a few of the relevant issues that need to be addressed by interdisciplinary researchers as we consider the future design and use of theoretically based and empirically grounded AIED systems toward the understanding, investigating, and fostering of metacognition.

Metacognitive pedagogy

In addition, there are pedagogical issues related to future work on metacognition and pedagogy that need to be addressed by researchers and designers. First, what metacognitive strategies are students knowledgeable about? How much practice have they had in using these strategies and are they successful in using them? Are they aware of whether they are using these strategies successfully? Can we expect novice or young students to dynamically and accurately monitor their cognitive and metacognitive processes?

Measures for assessing one's awareness of metacognition and metacognitive strategy use already exist (e.g., Metacognitive Awareness Inventory – MAI: Study 1 of Schraw and Dennison, 1994; Learning and Study Strategies Inventory – LASSI: Weinstein et al., 1987; Motivated Strategies for Learning Questionnaire – MSLQ: Pintrich and de Groot, 1990). However, these metrics are not being brought back into the implementation of AIED systems to provide more adaptive and individualized scaffolding and instruction. Furthermore, as many authors have pointed out, self-report instruments are non-dynamic and poor indicators of the processes they are designed to capture (Cromley & Azevedo, 2006; Jacobse & Harskamp, 2012; Perry, 2010; Schunk & Greene, 2018; Veenman et al., 2014; Winne et al., 2002). New metrics for measuring metacognition, especially those dynamical in nature, should be developed and integrated directly into AIED systems.

Second, researchers and designers should understand and assess how familiar students are with the tasks they are being asked to complete or learn about with AIED systems. Are they familiar with the various aspects of the context and the AIED systems they are being asked to use? That is, we question if some of the learning difficulties and lack of learning benefits might arise, not from the content difficulty, but rather the (meta)cognitive requirements to learn how to navigate and successfully use these systems on top of content. In other words, it is the delivery and the technology, not the instructional or pedagogical approaches AIED systems are employing.

Third, what are students' levels of prior knowledge? How do individual differences impact their knowledge acquisition and use of metacognitive strategies? What impact will prior knowledge and other individual differences have on students' ability to accurately and dynamically monitor and regulate?

Fourth, do students have the necessary declarative, procedural, and conditional knowledge of metacognitive and regulatory skills essential to learn with AIED systems? Are young students or novices able and sophisticated enough to verbally express utterances that represent (and are coded as or eventually classified in real time with NLP) monitoring processes (e.g., JOL, FOK) to be both coded by researchers and externalized to others (including avatars, intelligent virtual humans, and pedagogical agents) during collaborative tasks that involve negotiating, shared task understanding, shared mental model, joint attention and other aspects with AIED systems? Is non-verbal reporting (e.g., written or forced choice) as accurate as verbal reporting when measuring metacognitive processes?

Fifth, what is the "right" level of granularity for students to understand emerging, developing, and specific cognitive and metacognitive processes, and their roles in task performance while interacting either alone or in a team with AIED systems? How much (if any) and what types of scaffolding or direct instruction should be given about (meta)cognitive strategies and their implementation? Sixth, if the purpose of research is capturing and measuring real-time deployment of metacognitive processes, then what should the sampling frequency and timing be between observations? Relatedly, how do different measurement techniques (e.g., log files, utterances, eye movements) impact our ability to accurately measure and infer the presence of metacognitive-related processes – that is, distinguishing between metacognitive monitoring, judgments, and evaluations? Seventh, how many data channels (e.g., concurrent think-alouds alone vs. concurrent think-alouds in conjunction with eye-tracking, log files, and screen capture video clips of all human–machine interactions) are necessary to make valid and reliable inferences regarding the nature of temporally unfolding monitoring and regulatory processes while students use AIED systems? Are these channels additive in their capturing of processes or should the field take a more systems-directed approach with the measurement of metacognition within AIED systems? How do these processes relate to learning outcomes in complex and ill-structured tasks with AIED systems?

Lastly, how can contemporary, exploratory, and analytical tools accommodate additional trace data (e.g., video of the context, screen capture of human–machine interaction, non-verbal expressions, or gestures) to provide contextual information for enhancing the accuracy of results (Chapter 27.3 by Lane, this volume)?

Dynamics within AIED systems

Another issue not addressed by current AIED systems but which should be emphasized in future research and pedagogical efforts is the duration and valence associated with SRL processes as they are integral to examining the quality and nature of the temporally unfolding processes (see Azevedo et al., 2019). For example, if enacting a learning strategy, such as taking notes while using an ITS, takes over one minute to complete (followed by another SRL process) while a metacognitive judgment, such as a content evaluation related to the relevancy of multimedia materials embedded in an ITS, may last only two seconds (followed by another coded SRL process), then this potentially creates issues on unbalanced code density and inaccurate inferences about the processes, if not considered when analyzing process data.

Similarly, valence has emerged as another critical issue in examining metacognitive processes (see Azevedo & Dever, 2022; Greene & Azevedo, 2009, 2010). For example, certain metacognitive monitoring and regulatory processes, such as judgment of learning (e.g., negative JOL: "I do not understand this paragraph," and positive JOL: "I do understand this paragraph") need to be differentiated by adding valence. While both provide information about monitoring, including valence allows researchers to examine the micro-level feedback loops between metacognitive monitoring and control, and their use can be compared to theoretical assumptions. For example, it can be theoretically postulated that rereading would follow a negative JOL as it would be adaptive for students to reread the same text to try once more to understand something they indicated they did not understand initially. By contrast, one can postulate that self-testing processes could follow a positive JOL utterance, indicating that the student believes they understand the paragraph and are ready to test that understanding.

Based on current contributions to the field, these are only a few of the important methodological issues that future metacognitive research in the fields of educational and cognitive psychology, learing sciences, and modeling and simulation should address in order to ensure AIED systems are effective for improving learning.

CONCLUSION

Metacognition is a critical component of AIED systems. The field has grown immensely recently due to interdisciplinary advances, allowing researchers, designers, and educators to measure and infer enacted metacognitive processes *during* learning, problem solving, reasoning, and performance with different types of AIED systems. A major contribution has been strategically using trace data methodologies designed to capture real-time monitoring and regulatory processes during learning as AIED systems are designed to be both research and learning tools. In addition, advances in computing, engineering, statistical sciences, and AI are transforming the types of analyses conducted on metacognition both prior to and following learning but also, most importantly, *during* learning. These analyses utilize machine-learning techniques that have the potential to provide real-time, individualized, adaptive scaffolding and feedback for addressing each student's specific learning needs. Future advances are expected to accelerate the potential of addressing metacognition with AIED systems. Techniques such as NLP and explainable AI (Putnam & Conati, 2019; Chapter 11 by Rus et al., this volume) will allow for even faster, seamless interactions between humans and AIED systems by supporting a student's direct expression and verbalization of their metacognitive processes (e.g., "I don't understand this diagram as it relates to the current learning goal"). This could allow students to interrogate artificial agents to meta-reason by explaining to students why they do not understand why the human is not capable of accurately monitoring their learning after repeated attempts at providing external metacognitive scaffolding. In sum, this chapter has briefly highlighted several key conceptual, theoretical, methodological, and pedagogical/instructional issues related to metacognition with AIED systems.

ACKNOWLEDGMENTS

This chapter was supported by funding from the National Science Foundation (DRL#1661202, DUE #1761178, DRL#1916417, DRL#1916417, IIS#1917728, and BCS#2128684). Any opinions, findings, conclusions, or recommendations expressed in this material are those of the authors and do not necessarily reflect the views of the National Science Foundation. The authors would like to thank Elizabeth Cloude and Daryn Dever for comments on earlier versions of this chapter.

NOTE

1. While we acknowledge the roles of neural, perceptual, affective, motivational, and social processes in AIED systems, our chapter focuses on metacognition.

REFERENCES

Aleven, V., & Koedinger, K. (2002). An effective metacognitive strategy: learning by doing and explaining with a computer-based Cognitive Tutor. *Cognitive Science, 26*, 147–179.

Aleven, V., Roll, I., McLaren, B., & Koedinger, K. (2016). Help helps, but only so much: Research on help seeking with intelligent tutoring systems. *International Journal of Artificial Intelligence in Education, 26*, 205–223.

Anderson, J. R., Boyle, C. F., Corbett, A. T., & Lewis, M. W. (1990). Cognitive modeling and intelligent tutoring. *Artificial Intelligence, 42*, 7–49.

Anderson, J. R., Corbett, A. T., Koedinger, K. R., & Pelletier, R. (1995). Cognitive tutors: Lessons learned. *Journal of the Learning Sciences, 4*, 167–207.

Ariel, R., Dunlosky, J., & Bailey, H. (2009). Agenda-based regulation of study-time allocation: When agendas override item-based monitoring. *Journal of Experimental Psychology: General, 138*(3), 432–447. doi: 10.1037/a0015928

Arroyo, I., Woolf, B., Burelson, W., Muldner, K., Rai, D., & Tai, M. (2014). A multimedia adaptive tutoring system for mathematics that address cognition, metacognition, and affect. *International Journal of Artificial Intelligence in Education, 24*, 387–426.

Azevedo, R. (2020). Reflections on the field of metacognition: issues, challenges, and opportunities. *Metacognition and Learning, 15*, 91–98.

Azevedo, R., & Aleven, V. (Eds.). (2013). *International handbook of metacognition and learning technologies* (Vol. 26). Springer.

Azevedo, R., Bouchet, F., Duffy, M., Harley, J., Taub, M., Trevors, G., Cloude, E., Dever, D., Wiedbusch, M., Wortha, F., & Cerezo, R. (2022). Lessons learned and future directions of MetaTutor: Leveraging multichannel data to scaffold self-regulated learning with an Intelligent Tutoring System. *Frontiers in Psychology, 13*, 813632. doi: 10.3389/fpsyg.2022.813632.

Azevedo, R., & Dever, D. (2022). Metacognition in multimedia learning. In R. Mayer & L. Fiorella (Eds.), *The Cambridge handbook of multimedia learning* (3rd ed.). Cambridge University Press.

Azevedo, R., & Gasevic, D. (2019). Analyzing multimodal multichannel data about self-regulated learning with advanced learning technologies: Issues and challenges. *Computers in Human Behavior, 96*, 207–210.

Azevedo, R., Harley, J., Trevors, G., Duffy, M., Feyzi-Behnagh, R., Bouchet, F., & Landis, R. (2013). Using trace data to examine the complex roles of cognitive, metacognitive, and emotional self-regulatory processes during learning with multi-agent systems. In *International handbook of metacognition and learning technologies* (pp. 427–449). Springer.

Azevedo, R., Johnson, A., Chauncey, A., & Burkett, C. (2011). Self-regulated learning with MetaTutor: Advancing the science of learning with MetaCognitive tools. In M. Khine & I. Saleh (Eds.), *New science of learning* (pp. 225–247). New York: Springer.

Azevedo, R., & Lajoie, S. P. (1998). The cognitive basis for the design of a mammography interpretation tutor. In *Proceedings of the Twentieth Annual Conference of the Cognitive Science Society: August 1–4, 1998, University of Wisconsin-Madison* (Vol. 20, p. 78). Lawrence Erlbaum Associates.

Azevedo, R., Martin, S. A., Taub, M., Mudrick, N. V., Millar, G. C., & Grafsgaard, J. F. (2016, June). Are pedagogical agents' external regulation effective in fostering learning with intelligent tutoring systems? In *International Conference on Intelligent Tutoring Systems* (pp. 197–207). Springer, Cham.

Azevedo, R., Moos, D. C., Greene, J. A., Winters, F. I., & Cromley, J. G. (2008). Why is externally facilitated regulated learning more effective than self-regulated learning with hypermedia? *Educational Technology Research and Development, 56*(1), 45–72.

Azevedo, R., Mudrick, N. V., Taub, M., & Bradbury, A. (2019). Self-regulation in computer-assisted learning systems. In J. Dunlosky & K. Rawson (Eds.), *Handbook of cognition and education* (pp. 587–618). Cambridge University Press.

Azevedo, R., & Taub, M. (2020). The challenge of measuring processes and outcomes during learning from multiple representations with advanced learning technologies. In P. Kendeou, P. Van Meter, A. List, & D. Lombardi (Eds.), *Handbook of learning from multiple representations and perspectives* (pp. 532–553). Cambridge University Press.

Azevedo, R., Taub, M., & Mudrick, N. V. (2018). Using multi-channel trace data to infer and foster self-regulated learning between humans and advanced learning technologies. In D. Schunk & Greene, J. A. (Eds.), *Handbook of self-regulation of learning and performance* (2nd ed., pp. 254–270). Routledge.

Azevedo, R., & Witherspoon, A. M. (2009). 17 self-regulated learning with hypermedia. In D. J. Hacker, J. Dunlosky, & A. C. Graesser (Eds.), *Handbook of metacognition in education* (pp. 319–339). Routledge.

Azevedo, R., Witherspoon, A., Graesser, A., McNamara, D., Chauncey, A., Siler, E., … & Lintean, M. (2009). MetaTutor: Analyzing self-regulated learning in a tutoring system for biology. *Frontiers in Artificial Intelligence and Applications, 200*, 635–637.

Bargh, J. A., & Schul, Y. (1980). On the cognitive benefits of teaching. *Journal of Educational Psychology, 72*(5), 593.

Benware, C. A., & Deci, E. L. (1984). Quality of learning with an active versus passive motivational set. *American Educational Research Journal, 21*(4), 755–765.

Biswas, G., Baker, R., & Paquette, L. (2018). Data mining methods for assessing self-regulated learning. In D. H. Schunk & J. A. Greene (Eds.), *Handbook of self-regulation of learning and performance* (2nd ed., pp. 388–404). Routledge.

Biswas, G., Leelawong, K., Schwartz, D., Vye, N., & The Teachable Agents Group at Vanderbilt. (2005). Learning by teaching: A new agent paradigm for educational software. *Applied Artificial Intelligence, 19*(3–4), 363–392.

Biswas, G., Segedy, J. R., & Bunchongchit, K. (2016). From design to implementation to practice a learning by teaching system: Betty's Brain. *International Journal of Artificial Intelligence in Education, 26*(1), 350–364.

Bjork, R. A., Dunlosky, J., & Kornell, N. (2013). Self-regulated learning: Beliefs, techniques, and illusions. *Annual Review of Psychology, 64*, 417–444.

Bouchet, F., Harley, J. M., & Azevedo, R. (2016, June). Can adaptive pedagogical agents' prompting strategies improve students' learning and self-regulation? In *International Conference on Intelligent Tutoring Systems* (pp. 368–374). Springer, Cham.

Bull, S. (2020, April-June). There are open learner models about! *IEEE Transactions on Learning Technologies, 13*, 425–448.

Burstein, J., Tetreault, J., & Madnani, N. (2013). The e-rater automated essay scoring system. In Mark D. Shermis & Jill Burstein (Eds.), *Handbook of automated essay evaluation: Current applications and new directions* (pp. 55–67). Routledge.

Chi, M. T., Siler, S. A., Jeong, H., Yamauchi, T., & Hausmann, R. G. (2001). Learning from human tutoring. *Cognitive science, 25*(4), 471–533.

Cloude, E. B., Taub, M., & Azevedo, R. (2018, June). Investigating the role of goal orientation: Metacognitive and cognitive strategy use and learning with intelligent tutoring systems. In *International Conference on Intelligent Tutoring Systems* (pp. 44–53). Springer, Cham.

Conati, C. (2016). Commentary on: "Toward computer-based support of MetaCognitive skills: A computational framework to coach self-explanation". *International Journal of Artificial Intelligence in Education, 26*(1), 183–192.

Cromley, J. G., & Azevedo, R. (2006). Self-report of reading comprehension strategies: What are we measuring? *Metacognition and Learning, 1*, 229–247. doi:10.1007/s11409-006-9002-5.

D'Mello, S., Lehman, B., Sullins, J., Daigle, R., Combs, R., Vogt, K., … & Graesser, A. (2010, June). A time for emoting: When affect-sensitivity is and isn't effective at promoting deep learning. In *International Conference on Intelligent Tutoring Systems* (pp. 245–254). Springer, Berlin, Heidelberg.

Dever, D. A., & Azevedo, R. (2020) Examining gaze behaviors and metacognitive judgments of informational text within game-based learning environments. In *International Conference on Artificial Intelligence in Education* (pp. 121–132). Springer, Cham.

Du Boulay, B., & Luckin, R. (2016). Modeling human teaching tactics and strategies for tutoring systems: 14 years on. *International Journal of Artificial Intelligence in Education, 26*, 393–404.

Duffy, M. C., & Azevedo, R. (2015). Motivation matters: Interactions between achievement goals and agent scaffolding for self-regulated learning within an intelligent tutoring system. *Computers in Human Behavior, 52*, 338–348.

Dunlosky, J., & Rawson, K. (Eds.). (2019). *The Cambridge handbook of cognition and education.* Cambridge University Press.

Dunlosky, J., & Tauber, S. K. (2011). Understanding people's metacognitive judgments: An isomechanism framework and its implications for applied and theoretical research. In T. J. Perfect & D. S. Lindsay (Eds.) *The Sage handbook of applied memory*, 444–464.

Efklides, A., Schwartz, B. L., & Brown, V. (2018). Motivation and affect in self-regulated learning: Does metacognition play a role? In D. H. Schunk & J. A. Greene (Eds.), *Educational psychology handbook series. Handbook of self-regulation of learning and performance* (pp. 64–82). Routledge/Taylor & Francis Group.

Feyzi-Behnagh, R., Azevedo, R., Legowski, E., Reitmeyer, K., Tseytlin, E., & Crowley, R. (2014). Metacognitive scaffolds improve self-judgments of accuracy on a medical intelligent tutoring system. *Instructional Science, 42*, 159–181.

Graesser, A. C. (2009). Cognitive scientists prefer theories and testable principles with teeth. *Educational Psychologist, 44*(3), 193–197.

Graesser, A. C., Person, N. K., & Magliano, J. P. (1995). Collaborative dialogue patterns in naturalistic one-to-one tutoring. *Applied Cognitive Psychology, 9*(6), 495–522.

Graesser, A. C., Wiley, J., Goldman, S. R., O'Reilly, T., Jeon, M., & McDaniel, B. (2007). SEEK Web tutor: Fostering a critical stance while exploring the causes of volcanic eruption. *Metacognition and Learning, 2*(2–3), 89–105.

Graesser, A. C., Hu, X., & Sottilare, R. (2018). Intelligent tutoring systems. In F. Fischer, C. E. Hmelo-Silver, S. R. Goldman, and P. Reimann (Eds.), *International handbook of the learning sciences* (pp. 246–255). Routledge.

Graesser, A. C., Rus, V., Hu, X. (2017). Instruction based on tutoring. In R. E. Mayer & P. A. Alexander (Eds.), *Handbook of research on learning and instruction* (pp. 460–482). Routledge Press.

Greene, J. A., & Azevedo, R. (2009). A macro-level analysis of SRL processes and their relations to the acquisition of a sophisticated mental model of a complex system. *Contemporary Educational Psychology, 34*(1), 18–29.

Greene, J. A., & Azevedo, R. (2010). The measurement of learners' self-regulated cognitive and metacognitive processes while using computer-based learning environments. *Educational Psychologist, 45*, 203–209.

Greene, J. A., Bolick, C. M., Jackson, W. P., Caprino, A. M., Oswald, C., & McVea, M. (2015). Domain-specificity of self-regulated learning processing in science and history digital libraries. *Contemporary Educational Psychology, 42*, 111–128.

Griffin, T. D., Mielicki, M. K., & Wiley, J. (2019). Improving students' metacomprehension accuracy. In J. Dunlosky & K. Rawson, K. (Eds.). *The Cambridge handbook of cognition and education* (pp. 619–646). Cambridge University Press.

Hacker, D., & Bol, L. (2019). Calibration and self-regulated learning: Making the connections. In J. Dunlosky & K. Rawson, K. (Eds.). *The Cambridge handbook of cognition and education* (pp. 647–677). Cambridge University Press.

Hadwin, A. F. (2021). Commentary and future directions: What can multi-modal data reveal about temporal and adaptive processes in self-regulated learning? *Learning & Instruction, 172*. doi: 10.1016/j.learninstruc.2019.101287

Harley, J., Bouchet, F., & Azevedo, R. (2018, June). Examining how students' typical studying emotions relate to those experienced while studying with an ITS. In *ITS 2018-14th International Conference on Intelligent Tutoring Systems* (Vol. 10858, pp. 434–437). Springer.

Harley, J. M., Taub, M., Azevedo, R., & Bouchet, F. (2018). "Let's set up some subgoals": Understanding human-pedagogical agent collaborations and their implications for learning and prompt and feedback compliance. *IEEE Transactions on Learning Technologies, 11*, 54–66.

Heidig, S., & Clarebout, G. (2011). Do pedagogical agents make a difference to student motivation and learning? *Educational Research Review, 6*(1), 27–54.

Jackson, G. T., Davis, N. L., & McNamara, D. S. (2011, June). Students' enjoyment of a game-based tutoring system. In *International Conference on Artificial Intelligence in Education* (pp. 475–477). Berlin, Heidelberg: Springer.

Jackson, G. T., & McNamara, D. S. (2013). Motivation and performance in a game-based intelligent tutoring system. *Journal of Educational Psychology, 105*(4), 1036.

Jacobse, A. E., & Harskamp, E. G. (2012). Towards efficient measurement of metacognition in mathematical problem solving. *Metacognition and Learning, 7*, 133–149. doi:10.1007/s11409-012-9088-x.

Johnson, W. L., & Lester, J. C. (2016). Face-to-face interaction with pedagogical agents, twenty years later. *International Journal of Artificial Intelligence in Education, 26*(1), 25–36.

Kim, Y., & Baylor, A. L. (2016). Based design of pedagogical agent roles: A review, progress, and recommendations. *International Journal of Artificial Intelligence in Education, 26*(1), 160–169.

Koedinger, K., & Aleven, V. (2016). An interview reflection on "Intelligent tutoring goes to school in the big city". *International Journal of Artificial Intelligence in Education, 26*, 13–24.

Koriat, A. (2015). When two heads are better than one and when they can be worse: The amplification hypothesis. *Journal of Experimental Psychology: General, 144*(5), 934.

Kumar, S., Dasgupta, I., Cohen, J. D., Daw, N. D., & Griffiths, T. L. (2020). Meta-learning of compositional task distributions in humans and machines. arXiv preprint arXiv:2010.02317.

Lajoie, S. P. (2020). Student modeling for individuals and groups: the BioWorld and HOWARD platforms. *International Journal of Artificial Intelligence in Education*, 1–16.

Lajoie, S. P., & Azevedo, R. (2006). Teaching and learning in technology-rich environments. In P. A. Alexander & P. H. Winne (Eds.), *Handbook of educational psychology* (pp. 803–821). Lawrence Erlbaum Associates Publishers.

Lake, B. M. (2019). Compositional generalization through meta sequence-to-sequence learning. *Advances in Neural Information Processing Systems, 32*.

Leelawong, K., & Biswas, G. (2008). Designing learning by teaching agents: The Betty's Brain system. *International Journal of Artificial Intelligence in Education, 18*(3), 181–208.

Magliano, J. P., Todaro, S., Millis, K., Wiemer-Hastings, K., Kim, H. J., & McNamara, D. S. (2005). Changes in reading strategies as a function of reading training: A comparison of live and computerized training. *Journal of Educational Computing Research, 32*(2), 185–208.

Matsuda, N., Griger, C. L., Barbalios, N., Stylianides, G. J., Cohen, W. W., & Koedinger, K. R. (2014, June). Investigating the effect of meta-cognitive scaffolding for learning by teaching. In *International Conference on Intelligent Tutoring Systems* (pp. 104–113). Cham: Springer.

Matsuda, N., Weng, W., & Wall, N. (2020). The effect of metacognitive scaffolding for learning by teaching a teachable agent. *International Journal of Artificial Intelligence in Education, 30*, 1–37.

Matsuda, N., Yarzebinski, E., Keiser, V., Raizada, R., Stylianides, G. J., Cohen, W. W., & Koedinger, K. R. (2011, June). Learning by teaching SimStudent – An initial classroom baseline study comparing with Cognitive Tutor. In *International Conference on Artificial Intelligence in Education* (pp. 213–221). Berlin, Heidelberg: Springer.

McCarthy, K., Likens, A., Johnson, A., Guerrero, T., & McNamara, D. (2018). Metacognitive overload!: Positive and negative effects of metacognitive prompts in an intelligent tutoring system. *International Journal of Artificial Intelligence in Education, 28*, 420–438.

McNamara, D. S. (2004). SERT: Self-explanation reading training. *Discourse Processes, 38*(1), 1–30.

McNamara, D. S., Boonthum, C., Kurby, C. A., Magliano, J., Pillarisetti, S., & Bellissens, C. (2009). Interactive paraphrase training: The development and testing of an iSTART module. In V. Dimitrova, R. Mizoguchi, & B. du Boulay (Eds.) *Artificial intelligence in education* (pp. 181–188). Springer.

McNamara, D. S., O'Reilly, T., Rowe, M., Boonthum, C., & Levinstein, I. B. (2007). iSTART: A web-based tutor that teaches self-explanation and metacognitive reading strategies. *Reading comprehension strategies: Theories, interventions, and technologies*, 397–421.

Mudrick, N. V., Azevedo, R., & Taub, M. (2019). Integrating metacognitive judgments and eye movements using sequential pattern mining to understand processes underlying multimedia learning. *Computers in Human Behavior, 96*, 223–234.

Mudrick, N. V., Taub, M., & Azevedo, R. (2018). MetaMentor: An interactive system that uses visualizations of students' real-time cognitive, affective, metacognitive, and motivational self-regulatory processes to study human tutors' decision making. In S. Craig (Ed.), *Tutoring and intelligent tutoring systems* (pp. 157–184). Nova Science Publishers.

Nelson, T. O. (1990). Metamemory: A theoretical framework and new findings. In *Psychology of learning and motivation* (Vol. 26, pp. 125–173). Academic Press.

Nye, B., Graesser, A., & Hu, X. (2014). AutoTutor and family; A review of 17 years of natural language tutoring. *International Journal of Artificial Intelligence in Education, 24*, 427–469.

O'Reilly, T., Best, R., & McNamara, D. S. (2004). Self-explanation reading training: Effects for low-knowledge readers. In *Proceedings of the Annual Meeting of the Cognitive Science Society* (Vol. 26, No. 26).

Page, E. B. (2003). Project Essay Grade: PEG. In M. D. Shermis & J. Burstein (Eds.), *Automated essay scoring: A cross-disciplinary perspective* (pp. 43–54). Lawrence Erlbaum Associates Publishers.

Penttinen, M., Anto, E., & Mikkilä-Erdmann, M. (2013). Conceptual change, text comprehension and eye movements during reading. *Research in Science Education, 43*(4), 1407–1434.

Perry, N. E. (2010). Introduction: Using qualitative methods to enrich understandings of self-regulated learning. *Educational Psychologist, 37*, 1–3.

Pintrich, P. R. (2002). The role of metacognitive knowledge in learning, teaching, and assessing. *Theory into Practice, 41*(4), 219–225.

Pintrich, P. R., & de Groot, E. V. (1990). Motivated strategies for learning questionnaire. Retrieved from PsycTESTS. doi:10.1037/t09161-000.

Porayska-Pomsta, K. (2016). AI as a methodology for supporting educational praxis and teacher metacognition. *International Journal of Artificial Intelligence in Education, 26*(2), 679–700.

Putnam, V., & Conati, C. (2019, March). Exploring the need for explainable artificial intelligence (XAI) in intelligent tutoring systems (ITS). In *IUI Workshops* (Vol. 19).

Roll, I., Aleven, V., McLaren, B. M., & Koedinger, K. R. (2007, June). Can help seeking be tutored? Searching for the secret sauce of metacognitive tutoring. In *Proceedings of the 2007 conference on Artificial Intelligence in Education: Building Technology Rich Learning Contexts That Work* (pp. 203–210).

Roll, I., Wiese, E. S., Long, Y., Aleven, V., & Koedinger, K. R. (2014). Tutoring self-and co-regulation with intelligent tutoring systems to help students acquire better learning skills. *Design Recommendations for Intelligent Tutoring Systems, 2*, 169–182.

Roll, I., & Wylie, R. (2016). Evolution and revolution in artificial intelligence in education. *International Journal of Artificial Intelligence in Education, 26*(2), 582–599.

Rosenshine, B., Meister, C., & Chapman, S. (1996). Teaching students to generate questions: A review of the intervention studies. *Review of Educational Research, 66*(2), 181–221.

Saleh, A., Yuxin, C., Hmelo-Silver, C. E., Glazewski, K. D., Mott, B. W., & Lester, J. C. (2020). Coordinating scaffolds for collaborative inquiry in a game-based learning environment. *Journal of Research in Science Teaching, 57*(9), 1490–1518.

Schraw, G., & Dennison, R. S. (1994). Assessing metacognitive awareness. *Contemporary Educational Psychology, 19*, 460–475. doi:10.1006/ceps.1994.1033.

Schroeder, N. L., Adesope, O. O., & Gilbert, R. B. (2013). How effective are pedagogical agents for learning? A meta-analytic review. *Journal of Educational Computing Research, 49*(1), 1–39.

Schroeder, N. L., Romine, W. L., & Craig, S. D. (2017). Measuring pedagogical agent persona and the influence of agent persona on learning. *Computers & Education, 109*, 176–186.

Schunk, D., & Greene, J. (2018). *Handbook of self-regulation of learning and performance* (2nd edition). Routledge.

Self, J. (2016). The birth of IJAIED. *International Journal of Artificial Intelligence in Education, 28*, 4–12.

Shea, N., Boldt, A., Bang, D., Yeung, N., Heyes, C., & Frith, C. (2014). Supra-personal cognitive control and metacognition. *Trends in Cognitive Sciences, 18*(4), 186–193.

Sonnenberg, C., & Bannert, M. (2019). Using process mining to examine the sustainability of instructional support: How stable are the effects of metacognitive prompting on self-regulatory behavior? *Computers in Human Behavior, 96*, 259–272.

Sottilare, R., Burke, C., Salas, E., Sinatra, A., Johnston, J., & Gilbert, S. (2018). Designing adaptive instruction for team: A meta-analysis. *International Journal of Artificial Intelligence in Education, 28*, 225–264.

Suleman, R., Mizoguchi, R., & Ikeda, M. (2016). A new 2perspective on negotiation-based dialog to enhance metacognitive skills in the context of open learner models. *International Journal of Artificial Intelligence in Education, 26*, 1069–1115.

Tarricone, P. (2011). *The taxonomy of metacognition.* Psychology Press.

Taub, M., & Azevedo, R. (2019). How does prior knowledge influence fixations on and sequences of cognitive and metacognitive SRL processes during learning with an ITS? *International Journal of Artificial Intelligence in Education, 29*, 1–28.

Taub, M., Azevedo, R., Bouchet, F., & Khosravifar, B. (2014). Can the use of cognitive and metacognitive self-regulated learning strategies be predicted by learners' levels of prior knowledge in hypermedia-learning environments? *Computers in Human Behavior, 39*, 356–367.

Taub, M., Azevedo, R., Rajendran, R., Cloude, E. B., Biswas, G., & Price, M. J. (2019). How are students' emotions related to the accuracy of cognitive and metacognitive processes during learning with an intelligent tutoring system? *Learning and Instruction*, 101200.

Trevors, G., Duffy, M., & Azevedo, R. (2014). Note-taking within MetaTutor: Interactions between an intelligent tutoring system and prior knowledge on note-taking and learning. *Educational Technology Research and Development, 62*(5), 507–528.

Van Kleef, G. A. (2009). How emotions regulate social life: The emotions as social information (EASI) model. *Current Directions in Psychological Science, 18*(3), 184–188.

VanLehn, K. (2016a). Regulative loops, step loops and task loops. *International Journal of Artificial Intelligence in Education, 26*, 107–112.

VanLehn, K. (2016b). Reflections on Andes' Goal-free User Interface. *International Journal of Artificial Intelligence in Education, 26*(1), 82–90.

Veenman, M. V. (2015). Metacognition. In P. Afflerbach (Ed.), *Handbook of individual differences in reading* (pp. 44–58). Routledge.

Veenman, M. V., Bavelaar, L., De Wolf, L., & Van Haaren, M. (2014). The on-line assessment of metacognitive skills in a computerized learning environment. *Learning and Individual Differences, 29*, 123–130.

Weinstein, C. E., Schulte, A., & Palmer, D. R. (1987). *The learning and study strategies inventory.* H&H Publishing.

Wiedbusch, M. D., & Azevedo, R. (2020, June). Modeling metacomprehension monitoring accuracy with eye gaze on informational content in a multimedia learning environment. In *ACM Symposium on Eye Tracking Research and Applications* (pp. 1–9).

Wiedbusch, M. D., Kite, V., Yang, X., Park, S., Chi, M., Taub, M., & Azevedo, R. (2021). A theoretical and evidence-based conceptual design of MetaDash: An intelligent teacher dashboard to support teachers' decision making and students' self-regulated learning. In *Frontiers in Education* (Vol. 6, p. 14). Frontiers.

Winne, P. H. (2017). Learning analytics for self-regulated learning. In C. Lang, G. Siemens, A. Wise & D. Gasevic (Eds.), *Handbook of learning analytics* (pp. 241–249). The Society for Learning Analytics Research.

Winne, P. H. (2018). Cognition and metacognition within self-regulated learning. In D. Schunk & J. A. Greene, (Eds.), *Handbook of self-regulation of learning and performance* (2nd ed., pp. 254–270). Routledge.

Winne, P. H. (2019). Paradigmatic dimensions of instrumentation and analytic methods in research on self-regulated learning. *Computers in Human Behavior, 96*, 285–289.

Winne, P. H. (2020). Construct and consequential validity for learning analytics based on trace data. *Computers in Human Behavior, 112*, 106457.

Winne, P. H., & Azevedo, R. (2022). Metacognition. In K. Sawyer (Ed.), *Cambridge Handbook of the learning sciences* (3rd ed., pp. 93–113). Cambridge, MA: Cambridge University Press.

Winne, P. H., & Hadwin, A. F. (1998). Studying as self-regulated learning, In D. J. Hacker, J. Dunlosky, & A. Graesser (Eds.), *Metacognition in educational theory and practice.* Lawrence Erlbaum Associates Publishers.

Winne, P. H., & Hadwin, A. F. (2008). The weave of motivation and self-regulated learning. In D. H. Schunk & B. J. Zimmerman (Eds.), *Motivation and self-regulated learning: Theory, research, and applications* (pp. 297–314). Lawrence Erlbaum Associates Publishers.

Winne, P. H., & Jamieson-Noel, D. (2002). Exploring students' calibration of self-reports about study tactics and achievement. *Contemporary Educational Psychology, 27*(4), 551–572.

Woolf, B. (2009). *Building intelligent interactive tutors student-centered strategies for revolutionizing e-learning.* Morgan Kaufmann.

Zimmerman, B. J., & Moylan, A. R. (2009). Self-regulation: Where metacognition and motivation intersect. In *Handbook of metacognition in education* (pp. 311–328). Routledge.

5. Theories of affect, meta-affect, and affective pedagogy

Ivon Arroyo, Kaśka Porayska-Pomsta and Kasia Muldner

INTRODUCTION

When a student gets a low mark on a school exam, they may blame themselves for it, and experience negative emotions such as shame and guilt. Alternatively, a student may consider that the test was unfairly hard, and may instead experience anger, frustration, and/or helplessness. Another student may instead feel apathy, as they don't care about grades. The specific affective reactions of students might motivate them to redouble efforts in the next test, change studying habits, or give up on attempting to do well in the course altogether. Note that students experience, interpret, and react to the same academic situation in a multitude of different ways. Why such a variety of responses exists is a complex question that has been the subject of study in several cognate disciplines, including cognitive and developmental psychology and neuroscience, education research, the learning sciences, and AIED.

This chapter explores some of those theories and exemplifies how they have been used in AIED research. We address three major categorizations of affective experiences, namely emotion, motivation, and emotion/motivation regulation. This is because the term "affect" has been used as a generic term to refer to an umbrella of emotional and motivational experiences. At the most basic definition, *emotions* are internal experiences related to the pleasantness or unpleasantness of an experience (valence), that may produce a variety of physiological reactions (arousal) and physical manifestations such as facial and bodily expressions (Shuman & Scherer, 2014). For instance, when a person is surprised, they may open their eyes and mouth, activating their nervous system to the experience of surprise. When a person is either sad or bored, their facial muscles tend to relax, with mouth and eye corners pointing down (Ekman, 1972), showing a low level of physiological arousal.

Motivation instead refers to more stable affective predispositions, such as the general appreciation of a subject as being liked, worth pursuing, or about me being good at a certain subject or not. Another term is meta-affect, a construct used to refer to the various levels of awareness and regulation of a person's emotions and motivations (DeBellis & Goldin, 2006). It also refers to affect about affect, affect about and within cognition about affect, and the individual's monitoring of affect through cognition (thinking about the direction of one's feelings). Meta-affect relates to a person's realizations and reactions to their own affective experiences (e.g. the realization that thinking about exam preparation makes them anxious).

All these constructs, along with the mechanisms that regulate them, will be described and examined within this chapter through a review and summary of the key theories that have been proposed to explain them. Table 5.1 lays out the structure of the chapter. We discuss the two constructs of motivation and emotion in education, along with their differences, and examine these constructs from a multidisciplinary perspective, including educational,

Table 5.1   *Layout of the chapter*

Section	Subsection	Main Sub-Areas
Emotion	Early Theories	• Ekman Theory of Emotion • OCC Theory of Emotion
	Control-Value Theory of Emotion in Education	• Subjective control and value • Three-dimensional taxonomy of emotions • Implications for pedagogy
	Distinguishing Emotions from Other Affective Categories	• The distinguishing features of emotions • Emotions vs. moods • Emotions vs. attitudes and emotions vs. preferences
	Neuroscience of Emotions in Education	• Emotional thought • Implications for pedagogy • Introspective vs. extrospective processes • Implications for pedagogy • The social brain
	Past AIED Research, New Opportunities and Pitfalls for Research in AIED	
Motivation	Motivational Theories Related to Education	• Early theories • Expectancy-value theory • Implications for pedagogy • Intrinsic and extrinsic motivation • Attributional processes • Goals and growth mindset • Implications for pedagogy • Passion for long-term goals
	Past AIED Research, New Opportunities and Pitfalls for Research in AIED	
Meta-Emotion and Meta-Motivation Theories	Emotion Regulation Theories Related to Education	• Gross's Process Model of Emotion Regulation
	Motivation Regulation Theories Related to Education	• Strategies for motivation regulation
	What Causes Students to Regulate Their Emotions and/or Motivation?	• Implications for pedagogy
	Past AIED Research, New Opportunities and Pitfalls for Research in AIED	
Discussion and Conclusion		

affective neuroscience in education, and AIED research and practices. Last, we also cover meta-affect, a student's awareness and regulation of their own affective experiences.

Each section highlights major theories of the three affective areas (emotion, motivation, and regulation), but not only that. We also address how these theories impact learning and educational outcomes, and the major implications that the theories have on pedagogy for any kind of learning environment. At the end of each section, we discuss major implications, opportunities for research, and pitfalls for past and future research in AIED. This includes examples of efforts made by the AIED community to automatically understand, assess and respond to students' affect and lay out opportunities for future research in AIED.

EMOTION

Researchers from diverse disciplines widely recognize that emotions are primary to action and human learning. Emotions determine not only how we are able to engage in learning, but also whether we can be motivated to learn in the first place, and whether we can reason, remember and construct knowledge (e.g. Yerkes & Dodson, 1908). At a fundamental level, emotions are a person's physio-biological reactions to the environment, which operate according to some basic evolutionary nature-universal templates: negative emotions typically lead to avoidance behaviors (e.g. fright or flight), whereas positive emotions lead to approach behaviors (love–nurture) (Shuman and Scherer, 2014). These template-based behaviors can be readily explained by reference to basic survival mechanics that are inherent in our neuro-biological system design (Immordino-Yang, 2015).

The study of emotions in education and in human formal learning is relatively new, mainly because, for centuries, emotions have been considered a hindrance to rational thinking (Shuman and Sherer, 2014; Mandler, 1989). However, the relatively recent work on the nature and role of emotions in education (see Pekrun, 2006; Pekrun et al., 2007, 2012) along with the emerging affective neuroscience in education studies (see Immordino-Yang, 2016; Immordino-Yang and Damasio, 2007) provide both theoretical conceptualizations and growing empirical evidence of the profound influence that emotional experiences cast over people's ability to engage in learning in the short and long terms. This research suggests that these basic behavioral templates, involved in the survival mechanisms mentioned earlier, can also be found in complex situations, such as human learning in general and in formal learning in particular. Nevertheless, such behavioral templates tend to be harder to identify in learning than in basic survival reactions. This is due to the complex relationship between the causes of emotional reactions in learning contexts (e.g. hidden sociocultural and/or personality-based causes vs. directly observable fright-inducing stimuli), and the high-level neurocognitive processes involved in learning, such as deliberative executive function-driven actions, as required for problem solving, as opposed to automatic reptilian reactions of the fright–flight kind.

Key Questions for Emotion-Focused Research in Education

Key questions for research related to emotions and learning include (1) what defines emotions? (2) how can emotions be differentiated from other affective phenomena such as a person's mood or motivation? and (3) what emotions are relevant to learning and why? Distinguishing between the different affective categories is particularly important in education-oriented disciplines such as the Learning Sciences and AIED, which focus on developing and evaluating interventions to transform behavior and enable learning. Specifically, understanding the difference between short-lasting emotional states, such as anxiety about a specific math exam, and long-lasting emotional traits, such as persistent fearful predisposition about formal learning, will impact what underlying learning support may be needed (e.g. immediate feedback vs. longer-term support strategy). Making such a distinction is also important in selecting appropriate methods to identify and study the specific affective experiences (see e.g. Porayska-Pomsta et al., 2013). Knowing which emotions are particularly important in education is useful for understanding more precisely what barriers and openings for learning are inherent to individual students, and for tailoring the learning environments accordingly.

Early Theories

Many theories were proposed in the twentieth century that attempted to classify and explain emotions, and their origin. One of the most noteworthy was Ekman's Theory of Emotion, which proposed six basic emotions: fear, anger, joy, sadness, disgust, and surprise (Ekman et al., 1972; Ekman, 1999). His important contribution was that he associated universal physiological facial expressions with these basic emotions, coming from a Darwinian natural selection perspective.

The OCC (Ortony, Clore & Collins) Theory of Emotion (Ortony et al., 1988) is one of several appraisal theories that arose in the 1980s that have tried to frame and categorize emotions in general. It distinguishes 22 emotion types, differentiating those that have a focus on the *outcomes of events* (e.g. sadness and pity), from emotions that concern the agency of actions (e.g. pride and shame), and from emotions focused on the *attributes of objects* (e.g. disgust, love).

Control-Value Theory of Emotion in Education

The *Control-Value Theory* of achievement (henceforth, CVT) proposed by Pekrun (2006) is one of the key accounts of why particular emotions arise during formal learning and how such emotions relate to learners' motivation and actions. CVT offers a detailed account and an integrative framework that explains the mechanics involved in academic emotional experiences. The theory has served to define, examine and cater for emotional experiences of learners across numerous approaches within the Learning Sciences and the AIED community. The theory is so called because it assumes that at a high level of description, learners experience specific emotions depending on (1) how much control they feel they have over their academic activities and outcomes (subjective control) and (2) what importance they assign to those activities and outcomes (subjective value).

Subjective control and value

Subjective control is dependent on causal expectancies and attributions that lead to particular appraisals of control that students think they have over their activities and outcomes. In his earlier work, Pekrun (1988) defined three types of attributions that learners make and that arise from expectancies related to (1) *action control* (learners' belief that they are able to initiate actions), (2) *action outcome* (learners' belief that their actions will lead to expected outcomes) and (3) *situation outcome* (learners' beliefs that a particular situation is likely to naturally result in expected outcomes regardless of their own effort). In most learning scenarios, it is the first two categories that play the predominant role in the appraisal of subjective control.

Subjective value is defined in terms of intrinsic and extrinsic values of activities and outcomes. As in the context of motivation – a consequent of emotions – intrinsic value arises from a person's natural interest in or appreciation of activities, such as an interest in mathematics or appreciation of art, regardless of whether or not such activities lead to outcomes such as securing good grades or being able to produce a museum-worthy painting. In contrast, extrinsic value is tightly coupled with the perceived utility of activities (e.g. the value of studying for exams for securing good grades) and outcomes (e.g. the value of good grades for securing a job).

According to the CVT, depending on individuals and circumstances, there are different possible patterns of the control and value appraisals, which will lead to different academic emotions being foregrounded in an individual's experiences.

Three-dimensional taxonomy of emotions
CVT characterizes all academic emotions along a three-dimensional taxonomy of (1) object focus, (2) valence and (3) activation.

Object focus of emotions
Object focus is a directional dimension, which encapsulates the observation that, as with all emotions, academic emotions are directed toward something. As already mentioned, academic emotions can be directed towards either activities or outcomes, that is, the objects of the emotional experiences. The specific activities and outcomes that are particular to education, such as tests, grades, or subject-related tasks, help us to distinguish between the emotions that are specific to academic contexts, such as anxiety about the outcome of a math test, and broader emotional experiences, such as fear of harm under some physically threatening circumstances.

Outcome emotions can be directed towards *retrospective outcomes* (i.e. those that have already been achieved, for example, pride at getting a high grade on a math test) or *prospective outcomes* (i.e those that are yet to happen, e.g. anxiety about a future math test). The temporal aspect of the outcome-focused emotions dictates the specific emotions that are being experienced (e.g. pride, joy, gratitude for having achieved something, i.e. the past outcomes, vs. anxiety, hope, or anticipation toward something that is yet to happen, i.e. the future outcomes). The level of *perceived control* and the *valence of focus* (positive, negative, or neutral) will also influence the specific emotions experienced. For example, a high level of subjective control coupled with positive focus will likely result in anticipatory joy towards a prospective outcome (e.g. exam results); low subjective control (which may also be equated with partial predictability of the possible outcome), coupled with negative focus, is likely to lead to anxiety, whereas when coupled with positive focus, it is likely to result in hope. Note that the level of subjective control is not relevant to retrospective outcomes, since such emotions relate to outcomes that have been accomplished already and, thus, are no longer controllable.

Another aspect of outcome-related emotions is that they can either involve elaborate cognitive mediation, which renders them *control-dependent* emotions, or they can arise because of impulsive reactions to a situation in which success or failure has been experienced – there are *control-independent* emotions. Such control-independent emotions usually include *joy, contentment* (if success is experienced), *disappointment* (in the absence of occurrence of success), *sadness* and *frustration* in the context of failure, and *relief* in the absence of failure. Emotions such as *pride, shame, gratitude*, or *anger* can all be attributed to the success or failure resulting from actions by self (*pride, shame*), by others (*gratitude, anger*), or from situational factors.

Like outcome emotions, activity emotions are tightly linked with the perceived control dimension – in this case the perceived control over an activity – and with the value attributed to the activity. *Enjoyment* results from a highly controllable and positively valued activity; *anger* is likely to result from a high level of perceived control and negatively valued activity; whereas low controllability and positive value attributions towards an activity are likely to lead to *frustration*. Neutral attributions of control and value tend to lead to *boredom*.

Object focus of emotions also allows us to define specific *types* of academic emotions, which in turn allows us to identify the emotions that correspond to a given type. In particular, Pekrun and Stephens (2010) identified four types of academic emotions depending on their object focus: (1) achievement; (2) specific topic studied; (3) social relationships; and (4) epistemics. As already discussed, *achievement emotions*, such as contentment, anxiety, and frustration, are linked to activities (e.g. homework, taking a test) and outcomes (e.g. success/ failure). *Topic emotions* may involve sympathy and empathy for a character in a story and thus relate to a particular learning topic. *Social emotions*, such as pride or shame, reflect the fact that educational activities are socially situated and that there may be particular social expectations associated with learning (e.g. to prepare for exams, where failure to do so might give rise to shame vis-à-vis social expectations). *Epistemic emotions* arise primarily from cognitive information processing, such as surprise and curiosity when novelty is encountered, or confusion, when the student experiences an impasse (Pekrun et al., 2017; Vogl et al., 2020). This taxonomy of academic emotions presupposes a large set of affective states that are universally relevant across different educational contexts, such as lectures, homework, tests, and so on. Distinguishing between different object foci is important to deciding which contextual aspects of students' emotional experiences to include in the interpretation of those experiences (either in traditional educational settings or in an AIED system), and what specific support strategies and feedback may be best, and over what timescale.

Valence of emotions
Valence of emotions refers to the value (positive, negative, or neutral) that emotions can adopt and is directly linked to the valence of object focus as described above. This is an important dimension which impacts on students' motivation to act and on the type of actions they may take.

As was observed earlier, positive emotions tend to lead to nurturing behaviors (e.g. building social relationships or collaborations), whereas negative emotions tend to lead to avoidance behaviors (e.g. procrastination). Valence of emotional experiences will also likely affect students' ability to self-regulate, plan and strategize, which in turn will impact engagement and performance (Yerkes and Dodson, 1908; Immordino-Yang, 2016; Immordino-Yang and Damasio, 2007). Negative emotions such as anxiety may inhibit self-regulation and higher-order processes involved in metacognitive engagement, as well as motivation to act or even to communicate in the first place (Cohen, 2011; Van Ameringen et al., 2003; Pekrun, 1988; Pekrun, 2010; Baker, 2010). By contrast, positive emotions may lead to enhanced self-regulation, motivation, and social communication. Neuroscience research suggests that valence of emotional experiences can impact core cognitive capacities that are foundational to learning and self-regulation, such as memory, attention, cognitive flexibility, and inhibitory control (see Gomes et al., 2013; Frenzel et al., 2009). Again, negative emotions, such as anxiety and hopelessness, tend to hinder those capacities, whereas positive emotions tend to support healthy functioning of those capacities.

Activation of emotions
Activation of emotions refers to their intensity. Pekrun (1988) defined the intensity of emotions as a *multiplicative function of controllability and value*. Under this definition, the emotional

intensity is positively correlated with controllability for positive emotions (i.e. the higher the controllability, the more intense the positive emotions) and with uncontrollability for negative emotions (i.e. the less controllable the outcomes and activities, the more negative the emotions are). Furthermore, the intensity of the emotions experienced will be further affected by the increasing perceived value of the activity and outcomes, that is, the more highly a student values an activity or outcome, the more relevant the activity or outcome is to the student, and the more intense their emotions will be. Within the CVT framework, the intensity of the emotion experienced is thought to be a function of the degree of subjective value of an activity or outcome, such as belief in the importance of success or failure in an exam. Thus, the perceived value of a subject or a situation has a moderating effect on both the intensity and the type of emotions experienced. Activities or outcomes that are valued positively will tend to lead to positive emotions and vice versa; if they are valued negatively, they will tend to lead to negative emotions.

Implications for pedagogy

Considering the importance of positive emotions to learning, much of the pedagogical implications both with and without technology, and research within AIED and the Learning Sciences, focuses on developing approaches, strategies, and applications that foster positive emotional experiences during learning and practice scenarios. Nevertheless, it is important to note that not all negative emotions are detrimental to learning. Research shows that a battery of negative and positive emotions, namely frustration and surprise, and the epistemic emotions of confusion and curiosity, are often key to knowledge exploration, learning and to students' motivation to persevere (Vogl et al., 2020; Vogl et al., 2019; Baker et al., 2010; Craig, et al., 2004; D'Mello et al., 2014), especially if it is coupled with a value goal orientation. Furthermore, both positive and negative emotions can have a detrimental effect if they are experienced in extreme forms, that is, if their *activation level* is either too high or too low (see Yerkes & Dodson (1908) for negatively valenced emotions; see Gupta et al. (2016) for positively valenced emotions). Other research regarding negative emotions focuses on strategies to help students resolve those emotions, and how to take actions to regulate them and the environments and situations in which they occur (see the final section of this chapter on self-regulation of emotions).

Distinguishing Emotions from Other Affective Categories

The CVT framework offers a clear account of how academic emotions arise and of the different types of emotions that are specifically relevant to formal learning environments. In this sense, the framework aims explicitly to offer a unified theory of academic emotions. However, it is important to note that within the broad research studies of emotions in learning, there are also significant differences in accounting for academic emotions, which are typically reflected in the levels of specificity at which emotions and the neighboring constructs, such as moods, attitudes, preferences and affective dispositions, are being described (Scherer, 2005). Even within CVT, the distinction is often blurred between low-level emotional experiences, such as those that might be captured at the physiological level, and those that involve higher-order cognitive processes. For example, is boredom unequivocally an emotion or is it a motivational state? Being able to distinguish between emotions and other affective categories is useful for addressing the question of the role that emotions play in academic learning (Shuman and Scherer, 2014).

Depending on the discipline within which emotions are being studied, in different theoretical accounts affective phenomena such as emotions, feelings, moods, and motivation may be grouped under one umbrella. Alternatively, they may be treated as forming distinct categories of experiences requiring specialized methodological approaches to be studied, which in turn has implications for how knowledge developed about them may be operationalized in practice, including in front-line teaching (Pekrun, 2012) and in the design and deployment of Artificial Intelligence in Education systems (Porayska-Pomsta et al., 2013). Broadly speaking, educational research tends to compound the non-cognitive constructs under the general term of affect, whereas emotion-focused research in psychology, neuroscience, and latterly affective computing tend to separate between those constructs in order to distinguish between emotional experiences that can be observed and measured objectively (e.g. at a biophysiological level) and those that require further qualitative interpretations in context (e.g. feelings, moods, motivational states, personality-dependent emotion tendencies). In the context of AIED, the need for greater granularity of description adopted in the psychological sciences is preferred, since it allows for precision and formal representation assessment and manipulation of the constructs of interest.

The distinguishing features of emotions

Different affective phenomena range from persistent personality predispositions (e.g. predisposition to experience negative emotions), prolonged mood states (e.g. depression), intermediate-length mood states (e.g. feeling low because I am not having a good day), to transient emotions (e.g. frustration from being stuck), to rapid reflexive responses (e.g. startled) (Porayska-Pomsta et al., 2013; Barrett et al., 2007; Ekman, 1972; Izard et al., 2010; Rosenberg, 1998; Russell, 2003).

Emotions are thought to be multi-componential episodes which are elicited by a variety of stimuli. These stimuli can be real occurrences, or they can be remembered or imagined. Although these stimuli do not have to be consciously observed, the key distinguishing feature of emotions is that they are always *about* something (i.e. emotions always have an object or event focus). Another distinguishing feature between emotions and other affective experiences is that emotions are relatively short-lived and can fluctuate (typically less than 15 minutes for common fear and between 15 and 60 minutes for anger and joy – see Scherer et al. (1986) and Verduyn et al., 2009), with the specific duration and nature of the emotions experienced being determined by the changing relationship between the individual and the object of focus. The sources of such changes can involve the object itself (e.g. the teacher may give an easier test), the individual (e.g. the student may have prepared for a test), the relationship between the individual and the object (e.g. the student drops out from a course), or habituation (e.g. the student became used to taking tests). Finally, what also distinguishes emotions from other affective categories is their structure, which is made up of five key components, including *subjective feeling* ("I am scared"), *motor component* (facial expressions, posture, body language, etc.), *physiological component* ("I feel jittery"), *action tendency* ("I don't want to be here") and *appraisal components* ("I'm not prepared for this test") (Shuman and Sherer, 2014; Kleinginna and Kleinginna, 1981; Pekrun, 2014).

These different emotion components are associated with different, mutually supporting functions (Schuman and Sherer, 2014). Examining those functions allows us to distinguish clearly between emotions from other affective phenomena, such as moods, attitudes, preferences, and affect dispositions, which in turn serves to develop approaches to measuring emotions and for adaptively tailoring the pedagogical supports within AIED systems.

Emotions vs. moods

Emotions are distinguished from moods mainly by their shorter duration, by the fact that they always have an event/object focus, and that their object is appraised. In contrast, moods are lingering experiences which often do not have a specific object (e.g. one can be in a bad mood for no apparent reason).

Emotions vs. attitudes and emotions vs. preferences

Given that the differences between emotions and preferences are similar to the ones identified between emotions and attitudes, we present those differences together. The key difference between *attitudes* and *preferences* lies in their causes, with attitudes being strongly influenced by sociocultural factors, whereas preferences are tightly linked to personality and habits (Ibrahimoglu et al., 2013). As in the case of moods, attitudes and preferences are longer-lasting phenomena than emotions. The fact is that emotions, attitudes, and preferences all consist of cognitive, affective, and motivational components, which can make them appear very similar. However, these components are different in nature for emotions vs. attitudes, and for emotions vs. preferences.

Specifically, the cognitive component of attitudes involves beliefs about an attitude object and, in contrast to emotion object focus, these beliefs do not have to be triggered by a memory of, or actual, or imagined attitude object. For example, one may believe that a particular group of students is bad at mathematics without having actually met anyone in that group. Furthermore, the affective component of attitudes is more general and less nuanced than that of emotions, and consists mainly of general valence and a tendency towards approach avoidance. Finally, the relationship between attitudes and preferences, respectively, and behavior seems much less direct than in the case of emotions, insofar as neither attitudes nor preferences may be good predictors of specific behaviors. For example, a student's belief that a particular group of students is bad at math might not prevent them from asking a specific student from that group for help.

One implication of the multi-componential structure of emotions is that these components can be measured at different levels of analysis, involving different measurement paradigms, from self-reports, observations, and physiological sensing to brain activity monitoring.

Neuroscience of Emotions in Education

Affective neuroscience research has flourished recently, with evidence of the intertwined nature of emotions, cognition, decision making, and social functioning being most notably offered by Antonio Damasio (2005). Following from this work, Immordino-Yang provided seminal, affective neuroscience evidence, linking it directly to educational practices (Immordino-Yang & Damasio, 2007; Immordino-Yang, 2015). Given the growing importance and availability of neuroscience research, we review the key insights emerging from affective neuroscience that are of relevance to AIED, as a way of highlighting new theoretical, empirical, and practical implications for AIED research. The interested reader is referred to Immordino-Yang (2015) for a detailed elaboration of the key findings in the field and further links to supporting studies.

Our understanding of the neurobiological brain processes involved in learning is particularly valuable in further illustrating the critical importance of emotions to learning, to validating many aspects of the theoretical accounts such as Pekrun's Control Value Theory discussed earlier, and in showing how cognition, rationality, and decision making are fundamentally reliant on healthy emotional functioning. In a systematic and precise way not previously afforded by either the theoretical or empirical accounts of emotions, the affective neuroscience research demonstrates how emotions are both needed for and are an outcome of our social brains and the social behaviors that ensue as a consequence thereof. Affective neuroscience in education is a fledgling discipline of growing importance not only to what we consider traditional educational practices, but increasingly to technology-supported teaching and learning, including AIED. Whilst the research questions asked within neuroscience and AIED have a different point of origin and emphasis, the aims of the two fields are complementary in nature. In particular, AIED broadly asks questions about what kind of adaptive and AI-enhanced environments promote more efficient and effective learning, whereas neuroscience inquires about how neural systems enable some students to experience such environments as motivating, and how perception and learning are altered as a result. In this context, affective neuroscience and the insights that it offers enable an exploration and rethinking of educational practices of the future with a degree of formal precision required within the AIED field.

Emotional thought

Emotional thought is a construct proposed by Immordino-Yang and Damasio (2007) to refer to the large overlap between cognition and emotion processes involved in human learning, memory, and decision making in both social and nonsocial contexts. The evidence emerges from examining the neurobiological correlates of human behavior, as shown through a growing body of studies with patients suffering from certain damage to the brain, by comparing them to normally functioning individuals without that damage. For example, work with patients with damage to the ventromedial prefrontal cortex (vmPF) – an area of the brain linked to induction of social emotions, nonconscious induction of somatic responses, such as sweating, associated with sense of risk and modulation of the parasympathetic aspects of autonomic nervous systems of importance to calming of the heart rate – shows that without emotions, all decisions are equal and equally meaningless. Although the theoretical knowledge that such patients possess remains intact, their ability to contextualize and apply such knowledge to the specifics of given situations is impaired, often leading them to make decisions that are disadvantageous to them and preventing them from learning from their mistakes (Damasio, 2005). Recent affective neuroscience work debunks the traditional explanations of these forms of impairments resulting from damage to the patients' logical reasoning, by providing clear evidence of the specific disturbances observed occurring due to diminished resonance of emotional reactions in general, and social emotions such as compassion, embarrassment, and guilt in particular (Damasio, 1994; Damasio et al., 1990; Beadle et al., 2018).

At a high level of description, the emotional thought construct reflects the observation that emotions play a critical role in governing behavior and, in particular, in governing rational thought by helping people recruit memories and skills that are relevant to whatever task they are attending. At a low level of description and supported through specific empirical studies (see Damasio, 1994), the construct spotlights cognition as being both influenced by and subsumed within the process of emotion. The neurobiological perspective reveals to us that the body influences the mind as much as the mind influences the body. Within this perspective, emotions lead a basic form of decision making, functioning in service of our brains' original purpose to manage our bodies and mind in order to sustain life and to live happily in a world involving other people. Thus, in this biology-based view, homeostasis – a universal biological process necessary for sustaining life – is seen as essentially an emotional goal that persists and becomes apparent under increasingly more complex circumstances, such as those involved in academic learning.

More specifically to education, the emotion processes of attention focusing, recruiting relevant memories and learning associations between events and their outcomes, all of which are considered central to academic learning, reflect basic survival and decision-making mechanics, alongside valence dimensions that (quite literally) move us to action (Immordino-Yang and Sylvan, 2010). In other words, cognition functions in the service of life-regulating goals which are implemented by the machinery of emotion processes and are evaluated in specific sociocultural contexts.

Implications for pedagogy
There are two implications for educational practice and for the design of AIED systems, which emerge from the assumption of the construct of emotional thought as a dominant force in human cognition. The first implication is that neither learning nor recall happens in a purely rational domain, divorced from emotions, even if eventually our knowledge tends to transform into moderately rational and unemotional forms. The second implication is the importance of the environment in which not only emotions are recognized, acknowledged, and responded to (the predominant emphasis in AIED and other more traditional teaching contexts), but which actively orchestrate for emotions to be induced and utilized by learners as tools for meaningful engagement with the learning experiences, skills, and content.

Introspective vs. extrospective processes
One of the more compelling examples of learning environment designs that may induce and reinforce emotion processes is one which purposefully caters to rest and introspection as an essential part of learning. In particular, brain studies related to the social emotions of admiration and compassion revealed a strong dependence of emotion processes on people's attention to self, which is achieved during the so-called default mode (DM) of the brain. DM is a brain function which is induced spontaneously during rest, daydreaming, and other non-attentive (though awake) mental states (Smallwood et al., 2021). DM has been implicated in a number of processes of importance to academic learning, including in tasks involving self-awareness, reflection, recall of personal memories, imagining the future, emotions about people, social situations, and moral judgments (Gilbert and Wilson, 2007; Spreng and Grady, 2010). Key findings from studies looking at the quality of the connectivity of the DM network in individuals suggest a positive correlation between stronger DM connectivity at rest and higher scores on cognitive abilities scores such as reading comprehension, divergent thinking, and memory (Song et al., 2009; Van Den Heuven et al. 2009). Additionally, better cognitive abilities for connecting between disparate pieces of information in people with higher IQ have been found to be underpinned by greater efficiency and coordination between frontal and parietal DM regions during rest (van den Heuven, 2009).

Research focusing on the DM of the brain shows not only that the emotional health of individuals depends on strong DM connectivity, but also that emotional health functioning and consequent increased cognitive capacities rely on *toggling* between DM and neural networks that are responsible for maintaining and focusing attention toward the environment. Efficient toggling between those two systems has been shown to predict better reading and memory abilities. Essentially, such toggling coordinates the co-dependence and co-regulation between the systems within the brain that are responsible for "looking-in" (during task-negative states during rest) and those that are responsible for "looking-out" (during task-positive states during active engagement). Without the healthy functioning of one of those systems, the other cannot function well, and the functioning of one has been found to predict the functioning of the other.

Implications for pedagogy
The implications for education and by extension for the design of AIED systems relate to the emphasis that we might place on training introspection, with evidence suggesting that this may alter the functioning of the DM in individuals and improve skills for sustained attention. Another implication is that constant demands on learners to engage in attention-grabbing activities without adequate opportunities to rest, daydream, and reflect might be detrimental to healthy development, emotional functioning, and ultimately to their cognitive capacities. The neuroscience findings raise questions about both within-AIED systems design, such as how might we tailor such systems to explicitly support and encourage strengthening of the DM networks and the coordination between DM and active engagement through the interaction between learners and AIED systems, and further, how AIED systems might need to be integrated into broader educational practices to help take account of the findings just presented.

The social brain
While emotion is the organizing mechanic of behavior and skills, the learning and evaluation of behavior and skills take place largely in a social context. In essence, skills, as seen through the prism of cognitive neuroscience, are considered to be flexible repertoires of goal-directed representations built from convergence of actions ("what I did and thought") and perceptions ("what outcomes I noticed and how it made me feel/think") that are contextually relevant. In line with cognitive theories of development (Piaget, 1971), and broader theories of intelligence (see Legg and Hutter, 2005), learning is understood to involve cycles of perception and action, whereby perception is instantiated in the brain as sensory processing and action – as motor planning and representation. The iterative, recursive process, involving dynamic feedback loops between what a person perceives and how they act, think, and feel, that bring together the perceptual and motor representations in the brain, forms a major component of learning and memory, and social interaction and learning, respectively.

Thus, one critical aspect of skill development as just described is that people construct their skills in large part by learning from others. A key prerequisite of learning from others is the perceived transparency of the context and the goals of other people's actions. Specifically, research shows that if the actions and goals of others are understood by us, the same association areas in the brain that are activated when our own perception and motoric representations converge (implemented through emotion processes) are also activated when we observe the convergence processes in others. This is in essence the mirror property of the brain that is hypothesized to form the basic biological mechanism by which people internalize and learn from other people's thoughts and actions (Oberman & Ramachandran, 2007). Increasing evidence shows that if people do not recognize that another's actions are goal-directed, mirror systems will not be activated and the convergence will not take place, with appropriate appraisal and actions, along with the emotional reactions that learners implicitly attach to the outcomes of the actions perceived also being hindered. One implication for educational practice is to ensure transparency of goals to help learners navigate through their learning experiences and, by extension, to help them develop a sense of relevance of their (learning) environment to them. Linking to the observations of the importance of the environment in which emotional thought is elicited and nurtured as a prerequisite of cognitive abilities, in the context of AIED there is a need for a greater investment in developing environments where the goal-directness is also transparent to learners. Considering learning with AIED environments, as happens through a brain–computer interface, might help the community prioritize and tailor more precisely the designs of such environments, such as in terms of what is being measured and how.

Past AIED Research, New Opportunities, and Pitfalls for Research in AIED

One important part of AIED research focuses on using learning software systems as testbeds to learn about how people learn with AIED systems, and, in this case, to understand how student emotions occur during the learning process as students interact with learning technologies. This process involves collecting data from students at a fine-grained level (logs that represent student actions within the software), including some methodology to assess their emotions as they occur. These rich data are later used to create empirical models that predict student emotions, with the purpose of understanding how these emotions unfold and in which situations. Some of that research has focused not only on how emotions arise, but also how they develop and change into other emotions within the contexts in which they occur (see D'Mello et al., 2009).

Research on emotion prediction has varied in many ways. For instance, research has varied in the methodologies used to create the models, some of it using physiological sensors (Arroyo et al., 2009; Henderson et al., 2020), while some have gone sensor-less (Baker et al., 2020; Wixon et al., 2014). Research has varied in methodologies to determine what is ground truth, that is, what is the true emotion the student is experiencing. Some researchers have relied on their own perceptions, by observing and coding the emotions that students appear to exhibit (Ocumpaugh et al., 2012), while other researchers have relied on students themselves reporting how they feel, the emotions they are currently experiencing or what they have recently experienced, either during the learning session with a tutoring system (Arroyo et al., 2014, 2009) or retrospectively, asking how students were feeling in specific moments as they were using the learning technology after watching a video of the student's face (D'Mello et al., 2007).

There is always an opportunity to improve the models of affective states, making them more accurate at predicting an emotion thanks to new AI techniques (e.g. deep learning) or to finding new ways to increase the bandwidth to reach the students' behavior (e.g. computer vision or sensors). However, one of the pitfalls is that, even if the predictions are almost perfect according to some metrics, there will always be the problem of knowing what the true emotion of the student really is. Is it the one that the student self-reports? The one that is observed by trained researchers or teachers? Or the one diagnosed according to some physiological measurements? In general, even if predictive models (detectors, classifiers) reach high levels of accuracy at guessing the affective state of the student, according to statistical or machine-learning metrics, what the true emotion label is (the ground-truth) might never be perfect, as emotions are internal experiences and there might not be common agreement between what a student self-reports, an observer perceives for an emotion, or what physiological indicators might suggest. There are also individual differences between how students experience and express emotions, and even analyzing how emotions in education vary across cultures is an opportunity for research. In many ways, the prediction of an emotional category depends on what the learning technology and its designers decide to do with it, and whether the combination of the affective prediction and the pedagogical policies of when and how to intervene is emotion sensitive.

In other words, beyond mere understanding of how emotions unfold within learning technologies, a major purpose of AIED research should be to feed these models back into AIED systems to scaffold and support students, given that emotions are automatically predicted by the AIED system. Past research in AIED has focused more on the assessment of emotions than on the question of how knowing a student's affective state could impact what a digital tutor does with it. This prescriptive, interventionist approach assumes the AIED system takes the role of the teacher, acting maybe as a conversational tutor that talks to the student about their emotions, their frustrations, the material, help-seeking attitudes, and even that attempt to instill a growth mindset. Some of this important research on "closing the loop" and taking action depending on a student's affective state has used pedagogical agents, who for instance may empathize with the student (Karumbaiah et al., 2017). Other approaches have not used effective pedagogical agents, but instead have had the software react to students' negative emotions, intervening in a metacognitive fashion and prompting students to self-regulate and self-evaluate (Muldner et al., 2015). More research is needed in this area and there is definitely an opportunity for further research.

It is important to also note that some AIED research has been interventionist, as described before, but has not necessarily attempted to automatically assess a student's emotional states at the same time; instead, some research has evaluated the impact of pedagogical agents on promoting positive student affective states in general (Lester et al., 1997) without necessarily reacting adaptively to students' affective states, but to cognitive states, for instance. Many of these approaches have provided positive and moderately positive results, in that they can manage to improve students' affective states inside of the tutoring system (see Karumbaiah et al, 2017; D'Mello & Graesser, 2013). Figure 5.1 shows an example in the MathSpring AIED system (Arroyo et al, 2014), where affective learning companions address both affect and motivation. Another opportunity for further research is to attempt to understand the long-term effect of affective interventions, such as for how long the positive affective states last and persist, and how they transfer outside of the digital learning environments and into more traditional learning environments of the classroom, for instance.

Last, one less-explored opportunity is using student emotion predictions to inform, support, and scaffold as opposed to students, to understand their students at an emotional level and have software make recommendations on how the teacher could approach the student, showing affective dashboards that are specifically targeted for the teachers. This would be a prescriptive, interventionist approach that would support the instructor instead of the student (e.g. Gupta et al., 202, Ghasem Aghaei et al., 2020).

MOTIVATION

As specified earlier, there is a wide variety of terms to refer to affective experiences. The term *motivation* refers to an internal process that pushes or pulls the individual toward specific actions, and this push or pull is related to some external event. For instance, the phrase "what

Figure 5.1   *Learning companions in the MathSpring tutoring system empathize with the student, acknowledging and mirroring their frustration after the student has reported it (addressing emotion, left and middle) and then training growth mindset (addressing motivation, right)*

motivates me in school is the desire to please my parents" refers to the desire to achieve an outcome involving other people. As a second example, the phrase "what motivates me in school is my desire to learn something new and different" refers to the desire to achieve an outcome involving an inner pull of curiosity, maybe a lack of fear to fail.

The fundamental question in motivation research in education is what *causes* students' behavior. The study of motivation regards both why a person starts to carry out a certain activity, whether behavior is sustained over time, and the reasons why behavior is directed toward some goals or activities, and away from others. Research on motivation also investigates why a certain behavior stops, or changes direction. In general, we can say that research in motivation regards understanding the "drive," the "will," the "wish," the "need," or the "want" of a person to pursue or avoid specific goals and concrete actions (Dreikurs, 2000).

In the case of education and the learning sciences, motivation theory studies why students decide to approach and pursue specific courses, careers, as well as educational activities. Once an educational activity has started, and the student engages with it, the motivational drive also regulates a student's decision to sustain their engagement with the activity, or withdraw from it in a variety of ways.

Motivational Theories Related to Education

A wide variety of motivational theories exist, targeting different kinds of motivations, and what shapes students' motives. We summarize the key theories of motivation in education, and their implications for pedagogy in adaptive learning technologies and AIED systems.

Early theories

Atkinson's theory (1957) was one of the first motivation theories in education. He proposed that people's behavior depended on the combination of motives, probability of success, and incentive value. He established that two major motivations regarding academic achievement are the motive to *approach success* and the motive to *avoid failure*. His theory was important because it moved away from stimulus-response paradigms that were typical in psychology at the time to more complex explanations for what causes behaviors. These ideas about motivation as approach/avoidance are still held after decades; for instance, Lepper and Henderlong (2000) defined motivation as a student's drive (or lack thereof) to pursue means to achieve goals, the approach or avoidance of a task.

Expectancy-value theory

Extending Atkinson's theory of motivation as approach or avoidance, Eccles (1993) and Eccles and Wigfield (2002) posited that two important predictors of achievement and the pull towards or push away from academic behavior are *expectancy of success* and *subjective task value*. Much of this work was in relation to mathematics education, and in particular the relationship between students' motivation in mathematics classes and students' achievement.

Studies with junior high and college students have shown that when students have higher expectancy of success, especially self-competence beliefs, they engage more with the material, using more cognitive and metacognitive strategies (Pintrich, 1999).

Instruments were created to assess expectancy of success (e.g. "How well do you think you will do in your next math test?"), task-specific self-concept (e.g. "How good at math are you?"), and perceptions of task difficulty (e.g. "Compared with other subjects, how difficult is math for you?"). Survey instruments were also developed to assess task-value beliefs, in particular trying to understand a student's attainment value or importance (e.g. "How important is it to you to get good grades in math?"), general interest in the subject (e.g. "How much do you like doing math?"), utility value (e.g. "How useful is what you learn in math at school for your daily life outside school?"), and perceived costs (e.g. "Is the amount of effort it will take you to do well in math class this year worthwhile to you?").

Implications for pedagogy

This research suggests that one of the ways to maximize student achievement is to encourage students to believe that they can succeed if they put in the effort, and if educators can manage to improve their self-competence beliefs – both in classrooms and within learning technologies. If this is achieved, the student should be willing to continue working and persevere, even if it implies asking for help (either from the computer, a human teacher, or a classmate/pal).

Intrinsic and extrinsic motivation

For much of the twentieth century, researchers have investigated *intrinsic* motivation, meaning the desire to behave in specific ways for no reason other than sheer enjoyment, challenge, pleasure, or interest (Harter, 1981; Deci, 1971). This is in contrast to a heavy reliance on *extrinsic incentives* that were typical of the rewards/punishments research of the Skinner era (Skinner, 1953, 1963), where the research focused on how humans and animals would respond, given a particular stimulus.

Studies have shown positive correlations between intrinsic motivation and academic achievement (e.g. Gottfried, 1990; Harter & Connell, 1984; Henderlong & Lepper, 1997).

It is certainly not surprising that students perform better in school to the extent that they pursue challenges, are curious or interested in their schoolwork, and desire to master tasks. Meanwhile, there is a negative relationship between performance and extrinsic motivation. For instance, students may report a desire for easy work in an aim to get good grades, and later perform worse on standardized tests.

Much of the research on extrinsic and intrinsic motivation found that there are age differences in motivation for school, with lower levels of intrinsic motivation for older (middle school) versus younger (elementary school) children (see Lepper et al., 2005; Eccles, 1997). This finding is concerning and a real societal problem. Not only do children lose their enjoyment of the learning process as they get older, but the systems of extrinsic incentives and constraints that schools employed in the studies to keep students on track did not effectively compensate for the decline in intrinsic motivation (Royer & Walles, 2007).

Harter (1981) designed instruments, namely questionnaires, to assess intrinsic versus extrinsic motivation as contrasting ends of a single dimension. Later, researchers realized that this contrast is not always necessary or appropriate in the average classroom. Lepper and colleagues (2000) proposed separate scales to measure intrinsic and extrinsic motivation and found the two scales to be only moderately positively correlated with each other, implying that students could be both intrinsically and extrinsically motivated. One typical item to measure extrinsic motivation is "I work on problems because I'm supposed to," whereas a typical item to measure intrinsic motivation is "I work on problems to learn how to solve them" (Lepper et al., 2005).

Attributional processes

An important part of understanding students' motives for how they behave is to ask them why they acted in a certain way. This approach enables researchers to understand what students attribute as causes for their behaviors, as well as their affective experiences. Attribution theory studies the process by which individuals explain the causes of their behaviors and events that happen to them.

Some of the most important research in this area was done by Bernard Weiner (Weiner, 1986), who proposed that individuals' reactions to a situation depend on their perceptions or attributions as to why they have succeeded or failed at an activity (thinking of the past) or why they will succeed or fail (considering the future). When a student's causal attributions lead to positive affect and high expectancy of future success, such attributions will result in greater motivation (greater willingness to approach similar achievement tasks in the future) than those personal reasons (attributions) that produce negative affect and low expectancy of future success. Eventually, such affective and cognitive assessments influence future behavior when individuals encounter similar situations.

Weiner proposed that these justifications, perceptions and attributions that a student gives in a particular situation depend on their appraisals of stability of the situation (is it stable or unstable? Will it continue or not?), their locus of control (internal or external, who is responsible for the situation? Me or the outside world?), and their controllability of the situation (can I control the situation or not?).

Attribution theory interacts and intersects with expectancy-value theory mentioned above. For example, perceptions of stability of the situation (e.g. will my low ability stay the same?) influences the individual's expectancy about their future (the individual's expectation to succeed). In addition, perceptions of control are related to the individual's persistence on mission (e.g. the perception of not being in control of a situation could make a student quit or avoid studying). This theory also intersects with emotion theories presented in this chapter. For instance, the locus of control (who is to blame or praise, the student herself or other people) influences emotional responses to the outcome (for instance, upon the same good grade on a test, a student could feel proud – because they are internally responsible for it – or relieved – because they think they were lucky, or that the teacher gave an easy test).

Goals and growth mindset

An important area of research has investigated the role of goals and goal orientation in students' motivations. Students have different achievement goals when they are involved in academic activities. Two key types of achievement goals are *mastery goals* and *performance goals* (Elliott & Dweck, 1988). *Mastery goals* focus on the desire to master the material at hand, resulting in better learning (Somuncuoglu & Yildirim, 1999). On the other hand, performance goals are concerned with external factors – grades, impressing the teacher, or avoiding other people's perception of failure or inability (Elliott & Dweck, 1988). Actually, performance goals can be broken down even further, into three subsets: (a) goals that are linked to validating an aspect of self (e.g. one's ability), (b) goals that are explicitly normative in nature, and (c) goals that are simply focused on obtaining positive outcomes (i.e. doing well). It is the first form that was linked to impairment in achievement in some predictive models, but it has tended to be the second two forms (b and c) that have been associated with positive outcomes, such as higher grades (Grant & Dweck, 2003).

Performance and mastery goals have been measured through surveys, and with specific questions that give students choices. For instance, an option for students that measured performance goals was: "In this box we have problems of different levels. Some are hard, some are easier. If you pick this box, although you won't learn new things, it will really show me what kids can do." An item that measured mastery goals (also called learning goals) referred to: "If you pick the task in this box, you'll probably learn a lot of new things. But you'll probably make a bunch of mistakes."

Later, Elliot and colleagues proposed that the original mastery and performance goals be revised to distinguish between approach and avoidance (Elliot & Church, 1997; Elliot & Harackiewicz, 1996), and created an instrument to measure these four categories, namely: (1) mastery approach, (2) mastery avoidance, (3) performance approach, and (4) performance avoidance (Elliot & McGregor, 2001). Students who have *mastery approach* goals want to learn and improve. An example of a mastery approach item is: "I want to learn as much as possible from this class" and would be willing to seek help even if it implies exposing what they don't know to their teacher or others. A student that has *performance approach* goals cares about doing better than other students or showing what they know. Learners who have a performance approach goal orientation are extrinsically motivated. A student that has *mastery avoidance* goals is motivated to avoid situations in which they are unable to learn. When students have mastery avoidance goals, they tend to worry about their inability to master the task. An example of a mastery avoidance item is: "I worry that I may not learn all that I possibly could in this class." Last, a student who has *performance avoidance* goals is focused on avoiding failure in front of others. An example of a performance-avoidance item is: "My goal in this class is to avoid performing poorly."

Dweck's research on goal orientation evolved into the growth mindset theory (Dweck, 2002). This theory suggests that students who view their intelligence as an immutable internal characteristic tend to shy away from academic challenges, whereas students who believe that intelligence can be increased through effort and persistence tend to seek out academic challenges. Students who are praised for their *effort* are much more likely to view intelligence as being *malleable*; as a result, their self-esteem remains stable regardless of how hard they may have to work to succeed at a task. Additionally, praise for effort encourages perseverance.

Implications for pedagogy
Dweck's research suggests that delivering messages to students that intelligence is malleable, that perseverance and practice are needed to learn, that making mistakes is an essential part of learning and that failure is not due to a lack of innate ability can make students sustain their effort and their perseverance. These are interventions that target a student's intrinsic values, as they are targeting students' deep beliefs about themselves as learners, about the meaning of mistakes, and their interpretation and value of their own actions and their consequences. Some large-scale studies have shown that students who are trained to have a growth mindset consequently improve their achievement within learning technologies (Arroyo et al., 2014; Karumbiah et al., 2017). The traditional way for a learning technology to respond to students is to provide feedback for correctness on their work such as congratulating them verbally or with a "thumbs-up" gesture when the work is correct. A complimentary, alternative approach relates to praising their effort and training growth mindset based on students' effort (Dweck, 2002) to improve engagement, grades, and SRL and to set mastery-learning goals for themselves (see Burnette et al., 2013; Arroyo et al., 2014).

Passion for long-term goals
Angela Duckworth's theory of GRIT proposes that certain traits and dimensions of character other than intelligence are strong determinants of a person's unique path toward success despite setbacks. Duckworth (2016) identified grit as a trait of anyone who works hard and displays perseverance and passion for long-term goals (Duckworth et al., 2007). Educational researchers have turned their attention toward examining grit, how it changes and how it is related to other learning constructs such as effort, interest, and engagement (Von Culin et al., 2014; Wolters & Hussain, 2015). Grit has been measured using an 8- to 12-item scale representing two constructs: consistency of interests and perseverance (Duckworth & Quinn, 2009).

The long-term nature of grit is what differentiates it from similar constructs such as self-control and conscientiousness (Sumpter, 2017). Grit has been conceived as a very stable, domain-general inclination to maintain consistent, focused interest and effort for personally important and challenging goals. Unlike traditional measures of performance, grit is not tied to intelligence as a predictor of success, with grit found to be independent from IQ score (Duckworth & Quinn, 2009).

Past AIED Research, New Opportunities, and Pitfalls for Research in AIED

At least since the emergence of student-centered approaches to learning, educators have attempted to create learning environments that are motivating to students. It is clear to educators that it is very hard to learn without students feeling the drive for learning. It also has been clear that, ideally, we want to instill an intrinsic motivation for learning in students, beyond an extrinsic motivation, which is often not easy to do.

Learning technologies that align with students' personal and age-related interests are best for learning. For instance, game-based digital learning environments have been in vogue for decades (Tobias et al., 2014; Tobias & Fletcher, 2012). In this case, the system is designed to align with the interests of students, capture their engagement, and hopefully improve learning further, thanks to the exploration allowed, rewards, and other game features (Plass et al., 2015; Spires et al., 2011).

AIED systems are sometimes used as testbeds to learn about human learning. One such example could be to assess motivation towards the subject being taught, through surveys, before being exposed to the software. Later, researchers can analyze how a variety of motivational profiles predispose a student to behave in specific ways within the learning session. This regards building systems that model, predict, and understand a student's motivation and how this influences behavior within learning environments.

Because the factors around students' motivation are relatively stable in students and measured via surveys, only some AIED research has focused on automatically detecting motivational goals or intentions from student behaviors in a learning software (Contai & MacLaren, 2005, Arroyo et al, 2010).

However, learning technologies have attempted to understand and predict students' cognitive engagement within tutoring systems and other digital learning environments and how to maintain it, which might oscillate within a learning session with a tutoring system or some other learning system. This is related to motivation in that if a student feels the pull toward the learning activity, then cognitive engagement is more likely, and vice versa for students who are not drawn to the academic activity. Much work has been done regarding student disengagement and detecting when students lose focus and start having nonoptimal behaviors such as "gaming the system" (Baker et al., 2008), which is a form of avoidance of academic work.

Other research has attempted to understand productive uses of the software, including ideal behaviors of a student as opposed to nonproductive ones. For instance, engagement has resulted in modeling students' behavior during help seeking (Aleven et al., 2006; Roll et al., 2011), which is a crucial productive interaction toward learning at a critical moment of confusion or unknowing.

Last, research on AIED systems can attempt to scaffold or address a student's expectation of success, liking, or value of the subject, for instance by connecting the subject at hand to other topics that students are interested in depending on their age (e.g. video games or endangered species). This prescriptive, interventionist approach to attempt to adaptively intervene and measure a student's improvement in their motivation toward the domain or toward learning in general has been less common in AIED research per se, and is an opportunity for future research, with a few exceptions (see Beal et al., 2000; Rebolledo-Mendez et al., 2011)

META-EMOTION AND META-MOTIVATION THEORIES

Motivation and emotion within learning environments are both typically accompanied by meta-level mental processes, termed meta-affect (DeBellis & Goldin, 2006), that refers to affect about affect, and affect about and within cognition that may again be about affect, the monitoring of affect and the regulation of affect.

Because this is a new area of research, the opportunities for research in this area are vast. Research has focused on students' awareness of their emotions (Arguedas et al., 2016), and on how to support students to become aware of their emotions in e-learning environments (see Feidakis et al., 2014). Other research has focused on feelings about metacognition, or so-called "metacognitive feelings" (Eflkides, 2006), such as confidence and the feeling of knowing (Vogl, Pekrun, Loderer, 2021). These are all novel, worthy new areas of research; however, in this section, we particularly focus on the regulatory processes broadly speaking, i.e. in the attempts to regulate either emotion or motivation to influence the student's emotional and/or motivational states (Gross 2015; Wolters 2003).

The source of this affective regulation can be *intrinsic*, namely a conscious goal on the part of the student to regulate their emotion or motivation (Wolters 2003), or *extrinsic*, such as a teacher or tutoring system aiming to help a student with their regulation (Gross, 2015). Both emotion regulation and motivation regulation are important because, as established above, emotions and motivation impact student learning and educational outcomes in general (see sections on "Emotion" and "Motivation"). However, emotion regulation and motivation regulation are still relatively understudied, with some notable exceptions described next.

Emotion Regulation Theories Related to Education

A prominent model of how students regulate their own emotions is Gross's Process Model of Emotion Regulation (PMER) (Gross, 2015). Previous sections in this chapter have described research that theorizes how emotions arise, depending on appraisals of a situation (e.g. section on "Control-Value Theory of Emotion in Education"). Building on those theories, Gross's theory is grounded in a four-stage temporal model of how emotions arise. Briefly, Gross proposes that a situation first occurs (stage 1) that elicits attention from the student (stage 2), which results in a cognitive appraisal (stage 3) and subsequently in an emotional experience (stage 4). Each of these four stages related to emotion generation provides opportunities for emotion regulation through corresponding strategies, as follows:

1. Situation selection and modification strategies involve choosing situations and changing features of educational situations, respectively. Thus, these two categories of strategies involve *changing one's environment* with the aim of affecting the subsequent emotion elicited by the environment. For instance, students can choose to study in a group rather than alone to reduce their anxiety about a challenging domain that is being learned.
2. Attentional deployment strategies direct attention, with the goal of influencing emotion. Thus, this category of strategies changes how one *perceives* the environment. For instance, a student can choose to shift their attention away from the teacher who is delivering a difficult lecture in order to cope, causing anxiety to turn into a positive emotional experience due to happy off-task memories.
3. Cognitive appraisal strategies involve modifying the student's assessment of the situation with the aim of changing the subsequent emotion. Consequently, this set of strategies targets how one *represents* the environment and associated states internally. An example involves reducing anxiety about a test by reappraising the situation as not vital (e.g. "the test is only worth 15% of my grade so I won't worry too much").
4. Response modulation strategies target the emotion directly once it is experienced, using either internal (mental suppression of the emotion) or external means (e.g. breathing exercises to reduce anxiety).

The examples provided above center around anxiety but the strategies from each category can be applied to regulate a range of emotions, and particularly for negative valence emotions as these are the ones that might be more important to support students in handling and regulating (e.g. frustration, anxiety, etc.). In general, there are many opportunities to regulate emotion during learning, and these opportunities arise throughout and after the emotion-generation process. While in the PMER model the majority of strategies involve regulating an emotion before it is experienced, Gross acknowledges that the situations in which emotions arise (and may be regulated) are often more nuanced and cyclical. For instance, a student could experience frustration while working on problems and use the *situation modification* strategy to alleviate it, by working with a friend.

Gross's model provides a comprehensive framework by organizing emotion regulation strategies according to where and when in the emotion generation process they can be initiated. However, PMER is a general theory and thus does not take into account factors specific to learning situations. Fortunately, Harley et al. (2019) have recently addressed this gap by synthesizing the PMER framework by Gross and the control-value theory of emotion described in previous sections. Harley and colleagues extended the original framework with examples of how each of the aforementioned categories of emotion regulation strategies can be realized in achievement settings.

Harley and colleagues also refined the *situation-related* emotion regulation strategies by adding considerations related to context. For instance, regarding individual versus social contexts, Harley et al. (2019) propose that students in individual settings have more flexibility in selecting regulation strategies; in social settings, strategies may be more constrained and students not only have to regulate their own emotions, but potentially other students' as well in order to maintain positive group dynamics.

Considerations regarding low- versus high-stakes situations were also differentiated. For instance, high-stakes situations (such as exams) do not afford as much flexibility for emotion regulation strategy selection in comparison with low-stakes situations, such as classroom activities. High-stakes situations such as tests also involve more intense emotions, which may impact the effectiveness of certain regulation strategies.

Implications for pedagogy

Students could and should be supported to be aware of and to regulate academic emotions that would impede learning (e.g. confusion, frustration, anxiety, and boredom). School systems are increasingly becoming aware of the importance of emotion regulation in education. For instance, schools in the United States are increasingly training teachers with programs such as Social Emotional Learning (SEL) as part of CASEL (Collaborative for Academic for Social and Emotional Learning). SEL is described as the process through which children and adults acquire and effectively apply the knowledge, attitudes, and skills they need to understand and manage emotions, set and accomplish positive goals, feel and show empathy for others, establish and maintain positive relationships and make responsible decisions. SEL curricula teach self-awareness, self-management, social awareness, relationship skills, and responsible decision making so that first teachers, and then their students, can understand and manage their behaviors, understand and relate to the perspectives of others, and make sound personal and social choices (Elias et al., 2006; Domitrovich et al., 2017).

Motivation Regulation Theories Related to Education

Broadly speaking, motivation refers to a student's willingness to engage in an activity and/ or the processes that impact motivation, and in our case, the drive to engage with learning activities (see section on "Motivation"). Here, we use Wolter's (2003) framework to describe motivation regulation strategies.

One strategy for motivation regulation involves *emotion regulation*, where students aim to modify their emotion in order to stay engaged and on task. In particular, interest is commonly cited as an antecedent of motivation (Hidi, 2006; Wolters, 2003), and thus if students can manage to regulate their interest level, they can stay motivated and on-task. One way to increase interest is by gamifying repetitive or boring tasks (Sansone et al., 2012), a form of *situation modification*. Other emotions also play a role in motivating students. For instance, students sometimes rely on fear of failure to regulate motivation for study strategies and persist in academic tasks (Webster & Hadwin, 2015).

As with emotion regulation, motivation regulation can involve *situation selection and modification*. For instance, students can *recognize* they are less motivated to study in loud, distracting environments and so they choose to work in a quiet library (situation selection). A second category of motivation regulation strategies relates to *efficacy management*. For instance, one subclass of these strategies is efficacy self-talk, where students try to motivate their engagement in academic activities with self-directed comments aimed to boost their belief in their own efficacy (e.g. "You can do it"). Harley et al. (2019) classified some efficacy strategies as a form of cognitive appraisal (e.g. "I have the ability to finish this reading") to improve positive emotions. A contrasting but related strategy involves students using *defensive pessimism* to motivate themselves to engage in a task (e.g. to study for a test by highlighting to themselves how unprepared they are or removing pressure by using low-efficacy self-talk, such as "I am not good at this so won't do a good job anyway, but it has to get done").

Other motivation strategies described by Wolters (2003) do not overlap with emotion regulation strategies reported by Harley et al. (2019), because they do not involve regulating emotions per se. Instead, they involve regulating related constructs that impact motivation. In any case, we acknowledge that motivation regulation strategies are likely to also impact emotions (and so are indirectly a form of motivation regulation), and vice versa, with emotion regulation also impacting motivation.

A common motivational strategy pertains to *self-consequating*, which involves setting rewards or punishments for finishing/not finishing a task (e.g. bargaining with oneself, such as "If I study for an hour, I can watch TV"). Students often use this type of regulation to motivate studying (Webster and Hadwin, 2015). A related strategy pertains to *goal-oriented self-talk*, where students *set achievement goals* that provide reasons for engaging in a learning activity. Goals include performance or mastery achievement goals (see section on "Goals and growth mindset"), for instance to engage in an academic task to beat other students or to expand one's knowledge. Similarly to achievement goals, *attributions* and beliefs about oneself and what is being learned impact not only motivational states (see section on "Attributional processes") but also motivation regulation. One way students realize this type of control is through consciously modifying their attributions from maladaptive ones (e.g. "I did poorly on the test because I can't do math") to adaptive ones ("I did poorly because I did not study enough"). Such shifts in attributions can help inspire students to engage in learning tasks to help them succeed.

What Causes Students to Regulate Their Emotions and/or Motivation?

Gross (2015) proposes that emotion regulation is initiated by a three-prong process, which we propose also applies to motivation. First, the state (emotional, motivational) being instantiated is recognized and a goal is set to regulate that state. The recognition and goal initiation processes can be hindered by lack of awareness (Gross, 2015) as well as individual beliefs, such as that emotional/motivational states are immutable and so cannot be regulated (Kappes & Schikowski, 2013). If a regulation goal is successfully initiated, the second stage of regulation occurs, in which the strategy to modify the target state is selected. Doing so requires identifying potential strategies, evaluating them according to the target criteria (such as its utility or feasibility of implementation), and choosing the winning strategy. This second stage may be hindered by lack of knowledge about potential strategies, inaccurate valuation judgments about candidate strategies, and low self-efficacy beliefs about one's ability to implement a given strategy, resulting in reduced motivation to attempt regulation. The third and final stage of regulation involves implementation of the selected strategy. Doing so requires adapting a general strategy to the constraints of the current situation.

Implications for pedagogy

Teachers play an important role in keeping learning activities interesting, to support students' motivation (Rotgans & Schmidt, 2011) as a form of extrinsic regulation of students' motivation. In e-learning environments, gamification has been used as a tool to maintain student engagement (Dermeval & Bittencourt, 2020; Gonzalez et al., 2014). There is a vast opportunity to have e-learning systems teach students to support their awareness and regulation of their own motivation in the ways described above, supporting an *intrinsic* self-regulation process.

Past AIED Research, New Opportunities, and Pitfalls for Research in AIED

As described above, there are various strategies for students to regulate their emotions and motivations. Which ones are most effective? To date, research in educational psychology has focused on ways to regulate students' test anxiety (Brady et al., 2018; Brunyé et al., 2013), with interventions focusing on cognitive reappraisal and response modulation strategies like breathing techniques. In general, appraisal is believed to be an effective regulation strategy, while suppression has not proved effective (McRae, 2016). While these results are informative, there is currently little work on if and how they transfer to contexts involving tutoring systems.

Price et al. (2018) investigated the relationships between appraisal, suppression, and emotion in the context of tutoring systems and a new context, namely a learning one (as opposed to the traditionally emphasized test-taking context). The findings showed that students who tended to cognitively reappraise and not suppress emotion reported lower negative emotions. However, given an experimental design was not used, the directionality of this effect cannot be determined (i.e. do students who experience less negative emotions engage in lower suppression or vice versa).

In general, less is known about how students regulate emotions and motivation in other, non-test contexts and the utility of interventions to help them regulate in such contexts. Here, we focus on the role tutoring systems can play in terms of regulation. There are indeed tutoring systems that aim to regulate student emotions and motivational states, as well as promote ones good for learning. Such systems take over the regulation function through various interventions, such as by providing students with easier problems to reduce frustration (Arroyo et al., 2014), emotional design to improve affect (Mayer & Estrella 2014), and with affect-adapted messages to regulate student emotion (D'Mello et al., 2010). While these interventions can implicitly regulate emotion and motivation, we conjecture that they are unlikely to help students achieve the regulation on their own, unless regulation strategies are explicitly taught. Providing explicit personalized regulation support in a tutoring system requires (1) modeling of students' regulation strategies and (2) interventions and advice for regulation tailored to the model information. As far as modeling, while there has been substantial work on modeling student emotions (subsection under "Motivation" on "Past AIED Research, New Opportunities and Pitfalls for Research in AIED"), there has been little research on emotion and motivation regulation modeling. Doing so would require modeling not only the target states of emotion and/or motivation but also the strategies needed to regulate them, including students' effectiveness at using those strategies. Likewise, work on regulation interventions that aim to help students regulate their own emotions (rather than have the tutoring system do it) is very limited. One promising area of work that we now review corresponds to visualization tools, which, depending on the application, may implement emotion/motivation modeling and may provide explicit regulation interventions.

Visualization is a graphical representation of an individual's states, typically collected over a period of time (from hours to days). Some work to date has targeted emotion visualization (see Ruiz et al., 2016) via dashboards and user models that automatically recognize emotion and display it to the student. Because there could be a great deal of emotion data, the goal of visualization is to help the user process the data in an effective way (e.g. one that promotes regulation). This method can help to focus the user's attention on features in their emotional data and thus correspond to the attentional deployment stage in Gross's hierarchy.

Broadly speaking, emotion visualization is a growing field (Rivera-Pelayo et al., 2017; Hollis et al., 2015), driven by advances in tracking devices like Fitbits that collect a great deal of data and are now beginning to include emotional information in that collection (Hollis et al., 2015). Within AIED, there have been recent calls for the need to include emotion visualization tools in tutoring systems (Azevedo et al., 2017), although to date there are only a handful of systems that do so. One example is from the work by Ruiz and colleagues (2016), who used a user-centered approach to test the usability of various emotion visualization methods with high school students. Students self-reported believing the visualization helped them reflect on their emotions, the first step needed for emotion regulation. More broadly in the adaptive system community, there has been interest in using emotion visualization tools as assistive devices for individuals with autism spectrum disorder (ASD). For instance, the emotional hearing aid is a tool that recognizes emotion in others and helps its user respond appropriately to that emotion (Kaliouby and Robinson, 2005). More recently, Washington et al. (2017) used Google Glass technology to devise an emotion recognition system for children with ASD. The application includes a review system that allows parents and their children to review the child's emotional episodes. Based on a qualitative analysis, some parents reported that reviewing emotions helped their child reflect on them and improve their emotional responses, to exhibit increased emotion regulation.

To date, there has been little work on how to help students learn to regulate their emotional and motivational states and primary research is needed on which strategies are effective. ITSs are well positioned for this work as they can be used as testbeds for interventions. To illustrate, ASSISTments (Heffernan & Heffernan, 2014) is an online platform for students to practice math, which also allows researchers to create problems for students to work on along with corresponding answers and hints, as well as to design experiments and test the effect of pedagogical interventions. Once the studies are designed, teachers can sign up to use them in their classrooms. This platform allows researchers to test hypotheses in authentic settings without taking students away from their regular activities. To date, the interventions have focused on cognitive factors, but there have been exceptions (e.g. testing whether humor in lessons helps learning).

As noted above, students may fail to regulate because they are not aware of their emotions and/or motivation. Thus, a second opportunity relates to the modeling of emotion regulation and motivation regulation, subsequently providing students access to these models to prompt reflection and regulation. The modeling of regulation also affords the opportunity to provide personalized instruction, where tutoring systems use the model's assessment to tailor interventions. Here we can borrow from strategies used to model metacognitive behaviors, including data mining techniques (see Azevedo et al., 2018). This opportunity does not come without its challenges, as it requires not only the modeling of emotion and motivation but additional students' regulation strategies of those states. Moreover, evaluation of such models will be a challenge given the associated measurement challenges. In order to assess a model a "gold standard" is needed, namely the true value of the state the model is aiming to assess. To date, there are guidelines on ways to accomplish this for evaluating models of emotion (Porayska-Pomsta et al., 2013) but less is known about how to obtain the gold standard for states related to regulation, as required for model evaluation. A related challenge relates to identifying what regulation strategies to model and at what level of granularity.

A third opportunity lies in using learning technologies to train teachers about emotion and motivation regulation (programs such as Social Emotional Learning), so that they can better understand the affective scenarios that their students might encounter and understand how to support them or teach them self-regulation strategies. Affective and engagement dashboards such as the ones created by Arroyo and colleagues (Gupta et al., 2021) could be shared with students to promote reflection and encourage self-regulation. In turn, Azevedo et al. (2017) presented a conceptual framework that addresses the learning of self-regulation; they proposed using cognitive, affective, and metacognitive processes of the individual student and other students, through data visualizations (e.g. showing eye-movement behaviors, facial expressions of emotions, physiological arousal) to facilitate learner monitoring and regulation of their emotions. However, this kind of research is still in its infancy.

According to Domitrovich et al. (2017), teaching such socio-emotional learning interventions in schools has long-term positive outcomes because socio-emotional abilities (a) associate with social, behavioral, and academic outcomes that are important for healthy development; (b) predict important life outcomes in adulthood; (c) can be improved with feasible and cost-effective interventions; and (d) play a critical role in the behavior change process of students (Durlak, 2015).

DISCUSSION AND CONCLUSION

A breadth of research has been done to understand how students' behaviors are shaped by their emotions and motives within academic achievement settings. As mentioned in previous sections, emotion and motivation are different, in that the former are affective experiences that result from appraisals of control and value of a situation, while research about motivation has regarded understanding how situations and contexts influence and ultimately determine the push toward or pull away from an academic situation or task. In addition, while motivations can and do shift, emotions generally tend to be more fluctuating, even within one learning situation. A student might be confused or frustrated when solving a math problem, but not anymore when solving a second problem, and instead feel relief, hope, or excitement when a message pops up telling them they have mastered the concept, or a pedagogical agent talks to them.

To illustrate how learning technologies might be aware of and capitalize on research on emotion, meta-emotion, motivation, and regulation, we return to one of the examples from the beginning of the chapter. In this example, students are experiencing a variety of emotional and motivational states.

Sam logs in to an online mathematics learning software that shows math problems and a digital humanoid tutor agent on the side of the screen. As Sam works through the daily assignment, Sam receives hints for many answers until he gets the problems right. While the problems remain easy, he becomes bored and begins to skip through problems without even reading them. The tutor says "You seem bored. Would you like more challenging problems?" Sam says "Yes," which results in more challenging material being presented; however, it then becomes too difficult. He first becomes confused, then frustrated, thinking he cannot succeed. The tutor detects frustration and talks to Sam in an empathetic and supportive way. It says: "I know that these problems can sometimes be frustrating but getting frustrated means that there is an opportunity for you to learn something new. Let's look at some more hints; if you still don't understand them, I can pair you with another student to discuss the problem with." After presenting additional hints, the agent pairs Sam with another student through Chat, who is also solving the same problem. Isabella was pleased to speak with someone who is also working on the same problem, and together they can talk through the problem aloud, clear the confusion and eventually solve the math problem. The pedagogical agent congratulates both on their shared work and effort.

Several strategies were presented here to illustrate how an AIED system might assess and intervene in response to a combination of cognitive and affective states. Some of these strategies have been shown to be effective in previous research. There are many more opportunities in terms of using AIED systems as testbeds to understand how people learn and particularly how emotion and motivation might interact with each other. Additionally, opportunities for research exist on how to support teachers, particularly in identifying and working with students through affective and motivational scenarios.

We have spoken before about differences between motivation and emotion. In addition to conceptual differences, there are also differences in research methods across motivation, emotion, and affect regulation. Research methods for motivation have generally been in the form of subjective surveys that students fill out. Research methods for emotions have sometimes consisted of subjective questionnaires after and/or before the learning activity in question, but, more frequently, students have been prompted to report their emotions in-between learning activities (see Arroyo et al., 2014; Pekrun et al., 2017). More frequently, emotions have been assessed using sensors, or computer vision facial expression detectors, or assessed by having human coders annotate what they note about students' expressions of emotions (Baker et al., 2020) or inferred from data logs of students interacting with the technology.

These differences in research methods might be explained by the expertise of the people carrying out the research. While educational psychology research has relied on coarse-grained level measures, such as surveys, the AIED community has relied on much more fine-grained digital logs or "just-in-time" computer-based assessments as specific situations occur in the student–software interaction. This has allowed a much finer-grained level of analysis, relying not only on changes across individuals, but also within individuals, as their learning progresses.

Let us point out that the AIED community's focus is not necessarily better, but complementary. While AIED research has had a much higher level of detail than other areas, one drawback of AIED research has been to look at momentary changes in emotions/motivational states due to interventions, or within the length of a few sessions of use of a learning technology. Looking at long-term changes, from year to year, is something that educational psychologists are more used to, and is still much on the agenda, as another opportunity for AIED research to continue to push the agenda in innovative research at the intersection of education and technology.

REFERENCES

Aleven, V., McLaren, B., Roll, I., & Koedinger, K. (2006). Toward Meta-Cognitive Tutoring: A Model of Help Seeking with a Cognitive Tutor. *International Journal of Artificial Intelligence in Education*, 1, 101–128.

Arguedas, M., Daradoumis, T., & Xhafa, F. (2016). Analyzing How Emotion Awareness Influences Students' Motivation, Engagement, Self-Regulation and Learning Outcome. *Educational Technology & Society*, 19(2), 87–103.

Arroyo, I., Cooper, D.G., Burleson, W., Woolf, B.P., Muldner, K., & Christopherson, R. (2009). Emotion Sensors Go to School. *Proceedings of the 14th International Conference on Artificial Intelligence in Education*. IOS Press.

Arroyo, I., Cooper, D.G., Burleson, W., & Woolf, B.P. (2010). Bayesian Networks and Linear Regression Models of Students' Goals, Moods, and Emotions. In *Handbook of Educational Data Mining*. Chapman & Hall/CRC Data Mining and Knowledge Discovery Series.

Arroyo, I., Woolf, B.P., Burleson, W., Muldner, K., Rai, D., & Tai, M. (2014). A Multimedia Adaptive Tutoring System for Mathematics that Addresses Cognition, Metacognition and Affect. *International Journal on Artificial Intelligence in Education*. Special Issue on "Landmark AIED Systems for STEM Learning".

Atkinson, J.W. (1957). Motivational Determinants of Risk-Taking Behavior. *Psychological Review*, 64(6, Pt.1), 359–372.

Azevedo, R., Millar, G.C., Taub, M., Mudrick, N.V., Bradbury, A.E., & Price, M.J. (2017). Using Data Visualizations to Foster Emotion Regulation During Self-Regulated Learning with Advanced Learning Technologies: A Conceptual Framework. *Proceedings of the Seventh International Learning Analytics & Knowledge Conference*.

Azevedo, R., Taub, M., & Mudrick, N.V. (2018). Understanding and Reasoning about Real-Time Cognitive, Affective, and Metacognitive Processes to Foster Self-Regulation with Advanced Learning Technologies. In D.H. Schunk & J.A. Greene (eds.), *Handbook of Self-Regulation of Learning and Performance*, pp. 254–270. Routledge/Taylor & Francis Group.

Baker, R., Walonoski, J., Heffernan, N., Roll, I., Corbett, A., & Koedinger, K. (2008). Why Students Engage in "Gaming the System" Behavior in Interactive Learning Environments. *Journal of Interactive Learning Research*, 19(2), 185–224.

Baker, R.S.J.d., D'Mello, S.K., Rodrigo, M.M.T., & Graesser, A.C. (2010). Better to Be Frustrated Than Bored: The Incidence, Persistence, and Impact of Learners' Cognitive-Affective States During Interactions with Three Different Computer-Based Learning Environments. *International Journal of Human-Computer Studies*, 68(4), 223–241.

Baker, R.S., Ocumpaugh, J.L., & Andres, J.M.A.L. (2020). BROMP Quantitative Field Observations: A Review. In R. Feldman (ed.), *Learning Science: Theory, Research, and Practice*, pp. 127–156. McGraw-Hill.

Barrett, L., Mesquita, B., Ochsner, K., & Gross, J. (2007). The Experience of Emotion. [Review]. *Annual Review of Psychology*, 58, 373–403.

Beadle, J.N., Paradiso, S., & Tranel, D. (2018). Ventromedial prefrontal cortex is critical for helping others who are suffering. *Frontiers in Neurology*, 9, 288.

Beal, C.R., Woolf, B.P., Beck, J.E., Arroyo, I., Schultz, K., & Hart, D.M. (2000). Gaining Confidence in Mathematics: Instructional Technology for Girls. *Proceedings of International Conference on Mathematics/Science Education and Technology*, pp. 57–64.

Brady, S.T., Hard, B.M., & Gross, J.J. (2018). Reappraising Test Anxiety Increases Academic Performance of First-Year College Students. *Journal of Educational Psychology*, 110(3), 395–406. doi: 10.1037/edu0000219

Brunyé, T., Mahoney, C., Giles, G., Rapp, D., Taylor, H., & Kanarek, R. (2013). Learning to Relax: Evaluating Four Brief Interventions for Overcoming the Negative Emotions Accompanying Math Anxiety. *Learning and Individual Differences*, 27, 1–7, doi: 10.1016/j.lindif.2013.06.008.

Burnette, J.L., O'Boyle, E.H., VanEpps, E.M., Pollack, J.M., & Finkel, E.J. (2013). Mind-Sets Matter: A Meta-Analytic Review of Implicit Theories and Self-Regulation. *Psychological Bulletin*, 139(3), 655–701, 2013.

Cohen, R.A. (2011). Yerkes–Dodson Law. In J.S. Kreutzer, J. DeLuca, & B. Caplan (eds.), *Encyclopedia of Clinical Neuropsychology*. Springer.

Craig, S., Graesser, A., Sullins, J., & Gholson, B. (2004). Affect and Learning: An Exploratory Look into the Role of Affect in Learning with AutoTutor. *Journal of Educational Media*, 29 (3), 241–250. doi: 10.1080/1358165042000283101

D'Mello, S., Lehman, B., Sullins, J., Daigle, R., Combs, R., Vogt, K., Perkins, L., & Graesser, A. (2010). A Time for Emoting: When Affect-Sensitivity Is and Isn't Effective at Promoting Deep Learning. In V. Aleven, J. Kay, & J. Mostow (eds.), *Intelligent Tutoring Systems*. ITS 2010. Lecture Notes in Computer Science, Vol. 6094. Berlin, Heidelberg: Springer.

D'Mello, S.K., & Graesser, A. (2013). AutoTutor and Affective Autotutor: Learning by Talking with Cognitively and Emotionally Intelligent Computers that Talk Back. *ACM Transactions on Interactive Intelligent Systems*, 2(4), 23:1–23:39.

D'Mello, S.K., Picard, R.W., & Graesser, A.C. (2007). Towards an Affect-Sensitive AutoTutor. Special issue on Intelligent Educational Systems – *IEEE Intelligent Systems*, 22(4), 53–61.

D'Mello, S.K., Person, N., & Lehman, B.A. (2009). Antecedent-Consequent Relationships and Cyclical Patterns between Affective States and Problem Solving Outcomes. In V. Dimitrova, R. Mizoguchi, B. du Boulay, & A. Graesser (eds.), *Proceedings of 14th International Conference on Artificial Intelligence in Education*, pp. 57–64. Amsterdam: IOS Press.

D'Mello, S.K., Lehman, B., Pekrun, R., & Graesser, A. (2014). Confusion Can Be Beneficial for Learning. *Learning and Instruction*, 29, 153–170.

Damasio, A. (2005). *Descartes' Error: Emotion, Reason, and the Human Brain*. Penguin Books.

Damasio, A.R. (1994). Descartes' Error and the Future of Human Life. *Scientific American*, 271(4), 144–144.

Damasio, A.R, Tranel, D., & Damasio, H. (1990). Individuals with Sociopathic Behavior Caused by Frontal Damage Fail to Respond Autonomically to Social Stimuli. *Behavioural Brain Research*, 41(2), 81–94.

DeBellis, V.A., & Goldin, G.A. (2006). Affect and Meta-Affect in Mathematical Problem Solving: A Representational Perspective. *Educational Studies in Mathematics*, 63, 131–147.

Deci, E.L. (1971). Effects of Externally Mediated Rewards on Intrinsic Motivation. *Journal of Personality and Social Psychology*, 18, 105–115.

Dermeval, D., & Bittencourt, I.I. (2020). Co-Designing Gamified Intelligent Tutoring Systems with Teachers. *Brazilian Journal of Computers in Education (Revista Brasileira de Informática na Educação – RBIE)*, 28, 73–91. doi: 10.5753/RBIE.2020.28.0.73

Domitrovich, C.E., Durlak, J., Staley, K.C., & Weissberg, R.P. (2017). Social-Emotional Competence: An Essential Factor for Promoting Positive Adjustment and Reducing Risk and School Children. *Child Development*, 88, 408–416.

Duckworth, A. (2016). *Grit: The Power of Passion and Perseverance* (Vol. 234). Scribner.

Duckworth, A.L., & Quinn, P.D. (2009). Development and Validation of the Short Grit Scale (Grit–S). *Journal of Personality Assessment*, 91(2), 166–174.

Duckworth, A.L., Peterson, C., Matthews, M.D., & Kelly, D.R. (2007). Grit: Perseverance and Passion for Long-Term Goals. *Journal of Personality and Social Psychology*, 92(6), 1087–1101.

Durlak, J.A. (ed.). (2015). *Handbook of Social and Emotional Learning: Research and Practice*. Guilford Publications.

Dweck, C. (2002). Chapter 3 – Messages That Motivate: How Praise Molds Students' Beliefs, Motivation, and Performance (in Surprising Ways). In *Improving Academic Achievement: Impact of Psychological Factors on Education*, pp. 37–60. Academic Press.

Eccles, J.S., & Wigfield, A. (2002). Motivational Beliefs, Values and Goals. *Annual Review of Psychology*, 53(1), 109–132. doi: 10.1146/annurev.psych.53.100901.135153

Eflkides, A. (2006). Metacognition and Affect: What Can Metacognitive Experiences Tell Us about the Learning Process? *Educational Research Review*, 1(1): 3–14. doi: 10.1016/j.edurev. 2005.11.001

Ekman, P. (1999). Basic Emotions. In Dalgleish and Power (eds.), *Handbook of Cognition and Emotion*. Wiley and Sons Ltd.

Ekman, P., Friesen, W., & Ellsworth, P. (1972). *Emotion in the Human Face: Guidelines for Research and an Integration of Findings*. Pergamon Press Inc.

Elias, M.J., O'Brien, M.U., & Weissberg, R.P. (2006). Transformative Leadership for Social and Emotional Learning. *Principal Leadership*, 7, 10–13.

Elliott, E.S., & Dweck, C.S. (1988). Goals: An Approach to Motivation and Achievement. *Journal of Personality and Social Psychology*, 54(1), 5–12.

Elliot, A.J., & Church, M.A. (1997). A Hierarchical Model of Approach and Avoidance Achievement Motivation. *Journal of Personality and Social Psychology*, 72(1), 218.

Elliot, A.J., & Harackiewicz, J.M. (1996). Approach and Avoidance Achievement Goals and Intrinsic Motivation: A Mediational Analysis. *Journal of Personality and Social Psychology*, 70(3), 461.

Elliot, A.J., & McGregor, H.A. (2001). A 2×2 Achievement Goal Framework. *Journal of Personality and Social Psychology*, 80(3), 501.

Feidakis, M., Daradoumis, T., Caballé, S., Conesa, J., & Conesa, J. (2014). Embedding Emotion Awareness into e-Learning Environments. *International Journal of Emerging Technologies in Learning (iJET)*, 9(7), 39–46.

Frenzel, A.C., Goetz, T., Lüdtke, O., Pekrun, R., & Sutton, R. (2009). Emotional Transmission in the Classroom: Exploring the Relationship between Teacher and Student Enjoyment. *Journal of Educational Psychology*, 101, 705–716.

Gilbert, D.T., & Wilson, T.D. (2007). Prospection: Experiencing the Future. *Science*, 317(5843), 1351–1354.

Gomes, C.F.A., Brainerd, C.J., & Stein, L.M. (2013). Effects of Emotional Valence and Arousal on Recollective and Nonrecollective Recall. *Journal of Experimental Psychology: Learning, Memory, and Cognition*, 39(3), 663–677. doi: 10.1037/a0028578

Gottfried, A.E. (1990). Academic Intrinsic Motivation in Young Elementary School Children. *Journal of Educational Psychology*, 82(3), 525–538.

Grant, H., & Dweck, C. (2003). Clarifying Achievement Goals and Their Impact. *Journal of Personality and Social Psychology*, 85(3), 541–553.

Gross, J.J. (2015). Emotion Regulation: Current Status and Future Prospects. *Psychological Inquiry*, 26(1), 1–26. doi:/10.1080/ 1047840X.2014.940781

Gupta, A., Menon, N., Lee, W., Rebelsky, W., Allesio, D., Murray, T., Woolf, B., Whitehill, J., & Arroyo, I. (2021). Affective Teacher Tools: Affective Class Report Card and Dashboard. *Proceedings of the International Conference on Artificial Intelligence in Education*, pp. 78–189. Springer.

Gupta, R., Hur, Y.-J., & Lavie, N. (2016). Distracted by Pleasure: Effects of Positive Versus Negative Valence on Emotional Capture Under Load. *Emotion*, 16(3), 328–337. doi: 10.1037/emo0000112

Harley, J., Pekrun, R., Taxer, J., & Gross, J. (2019). Emotion Regulation in Achievement Situations: An Integrated Model. *Educational Psychologist*, 54(2), 106–126. doi: 10.1080/00461520.2019.1587297

Harter, S. (1981). A New Self-Report Scale of Intrinsic Versus Extrinsic Orientation in the Classroom: Motivational and Informational Components. *Developmental Psychology*, 17, 300–312.

Harter, S., & Connell, J.P. (1984). A Model of Children's Achievement and Related Self-Perceptions of Competence, Control, and Motivational Orientation. *Advances in Motivation and Achievement*, 3, 219–250.

Heffernan, N.T., & Heffernan, C.L. (2014). The ASSISTments Ecosystem: Building a Platform that Brings Scientists and Teachers Together for Minimally Invasive Research on Human Learning and Teaching. *International Journal of Artificial Intelligence in Education*, 24, 470–497. doi: 10.1007/s40593-014-0024-x

Henderlong, J., & Lepper, M.R. (1997). Conceptions of Intelligence and Children's Motivational Orientations: A Developmental Perspective. In *Biennial Meeting of the Society for Research in Child Development*, Washington, DC.

Henderson, N., Rowe, J., Paquette, L., Baker, R., & Lester, J. (2020). Improving Affect Detection in Game-Based Learning with Multimodal Data Fusion. *Proceedings of the International Conference on Artificial Intelligence in Education 2020*. LNCS 12163.

Hidi, S. (2006). Interest: A Unique Motivational Variable. *Educational Research Review*, 1, 69–82. doi: 10.1016/j.edurev.2006.09.001.

Hollis, V., Konrad, A., & Whittaker, S. (2015). Change of Heart: Emotion Tracking to Promote Behavior Change. *Proceedings of the 33rd Annual ACM Conference on Human Factors in Computing Systems*, pp. 2643–2652.

Ibrahimoglu, N., Unaldi, I., Samancioglu, M., & Baglibel, M. (2013). The Relationship Between Personality Traits and Learning Styles: A Cluster Analysis. *ASIAN Journal of Management Sciences and Education*, 2(3).

Immordino-Yang, M.H. (2015). *Emotions, Learning, and the Brain: Exploring the Educational Implications of Affective Neuroscience.* The Norton Series on the Social Neuroscience of Education. W.W. Norton & Company.

Immordino-Yang, M.H. (2016). *Emotions, Learning and the Brain: Exploring the Educational Implications of Affective Neuroscience.* W.W. Norton & Company.

Immordino-Yang, M.H. & Damasio, A.R. (2007). We Feel Therefore We Learn: The Relevance of Affective and Social Neuroscience to Education. *Mind, Brain and Education*, 1(1), 3–10.

Immordino-Yang, M.H., & Sylvan, L. (2010). Admiration for Virtue: Neuroscientific Perspectives on a Motivating Emotion. *Contemporary Educational Psychology*, 35(2), 110–115.

Izard, C.E., Woodburn, E.M., & Finlon, K.J. (2010). Extending Emotion Science to the Study of Discrete Emotions in Infants. *Emotion Review*, 2(2), 134–136.

Kaliouby, R.E., & Robinson, P. (2005). The Emotional Hearing Aid: An Assistive Tool for Children with Asperger Syndrome. *Universal Access in the Information Society*, 4, 121–134.

Kappes, A., & Schikowski, A. (2013). Implicit Theories of Emotion Shape Regulation of Negative Affect. *Cognition & Emotion*, 27(5), 952–960. doi: 10.1080/02699931.2012.753415

Karumbaiah, S., Lizarralde, R., Allessio, D., Woolf, B., & Arroyo, I. (2017). Addressing Student Behavior and Affect with Empathy and Growth Mindset. In A. Hershkovitz & L. Paquette (eds.), *10th International Conference on Educational Data Mining.* Springer International Publishing.

Kleinginna, P.R., & Kleinginna, A.M. (1981). A Categorized List of Emotion Definitions, with Suggestions for a Consensual Definition. *Motivation and Emotion*, 5(4), 345–379.

Legg, S., & Hutter, M. (2005). A Universal Measure of Intelligence for Artificial Agents. *IJCAI'05: Proceedings of the 19th International Joint Conference on Artificial Intelligence.* Morgan Kaufmann Publishers Inc., pp. 1509–1510.

Lepper, M.R., & Henderlong, J. (2000). Turning "Play" into "Work" and "Work" into "Play": 25 Years of Research on Intrinsic versus Extrinsic Motivation. *Intrinsic and Extrinsic Motivation*, 257–307.

Lepper, M.R., Henderlong Corpus, J., & Iyengar, S.S. (2005). Intrinsic and Extrinsic Motivational Orientations in the Classroom: Age Differences and Academic Correlates. *Journal of Educational Psychology*, 97(2), 184–196.

Lester, J.C., Converse, S.A., Kahler, S.E., Barlow, S.T., Stone, B.A., & Bhogal, R.S. (1997). The Persona Effect: Affective Impact of Animated Pedagogical Agents. In *Proceedings of the ACM SIGCHI Conference on Human Factors in Computing Systems* (pp. 359–366).

Mandler, G. (1989). Affect and Learning: Causes and Consequences of Emotional Interactions. In D.B. McLeod (ed.), *Affect and Mathematical Problem Solving* (pp. 3–19). Springer.

Mayer, R., & Estrella, G. (2014). Benefits of Emotional Design in Multimedia Instruction. *Learning and Instruction*, 33, 12–18.

McRae, K. (2016). Cognitive Emotion Regulation: A Review of Theory and Scientific Findings. *Current Opinion in Behavioral Sciences*, 10, 119–124. doi: 10.1016/j.cobeha.2016.06.004

Muldner, K., Wixon, M., Rai, D., Burleson, W., Woolf, B., & Arroyo, I. (2015). Exploring the Impact of a Learning Dashboard on Student Affect. *Proceedings of the International Conference on Artificial Intelligence in Education.* Springer-Verlag, Berlin, Heidelberg.

Oberman, L.M., & Ramachandran, V.S. (2007). The Simulating Social Mind: The Role of the Mirror Neuron System and Simulation in the Social and Communicative Deficits of Autism Spectrum Disorders. *Psychological Bulletin*, 133(2), 310–327. doi: 10.1037/0033-2909.133.2.310

Ocumpaugh, J., Baker, R., & Rodrigo, M. (2012). Baker-Rodrigo Observation Method Protocol (BROMP) 1.0. Training Manual Version 1.0 (PDF). EdLab.

Ortony, A., Clore, G.L., & Collins, A. (1988). *The Cognitive Structure of Emotions.* Cambridge University Press.

Pekrun, R. (1988). Anxiety and Motivation in Achievement Settings: Towards a Systems-Theoretical Approach. *International Journal of Educational Research*, 12(3), 307–323, doi: 10.1016/0883-0355 (88)90008-0.

Pekrun, R. (2006). The Control-Value Theory of Achievement Emotions: Assumptions, Corollaries, and Implications for Educational Research and Practice. *Educational Psychology Review*, 18(4), 315–341. doi: 10.1007/s10648-006-9029-9

Pekrun, R. (2014). Emotions and Learning. *Educational Practices Series*, 24(1), 1–31.

Pekrun, R., Frenzel, A.C., Goetz, T., & Perry, R.P. (2007). The Control-Value Theory of Achievement Emotions: An Integrative Approach to Emotions in Education. Chapter 2. In Paul A. Schutz & Reinhard Pekrun (eds.), *Emotion in Education*, pp. 13–36. Academic Press.

Pekrun, R., & Stephens, E.J. (2010). Achievement Emotions: A Control-Value Approach. *Social and Personality Psychology Compass*, 4(4), 238–255.

Pekrun, R., Vogl, E., Muis, K.R, & Sinatra, G.M. (2017). Measuring Emotions During Epistemic Activities: The Epistemically-Related Emotion Scales. *Cognition and Emotion*, 31(6), 1268–1276. doi: 10.1080/02699931.2016.1204989

Piaget, J. (1971). The Theory of Stages in Cognitive Development. In D.R. Green, M.P. Ford, & G.B. Flamer (eds.), *Measurement and Piaget*. McGraw-Hill.

Pintrich, P.R. (1999). The Role of Motivation in Promoting and Sustaining Self-Regulated Learning. *International Journal of Education Research*, 31(6), 459–470.

Plass, J., Homer, B., & Kinzer, C. (2015). Foundations of Game-Based Learning. *Educational Psychologist*, 50(4), 258–283. doi: 10.1080/00461520.2015.1122533

Porayska-Pomsta, K., Mavrikis, M., D'Mello, S.K., Conati, C., & Baker, R. (2013). Knowledge Elicitation Methods for Affect Modelling in Education. *International Journal of Artificial Intelligence in Education*, 22, 107–140.

Price, M.J., Mudrick, N.V., Taub, M., & Azevedo, R. (2018). The Role of Negative Emotions and Emotion Regulation on Self-Regulated Learning with MetaTutor. In R. Nkambou, R. Azevedo, & J. Vassileva (eds.), *Intelligent Tutoring Systems*. ITS 2018. Lecture Notes in Computer Science, vol 10858. Springer, Cham.

Rebolledo-Mendez, G., Luckin, R., & Du Boulay, B. (2011). Designing Adaptive Motivational Scaffolding for a Tutoring System. In R. Calvo and S. D'Mello (eds.), *New Perspectives on Affect and Learning Technologies*, pp. 155–168. Springer.

Rivera-Pelayo, V., Fessl, A., Müller, L., & Pammer, V. (2017). Introducing Mood Self-Tracking at Work: Empirical Insights from Call Centers. *ACM Transactions on Computer-Human Interaction*, 24(1), Article 3, 28 p. doi: 10.1145/3014058

Roll, I., Aleven, V., McLaren, B., & Koedinger, K. (2011). Improving Students' Help-Seeking Skills Using Metacognitive Feedback in an Intelligent Tutoring System. *Learning and Instruction*, 21(2), 267–280.

Rosenberg, E.L. (1998). Levels of Analysis and the Organization of Affect. *Review of General Psychology*, 2(3), 247–270.

Rotgans, J., & Schmidt, H. (2011). The Role of Teachers in Facilitating Situational Interest in an Active-Learning Classroom. *Teaching and Teacher Education*, 27(1), 37–42.

Royer, J.M., & Walles, R. (2007). Influences of Gender, Motivation and Socioeconomic Status on Mathematics Performance. In D.B. Berch and M.M.M. Mazzocco (eds.), *Why Is Math So Hard for Some Children*, pp. 349–368. Paul H. Brookes Publishing Co.

Ruiz, S., Charleer, S., Urretavizcaya, M., Klerkx, J., Fernández-Castro, I., & Duval, E. (2016). Supporting Learning by Considering Emotions: Tracking and Visualization a Case Study. *Proceedings of the Sixth International Conference on Learning Analytics & Knowledge (LAK '16)*. Association for Computing Machinery, New York, pp. 254–263.

Russell, J.A. (2003). Core Affect and the Psychological Construction of Emotion. *Psychological Review*, 110(1), 145.

Sansone, C., Smith, J., Thoman, D., & MacNamara, A. (2012). Regulating Interest When Learning Online: Potential Motivation and Performance Trade-Offs. *The Internet and Higher Education*, 15(3), 141–149. doi: 10.1016/j.iheduc.2011.10.004.

Smallwood, J., Bernhardt, B.C., Leech, R., Bzdok, D., Jefferies, E., & Margulies, D.S. (2021). The Default Mode Network in Cognition: A Topographical Perspective. *Nature Reviews Neuroscience*, 22(8), 503–513.

Scherer, K.R., Wallbott, H.G., & Summerfield, A.B. (1986). *Experiencing Emotion: A Cross Cultural Study*. Cambridge University Press.

Shuman, V., & Scherer, K.R. (2014). Concepts and Structures of Emotions. In R. Pekrun & L. Linnenbrink-Garcia (eds.), *International Handbook of Emotions in Education*, Educational Psychology Handbook Series, pp. 13–35.

Skinner, B.F. (1953). *Science and Human Behavior.* Macmillan.

Somuncuoglu, Y., & Yildirim, A. (1999). Relationship between Achievement Goal Orientations and the Use of Learning Strategies. *The Journal of Educational Research*, 92(5), 267–277.

Song, M., Liu, Y., Zhou, Y., Wang, K., Yu, C., & Jiang, T. (2009). Default Network and Intelligence Difference. *IEEE Transactions on Autonomous Mental Development*, 1(2), 101–109.

Spires, H.A., Rowe, J.P., Mott, B.W., & Lester, J.C. (2011). Problem Solving and Game-Based Learning: Effects of Middle Grade Students' Hypothesis Testing Strategies on Learning Outcomes. *Journal of Educational Computing Research*, 44(4), 453–472.

Spreng, R.N., & Grady, C.L. (2010). Patterns of Brain Activity Supporting Autobiographical Memory, Prospection, and Theory of Mind, and Their Relationship to the Default Mode Network. *Journal of Cognitive Neuroscience*, 22(6), 1112–1123.

Sumpter, A.L. (2017). *Grit and Self-Control: Independent Contributors to Achievement Goal Orientation and Implicit Theories of Intelligence* (Doctoral dissertation, Ohio Dominican University).

Tobias, S., & Fletcher, J.D. (2012). Reflections on "A Review of Trends in Serious Gaming". *Review of Educational Research*, 82(2), 233–237. doi: 10.3102/0034654312450190

Tobias S., Fletcher J.D., & Wind A.P. (2014). Game-Based Learning. In J. Spector, M. Merrill, J. Elen, & M. Bishop, (eds.), *Handbook of Research on Educational Communications and Technology*. Springer.

Van Ameringen, M., Mancini, C., Farvolden, P. (2003) The Impact of Anxiety Disorders on Educational Achievement. *Journal of Anxiety Disorders*, 17(5), 561–571. doi: 10.1016/S0887-6185(02)00228-1

Van Den Heuvel, M.P., Stam, C.J., Kahn, R.S., & Pol, H.H. (2009). Efficiency of Functional Brain Networks and Intellectual Performance. *Journal of Neuroscience*, 29(23), 7619–7624.

Verduyn, P., Delvaux, E., Van Coillie, H., Tuerlinckx, F., & Van Machelen, I. (2009). Predicting the Duration of Emotional Experience: Two Experience Sampling Studies. *Emotion*, 9, 83–91.

Vogl, E., Pekrun, R., Murayama, K., Loderer, K., & Schubert, S. (2019). Surprise, Curiosity, and Confusion Promote Knowledge Exploration: Evidence for Robust Effects of Epistemic Emotions. *Frontiers in Psychology*. doi: 10.3389/fpsyg.2019.02474

Vogl, E., Pekrun, R., Murayama, K., & Loderer, K. (2020). Surprised–Curious–Confused: Epistemic Emotions and Knowledge Exploration. *Emotion*, 20(4), 625–641. doi: 10.1037/emo0000578

Vogl, E., Pekrun, R., & Loderer, K. (2021). Epistemic Emotions and Metacognitive Feelings. doi: 10.1007/978-3-030-51673-4_3

Von Culin, K.R., Tsukayama, E., & Duckworth, A.L. (2014). Unpacking Grit: Motivational Correlates of Perseverance and Passion for Long-Term Goals. *The Journal of Positive Psychology*, 9(4), 306–312.

Washington, P., Voss, C., Kline, A., Haber, N., Daniels, J., Fazel, A., De, T., Feinstein, C., Winograd, T., & Wall, D. (2017). SuperpowerGlass: A Wearable Aid for the At-Home Therapy of Children with Autism. *Proceeding of ACM Interactive, Mobile, Wearable and Ubiquitous Technologies*, 1, 112:1–112:22.

Webster, E.A., & Hadwin, A.F. (2015). Emotions and Emotion Regulation in Undergraduate Studying: Examining Students' Reports from a Self-Regulated Learning Perspective. *Educational Psychology*, 35(7), 794–818. doi: 10.1080/01443410.2014.895292

Weiner, B. (1986). An Attributional Theory of Achievement Motivation and Emotion. In *An Attributional Theory of Motivation and Emotion*. SSSP Springer Series in Social Psychology. Springer.

Wixon, M., Arroyo, I., Muldner, K., Burleson, W., Rai, D., & Woolf, B.P. (2014). The Opportunities and Limitations of Scaling Up Sensor-Free Affect Detection. In J. Stamper, Z. Pardos, M. Mavrikis, & B.M. McLaren (eds.), *Proceedings of the 7th International Conference on Educational Data Mining*, pp. 145–152.

Wolters, C. (2003). Regulation of Motivation: Evaluating an Underemphasized Aspect of Self-Regulated Learning. *Educational Psychologist*, 38(4), 189–205. doi: 10.1207/S15326985EP3804_1

Wolters, C.A., & Hussain, M. (2015). Investigating Grit and Its Relations with College Students' Self-Regulated Learning and Academic Achievement. *Metacognition and Learning*, 10(3), 293–311.

Yerkes R.M., & Dodson J.D. (1908). The Relation of Strength of Stimulus to Rapidity of Habit-Formation. *Journal of Comparative Neurology and Psychology*, 18(5), 459–482. doi: 10.1002/cne.920180503

6. Scrutable AIED

Judy Kay, Bob Kummerfeld, Cristina Conati,
Kaśka Porayska-Pomsta and Ken Holstein

INTRODUCTION

As technology takes an increasing role in our lives, there has been a growing call to ensure that people can understand and control it. This is reflected in the media and in fast-changing legislation, notably the European Union's General Data Protection Regulation (GDPR)[1] and the call for appropriate management of, and access to, learning data, such as Family Education Rights and Privacy Act (FERPA).[2] Meanwhile, there has been an explosion of research on how to build AI systems that are fair, accountable, transparent and ethical (FATE).[3] One key concern of the public and these research communities relates to the ways that personalisation can be used and misused with nudges, dark patterns, technocognition and other forms of data collection and use that people are unaware of (Eslami et al., 2019; Kozyreva et al., 2020).

A starting point for giving learners greater agency is to acknowledge that educational systems are so complex that even the designers and developers who build them cannot really understand them fully, or anticipate how they might behave under various circumstances (Holstein et al., 2020; Subramonyam et al., 2021; Yang et al., 2020). In spite of that complexity, we argue that it is both important and feasible to create AIED systems with interfaces that are scrutable, because they enable learners to understand at least some key aspects of the way they work (Eslami et al., 2015, 2019; Wang et al., 2019).

A typical dictionary definition of *scrutable* is: "capable of being understood by careful study or investigation".[4] We operationalise scrutability in AIED with questions a user may want to be able to answer about a learning system. For example, suppose Alice is working on a problem in a personalised teaching system. She is surprised to suddenly see a hint with information (which we call X). She considers that she already knows X. Here are some questions she may want to answer:

- "Does the system "know" that I already know X?"
- "Why did the system give me that hint at this time?"

The first question essentially asks about the system's model of Alice's knowledge – whether the system models Alice's knowledge of X. If the system had chosen the hint because it modelled her as not knowing X, the answer to the second question involves: (1) details of the learner model for X; and (2) the method used to select that hint at that time. Suppose that the system provided a scrutiny interface that enabled Alice to answer both these questions, she may then go on to ask:

- "Why does the system "believe" that I do not know X?"

Suppose the answer to this question is that camera data indicates Alice was confused when she read about X and she answered a question about X incorrectly. Alice may now want to know:

- *"How can I tell the system I already knew X?"*
- *"How can I tell the system not to use camera data?"*

We have italicised these questions as they go beyond scrutinising how the system operates to a form of user control.

The next section explains how scrutability relates to the many similar terms and why distinguishing between these terms matters. Then, we show how scrutability needs to be considered in the design of each element in the architecture of AIED systems. This is crucial for integrating scrutability into the whole enterprise of engineering learning systems. From these foundations, we present a learner-centred and testable way to operationalise the various layers of scrutability. We do this with an approach from human–computer interaction (HCI), in terms of a set of "benchmark" questions, like the examples above, that would enable a learner to ask of a highly scrutable system. Not all the questions need to be supported in every system; system designers should consider the list and decide which to build into the design of their AIED systems, based on the specific features, pedagogical and interaction goals of their systems. Then, evaluation of those systems should include user studies to test if learners can work out how to answer these questions (usability) and whether learners bother to scrutinise the system through such questions. We illustrate these ideas with two case studies. We then outline the reasons why scrutability is particularly important in educational technology and conclude with a set of principles for designing scrutable AIED systems and a research agenda.

SCRUTABILITY IN THE FATE LANDSCAPE

There has been an explosion of research in the broad area of fair, accountable, transparent, explainable, ethical (FATE) systems. This has produced a large and growing body of literature that uses many terms for the broad idea of *transparency*, which in turn, are used in different ways by different researchers. We now explain how the term *scrutability* fits into this landscape and why we use it to describe a goal that is important and that AIED system builders can realistically implement.

Figure 6.1 shows how scrutability relates to some of the many other widely used terms in this space. The upper four boxes are user-centred terms. The two across the bottom are machine-centred – the left one has Explainable AI (also called XAI) (Arrieta et al., 2020), which describes what the *machine* does. The other machine-centred box has the terms *transparent* and *glass box*. These may be attributes of an explainable system. The arrow in the figure indicates that XAI aims to achieve transparency.

Transparency implies low user effort – just as you can look through a clean glass window, barely aware that it is there, to see what is beyond. While you may be able to observe what is beyond, you still may have trouble understanding it. In practice, educational technology is typically too complex for a person to easily understand how the whole system works, even when they can see some details of the elements of data and algorithms. So, transparency fails to reflect the substantial effort a learner needs to make to understand an AIED system,

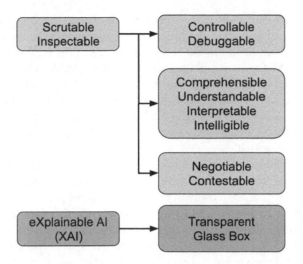

Notes: Terms in the top four boxes are human centred – the bottom pair are machine centred

Figure 6.1   *Placing scrutability within the landscape of related terms in the AI, human–computer interaction and FATE literature*

which may not add in any meaningful way to how they interact with the system or can benefit from it. Other domains, such as medicine, pharmacological and food industries, offer some useful examples of transparency practices deriving from similar challenges. These domains are also very complex domains with much technical knowledge that might be out of reach to non-specialists. The basic transparency requirements in those contexts involve declarations of the (active) ingredients, their intended benefits and potential side effects. The transparency practices in those domains also involve an accountability trail which includes both who is ultimately responsible for the safety of the products/interventions and how to report any potential issues. Similar practices are non-existent in AI in Education or broader EdTech domains.

While in the context of educational technologies it might be tempting to focus on explaining the algorithms and the complex design and operation of such systems, as demonstrated in those other domains, such a focus may be misplaced insofar as it might not inform the user about the intended goals/benefits of those systems, the underlying measures by which a system evaluates its success, or the systems' limitations including what it cannot measure and where there is an uncertainty in its inferences. We argue that it is being transparent about the system's goals, measurements methods and its limitations that represent the necessary, even if not always sufficient, transparency requirements for the intended users of such systems (see also Chapter 26 by Porayska-Pomsta et al. in this volume for a related discussion). As in the other domains, these necessary requirements do not preclude the need for transparency about the technical details that may be required by specialist stakeholders. Thus, they do not guarantee sufficiency of scrutability under all circumstances.

We now turn to the many user-centred terms. The top left box, with *scrutable* and *inspectable*, relates to what a user does. The key difference between these terms is that scrutable better reflects the user effort to carefully examine (scrutinise) what may be many parts of a system, from the data capture through to potentially sophisticated processing by AI algorithms. This highlights that design of scrutable AIED systems must have a strong HCI and interface focus that runs in parallel with design of the rest of the AI and system.

The top right box has the terms *controllable* and *debuggable*. These can be undertaken by a user after they have scrutinised and understood at least some parts of the system. Consider the example we introduced above where the student thinks they know X but the learner model indicates they do not. From the learner's perspective this is a bug which they may want to correct. Equally, they may want to control the system by changing this aspect. In a debuggable or controllable system, the learner can make this change. This indicates more learner agency than a negotiable system. With complete learner control, they tell the system they know X and the model is changed accordingly. Some may argue that it is risky to give the learner such control. However, in the user-control perspective of Personis-based systems (Kay, 2000; Assad et al., 2007), users could provide evidence, such as that they know X and this is simply "accreted" along with other evidence for the user's knowledge of X; all that was interpreted as needed by the application. We return to this below.

The next box at the right has four terms that relate to the target cognitive state of the user. For example, we may demonstrate that a system is "understandable" if users can correctly explain how it works. Indeed, these terms, particularly the term "intelligible," come from the HCI research community (Abdul et al., 2018; Lim et al., 2009; Vaughan and Wallach, 2020). It follows then that evaluating aspects like understandability requires user studies which assess whether, and how well, people actually could understand it. The figure shows that users need to scrutinise or inspect aspects of the system to learn enough to achieve the cognitive states associated with these terms.

We now turn to the third user-centred box at the right, with *Negotiable* and *Contestable*. A body of AIED work has focused on negotiable learner models (Baker, 1993; Bull et al., 1995; Holstein et al., 2019b). These offer the student an interface to (1) see that the learner model "believes" they do not know X, (2) the student can contest this, and (3) start the "negotiation" process where the system provides an assessment task – if the student does this correctly, the system changes its model (or if the student cannot do it, they may reflect and realise the model is correct). Notably, this approach had the system in control. A similar notion is captured by the term *contestability*, that is, "the [user's] ability to contest, appeal, or challenge algorithmic decisions" (Lyons et al., 2021) and used in emerging legal guidelines (Jobin et al., 2019). This refers to a loosely defined notion which may be operationalised in the future. It refers to what the user does, and so it is user centred.

In summary, this section has reviewed some of the many terms that appear in the FATE literature. *Transparency* has become the umbrella term, as reflected in its use in the acronym, FATE. Reflecting the importance of this topic for AIED, Porayska-Pomsta et al. (see Chapter 26) discuss broad dimensions of ethics in AIED. Scrutability relates to one of the core aspects, which they describe as "explicability" and as transparency of the way the system works and accountability in terms of who is responsible for how AI works. It also links with the broad perspectives such as discrimination, governance and ethics in Chapter 25 (Williamson et al.). Figure 6.1 shows the particular role of scrutability. It is also a foundation for users to be able to assess whether they can *trust* a system. It should be a driver for system builders to be *accountable* for their AIED design. We have presented this landscape to highlight the reason why we chose the term *scrutability*, because it is user-centred and highlights the user effort required.

ARCHITECTURE OF LEARNING SYSTEMS FOR SCRUTABILITY AND CONTROL

This section presents the main elements in personalised learning systems. Figure 6.2 shows them in a high-level architecture with seven boxes: the top pair of boxes has data elements, the middle pair has learner models and the bottom three show systems which the user interacts with. From the learner's perspective, interfaces are the system. The purpose of scrutability is to enable the learner to delve into the details of each box. This section explains the overall architecture and the next section deals with supporting scrutiny of its key elements.

The bottom-left interface box is the *Learning System.* In current widely used software, this is all that the learner sees and uses. Figure 6.2 shows that the learning system may use two forms of learner models. First, and common to most learning software, is the *Individual Learner Model* (at the middle left). This is built from learning data shown in the top box. It can also be changed by the learning system. Secondly, the learning system may use an *Aggregate Learner Model*, the middle-right box. It can be built from aggregated data from many individual learners, for example log data from all users of a massive open online course (MOOC). It can also be built by aggregating individual learner models from many users of a teaching system.

Unfortunately, most literature on learner modelling simply uses the term "learner model" for both the individual and aggregate models. To deal with scrutability, it is important to distinguish them, especially to take account of the privacy of personal data. The literature also refers to learner models by other terms, with "student model" as a synonym. The term "user model" is broader. The literature has some differences in the definition of just what is modelled for each of these. Some researchers reserve the term "learner model" for the learner's knowledge and misconceptions. Others use it for the full range of possibilities that "systems

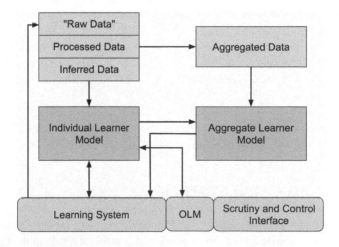

Notes: The bottom three boxes are the interfaces the learner sees and uses. The two middle boxes are learner models and the top boxes represent data. We distinguish individual and aggregate learner models even though the literature typically calls both "learner models"

Figure 6.2   *Key interfaces and architecture of a scrutable learning system*

model," such as the learner's preferences (e.g., interest in music), attributes (e.g., self-confidence), goals (e.g., want to gain deep knowledge) as well as knowledge and misconceptions that are the core of learner models. This chapter treats all three terms as synonyms and defines them to include all that is modelled.[5]

Figure 6.2 shows how the aggregate learner model may be built from two main sources of information. One is the individual learner models of many learners. The other path is from the data of individuals, aggregated first and then transformed into an aggregate learner model. In either case, aggregate models can be based on thousands of learners. Building them is a focus of Educational Data Mining (EDM) research and they may be built with sophisticated machine learning and data mining. Such aggregate models can be powerful tools for learning systems. For example, they can predict an individual learner's trajectory by matching that learner's history with the model. This is akin to the way a human teacher draws on their experience from teaching many previous students to interpret the progress of the current individual and to inform their decisions about how to teach that student.

Both individual and aggregate learner models represent the system's beliefs about learners. The flows in Figure 6.2 show two roles for these learner models. To guide personalisation of the teaching, the learner model needs enough detail for the learning system to interpret learner actions and drive personalisation of teaching actions. The second use is for the Open Learner Model (OLM), which provides the learner with an interface for the system's underlying learner model. OLMs have been part of many AIED systems; for example, the early Cognitive Tutors had a skill-meter that enabled a student to see their learning progress (Corbett and Anderson, 1994). There have now been many studies that have demonstrated their learning benefits, as recently reviewed (Bull, 2020).

A body of work has created Learner Models and OLMs that are not tied to a single AIED system. Bull called these independent OLMs (Bull et al., 2007). These can be long-term and may be used by multiple teaching systems (Cook and Kay, 1994; Kay and Kummerfeld, 2013). This matches the way that a human teacher remembers a student over time and can use their own mental model of the student to teach different topics and in different contexts. The underlying model may also be created purely to drive an OLM that shows a user their learning progress. Importantly, the OLM serves learning roles, notably supporting important metacognitive processes (Bull, 2020; Bull and Kay, 2013, 2016), such as self-monitoring, self-reflection and planning.

Figure 6.2 also shows a scrutiny and control interface. This needs to be designed, along with the learning system and all the other elements in the architecture, so that a learner will be able to scrutinise and control some or all of these aspects of the system.

ELEMENTS WITHIN AIED SYSTEMS

We now drill down into detailed elements in Figure 6.2 to consider how designers of AIED systems can incorporate the design of the scrutiny and control interface in the figure. Although the figure shows no connection lines between it and any other box, it is an interface onto those boxes and so could link to any or all of them. Throughout the history of AIED systems, the design of each part of a system has been driven by a trade-off between two main aspects, the teaching and learning goals and pragmatics. We now add two more goals for the designer, scrutability and control. To achieve scrutability, system designers should systematically consider how to enable learners to answer key questions about each box in Figure 6.2. Much FATE and AI research has focused on sophisticated machine learning. It is challenging to create these for scrutability. Such work is most relevant to the aggregate learner modelling and possibly also in parts of the learning system. Even there, very simple models are likely to be quite effective for domains like education (Kahneman et al., 2021). However, in terms of the overall picture in Figure 6.2, that is a very minor part of scrutability from a whole-system perspective. We now discuss how this offers ways to build practical and useful systems that can easily support some levels of scrutiny and control of some of the elements.

"Raw Data"

This is the first element in the learning data box (at the top left of Figure 6.2). We use quotes around "raw data" in line with the reasoning that this data is not raw – rather it is designed by people who create the system (Gitelman, 2013). There are many design decisions about what to capture. For example, more data from multiple sources, such as eye-tracking or vision-based emotion tracking, may seem useful in supporting a high-quality learner model. But the designer needs to consider how the potential benefits compare with disadvantages such as the additional complexity of the teaching system, potential privacy and ethical concerns, and whether learners, teachers, parents and other stakeholders would find them acceptable (Holstein et al., 2019b). It is useful for the designer to consider the following classes of raw data (Kay and Kummerfeld, 2013):

- Low-level *observational* data, such as clicks, mouse-overs or touches;
- Higher-level *observational data*, such as the learner's answers in assessment tasks;
- *Direct* data given by the learner about themselves, such as answers to questions such as, "How well do you know X?", "Do you want extra historical background information?";
- Details of what the system has *told* the learner, such as what hints have been provided or what content has been presented to the learner.

As a user of the AIED system, a learner can readily appreciate the differences between these classes of data. One form of scrutiny interface can show learners which of the above classes of data is collected about them. Once the designer is thinking in terms of scrutability and learner control, it would be natural for them to document the rationale for capturing each form of data along with how it is used. This could be available at the scrutiny interface which could also invite the learner to control whether a data source is used or not. Continuing the example above, if camera-based eye-tracking or emotion-tracking can be used by the system, the scrutiny and control interface could enable the learner to realise this and understand their use, and to then decide whether to allow them (Holstein et al., 2019b). Taking one other example, a learner may not want data from certain assessment tasks used for various reasons, such as having had help from a friend when they did them, making them inaccurate. Of course, this may mean a real loss for personalisation, something the scrutiny interface would need to make clear.

Processed Data

Within the top left data box in Figure 6.2, this element is the basic processing of the raw data. For example, if the designer wants to collect data about the time the learner spent on each task, they may apply thresholds to remove outliers, both those too short for serious engagement or so long that the learner has likely been distracted from the task. Of course, the presence of outliers might be separately used to model aspects such as learner engagement and focus. This is where the designer accounts for the typically incomplete and noisy nature of the data available. Details of the steps used could be available at the scrutiny interface.

Inferred Data

The data analysis step uses the raw and processed data to infer new data. This may be a very simple parameter, such as a moving average or a count of the number of correctly completed tasks. It may also be quite a sophisticated process, that may make use of external aggregate data models and machine learning. AIED has long distinguished slips from errors during learner interaction; this involves defining thresholds for interpreting learning data. The scrutiny and control interface could present this information.

Long-term individual learner model

The long-term user model layer is the representation that persists between sessions of use. For example, in a semester-long course, it may track the learning progress over the full semester. In lifelong and life-wide learning, such as using a wearable activity tracker in conjunction with a coaching system, this model could have data from several years, so that a suitable interface, such as iStuckWithIt (Tang and Kay, 2018), could help the learner discover changes they had failed to notice and identify factors triggering the change as a foundation for finding strategies to help them meet their goals. The system designer needs to take particular care about the management of such long-term models in terms of the location of the data store and the learner's control over it.

Flows of individual learning data and learner model

To this point, we have discussed the two boxes in Figure 6.2 for individual learning data and the individual learner model. To date, these have received relatively less attention in the broader XAI and FATE literature (Anik and Bunt, 2021; Ehsan et al., 2021; Hutchinson et al., 2021). In practice, they are very important since each layer impacts subsequent ones. Importantly, both these boxes can share a student's data or learning model to construct the aggregated data and models. The scrutiny and control interface should ensure the learner can know about this and control it.

The elements within the learning system

In much AI work (Woolf, 2010), the learning system has four key elements. One of these is the learner models that drive personalisation. We treated these in detail above. The learning system box in Figure 6.2 covers the three others: domain expertise, which determines *what* to teach; pedagogic expertise, which determines *how* to teach; and the interface, which may take many forms, such as conventional keyboard and mouse on a desktop, mobile devices, smart watches and other wearables, gesture interaction, natural language as text or speech and haptics.

When the learning systems make use of an individual learner model, they may use different interpretations of that model. A learner model representation to support this has: (Kay and Kummerfeld, 2013):

- *Components* modelled, for example, a knowledge-component X models the learner's knowledge of X;

- *Evidence*, from processed learning data, for example, a correct answer to a problem on X;
- *Resolver*, a process that interprets the available evidence about X to resolve a value if the learner knows X.

So, for example, a mastery-based teaching system teaches a topic X until the learner model indicates the student has mastered X; only then can the system move on to the next topic. So its resolver interprets the evidence about X as indicating mastery or not. But another teaching system may need to interpret the same set of evidence about X as a score out of 5. We could build systems that allow the learner control over the resolver. For example, in a formal setting, students might be offered a choice between two resolvers for a knowledge component, X: a pass-resolver which rates X as known well enough for pass-level performance and another distinction-resolver that only rates X as known if the evidence indicates the student is performing at a distinction level. This section has used examples about modelling learners' knowledge, but the same approach applies to other aspects such as preferences, goals and attributes.

Summary

There are two high-level insights to take from this analysis of the elements in Figure 6.2. First, it reflects the complexity of AIED systems. This is reflected in the many elements within the boxes in Figure 6.2. Adding to the complexity, several elements interact. Some are indicated in the lines in the figure. Beyond that, Figure 6.2 emphasises the data and learner model elements that are common to many AIED systems. Beyond that, each learning system element can be complex, and they may have quite different subelements that interact in complex ways. This makes it challenging even for system developers to build a deep and holistic understanding of the full system because that requires detailed knowledge of all the elements and their inter-dependencies. Even if each part is simple in itself, the whole picture is hard for a person to really understand – if some parts are complex, this is even more difficult. This may seem daunting. Fortunately, the second key insight is that learners may gain a great deal from being able to scrutinise just parts of the system.

Several chapters in this book link to various parts of the architecture of Figure 6.2. Chapter 12 (Blessing et al.) describes authoring systems for sophisticated intelligent tutoring systems. These support teachers and designers in creation of each element in the architecture. Chapter 5 (Arroyo et al.) deals with affective AIED systems. These may use wearables or camera sensors to collect data for a model of a learner's emotion. Assessment, core for learning modelling, is discussed in Chapter 21 (Ying Fang et al.). This includes stealth assessments.

Several chapters discuss aspects of learning modelling, which covers several elements of Figure 6.2. Chapter 27.7 (Mizoguchi) considers cultural awareness. Chapter 7 (Aleven et al.) considers domain modelling; this is tightly interdependent with the learner model ontology. Forms of aggregate learner modelling are treated in Chapter 13 (Mao et al.) on temporal learner modelling and in Chapter 8 (Conati and Lallé) on learner modelling in open-ended learning environments based on FUMA (Framework for User Modeling and Adaptation). FUMA has two paths, one called *behaviour discovery*, which matches the aggregate learner modelling in Figure 6.2, and the other, *user classification*, is the part of the learning system that uses learning data, from learning activities and assessments, the individual learner model and the aggregate learner model. Chapter 15 on learning analytics for teachers (Pozdniakov et al.) involves the elements of aggregate learner modelling in our architecture.

EXAMPLES OF SCRUTINY INTERFACES

We now present two examples that provide very different forms of scrutability. The first is a particularly simple but also very valuable form of scrutability. The second illustrates a far more complex case which enables the learner to scrutinise a much more complex set of reasoning in a personalised teaching system.

Example of OLM-Supporting Scrutiny of Its Learning Data Sources

Figure 6.3 shows an OLM for a programming subject (Guerra-Hollstein et al., 2017; Somyürek et al., 2020). The top row of cells (colour-coded green in the actual interface) shows this learner's progress overall and for each of the set of learning topics. The intensity of the green colour shows the level of mastery. The bottom row of cells shows the corresponding information for the class (colour-coded blue in the actual interface). The middle row helps the learner see the differences between the two: it becomes green if the learner is ahead of the class, and blue if the class is ahead.

The cell labelled *Loops For* has a diamond because the student has clicked it to reveal the details of the "raw data" sources for the learner model. This enables the learner to scrutinise the system to determine the reason for the rating of their knowledge on this component of the model. The student would know about the *Quizzes*, *Examples* and *Annotated Examples* referred to in this detailed view. This could provide a valuable source of information for the student. From a learning perspective, the scrutiny of these details could enable them to work on the aspects that have low scores. From a FATE perspective, they could decide whether they trust these scores. For example, if the student had a lot of help with the quizzes, they could take that into account in judging the accuracy of their model. This example illustrates a case of added value of scrutability, where the learner can see what the "raw data" sources are.

Example of Scrutability of Learning System Reasoning

The second example has been chosen to illustrate a personalised teaching system which provides an interface that has detailed explanations of its actions (Conati et al., 2021). This is the Adaptive CSP applet, an open learning environment that leverages the FUMA framework described in Chapter 8 (Conati and Lallé) to provide personalized hints to students who are predicted to need help to learn well from the environment. Figure 6.4 shows a screen where the learner can see a detailed explanation of the reasons why they were given a hint.

This is an example of a scrutiny and control interface, as described in Figure 6.2. In this case, the explanation mentions "tracking your actions" and of these, it mentions "Using Reset 4 times" (the "raw data" of 2). The explanation also refers to "various patterns" which come from the long-term user model. For more details, see the FUMA's Behaviour Discovery phase in Chapter 8 (Conati and Lallé). The text also refers, in rather general terms, to the system reasoning that caused the hint to appear and there is a figure to provide a conceptual model of the process as well as the text.

Figure 6.5 shows another example screen for this system, in this case for the system which rated this student as "low learning". For more details, see the FUMA's User Classification phase in Chapter 8 (Conati and Lallé). This is all at the *data layers* of Figure 6.2. It illustrates a case where the explanation is quite detailed and so the student would need to invest some effort to read it carefully and try to understand it. The bottom of the screen has links to

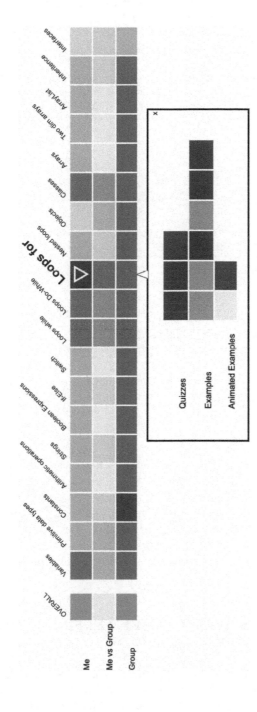

Notes: Darker cells indicate greater mastery

Source: Guerra-Hollstein et al., 2017

Figure 6.3   *Example of an OLM that provides scrutability of the main classes of raw data that have been used to determine the value of each knowledge component*

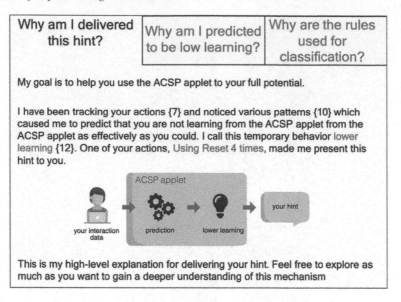

Source: Conati et al., 2021

Figure 6.4   *Screenshot of adaptive CSP where the learner can study the answer to the question "Why am I delivered this hint?"*

additional aspects. These, too, would require some time and effort for a student to scrutinise, especially as they need to integrate that additional information into the mental model they build for these processes.

Summary

This section has briefly introduced two examples of scrutiny and control interfaces. The first is part of an OLM and provides just details of the "raw data" used for the system's reasoning. This has had authentic use in several studies. The scrutability provides a clear link to ways that a learner can do the quizzes and study the two forms of examples to learn more about topics. The second example provides insights into a more complex set of system reasoning about personalised teaching and the learner model. For both, the learner would need to take a break from their main learning activity and invest some time and effort to scrutinise these details with respect to how these systems work.

BENCHMARK QUESTIONS: USER-CENTRED DEFINITION OF SCRUTABILITY AND CONTROL

We now introduce a core contribution of this paper, the notion of "benchmark questions" to drive the design of a scrutable system. We first present a small set of questions a learner may want to answer and show how these relate to the elements of Figure 6.2. These illustrate how

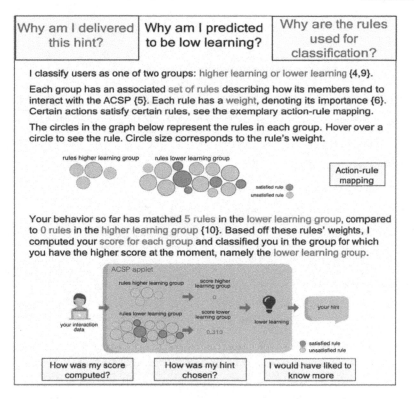

Source: Conati et al., 2021

Figure 6.5   *Screenshot of adaptive CSP where the learner can study the answer to the question "Why am I predicted to be low learning?"*

an AIED designer should consider how to integrate scrutability into their design process. We then present a fuller set of questions for designers to use as a checklist. This builds on work on scrutable user models (Kay, 1998, 2006), context-aware systems (Lim et al., 2009) and intelligent user interfaces (Eiband et al., 2020).

Figure 6.6 has seven benchmark questions, with columns showing the mapping to elements of Figure 6.2. The first question gives minimal, easily implemented but useful scrutability. We illustrate this in relation to the Open Learner Model interface in Figure 6.3, the first example in the fifth section. The screenshot shows how the learner can scrutinise a topic-cell to find that this is based on three data sources (quizzes, examples and animated examples). This can answer the first question at a high level. If the learner can click down to details of the quizzes, that gives a fine-grained answer. The learner is then able to change their OLM (Question 3), for example, by doing a quiz.

In general, raw data is the foundation for all later reasoning. Making its details scrutable means the learner can consider it along with aspects they know about, but the system does not (for example, they were unwell when they did Quiz 1, or they had a friend helping them with

Question	Raw Data	Data after cleaning	Inferred data	Learner model	Interpretation	Learning system
1 What data does the system collect about me?	✓					
2 Why does this system "believe" I know X? Or like Y?	✓	✓	✓	✓	✓	✓
3 *How do I change any of the above processes?*	✓	✓	✓	✓	✓	✓
4 Why did the system do A?				✓	✓	✓
5 *How can I tell the system I found A unhelpful?*				✓	✓	✓
6 Does my data go outside this system?	✓	✓	✓	✓	✓	✓
7 If so, where does it go?	✓	✓	✓	✓	✓	✓

Notes: Columns are for elements the learner scrutinises to answer each question. Most are for scrutiny, with the last two (italicised) for control

Figure 6.6   Illustrative benchmark questions mapped to the elements in Figure 6.2

Quiz 2). There are many other cases where the learner may have views or knowledge that mean they do not want certain raw data used. For example, if a camera is used to track their attention, they may consider that it is unreliable or they simply may not want that tracking used by the system.

Where the first question is minimal, a comprehensive answer to the second question involves all the elements in Figure 6.2. A designer should consider all of them but may decide to support just some. We illustrate the comprehensive answer in terms of the first example in the fifth section. The interface in Figure 6.3 is a form of learning system. We have already explained how scrutiny of the *raw data* can be supported (mapping to the first tick). Suppose it only uses assessment data less than one month old – this *data cleaning* detail can be made available to the learner. This could well resolve what would otherwise be a mysterious change in the system behaviour when older data are discarded. Each coloured cell in Figure 6.3 is *inferred data*: it is a small integer that determines the colour of the cell. The *OVERALL* cells have also been inferred, in this case from fine-grained learning data to higher-level data the learning system needs (Kay and Lum, 2005). This is a very common form of inference where each learning activity and assessment is about a subtopic of the main learning goals of the system. A scrutiny interface would enable a learner to discover how their competence on the higher-level topic is inferred. The next column is for the *learner model*, and scrutiny of this means the learner could discover what is modelled and how. For example, if the Figure 6.3 example were based on a Personis model (Kay and Kummerfeld, 2013), the scrutiny interface could take the learner to each modelled component, the evidence the model has stored about it and details of the multiple resolver processes to interpret that evidence. The OLM interface in the figure may show just a subset of these components. Of course, this OLM learning interface uses just one resolver. Question 3 is about making changes to any of the processes just described. An interface that enables a student to scrutinise the details to answer any of the elements of Question 2 could have an associated control interface.

Question 4 has ticks for the elements that correspond to ACSP, the second example in the last section. This has a scrutiny interface that enables the learner to find why a particular hint was given by the system, as well as the details of the learner model (low learning level in Figures 6.4 and 6.5) and the inference. Question 5, on user control, is similar to the lower right button, "I would have liked to know more" in Figure 6.5.

Questions 6 and 7 refer to data privacy associated with each element. They just mean that the learner can discover whether their personal data leave the learning system and, if so, which parts go where.

The set of benchmark questions above was chosen to illustrate the mapping from the user questions to the Figure 6.2 elements. Figure 6.7 has a longer list organised around the main elements and flows in Figure 6.2. Designers can use this as a checklist: for each question, they can document if they support it, or not, and their rationale. These questions serve three roles:

1. A user-centred way to *document* the extent of support for scrutability, and control in a particular learning system;
2. Drivers for *test-driven development* (TDD) (Beck, 2003) of scrutable AIED systems;

Question	Examples of answers
Individual data elements	
What "raw data" is collected about me?	details of video, physiological data, interface clicks, assessments
What processed data is kept?	video is discarded after analysis but all assessment results are kept.
What inferred data is kept?	video is analysed to infer if the learner is frustrated and this is stored as per-minute frustrating-ratings.
How do I control this inflow? i.e. add/remove a data source.	disable use of video
How do I volunteer raw data?	my self-assessment of knowledge, mood, frustration, fatigue
Individual learner model	
What is modelled about me?	knowledge components on loops as in Figure 6.3
How does the modelling process work?	as in Figure 6.3, this is the quizzes etc
How do I add/alter/remove an inference process?	disable use of quizzes
How do I control the interpretation of evidence about a component?	set a higher standard for full mastery
Flow of data from the individual to aggregate data stores and learner models	
Where does my data go?	to a whole state database
Where does my user model go?	to a whole state database
How do I control this? add/stop export?	stop sharing
Learning system	
How does this system use my learner model?	
How does it use aggregate learner models?	**illustrated**
What is personalised in its teaching?	**in**
Why did it do X?	**Figures 4 and 5**

Notes: Columns are for elements the learner scrutinises to answer each question. Most are for scrutiny, with italics for those that go beyond just scrutiny, and involve control

Figure 6.7   *Benchmark questions for use by designers of AIED systems to define the level of scrutability and control, and to drive design and evaluation*

3. In *user studies* to evaluate the effectiveness of a scrutiny interface following best practice in user experience (Hartson and Pyla, 2018).

The first role highlights that scrutability can be useful even if it only enables learners to answer some of the questions. The second role is about integrating scrutability into the design of the whole system. Finally, these questions are templates for user studies that assess whether learners can actually use the scrutiny and control interface.

For completeness, we present benchmark questions for an Open Learner Model (Kay and Kummerfeld, 2019).

1. Am I making progress?
2. Am I meeting my own goals – over the short and long term?
3. Am I meeting external goals? For example, teacher expectations, whole class performance, relevant subgroup performance.
4. What changes might help me reach my goals?
5. What is the meaning of the data and components modelled?
6. Can I trust the accuracy of the model?

These support metacognitive processes of self-monitoring (all but Q4), reflection (all but Question 1) and planning (Questions 4–6). These are important both for learning and as a potential trigger for scrutiny and control.

At this point, we briefly consider whether learners would bother to scrutinise and control an AIED system. An early study of an authentic evaluation of a scrutable teaching system (Czarkowski and Kay, 2002; Kay and Kummerfeld, 2013) shows students did so. Their system taught about aspects of the Unix file system and students were required to use this for a homework task. The researchers had introduced some errors in the personalisation to see if students would scrutinise the system to track these down. They did not. In follow-up interviews, students who had noticed the errors said they were used to software that had bugs. However, after each of the short quizzes in the system, students did scrutinise the system, exploring their learner model and the personalisation based on it. Some students changed their model to alter the personalisation. Some also explored ways to directly control the personalisation. Two key findings were that students had learnt to expect errors in systems and that they did take time to scrutinise the system and they did this after the quizzes.

Further evidence that students are willing to leverage scrutability tools comes from the evaluation of the explanations for the hints generated by the Adaptive CSP, shown in Figures 6.4 and 6.5 (Conati et al., 2021). Of the 30 participants who had access to the hints' explanations in this study, only six participants did not access them, stating as the reason that the hints they received were clear enough, or that they were not wanted in the first place. The remaining 24 participants accessed the explanations. These participants received on average 2.6 hints, and the ratio of explanation initiations over the number of hints received was 0.75 on average (standard deviation, SD = 0.28). On average, explanations were initiated for three-quarters of the hints received, indicating that some participants were eager to view explanations and went back to the explanations for subsequent hints. Participants spent an average of 63 s in the explanation interface, with a notable SD of 53.3 s and a range between 4.7 s and 191 s. The total time spent had a correlation coefficient of $r = 0.41$ with the number of hints received, indicating that this factor does not fully explain the time spent with the explanations.

THE DISTINCTIVE NATURE OF SCRUTABILITY IN AIED

Educational AI systems have attracted little attention to date in the broader literature on FATE and XAI (Conati et al., 2018). Yet, they have three distinctive features. First, we can, and should, draw on a huge body of research on education when designing AIED systems. Several chapters in this book link AIED to relevant educational theory – for example, Chapter 9 (Aleven et al.) on instructional processes and Chapter 4 (Azevedo and Wiedbusch) on meta-cognition. The scrutiny interface should provide information that reflects the education theory underpinning design decisions.

Secondly, educational contexts bring distinctive limitations to the quality of raw data. This has important implications for all the other elements in Figure 6.2 and distinctive challenges for system builders. These apply to every element of the architecture. Consider the raw data available for modelling the learner's knowledge of a topic X. This is limited by factors such as the amount of time that a student could be asked to spend on assessment tasks. It is also noisy on many levels that the AIED system cannot account for. These include the potential for students to have help with tasks (inflating their apparent knowledge) or they may be in a noisy, distracting classroom (reducing their performance). Such inaccuracy and noise affect all elements that rely on the raw data. A classroom teacher may want an AIED system to use aggregate learner models just for their class. This means that the dataset is quite small compared with large-data AI. At the other extreme, where learning data from thousands of students is aggregated, there are different limitations. For example, detailed attributes of the students may be too sensitive to share in such datasets, impoverishing the aggregate learner model.

The third and most important feature of scrutability in education is that a scrutiny and control interface has the potential to provide valuable learning benefits. This is in addition to the benefits that broader FATE and XAI research identify for general AI systems. Examples of these are that a scrutable system may:

- Enable others to understand the AIED designer's view of the key modelling and teaching processes – in education, this is not just a matter of ensuring *accountability* but it should also improve the student's understanding of the purpose of the system and this should help them understand what it was designed to teach them;
- Enable the learner to determine how much to trust the system's personalisation – this is important in education where we know that most AIED systems have limited information about the learner's actual knowledge, and where learners and other stakeholders often have access to system-external knowledge that is important for assessing the validity of various data sources;
- Encourage accountability of the designers for pedagogic decisions – these decisions should be based on solid educational research, and this should be documented as part of the design;
- Enable the learner to be a partner in the modelling process – this supports the design perspective that AIED systems should be collaborative endeavours between the learner and the system;

- Facilitate learner autonomy and responsibility – this is in line with a principle of designing AIED systems so that they confirm the role of the machine as an aid to the learner;
- Help learners become more self-aware, particularly because they can access their learner model and its representation of their learning progress – in AIED, this has the potential to support self-regulated learning and facilitate metacognitive processes that have resulted in learning benefits. Chapter 4 (Azevedo and Wiedbusch) presents theories of metacognition and how these link to learning systems.

These aspects link to many classes of learning systems described in this book. For example, game-based systems (Chapter 20 by McLaren and Nguyen) are designed to be highly immersive. That immersion could be complemented by scaffolded metacognitive activities at a scrutiny and control interface. This could also offer learners opportunities to experiment with ways to tune the game play to gain understanding of their learning. Pedagogic interface agents (Chapter 27.3 by Lane) have the potential to address the distinctive needs of different learners. Such personalisation relies on the model of the individual learner, along with teaching strategies and assumptions about the best way to address different needs. A scrutiny interface could offer learners a way to take an active role in addressing the limits of the model and teaching strategy. Holstein and Olsen (Chapter 14) discuss human–AI collaboration for classroom orchestration. Scrutability and control are at the core of human–AI collaboration because both the human and the AI need to build models of each other in order to collaborate. Scrutability is, in essence, a mechanism for people to build a mental model of the way that the AIED system works.

Together, the aspects described in this section may make AIED the ideal crucible for scrutability research. It may well have the right forcing functions for important progress in creating scrutiny and control interfaces that are actually usable and understandable to naïve users. This aligns with the drivers for AIED, who have long pushed the envelope to support learning. The defining features of AIED contexts, the nature of learning and the noise in its data and models are distinctive and challenging.

DISCUSSION AND RESEARCH AGENDA

This discussion first outlines principles for building AIED systems that support scrutability and control. These provide a starting point as well as a research agenda for making it faster and easier to create AIED systems that are scrutable.

Pragmatic and Valuable Scrutability

Our Figure 6.6 architecture shows the many elements of an advanced teaching system. We have explained how designers of AIED systems can consider integrating scrutability into any or all of them. While designers need to be mindful of that whole picture, we now present principles for minimalist scrutability that is practical to implement and explain how even that level of scrutability is valuable.

Designers should account for "raw data" as it is foundational
The "raw data", as we can see in Figure 6.2, is the ground upon which all later stages of processing, modelling and personalisation are built. It also makes this layer a critical part of

scrutability (Holstein et al., 2019a). Taking a design perspective of data (Feinberg, 2017) means that these very foundations of AIED systems should have scrutability as a design goal. This is part of an urgent need for "data excellence in AI" (Sambasivan et al., 2021), meaning that real care is taken in its systematic design and documentation processes. Incorporating design for scrutability could be a valuable part of that data design process since it requires designers to provide explanations that enable learners to understand what data are collected about them; this should include an explanation about the reason it is needed and useful and it could include information about its limitations. A scrutiny interface with this information would be a perfect jumping-off point for the learner to be invited to provide additional raw information about themself. For example, they could self-assess their knowledge, share their goals. This would invite AIED design perspectives that make use of such information.

Design for incomplete, noisy, uncertain and misleading data
All sources of learning data have limitations for the goal of building a learner model, and then using this to drive personalisation. For example, consider the data from a set of assessment tasks designed to determine how well the learner knows X. This has many limitations such as: the learner may have done the task with a friend helping them; they may have been working in a distracting environment, such as many classrooms; they may have been feeling unwell; they may misinterpret part of the interface; they may make a slip and inadvertently select the wrong menu item or mistype answers. Beyond these situational factors, there are limitations that follow from the design of a system and limits in the actual data collection. Sensing devices may be inaccurate. For example, the learner may not trust a camera-based system of mind-wandering or emotion. Design of assessment is a trade-off between accuracy and pragmatics. For example, a designer needs to decide how many assessments to use, taking account of the time the learner should spend, the effort of building more assessments and the accuracy of the reasoning about the mastery of X. AIED designers should document the limitations that they are aware of for the learning data they capture.

Start with scrutability of data elements
Given the key role of raw data as the foundation for all later layers and the nature of that data as just discussed, an obvious starting point for scrutability is to enable learners to determine what raw data is captured. A simple way to do this is to keep a description of each data source, where this includes details of how it is collected and the designer's rationale for its collection (Anik and Bunt, 2021; Ehsan et al., 2021; Gebru et al., 2018; Hutchinson et al., 2021). In the section above, Benchmark Questions: User-Centred Definition of Scrutability and Control, we worked through the cascade from raw data, data that are cleaned and inferences that create new data, such as reasoning from fine-grained to high-level aspects of learning. The simplest level of scrutability could provide details of the raw data. Doing so should put modest demands on the interface design and the learner's time.

Scrutability Design Mindset

By designing AIED systems with scrutability in mind, designers will document their justification for each element. This makes for accountable-design thinking. For the base element, "raw data" layer, this means the designer should consider the value and accuracy of each data source. They could also consider, at design time, how to create interfaces that help the learner understand this and decide if the system should be allowed to use it.

Scrutability Driving Simplicity When It Is Sufficient

Each element in Figure 6.2 contributes to complexity. Designers can strive to make each no more complex than it needs to be. One important place to consider simplicity is in the machine-learning and data-mining algorithms. Before using a sophisticated algorithm, especially one that is harder for the user to scrutinise, there should be careful analysis of the performance benefit it offers over simpler algorithms. In a 2019 analysis of recommender deep-learning algorithms in papers published at top conferences, Dacrema, Cremonesi and Jannach (2019), found that six of the seven they could readily reproduce were often outperformed by simpler methods. A similar case occurred in 2020, for Task 3 of the NeurIPS Education Challenge, one of the equal-first place solutions (McBroom and Paassen, 2020) to the task of automatic ranking of mathematics questions according to their quality. This achieved 80% agreement with expert ratings with a very simple method based on student confidence ratings when tackling the question. More sophisticated modelling programs performed better on the training data but not on the test data. Even if more sophisticated algorithms outperform simpler ones, scrutability thinking calls for a carefully assessment of the meaningfulness of the difference. In a domain like education, with all the noise in data collection and reasoning, statistically significant but modest differences may not be meaningful. With a scrutability mindset, AIED system builders should carefully assess and document their choice of machine-learning algorithms.

Scrutability Integrated Into Learning

Clearly, the core role of AIED systems is to enable their users to learn. In terms of the architecture in Figure 6.2, learners will spend most of their time at the learning system interface. We now consider ways to make scrutability fit usefully into the learning process.

Recognise That Learners Have Considerable Agency: Scrutable Systems Can Be Partners

Learners have considerable agency at many levels. It is the learner who decides to concentrate, or not, to engage with the learning activities, or not or to try to game the system. With inscrutable systems, inquisitive learners may play with the system to try to see how it works. A philosophy of scrutable and controllable systems recognises this and calls for design of learning systems that are a partner for the learner. In learning outside formal classrooms, the learner needs to take responsibility for their learning. If they want to control a system, for example, by modifying their learner model to indicate they know X, it seems arrogant of a system designer to presume that their system always "knows" better than the learner. Of course, if learners can make such changes, the interface design must make it easy for the learner to also undo changes.

Teachable Moments for Metacognitive Activities at the Scrutiny and Control Interface

A scrutability mindset calls for designers to consider when and how to integrate scrutiny activities into learning. For example, when the learner has just completed an assessment task, that can be a time for them to pause and reflect. This has been explored in the case of OLMs, for example by Long and Aleven (2017). In a scrutable teaching system (Czarkowski and Kay, 2002; Kay and Kummerfeld, 2013), students chose to scrutinise the personalisation processes and the learner model after the quizzes. When the learning system is used as part of formal classroom teaching, the teacher can orchestrate use of the system to make time for students to use the scrutiny interfaces. This could include activities to help students learn how to make use of the information available in a way that matches their level and fits with the broader classroom context. With the extensive and growing use of learning systems in education, the designer of one system cannot know about the many potential contexts of use. A scrutiny interface can be part of classroom activities that bridge the gaps between the system and the context of use.

Standard scrutiny and control interfaces

This is key to reducing the burden on learners and AIED developers (Kaur et al., 2020). From the *learner*'s perspective, scrutiny at a familiar interface is much easier. From the AIED *designer* perspective, standard toolkits and methods reduce their work. A promising starting point is to do this for selected benchmark questions, notably those related to "raw data".

This is a two-way process since we also need to educate users to know that they should expect scrutiny interfaces that enable them to find at least partial answers to the benchmark questions. The particular needs of education mean that we should aim to create toolkits that make it easier for designers to create these scrutiny interfaces and that link explicitly to the pedagogical best practices to which AIED systems aspire. From the *learner*'s perspective, we need to acknowledge the challenges any person has in understanding the whole of a system, even after they have carefully reviewed each of the parts, in terms of each of the layers in Figure 6.2. Recognition of this is even more significant in light of the principle above, that learning is the core goal; this limits the time a learner can devote to scrutiny and control.

Scaffold learners to understand uncertainty

Given the uncertainty and limited accuracy of input data, it follows that all computation based on it only amplifies these factors. Of course, the AIED designer needs to consider this but, in addition, scrutiny interfaces should disclose known limits to accuracy. There is a growing body of work on visualisation of uncertainty, the need for it and challenges for designers and users (Correll, 2019). Some important work has explored this in AIED (Al-Shanfari et al., 2020), where the learner's own uncertainty and that of the system are presented on the interface. People find it challenging to understand uncertainty (Epstein, 1999) and so, an important direction is the design of interfaces that enable learners to understand it. Given the principle above, of infrequent use of scrutiny interfaces, one promising research direction is the creation of scaffolding to help the learner understand the uncertainty in the AIED system and its implications.

Summary

Each of the principles points to a part of a rich research agenda. For example, we need validated guidelines and tools that can provide systematic ways to carefully design the "raw data" of AIED systems and document the rationale so that this is available for scrutiny by users of these systems. A key for such research is both to serve the particular needs of educational settings and to harness the features of these settings to create frameworks, tools and practices that can support scrutiny and control in AIED.

SUMMARY AND CONCLUSIONS

This chapter has described a pragmatic, system builder's perspective of AIED, which accounts for the FATE dimensions of the AIED system, in terms of their transparency and accountability, with the potential to also enable the learner to assess the fairness. We began by explaining the choice of the term scrutability, rather than the many other terms. We then introduced the notion of a scrutiny and control interface as a new part of the Figure 6.2 architecture of an AIED system. That section of the paper also highlighted the special role of the raw data and individual and aggregate learner models and how these can support simple forms of scrutability. We drilled down into the elements of personalised systems in Figure 6.2 to highlight the inherent complexity of AIED systems. This adds to characterisation of scrutability as both complex but also involving many parts. This, in turn, highlights the fact that scrutability is not an all-or-nothing endeavour. The AIED system designer needs to carefully consider how to design these elements and the implications of that design for creating scrutiny interfaces. We illustrated this in two case studies. Then we introduced the "benchmark questions" that can be used in test-driven design of AIED systems, with a scrutability mindset. From this foundation, we highlighted the particular nature of AIED systems that makes FATE for AIED distinctive. Finally, we introduced a set of principles for use in design for scrutability and control in AIED.

To keep this chapter simpler, we have made the learner the focus. Of course, there are many other key stakeholders, including peers, collaborators, teachers, parents and administrators of educational institutions as well as those responsible for education and training systems within states and countries. We acknowledge that there may be very different needs and drivers for the design of effective support for scrutiny by each of these groups, in the various contexts where they operate. The benchmark questions involve the same elements and system architecture. But new questions need to be determined. We also decided not to discuss systems with bugs, ones created either with intentional lies or unintended ones.

We have briefly discussed when and how scrutiny can fit into and aid learning, although we need more work on how students do, indeed, scrutinise (Kay and Kummerfeld, 2013). There is also a wealth of evidence that learners are very interested in OLMs (Bull, 2020), and the decades of work on OLMs provide a valuable foundation for work on scrutability and scrutable AIED.

NOTES

1. https://gdpr-info.eu/
2. www2.ed.gov/policy/gen/guid/fpco/ferpa/index.html
3. This is reflected in the many papers in AI venues and specialised conferences such as FAccT https://facctconference.org/ and ARIES www.aies-conference.com
4. www.dictionary.com/browse/scrutable We also note that this word is rarely used. However, the word "inscrutable" is used more often, for example, to describe people when we cannot understand what they are thinking.
5. To make things worse, there are more terminological inconsistencies across the literature. For example, in HCI, the user model may be used to refer to a designer's mental model of the user. See also Kay and Kummerfeld (2019).

REFERENCES

Abdul, A., Vermeulen, J., Wang, D., Lim, B. Y., and Kankanhalli, M. (2018). Trends and trajectories for explainable, accountable and intelligible systems: An HCI research agenda. In *Proceedings of the 2018 CHI conference on human factors in computing systems*, pp. 1–18.

Al-Shanfari, L., Epp, C. D., Baber, C., and Nazir, M. (2020). Visualising alignment to support students' judgment of confidence in open learner models. *User Modeling and User-Adapted Interaction*, 30(1):159–194.

Anik, A. I. and Bunt, A. (2021). Data-centric explanations: Explaining training data of machine learning systems to promote transparency. In *Proceedings of the 2021 CHI Conference on Human Factors in Computing Systems*, pp. 1–13.

Arrieta, A. B., Díaz-Rodríguez, N., Del Ser, J., Bennetot, A., Tabik, S., Barbado, A., García, S., GilLópez, S., Molina, D., Benjamins, R., et al. (2020). Explainable artificial intelligence (XAI): Concepts, taxonomies, opportunities and challenges toward responsible AI. *Information Fusion*, 58:82–115.

Assad, M., Carmichael, D. J., Kay, J., and Kummerfeld, B. (2007). Personisad: Distributed, active, scrutable model framework for context-aware services. In *International Conference on Pervasive Computing*, pp. 55–72. Springer.

Baker, M. (1993). Dialogic learning: Negotiation and argumentation as mediating mechanisms. *Invited paper, in Proceedings of AI-ED'93: World Conference on Artificial Intelligence in Education*, pp. 4–11.

Beck, K. (2003). *Test-driven development: by example*. Addison-Wesley Professional.

Bull, S. (2020). There are open learner models about! *IEEE Transactions on Learning Technologies*, 13(2):425–448.

Bull, S., Brna, P., and Pain, H. (1995). Extending the scope of the student model. *User Modeling and User-Adapted Interaction*, 5(1):45–65.

Bull, S. and Kay, J. (2013). Open learner models as drivers for metacognitive processes. In *International Handbook of Metacognition and Learning Technologies*, pp. 349–365. Springer.

Bull, S. and Kay, J. (2016). Smili :-): A framework for interfaces to learning data in open learner models, learning analytics and related fields. *International Journal of Artificial Intelligence in Education*, 26(1):293–331.

Bull, S., Mabbott, A., and Abu Issa, A. S. (2007). Umpteen: Named and anonymous learner model access for instructors and peers. *International Journal of Artificial Intelligence in Education*, 17(3):227–253.

Conati, C., Barral, O., Putnam, V., and Rieger, L. (2021). Toward personalized xai: A case study in intelligent tutoring systems. *Artificial Intelligence*, 103503.

Conati, C., Porayska-Pomsta, K., and Mavrikis, M. (2018). AI in education needs interpretable machine learning: Lessons from open learner modelling. *arXiv preprint arXiv:1807.00154*.

Cook, R. and Kay, J. (1994). The justified user model: a viewable, explained user model. In *Proceedings of the Fourth International Conference on User Modeling*.

Corbett, A. T. and Anderson, J. R. (1994). Knowledge tracing: Modeling the acquisition of procedural knowledge. *User modeling and user-adapted interaction*, 4(4):253–278.

Correll, M. (2019). Ethical dimensions of visualization research. In *Proceedings of the 2019 CHI Conference on Human Factors in Computing Systems*, pp. 1–13.

Czarkowski, M. and Kay, J. (2002). A scrutable adaptive hypertext. In *International Conference on Adaptive Hypermedia and Adaptive Web-Based Systems*, pp. 384–387. Springer.

Dacrema, M. F., Cremonesi, P., and Jannach, D. (2019). Are we really making much progress? A worrying analysis of recent neural recommendation approaches. In *Proceedings of the 13th ACM Conference on Recommender Systems*, RecSys '19, pp. 101–109, New York. Association for Computing Machinery.

Ehsan, U., Liao, Q. V., Muller, M., Riedl, M. O., and Weisz, J. D. (2021). Expanding explainability: Towards social transparency in AI systems. In *Proceedings of the 2021 CHI Conference on Human Factors in Computing Systems*, pp. 1–19.

Eiband, M., Buschek, D., and Hussmann, H. (2020). How to support users in understanding intelligent systems? structuring the discussion. *arXiv preprint arXiv:2001.08301*.

Epstein, L. G. (1999). A definition of uncertainty aversion. *The Review of Economic Studies*, 66(3):579–608.

Eslami, M., Aleyasen, A., Karahalios, K., Hamilton, K., and Sandvig, C. (2015). Feedvis: A path for exploring news feed curation algorithms. In *Proceedings of the 18th ACM Conference Companion on Computer Supported Cooperative Work & Social Computing*, pp. 65–68.

Eslami, M., Vaccaro, K., Lee, M. K., Elazari Bar On, A., Gilbert, E., and Karahalios, K. (2019). User attitudes towards algorithmic opacity and transparency in online reviewing platforms. In *Proceedings of the 2019 CHI Conference on Human Factors in Computing Systems*, pp. 1–14.

Feinberg, M. (2017). A design perspective on data. In *Proceedings of the 2017 CHI Conference on Human Factors in Computing Systems*, pp. 2952–2963.

Gebru, T., Morgenstern, J., Vecchione, B., Vaughan, J. W., Wallach, H., Daumé III, H., and Crawford, K. (2018). Datasheets for datasets. *arXiv preprint arXiv:1803.09010*.

Gitelman, L. (2013). *Raw data is an oxymoron*. MIT Press.

Guerra-Hollstein, J., Barria-Pineda, J., Schunn, C. D., Bull, S., and Brusilovsky, P. (2017). Fine-grained open learner models: Complexity versus support. In *Proceedings of the 25th Conference on User Modeling, Adaptation and Personalization*, pp. 41–49.

Hartson, R. and Pyla, P. S. (2018). *The UX book: Agile UX design for a quality user experience*. Morgan Kaufmann.

Holstein, K., Harpstead, E., Gulotta, R., and Forlizzi, J. (2020). Replay enactments: Exploring possible futures through historical data. In *Proceedings of the 2020 ACM Designing Interactive Systems Conference*, pp. 1607–1618.

Holstein, K., McLaren, B. M., and Aleven, V. (2019a). Co-designing a real-time classroom orchestration tool to support teacher–AI complementarity. *Journal of Learning Analytics*, 6(2):27–52.

Holstein, K., McLaren, B. M., and Aleven, V. (2019b). Designing for complementarity: Teacher and student needs for orchestration support in AI-enhanced classrooms. In *International Conference on Artificial Intelligence in Education*, pp. 157–171. Springer.

Hutchinson, B., Smart, A., Hanna, A., Denton, E., Greer, C., Kjartansson, O., Barnes, P., and Mitchell, M. (2021). Towards accountability for machine learning datasets: Practices from software engineering and infrastructure. In *Proceedings of the 2021 ACM Conference on Fairness, Accountability, and Transparency*, pp. 560–575.

Jobin, A., Ienca, M., and Vayena, E. (2019). The global landscape of AI ethics guidelines. *Nature Machine Intelligence*, 1(9):389–399.

Kahneman, D., Sibony, O., and Sunstein, C. R. (2021). *Noise: A flaw in human judgment*. Little, Brown.

Kaur, H., Nori, H., Jenkins, S., Caruana, R., Wallach, H., and Wortman Vaughan, J. (2020). Interpreting interpretability: Understanding data scientists' use of interpretability tools for machine learning. In *Proceedings of the 2020 CHI Conference on Human Factors in Computing Systems*, pp. 1–14.

Kay, J. (1998). *A scrutable user modelling shell for user-adapted interaction*. PhD thesis, Basser Department of Computer Science, Faculty of Science, University of Sydney.

Kay, J. (2000). Stereotypes, student models and scrutability. In *International Conference on Intelligent Tutoring Systems*, pp. 19–30. Springer.

Kay, J. (2006). Scrutable adaptation: Because we can and must. In *International Conference on Adaptive Hypermedia and Adaptive Web-Based Systems*, pp. 11–19. Springer.

Kay, J. and Kummerfeld, B. (2013). Creating personalized systems that people can scrutinize and control: Drivers, principles and experience. *ACM Transactions on Interactive Intelligent Systems (TiiS)*, 2(4):1–42.

Kay, J. and Kummerfeld, B. (2019). From data to personal user models for life-long, life-wide learners. *British Journal of Educational Technology*, 50(6):2871–2884.

Kay, J. and Lum, A. (2005). Exploiting readily available web data for scrutable student models. In *AIED*, pp. 338–345.

Kozyreva, A., Lewandowsky, S., and Hertwig, R. (2020). Citizens versus the internet: Confronting digital challenges with cognitive tools. *Psychological Science in the Public Interest*, 21(3):103–156.

Lim, B. Y., Dey, A. K., and Avrahami, D. (2009). Why and why not explanations improve the intelligibility of context-aware intelligent systems. In *Proceedings of the SIGCHI Conference on Human Factors in Computing Systems*, pp. 2119–2128.

Long, Y. and Aleven, V. (2017). Enhancing learning outcomes through self-regulated learning support with an open learner model. *User Modeling and User-Adapted Interaction*, 27(1):55–88.

Lyons, H., Velloso, E., and Miller, T. (2021). Conceptualising contestability: Perspectives on contesting algorithmic decisions. *Proceedings of the ACM on Human-Computer Interaction*, 5(CSCW1):1–25.

McBroom, J. and Paassen, B. (2020). Assessing the quality of mathematics questions using student confidence scores. In *1st NeurIPS Education Challenge*, 3pp. NeurIPS 2020.

Sambasivan, N., Kapania, S., Highfill, H., Akrong, D., Paritosh, P., and Aroyo, L. M. (2021). "Everyone wants to do the model work, not the data work": Data cascades in high-stakes AI. In *Proceedings of the 2021 CHI Conference on Human Factors in Computing Systems*, CHI '21, New York. Association for Computing Machinery.

Somyürek, S., Brusilovsky, P., and Guerra, J. (2020). Supporting knowledge monitoring ability: open learner modeling vs. open social learner modeling. *Research and Practice in Technology Enhanced Learning*, 15(1):1–24.

Subramonyam, H., Seifert, C., and Adar, E. (2021). ProtoAI: Model-informed prototyping for AI-powered interfaces. In *26th International Conference on Intelligent User Interfaces*, pp. 48–58.

Tang, L. M. and Kay, J. (2018). Scaffolding for an OLM for long-term physical activity goals. In *Proceedings of the 26th Conference on User Modeling, Adaptation and Personalization*, pp. 147–156.

Vaughan, J. W. and Wallach, H. (2020). A human-centered agenda for intelligible machine learning. *Machines We Trust: Getting Along with Artificial Intelligence*.

Wang, D., Yang, Q., Abdul, A., and Lim, B. Y. (2019). Designing theory-driven user-centric explainable AI. In *Proceedings of the 2018 CHI Conference on Human Factors in Computing Systems*, pp. 1–15.

Woolf, B. P. (2010). *Building intelligent interactive tutors: Student-centered strategies for revolutionizing e-learning*. Morgan Kaufmann.

Yang, Q., Steinfeld, A., Rosé, C., and Zimmerman, J. (2020). Re-examining whether, why, and how human-AI interaction is uniquely difficult to design. In *Proceedings of the 2018 CHI Conference on Human Factors in Computing Systems*, pp. 1–13.

PART III

THE ARCHITECTURE AND DESIGN OF AIED SYSTEMS

7. Domain modeling for AIED systems with connections to modeling student knowledge: a review

Vincent Aleven, Jonathan Rowe, Yun Huang and Antonija Mitrovic

INTRODUCTION

A central component of many AIED systems is a "domain model," that is, a representation of knowledge of the domain of instruction. The system uses the model in many ways to provide instruction that adapts to learners. Not all AIED systems have an elaborate domain model, but in those that do, the domain model is central to the system's functioning. In fact, domain models fulfill so many important functions within AIED systems that entire classes of AIED systems are defined in terms of the types of domain model they use (such as model-tracing tutors, constraint-based tutors, example-tracing tutors, and issue-based approaches to building tutoring systems). Across AIED projects, systems, and paradigms, the types of domain models used span the gamut of AI representations. AIED systems use their domain models for many different purposes, chief among them assessing student work, which is foundational for other functionality.

This chapter reviews major approaches to domain modeling used in AIED systems and briefly touches on the corresponding student models and the way they are used to track an individual student's knowledge growth. (We do not discuss student models that target other aspects, such as affect, motivation, self-regulation, or metacognition.) We discuss, in turn: rule-based models, constraint-based models, Bayesian networks, machine-learned models, text-based models, generalized examples, and knowledge spaces. These types of models have been studied extensively in AIED research and have been the foundation for many AIED systems that have been proven to be effective in enhancing student learning or other aspects of the student experience. A number of these approaches are now used in AIED systems that are used on a wide scale in educational practice. The chapter discusses how these approaches support key aspects of an AIED system's behavior and enable the system to adapt aspects of its instruction to individual student variables. We also highlight challenges that occur when applying the different approaches. We look at the use of machine learning and data-driven methods to create or refine domain models, so they better account for learning data and support more effective adaptive instruction. As well, we make note of connections between a system's domain model and other key components, including the system's student model. We base this discussion on traditional views of intelligent tutoring systems (ITSs), which divide the system's architecture into four main components: a domain model, a student model, a pedagogical model, and a problem-solving environment. We focus on systems that support *individual learning.* Other types of AIED systems are covered in other chapters.

What Do We Mean by a Domain Model?

The domain model of an AIED system captures knowledge in the given task domain, including concepts, skills, strategies, tactics, or constraints. In many cases, it captures the knowledge that the system aims to help students learn. A domain model in an AIED system normally contains the ideal knowledge that experts have. It may optionally contain representations of incorrect knowledge that novices in the domain tend to exhibit, such as bugs, mal-rules, and misconceptions. In addition, a domain model may capture prerequisite relations and other relations between the knowledge components represented in the model, as well as relations between knowledge components and practice problems or steps of practice problems, also referred to as "items." This definition is grounded in older definitions of the domain model but is broader (see Burns & Capps, 1988; Holmes, Bialik, & Fadel, 2019; Pelánek, 2017; Sottilare et al., 2016).

It may help to distinguish between a domain model and a student model, another central component of many AIED systems, also known as a learner model. Whereas a domain model captures general domain knowledge, a student model represents an individual student's current learning state. Exactly what state is captured, how it is represented, and how it is kept up to date varies across AIED systems. A student model often captures a student's current level of mastery of the knowledge targeted in the instruction, and may capture other aspects as well (e.g., a student's affective or motivational state, their skill at self-regulation, etc.). To model individual students' knowledge state, the student model is often an "overlay" on the domain model, in the sense that it records the student's status with respect to key elements in the domain model. In other cases, the student and domain model are components within a single integrated model (see Bayesian networks and machine learning paradigms discussed below).

Mainly for purposes of student modeling, it has turned out to be fruitful to view domain models as "knowledge component models," or "KC models" for short (Aleven & Koedinger, 2013; Koedinger et al., 2010). Knowledge components (KCs) are units of knowledge whose existence can be inferred from student performance on a set of related tasks (Koedinger et al., 2012). A KC model breaks up the overall knowledge to be learned into units that reflect students' psychological reality (as evidenced by the fact that they lead to accurate performance predictions). A KC model also maps items (e.g., problem steps, problems) to KCs, indicating which KCs are needed for correct performance on the item. In its simplest form, a KC model is a KC-to-item mapping, or KC x item matrix (a Q-Matrix; Koedinger et al., 2010; Tatsuoka, 1983). This mapping enables a tutoring system to track students' knowledge growth (namely of specific KCs) based on their problem-solving performance. Increasingly, data-driven methods are being used to create and refine KC models (Huang et al., 2021). The KC-modeling perspective is compatible with many of the domain modeling paradigms used in AIED (e.g., rules and constraints can be viewed as KCs learned by students, without considering their specific representation). For more information about student modeling, the interested reader may consult reviews by Desmarais and Baker (2012) and Pelánek (2017).

Although the domain models used in AIED systems are not fundamentally different from those in many other AI systems, they do emphasize certain modeling issues over others. For example, amid the great variety of AIED domain models, there is a premium on having models that capture human ways of reasoning and that can accommodate different ways of reasoning about the same problem. Moreover, it helps if models are interpretable and explainable. An *interpretable* model is one that maps inputs to outputs in a manner that naturally aligns with human ways of understanding or reasoning. An *explainable* model is one for which we have external processes that align the model's state and inferences with human ways of reasoning (Adadi & Berrada, 2018). For example, deep neural networks are not interpretable, but there is work (outside of AIED) on generating natural language explanations that coincide with the classifications of deep neural networks, which bring some transparency to the model (Park et al., 2018). Explainable models can support instructional functions that black box (i.e., non-interpretable) models cannot, such as explaining a reasoning process to learners. Explainable models may also contribute to theory formation more readily. The point that AIED systems both benefit from interpretable and explainable representations of domain knowledge *and* can be a force driving technology design toward greater explainability and interpretability goes back at least to Wenger's (1987) book. It is still true today.

Why Do AIED Systems Have Domain Models?

Before describing different domain modeling paradigms, we consider the many purposes for which domain models are used in AIED systems, to guide later discussion. We look specifically at the adaptive instructional behaviors that they enable or for which they have an auxiliary role, corresponding to the columns in Table 7.1.

Assessing student work

In all the AIED domain modeling paradigms we surveyed, a key function of the domain model is to assess student work, although there is substantial variability in *how*. We use the term "student work" to denote attempted problem solutions, partial solutions, and attempts at problem steps. An assessment may be a determination that the student work is correct, accurate, or of high quality by the standards of the given domain, or it may be based on other, richer classifications of student work's desirable and undesirable qualities, or it may focus on detecting specific qualities or issues. The assessment is often the foundation for other instructional behaviors of the AIED system. Assessment by AIED systems is typically *formative* in nature; its main purpose is to enable and support instructional behavior that helps students improve.

Assessing student knowledge

Domain models often have an auxiliary role in a system's assessment of a student's knowledge growth over time, a central concern in the realm of student modeling. A domain model often helps to analyze student work in terms of KCs. Specifically, given a piece of student work, the domain model helps "diagnose" which KCs the student may have used, mis-used, or mistakenly not used in generating that piece of work. This information is then used to update estimates of the student's knowledge state, using any of the many established student modeling methods or models that have come out of AIED and Educational Data Mining (EDM) research (Desmarais & Baker, 2012; Pavlik et al., 2013; Pelánek, 2017). As discussed, to this end, the student model and domain model often break up the knowledge to be learned into the same set of KCs, as one way in which domain modeling and student modeling tend to be closely interrelated. The domain model and student model are often separate software components, but it is also possible that the domain and student modeling components of an AIED system are integrated together within a single model, as is the case for example in Bayesian networks for stealth assessment (Shute et al., 2016).

Table 7.1   *Domain model functions*

Paradigms	Assess and model student work	Generate feedback on student work	Demonstrate how to solve problems	Modeling and recognizing student errors	Assess and model student knowledge	Select problems
Rules	Yes (Anderson, Corbett, Koedinger, & Pelletier, 1995)	Yes (Anderson, Corbett, Koedinger, & Pelletier, 1995)	Yes (Anderson, Corbett, Koedinger, & Pelletier, 1995)	Optional (McKendree, 1990)	Auxiliary (Corbett & Anderson, 1995)	Auxiliary (Corbett, McLaughlin, & Scarpinatto, 2000)
Constraints	Yes (Mitrovic & Ohlsson, 1999)	Yes (Mitrovic & Ohlsson, 1999)	No	Contrary to fundamental assumptions	Auxiliary (Mitrovic & Ohlsson, 2016)	Auxiliary (Mitrovic & Ohlsson, 2016)
Generalized Examples (Behavior Graphs)	Yes (Aleven et al., 2016)	Yes (Aleven et al., 2016)	Yes (Aleven et al., 2016)	Optional (Aleven et al., 2016)	Auxiliary (Corbett & Anderson, 1995)	Auxiliary (Corbett, McLaughlin, & Scarpinatto, 2000)
Bayesian Networks	Yes (Conati et al., 2002)	Yes (Conati et al., 2002)	Yes (Conati et al., 2002)	Optional (Stacey et al., 2003)	Yes (Millán & Pérez-de-la-Cruz, 2002)	Yes (Mayo & Mitrovic, 2001)
Supervised Learning	Yes (Gobert et al., 2013)	Yes (Li, Gobert, Dickler, & Moussavi, 2018)	Yes (MacLellan & Koedinger, 2020)	Yes (Michalenko, Lan, & Baraniuk, 2017)	Yes (Min et al., 2020)	Open issue
Unsupervised Learning	Yes (Käser & Schwartz, 2020)	Open issue	Open issue	Yes (Shi et al., 2021)	Open issue	Auxiliary
Reinforcement Learning	Yes (Rafferty et al., 2015)	Yes (Rafferty, Jansen, & Griffiths, 2016)	Yes (Barnes & Stamper, 2008)	Auxiliary (Barnes & Stamper, 2008)	Yes (Rafferty et al., 2015)	Yes (Beck, Woolf, & Beal, 2000)

Providing formative feedback to students

A key function of many AIED systems is to give students feedback on their work, for example as part of a coaching strategy (Chapter 9 by Aleven et al.). The purpose of this feedback is typically to help students learn; in this sense, the feedback is "formative" (Shute, 2008). The notion of feedback is often divided into three main categories: correctness feedback, knowledge of results, and elaborated feedback (Kluger & DeNisi, 1996; van der Kleij et al., 2015). Correctness feedback indicates whether the work is correct or not, or it signals the degree of correctness. Knowledge of results means providing a correct answer or solution. Elaborated feedback provides further information regarding correct/incorrect aspects. The latter category of feedback may state desirable and undesirable properties of the student's work, or how it might be improved. Generating feedback is facilitated by having an interpretable or explainable domain model, as discussed below.

Recognizing student errors

AIED systems sometimes provide *error-specific feedback*, a form of elaborated feedback that comments on specific errors or misconceptions reflected in the student's work. The feedback might say, for example, how or why student work is wrong, or how an error might be fixed. One way to generate error-specific feedback in an AIED system is to model common erroneous knowledge into the system's domain model (e.g., bugs, mal-rules, and misconceptions). The empirical evidence regarding the pedagogical value of error-specific feedback, however, is not elaborate and is mixed (Lodder et al., 2021; McKendree, 1990; Sleeman et al., 1989; VanLehn, 1990; VanLehn et al., 2021), which is perhaps a key reason that such feedback tends to be treated as optional in AIED systems (see Table 7.1). Then again, error-specific feedback is often viewed as an attractive feature of AIED systems. Thus, there is more to be learned in the field of AIED about the topic of error-specific feedback.

Demonstrate how to solve problems to provide next-step hints

Some AIED systems can use their domain models to demonstrate problem solutions (i.e., the domain model can solve problems), which enables them to generate next-step hints for students. These hints suggest what the student might do next and may include information such as how in general one might determine the next step and why that is a correct thing to do (e.g., in terms of domain-specific principles). Hints may be offered either at the student's request or proactively by the system. Their purpose is to help students better acquire the knowledge to be learned and to help them avoid floundering (e.g., help them avoid a fruitless search for a solution or step when they lack the knowledge). Next-step hints are different from feedback in that they do not provide an assessment of student work.

Selecting individualized learning content

The domain model often plays an auxiliary role in another key function of AIED systems, namely selecting or sequencing learning content (e.g., problems, tasks, textbook pages) for students on an individualized basis. This choice is often based on variables in the student model, in particular students' mastery of knowledge components, sometimes in combination with other variables (e.g., personal interest, affect). The content selection process or algorithm is outside of the domain model per se; it is viewed as part of a pedagogical model. The domain model helps in the first place by assessing student knowledge, as described above. As well, some domain models represent prerequisite relations between knowledge components, so that a selection algorithm can sequence learning materials in accordance with these relations.

Designing new learning content

A final important function of domain models is to guide the design and redesign of content for AIED systems. A domain model can help with many aspects of content including inventing new tasks (Huang et al., 2021; Koedinger & McLaughlin, 2010; Koedinger et al., 2013), new hint messages (Liu & Koedinger, 2017) or new contrasting cases (Roll et al., 2010; Schwartz et al., 2011). An initial KC model (based, ideally, on empirical cognitive task analysis) can guide designers in creating initial versions of these content elements. Iterations may follow once cohorts of students have used the system and log data are available to feed data-driven approaches to KC model refinement. As a simple example, the pool of problems that an AIED system can assign to students must provide sufficient coverage of each KC, so that students can get sufficient practice with each. Similarly, the system's hints will likely be designed to closely track the KCs (e.g., with hint templates attached to specific KCs). When the KC model changes (e.g., when a process of data-driven model refinement discovers new KCs), these aspects need to be revised and a refined model can provide much guidance (see Huang et al., 2021).

DOMAIN MODELING PARADIGMS

We review four major paradigms for domain modeling in AIED systems: rules, constraints, Bayesian networks, and machine learning. We also briefly describe several other paradigms: labeled example solutions (including behavior graphs), knowledge spaces, and domain modeling in textbooks.

Rules

Production rules remain a popular formalism for representing domain knowledge in AIED systems. The use of rule-based models in AIED systems is grounded both in AI work on production rule systems (Brownston et al., 1985; Davis & King, 1984) and in cognitive science work that uses rules to represent aspects of human cognition and human problem solving (Anderson, 1993; Newell & Simon, 1972). In this knowledge representation paradigm, domain knowledge is expressed as a set of IF-THEN rules. Each rule ties one or more (mental or observable) problem-solving actions (the THEN-part) to the conditions under which they are appropriate (the IF-part). Rule-based models, which may comprise hundreds of rules, are executable and capable of solving problems in the given task domain. They can be viewed as simulations of expert (and student) problem solving in the given task domain. Rule-based models used in AIED systems typically represent the knowledge that the system is designed to help students learn. For simple examples, see Koedinger and Corbett (2006) and Aleven (2010). For a more elaborate example, see Aleven (2010).

Rule-based domain models have been used extensively in model-tracing tutors, a widely used type of AIED system grounded in cognitive science and cognitive modeling (Anderson et al., 1995). Model-tracing tutors guide students as they solve complex problems, that is, problems that have multiple possible solution paths, each with multiple steps. Many model-tracing tutors have been described in the AIED literature, including Cognitive Tutors for middle-school and high-school mathematics (Koedinger & Corbett, 2006), the Genetics Tutor (Corbett et al., 2010), Cognitive Tutors for Lisp, Pascal, and Prolog programming (Anderson et al., 1989; Anderson et al., 1993), Lynnette (middle-school equation solving;

Long & Aleven, 2014), MATHia (middle- and high-school mathematics; Ritter et al., 2007), Andes (physics; VanLehn et al., 2005), SlideTutor (skin pathology; Crowley & Medvedeva, 2006), and MATHESIS (high-school algebra; Sklavakis & Refanidis, 2013). Model-tracing tutors for mathematics learning are being used widely in American mathematics learning (Ritter et al., 2007). There is substantial evidence that model-tracing tutors can help students learn very effectively (for an overview, see Koedinger & Aleven, 2007), including a large-scale study that found a doubling of the amount of learning within a school year due to the Cognitive Tutor Algebra curriculum (Pane et al., 2014; but also see Pane et al., 2010).

Model tracing tutors use their rule-based models for many of the functions described above: assessing student work, providing hints and feedback, interpreting student problem solving in terms of knowledge components, and guiding content design. To support these functions, model-tracing tutors use their rule-based model to maintain a live, up-to-date, step-by-step reconstruction of a student's problem-solving process, in sync with the student's solution (as the student is working with the tutoring system). For this approach to work, the model must capture *all* reasonable ways of solving problems that students might use, one way in which rule-based models used in AIED systems differ from those used in many other AI applications. A model-tracing tutor can also use its domain model to generate next-step hints at any point in a student's problem-solving process. To do so, the tutor finds an applicable rule (i.e., one that could generate the next step from the current problem state) and generates an explanation of that step (and why that is a correct or good step to take) using the rule's hint template. For this approach to yield understandable next-step advice, the rules must capture human approaches to problem solving. In this sense, the rules must be explainable. From the perspective of Cognitive Tutors, rules are a key analytical tool for understanding student reasoning and learning in a given task domain. They can be used to summarize results of cognitive task analysis activities, which can be an important step in designing an intelligent tutoring system (Baker et al., 2007; Lovett, 1998; Means & Gott, 1988; Tofel-Grehl & Feldon, 2013). The model-tracing process as described feeds into the tutor's long-term student modeling process. Following any student step, it identifies which rule(s) a student applied or should have applied but did not. This information enables the tutor to track the probability that the given student masters each of the key rules in the model, for example using a model such as Bayesian Knowledge Tracing (Corbett & Anderson, 1995).

We illustrate the main idea behind model tracing with a simple example provided by Ken Koedinger. As mentioned, a key challenge in model tracing is that any given problem may be solved in multiple ways, captured in the model. Of these many solution paths, the model must follow the one that the given student is using for the given problem. It does so in a step-by-step manner. For example, even basic equations (such as the one in Figure 7.1) can be solved in different ways. Assume a model for basic equation solving with the three rules shown at the top of Figure 7.1. Two of the rules represent correct student strategies, and one represents an erroneous strategy. Note all three rules have the same IF-part, so they apply to the same set of problem states. The letters a, b, c, and d represent variables that can match specific numbers in the problem state. Whenever the student attempts the next problem step, the model tracer searches the space of possible next steps generated by its rule model to see if the student step is among the model-generated steps. In our example, in the given problem state (i.e., $3(2x - 5) = 9$), our three rules apply. The model tracer (searching through the set of applicable rules) will find three possible next steps, namely two correct steps and an error, shown at

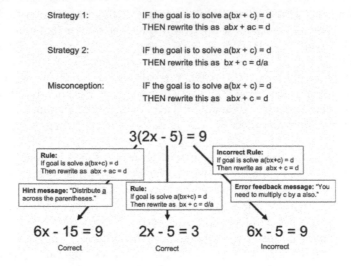

Strategy 1:   IF the goal is to solve a(bx + c) = d
                     THEN rewrite this as abx + ac = d

Strategy 2:   IF the goal is to solve a(bx + c) = d
                     THEN rewrite this as bx + c = d/a

Misconception: IF the goal is to solve a(bx + c) = d
                     THEN rewrite this as abx + c = d

$3(2x - 5) = 9$

Rule:
If goal is solve a(bx+c) = d
Then rewrite as abx + ac = d

Incorrect Rule:
If goal is solve a(bx+c) = d
Then rewrite as abx + c = d

Hint message: "Distribute a across the parentheses."

Rule:
If goal is solve a(bx+c) = d
Then rewrite as bx + c = d/a

Error feedback message: "You need to multiply c by a also."

$6x - 15 = 9$ $2x - 5 = 3$ $6x - 5 = 9$
Correct   Correct   Incorrect

Figure 7.1   Model tracing in action

the bottom of Figure 7.1. If the student's input is one of the correct transformations, the tutor accepts it as correct and applies the matching rule to move the state of the rule-based model forward. By contrast, if the student's input is the incorrect transformation (i.e., $6x - 5 = 9$), the tutoring system presents an error message based on the erroneous rule, generated using a hint template attached to the rule. If the student's input is anything else, the tutor flags it as incorrect, without specific error feedback. This way, the model stays in sync with the student. Finally, if the student requests a hint in the given situation, the tutor will recommend a step generated by one of the rules (the one with highest priority), again using a template attached to the rule. Incidentally, rules that represent incorrect problem-solving behavior are not strictly required in model-tracing tutors. They enable the tutoring system to provide elaborated error-specific feedback.

This example is a simplification in that the model has very few rules that apply to only a narrow range of problem states. The rule-based models in model-tracing tutors, by contrast, can have hundreds of rules that apply to a wide range of problem states. A second way in which this example is a simplification is that each problem-solving step is modeled by a single rule, whereas, in the more general case, a problem-solving step may result from a *sequence* of rule applications—any number of them, in fact. In the general case, therefore, the model tracer has more searching to do to find the possible model-generated next steps against which to compare the student's next step.

Over the years, rule-based models in AIED have been used for purposes other than modeling domain knowledge to be learned. For example, rule-based models have been used to capture—and provide tutoring regarding—strategy aspects of (algebra) problem solving (Ritter, 1997), aspects of self-regulated learning, such as help seeking (Aleven et al., 2006a) and error correction (Mathan & Koedinger, 2005), as well as collaboration skills (Walker et al., 2014). Various projects have also used rules to model pedagogical knowledge (Aleven et al., 2017; Heffernan et al., 2008; Roll et al., 2010), illustrating the versatility of rules as a representational paradigm for AIED systems.

Challenges

A key challenge is that it is hard to create rule-based models of problem solving. This process requires cognitive task analysis, cognitive modeling, and AI programming. To address this challenge, a considerable amount of AIED work has focused on developing efficient authoring tools (see Chapter 12 by Blessing et al.), use of interactive machine learning to develop rule-based models (see below), and non-programmer AIED paradigms that can achieve some of the same tutoring behaviors with easier-to-create knowledge representations (e.g., example-tracing tutors [Aleven et al., 2016]; see below). This work is still moving forward. A second critique that is sometimes leveraged against tutoring systems with rule-based models is that they might be limited to STEM domains or domains with clear correctness criteria. Although many AIED projects with rule-based domain models have indeed focused on STEM domains, other domains have been explored as well (e.g., medical diagnosis; Crowley & Medvedeva, 2006). As well, clear correctness criteria can sometimes be identified in domains not initially thought to be amenable to rule-based modeling (Means & Gott, 1988; Tofel-Grehl & Feldon, 2013). It may be challenging, however, to create model-tracing tutors in ill-defined domains (Lynch et al., 2009) or domains with natural language interactions (see Chapter 11 by Rus et al.). A third critique has been that the pedagogical approach of model-tracing tutors (tutored problem solving) tends to be limited. While this critique may not fully value the important role of deliberate practice and learning to solve recurrent problems in many domains (Koedinger & Aleven, 2021), it is important to note that rule-based tutors are often combined with other instructional approaches, such as example-based learning, collaborative learning or standard classroom instruction (e.g., Koedinger & Corbett, 2006; Olsen et al., 2019; Salden et al., 2010).

Constraints

Another popular formalism for representing domain knowledge in AIED systems is constraints (Mitrovic, 2010; Mitrovic & Ohlsson, 2006; Ohlsson & Mitrovic, 2007). In Constraint-Based Modeling (CBM), the domain model consists of a set of constraints on ideal solutions. In comparison to rule-based cognitive models, which capture procedural knowledge, constraint-based domain models capture the declarative knowledge of a specific instructional domain. Constraints capture features of correct solutions; they specify what ought to be so.

Numerous constraint-based tutors have been developed, some of which are SQL-Tutor, an ITS for the Structured Query Language (SQL) (Mitrovic, 1998; Mitrovic & Ohlsson, 1999), and EER-Tutor, an ITS teaching conceptual database design using the Enhanced Entity-Relationship model (EER)(Mitrovic, 2012). Constraints have not only been used to represent domain principles, but also to model collaboration (Baghaei et al., 2007) and metacognitive strategies such as self-explanation (Weerasinghe & Mitrovic, 2006), and have even been used for rehabilitation of prospective memory of stroke patients (Mitrovic et al., 2016).

The theoretical foundation for CBM comes from Ohlsson's Theory of Learning from Performance Errors (Ohlsson, 1996). This theory says that both declarative and procedural knowledge is necessary for good performance, but the theory focuses on declarative knowledge, represented as a set of constraints on solutions. People make mistakes when they do not have adequate procedural knowledge (either missing or incorrect). Constraints are used to identify mistakes and to repair incorrect production rules. This theory explains how it is possible for a person to know that he/she made a mistake even though they do not have correct procedural knowledge. The role of conceptual knowledge is to identify mistakes.

A constraint consists of two conditions. The relevance condition consists of one or more tests applied to students' solutions to see whether a constraint is relevant or not. If a constraint is relevant for a particular solution, its satisfaction condition specifies another list of tests which the solution must meet to be correct. An example of a constraint is: if you are driving a car in New Zealand, you should be on the left-hand side of the road. The relevance condition specifies that this constraint is applicable to situations when a person is driving a car in New Zealand; the satisfaction condition imposes a test on the side of the road the person is driving on. Correct solutions violate no constraints. Constraint violation signals errors in the solution.

We provide some constraints from SQL-Tutor, which contains 700+ constraints related to the use of the SQL Select statement. We present the constraints in the English form; the interested reader is referred to Mitrovic (1998), Mitrovic (2003) and Mitrovic and Ohlsson (1999) to see how the constraints were implemented in Lisp.

1) Every solution must contain the SELECT clause.
2) Every solution must contain the FROM clause.
3) If the solution contains the HAVING clause, the GROUP BY clause also needs to be specified.
4) If the solution contains the JOIN keyword, the FROM clause must specify the names of tables to be joined.
5) If the FROM clause of the student's solution contains a join condition, and the ideal solution requires the join condition between the same two tables, the join condition the student specified needs to use the correct join attributes.
6) If the ideal solution contains a search condition using the Between predicate and two constants, the student's solution should also contain a matching condition or alternative two conditions, using the same attribute and corresponding constants.

Some constraints are syntactic (such as constraints 1–4), meaning they check the syntax of the submitted Select statement. Constraints 1 and 2 do not contain the "if" part; they are relevant for all solutions, as the SELECT and FROM clauses are mandatory in SQL. On the other hand, constraints 3 and 4 have relevance conditions that restrict the set of solutions for which these constraints are relevant. If the relevance condition is met, the satisfaction condition is evaluated against the solution.

SQL-Tutor also contains semantic constraints (see example constraints 5 and 6); these constraints check whether the submitted solution is a correct solution for the particular problem. The semantics of the solution is captured by the ideal solution, which is defined by the teacher. Although many problems in SQL have multiple correct solutions, only one ideal solution is stored in SQL-Tutor per problem; the other correct solutions are recognized by the system automatically as there are constraints that check for alternative ways of solving the same problem (Mitrovic, 2003). This makes adding new problems very simple: the author needs to provide the text of the problem and one correct solution only.

Semantic constraints check whether the student's solution is correct by matching it to the constraints and the ideal solution. For example, constraint 5 checks that the student has used the correct attributes to join two tables which are also used in the ideal solution. Constraint 6, on the other hand, is relevant for those problems that require a search condition checking that the value of an attribute is between two specified values; for example, a range search like "Year between 2000 and 2022." For the student's solution to be correct, it should also contain a matching range search; alternative correct solutions need to contain two comparison conditions using the correct constants (e.g., "Year > 1999 and Year < 2023").

The space of correct knowledge can be big, but the space of incorrect knowledge is huge. CBM does not model incorrect knowledge; on the contrary, constraints only capture features of correct solutions. The abstraction used is the sets of equivalent states of the problem space. Each equivalence set corresponds to one constraint, which specifies one aspect of a domain principle; basically, an equivalence set of problem states is the set of solutions which all use the same domain principle. The whole set of states is represented via a single constraint. All solutions that require that constraint must satisfy it to be correct. Otherwise, there is a mistake in the student's solution. This makes CBM applicable to ill-defined tasks, such as design (Mitrovic & Weerasinghe, 2009). The domain model in such cases captures what is known about good solutions; the aspects which are not crucial are not checked. We refer to CBM as the "innocent until proven guilty" approach; if the student's solution does not violate any constraints, it is deemed correct.

In constraint-based tutors, the student model is represented as an overlay on the constraint set. The short-term student model is the result of diagnosing the solution the student submitted and consists of the set of satisfied and potentially violated constraints. The long-term model of the student's knowledge is represented in terms of the student's knowledge of individual constraints. There have also been extensions of the long-term model using Bayesian networks (Mayo & Mitrovic, 2001).

Constraints are evaluative in nature, as opposed to production rules which are generative (i.e., each rule generates an action to be performed to solve the problem). Constraints are modular and can be applied in parallel to diagnose the student's solution. This diagnosis consists of matching the student's solution to the constraint set and the ideal solution. The result is the set of matched constraints and, if the solution contains mistakes, a set of violated constraints. Each violated constraint represents a tiny part of the domain and is used to generate feedback for the student. In constraint-based tutors, each constraint typically has one or more feedback messages. These messages can be used to provide negative feedback (i.e., feedback on errors), with a gradually increasing level of detail. Messages attached to constraints can also be used to provide positive feedback, which are given to the student when the student masters a new piece of knowledge (e.g., using the constraint correctly for the first time), when the student overcomes impasses (e.g., satisfying a constraint after making a series of mistakes), or when the student solves a challenging problem (Mitrovic et al., 2013).

All constraint-based tutors match the student's solution to the constraints and the ideal solution. Depending on the instructional domain, the ideal solution may need to be stored (in the case of design tasks, where there is no problem solver), or it can be generated on the fly (for procedural tasks). When developing constraints, the level of granularity is crucial; constraints need to be very specific, so that feedback messages can be useful. If constraints are written on a very abstract level, the feedback messages would not be useful to students. Our general advice for writing constraints is to think about what a human teacher would say to the student if the constraint is violated. In addition to writing constraints manually, there is also ASPIRE, an authoring system (Mitrovic et al., 2009; Suraweera et al., 2010). ASPIRE requires the teacher to specify a simple domain ontology, the structure of solutions in terms of ontology concepts, and to provide examples of solved problems. Based on that information, ASPIRE induces a set of constraints for evaluating students' answers (see Chapter 12 by Blessing et al.).

Challenges

Like rule-based AIED systems, the key challenge for constraint-based tutors is the development of the constraint set. This process requires domain knowledge, pedagogical expertise (for specifying the hint messages attached to constraints) and AI programming. The ASPIRE authoring system (Mitrovic et al., 2009) automates a lot of the functionality for generating a constraint set, but pedagogical expertise is still necessary.

Bayesian Networks

Bayesian Networks (BNs) are a powerful AI formalism for reasoning with uncertainty, combining principles from graph theory and probability theory (Pearl, 1988; Russell & Norvig, 2020). BNs have been used in a broad range of task domains (e.g., medical diagnosis), and became actively used in the AIED field for domain modeling and student modeling in the early 1990s. A BN is a probabilistic model, often depicted as a directed graph, where nodes represent random variables and directed edges between the nodes represent dependencies between the variables. Central to BNs is the notion of conditional independence, which allows the joint probability of variables to be computed by multiplying the conditional probabilities of each variable given its parents. An attractive property of BNs is that they allow for two kinds of reasoning with uncertainty within a single integrated framework: diagnosis (i.e., identifying likely causes, given effect observations), and prediction (i.e., predicting the likely effect, given the current beliefs of the causes). In AIED systems, diagnosis typically involves inferring a student's knowledge of KCs (or other latent states, such as goals or plans) targeted in the instruction, given the student's performance. Diagnosis is instrumental to assessment and student modeling. Prediction involves predicting a student's performance based on the current estimates of the student's knowledge levels, which could be used to realize functions such as adaptive content selection or hint selection. In both forms of reasoning, uncertainty arises due to noise in student behaviors (e.g., guessing without knowing the KC) and noise in domain model specifications (e.g., a KC not being identified).

BNs used in AIED support a range of functionality, including knowledge assessment or student modeling (Millán & Pérez-de-la Cruz, 2002), modeling students' misconceptions (Stacey et al., 2003), solution plan recognition (Conati et al., 2002), error or hint message selection (Conati et al., 2002; Mayo & Mitrovic, 2001) and problem selection (Ganeshan et al., 2000; Huang, 2018; Mayo & Mitrovic, 2001). The BN paradigm is a good choice for domain modeling and student modeling for several reasons. First, BNs handle reasoning with uncertainty based on sound mathematical theories. Second, BNs afford high expressiveness. They can be used to create models that integrate domain knowledge with other kinds of student variables (e.g., metacognitive skills and affective states). Third, BNs naturally integrate domain modeling, student modeling, and aspects of pedagogical modeling in a single framework. Finally, BNs provide a principled way to utilize prior domain knowledge and integrate new data with prior knowledge. A more thorough introduction can be found elsewhere (Millán et al., 2010).

There have been many successful cases of utilizing BNs in domain modeling for AIED systems. One prominent example is the Andes tutoring system for physics (Conati et al., 2002). In Andes, a BN that integrates domain modeling and student modeling enables step-by-step problem-solving support tailored to each student's knowledge and strategy choices. As shown in Figure 7.2, Andes' BN consists of a domain-general component that models students' long-term knowledge shared across problems, and a task-specific component that models possible correct solution paths specific to each problem. In the domain-general component, *Rule* nodes

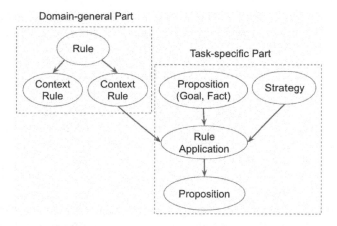

Figure 7.2   The basic structure of Andes' BN-based domain and student model

represent knowledge in a general form (e.g., being able to apply F=ma in all possible contexts) while *Context Rule* nodes represent knowledge in context-specific forms (e.g., being able to apply F=ma in a specific context). In the task-specific component of the BN, a *Rule Application* node represents an application of a specific rule (KC) in a problem (e.g., the application of F=ma in the current problem). A *Proposition* node represents a goal (e.g., try F=ma to solve the problem) or a fact (e.g., block A is selected as the body). *Strategy* nodes, finally, can be used to model different, mutually exclusive, correct solutions. *Rule Application* nodes connect *Context Rule* nodes, *Proposition* nodes, and *Strategy* nodes to newly derived *Proposition* nodes. All nodes can have true or false values. Depending on the node type, the probability of a node taking on a true value represents a student's knowledge level or the likelihood that the given student will either infer a goal/fact or choose a strategy. Uncertainty is handled by assuming a small probability of slipping or guessing in the conditional probabilities for *Rule Application* or *Proposition* nodes. Once the structure and parameters of Andes' BN have been specified (expert engineered), the BN is used to estimate how likely it is that a student can derive a goal/fact, will choose a specific strategy, or will apply a specific rule (KC). The BN updates these estimations after each observed student action. These estimations drive tutorial interventions such as selecting a hint topic, providing mini lessons for weakly mastered KCs, and selecting problems with desirable difficulties. For example, when a student requests a hint, Andes figures out what goal the student is likely trying to achieve (i.e., plan recognition) by comparing the probabilities of related goals for the most recent student action. It then looks for a related rule application with a low probability and finally makes the relevant knowledge the focus of the hint.

Classroom evaluations of Andes demonstrated that students who used Andes for their homework significantly improved their learning compared with students who used pencil and paper for their homework, reaching effect sizes of 1.2 (conceptual components) and 0.7 (algebraic components) on experimenter-designed tests and 0.3 on standardized tests (VanLehn et al., 2005). VanLehn et al. (2005) pointed out that Andes' key feature appears to be the grain-size of interaction (i.e., on a step level rather than on a problem level). Other examples of the use of BNs in AIED systems include the CAPIT tutor for English capitalization and punctuation (Mayo & Mitrovic, 2001) and Cognitive Tutors for algebra (Ritter et al., 2007), where classroom evaluations demonstrated that systems using BN-based domain modeling (and student modeling) yielded greater student learning outcomes or efficiency compared with systems that used alternative modeling or traditional classroom instruction.

We classify existing cases of utilizing BNs in AIED systems into four types, based on several past reviews (Desmarais & Baker, 2012; Millán et al., 2010; Pelánek, 2017): *Prerequisite, Granularity, Solution, and Independence*. In Prerequisite BNs, the edges between nodes denote prerequisite relations between KCs. Such networks can help better sequence learning materials and increase the efficiency and accuracy of knowledge assessment (Carmona et al., 2005; Käser et al., 2014; Reye, 1996). In Granularity BNs, nodes and edges are organized in a hierarchy to decompose domain knowledge into different levels of detail (e.g., a topic and a subtopic). They allow for knowledge assessment at different levels. Granularity BNs have been investigated in several prior projects (Collins et al., 1996; Millán & Pérez-de-la Cruz, 2002; Mislevy & Gitomer, 1995). Another type is Solution BNs, which represent problem solution paths in conjunction with knowledge levels. For example, Andes' task-specific part of the BN corresponds to a solution graph composed of goals, facts, rule applications, context rules, and strategies, allowing for knowledge assessment and plan recognition for generating hints and instructions (Conati et al., 2002). In Independence BNs, independence among KCs is assumed. An example is Bayesian Knowledge Tracing (BKT; Corbett & Anderson, 1995) where knowledge estimation of a KC is independent of that of other KCs. BKT models knowledge dynamically with a dynamic Bayesian network (DBN) with key structure repeated at each time slice and with additional edges connecting the same types of knowledge nodes across time slices. Another kind of Independence BN uses a flat structure in which there is only one layer of KCs and there are no edges among KCs (Huang et al., 2017).

To reduce the number of parameters for ease of BN construction and inference, logic gates (Noisy-AND or Leaky-OR) can be used (Conati et al., 2002; Huang et al., 2017). There are other variations, such as integration with decision theory (Mayo & Mitrovic, 2001; Murray et al., 2004), complex dynamic BNs in narrative-centered learning environments (Rowe & Lester, 2010), logistic regression models for efficient modeling of subskills (González-Brenes et al., 2014; Xu & Mostow, 2012), and modeling integrative KCs that integrate or must be integrated with other KCs to produce behaviors (Huang et al., 2017).

There are three main approaches for creating or refining a BN-based domain (and student) model: expert-engineered, automated, or mixed approaches. (Mayo and Mitrovic (2001) use the terms expert-centric, data-centric, and efficiency-centric approaches, respectively.) Most of the work in AIED falls into the category of expert-engineered approaches where an expert specifies directly or indirectly the structure and parameters of the BN (Conati et al., 2002; Mislevy & Gitomer, 1995). Some research took an automated approach where the BN structure and parameters are learned primarily from data (Chen et al., 2016; Mayo & Mitrovic, 2001). Other research applied a mixed approach, where several BNs are specified first based on domain knowledge and then compared in terms of predictive accuracy on collected data (Pardos, Heffernan, Anderson, & Heffernan, 2006), or a BN is partially learned from data and then refined by experts (Vomlel, 2004). To evaluate a BN for domain modeling, data-driven evaluations on simulated datasets (Conati et al., 2002; Mayo & Mitrovic, 2001; Millán & Pérez-de-la Cruz, 2002) or real-world datasets (Huang, 2018; Pardos et al., 2006), as well as classroom studies (Conati et al., 2002; Huang, 2018; Mayo & Mitrovic, 2001), have been conducted.

Challenges

There are several concerns or challenges regarding the use of the BN paradigm for domain modeling in AIED systems. In cases where BNs are constructed by expert engineering, the process can be time-consuming and error-prone. Although many data-driven approaches have been devised to address this issue, fully automated methods for learning BNs (structure or parameters) in many cases are still computationally expensive and require a substantial amount of data to reach acceptable accuracy (Millán et al., 2010). Several issues that are relevant to many machine learning models also apply here. One is the model degeneracy issue where parameters learned from data conflict with the model's conceptual meaning, such as a student being more likely to get a correct answer if they do not know a skill than if they do (Baker et al., 2008; Huang, 2018; Huang et al., 2015). Another is the identifiability issue where the same data can be fit equally well by different parameters, resulting in different system behaviors (Beck & Chang, 2007; Huang et al., 2015), or different interpretations of effects of system features (Huang et al., 2015). To address this, constraints or prior distribution of parameters could be imposed when fitting parameters (Beck & Chang, 2007; Huang, 2018). More elaboration of these issues can be found in *Challenges* in the next machine learning section.

Machine Learning

Machine learning (ML) techniques are widely used in AIED systems, and they play an important role in domain modeling (Koedinger et al., 2013). Machine learning and domain representations intersect in two primary ways. First, domain knowledge is often encoded in the input representations used by machine learning models in AIED systems. These representations of domain knowledge are used to enhance the models' predictive effectiveness across a range of AIED tasks, such as assessing student knowledge (González-Brenes et al., 2014; Min et al., 2020), recognizing student affect (Jiang et al., 2018) or making pedagogical decisions (Rowe & Lester, 2015; Shen, Mostafavi et al., 2018), among others. In many cases, these applications are distinct from the task of modeling knowledge in a given domain itself. When data are provided to a machine learning algorithm, they are typically encoded using a factored representation known as a feature vector (Russell & Norvig, 2020). The attributes in this feature vector representation may indirectly encode information about knowledge in the domain, such as the current problem-solving context or characteristics of expert problem-solving behavior (Geden et al., 2021; Gobert et al., Baker, 2013; Rowe & Lester, 2015). The input feature representations utilized by machine learning models can be either manually engineered or learned automatically as typified by applications of deep neural networks (Jiang et al., 2018; Min et al., 2016).

The second way in which ML and domain representations intersect is in using ML to create or refine a model of domain knowledge itself. This latter approach encompasses a range of different modeling tasks within AIED systems. For example, ML techniques have been used to model effective inquiry strategies (Gobert et al., 2013; Käser & Schwartz, 2020), discover or refine skill models (Boros et al., 2013; Cen et al., 2006; Desmarais & Naceur, 2013; Lindsey et al., 2014; Huang et al., 2021), detect student misconceptions (Michalenko et al., 2017; Shi et al., 2021), and generate automated next-step hints based upon prior students' learning behaviors (Barnes & Stamper, 2008).

Several families of ML algorithms have been examined for domain modeling in AIED systems, including supervised learning, unsupervised learning, and reinforcement learning techniques. We briefly discuss each of these families and provide examples showing how they have been used for domain modeling in AIED. An issue that merits acknowledgment is the relationship between ML approaches for *domain modeling* and *student modeling*. These tasks are often closely related. In some cases, they may coexist within a single model, as we already saw with Bayesian Networks, described in the previous section. In the current section, we focus on work that applies ML to capture data-driven models of target knowledge, skills, and strategies in a particular task domain and/or learning environment. As discussed previously, we distinguish this from work investigating models that capture students' current learning states, which we regard as student modeling.

Supervised learning

Supervised learning is a family of ML techniques that involve training a model on labeled data in order to classify or predict the outcome associated with a new, as yet unseen input (Bishop, 2006; Russell & Norvig, 2020). Supervised learning encompasses a range of algorithmic techniques, including linear models, decision trees, kernel machines, probabilistic graphical models, deep neural networks, and ensemble techniques. A related paradigm is semi-supervised learning, which augments the supervised learning process by combining a small amount of labeled data with a large amount of unlabeled data during training in order to improve model predictions (Van Engelen & Hoos, 2020). Semi-supervised learning has been used to identify learning outcomes and prerequisites from educational texts (Labutov et al., 2017) and predict student performance on assessments (Livieris et al., 2019).

An important domain modeling task is automated model discovery (Cen et al., 2006; Chaplot et al., 2018; Koedinger et al., 2012). Automated model discovery is a form of cognitive model optimization that applies data-driven techniques to refine computational representations of knowledge and skills targeted for learning in a particular domain. For example, Learning Factors Analysis (LFA) is a semi-automated method for refining a cognitive domain model that combines multiple logistic regression and combinatorial search (Cen et al., 2006). The fit of a multiple logistic regression model to students' problem-solving data serves as a heuristic to guide a search for an improved domain representation. The search involves iteratively decomposing problem-solving skills (KCs) based on expert-defined difficulty factors to obtain a refined domain model that better fits the student data. In LFA, supervised learning supports a procedure for discovering (or refining) what the KCs in a domain model *are*. Supervised learning is not used to directly infer relations between KCs and/or student actions, but rather to guide a search process that reveals them. LFA and related techniques have been investigated with a range of algorithmic variations and AIED systems (Koedinger et al., 2012; Huang et al., 2021).

Supervised learning has also been used to model domain-specific strategies by training models with annotated datasets consisting of student learning interactions. Gobert and colleagues used supervised learning to devise models of students' inquiry processes in the Inq-ITS intelligent tutoring system (Gobert et al., 2013). Specifically, they utilized a combination of text replay tagging and decision tree classifiers to create ML-based detectors for automatically recognizing when students demonstrate the skill of designing controlled experiments within science microworlds. Similar techniques have also been used to model other facets of student interaction with AIED systems, such as detecting student affect (Jiang et al., 2018) and gaming the system (Baker et al., 2010; Paquette & Baker, 2019), which highlight the close connection between ML approaches to domain modeling and student modeling.

Work by Gobert et al. (2013) offers an example of how supervised learning can be used to create a domain model to assess student inquiry processes. (Their Inq-ITS system, on which this example is based, is mentioned briefly in the section "Exploratory Learning" of Chapter 9 (Aleven et al.).) Figure 7.3 provides a high-level illustration of the major steps involved. The first step is collecting log data from student interactions with an AIED system. Gobert and colleagues use data from 148 eighth-grade students collected during a classroom implementation of the Inq-ITS web-based tutor. In Inq-ITS's phase change microworld, students are given the task of determining which variables (e.g., container size, heat level, substance amount) affect different properties of a substance's phase change. Students proceed through a series of inquiry phases—exploring the simulation, using built-in tools to generate hypotheses, conducting simulated experiments, analyzing data—to complete the task. Students' interactions with Inq-ITS are time-stamped and logged to produce a low-level, sequential record of students' inquiry behaviors in the science microworld. Next, students' logs are segmented into meaningful sets of student actions, called clips, to be annotated by human coders. Each clip is tagged with one of ten possible inquiry skill labels, capturing productive inquiry behaviors such as "Designed Controlled Experiments," "Tested Stated Hypothesis," and "Used Data Table to Plan," as well as undesirable inquiry behaviors such as "Never Changed Variables" and "No Activity" (Sao Pedro et al., 2013). Two coders each assign a single label to each clip for a subset of clips. The subset of clips is used to establish interrater agreement, and, after establishing close agreement, the coders split up the remaining clips to be coded separately.

Next, the student log data is processed to distill features that will serve as input for machine learning. Gobert et al. (2013) distilled 12 predictor features from the student log data for each tagged clip: *all actions count, complete trials count, total trials count,* and so forth. For each tagged clip, the predictor features are combined into a vector with the "ground truth labels" from human coders appended. The set of feature vectors and their associated labels serve as the dataset for creating the machine learning model to detect student design of controlled experiments.

The dataset is then split into separate training, validation, and test sets. A widely used approach for model evaluation in supervised learning is called *cross-validation*, which involves repeatedly splitting a dataset into separate subsets for training and validation and alternately using each data point as either training data or validation data (Russell & Norvig, 2020). In cross-validation, training sets are used to tune the machine learning model's parameters, and

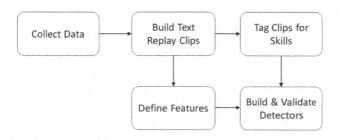

Source: Adapted from Gobert et al. (2013)

Figure 7.3　　*Steps for creating a domain model to detect the skill of designing controlled experiments using supervised learning*

validation sets are used to test the model's predictive performance on data not used in training. In the work of Gobert and colleagues (Gobert et al., 2013), the training data was provided as input to a J48 decision tree algorithm (Quinlan, 1993). In this algorithm, a decision tree is created by repeatedly dividing the data based on the values of different input features and by inducing a set of decision rules to predict clip labels based on the input features' values. The result is a tree-like data structure that has both internal nodes and leaf nodes, each associated with a decision rule, that collectively make up the decision criteria for classifying an input clip. As a final step during model creation, Gobert et al. (2013) reduced the set of input features by applying a standard feature selection technique called backward elimination search (Chandrashekar & Sahin, 2014).

The best-performing decision tree model that emerged from this process had, at its root, a decision rule about the number of adjacent controlled trials with repeats; if a student never ran two controlled experiments in a row, the model produced a high confidence prediction that the student did not know how to design a controlled experiment. If the student ran at least two controlled experiments in a row, the model utilized several additional features to determine how to classify knowledge of this skill. An example decision tree rule from Gobert et al. (2013) is shown in Box 7.1.

BOX 7.1: EXAMPLE DECISION RULE IN J48 DECISION TREE FOR DETECTING THE SKILL OF DESIGNING CONTROLLED EXPERIMENTS IN THE INQ-ITS TUTORING SYSTEM

IF count of adjacent controlled experiments (with repeats) = 1 AND

count of simulation variable changes ≤ 2 AND

count of pairwise controlled experiments (with repeats) > 1 AND

complete trials count > 2

THEN predict that the clip is a demonstration of designing controlled experiments with 74% confidence.

Source: Reproduced from Gobert et al. (2013)

After creating a domain model using supervised learning, as described above, the resulting model can be integrated back into the run-time AIED system. Specifically, the AIED system is extended to include support for distilling the predictor features utilized as input by the machine learning model (e.g., J48 decision tree) in real-time as students perform learning actions. The distilled features are assembled and provided as input to the trained model, which then produces a prediction, such as whether the student has demonstrated knowledge of how to design controlled experiments. These predictions can be used to drive decisions about adaptive support, problem selection, or other pedagogical functions of student modeling.

Another application of supervised learning for domain modeling in AIED systems is automated goal recognition, which is the task of inferring an agent's higher-order goal (or goals) based upon a series of observations of their lower-level actions in a learning environment (Sukthankar et al., 2014). A broad range of ML techniques have been used for automated goal recognition in AIED systems, including probabilistic models (Mott et al., 2006), deep-learning techniques (Min et al., 2016), and statistical relational learning methods that combine

ML with logic-based representations (Ha et al. 2011). Like the work by Gobert et al. (2013), ML-based goal recognition provides a framework for devising models that encode the relationships between low-level actions and higher-order cognitive processes, such as goal setting or strategy use.

Unsupervised learning

Unsupervised learning techniques are widely used to analyze student data in AIED systems. Unsupervised learning is a family of ML techniques for capturing generalizable patterns or groups in unlabeled datasets (Bishop, 2006). A key application of unsupervised learning is discovering patterns in student strategy use, an application that blends elements of domain modeling and student modeling. For example, Käser and Schwartz (2020) clustered students into different groups based on their inquiry strategies in an open-ended learning environment for middle-school physics education called TugLet. Although Käser and Schwartz (2020) used a rule-based model of knowledge of motion and forces in TugLet, they utilized clustering analysis to model inquiry strategies. Clustering analysis revealed several patterns of student behavior that could be interpreted in terms of effective and ineffective inquiry strategies in TugLet. For example, one cluster was associated with efficient, systematic testing behavior using TugLet's simulation-based exploration mode. Another cluster was associated with an inefficient trial-and-error process, which included little use of TugLet's exploration mode. In total, seven clusters were identified, and they were validated using a separate validation dataset collected from a different public middle school. Findings showed a high level of cluster agreement between the two datasets, although the distribution of clusters was different (Käser & Schwartz, 2020). Notably, the analysis also revealed a new, positive inquiry strategy—keep it simple to isolate equivalence of units—which had not yet been described in the literature.

Clustering analysis has also been used to identify student error patterns and misconceptions in specific domains. Shi and colleagues (2021) used student program code data from an introductory computing course to train a neural embedding-based representation of student code called code2vec. This representation was then used to identify clusters of student mistakes using Density-Based Spatial Clustering of Applications with Noise (DBSCAN) (Ester et al., 1996). The resulting clusters were interpreted by domain experts to identify common misconceptions exemplified in students' unsuccessful code. A case study of three clusters suggested that the approach revealed novel and meaningful misconceptions that would not have been easily discovered using traditional clustering methods (Shi et al., 2021).

Unsupervised learning techniques also play a role in acquiring domain knowledge representations for use by *simulated students*. For example, the SimStudent teachable agent, which is integrated with the APLUS learning by teaching platform, leverages a combination of inductive logic programming and learning by demonstration to learn rule-based domain model representations from demonstrations (e.g., feedback and hints) provided by ITS authors and students (Matsuda et al., 2020; Matsuda et al., 2013). SimStudent engages in a hybrid machine learning process that combines elements of both supervised and unsupervised learning. Demonstrations provided by students (a form of supervision) are used to generate production rules, each representing a skill, that together constitute SimStudent's model of the domain. Unsupervised representation learning algorithms that encode "deep features" in algebra equation solving have also been integrated with SimStudent, reducing the knowledge engineering requirements associated with constructing these types of agents (Li et al., 2015). Work on SimStudent has also been extended toward the creation of the Apprentice Learner

Architecture, which enables interactive machine-learning-based authoring paradigms for the creation of AIED systems across a range of knowledge types and domains (MacLellan & Koedinger, 2020; Weitekamp et al., 2020).

An important property of student behavior in many AIED systems is its sequential nature. Sequence mining has been found to be effective for detecting patterns in learner behavior that unfold over time within open-ended learning environments. Kinnebrew et al. (2013) developed a differential sequence mining framework to distinguish between productive and unproductive learning behaviors in Betty's Brain, a learning-by-teaching platform for middle-school mathematics and science education. They identified sequential patterns in students' metacognitive activities, such as taking quizzes or reading relevant resources to monitor aspects of their solutions, that were distinct between high- and low-performing groups of students, or between productive and unproductive phases of learning. Taub et al. (2018) used a similar approach to extract patterns in students' scientific reasoning processes (e.g., sequences of relevant and irrelevant testing behaviors) during inquiry-based learning in a game-based learning environment. A key use case for these patterns is to refine the design of metacognitive strategy feedback that is specific to a particular domain and learning environment. Other work has utilized principal component analysis (PCA) to filter students' problem-solving sequences to devise time series representations of learner behavior in open-ended learning environments (Reilly & Dede, 2019; Sawyer et al., 2018). Using PCA-based representations of expert problem solving, this approach enables entire trajectories of student problem-solving behaviors to be efficiently compared with expert problem-solving trajectories. The distance between student trajectories and expert trajectories has been found to be predictive of student learning gains (Sawyer et al., 2018). Again, these examples are illustrative of the close relationship between domain modeling and student modeling in many applications of ML (and data mining) within AIED.

Reinforcement learning

Recent years have seen growing interest in leveraging reinforcement learning to model and support students' learning processes (Doroudi et al., 2019). Reinforcement learning is a family of ML techniques that focus on sequential decision making under uncertainty (Sutton & Barto, 2018). Rather than being trained upon a set of labeled data, reinforcement learning typically involves a process of learning by experience where an ML agent explores alternative courses of action with the goal of maximizing the accumulated reward over time. Much of the work on reinforcement learning in AIED has focused on pedagogical models (Ausin et al., 2020; Beck et al., 2000; Rowe & Lester, 2015), but reinforcement learning techniques have also been used to model structured domains, such as logic proofs and algebra equation solving. Barnes and Stamper (2008) leveraged a Markov decision process (MDP) formalism to model logic proof solving in the DeepThought intelligent tutoring system. By mining data from previous students' interactions, their MDP-based domain representation could be used to automatically generate contextual hints by matching the current state of a student's proof attempt and selecting the next action that is optimal with respect to the MDP's reward function. The result was a system that would recommend solution paths (i.e., proof steps) that were taken in successful proofs by previous students. An additional benefit of this approach is that the hint generation model can continue to improve as new student data is collected; the domain model is enriched as more students interact with the system.

Rafferty and Griffiths (2015) utilized inverse reinforcement learning to interpret students' freeform algebra equation-solving steps to assess student knowledge. Their approach, which is based upon Bayesian inverse planning, enables the interpretation of students' equation-solving processes regardless of whether a structured or freeform interface is used by the learning environment. Rafferty and Griffiths (2015) modeled equation transformations as a Markov decision process, and they utilized inverse planning to approximate a posterior distribution over the space of hypotheses representing possible learner understandings in the algebra equation- solving domain. In related work, Rafferty et al. (2016) used inverse planning to provide automated feedback on students' equation-solving choices. Results from a study indicated that the feedback yielded pre-performance to post-performance improvements, and learners who received feedback on skills that were far from mastery showed greater improvement than students who received feedback on already-mastered skills.

How to create domain models using machine learning

There are software toolkits that are freely available to facilitate the creation of ML-based domain models, but current tools are not specific to domain model creation for use in AIED systems. Several popular tools provide graphical user interfaces for training, validating, and testing ML algorithms, such as RapidMiner (Kotu & Deshpande, 2014) and Weka (Hall et al., 2009). Similarly, research on deep learning applications has been accelerated by the availability of popular software packages for R (e.g., caret) and Python (e.g., TensorFlow, Keras, PyTorch, and ScikitLearn). A prerequisite for the application of ML techniques is the availability of cleaned, formatted data to train and validate models. Given the widespread availability of free ML toolkits, much of the work in creating ML-based models in AIED systems is in the acquisition and formatting of data, formulation of the ML task, and engineering of feature representations. Shared data repositories, such as DataShop and LearnSphere, provide datasets, analysis tools, and visualizations that can serve to reduce the burden of data acquisition and formatting (Koedinger et al., 2010; Koedinger et al., 2017). Furthermore, many ML toolkits provide implementations of common feature selection algorithms, which further reduce the burden of manually creating effective feature representations in ML-based domain models. Although these resources are useful, the development of authoring tools that specifically focus on the creation of ML-based domain models is a promising direction for future research.

Challenges

Machine learning provides a useful means for automatically modeling domain knowledge in AIED systems, but it also raises several important challenges. First, ML assumes the availability of significant data for training and validation. Sufficient data to produce a high-quality model may not always be available, or the available data may not be ideally distributed (e.g., a non-randomized problem order), especially early in the development of an AIED system or in domains that are not conducive to formalization using ML techniques. Second, ML approaches to domain modeling raise important questions related to fairness and transparency. Recent years have seen growing attention to the issue of encoded bias in ML (Gardner et al., 2019). In domain modeling, a biased model has the potential to cause harm to students if they are improperly judged to be engaged in "incorrect" learning behaviors because those behavior patterns were not included in the data used to train the model.

A related issue is transparency. Machine learning often produces models that are effectively a "black box" consisting of many thousands (or more) parameters that are difficult to interpret or explain. Lack of transparency, including weak interpretability and/or explainability, in a domain model is likely to reduce the level of trust that is imparted upon it, reduce what scientific insights can be gained from the model, and perhaps even reduce its utility for instruction. This issue points toward the opportunity for developing *explanatory models* within AIED systems, which provide insights about learners and the learning process that are interpretable and actionable in addition to being accurate (Rosé et al., 2019).

A third challenge is the issue of semantic model degeneracy, which refers to situations where the parameters induced for an ML-based domain model conflict with theoretical or conceptual understandings of the domain (Baker et al., 2008; Doroudi & Brunskill, 2017). This issue is closely related to concerns of model plausibility, identifiability, and consistency (Huang et al., 2015). An example occurs in work by Gobert et al. (2013), described above, in which they initially observed that ML-based detectors of students' inquiry skills (e.g., designing controlled experiments) omitted key features considered theoretically important to the behavior, such as the number of controlled comparisons that a student made in his/her data set. This observation resulted in the adoption of a modified approach to their text replay tagging procedure and the use of different datasets for training, refining, and testing their machine learning model to improve its construct validity. This form of model degeneracy may reflect an issue in the distribution of the training data, or some other source of bias rather than properties of an ML model or an optimization algorithm. In general, however, ML-based models are more prone to degeneracy issues than the other major paradigms discussed in this chapter where domain experts are more heavily involved in the creation or refinement of domain models.

Despite these limitations, machine learning provides a range of useful tools and techniques for domain modeling in AIED systems. Furthermore, applications of ML intersect with many of the other paradigms outlined in this chapter, giving rise to hybrid systems that draw upon multiple paradigms to devise computational models of domain knowledge that inform the adaptive pedagogical functionalities of AIED systems.

Domain Modeling for Intelligent Textbooks

Domain modeling has supported a wide range of intelligent or adaptive online textbooks, which have a long history in personalized web-based learning (Brusilovsky & Pesin, 1998; Henze & Nejdl, 1999; Kavcic, 2004; Melis et al., 2001; Weber & Brusilovsky, 2001). Intelligent or adaptive textbooks can guide students to the most relevant content based on student modeling (Huang et al., 2016; Thaker et al., 2018), content recommendation (Kavcic, 2004; Sosnovsky et al., 2012), knowledge-adapted content presentation (Melis et al. 2001), and adaptive navigation support (Brusilovsky & Eklund, 1998; Brusilovsky & Pesin 1998; Henze & Nejdl, 1999; Weber & Brusilovsky, 2001), such as a "traffic light" approach to annotate links as content for which the student is deemed ready or not ready (Brusilovsky et al., 1996, 1998). A domain model in an intelligent textbook typically consists of a KC-to-item mapping which specifies domain concepts presented on a page or a section (i.e., an item), and sometimes also specifies the prerequisite concepts required to understand the current page or section. Domain models in intelligent textbooks are used mainly to assess student knowledge (Huang et al., 2016) and guide students to the right content (Brusilovsky & Eklund, 1998; Brusilovsky & Pesin 1998; Henze & Nejdl, 1999); a few also assess student work and provide problem-solving support

(Weber & Brusilovsky 2001). Many studies have confirmed the effectiveness of personalization approaches based on domain and student modeling for student learning with online textbooks (Brusilovsky & Eklund, 1998; Davidovic et al., 2003; Weber & Brusilovsky, 2001).

Domain modeling in intelligent textbooks has evolved from manual indexing by domain experts to the more recent automatic extraction using ML and text mining (i.e., natural language processing) techniques. Several studies demonstrated the effectiveness of personalization approaches built based on manually-indexed domain models in early adaptive textbooks (Brusilovsky & Eklund 1998; Davidovic et al., 2003; Weber & Brusilovsky 2001). To reduce the cost of expert labeling, a research stream focused on open corpus adaptive educational hypermedia (Brusilovsky & Henze, 2007) has explored automatic methods that borrow from information retrieval and semantic web models (Dolog & Nejdl, 2003; Sosnovsky & Dicheva, 2010) to build various kinds of models of educational documents. More recently, automatic methods have been developed for identifying prerequisite concepts (Agrawal et al., 2014; Labutov et al., 2017), building prerequisite structures (Chaplot et al., 2016), and building concept hierarchies (Wang et al., 2015). Chau et al. (2020) provide a comprehensive, offline evaluation of various automatic concept extraction methods and a review of domain modeling for adaptive textbooks.

A notable challenge is the evaluation of domain models used in intelligent textbooks. Early empirical evaluations in this field typically compared an adaptive system with a non-adaptive system, demonstrating benefits of a whole adaptivity "package" such as a combination of the domain model, student model, and adaptive navigation support (Brusilovsky & Eklund, 1998; Weber & Brusilovsky, 2001). There is still a lack of empirical or data-driven evaluations that isolate the contribution of domain models. Another challenge is a lack of high-quality labeled data to train and evaluate domain models for intelligent textbooks. Most automatic methods in this field rely on labeled data provided by domain experts for supervised or semi-supervised learning tasks, yet labeling domain concepts is a very time-consuming and difficult task.

Examples and Generalized Examples

Several types of AIED systems use problem-solving examples or generalized versions of such examples as their main representation of domain knowledge. These systems typically assess student work by comparing them against stored examples. To this end, they employ a flexible matching process for finding a relevant example and mapping it to the student solution. Given that there may be great variability in student solutions, matching literally against stored examples might not be effective.

Example-tracing tutors, a widely-used paradigm for creating AIED tutoring systems, use "behavior graphs" as their representation of domain knowledge (Aleven et al., 2016). Behavior graphs are generalized examples of step-by-step solution *processes* within a given problem. The nodes in these graphs represent problem states, the links represent problem-solving steps. Different paths in a behavior graph capture different ways of solving a given problem. (Thus, behavior graphs can handle problems with multiple different solution paths, although if the number of such paths is very large in a problem, they become unwieldy.) An example-tracing algorithm flexibly matches a student's problem-solving steps, one-by-one, against the graph, to track which path(s) the student might be following. The process of example tracing is analogous to model tracing, described in the current chapter, above. Just as the model-tracing algorithm tracks which solution path the student is following from among the many solutions paths the rule model could generate, the example-tracing algorithm tracks which solution path the student is on from among the multiple possible solution paths captured in the given behavior graph. With dedicated authoring tools, an author can create behavior graphs through programming by demonstration, without having to write code. With the same tools, the author can also indicate how a graph generalizes, so it can be used to recognize, as correct, a wide range of student problem-solving behavior. Many example-tracing tutors have been built and found to be effective in helping students learn in real educational settings (Aleven et al., 2016). Interestingly, behavior graphs have a long history in cognitive science (Newell & Simon, 1972) that predates their use in AIED systems, another way in which the fields of AIED and cognitive science are connected.

Other AIED systems use examples of *solutions* (rather than solution paths) as a key store of domain knowledge. We have already encountered one instance: constraint-based tutors use stored examples of solutions in order to help students learn. As another instance, a programming tutor by Rivers and Koedinger (2017) uses a large store of student Python programs to interpret student work and provide hints for how to fix or complete programs. Much emphasis in this work is on creating a process for converting students' program code to an abstract, canonical representation. Doing so decreases the number of examples that need to be stored and increases the probability of finding a match for any given student program.

In a different way of using examples, several AIED systems support students in studying worked examples as part of their instructional approaches, often eliciting self-explanations from students, with feedback from the system (see Conati & VanLehn, 2000; Adams et al., 2014, MacLaren et al., 2016; Zhi et al., 2019; Chen et al., 2020; also Chapter 9 by Aleven et al.). Some systems are capable of adaptively selecting or fading worked examples (i.e., gradually transitioning to problem solving), based on measures of students' knowledge or knowledge growth (Goguadze et al., 2011; Salden et al., 2010). In these methods for selecting or fading examples on an individualized basis, the domain model, student model, and pedagogical model all work together.

Knowledge Spaces

Another paradigm in domain modeling and student modeling is based on the theory of *knowledge spaces* (Doignon & Falmagne, 1985, 2012). In this paradigm, domain knowledge is represented by a network of interconnected items. These items correspond to the problem types in the given educational domain. The relations between items are precedence relations between problem types, which may be due to the prerequisite structure of the domain or the order in which problem types are taught (Falmagne et al., 2006). A student's knowledge state is represented as a subset of these items, namely, the items that the student is assumed to have mastered. The knowledge spaces paradigm could be viewed as overlapping with the Bayesian network paradigm in that a knowledge structure in knowledge spaces theory can be described as a Bayesian network without hidden nodes, where each of the nodes maps to a concrete class of problems (Desmarais & Pu, 2005). This paradigm emphasizes tailoring and selecting the right learning content based on estimated student competence.

Systems based on the knowledge spaces theory include the widely used ALEKS mathematics tutor (Falmagne et al., 2006) and the Catalyst or MCWeb system for chemistry (Arasasingham et al., 2011, 2005). A recent meta-analysis (Fang et al., 2019) revealed that ALEKS was as effective as, but not better than, traditional classroom teaching. Also, a study by Arasasingham et al. (2005) found that the MCWeb system improved learning outcomes in chemistry. Students who used MCWeb for their homework performed significantly better in subsequent assessments, compared with students who carried out homework from their text-books. However, it's unclear whether the improvement was from the multiple representation mechanism used in the system, or the knowledge spaces model itself.

Knowledge spaces are often human engineered, but they need to be refined with data to enhance accuracy (Falmagne et al., 2006; Pavlik et al., 2013). Typically, a large amount of data is needed to infer a complete set of precedence relations. Partial Order Knowledge Structures (POKS) have been developed to address challenges of inferring the AND/OR precedence relations from data alone (Desmarais et al., 2006; Desmarais & Pu, 2005). Another issue is that this paradigm does not model domain knowledge in terms of cognitive structures (e.g., concepts, skills). Without such information, it is hard to differentiate problems that share some knowledge demands but differ in other knowledge demands, which would seem to hamper accurate knowledge estimation or recommendations. There is some work to extend the frame-work to include skills as well (Heller et al., 2006). For a more thorough review of this para-digm, readers can refer to reviews by Desmarais and Baker (2012) or by Pavlik et al. (2013).

Other Types of Domain Models

We briefly discuss several other types of domain models that have been demonstrated to be effective in AIED systems, even if they have not quite seen the same amount of research or widespread use as the paradigms discussed above: domain ontologies, concept maps, case-based models, qualitative models of physical systems, models of inquiry processes, and issue-based models.

First, a substantial amount of work within the field of AIED has focused on using *domain ontologies* within AIED systems (see Lenat & Durlach, 2014). These ontologies provide a hierarchical ordering of domain concepts. For example, the SlideTutor system uses domain knowledge represented as an ontology. This representation is used for visual classification problem solving in surgical pathology, in combination with a rule-based model (Crowley et al., 2003; Crowley & Medvedeva, 2006). Separating declarative knowledge (represented in the system's ontology) and procedural knowledge (represented as rules) facilitates system exten-sions (e.g., modeling additional medical visual classification tasks) and reusability of knowl-edge representations. Ontologies have also been used for domain model alignment between various AIED systems to enable the exchange of student models. For example, Sosnovsky et al. (2009) discuss how AIED systems based on different formalisms can exchange assess-ments of student work using ontology mapping. The ontology served as a mediator between the set of constraints in SQL-Tutor and SQL-Guide, an adaptive hypermedia system in which the student model is represented as an overlay on the ontology.

Second, a number of AIED systems use *concept maps* (Novak, 1996) and *conceptual graphs* (Sowa, 1994) as domain models. Concept maps are graphs that represent domain concepts and relations between them, with domain-specific labels, to capture conceptual and propositional knowledge of a domain (Martínez-Maldonado et al., 2010). In a number of AIED systems, the students' main learning activity is to construct a concept map as a representation of his/her domain knowledge. They may receive assistance from the system (e.g., the Betty's Brain sys-tem from Biswas et al., 2005) or from a teacher, in turn supported by an analytics system (e.g., Martinez-Maldonado et al., 2014). Another approach involves the student in building a stu-dent model, represented as a conceptual graph, collaboratively with the STyLE-OLM system (Dimitrova, 2003; Dimitrova & Brna, 2016), to improve the accuracy of the student model, and at the same time promote metacognitive skills such as reflection and self-assessment.

Concept maps have also been used to provide some guidance to students during inquiry activities (Hagemans et al., 2013). All these approaches capitalize on the idea that concept maps or conceptual graphs are highly interpretable ways of organizing domain knowledge. The system often assesses the student's work by comparing the student's evolving model against a stored expert model but may also assess student work in terms of whether their process of building and testing the model, given resources, is sound and coherent.

Third, some AIED systems have *case-based domain models*, which capture processes of reasoning with cases. Some AIED systems support students in domains where experts naturally reason with cases. In such domains, rules may be "weak" or too abstract to give much direct guidance (i.e., these may be ill-defined domains); therefore, reasoning with cases is a natural supplement or even a substitute for reasoning with rules (Lynch et al., 2009). Examples of such systems are CATO (Aleven, 2003) and LARGO (Pinkwart et al., 2009) in the domain of legal reasoning. Some systems use case-based reasoning processes as part of their pedagogical approach (Gauthier et al., 2007; Schank, 1990), although that is outside the scope of the current chapter.

Fourth, some AIED work has focused on systems that use various types of "qualitative models" as domain models (Bredeweg & Forbus, 2016; Bredeweg et al., 2013; Joyner et al., 2013). Betty's Brain, mentioned above, could also be viewed as falling into this category (Biswas et al., 2016). Typically, these models capture phenomena in the natural world (e.g., models of biological or ecological systems, models of how physical devices work, or other forms of causal models). They are networks that capture causal influences among variables; unlike concept maps or conceptual graphs, discussed above, these networks can support inference generation. Oftentimes, they are used in AIED systems in which the student's task is to build a model (e.g., of a natural phenomenon), with guidance from the system. In some systems, the qualitative models are executable, so that students can test their models against data (e.g., to see if they account for data about the model phenomenon).

Fifth, relatedly, some AIED systems use *models of inquiry processes* to support students as they carry out such processes, such as the Inq-ITS system from Gobert et al. (2013) and Käser & Schwartz's (2020) work with the TugLet game. These models capture how to gather evidence and design experiments and are used to assess student work and knowledge of inquiry skills; the models used in Inq-ITS are described above, in the section in this chapter on machine learning. In some instances, models of inquiry processes have been found to generalize across different science topics (Gobert et al., 2013). More information about the nature of these systems and their domain models can be found in Chapter 9 by Aleven et al.

Finally, some systems use an *issue-based approach*. They use a domain model that captures specific "issues" within the given task domain, which include both desirable aspects and shortcomings of work that are common among novices. Having a representation of issues enables the system to provide useful adaptive feedback on student work, without the need for a complete domain model. Systems of this kind are often characterized by a coaching style that minimizes the amount of intervention (Burton & Brown, 1982). An issue-based approach may be particularly appropriate in domains where AI models have limited scope or are not sophisticated enough to fully evaluate students' work. The LARGO system of Pinkwart et al. (2009) illustrates this approach. Using LARGO, students diagram out oral argument exchanges before the US Supreme Court. The LARGO system provides feedback based on a representation of argument issues that were not themselves meant to be a complete model of the kind of legal argumentation being analyzed. As an additional example, some analytics-based tools that provide alerts regarding student work to teachers (e.g., VanLehn et al., 2021) can also be viewed as falling under this category.

New Trends

We briefly review two lines of research related to domain modeling that have come to the foreground since 2015: the application of text mining techniques for discovering and refining domain models from text and the use of crowdsourcing for building domain models.

A new trend in AIED research is discovering and refining domain models from text utilizing text mining techniques. The availability of large amounts of digital text-based learning content and advances in computational linguistics create numerous opportunities for automated discovery or improvement of domain models (for example, a Q-matrix or prerequisite structures) based on text mining. This trend goes beyond the textbook context mentioned in our previous section and involves broader contexts such as Wikipedia (Gasparetti et al., 2015), MOOC lecture transcripts (Alsaad et al., 2018), and conversational interactions with learners (see Chapter 11 by Rus et al. for text-based domain modeling in AutoTutor systems). Some of the approaches used only textual content (Alsaad et al., 2018; Gasparetti et al., 2015; Pardos & Dadu, 2017), while others used a combination of textual and student performance data (Chaplot et al., 2016; Chen et al., 2018; Matsuda et al., 2015). Various text mining techniques have been shown to be effective, as evaluated by predictive performance in prediction tasks. For example, Pardos and Dadu (2017) applied a skip-gram model (a neural network commonly known as word2vec) to model both the content of a problem and problems around it and reached a 90% accuracy in predicting the missing skill from a KC model. Michalenko et al. (2017) utilized word embeddings to detect misconceptions from students' textual responses to open-response questions. Other text mining techniques have also been applied, such as semantic analysis for identifying relevant Wikipedia concepts in text-based learning objects (Gasparetti et al., 2015), named entity recognition for extracting educational concepts in curriculum standards (Chen et al., 2018), and correlational topic modeling for identifying topics by analyzing the content of mathematics problems (Slater et al., 2017).

Another new trend that has received increasing attention in recent years is crowdsourcing domain models. This work is situated in the broader ongoing research into crowdsourcing explanations, feedback, and other pedagogical interactions (Heffernan et al., 2016; Williams et al., 2016). For example, crowdsourcing has been used to identify KCs in the domains of mathematics and English writing; it was found that roughly one-third of the crowdsourced KCs directly matched those generated by domain experts (Moore et al., 2020). *Learnersourcing* is a form of crowdsourcing where learners collectively contribute novel content for future learners while they are engaged in a meaningful learning experience themselves (Kim, 2015). One active line of learningsourcing research is in video learning, including subgoal label generation (Weir et al., 2015), solution structure extraction (Kim, 2015), and concept map generation (Liu et al., 2018) from educational videos. Several studies found that learner-generated labels or content can be comparable in quality to expert-generated ones (Liu et al., 2018; Weir et al., 2015), and that the learnersourcing workflow did not detract learners from the learning experience (Weir et al., 2015). Learnersourcing was also used for understanding large-scale variation in student solutions in programming and hardware design, and has proven valuable for both teachers and students (Glassman & Miller, 2016).

DISCUSSION

Our review of AIED domain modeling paradigms, summarized in Tables 7.1 and 7.2, shows an astounding richness. Many domain modeling paradigms for AIED systems have been explored, developed, and proven to be useful. Within each paradigm, multiple systems have been built and have been found to be effective in helping students learn in real educational settings.

The use of domain models in AIED systems offers many advantages, as described above and summarized in Table 7.1. A domain model enables a system to provide adaptive step-level guidance to students within complex problem-solving activities, which enables the system to support student learning more effectively than systems without step-level support (VanLehn, 2011) and to guide students during richer problem-solving experiences. Domain models can be the basis for student modeling and hence for many forms of adaptivity within AIED systems, including personalized mastery learning. As well, domain models can be used to guide the design of many aspects of AIED systems. Finally, some have argued that the use of domain models may promote interoperability between system components and systems (Sottilare et al., 2016, Chapter 4). Although domain models are key in many effective AIED systems, it should be noted that several adaptive instructional systems, including some widely used ones, do not have a strong domain model, for example ASSISTments (Heffernan & Heffernan, 2014), MathSprings (Arroyo et al., 2014), Khan Academy (Kelly & Rutherford, 2017), and Duolingo (von Ahn, 2013). Without domain models, these systems provide simple practice problems with immediate feedback and forms of personalized task selection, which can be effective for learners. These systems, however, cannot support the greater adaptivity and more complex problem solving afforded by a domain model.

Although, as Table 7.1 attests, there is substantial overlap in the functionality supported by the different domain modeling paradigms, some interesting differences emerge as well. Such differentiation across AIED paradigms is attractive, for example because it gives the AIED system developer different tools in their toolkit. For example, the AIED domain modeling paradigms differ in the degree to which they can readily handle problems that have large solution spaces. In such problems (e.g., computer programming or solving algebraic equations), there is great variability in student solutions, even among the correct solutions, or the steps that lead to correct solutions. Constraint-based tutors and model-tracing tutors deal well with such domains. On the other hand, example-tracing tutors are not well-suited to practice problems with large solution spaces, although they can still handle problems with multiple alternative solution paths. In addition, although BNs in theory could be constructed to support domain modeling with vast solution spaces, the construction of such BNs may be labor intensive if done by human engineering, or challenging in terms of both computational efficiency and accuracy if done by automated methods. Systems that rely on stores of examples have the potential to handle large solution spaces, although doing so might require sophisticated canonicalization and matching approaches (e.g., Rivers & Koedinger, 2017). Advances in machine learning have shown promise to tackle some of these challenges.

Different domain modeling paradigms assess student work in different ways. In some paradigms (e.g., model-tracing tutors, BNs in Andes), the domain model captures general problem-solving knowledge, which enables the system to simulate the process of solving problems and to assess student solutions steps by comparing them against solution steps or processes generated by the model. In other paradigms (e.g., constraint-based tutors), the domain model

Table 7.2 Strengths and weaknesses of AIED domain modeling paradigms

Paradigms	Can handle large solution spaces	Amenable to machine learning or data-driven refinement	Ease of authoring/authoring tools exist	Requiring data to develop	Model identifiability and/or degeneracy issues	Interpretability
Rules	Yes	Yes, SimStudent can learn rules. Many methods for data-driven KC model refinement	CTAT, SimStudent	Cognitive task analysis upfront recommended	N/A	Yes
Constraints	Yes	Yes	Requires domain knowledge/ASPIRE	No data required (though can use data if you have it)	N/A	Yes
Behavior Graphs	No	Many methods for data-driven KC model refinement.	CTAT—non-programmer authoring	Cognitive task analysis upfront recommended	N/A	Yes
Bayesian Networks	Hard	Yes	Yes, but not integrated with ITS authoring	Yes	Yes	Yes
Supervised Learning	Hard	—	Yes, but not integrated with ITS authoring	Yes	Yes	Depends
Unsupervised Learning	Yes	—	Yes, but not integrated with ITS authoring	Yes	No. No conceptual assumptions.	Depends
Reinforcement Learning	Yes	—	Yes, but not integrated with ITS authoring	Yes	In principle, yes.	Depends

captures knowledge for assessing solutions and partial solutions. This approach enables the system to provide rich feedback on student work without the ability to generate problem solutions. Issue-based approaches capture knowledge for evaluating specific solution aspects (e.g., identifying inquiry strategies or recognizing common issues or undesirable properties of student work) without fully evaluating a complete solution (issue-based approaches or some ML approaches). Finally, some example-based approaches store solutions or solution paths, and have smart, flexible ways of comparing student solutions to stored solutions, so as to provide feedback and hints (Aleven et al., 2016; Rivers & Koedinger, 2017; Stamper et al., 2013).

Relatedly, across domain models, we see some differences in the type of formative feedback that the systems can give to students. As mentioned, formative feedback is a key function of domain models. Many domain modeling approaches evaluate the overall quality of the student's work (e.g., correctness of the entire solution), but others (e.g., issue-based approaches and some ML approaches) focus only on specific aspects of solutions, without the intent of assessing the overall quality of student work. An issue-based approach may be appropriate in domains where AI/ML has not advanced to the point that complete evaluation of solution quality is possible (e.g., complex, open-ended domains; Lynch et al., 2009). Another difference in tutoring behaviors is in the specificity of next-step hints. Model-tracing tutors and example-tracing tutors can always suggest a specific next step (together with reasons why). On the other hand, constraint-based tutors provide hints that state missing solution elements, or extra elements; they can also present example solutions to students. A final observation is that most domain modeling paradigms allow for modeling of errors or misconceptions for the purpose of providing error-specific feedback to students, though without strictly requiring it.

Although, as mentioned, creating a domain model is labor intensive, various developments make doing so easier, including the development of AIED authoring tools, the vastly increased use of ML in creating AIED systems, and (in a very recent development) the use of crowd-sourcing (Williams et al., 2016; Yang et al., 2021). AIED authoring tools have long existed for established domain modeling paradigms such as rules (Aleven et al., 2006b; Koedinger et al., 2003), constraints (Mitrovic et al., 2009; Suraweera et al., 2010), and behavior graphs (Aleven et al., 2016). A number of these projects involve machine learning to support non-programmers in creating domain models for use in AIED systems (Matsuda et al., 2015; Mitrovic et al., 2009), often integrated with other authoring functions (e.g., tutor interfaces, student models, etc.). We see an on-going trend toward the use of ML to facilitate representation learning (Li et al., 2018), factoring interactive learning approaches to domain knowledge (MacLellan & Koedinger, 2020), and addressing human–computer interaction aspects (Weitekamp et al., 2020). We also see opportunities for further integration, both between AIED domain modeling paradigms and with existing general AI/ML toolkits, to facilitate experiments with AIED systems.

The use of machine learning to create domain models has grown dramatically in recent years. Machine learning has been used to create domain models that range in focus from specific aspects of student work (e.g., Gobert et al., 2013) to more general models of problem-solving knowledge within a specific domain (e.g., Barnes & Stamper, 2008). A broad range of machine learning techniques have also been used across different domain modeling tasks, including supervised learning, unsupervised learning, and reinforcement learning methods. Interestingly, machine learning is not tied to a particular computational representation or formalism. Rather, machine learning can be used to create domain models (and student models) with a broad range of representations, including the major paradigms discussed in this chapter (e.g., rules, constraints, Bayesian networks, etc.) as well as others. In fact, data-driven techniques for creating or refining domain models, which are informed by machine learning, have proven useful across all domain modeling paradigms (see Table 7.2). The data-driven methods used in AIED research differ starkly with respect to the amount of data needed. Some paradigms depend on the availability of large amounts of data right from the start (i.e., many ML approaches). Others can operate while requiring less or even no data initially (e.g., interactive ML or qualitative cognitive task analysis; Clark et al., 2007). Some require limited data for the initial creation of a model, but require more data later (e.g., for data-driven refinement). We see great promise for approaches and tools that integrate data-driven improvement and authoring of AIED systems, a challenge (and an opportunity!) for the field.

The review highlights many connections and dependencies between an AIED system's domain model and its student model, traditionally considered to be separate modules. These two models tend to be closely coupled and sometimes fully integrated. For example, overlay models and KC modeling are ways of tightly linking domain models and student models. As another example, BNs have been applied in an AIED system (VanLehn et al., 2005) in a manner that elegantly blends domain modeling with student modeling. Another interesting connection is seen where ML-based domain models are trained from student learning data, or when a KC model is refined using log data from a tutoring system.

An interesting issue arises regarding the *practice* of AIED: given that professional AIED designers, developers, and learning engineers have multiple domain modeling paradigms to choose from, how should they select the most appropriate paradigm for any given AIED development project or the most appropriate combination of paradigms (see Roll et al., 2010)? So far, the field of AIED has not produced a strong, evidence-based set of guidelines; generating such guidelines is a great challenge because research studies comparing different domain modeling paradigms are very hard to do. Based on our review, some relevant factors that influence this choice may be:

1) The desired behavior of the tutoring system. We noted some differences with respect to whether feedback is based on a full evaluation of correctness or focuses on specific issues only, the specificity of next-step advice, and whether error feedback is accommodated.
2) Whether the tutored tasks have large solution spaces. We noted some differences among the domain modeling paradigms in how well they deal with large solution spaces.
3) Whether one has confidence that AI can do a good enough job either in generating or fully evaluating solutions. We noted some differences among the paradigms in this regard as well. This factor may correlate with how well- or ill-defined the domain is.
4) The skill and experience of the design and development team (e.g., whether they have experience with the given modeling paradigm).
5) The availability of dedicated authoring tools or the demonstrated use of ML techniques to facilitate building the system.

To conclude, domain models are a key feature of many AIED systems. They support many of the behaviors that distinguish AIED systems from other educational technologies. AIED systems use a very wide range of AI knowledge representations. We hope that this chapter succeeds in highlighting that great richness, as well as the many advantages that derive from having a domain model.

REFERENCES

Adadi, A., & Berrada, M. (2018). Peeking inside the black-box: A survey on explainable artificial intelligence (XAI). *IEEE Access, 6*, 52138–52160.

Adams, D. M., McLaren, B. M., Durkin, K., Mayer, R. E., Rittle-Johnson, B., Isotani, S., & van Velsen, M. (2014). Using erroneous examples to improve mathematics learning with a web-based tutoring system. *Computers in Human Behavior, 36*, 401–411.

Agrawal, R., Gollapudi, S., Kannan, A., & Kenthapadi, K. (2014). Study Navigator: An algorithmically generated aid for learning from electronic textbooks. *Journal of Educational Data Mining, 6*(1), 53–75.

Aleven, V. (2003). Using background knowledge in case-based legal reasoning: A computational model and an intelligent learning environment. *Artificial Intelligence, 150*(1–2), 183–237.

Aleven, V. (2010). Rule-based cognitive modeling for intelligent tutoring systems. In R. Nkambou, J. Bourdeau, & R. Mizoguchi (Eds.), *Advances in intelligent tutoring systems* (pp. 33–62). Berlin, Germany: Springer.

Aleven, V., Connolly, H., Popescu, O., Marks, J., Lamnina, M., & Chase, C. (2017). An adaptive coach for invention activities. *International conference on artificial intelligence in education* (pp. 3–14). Cham, Switzerland: Springer.

Aleven, V., & Koedinger, K. R. (2013). Knowledge component (KC) approaches to learner modeling. *Design Recommendations for Intelligent Tutoring Systems, 1*, 165–182.

Aleven, V., McLaren, B., Roll, I., & Koedinger, K. (2006a). Toward meta-cognitive tutoring: A model of help seeking with a Cognitive Tutor. *International Journal of Artificial Intelligence in Education, 16*(2), 101–128.

Aleven, V., McLaren, B. M., Sewall, J., & Koedinger, K. R. (2006b). The Cognitive Tutor Authoring Tools (CTAT): Preliminary evaluation of efficiency gains. *International conference on intelligent tutoring systems* (pp. 61–70). Berlin, Heidelberg, Germany: Springer.

Aleven, V., McLaren, B. M., Sewall, J., van Velsen, M., Popescu, O., Demi, S., … Koedinger, K. R. (2016). Example-tracing tutors: Intelligent tutor development for non-programmers. *International Journal of Artificial Intelligence in Education, 26*(1), 224–269. doi:10.1007/s40593-015-0088-2.

Alsaad, F., Boughoula, A., Geigle, C., Sundaram, H., & Zhai, C. (2018). Mining MOOC lecture transcripts to construct concept dependency graphs. *Proceedings of the 11th International Conference on Educational Data Mining* (pp. 467–473).

Anderson, J. R. (1993). *Rules of the mind*. Hillsdale, NJ: Erlbaum.

Anderson, J. R., Conrad, F. G., & Corbett, A. T. (1989). Skill acquisition and the LISP tutor. *Cognitive Science, 13*(4), 467–505.

Anderson, J. R., Conrad, F. G., Corbett, A.T., Fincham, J.M., Hoffman, D., & Wu, Q. (1993). Computer programming and transfer. In J. R. Anderson (Ed.), *Rules of the mind* (pp. 205–233). Hillsdale, NJ: Lawrence Erlbaum Associates.

Anderson, J. R., Corbett, A. T., Koedinger, K. R., & Pelletier, R. (1995). Cognitive tutors: Lessons learned. *The Journal of the Learning Sciences, 4*(2), 167–207.

Arasasingham, R. D., Martorell, I., & McIntire, T. M. (2011). Online homework and student achievement in a large enrollment introductory science course. *Journal of College Science Teaching, 40*, 70–79.

Arasasingham, R. D., Taagepera, M., Potter, F., Martorell, I., & Lonjers, S. (2005). Assessing the effect of web-based learning tools on student understanding of stoichiometry using knowledge space theory. *Journal of Chemical Education, 82*, 1251–1262.

Arroyo, I., Woolf, B. P., Burelson, W., Muldner, K., Rai, D., & Tai, M. (2014). A multimedia adaptive tutoring system for mathematics that addresses cognition, metacognition and affect. *International Journal of Artificial Intelligence in Education, 24*(4), 387–426.

Ausin, M. S., Maniktala, M., Barnes, T., & Chi, M. (2020). Exploring the impact of simple explanations and agency on batch deep reinforcement learning induced pedagogical policies. In I. I. Bittencourt, M. Cukurova, K. Muldner, R. Luckin & E. Millán (Eds.), *Proceedings of the International Conference on Artificial Intelligence in Education* (pp. 472–485). Cham, Switzerland: Springer.

Baghaei, N., Mitrovic, A., & Irwin, W. (2007). Supporting collaborative learning and problem-solving in a constraint-based CSCL environment for UML class diagrams. *International Journal of Computer-Supported Collaborative Learning, 2*(2), 159–190.

Baker, R., Corbett, A., & Aleven, V. (2008). More accurate student modeling through contextual estimation of slip and guess probabilities in Bayesian knowledge tracing. *International Conference on Intelligent Tutoring Systems* (pp. 406–415). Berlin, Heidelberg, Germany: Springer.

Baker, R., Corbett, A. T., & Koedinger, K. R. (2007). The difficulty factors approach to the design of lessons in intelligent tutor curricula. *International Journal of Artificial Intelligence in Education*, *17*(4), 341–369.

Baker, R., Mitrovic, A., & Mathews, M. (2010). Detecting gaming the system in constraint-based tutors. In de Bra, P., Kobsa, A., Chin, D. (Eds.), *Proceedings of the 18th International Conference on User Modeling, Adaptation, and Personalization* (pp. 267–278). Berlin, Heidelberg, Germany: Springer.

Barnes, T., & Stamper, J. (2008). Toward automatic hint generation for logic proof tutoring using historical student data. In Woolf, B., Aïmeur, E., Nkambou, R., Lajoie, S. (Eds.), *Proceedings of the 9th International Conference on Intelligent Tutoring Systems* (pp. 373–382). Berlin, Heidelberg, Germany: Springer.

Beck, J. E., & Chang, K. M. (2007). Identifiability: A fundamental problem of student modeling. *International Conference on User Modeling* (pp. 137–146). Berlin, Heidelberg, Germany: Springer.

Beck, J., Woolf, B. P., & Beal, C. R. (2000). ADVISOR: A machine learning architecture for intelligent tutor construction. In H. Kautz & B. Porter (Eds.), *Proceedings of the 17th National Conference on Artificial Intelligence* (pp. 552–557). Menlo Park, CA: AAAI.

Bishop, C. M. (2006). *Pattern recognition and machine learning*. New York: Springer.

Biswas, G., Leelawong, K., Schwartz, D., Vye, N., & The Teachable Agents Group at Vanderbilt. (2005). Learning by teaching: A new agent paradigm for educational software. *Applied Artificial Intelligence*, *19*(3–4), 363–392.

Biswas, G., Segedy, J. R., & Bunchongchit, K. (2016). From design to implementation to practice a learning by teaching system: Betty's Brain. *International Journal of Artificial Intelligence in Education*, *26*(1), 350–364.

Boroš, P., Nižnan, J., Pelánek, R., & Řihák, J. (2013). Automatic detection of concepts from problem solving times. *Proceedings of 16th International Conference on Artificial Intelligence in Education* (pp. 595–598).

Bredeweg, B., & Forbus, K. D. (2016). Qualitative representations for education. In R. A. Sottilare et al. (Eds.), *Design recommendations for intelligent tutoring systems: Volume 4—Domain modeling* (pp. 57–68). Orlando, FL: US Army Research Laboratory.

Bredeweg, B., Liem, J., Beek, W., Linnebank, F., Gracia, J., Lozano, E., ... & Mioduser, D. (2013). DynaLearn–An intelligent learning environment for learning conceptual knowledge. *AI Magazine*, *34*(4), 46–65.

Burton, R. R., & Brown, J. S. (1982). An investigation of computer coaching for informal learning activities. In R. R. Burton, J. S. Brown & D. Sleeman (Eds.), *Intelligent Tutoring Systems* (pp. 79–98). New York: Academic Press.

Brownston, L., Farrell, R., Kant, E., & Martin, N. (1985). *Programming expert systems in OPS5: An introduction to rule-based programming*. Addison-Wesley Longman.

Brusilovsky, P., & Eklund, J. (1998). A study of user model based link annotation in educational hypermedia. *Journal of Universal Computer Science*, *4*(4), 429–448.

Brusilovsky, P., & Henze, N. (2007). Open corpus adaptive educational hypermedia. *The adaptive web* (pp. 671–696). Berlin, Heidelberg, Germany: Springer.

Brusilovsky, P., & Pesin, L. (1998). Adaptive navigation support in educational hypermedia: An evaluation of the ISIS-Tutor. *Journal of Computing and Information Technology*, *6*(1), 27–38.

Brusilovsky, P., Schwarz, E., & Weber, G. (1996). ELM-ART: An intelligent tutoring system on the world-wide web. In C. Frasson, G. Gauthier, & A. Lesgold (Eds.), *The Third International Conference on Intelligent Tutoring Systems* (pp. 261–269). Springer.

Burns, H., & Capps, C. (1988). Foundations of Intelligent Tutoring Systems: An introduction. In M. Polson & J. Richardson (Eds.), *Foundations of Intelligent Tutoring Systems* (pp. 1–19). Hillsdale, NJ: Lawrence Erlbaum Associates.

Carmona, C., Millán, E., Pérez-de-la-Cruz, J. L., Trella, M., & Conejo, R. (2005). Introducing prerequisite relations in a multi-layered Bayesian student model. *International Conference on User Modeling* (pp. 347–356). Berlin, Heidelberg, Germany: Springer.

Cen, H., Koedinger, K., & Junker, B. (2006). Learning Factors Analysis–A general method for cognitive model evaluation and improvement. *Proceedings of the 8th International Conference on Intelligent Tutoring Systems* (pp. 164–175). Berlin, Heidelberg, Germany: Springer.

Chandrashekar, G., & Sahin, F. (2014). A survey on feature selection methods. *Computers & Electrical Engineering*, *40*(1), 16–28.

Chaplot, D. S., MacLellan, C., Salakhutdinov, R., & Koedinger, K. (2018). Learning cognitive models using neural networks. *Proceedings of the 19th International Conference on Artificial Intelligence in Education* (pp. 43–56). Cham, Switzerland: Springer.

Chaplot, D. S., Yang, Y., Carbonell, J., & Koedinger, K. R. (2016). Data-driven automated induction of prerequisite structure graphs. *Proceedings of the 9th International Conference on Educational Data Mining* (pp. 318–323). Raleigh, NC.

Chau, H., Labutov, I., Thaker, K., He, D., & Brusilovsky, P. (2020). Automatic concept extraction for domain and student modeling in adaptive textbooks. *International Journal of Artificial Intelligence in Education*, *31*(4), 820–846.

Chen, Y., González-Brenes, J. P., & Tian, J. (2016). Joint discovery of skill prerequisite graphs and student models. *Proceedings of the 9th International Conference on Educational Data Mining* (pp. 46–53).

Chen, P., Lu, Y., Zheng, V. W., Chen, X., & Li, X. (2018). An automatic knowledge graph construction system for K-12 education. *Proceedings of the Fifth Annual ACM Conference on Learning at Scale* (pp. 1–4). London, United Kingdom.

Chen, X., Mitrovic, A., & Mathews, M. (2020). Learning from worked examples, erroneous examples, and problem solving: Toward adaptive selection of learning activities. *IEEE Transactions on Learning Technologies*, *13*(1), 135–149.

Clark, R. E., Feldon, D., van Merriënboer, J., Yates, K., & Early, S. (2007). Cognitive task analysis. In J. M. Spector, M. D. Merrill, J. J. G. van Merriënboer & M. P. Driscoll (Eds.), *Handbook of research on educational communications and technology* (3rd ed., pp. 577–593). Lawrence Erlbaum Associates.

Collins, J., Greer, J., & Huang, S. (1996). Adaptive assessment using granularity hierarchies and Bayesian Nets. In C. Frasson, G. Gauthier & A. Lesgold (Eds.), *Proceedings of the 3rd International Conference on Intelligent Tutoring Systems* (pp. 569–577). Springer-Verlag.

Conati, C., Gertner, A. & VanLehn, K. (2002). Using Bayesian networks to manage uncertainty in student modeling. *User Modeling and User-Adapted Interaction*, *12*(4), 371–417.

Conati, C., & VanLehn, K. (2000). Toward computer-based support of meta-cognitive skills: A computational framework to coach self-explanation. *International Journal of Artificial Intelligence in Education*, *11*, 389–415.

Corbett, A., & Anderson, J. R. (1995). Knowledge tracing: Modeling the acquisition of procedural knowledge. *User modeling and user-adapted interaction*, *4*(4), 253–278.

Corbett, A., Kauffman, L., MacLaren, B., Wagner, A., & Jones, E. (2010). A cognitive tutor for genetics problem solving: Learning gains and student modeling. *Journal of Educational Computing Research*, *42*(2), 219–239.

Corbett, A., McLaughlin, M., & Scarpinatto, K. C. (2000). Modeling student knowledge: Cognitive tutors in high school and college. *User Modeling and User-Adapted Interaction*, *10*(2), 81–108.

Crowley, R., & Medvedeva, O. (2006). An intelligent tutoring system for visual classification problem solving. *Artificial Intelligence in Medicine*, *36*(1), 85–117.

Crowley, R., Medvedeva, O., & Jukic, D. (2003). SlideTutor: A model-tracing intelligent tutoring system for teaching microscopic diagnosis. *Proceedings of the 11th International Conference on Artificial Intelligence in Education* (pp. 157–164).

Davidovic, A., Warren, J., & Trichina, E. (2003). Learning benefits of structural example-based adaptive tutoring systems. *IEEE Transactions on Education*, *46*(2), 241–251.

Davis, R., & King, J. J. (1984). The origin of rule-based systems in AI. In B. G. Buchanan & E. H. Shortliffe (Eds.), *Rule-based expert systems: The MYCIN experiments of the Stanford Heuristic Programming Project* (pp. 20–51). Boston, MA: Addison-Wesley.

Desmarais, M. C., & Baker, R. S. (2012). A review of recent advances in learner and skill modeling in intelligent learning environments. *User Modeling and User-Adapted Interaction*, *22*(1–2), 9–38.

Desmarais, M. C., Meshkinfam, P., & Gagnon, M. (2006). Learned student models with item to item knowledge structures. *User Modeling and User-Adapted Interaction*, *16*(5), 403–434.

Desmarais, M. C., & Naceur, R. (2013). A matrix factorization method for mapping items to skills and for enhancing expert-based Q-matrices. *Proceedings of the 16th International Conference on Artificial Intelligence in Education* (pp. 441–450). Berlin, Heidelberg, Germany: Springer.

Desmarais, M. C. & Pu, X. (2005). A Bayesian student model without hidden nodes and its comparison with Item Response Theory. *International Journal of Artificial Intelligence in Education*, *15*, 291–323.

Dimitrova, V. (2003). STyLE-OLM: interactive open learner modelling. *International Journal of Artificial Intelligence in Education*, *13*, 35–78.

Dimitrova, V., & Brna, P. (2016). From interactive open learner modelling to intelligent mentoring: STyLE-OLM and beyond. *International Journal of Artificial Intelligence in Education*, *26*(1), 332–349.

Doignon, J. P., & Falmagne, J. C. (1985). Spaces for the assessment of knowledge. *International Journal of Man-Machine Studies*, *23*(2), 175–196.

Doignon, J. P., & Falmagne, J. C. (2012). *Knowledge spaces*. Springer Science & Business Media.

Dolog, P., & Nejdl, W. (2003). Challenges and benefits of the semantic web for user modelling. *Proceedings of the Workshop on Adaptive Hypermedia and Adaptive Web-Based Systems (AH2003) at 12th International World Wide Web Conference*. Budapest, Hungary.

Doroudi, S., Aleven, V., & Brunskill, E. (2019). Where's the reward? A review of reinforcement learning for instructional sequencing. *International Journal of Artificial Intelligence in Education*, *29*(4), 568–620.

Doroudi, S., & Brunskill, E. (2017). The misidentified identifiability problem of Bayesian knowledge tracing. In X. Hu, T. Barnes, A. Hershkovitz & L. Paquette (Eds.), *Proceedings of the 10th International Conference on Educational Data Mining* (pp. 143–149).

Ester, M., Kriegel, H., Sander, J., & Xu, X. (1996). A density-based algorithm for discovering clusters in large spatial databases with noise. In E. Simoudis, J. Han & U. Fayyad (Eds.), *Proceedings of the 2nd International Conference on Knowledge Discovery and Data Mining* (pp. 226–231). Palo Alto, CA: AAAI.

Falmagne, J. C., Cosyn, E., Doignon, J. P., & Thiéry, N. (2006). The assessment of knowledge, in theory and in practice. In R. Missaoui & J. Schmid (Eds.), *International Conference on Formal Concept Analysis (ICFCA), Lecture Notes in Computer Science* (pp. 61–79). Berlin, Heidelberg, Germany: Springer.

Fang, Y., Ren, Z., Hu, X., & Graesser, A. C. (2019). A meta-analysis of the effectiveness of ALEKS on learning. *Educational Psychology*, *39*(10), 1278–1292.

Ganeshan, R., Johnson, W. L., Shaw, E., & Wood, B. P. (2000). Tutoring diagnostic problem solving. In G. Gauthier, C. Frasson & K. VanLehn (Eds.), *Proceedings of the 5th International Conference on Intelligent Tutoring Systems* (pp. 33–42). Berlin, Heidelberg, Germany: Springer.

Gardner, J., Brooks, C., & Baker, R. (2019). Evaluating the fairness of predictive student models through slicing analysis. *Proceedings of the 9th International Conference on Learning Analytics & Knowledge* (pp. 225–234). New York: ACM.

Gasparetti, F., Limongelli, C., & Sciarrone, F. (2015). Exploiting Wikipedia for discovering prerequisite relationships among learning objects. *International Conference on Information Technology Based Higher Education and Training (ITHET)* (pp. 1–6).

Gauthier, G., Lajoie, S., Richard, S. & Wiseman, J. (2007). Mapping and validating diagnostic reasoning through interactive case creation. In T. Bastiaens & S. Carliner (Eds.), *Proceedings of E-Learn 2007—World Conference on E-Learning in Corporate, Government, Healthcare, and Higher Education* (pp. 2553–2562). Quebec City, Canada: Association for the Advancement of Computing in Education (AACE).

Geden, M., Emerson, A., Carpenter, D., Rowe, J., Azevedo, R., & Lester, J. (2021). Predictive student modeling in game-based learning environments with word embedding representations of reflection. *International Journal of Artificial Intelligence in Education*, *31*(1), 1–23.

Glassman, E. L., & Miller, R. C. (2016). Leveraging learners for teaching programming and hardware design at scale. *Proceedings of the 19th ACM Conference on Computer Supported Cooperative Work and Social Computing Companion* (pp. 37–40).

Gobert, J. D., Pedro, M. S., Raziuddin, J., & Baker, R. S. (2013). From log files to assessment metrics: Measuring students' science inquiry skills using educational data mining. *Journal of the Learning Sciences, 22*(4), 521–563.

Goguadze, G., Sosnovsky, S. A., Isotani, S., & McLaren, B. M. (2011). Evaluating a Bayesian student model of decimal misconceptions. *International Conference on Educational Data Mining* (pp. 301–306).

González-Brenes, J., Huang, Y., & Brusilovsky, P. (2014). General features in knowledge tracing to model multiple subskills, temporal item response theory, and expert knowledge. *Proceedings of the 7th International Conference on Educational Data Mining* (pp. 84–91).

Ha, E. Y., Rowe, J., Mott, B., & Lester, J. (2011). Goal recognition with Markov logic networks for player-adaptive games. *Proceedings of the 7th Annual AAAI Conference on Artificial Intelligence and Interactive Digital Entertainment* (pp. 32–39). Menlo Park, CA: AAAI.

Hagemans, M. G., van der Meij, H., & de Jong, T. (2013). The effects of a concept map-based support tool on simulation-based inquiry learning. *Journal of Educational Psychology, 105*(1), 1–24.

Hall, M., Frank, E., Holmes, G., Pfahringer, B., Reutemann, P., & Witten, I. H. (2009). The WEKA data mining software: An update. *ACM SIGKDD Explorations Newsletter, 11*(1), 10–18.

Heffernan, N. T., & Heffernan, C. L. (2014). The ASSISTments ecosystem: Building a platform that brings scientists and teachers together for minimally invasive research on human learning and teaching. *International Journal of Artificial Intelligence in Education, 24*(4), 470–497.

Heffernan, N. T., Koedinger, K. R., & Razzaq, L. (2008). Expanding the model-tracing architecture: A 3rd generation intelligent tutor for algebra symbolization. *International Journal of Artificial Intelligence in Education, 18*(2), 153–178.

Heffernan, N. T., Ostrow, K. S., Kelly, K., Selent, D., van Inwegen, E. G., Xiong, X., & Williams, J. J. (2016). The future of adaptive learning: Does the crowd hold the key? *International Journal of Artificial Intelligence in Education, 26*(2), 615–644.

Heller, J., Steiner, C., Hockemeyer, C., & Albert, D. (2006). Competence-based knowledge structures for personalised learning. *International Journal on E-learning, 5*(1), 75–88.

Henze, N., & Nejdl, W. (1999). Adaptivity in the KBS hyperbook system. *The 2nd Workshop on Adaptive Systems and User Modeling on the WWW.*

Holmes, W., Bialik, M., & Fadel, C. (2019). *Artificial intelligence in education: Promises and implications for teaching and Learning.* Boston, MA: The Center for Curriculum Redesign.

Huang, Y. (2018). *Learner modeling for integration skills in programming* (Doctoral dissertation). University of Pittsburgh, Pittsburgh, PA.

Huang, Y., González-Brenes, J. P., & Brusilovsky, P. (2015). Challenges of using observational data to determine the importance of example usage. *International Conference on Artificial Intelligence in Education* (pp. 633–637). Cham, Switzerland: Springer.

Huang, Y., González-Brenes, J. P., Kumar, R., & Brusilovsky, P. (2015). A framework for multifaceted evaluation of student models. *Proceedings of the 8th International Conference on Educational Data Mining* (pp. 203–210).

Huang, Y., Guerra-Hollstein, J. P., Barria-Pineda, J., & Brusilovsky, P. (2017). Learner modeling for integration skills. *Proceedings of the 25th Conference on User Modeling, Adaptation and Personalization* (pp. 85–93).

Huang, Y., Lobczowski, N. G., Richey, J. E., McLaughlin, E. A., Asher, M. W., Harackiewicz, J., … Koedinger, K. R. (2021). A general multi-method approach to data-driven redesign of tutoring systems. *Proceedings of the 11th International Conference on Learning Analytics and Knowledge* (pp. 161–172).

Huang, Y., Yudelson, M., Han, S., He, D., & Brusilovsky, P. (2016). A framework for dynamic knowledge modeling in textbook-based learning. *Proceedings of the 2016 conference on User Modeling, Adaptation and Personalization* (pp. 141–150).

Jiang, Y., Bosch, N., Baker, R. S., Paquette, L., Ocumpaugh, J., Andres, J. M. A. L., … Biswas, G. (2018). Expert feature-engineering vs. deep neural networks: Which is better for sensor-free affect detection? *Proceedings of the 19th International Conference on Artificial Intelligence in Education* (pp. 198–211). Springer, Cham.

Joyner, D. A., Majerich, D. M., & Goel, A. K. (2013). Facilitating authentic reasoning about complex systems in middle school science education. *Procedia Computer Science, 16*, 1043–1052.

Käser, T., Klingler, S., Schwing, A. G., & Gross, M. (2014). Beyond knowledge tracing: Modeling skill topologies with Bayesian networks. *International Conference on Intelligent Tutoring Systems* (pp. 188–198).

Käser, T., & Schwartz, D. L. (2020). Modeling and analyzing inquiry strategies in open-ended learning environments. *International Journal of Artificial Intelligence in Education*, *30*(3), 504–535.

Kavcic, A. (2004). Fuzzy user modeling for adaptation in educational hypermedia. *IEEE Transactions on Systems, Man, and Cybernetics, Part C (Applications and Reviews)*, *34*(4), 439–449.

Kelly, D. P., & Rutherford, T. (2017). Khan Academy as supplemental instruction: A controlled study of a computer-based mathematics intervention. *The International Review of Research in Open and Distributed Learning*, *18*(4). doi: 10.19173/irrodl.v18i4.2984

Kim, J. (2015). *Learnersourcing: Improving learning with collective learner activity* (Doctoral dissertation). Massachusetts Institute of Technology, Cambridge, MA.

Kinnebrew, J. S., Loretz, K. M., & Biswas, G. (2013). A contextualized, differential sequence mining method to derive students' learning behavior patterns. *Journal of Educational Data Mining*, *5*(1), 190–219.

Kluger, A. N., & DeNisi, A. (1996). The effects of feedback interventions on performance: A historical review, a meta-analysis, and a preliminary feedback intervention theory. *Psychological Bulletin*, *119*(2), 254.

Koedinger, K. R., & Aleven, V. (2007). Exploring the assistance dilemma in experiments with Cognitive Tutors. *Educational Psychology Review*, *19*(3), 239–264.

Koedinger, K. R., & Aleven, V. (2021). Multimedia learning with cognitive tutors. To appear in R. E. Mayer & L. Fiorella (Eds.), *The Cambridge handbook of multimedia learning* (3rd ed). Cambridge, UK: Cambridge University Press.

Koedinger, K. R., Aleven, V., & Heffernan, N. (2003). Toward a rapid development environment for Cognitive Tutors. *Proceedings of the International Conference on Artificial Intelligence in Education* (pp. 455–457).

Koedinger, K. R., Baker, R. S., Cunningham, K., Skogsholm, A., Leber, B., & Stamper, J. (2010). A data repository for the EDM community: The PSLC DataShop. *Handbook of Educational Data Mining*, *43*, 43–56.

Koedinger, K. R., Brunskill, E., Baker, R. S., McLaughlin, E. A., & Stamper, J. (2013). New potentials for data-driven intelligent tutoring system development and optimization. *AI Magazine*, *34*(3), 27–41.

Koedinger, K. R., & Corbett, A. T. (2006). Cognitive Tutors: Technology bringing learning sciences to the classroom. In R. K. Sawyer (Ed.), *The Cambridge handbook of the learning sciences* (pp. 61–78). New York: Cambridge University Press.

Koedinger, K. R., Corbett, A. T., & Perfetti, C. (2012). The Knowledge-Learning-Instruction framework: Bridging the science-practice chasm to enhance robust student learning. *Cognitive Science*, *36*(5), 757–798.

Koedinger, K., Liu, R., Stamper, J., Thille, C., & Pavlik, P. (2017). Community based educational data repositories and analysis tools. *Proceedings of the Seventh International Conference on Learning Analytics & Knowledge* (pp. 524–525).

Koedinger, K., & McLaughlin, E. (2010). Seeing language learning inside the math: Cognitive analysis yields transfer. *Proceedings of the Annual Meeting of the Cognitive Science Society*, *32*(32), 471–476.

Koedinger, K. R., McLaughlin, E. A., & Stamper, J. C. (2012). Automated student model improvement. *Proceedings of the 5th International Conference on Educational Data Mining* (pp. 17–24).

Koedinger, K.R., Stamper, J.C., McLaughlin, E.A., & Nixon, T. (2013). Using data-driven discovery of better student models to improve student learning. In H.C. Lane, K. Yacef, J. Mostow & P. Pavlik (Eds.), *International Conference on Artificial Intelligence in Education* (pp. 421–430). Berlin, Heidelberg, Germany: Springer.

Kotu, V., & Deshpande, B. (2014). *Predictive analytics and data mining: Concepts and practice with rapidminer*. Morgan Kaufmann.

Labutov, I., Huang, Y., Brusilovsky, P., & He, D. (2017). Semi-supervised techniques for mining learning outcomes and prerequisites. *Proceedings of the 23rd ACM SIGKDD International Conference on Knowledge Discovery and Data Mining* (pp. 907–915).

Lenat, D. B., & Durlach, P. J. (2014). Reinforcing math knowledge by immersing students in a simulated learning-by-teaching experience. *International Journal of Artificial Intelligence in Education*, *24*(3), 216–250.

Lindsey, R. V., Khajah, M., & Mozer, M. C. (2014). Automatic discovery of cognitive skills to improve the prediction of student learning. In Z. Ghahramani, M. Welling, C. Cortes, N. Lawrence & K.

Q. Weinberger (Eds.), *Proceedings of the 28th International Conference on Advances in Neural Information Processing Systems* (pp. 1386–1394).

Li, H., Gobert, J., Dickler, R., & Moussavi, R. (2018). The impact of multiple real-time scaffolding experiences on science inquiry practices. *International Conference on Intelligent Tutoring Systems* (pp. 99–109). Springer, Cham.

Li, N., Matsuda, N., Cohen, W. W., & Koedinger, K. R. (2015). Integrating representation learning and skill learning in a human-like intelligent agent. *Artificial Intelligence, 219*, 67–91.

Liu, C., Kim, J., & Wang, H. C. (2018). Conceptscape: Collaborative concept mapping for video learning. *Proceedings of the 2018 CHI Conference on Human Factors in Computing Systems* (pp. 1–12).

Liu, R., & Koedinger, K. R. (2017). Closing the loop: Automated data-driven cognitive model discoveries lead to improved instruction and learning gains. *Journal of Educational Data Mining, 9*(1), 25–41.

Livieris, I. E., Drakopoulou, K., Tampakas, V. T., Mikropoulos, T. A., & Pintelas, P. (2019). Predicting secondary school students' performance utilizing a semi-supervised learning approach. *Journal of Educational Computing Research, 57*(2), 448–470.

Lodder, J., Heeren, B., Jeuring, J., & Neijenhuis, W. (2021). Generation and use of hints and feedback in a Hilbert-style axiomatic proof tutor. *International Journal of Artificial Intelligence in Education, 31*(1), 99–133.

Long, Y., & Aleven, V. (2014). Gamification of joint student/system control over problem selection in a linear equation tutor. In S. Trausan-Matu, K. E. Boyer, M. Crosby, & K. Panourgia (Eds.), *Proceedings of the 12th International Conference on Intelligent Tutoring Systems, ITS 2014* (pp. 378–387). New York: Springer.

Lovett, M. C. (1998). Cognitive task analysis in service of intelligent tutoring system design: A case study in statistics. In *International Conference on Intelligent Tutoring Systems* (pp. 234–243). Berlin, Heidelberg, Germany: Springer.

Lynch, C., Ashley, K. D., Pinkwart, N., & Aleven, V. (2009). Concepts, structures, and goals: Redefining ill-definedness. *International Journal of Artificial Intelligence in Education, 19*(3), 253–266.

MacLellan, C. J., & Koedinger, K. R. (2020). Domain-general tutor authoring with Apprentice Learner models. *International Journal of Artificial Intelligence in Education*.

Martinez-Maldonado, R., Clayphan, A., Yacef, K., & Kay, J. (2014). MTFeedback: Providing notifications to enhance teacher awareness of small group work in the classroom. *IEEE Transactions on Learning Technologies, 8*(2), 187–200.

Martínez-Maldonado, R., Kay, J., & Yacef, K. (2010, November). Collaborative concept mapping at the tabletop. In *ACM International Conference on Interactive Tabletops and Surfaces* (pp. 207–210).

Mathan, S. A., & Koedinger, K. R. (2005). Fostering the intelligent novice: Learning from errors with metacognitive tutoring. *Educational Psychologist, 40*(4), 257–265.

Matsuda, N., Cohen, W. W., & Koedinger, K. R. (2015). Teaching the teacher: Tutoring SimStudent leads to more effective cognitive tutor authoring. *International Journal of Artificial Intelligence in Education, 25*(1), 1–34.

Matsuda, N., Furukawa, T., Bier, N., & Faloutsos, C. (2015). Machine beats experts: Automatic discovery of skill models for data-driven online course refinement. *Proceedings of the 8th International Conference on Educational Data Mining* (pp. 101–108).

Matsuda, N., Weng, W., & Wall, N. (2020). The effect of metacognitive scaffolding for learning by teaching a teachable agent. *International Journal of Artificial Intelligence in Education*, 1–37.

Matsuda, N., Yarzebinski, E., Keiser, V., Raizada, R., Cohen, W. W., Stylianides, G. J., & Koedinger, K. R. (2013). Cognitive anatomy of tutor learning: Lessons learned with SimStudent. *Journal of Educational Psychology, 105*(4), 1152–1163.

Mayo, M., & Mitrovic, A., (2001) Optimising ITS behaviour with Bayesian networks and decision theory. *International Journal on Artificial Intelligence in Education, 12*(2), 124–153.

McKendree, J. (1990). Effective feedback content for tutoring complex skills. *Human-Computer Interaction, 5*(4), 381–413.

McLaren, B. M., van Gog, T., Ganoe, C., Karabinos, M., & Yaron, D. (2016). The efficiency of worked examples compared to erroneous examples, tutored problem solving, and problem solving in computer-based learning environments. *Computers in Human Behavior, 55*, 87–99.

Means, B., & Gott, S. P. (1988). Cognitive task analysis as a basis for tutor development: Articulating abstract knowledge representations. In J. Psotka, L. D. Massey & S. A. Mutter (Eds.), *Intelligent tutoring systems: Lessons learned* (pp. 35–57). Lawrence Erlbaum Associates.

Melis, E., Andres, E., Büdenbender, J., Frischauf, A., Goguadze, G., Libbrecht, P., ... & Ullrich, C. (2001). ActiveMath: A generic and adaptive web-based learning environment. *International Journal of Artificial Intelligence in Education*, *12*(4), 385–407.

Michalenko, J. J., Lan, A. S., & Baraniuk, R. G. (2017). Data-mining textual responses to uncover misconception patterns. *Proceedings of the Fourth ACM Conference on Learning @ Scale* (pp. 245–248).

Millán, E., Loboda, T., & Pérez-De-La-Cruz, J. L. (2010). Bayesian networks for student model engineering. *Computers & Education*, *55*(4), 1663–1683.

Millán, E., & Pérez-de-la Cruz, J.-L. (2002). A Bayesian diagnostic algorithm for student modeling and its evaluation. *User Modeling and User-Adapted Interaction*, *12*(2), 281–330.

Min, W., Frankosky, M., Mott, B., Rowe, J., Smith, A., Wiebe, E., ... Lester, J. (2020). DeepStealth: Game-based learning stealth assessment with deep neural networks. *IEEE Transactions on Learning Technologies*, *13*(2), 312–325.

Min, W., Mott, B., Rowe, J., Liu, B., & Lester, J. (2016). Player goal recognition in open-world digital games with long short-term memory networks. *Proceedings of the 25th International Joint Conference on Artificial Intelligence* (pp. 2590–2596).

Mislevy, R. J., & Gitomer, D. H. (1995). The role of probability-based inference in an intelligent tutoring system. *ETS Research Report Series*, *1995*(2), i-27.

Mitrovic, A. (1998). Experiences in implementing constraint-based modeling in SQL-Tutor. In B. Goettl, H. Halff, C. Redfield & V. Shute (Eds.), *Proceedings of the International Conference on Intelligent Tutoring Systems* (pp. 414–423). Springer.

Mitrovic, A. (2003). An intelligent SQL tutor on the Web. *International Journal of Artificial Intelligence in Education*, *13*(2–4), 173–197.

Mitrovic, A. (2010). Modeling domains and students with constraint-based modeling. In R. Nkambou, J. Bordeaux & R. Mizoguchi (Eds.), *Advances in Intelligent Tutoring Systems. Studies in Computational Intelligence* (pp. 63–80). Berlin, Heidelberg, Germany: Springer.

Mitrovic, A. (2012). Fifteen years of constraint-based tutors: What we have achieved and where we are going. *User Modeling and User-Adapted Interaction*, *22*(1–2), 39–72.

Mitrovic, A., Koedinger, K., & Martin, B. (2003). A comparative analysis of cognitive tutoring and constraint-based modelling. In P. Brusilovsky, A. Corbett & F. de Rosis (Eds.), *Proceedings of the 9th International Conference on User Modeling* (pp. 313–322). Berlin, Heidelberg, Germany: Springer.

Mitrovic, A., Martin, B., Suraweera, P., Zakharov, K., Milik, N., Holland, J., & McGuigan, N. (2009). ASPIRE: An authoring system and deployment environment for constraint-based tutors. *International Journal of Artificial Intelligence in Education*, *19*(2), 155–188.

Mitrovic, A., Mathews, M., Ohlsson, S., Holland, J., & McKinlay, A. (2016). Computer-based post-stroke rehabilitation of prospective memory. *Journal of Applied Research in Memory and Cognition*, *5*(2), 204–214.

Mitrovic, A., & Ohlsson, S. (1999). Evaluation of a constraint-based tutor for a database language. *International Journal of Artificial Intelligence in Education*, *10*(3–4), 238–256.

Mitrovic, A., & Ohlsson, S. (2006). Constraint-based knowledge representation for individualized instruction. *Computer Science and Information Systems*, *3*(1), 1–22.

Mitrovic, A., Ohlsson, S., & Barrow, D. (2013). The effect of positive feedback in a constraint-based intelligent tutoring system. *Computers & Education*, *60*(1), 264–272.

Mitrovic, A., & Weerasinghe, A. (2009). Revisiting the ill-definedness and consequences for ITSs. In V. Dimitrova, R. Mizoguchi, B. du Boulay, A. Graesser (Eds.), *Proceedings of the 14th International Conference on Artificial Intelligence in Education* (pp. 375–382).

Moore, S., Nguyen, H. A., & Stamper, J. (2020). Towards crowdsourcing the identification of knowledge components. *Proceedings of the Seventh ACM Conference on Learning@ Scale* (pp. 245–248).

Mott, B., Lee, S., & Lester, J. (2006). Probabilistic goal recognition in interactive narrative environments. In Gil, Y. & Mooney, R. (Eds.), *Proceedings of the Twenty-First National Conference on Artificial Intelligence* (pp. 187–192).

Murray, R. C., VanLehn, K., & Mostow, J. (2004). Looking ahead to select tutorial actions: A decision-theoretic approach. *International Journal of Artificial Intelligence in Education*, *14*(3, 4), 235–278.

Newell, A., & Simon, H. A. (1972). *Human problem solving*. Englewood Cliffs, NJ: Prentice-Hall.

Novak, J. D. (1996). Concept mapping: A tool for improving science teaching and learning. *Improving Teaching and Learning in Science and Mathematics*, 32–43.

Ohlsson, S. (1996). Learning from performance errors. *Psychological Review*, *103*(2), 241.

Ohlsson, S., & Mitrovic, A. (2007). Fidelity and efficiency of knowledge representations for intelligent tutoring systems. *Technology, Instruction, Cognition and Learning*, *5*(2), 101–132.

Olsen, J. K., Rummel, N., & Aleven, V. (2019). It is not either or: An initial investigation into combining collaborative and individual learning using an ITS. *International Journal of Computer-Supported Collaborative Learning*, *14*(3), 353–381.

Pane, J. F., Griffin, B. A., McCaffrey, D. F., & Karam, R. (2014). Effectiveness of Cognitive Tutor Algebra I at scale. *Educational Evaluation and Policy Analysis*, *36*(2), 127–144.

Pane, J. F., McCaffrey, D. F., Slaughter, M. E., Steele, J. L., & Ikemoto, G. S. (2010). An experiment to evaluate the efficacy of cognitive tutor geometry. *Journal of Research on Educational Effectiveness*, *3*(3), 254–281.

Paquette, L., & Baker, R. (2019). Comparing machine learning to knowledge engineering for student behavior modeling: A case study in gaming the system. *Interactive Learning Environments*, *27*(5–6), 585–597.

Pardos, Z. A., & Dadu, A. (2017). Imputing KCs with representations of problem content and context. *Proceedings of the 25th Conference on User Modeling, Adaptation and Personalization* (pp. 148–155).

Pardos, Z. A., Heffernan, N. T., Anderson, B., & Heffernan, C. L. (2006). Using fine-grained skill models to fit student performance with Bayesian networks. *Proceedings of the Workshop in Educational Data Mining held at the 8th International Conference on Intelligent Tutoring Systems*. Taiwan, China.

Park, D. H., Hendricks, L. A., Akata, Z., Rohrbach, A., Schiele, B., Darrell, T., & Rohrbach, M. (2018). Multimodal explanations: Justifying decisions and pointing to the evidence. *Proceedings of the IEEE Conference on Computer Vision and Pattern Recognition* (pp. 8779–8788).

Pavlik, P.I ., Brawner, K., Olney, A., & Mitrovic, A. (2013). A review of student models used in intelligent tutoring systems. In R. A. Sottilare, A. Graesser, X. Hu & H. Holden (Eds), *Design Recommendations for Intelligent Tutoring Systems*, *1*, 39–68. Orlando, FL: US Army Research Laboratory.

Pearl, J. (1988). *Probabilistic reasoning in intelligent systems: Networks of plausible inference*. Morgan Kaufmann.

Pelánek, R. (2017). Bayesian knowledge tracing, logistic models, and beyond: An overview of learner modeling techniques. *User Modeling and User-Adapted Interaction*, *27*(3–5), 313–350.

Pinkwart, N., Ashley, K., Lynch, C., & Aleven, V. (2009). Evaluating an intelligent tutoring system for making legal arguments with hypotheticals. *International Journal of Artificial Intelligence in Education*, *19*(4), 401–424.

Quinlan, J. R. (1993). *C4.5: Programs for machine learning*. San Mateo, CA: Morgan Kaufmann.

Rafferty, A. N., & Griffiths, T. L. (2015). Interpreting freeform equation solving. *Proceedings of the 17th International Conference on Artificial Intelligence in Education* (pp. 387–397). Springer, Cham.

Rafferty, A. N., Jansen, R., & Griffiths, T. L. (2016). Using inverse planning for personalized feedback. In T. Barnes, M. Chi & M. Feng (Eds.), *Proceedings of the 9th International Conference on Educational Data Mining* (pp. 472–477).

Reilly, J. M., & Dede, C. (2019). Differences in student trajectories via filtered time series analysis in an immersive virtual world. *Proceedings of the 9th International Conference on Learning Analytics & Knowledge* (pp. 130–134).

Reye, J. (1996). A belief net backbone for student modelling. *Proceedings of the International Conference on Intelligent Tutoring Systems* (pp. 596–604). Berlin, Heidelberg, Germany: Springer.

Ritter, S. (1997). Communication, cooperation and competition among multiple tutor agents. In B. du Boulay & R. Mizoguchi (Eds.), *Artificial Intelligence in Education, Proceedings of AI-ED 97 World Conference* (pp. 31–38). Amsterdam, Netherlands: IOS Press.

Ritter, S., Anderson, J. R., Koedinger, K. R., & Corbett, A. (2007). Cognitive Tutor: Applied research in mathematics education. *Psychonomic Bulletin & Review*, *14*(2), 249–255.

Rivers, K., & Koedinger, K. R. (2017). Data-driven hint generation in vast solution spaces: A self-improving Python programming tutor. *International Journal of Artificial Intelligence in Education*, *27*(1), 37–64.

Roll, I., Aleven, V., & Koedinger, K. R. (2010). The invention lab: Using a hybrid of model tracing and constraint-based modeling to offer intelligent support in inquiry environments. In *International Conference on Intelligent Tutoring Systems* (pp. 115–124). Berlin, Heidelberg, Germany: Springer.

Rosé, C. P., McLaughlin, E. A., Liu, R., & Koedinger, K. R. (2019). Explanatory learner models: Why machine learning (alone) is not the answer. *British Journal of Educational Technology, 50*(6), 2943–2958.

Rowe, J., & Lester, J. (2010). Modeling user knowledge with dynamic Bayesian networks in interactive narrative environments. *Proceedings of the Sixth Annual Artificial Intelligence and Interactive Digital Entertainment* (pp. 57–62).

Rowe, J. & Lester, J. (2015). Improving student problem solving in narrative-centered learning environments: A modular reinforcement learning framework. Proceedings *of the Seventeenth International Conference on Artificial Intelligence in Education* (pp. 419–428).

Russell, S., & Norvig, P. (2020). *Artificial intelligence: A modern approach* (Fourth Edition). Pearson.

Salden, R. J., Aleven, V., Schwonke, R., & Renkl, A. (2010). The expertise reversal effect and worked examples in tutored problem solving. *Instructional Science, 38*(3), 289–307.

Salden, R. J., Koedinger, K. R., Renkl, A., Aleven, V., & McLaren, B. M. (2010). Accounting for beneficial effects of worked examples in tutored problem solving. *Educational Psychology Review, 22*(379–392). doi: 10.1007/s10648-010-9143-6.

Sao Pedro, M. A., Baker, R., Gobert, J. D., Montalvo, O., & Nakama, A. (2013). Leveraging machine-learned detectors of systematic inquiry behavior to estimate and predict transfer of inquiry skill. *User Modeling and User-Adapted Interaction, 23*(1), 1–39.

Sawyer, R., Rowe, J., Azevedo, R., & Lester, J. (2018). Filtered time series analyses of student problem-solving behaviors in game-based learning. *Proceedings of the Eleventh International Conference on Educational Data Mining* (pp. 229–238).

Schank, R. C. (1990). Case-based teaching: Four experiences in educational software design. *Interactive Learning Environments, 1*(4), 231–253.

Schwartz, D. L., Chase, C. C., Oppezzo, M. A., & Chin, D. B. (2011). Practicing versus inventing with contrasting cases: The effects of telling first on learning and transfer. *Journal of Educational Psychology, 103*(4), 759.

Shen, S., Mostafavi, B., Barnes, T., & Chi, M. (2018). Exploring induced pedagogical strategies through a Markov decision process framework: Lessons learned. *Journal of Educational Data Mining, 10*(3), 27–68.

Shi, Y., Shah, K., Wang, W., Marwan, S., Penmetsa, P., & Price, T. (2021). Toward semi-automatic misconception discovery using code embeddings. *Proceedings of the 11th International Conference on Learning Analytics and Knowledge* (pp. 606–612).

Shute, V. J. (2008). Focus on formative feedback. *Review of Educational Research, 78*(1), 153–189.

Shute, V. J., Wang, L., Greiff, S., Zhao, W., & Moore, G. (2016). Measuring problem solving skills via stealth assessment in an engaging video game. *Computers in Human Behavior, 63*, 106–117.

Sklavakis, D., & Refanidis, I. (2013). Mathesis: An intelligent web-based algebra tutoring school. *International Journal of Artificial Intelligence in Education, 22*(4), 191–218.

Slater, S., Baker, R., Almeda, M. V., Bowers, A., & Heffernan, N. (2017). Using correlational topic modeling for automated topic identification in intelligent tutoring systems. *Proceedings of the Seventh International Learning Analytics & Knowledge Conference* (pp. 393–397).

Sleeman, D., Kelly, A. E., Martinak, R., Ward, R. D., & Moore, J. L. (1989). Studies of diagnosis and remediation with high school algebra students. *Cognitive Science, 13*(4), 551–568.

Sosnovsky, S., & Dicheva, D. (2010). Ontological technologies for user modelling. *International Journal of Metadata, Semantics and Ontologies, 5*(1), 32–71.

Sosnovsky, S., Brusilovsky, P., Yudelson, M., Mitrovic, A., Mathews. M., & Kumar, A. (2009). Semantic integration of adaptive educational systems. In T. Kuflik, S. Berkovsky, F. Carmagnola & D. Heckmann (Eds.), *Advances in Ubiquitous User Modelling: Revised Selected Papers, Springer LCNS*, 5830, 134–158.

Sosnovsky, S., Hsiao, I. H., & Brusilovsky, P. (2012). Adaptation "in the wild": Ontology-based personalization of open-corpus learning material. In *European Conference on Technology Enhanced Learning* (pp. 425–431). Berlin, Heidelberg, Germany: Springer.

Sottilare, R. A., Graesser, A. C., Hu, X., Olney, A., Nye, B., & Sinatra, A. M. (Eds.). (2016). *Design recommendations for Intelligent Tutoring Systems: Volume 4-Domain Modeling* (Vol. 4). Orlando, FL: US Army Research Laboratory.

Sowa, J. (1994). *Conceptual structures: Information processing in mind and machine.* Boston, MA: Addison-Wesley.

Stacey, K., Sonenberg, E., Nicholson, A., Boneh, T., & Steinle, V. (2003). A teaching model exploiting cognitive conflict driven by a Bayesian network. *International Conference on User Modeling* (pp. 352–362). Berlin, Heidelberg, Germany: Springer.

Stamper, J., Eagle, M., Barnes, T., & Croy, M. (2013). Experimental evaluation of automatic hint generation for a logic tutor. *International Journal of Artificial Intelligence in Education, 22*(1–2), 3–17.

Sukthankar, G., Geib, C., Bui, H. H., Pynadath, D., & Goldman, R. P. (Eds.). (2014). *Plan, activity, and intent recognition: Theory and practice.* San Francisco, CA: Morgan Kaufman.

Suraweera, P., Mitrovic, A., & Martin, B. (2010). Widening the knowledge acquisition bottleneck for constraint-based tutors. *International Journal on Artificial Intelligence in Education, 20*(2), 137–173.

Sutton, R. S., & Barto, A. G. (2018). *Reinforcement learning: An introduction.* Cambridge, MA: MIT Press.

Tatsuoka, K. K. (1983). Rule space: An approach for dealing with misconceptions based on item response theory. *Journal of Educational Measurement, 20*(4), 345–354.

Taub, M., Azevedo, R., Bradbury, A., Millar, G., & Lester, J. (2018). Using sequence mining to reveal the efficiency in scientific reasoning during STEM learning with a game-based learning environment. *Learning and Instruction, 54*, 93–103.

Thaker, K., Huang, Y., Brusilovsky, P., & Daqing, H. (2018). Dynamic knowledge modeling with heterogeneous activities for adaptive textbooks. *The 11th International Conference on Educational Data Mining* (pp. 592–595).

Tofel-Grehl, C., & Feldon, D. F. (2013). Cognitive task analysis–based training: A meta-analysis of studies. *Journal of Cognitive Engineering and Decision Making, 7*(3), 293–304.

van der Kleij, F. M., Feskens, R. C., & Eggen, T. J. (2015). Effects of feedback in a computer-based learning environment on students' learning outcomes: A meta-analysis. *Review of Educational Research, 85*(4), 475–511.

Van Engelen, J. E., & Hoos, H. H. (2020). A survey on semi-supervised learning. *Machine Learning, 109*(2), 373–440.

VanLehn, K. (1990). *Mind bugs: The origins of procedural misconceptions.* Cambridge, MA: MIT Press.

VanLehn, K. (2011). The relative effectiveness of human tutoring, intelligent tutoring systems, and other tutoring systems. *Educational Psychologist, 46*(4), 197–221.

VanLehn, K., Burkhardt, H., Cheema, S., Kang, S., Pead, D., Schoenfeld, A., & Wetzel, J. (2021). Can an orchestration system increase collaborative, productive struggle in teaching-by-eliciting classrooms? *Interactive Learning Environments, 29*(6), 987–1005.

VanLehn, K., Lynch, C., Schulze, K., Shapiro, J. A., Shelby, R., Taylor, L., ... Wintersgill, M. (2005). The Andes physics tutoring system: Lessons learned. *International Journal of Artificial Intelligence in Education, 15*(3), 147–204.

Vomlel, J. (2004). Bayesian networks in educational testing. *International Journal of Uncertainty, Fuzziness and Knowledge Based Systems, 12*, 83–100.

Von Ahn, L. (2013). Duolingo: learn a language for free while helping to translate the web. *Proceedings of the 2013 International Conference on Intelligent User Interfaces* (pp. 1–2).

Walker, E., Rummel, N., & Koedinger, K. R. (2014). Adaptive intelligent support to improve peer tutoring in algebra. *International Journal of Artificial Intelligence in Education, 24*(1), 33–61.

Wang, S., Liang, C., Wu, Z., Williams, K., Pursel, B., Brautigam, B., ... Giles, C. L. (2015). Concept hierarchy extraction from textbooks. *Proceedings of the 2015 ACM Symposium on Document Engineering* (pp. 147–156).

Weber, G., & Brusilovsky, P. (2001). ELM-ART: An adaptive versatile system for web-based instruction. *International Journal of Artificial Intelligence in Education, 12*, 351–384.

Weerasinghe, A., & Mitrovic, A. (2006). Facilitating deep learning through self-explanation in an open-ended domain. *International Journal of Knowledge-based and Intelligent Engineering Systems, 10*(1), 3–19.

Wenger, E. (1987). *Artificial intelligence and tutoring systems: Computational and cognitive approaches to the communication of knowledge.* Los Altos, CA: Morgan Kaufmann.

Weir, S., Kim, J., Gajos, K. Z., & Miller, R. C. (2015). Learnersourcing subgoal labels for how-to videos. *Proceedings of the 18th ACM Conference on Computer Supported Cooperative Work & Social Computing* (pp. 405–416).

Weitekamp, D., Harpstead, E., & Koedinger, K. R. (2020). An interaction design for machine teaching to develop AI tutors. *Proceedings of the 2020 CHI Conference on Human Factors in Computing Systems* (pp. 1–11).

Williams, J. J., Kim, J., Rafferty, A., Maldonado, S., Gajos, K. Z., Lasecki, W. S., & Heffernan, N. (2016). Axis: Generating explanations at scale with learnersourcing and machine learning. *Proceedings of the Third (2016) ACM Conference on Learning@ Scale* (pp. 379–388).

Yang, K. B., Nagashima, T., Yao, J., Williams, J. J., Holstein, K., & Aleven, V. (2021). Can crowds customize instructional materials with minimal expert guidance? Exploring teacher-guided crowdsourcing for improving hints in an AI-based tutor. *Proceedings of the ACM on Human-Computer Interaction*, *5*(CSCW1), 1–24.

Xu, Y., & Mostow, J. (2012). Comparison of methods to trace multiple subskills: Is LR-DBN best? *Proceedings of the 5th International Conference on Educational Data Mining* (pp. 41–48).

Zhi, R., Price, T. W., Marwan, S., Milliken, A., Barnes, T., & Chi, M. (2019). Exploring the impact of worked examples in a novice programming environment. *Proceedings of the 50th ACM Technical Symposium on Computer Science Education* (pp. 98–104).

8. Student modeling in open-ended learning environments

Cristina Conati and Sébastien Lallé

INTRODUCTION

There is extensive evidence that AI-based educational technology can effectively provide personalized support to help students learn problem solving skills in a variety of domains (Koedinger et al., 1997; VanLehn, 2011; Woolf, 2008). In contrast, until recently there has been little focus on AI-based environments to support educational activities that are more open-ended and exploratory in nature, such as learning from interactive simulations or playing educational games. These activities are becoming increasingly widespread, especially in the context of MOOCs (Massive Open On-Line Courses) and other forms of self-directed learning, because they can increase motivation and foster grounded skills acquisition. However, not all students have the cognitive and metacognitive skills to learn effectively from these activities, calling for AI-driven learning environments that can provide adaptive support for open-ended exploratory learning to those students who need it, while interfering as little as possible with the unconstrained nature of the interaction.

Providing such adaptive support is challenging because it requires student models that can track and assess open-ended behaviors for which there may be no clear definition of correctness or efficacy. The student models may also need to capture traits and states that cause the student's need for support and that are beyond those traditionally addressed by student models for problem solving, such as the metacognitive skills required to learn from unstructured activities and affective states that can impact a student's drive and motivation for self-directed exploration. Researchers have focused on two main approaches to tackle these challenges in student modeling for learning environment that support open-ended exploration (Open-Ended Learning Environments or OELEs from now on), which we will denote as *knowledge-based* and *data-driven*. In knowledge-based approaches, the student models are based on a detailed analysis of the target exploratory interaction, task domain, and relevant user cognitive and metacognitive abilities, whereas data-driven approaches rely on data mining and machine learning techniques to automatically infer a student's relevant traits and states from data. This chapter will review advances in student modeling research with the two approaches, as well as attempts to combine them (denoted as *hybrid approaches*). We will start by providing examples of OELEs.

OPEN-ENDED LEARNING ENVIRONMENTS (OELES)

Many successful Intelligent Tutoring Systems (ITS) for problem solving provide personalized support by modeling desirable sequences of steps to solve a problem and how these steps relate to relevant domain knowledge (see Chapter 7 by Aleven et al.). They then compare a student's problem solving steps to these solutions, and provide help and feedback when mismatches are detected. In contrast, OELEs do not guide student activities in a directed or step-by-step fashion, but rather let the students be in charge of leading the interaction. This approach stems from constructivist theories, especially the idea that "understanding is best achieved when it is individually driven by, or constructed by, the learner" (Hill & Land, 1998), which is operationalized in OELEs via unrestricted exploration, concrete manipulation, and self-regulation (Hannafin, 1995). One key objective of OELEs is letting students iteratively build and revise their understanding of the target learning principles, by exposing them to different configurations, parameters, contexts, and/or points of view related to those principles. Another key objective is fostering the metacognitive, self-regulatory, and inquiry skills required to learn, by letting the students drive and monitor their exploration of the learning material. The open-ended nature of the resulting interactions makes it challenging to foresee and model *a priori* all the strategies that the students will use and the behaviors they will generate, as the space of possible behaviors is often too vast for exhaustive modeling. In this section, we will provide an overview of some of the most widespread types of OELEs used in recent research, namely self-regulated hypermedia, interactive simulations, and game-based learning environments. Then, in the rest of the chapter, we will introduce approaches that have been proposed to address this challenge.

Self-regulation and exploration are typically fostered in hypermedia and online courses such as MOOCs, where students have the opportunity to decide both the order in which they access the available resources and activities, as well as the effort they dedicate to them. As a result, extensive research has shown that students pursue different goals and exhibit very diverse strategies to browse the content of the MOOC and engage in the available activities such as quizzes (e.g., Boroujeni & Dillenbourg, 2018). Other OELEs that provide content organized as hypermedia, even if much narrower in scope than MOOCs, are based on self-regulated content-browsing paradigms similar to MOOCs such as MetaTutor (Azevedo et al., 2013) and Betty's Brain (Biswas et al., 2016), already introduced in Chapter 4 by Azevedo and Wiedbusch. For instance, Betty's Brain lets the students freely explore hypermedia-based instructional material to learn as much as possible about scientific topics, such as the impact of deforestation on climate change. In Betty's Brain, the students are also invited to organize their knowledge into causal maps, as shown in Figure 8.1, where the student added a causal link ("produces") between the concepts of "fossil fuel use" and "carbon dioxide." Students can freely design and revise their causal maps as they go through the learning material until they are satisfied with it.

Beyond hypermedia-based OELEs, interactive learning simulations are highly exploratory OELEs that allow students to proactively experiment with concrete examples of concepts and processes they have learned in theory. For example, Circuit Construction Kit (CCK) is a simulation from the PhET suite of interactive simulations for science developed at the University of Colorado Boulder (https://phet.colorado.edu). CCK emulates a science lab (see Figure 8.2) where students can construct and test circuits using a large set of components (batteries, resistors, light bulbs, and measuring instruments) to experiment with several principles of electricity (e.g., Ohm's law). The students select and connect electric components in the design scene (as shown in the middle part of Figure 8.2), and they can change several properties of the circuit and components via the right panel shown in Figure 8.2. Students can also test their circuit and get visual feedback of its outcome (e.g., fire, lighted bulb). This type of simulation allows capturing very fine-grained student behaviors, namely how they manipulate each of the components, tools, and objects available in the CCK interface.

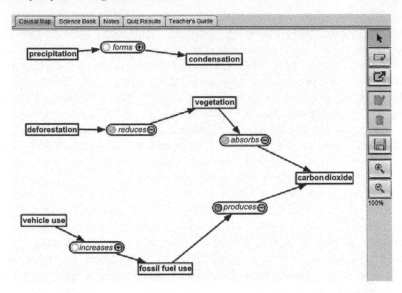

Figure 8.1   Sample concept map in Betty's Brain

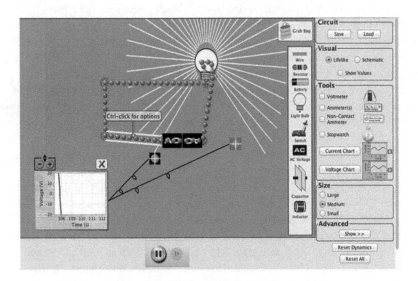

Figure 8.2   The CCK simulation (PhET Interactive Simulations)

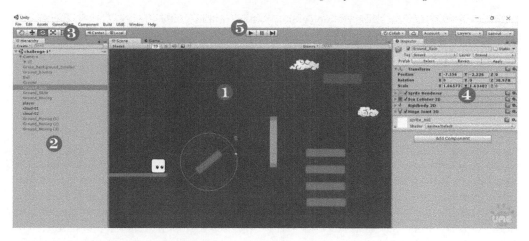

Source: UME Academy, www.ume.academy/

Figure 8.3 Unity-CT

Game-based learning (see Chapter 20 by McLaren & Nguyen) often lets the students explore the gaming resources at will, thus falling in the range of OELEs. For instance, several researchers studied how students can learn the fundamentals of programming and Computational Thinking (CT) by designing games (Asbell-Clarke et al., 2021; Emerson et al., 2020; Lallé et al., 2021; Price et al., 2017; Zhang et al., 2020). One such OELE is Unity-CT (Lallé et al., 2021), where students learn how to design a platformer game with Unity, a popular game engine (see Figure 8.3). Unity allows students to freely build games via an interactive scene view (Figure 8.3, 1) in which students can manipulate the objects of their games and modify their properties (Figure 8.3, 2–4). Lastly, students can execute and thus test their game at will, by clicking the Run button (Figure 8.3, 5).

KNOWLEDGE-BASED APPROACHES FOR STUDENT MODELING IN OELEs

Knowledge-based approaches to student modeling for providing adaptive support in OELEs are based on a detailed analysis of the target exploratory interaction, task domain, and relevant user cognitive processes. This detailed analysis is used to design fine-grained student models that explicitly represent the relation between user interface actions, exploration effectiveness, student knowledge, learning, and, in some cases, the metacognitive processes that can be relevant for a successful interaction with the OELE.

Early research in this area focused on purely knowledge-based student models. To facilitate the design of such expert models – a difficult task even in simple problem solving activities – Mislevy et al. (2006) proposed the Evidence-Centered Design (ECD) framework. This framework allows experts to create robust assessments by modeling in particular the relationships among domain concepts, the knowledge and skills to be assessed, and the tasks and observations that can drive the assessment. ECD has been used in particular in an interactive game meant to foster inquiry skills, model game scenarios, and guide the students in these scenarios by providing decision points in which the students need to choose how to proceed in the inquiry process by selecting one of a set of available options (Clarke-Midura et al., 2012). This helps the assessment tool to reduce the space of possible student behaviors to monitor and map the student choices onto the assessment of skills. Results showed that the assessment tool significantly improved learning performance with the interactive game.

Another example of knowledge-based student modeling for OELE is the original student model in ACE (Adaptive Coach for Exploration) (Bunt & Conati, 2003; Bunt et al., 2004), an OELE that supports active exploration in an interactive simulation for helping students understand concepts related to mathematical functions (e.g., the relation between input and output). Through its student model, ACE detects when a student is not exploring the simulation effectively and infers specific student difficulties that call for help, such as not testing a wide enough range of input values to fully understand the function's behavior. The student model is a Dynamic Bayesian Network (DBN) that represents the relation among different simulation "cases" that the student can initiate, the domain knowledge each case connects to, and whether the student self-explains (i.e., reasons about) each case that they initiate, as opposed to just executing them superficially. The model also includes nodes that represent how all these aspects reflect good exploration and related learning. The hints provided by ACE recommend relevant exploratory behaviors that the students have not used yet, based on the state of their Bayesian network. A user study showed that these recommendations can increase learning outcomes (Bunt & Conati, 2003; Bunt et al., 2004).

HYBRID APPROACHES

Knowledge-based approaches can be integrated with data-driven aspects to form "hybrid models" that leverage data mining and machine learning to refine the models based on the input of domain experts by taking advantage of available student data, as showcased in this section.

Leveraging student data is very suitable to learn the weights and parameters of knowledge-based models, especially the parameters of probabilistic models that can be hard for experts to quantify, as done for example for the ACE student model (Conati & Merten, 2007) discussed above, and in the Teleos simulation for surgery (Lallé & Luengo, 2011). Specifically, the ACE student model was extended to include evidence of whether students *self-explained* each case they explored, where self-explanation involves clarifying and elaborating the available instructional material in terms of the underlying domain knowledge (Chi et al., 1994). Evidence for self-explanation in the extended ACE student model consists of how much time elapsed before the student moved to a new case, and how they looked at the outcomes of the current case on the screen, as captured by an eye-tracker (Conati & Merten, 2007). The conditional probabilities linking this evidence to self-explanation in the DBN of ACE were learned from data collected from a user study designed *ad hoc* for this purpose. An empirical evaluation of this extended model showed that it was more accurate at assessing student exploration and learning than the original model without explicit evidence for self-explanation. In Teleos, an exploratory learning simulation for surgery where students can practice vertebrae surgery on 3D clinical cases (Minh Chieu et al., 2010), parameter learning was used to fine-tune the weights of a DBN. The DBN is meant to assess how specific behaviors are linked to the acquisition of a predefined set of surgical knowledge, and was designed in collaboration with surgeons and educational psychologists. The design of the DBN required extensive interviews with experts to elicit how the domain knowledge related to key behaviors in the learning activities. For instance, the knowledge required to insert a surgical tool between cervical vertebrae is linked to several behaviors, such as taking both front and side X-rays and not hitting the spine. The weights of the DBN were fine-tuned based on data collected from both experts and novices, based on the frequency of the target behaviors modeled in the network and their outcome on the simulator (Lallé & Luengo, 2011). The DBN was also evaluated with the help of the surgeons, who provided their own assessment of the surgical knowledge of their interns by observing how they operate with Teleos. Results showed that the experts' assessments overall match the DBN inferences.

Another hybrid approach is in using the output of a purely knowledge-based model to inform a data-driven student model, as done in MetaHistoReasoning (Poitras & Lajoie, 2014). The role of the data-driven models is thus to enhance the predictive power of the initial knowledge-based model. Specifically, Poitras & Lajoie (2014) leveraged input from history teachers to generate a knowledge-based model consisting of rules that define how to predict the acquisition of inquiry skills in an exploratory hypermedia, where the students freely browse historical sources, interviews, and texts to investigate the cause of controversial historical events. The rules designed by the experts are meant to map specific student behaviors with the hypermedia to inquiry skills; for instance, highlighting and annotating important claims in a document is mapped onto identifying the cause of a historical event. The number of expert rules satisfied by a student was then used to inform a machine learning classifier aimed at predicting the student's performance on a post-test. Results showed that the classifiers achieved up to 75% accuracy against a balanced baseline, showing that the rules capture behaviors that are predictive of learning performance.

Expert knowledge can also be provided in the form of models of desired solutions and strategies that can then be automatically compared with the students' solutions, as done in Betty's Brain (Biswas et al., 2016) and CTSiM (Computational Thinking in Simulation and Modeling) (Basu et al., 2017). Because OELEs typically offer a large behavior space, the experts in these works focused on modeling only a few behaviors and strategies they deemed relevant for learning. Specifically, in Betty's Brain, this approach was used to cluster students based on their browsing behaviors with the material and correct/incorrect changes in the causal maps. This was made possible because experts provided desired causal maps for the science topics covered by Betty's Brain, which were used to assess the correctness of changes made by the students in their own causal maps. They could then analyze these clusters to identify the salient behaviors in the clusters that were associated with more correct changes in the causal maps (Biswas et al., 2016). Basu et al. (2017) also used an expert model of desired solutions, along with an expert model of efficient strategies captured as a series of actions performed in the CTSiM environment meant to foster computational thinking during model building activities, such as modeling a car's speed based on its mass and engine force. The students' solutions are evaluated against that of the experts, and a sequence mining algorithm is applied to the student behaviors to detect whether and when the students exhibit the strategies modeled by the experts. The outcome of this model is used to drive the delivery adaptive support in the form of a mixed-initiative conversational dialog initiated by a virtual agent. An evaluation showed positive results in terms of learning outcomes and engagement.

Whereas in the above hybrid models, experts are directly involved in the definition of the model's components and structure, an alternative hybrid approach is to leverage experts to label the data generated by the students with the OELE, and then build the student model by training machine learning models that can predict the expert labels from interaction data. Hence, the experts do not build the student models, but provide the labels necessary for learning from data. The main difficulty with this approach is in getting a sufficiently large amount of hand-labeled data from the experts to train accurate models, which can be a daunting task. For instance, in Asbell-Clarke et al. (2021), teachers watched recordings of students' interaction with the Zoombinis learning game, which is meant to foster computational thinking, to label instances in the data when students leveraged a computational thinking concept. These labels were used to create clusters that modeled students who exhibit similar usages of computational thinking concepts, and also successfully built predictors meant to detect these usages solely from the student behaviors in the games. Cock et al. (2021) investigated how to build classifiers for the early prediction of conceptual understanding based on interaction data of students with the CCK simulation. Teachers generated labels in CCK by rating the student's level of understanding of electricity concepts based on the circuits they create. Cock et al. (2021) leveraged student interaction data with CCK to predict these labels by training machine learning classifiers. Results showed that the built classifiers can reliably detect students who have poor understanding of specific concepts.

Finally, input from experts can also be used to inform the selection of relevant features to train student models from data (e.g., Baker et al., 2016).

DATA-DRIVEN APPROACHES

The knowledge-based and hybrid approaches discussed above have the advantage of providing a detailed representation of the different aspects that generate effective exploration and learning in OELEs (or lack thereof), and thus are well suited to inform adaptive interventions that target the specific causes of a student's suboptimal learning from an OELE. However, these models have the drawbacks typical of knowledge-based approaches: they are very labor intensive to build and difficult to generalize, because they are based on human experts' detailed analysis of the target system and task domain. Although hybrid approaches can alleviate some of these difficulties, they still require extensive expert involvement to provide the initial knowledge-driven student models to be refined from data, or to label the available student data and solutions. To overcome these limitations, researchers have investigated approaches that derive student models solely from interaction data with the OELE, without requiring extensive labeling or expert knowledge to define model structure (although such knowledge might still be needed for identifying suitable features). In the rest of this section, we provide several examples of data-driven approaches.

Extensive work in this area has been done for MOOCs, which are very suitable for purely data-driven approaches because they typically engage thousands of students across a wide range of learning domains, thus generating large datasets. Several studies have leveraged MOOC data to mine student behaviors and cluster together groups of students that behave similarly (Athira et al., 2015; Boroujeni & Dillenbourg, 2018; Liu et al., 2017; Liu & Xiu, 2017; Wen & Rosé, 2014), to identify the strategies that students use to browse the content and gain a better overall understanding of how this relatively new form of instruction works (or does not) in practice. Interestingly, some of the strategies identified in this work revealed counterintuitive behaviors such as taking the quizzes before watching the educational content, or attending to the content without doing the quizzes (Boroujeni & Dillenbourg, 2018). Other studies of MOOCs have focused on building student models that can predict information about the students that is relevant for adaptation, especially dropout (Gardner et al., 2019; Li et al., 2016; Liang et al., 2016). Extensive work has shown that early prediction of dropout is possible by using interaction data from the first days of the courses, with high predictive accuracy values of greater than 80% (Andres et al., 2018; Li et al., 2016; Liang et al., 2016). These student models have been used to provide adaptive interventions meant to increase retention. For example, Feng et al. (2019) found that sending targeted emails to students predicted to be at risk of dropping out can significantly reduce the dropout rate. Davis et al. (2017) provided targeted encouragements in the MOOC interface to students predicted to be disengaged, with positive results in terms of course completion. Interaction data with specific MOOC resources have been used for more fine-grained analysis. For instance, Brinton et al. (2016) and Brinton and Chiang (Brinton et al., 2016) used interaction data collected during video watching (pausing, fast forwarding…) to predict performance on quizzes, but did not use the models to adapt the interface. Other work (Kardan et al., 2017; Yang et al., 2014) used the students' social behaviors in the forum (number of posts, number of replies, length of posts) to predict engagement and suggest to them to post on a forum they might be interested in.

Less data-driven research exists for simulations and design activities, which is the focus of FUMA (Framework for User Modeling and Adaptation) (Conati & Kardan, 2013; Kardan & Conati, 2011, 2015). FUMA uses clustering and association rule mining on existing data of students interacting with a target OELE to discover classes of exploratory behaviors conducive or detrimental to learning (Figure 8.4, "Behavior Discovery"). Specifically, in FUMA, the interaction data are pre-processed into feature vectors and fed into a clustering algorithm to identify students with similar interaction behaviors. The resulting clusters are then statistically analyzed in attempts to identify groups of students with different learning outcomes. If

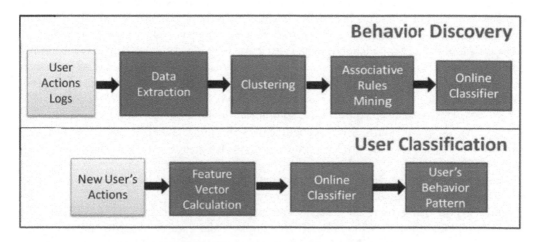

Source: Department of Computer Science, The University of British Columbia (Kardan & Conati, 2011)

Figure 8.4   *Overview of FUMA*

significant, the distinctive behaviors in each cluster are automatically identified via association rule mining. Next, the clusters and association rules are used to build supervised classifiers that predict in real time whether a student is learning from the exploratory interaction and, if not, what are the behaviors responsible for this outcome (Figure 8.4, "User Classification"). These behaviors can then be used to generate personalized hints that guide a student toward more effective usage of the tools and affordances available in the OELE.

A key asset of FUMA is that it is a generic framework that can be leveraged to derive student models for different forms of OELEs, as shown in several existing applications of FUMA. FUMA has been applied to two interactive simulations, the Constraint Satisfaction Problems applet (CSP applet) to support learning about the AC3 algorithm for constraint satisfaction (Kardan & Conati, 2011) and the CCK simulation for electric circuits described in a previous section. FUMA has then been applied to Unity-CT, also described in a previous section (Lallé et al., 2021), and to four different MOOCs (Lallé & Conati, 2020). In all of these OELEs, results showed that FUMA identified clusters of students with significantly different levels of learning performance, solely by mining interaction behaviors represented in terms of summative statistics on the usage of the available interface actions. FUMA then classified unseen students to the cluster corresponding to their learning performance with 80 to 85% accuracy, which was significantly higher than chance and other standard classifiers (e.g., random forests, support vector machines, as well as classifiers learned not from student behaviors but from labels of student learning performance). A user study (Kardan & Conati, 2015) also showed that a version of the CSP simulation augmented with adaptive support provided by FUMA improved student learning, compared to no support or support provided at random. A follow-up study (Conati et al., 2021) showed that giving students automatic explanations about why they received a specific hint from FUMA increased the students' trust in the adaptive support and willingness to receive it. The explanations also further improved learning for students with specific personality traits. These explanations describe to the student why FUMA predicted that they are not learning as well as they could from the CSP applet, based on the association rules they broke (see more details on the explanations in Conati et al. (2021) and Chapter 6 by Kay et al. in this handbook). Such explanation is possible because FUMA was intentionally designed to generate interpretable student models that can drive the design of adaptive support. For example, one of the rules learned by FUMA is that students who infrequently manipulate specific game objects in the Unity-CT learning environment had lower learning performance, a behavior that an instructor can reflect upon. As a matter of fact, this interpretability has been formally evaluated with Unity-CT (Lallé et al., 2021), where experienced instructors were asked *a posteriori* to process all of the association rules generated by FUMA and report whether they can recognize the behaviors captured by the rules as indicative of learning performance. The instructors also reflected on how the rules capture behaviors that they have observed in the classroom, as well as mapping the rules to actionable adaptive support to be provided during the activities with Unity-CT. Results showed that the instructors could interpret most rules and had strong agreement with their interpretation.

Apart from FUMA, there have been other attempts of data-driven student modeling for game-based OELEs, namely the SPRING framework (Falakmasir et al., 2016) and in Crystal Island (Geden et al., 2021). SPRING was designed to predict students' learning performance from their actions in learning games (e.g., move character, grab object, drop object). SPRING uses Hidden Markov Models (HMMs) where the latent variables are from a student's performance in a post-test. The HMMs are fitted by computing the probabilities that sequences of student actions lead to high vs. low performance. SPRING has been evaluated on a set of mini-games where students must leverage mathematical knowledge to progress in the game environments and showed that students' performance on a post-test can be reliably predicted. In Crystal Island (Geden et al., 2021), a game-based OELE in the domain of eighth-grade microbiology, a recurrent neural architecture was used to successfully predict student learning performance on a post-test, by combining the sequence of a student's actions in the environment and textual description submitted by the students on their progress. Both these works needed to obtain the student's performance labels, unlike FUMA that can work in a completely unsupervised way when these labels are not available.

DISCUSSION AND CONCLUSIONS

The data-driven student models described in the previous section are "shallow" in the sense that they can detect student behaviors that require feedback, but cannot assess any of the cognitive, metacognitive, and affective factors that underlie them. Thus, the feedback that these shallow models enable is shallow in turn, meaning that it can flag suboptimal behaviors and possibly suggest better alternatives, but it cannot address any of the underlying causes. For instance, the FUMA student model for the CSP applet mentioned in the previous section (Kardan & Conati, 2015) learned that students who often use a functionality to tell the AC3 algorithm which constraints to work on tend to learn well from the system. The opposite is true for students who seldom use this functionality. Thus, if FUMA detects that a student is not using this functionality much, it generates prompts to encourage its usage, but it cannot go beyond that. Although there are results showing that this shallow feedback is already enough to improve learning (Kardan & Conati, 2015), the question remains as to what would be the added value of a model that can assess cognitive and metacognitive factors, rather than just behavioral ones.

These cognitive factors include the student's knowledge of relevant domain concepts and skills (in the case of the CSP applet, the various components of a CSP problem and of the AC-3 algorithm). Having a student model that has an explicit representation of the connection between a student's interaction behaviors and their underlying domain knowledge allows using the observed behaviors to perform knowledge assessment. Knowledge assessment can then be used to provide richer, adaptive interventions that go beyond strictly behavioral suggestions, such as re-teaching skills that the student model indicates to be poorly understood. In the CSP applet, for instance, a student may not perform direct arc clicks because she does not understand how the arcs are selected by AC-3. If the student model can make this inference, it can also trigger an intervention to explain to the student that arc selection can be made randomly since selection order does not affect the outcome of arc consistency. Creating the connections between knowledge and behavior, however, is usually a laborious and time-consuming process, even in relatively well-understood problem solving domains (e.g., Kodaganallur et al., 2005). Having a data-driven approach like FUMA isolate the behaviors that are important for learning (or lack thereof) in open-ended interactions may facilitate this knowledge engineering process.

Metacognitive factors that may be useful in a student model for exploratory open-ended interactions include self-explanation, as was the case for the ACE student model described earlier (Conati & Merten, 2007), as well as other self-regulatory processes that can help students structure their learning, such as self-monitoring, goal setting and summarizing (Winne, 2011). Having this metacognitive information in the student model can support feedback that explicitly targets these metacognitive skills. For instance, if a student model represents a student's self-explanation tendency, its defining behaviors, and its connection with exploration effectiveness, as in Conati & Merten (2007), then it can generate feedback that explicitly targets this metacognitive skill by explaining what it involves and why it is useful (Conati, 2004). Although there are some OELEs that provide feedback for metacognition (see Chapter 3 by Ohlsson in this handbook), they do not specifically model relevant metacognitive skills, and thus the feedback they provide is less targeted than what could be provided when having metacognitive components in the model. But once again, the process of building knowledge-driven metacognitive student models is very laborious. In Conati & Merten (2007), this process involved explicitly representing the connections between exploration and self-explanation in a Bayesian network, as well as the connections between self-explanation and its predictors (action latency and gaze patterns). The conditional probabilities defining these connections were learned from interaction and gaze data that was hand-labeled for instances of self-explanation by means of laborious protocol analysis. The gaze information tracked by this model relates to the occurrence of a simple gaze pattern that was easily defined *a priori* as an indication of self-explanation. This gaze pattern consists of a gaze shift between the panel where the student can manipulate a function's parameters and a panel that shows the corresponding effects in the function graph. However, this approach of pre-identifying reliable indicators for self-explanation may not scale up to more complex learning environments. Furthermore, even when patterns can be specified, they generally are task specific and may not directly transfer to a different OELE. The relevant patterns could be learned from data, but this approach would require a large dataset with gaze data and labels for self-explanations, which is extremely difficult and time consuming to collect.

We expect that shallower, though faster to build, behavior-based data-driven student models for OELEs will become more and more prominent as the increased popularity of online learning tools, further boosted by the COVID pandemic, will facilitate the collection of large amounts of data. The availability of large datasets may also allow researchers to use powerful deep-learning methods to derive the models, as discussed in the previous section for predicting learning performance in Crystal Island (Geden et al., 2021). However, although deep-learning methods are often more accurate than more traditional machine learning approaches, they tend to be much less interpretable, making it very difficult to have scrutable and explainable models, as advocated in Chapter 6 by Kay et al. in this handbook.

The hybrid approaches described in this chapter that combine knowledge-based and data-driven approaches could address in part the lack of scrutability of the data-driven models as they still include some levels of interpretable expert knowledge. However, so far, no hybrid approaches have been proposed to learn from data the aforementioned underlying cognitive and metacognitive factors relevant for providing "deeper" personalized support. Specifically, several hybrid approaches aim at fine-tuning an existing expert model for knowledge assessment, for example, learning the many parameters of graph-based probabilistic models as in ACE (Conati & Merten, 2007), however the experts still provide an initial mapping between the relevant underlying factors and observed behaviors and strategies. Instead, other hybrid approaches use expert-based assessment of the correctness of students' behaviors and solutions, which can serve as predictive targets for data-driven models as has been done with

Betty's Brain (Biswas et al., 2016) and Zoombinis (Asbell-Clarke et al., 2021), however, without modeling the relevant cognitive and metacognitive factors. Further research is needed to understand whether and how hybrid approaches could leverage student data to ease and speed up the design of knowledge-based models.

In summary, moving forward, as for many other AI applications, a driving research question in student modeling for OELE should be how to strike the right balance between having models that can support rich feedback on the important aspects of learning by exploration and can be understood by their users, and the cost of building these models. As is the case for AI at large, an important avenue of investigation is to continue exploring the pros and cons of fully knowledge-based, fully data-driven and the spectrum of combinations in between as done in some of the OELE research described in this chapter, as well as in other areas of AIED (e.g., Chapter 13 by Mao et al., Chapter 7 by Aleven et al., and Chapter 15 by Pozdniakov et al. in this handbook).

REFERENCES

Andres, J. M. L., Baker, R. S., Gašević, D., Siemens, G., Crossley, S. A., & Joksimović, S. (2018). Studying MOOC completion at scale using the MOOC replication framework. *Proceedings of the 8th International Conference on Learning Analytics and Knowledge*, 71–78. Sydney, Australia: ACM.

Asbell-Clarke, J., Rowe, E., Almeda, V., Edwards, T., Bardar, E., Gasca, S., Baker, R. S., & Scruggs, R. (2021). The development of students' computational thinking practices in elementary-and middle-school classes using the learning game, Zoombinis. *Computers in Human Behavior, 115*, 106587. doi: 10.1016/j.chb.2020.106587

Athira, L., Kumar, A., & Bijlani, K. (2015). Discovering learning models in MOOCs using empirical data. In *Emerging Research in Computing, Information, Communication and Applications* (pp. 551–567). Springer.

Azevedo, R., Harley, J., Trevors, G., Duffy, M., Feyzi-Behnagh, R., Bouchet, F., & Landis, R. (2013). Using trace data to examine the complex roles of cognitive, metacognitive, and emotional self-regulatory processes during learning with multi-agent systems. In *International Handbook of Metacognition and Learning Technologies* (pp. 427–449). Springer.

Baker, R. S., Clarke-Midura, J., & Ocumpaugh, J. (2016). Towards general models of effective science inquiry in virtual performance assessments. *Journal of Computer Assisted Learning, 32*(3), 267–280. doi: 10.1111/jcal.12128

Basu, S., Biswas, G., & Kinnebrew, J. S. (2017). Learner modeling for adaptive scaffolding in a computational thinking-based science learning environment. *User Modeling and User-Adapted Interaction, 27*(1), 5–53. doi: 10.1007/s11257-017-9187-0

Biswas, G., Segedy, J. R., & Bunchongchit, K. (2016). From design to implementation to practice a learning by teaching system: Betty's Brain. *International Journal of Artificial Intelligence in Education, 26*(1), 350–364. doi: 10.1007/s40593-015-0057-9

Boroujeni, M. S., & Dillenbourg, P. (2018). Discovery and temporal analysis of latent study patterns in MOOC interaction sequences. *Proceedings of the 8th International Conference on Learning Analytics and Knowledge*, 206–215. Sydney, Australia: ACM.

Brinton, C. G., Buccapatnam, S., Chiang, M., & Poor, H. V. (2016). Mining MOOC clickstreams: Video-watching behavior vs. In-video quiz performance. *IEEE Transactions on Signal Processing, 64*(14), 3677–3692. doi: 10.1109/TSP.2016.2546228

Bunt, A., & Conati, C. (2003). Probabilistic student modelling to improve exploratory behaviour. *User Modeling and User-Adapted Interaction, 13*(3), 269–309. doi: 10.1023/A:1024733008280

Bunt, A., Conati, C., & Muldner, K. (2004). Scaffolding self-explanation to improve learning in exploratory learning environments. *Proceedings of the 7th International Conference on Intelligent Tutoring Systems*, 656–667. Maceió, AL, Brazil: Springer.

Chi, M. T., De Leeuw, N., Chiu, M.-H., & LaVancher, C. (1994). Eliciting self-explanations improves understanding. *Cognitive Science, 18*(3), 439–477. doi: 10.1016/0364-0213(94)90016-7

Clarke-Midura, J., Code, J., Zap, N., & Dede, C. (2012). Assessing science inquiry: A case study of the virtual performance assessment project. In *Cases on Inquiry through Instructional Technology in Math and Science* (pp. 138–164). IGI Global.

Cock, J., Marras, M., Giang, C., & Käser, T. (2021). Early prediction of conceptual understanding in interactive simulations. *Proceedings of the 14th International Conference on Educational Data Mining*. Paris, France: IEDMS.

Conati, C. (2004). Toward comprehensive student models: Modeling meta-cognitive skills and affective states in ITS. *Proceedings of the 7th International Conference on Intelligent Tutoring Systems*, 902–902. Macció, AL, Brazil: Springer.

Conati, C., Barral, O., Putnam, V., & Rieger, L. (2021). Toward personalized XAI: A case study in intelligent tutoring systems. *Artificial Intelligence, 298*, 103503. doi: 10.1016/j.artint.2021.103503

Conati, C., & Kardan, S. (2013). Student modeling: Supporting personalized instruction, from problem solving to exploratory open ended activities. *AI Magazine, 34*(3), 13–26.

Conati, C., & Merten, C. (2007). Eye-tracking for user modeling in exploratory learning environments: An empirical evaluation. *Know.-Based Syst., 20*(6), 557–574. doi: 10.1016/j.knosys.2007.04.010

Davis, D., Jivet, I., Kizilcec, R. F., Chen, G., Hauff, C., & Houben, G.-J. (2017). Follow the successful crowd: Raising MOOC completion rates through social comparison at scale. *Proceedings of the 7th International Learning Analytics & Knowledge Conference*, 454–463. Vancouver, BC, Canada: ACM.

Emerson, A., Geden, M., Smith, A., Wiebe, E., Mott, B., Boyer, K. E., & Lester, J. (2020). Predictive student modeling in block-based programming environments with Bayesian hierarchical models. *Proceedings of the 28th Conference on User Modeling, Adaptation and Personalization*, 62–70. Genoa, Italy: ACM.

Falakmasir, M. H., Gonzalez-Brenes, J. P., Gordon, G. J., & DiCerbo, K. E. (2016). A data-driven approach for inferring student proficiency from game activity logs. *Proceedings of the 3rd (2016) ACM Conference on Learning @ Scale*, 341–349. New York: ACM.

Feng, W., Tang, J., & Liu, T. X. (2019). Understanding dropouts in MOOCs. *Proceedings of the 33rd AAAI Conference on Artificial Intelligence*, 517–524. Honolulu, HI: AAAI Press.

Gardner, J., Yang, Y., Baker, R. S., & Brooks, C. (2019). Modeling and experimental design for MOOC dropout prediction: A replication perspective. *Proceedings of the 12th International Conference on Educational Data Mining*, 49–58. Montreal, QC, Canada: IEDMS.

Geden, M., Emerson, A., Carpenter, D., Rowe, J., Azevedo, R., & Lester, J. (2021). Predictive student modeling in game-based learning environments with word embedding representations of reflection. *International Journal of Artificial Intelligence in Education, 31*(1), 1–23. doi: 10.1007/s40593-020-00220-4

Hannafin, M. J. (1995). Open-ended learning environments: Foundations, assumptions, and implications for automated design. In R. D. Tennyson & A. E. Barron (Eds.), *Automating Instructional Design: Computer-Based Development and Delivery Tools* (pp. 101–129). Berlin, Heidelberg: Springer. doi: 10.1007/978-3-642-57821-2_5

Hill, J. R., & Land, S. M. (1998). Open-ended learning environments: A theoretical framework and model for design. *Proceedings of Selected Research and Development Presentations at the National Convention of the Association for Educational Communications and Technology*, 167–178. St. Louis, MO: AECT.

Kardan, S., & Conati, C. (2011). A framework for capturing distinguishing user interaction behaviors in novel interfaces. *Proceedings of the 4th International Conference on Educational Data Mining*, 159–168. Eindhoven, The Netherlands: IEDMS.

Kardan, S., & Conati, C. (2015). Providing adaptive support in an interactive simulation for learning: An experimental evaluation. *Proceedings of the 33rd Annual ACM Conference on Human Factors in Computing Systems*, 3671–3680. Seoul, South Korea: ACM.

Kardan, A., Narimani, A., & Ataiefard, F. (2017). A hybrid approach for thread recommendation in MOOC forums. *International Journal of Social, Behavioral, Educational, Economic, Business and Industrial Engineering, 11*(10), 2360–2366.

Kodaganallur, V., Weitz, R. R., & Rosenthal, D. (2005). A comparison of model-tracing and constraint-based intelligent tutoring paradigms. *International Journal of Artificial Intelligence in Education*, *15*(2), 117–144.

Koedinger, K. R., Anderson, J. R., Hadley, W. H., & Mark, M. A. (1997). Intelligent tutoring goes to school in the big city. *International Journal of Artificial Intelligence in Education*, *8*(1), 30–43.

Lallé, S., & Conati, C. (2020). A data-driven student model to provide adaptive support during video watching across MOOCs. *Proceedings of the 21st International Conference on Artificial Intelligence in Education*, 282–295. Ifrane, Morocco: Springer.

Lallé, S., & Luengo, V. (2011). Learning parameters for a knowledge diagnostic tools in orthopedic surgery. *Proceedings of the 4th International Conference on Educational Data Mining*, 369–370. Eindhoven, The Netherlands: IEDMS.

Lallé, S., Yalcin, N., & Conati, C. (2021). Combining data-driven models and expert knowledge for personalized support to foster computational thinking skills. *Proceedings of the 11th ACM International Conference on Learning Analytics & Knowledge*, 375–385. Irvine, CA: ACM.

Li, W., Gao, M., Li, H., Xiong, Q., Wen, J., & Wu, Z. (2016). Dropout prediction in MOOCs using behavior features and multi-view semi-supervised learning. *Proceedings of the International Joint Conference on Neural Networks*, 3130–3137. Vancouver, BC: IEEE.

Liang, J., Yang, J., Wu, Y., Li, C., & Zheng, L. (2016). Big data application in education: Dropout prediction in Edx MOOCs. *Proceedings of the IEEE 2nd International Conference on Multimedia Big Data*, 440–443. Taipei, Taiwan: IEEE.

Liu, S., Hu, Z., Peng, X., Liu, Z., Cheng, H. N., & Sun, J. (2017). Mining learning behavioral patterns of students by sequence analysis in cloud classroom. *International Journal of Distance Education Technologies*, *15*(1), 15–27. doi: 10.4018/IJDET.2017010102

Liu, T., & Xiu, L. I. (2017). Finding out reasons for low completion in MOOC environment: An explicable approach using hybrid data mining methods. *DEStech Transactions on Social Science, Education and Human Science*, *15*(1), 15–27. doi: 10.12783/dtssehs/meit2017/12893

Minh Chieu, V., Luengo, V., Vadcard, L., & Tonetti, J. (2010). Student modeling in complex domains: Exploiting symbiosis between temporal Bayesian networks and fine-grained didactical analysis. *International Journal of Artificial Intelligence in Education*, *20*(3), 269–301.

Mislevy, R. J., & Haertel, G. D. (2006). Implications of evidence-centered design for educational testing. *Educational Measurement: Issues and Practice*, *25*(4), 6–20. doi: 10.1111/j.1745-3992.2006.00075.x

Poitras, E. G., & Lajoie, S. P. (2014). Developing an agent-based adaptive system for scaffolding self-regulated inquiry learning in history education. *Educational Technology Research and Development*, *62*(3), 335–366. doi: 10.1007/s11423-014-9338-5

Price, T. W., Dong, Y., & Lipovac, D. (2017). iSnap: Towards intelligent tutoring in novice programming environments. *Proceedings of the 2017 ACM SIGCSE Technical Symposium on Computer Science Education*, 483–488.

VanLehn, K. (2011). The relative effectiveness of human tutoring, intelligent tutoring systems, and other tutoring systems. *Educational Psychologist*, *46*(4), 197–221. doi: 10.1080/00461520.2011.611369

Wen, M., & Rosé, C. P. (2014). Identifying latent study habits by mining learner behavior patterns in massive open online courses. *Proceedings of the 23rd ACM International Conference on Information and Knowledge Management*, 1983–1986. Shanghai, China: ACM.

Winne, P. H. (2011). A cognitive and metacognitive analysis of self-regulated learning. In *Handbook of Self-Regulation of Learning and Performance* (pp. 15–32). Routledge.

Woolf, B. P. (2008). *Building Intelligent Interactive Tutors: Student-Centered Strategies for Revolutionizing e-Learning*. Morgan Kaufmann.

Yang, D., Piergallini, M., Howley, I., & Rose, C. (2014). Forum thread recommendation for massive open online courses. *Proceedings of the 7th International Conference on Educational Data Mining*, 257–260. London, UK: IEDMS.

Zhang, N., Biswas, G., McElhaney, K. W., Basu, S., McBride, E., & Chiu, J. L. (2020). Studying the interactions between science, engineering, and computational thinking in a learning-by-modeling environment. *Proceedings of the 21st International Conference on Artificial Intelligence in Education*, 598–609. Ifrane, Morocco: Springer.

9. Six instructional approaches supported in AIED systems

Vincent Aleven, Manolis Mavrikis, Bruce M. McLaren, Huy A. Nguyen, Jennifer K. Olsen and Nikol Rummel

INTRODUCTION

The current chapter reviews how AIED systems support six common instructional approaches, namely:

- *Learning from problem solving* – where students develop skills and knowledge through deliberate practice in solving complex problems;
- *Learning from examples* – where students learn by studying and explaining worked-out solutions to problems;
- *Exploratory learning* – where students engage in open-ended exploration of a task, task domain or set of phenomena;
- *Collaborative learning* – where students work together on learning activities;
- *Game-based learning* – where students work in a game or gamified environment for engaged and motivated learning; and
- *Learning by teaching* – where students train or teach a computer-based agent and learn as a result.

An instructional approach is a method of instruction based on instructional theory (e.g., Reigeluth et al., 1994; Reigeluth, 1999). The theory guides the design of the instruction and lends coherence to the choice of instructional goals, the nature of the tasks that learners carry out, and the nature of the support they receive as they carry out these tasks. du Boulay (2019) uses the term "pedagogy." Any given instructional approach may be implemented in different ways, with variation in many of its instructional features, while staying true to its theoretical foundation. There are several reasons why many instructional approaches are being used in educational practice. First, it may be that different types of knowledge (e.g., facts, concepts, procedures, strategies, beliefs) might be better learned with different approaches (Koedinger et al., 2012). However, with a few exceptions (Mavrikis et al., 2022; Mullins et al., 2011), the scientific understanding of this relationship is incomplete, and more research is required. Second, in some instructional approaches (e.g., collaborative learning or exploratory learning), students engage in learning processes that in themselves are valuable to learn. Third, some instructional approaches may support greater engagement and motivation. Finally, many teachers and students may prefer variability in their learning activities.

We selected the six approaches listed above because they have been widely studied within the AIED community. For each approach, AIED implementations have proven to be effective in helping students learn. It is hard to do justice, however, in a single chapter, to the full range of instructional approaches that have been implemented and studied within the field of AIED. Our sampling of instructional approaches is not comprehensive. Other chapters in the current volume review other approaches that have been studied, including those focused on metacognition and self-regulated learning (Chapter 4 by Azevedo & Wiedbusch) and those based on natural language technologies (Chapter 11 by Rus et al.). Also, instructional approaches such as project-based learning (Blumenfeld et al., 1991; Chen & Yang, 2019; Krajcik & Blumenfeld, 2006) and productive failure (Darabi et al., 2018; Kapur & Rummel, 2012) are not strongly represented in AIED. Therefore, we do not review these approaches in the current chapter.

The instructional approaches that we review came into being outside the field of AIED. Only later they were implemented using AIED technologies. Therefore, a key question in our chapter is: What are the advantages of employing AIED technologies in the implementation of these instructional approaches? To take a systematic approach to this question, we take guidance from two established conceptual frameworks that deal with technology-enhanced learning. One framework distinguishes *levels of instructional assistance* (Soller et al., 2005; VanLehn, 2016), the second categorizes ways that assistance can be *adaptive* to students' needs (Aleven et al., 2017). Use of these two conceptual frameworks helps focus the discussion on two key dimensions of AIED support for learners. Combining these two frameworks helps us see what trends might exist across AIED implementations of these instructional approaches and helps us see commonalities and differences in how AIED supports or enhances them. Although there may not be a single right choice of the conceptual frameworks one might use in a review such as the current one, we believe our choice of frameworks is appropriate and helpful for several reasons: First, the two frameworks each focus on a (different) key dimension of technology-enhanced learning. Second, they are broad enough to accommodate our six instructional approaches, which is not the case for all instructional theories. For example, theories of deliberate practice (Ericsson et al., 1993) have little to say about game-based, collaborative, or exploratory learning. Third, compared to other broad conceptual frameworks for instruction, such as the Knowledge-Learning-Instruction (KLI) framework (Koedinger et al., 2012; Koedinger et al., 2013) and the Interactive, Constructive, Active, and Passive (ICAP) framework (Chi & Wiley, 2014; Chi et al., 2018), the ones we selected focus more strongly on technology-enhanced learning.

The chapter is structured as follows. We first briefly review the two conceptual frameworks mentioned above, to make the chapter self-contained. We then describe AIED implementations of each of the reviewed instructional approaches and relate them to the two frameworks. We also consider other key information regarding each instructional approach, such as relevant psychological or instructional theory, the kinds of learning objectives the approach seeks to support, examples and variations of the approach presented in the AIED literature, empirical results, and the kind of tools that have been developed to support *teachers*. In our discussion section, we synthesize trends across the approaches to get a sense of what AIED brings to the table.

Conceptual Background

We briefly describe the two established conceptual frameworks that we use to understand how AIED systems support different instructional approaches. The goal is to explain the conceptual lenses we use in this chapter to look at the different instructional approaches.

Levels of assistance

The first of these frameworks focuses on the level of assistance given to learners, a key concern in instructional design (cf. Koedinger & Aleven, 2007). The framework was first set forth by Soller et al. (2005) and later adapted, expanded, and generalized by VanLehn (2016). We refer to it as the "S/vL" framework and follow VanLehn's (2016) presentation of it, with slight modifications described below. Although the framework was originally conceived of as describing computer-supported collaborative learning (CSCL) only, VanLehn (2016) convincingly argues that it applies just as well to many other instructional approaches. In this framework, a computer-based learning environment is viewed as a loop in which students (working individually or collaboratively) perform a task. As they do so, a system gathers data about their performance, analyzes the data, and provides support based on that analysis. The loop is called a "collaboration management cycle" by Soller et al. (2005) and a "regulative loop" by VanLehn (2016). The support offered to students within this loop is classified into four broad categories, described by VanLehn (2016) as follows (we change some of the terms used; our new terms are shown below in square brackets):

> The regulative loop involves both a comparison of the [students' task] performance against some gold standard and an adjustment to the students' knowledge that brings their performance closer to the gold standard. Computer systems can take over varying amounts of this loop:
>
> - If the students execute the whole regulative loop themselves, the activity is called *[self/ co-regulation]*.
> - If the system monitors the students' performance and presents it back to the students, then the activity is called *mirroring*.
> - If the system both monitors the students' performance, compares it to a gold standard and reports the comparison to the students, then the activity is called *[formative feedback]*.
> - If the system monitors the performance, compares it to a gold standard, and generates some advice to the students or modifies the task or context, then the activity is called *coaching*.
>
> (VanLehn, 2016, p. 108)

Although Soller et al. (2005) and VanLehn (2016) characterize these categories as phases in a regulative loop, they can usefully be viewed as increasingly greater levels of instructional assistance (cf. Koedinger & Aleven, 2007). We consider them as such in the current chapter. The first of these levels, *self/co-regulation*, refers to learner performances with no support except possibly static instructions regarding what to do (e.g., a collaboration script, in the case of collaborative learning activities; Dillenbourg, 2002). Although VanLehn (2016) uses the term "self-regulation," we prefer the term "self/co-regulation" and use it throughout this chapter, to acknowledge perspectives that focus on the joint regulation of learners working collaboratively (e.g., Hadwin et al., 2018). In this chapter, we do not say much about the category of self/co-regulation, as we focus on how AIED supports learning and not on how students learn without such support. *Mirroring* represents the lowest level of assistance found within AIED systems. In its original conception by Soller et al. (2005), mirroring appears to be concerned mainly with presenting various forms of *process* data to learners. However, AIED systems support other forms of mirroring as well. For example, as discussed below, Open Learner Models (Bull & Kay, 2008, 2016; Bull, 2020), a staple of many AIED systems, can be viewed as mirroring a student's learning state. *Formative feedback*, the next level of assistance, presents a comparison of the learner's performance against an appropriate standard. Although VanLehn (2016) uses the term "formative *assessment*," we prefer the term "formative *feedback*," because this term denotes the interactions between the system and the learner, consistent with how the other assistance levels are named. Formative feedback encompasses many different forms of feedback. The term "formative" indicates that the feedback aims to help students learn and improve, rather than providing any kind of definitive evaluation of their skill or knowledge. Fourth, *coaching* is the highest level of support in the S/vL framework. Coaching often involves giving feedback to students. In that sense, coaching envelopes the previous level, formative feedback. However, it goes beyond formative feedback in that it also encompasses advice regarding what comes next, including what the next step or goal within a given learning activity might be, or what learning activity to take on next.

VanLehn (2016) adds important extensions. First, in designing and analyzing instructional support, it is important to consider the different objectives of the instruction (VanLehn, 2016), a point supported by other conceptual frameworks for instruction as well (e.g., Rummel, 2018). In many instructional interventions, there are multiple learning objectives. For example, an AIED system that supports problem-solving practice may aim to help students acquire both domain knowledge *and* certain self-regulatory skills (e.g., help seeking; Roll et al., 2011). Similarly, an AIED system that supports collaborative learning may aim to help students acquire domain knowledge *and* strengthen collaboration skills. And so forth. In each of these instances, the different instructional objectives may require different levels of support, a key instructional design challenge. Furthermore, as VanLehn (2016) and du Boulay (2019) point out, to make sure adaptive learning technologies are effective in classrooms, it is important to consider the role of the teacher or other classroom instructor(s). Similarly, we see advantages in conceptualizing the classroom ecosystem as a synergistic student–teacher–AI partnership (e.g., Holstein et al., 2020).

Adaptivity

The ability to adapt instruction to learners' needs is often viewed as a hallmark of what AIED systems do. Following Aleven et al. (2017), we consider instruction to be adaptive to the degree that it takes into account (in its instructional choices) that learners are different in many ways and that they constantly change as they learn (e.g., by building up understanding or developing skills, interests, new ways of self-regulating their learning, and so forth). In addition, instruction is adaptive to the degree that it is designed with a deep understanding of common challenges that learners face within a given task domain. These three aspects of adaptivity have in common that, instead of asking the learners to change to match the instructional environment, we change the instructional environment to align with the needs of the learner (Plass & Pawar, 2020).

The Adaptivity Grid (Aleven et al., 2017) breaks down the broad concept of adaptivity along two main dimensions: What features of the instruction are being adapted? In response to what student variables are they being adapted? Regarding the first question, the Adaptivity Grid distinguishes three broad categories of adaptation processes, which differ in the time-scale at which the adaptation happens. Instruction can be adapted dynamically, at student run time, either within tasks (step-loop adaptivity; short timescale) or with respect to the choice of tasks (task-loop adaptivity; medium timescale). As a third category, instruction can be adapted at design time, that is, in-between uses of the system, based on offline analysis of data from the instructional system (design-loop adaptivity; long timescale). This third type of adaptivity focuses on updating the system so it better helps learners tackle challenges that *all* learners face (Huang et al., 2021). The distinction between a system's task loop and its step loop is based on VanLehn's (2006; 2016) notion of regulative loops. In step-loop adaptivity, the system varies elements of its support at the level of problem steps, such as prompts, hints, feedback, whether a step is given as a worked-out step for the student to explain or as an open step for the student to solve, and so forth. In task-loop adaptivity, the choice of the next task (for a given student, at a given moment in their learning process) may be based adaptively on attributes such as knowledge required, effort required, the content's topic, and so forth. As its second dimension (in response to what student variables is the instruction being adapted?), the Adaptivity Grid distinguishes five broad psychological realms. Within each, many variables can be discerned to which instruction could be (and has been) made to adapt. Four of these realms have proven to be a fruitful basis for adaptive instruction: knowledge growth, errors/strategies, motivation/affect, and self-regulation (Aleven et al., 2017). The two dimensions together make up a 3×5 matrix, the Adaptivity Grid, capturing a very large, open-ended, and constantly evolving design space for adaptivity in learning technologies. Many forms of adaptivity that have been studied within the field of AIED can readily be classified into this grid (Aleven et al., 2017).

AIED IMPLEMENTATIONS OF THE SIX INSTRUCTIONAL APPROACHES

We review AIED implementations of the six instructional approaches, listed above, through the lens of the two conceptual frameworks just introduced. Our overarching goal is to get a sense of what AIED brings to the table. What is it that AIED implementations of these approaches offer that other implementations, with or without technology, do not bring, or bring only to a lesser degree? Thus, we consider whether different instructional approaches tend to be implemented with different levels of assistance and different forms of adaptivity. In describing each instructional approach, we also address several other important themes, including a brief characterization of the approach (what are its essential properties?), relevant psychological or instructional theory, the kinds of learning objectives the approach seeks to support, examples and variations of the approach presented in the AIED literature, empirical results reported in the AIED literature regarding the effectiveness of the approach in supporting beneficial student or teacher experiences and learning, and finally, the kind of support that AIED systems give to *teachers*. This latter topic is covered in greater depth in Chapter 14 by Holstein and Olsen.

Learning from Problem Solving

A large amount of AIED research has focused on supporting learners as they engage in problem-solving practice. Systems that support problem solving, often referred to as "intelligent tutoring systems" (ITSs), provide the highest level of support in the S/vL framework (i.e., coaching), often with multiple forms of adaptivity, in terms of the Adaptivity Grid. AIED systems for tutored problem solving aim to help students acquire complex problem-solving knowledge, often a combination of skill and conceptual understanding (Crooks & Alibali, 2014). Six meta-reviews in leading educational journals summarize the strong evidence that these systems can substantially enhance the learning of students at many educational levels, compared with other forms of instruction (Kulik & Fletcher, 2015; Ma et al., 2014; Steenbergen-Hu & Cooper, 2013, 2014; VanLehn, 2011; Xu et al., 2019).

Tutored problem solving is grounded in a variety of theoretical perspectives, such as theories of scaffolding (Wood et al.,1976) and theories of deliberate practice (Koedinger & Aleven, 2022; Ericsson et al., 1993). Specific lines of work are grounded as well in cognitive science theory, including the ACT-R theory of cognitive and learning (Anderson, 1993), the KLI framework, which links knowledge, learning, and instruction (Koedinger et al., 2012) and the theory of constraint-based modeling (Ohlsson, 1992). As well, VanLehn's (2006; 2016) cataloging of the behavior of tutoring systems (extended by Aleven & Sewall, 2016) provides a useful conceptual framework, as well as a set of "Cognitive Tutor principles" formulated by Anderson et al. (1995), based on their experience building many problem-solving tutors.

The field of AIED has created many effective systems that support tutored problem solving. First, Cognitive Tutors are an approach grounded in cognitive theory and rule-based cognitive modeling (Anderson et al., 1995). Tutors of this type have been built for a variety of task domains including programming (Anderson et al.,1992), middle-school and high-school mathematics (Koedinger et al., 1997; Long & Aleven, 2017b; Ritter et al., 2007), and genetics (Corbett et al., 2010). Cognitive Tutors for mathematics were possibly the first AIED systems to be used regularly in schools (Koedinger et al., 1997; Koedinger & Aleven, 2016). In many studies, they have been shown to enhance student learning compared with other mathematics curricula without AIED components (Pane et al., 2014; Ritter et al., 2007; but also see Pane et al., 2010). They also have proven to be commercially successful.

Another widely researched and commercially successful AIED implementation of tutored problem solving is called "constraint-based tutors" (Mitrovic, 2012; Mitrovic & Ohlsson, 2016). Constraint-based tutors are grounded in cognitive science research on "constraint-based modeling" (Ohlsson, 1992), where target knowledge is captured as a set of constraints that problem solutions must satisfy. Constraint-based tutors have been developed for a wide variety of domains (Mitrovic & Ohlsson, 2016), including Structured Query Language (SQL) queries, database modeling, Unified Modeling Language (UML) class diagrams, Java programming, data normalization, and capitalization and punctuation (Mayo et al., 2000). They have been shown to be effective in enhancing student learning (Mitrovic & Holland, 2020; Mitrovic & Suraweera, 2016).

Other notable AIED systems for tutored problem solving include the Andes system for physics problem solving (VanLehn et al., 2005) and the many example-tracing tutors built with the Cognitive Tutor Authoring Tools (Aleven et al., 2016), including tutors for middle-school mathematics (Aleven et al., 2009; Aleven & Sewall, 2016), stoichiometry (McLaren, 2011) and fractions (Rau et al., 2013). Further back in time, ActiveMath (Melis et al., 2001), Sherlock (Lesgold et al., 1992) and ELM-ART (Brusilovsky et al., 1996) supported complex problem solving. Several current AIED systems support students in solving simpler problems, without much adaptivity in their step loops, including ALEKS (Fang et al., 2019; Phillips et al., 2020), ASSISTments (Heffernan & Heffernan, 2014), Duolingo (Jiang et al., 2020; Teske, 2017), Khan Academy (Kelly & Rutherford, 2017) and MathSpring (Arroyo et al., 2014), Many other systems have been built and described in the AIED literature.

AIED systems for tutored problem solving are often characterized as adaptive coaches, in terms of the S/vL framework. Typically, this type of system presents a problem-solving environment, with a user interface designed to "make thinking visible" (Anderson et al., 1995) and often with representational tools for students to use (Koedinger & Sueker, 1996). The system follows along as the student solves problems in this interface; it provides detailed guidance. Its coaching can be characterized as "directive" in nature (our term). By that term we mean that the system provides correctness feedback and insists on correct solutions. Below we contrast this form of coaching to more "suggestive" approaches that provide helpful feedback and suggestions but may not communicate fully whether a solution is correct or strongly steer students toward correct solutions. The coaching of AIED systems often exhibits several forms of step-level adaptivity, such as adaptive prompts for problem steps, correctness feedback on the student's attempts at problem steps, error-specific feedback messages (which explain why the step is wrong, sometimes with hints for how to fix it), and next-step hints (i.e., advice as to what to do next when a student is stuck). In this manner, the system adapts to the student's strategy within the given problem and the specific errors that the student makes.

Additionally, in their task loop, AIED systems for tutored problem solving often support mastery learning. In mastery learning, a student must demonstrate mastery of the learning objectives of one curricular unit before moving on to the next, as one way of personalizing instruction. Mastery learning first came into being outside of AIED. Even without technology, it has proven to be more effective than standard classroom instruction (e.g., Kulik et al., 1990). Implementations of mastery learning in AIED systems have additional benefits, compared with non-technology approaches. No separate assessment activities are needed to ascertain whether a student has mastered targeted learning objectives; the AIED system, as part of its coaching, continuously assesses students. In addition, because an AIED system often tracks students' knowledge growth with respect to very fine-grained knowledge components, it can select problems that target a student's knowledge needs with great specificity, which may help students learn efficiently. In terms of the Adaptivity Grid, mastery learning is a key way of adjusting to students' knowledge growth in the task loop. Support for mastery learning has been shown to enhance the effectiveness of AIED systems for tutored problem solving (Corbett et al., 2000; Ritter et al., 2016; but see Doroudi et al., 2019). The self-paced nature of mastery learning that is typical of AIED systems (with each student proceeding at their own pace) does, however, present challenges with respect to classroom management that the field of AIED has not yet fully solved (Phillips et al., 2020; Ritter et al., 2016; Sales & Pane, 2020).

As an additional form of support, AIED systems for tutored problem solving often feature an Open Learner Model (OLM; Bull, 2020; Bull & Kay, 2016). Typically, an OLM visualizes the system's representation of the student's learning state for the student to scrutinize (Kay, 2021; see also Chapter 6 by Kay et al.). For example, the system may show a visualization of its assessment of the student's mastery of the knowledge components targeted in the instruction. In terms of the S/vL framework, OLMs *mirror* information back to the student; this information can be viewed as *formative feedback* on the students' learning over time, based on the system's continuous assessment of student work. Evidence from a small number of studies shows that an OLM can help students learn better, compared with not having an OLM (Long & Aleven, 2017b; Mitrovic & Martin, 2007).

Design-loop adaptivity has also proven to be effective in improving systems so they yield more effective learning (Aleven et al., 2017; Huang et al., 2021). This work often focuses on the data-driven refinement of the knowledge component models underlying the instruction, followed by redesign of the tutoring system, so that it is more effective for many students.

AIED research has explored and tested many variations of the coaching behaviors to support tutored problem solving. There is a very large body of empirical research on this topic. Here we only have space to list some of the main variations that have been investigated. First, within the system's *step loop*, AIED research has tested formative feedback with elements of student control (as opposed to the more typical fully system-controlled feedback), including feedback given at the student's request (Corbett & Anderson, 2001; Schooler & Anderson, 1990) and feedback that (compared to immediate feedback) is slightly delayed so as to give students a chance to catch and fix their errors before receiving feedback (Mathan & Koedinger, 2005). As well, AIED research has studied effects of different feedback content. Several studies have found advantages of grounded feedback (also known as situational feedback), which does not directly communicate the correctness of student work, but instead, communicates consequences of student attempts (correct or incorrect) in a form or representation that is familiar or intuitive to students (Nathan, 1988; Wiese & Koedinger, 2017). It is left up to the student to infer, from the grounded feedback, whether and how the attempt needs to be improved. Other studies found positive effects of goal-directed feedback (McKendree, 1990), error-directed feedback (Gusukuma et al., 2018), positive feedback that adapts to students' uncertainty (Mitrovic et al., 2013), positive feedback that focuses on the conclusion of learning objectives (Marwan et al., 2020), and feedback focused on domain principles (Mitrovic & Martin, 2000). Similarly, some research has studied variations of the content of the next-step hints, including principle-based hints (Aleven et al., 2016) and "bottom-out hints" (i.e., hints that directly give the next step; Stamper et al., 2013). As with feedback, research has studied both hints given at the student's request and hints given proactively by the system (see Maniktala et al., 2020).

Other features that have been found effective in AIED implementations of tutored problem solving are support for self-explanation (Aleven & Koedinger, 2002; Conati & VanLehn, 2000) and the use of multiple representations (Azevedo & Taub, 2020; Rau et al., 2013; Rau et al., 2015; Nagashima et al., 2021). Some systems adaptively break down problems into steps, in response to student difficulty (Heffernan et al., 2008), rather than (as is typical in AIED systems for tutored problem solving) right from the start. This way, the student has a chance to decompose problems themselves, without the system always taking over that important aspect of problem solving. Other work explored advantages of after-action review, also known as post-problem reflection, or reflective follow-up, where students are supported in reflecting on their problem solution (Katz et al., 2003; Katz et al., 1997). Some AIED systems "fade" their support as the learner gains proficiency (Collins et al., 1989; Jordan et al., 2018; Salden et al., 2010). Although it is often assumed that the fading of scaffolding is important in tutored problem solving (Collins et al., 1989; VanLehn et al., 2000; Wood et al., 1976), it is fair to say that this topic is underexplored in the field of AIED; there is limited scientific knowledge on which to base the design of fading mechanisms. As a final variation of tutoring behavior within an AIED system's step loop, some work focused on supporting aspects of self-regulated learning or metacognition in the context of problem solving (Koedinger et al., 2009; Long & Aleven, 2016, 2017; Roll et al., 2011; see also Chapter 4 by Azevedo & Wiedbusch).

Additionally, many variations of the systems' *task loop* have been developed and tested. For example, a large amount of work has focused on refining the methods for personalized mastery learning used in AIED systems, such as Cognitive Mastery based on Bayesian Knowledge Tracing (Corbett & Anderson, 1995), often by creating more accurate methods for estimating a student's knowledge state or predicting performance (Pelánek, 2017). As a second variation in the task loop of systems for tutored problem solving, a significant amount of work has focused on studying combinations of problem solving and worked example studying, including adaptive combinations. This work is described below in the next section, "Learning from Examples."

Recent AIED research has focused on designing tools to help teachers better guide students in their (the students') work with problem-solving tutors. Different projects explored tools associated with different use scenarios, including real-time support for teachers (i.e., support for teachers as they help students *during* their work with tutoring software) (Holstein et al., 2018), support for in-class discussion of homework carried out with AIED tutoring systems (Kelly et al., 2013), and support for tailoring lesson plans based on analytics from a tutoring system (Xhakaj et al., 2017). One study (Holstein et al., 2018) demonstrated that a teacher awareness tool, working in conjunction with an AI system for tutored problem solving, can help students learn better, especially those students who have most to learn; see also Chapter 15 by Pozdniakov et al.

Learning from Examples

A substantial amount of work in the field of AIED has focused on providing adaptive support for learning from (interactive) examples. In this instructional approach, students are given a problem with a step-by-step solution and asked to study the solution. Typically, these examples are of the same type as the problems that students eventually will learn to solve themselves. Oftentimes, learning from examples is combined with learning from problem solving. Typically, students are prompted to explain the solution steps in terms of underlying domain concepts, problem-solving principles, or problem-solving goals. Most of the time, students are given examples that show correct problem solutions but some interesting work (both within and outside of AIED) has shown that having students explain example solutions with errors (often referred to as "erroneous examples") can be effective as well (Adams et al., 2014; Booth et al., 2013; McLaren et al., 2016). Example studying tends to be particularly effective in helping students acquire conceptual understanding and promoting conceptual transfer (Renkl, 2014).

AIED work on learning from examples builds upon the extensive literature in cognitive and educational psychology on learning from examples (Renkl, 2014), self-explanation (Wylie & Chi, 2014), and "expertise reversal" (Kalyuga, 2007). Much past work on worked examples is grounded in cognitive load theory (Mayer & Moreno, 2003; Sweller, 2020). A key finding in this literature is that studying many worked examples early on during skill acquisition, followed by problem-solving exercises, is a highly effective combination of instructional approaches (expertise reversal; Kalyuga, 2007). Therefore, AIED implementations of example studying often combine support for studying examples with tutored problem solving (as described in the previous section). Some gradually fade out examples as the student gains competence in explaining the examples (Salden et al., 2010) or interleave examples and problems (McLaren et al., 2008). Another key finding in literature on example studying is that students learn the most when they self-explain the steps of example solutions (Renkl, 2014; Wylie & Chi, 2014). Therefore, AIED systems that support example studying often prompt students to provide explanations; they also provide formative feedback on these explanations. AIED systems use a variety of input formats for explanations: some systems offer menus from which explanations can be selected or structured interfaces for piecing together explanations (e.g., Aleven & Koedinger, 2002; Conati & VanLehn, 2000), whereas others let students type explanations in their own words and provide feedback on the typed explanations (Aleven et al., 2004).

In line with past work on expertise reversal (Kalyuga, 2007), work within AIED has found advantages of combining worked examples with tutored problem solving (Hosseini et al.,

2020; Liu et al., 2016; McLaren et al., 2016; McLaren et al., 2008; Olsen et al., 2019; Salden et al., 2010; Salden et al., 2010; Zhi et al., 2019). One study found, by contrast, that an all-examples condition (without any problem solving) was most beneficial (McLaren & Isotani, 2011). This work goes beyond mere replication of earlier results in the cognitive and educational psychology literature in that it finds that worked examples tend to be effective even when added to problem-solving activities in learning environments that (in contrast with those studied earlier) have high levels of assistance (Salden et al., 2010). In addition, some AIED work has confirmed the importance of supporting self-explanation in this context (Conati & VanLehn, 2000; McLaren et al., 2012; Richey et al., 2019), in line with earlier work on cognitive and educational psychology (e.g., Renki, 2014).

In terms of the S/vL framework, AIED systems for studying examples offer assistance in the form of formative feedback and other forms of coaching. Their feedback typically focuses on the correctness of students' explanations; they typically insist on correct explanations from students, before allowing the student to move on to the next example or problem. They often provide hints regarding how to explain example steps (e.g., what the underlying problem-solving principle might be and how it might apply to the step at hand). Another aspect of their coaching is the selection of examples, sometimes in a manner that adapts to students' knowledge growth, as discussed in the next paragraph.

AIED systems that support example studying have implemented different forms of adaptivity. In their step loop, some systems give adaptive feedback on students' explanations of example steps (Salden et al., 2010). One system adaptively selects example steps to explain based on an individual student's knowledge state, so students are only asked to explain steps for which they have limited knowledge – from which they have most to gain (Conati & VanLehn, 2000). In their task loop, one system adaptively fades worked examples, gradually transitioning from presenting worked examples to presenting open problems for students to solve in a personalized way (Salden et al., 2010). The example-fading procedure takes into account a student's state of explanatory knowledge, evidenced by their performance on example explanation steps. Another system adaptively selects erroneous examples based on students' errors (Goguadze et al., 2011). Finally, one project focused on a form of design-loop adaptivity, in that they created a pool of erroneous examples based on analysis of student errors in log data from an ITS (Adams et al., 2013).

A practical takeaway from this work is that AIED systems for tutored problem solving should support studying examples. Interesting open questions are what the ideal mix of examples and problems might be and how the ideal mix might vary by, for example, student and situation (Salden et al., 2010).

Exploratory Learning

Under the broad category of exploratory learning, we include a variety of approaches and systems that encourage students to explore a knowledge domain or engage in inquiry and experimentation as part of the learning process. We group together several related approaches such as discovery, exploratory, or inquiry learning (see Alfieri et al., 2011; Rieber et al., 2004; Quintana et al., 2004; van Joolingen, 1999). Digital tools associated with these approaches range from simulators to virtual labs, and from microworlds to task-specific virtual manipulatives or other open-ended environments. We refer to them collectively as exploratory learning environments (ELEs). Several provide coaching for learners as they carry out their explorations.

AIED support in this context is aimed at helping students acquire domain-specific conceptual knowledge or other high-level skills such as inquiry, problem solving in general or self-regulated learning. For STEM in particular, ELEs provide learners with opportunities to engage with a domain and explore a range of possibilities that would otherwise be difficult to experience directly. The main theoretical basis for this work is constructionism (or "framework of action" as described in DiSessa & Cobb, 2004), which puts exploratory learning at its core but also emphasizes that students learn most effectively by not only exploring but also by making and sharing artifacts (Harel & Papert, 1991). For example, mathematical microworlds and interactive science simulations allow students to explore key concepts through the structure of objects within the environment. Especially in mathematics, students are encouraged to explore external representations that make such concepts concrete and accessible (Hoyles, 1993; Thompson, 1987). For example, dynamic geometry environments such as the widely used Geogebra (http://geogebra.org/) make external representations available for exploration (Healy & Kynigos, 2010). Other topic-specific microworlds have been researched as well in the field of mathematics education (Noss et al., 2009), including microworlds for algebra (Mavrikis et al., 2013) and fractions (FractionsLab; Hansen et al., 2016; Mavrikis et al., 2022). Similarly, in ELEs for science learning, learners can manipulate variables or observe outcomes in order to answer "what if" questions, or understand the model underlying the simulation (McLaren et al., 2012; Roll et al., 2018). Characteristic examples are the PhET simulations (Wieman, Adams, & Perkins, 2008), which are designed specifically to provide opportunities for experimentation. In some ELEs, students learn by building executable models of scientific phenomena, running the models, observing the consequences (e.g., by analyzing data generated by running the model), and revising their models as needed (Biswas et al., 2016; Bredeweg et al., 2016; Joyner & Goel, 2015).

Research in AIED has been trying to address the lack of instructional support for which constructionist-oriented approaches have often been criticized (Kirschner et al., 2006; Mayer, 2004). The lack of support is particularly detrimental in classrooms where one-to-one support from a teacher is not practical (Mavrikis et al., 2019). The goal in AIED systems that support exploratory learning, therefore, is to guide students toward effective explorations and inquiry without compromising the exploratory nature of the learning processes.

At a high level, the support offered to students within ELEs has many similarities with that in the tutored problem-solving approaches presented earlier, in that the system acts as a coach and provides feedback. However, the support in ELEs operates at a different level of granularity and is suggestive rather than directive, compared with ITSs. It is closer to what Elsom-Cook (1988) described as "guided discovery." Compared with tutored problem solving, the interfaces of ELEs tend to be more open-ended and are not typically designed to prompt and make visible a learner's step-level thinking in answering a structured problem. The problems that learners tackle are more open ended and in most cases ill defined (see Lynch et al., 2009). Due to the open-ended nature of the interaction, it is more difficult to model the learner and to model effective inquiry or exploration processes, particularly because the knowledge that the learner is expected to develop is an outcome of the process of exploration. The fact that in exploratory learning there are often no right or wrong answers makes it much harder to apply commonly used techniques in AIED for tracking student knowledge growth, such as Bayesian Knowledge Tracing (BKT) (Corbett & Anderson, 1995; Käser & Schwartz, 2020). Consequently, very few ELEs employ a learner model that captures students' knowledge state. Rather, ELEs tend to focus on analyzing students' interactions with the environment (e.g., aspects of their inquiry process) and the outcomes without making inferences about a student's knowledge state. For example, Cocea et al. (2009) present a case-based knowledge representation to model learner behavior as simple cases and collection of cases (i.e., strategies). Mavrikis et al. (2010) advocate modeling "ways of thinking" or other complex cognitive skills as manifested in the ELE (e.g., through a series of actions similar to the cases above) and provide a layered conceptual model for ELEs. Other notable learner models in ELEs include Bunt and Conati (2003) and Cocea and Magoulas (2017).

The results of the modeling process are used to recognize learners' interactions within a range of possibilities or feed into other reasoning and analysis techniques, in an attempt to guide or coach the student toward effective inquiry or exploration of the environment and/or completing the task at hand (Gutierrez-Santos et al., 2012). As such, in contrast with feedback in tutored problem solving, there is less emphasis on the correctness of answers. Mavrikis et al. (2012) provide a framework of pedagogical strategies for supporting students' exploration in ELEs based on both empirical evidence and theoretical perspectives. These strategies vary from supporting interaction with the digital environment (e.g., by drawing attention to its affordances) to encouraging goal-orientation (e.g., by supporting students to set and work towards explicit goals) to domain-specific strategies (e.g., inducing cognitive conflict or showing counterexamples).

Commercial successes in this area include Inq-ITS, an ITS for scientific inquiry for late primary or early secondary students (Gobert et al., 2013). Using Inq-ITS, students manipulate simulations, formulate hypotheses, conduct experiments, and collect data, for example, by changing the values of parameters in a simulation. In order to assess student work and coach students, the environment makes inferences about students' inquiry skills using models that can detect if students are carefully testing hypotheses and conducting controlled experiments (Gobert et al., 2013). (How these models were created using machine learning is described in Chapter 7 by Aleven et al.). An earlier ELE is Smithtown (Shute & Glaser, 1990), a simulation where students change parameters in a hypothetical town to experiment with changes in market supply and demand. Smithtown models students' microeconomic knowledge and their scientific inquiry skills. In mathematics, FractionsLab (Hansen et al., 2016; Mavrikis et al., 2022) and eXpresser (Mavrikis et al., 2013) are intelligent ELEs. These systems typically provide feedback (using rule-based engines) that does not interrupt the learner as long as they are not manifesting some problematic interaction toward their goal that might be defined based on a given task. The goal is often to encourage effective exploration. Some systems employ a strong model of inquiry to evaluate student inquiry and give correctness feedback, including TED, a tutor for experimental design (Siler et al., 2010), and EarthShake, a mixed-reality environment for young children that supports a predict–explain–observe–explain cycle of exploration, with strong benefits for student learning (Yannier et al., 2020).

In some systems, students can ask for support (e.g., by means of a help button). These systems may still intervene proactively (at the system's initiative) when the system detects that a user has deviated a lot from the expected interaction. For example, the most common type of feedback in simulation environments, such as Smithtown, targets a behavior such as repeatedly changing several variables at once (thus violating a key maxim of scientific inquiry, that experimental conditions should differ only by the independent factors whose effect one is testing). It responds by suggesting alternative strategies (e.g., controlling a single variable at a time; see Shute & Glaser, 1990). Similarly, in mathematical constructions (such as in eXpresser or GeoGebra), a common strategy is to draw attention to the lack of generality of a construction by "messing it up" and helping students distinguish variants and invariants that emerge directly from their own actions (Mavrikis et al., 2013). Some systems provide feedback that targets students' motivation and effort that is separate or additional to domain- or task-specific feedback. Examples include the affective support provided in FractionsLab (Grawemeyer et al., 2017) or the motivation and problematizing support in the Invention Coach (Chase et al., 2019).

Lastly, like tutored problem solving, an emerging area is teacher dashboards and other Teacher Assistance tools (Mavrikis et al., 2019). The combination of intelligent analysis of interaction data from ELEs and the targeted design of tools for teachers has been shown to support classroom orchestration through, for example, increased awareness (Amir & Gal, 2013; Dickler et al., 2021) or support for grouping students according to their ELE construc- tions (Gutierrez-Santos et al., 2017). This is important because even effective AIED imple- mentations of these systems will not be able to fully automate the desired support for students; it is therefore important to support teachers to use ELEs in the classroom and to take decisions based on students' interactions (Mavrikis et al., 2019).

Collaborative Learning

Collaborative learning can be defined as "a situation in which two or more people learn or attempt to learn something together" (Dillenbourg, 1999, p. 1). In this section, we provide an overview; for a more detailed review of collaborative learning in AIED, see Chapter 19 by Martinez-Maldonado et al. In collaborative learning settings, learning results from interaction between the learners (for an overview, see Chi & Wylie, 2014). Although different theoretical perspectives posit different interaction processes as being central to learning (Slavin, 1996), all collaborative learning settings encourage learners to engage in interaction that leads to constructing new knowledge together, with both the construction and the togetherness being key (Stahl et al., 2006). King (2007) provides a list of activities during collaborative learning that can promote learning when they occur, such as verbalizing and clarifying thoughts, mak- ing connections between concepts explicit, and reconciling cognitive discrepancies that arise from opposing perspectives. These activities can, for example, take place in pairs (dyads) of students (e.g., in reciprocal teaching; Rosenshine & Meister, 1994), in small groups of learn- ers (e.g., in a jigsaw script; Aronson, 2002) or with the whole class (e.g., using a wiki-writing approach; Larusson & Alterman, 2009). Several meta-analyses have shown that collabora- tive learning yields better learning outcomes than when students learn individually (Hattie, 2009; Pai et al., 2015) and that dedicated computer support can additionally enhance student learning (Chen et al., 2018). The field of computer-supported collaborative learning (CSCL) is based on the idea of facilitating or supporting collaborative learning by means of digital tools (Stahl et al., 2006). Often these tools provide targeted support in the form of a "script" that guides the collaboration by providing a set of roles, activities, or interactions for the students to follow. However, even with computer support that can help to guide and scaffold students' collaborative processes, a one-size-fits-all approach to support can lead to over- or under-scripting, which in turn can inhibit learning (Dillenbourg, 2002). *Adaptive* scripting can address these concerns by personalizing the collaboration support based on the charac- teristics of the individual learners (Fischer et al., 2013; Vogel et al., 2021; Wang et al., 2017). More generally, adaptive needs-tailored support is a strength that AIED brings to collabora- tive learning approaches.

To account for the breadth of support for collaborative learning, previous research has reviewed adaptive, collaborative systems to identify several dimensions along which the adaptivity can vary (Magnisalis et al., 2011; Walker et al., 2009). These dimensions are summarized in a framework for CSCL developed by Rummel (2018). As captured in this framework, adaptation can occur before, during, or after a collaborative learning activity; an example of the former is adaptive group formation (Amarasinghe et al., 2017). In the current section, we focus on the support that is given *during* the collaborative activity. For the adaptation that occurs during collaborative learning, we focus on the target of the support (i.e., cognitive, metacognitive, social, affective, and motivational processes) as a key influence on the modeling needed to support the adaptivity. A system can provide adaptive support for one or more of these targets while providing either no support or fixed support for the other aspects.

The combination of AIED and collaborative learning began with the promise of extending traditional ITSs, designed for individual learning, to adaptively support collaboration (see Diziol et al., 2010; Lesgold et al., 1992). This goal made cognitive support (i.e., support focused on learning domain knowledge) a key aspect of the system and provided some of the same support and modeling as described in the section on problem solving. It appears, however, that models for tracking knowledge growth need to distinguish between individual and collaborative opportunities (Olsen et al., 2015). As early as 1992, Lesgold and colleagues (1992) investigated how to support collaborative learning within ITSs. In the intervening years, researchers have extended several ITSs to include collaboration support within such domains as algebra (Walker et al., 2014), fractions (Olsen et al., 2019), chemistry (Rau & Wu, 2017), and computer science (Harsley et al., 2017). For example, the Fractions Tutor (Rau et al., 2013) was extended to provide fixed (i.e., non-adaptive) collaboration support directly to the students through distributed roles (i.e., different students had different responsibilities and/ or access to different information, so as to encourage collaboration), in addition to the adaptive cognitive support typical of an ITS through on-demand hints and feedback (Olsen et al., 2019). The collaboration support in this tutor version was fixed in that it supported different roles with different affordances in the interface (information, available actions) but did not respond to how students were actually collaborating.

On the other hand, systems can also provide adaptive support targeting the collaboration process. The data that are used in these systems vary greatly. For example, systems that use screen-based or robotic conversational agents may focus on the dialog occurring between the students by modeling students' conversational patterns (Adamson et al., 2014; Rosenberg-Kima et al., 2020). Researchers have also used log data from the system to provide adaptive support around collaborative actions. For instance, in a tabletop interface, the touch interaction patterns of the group can be used to facilitate the collaboration by having students vote on actions that will impact the global state of the project or lock out actions for a user to encourage a group focus (Evans et al., 2019). As another example, the COLLER system provided support to students around the collaborative process through a pedagogical agent by tracking problem solutions and participation (Constantino-Gonzalez et al., 2003).

At this point in time, only a small number of studies have tested the value of adaptive collaboration support by comparing adaptive and non-adaptive versions of collaboration support within the same system. For example, a study by Walker et al. (2011) found that an adaptive script supported higher levels of collaboration – but not individual learning gains – than a fixed script. Another example of a comparison that was successful was in LAMS where students who received adaptive rather than fixed prompts for discussion around missing keywords had higher knowledge acquisition (Karakostas & Demetriadis, 2014). This type of study is rare, however. Most researchers focused their evaluation studies on comparing students working individually to collaboratively.

In the tradition of ITSs, most AI support for collaborative learning has been directed at supporting students directly. However, recently the focus has turned to teachers. In the context of collaborative learning and CSCL, the teacher plays a large role in making sure the types of interactions that occur between students are effective for learning (Kaendler et al., 2015; Van Leeuwen & Janssen, 2019). It is, however, a demanding task for the teacher to monitor multiple groups at the same time and provide adequate support at any given moment without disrupting the collaborative process. A possible way to aid teachers in this task is by providing them with information about their collaborating students, collected automatically (i.e., analytics) (Van Leeuwen & Rummel, 2019). The assumption is that by enhancing teachers' understanding or diagnosis of the collaborating activities of their students, teachers can provide more adequate support, and in turn enhance the effectiveness of the collaboration. It is thus assumed that such tools aid the teacher to *orchestrate* student collaboration, in the sense of coordinating the learning situation by managing and guiding the activities within the collaborating groups (Prieto et al., 2011).

When we consider how this support fits into our frameworks, we can see a range of support provided. As the S/vL framework began in a collaborative setting, it may come as no surprise that the support provided spans the categories captured in this framework. Mirrored information can include both the social level (such as who is contributing and how much; Bachour et al., 2008; Strauß & Rummel, 2021) and cognitive level (such as who knows what information; Janssen & Bodemer, 2013). For formative feedback, some collaborative learning systems have given formative feedback on domain-level work. Finally, coaching systems are common in more adaptive systems that provide advice (as an example, Karakostas & Demetriadis, 2014). In terms of the Adaptivity Grid, much of the adaptivity occurs at the step and task levels, which may roughly correspond to the idea of micro and macro scripting, where micro scripts influence the interaction processes and macro scripts guide the learning activities and conditions (Häkkinen & Mäkitalo-Siegl, 2007).

Despite the examples in this section, much of the work that focuses on social support (i.e., collaboration support) as the target is still developing methods that can be used to track the state of students' interaction and provide adaptive recommendations. For example, in the field of multi-modal learning analytics, much of the focus has been on developing new models of the learning process (Chng et al., 2020; Olsen et al., 2020). As one explanation, in the context of collaboration, it is difficult to provide automated, adaptive support as discussed by Walker et al. (2009). Although promising steps have been made concerning adaptive collaboration support, it remains challenging to automatically determine the appropriate support at any single time point because there are several levels on which assistance needs to be delivered during student collaboration. Furthermore, depending on the data used to assess the collaboration, it can be difficult to collect and analyze those data in real time, such as for speech data. This is not to say that AIED cannot make progress in providing social support. One solution is to consider how to combine adaptive support provided directly to the student and that provided to the teacher where the teacher may be able to facilitate the last 10% of support.

Game-Based Learning

Learning games were originally conceived as a novel and motivational learning platform (Castell & Jenson, 2003; Gros, 2007) with their effectiveness eventually supported by various studies and meta-analyses (e.g., Clark et al., 2016; Ke, 2016; Mayer, 2019; Hussein et al., 2022). In many cases, students' interactions with a learning game environment are fundamentally different from those of other platforms, such as intelligent tutors. For example, in the game *Crystal Island* (Lester et al., 2013; Sawyer et al., 2017), students learn about microbiology by solving a realistic problem involving disease diagnoses, interacting with non-player characters (also called "pedagogical agents" or "learning companions") as they proceed. In *AutoThinking* (Hooshyar et al., 2021), students learn programming not by writing code but by controlling a mouse to evade two cats in a maze. Thus, game-based learning qualifies as its own instructional approach, with an emphasis on immersing students in fantasy (or virtual) environments that are game-like. More formally, we define a digital learning game as an interactive, computer-based system in which users (i.e., players) engage in activities involving fun, challenge, and/or fantasy, in which instructional and entertainment goals are part of the system, and in which predefined rules guide game play. An expanded definition and description of game-based learning can be found in Chapter 20 by McLaren and Nguyen.

In recent years, game-based learning has increased in general interest and prominence due to at least two key developments. First, more and more children are playing digital games (Lobel et al., 2017). For example, some reports have stated that as many as three-quarters of American children play digital games (NPD Group, 2019). Second, a variety of researchers (Chi & Wylie, 2014; Gee, 2003; Mayer, 2014; Plass et al., 2015; Prensky, 2006; Shute et al., 2015) have focused on the relationship between engagement and learning, and digital games have clearly been shown to prompt engagement in young learners. Much of this work is grounded in Czikszentmihalyi's theory of *flow* (1990), which proposes that people learn best when they are so engaged in an activity that they lose their sense of time and place and engage in activities for the simple joy of it, not for external rewards. There are other theories that are often cited in connection with game-based learning, as well, such as intrinsic motivation (Malone, 1981; Malone & Lepper, 1987) and self-determination theory (Deci & Ryan, 1985; Ryan et al., 2006).

The AIED community in particular has ramped up research on digital learning games over the past 15 years (see Arroyo et al., 2013, Arroyo et al., 2014; Benton et al., 2021; Conati et al., 2013; Easterday et al., 2017; Hooshyar et al., 2021; Jacovina et al., 2016; Johnson, 2010; Lester et al., 2013; Lomas et al., 2013; Long & Aleven, 2017a; McLaren et al., 2017; Shute et al., 2019; Wang et al., 2022). We have found it useful to divide the existing AIED digital learning games into four general categories. These categories have elements of the S/vL framework previously discussed.

1. *AI-based Adaptation games.* These are games that use AI to adapt in real time during gameplay. These games provide personalized support to students in the form of adapted problems, hints, and error messages. Thus, this category of games is aligned with the "coaching" level of the S/vL framework.
2. *AI-based Decision Support games.* These are digital learning games that instead of (or in addition to) automatically adapting to students, as in *AI-based Adaptation*, provide a dashboard with information on students' growth and progress, or make recommendations based on this information (e.g., Hou et al., 2020). This category of games is aligned with the "mirroring" and "coaching" levels of the S/vL framework.
3. *AI Character Interaction games.* Other AIED digital learning games use an AI-driven non-player character (NPC) to support student learning. These NPCs are often called pedagogical agents or learning companions.

4. *Games that use Learning Analytics (LA) and/or Educational Data Mining (EDM) for player analysis and/or improvement.* Perhaps the most prominent use of AI in digital learning game research has not been the actual integration of AI into real-time gameplay but rather the use of machine-learning techniques to do *post-hoc* analyses. This kind of analysis has been done either to better understand how students interact with games or to iteratively improve the games (i.e., a form of design-loop adaptivity in terms of the Adaptivity Grid).

In what follows, we provide examples of games and research that has been done in each of the above categories, as well as some thoughts on the future of AIED digital learning games. This review is necessarily brief; for a more elaborate discussion, see Chapter 20 by McLaren and Nguyen.

In the category of *AI-based Adaptation games*, there have primarily been games that have focused on adapting to support student mastery and/or to stay within a student's zone of proximal development (Vygotsky, 1978). For example, *MathSpring* (Arroyo et al., 2013, 2014) is a math learning game for fourth to seventh graders that adapts problem selection based on three dimensions of student behavior: attempts to solve a problem, help requested and time to answer (task-loop adaptivity). *MathSpring* also adapts based on student affect. *MathSpring* has led to improved performance in mathematics and improved engagement and affective outcomes for students overall but more specifically for females and low-achieving students. Another game that adapts to support mastery is *Prime Climb* (Conati et al., 2013), in which pairs of fifth- and sixth-grade students work together in solving number factorization problems by climbing a series of "number mountains," composed of numbered hexagons. The student model of *Prime Climb* uses a probabilistic algorithm to assess each student's factorization skills and then, in turn, uses this assessment to present adaptive hints at incrementally increasing levels of detail to support learning (step-loop adaptivity). Another example, one that is focused on adapting for a combination of fun and learning (rather than just learning) is *AutoThinking* (Hooshyar et al., 2021), a single-player game designed to promote elementary students' skills and conceptual knowledge in computational thinking (CT). The player takes the role of a mouse that is trying to collect cheese pieces in a maze to score as many points as possible, while at the same time avoiding two cats. To this end, the player writes "programs" using icons representing programming steps to create solutions to evade two (non-player) cats. Using a Bayesian Network algorithm, one of the two cats adapts to try to promote game fun and learning. The smart cat adaptively chooses between different algorithms that vary in how close the cat tends to get to the mouse. In a classroom study, *AutoThinking* improved students' CT skills and conceptual knowledge more than a more conventional, computer-based approach. Other key AI-based adaptive games that have been developed and experimented with include *Navigo* (Benton et al., 2021), *iStart-2* (Jacovina et al., 2016), and *Policy World* (Easterday et al., 2017).

AI-based Decision Support games also use adaptation algorithms but, as mentioned, typically for the purpose of collecting recommendations to present to students to make their own decisions rather than making automated decisions for them. In terms of the S/vL framework, we view recommending as a form of coaching, where the learner is in control of whether to follow the recommendation or not. These games are designed to support self-regulated learning, the notion that students, perhaps with some guidance and scaffolding, can make effective instructional decisions for themselves. A good example of this category of games is *Decimal Point* (McLaren et al., 2017; Hou et al., 2020; 2022), a single-player game that helps fifth- and sixth-grade kids learn decimals and decimal operations. *Decimal Point* is based on an amusement park metaphor, with a series of mini-games within it, each mini-game focused on a common decimal misconception. The original game was found to lead to better learning than a comparable computer-based tutoring system (McLaren et al., 2017). A variant of the game provided an adaptive recommender system that used Bayesian Knowledge Tracing (BKT; Corbett & Anderson, 1995) to make game suggestions (Hou et al., 2020; 2022). In a study comparing the Bayesian-supported dashboard, focused on skills, versus an enjoyment-focused dashboard, Hou et al. found that the enjoyment-focused group learned more efficiently, and that females had higher learning gains than males across all conditions.

Another game that provides a recommender is *Physics Playground* (Shute et al., 2019), a single-player, physics learning game designed to enhance physics understanding. The goal of *Physics Playground* is to solve problems related to hitting a balloon with a ball using as support a variety of tools provided in the game environment. To encourage student performance and use of learning supports, the authors added an incentive and recommendation system called *My Backpack* based on a "stealth assessment" of students' physics concepts and skills, as well as a space to customize game play. Students can use the My Backpack feedback to help them choose their next activity, that is, students can get task-loop adaptive recommendations from the game. Studies with the *Physics Playground* have indicated that students both learn the target skills and enjoy the game. There have been other *AI-based Decision Support* games – or gamified instructional tools – such as *Lynnette*, a mathematics intelligent tutor that Long and Aleven (2016) extended with game mechanics (i.e., badges, achievements) to "share" control of problem selection between student and system. A classroom experiment found that gamified shared control over problem selection led to better learning outcomes than full system control.

In the category of *AI Character Interaction*, learning game research has taken advantage of modern game frameworks (e.g., Unity) and advances in natural language processing to build realistic in-game characters (Non-Player Characters or NPCs) that can interact and learn with the student. Games in this category can foster an immersive learning experience while reducing the social anxiety associated with typical classroom activities (Bernadini et al., 2014). Perhaps the two most prominent AIED games in this category are *the Tactical Language and Cultural Training System* (*TLCTS*; Johnson, 2010; Johnson & Lester, 2018) and *Crystal Island* (Johnson, 2010; Lester et al., 2013; Sawyer et al., 2017). *TLCTS* is a game and virtual learning environment for helping learners master a foreign language and unfamiliar cultural traditions (Johnson, 2010). *TLCTS* has been used to help learners, predominantly military personnel, with Arabic, Chinese, and French, as well as other languages and cultures. Learners control a game character that interacts with NPCs. They do this by giving voice commands in the target language. The NPCs intelligently interact with learners in genuine cultural situations, so the learners can learn and understand both language and culture. Three studies with *TLCTS*, in which knowledge of Arabic and the Iraqi culture were the focus, showed that learners significantly increased their understanding of Arabic. Participants in two of the studies also reported significant increases in speaking and listening self-efficacy. A second prominent line of research in this category is *Crystal Island* (Lester et al. 2013), a narrative-based game for learning microbiology. In the game, the student plays the role of a medical agent who investigates an infectious disease plaguing the island's inhabitants. They can interact with a wide range of environmental objects and NPCs to collect data and form hypotheses. Results from several studies of the game identified a consistent learning benefit, while also shedding light on central learning game topics such as agency, affect, and engagement (Sawyer et al., 2017; Sabourin et al., 2013). Other games that have deployed NPCs to support learning include the computer science learning game *TurtleTalk* (Jung et al., 2019) and the conceptual math game *Squares Family* (Pareto, 2009; 2014), which also uses a teachable agent to support learning (see the next section).

The final category of AI applied to digital learning games is *Games that use Learning Analytics (LA) and/or Educational Data Mining (EDM) for player analysis and/or improvement*. Here, data mining, often using machine learning, and learning analytics, commonly with techniques used to analyze log data from ITSs, are used to assess student behavior post-play and/or to iteratively revise and improve games (a form of design-loop adaptivity, in terms of the Adaptivity Grid). For example, Baker et al. (2007) used learning curve techniques to model the acquisition of skills in the game *Zombie Division* (Habgood & Ainsworth, 2011) to help with game (re)design. Likewise, Harpstead and Aleven (2015) employed learning curve analysis to help in identifying student strategies and, consequently, redesigning the game *Beanstalk*. An important vein of research in this category has been using data mining to identify student affect. This is important given the key hypothesis behind digital learning games, that engagement is a mediator that leads to student learning. For instance, *Physics Playground* (Shute et al., 2015) was analyzed using structural equation modeling; it was discovered that in-game performance can be predicted by pretest data, frustration, and engaged concentration. Several of the games previously mentioned have also been the subject of EDM and LA analyses, both of student behavior and student affect, including *Decimal Point* (Nguyen et al., 2020), *Prime Climb* (Conati & Zhou, 2002), and *Crystal Island* (Sabourin et al., 2013; Sawyer et al., 2017).

As mentioned, there are several parallels between the above game categories and the S/vL framework. For example, to maintain engagement, games commonly provide feedback on players' actions, in the form of in-game credits or interface changes, a form of *mirroring*. Game-based adaptivity, where the game dynamically adjusts its difficulty to match the student's performance, is likewise analogous to *coaching* in tutoring systems. Finally, games with AI-based decision support both provide *formative feedback* and foster *self/co-regulation* in students. All in all, these similarities indicate that, despite their game-based nature, digital learning games can provide a rich, learning experience, structured sometimes like a formal tutoring system (see Easterday et al., 2017). At the same time, learning games also enable a much wider range of student–system interactions (e.g., through AI-powered game characters or immersive environments), whose potential learning benefits open up a promising area of future research. Furthermore, while learning games typically allow students to progress at their own pace, there is potential in developing teacher-focused tools to leverage the teacher's expertise in helping students self-regulate while playing.

Learning-by-Teaching

In *learning-by-teaching*, one student provides guidance to another as they both learn a topic (Lachner et al., 2021). It is thus a form of collaborative learning. There is no assumption (as one might perhaps expect) that the student in the role of teacher has fully mastered the material. Rather, both students are often peers within the same social group, working on the same learning objectives (Duran, 2017). Learning-by-teaching shares much of its theoretical grounding with collaborative learning, in that students benefit from building and articulating knowledge (Roscoe & Chi, 2007). When students prepare for teaching, they often gain a deeper understanding of the materials (Biswas et al., 2004). During the teaching, they engage in further learning through structuring, taking responsibility, and reflecting.

In AIED systems that support learning-by-teaching, the role of the "tutored student" is taken on either by another human (e.g., in peer tutoring; Walker et al., 2011) or by the system (e.g., with simulated students such as teachable agents; Blair et al., 2007). The system supports the learning process by scaffolding the teaching process, by building intelligence into the simulated student, or by doing both. In this section, we discuss both types of support. We also look at the factors that influence their impact.

AIED systems that support peer tutoring (among human peers) closely resemble those discussed in the section on collaborative learning in that they provide support for the communication within the group. They also typically provide help-giving assistance, that is, assistance regarding how one student might effectively help another student learn. For example, the *Adaptive Peer Tutoring Assistant (APTA)* provided the student instructor with adaptive resources including help-giving hints tailored to the problem and feedback tailored to the help that the student instructor had provided (Walker et al., 2011). An empirical study found that, compared with fixed support, this adaptive support improved the conceptual help provided by the student instructor. Recently, researchers have begun to expand this adaptive support to rapport. Students in high-rapport dyads (i.e., students who get along well) tend to provide more help and prompt for more explanations than those in low-rapport dyads (Madaio et al., 2018). The level of rapport can be detected automatically, which may allow for adaptive support within peer-tutoring systems that varies based on the students' current level of rapport (Madaio et al., 2017). AIED systems with simulated students may provide adaptive coaching to support the human student (in the teacher role) in becoming better tutors, as is the case in Betty's Brain (Kinnebrew et al., 2014). As these examples illustrate, the support provided in these systems to help students become better tutors is similar to the type of support that is provided in other AIED systems that support collaborative learning, discussed above in the section on collaborative learning.

A significant amount of AIED research has focused on the creation and study of learning-by-teaching systems in which the human student teaches simulated students. Although the student in the teaching role is aware that the simulated student is not a human, there are still motivational advantages for the student in the teaching role. Being responsible for someone else's learning, as students are in learning-by-teaching scenarios, can lead to greater motivation compared to being responsible for one's own learning (Chase et al., 2009). This phenomenon has been dubbed the "protégé effect" (Chase et al., 2009). A central capability of AIED systems is that the simulated student often can actually learn (using machine learning) or can reason with the information given by the human student (using AI inferencing methods), a unique advantage of AIED implementations. Feedback to the student instructor is often provided through the behavior of the simulated student such as how it performs in solving problems or on a quiz. The system learns and models productive learner behaviors allowing for adaptivity to the student instructor's behaviors (Blair et al., 2007). In other words, the simulated student will show learning that is dependent on what the student instructor teaches them.

The AIED field has produced several systems that support learning-by-teaching with simulated students, often called "teachable agents." For example, *Betty's Brain* (Biswas et al., 2005, 2016) has the student instructor "teach" Betty, an AI-driven teachable agent, about scientific phenomena. Betty uses a causal map of a task domain constructed by the student to reason about a given problem and answer quiz questions. The questions Betty can answer and how she reasons about the problem depends on how the (human) student has taught her (i.e., the causal map they constructed) and thus provides situational feedback. This feedback provides an incentive for the student to update the map in light of Betty's incorrect answers to quiz questions, so Betty can do better on the next quiz. Studies with Betty's Brain have found strong learning gains in multiple-choice and short-answer item questions but not in causal reasoning and other conceptual casual information (Segedy et al., 2015). Similarly, in *SimStudent* (Matsuda et al., 2011), the student instructor teaches by choosing a math problem for the simulated student to work through. As the simulated student attempts to solve the problem, the human student provides correctness feedback and correct answers when the simulated student is stuck. The simulated student learns a rule-based model based on this information and gradually becomes better at the task. Studies with SimStudent have shown limited benefits when students have low prior knowledge compared to tutored problem solving. In another system that supports learning by teaching with a simulated student, *Bella* (Lenat & Durlach, 2014), the main goal of the interactions between the human students and the teachable agent is for the system to learn about the knowledge of the human student. Although Elle (the teachable agent) appears to the human students to be learning, in reality, Elle learns from the system, which is different from the simulated students that we have previously discussed. Learning by teaching can also take place in digital learning games in which the human student tutors the simulated student on how to play the game (Pareto, 2014) and within classification tasks, such as in *Curiosity Notebook* (Law et al., 2020).

In the above examples, the simulated students take the form of virtual agents. However, researchers have also expanded to physical forms with the use of robots. Using robots, as opposed to virtual agents, allows the simulated student to interact with the physical space and to use gestures. For example, the *Co-writer* project (Hood et al., 2015) incorporates feedback from user demonstrations of how to write letters to learn the appropriate shapes, allowing the system to adapt to the writing input from the student instructor. As writing is a very physical activity, this interaction allows the robot to simulate realistic writing skills. In the *Co-reader* project (Yadollahi et al., 2018), human students taught the robot to read using a physical book that the robot could gesture toward. The pointing gestures of the robot were beneficial for student learning. Robots can also support language learning by having students use gestures and physical items to teach the robot by making associations with different words (Tanaka et al., 2015).

AIED research has also investigated how different features of the simulated students impact learning of the human student that teaches them. When agents engage in reciprocal feedback, there is a positive impact on learning (Okita & Schwartz, 2013). Furthermore, students learn more when there is greater rapport with the agent (Ogan et al., 2012) and the rapport and learning increase when agents speak socially and adapt to match the learner's pitch and loudness than when they just adapt (Lubold et al., 2019). Also, when the simulated student asks deep follow-up questions, students with low prior knowledge gain greater conceptual knowledge (Shahriar & Matsuda, 2021). Although many types of support and interactions have been assessed in teachable agents, adaptive agents have rarely been compared with fixed agents or human peers.

When we consider learning by teaching within our two conceptual frameworks, the support given to the students tends to focus on domain support, unlike with collaborative learning where students may also be provided with social support. In addition, students may be given coaching support on how to tutor, as in *Betty's Brain* (Kinnebrew et al., 2014) and *APTA* (Walker et al., 2011). This type of support is often at the step level. Due to the set-up of learning-by-teaching, students also get formative feedback based on the tutee's performance. As this feedback often occurs at the end of a problem or on a test/quiz, it is more often within the task loop. It can be viewed as situational feedback – the human tutor needs to figure out how to help the tutee do better based on the quiz results. Some systems (e.g., *Betty's Brain*) provide coaching in this regard.

DISCUSSION

In this chapter, we review AIED implementations of six instructional approaches that have been well studied within the field of AIED, using two conceptual frameworks to guide our comparison, Soller et al.'s (2006) assistance levels, as modified by VanLehn (2016), and the Adaptivity Grid (Aleven et al., 2017). Our review finds a rich variety in how these instructional approaches are conceptualized and implemented as AIED systems.

Let us now turn to our question: what does AIED bring to the table and how does AIED enable and enrich implementations of these six instructional approaches? To address this question, we synthesize the findings from our discussion so far, by looking for trends across the different instructional approaches. In doing so, we continue to take guidance from the two conceptual frameworks we have used throughout this chapter. Specifically, we ask: within and across instructional approaches, what assistance levels, as defined in the S/vL framework, are common in the AIED state-of-the-art, and (how) does AIED help in implementing them? Within and across instructional approaches, what range of adaptivity, as defined in the Adaptivity Grid, do we see within the AIED state-of-the-art? How does AIED help?

Levels of Assistance in the Instructional Approaches

We look at how the levels of assistance found in AIED systems vary depending on the instructional approach. We are not aware of any prior work that has addressed this question. Our review finds that, for each of the six reviewed instructional approaches, AIED systems provide adaptive coaching as their main form of assistance. They often provide formative feedback as an integral part of coaching, with mirroring being prevalent as well.

Across instructional approaches and AIED systems, we find many variations of *coaching*. As we were doing our review, we found it useful to distinguish between *more directive* and *more suggestive forms of coaching*. We see these notions as endpoints of a continuum. We do not provide necessary and sufficient conditions for these notions, but rather provide archetypal examples, sketched with a broad brush. We see this distinction as preliminary, albeit informed by a substantial amount of AIED literature. More precise definition is left for future work.

In *more directive coaching*, the AIED system tends to provide a high degree of structure within the learner's task. It is capable of fully evaluating the correctness or quality of student work, and the system's coaching focuses squarely on guiding students efficiently toward correct or high-quality work. The system may insist that students generate correct work (e.g., that they solve each problem correctly before moving to the next problem), while providing ample (step-level) guidance to the student such as hints and correctness feedback. To help students efficiently master the targeted skills or knowledge (i.e., individualized mastery learning), the system may require that students demonstrate mastery of one topic before moving on to the next. It may select problems for students to help them with these goals. This type of tutoring is typically made possible by a strong domain model (see Chapter 7 by Aleven et al.).

In *more suggestive coaching*, by contrast, the system's coaching is milder and not as demanding. The system can recognize a certain limited set of desirable or undesirable qualities in the student's work (i.e., in the process or product of the work), and can generate advice and feedback accordingly. However, systems that operate suggestive coaching often do not have a strong model of the targeted skills or knowledge. Their coaching does not focus strongly on (full, overall) solution correctness or quality, either because the system (lacking a strong domain model) is not capable of assessing it, or because, within the given instructional approach, evaluating and assessing is viewed as part of the student's task. As examples of more suggestive coaching, in collaborative learning, the system might look at whether the contributions to an on-going dialog are evenly divided among the participating students, on the assumption that an even distribution might result in the most learning for these students. The system might provide formative feedback or mirroring based on that information, without being capable of fully understanding the dialog and without assessing who is saying insightful things in the dialog. Similarly, a system for exploratory or inquiry learning, after the student has induced a general rule or conclusion from their explorations or inquiry, might show a counterexample that contradicts the student's rule, but it may leave it up to the student to recognize it as a counterexample and to figure out whether to repair their general rule, as doing so is viewed as an essential part of inquiry. As a final example, in an argumentation game, when a student's argument was not successful in convincing a judge or jury (within the game), that might be so because the argument position that the student was given the task of defending was inherently weak, or because the student failed to make the best possible argument. It may be up to the student to figure that out, as part of the instructional goals.

Before diving in, let us make two final comments regarding these two coaching styles. First, as mentioned, our distinction is just a first cut at trying to characterize differences in coaching, albeit one that is in tune with a wide range of AIED literature. We see a need for a nuanced, multi-faceted taxonomy of coaching, possibly with many more categories than our two, although we do not attempt to provide one in the current chapter. Second, we are not the first to try to characterize coaching styles. Our notions bear some semblance to the contrasting notions of tutoring (e.g., Anderson et al., 1995) versus issue-based coaching (e.g., Burton & Brown, 1979), respectively, that have a long history in AIED. As well, they connect to notions in other frameworks such as "directivity" and "coercion" (Rummel, 2018), or guidance versus information (Porayska-Pomsta, Mavrikis, & Pain, 2008), or learner control (Kay, 2001). We leave exploring connections with other frameworks as an interesting area for future work.

Our review finds that the directiveness of an AIED system's coaching tends to vary both with the system's main instructional approach and with the type of learning goals that the system aims to support. More directive coaching is found, first and foremost, in AIED systems *for tutored problem solving.* Many AIED systems for *example-based learning* also exhibit forms of directive coaching, for example, by providing feedback on students' explanations of example steps and by insisting on correct explanations (Conati & VanLehn, 2000; Salden et al., 2010; McLaren et al., 2008). Some AIED systems that support *game-based learning*, in particular those that guide students during problem-solving activities (see Conati et al., 2013; McLaren et al., 2017; Shute et al., 2015, 2019) have elements of directive coaching similar to those used in problem-solving tutors. Some of the directive coaching in game-based learning comes in the form of context-specific hints (Arroyo et al., 2014; Conati et al., 2013; Easterday et al., 2017; McLaren et al., 2022) or feedback (Easterday et al., 2017; Habgood & Ainsworth, 2011). Even systems for game-based learning that do not directly derive from tutoring systems (see Lester et al., 2013; Johnson, 2010) apply principles from tutoring, supporting more directive coaching. On the other hand, making recommendations (e.g., for the next task the student could take on), as many games do, should be viewed as a more suggestive (less directive) form of coaching.

Suggestive coaching approaches are found in AIED systems for *exploratory learning, collaborative learning*, and *learning-by-teaching*. The main goal behind coaching approaches in systems that support *exploratory learning* tends to be to support students in exploring effectively, while honoring the exploratory nature of the activity. In contrast to more directive coaching, feedback in these systems may not tell the student whether their exploration processes are "correct." Instead, these systems may prompt students to demonstrate strategies that are more likely to lead to conceptual understanding or provide opportunities for developing higher cognitive skills such as inquiry. Often, these systems coach without a strong model of inquiry or exploration. There are exceptions, however. Some AIED systems do more directive coaching (e.g., provide correctness feedback) during exploratory tasks (Gobert et al., 2013; Grawemeyer, 2017; McLaren et al., 2012; Siler et al., 2010). Similarly, AIED systems for *collaborative learning* tend to implement suggestive coaching aimed at helping students learn productive collaborative behaviors (which in the section above is referred to as "social support"), for example, with prompts or alerts that adapt to aspects of social interaction such as who is talking too much or too little (Dillenbourg & Fischer, 2007). AIED systems that support collaborative learning often do not have strong models of collaboration; some (e.g., APTA; Walker et al., 2011) conduct coaching based on a minimal model or an issue-based approach. These systems tend to combine suggestive coaching of collaborative behaviors with more directive coaching at the domain level (which in the section above is referred to as "cognitive support"), especially in projects that worked on individual learning first and then segued to support of collaborative learning (Baghaei et al., 2007; Olsen et al., 2019; Walker et al., 2011). Finally, systems that support *learning-by-teaching* have yielded some interesting forms of suggestive coaching. Some systems have tutor agents that coach the student in the role of tutor with the aim of helping them improve their tutoring strategies (Biswas et al., 2016; Leelawong & Biswas, 2008; Matsuda et al., 2011). Note that while most AIED learning games are firmly in the directive coaching category, as previously discussed, some do have more open-ended game structures for which more suggestive coaching is more appropriate (see Lester et al., 2013).

Moving to the next assistance level within the S/vL framework, *formative feedback* is plentiful in AIED systems, most often as an integral and central element of coaching. Strong correctness feedback is often a key element of *directive coaching*, for example in AIED systems that support *tutored problem solving, example-based learning* and *game-based learning*. These systems sometimes also provide elaborated error-specific feedback, as part of a directive coaching strategy. Some systems that support collaborative learning give correctness feedback on the domain-level aspects of students' work. On the other hand, formative feedback in AIED systems for exploratory learning and collaborative learning tends to focus on a limited set of desirable or undesirable aspects of student work (rather than providing a complete valuation of correctness), as part of a suggestive coaching strategy. Systems for *exploratory learning* sometimes give formative feedback when there are specific tasks/goals (sometimes, what to explore is left up to the student and the system does not know), or in response to a student's request for additional support. Sometimes, an inherent part of the coaching strategy is to *withhold* formative feedback, so as not to spoil the exploratory nature of the learning process. Similarly, when systems that support collaborative learning give formative feedback on collaboration, it is not strongly directive. Interestingly, "situational feedback" (Nathan, 1998) in both *games* and in systems for *learning-by-teaching* could be viewed as more suggestive coaching. Rather than providing correctness information, the system shows the student the consequences of their actions in the simulated world that the student is working in. It is up to the student to make sense of these consequences and infer how to improve their knowledge and work.

Regarding the third level of the S/vL framework, *mirroring* is a common form of assistance in AIED systems, across instructional approaches. We see two forms of mirroring in AIED systems. First, OLMs (a staple of *problem-solving tutors*, but present in other types of AIED systems as well, such as learning games) mirror the student *state*, as estimated by the system and captured in the system's student model, such as, for example, their (ever-changing) state of knowledge. In other words, the OLM may visualize how well a student, at any given point in time, masters targeted knowledge components. As discussed, a few empirical studies have tested whether OLMs of this type can support effective reflection and greater learning and have confirmed that they can (Long & Aleven, 2017b; Mitrovic & Martin, 2007). Second, many AIED systems support mirroring of *process* data, displaying, for example, how many problems a student has completed or how much time the student has spent. Systems that support *problem solving* often provide a variety of reports to students (e.g., Arroyo et al., 2014). Also, some studies focused on visualizations within the tutor interface itself, including visualizations of learning behaviors such as "gaming the system" (Baker et al., 2006; Walonoski & Heffernan, 2006). Furthermore, AIED systems that support *collaborative learning* may display or visualize the distribution of talk among the collaborating partners or the distribution of actions within the learning software among the team members. Often, the mirrored information is presented on a student dashboard or awareness tool (e.g., De Groot et al., 2007; McLaren et al., 2010). Mirroring of multimodal analytics is increasingly common, especially in collaborative learning (see Echeverria et al., 2019; Schneider & Pea, 2013). Some systems that support *exploratory learning* also mirror process data. As well, *games for learning* have long had dashboards (showing a student's advancement through the game's levels, for example), sometimes combined with suggestions or nudges for moving to the next level (see Hou et al., 2020; 2022; Long & Aleven, 2014).

Regarding teacher tools – as mentioned, a strong focus in current AIED research – we summarize for which instructional approaches such tools have been explored. A more in-depth treatment of teacher support tools can be found in Chapter 14 by Holstein and Olsen and Chapter 15 by Pozdniakov et al. Teacher awareness tools are starting to become available in AIED systems for *problem solving* and *collaborative learning*. In the former, the tool can inform the teacher of students' progress and struggle as they (the students) are working through the tutoring system's problem sets. In the latter, the focus tends to be on collaboration analytics. Having a teacher in the loop may compensate for not having strong models of collaboration (see De Groot et al., 2007). Teacher tools are also emerging in systems for *exploratory learning*. Teacher tools in such systems may mirror aspects of students' exploratory processes to teachers and (analogous to teacher tools for collaborative learning) may compensate for not having strong models of inquiry or exploration. Although, with a few exceptions (Gauthier et al., 2022), there are not many dedicated teacher tools integrated into AIED systems for *game-based learning* and *learning-by-teaching*, such tools have the potential to be highly useful.

Adaptivity in the Instructional Approaches

Looking at the six instructional approaches through the lens of the Adaptivity Grid (Aleven et al., 2017), our review finds many interesting examples of adaptivity in AIED systems, confirming the notion that adapting to students' needs is a central property of AIED systems and confirming earlier findings that adaptivity is a multifaceted concept. The current discussion highlights some forms of adaptivity not discussed in earlier reviews (e.g., Aleven et al., 2017) and contributes some new insights into how AIED systems' adaptivity tends to vary with their instructional approach. We also note that, interestingly, quite a few AIED systems combine multiple forms of adaptivity (e.g., adaptivity in the task loop and in the step loop, or different forms of adaptivity applied to different instructional goals). It has been shown empirically that, in some cases, combining several forms of adaptivity within a single system can be synergistic (see Corbett, 2001), although there is limited scientific knowledge regarding what forms of adaptivity work well together.

We first consider forms of *step-loop adaptivity* in the different instructional approaches that we studied, typically as part of their coaching strategy. As mentioned, step-loop adaptivity comprises adaptations at a small grain size and timescale, namely, within a given problem, at the level of problem steps. In systems that support *problem solving*, we often find forms of step-loop adaptivity as part of a directive coaching strategy, including step-level correctness feedback and hints that adapt to students' errors and strategies. We also came across some forms of step-loop adaptivity that are less typical, such as adapting feedback to student uncertainty (Mitrovic et al., 2013) and adaptive scaffolding in response to students' errors, for example by breaking down a problem into steps when a student makes an error (see Heffernan & Heffernan, 2014).

Similarly, in the support given by AIED systems for *example studying*, also characterized by directive coaching, we find interesting forms of step-loop adaptivity, including formative feedback that adapts to students' errors (typically, feedback on explanations) and the selection of example steps within a given worked-out example that a student is prompted to explain, based on their (estimated) state of knowledge (Conati & VanLehn, 2000). This way, the student's efforts can focus on explaining steps that involve knowledge that the student is yet to master.

We also find forms of step-loop adaptivity in systems for *exploratory learning*, whose coaching tends to be suggestive in nature. Systems for exploratory learning often provide a simulated world that adaptively responds to student interactions (e.g., manipulating variables, querying a model or simulation of the phenomena being explored, posing what if questions, or creating and running executable models). This form of adaptivity is not captured in the Adaptivity Grid but is a key part of the functionality of these systems and the way learners interact with them. Additionally, systems for *exploratory learning* often provide adaptive feedback aimed at the *process* of exploration or inquiry. The feedback may point out certain desirable or undesirable properties of student work, to encourage effective exploration or inquiry. By contrast, a few systems in this category employ a strong model of inquiry to provide directive (and adaptive) coaching in the step loop (Gobert et al., 2013; Grawemeyer, 2016; Siler et al., 2010).

Systems for *collaborative learning* may provide adaptive support during a task targeting different processes (cognitive, metacognitive, social, affective, and motivational) with different forms of adaptive support. Conversational agents may provide collaboration support in a manner that adapts to ongoing conversations between collaborating students, as a form of step-loop adaptivity. This form of coaching is sometimes combined with more directive coaching at the domain level, for example in systems that support collaborative problem solving. These systems may have some of the forms of step-level adaptivity described above.

Several *digital learning games* also implement forms of step-loop adaptivity, sometimes as part of directive coaching, including hints whose level of detail adapts to students' knowledge (e.g., Conati et al., 2013; Lesgold et al., 1992). Furthermore, some games, in their step loop, adapt to student affect (Conati et al., 2013; Arroyo et al., 2013, 2014) or adapt to a combination of fun and learning (Hooshyar et al., 2021). A key form of adaptive step-level support is situational feedback: the consequences of student actions are shown in the game world. The consequences are contingent on – or adapt to – the actions. As mentioned under exploratory learning above, this form of adaptivity is not captured well in the Adaptivity Grid.

In systems for *learning-by-teaching*, we see several interesting and unusual forms of step-loop adaptivity. First, a simulated student's answers to questions and its performance on quizzes is a form of (adaptive) situational feedback. Even the gestures of teachable robots may function as situational feedback. In addition, AIED systems for learning-by-teaching provide adaptive feedback on the teaching or tutoring by the (human) student, tailored to the problem and with feedback tailored to the help that the student instructor had provided. An interesting novel idea (though one that appears not to have been implemented yet at the time of this writing) is to create adaptive support for peer tutoring that varies based on the students' current level of rapport (Madaio et al., 2017).

Let us now turn to *task-loop adaptivity*, that is, adaptations in the choice and sequencing of learning activities or problems. Task-loop adaptivity tends to be more typical of directive coaching, perhaps because typical forms of it (e.g., individualized mastery learning) depend on being able to assess the correctness of students' solutions (e.g., in Bayesian Knowledge Tracing; Corbett & Anderson, 1995). Indeed, individualized mastery learning remains a key form of task-loop adaptivity of AIED systems that support *problem solving*. We also find task-loop adaptivity in systems that support *example studying*, such as adaptive selecting of erroneous examples so they match specific student errors (Goguadze et al., 2011) and the adaptive fading from examples to open problems based on growth in a student's explanation knowledge (Salden et al., 2010). Adaptive task selection is also found in several *digital learning games*, often presented to the student in the form of recommendations, a suggestive form of coaching (Hou et al., 2022), compared to the directive approaches found in typical implementations of individualized mastery learning. We also see forms of "hybrid task-loop adaptivity" in which the system adapts its task-level decisions based on a combination of student variables, such as measures of recent performance, effort, and affect; these approaches have been explored both in *games* (Arroyo et al., 2013, 2014; Conati et al., 2013; Hooshyar et al., 2021) and in systems that support *exploratory learning* (Mavrikis et al., 2022).

Finally, we turn to *design-loop adaptivity*. In design-loop adaptivity, as mentioned, a system is updated (by its designers) based on analysis of data collected during previous use of the system. Where past reviews (Aleven et al., 2017; Aleven & Koedinger, 2013) have highlighted instances of *design-loop adaptivity* in AIED systems for *problem solving* and *example studying*, the current review finds additional interesting instances of design-loop adaptivity in *digital learning games* and in systems that support *exploratory learning*. As discussed, it is becoming increasingly common that digital learning games are updated based on analysis of log data or game analytics. Our review in fact defines an entire category of games for which design-loop adaptivity is a distinguishing characteristic. Interestingly, some work on design-loop adaptivity in games has focused on exploring and adapting to student affect. As an example of design-loop adaptivity applied to *exploratory learning*, the model of scientific inquiry used in the Inq-ITS system to provide feedback was created by applying machine learning to log data from the inquiry environment (Gobert et al., 2013). The development of Inq-ITS coaching model is described in Chapter 7 by Aleven et al.

CONCLUSION

Our review applies two established, complementary conceptual frameworks, Soller et al.'s (2006) assistance levels, as modified by VanLehn (2016), and the Adaptivity Grid (Aleven et al., 2017), to compare AIED implementations of six instructional approaches. For each, we find a rich variety in the ways AIED systems assist learners and adapt their instruction to learners' needs. Increasingly, AIED systems are also designed to support teachers' needs, an important addition to past research.

Across instructional approaches, adaptive coaching is the most frequent form of assistance. Formative feedback is highly frequent as well, typically as part of adaptive coaching, and a great many AIED systems support mirroring. Adaptive coaching is what sets AIED apart from many other forms of instructional technology. AIED implementations of the different instructional approaches vary in their assistance levels and adaptivity. To the best of our knowledge, the relation between instructional approach and the forms of assistance and adaptation has not been explored in prior reviews. Given the great variety in how adaptive coaching is implemented in today's AIED systems, we find it useful to distinguish between two "flavors," which we call more directive and more suggestive coaching. Directive coaches focus strongly on – and may even insist on – correctness and mastery of knowledge. Suggestive coaches provide helpful feedback but without a full evaluation of correctness, either because the system does not have strong enough knowledge to do so, or because a suggestive coaching strategy is viewed as more compatible with the given instructional approach. We note that our distinction is only preliminary. More conceptual work is needed to describe the richness of coaching. The field of AIED may benefit from a more fine-grained taxonomy of coaching, a very interesting challenge for future work.

Our review highlights many forms of adaptivity, including forms of adapting to student affect, collaboration, and rapport, often in combination with other student variables (i.e., hybrid adaptivity in the terminology of Aleven et al., 2017). The design space for adaptivity in learning technologies is open-ended and constantly evolving. The scientific understanding of what forms of adaptivity are most helpful to learners may be a unique contribution of AIED to the field of technology-enhanced learning. Our review also finds that supporting multiple instructional goals within a single AIED is more common in AIED systems than we expected. Doing so poses a challenging design problem. We expect the field will produce new forms of adaptivity, for example, to help (dynamically) balance support for different instructional goals.

As our review indicates, a great amount of empirical research has documented the effectiveness of AIED implementations of all six instructional approaches, often by means of studies conducted in real educational settings (schools, university courses, academic online learning environments, etc.). Although the amount of empirical evidence that has been produced varies substantially across instructional approaches, all instructional approaches have proven to be effective in empirical studies.

By providing effective adaptive assistance, AIED has the potential to render feasible, at scale, the use of instructional approaches that (without AIED support) might require too much instructor involvement to be fit for use in classrooms or use by larger numbers of students. We are already seeing that kind of scaling in educational practice for AIED implementations of tutored problem solving. However, we see a great opportunity and great promise in bringing AIED implementations of the other instructional approaches reviewed to scale.

REFERENCES

Adams, D., McLaren, B. M., Durkin, K., Mayer, R.E., Rittle-Johnson, B., Isotani, S., & Van Velsen, M. (2014). Using erroneous examples to improve mathematics learning with a web-based tutoring system. *Computers in Human Behavior, 36*, 401–411. doi: 10.1016/j.chb.2014.03.053

Adams, D., McLaren, B.M., Mayer, R.E., Goguadze, G., & Isotani, S. (2013). Erroneous examples as desirable difficulty. In H. C. Lane, K. Yacef, J. Mostow, & P. Pavlik (Eds.), *Proceedings of the 16th International Conference on Artificial Intelligence in Education (AIED 2013)* (pp. 803–806). Springer.

Adamson, D., Dyke, G., Jang, H., & Rosé, C. P. (2014). Towards an agile approach to adapting dynamic collaboration support to student needs. *International Journal of Artificial Intelligence in Education, 24*(1), 92–124. doi: 10.1007/s40593-013-0012-6

Aleven, V., & Koedinger, K. R. (2000). Limitations of student control: Do students know when they need help? In G. Gauthier, C. Frasson, & K. VanLehn (Eds.), *Proceedings of the 5th International Conference on Intelligent Tutoring Systems, ITS 2000* (pp. 292–303). Berlin: Springer Verlag.

Aleven, V. A., & Koedinger, K. R. (2002). An effective metacognitive strategy: Learning by doing and explaining with a computer-based cognitive tutor. *Cognitive Science, 26*(2), 147–179. doi: 10.1207/s15516709cog2602_1

Aleven, V., & Koedinger, K. R. (2013). Knowledge component approaches to learner modeling. In R. Sottilare, A. Graesser, X. Hu, & H. Holden (Eds.), *Design recommendations for adaptive intelligent tutoring systems* (Vol. I, Learner Modeling, pp. 165–182). Orlando, FL: US Army Research Laboratory.

Aleven, V., McLaren, B. M., & Sewall, J. (2009). Scaling up programming by demonstration for intelligent tutoring systems development: An open-access web site for middle school mathematics learning. *IEEE Transactions on Learning Technologies, 2*(2), 64–78. doi: 10.1109/TLT.2009.22

Aleven, V., McLaren, B. M., Sewall, J., Van Velsen, M., Popescu, O., Demi, S., Ringenberg, M., & Koedinger, K. R. (2016). Example-tracing tutors: Intelligent tutor development for non-programmers. *International Journal of Artificial Intelligence in Education, 26*(1), 224–269. doi: 10.1007/s40593-015-0088-2

Aleven, V., McLaughlin, E. A., Glenn, R. A., & Koedinger, K. R. (2017). Instruction based on adaptive learning technologies. In R. E. Mayer & P. Alexander (Eds.), *Handbook of research on learning and instruction* (2nd ed., pp. 522–560). New York: Routledge.

Aleven, V., Ogan, A., Popescu, O., Torrey, C., & Koedinger, K. (2004). Evaluating the effectiveness of a tutorial dialogue system for self-explanation. In J. C. Lester, R. M. Vicario, & F. Paraguaçu (Eds.), *Proceedings of Seventh International Conference on Intelligent Tutoring Systems, ITS 2004* (pp. 443–454). Berlin: Springer Verlag.

Aleven, V., Roll, I., McLaren, B. M., & Koedinger, K. R. (2016). Help helps, but only so much: Research on help seeking with intelligent tutoring systems. *International Journal of Artificial Intelligence in Education, 26*(1), 205–223. doi: 10.1007/s40593-015-0089-1

Aleven, V., & Sewall, J. (2016). The frequency of tutor behaviors: A case study. In A. Micarelli, J. Stamper, & K. Panourgia (Eds.), *Proceedings of the 13th International Conference on Intelligent Tutoring Systems, ITS 2016* (pp. 396–401). Cham, Switzerland: Springer.

Alfieri, L. Brooks, P., Aldrich, N., & Tenenbaum,H. (2011). Does discovery-based instruction enhance learning? *Journal of Educational Psychology, 103*(1), 1–18. doi: 10.1037/a0021017

Amarasinghe, I., Hernández-Leo, D., & Jonsson, A. (2017). Intelligent group formation in computer-supported collaborative learning scripts. In M. Chang, N. Chen, R. Huang, Kinshuk, D. G. Sampson, &

R. Vasiu (Eds.), *Proceedings of the 2017 IEEE 17th International Conference on Advanced Learning Technologies (ICALT)* (pp. 201–203). Los Alamitos, CA: IEEE.

Amir, O., & Gal, Y. (2013). Plan recognition and visualization in exploratory learning environments. *ACM Transactions on Interactive Intelligent Systems, 3*(3), 1–23. doi: 10.1145/2533670.2533674

Anderson, J. R. (1993). *Rules of the mind.* New York: Taylor & Francis.

Anderson, J. R., Corbett, A. T., Koedinger, K. R., & Pelletier, R. (1995). Cognitive Tutors: Lessons learned. *The Journal of the Learning Sciences, 4*(2), 167–207. doi: 10.1207/s15327809jls0402_2

Anderson, J. R., Corbett, A. T., Fincham, J. M., Hoffman, D., & Pelletier, R. (1992). General principles for an intelligent tutoring architecture. In V. Shute & W. Regian (Eds.), *Cognitive Approaches to Automated Instruction* (pp. 81–106). Hillsdale, NJ: Erlbaum.

Aronson, E. (2002). Building empathy, compassion, and achievement in the jigsaw classroom. In J. Aronson (Ed.), *Improving academic achievement: Impact of psychological factors on education* (pp. 209–225). Cambridge, MA: Academic Press.

Arroyo, I., Burleson, W., Tai, M., Muldner, K., & Woolf, B. P. (2013). Gender differences in the use and benefit of advanced learning technologies for mathematics. *Journal of Educational Psychology, 105*(4), 957–969. doi: 10.1037/a0032748

Arroyo, I., Woolf, B. P., Burleson, W., Muldner, K., Rai, D., & Tai, M. (2014). A multimedia adaptive tutoring system for mathematics that addresses cognition, metacognition and affect. *International Journal of Artificial Intelligence in Education, 24*(4), 387–426. doi: 10.1007/s40593-014-0023-y

Azevedo, R., & Taub, M. (2020). The challenge of measuring processes and outcomes while learning from multiple representations with advanced learning technologies. In P. Van Meter, A. List, G. Lombardi, & P. Kendeou (Eds.), *Handbook of learning from multiple representations and perspectives* (pp. 532–553). Routledge.

Bachour, K., Kaplan, F., & Dillenbourg, P. (2008). Reflect: An interactive table for regulating face-to-face collaborative learning. In P. Dillenbourg & M. Specht (Eds.), *Proceedings of the 3rd European Conference on Technology Enhanced Learning: Times of convergence: Technologies across learning contexts* (pp. 39–48). Berlin, Heidelberg: Springer.

Baghaei, N., Mitrovic, A., & Irwin, W. (2007). Supporting collaborative learning and problem-solving in a constraint-based CSCL environment for UML class diagrams. *International Journal of Computer-Supported Collaborative Learning, 2*(2), 159–190. doi: 10.1007/s11412-007-9018-0

Baker, R. S. J. d., Corbett, A. T., Koedinger, K. R., Evenson, S., Wagner, A. Z., Naim, M., Raspat, J., Baker, D. J., & Beck, J. E. l. (2006). Adapting to when students game an intelligent tutoring system. In M. Ikeda, K. D. Ashley, & T. W. Chan (Eds.), *Proceedings of the 8th International Conference on Intelligent Tutoring Systems, ITS 2006* (pp. 392–401). Berlin: Springer.

Baker, R. S. J. d., Habgood, M. P. J., Ainsworth, S. E., & Corbett, A. T. (2007). Modeling the acquisition of fluent skill in educational action games. In C. Conati, K. McCoy, & G. Paliouras (Eds.), *Proceedings of User Modeling 2007, 11th International Conference, UM 2007* (Lecture Notes in Computer Science, vol. 4511, pp. 17–26). Berlin, Heidelberg: Springer.

Benton, L., Mavrikis, M., Vasalou, M., Joye, N., Sumner, E., Herbert, E., Revesz, A., Symvonis, A. & Raftopoulou, C. (2021). Designing for "challenge" in a large-scale adaptive literacy game for primary school children. *British Journal of Educational Technology, 52*(5), 1862–1880. doi: 10.1111/bjet.13146

Bernardini, S., Porayska-Pomsta, K., & Smith, T. J. (2014). ECHOES: An intelligent serious game for fostering social communication in children with autism. *Information Sciences, 264*, 41–60. doi: 10.1016/j.ins.2013.10.027

Biswas, G., Leelawong, K., Belynne, K., & Adebiyi, B. (2005). Case studies in learning by teaching behavioral differences in directed versus guided learning. In B. G. Bara, L. Barsalou, & M. Bucciarelli (Eds.), *Proceedings of the 27th Annual Conference of the Cognitive Science Society* (pp. 828–833). Mahwah, NJ: Erlbaum.

Biswas, G., Leelawong, K., Belynne, K., Viswanath, K., Vye, N., Schwartz, D., & Davis, J. (2004). Incorporating self regulated learning techniques into learning by teaching environments. In K. Forbus, D. Gentner, & T. Regier (Eds.), *Proceedings of the 26th Annual Meeting of the Cognitive Science Society* (pp. 120–125). Mahwah, NJ: Erlbaum.

Biswas, G., Segedy, J. R., & Bunchongchit, K. (2016). From design to implementation to practice – A learning by teaching system: Betty's Brain. *International Journal of Artificial Intelligence in Education, 26*(1), 350–364. doi: 10.1007/s40593-015-0057-9

Blair, K., Schwartz, D. L., Biswas, G., & Leelawong, K. (2007). Pedagogical agents for learning by teaching: Teachable agents. *Educational Technology*, *47*, 56–61.

Blumenfeld, P. C., Soloway, E., Marx, R. W., Krajcik, J. S., Guzdial, M., & Palincsar, A. (1991). Motivating project-based learning: Sustaining the doing, supporting the learning. *Educational Psychologist*, *26*(3), 369–398. doi: 10.1207/s15326985ep2603&4_8

Booth, J. L., Lange, K. E., Koedinger, K. R., & Newton, K. J. (2013). Using example problems to improve student learning in algebra: Differentiating between correct and incorrect examples. *Learning and Instruction*, *25*, 24–34. doi: 10.1016/j.learninstruc.2012.11.002

Bredeweg, B., Liem, J., & Nicolaou, C. (2016). Assessing learner-constructed conceptual models and simulations of dynamic systems. In K. Verbert, M. Sharples, & T. Klobučar (Eds.), *Proceedings of the 11th European Conference on Technology Enhanced Learning, EC-TEL 2016* (pp. 357–362). Cham, Switzerland: Springer.

Brusilovsky, P., Schwarz, E., & Weber, G. (1996). ELM-ART: An intelligent tutoring system on the World Wide Web. In C. Frasson, G. Gauthier, & A. Lesgold (Eds.), *Proceedings of the Third International Conference on Intelligent Tutoring Systems, ITS '96* (pp. 261–269). Berlin: Springer.

Bull, S. (2020). There are open learner models about! *IEEE Transactions on Learning Technologies*, *13*(2), 425–448. doi: 10.1109/TLT.2020.2978473

Bull, S., & Kay, J. (2008). Metacognition and open learner models. In I. Roll, & V. Aleven (Eds.), *Proceedings of the Workshop on Metacognition and Self-Regulated Learning in Educational Technologies (SRL@ET), held in conjunction with ITS 2008* (pp. 7–20). Montreal, Canada. https://citeseerx.ist.psu.edu/viewdoc/download?doi=10.1.1.217.4070&rep=rep1&type=pdf

Bull, S., & Kay, J. (2016). SMILI☺: A framework for interfaces to learning data in open learner models, learning analytics and related fields. *International Journal of Artificial Intelligence in Education*, *26*(1), 293–331. doi: 10.1007/s40593-015-0090-8

Bunt, A., & Conati, C. (2003). Probabilistic student modeling to improve exploratory behaviour. *Journal of User Modeling and User-Adapted Interaction*, *13*(3), 269–309 doi: 10.1023/A:1024733008280

Burton, R. R., & Brown, J. S. (1979). An investigation of computer coaching for informal learning activities. *International Journal of Man-Machine Studies*, *11*(1), 5–24.

Castell, S. D., & Jenson, J. (2003). Serious play: Curriculum for a post-talk era. *Journal of the Canadian Association for Curriculum Studies*, *35*(6), 649–665. doi: 10.1080/0022027032000145552

Chase, C. C., Chin, D. B., Oppezzo, M. A., & Schwartz, D. L. (2009). Teachable agents and the protégé effect: Increasing the effort towards learning. *Journal of Science Education and Technology*, *18*(4), 334–352. doi: 10.1007/s10956-009-9180-4

Chase, C. C., Connolly, H., Lamnina, M., & Aleven, V. (2019). Problematizing helps! A classroom study of computer-based guidance for invention activities. *International Journal of Artificial Intelligence in Education*, *29*(2), 283–316. doi: 10.1007/s40593-019-00178-y

Chen, J., Wang, M., Kirschner, P. A., & Tsai, C. C. (2018). The role of collaboration, computer use, learning environments, and supporting strategies in CSCL: A meta-analysis. *Review of Educational Research*, *88*(6), 799–843. doi: 10.3102/0034654318791584

Chen, C. H., & Yang, Y. C. (2019). Revisiting the effects of project-based learning on students' academic achievement: A meta-analysis investigating moderators. *Educational Research Review*, *26*, 71–81.

Chi, M. T. H., & Wylie, R. (2014). The ICAP framework: Linking cognitive engagement to active learning outcomes. *Educational Psychologist*, *49*(4), 219–243. doi: 10.1080/00461520.2014.965823

Chi, M. T. H., Adams, J., Bogusch, E. B., Bruchok, C., Kang, S., Lancaster, M., … Yaghmourian, D. L. (2018). Translating the ICAP theory of cognitive engagement into practice. *Cognitive Science*, *42*(6), 1777–1832. doi: 10.1111/cogs.12626

Chng, E., Seyam, M. R., Yao, W., & Schneider, B. (2020). Using motion sensors to understand collaborative interactions in digital fabrication labs. In I. Bittencourt, M. Cukurova, K. Muldner, R. Luckin, & E. Millán (Eds.), *Proceedings of the 21st International Conference on Artificial Intelligence in Education* (pp. 118–128). Cham, Switzerland: Springer.

Clark, D. B., Tanner-Smith, E., & Killingsworth, S. (2016). Digital games, design, and learning: A systematic review and meta-analysis. *Review of Educational Research*, *86*(1), 79–122. doi: 10.3102/0034654315582065.

Cocea, M., Gutierrez-Santos, S., & Magoulas, G. (2009). Enhancing modelling of users' strategies in exploratory learning through case-base maintenance. In *Proceedings of 14th UK Workshop on Case-Based Reasoning (UKCBR 2009)* (pp. 2–13). Cambridge, UK: BCS SGAI.

Cocea, M., & Magoulas, G. D. (2017). Design and evaluation of a case-based system for modelling exploratory learning behavior of math generalization. *IEEE Transactions on Learning Technologies*, *10*(4), 436–449. doi: 10.1109/TLT.2017.2661310

Collins, A., Brown, J. S., & Newman, S. E. (1989). Cognitive apprenticeship: Teaching the crafts of reading, writing, and mathematics. In L. B. Resnick (Ed.), *Knowing, learning, and instruction: Essays in honor of Robert Glaser* (pp. 453–494). Hillsdale, NJ: Lawrence Erlbaum Associates, Inc.

Conati, C., Jaques, N., & Muir, M. (2013). Understanding attention to adaptive hints in educational games: An eye-tracking study. *International Journal of Artificial Intelligence in Education*, *23*, 131–161. doi: 10.1007/s40593-013-0002-8

Conati, C., & Vanlehn, K. (2000). Toward computer-based support of meta-cognitive skills: A computational framework to coach self-explanation. *International Journal of Artificial Intelligence in Education*, *11*(4), 389–415. doi: 10.1007/s40593-015-0074-8

Conati, C., & Zhou, X. (2002). Modeling students' emotions from cognitive appraisal in educational games. In S. A. Cerri, G. Gouardères, & F. Paraguaçu (Eds.), *Proceedings of the 6th International Conference on Intelligent Tutoring Systems, ITS 2002* (pp. 944–954). Berlin, Heidelberg, New York: Springer-Verlag.

Constantino-Gonzalez, M., Suthers, D. D., & de los Santos, J. G. E. (2003). Coaching web-based collaborative learning based on problem solution differences and participation. *International Journal of Artificial Intelligence in Education*, *13*(2–4), 263–299.

Corbett, A. (2001). Cognitive computer tutors: Solving the two-sigma problem. In M. Bauer, P. J. Gmytrasiewicz, & J. Vassileva (Eds.), *UM '01: Proceedings of the 8th International Conference on User Modeling* (pp. 137–147). Berlin, Heidelberg: Springer-Verlag.

Corbett, A. T., & Anderson, J. R. (1995). Knowledge tracing: Modeling the acquisition of procedural knowledge. *User Modeling and User-Adapted Interaction*, *4*(4), 253–278. doi: 10.1007/BF01099821

Corbett, A. T., & Anderson, J. R. (2001). Locus of feedback control in computer-based tutoring: Impact on learning rate, achievement and attitudes. In J. Jacko & A. Sears (Eds.), *CHI '01: Proceedings of the SIGCHI Conference on Human Factors in Computing Systems* (pp. 245–252). New York: ACM.

Corbett, A., Kauffman, L., Maclaren, B., Wagner, A., & Jones, E. (2010). A Cognitive Tutor for genetics problem solving: Learning gains and student modeling. *Journal of Educational Computing Research*, *42*(2), 219–239. doi: 10.2190/EC.42.2.e

Corbett, A., McLaughlin, M., & Scarpinatto, K. C. (2000). Modeling student knowledge: Cognitive tutors in high school and college. *User Modeling and User-Adapted Interaction*, *10*(2), 81–108. doi: 10.1023/A:1026505626690

Crooks, N. M., & Alibali, M. W. (2014). Defining and measuring conceptual knowledge in mathematics. *Developmental Review*, *34*(4), 344–377. doi: 10.1016/j.dr.2014.10.001

Czikszentmihalyi, M. (1990). *Flow: The psychology of optimal experience.* Harper & Row.

Darabi, A., Arrington, T. L., & Sayilir, E. (2018). Learning from failure: A meta-analysis of the empirical studies. *Educational Technology Research and Development*, *66*(5), 1101–1118.

Deci, E. L., & Ryan, R. M. (1985). *Intrinsic motivation and self-determination in human behavior.* Plenum.

De Groot, R., Drachman, R., Hever, R., Schwarz, B., Hoppe, U., Harrer, A., De Laat, M., Wegerif, R., McLaren, B.M., & Baurens, B. (2007). Computer supported moderation of e-Discussions: The ARGUNAUT approach. In C. A. Chinn, G. Erkens, & S. Puntambekar (Eds.), *Mice, Minds and Society, Proceedings of the Conference on Computer Supported Collaborative Learning, CSCL-07* (Vol. 8, pp. 165–167). New Brunswick, NJ, USA: International Society of the Learning Sciences, Inc.

Dickler, R., Adair, A., Gobert, J., Hussain-Abidi, H., Olsen, J., O'Brien, M., & Pedro, M. S. (2021). Examining the use of a teacher alerting dashboard during remote learning. In I. Roll, D. McNamara, S. Sosnovsky, R. Luckin, & V. Dimitrova (Eds.), *Proceedings of the 22nd International Conference on Artificial Intelligence in Education, AIED 2021* (pp. 134–138). Cham, Switzerland: Springer International Publishing.

Dillenbourg, P. (1999). What do you mean by "collaborative learning?" In P. Dillenbourg (Ed.), *Collaborative learning: Cognitive and computational approaches* (pp. 1–16). Amsterdam, the Netherlands: Pergamon, Elsevier Science.

Dillenbourg, P. (2002). Overscripting CSCL: The risks of blending collaborative learning with instructional design. In P. A. Kirschner (Ed.), *Three worlds of CSCL. Can we support CSCL?* (pp. 61–91). Heerlen, the Netherlands: Open Universiteit Nederland.

Dillenbourg, P., & Fischer, F. (2007). Computer-supported collaborative learning: The basics. *Zeitschrift für Berufs- und Wirtschaftspädagogik*, *21*, 111–130.

DiSessa, A. A., & Cobb, P. (2004). Ontological innovation and the role of theory in design experiments. *The Journal of the Learning Sciences*, *13*(1), 77–103. doi: 10.1207/s15327809jls1301_4

Diziol, D., Walker, E., Rummel, N., & Koedinger, K. (2010). Using intelligent tutor technology to implement adaptive support for student collaboration. *Educational Psychology Review*, *22*(1), 89–102. doi: 10.1007/s10648-009-9116-9

Doroudi, S., Aleven, V., & Brunskill, E. (2019). Where's the reward? A review of reinforcement learning for instructional sequencing. *International Journal of Artificial Intelligence in Education*, *29*(10), 568–620. doi: 10.1007/s40593-019-00187-x

du Boulay, B. (2019). Escape from the Skinner Box: The case for contemporary intelligent learning environments. *British Journal of Educational Technology*, *50*(6), 2902–2919. doi: 10.1111/bjet.12860

Duran, D. (2017). Learning-by-teaching. Evidence and implications as a pedagogical mechanism. *Innovations in Education and Teaching International*, *54*(5), 476–484. doi: 10.1080/14703297.2016.1156011

Elsom-Cook, M. T. (1988). Guided discovery tutoring and bounded user modelling. In J. A. Self (Ed.), *Artificial Intelligence and Human Learning: Intelligent Computer-Aided Instruction*. Chapman and Hall.

Easterday, M. W., Aleven, V., Scheines, R. & Carver, S. M. (2017). Using tutors to improve educational games: A cognitive game for policy argument. *Journal of the Learning Sciences*, *26*(2), 226–276. doi: 10.1080/10508406.2016.126928

Echeverria, V., Martinez-Maldonado, R., & Buckingham Shum, S. (2019). Towards collaboration translucence: Giving meaning to multimodal group data. In S. Brewster, G. Fitzpatrick, A. Cox, & V. Kostakos (Eds.), *CHI '19: Proceedings of the 2019 CHI Conference on Human Factors in Computing Systems* (pp. 1–16). New York: ACM.

Ericsson, K. A., Krampe, R. T., & Tesch-Römer, C. (1993). The role of deliberate practice in the acquisition of expert performance. *Psychological Review*, *100*(3), 363–406. doi: 10.1037//0033-295X.100.3.363

Evans, A., Davis, K., & Wobbrock, J. (2019). Adaptive Support for Collaboration on Tabletop Computers. In K. Lund, G. P. Niccolai, E. Lavoué, C. Hmelo-Silver, G. Gweon, & M. Baker (Eds.), *A wide lens: Combining embodied, enactive, extended, and embedded learning in collaborative settings, 13th International Conference on Computer Supported Collaborative Learning, CSCL 2019* (vol. 1, 176–183). Lyon, France. International Society of the Learning Sciences.

Fang, Y., Ren, Z., Hu, X., & Graesser, A. C. (2019). A meta-analysis of the effectiveness of ALEKS on learning. *Educational Psychology*, *39*(10), 1278–1292. doi: 10.1080/01443410.2018.1495829

Fischer, F., Kollar, I., Stegmann, K., & Wecker, C. (2013). Toward a script theory of guidance in computer-supported collaborative learning. *Educational Psychologist*, *48*(1), 56–66.

Gee, J. P. (2003). *What video games have to teach us about learning and literacy*. London: Palgrave Macmillan.

Gauthier, A., Mavrikis, M., Benton, L., & Vasalou, A. (2022) Adoption and usage challenges of a learning analytics dashboard for game-based learning: Design and implementation implications. To appear in the *Practitioner Track Proceedings of the 12th International Conference on Learning Analytics and Knowledge (LAK'22)*.

Gobert, J., Sao Pedro, M., Raziuddin, J., & Baker, R. S. (2013). From log files to assessment metrics for science inquiry using educational data mining. *Journal of the Learning Sciences*, *22*(4), 521–563. doi: 10.1080/10508406.2013.837391

Goguadze, G., Sosnovsky, S., Isotani, S., & McLaren, B. M. (2011). Evaluating a Bayesian student model of decimal misconceptions. In M. Pechenizkiy, T. Calders, C. Conati, S. Ventura, C. Romero, & J. Stamper (Eds.), *Proceedings of the 4th International Conference on Educational Data Mining (EDM 2011)* (pp. 301–306). Worcester, MA: International Educational Data Mining Society.

Grawemeyer, B., Mavrikis, M., Holmes, W., Gutiérrez-Santos, S., Wiedmann, M., & Rummel, N. (2017). Affective learning: Improving engagement and enhancing learning with affect-aware feedback. *User Modeling and User-Adapted Interaction*, *27*, 119–158. doi: 10.1007/s11257-017-9188-z

Gros, B. (2007). Digital games in education: The design of games-based learning environments. *Journal of Research on Technology in Education*, *40*(1), 23–38.

Gutierrez-Santos, S., Mavrikis, M., Geraniou, E., & Poulovassilis, A. (2017). Similarity-based grouping to support teachers on collaborative activities in an exploratory mathematical microworld. *IEEE Transactions on Emerging Topics in Computing*, *5*(1), 56–68. doi: 10.1109/TETC.2016.2533318

Gutierrez-Santos, S., Mavrikis, M., & Magoulas, G. D. (2012). A separation of concerns for engineering intelligent support for exploratory learning environments. *Journal of Research and Practice in Information Technology*, *44*(3), 347–360.

Gusukuma, L., Bart, A. C., Kafura, D., & Ernst, J. (2018). Misconception-driven feedback: Results from an experimental study. In L. Malmi, A. Korhonen, R. McCartney, & A. Petersen (Eds.), *Proceedings of the 2018 ACM Conference on International Computing Education Research, ICER '18* (pp. 160–168). New York: ACM.

Habgood, M. P. J., & Ainsworth, S. (2011). Motivating children to learn effectively: Exploring the value of intrinsic integration in educational games. *Journal of the Learning Sciences*, *20*(2), 169–206. doi: 10.1080/10508406.2010.50802

Hadwin, A., Järvelä, S., & Miller, M. (2018). Self-regulation, co-regulation, and shared regulation in collaborative learning environments. In D. H. Schunk & J. A. Greene (Eds.), *Handbook of self-regulation of learning and performance* (pp. 83–106). New York: Routledge/Taylor & Francis Group.

Häkkinen, P., & Mäkitalo-Siegl, K. (2007). Educational perspectives on scripting CSCL. In F. Fischer, I.Kollar, H. Mandl, & J. M. Haake (Eds.), *Scripting computer-supported collaborative learning* (pp. 263–271). Boston, MA: Springer.

Hansen, A., Mavrikis, M., & Geraniou, E. (2016). Supporting teachers' technological pedagogical content knowledge of fractions through co-designing a virtual manipulative. *Journal of Mathematics Teacher Education*, 19(2–3), 205–226. doi: 10.1007/s10857-016-9344-0

Harel, I., & Papert, S. (1991). *Constructionism*. Ablex Publishing Corporation.

Harpstead, E., & Aleven, V. (2015). Using empirical learning curve analysis to inform design in an educational game. In A. L. Cox, P. Cairns, R. L. Mandryk, & D. Johnson (Eds.), *Proceedings of the ACM SIGCHI Annual Symposium on Computer-Human Interaction in Play, CHIPLAY '15* (pp. 197–207). New York: ACM.

Harsley, R., Di Eugenio, B., Green, N., & Fossati, D. (2017). Enhancing an intelligent tutoring system to support student collaboration: Effects on learning and behavior. In E. André, R. Baker, X. Hu, Ma. M. T. Rodrigo, & B. du Boulay (Eds.), *Proceedings of the 18th International Conference on Artificial Intelligence in Education, AIED 2017* (pp. 519–522). Cham, Switzerland: Springer.

Hattie, J. (2009). *Visible learning: A synthesis of over 800 meta-analyses relating to achievement*. Routledge.

Healy, L., & Kynigos, C. (2010). Charting the microworld territory over time: design and construction in mathematics education. *ZDM Mathematics Education*, *42*, 63–76. doi: 10.1007/s11858-009-0193-5

Heffernan, N. T., & Heffernan, C. L. (2014). The ASSISTments ecosystem: Building a platform that brings scientists and teachers together for minimally invasive research on human learning and teaching. *International Journal of Artificial Intelligence in Education*, *24*(4), 470–497. doi: 10.1007/s40593-014-0024-x

Heffernan, N. T., Koedinger, K. R., & Razzaq, L. (2008). Expanding the model-tracing architecture: A 3rd generation intelligent tutor for algebra symbolization. *International Journal of Artificial Intelligence in Education*, *18*(2), 153–178.

Holstein, K., Aleven, V., & Rummel, N. (2020). A conceptual framework for human–AI hybrid adaptivity in education. In I. Bittencourt, M. Cukurova, K. Muldner, R. Luckin, & E. Millán (Eds.), *Proceedings, 21th International Conference on Artificial Intelligence in Education, AIED 2020* (pp. 240–254). Cham, Switzerland: Springer.

Holstein, K., McLaren, B. M., & Aleven, V. (2018). Student learning benefits of a mixed-reality teacher awareness tool in AI-enhanced classrooms. In C. P. Rosé, R. Martínez-Maldonado, H. U. Hoppe, R. Luckin, M. Mavrikis, K. Porayska-Pomsta, B. McLaren, & B. du Boulay (Eds.), *Proceedings, 19th International Conference on Artificial Intelligence in Education, AIED 2018* (Part 1, pp. 154–168). Cham, Switzerland: Springer.

Hood, D., Lemaignan, S., & Dillenbourg, P. (2015). When children teach a robot to write: An autonomous teachable humanoid which uses simulated handwriting. In J. A. Adams, W. Smart, B. Mutlu, & L. Takayama (Eds.), *Proceedings of the Tenth Annual ACM/IEEE International Conference on Human-Robot Interaction* (pp. 83–90). New York: ACM.

Hooshyar, D., Malva, L., Yang, Y., Pedaste, M., Wang, M., & Lim, H. (2021). An adaptive educational computer game: Effects on students' knowledge and learning attitude in computational thinking. *Computers in Human Behavior*, *114*, Article 106575. doi: 10.1016/j.chb.2020.106575

Hosseini, R., Akhuseyinoglu, K., Brusilovsky, P., Malmi, L., Pollari-Malmi, K., Schunn, C., & Sirkiä, T. (2020). Improving engagement in program construction examples for learning Python programming. *International Journal of Artificial Intelligence in Education, 30*(2), 299–336. doi: 10.1007/s40593-020-00197-0

Hou, X., Nguyen, H. A., Richey, J. E., Harpstead, E., Hammer, J., & McLaren, B. M. (2022). Assessing the effects of open models of learning and enjoyment in a digital learning game. *International Journal of Artificial Intelligence in Education, 32*, 120–150. doi: 10.1007/S40593-021-00250-6

Hou, X., Nguyen, H.A., Richey, J.E., & McLaren, B.M. (2020). Exploring how gender and enjoyment impact learning in a digital learning game. In I. Bittencourt, M. Cukurova, K. Muldner, R. Luckin, & E. Millán (Eds.), *Proceedings of the 21st International Conference on Artificial Intelligence in Education. AIED 2020.* Lecture Notes in Computer Science (LNCS, vol. 12163, pp. 255–268). Springer, Cham.

Hoyles, C. (1993). Microworlds/Schoolworlds: The transformation of an innovation. In C. Keitel & K. Ruthven (Eds.), *Learning from computers: Mathematics education and technology* (pp. 1–17). Berlin: Springer-Verlag.

Huang, Y., Lobczowski, N. G., Richey, J. E., McLaughlin, E. A., Asher, M. W., Harackiewicz, J. M., Aleven, V. A. W. M. M., & Koedinger, K. R. (2021). A general multi-method approach to data-driven redesign of tutoring systems. In M. Scheffel, N. Dowell, S. Joksimovic, G. Siemens (Eds.), Proceedings *LAK21: 11th International Learning Analytics and Knowledge Conference* (pp. 161–172). New York: ACM.

Hussein, M. H., Ow, S. H., Elaish, M. M., & Jensen, E. O. (2022). Digital game-based learning in K-12 mathematics education: A systematic literature review. *Education and Information Technologies, 27,* 2859–2891. https://doi.org/10.1007/s10639-021-10721-x

Jacovina, M. E., Jackson, G. T., Snow, E. L., & McNamara, D. S. (2016). Timing game-based practice in a reading comprehension strategy tutor. In A. Micarelli, J. Stamper, & K. Panourgia (Eds.), *Proceedings of the 13th International Conference on Intelligent Tutoring Systems (ITS 2016)* (pp. 59–68). Cham, Switzerland: Springer.

Janssen, J., & Bodemer, D. (2013). Coordinated computer-supported collaborative learning: Awareness and awareness tools. *Educational Psychologist, 48*(1), 40–55. doi: 10.1080/00461520.2012.749153

Jiang, X., Rollinson, J., Plonsky, L., & Pajak, B. (2020). *Duolingo efficacy study: Beginning-level courses equivalent to four university semesters. Duolingo Research Report DRR-20-04.* https://www.duolingo.com/efficacy

Johnson, W. L. (2010). Serious use of a serious game for language learning. *International Journal of Artificial Intelligence in Education 20*(2), 175–195.

Johnson, W. L., & Lester, J. (2018). Pedagogical agents: Back to the future. *AI Magazine 39*(2), 33–44. doi: 10.1609/aimag.v39i2.2793

Jordan, P., Albacete, P., & Katz, S. (2018). A comparison of tutoring strategies for recovering from a failed attempt during faded support. In C. P. Rosé, R. Martínez-Maldonado, H. U. Hoppe, R. Luckin, K. Mavrikis, K. Porayska-Pomsta, B. McLaren, & B. du Boulay (Eds.), *Proceedings, 19th International Conference on Artificial Intelligence in Education, AIED 2018* (pp. 212–224). Cham, Switzerland: Springer.

Joyner, D. A., & Goel, A. K. (2015). Improving inquiry-driven modeling in science education through interaction with intelligent tutoring agents. In O. Brdiczka, P. Chau, G. Carenini, S. Pan, & P. O. Kristensson (Eds.), *IUI '15: Proceedings of the 20th International Conference on Intelligent User Interfaces* (pp. 5–16). New York: ACM.

Jung, H., Kim, H.J. So, S., Kim, J., & Oh, C. (2019). TurtleTalk: An educational programming game for children with voice user interface. In S. Brewster, G. Fitzpatrick, A. Cox, & V. Kostakos (Eds.), *CHI'19 Conference on Human Factors in Computing Systems Extended Abstracts* (pp. 1–6). New York: ACM.

Kaendler, C., Wiedmann, M., Rummel, N., & Spada, H. (2015). Teacher competencies for the implementation of collaborative learning in the classroom: A framework and research review. *Educational Psychology Review, 27*(3), 505–536. doi: 10.1007/s10648-014-9288-9

Kalyuga, S. (2007). Expertise reversal effect and its implications for learner-tailored instruction. *Educational Psychology Review, 19*(4), 509–539. doi: 10.1007/s10648-007-9054-3

Karakostas, A., & Demetriadis, S. (2014). Adaptive vs. fixed domain support in the context of scripted collaborative learning. *Journal of Educational Technology & Society, 17*(1), 206–217.

Käser, T., & Schwartz, D. L. (2020). Modeling and analyzing inquiry strategies in open-ended learning environments. *International Journal of Artificial Intelligence in Education*, *30*(3), 504–535. doi: 10.1007/s40593-020-00199-y

Kapur, M., & Rummel, N. (2012). Productive failure in learning from generation and invention activities. *Instructional Science*, *40*(4), 645–650. doi: 10.1007/s11251-012-9235-4

Katz, S., Allbritton, D., & Connelly, J. (2003). Going beyond the problem given: How human tutors use post-solution discussions to support transfer. *International Journal of Artificial Intelligence in Education*, *13*(1), 79–116.

Katz, S. N., Hall, E., & Lesgold, A. (1997). Cognitive task analysis and intelligent computer-based training systems: Lessons learned from coached practice environments in Air Force avionics. Paper presented at the Annual Meeting of the American Educational Research Association, Chicago, IL.

Kay, J. (2001). Learner control. *User Modeling and User-adapted Interaction*, *11*(1), 111–127. doi: 10.1023/A:1011194803800

Kay, J. (2021). Scrutability, control and learner models: Foundations for learner-centred design in AIED. In I. Roll, D. McNamara, S. Sosnovsky, R. Luckin, & V. Dimitrova (Eds.), *Proceedings of the 22nd International Conference on Artificial Intelligence in Education, AIED 2021* (pp. 3–8). Cham, Switzerland: Springer.

Ke, F. (2016). Designing and integrating purposeful learning in game play: A systematic review. *Educational Technology Research and Development*, *64*(2), 219–44. doi: 10.1007/s11423-015-9418-1

Kelly, K., Heffernan, N., Heffernan, C., Goldman, S., Pellegrino, J., & Goldstein, D. S. (2013). Estimating the effect of web-based homework. In H. C. Lane, K. Yacef, J. Mostow, & P. Pavlik (Eds.), Proceedings of the 16th International Conference on Artificial Intelligence in Education AIED 2013 (pp. 824–827). Berlin, Heidelberg: Springer.

Kelly, D. P., & Rutherford, T. (2017). Khan Academy as supplemental instruction: A controlled study of a computer-based mathematics intervention. *The International Review of Research in Open and Distributed Learning*, *18*(4), 70–77. doi: 10.19173/irrodl.v18i4.2984

King, A. (2007). Scripting collaborative learning processes: A cognitive perspective. In F. Fischer, I. Kollar, H. Mandl, & J. M. Haake (Eds.), *Scripting Computer-Supported Collaborative Learning: Cognitive, Computational and Educational Perspectives* (pp. 13–37). New York: Springer.

Kinnebrew, J. S., Segedy, J. R., & Biswas, G. (2014). Analyzing the temporal evolution of students' behaviors in open-ended learning environments. *Metacognition and Learning*, *9*(2), 187–215. doi: 10.1007/S11409-014-9112-4

Kirschner, P., Sweller, J., & Clark, R. (2006). Why minimal guidance during instruction does not work: An analysis of the failure of constructivist, discovery, problem-based, experiential, and inquiry-based teaching. *Educational Psychologist*, *41*(2), 75–86. doi: 10.1207/s15326985ep4102_1

Koedinger, K. R., & Aleven, V. (2007). Exploring the assistance dilemma in experiments with Cognitive Tutors. *Educational Psychology Review*, *19*(3), 239–264. doi: 10.1007/s10648-007-9049-0

Koedinger, K. R., & Aleven, V. (2016). An interview reflection on "Intelligent tutoring goes to school in the big city." *International Journal of Artificial Intelligence in Education*, *26*(1), 13–24. doi: 10.1007/s40593-015-0082-8

Koedinger, K. R., & Aleven, V. (2022). Multimedia learning with Cognitive Tutors. In R. Mayer & L. Fiorella (Eds.), *The Cambridge handbook of multimedia learning: Third Edition* (pp. 439–451). Cambridge, New York: Cambridge University Press.

Koedinger, K. R., Aleven, V., Roll, I., & Baker, R. (2009). In vivo experiments on whether supporting metacognition in intelligent tutoring systems yields robust learning. In D. J. Hacker, J. Dunlosky, & A. C. Graesser (Eds.), *Handbook of metacognition in education* (pp. 897–964). The Educational Psychology Series. New York: Routledge.

Koedinger, K. R., Anderson, J. R., Hadley, W. H., & Mark, M. A. (1997). Intelligent tutoring goes to school in the big city. *International Journal of Artificial Intelligence in Education*, *8*(1), 30–43.

Koedinger, K. R., Booth, J. L., & Klahr, D. (2013). Instructional complexity and the science to constrain it. *Science*, *342*(6161), 935–937. doi: 10.1126/science.1238056

Koedinger, K. R., Corbett, A. T., & Perfetti, C. (2012). The Knowledge-Learning-Instruction framework: Bridging the science-practice chasm to enhance robust student learning. *Cognitive Science*, *36*(5), 757–798. doi: 10.1111/j.1551-6709.2012.01245.x

Koedinger, K. R., & Sueker, E. L. (1996). PAT goes to college: Evaluating a Cognitive Tutor for developmental mathematics. In D. C. Edelson & E. A. Domeshek (Eds.), *Proceedings of the*

1996 International Conference on the Learning Sciences, ICLS '96 (pp. 180–187). Charlottesville, VA: Association for the Advancement of Computing in Education.

Krajcik, J. S., & Blumenfeld, P. C. (2006). Project-based learning. In K. Sawyer (Ed.), *The Cambridge handbook of the learning sciences* (pp. 317–34). Cambridge, MA: Cambridge University Press.

Kulik, C. L. C., Kulik, J. A., & Bangert-Drowns, R. L. (1990). Effectiveness of mastery learning programs: A meta-analysis. *Review of Educational Research, 60*(2), 265–299. doi: 1170612

Kulik, J. A., & Fletcher, J. D. (2015). Effectiveness of intelligent tutoring systems. *Review of Educational Research, 86*(1), 42–78. doi: 10.3102/003465431558142

Lachner, A., Hoogerheide, V., van Gog, T., & Renkl, A. (2021). Learning-by-teaching without audience presence or interaction: When and why does it work? *Educational Psychology Review, 34,* 575–607. doi: 10.1007/s10648-021-09643-4

Larusson, J. A., & Alterman, R. (2009). Wikis to support the "collaborative" part of collaborative learning. *International Journal of Computer-Supported Collaborative Learning, 4*(4), 371–402. doi: 10.1007/s11412-009-9076-6

Law, E., Baghaei Ravari, P., Chhibber, N., Kulic, D., Lin, S., Pantasdo, K. D., ... & Dillen, N. (2020). Curiosity Notebook: A platform for learning by teaching conversational agents. In R. Bernhaupt et al. (Eds.), *CHI EA '20: Extended Abstracts of the 2020 CHI Conference on Human Factors in Computing Systems* (pp. 1–9). New York: ACM.

Leelawong, K., & Biswas, G. (2008). Designing learning by teaching agents: The Betty's Brain system. *International Journal of Artificial Intelligence in Education, 18*(3), 181–208.

Lenat, D. B., & Durlach, P. J. (2014). Reinforcing math knowledge by immersing students in a simulated learning-by-teaching experience. *International Journal of Artificial Intelligence in Education, 24*(3), 216–250. doi: 10.1007/s40593-014-0016-x

Lesgold, A., Katz, S., Greenberg, L., Hughes, E., & Eggan, G. (1992). Extensions of intelligent tutoring paradigms to support collaborative learning. In S. Dijkstra, H. P. M. Krammer, & J. J. G. van Merriënboer (Eds.), *Instructional models in computer-based learning environments* (pp. 291–311). Springer.

Lesgold, A., Lajoie, S., Bunzo, M., & Eggan, G. (1992). SHERLOCK: A coached practice environment for an electronics troubleshooting job. In J. H. Larkin & R. W. Chabay (Eds.), *Computer-assisted instruction and intelligent tutoring systems: Shared goals and complementary approaches* (pp. 201–238). Hillsdale, NJ: Lawrence Erlbaum Associates, Inc.

Lester, J. C., Ha, E. Y., Lee, S. Y., Mott, B. W., Rowe, J. P., & Sabourin, J. L. (2013). Serious games get smart: Intelligent game-based learning environments. *AI Magazine, 34*(4), 31–45. doi: 10.1609/aimag.v34i4.2488.

Liu, Z., Mostafavi, B., & Barnes, T. (2016). Combining worked examples and problem solving in a data-driven logic tutor. In A. Micarelli, J. Stamper, & K. Panourgia (Eds.), *Proceedings of the 13th International Conference on Intelligent Tutoring Systems, ITS 2016* (pp. 347–353). Cham, Switzerland: Springer.

Lobel, A., Engels, R.C.M.E., Stone, L.L., Burk, W.J., & Granic, I. (2017). Video gaming and children's psychosocial well-being: A longitudinal study. *Journal of Youth and Adolescence, 46*(4), 884–897. doi: 10.1007/s10964-017-0646-z.

Lomas, D., Patel, K., Forlizzi, J.L., Koedinger, K.R. (2013). Optimizing challenge in an educational game using large-scale design experiments. In W. E. Mackay, S. Brewster, & S. Bødker (Eds.), *CHI '13: Proceedings of the SIGCHI Conference on Human Factors in Computing Systems* (pp. 89–98). New York: ACM.

Long, Y., & Aleven, V. (2014). Gamification of joint student/system control over problem selection in a linear equation tutor. In S. Trausan-Matu, K. E. Boyer, M. Crosby, & K. Panourgia (Eds.), *Proceedings of the 12th International Conference on Intelligent Tutoring Systems, ITS 2014* (pp. 378–387). New York: Springer.

Long Y., & Aleven, V. (2016). Mastery-oriented shared student/system control over problem selection in a linear equation tutor. In: A. Micarelli, J. Stamper, & K. Panourgia (Eds.), *Proceedings of the 13th International Conference on Intelligent Tutoring Systems, ITS 2016* (pp. 90–100). Springer, Cham.

Long, Y., & Aleven, V. (2017a). Educational game and intelligent tutoring system: A classroom study and comparative design analysis. *ACM Transactions on Computer-Human Interaction (TOCHI), 24*(3), 1–27. doi: 10.1145/3057889

Long, Y., & Aleven, V. (2017b). Enhancing learning outcomes through self-regulated learning support with an open learner model. *User Modeling and User-Adapted Interaction, 27*(1), 55–88. doi: 10.1007/s11257-016-9186-6

Lubold, N., Walker, E., Pon-Barry, H., & Ogan, A. (2019). Comfort with robots influences rapport with a social, entraining teachable robot. In: S. Isotani, E. Millán, A. Ogan, P. Hastings, B. McLaren, & R. Luckin (Eds.), *Proceedings, 20th International Conference on Artificial Intelligence in Education, AIED 2019* (pp. 231–243). Cham, Switzerland: Springer.

Lynch, C., Ashley, K., Pinkwart, N., & Aleven, V. (2009). Concepts, structures, and goals: Redefining ill-definedness. *International Journal of Artificial Intelligence in Education*, 19(3), 253–266.

Ma, W., Adesope, O. O., Nesbit, J. C., & Liu, Q. (2014). Intelligent tutoring systems and learning outcomes: A meta-analysis. *Journal of Educational Psychology*, 106(4), 901–918. doi: 10.1037/a0037123

Madaio, M., Lasko, R., Ogan, A., & Cassell, J. (2017). Using temporal association rule mining to predict dyadic rapport in peer tutoring. In X. Hu, T. Barnes, A. Hershkovitz, & L. Paquette (Eds.), *Proceedings of the 10th International Conference on Educational Data Mining* (pp. 318–323). Worcester, MA: Educational Data Mining Society.

Madaio, M., Peng, K., Ogan, A., & Cassell, J. (2018). A climate of support: A process-oriented analysis of the impact of rapport on peer tutoring. In Kay, J. and Luckin, R. (Eds.) *Rethinking learning in the digital age: Making the learning sciences count, 13th International Conference of the Learning Sciences, ICLS 2018* (vol. 1, pp. 600–607). London, UK: International Society of the Learning Sciences.

Magnisalis, I., Demetriadis, S., & Karakostas, A. (2011). Adaptive and intelligent systems for collaborative learning support: A review of the field. *IEEE Transactions on Learning Technologies*, 4(1), 5–20. doi: 10.1109/TLT.2011.2

Malone, T. W. (1981). Toward a theory of intrinsically motivating instruction. *Cognitive Science*, 5, 333–369. doi: 10.1207/s15516709cog0504_2

Malone, T.W. & Lepper, M.R. (1987). Making learning fun: A taxonomy of intrinsic motivations for learning. In R.E. Snow & M.J. Farr (Eds.), *Aptitude, learning, and instruction: Volume 3: Conative and affective process analyses* (pp. 223–253). New York: Routledge.

Maniktala, M., Cody, C., Barnes, T., & Chi, M. (2020). Avoiding help avoidance: Using interface design changes to promote unsolicited hint usage in an intelligent tutor. *International Journal of Artificial Intelligence in Education*, 30(4), 637–667. doi: 10.1007/s40593-020-00213-3

Marwan, S., Gao, G., Fisk, S., Price, T. W., & Barnes, T. (2020). Adaptive immediate feedback can improve novice programming engagement and intention to persist in computer science. In A. Robins, A. Moskal, A. J. Ko, & R. McCauley (Eds.), *Proceedings of the 2020 ACM Conference on International Computing Education Research* (pp. 194–203). New York: ACM. doi: 10.1145/3372782.3406264

Mathan, S. A., & Koedinger, K. R. (2005). Fostering the intelligent novice: Learning from errors with metacognitive tutoring. *Educational Psychologist*, 40(4), 257–265. doi: 10.1207/s15326985ep4004_7

Matsuda, N., Yarzebinski, E., Keiser, V., Raizada, R., Stylianides, G. J., Cohen, W. W., & Koedinger, K. R. (2011). Learning by teaching SimStudent–An initial classroom baseline study comparing with Cognitive Tutor. In G. Biswas, S. Bull, J. Kay, & T. Mitrovic (Eds.), *Proceedings of the 15th International Conference on Artificial Intelligence in Education, AIED 2011* (pp. 213–221). Berlin, Heidelberg: Springer.

Mavrikis, M., Geraniou, E., Gutierrez Santos, S., & Poulovassilis, A. (2019). Intelligent analysis and data visualisation for teacher assistance tools: The case of exploratory learning. *British Journal of Educational Technology*, 50, 2920–2942. doi: 10.1111/bjet.12876

Mavrikis, M., Gutierrez-Santos, S., Geraniou, E., & Noss, E. (2012). Design requirements, student perception indicators and validation metrics for intelligent exploratory learning environments. *Personal and Ubiquitous Computing*, 17(8), 1605–1620. doi: 10.1007/s00779-012-052.

Mavrikis, M., Gutierrez-Santos, S., Pearce-Lazard, D., Poulovassilis, A. & Magoulas, G. (2010). Layered Learner Modelling in ill-defined domains: Conceptual model and architecture in MiGen. In C. Lynch, K. Ashley, A. Mitrovic, V. Dimitrova, N. Pinkwart, & V. Aleven (Eds.), *Proceedings of Workshop on Intelligent Tutoring Technologies for Ill-Defined Problems and Ill-Defined Domains*, at ITS 2010 (pp. 53–60). Retrieved from http://citeseerx.ist.psu.edu/viewdoc/download?doi=10.1.1. 702.7771&rep=rep1&type=pdf

Mavrikis, M., Noss, R., Hoyles, C., & Geraniou, E. (2013). Sowing the seeds of algebraic generalization: Designing epistemic affordances for an intelligent microworld. *Journal of Computer Assisted Learning*, 29(1), 68–84. doi: 10.1111/j.1365-2729.2011.00469.x

Mavrikis, M., Rummel, N. Wiedmann, M., Loibl, K., Mazziotti, C., & Holmes, W. (2022). Combining exploratory learning with structured practice educational technologies to foster both conceptual and procedural fractions knowledge. *Journal of Educational Technology Research & Development*, 70, 691–712. doi: 10.1007/s11423-022-10104-0.

Mayer, R. E., & Moreno, R. (2003). Nine ways to reduce cognitive load in multimedia learning. *Educational Psychologist, 38*(1), 43–52. doi: 10.1207/S15326985EP3801_6

Mayer, R. E. (2014). *Computer games for learning: An evidence-based approach.* MIT Press.

Mayer, R. E. (2004). Should there be a three-strikes rule against pure discovery learning? *American Psychologist, 59*(1), 14–19. doi: 10.1037/0003-066X.59.1.14

Mayer, R. E. (2019). Computer games in education. *Annual Review of Psychology, 70*, 531–549. doi: 10.1146/annurev-psych-010418-102744

Mayo, M., Mitrovic, A., & McKenzie, J. (2000). CAPIT: An intelligent tutoring system for capitalisation and punctuation. In *Proceedings International Workshop on Advanced Learning Technologies. IWALT 2000. Advanced Learning Technology: Design and Development Issues* (pp. 151–154). Los Alamitos, CA: IEEE.

McKendree, J. (1990). Effective feedback content for tutoring complex skills. *Human-computer interaction, 5*(4), 381–413.

McLaren, B. M., Adams, D. M., Mayer, R. E., & Forlizzi, J. (2017). A computer-based game that promotes mathematics learning more than a conventional approach. *International Journal of Game-Based Learning (IJGBL), 7*(1), 36–56. doi: 10.4018/IJGBL.2017010103

McLaren, B. M., DeLeeuw, K. E., & Mayer, R. E. (2011). Polite web-based intelligent tutors: Can they improve learning in classrooms? *Computers & Education, 56*(3), 574–584. doi: 10.1016/j.compedu.2010.09.019.

McLaren, B. M., Farzan, R., Adams, D .M., Mayer, R. E., & Forlizzi, J. (2017). Uncovering gender and problem difficulty effects in learning with an educational game. In E. André, R. Baker, X. Hu, M.M.T. Rodrigo, & B. du Boulay (Eds.). *Proceedings of the 18th International Conference on Artificial Intelligence in Education (AIED 2017).* LNAI 10331 (pp. 540–543). Cham, Switzerland: Springer.

McLaren, B. M. & Isotani, S. (2011). When is it best to learn with all worked examples? In G. Biswas, S. Bull, J. Kay, & A. Mitrovic (Eds.), *Proceedings of the 15th International Conference on Artificial Intelligence in Education, AIED-2011* (pp. 222–229). Berlin, Heidelberg: Springer.

McLaren, B. M., Lim, S., & Koedinger, K. R. (2008). When and how often should worked examples be given to students? New results and a summary of the current state of research. In B. C. Love, K. McRae, & V. M. Sloutsky (Eds.), *Proceedings of the 30th Annual Conference of the Cognitive Science Society* (pp. 2176–2181). Austin, TX: Cognitive Science Society.

McLaren, B. M., Richey, J. E., Nguyen, H. A., & Hou, X. (2022). How instructional context can impact learning with educational technology: Lessons from a study with a digital learning game. *Computers & Education, 178.* doi: 10.1016/j.compedu.2021.104366

McLaren, B. M., Scheuer, O., & Mikšátko, J. (2010). Supporting collaborative learning and e-Discussions using artificial intelligence techniques. *International Journal of Artificial Intelligence in Education (IJAIED) 20*(1), 1–46. doi: 10.3233/JAI-2010-0001

McLaren, B. M., Timms, M., Weihnacht, D., & Brenner, D. (2012). Exploring the assistance dilemma in an inquiry learning environment for evolution theory. In *Proceedings of the Workshop on Intelligent Support for Exploratory Environments 2012: Exploring, Collaborating and Learning Together at the 11th International Conference on Intelligent Tutoring Systems (ITS 2012).*

McLaren, B. M., van Gog, T., Ganoe, C., Karabinos, M., & Yaron, D. (2016). The efficiency of worked examples compared to erroneous examples, tutored problem solving, and problem solving in computer-based learning environments. *Computers in Human Behavior, 55*, 87–99. doi: 10.1016/j.chb.2015.08.038

Melis, E., Andres, E., Büdenbender, J., Frischauf, A., Goguadze, G., Libbrecht, P., Pollet, M., & Ullrich, C. (2001). ActiveMath: A generic and adaptive web-based learning environment. *International Journal of Artificial Intelligence in Education, 12*(4), 385–407.

Mitrovic, A. (2012). Fifteen years of constraint-based tutors: what we have achieved and where we are going. *User Modeling and User-Adapted Interaction, 22*(1), 39–72. doi: 10.1007/s11257-011-9105-9

Mitrovic, A., & Holland, J. (2020). Effect of non-mandatory use of an intelligent tutor system on students' learning. In I. Bittencourt et al. (Eds.), *Proceedings of the International Conference on Artificial Intelligence in Education, AIED 2020* (pp. 386–397). Cham, Switzerland: Springer

Mitrovic, A., & Ohlsson, S. (2016). Implementing CBM: SQL-Tutor after fifteen years. *International Journal of Artificial Intelligence in Education, 26*(1), 150–159, doi: 10.1007/s40593-015-0049-9

Mitrovic, A., & Martin, B. (2000). Evaluating the effectiveness of feedback in SQL-Tutor. Proceedings of the International Workshop on Advanced Learning Technologies. IWALT 2000. Advanced Learning Technology: Design and Development Issues (pp. 143–144). Los Alamitos, CA: IEEE.

Mitrovic, A., & Martin, B. (2007). Evaluating the effect of open student models on self-assessment. *International Journal of Artificial Intelligence in Education*, *17*(2), 121–144.

Mitrovic, A., Ohlsson, S., & Barrow, D. K. (2013). The effect of positive feedback in a constraint-based intelligent tutoring system. *Computers & Education*, *60*(1), 264–272. doi: 10.1016/j.compedu.2012.07.002

Mitrovic, A., & Suraweera, P. (2016). Teaching database design with constraint-based tutors. *International Journal of Artificial Intelligence in Education*, *25*(4), 448–456. doi: 10.1007/s40593-015-0084-6

Mullins, D., Rummel, N., & Spada, H. (2011). Are two heads always better than one? Differential effects of collaboration on students' computer-supported learning in mathematics. *International Journal of Computer-Supported Collaborative Learning*, *6*(3), 421–443. doi: 10.1007/s11412-011-9122-z

Nagashima, T., Bartel, A. N., Yadav, G., Tseng, S., Vest, N. A., Silla, E. M., Alibali, M. W., & Aleven, V. (2021). Using anticipatory diagrammatic self-explanation to support learning and performance in early algebra. In E. de Vries, Y. Hod, & Ahn (Eds.), *Proceedings of the 15th International Conference of the Learning Sciences – ICLS 2021* (pp. 474–481). Bochum, Germany: International Society of the Learning Sciences.

Nathan, M. J. (1998). Knowledge and situational feedback in a learning environment for algebra story problem solving. *Interactive Learning Environments*, *5*(1), 135–159.

Nguyen, H. A, Hou, X., Stamper, J., & McLaren, B. M. (2020). Moving beyond test scores: Analyzing the effectiveness of a digital learning game through learning analytics. In A. N. Rafferty, J. Whitehill, C. Romero, & V. Cavalli-Sforza (Eds), *Proceedings of the 13th International Conference on Educational Data Mining* (pp. 487–495). Worcester, MA: International Educational Data Mining Society.

Noss, R., Hoyles, C., Mavrikis, M., Geraniou, E., Gutierrez-Santos, S., & Pearce, D. (2009). Broadening the sense of "dynamic": a microworld to support students' mathematical generalisation. *ZDM Mathematics Education 41*, 493–503. doi: 10.1007/s11858-009-0182-8

NPD Group (2019). Retail Tracking Service, 2019 Entertainment Survey. https://igda-website.s3.us-east-2.amazonaws.com/wp-content/uploads/2019/10/16161928/NPD-2019-Evolution-of-Entertainment-Whitepaper.pdf

Ogan, A., Finkelstein, S., Mayfield, E., D'Adamo, C., Matsuda, N., & Cassell, J. (2012). "Oh dear Stacy!" Social interaction, elaboration, and learning with teachable agents. In J. A. Konstan, E. H. Chi, & K. Höök (Eds.), *CHI '12: Proceedings of the SIGCHI Conference on Human Factors in Computing Systems* (pp. 39–48). New York: ACM. doi: 10.1145/2207676.2207684

Ohlsson, S. (1992). Constraint-based student modelling. *Journal of Interactive Learning Research*, *3*(4), 429. doi: 10.3991/ijet.v13i01.7397

Okita, S. Y., & Schwartz, D. L. (2013). Learning by teaching human pupils and teachable agents: The importance of recursive feedback. *Journal of the Learning Sciences*, *22*(3), 375–412.

Olsen, J. K., Aleven, V., & Rummel, N. (2015). Predicting student performance in a collaborative learning environment. In O. C. Santos et al. (Eds.), *Proceedings of the 8th International Conference on Educational Data Mining* (pp. 211–217). Worcester, MA: Educational Data Mining Society.

Olsen, J. K., Rummel, N., & Aleven, V. (2019). It is not either or: An initial investigation into combining collaborative and individual learning using an ITS. *International Journal of Computer-Supported Collaborative Learning*, *14*(3), 353–381. doi: 10.1007/s11412-019-09307-0

Olsen, J. K., Sharma, K., Rummel, N., & Aleven, V. (2020). Temporal analysis of multimodal data to predict collaborative learning outcomes. *British Journal of Educational Technology*, *51*(5), 1527–1547. doi: 10.1111/bjet.12982

Pai, H. H., Sears, D. A., & Maeda, Y. (2015). Effects of small-group learning on transfer: A meta-analysis. *Educational Psychology Review*, *27*(1), 79–102. doi: 10.1007/s10648-014-9260-8

Pane, J. F., Griffin, B. A., McCaffrey, D. F., & Karam, R. (2014). Effectiveness of Cognitive Tutor Algebra I at scale. *Educational Evaluation and Policy Analysis*, *36*(2), 127–144. doi: 10.3102/0162373713503748

Pane, J. F., McCaffrey, D. F., Slaughter, M. E., Steele, J. L., & Ikemoto, G. S. (2010). An experiment to evaluate the efficacy of Cognitive Tutor Geometry. *Journal of Research on Educational Effectiveness*, *3*(3), 254–281. doi: 10.1080/19345741003681189

Pareto, L. (2009). Teachable agents that learn by observing game playing behaviour. In S. D. Craig, D. Dicheva, A. Ogan, & H. C. Lane (Eds.), *AIED 2009: 14th International Conference on Artificial Intelligence in Education, Workshop Proceedings* (Volume 3: Intelligent Educational Games; pp. 31–40). Brighton, UK: International AIED Society.

Pareto, L. (2014). A teachable agent game engaging primary school children to learn arithmetic concepts and reasoning. *International Journal of Artificial Intelligence in Education, 24*(3), 251–283. doi: 10.1007/s40593-014-0018-8

Pelánek, R. (2017). Bayesian knowledge tracing, logistic models, and beyond: An overview of learner modeling techniques. *User Modeling and User-Adapted Interaction, 27*(3), 313–350. doi: 10.1007/s11257-017-9193-2

Phillips, A., Pane, J. F., Reumann-Moore, R., & Shenbanjo, O. (2020). Implementing an adaptive intelligent tutoring system as an instructional supplement. *Educational Technology Research and Development, 68*(3), 1409–1437. doi: 10.1007/s11423-020-09745-w

Plass, J. L., Homer, B. D., & Kinzer, C. K. (2015). Foundations of game-based learning. *Educational Psychologist, 50*(4), 258–283. doi: 10.1080/00461520.2015.1122533

Plass, J. L., & Pawar, S. (2020). Toward a taxonomy of adaptivity for learning. *Journal of Research on Technology in Education, 52*(3), 275–300. doi: 10.1080/15391523.2020.1719943

Porayska-Pomsta, K., Mavrikis, M., & Pain, H. (2008). Diagnosing and acting on student affect: the tutor's perspective. *User Modeling and User-Adapted Interaction, 18*(1), 125–173.

Prensky, M. (2006). *Don't bother me, Mom, I'm learning! How computer and video games are preparing your kids for 21st century success and how you can help.* St. Paul, MN: Paragon House.

Prieto, L. P., Holenko Dlab, M., Gutiérrez, I., Abdulwahed, M., & Balid, W. (2011). Orchestrating technology enhanced learning: a literature review and a conceptual framework. *International Journal of Technology Enhanced Learning, 3*(6), 583–598.

Quintana, C., Reiser, B. J., Davis, E. A., Krajcik, J., Fretz, E., Duncan, R. G., Kyza, E., Edelson, D., & Soloway, E. (2004). A scaffolding design framework for software to support science inquiry. *The Journal of the Learning Sciences, 13*(3), 337–386. doi: 10.1207/s15327809jls1303_4

Rau, M. A., Aleven, V., & Rummel, N. (2013). Interleaved practice in multi-dimensional learning tasks: Which dimension should we interleave? *Learning and Instruction, 23*, 98–114. doi: 10.1016/j.learninstruc.2012.07.003

Rau, M. A., Michaelis, J. E., & Fay, N. (2015). Connection making between multiple graphical representations: A multi-methods approach for domain-specific grounding of an intelligent tutoring system for chemistry. *Computers & Education, 82*, 460–485. doi: 10.1016/j.compedu.2014.12.009

Rau, M. A, & Wu, S. (2017). Educational technology support for collaborative learning with multiple visual representations in chemistry. In B. K. Smith, M. Borge, E. Mercier, & K. Y. Lim (Eds.), *Proceedings of the 12th International Conference on Computer-Supported Collaborative Learning, CSCL 2017* (Vol. 1, pp. 79–86). Philadelphia, PA: International Society of the Learning Sciences.

Reigeluth, C. M. (1999). What is instructional design theory and how is it changing? In C. M. Reigeluth (Ed.), *Instructional design theories and models: A new paradigm of instructional theory* (Vol. 2, pp. 5–29). Mahwah, NJ: Lawrence Erlbaum Associates.

Reigeluth, C. M., Bunderson, C. V. & Merrill, M. D. (1994) Is there a design science of instruction? In M. D. Merrill & D. G. Twitchell (Eds.), *Instructional design theory* (pp. 5–16). Englewood Cliffs, NJ: Educational Technology Publications.

Reiser, B. J. (2004). Scaffolding complex learning: The mechanisms of structuring and problematizing student work. *The Journal of the Learning Sciences, 13*(3), 273–304. doi: 10.1207/s15327809jls1303_2

Renkl, A. (2014). Toward an instructionally-oriented theory of example-based learning. *Cognitive science, 38*(1), 1–37. doi: 10.1111/cogs.12086

Richey, J. E., Andres-Bray, J. M. L., Mogessie, M., Scruggs, R., Andres, J. M., Star, J. R., ... & McLaren, B. M. (2019). More confusion and frustration, better learning: The impact of erroneous examples. *Computers & Education, 139*, 173–190. doi: 10.1016/j.compedu.2019.05.012

Rieber, L. P., Tzeng, S.-C., & Tribble, K. (2004). Discovery learning, representation, and explanation within a computer-based simulation: Finding the right mix. *Learning and Instruction*, *14*(3), 307–323. doi: 10.1016/j.learninstruc.2004.06.008

Ritter, S., Anderson, J. R., Koedinger, K. R., & Corbett, A. (2007). Cognitive Tutor: Applied research in mathematics education. *Psychonomic Bulletin & Review*, *14*(2), 249–255.

Ritter, S., Yudelson, M., Fancsali, S. E., & Berman, S. R. (2016). How mastery learning works at scale. In J. Haywood, V. Aleven, J. Kay & I. Roll (Eds.), *Proceedings of the Third (2016) ACM Conference on Learning @ Scale* (pp. 71–79). New York: ACM.

Roll, I., Aleven, V., McLaren, B. M., & Koedinger, K. R. (2011). Improving students' help-seeking skills using metacognitive feedback in an intelligent tutoring system. *Learning and instruction*, *21*(2), 267–280. doi: 10.1016/j.learninstruc.2010.07.004

Roll, I., Butler, D., Yee, N., Welsh, A., Perez, S., Briseno, A., Perkins, K., & Bonn, D. (2018). Understanding the impact of guiding inquiry: The relationship between directive support, student attributes, and transfer of knowledge, attitudes, and behaviours in inquiry learning. *Instructional Science*, *46*(1), 77–104. doi: 10.1007/s11251-017-9437-x

Roscoe, R. D., & Chi, M. T. (2007). Understanding tutor learning: Knowledge-building and knowledge-telling in peer tutors' explanations and questions. *Review of Educational Research*, *77*(4), 534–574. doi: 10.3102/0034654307309920

Rosenberg-Kima, R. B., Koren, Y., & Gordon, G. (2020). Robot-supported collaborative learning (RSCL): Social robots as teaching assistants for higher education small group facilitation. *Frontiers in Robotics and AI*, *6*, Article 148. doi: 10.3389/frobt.2019.00148

Rosenshine, B., & Meister, C. (1994). Reciprocal teaching: A review of the research. *Review of Educational Research*, *64*(4), 479–530. doi: 10.3102/00346543064004479

Rummel, N. (2018). One framework to rule them all? Carrying forward the conversation started by Wise and Schwarz. *International Journal of Computer-Supported Collaborative Learning*, *13*(1), 123–129. doi: 10.1007/s11412-018-9273-2

Ryan, R. M., Rigby, C. S., & Przybylski, A. (2006). The motivational pull of video games: A self-determination theory approach. *Motivation and Emotion*, *30*(4), 344–360. doi: 10.1007/s11031-006-9051-8

Sabourin, J. L., Shores, L. R., Mott, B. W., & Lester, J. C. (2013). Understanding and predicting student self-regulated learning strategies in game-based learning environments. *International Journal of Artificial Intelligence in Education*, *23*, 94–114. doi: 10.1007/s40593-013-0004-6.

Salden, R. J. C. M., Aleven, V. A. W. M. M., Schwonke, R., & Renkl, A. (2010). The expertise reversal effect and worked examples in tutored problem solving: Benefits of adaptive instruction. *Instructional Science*, *38*(3), 289–307. doi: 10.1007/s11251-009-9107-8

Salden, R. J., Koedinger, K. R., Renkl, A., Aleven, V., & McLaren, B. M. (2010). Accounting for beneficial effects of worked examples in tutored problem solving. *Educational Psychology Review*, *22*(4), 379–392. doi: 10.1007/s10648-010-9143-6

Sales, A. C., & Pane, J. F. (2020). The effect of teachers reassigning students to new Cognitive Tutor sections. In A. N. Rafferty, J. Whitehill, C. Romero, & V. Cavalli-Sforza (Eds.), *Proceedings of the 13th International Conference on Educational Data Mining* (pp. 202–211). Worcester, MA: International Educational Data Mining Society.

Sawyer, R., Smith, A., Rowe, J., Azevedo, R., & Lester, J. (2017). Is more agency better? The impact of student agency on game-based learning. In: E. André, R. Baker, X. Hu, M. M. T. Rodrigo, & B. du Boulay (Eds.), *Proceedings of the 18th International Conference on Artificial Intelligence in Education, AIED 2017* (LNCS, vol. 10331, pp. 335–346). Cham, Switzerland: Springer.

Schneider, B., & Pea, R. (2013). Real-time mutual gaze perception enhances collaborative learning and collaboration quality. *International Journal of Computer-Supported Collaborative Learning*, *8*(4), 375–397. doi: 10.1007/s11412-013-9181-4

Schooler, L. J., & Anderson, J. R. (1990). The disruptive potential of immediate feedback. In M. Piattelli-Palmarini (Ed.), *Proceedings of the Twelfth Annual Conference of the Cognitive Science Society* (pp. 702–708). Hillsdale, NJ: Erlbaum.

Segedy, J. R., Kinnebrew, J. S., & Biswas, G. (2015). Using coherence analysis to characterize self-regulated learning behaviours in open-ended learning environments. *Journal of Learning Analytics*, *2*(1), 13–48. doi: 10.18608/jla.2015.21.3

Shahriar, T., & Matsuda, N. (2021). "Can you clarify what you said?": Studying the impact of tutee agents' follow-up questions on tutors' learning. In I. Roll, D. McNamara, S. Sosnovsky, R. Luckin, & V. Dimitrova (Eds.), *Proceedings of the 22nd International Conference on Artificial Intelligence in Education, AIED 2021* (pp. 395–407). Cham, Switzerland: Springer.

Shute, V. J., D'Mello, S., Baker, R., Cho, K., Bosch, N., Ocumpaugh, J., Ventura, M. & Almeda, V. (2015). Modeling how incoming knowledge, persistence, affective states, and in-game progress influence student learning from an educational game. *Computers & Education, 86* (2015) 224–235. doi: 10.1016/j.compedu.2015.08.001

Shute, V. J., & Glaser, R. (1990). A large-scale evaluation of an intelligent discovery world: Smithtown. *Interactive Learning Environments, 1*(1), 51–77. doi: 10.1080/1049482900010104

Shute, V. J., Rahimi, S., & Smith, G. (2019). Chapter 4: Game-based learning analytics in physics playground. In A. Tlili &M. Chang (Eds.), *Data Analytics Approaches in Educational Games and Gamification Systems* (pp. 69–93). Singapore: Springer.

Siler, S., Klahr, D., Magaro, C., Willows, K., & Mowery, D. (2010). Predictors of transfer of experimental design skills in elementary and middle school children. In V. Aleven, J. Kay, & J. Mostow (Eds.), *Proceedings of the 10th International Conference on Intelligent Tutoring Systems, ITS 2010* (Vol. 2, pp. 198–208). Berlin, Heidelberg: Springer-Verlag.

Slavin, R. E. (1996). Research on cooperative learning and achievement: What we know, what we need to know. *Contemporary Educational Psychology, 21*(1), 43–69. doi: 10.1006/ceps.1996.0004

Soller, A., Martinez, A., Jermann, P., & Muehlenbrock, M. (2005). From mirroring to guiding: A review of state of the art technology for supporting collaborative learning. *International Journal of Artificial Intelligence in Education, 15*(4), 261–290.

Stahl, G., Koschmann, T., & Suthers, D. (2006). Computer-supported collaborative learning: An historical perspective. In R. K. Sawyer (Ed.), *Cambridge handbook of the learning sciences* (pp. 409–426). Cambridge, MA: Cambridge University Press.

Stamper, J., Eagle, M., Barnes, T., & Croy, M. (2013). Experimental evaluation of automatic hint generation for a logic tutor. *International Journal of Artificial Intelligence in Education, 22*(1–2), 345–352. doi: 10.1007/978-3-642-21869-9_45

Steenbergen-Hu, S., & Cooper, H. (2013). A meta-analysis of the effectiveness of intelligent tutoring systems on K–12 students' mathematical learning. *Journal of Educational Psychology, 105*(4), 970–987. doi: 10.1037/a003244

Steenbergen-Hu, S., & Cooper, H. (2014). A meta-analysis of the effectiveness of intelligent tutoring systems on college students' academic learning. *Journal of Educational Psychology, 106*(2), 331–347. doi: 10.1037/a003475

Strauß, S., & Rummel, N. (2021). Promoting regulation of equal participation in online collaboration by combining a group awareness tool and adaptive prompts. But does it even matter? *International Journal of Computer-Supported Collaborative Learning, 16*, 67–104. doi: 10.1007/s11412-021-09340-y

Sweller, J. (2020). Cognitive load theory and educational technology. *Educational Technology Research and Development, 68*(1), 1–16. doi: 10.1007/s11423-019-09701-3

Tanaka, F., Isshiki, K., Takahashi, F., Uekusa, M., Sei, R., & Hayashi, K. (2015). Pepper learns together with children: Development of an educational application. In *2015 IEEE-RAS 15th International Conference on Humanoid Robots (Humanoids)* (pp. 270–275). Los Alamitos, CA: IEEE.

Teske, K. (2017). Duolingo. *CALICO Journal, 34*(3), 393–401. doi: 10.1558/cj.32509

Thompson, P. W. (1987). Mathematical microworlds and intelligent computer-assisted instruction. In G. Kearsley (Ed.), *Artificial intelligence and instruction: Applications and methods* (pp. 83–109). Boston, MA: Addison-Wesley Longman Publishing Co., Inc.

van Joolingen, W. (1999). Cognitive tools for discovery learning. *International Journal of Artificial Intelligence in Education, 10*(3), 385–397.

van Leeuwen, A., & Janssen, J. (2019). A systematic review of teacher guidance during collaborative learning in primary and secondary education. *Educational Research Review, 27*, 71–89. doi: 10.1016/j.edurev.2019.02.001

van Leeuwen, A., & Rummel, N. (2019). Orchestration tools to support the teacher during student collaboration: A review. *Unterrichtswissenschaft, 47*(2), 143–158. doi: 10.1007/s42010-019-000 52-9

VanLehn, K. (2006). The behavior of tutoring systems. *International Journal of Artificial Intelligence in Education*, *16*(3), 227–265.

VanLehn, K. (2011). The relative effectiveness of human tutoring, intelligent tutoring systems, and other tutoring systems. *Educational Psychologist*, *46*(4), 197–221. doi: 10.1080/00461520.2011.611369

VanLehn, K. (2016). Regulative loops, step loops and task loops. *International Journal of Artificial Intelligence in Education*, *26*(1), 107–112. doi: 10.1007/s40593-015-0056-x

VanLehn, K., Freedman, R., Jordan, P., Murray, C., Osan, R., Ringenberg, M., Rosé, C., Schulze, K., Shelby, R., Treacy, D, Weinstein, A., & Wintersgill, M. (2000). Fading and deepening: The next steps for Andes and other model-tracing tutors. In Gauthier, G., Frasson, C., & VanLehn, K. (Eds.), *Intelligent Tutoring Systems: 5th International Conference* (LNCS Vol. 1839, pp. 474–483). Berlin, Heidelberg: Springer.

VanLehn, K., Lynch, C., Schulze, K., Shapiro, J. A., Shelby, R., Taylor, L., Treacy, D., Weinstein, A., & Wintersgill, M. (2005). The Andes physics tutoring system: Lessons learned. *International Journal of Artificial Intelligence in Education*, *15*(3), 147–204.

Vogel, F., Weinberger, A., & Fischer, F. (2021). Collaboration scripts: Guiding, internalizing, and adapting. In U. Cress, C. Rosé, A. F. Wise, & J. Oshima (Eds.), *International Handbook of Computer-Supported Collaborative Learning* (pp. 335–352). Cham, Switzerland: Springer.

Vygotsky, L.S. (1978). *Mind in society: The development of higher psychological processes.* Cambridge: Harvard University Press.

Walker, E., Rummel, N., & Koedinger, K. R. (2009). CTRL: A research framework for providing adaptive collaborative learning support. *User Modeling and User-Adapted Interaction*, *19*(5), 387–431. doi: 10.1007/s11257-009-9069-1

Walker, E., Rummel, N., & Koedinger, K. R. (2011). Designing automated adaptive support to improve student helping behaviors in a peer tutoring activity. *International Journal of Computer-Supported Collaborative Learning*, *6*(2), 279–306. doi: 10.1007/s11412-011-9111-2

Walker, E., Rummel, N., & Koedinger, K. R. (2014). Adaptive intelligent support to improve peer tutoring in algebra. *International Journal of Artificial Intelligence in Education*, *24*(1), 33–61. doi: 10.1007/s40593-013-0001-9

Walonoski, J. A., & Heffernan, N. T. (2006). Detection and analysis of off-task gaming behavior in intelligent tutoring systems. In M. Ikeda, K. Ashley, & T. W. Chan (Eds.), *Proceedings of the Eighth International Conference on Intelligent Tutoring Systems* (pp. 382–91). Berlin: Springer.

Wang, N., Greenwald, E., Montgomery, R., & Leitner, M. (2022). ARIN-561: An educational game for learning artificial intelligence for high-school students. In *Posters and Late Breaking Results, Workshops, and Tutorials, Industry and Innovation Tracks, Practitioners' and Doctoral Consortium: 23rd International Conference on Artificial Intelligence in Education* (pp. 528–531). Springer, Cham.

Wang, X., Kollar, I., & Stegmann, K. (2017). Adaptable scripting to foster regulation processes and skills in computer-supported collaborative learning. *International Journal of Computer-Supported Collaborative Learning*, *12*(2), 153–172. doi: 10.1007/s11412-017-9254-x

Wieman, C. E., Adams, W. K., & Perkins, K. K. (2008). PhET: Simulations that enhance learning. *Science*, *322*(5902), 682–683. doi: 10.1126/science.1161948

Wiese, E. S., & Koedinger, K. R. (2017). Designing grounded feedback: Criteria for using linked representations to support learning of abstract symbols. *International Journal of Artificial Intelligence in Education*, *27*(3), 448–474. doi: 10.1007/s40593-016-0133-9

Wood, D., Bruner, J. S., & Ross, G. (1976). The role of tutoring in problem solving. *Journal of Child Psychology and Psychiatry*, *17*(2), 89–100. doi: 10.1111/j.1469-7610.1976.tb00381.x

Wylie, R., & Chi, M. T. (2014). The self-explanation principle in Multimedia Learning. In R. Mayer (Ed.), *The Cambridge handbook of multimedia learning* (Cambridge Handbooks in Psychology, pp. 413–432). Cambridge University Press.

Xhakaj, F., Aleven, V., & McLaren, B. M. (2017). Effects of a dashboard for an intelligent tutoring system on teacher knowledge, lesson planning, lessons, and student learning. In É. Lavoué, H. Drachsler, K. Verbert, J. Broisin, & M. Pérez-Sanagustín (Eds.), *Proceedings of the 12th European Conference on Technology-Enhanced Learning, EC-TEL 2017* (pp. 315–329). Cham, Switzerland: Springer.

Xu, Z., Wijekumar, K., Ramirez, G., Hu, X., & Irey, R. (2019). The effectiveness of intelligent tutoring systems on K-12 students' reading comprehension: A meta-analysis. *British Journal of Educational Technology*. doi: 10.1111/bjet.12758

Yadollahi, E., Johal, W., Paiva, A., & Dillenbourg, P. (2018). When deictic gestures in a robot can harm child-robot collaboration. In M. N. Giannakos, L. Jaccheri, & M. Divitini (Eds.), *Proceedings of the 17th ACM Conference on Interaction Design and Children* (pp. 195–206). New York: ACM.

Yannier, N., Hudson, S. E., & Koedinger, K. R. (2020). Active learning is about more than hands-on: A mixed-reality AI system to support STEM education. *International Journal of Artificial Intelligence in Education*, *30*(1), 74–96. doi: 10.1007/s40593-020-00194-3

Zhi, R., Price, T. W., Marwan, S., Milliken, A., Barnes, T., & Chi, M. (2019). Exploring the impact of worked examples in a novice programming environment. In E. K. Hawthorne, M. A. Pérez-Quiñones, S. Heckman, & J. Zhang (Eds.), *SIGCSE '19: Proceedings of the 50th ACM Technical Symposium on Computer Science Education* (pp. 98–104). New York: ACM.

10. Theory-driven design of AIED systems for enhanced interaction and problem-solving

Susanne P. Lajoie and Shan Li

In this chapter, we consider AIED systems as AI-supported interfaces for education. For the purpose of simplicity in expression, we use the terms "AI interfaces" and "AIED systems" interchangeably. Interface design is typically defined as "the creation of environments for enhanced interaction and problem solving" (Hooper, 1986, p. 9). According to Hooper (1986), a primary consideration in the design of an interface is that "it works, that it fulfills the purposes for which it was intended" (p. 10). This understanding resonates with the contemporary focus on the design of interfaces that support the enhancement of learning experience, the acquisition of true expertise, self-regulation, collaboration, and decision making. We acknowledge the crucial role of interfaces, and consider the form and functionality of interfaces to be of tantamount importance to users who interact with a system or environment that responds to their actions (Bennett & Flach, 2011). Based on these considerations, we focus on the current and emerging forms of interfaces and their functionalities rather than their aesthetics.

Norman (1986), in his well-known work on the prescriptions for design principles, noted that:

> It takes at least three kinds of special knowledge to design an interface: first, knowledge of design, of programming and of the technology; second, knowledge of people, of the principles of mental computation, of communication, and of interaction; and third, expert knowledge of the task that is to be accomplished. Most programmers and designers of computer systems have the first kind of knowledge, but not the second or third. (p. 60)

In this chapter, we focus on what Norman (1986) refers to as the second and third kind of knowledge needed for interface design. Consequently, we do not delve into specific design processes and components given the vastness and variability of the literature. Instead, our particular focus will be on the functional design of interfaces from a learning sciences perspective. Specifically, we discuss how learning theories and models can assist in the creation of effective interfaces for learning and teaching, which addresses Norman's call to consider the person, how they think, communicate, and interact, along with knowledge of the task that needs to be accomplished. This chapter presents a brief review of some, but not all, of the theories that address knowledge of how people learn, along with examples of their applications in specific systems. We review the developments in AI that are leading to new functionalities and modalities in AIED systems. We conclude the chapter with some eye-gazing toward future developments in the field of AIED that will advance interface designs.

THEORIES THAT CAN INFLUENCE THE DESIGN OF LEARNING AND TEACHING INTERFACES

The underlying mechanisms and design principles that dictate how learning and engagement can be enhanced in AIED learning and teaching environments have been the focus of continued research for many years. Although generalizable design guidelines are a matter of considerable debate, there is some agreement among learning scientists regarding learning theories and frameworks that promote learning and engagement with AIED systems (see Lajoie & Azevedo, 2006; Lajoie & Poitras, 2017, forthcoming).

It is beyond the scope of this chapter to address the evolution of learning theories and their influence on the design of AIED systems, however, Mayer (1996) provides an in-depth review of how such theories influence the learner and the teacher. Each theory, be it information processing theory, constructivist or social constructivist theories of learning, can influence the design of the interface based on assumptions of how learners learn. For example, information processing principles are based on the assumption that one could break down a task into a series of cognitive steps and rules that computers could model and then tutor learners on the appropriate sequence of steps and provide feedback when an impasse occurred (van Lehn, 2011). This assumption underlies many intelligent tutoring systems. The interface in this case would be designed based on expert knowledge of the task itself, as well as knowledge of the mental computations needed to successfully solve the task. The interface would present opportunities for learners to engage in such steps so that appropriate tutoring could occur.

In the section below, we speak to the importance of specific learning models, followed by examples of how these models are used in various AIED interface designs. The theories and interfaces described are by no means exhaustive. Rather, they are presented as examples of how interfaces can be designed to support situated learning, cognitive apprenticeships, development of expertise, self regulated learning, positive affect, and collaborative learning. Furthermore, these theories are not mutually exclusive.

Situated Learning: Learning in Context

When learning is situated in meaningful activities, it becomes contextualized and easier to remember and apply since the uses of knowledge are more obvious than facts that are learned in isolation of how to use such knowledge (Clancey, 1997; Greeno, 1998). Situating learning in complex contexts provides more opportunities for integrating information from multiple sources. Some sources are social in nature, where learners construct new knowledge by sharing perspectives with those who are learning with them. Learning by doing and experiencing things helps construct new meaning (Dewey, 1938).

Cognitive Apprenticeship

The cognitive apprenticeship model of learning (Collins et al., 1989) embodies the concept of situating learning as it helps learners by situating them in meaningful real-world activities within a specific learning or practice community. Traditional apprenticeships, such as learning to be a chef, require new members to legitimately practice skills that are required, and to learn by observing and being mentored by those who are proficient in their domains. Cognitive apprenticeships are built on these same principles but are more complex since they require modeling expert thoughts as well as strategies and actions. Whereas one can observe a chef's actions as they prepare a crème brûlée, one cannot observe a physician's diagnostic reasoning ability without methods that externalize that physician's thought processes. Therefore, expert modeling of a task is a prerequisite for cognitive apprenticeship so that students can observe and develop a conceptual understanding of the problem-solving process. Such modeling requires domain knowledge, or expert knowledge of the task that is to be accomplished along with knowledge of how experts solve the task. Teaching methods are created, using such knowledge, to scaffold novices as they learn to solve the task at hand.

Cognitive apprenticeships are similar to traditional apprenticeships where new learners start at the periphery of the activity and gradually acquire new knowledge as they participate in the community of practice with those that help scaffold their knowledge development. Once students articulate this new knowledge, the experts (human or computer) fade their assistance and learners can independently practice on their own. By sharing one's perspectives with others, students can learn to critically evaluate their own understanding.

The cognitive apprenticeship framework offers advice for designing content, teaching methods, and sequencing of instruction. Instructional content should teach what experts know and how they solve problems. Teaching methods should model expert knowledge and coach students with appropriate levels of scaffolding so they can solve problems. Once students demonstrate success, scaffolding is gradually faded. Students are expected to articulate and reflect on their own problem-solving abilities. Instruction is sequenced to provide optimal levels of challenge to maintain student motivation. Finally, learning is situated in the culture of practice.

Expertise

As we saw above, expert models of performance for a particular domain must be identified and reified to help learners deliberately practice the correct skills that will lead to success in a particular context (Ericsson et al., 1993). Deliberate practice is often accomplished with the assistance of a tutor, coach, or mentor. Paving the road to competence in a specific domain involves providing a path for novices to follow (Lajoie, 2003). Expertise is domain specific but experts share commonalities: they are able to quickly identify relevant information, perform in a consistently superior manner, are consistently fast and accurate, able to identify meaningful patterns, have superior memories specific to their field, and have better self-monitoring or self-regulation skills (Chi et al., 1988). Helping learners toward such competencies can assist them in their learning goals and outcomes.

Self-Regulation

Self-regulation is central to learning and it is a multicomponential process that involves cognitive, affective, behavioral, motivational, and metacognitive components (Azevedo et al., 2019). Thinking about what to do next in a problem-solving context is affected by prior knowledge, emotions around the topic of learning, motivation to pursue the topic, and ability to perform and reflect on one's performance. In addition to these internal factors, self-regulation is influenced by external factors, be that the artifacts in the environment and/or the people you engage with to solve a problem (Winne & Hadwin, 1998).

Affect

Learning, performance, and achievement can be influenced by an array of emotions, including enjoyment, hope, pride, relief, anger, anxiety, shame, frustration, boredom, and hopelessness (Pekrun et al., 2018; Pekrun & Linnenbrink-Garcia, 2014). Positive emotions can enhance learning whereas negative ones can hinder learning. Consequently, emotional regulation is essential during learning since emotions before, during, and after a task (Pekrun et al., 2002) influence current and future learning outcomes. Harley et al. (2019) presented an integrated model of how emotions and emotion regulation can be considered jointly, by considering Pekrun's control value theory of emotions (2018) along with Gross's (2015) process model of specific emotion regulation strategies, that, when taken together, can reveal their joint effects on achievement and performance.

Collaboration

Learning in formal and informal settings often requires collaboration and communication skills and social emotional competencies (Järvelä & Hadwin, 2013) that help learners when challenges or obstacles occur in a group- or team-related task. Multiple perspective taking can lead to more informed decisions and promote scientific discourse and inquiry.

This short sampling of theories that influence learning can be used when considering interface design decisions. These theories often overlap, as do the goals of instruction and the learning objectives that the technology is designed to support. The following section provides a few examples of how learning theories can be embodied in interface design.

THEORY-DRIVEN INTERFACES: SOME EXAMPLES

The development of artificial intelligence, along with the proliferation of teaching and learning theories, opens up new opportunities for building innovative interfaces (see Chapter 5 by Arroyo et al. and Chapter 4 by Azevedo and Wiedbusch in this handbook). In this section, we describe the various interfaces applied to AIED teaching and learning environments with a view to illustrating how interface design can support learning.

Computer Simulations for Situating Learning in Authentic Contexts

When learning is situated in authentic contexts embedded with meaningful problem-solving scenarios and activities, there are opportunities for students to consider knowledge as a tool to address real-life problems rather than scattered facts and procedures (Herrington & Oliver, 2000; Lajoie, 2014). Computer simulations, which center on the theoretical or simplified modeling of real-world components, phenomena, or processes, provide students with a powerful means to address authentic problems in school settings (Smetana & Bell, 2012; Lajoie, 2022. In addition to its advantages of authenticity and real-time interactivity, computer simulation usually allows students to manipulate aspects of the simulated model that would otherwise be dangerous, impractical, or even impossible in a real-world context. As Lajoie (2022) states "simulations can feel real, embedding the learner or trainee in an activity that provides sustained practice opportunities on meaningful tasks that are valued, since they mimic realistic situations" (p. 464). She elaborates that there are many types of simulations; those that provide deliberate practice opportunities on technical skills, communication skills, or decision making. Typical examples of computer simulations include animations, visualizations, and interactive laboratories (Smetana & Bell, 2012), and there are increasing numbers of advanced computer simulations that include immersive virtual worlds where learners learn in such contexts (Chen et al., 2003; Dede, 2008). Each type of simulation would require its own interface.

Intelligent Tutoring Systems

Intelligent tutoring systems (ITSs) are grounded in AI techniques and cognitive theory and are designed to engage learners in various types of cognitive processing with the goal of increasing positive learning outcomes. ITSs are based on a model of the domain (expert model), knowledge of the learner (student model), and knowledge of teaching strategies (tutor) (Psotka et al., 1988; Shute et al., 2000; Shute & Psotka, 1996; see also Chapter 7 by Aleven et al. in this handbook). These models are used to diagnose student difficulties and provide dynamic feedback to the learner in response to the diagnosis. For example, Anderson's ACT-R theory (Anderson, 1983), used to design ACT-R tutors, is based on the premise that human cognition reflects the complex composition of basic elements and principles that can be decomposed and taught to individuals through computer tutors. ACT-R tutors are among the most successful ITSs and have been evaluated in well-structured domains such as geometry, algebra, and lisp programming (Anderson et al., 1995; Koedinger & Corbett, 2006). Other learning theories have also guided the design of ITSs. Ohlsson's (1996) theory suggests we learn from performance errors, and his approach led to the design of constraint-based modeling (see Mitrovic, 2012 for a review of the success of constraint-based tutors). Constraint-based tutors represent knowledge in the form of constraints of what ought to be so, rather than generating problem-solving paths.

Ill structured problems may require flexibility in tutoring approaches and a different learning theory. Cognitive apprenticeship models work well for ill-structured problems, situating the learning in real-world contexts and scaffolding the learner when needed.

BioWorld (Lajoie, 2009) is an ITS that uses a cognitive apprenticeship model to guide its design. It provides models of expertise and scaffolding to support the deliberate practice of diagnostic reasoning skills in a simulated real-world context (i.e., virtual hospital and patients).

BioWorld's interface allows students to perform meaningful cognitive tasks that would otherwise be out of their reach, and support the sharing of cognitive load so that students can focus on higher-order thinking skills in learning or problem solving (Lajoie, 2014). Figure 10.1 presents an example of the initial interface where students are situated in an authentic diagnostic setting where they are presented with a virtual patient case that includes a description of the pateint's history, symptoms, etc. The interface permits students to formulate differential diagnoses (since physicians commonly consider multiple diagnoses simultaneously) and encourages them to collect and post evidence from the patient description that supports each diagnosis (i.e., exploration). In this manner, students are encouraged to highlight their goals in solving the case by highlighting specific hypotheses/diagnoses, and to reflect on them as they collect information about the patient (i.e., reflection). Students' declarative and/or factual knowledge about specific diseases is supported with an online library that presents information about symptoms, terminology, and diagnostic tests, as well as treatments. Procedural knowledge, of how to do something, is supported in the interface as well (i.e., scaffolding). Students can conduct a diagnostic test on the patient and see the results of their test instantly. Test results can determine the next actions. Conceptual understanding is supported through the case summary tool, where students explain how they solved the case to the next physician who will see the patient's case (i.e., articulation). Finally, student trajectories toward expertise are supported with assistance throughout problem solving but also after a final diagnosis is submitted. Specifically, expert modeling of the task is embedded in the interface design of the BioWorld system, whereby students compare their solution path with that of an expert to

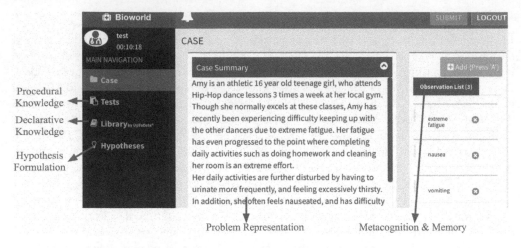

Figure 10.1   BioWorld interface

determine how they might refine their diagnostic reasoning (i.e., modeling and reflection). Delaying expert modeling has been proven to be particularly effective by recent research (Collins & Kapur, 2014; Kapur, 2008), given that students have attempted to generate their own ideas and strategies for accomplishing the task beforehand. In summary, BioWorld promotes diagnostic reasoning by integrating cognitive apprenticeship methods into its interface design and by providing students with apprenticeship-like learning experiences.

Virtual Environments to Support Self-Regulated Learning

Interfaces of virtual environments have the advantage of situating learning experiences in authentic contexts; however, virtual environments can be disorienting or even upsetting for learners if they lack skills in self-regulated learning (SRL). Therefore, many educational researchers have begun emphasizing either the scaffolding of SRL activities or the training of SRL skills when designing virtual environments (Azevedo et al., 2010; Azevedo & Gašević, 2019; Graesser & McNamara, 2010; Lajoie, 2020).

Azevedo et al. (2010) designed *MetaTutor*, a hypermedia learning environment, designed to support self-regulated learning as students acquire an understanding of science topics. *MetaTutor* is designed to detect, model, trace, and foster students' self-regulatory processes during learning. In *MetaTutor*, students receive training on SRL processes prior to the learning of various human body systems. Students can highlight the SRL processes they are about to use during learning to enhance their metacognitive awareness. Azevedo and colleagues (2019) have extended *MetaTutor* to include intelligent pedagogical agents that are embedded within the *MetaTutor* interface, to assist students in learning to self-regulate while reading about complex systems. Pedagogical agents are computerized characters that can be assigned different roles to facilitate instruction to the learners (Craig et al., 2002; Schroeder et al., 2013). In MetaTutor, each agent has a specific goal of scaffolding a specific self-regulatory strategy. For instance, Pam the Planner, Sam the Strategizer, Mary the Monitor, Gavin the Guide (see Figure 10.2) each have a specific role in guiding the learner in their reading. These animated pedagogical agents serve as external regulatory agents to promote students'

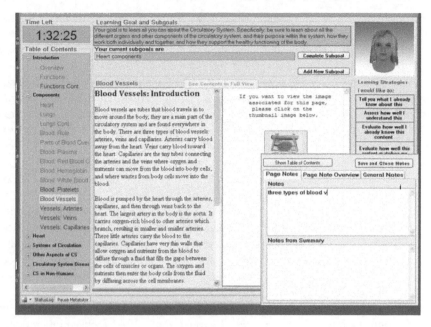

Figure 10.2   Screenshot of MetaTutor's interface with Mary the Monitor

self-regulatory processes in learning. Empirical evidence from the *MetaTutor* project reveals that key self-regulatory processes during learning with hypermedia are critical to students' performance (Azevedo et al., 2010; 2019). Moreover, externally facilitated regulated learning is more effective than self-regulated learning with hypermedia (Azevedo et al., 2008). In this example, the interface presents learners with hypermedia access to domain knowledge as well as pedagogical agents designed to scaffold learners in SRL strategies as they acquire new knowledge through reading about the circulatory system.

Pedagogical Agents and AI Dialogue Systems

As we saw in *MetaTutor*, pedagogical agents can play an important role in supporting learning. Pedagogical agent research has a strong foundation of using traditional psychological theories of human cognition (Schroeder et al., 2013) and metacognition (see Chapter 4 by Azevedo & Wiedbusch in this handbook) to guide their design. In a meta-analytic review of pedagogical agents for learning, Schroeder et al. (2013) found that the design and implementation of pedagogical agents are driven by social agency theory (Atkinson et al., 2005), cognitive load theory (Sweller, 1994), and split-attention of modality principles of multimedia learning (Mayer, 2002), as well as by the presence principle. They state that pedagogical agents are not necessarily artificially intelligent, given that pedagogical agents, by definition, are on-screen characters that facilitate instruction to learners (Shroeder, 2013). However, pedagogical agents can be designed to be artificially intelligent by leveraging AI techniques such as user modeling and natural language processing (NLP), to create dialogue-based tutoring systems (see Chapter 11 by Rus et al. in this handbook). In this way, interactions with pedagogical agents feel more natural and are being incorporated into an increasing number of AI dialogue systems (D'Mello & Graesser, 2010; Graesser & McNamara, 2010; Schroder et al., 2011; see also Chapter 14 by Holstein and Olsen in this handbook). Furthermore, a class of AI dialogue systems guided by both self-regulated learning and emotion theories are being developed to promote human–computer interactions (HCIs) that lead to deeper levels of understanding. For instance, *AutoTutor* is a computer tutor with pedagogical agents that hold conversations with students in natural language (Graesser & McNamara, 2010). The dialogues in *AutoTutor* are organized around difficult questions and problems that require reasoning and explanations in the answers. Therefore, SRL is crucial to students' performance. Although *AutoTutor* does not train students on SRL strategies directly, students' use of metacognition and SRL strategies can be extracted from their discourse and discourse moves with the *AutoTutor*. As such, these data can be analyzed to reveal how students control, monitor, and reflect on their conversations with the pedagogical agent (Graesser & McNamara, 2010). Although there is no guarantee on the induction and acquisition of SRL strategies in learning with *AutoTutor*, the interface does present opportunities for students to reflect on what they know and do not know. In addition, *AutoTutor* automatically detects learner emotions based on multimodal multichannel data such as dialogue patterns, speech patterns, facial features, and body language (D'Mello & Graesser, 2010; Graesser & McNamara, 2010), thereby increasing our understanding of how learning occurs.

The research of Schroder et al. (2011) provided another example of the seamless interaction in AI dialogue systems. To be specific, Schroder et al. (2011) focused on emotional and nonverbal aspects of HCIs and built a real-time interactive multimodal dialogue system of "Sensitive Artificial Listener (SAL)" based on the research on emotion detection. In essence, SAL is a virtual agent that has the capabilities to perceive and produce emotional and nonverbal behaviors needed to sustain a naturally flowing conversation. In a human-to-computer dialogue setting, SAL analyzes human behaviors (i.e., acoustic features, head movements, and facial expressions) based on its emotion recognition and feature extraction systems. The virtual agent then determines how it should respond with appropriate emotional and nonverbal behaviors. Specifically, SAL chooses one of the four characters (i.e., aggressive Spike, cheerful Poppy, gloomy Obadiah, and pragmatic Prudence) to sustain a conversation, where the character will try to be an active speaker and listener using multimodal verbal utterances and feedback signals. For instance, a SAL character could "simply nod, or nod and smile, or nod, smile, and say m-hm" to communicate its agreement in a conversation (Schroder et al., 2011, p. 175). These types of interfaces enhance the quality of the human–computer interface and interactions.

Immersive Virtual Environments

The technological breakthrough in virtual reality (VR), augmented reality (AR), and mixed reality (MR) has also enriched the interfaces of AIED systems. VR refers to a computer-simulated reality, which replicates a physical, real-world environment on computers and allows users to interact with the virtual environment. AR is a type of interactive, reality-based display environment, where the user's real-world experience is enhanced/augmented by computer-generated sensory input such as text, sound, video, and graphics (Carmigniani et al., 2011; Tang et al., 2020). MR is a type of hybrid environment where real-world elements and digital objects co-exist and interact in real time (Pan et al., 2006; Tang et al., 2020). In the context of teaching and learning, the interfaces of VR, AR, and MR exploit the affordances of real-world scenarios, which provide students with a relatively deeply situated experience compared with traditional computer simulations (Clarke et al., 2008; Harley et al., 2020; Squire & Klopfer, 2007).

Virtual reality (VR) interfaces
VR interfaces are perhaps the most-used immersive systems for teaching and learning over the last thirty years (Slater, 2018). The Tactical Language and Culture Training System (TLCTS) (Johnson & Valente, 2009) is a good example of a VR environment that situates users in a social simulation context to learn foreign languages and cultures. Specifically, the TLCTS provides learners with a three-dimensional virtual world that simulates a target culture, whereby learners practice language by engaging in a scenario-based Mission Game. Moreover, the TLCTS gives learners extensive conversational practice as they interact with a virtual tutor, who can demonstrate adaptive behaviors with AI techniques. For instance, the virtual tutor can give appropriate corrective feedback on pronunciation, grammatical forms, cultural pragmatics, or word choice, if the TLCTS system recognizes an error in learners' utterances.

Augmented reality (AR) interfaces
AR interfaces have the capacity to "situate learners in emotionally compelling, cognitively complex problem-solving contexts" (Squire & Klopfer, 2007, p. 374); therefore, a number of theories account for the design of AR interfaces such as the control-value theory of achievement emotions (Harley et al., 2020; Pekrun, 2006), situated learning theory, problem-based learning, inquiry-based learning, learning as doing, and learning through games. For instance, *Environmental Detectives* is an augmented reality simulation game in which a simulation of an environmental disaster (i.e., chemical spill) is superimposed on a real-world watershed (Squire & Klopfer, 2007). Squire and Klopfer (2007) state that they used the situated model of cognition to design this AR game for scientific inquiry learning. In *Environmental Detectives*, students play the role of environmental engineers to investigate the simulated chemical spill by combining the information from both the real world and the AR world. As students experience the real-world environment such as bodies of water, fences, and tree cover, they use virtual tools to sample chemical concentrations in the groundwater on their handheld computers. Students can also interview virtual experts on toxicology or hydrology who are located at various sites. Students identify the location and severity of the spill, and ultimately propose a viable remediation plan. Moreover, the plan must consider other similar cases, local environmental conditions, as well as political, financial, and practical trade-offs. Findings from two empirical studies conducted by Squire and Klopfer (2007) suggested that AR games provide authentic environments for solving complex problems but more scaffolding of learners' behaviors and thinking is needed.

Another gap in the nascent AR literature is the role of emotion in enhancing or hindering the learning process (Harley et al., 2020; Wu et al., 2013). In an effort to address this gap, Harley et al. (2016) examined students' emotions with a location-based AR app designed to support learning of historical knowledge and reasoning (see Figure 10.3). The design of the AR interface was guided by the control-value theory of achievement emotions (Harley et al., 2020; Pekrun, 2006; Pekrun et al., 2002), situating the learner in a physical environment that was controlled by their movements and interactions using the interface. Harley et al. (2016) found that students experienced more enjoyment and less boredom when physically exploring the historical site with the AR app than learning the same material with multimedia in

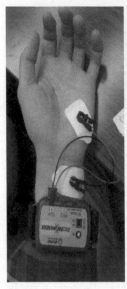

Source: Harley et al., 2016

Figure 10.3   The interfaces of the location-based AR app

laboratory settings. Clearly the AR technology *per se* and the experience of field investigation could induce positive emotions. More studies are needed to shed light on the relationships between AR interfaces and achievement emotions.

Mixed-reality (MR) interfaces
The affordances of mixed-reality techniques include the emergence of new forms of interfaces along with the incorporation of innovative teaching and learning theories. When designing the mixed-reality learning environment of the Situated Multimedia Arts Learning Lab (SMALLab), Birchfield et al. (2008) integrated three themes that align HCI and education research: *embodiment, multimodality*, and *composition*. The three themes were integrated into a new theoretical and technological framework for learning, and the effectiveness of the framework in guiding the design of SMALLab and in developing related curriculums has been verified in diverse pedagogical programs (Birchfield et al., 2008). Specifically, the theme of *embodiment* originates from an embodied cognition perspective, which argues that perception, cognition, and action "occur simultaneously and are closely intertwined" (Birchfield et al., 2008, p. 2; Wilson, 2002). MR interfaces provide learners with a bodily-kinesthetic sense as they physically interact with surrounding environments, whereby learners make meaningful connections between cognition, action, and physical objects. In this regard, MR interfaces offer opportunities for embodied interactions, enabling learners to deepen their thinking and learning. Moreover, MR interfaces provide learners with multi-sensory learning environments, which underscore the use of multiple models of information representation to improve learning performance (Birchfield et al., 2008). As claimed by Birchfield et al. (2008), *multimodality*, referring to visual, sonic, haptic, and kinesthetic

information and their interactions, was well represented in SMALLab and many other mixed-reality spaces.

From a learning sciences perspective, the design of MR interfaces also needs to embrace the idea of *composition*, which emphasizes a social constructivist approach to learning and teaching. In particular, MR interfaces should allow learners to creatively explore new modes of interaction to address open-ended problems (Birchfield et al., 2008). Mixed-reality interfaces in medicine are starting to address this through the use of high-fidelity simulators that provide deliberate practice opportunities of surgical skills or ultrasound probe handling for specific diagnostic tasks. Combining mannequin-based simulators with haptic devices and augmented reality has proven to be an excellent way to design situated learning opportunities that are supported by haptic interactions, realistic visualizations, and materials that simulate the real world along with supplemental declarative knowledge that is provided through augmented reality with HoloLens or mobile technologies (for examples, see Mirchi et al., 2020; Platts et al., 2011; Vassiliou et al., 2005).

Multi-User Virtual Environments (MUVEs) to Support Collaborative Learning

Collaborative learning situations require interfaces to support collaborative learning activities. MUVEs present technological interfaces that enable collaborative and immersive learning in complex virtual worlds (Clarke et al., 2008; Dede, 2008; Ketelhut et al., 2010). The interface allows instructional designers to create shared learning experiences, enabling students to construct meaning collaboratively in simulated situations where they can socially regulate their learning (Chen et al., 2003; Dede, 2008; Järvelä et al., 2019). In addition, the interface facilitates novel forms of communication among avatars (Dede, 2008). A number of studies have demonstrated positive learning gains using MUVEs. For example, Clarke et al. (2008) found that students' performance was improved in River City, a MUVE designed for middle-grade students to learn scientific inquiry and twenty-first-century skills. In the River City MUVE, students work collaboratively to identify the causes of illness as they travel through a historically accurate nineteenth-century virtual city (Ketelhut et al., 2010). Students collect evidence by visiting different places in the city, talking to various residents, and leveraging the affordances of virtual scientific instruments such as microscopes in this simulated setting. Moreover, students can manipulate certain environmental factors in order to develop and test their hypotheses. In short, the River City represents an example of computer simulations for authentic collaborative inquiry learning, which could promote deep learning and high levels of student engagement (Ketelhut et al., 2010).

Crystal Island: EcoJourneys (Saleh et al., 2020) is another MUVE designed to support collaborative inquiry learning through problem-based learning (PBL). In Crystal Island: EcoJourneys, students work closely to solve an authentic aquatic ecosystem problem related to fish farming that occurs on an island in the Philippines. In particular, students work in groups to provide an explanation for why the fish are sick by exploring the game-based learning environment and interacting with in-game characters and objects. The game environment is designed to engage students in two inquiry phases, that is, the investigation phase and brainstorming phase (see Figure 10.4). In addition, Saleh et al. (2020) designed several hard and soft scaffolds. Hard scaffolds are static supports that can be anticipated and planned in advance, based upon typical student difficulties with a task, whereas soft scaffolds are dynamic, situation-specific aids provided by humans or computers (Brush & Saye, 2002). In Eco-Journey, the hard scaffolds consisted of to-do lists, notebooks, and pre-planned worksheets designed to

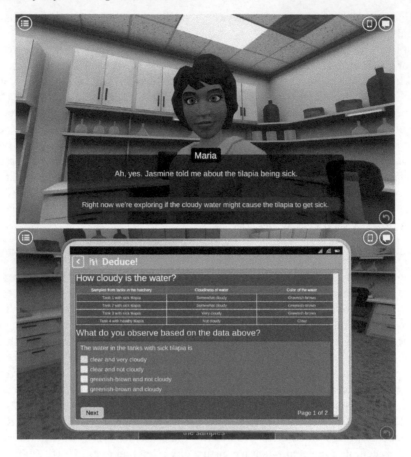

Figure 10.4   Crystal Island EcoJourneys: AI interface designs to promote collaboration

support students' investigation of the problem. Soft scaffolds were presented in a text-based chat tool that was dynamic and situation specific. During the brainstorming phase, both hard and soft scaffolds were provided. Saleh et al. (2020) examined how hard and soft scaffolds supported the problem based learning (PBL) inquire cycle and accountable talks, respectively. They found that these scaffolds were effective in promoting students' engagement in collaborative inquiry.

Another example of a MUVE is Quest Atlantis (QA), which provides children with the practice of social commitments and the opportunities for scientific inquiry as they take on a central role to solve social issues in an emerging story (Barab et al., 2007). It is noteworthy that QA is designed to support scaffolding and apprenticeship activities in which children with more knowledge or experience guide novice players to accomplish the tasks. As noticed by Barab et al. (2007), the scaffolding and apprenticeship activities contribute substantially to the experiences of all participants, and eventually foster a culture of collaboration. Given that QA follows a socially responsive design with a focus on gender representation, Barab et al. (2007) examined gender difference in metacognition. They found that girls demonstrated significantly greater depth and frequency of metacognition than boys when reflecting on their responses to the QA problem scenarios, although both genders engaged with QA activities.

Intelligent Visual Interfaces

Learning analytics and affective visualization have gained increasing attention from researchers in the recent development of intelligent user interfaces. Learning analytics help improve student modeling in terms of behavior, cognition, metacognition, and emotion, and ultimately provides students with adaptive and individualized learning supports. Moreover, learning analytics empower instructors to pinpoint key information about the learning or problem-solving process from visual displays, whereby they identify patterns and develop an understanding of when and how to intervene to achieve optimal effects (Lajoie, 2020). Martinez-Maldonado et al. (2015) speak about the difficulty teachers have in orchestrating appropriate feedback in a timely manner to groups of students. Their research provides empirical data on how technology can be used to automatically alert teachers about significant events that occur in groups so that feedback can be presented as needed. There is an abundance of literature on dashboards that can be used to facilitate both the learner and the teacher. However, for the purpose of illustration, we present only a few examples.

A dashboard can generally be defined as "a visual display of the most important information … consolidated and arranged on a single screen so the information can be monitored at a glance" (Few, 2006, p. 34). Such information can be used by learners to reflect on their own knowledge or it can be used by teachers to inform their decision making on where students need assistance (Verbert et al., 2013, p. 3).

As an example, a learning analytic (LA) dashboard is embedded in the HOWARD (Helping Other with Augmentation and Reasoning Dashboard) platform, an asynchronous online collaborative learning environment designed for medical students to learn the optimal way of delivering bad news to patients (Lajoie, 2020; Zheng et al., 2021). The LA dashboard interface provides instructors with four types of visualizations which include conversation explorer, social network analysis, task progress view, and activity view (see Figure 10.5). The four visualization features demonstrate the information of the overall participation level of individual students, group interactions, task progress of each individual, and each student's trajectories of participation, respectively (Lajoie, 2020). In short, the design of the LA dashboard emphasizes data visualization of students' participation, learning behaviors, and cognitive activities, and teachers can interact with these visualizations to reflect on student progress and thereby make decisions about when and where to intervene.

Research on affective visualization is emerging, given that a growing body of educational studies with a focus on advanced learning technologies have underlined the role of emotions in students' learning (Harley et al., 2016; Lajoie et al., 2020). As an illustration, GhasemAghaei et al. (2016) developed a dashboard for instructors to monitor students' emotions in e-learning, based on the MADE (Multimodal Affect for Design and Evaluation) framework (GhasemAghaei et al., 2015). The MADE framework emphasizes the importance of bridging the elements of learning objective, cognitive strategy, affective strategy, quasi-sensory, and multiple sensory modalities together when designing interactive systems for teaching and learning (GhasemAghaei et al., 2015). In order to accomplish a learning goal, students cognitively and emotionally engage in learning with interactive learning environments that leverage information acquisition through quasi-sensory and multiple sensory modalities such as visual, acoustic, and haptic senses. The MADE framework, along with

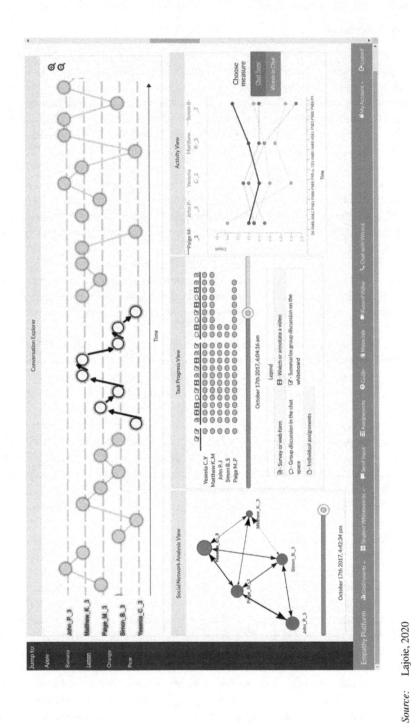

Source: Lajoie, 2020

Figure 10.5   The interface of HOWARD dashboard

the theories of emotion and computer vision techniques, guided the design of the MADE Teacher's Dashboard, which provided a novel visualization of students' emotional states in learning (GhasemAghaei et al., 2016). On the dashboard, teachers can monitor the fluctuation of students' emotions as they accomplish various tasks. In addition, teachers can provide different types of affective feedback (e.g., applause or clapping, cheering sound, praising text messages) based on learning events and students' preferences. It is important to note that not all students are comfortable with sharing their emotional states with teachers. Holstein et al. (2019) found that US middle-school students are not always comfortable with the notion that the system would gauge their affective or emotional state, and forward that information to teachers. Privacy of information, be it cognitive or affective information, will need to remain at the forefront of ethical computing decisions.

As we have demonstrated, AI interfaces can take on many different forms, depending on the theory guiding their design and the purpose of instruction. The interfaces described in this chapter are by no means exhaustive. However, examples of interfaces designed to support situated learning, cognitive apprenticeships, development of expertise, self-regulated learning, positive affect, and collaborative learning were discussed. Technological interfaces can vary with respect to their purposes in facilitating teaching and learning and the affordances they present in terms of modeling, adaptation, visualization, and seamlessness of HCI. We review some of the benefits of AI interfaces for education below.

AI INTERFACES FOR EDUCATION: THE PRESENT AND FUTURE

The integration of AI in the design and use of intelligent interfaces has been changing the landscapes of educational research, instruction, and learning. AI interfaces bring together the interdisciplinary field of learning sciences and AI techniques to simulate, model, and infer human mind and behaviors, which make them think humanly and act rationally. In particular, one potential of AI interfaces is that they can keep learning from their accumulated data through machine-learning and deep-learning algorithms such as neural networks. Therefore, they are "growing" to be smart enough to provide students with adaptive and individualized learning experience. Using natural language processing techniques, AI interfaces also offer unique interaction experiences since the interfaces could respond more naturally, through voice and actions, to students' needs.

AI interfaces are unique in that they can support the automatic detection of students' mental states and emotions. As an example, D'Mello et al. (2017) presented an *analytic, automated* approach to measure engagement at a fine-grained temporal resolution, taking advantage of *advanced* machine-learning techniques. The advanced, analytic, and automated (AAA) approach, as claimed by D'Mello et al. (2017), has a solid theoretical foundation of embodied theories of cognition and affect as well as methodological novelties regarding the use of behavioral and psychological signals to infer mental states with advanced computational techniques. In a review of 15 case studies featuring the AAA approach to measuring engagement, D'Mello et al. (2017) concluded that the research on students' engagement in learning could be fundamentally transformed when the AAA approach was integrated into digital learning environments. Perhaps the most mature technology available for AI interfaces is emotion detection and recognition. As an example, D'Mello and Graesser (2010) developed *AutoTutor*, which included a semi-automated affect detector to reveal students' affective states from conversational cues, body language, and facial behaviors as they held conversations with the tutor while solving challenging questions. The Sensitive Artificial Listener (SAL) is another example of AI used to automatically detect and interact with individuals based on automatically recognizing human emotions based on their voices, head movements, and facial expressions and interacting using a real-time interactive multimodal dialogue system (Schroder et al., 2011).

As we move to the future, we anticipate that student modeling and diagnostic assessments of learning and affect will be enriched by learning analytics as well as by increases in the automatic multimodal recognition systems used to decide dynamically on appropriate types of feedback and scaffolding to the learner. Advances in multimodal data collection techniques that include system log files, physiological sensor data, behavioral posture, haptic and expression data, EEG, eye trackers, and so on, are all leading to more nuanced assessments of cognition, metacognition, motivation, and affect, determining better triggers for effective scaffolding of learners (Azevedo & Gašević, 2019). For example, the *MetaTutor* environment allows researchers to model, prompt, and support students' SRL processes, which include the behavioral, cognitive, metacognitive (e.g., feeling of knowing, and judgment of learning), motivational, and affective aspects of learning (Azevedo et al., 2010). A crucial objective of the *MetaTutor* project is to "determine which and how many learner variables must be traced to accurately infer the students' needs for different types of feedback" (Azevedo et al., 2010, p. 242). Perhaps new interface designs can consider how sensor data can be collected and integrated with specific learning events.

Moreover, AI interfaces facilitate the development of expertise, given that the interfaces have the capability to assess and promote changes in competence based on the models of different learning trajectories toward expertise (Lajoie, 2003). AI techniques such as decision tree, process mining, Hidden Markov models, and Bayesian networks lead to another level of student assessment regarding automated discovery of learning or problem-solving patterns. For instance, Lajoie et al. (2021) used sequential data mining techniques to examine patterns of SRL behaviors and emotions as students diagnosed virtual patients in BioWorld (Lajoie, 2009). The differences between high and low performers in sequential occurrences of SRL activities and affective states provided researchers with a nuanced understanding of how performance differences occurred.

In addition, AI techniques empower information visualization and the design of interactive visual interfaces in AIED systems. The potential offered by information visualization includes: (a) an increase in cognitive resources by decreasing cognitive load; (b) a decrease in the need to search for information; (c) increased pattern recognition; (d) easier perception of relationships, and; (e) increased ability to explore and manipulate the data (Vaitsis et al., 2016). As an example, Li et al. (2020) viewed students' learning or problem-solving processes as networks of mutually interacting SRL behaviors based on a network perspective. The visualization of the dynamic interactions between SRL behaviors in a network architecture provides an intuitive understanding of how different SRL behaviors augment or blunt each other. In addition, Li et al. (2020) built SRL networks for each performance group (i.e., unsuccessful, success-oriented, and mastery-oriented groups), whereby instructors could visually pinpoint the differences in SRL processes among different performance groups. As such, instructors can identify optimal learning or problem-solving trajectories and provide interventions when an undesirable behavioral pattern occurs. In fact, researchers have taken further steps to integrate different types of visualizations in an online dashboard to support analytical reasoning and decision making by learners and instructors. Such examples include, but are not limited to, the Learning Analytics (LA) dashboard (Lajoie, 2020; Zheng et al., 2021) and the MADE Teacher's dashboard (GhasemAghaei et al., 2016).

Challenges

While AI-driven interfaces take advantage of cutting-edge technologies, they can be difficult to develop, maintain, and implement, especially when taking local constraints and the various needs of learners with different levels of technological competence into consideration. In addition, instructors may feel overwhelmed or perplexed with AI-driven interfaces, given that the inputs and the modeling or decision-making processes are usually not visible to them. These challenges need to be remedied to have more uptake of these innovative approaches to learning and instruction. In a meta-analysis of 25 years of research in intelligent user interfaces, Völkel et al. (2020) identified 117 occurrences of challenges in designing intelligent technology with clusters of obstacles around the presentation of the interface, technical challenges of when, where, and how to integrate intelligence, and challenges related to trust, confidence, reliance, privacy, usability, and usefulness. We see additional challenges relating to what Pinkwart (2016) called *intercultural* and *global dimensions* of AIED. There is no one-size-fits-all solution due to language factors as well as the variety of learning and educational cultures. Future AI interfaces must consider these cultural variables so that they are not perceived as biased.

Finally, there is still a large gap between theory and application. There is no "how to" book that can present prescriptions for best interface designs since, as stated earlier, the design is dependent on the learning objectives and task contexts. However, this gap could be reduced if disciplines worked together to design new interfaces. Learning scientists, instructional designers, educational technology specialists, computer scientists, and engineers could form teams with content experts to jointly design better learning and teaching interfaces. Without joining forces, each discipline will continue to come at the task with its own lens and fractures will remain in communicating important concepts that can move the field forward.

REFERENCES

Anderson, J. R. (1983). *The architecture of cognition.* Cambridge, MA: Harvard University Press.

Anderson, J. R., Corbett, A. T., Koedinger, K. R., & Pelletier, R. (1995). Cognitive tutors: Lessons learned. *Journal of the Learning Sciences, 4*(2), 167–207.

Atkinson, R. K., Mayer, R. E., & Merrill, M. M. (2005). Fostering social agency in multimedia learning: Examining the impact of an animated agent's voice. *Contemporary Educational Psychology, 30*(1), 117–139.

Azevedo, R., & Gašević, D. (2019). Analyzing multimodal multichannel data about self-regulated learning with advanced learning technologies: Issues and challenges. *Computers in Human Behavior, 96*, 207–210. doi: 10.1016/j.chb.2019.03.025

Azevedo, R., Johnson, A., Chauncey, A., & Burkett, C. (2010). Self-regulated learning with MetaTutor: Advancing the science of learning with metacognitive tools. In M. S. Khine & I. M. Saleh (Eds.), *New science of learning: Cognition, computers and collaboration in education* (pp. 225–247). New York: Springer.

Azevedo, R., Moos, D. C., Greene, J. A., Winters, F. I., & Cromley, J. G. (2008). Why is externally-facilitated regulated learning more effective than self-regulated learning with hypermedia? *Educational Technology Research and Development, 56*(1), 45–72.

Azevedo, R., Mudrick, N. V., Taub, M., & Bradbury, A. E. (2019). Self-regulation in computer-assisted learning systems. In J. Dunlosky & K. A. Rawson (Eds.), *The Cambridge handbook of cognition and education* (pp. 587–618). Cambridge, UK: Cambridge University Press.

Barab, S., Dodge, T., Tuzun, H., Job-Sluder, K., Jackson, C., Arici, A., Job-Sluder, L., Carteaux Jr, R., Gilbertson, J., & Heiselt, C. (2007). The Quest Atlantis project: A socially-responsive play space for learning. In B. E. Shelton & D. A. Wiley (Eds.), *The design and use of simulation computer games in education* (pp. 159–186). Rotterdam, The Netherlands: Sense Publishers.

Bennett, K. B., & Flach, J. M. (2011). A framework for ecological interface design (EID). In K. B. Bennett & J. M. Flach (Eds.), *Display and interface design: Subtle science, exact art* (1st ed., pp. 109–140). Boca Raton, FL: CRC Press.

Birchfield, D., Thornburg, H., Megowan-Romanowicz, M. C., Hatton, S., Mechtley, B., Dolgov, I., & Burleson, W. (2008). Embodiment, multimodality, and composition: convergent themes across HCI and education for mixed-reality learning environments. *Advances in Human-Computer Interaction*, 1–19. doi.org/10.1155/2008/874563

Brush, T. A., & Saye, J. W. (2002). A summary of research exploring hard and soft scaffolding for teachers and students using a multimedia supported learning environment. *The Journal of Interactive Online Learning*, *1*(2), 1–12.

Carmigniani, J., Furht, B., Anisetti, M., Ceravolo, P., Damiani, E., & Ivkovic, M. (2011). Augmented reality technologies, systems and applications. *Multimedia Tools and Applications*, *51*(1), 341–377.

Chen, J. X., Yang, Y., & Loffin, B. (2003). Muvees: A PC-based multi-user virtual environment for learning. *IEEE Virtual Reality*, 163–170. doi: 10.1109/VR.2003.1191135

Chi, M.T.H., Glaser, R., & Farr, M. (1988). *The nature of expertise*. Hillsdale, NJ: Erlbaum. pp. xv–xxxvi.

Clancey, W. (1997). *Situated cognition: On human knowledge and computer representations*. Cambridge, MA: Cambridge University Press.

Clarke, J., Dede, C., & Dieterle, E. (2008). Emerging technologies for collaborative, mediated, immersive learning. In J. Voogt & G. Knezek (Eds.), *International handbook of information technology in primary and secondary education* (pp. 901–909). Cham, Switzerland: Springer.

Collins, A., Brown, J. S., and Newman, S. E. (1989). Cognitive apprenticeship: teaching the craft of reading, writing, and mathematics. In L. Resnick (Ed.) *Knowing, learning, and Instruction: Essays in honor of Robert Glaser* (pp. 453–494). Hillsdale, NJ: Lawrence Erlbaum Associates.

Collins, A., & Kapur, M. (2014). Cognitive apprenticeship. In R. K. Sawyer (Ed.), *The Cambridge handbook of the learning sciences* (2nd ed., pp. 109–127). Cambridge, UK: Cambridge University Press.

Craig, S. D., Gholson, B., & Driscoll, D. M. (2002). Animated pedagogical agents in multimedia educational environments: Effects of agent properties, picture features and redundancy. *Journal of Educational Psychology*, *94*(2), 428.

D'Mello, S., Dieterle, E., & Duckworth, A. (2017). Advanced, analytic, automated (AAA) measurement of engagement during learning. *Educational Psychologist*, *52*(2), 104–123. doi: 10.1080/00461520.2017.1281747

D'Mello, S. K., & Graesser, A. (2010). Multimodal semi-automated affect detection from conversational cues, gross body language, and facial features. *User Modeling and User-Adapted Interaction*, *20*(2), 147–187.

Dede, C. (2008). Theoretical perspectives influencing the use of information technology in teaching and learning. In J. Voogt & G. Knezek (Eds.), *International handbook of information technology in primary and secondary education* (pp. 43–62). Cham, Switzerland: Springer.

Dewey, J. (1938). *Experience and education*. New York: Collier Books.

Ericsson, K.A., Krampe, R.T., & Tesch-Romer, C. (1993). The role of deliberate practice in the acquisition of expert performance. *Psychological Review*, *100*(3), 363–406.

Few, S. (2006). *Information dashboard design: The effective visual communication of data*. Sebastopol, CA: O'Reilly Media.

GhasemAghaei, R., Arya, A., & Biddle, R. (2015). The MADE framework: multimodal software for affective education. *EdMedia+ Innovate Learning*, 1861–1871.

GhasemAghaei, R., Arya, A., & Biddle, R. (2016). A dashboard for affective E-learning: Data visualization for monitoring online learner emotions. *EdMedia+ Innovate Learning*, 1536–1543.

Graesser, A., & McNamara, D. (2010). Self-regulated learning in learning environments with pedagogical agents that interact in natural language. *Educational Psychologist, 45*(4), 234–244.

Greeno, J. (1998). The situativity of knowing, learning, and research. *American Psychologist, 53*(1), 5–26.

Gross, J. (2015). Emotion regulation: Current status and future prospects. *Psychological Inquiry, 26*, 1–26.

Harley, J. M., Lajoie, S. P., Haldane, C., McLaughlin, B., & Poitras, E. G. (2020). Beyond historical books, names and dates: Leveraging augmented reality to promote knowledge, reasoning, and emotional engagement. In V. Geroimenko (Ed.), *Augmented reality in education* (pp. 199–216). Cham, Switzerland: Springer.

Harley, J. M., Pekrun, R., Taxer, J. L., & Gross, J. J. (2019). Emotion regulation in achievement situations: An integrated model. *Educational Psychologist, 54*(2), 106–126.

Harley, J. M., Poitras, E. G., Jarrell, A., Duffy, M. C., & Lajoie, S. P. (2016). Comparing virtual and location-based augmented reality mobile learning: emotions and learning outcomes. *Educational Technology Research and Development, 64*(3), 359–388.

Herrington, J., & Oliver, R. (2000). An instructional design framework for authentic learning environments. *Educational Technology Research and Development, 48*(3), 23–48.

Holstein, K., McLaren, B. M., & Aleven, V. (2019). Designing for complementarity: Teacher and student needs for orchestration support in AI-enhanced classrooms. In S. Isotani, E. Millán, A. Ogan, P. Hastings, B. McLaren & R. Luckin (Eds.), *Proceedings, 20th International Conference on Artificial Intelligence in Education, AIED* (pp. 157–171). Cham, Switzerland: Springer.

Hooper, K. (1986). Architectural design: An analogy. In D. A. Norman & S. Draper (Eds.), *User centered system design: New perspectives on human-computer interaction* (1st ed., pp. 9–24). Boca Raton, FL: CRC Press.

Järvelä, S., & Hadwin, A. F. (2013). New frontiers: Regulating learning in CSCL. *Educational Psychologist, 48*(1), 25–39.

Järvelä, S., Järvenoja, H., & Malmberg, J. (2019). Capturing the dynamic and cyclical nature of regulation: Methodological Progress in understanding socially shared regulation in learning. *International Journal of Computer-Supported Collaborative Learning, 14*(4), 425–441.

Johnson, W. L., & Valente, A. (2009). Tactical language and culture training systems: Using AI to teach foreign languages and cultures. *AI Magazine, 30*(2), 72.

Kapur, M. (2008). Productive failure. *Cognition and Instruction, 26*(3), 379–424.

Ketelhut, D. J., Clarke, J., & Nelson, B. C. (2010). The development of River City, a multi-user virtual environment-based scientific inquiry curriculum: historical and design evolutions. In M. J. Jacobson & P. Reimann (Eds.), *Designs for learning environments of the future* (pp. 89–110). Cham, Switzerland: Springer.

Koedinger, K. R., & Corbett, A. T. (2006). Cognitive tutors: Technology bringing learning sciences to the classroom. In R. K. Sawyer (Ed.), *The Cambridge handbook of the learning sciences* (pp. 61–78). New York: Cambridge University Press.

Lajoie, S. P. (2003). Transitions and trajectories for studies of expertise. *Educational Researcher, 32*(8), 21–25. doi: 10.3102/0013189X032008021

Lajoie, S. P. (2009). Developing professional expertise with a cognitive apprenticeship model: Examples from Avionics and Medicine. In K. A. Ericsson (Ed.), *Development of professional expertise: Toward measurement of expert performance and design of optimal learning environments* (pp. 61–83). Cambridge, UK: Cambridge University Press.

Lajoie, S. P. (2014). Multimedia learning of cognitive processes. In R. E. Mayer (Ed.), *The Cambridge handbook of multimedia learning* (2nd ed., pp. 623–646). Cambridge, UK: Cambridge University Press.

Lajoie, S. P. (2020). Student modeling for individuals and groups: the BioWorld and HOWARD platforms. *International Journal of Artificial Intelligence in Education,* 1–16. doi: 10.1007/s40593-020-00219-x

Lajoie, S. P. (2022). Multimedia learning with simulation. In R. Mayer & L. Fiorella (Eds.), *Cambridge handbook of multimedia learning* (3rd ed.) (pp. 461–471). New York: Cambridge University Press.

Lajoie, S. P., & Azevedo, R. (2006). Teaching and learning in technology-rich environments. In P. Alexander and P. Winne (Eds.), *Handbook of educational psychology* (2nd ed.) (pp. 803–821). Mahwah, NJ: Erlbaum.

Lajoie, S. P., & Poitras, E. (forthcoming). Technology rich learning environments: Theories and methodologies for understanding solo and group learning. In K. Muis & P. Schutz (Eds.). *Handbook of educational psychology* (4th ed.). New York: Routledge.

Lajoie, S. P., & Poitras, E. (2017). Crossing disciplinary boundaries to improve technology rich learning. *Teachers College Record*, *119*(3), 1–30.

Lajoie, S. P., Pekrun, R., Azevedo, R., Leighton, J. P. (2020). Understanding and measuring emotions in technology-rich learning environments. *Journal of Learning and Instruction*, *70*, 1–6. doi: https://doi.org/10.1016/j.learninstruc.2019.101272

Lajoie, S. P., Zheng, J., Li, S., Jarrell, A., & Gube, M. (2021). Examining the interplay of affect and self regulation in the context of clinical reasoning. *Learning and Instruction*, *72*, 1–14. doi: 10.1016/j.learninstruc.2019.101219

Li, S., Du, H., Xing, W., Zheng, J., Chen, G., & Xie, C. (2020). Examining temporal dynamics of self-regulated learning behaviors in STEM learning: A network approach. *Computers & Education*, *158*, 103987. doi: 10.1016/j.compedu.2020.103987

Martinez-Maldonado, R., Clayphan, A., Yacef K., & Kay, J. (2015). MTFeedback: Providing notifications to enhance teacher awareness of small group work in the classroom. *IEEE Transactions on Learning Technologies*, *8*(2), 187–200. doi: 10.1109/TLT.2014.2365027.

Mayer, R. E. (1996). Learners as information processors: Legacies and limitations of educational psychology's second. *Educational Psychologist*, *31*(3–4), 151–161. doi: 10.1080/00461520.1996.9653263

Mayer, R. E. (2002). Multimedia learning. *Psychology of Learning and Motivation*, *41*, 85–139.

Mirchi, N., Bissonnette, V., Yilmaz, R., Ledwos, N., Winkler-Schwartz, A., & Del Maestro, R.F. (2020). The virtual operative assistant: An explainable artificial intelligence tool for simulation based training in surgery and medicine. *PLoS ONE*, *15*(2): e0229596. doi: 10.1371/journal.pone.0229596

Mitrovic, A. (2012). Fifteen years of constraint-based tutors: What we have achieved and where we are going. *User Modeling and User-Adapted Interaction*, *22*(1), 39–72. doi: 10.1007/s11257-011-9105-9

Norman, D. A. (1986). Cognitive engineering. In D. Norman & S. Draper (Eds.), *User centered system design: New perspectives on human-computer interaction* (1st ed., pp. 31–61). Boca Raton, FL: CRC Press.

Ohlsson, S. (1996). Learning from performance errors. *Psychological Review*, *103*, 241–262.

Pan, Z., Cheok, A. D., Yang, H., Zhu, J., & Shi, J. (2006). Virtual reality and mixed reality for virtual learning environments. *Computers & Graphics*, *30*(1), 20–28.

Pekrun, R. (2006). The control-value theory of achievement emotions: Assumptions, corollaries, and implications for educational research and practice. *Educational Psychology Review*, *18*(4), 315–341. doi: 10.1007/s10648-006-9029-9

Pekrun, R., & Linnenbrink-Garcia, L. (2014). *International handbook of emotions in education*. New York: Routledge.

Pekrun, R., Goetz, T., Titz, W., & Perry, R. P. (2002). Academic emotions in students' self-regulated learning and achievement: A program of qualitative and quantitative research. *Educational Psychologist*, *37*(2), 91–105.

Pekrun, R., Muis, K., Frenzel, A., & Goetz, T. (2018). *Emotions at school*. New York: Routledge.

Pinkwart, N. (2016). Another 25 years of AIED? Challenges and opportunities for intelligent educational technologies of the future. *International Journal of Artificial Intelligence in Education*, *26*(2), 771–783.

Platts, D., Anderson, B., Forshaw, T., & Burstow, D. (2011). Use of an echocardiographic mannequin simulator for early-sonographer training. *Heart, Lung and Circulation*, *20*, S199–S200.

Psotka, J., Massey, L. D., & Mutter, S. A. (Eds.). (1988). *Intelligent tutoring systems: Lessons learned*. Hillsdale, NJ: Lawrence Erlbaum Associates, Inc.

Saleh, A., Chen, Y., Hmelo-Silver, C., E., Glazewski, K. D., Mott, B.W., & Lester, J. C. (2020). Coordinating scaffolds for collaborative inquiry in a game-based learning environment. *Journal of Research in Science Teaching*, *57*(9), 1490–1518.

Schroder, M., Bevacqua, E., Cowie, R., Eyben, F., Gunes, H., Heylen, D., Ter Maat, M., McKeown, G., Pammi, S., & Pantic, M. (2011). Building autonomous sensitive artificial listeners. *IEEE Transactions on Affective Computing*, *3*(2), 165–183.

Schroeder, N. L., Adesope, O. O., & Gilbert, R. B. (2013). How effective are pedagogical agents for learning? A meta-analytic review. *Journal of Educational Computing Research*, *49*(1), 1–39.

Shute, V., Lajoie, S. P., & Gluck, K. (2000). Individual and group approaches to training. In S. Tobias & H. O'Neill (Eds.), *Handbook on training* (pp. 171–207). Washington, DC: American Psychological Association.

Shute, V., & Psotka, J. (1996). Intelligent tutoring system: Past, present, and future. In D. Jonassen (Ed.), *Handbook of research for educational communications and technology* (pp. 570–600). New York: Macmillan.

Slater, M. (2018). Immersion and the illusion of presence in virtual reality. *British Journal of Psychology*, *109*(3), 431–433.

Smetana, L. K., & Bell, R. L. (2012). Computer simulations to support science instruction and learning: A critical review of the literature. *International Journal of Science Education*, *34*(9), 1337–1370.

Squire, K., & Klopfer, E. (2007). Augmented reality simulations on handheld computers. *Journal of the Learning Sciences*, *16*(3), 371–413.

Sweller, J. (1994). Cognitive load theory, learning difficulty, and instructional design. *Learning and Instruction*, *4*(4), 295–312.

Tang, Y. M., Au, K. M., Lau, H. C. W., Ho, G. T. S., & Wu, C. H. (2020). Evaluating the effectiveness of learning design with mixed reality (MR) in higher education. *Virtual Reality*, *24*, 797–807.

Vaitsis, C., Hervatis, V., & Zary, N. (2016). Introduction to big data in education and its contribution to the quality improvement processes. In S. V. Soto, J. Luna, & A. Cano (Eds.), *Big data on real-world applications* (Vol. 113, p. 58). InTechOpen.

Van Lehn, K. (2011). The relative effectiveness of human tutoring intelligent tutoring systems and other tutoring systems. *Educational Psychologist*, *46*, 197–221.

Vassiliou, M. C., Feldman, L. S., Andrew, C. G., et al. (2005). A global assessment tool for evaluation of intraoperative laparoscopic skills. *American Journal of Surgery*, *190*, 107–13.

Verbert, K., Duval, E., Klerkx, J., Govaerts, S., & Santos, J. (2013). Learning analytics dashboard applications. *American Behavioral Scientist*, *57*(10), 1500–1509. doi: 10.1177/0002764213479363

Völkel, S. T., Schneegass, C., Eiband, M., & Buschek, D. (2020). What is "intelligent" in intelligent user interfaces? A meta-analysis of 25 years of IUI. *Proceedings of the 25th International Conference on Intelligent User Interfaces*, 477–487.

Wilson, M. (2002). Six views of embodied cognition. *Psychonomic Bulletin & Review*, *9*(4), 625–636.

Winne, P. H., & Hadwin, A. (1998). Studying as self-regulated learning. In D. J. Hacker, J. Dunlosky, & A. Graesser (Eds.), *Metacognition in educational theory and practice* (pp. 277–304). Hillsdale, NJ: Erlbaum.

Wu, H.-K., Lee, S. W.-Y., Chang, H.-Y., & Liang, J.-C. (2013). Current status, opportunities and challenges of augmented reality in education. *Computers & Education*, *62*, 41–49.

Zheng, J., Huang, L., Li, S., Lajoie, S. P., Chen, Y., & Hmelo-Silver, C. E. (2021). Self-regulation and emotion matter: A case study of instructor interactions with a learning analytics dashboard. *Computers & Education*, *161*, 104061.

11. Deeper learning through interactions with students in natural language

Vasile Rus, Andrew M. Olney and Arthur C. Graesser

Interacting with students in natural language has many advantages. It encourages deeper, conceptual learning as students are required to explain their reasoning and reflect on their basic approach to solving a problem. It also provides deeper insights into the learning process by revealing students' reasoning and mental model construction processes, including potential misconceptions, thereby enabling better detection of opportunities to scaffold students' learning by providing immediate corrective feedback. Conceptual reasoning is more challenging and beneficial than mechanical application of mathematical formulas or other abstract schemas (Halloun & Hestenes, 1985; Hake, 1998). Furthermore, natural language interactions give students the opportunity to develop the language of their target professional communities and therefore much-needed communication skills. When conversational AI systems for learning are augmented with virtual agents, they have affordances to social agency which allegedly leads to more engaging, satisfying, and effective learning experiences.

Interactions in natural language come in a variety of forms. In simple designs, the student simply selects from a set of alternative options, explanations, or answers presented in natural language or produces words in fill-in-the-blank presentations. In more complex designs, there is a full-blown conversational interaction between the student and the system. This chapter primarily focuses on dialogue-based intelligent tutoring systems (ITSs) that involve collaborative problem-solving activities; while most of the discussion focuses on one-on-one tutoring, we have in mind more general ITSs where one or more tutoring agents may interact with one or more students (for a more general discussion of collaborative learning, see Chapter 19 by Martinez-Maldonado et al.). We review prior work in this area, note current challenges, and discuss potential solutions based on recent advances in Artificial Intelligence.

THEORETICAL FOUNDATIONS

Conversational ITSs are built on a number of theoretical foundations that address fundamental issues such as the nature of knowledge, knowledge representation, and knowledge acquisition as we describe in this section.

Deep, Conceptual Knowledge

A contrast is frequently made between shallow versus deep knowledge, skills, and learning (Bransford et al., 2000; Chi, 2009; Graesser, 2020; Hattie & Donoghue, 2016; Millis et al., 2019). There is no sharp boundary between shallow and deep knowledge but Graesser (2020) identified some examples of each. Shallow knowledge of a subject matter includes recognition of key terms, their features, simple definitions, and routine skills and procedures to complete specific tasks. Deep knowledge is required when students comprehend difficult technical material, build mental models of complex systems, solve challenging problems, justify claims with evidence and logical arguments, identify inaccurate information, resolve contradictions, quantify ideas precisely, and build new artifacts. It is more difficult, and often less enjoyable, to acquire deep knowledge than shallow knowledge so there is a tendency to settle for shallow knowledge of a subject matter unless deep knowledge is needed to overcome obstacles in school, employment, or life. Higher-paying jobs in the twenty-first century require deep knowledge and also the ability to collaborate with others while solving complex problems (Autor et al., 2003; Carnevale & Smith, 2013).

Pedagogical Approaches to Acquiring Deep Knowledge

There are two basic pedagogical approaches to meeting the demand of acquiring deep knowledge and solving difficult problems. The first approach is to design pedagogical activities that encourage the student to mentally build *self-explanations* of the difficult material being learned. This can be as simple as instructing the students to think aloud (Chi et al., 1989; McNamara, 2004) or answer why, how, or other questions (Magliano et al., 1999) as they read texts, lessons, or solutions to problems. The student attempts to understand the material and use their prior knowledge to make inferences that explain the explicit content. The hope is that the mental model that is built subjectively (that's why it is called a *self*-explanation) is of sufficiently high quality that it will reasonably match an ideal explanation. Of course, some complex systems are so complex that it is debatable what an ideal explanation would be. As the student generates self-explanations on many texts and problems to solve, they would be expected to construct mental models over time that are closer to the ideal explanation.

The second pedagogical approach is to have a group of individuals attempt to construct explanations and, more generally, interpretations of the world that are vetted among the members of a group. The *socio-constructivist* approach, which has strong alliances with the tradition of Vygotsky (1978), emphasizes the importance of social practice, language, and activities in constructing representations of the learning material. Disagreements periodically arise among members of the community of practice so there is the opportunity to discuss and debate what ideas mean, the causes of events, and plausible shared mental models of the subject matter. Members of the community adopt a mindset that guides their interpretations of learning materials and actions to pursue. Pedagogical designs with collaborative learning and problem solving are good examples of pedagogical approaches that encourage the socio-cultural construction of knowledge. As with self-explanations, the hope is that the socio-cultural knowledge increasingly matches ideal/ mastery knowledge as the experiences of the learning communities mature over time.

The Role of Natural Language in Knowledge Representation and Acquisition

Natural language understanding, generation, and interaction play a fundamental role in the two pedagogical approaches that implement self-explanations and the socio-constructivist approaches. This is due to the tight relationship in our brains among natural language, knowledge representation, and reasoning. Natural language also plays a key role in social interactions, transfer of knowledge, collaboration, and coordination of teamwork that is often necessary to solve complex tasks that a single person cannot possibly solve. Consequently, conversational ITSs have some key advantages over other types of ITSs. They encourage deep learning as students are required to explain their reasoning and reflect on their basic approach to solving a problem. As already noted, conceptual reasoning is presumably more challenging and beneficial than mechanical application of mathematical formulas. Furthermore, conversational ITSs have the potential of giving students the opportunity to learn the language of professionals in a target domain (Mohan et al., 2009; Shaffer, 2017). For instance, a student with a shallow understanding of a science topic uses more informal language with mundane reasoning rather than scientific explanations. The role of science training in general is to also help students acquire the language of science.

Animated Pedagogical Agents

The impact of conversational ITSs allegedly can be augmented by the use of animated conversational agents that have become more popular in contemporary advanced learning environments (Graesser, 2020; Johnson & Lester, 2016; Nye et al., 2014; Rus et al., 2013). The animated agents interact with students and help them learn by either modeling good pedagogy or by holding a conversation with the students. Both single agents and ensembles of agents can be carefully choreographed to mimic virtually any activity or social situation: curiosity, inquiry learning, negotiation, interrogation, arguments, empathetic support, helping, and so on. Agents not only enact these strategies, individually or in groups, but can also think aloud while they do so (McNamara et al., 2004).

The number of agents interacting with the student has been an important consideration in the design of agent-based systems. In a *dialogue*, a single agent interacts with a single human, as in the case of the original *AutoTutor* (Graesser, 2016). In a *trialogue*, there is a three-party conversation among, for instance, two computer agents and a human student. The two agents take on different roles, but often serve as tutors and peers of the student. There are alternative trialogue designs that address different pedagogical goals for particular classes of students (Graesser et al., 2017; Swartout et al., 2010). For example, students can observe two agents interacting so that the student can model the actions and thoughts of an ideal agent. Agents can argue with each other over issues and ask what the student's position is on the argument (D'Mello et al., 2014; Lehman & Graesser, 2016). A tutor agent can put a student against a peer agent in a game scenario in order to enhance motivation (Millis et al., 2017). It is also possible for a single agent to communicate with a small group of students to facilitate group learning and problem solving.

Agent-based systems have also been used in assessment in addition to learning. In particular, components of *AutoTutor* trialogues have been developed at Educational Testing Service (ETS) in assessments of reading, writing, science, and mathematics (Zapata-Rivera et al., 2014). Collaborative problem solving has been assessed by *tetralogues* that have two agents interacting with two humans (Liu et al., 2015). Agents were also used in the *Programme for International Student Assessment* (PISA), an international assessment of collaborative problem solving, in 2015 (Graesser et al., 2018; OECD, 2017).

Although agent-based systems have been used in assessment contexts, in this chapter we focus on the use of conversational agents in the context of tutoring. We have organized the chapter into two sections. In the first section, we discuss the structure of *tutorial dialogues* whereas in the second section we discuss solutions to key tasks based on recent advances in AI. But first, we provide a brief history.

A BRIEF HISTORY OF ITSs WITH NATURAL LANGUAGE INTERACTION

The vision of developing an ITS with natural language capabilities has a history of at least 50 years (see Chapter 2 by McCalla for a broader history that includes ITSs). Many recall

Stanley Kubrick's 1968 film *2001: A Space Odyssey*, which had a HAL computer (IBM minus one letter) that communicated with people in natural language. Interestingly, systems surprisingly ended up being developed around 2001 that fulfilled that vision, although they were far from perfect. One early system was called SCHOLAR (Carbonell, 1970; Carbonell & Collins, 1973; Collins et al., 1975), which tutored students by asking questions about South American geography. The system had a semantic network with a structured taxonomy (node concepts connected hierarchically by is-a links, with distinctive properties connected to nodes), which was very popular in AI and cognitive science at that time. The system asked and attempted to answer student questions by consulting the network and implementing deductive and abductive reasoning. Unfortunately, there were several challenges in handling tutorial dialogue so the system was primarily a demonstration prototype that illustrated what was possible in a tutoring system with mundane reasoning. One challenge was that the syntactic parsers were limited, so many student queries could not be handled unless the questions were highly structured. A second problem was that semantic networks were very limited in the knowledge that was needed to cover a subject matter. Semantic networks do not cover causal events in scientific mechanisms or actions in scripted activities, for example.

CIRCSIM tutor (Evens & Michael, 2006) was an attempt to build an NLP tutor about scientific mechanisms, in this case the circulatory system and functioning of the heart. The system would ask questions about what would happen in the circulatory system under specific conditions, with a simulation of the ideal model. The dialogue would ask questions that required short natural language descriptions, such as a word or a phrase. At that time, interpretation of words, noun-phrases, and simple propositions was the best that the ITS with NLP could handle reliably. The system could not handle turns of students with multiple sentences and discourse interactions with multiple turns.

AutoTutor (Graesser, 2016; Graesser et al., 2004) was one of the first NLP-based ITS systems that attempted to handle multi-sentence turns and multi-turn interactions between the human student and tutor agent. The student and tutor agents co-constructed explanations in natural language when prompted with difficult questions or problems to solve. The student's responses over multiple turns were continuously compared with ideal answers (called expectations) and potential misconceptions. *AutoTutor* classified student contributions with a statistical parser that discriminated student statements (assertions), questions, expressive comments, metacognitive expressions (e.g., "I'm lost"), versus short responses (yes, no, etc.). *AutoTutor* made semantic comparisons between student contributions over multiple turns and the expectations and misconceptions, using a variety of semantic evaluation approaches, such as Latent Semantic Analysis (Landauer et al., 2007) and regular expressions (Jurafsky & Martin, 2008). *AutoTutor* provided feedback on the quality of the students' contributions as well as prompts and hints to get the student to express more ideas. *AutoTutor* was found to improve learning of computer literacy and physics at a level comparable to human tutors and much better than students' reading text for an equivalent amount of learning time (Graesser et al., 2004; VanLehn et al., 2007; Nye et al., 2014). There were also versions of *AutoTutor* that accommodated speech input (D'Mello et al., 2011), interactions with simulation environments (Graesser et al., 2005), and the detection of student emotions and adaptive responses to such emotions (D'Mello & Graesser, 2012). Unfortunately, *AutoTutor* has been beset with a number of limitations. It takes substantial time and resources to author content for *AutoTutor* to anticipate different paths of conversational interaction and also have grounded connections with external media (e.g., graphics, tables, simulations). *AutoTutor* was also not capable of handling any question a student would ask, with students being uninspired by *AutoTutor* responses such as "That's a good question but I can't answer it", or "How would you answer the question?", or "Let's go on". *AutoTutor* also had errors in speech act classification of student responses and semantic evaluation of student answers although the computations were almost on a par with human expert judgments.

Advances in NLP-based ITS evolved around the time of *AutoTutor*, some of which were inspired by this system (Nye et al., 2014). A major goal of these systems is to train students on subject matter and skills by holding a conversation in natural language. The systems were also validated by showing learning gains and/or promising motivational variables. For example, *My-Science-Tutor* helps students in school learn about science topics with speech input (Ward et al., 2013). *Writing-Pal* helps students write persuasive essays (Roscoe & McNamara, 2013). Other conversation-based systems include *ITSPOKE* (Litman et al., 2006), *Why2* (VanLehn et al., 2007), *Mission Rehearsal* (Gratch et al., 2002), *DC-Trains* (Pon-Barry et al., 2004), *Enskill* (Johnson, 2019), *GuruTutor* (Olney et al., 2012) and *DeepTutor* (Rus et al., 2013).

GENERAL ITS FRAMEWORK

The behavior of any ITS, conversational or not, can be described in a simple way using VanLehn's (2006) two-loop framework. According to VanLehn, ITSs can be described in broad terms as running two loops: the outer loop, which selects the next task to work on, and the inner loop, which manages the student–system interaction while the student works on a particular task. The outer loop is usually just an iteration over the set of existing tasks (i.e., main questions or problems) or can be guided by stronger theoretical foundations such as Learning Progressions (Rus et al., 2013). The inner loop of an ITS monitors students' performance through embedded assessment, updates its model of students' levels of understanding (i.e., the student model), and uses the updated student model to provide appropriate scaffolding in the form of feedback and other scaffolds such as correcting misconceptions. The two-loop framework is a simplified view of ITS behavior. Rus et al. (2014, 2016) detailed a number of other important loops such as the sub-step loop and the curriculum loop.

In dialog-based ITSs, embedded assessment relies heavily on language understanding algorithms as students' responses are natural language utterances. Language processing algorithms in dialogue ITSs have relied on co-occurrence methods such as Latent Semantic Analysis (LSA; Landauer et al., 2007), inverse weighted word frequency overlap, and regular expressions. Recent advances in semantic representations and natural language processing methods based on deep neural networks are now used, as described later.

The three major advances in conversational ITSs described later in this chapter will have direct impact on both the outer and inner loops of ITSs and will lead to improvements in core tasks handled by ITSs: comprehensive student models, more accurate auto-assessment methods, and more scalable development processes. Advances in these core tutoring tasks will move state-of-the-art conversational ITSs closer to implementing fully adaptive tutoring, which implies tailoring instruction to each individual student at both macro- and micro-level based on comprehensive student models, improved tutorial dialogue, user satisfaction, learning effectiveness, and more scalable ITS development processes across topics and domains.

Effectiveness of Conversational ITSs in Improving Learning

In some early assessments of conversational ITSs, *Why-Atlas* and *Why-AutoTutor* had student learning gains as high as an impressive 1.64 effect size when compared with students learning the same content by reading textbook sections on the topic on Newtonian physics with no personalized feedback, a one-size-fits-all approach (VanLehn et al., 2007). Graesser et al. (2001) reported more modest effect sizes in learning gains (between 0.3 and 0.9 standard deviation units) when compared with students reading text content in the training of computer literacy and physics. Nye et al. (2014) reported a similar range in effect sizes for a much larger number of conversational ITSs. Of course, not all results are so rosy. Some experimental conditions and groups of students investigated by VanLehn et al. (2007) showed little or no improvement. The true impact of conversational ITSs on learning is still not settled empirically (see Paladines & Ramirez, 2020, for a recent review).

How Much Farther Can ITSs' Effectiveness Improve?

Due to their interactive nature, conversational ITSs fall within the constructive and interactive dimensions of the Interactive > Constructive > Active > Passive (ICAP) framework (Chi & Wylie, 2014). They engage students in constructive and interactive activities rather than resorting to the mere delivery of information through text and other modalities that involve natural language, such as videos with spoken/voice-over or subtitles. Conversational ITSs engage students in interactive collaborative problem-solving activities, prompting students to construct responses at different levels of granularity (task level, step level, or sub-step level) depending on students' needs for scaffolding. The knowledge, skills, and mastery levels of the student are inferred by automatically assessing the answers provided by the students. This fine-grain student profile affords the ITS to provide adequate feedback and plan the next pedagogical move. Sub-step level interaction is deemed more interactive than (logical) step level which in turn is deemed more interactive than task level (VanLehn, 2011). That is, the interactivity increases if the tutor–student interaction moves from task level to sub-step level interactions. Two questions follow naturally: (1) If interactivity increases, can effectiveness of such instructional activities keep increasing? and (2) Is there a ceiling and if so what is it?

Up to a decade ago, the conventional wisdom speculated that as interactivity of tutoring increases, the effectiveness of tutoring should keep increasing. Because sub-step-level interaction focuses on atomic pieces of knowledge whereas step-level interaction on logical steps (of a solution to a problem, for instance), the implication is that focusing on atomic knowledge components is better. Based on a meta-review analysis, VanLehn (2011) reported that as interactivity of tutoring increases, the effectiveness of human and computer tutors empirically plateaus at some point, notably the sub-step level. This is not surprising since interactivity, as defined by VanLehn (2011), cannot keep increasing beyond the sub-step level as at this level the focus is on atomic knowledge which cannot be further subdivided as a way to increase interactivity further. One possible way to increase the granularity of knowledge would be to present that concept in different contexts as there are subtle aspects of, say, a particular concept that vary from context to context, similar to the meaning of a word which can have subtle differences in different contexts which is why true synonymy between words is rare. Nevertheless, VanLehn's interactivity plateau finding challenged ITS developers to find new approaches to further increase computer tutors' effectiveness, which we highlighted in Rus et al. (2013) and address later in this chapter.

We strongly believe that there is much room to improve the effectiveness of current computer tutors by addressing limitations of current state-of-the-art systems. Consequently, this chapter outlines several promising opportunities to improve current ITSs and push their effectiveness beyond the interactivity plateau. In particular, we suggest the focus be on improving the quality of tutorial interactions as opposed to the level (quantity/granularity) of interactions. We also address limitations of the capabilities and true potential of current conversational ITSs that can be attributed to their past limited scalability across domains and topics, which has frequently narrowed their evaluations to small-scale studies compared to non-conversational ITSs. *How far can the effectiveness be increased beyond the interactivity plateau*? We answer this question by looking at prior research of high-achievers in a particular domain – see below. As already noted, there are some limitations imposed by the nature of knowledge which can only be broken down to a certain degree until an atomic level is reached but also, as noted later, by the nature of learning and learners, for example, cognitive load and motivation. There are also technological limitations at this moment which we address, such as limitations with respect to understanding natural language. The related question we highlight is whether there is a theoretical limit to ITS improvements, for example, assuming technological and motivation limitations are addressed, or if there is limit to achievement in a domain in general: *Is there a theoretical or empirically suggested ceiling?* We make an argument next that research on learning habits and trajectories of high-achievers suggests such a ceiling when considering the length and density of interactive and intense, deliberate learning sessions. The good news is that research suggests there is no long-term ceiling for improving the mastery of a given domain.

A Suggested Ceiling for the Length and Density of Interactive, Intense Learning Sessions

As already noted, interactive instructional activities are the most effective and desired type of learning activities according to the ICAP framework (Chi & Wylie, 2014). Chi and Wylie argue they not only lead to higher cognitive engagement but also more inferences and corrections of flawed mental models. However, there are valid questions about the density of such intensively interactive learning sessions and about the length of such sessions that include intense cognitive activities. Indeed, one-on-one interactive instructional sessions with an expert or significantly more knowledgeable other, that is, tutoring, are probably among the most intense interactive learning activities because the students must be fully engaged and pay attention all the time as opposed to other forms of instruction such as lecturing/monologue, in which the student may or may not choose to pay attention (VanLehn et al., 2007). The higher cognitive engagement during tutoring, which is the result of high attention and interactivity, leads to high cognitive load (or even overload). Engaging in such highly interactive and cognitively intense learning activities may not be sustainable over lengthy sessions (learning episodes) and over many such sessions within a given time frame (e.g., a day or a week), that is, the density of learning episodes per period of time.

Meta-analyses of high-achievers in a particular domain indicate that it takes sustained, deliberate practice over many years to master a domain and that there are limitations about the length and the density of learning episodes within a given period of time such as a day or a week (Ericsson et al., 1993). The timing of those episodes within a day (e.g., morning or after a nap) or within a week are important as well because they should be scheduled when students are well rested and attentive. Limits of a single, highly interactive learning session/ episode has also been reported to have diminishing returns as the session is prolonged (Kopp et al., 2012). This implies there is a limit for the density of such highly interactive and deliberate learning episodes (i.e., the number of episodes over a period of time such as a day or a week) and for the duration of each individual learning episode. Being aware of such limits could inform both human and computer tutors what may be possible or expected (short term and long term) from tutorial interactions. For instance, for average students, tutors should not expect to push for more and longer sessions than those just discussed as these were inferred from research on high achievers and therefore be regarded as upper limits. The good news is that there is no apparent limitation in how much one can achieve with sustained, intense effort spread over long periods of time, that is, mastery keeps increasing over long periods of time (Ericsson et al., 1993).

It should be noted that other factors play an important role in the level of engagement during a session. For instance, motivation, affect, and meta-cognition play important roles in both short-term and long-term spans of time. Accounting for all these and other variables is the essence of what we call a *comprehensive student model*. Such a model is needed to move tutoring/instruction beyond the currently observed interactivity plateau and towards true or full adaptivity which we envision will help tutors, both human and computer based, and learners move closer to the theoretical limit. True adaptivity implies tutors would put the student in a zone of optimal concentration that targets relevant knowledge about the subject matter, at a pace that delivers the right challenges to the particular student at the right time (cognitive load management) and over long periods of time. That is, designing ITSs that promote deep conceptual learning over long periods of time through productive learning episodes requires bridging the gap between learning and liking, which are often at odds (Graesser, 2020).

OPPORTUNITIES TO IMPROVE CURRENT CONVERSATIONAL ITSs BASED ON RECENT ADVANCES IN ARTIFICIAL INTELLIGENCE

Conversational ITSs are not yet widely adopted due to a number of technological challenges related to natural language dialogue systems in general such as: (1) fundamentally challenging core AI tasks (natural language understanding and generation, knowledge representation and reasoning), (2) high expectations from such systems when it comes to the quality of natural language interactions, (3) challenges in scaling up the development of such systems across topics and domains, and (4) current limitations with respect to aligning natural language with other knowledge representations, such as structured source code, mathematical equations, or visual representations.

Nevertheless, it should be noted that conversational ITSs do have a major scalability advantage over other types of ITSs like constraint-based and model- or example-tracing tutors in the sense that much of human knowledge is encoded and communicated via natural language (as well as images, diagrams, or tables). This makes it easier for experts (e.g., domain or pedagogical experts), or even non-experts (Olney, 2018), to create artifacts needed by conversational ITSs. Furthermore, such ITSs can benefit from existing textbooks and other instructional materials to speed up the authoring of ITSs for new domains by using knowledge representations that are easily derived from natural language, for example, the so-called natural language-based knowledge representations (Rus, 2002).

Recent advances in Artificial Intelligence and in particular machine learning provide new promising tools to address many of the key challenges. We highlight in this chapter some of the most emerging and promising tools and illustrate how these new tools can help address key tasks in conversational ITSs such as assessment and scalability. This includes opportunities to move conversational ITSs beyond the interactivity plateau (more effective) and make them more widely adopted (more scalable): (1) comprehensive student models which in turn should lead to progress towards true or full adaptivity, (2) opportunities specific to conversational ITSs such as promising new automated methods based on novel semantic representations to assess student natural language responses, which are the norm in tutorial dialogue interactions, and (3) scaling up the development of such conversational ITSs across topics and domains which is possible through recent advances in automating the development of such systems.

Towards Comprehensive Student Models

The frontiers of our understanding, modeling, and scaffolding of student learning could accelerate if comprehensive student data were available. Ideally, ITSs would have a complete description of the student in order to tailor instruction to their needs. Not only would student data offer a more comprehensive view of the student but it would be up-to-date so that at any moment the student model would reflect the most recent student state.

A comprehensive student model is a key long-term goal of ITS developments of the future and in particular of the NSF-funded Learner Data Institute (LDI; Rus et al., 2020). A stepping stone towards that goal is student and learning *data convergence*, the collecting and aligning of comprehensive data about the same student across disciplines, skills, modalities, and psychological attributes (e.g., cognitive, metacognitive, emotional, motivational, behavioral, social) and about other aspects of the learning process, such as the learning and instructional strategies involved. We use the broad term "learning data" to refer to student/learner data, data about the learning and instruction process, and data about the overall learning and broader environment. Undoubtedly, full data convergence will be hard to achieve for various reasons such as privacy, security, equity and ethical reasons in addition to other challenges, technical or otherwise. However, the goal is to push the limits of what is possible, understand those limits, and act accordingly. Understanding the limits of data convergence will allow us to understand the limits of technology, what teachers/instructors and other stakeholders can do to compensate for those limitations, and how to best orchestrate the student–teacher–system partnership.

There are challenges in achieving data convergence. A starting point is to assess what student data is currently being collected and usable and to identify data needs from a learning science and engineering perspective. For instance, epistemic frame theory assumes that professionals develop epistemic frames, a network of skills, knowledge, identity, values, and epistemology (SKIVE elements) that are unique to that profession (Chesler et al., 2010). Engineers, for instance, share ways of understanding and doing (knowledge and skills), beliefs about which problems are worth investigating (values), characteristics that define them as members of the profession (identity), and ways of justifying decisions (epistemology). What kind of data and data analysis method are needed to obtain each student's SKIVE profile at any given moment?

The student data specification effort accounts for views from different stakeholders in the learning sciences, human–technology frontier, and data science opportunities to make the adoption and use of the systems by students and instructors effective and efficient. Raw data, including video, need to be processed in order to extract from it the higher-level constructs needed for capturing the learning process. For instance, students' emotions are inferred from raw sensor data such as faces (images) and/or physiological measurements. There are many aspects that need to be considered with collecting, processing, analyzing, storing, securing, and sharing education data: data fidelity, reliability, privacy, security, ethics, equity, intrusiveness, human subject research compliance, provenance, and exchangeability/sharing. Attempts to collect various types of student data have been made in previous major efforts, such as the LearnSphere/Datashop project and the *Generalized Intelligent Framework for Tutoring* project (Sottilare et al., 2018), as well as efforts in the recent AI Institute (Alexa for Education).

While prior efforts such as LearnSphere/DataShop have made progress towards building data infrastructure and capacity in education contexts, slow data convergence is a critical issue that hinders realizing the full potential of data and data science (and AI/Machine Learning) to transform the learning ecosystem. For instance, the DataShop metric reports show that most of the data is composed of datasets in the standard datashop format, of which there are about 3 500 (https://pslcdatashop.web.cmu.edu/ MetricsReport). While this might seem superficially large, the average number of observations per student is less than 400 from the large number of students (greater than 800 000) and is spread across more than 3 000 datasets, resulting in less than 260 students per dataset. By the same token, the recently released EduNet (Choi et al., 2020) contains data from 784 309 students preparing for the Test of English for International Communication at an average of 400.20 interactions per student. They do not cover STEAM+C topics and are limited to student performance data. That is, there is an "impoverished datasets" challenge in education, due to lack of big edu-data, that is, fine-grain student data from many students across many domains and timespans. To address this challenge, we proposed the development of LearnerNet (Rus et al., 2020), an "ImageNet" (Su et al., 2012) for learner modeling which could enable a transformation of our modeling and understanding of how learners learn, of how adaptive instructional systems can be made more capable of adapting to diverse learners, and fueling a better understanding of the learning ecosystem as a whole.

Big edu-data should include data about millions of students that is *fine-grain* (e.g., step/sub-step level information or detailed process data), *rich* (cognition, affect, motivation, behavior, social, epistemic), and *longitudinal* (across many grades). Big edu-data should be *deep* (e.g., about many students), *wide* (e.g., capture as many learning relevant aspects as possible, such as behavior, cognitive, social, emotional, epistemic, and motivational aspects), and *long* (being *long*-itudinal, across many grades or even lifetime). Convergence efforts will seek to "deepen" samples and "lengthen" timeframes of datasets that are (sometimes, but not always, already) "wide" in terms of features captured.

The LDI adopts the principle that the data owner (student/parent/guardian/teacher/school/developer/etc.) should be given a spectrum of options with respect to data sharing or, if deciding not to share, with respect to providing access to data. Indeed, access to student data is a complex issue. Individuals such as students (minors or adult students) and education technology developers may be reluctant to share data if they perceive the contribution as having only downsides, perhaps running afoul of regulation, enabling sanctions, or jeopardizing individual opportunities. Security and privacy risks discourage data owners from sharing data due to concerns of data abuse and data leaks and pose huge responsibilities to data collectors to protect data under regulations like FERPA.

A spectrum of solutions is needed to accommodate various attitudes that student data owners may have towards data ownership, security, and privacy. For instance, at one end of the spectrum there need to be solutions for students who do not wish to share their data or even provide access to it in any secure and privacy-preserving way. In that case, standalone education technologies are needed that can be downloaded on the student's device and which do not rely on and do not send any information to an outside location. The disadvantage is that the students will not be able to take advantage of updated tailored components of the education technology and therefore will not have access to the optimal learning experience and learning outcomes. Other students may be willing to provide access to some aggregate characteristics of the data (not necessarily share the data) and in return benefit from a better learning experience and better learning outcomes. In this case, students do not provide access to the actual data but rather can offer education developers and other interested parties access to certain characteristics or patterns of the data based on which the consumer of the data can generate new, synthetic data that matches the characteristics of the student data. At the other end of the spectrum, there are students willing to share their data with the education developer and also with other student data consumer for the benefit of everyone as long as there are checks and assurances that the data will not be misused or used for purposes other than to improve learning experiences and outcomes for everyone.

Once comprehensive student data is available, promising machine-learning theories such as neuro-symbolic theories can be used to identify patterns and infer student models, such as in the form of student embeddings, from deep (many students) and rich/complex data. Neuro-symbolic methods combine deep learning approaches which are very good at learning from large and complex data (LeCun et al., 2015; Schmidhuber, 2015; Salakhutdinov et al., 2019) with statistical relational learning approaches (Domingos & Lowd, 2009; Bach et al., 2017) that use symbolic logic to explicitly encode expertise/domain knowledge/theories.

Advanced Assessment Based on Recent Advances in AI, Machine Learning, and Natural Language Processing

We focus in this section on the assessment of natural language open responses as opposed to responses that require, for instance, drawing a diagram or selecting an answer from a set of given answers. Assessing such natural language student responses is a natural language understanding (NLU) task.

Computational approaches to NLU can be classified into three major categories: true-understanding, information extraction, and text-to-text similarity. Rus (2018) provides an overview of these categories of approaches by considering the nature of free student responses, opportunities, challenges, and state-of-the-art solutions. Here we summarize the most promising recent developments. However, first we would like to draw readers' attention to the important relationship between what we call micro-level assessment and macro-level assessment in conversational tutoring.

Assessment in many conversational ITSs is conducted at the logical step level (expectation or reference answer) which is often different from a standard knowledge component (KC; Koedinger et al., 2012). Knowledge components are expected to be intrinsic information packets that apply to different learning contexts and can be measured on mastery in these different contexts. However, the logical steps completed in particular tasks do not have simple mappings to the knowledge components; they may only refer to pieces of a KC and one step may refer to multiple KC's. When assessment in such ITSs need to be aligned to student performance in other ITSs that perform KC-level assessment then it is necessary to map logical steps to KCs. Due to the open/free structure of natural language statements (in contrast to structured or semi-structured information), it is not straightforward to easily identify KCs in free text student responses.

As an example, a typical assessment step in conversational tutors is comparing a student answer to a reference answer provided by an expert (i.e., we perform a semantic similarity operation) as shown below:

Reference Answer: *The forces from the truck and car are equal and opposite.*
Student Answer: *The magnitudes of the forces are equal and opposite to each other due to Newton's third law of motion.*

The question is whether there are one or more knowledge components (KCs) in the reference answer (logical step). Depending on the granularity of the domain model, one can argue there are two knowledge components: one referring to the magnitude of the opposing forces in Newton's third law and one referring to the direction of the forces. Consequently, there needs to be a mapping between steps in solving a particular problem and the more generic KCs.

Once mastery of such KCs has been detected, for example, using models such as Bayesian knowledge tracing (BKT; Corbett & Anderson, 1994), one can also infer a more overall mastery level as modeled by proficiency of a target domain, such as Newtonian Physics, using models such as Item Response Theory (IRT; Embretson & Reise, 2000). BKT focuses on KC-level assessment, which we may call micro-level assessment, whereas IRT focuses on macro-level assessment, that is, assessment across a number of KCs that together represent a domain of mastery. It is beyond the scope of this chapter to explore micro- and macro-level assessment. We just wanted to highlight the relationship between assessment of free student responses, which is our focus in this section, KCs, and micro- and macro-level assessment methods such as BKT and IRT, respectively.

We will focus next on recent advances with respect to algorithms that assess the correctness of natural language student answers by comparing them to reference answers.

Examples of compositional approaches to assessing students' short responses in conversational tutors

The principle of compositionality states that the meaning of a text can be determined by the meaning of its constituents and the rules used to combine them (Lintean & Rus, 2012, 2015). Compositional approaches rely on word-level and text-level meaning representations. Many such representations are distributional vector representations that rely on a statistical analysis of word co-occurrences in large collections of natural language texts, that is, a corpus such as Wikipedia articles (Ştefănescu et al., 2014a, b). Examples of distributional vector representations that have been explored for automatically assessing student responses in conversational tutors are latent semantic analysis (LSA; Landauer et al., 2007), Explicit Semantic Analysis (ESA; Gabrilovich & Markovitch, 2007) or Latent Dirichlet Allocation (LDA; Blei et al., 2003). Yet another major trend in the area of distributional vector-based representations is the new category of representations derived using deep neural networks. A typical example in this category is the *word2vec* representation developed by Mikolov et al. (2013). They trained a Recursive Neural Network (RNN) with local context (continuous n-grams or skip-grams) using a process in which the input word vectors are recursively adjusted until the target context words are accurately predicted given the input word. These representations were shown to capture syntactic and lexical semantic regularities, have superior compositionality properties, and enable more precise analogical reasoning using simple vector algebra (Mikolov et al., 2013; Pennington et al., 2014).

Methods that account for context

A major limitation of previous semantic similarity approaches to assessing freely generated student answers is the assumption that student answers are explicit, self-contained statements that can be used as they are when compared with benchmark, expert-generated reference answers. That is definitely not the case because student answers vary substantially in the amount of explicit information they contain due to differences in knowledge levels as well as verbal and cognitive abilities among students. Furthermore, the intrinsic nature of human conversation is such that utterances are heavily contextualized by the previous dialogue history. Indeed, the variation in explicit information is even more extreme in conversational tutoring environments where students make frequent use of the context, for example, dialogue history, and use context referring tools such as pronouns, other (vague) referring expressions, and ellipses.

One promising approach to account for context when assessing automatically student responses is the LSTM-based approach proposed recently to handle student answers in context (Maharjan et al., 2018). Specifically, context is accounted for by using LSTM (Long Short-Term Memory) layers that capture long-term dependencies between a target student answer and the previous context in which that answer was generated by the student. Furthermore, motivated by the impressive results of capsule networks in text classification and other NLP tasks, Ait-Khayi and Rus (2019) have introduced a Bi-GRU Capsule Networks model to automatically assess freely-generated student answers assessment within the context of dialogue-based ITSs.

Interpretable or explanation-based semantic similarity approaches

Consider a question asked by *DeepTutor* (Rus et al., 2013), an ITS for Newtonian Physics, and the corresponding ideal answer or expectation shown below.

> Question: *Because it is a vector, acceleration provides what two types of information?*
> Student Answer: *Acceleration gives magnitude.*
> Reference Answer: *Acceleration provides magnitude and direction.*

A short textual semantic similarity (STS) approach (Agirre et al., 2015, 2016; Maharjan et al., 2017) would most likely assign a similarity score of three (out of a maximum score of four, which means semantically equivalent) for the given student answer, meaning that the student response is missing important information. However, it does not explain which information is missing. If such explanatory functionality existed that could explain that the student is missing information about direction of the acceleration, an ITS could use this diagnostic information to generate a follow-up question such as: *What other type of information is provided by acceleration?*

One approach to add an explanatory layer in STS systems is to align text chunks, for example, phrases or clauses, in a given pair of texts and label them with semantic relation types and similarity scores, as proposed in the pilot interpretable Semantic Textual Similarity task (iSTS; Agirre et al., 2015). Indeed, interpretable alignment-based approaches first perform an alignment between words in one text versus words in the other texts while at the same time identifying semantic labels for aligned words (Banjade et al., 2016). The advantage of adding semantic relationships between the aligned words is that an explanation for the alignment can be provided based on these word-to-word semantic relationships. The set of semantic relationships used was proposed as part of the interpretable Semantic Textual Similarity (iSTS) task (Agirre et al., 2016), organized by SemEval, the leading semantic evaluation forum, and includes: EQUI (semantically equivalent), OPPO (opposite in meaning), SPE (one chunk is more specific than other), SIMI (similar meanings, but not EQUI, OPPO, SPE), REL (related meanings, but not SIMI, EQUI, OPPO, SPE), and NOALI (has no corresponding chunk in the other sentence). It should be noted that alignment-based methods typically focus on words, but other units of analysis can be adopted, such as chunks (Stefanescu et al., 2014).

Another approach is to use a concept map approach such as the one proposed by Maharjan and Rus (2019) to both assess and interpret freely generated student answers. Using the concept map approach, we break down a reference answer into one or more tuples which essentially means that we end up with finer-grain learning or knowledge components. That is, we can track students' knowledge at a finer grain level leading to subtler differences among different knowledge states. This has a more direct correspondence with other approaches to assessing and tracing students' knowledge that rely directly on KCs.

Scaling Up Conversational ITSs: Automating the Tutorial Dialogue Generation from Textbooks

Interactivity in conversational ITS is highly dependent on the diversity of tutor actions, which traditionally have been manually authored. A practical advantage of conversational tutoring systems is that they are easier to author than the other major types of ITS, like model- or example-tracing tutors (Aleven et al., 2016; Anderson et al., 1995) and constraint-based tutors (Mitrovic, 2012). This is perhaps best illustrated with early versions of *AutoTutor*, which did not represent domain knowledge in a formal representation like logic but rather in natural language; later versions did add regular expression representations to improve the semantic matches between student input and reference answers (Graesser, 2016), but several *AutoTutor* applications relied on natural language to represent the domain knowledge. Therefore, creating an *AutoTutor*-style ITS on new topics is a straightforward as creating sentences and questions in natural language, which may be accomplished using a variety of different natural language processing techniques. This section describes two broad approaches for automated authoring of conversational ITS from textbooks as well as several approaches for correcting any errors that may arise during the process. In what follows, we focus on a basic implementation of *AutoTutor* as representative of a conversational ITS so as to simplify presentation and improve transferability to other conversational ITS.

Authoring needs

There are two primary components that must be authored for a new topic, namely a vector space and a curriculum script. The vector space can be generated automatically using LSA or modern word embedding methods described earlier. The curriculum script defines the problems the tutor will pose, the answers to those problems, and the hints, prompts, and assertions (a bottom-out hint) used by the tutor to help guide students toward the correct answer. These curriculum script elements are implicitly hierarchical, such that each sentence of a correct answer has an associated set of hints, prompts, and assertions (hereafter referred to as questions). Therefore, from an authoring standpoint, there are only two primary needs: the correct answer and questions generated from each sentence of the correct answer. The problem statement can, in declarative domains like a textbook, simply be a gist-type question that is also generated from the correct answer, such as "What can you say about the features of RAM?"

Knowledge-poor approaches

A simple approach to authoring a correct answer and associated questions is to generate an extractive summary and use syntactic transformations and template-based methods for generating questions from that summary. Extractive summaries (Nenkova & McKeown, 2011) are summaries generated by identifying the most important sentences in a document, which can be accomplished using methods as simple as tf-idf (Salton et al., 1975) where the importance of a sentence is simply the sum of the importance of the words in it, weighting words by their relative rarity in a corpus. The most important sentences, either as a fixed number or a percentage, are then selected. Simple syntactic transformation methods can convert these sentences into questions, for example, "The capital of France is Paris" becomes "What is the capital of France?" and template methods can similarly be used, for example, "What can you say about Paris?" This approach is knowledge-poor because only surface properties of language are used, rather than representations of meaning. The advantage of this approach is that extractive summarization does not introduce grammatical errors, and, similarly, syntactic/template-based question generation typically does not introduce errors. The disadvantage of this approach is that extractive summarization operates on the sentence level, meaning that some unimportant information may be selected by virtue of being in a sentence with important information, and, similarly, important information may be lost because it was buried in a sentence that was less important overall. Additionally, the associated questions tend to be shallow in the sense that they are bounded by sentences in the text and so cannot address conceptual relationships that span multiple sentences. Knowledge-poor approaches thus support relatively low interactivity because they are tightly bound to the source text.

Knowledge-rich approaches

A more sophisticated approach maps natural language to a knowledge representation and then uses that knowledge representation to generate the correct answer and questions (Olney, Graesser, et al., 2012; Olney, Person, et al., 2012). While it may be possible to use first-order logic or similar representations, one fairly simple alternative popular in the NLP community is to use triples. A triple is a specific binary relationship between two entities, has robin-ISA-bird, robin-HAS_PART-red breast, and robin-EATS-worms. Triples have long been used in semantic networks, concept maps, and similar representations dating back to the early days of AI, and triples have been used in the last decade for extracting structured information from the web (Banko et al., 2007; Mitchell et al., 2018) as well as formalizing knowledge in Wikipedia (Bollacker et al., 2008; Vrandečić & Krötzsch, 2014). One way to extract triples from text is to use a semantic parser, that is, a parser that focuses on the verbs, or predicates, in a sentence and the semantic arguments of that verb, in addition to syntactic parsing (Johansson & Nugues, 2008). Going back to the example above, the sentence, "A robin is a bird with a red breast that eats worms" can be decomposed into the aforementioned triples so long as the arguments can be correctly identified, and the predicate appropriately mapped to the relation type of the triple. Notably in this example, "breast" is a nominal predicate mapping to a partonomy (Meyers et al., 2004) with a distant entity "robin," and "eats" similarly has "robin" as a distant entity. Once triples have been extracted from a textbook, for example at the page or section level, correct answer sentences can be generated by using the most connected entity on that page or another entity of interest, essentially by walking the connected set of triples, that is, robin-ISA-bird becomes "A robin is a bird". Because the complete correct answer, as a summary, is never shown to the student or otherwise used, it is not necessary to create a summary out of these sentences.

Question generation similarly manipulates triples, yielding three logical question types for each triple, for example, "What is a robin?", "What is a type of bird?", and "What can you say about the relationship between robins and birds?" The advantage of the knowledge-rich approach is that the summaries can be finely tailored to include only the desired information, and because triples can be aggregated across sentences, summaries can capture deeper conceptual relationships across the source text with similar implications for the questions. For example, the cerebrum and cerebellum are both parts of the brain and are potentially confused. A simple template strategy for question generation focusing on two siblings of a parent node can be used to generate questions like, "What's the difference between a cerebrum and a cerebellum?" (Olney, Graesser, et al., 2012; Olney, Person, et al., 2012); this type of strategy can be used to generate problems and correct answers as well. Knowledge-rich approaches, therefore, support a high level of interactivity where the knowledge in the text can be presented dynamically depending on the student's needs. The disadvantage of the knowledge-rich approach is that there are more places for errors to be introduced into the curriculum script, that is, at the triple extraction stage, the triple reasoning stage, and the triple-to-text stage.

Semi-automatic approaches

Knowledge-poor and knowledge-rich approaches can both be followed by a human correction phase. This section identifies three possible settings for correction: within an authoring tool, as a distributed task, and within a symmetric learning environment, which are discussed in turn. Authoring tools for ITS are a natural setting for semi-automated authoring. After items are automatically generated (e.g., summaries, questions, triples), a human expert can decide which to keep and optionally to correct errors as desired. Systems that have used this approach include the *Guru* ITS (Olney, D'Mello, et al., 2012) as well as non-conversational ITS like model-tracing tutors (Matsuda et al., 2015) and constraint-based tutors (Mitrovic et al., 2009). The correction process can also be scaled, at a cost, by distributing the correction task on online workplaces like Amazon Mechanical Turk. A free alternative under development, called BrainTrust, uses a symmetric learning task for correction, such that students in another learning environment correct the ITS representation by completing tasks in that environment (Olney, 2018). The key idea in this approach is to use reading comprehension activities enacted by students while they read a textbook to correct the summary and associated questions generated using one of the approaches mentioned above. In BrainTrust, students correct a virtual peer student who is summarizing, asking questions, creating concept maps, and predicting based on a passage in the textbook. What the virtual peer student says initially comes from the summary, questions, or triples generated by one of the approaches above but later comes from a corrected version of these produced by a previous student. In other words, students iteratively correct and improve upon other students' answers, with the twin goals of learning from the textbook and correcting a domain model for a conversational ITS. Our preliminary work suggests that BrainTrust meets both goals, though optimizing them simultaneously is a topic for future research. Semi-automated approaches hold the promise of scaling highly interactive, conversational ITS.

CONCLUSIONS

Natural language interaction during learning activities is one of the most promising, if not the most promising, form of instruction for deep conceptual understanding of complex topics, in particular STEM+C topics. They combine the effectiveness of interactive instructional activities, which, according to the ICAP framework, are the most effective, with the power of scaffolded self-explanations. This chapter presented an overview of the theoretical foundations and potential and current state-of-the-art of conversational ITSs.

More broadly, this chapter addressed three important questions in the AIED community: (1) if interactivity increases, can the effectiveness of such instructional activities keep increasing?; (2) Is there a ceiling and if so where is it?; and (3) how can we get close to the ceiling, with a focus, in our case, on conversational ITSs. We address the challenge of scaling up the development of conversational ITSs across domains. Regarding the first question, we suggested the interactivity cannot increase beyond sub-step level where the focus is on atomic pieces of knowledge and therefore the interactivity plateau is a natural consequence of the nature of knowledge and how much it can be broken down (it is more of an interactivity wall as once atomic level knowledge, i.e., indivisible, is reached, the interactivity cannot increase anymore, i.e., you hit an interactivity level wall). Since we already hit the interactivity wall, so to speak, the alternative to increasing tutoring's effectiveness could therefore be increasing the quality of the interaction, e.g., by developing better student models which in turn will lead to better feedback and consequently better learning. The natural follow-up question would be how much more can effectiveness increase beyond the interactivity plateau? Is there an upper limit or ceiling? For the second question, we provided an answer based on the assumption that the ceiling can be indicated by what high achievers do. Fortunately, there is such prior research on high achievers, based on which we suggest there is a limit to how many such intense interactions in natural language students can be engaged in during a particular period of time, which should inform the development of instructional strategies and of conversational ITSs. We presented three pathways (better student models, better assessment of freely generated responses, and automated authoring) to increasing the quality of the interaction which constitute an answer to the third question and to improve the cross-domain scalability of conversational ITSs.

The need for comprehensive student models cannot be overstated given the upstream nature of student modeling in instruction. Assuming all other elements are optimal (instructional strategies, domain model, interface), an incomplete and inaccurate student model will have undesirable impact on all the downstream components and therefore the overall effectiveness of any tutoring enterprise. That is, the tutor must have a clear, comprehensive image of who the student is before they can adapt instruction to each student's needs. Without such comprehensive student models, instruction cannot be tailored which would lead to suboptimal effectiveness and experiences. Using data and data science is a very promising approach to build comprehensive student models. Comprehensive student models will enable true adaptivity, that is, tailoring instruction to each individual student based on their unique characteristics, and lead to, for instance, better execution of instructional strategies and better timing and dosage of feedback.

Conversational ITSs' unique needs to manage dialogue interactions and to assess freely generated student responses (free text responses) add a level of complexity above and beyond other ITSs which makes the development of such systems more challenging. Conversational ITSs are a special category of conversational AI systems which are at the core of the Turing test (can a human discriminate between a human and computer communication partner?), the ultimate AI success test. The unique needs of conversational ITSs limit their widespread adoption (limited scalability across topics and domains). To address these challenges, we have presented in this chapter some promising new developments to solving the task of assessing students' freely generated responses and making conversational ITSs more scalable by automating as much as possible the development of such ITSs based on recent advances in AI, machine learning, and data science. Among the most promising developments, we highlighted the ones that rely on recent advances in AI, such as deep learning and more powerful natural language assessment methods that account for context and are interpretable. We also highlighted knowledge-poor and knowledge-rich approaches to scaling up the development of conversational ITSs. Each of those approaches can be followed by a human curation phase as a way to mitigate any shortcomings of the technology, thus reaching a good authoring cost-versus-quality balance.

Given the potential of natural language interactions for deep conceptual understanding and the recent AI and Data Science revolution, we believe there are new and exciting opportunities to developing effective and affordable conversational ITSs across many domains serving students of various backgrounds, anytime, anywhere.

ACKNOWLEDGMENTS

This material is based upon work supported by the National Science Foundation (1918751, 1934745), the Institute of Education Sciences (R305A190448, R305A200413), the Office of Naval Research (N00014 16 C 3027), the Navy Nuclear Power Training Command (W911NF-14-D-0005), and the US Army Combat Capabilities Development Command – Soldier Center (W911NF-12-2-0030).

REFERENCES

Agirre, E., Banea, C., Cardie, C., Cer, D., Diab, M., Gonzalez-Agirre, A., Guo, W., Lopez-Gazpio, I., Maritxalar, M., Mihalcea, R., Rigau, G., Uria, L., & Wiebe, J. (2015). SemEval-2015 Task 2: Semantic Textual Similarity, English, Spanish and Pilot on Interpretability. In *Proceedings of the 9th International Workshop on Semantic Evaluation* (SemEval 2015), Denver, CO, June. Association for Computational Linguistics.

Agirre, E., Gonzalez-Agirre, A., Lopez-Gazpio, I., Maritxalar, M., Rigau, G., & Uria, L. (2016). Semeval-2016 Task 2: Interpretable Semantic Textual Similarity. In *Proceedings of the 10th International Workshop on Semantic Evaluation* (SemEval 2016), San Diego, California, June, 2016.

Ait-Khayi, N., & Rus, V. (2019). BI-GRU Capsule Networks for Student Answers Assessment. In *Proceedings of The 2019 KDD Workshop on Deep Learning for Education (DL4Ed) in conjunction with the 25th ACM SIGKDD Conference on Knowledge Discovery and Data Mining* (KDD 2019), August 4–8, 2019, Anchorage, Alaska, USA.

Aleven, V., McLaren, B. M., Sewall, J., van Velsen, M., Popescu, O., Demi, S., Ringenberg, M., & Koedinger, K. R. (2016). Example-Tracing Tutors: Intelligent Tutor Development for Non-Programmers. *International Journal of Artificial Intelligence in Education*, 26(1), 224–269. https://doi.org/10.1007/s40593-015-0088-2.

Anderson, J. R., Corbett, A. T., Koedinger, K. R., & Pelletier, R. (1995). Cognitive Tutors: Lessons Learned. *The Journal of the Learning Sciences*, 4(2), 167–207.

Autor, D., Levy, F., & Murnane, R. J. (2003). The Skill Content of Recent Technological Change: An Empirical Exploration. *Quarterly Journal of Economics*, 118(4), 1279–1334.

Bach, S. H., Broecheler, M., Huang, B., & Getoor, L. (2017). Hinge-Loss Markov Random Fields and Probabilistic Soft Logic. *Journal of Machine Learning Research*, 18, 1–67.

Banjade, R., Maharjan, N., Niraula, N. B., & Rus, V. (2016). DT-Sim at Semeval-2016 Task 2: Interpretable Semantic Textual Similarity. In *Proceedings of the 10th International Workshop on Semantic Evaluation* (SemEval 2016), San Diego, California, June. Association for Computational Linguistics.

Banko, M., Cafarella, M. J., Soderland, S., Broadhead, M., & Etzioni, O. (2007). Open Information Extraction for the Web. *IJCAI*, 7, 2670–2676.

Blei, D. M., Ng, A. Y., & Jordan, M. I. (2003). Latent Dirichlet Allocation. *The Journal of Machine Learning Research*, 3, 993–1022.

Bollacker, K., Evans, C., Paritosh, P., Sturge, T., & Taylor, J. (2008). Freebase: A Collaboratively Created Graph Database for Structuring Human Knowledge. In *Proceedings of the 2008 ACM SIGMOD International Conference on Management of Data, 1247–1250*. https://doi.org/10.1145/1376616.1376746.

Bransford, D., Brown, A., & Cocking, R. (Eds.). (2000). *How People Learn: Brain, Mind, Experience, and School Committee on Developments in the Science of Learning*. Washington, DC: National Academy Press.

Carbonell, J. R. (1970). AI in CAI: Artificial Intelligence Approach to Computer Assisted Instruction. *IEEE Transactions on Man-Machine Systems*, 11(4), 190–202.

Carbonell, J. R., & Collins, A. (1973). Natural Semantics in Artificial Intelligence. In *Proceedings of Third International Joint Conference on Artificial Intelligence*, pp. 344–351.

Carnevale, A. P., & Smith, N. (2013). Workplace Basics: The Skills Employees Need and Employers Want [Editorial]. *Human Resource Development International*, 16(5), 491–501. https://doi.org/10.1080/13678868.2013.821267.

Chesler, N. C., Bagley, E., Breckenfeld, E., West, D., & Shaffer, D. W. (2010). A Virtual Hemodialyzer Design Project for First-Year Engineers: An Epistemic Game Approach. In *ASME 2010 Summer Bioengineering Conference* (pp. 585–586). American Society of Mechanical Engineers.

Chi, M. T. H. (2009). Active-Constructive-Interactive: A Conceptual Framework for Differentiating Learning Activities. *Topics in Cognitive Science*, 1, 73–105. https://doi.org/10.1111/j.1756-8765.2008.01005.x.

Chi, M. T. H., Bassok, M., Lewis, M., Reimann, P., & Glaser, R. (1989). Self-Explanations: How Students Study and Use Examples in Learning to Solve Problems. *Cognitive Science*, 13, 145–182.

Chi, M. T. H., & Wylie, R. (2014). The ICAP Framework: Linking Cognitive Engagement to Active Learning Outcomes. *Educational Psychologist*, 49, 219–243.

Choi, Y., Lee, Y., Shin, D., Cho, J., Park, S., Lee, S., Baek, J., Bae, C., Kim, B., & Heo, J. (2020). EdNet: A Large-Scale Hierarchical Dataset in Education. In I. Bittencourt, M. Cukurova, K. Muldner, R. Luckin, & E. Millán (Eds.), *Artificial Intelligence in Education. AIED 2020. Lecture Notes in Computer Science* (Vol. 12164). Cham: Springer. https://doi.org/10.1007/978-3-030-52240-7_13.

Collins, A., Warnock, E. H., Aiello, N., & Miller, M. (1975). Reasoning From Incomplete Knowledge. In D. Bobrow & A. Collins (Eds.), *Representation and Understanding*. New York: Academic Press.

Corbett, A. T., & Anderson, J. R. (1994). Knowledge Tracing: Modeling the Acquisition of Procedural Knowledge. *User Modeling and User-Adapted Interaction*, 4(4), 253–278.

D'Mello, S., Dowell, N., & Graesser, A. C. (2011). Does It Really Matter Whether Students' Contributions Are Spoken Versus Typed in an Intelligent Tutoring System With Natural Language? *Journal of Experimental Psychology: Applied*, 17, 1–17.

D'Mello, S., Lehman, S., Pekrun, R., & Graesser, A. (2014). Confusion Can Be Beneficial for Learning. *Learning and Instruction*, 29, 153–170.

D'Mello, S. K., & Graesser, A. C. (2012). AutoTutor and Affective AutoTutor: Learning by Talking With Cognitively and Emotionally Intelligent Computers That Talk Back. *ACM Transactions on Interactive Intelligent Systems*, 2(4), 1–38.

Domingos, P., & Lowd, D. (2009). Markov Logic: An Interface Layer for Artificial Intelligence. In *Morgan & Claypool*. San Rafael, CA.

Embretson, S. E., & Reise, S. (2000). *Item Response Theory for Psychologists*. Mahwah: Lawrence Erlbaum Associates, p. 376.

Ericsson, K. A., Krampe, R., & Tesch-Römer, C. (1993). The Role of Deliberate Practice in the Acquisition of Expert Performance. *Psychological Review*, 100(3), 363.

Evens, M. W., & Michael, J. (2006). *One-on-One Tutoring by Humans and Computers.* Mahwah: Lawrence Erlbaum Associates.

Gabrilovich, E., & Markovitch, S. (2007). Computing Semantic Relatedness Using Wikipedia-Based Explicit Semantic Analysis (PDF). In *Proceedings of the 20th Int'l Joint Conference on Artificial Intelligence (IJCAI)*, pp. 1606–1611.

Graesser, A., Lu, S. L., Jackson, G., Mitchell, H., Ventura, M., Olney, A., & Louwerse, M. (2004). AutoTutor: A Tutor With Dialogue in Natural Language. *Behavioral Research Methods, Instruments, and Computers*, 36, 180–193.

Graesser, A. C. (2016). Conversations With AutoTutor Help Students Learn. *International Journal of Artificial Intelligence in Education*, 26, 124–132.

Graesser, A. C. (2020). Learning Science Principles and Technologies With Agents That Promote Deep Learning. In R. S. Feldman (Ed.), *Learning Science: Theory, Research, and Practice* (pp. 2–33). New York: McGraw-Hill.

Graesser, A. C., Chipman, P., Haynes, B. C., & Olney, A. (2005). AutoTutor: An Intelligent Tutoring System With Mixed-Initiative Dialogue. *IEEE Transactions in Education*, 48, 612–618.

Graesser, A. C., Fiore, S. M., Greiff, S., Andrews-Todd, J., Foltz, P. W., & Hesse, F. W. (2018). Advancing the Science of Collaborative Problem Solving. *Psychological Science in the Public Interest*, 19, 59–92.

Graesser, A. C., Forsyth, C., & Lehman, B. (2017). Two Heads Are Better Than One: Learning From Agents in Conversational Trialogues. *Teachers College Record*, 119, 1–20.

Graesser, A. C., VanLehn, K., Rose, C. P., Jordan, P., & Harter, D. (2001). Intelligent Tutoring Systems With Conversational Dialogue. *AI Magazine*, 22(4), 39–41.

Gratch, J., Rickel, J., André, E., Cassell, J., Petajan, E., & Badler, N. (2002). Creating Interactive Virtual Humans: Some Assembly Required. *IEEE Intelligent Systems*, 17(4), 54–63.

Hake, R. (1998). Interactive Engagement Versus Traditional Methods: A Six-Thousand Student Survey of Mechanics Test Data for Introductory Physics Students. *American Journal of Physics*, 66, 64–74.

Halloun, I., & Hestenes, D. (1985). The Initial Knowledge State of College Physics Students. *American Journal of Physics*, 53(11), 1043–1055.

Hattie, J. A. C., & Donoghue, G. M. (2016). Learning Strategies: A Synthesis and Conceptual Model. *Nature Partner Journal: Science of Learning*, 1, 1–13. https://doi.org/10.1038/npjscilearn.2016.13.

Johansson, R., & Nugues, P. (2008). Dependency-Based Syntactic-Semantic Analysis With PropBank and NomBank. In *CoNLL '08: Proceedings of the Twelfth Conference on Computational Natural Language Learning* (pp. 183–187).

Johnson, W. L. (2019). Data-Driven Development and Evaluation of Enskill English. *International Journal of Artificial Intelligence in Education*, 29(3), 425–457. https://doi.org/10.1007/s40593-019-00182-2.

Johnson, W. L., & Lester, J. C. (2016). Face-to-Face Interaction With Pedagogical Agents, Twenty Years Later. *International Journal of Artificial Intelligence in Education*, 26(1), 25–36.

Jurafsky, D., & Martin, J. H. (2008). *Speech and Language Processing: An Introduction to Natural Language Processing, Computational Linguistics, and Speech Recognition.* Upper Saddle River, NJ: Prentice-Hall.

Koedinger, K. R., Corbett, A. C., & Perfetti, C. (2012). The Knowledge-Learning-Instruction (KLI) Framework: Bridging the Science-Practice Chasm to Enhance Robust Student Learning. *Cognitive Science*, 36(5), 757–798.

Kopp, K. J., Britt, M. A., Millis, K., & Graesser, A. C. (2012). Improving the Efficiency of Dialogue in Tutoring. *Learning and Instruction*, 22(5), 320–330.

Landauer, T., McNamara, D. S., Dennis, S., & Kintsch, W. (Eds.). (2007). *Handbook on Latent Semantic Analysis.* Mahwah, NJ: Erlbaum.

LeCun, Y., Bengio, Y., & Hinton, G. (2015). Deep Learning. *Nature*, 521, 426–444.

Lehman, B., & Graesser, A. C. (2016). Arguing Your Way Out of Confusion. In F. Paglieri (Ed.), *The Psychology of Argument: Cognitive Approaches to Argumentation and Persuasion.* London: College Publications.

Lintean, M., & Rus, V. (2012). Measuring Semantic Similarity in Short Texts Through Greedy Pairing and Word Semantics. In *Proceedings of the 25th International Florida Artificial Intelligence Research Society Conference*, Marco Island, FL.

Lintean, M., & Rus, V. (2015). An Optimal Quadratic Approach to Monolingual Paraphrase Alignment. In *Proceedings the 20th Nordic Conference on Computational Linguistics (NODALIDA 2015)*, Lithuania, Vilnius, 11–13 May 2015.

Litman, D., Rose, C., Forbes-Riley, K., VanLehn, K., Bhembe, D., & Silliman, S. (2006). Spoken Versus Typed Human and Computer Dialogue Tutoring. *International Journal of Artificial Intelligence in Education*, 16(2), 145–170.

Liu, L., Von Davier, A., Hao, J., Kyllonen, P., & Zapata-Rivera, D. (2015). A Tough Nut to Crack: Measuring Collaborative Problem Solving. In R. Yigal, S. Ferrara, & M. Mosharraf (Eds.), *Handbook of Research on Technology Tools for Real-World Skill Development* (pp. 344–359). Hershey, PA: IGI Global.

Magliano, J., Trabasso, T., & Graesser, A. C. (1999). Strategic Processing During Comprehension. *Journal of Educational Psychology*, 91, 615–629.

Maharjan, N., & Rus, V. (2019). Towards Concept Map Based Free Student Answer Assessment. In *Proceedings of the 32nd International Florida Artificial Intelligence Research Society Conference (FLAIRS 2019)*, Sarasota, FL, USA May 19–22, 2019.

Maharjan, N., Banjade, R., Gautam, D., Tamang, L. J., & Rus, V. (2017). DT_Team at SemEval-2017 Task 1: Semantic Similarity Using Alignments, Sentence-Level Embeddings and Gaussian Mixture Model Output. In *Proceedings of the 11th International Workshop on Semantic Evaluation (SemEval-2017)*.

Maharjan, N., Gautam, D., & Rus, V. (2018). Assessing Freely-Generated Student Answers in Tutorial Dialogues Using LSTM Models. In *Proceedings of the 19th International Conference on Artificial Intelligence in Education* (AIED 2019), London, United Kingdom, June 27–30, 2018.

Matsuda, N., Cohen, W. W., & Koedinger, K. R. (2015). Teaching the Teacher: Tutoring SimStudent Leads to More Effective Cognitive Tutor Authoring. *International Journal of Artificial Intelligence in Education*, 25(1), 1–34. https://doi.org/10.1007/s40593-014-0020-1.

McNamara, D. S. (2004). SERT: Self-Explanation Reading Training. *Discourse Processes*, 38, 1–30.

Meyers, A., Reeves, R., Macleod, C., Szekely, R., Zielinska, V., Young, B., & Grishman, R. (2004). The NomBank Project: An Interim Report. In A. Meyers (Ed.), *HLT-NAACL 2004 Workshop: Frontiers in Corpus Annotation* (pp. 24–31). Association for Computational Linguistics.

Mikolov, T., Sutskever, I., Chen, K., Corrado, G. S., & Dean, J. (2013), Distributed Representations of Words and Phrases and Their Compositionality. In *Advances in Neural Information Processing Systems* (pp. 3111–3119).

Millis, K., Forsyth, C., Wallace, P., Graesser, A. C., & Timmins, G. (2017). The Impact of Game-Like Features on Learning from an Intelligent Tutoring System. *Technology, Knowledge and Learning*, 22.

Millis, K., Long, D. L., Magliano, J. P., & Wiemer, K. (Eds.). (2019). *Deep Comprehension: Multidisciplinary Approaches to Understanding, Enhancing, and Measuring Comprehension*. New York: Routledge. https://doi.org/10.4324/9781315109503.

Mitchell, T., Cohen, W., Hruschka, E., Talukdar, P., Yang, B., Betteridge, J., Carlson, A., Dalvi, B., Gardner, M., Kisiel, B., Krishnamurthy, J., Lao, N., Mazaitis, K., Mohamed, T., Nakashole, N., Platanios, E., Ritter, A., Samadi, M., Settles, B., … Welling, J. (2018). Never-Ending Learning. *Communications of the ACM*, 61(5), 103–115. https://doi.org/10.1145/3191513.

Mitrovic, A. (2012). Fifteen Years of Constraint-Based Tutors: What We Have Achieved and Where We Are Going. *User Modeling and User-Adapted Interaction*, 22(1–2), 39–72.

Mitrovic, A., Martin, B., Suraweera, P., Zakharov, K., Milik, N., Holland, J., & Mcguigan, N. (2009). ASPIRE: An Authoring System and Deployment Environment for Constraint-Based Tutors. *International Journal of Artificial Intelligence in Education*, 19(2), 155–188.

Mohan, L., Chen, J., & Anderson, W. A. (2009). Developing a Multi-Year Learning Progression for Carbon Cycling in Socioecological Systems. *Journal of Research in Science Teaching*, 46(6), 675–698.

Nenkova, A., & McKeown, K. (2011). Automatic Summarization. *Foundations and Trends in Information Retrieval*, 5(2–3), 103–233.

Nye, B. D., Graesser, A. C., & Hu, X. (2014). AutoTutor and Family: A Review of 17 Years of Natural Language Tutoring. *International Journal of Artificial Intelligence in Education*, 24(4), 427–469.

OECD. (2017). *PISA 2015 Results (Volume V): Collaborative Problem Solving*. Paris: OECD Publishing.

Olney, A. M. (2018). Using Novices to Scale Up Intelligent Tutoring Systems. In *Interservice/Industry Training, Simulation, and Education Conference (I/ITSEC)*.

Olney, A. M., D'Mello, S. K., Person, N., Cade, W., Hays, P., Williams, C., Lehman, B., & Graesser, A. (2012). Guru: A Computer Tutor That Models Expert Human Tutors. In S. Cerri, W. Clancey, G. Papadourakis, & K. Panourgia (Eds.), *Intelligent Tutoring Systems* (Vol. 7315, pp. 256–261). Berlin/ Heidelberg: Springer.

Olney, A. M., Graesser, A. C., & Person, N. K. (2012). Question Generation From Concept Maps. *Dialogue and Discourse*, 3(2), 75–99.

Olney, A. M., Person, N. K., & Graesser, A. C. (2012). Guru: Designing a Conversational Expert Intelligent Tutoring System. In P. McCarthy, C. Boonthum-Denecke, & T. Lamkin (Eds.), *Cross-Disciplinary Advances in Applied Natural Language Processing: Issues and Approaches* (pp. 156–171). IGI Global.

Paladines, J., & Ramírez, J. (2020). A Systematic Literature Review of Intelligent Tutoring Systems With Dialogue in Natural Language. *IEEE Access*, 8, 164246–164267.

Pennington, J., Socher, R., & Manning, C. D. (2014). Glove: Global Vectors for Word Representation. In *Proceedings of the Empirical Methods in Natural Language Processing (EMNLP 2014)* (Vol. 12, pp. 1532–1543).

Pon-Barry, H., Clark, B., Schultz, K., Bratt, E. O., & Peters, S. (2004). Advantages of Spoken Language Interaction in Dialogue-Based Intelligent Tutoring Systems. In J. Lester, R. Vicari, & F. Paraguacu (Eds.), *Proceedings of Seventh International Conference on Intelligent Tutoring Systems* (pp. 390–400). Berlin/Heidelberg: Springer.

Roscoe, R. D., & McNamara, D. S. (2013). Writing Pal: Feasibility of an Intelligent Writing Strategy Tutor in the High School Classroom. *Journal of Educational Psychology*, 105(4), 1010–1025.

Rus, V. (2002). *Logic Form for WordNet Glosses and Application to Question Answering*. Computer Science Department, School of Engineering, Southern Methodist University, PhD Thesis, May 2002, Dallas, Texas.

Rus, V. (2018). Explanation-Based Automated Answer Assessment of Open Ended Learner Responses. In *Proceedings of the 14th International Scientific Conference eLearning and Software for Education*, Bucharest, Romania, April 19–20, 2018.

Rus, V., Conley, M., & Graesser, A. (2014). The DENDROGRAM Model of Instruction: On Instructional Strategies and Their Implementation in DeepTutor. In R. Sottilare (Ed.), *Design Recommendations for Adaptive Intelligent Tutoring Systems: Adaptive Instructional Strategies* (Vol. 2). Army Research Lab.

Rus, V., D'Mello, S., Hu, X., & Graesser, A. C. (2013). Recent Advances in Intelligent Systems With Conversational Dialogue. *AI Magazine*, 34, 42–54.

Rus, V., Fancsali, S. E., Bowman, D., Pavlik, P., Jr., Ritter, S., Venugopal, D., Morrison, D., & The LDI Team (2020). The Student Data Institute: Mission, Framework, & Activities. In *Proceedings of the First Workshop of the Student Data Institute - Big Data, Research Challenges, & Science Convergence in Educational Data Science, The 13th International Conference on Educational Data Mining (EDM 2020)*, 10–13 July, Ifrane, Morocco (Held Online).

Rus, V., & Stefanescu, D. (2016). Non-Intrusive Assessment of Students' Prior Knowledge in Dialogue-Based Intelligent Tutoring Systems. *Journal of Smart Learning Environments*, 3(2), 1–18.

Salakhutdinov, R. (2019). Integrating Domain-Knowledge into Deep Learning. In *Proceedings of the 25th ACM SIGKDD International Conference on Knowledge Discovery & Data Mining, KDD '19*, July 2019.

Salton, G., Wong, A., & Yang, C. S. (1975). A Vector Space Model for Automatic Indexing. *Communications of the ACM*, 18(11), 613–620. http://doi.acm.org/10.1145/361219.361220.

Schmidhuber, J. (2015). Deep Learning in Neural Networks: An Overview. *Neural Networks*, 61, 85–117.

Shaffer, D. W. (2017). *Quantitative Ethnography*. Madison, WI: Cathcart Press.

Sottilare, R. A., Baker, R. S., Graesser, A. C., & Lester, J. C. (2018). Special Issue on the Generalized Intelligent Framework for Tutoring (GIFT): Creating a Stable and Flexible Platform for Innovation in AIED Research. *International Journal of Artificial Intelligence in Education*, 28, 139–151.

Ştefănescu, D., Banjade, R., & Rus, V. (2014a). Latent Semantic Analysis Models on Wikipedia and TASA. In *The 9th International Conference on Language Resources and Evaluation*, 26–31 May, Reykjavik, Iceland.

Ştefănescu, D., Banjade, R., & Rus, V. (2014b). A Sentence Similarity Method Based on Parsing and Information Content. In *Proceedings of 15th International Conference on Intelligent Text Processing and Computational Linguistics (CICLing 2014)*, 6–12 April, Kathmandu, Nepal.

Su, H., Deng, J., & Fei-Fei, L. (2012). *Crowdsourcing Annotations for Visual Object Detection*. AAAI 2012 Human Computation Workshop, 2012.

Swartout, W., Traum, D., Artstein, R., Noren, D., Debevec, P., Bronnenkant, K., Williams, J., Leuski, A., Narayanan, S., Piepol, D., & Lane, C. (2010). Ada and Grace: Toward Realistic and Engaging Virtual Museum Guides. In J. Allbeck, N. Badler, T. Bickmore, C. Pelachaud, & A. Safonova (Eds.), *Intelligent Virtual Agents*. IVA 2010. Lecture Notes in Computer Science (Vol. 6356). Berlin, Heidelberg: Springer.

VanLehn, K. (2006). The Behavior of Tutoring Systems. *International Journal of Artificial Intelligence in Education*, 16(3), 227–265.

VanLehn, K. (2011). The Relative Effectiveness of Human Tutoring, Intelligent Tutoring Systems, and Other Tutoring Systems. *Educational Psychologist*, 46(4), 197–221.

VanLehn, K., Graesser, A. C., Jackson, G. T., Jordan, P., Olney, A., & Rose, C. P. (2007). When Are Tutorial Dialogues More Effective Than Reading? *Cognitive Science*, 31(1), 3–62.

Vrandečić, D., & Krötzsch, M. (2014). Wikidata: A Free Collaborative Knowledge Base. *Communications of the ACM*, 57(10), 78–85. https://doi.org/10.1145/2629489.

Vygotsky, L. S. (1978). *Mind in Society: The Development of Higher Psychological Processes*. Cambridge, MA: Harvard University Press.

Ward, W., Cole, R., Bolaños, D., Buchenroth-Martin, C., Svirsky, E., & Weston, T. (2013). My Science Tutor: A Conversational Multimedia Virtual Tutor. *Journal of Educational Psychology*, 105(4), 1115.

Woolf, B. P. (2009). *Building Intelligent Interactive Tutors: Student-Centered Strategies for Revolutionizing e-Learning*. Burlington, MA: Morgan Kaufman Publishers.

Zapata-Rivera, D., Jackson, G. T., & Katz, I. (2015). Authoring Conversation-Based Assessment Scenarios. In R. Sottilare, X. Hu, A. Graesser, & K. Brawner (Eds.), *Design Recommendations for Adaptive Intelligent Tutoring Systems* (Vol. 3, pp. 169–178). Orlando, FL: Army Research Laboratory.

12. Authoring tools to build AIED systems

Stephen Blessing, Stephen B. Gilbert and Steven Ritter

INTRODUCTION

An authoring tool is a software application that enables someone to create an experience for someone else. Strictly speaking, Microsoft Word, Google Docs, and other word processors are authoring tools for creating reading experiences, and the author's choices about length of paragraphs, complexity of words, heading and figure placement all affect the experience for the reader. Similarly, Microsoft PowerPoint, Google Slides, and other presentation applications are authoring tools for slide-based experiences, and Adobe Premier, Apple iMovie, and other video editing tools are authoring tools for video experiences. All the above experiences are typically linear, unfolding over time. Much like riding a roller coaster, there are not usually choices to be made as an end-user engages with them. Thus, despite the complexity of these authoring tools, with their hundreds of features, their output experiences usually have a simple linear form.

Authoring tools for AI-based educational systems, however, such as intelligent tutoring systems, chatbots, software agents, robots, or learning games, differ significantly in that the experiences they create are interactive, adaptive, and nonlinear. In this chapter, we are concerned with the authoring tools that create the "intelligence" of an Intelligent Tutoring System (ITS), and not with authoring tools that might deal with assessment, class orchestration, or academic integrity. In the systems described here, the experience of the learner depends on choices they make as they engage. The non-linear nature of the output has several consequences for authors. First, they must prepare for all possible situations in which the learner might find themselves, spanning the interaction space. Second, the authors must establish relationships between the experiences, if any. Perhaps situation 4 leads to either situation 5 or situation 7, in a choose-your-own-adventure style experience. Perhaps there are multiple paths to reach situation 5, but situation 7 can be reached only through situation 4, making 4 a prerequisite. This authoring activity consists of structuring the interaction space.

As a concrete example, consider the design of a museum exhibit on the water cycle. Museum visitors can choose how to experience the exhibit—which stations they engage and the order in which they approach them. Imagine we enter a room arranged in a rough circle, with different stations illustrating evaporation from oceans and lakes, precipitation from clouds, and groundwater infiltration. There is a small side room for glaciers. The exhibit author had to span the interaction space by preparing to engage users no matter where they are in the room and where they look. By structuring the interaction space in a circle, the author decided that the order in which visitors experienced the stations was not important, while still nudging (Thaler & Sunstein, 2021) the visitor into certain decisions. At the conclusion of the exhibit, however, the author wanted all visitors to reflect on how they personally engage with the water cycle, so the room's exit hallway offers a linear sequence of stations as visitors progress to the gift shop.

To provide an example within an ITS, a student using an equation solver ITS working on $3x + 4 = 13$ might elect to make explicit the step to subtract 4 from both sides, or they might simply input that 3x = 9. More substantially, in a programming tutor, one student might elect to solve a problem using an iterative approach, while another takes a recursive approach. All these approaches are valid and should be recognized by the systems, but having the ITSs recognize the multiple paths that students can take in solving problems, that non-linearity makes creating ITS authoring tools challenging.

Hierarchy of Interaction Granularity Tied to Domain

This museum example offers an opportunity to note that our analysis of interaction can occur at different levels of granularity that form a hierarchy. So far, the museum example described interaction at the higher level of the room and its stations, but said nothing about the interactions of people with the individual stations. Do visitors turn a knob on a tank to increase condensation? Enable a simulated rain cloud to form? This lower level of interaction granularity requires authoring as well, and illustrates that at a higher level, general principles of interaction design may apply, for example, "Give visitors some freedom to explore, but not more than four choices..." while at the lower level, the knowledge domain of the experience matters significantly. Therefore, the author of the higher-level exhibit structure might understand only the superficial concepts of the water cycle, while the author of each station's experience must understand the water cycle in depth. These differences in both the granularity of the interaction and the amount of discipline-specific knowledge required make it difficult to create a single authoring tool to support interactive experiences generally.

Kurt VanLehn (2006) described these granularity levels in the context of ITSs as the inner loop and the outer loop. In the outer loop, the system decides which problem-solving experience you will have next, somewhat like choosing which museum exhibit station you will visit. In the inner loop, the system offers interaction with the specific domain while solving the problem, for example, by offering hints or explanations of incorrect answers.

The complexity of the domain itself has a significant impact on both the experience and the authoring of that experience. If I want to create an AI-based educational system that teaches how to play the game checkers, the system will be far simpler than a system that teaches chess. In checkers, all the player's pieces are identical and are differentiated only by their position on the board. There are few rules, and few patterns of piece placements to recognize. In chess, on the other hand, the player has six different kinds of pieces, each with their own rules, and there are hundreds of patterns of piece arrangements to consider. These different levels of domain complexity affect the design of a good authoring tool, as well as the pedagogy used when teaching the respective games.

The pedagogical goals of the author also affect the complexity of the authoring experience. As anyone who has authored a quiz in Blackboard, Canvas, or Moodle has noticed, multiple choice questions are the simplest to create, but do not typically offer the most active learning experience. Designing an authoring tool that allows an author to create activities allowing learners to participate in creation and evaluation themselves is more complex than designing an authoring tool to create knowledge retrieval activities such as a multiple-choice quiz.

Who Are the Authors?

The author of an AI-based educational system might be one of several kinds of people: a teacher, a professional subject matter expert, or an instructional designer. Let us assume that we desire to create an instructional tool for teaching chemistry to high-school students. Based on extensive hours teaching students, the chemistry teacher will have experience with students' common conceptual errors, methods of helping them overcome those errors, and techniques of assessing their mastery of the required skills. However, teachers might have little experience codifying their knowledge of the chemistry learning process into a computational authoring tool. Professional subject matter experts, such as chemical engineers from a manufacturing facility, will have numerous chemistry examples to draw on from the real world, but may have less experience teaching a novice chemist about the basic principles of chemistry or using a computational authoring tool to address all the potential misunderstandings of those principles. A professional instructional designer, on the other hand, will have significant experience working with computational authoring tools to structure content, but little knowledge of chemistry. It is likely that to produce a good chemistry teaching tool, we will need a team of people with different skills.

A boundary object (Carlile, 2002) is something concrete that enables people with different backgrounds and goals to find common ground. The classic example is a blueprint, which enables a homeowner, an architect, and a construction engineer to discuss features of a future home even though their day-to-day goals and vocabulary differ dramatically. An authoring tool for an AI-based learning system will similarly have several types of users, and, ideally, it can provide boundary objects for different kinds of authors to discuss the learner's experience.

As noted by Gilbert et al. (2018), along with the teacher, subject matter expert, and instructional designer, there are other stakeholders in our learning system, who while not authors *per se*, will have advice and requirements on our system design. The software engineer who will be implementing the system will need to know the full range of interactivity that the system is expected to offer. The learning sciences expert, who may be familiar with theories and models from computer-assisted learning, can advise on the best pedagogies to use for each learning objective. If our learning system is to be used by multiple students simultaneously, e.g., a chemistry lab experience for a small group, a science-of-teams expert may bring knowledge from computer-supported collaborative learning (CSCL), computer-supported cooperative work (CSCW) and team cognition to the project. If we plan to deploy our system widely and gather data on students' misconceptions, an educational data mining or learning analytics expert will have advice for us on how to measure and structure those data. Finally, for the design of the system user interface itself, an expert in human–computer interaction or user-centered design could ensure that the system has high usability for the learners.

AUTHORING TOOLS FOR DIFFERENT TYPES OF ITSs

An authoring tool must provide a method for authors to create the learning experiences that they have envisioned for their students. It is unclear whether there is a best way to do this across domains, educational objectives, and pedagogies, but several different approaches are described below. All of these tools must take into account the issues discussed above: the level of the desired tutoring, the type of authors using it and their skill level, and what domain is being tutored. With these underlying differences in the resulting tutors, the authoring tools themselves take many different forms, with some of their interfaces being more text based and others more graphics based. The authoring tools described below allow authoring a variety of different types of domain models (see Chapter 7 by Aleven et al.), reflect different theories of learning and pedagogy (see Chapter 3 by Ohlsson), and in some cases allow the construction of varied student interfaces (see Chapter 10 by Lajoie and Li). Their main similarity is the ability of the author to encode the expert model, whatever form it may take, and make that as simple of a task as possible.

Model-Tracing Tutors

Model-tracing tutors aim to evaluate student action against an expert model—one that can solve the task presented to the student in the way, or one of the many ways, that an expert would solve the problem (see Chapter 7, Aleven et al.). As such, the primary challenge in authoring model-tracing tutors is to anticipate and respond to variation, such as the strategies that students use to solve problems. Consider a tutor for solving linear equations that asks students to show each step in solving the equation. A student might correctly solve the equation "$3x + 4 = 5$" by first writing "$3x = 1$" and then writing "$x = 1/3$." A different student might write "$x + 4/3 = 5/3$" and then "$x = 1/3$." A different student may mistakenly transform "$3x + 4 = 5$" into "$3x = 5$." The author of a model-tracing tutor must design the tutor in such a way that it appropriately responds to each of these students.

One of the challenges in authoring model-tracing tutors is categorizing steps as either correct, incorrect, or what VanLehn (2006) calls "intermediate correctness." Even in a domain as well defined as linear equation solving, such decisions arise often. For example, consider a student solving the equation "$-x = 5$" who transforms the equation into "$0 = 5 + x$" and then "$-5 = x$." The student arrives at the correct answer, and the solution demonstrates some sophistication and creativity, but it seems reasonable to wonder whether a student using this strategy really understands the meaning of "$-x$," particularly if the student solves equations like "$-2x = 5$" through a single-step transformation to "$x = -5/2$."

Given the necessity to anticipate how students might approach problem solving, how does the author of a model-tracing tutor provide the tutor with the ability to anticipate a wide enough range of student actions? We consider four approaches: knowledge engineering, generation, demonstration, and crowdsourcing.

The knowledge engineering approach (Anderson & Pelletier, 1991; Blessing et al., 2009) relies on observations and interviews of both experts and students in order to understand the range of strategies, both correct and incorrect, that might be encountered. The strategies observed are then coded into rules, which generalize the observed steps into patterns that apply to a wider range of problems. Doing so is largely a programming task involving specialized rule-based programming.

The generative approach (Weitekamp et al., 2020; MacLellan & Koedinger, 2020) substitutes AI-based simulated students for the observation of real students in the knowledge engineering approach, creating synthetic training data for the model. This approach uses techniques from knowledge engineering to build the AI model but, once such a model is built, it can generate a wide range of student behaviors. If the model is accurate, it will generate the range of strategies and errors that students are likely to exhibit.

In the programming-by-demonstration method, the tutor author uses the tutor interface, or a facsimile of it, to solve problems in various different ways. Some such systems (e.g., Blessing, 1997; Matsuda et al., 2015) can additionally generalize from the directly generated steps to broader rules that apply in different types of problems, in a manner similar to the generative approach. The Cognitive Tutor Authoring Tools (CTAT; Aleven et al., 2006) use demonstration to generate a behavior graph, which represents the possible solution paths which will be recognized by the tutor. However, this gets complicated with demonstrating large solution spaces and error paths.

Crowdsourcing is an extension of the demonstration method in which users of the tutor, rather than the authors (or beta users working closely with the authors), demonstrate solution techniques. Typically, a crowdsourcing approach will bootstrap a tutor developed using other methods, and, as usage of the system grows, the range of student behaviors recognized by the system expands (McLaren et al., 2004). In this way, crowdsourcing may also be seen as a method of data-driven improvement (see Chapter 16 by Brooks et al.). Other types of models also use a data-driven approach to creating the ITS. The Intelligent Teaching Assistant for Programming (Rivers & Koedinger, 2017) produces personalized hints based on reference solutions and these hints can change as the data changes. SourceCheck (Price et al., 2020) is another data-driven algorithm to produce hints in a programming tutor by data-driven means. The challenge with any of these data-driven approaches is reviewing the correctness of the model and ensuring it actually provides help to the student. One approach is to use a constraint-based tutoring approach to validate novel student strategies and incorporate them into the model-tracing tutor (Ritter, 1997; Gross et al., 2014).

Constraint-Based Tutors

Constraint-based tutors have student models that attempt to decrease ITS complexity by reducing what needs to be represented within the model (Mitrovic, 2012; Mitrovic et al., 2001; see Chapter 7 by Aleven et al.). Instead of representing the student's domain knowledge completely, constraint-based tutors focus on the correct knowledge and states that students can traverse. This notion is based on Ohlsson's theory examining performance errors (1996). As long as a student does not violate a constraint in their problem solution, then the tutor considers that solution correct. Constraint-based tutors, then, represent their knowledge as a set of state constraints, where each state constraint lists when that state is relevant and how it is satisfied. The operation of a basic constraint-based tutor boils down to pattern matching, as the system needs to check if a student's current state is captured by a constraint, and if so, does the student state satisfy that constraint. Such a representation allows for at least two related advantages: 1) no requirement for a runnable expert module, as the system just needs to check constraints, and 2) computational simplicity, as the basic tutor operation is pattern matching. Constraint-based tutors have been created for such domains as SQL (Mitrovic, 2003), grammar (Mayo & Mitrovic, 2001), and database modeling (Suraweera & Mitrovic, 2002).

Creating constraint-based tutors requires much effort, with an original estimate of one hour per constraint for the SQL-tutor, the first constraint-based tutor developed, with a person knowledgeable about both the domain and the tools used to create the tutor (Blessing et al., 2015). In order to ease the creation of these tutors, Mitrovic and her collaborators have developed two authoring tools for constraint-based tutors. The first, WETAS (Web-Enabled Tutoring Authoring System) allows for the creation of text-based tutoring systems (Martin & Mitrovic, 2002). The system supports the creation of a simple student interface and a way to author constraints. The student interacts with the tutor via a standard web browser. The designers re-implemented the original SQL-tutor using WETAS without issue, as well as created a new tutor, LBITS, that taught language concepts to primary school children. While no authoring performance measures were given for the SQL-tutor, the LBITS system had 315 constraints authored in five hours, and a total of 222 puzzles created in less than two days.

Building on the initial success of WETAS, the team constructed a new authoring tool for constraint-based tutors, ASPIRE (Authoring Software Platform for Intelligent Resources in Education; Mitrovic et al., 2009). ASPIRE automates much more of the work than WETAS did, particularly in terms of the domain model, including the automation of constraint authoring. The author creates the domain ontology in a web-based environment, where they also provide example problems and solutions. ASPIRE then automatically generates the syntactic and semantic constraints using a machine-learning algorithm. ASPIRE allows for problems to have multiple solutions and will assist the author in creating a tutor that correctly identifies correct student paths. ASPIRE also delivers the tutor in a web-based environment, though it can also communicate with an applet, eliminating the need for the student interface to be text-based like in WETAS. ASPIRE can also produce procedurally-based tutors, in which case the author will also need to create path constraints. ASPIRE has been used by non-ITS researchers to create substantial tutors, such as CIT, a tutor for teaching about capital investments in financial decision making (Mitrovic et al., 2009).

Agent-Based Tutors

We will consider two different types of agent-based intelligent tutors, those that involve pedagogical agents and those involving software agents that have been linked together in order to create the ITS. Authoring for either involves scripting how the agent reacts, toward either the learner or the other software components that comprise the system.

Pedagogical agents

The agent-based tutors that involve pedagogical agents have an on-screen avatar with which the learner interacts. These can motivate students by displaying a lifelike on-screen presence that provides instruction through a combination of speech, gestures, and other communicative acts. Such agents have been designed for middle-school science (Biswas et al., 2016), healthcare decision support (Morbini et al., 2014), and language and culture learning (Johnson et al., 2011). Sometimes the agent provides the instruction, but at other times the student instructs the agent, in order to experience learning by teaching (e.g., *Betty's Brain*; Biswas et al., 2016). Johnson and Lester (2016) provide a summary of research into these pedagogical agents.

A number of researchers have considered how to author these on-screen pedagogical agents. Some of these agents converse with the students purely through natural language dialog (e.g., *AutoTutor*; Nye et al., 2014). These systems will be considered more fully in the next section. Other authoring systems involve scripting interactions of the pedagogical agent, and students typically use on-screen menus and dialogs for interaction. These authoring systems will be considered here.

Lane et al. (2015) describe SitPed, the Situated Pedagogical Authoring System. The author uses an interface similar to what the students see in order to produce tutors that teach through an on-screen conversation, a series of branching choices made by the learner. A preliminary study showed a modest learning advantage for authoring using this tool versus the more traditional way of authoring such systems, such as a spreadsheet. An earlier version of this type of tool had been created for the Tactical Language Training System, discussed in Meron et al. (2007).

Some authoring systems used with pedagogical agents attempt to use previously created content (e.g., PowerPoints, PDFs, scripts, and others) to generate the script and actions used by the on-screen agent. This approach is used by both The Tools for Rapid Automated Development of Expert Models (TRADEM; Robson et al., 2013) and Text2Dialogue (Piwek et al., 2007). The Leonardo system uses a notebook metaphor along with an avatar to teach various elementary school science concepts (Smith et al., 2018). To allow their subject matter experts to participate more fully in creating and editing the curricular components, the team created an authoring tool, Composer (Lester et al., 2015). This tool improved the workflow as the team created the overall system.

In order to be effective, on-screen avatars need to behave in a realistic way with regard to their gestures, head movements, and other nonverbal behaviors. Cerebella (Lhommet &

Marsella, 2013) provides a way to automate the scripting of such behaviors. This could be accomplished by either providing Cerebella with information about the attitude and emotional state of the avatar, or the system could infer such information by analyzing the text. For systems that involve multiple on-screen agents, such as found in the Tactical Language Training System (Johnson et al., 2011), Si et al. (2005) created Thespian. Later work has emphasized the use of image schemas to link utterances with on-screen avatar actions (Ravenet et al., 2018).

Software agents

A different type of agent-based tutor involves linking different software agents together in order to create a complete ITS. As discussed in this volume, ITSs generally consist of multiple components (e.g., the interface the student interacts with, the expert and student models, pedagogical knowledge, etc.) with the expertise for creating these different pieces residing in several different people. Instead of all working together on one large, complete system, it may make more sense in terms of efficiency and cost to gather individual software agents and link them together in order to construct a full ITS. This particularly makes sense with the student interface, as different interfaces may be desired for different purposes, but perhaps the same pedagogical knowledge would largely apply to both of them (e.g., teaching statistics either using SPSS or JMP).

Ritter et al. (2003) argue that creating ITS authoring tools for a full system is misguided, and that individual authoring systems for the separate pieces would be a better use of resources and effort. They describe a system that allows the separate pieces to be hooked together. In particular, this system, Dormin, provides a scripting language to indicate interface actions done by the student to be transmitted for the expert model, and then for the expert model to approve or disapprove of those actions. As indicated above, this allows for the interface to be changed with little if any modification to the expert model. Later authors have also argued for such a system. Ramachandran et al. (2004) describe FlexiTrainer, a method for connecting up multiple intelligent agents that comprise a tutoring system. Cohn et al. (2015) discuss an automated way to link up various software agents, and describe an ITS for training unmanned aerial system personnel that uses such a method. The GIFT system, described below, is also designed with this modular approach in mind.

Dialog-Based Tutors

Problem-solving tutors, in which the student's goal is to complete a task, guided by a structured user interface, use the structure of the task as a way to constrain the space of solutions that the user might attempt (Koedinger & Anderson, 1993). Constraining this space, in turn, makes authoring these systems tractable. An alternative approach to tutoring focuses on dialog (Carbonell, 1970), an inherently less constrained solution space, since conversations might go in many directions (see Chapter 11 by Rus et al.). The challenge for the author of such systems is to direct the conversation back to a familiar and pedagogically productive place, which both satisfies educational goals and makes dialog-based tutors more tractable.

A large variety of dialog-based tutors are variants of *AutoTutor* (Nye et al., 2014). These tutors constrain the conversation base by setting "expectations" for student statements (Graesser, 2011). These expectations may, for example, reflect explanations of a scientific principle which the tutor wishes the student to express. Coupled with expectations is a set of misconceptions, which recognize common ways that the student's statement might differ from the expectations. A speech act classifier compares the student states to the set of expectations and misconceptions (Cai et al., 2011). The tutor's response is determined based on a set of discourse rules, which might, for example, "pump" the student for more information on an incomplete answer or provide feedback (Graesser, 2011).

Scripts control the behavior of such systems, and the authoring tools to assist in creating and maintaining these tutors derive from the Autotutor Script Authoring Tool (ASAT; Susarla et al., 2003). These tools allow authors to associate expectations and misconceptions with dialog moves. In ASAT-V (Cai et al., 2015), a visual authoring version of ASAT, a flowchart controls the progress through states of the conversation, such as greeting the student, asking questions and concluding the conversation.

Some dialog-based tutors integrate both verbal and non-verbal communication. For example, Alelo uses an internal tool called Tide to control dialog by pedagogical agents (Johnson, 2015). Authors use Tide to establish states in the conversations which represent both informational and attitudinal states. These states control both utterances and gestures. For example, an avatar may extend a hand in greeting or turn away from the student in frustration.

Authoring dialog trees representing the conversational flow in dialog-based tutors remains a difficult task, since there are potentially many branches to manage. Progress is being made in using artificial intelligence to generate concept maps that structure the domain model (Olney et al., 2012) and common misconceptions based on cognitive models of task performance (MacLellan & Koedinger, 2020), which can help automate building the structure of the dialog tree.

The GIFT Authoring System

The Generalized Intelligent Framework for Tutoring (GIFT), developed by the US Army, is an open-source software system designed to enable ITS authors to create tutors in any domain (Sottilare et al., 2012). It contains several modules that can be configured for the task, the domain, the learners, and the types of feedback that need to be provided. The GIFT learner module records skills mastered by the learner. The domain module contains the feedback that the tutor would give in response to common errors. The pedagogical module can be configured to choose the form of pedagogical intervention, perhaps based on the context or history of success by the learner. The communication module is configured to communicate with the learner's user interface. A 2018 special issue in IJAIED on GIFT (Sottilare et al., 2018) and Proceedings of the 2020 GIFT User Symposium (Goldberg, 2020) offer a good summary of the current usage of GIFT, ranging from marksmanship training, training for nuclear technicians, training for pilots, and team communication improvement.

A GIFT-based tutor can be a stand-alone software application, for example, a Unity app that communicates with GIFT via the GIFT Unity plugin or an automated PowerPoint lecture followed by a GIFT-powered post-test or survey. It could also be a browser-based application. GIFT includes various default plugins to work with existing military simulation and training applications like Virtual Battlespace Simulation (VBS), VR-Engage, ARES sandtable, and TC3 (vMedic), but it could work with any simulation if you can write a plugin for it. GIFT also allows connection with external sensors, such as the eMotive EEG headset or wrist-worn wearables. Tutor authors can also write a plugin themselves for a new sensor. GIFT has a built-in survey/quiz creation tool and can also embed simple Qualtrics surveys.

GIFT is quite unusual in authoring tools for supporting Intelligent Team Tutoring Systems (ITTSs) for small teams. Early work in this area used a manually crafted tutor structure in which there was a tutor for each team member and also a tutor for the team (Gilbert et al., 2018; Ouverson et al., 2021). A team of four, for example, would have five tutors. Thus each team member might receive both individual feedback, such as "Pat, focus on acknowledging every communication you receive," and team feedback, such as "Team, we all need to respond more quickly to each other." In the early configurations, the tutors acted independently of each other, that is, the team tutor did not know what the individual tutors were doing. This led to difficulties in reliably predicting how much total feedback any one team member would receive, since the feedback arrived from two independent sources. In 2020, GIFT released new features in its user interface for authoring ITSs (Goldberg et al., 2020) that allowed authors to configure the structure of a team, and when individual team members vs. the entire team receive feedback, helped address the feedback throughput challenge. In general, GIFT is built to be quite modular and extensible, and thus is quite powerful as an authoring tool. However, some software development work is required by authors who desire to extend GIFT to create a new learning experience.

CONCLUSION

Despite these advances in authoring tools for ITSs, the models remain relatively expensive to develop. This expense typically only makes sense in cases where the model will be used for a substantial amount of instruction. Such domains rely on large amounts of practice solving a wide variety of problems within the domain. But where do those problems come from?

To be viable, ITS models must be general enough to be applied to a wide range of problems. For example, in an equation-solving tutor, we would want the model to tutor not only "3x + 4 = 5" but also any equation of the form "ax + b = c" (and other forms as well). The generality of the model comes, in part, from including variables in the model. A tutor assisting a student with solving "3x + 4 = 5" might provide a hint like, "Subtract 4 from both sides." By treating the 4, the y-intercept, as a placeholder, this hint can generalize to other equations where the y-intercept is different. In this way, the model can be applied to a general class of problems.

For this approach to work, the tutor's model needs to know the values of the underlying variables for any problem. For a domain like equation solving, where the surface structure (the equation) is easily parsed, this is not a problem. But many problems show students problems which involve pictures, diagrams, or words, which are not easily parsed into a deep structure accessible to the model. Consider a word problem tutor. The student might be asked to solve the problem "To build a doghouse, you and your friends cut a 10-foot board into two boards. One of the boards is 4 feet longer than the other. How long is each board?" We might have a model that could tutor a student on this problem, given the underlying variables, but how does the model know the underlying variables?

Essentially, the student and the tutor "see" different things: the student sees the surface representation and the tutor "sees" the deep structure. The question in authoring is: how do we create a surface representation and a deep structure that are consistent? There are three possibilities, evident in the tools discussed above:

1. *AI*: Write software that perceives the surface structure and, from it, generates the deep structure. This is a sensible approach for equation solving, since equations can be completely and reliably parsed, and surface structures for equations of a particular class can be easily generated.

2. *Dual encoding*: Separately encode the surface representation and the deep structure. The problem author is responsible for writing the words of a word problem (or the diagrams and pictures for geometry problems) and, separately, encode data that are passed to the tutor—the deep structure. This approach is common with problems whose surface structure cannot be reliably parsed, as is the case with word problems. The danger in this approach is that it can be difficult to maintain consistency between the deep and surface structures. Ritter et al. (1998) developed a system where a partially reliable natural language parser identified possible mismatches between surface and deep structure, to be resolved by the problem author.

3. *Common source*: This technique uses parameters that can generate both the surface and deep structure at the same time. The relevant parameters used in the model of a class of problems represented by the doghouse problem are used both to encode the deep structure of the problem and (along with various linguistic parameters) to generate the wording of the problem that the student sees.

Future Directions

As indicated above, for ITSs to become more prevalent and commercially viable, usable authoring tools need to be created that can bridge this gap between what the student "sees" and what the problem author "sees," as this will allow non-cognitive scientists better entry into authoring. As authoring tools in other areas have become easier to use, such as in video editing, a wider audience has been able to create compelling user experiences. As discussed in the Introduction, unlike video editing, ITSs by their nature are non-linear experiences, consisting of both an inner loop where solutions are constructed step-by-step, and an outer loop that is concerned with problem sequencing. This adds complexity to the authoring, which influences what type of people may want to engage in the task of authoring, and at what level they do so. As the tools become easier to use, more people will engage at all the different levels of authoring, from editing problems, to creating problems, and then to authoring additional problem types.

As a possible look into what future ITS authoring tools look like, let us close by considering a recent video game authoring tool. Media Molecule released Dreams for the PlayStation 4 game console in early 2020. Dreams lets users create sophisticated games, on a par with those that have been commercially released, in part because it bridges the gap between player and programmer views of the system. Dreams allows users to interact with the system on multiple levels, from tweaking existing content to creating whole new game mechanics. It does all that with an easy-to-use interface, usable by just the standard PS4 game controller. Creating games used to be done only by those who knew how to write, compile, and deliver code—skills gained through thousands of hours of work and study. Dreams allows game creation to be done by almost anyone, with training provided by the tool itself. While game creation has obvious differences from authoring intelligent tutors, there are some similarities. Many games have a non-linear flow, require different types of elements to be authored (graphics, sounds, game logic), and some games have what could be considered inner and outer loops. Dreams allows different authors of differing ability levels to author or at least modify commercial-quality games of many different genres.

In short, Dreams allows budding game designers to more readily "see" what the player sees. The existence of Dreams, which allows non-programmers the ability to create sophisticated games, lends support to the goal of creating ITS authoring systems that will allow educators, subject matter experts, and instructional designers the ability to create high-quality ITSs for a variety of domains from which students can learn. A Dreams-style ITS authoring tool would support authors of various skill levels with the ability to perform different authoring tasks, from tweaking existing problems and tutors to creating entirely new tutors with a variety of different tutoring types.

REFERENCES

Aleven, V., McLaren, B. M., Sewall, J., & Koedinger, K. R. (2006, June). The cognitive tutor authoring tools (CTAT): Preliminary evaluation of efficiency gains. In *International Conference on Intelligent Tutoring Systems* (pp. 61–70). Berlin, Heidelberg: Springer.

Anderson, J. R., & Pelletier, R. (1991). A development system for model-tracing tutors. In *Proceedings of the International Conference of the Learning Sciences* (pp. 1–8). Evanston, IL.

Biswas, G., Segedy, J. R., & Bunchongchit, K. (2016). From design to implementation to practice a learning by teaching system: Betty's brain. *International Journal of Artificial Intelligence in Education*, 26(1), 350–364.

Blessing, S. B. (1997). A programming by demonstration authoring tool for model-tracing tutors. *International Journal of Artificial Intelligence in Education*, 8(3–4), 233–261.

Blessing, S. B., Aleven, V., Gilbert, S., Heffernan, N. T., Matsuda, N., & Mitrovic, A. (2015). Authoring example-based tutors for procedural tasks. In R. Sottilare, A. Graesser, X. Hu, & K. Brawner (Eds.), *Design Recommendations for Adaptive Intelligent Tutoring Systems* (Vol. 3, pp. 71–93). Orlando, FL: US Army Research Laboratory.

Blessing, S. B., Gilbert, S., Ourada, S., & Ritter, S. (2009). Authoring model-tracing cognitive tutors. *International Journal for Artificial Intelligence in Education*, 19, 189–210.

Cai, Z., Graesser, A., & Hu, X. (2015). ASAT: AutoTutor script authoring tool. In R. Sottilare, A. Graesser, X. Hu, & K. Brawner (Eds.), *Design Recommendations for Adaptive Intelligent Tutoring Systems* (Vol. 3, pp. 199–210). Orlando, FL: US Army Research Laboratory.

Cai, Z., Graesser, A. C., Forsyth, C., Burkett, C., Millis, K., Wallace, P., Halpern, D., & Butler, H. (2011). Trialog in ARIES: User input assessment in an intelligent tutoring system. In W. Chen & S. Li (Eds.), *Proceedings of the 3rd IEEE International Conference on Intelligent Computing and Intelligent Systems* (pp. 429–433). Guangzhou: IEEE Press.

Carbonell, J. R. (1970). AI in CAI: An artificial-intelligence approach to computer-assisted instruction. *IEEE Transactions on Man-Machine Systems*, 11(4), 190–202.

Carlile, P. R. (2002). A pragmatic view of knowledge and boundaries: Boundary objects in new product development. *Organization Science*, 13(4), 442–455.

Cohn, J., Olde, B., Bolton, A., Schmorrow, D., & Freeman, H. (2015). Adaptive and generative agents for training content development. *Design Recommendations for Adaptive Intelligent Tutoring Systems* (Vol. 3, pp. 161–168). Orlando, FL: US Army Research Laboratory.

Gilbert, S. B., Slavina, A., Dorneich, M. C., Sinatra, A. M., & Bonner, D. (2018). Creating a team tutor using GIFT. *International Journal for Artificial Intelligence in Education*, 28, 286–313.

Goldberg, B., Brawner, K., & Hoffman, M. (2020, May). The GIFT architecture and features update: 2020 edition. In *Proceedings of the 8th Annual Generalized Intelligent Framework for Tutoring (GIFT) Users Symposium (GIFTSym8)* (p. 11). US Army Combat Capabilities Development Command–Soldier Center.

Goldberg, B. S. (2020) *Proceedings of the Eighth Annual GIFT Users Symposium (GIFTSym)*. US Army Combat Capabilities Development Command – Soldier Center.

Graesser, A. C. (2011). Learning, thinking, and emoting with discourse technologies. *The American Psychologist*, 66(8), 743–757.

Gross, S., Mokbel, B., Paassen, B., Hammer, B., & Pinkwart, N. (2014). Example-based feedback provision using structured solution spaces. *International Journal of Learning Technology*, 9(3), 248–280.

Johnson, W. L. (2015). Constructing virtual role-play simulations. In R. Sottilare, A. Graesser, X. Hu, & K. Brawner (Eds.), *Design Recommendations for Adaptive Intelligent Tutoring Systems* (Vol. 3, pp. 211–226). Orlando, FL: US Army Research Laboratory.

Johnson, W. L., Friedland, L., Schrider, P., Valente, A., & Sheridan, S. (2011). The virtual cultural awareness trainer (VCAT): Joint knowledge online's (JKO's) solution to the individual operational culture and language training gap. In *Proceedings of ITEC 2011*. London: Clarion Events.

Johnson, W. L., & Lester, J. C. (2016). Face-to-face interaction with pedagogical agents, twenty years later. *International Journal of Artificial Intelligence in Education, 26*(1), 25–36.

Koedinger, K. R., & Anderson, J. R. (1993). Reifying implicit planning in geometry: Guidelines for model-based intelligent tutoring system design. *Computers as Cognitive Tools*, 15–46.

Lane, H. C., Core, M. G., Hays, M. J., Auerbach, D., & Rosenberg, M. (2015). Situated pedagogical authoring: Authoring intelligent tutors from a student's perspective. In *International Conference Artificial Intelligence in Education* (pp. 195–204). Springer International Publishing.

Lester, J., Mott, B., Rowe, J., & Taylor, R. (2015, July). Design principles for pedagogical agent authoring tools. In *Design Recommendations for Adaptive Intelligent Tutoring Systems* (Vol. 3, pp. 151–160). Orlando, FL: US Army Research Laboratory.

Lhommet, M., & Marsella, S. C. (2013). Gesture with meaning. In *Intelligent Virtual Agents* (Vol. 8108, pp. 303–312). Berlin, Heidelberg: Springer.

MacLellan, C. J., & Koedinger, K. R. (2020). Domain general tutor authoring with apprentice learner models. *International Journal of Artificial Intelligence in Education*. Advance online publication. DOI: 10.1007/s40593-020-00214-2.

Martin, B., & Mitrovic, A. (2002, December). Authoring web-based tutoring systems with WETAS. In *International Conference on Computers in Education* (pp. 183–187). New York: IEEE.

Matsuda, N., Cohen, W. W., & Koedinger, K. R. (2015). Teaching the teacher: Tutoring SimStudent leads to more effective cognitive tutor authoring. *International Journal of Artificial Intelligence in Education, 25*(1), 1–34.

Mayo, M., & Mitrovic, A. (2001). Optimising ITS behaviour with Bayesian networks and decision theory. *International Journal of Artificial Intelligence in Education, 12*, 124–153.

McLaren, B. M., Koedinger, K. R., Schneider, M., Harrer, A., & Bollen, L. (2004). Bootstrapping novice data: Semi-automated tutor authoring using student log files. In *Proceedings of the Workshop on Analyzing Student-Tutor Interaction Logs to Improve Educational Outcomes, Seventh International Conference on Intelligent Tutoring Systems (ITS-2004)*.

Meron, J., Valente, A., & Johnson, W. L. (2007). Improving the authoring of foreign language interactive lessons in the Tactical Language Training System. In *Workshop on Speech and Language Technology in Education*.

Mitrovic, A. (2003). An intelligent SQL tutor on the web. *International Journal of Artificial Intelligence in Education, 13*(2–4), 173–197.

Mitrovic, A. (2012). Fifteen years of constraint-based tutors: What we have achieved and where we are going. *User Modeling and User-Adapted Interaction, 22*(1–2), 39–72.

Mitrovic, A., Martin, B., Suraweera, P., Zakharov, K., Milik, N., Holland, J., & McGuigan, N. (2009). ASPIRE: An authoring system and deployment environment for constraint-based tutors. *International Journal of Artificial Intelligence in Education, 19*(2), 155–188.

Mitrovic, A., Mayo, M., Suraweera, P., & Martin, B. (2001, June). Constraint-based tutors: A success story. In *International Conference on Industrial, Engineering and Other Applications of Applied Intelligent Systems* (pp. 931–940). Berlin, Heidelberg: Springer.

Morbini, F., DeVault, D., Georgilla, K., Artstein, R., Traum, D., & Morency, L. (2014, June). A demonstration of dialogue processing in SimSensei kiosk. In *Proceedings of the SIGDIAL 2014 Conference* (pp. 254–256).

Nye, B. D., Graesser, A. C., & Hu, X. (2014). AutoTutor and family: A review of 17 years of natural language tutoring. *International Journal of Artificial Intelligence in Education, 24*(4), 427–469.

Ohlsson, S (1996). Learning from performance errors. *Psychological Review, 103*(2), 241–262.

Olney, A. M., Graesser, A. C., & Person, N. K. (2012). Question generation from concept maps. *Dialogue & Discourse, 3*(2), 75–99.

Ouverson, K., Ostrander, A., Walton, J., Kohl, A., Gilbert, S., Dorneich, M., Winer, E., & Sinatra, A. (2021). Analysis of communication, team situational awareness, and feedback in a three-person intelligent team tutoring system. *Frontiers in Cognitive Science*. Advance online publication. DOI: 10.3389/fpsyg.2021.553015.

Piwek, P., Hernault, H., Prendinger, H., & Ishizuka, M. (2007). T2D: Generating dialogues between virtual agents automatically from text. In C. Pelachaud, J. Martin, E. André, G. Chollet, K. Karpouzis, & D. Pelé (Eds.), *Intelligent Virtual Agents. IVA 2007. Lecture Notes in Computer Science* (Vol. 4722, pp. 161–174). Berlin, Heidelberg: Springer.

Price, T. W., Marwan, S., Winters, M., & Williams, J. J. (2020). An evaluation of data-driven programming hints in a classroom setting. In I. Bittencourt, M. Cukurova, K. Muldner, R. Luckin, & E. Millán (Eds.), *International Conference on Artificial Intelligence in Education* (pp. 246–251). Cham: Springer.

Ramachandran, S., Remolina, E., & Fu, D. (2004, August). FlexiTrainer: A visual authoring framework for case-based intelligent tutoring systems. In *International Conference on Intelligent Tutoring Systems* (pp. 848–850). Berlin, Heidelberg: Springer.

Ravenet, B., Pelachaud, C., Clavel, C., & Marsella, S. (2018). Automating the production of communicative gestures in embodied characters. *Frontiers in Psychology*, *9*, 1144.

Ritter, S. (1997). Communication, cooperation and competition among multiple tutor agents. In B. du Boulay & R. Mizoguchi (Eds.), *Artificial Intelligence in Education: Knowledge and Media in Learning Systems* (pp. 31–38). Amsterdam: IOS Press.

Ritter, S., Anderson, J., Cytrynowicz, M., & Medvedeva, O. (1998) Authoring content in the PAT algebra tutor. *Journal of Interactive Media in Education*, *98*(9). DOI: 10.5334/1998-9.

Ritter, S., Blessing, S. B., & Wheeler, L. (2003). Authoring tools for component-based learning environments. In *Authoring Tools for Advanced Technology Learning Environments* (pp. 467–489). Dordrecht: Springer.

Rivers, K., & Koedinger, K. R. (2017). Data-driven hint generation in vast solution spaces: A self-improving python programming tutor. *International Journal of Artificial Intelligence in Education*, *27*(1), 37–64.

Robson, R., Ray, F., & Cai, Z. (2013). Transforming content into dialogue-based intelligent tutors. In *Interservice/Industry Training, Simulation & Education Conference (I/ITSEC)* (Vol. 2013, No. 1). National Training Systems Association.

Si, M., Marsella, S. C., & Pynadath, D. V. (2005, July). Thespian: Using multi-agent fitting to craft interactive drama. In *Proceedings of the Fourth International Joint Conference on Autonomous Agents and Multiagent Systems* (pp. 21–28).

Smith, A., Leeman-Munk, S., Shelton, A., Mott, B., Wiebe, E., & Lester, J. (2018). A multimodal assessment framework for integrating student writing and drawing in elementary science learning. *IEEE Transactions on Learning Technologies*, *12*(1), 3–15.

Sottilare, R. A., Baker, R. S., Graesser, A. C., & Lester, J. C. (Eds.). (2018) Special issue on the generalized intelligent framework for tutoring (GIFT): Creating a stable and flexible platform for innovations in AIED research. *International Journal of Artificial Intelligence in Education*, *28*(2), 139–151.

Sottilare, R. A., Brawner, K. W., Goldberg, B. S., & Holden, H. K. (2012). *The Generalized Intelligent Framework for Tutoring (GIFT)*. Orlando, FL: US Army Research Laboratory–Human Research & Engineering Directorate (ARL-HRED).

Suraweera, P., & Mitrovic, A. (2002, June). KERMIT: A constraint-based tutor for database modeling. In *International Conference on Intelligent Tutoring Systems* (pp. 377–387). Berlin, Heidelberg: Springer.

Susarla, S., Adcock, A., Van Eck, R., Moreno, K., & Graesser, A. C. (2003). Development and evaluation of a lesson authoring tool for AutoTutor. In V. Aleven, U. Hoppe, J. Kay, R. Mizoguchi, H. Pain, F. Verdejo, & K. Yacef (Eds.), *AIED2003 Supplemental Proceedings* (pp. 378–387). Sydney: University of Sydney School of Information Technologies.

Thaler, R. H., & Sunstein, C. R. (2021). *Nudge: The Final Edition*. New Haven: Yale University Press.

VanLehn, K. (2006). The behavior of tutoring systems. *International Journal of Artificial Intelligence in Education*, *16*(3), 227–265.

Weitecamp, D., Harpstead, E., & Koedinger, K. R. (2020, April). An interaction design for machine teaching to develop AI tutors. In *CHI '20*, Honolulu, HI, USA.

PART IV

ANALYTICS

13. Continuous student modeling for programming in the classroom: challenges, methods, and evaluation

Ye Mao, Samiha Marwan, Preya Shabrina, Yang Shi, Thomas W. Price, Min Chi and Tiffany Barnes

INTRODUCTION

Within intelligent tutoring systems for complex, multi-step tasks, student modeling is widely applied to predict students' performance on future (inner-loop) problem-solving steps to enable adaptation to improve learning (VanLehn, 2006). As in many domains, programming problems often have many acceptable solutions and students are often left to solve them at their own pace (Blikstein, 2011; Emerson et al., 2019). Student modeling techniques such as Bayesian Knowledge Tracing (BKT) (Corbett & Anderson, 1994) and Deep Knowledge Tracing (DKT) (Piech et al., 2015) infer knowledge states by monitoring the correctness of applying a skill during each problem-solving step. However, this type of student modeling is particularly challenging in programming for three reasons. First, in many problems, there is no clear definition of a step (i.e. is a "step" a single edit, a line, a compilation, or something else?) Second, we may not have discrete labels for which skill(s) a student is practicing. Third and finally, correctness is not straightforward to assess. Even many automated techniques for inferring and refining skills from student work, such as Learning Factors Analysis (Cen et al., 2006) or Q-matrix learning (Barnes, 2005), first require that problem steps are clearly defined and assessed.

Historically, the challenge of defining, labeling, and assessing steps has been addressed through carefully authored expert models (Anderson & Reiser, 1985; Mitrovic et al., 2003; Gerdes et al., 2017). For example, constraint-based tutors may have hundreds of constraints which continually detect when skills are correctly or incorrectly applied in student code (Mitrovic et al., 2003). However, these models require extensive time and expertise, and may not generalize to new domains. For example, a production system for LISP (Anderson & Reiser, 1985) programming does not work for model tracing in Python programming. Thus, there is a need for automated approaches to automatically identify, detect, and assess skills in continuous domains like programming, and a new generation of data-driven student models that use prior student data to do so. Such data-driven approaches have been used in programming to generate automated hints and feedback (Rivers, 2017; Price et al., 2017a). However, in this chapter, we focus on how they can be used for the traditional student modeling tasks of predicting students' struggles, successes, and misconceptions in programming.

This chapter is organized as follows: the first two sections of this chapter introduce aspects of *Skill Discovery* and *Effective Modeling* for programming. For skill discovery, we discuss how we can discover and model skills during a single, complex programming problem without expert-authored labels, and how we can automatically assess a student's correctness on these skills as they work. Regarding effective modeling, we address how to leverage the temporal aspects of students' work within a given problem to model student performance and knowledge. And we also present how to address *data sparsity* through semi-supervised learning to deal with the common problem of small data sets in programming classes. A final section discusses the *evaluation* of a data-driven programming ITS and future research directions.

SKILL DISCOVERY FOR PROGRAMMING

In programming, students are usually given a set of requirements and objectives to achieve with a program, and even for very simple programs there are often hundreds of potential correct solutions. Student modeling can and should leverage the rich structure of student problem-solving data, including actions and time, to accurately predict student success. However, these action and time data are typically not labeled with Knowledge Components (KCs) (Koedinger et al., 2010), as it is extremely challenging to determine what part of a student program corresponds to which skill a student is practicing. Therefore, we have explored two ways to discover the skills that students may be applying while writing programs: one based on features, and the other based on machine learning.

Feature-Based Methods

In programming environments, a student's work is typically represented as a programming trace, which consists of a series of *code states*, that is, snapshots of student code, as it changes over time (Price et al., 2017a). However, because of the large number of ways any programming objective can be implemented, any state representation that consists mainly of student code results in very large, poorly connected state spaces (Jin et al., 2012; Price & Barnes, 2015), which makes it difficult to compare students and apply data-driven methods. As a result, prior research has focused on utilizing other features, such as hint usage and interface interactions, to evaluate student learning outcomes (Emerson et al., 2019), or creating meaningful states by transforming students' fine-grained log files into fixed feature sets for various student modeling tasks (Zhi et al., 2018; Peddycord et al., 2014).

The research in this section was performed in the context of iSnap, a block-based programming environment used in an introductory computer science course for non-majors at a public university in the United States (Price et al., 2017a). iSnap extends Snap! by providing students with data-driven hints derived from historical, correct student solutions (Price et al., 2017c). Additionally, iSnap logs all student actions while programming (e.g. adding or deleting a block), as a trace, allowing researchers to study the sequences of student programming actions and the time taken for each action. While iSnap and most block-based languages were created for novice programming, they still have large, poorly connected code state spaces even for small programming problems. To illustrate the challenge of skill discovery in the programming domain, we present the Squiral programming problem as an example, derived from the Beauty and Joy of Computing introductory computer science curriculum (Garcia et al., 2015). The Squiral problem description asks students to create a procedure (i.e. a method) with one parameter, "r", that draws a square-shaped spiral with "r" rotations. Figure 13.1 shows an example solution to Squiral and its visual program output.

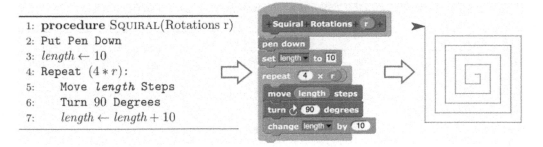

```
1:  procedure SQUIRAL(Rotations r)
2:  Put Pen Down
3:  length ← 10
4:  Repeat (4 * r):
5:      Move length Steps
6:      Turn 90 Degrees
7:      length ← length + 10
```

Figure 13.1   A pseudocode Squiral solution (left), a solution sample in iSnap (middle), and the Squiral problem output (right)

Data-Driven Features

We first present our unsupervised data-driven feature detection (DDFD) algorithm for skill discovery (Zhi et al., 2018). DDFD learns student code features based on hierarchical clustering to find meaningful features of student programs. Such features, such as having a loop or using a variable, are different from unit tests because they can be present in incomplete or unrunnable code, and they can be created to align with any programming language. Additionally, these features are different from skills or knowledge components (KCs) because they describe assignment-specific properties of the code, not assignment-general components of expert competence. As such, we apply them primarily to student modeling *within* a given problem. Zhi et al. (2018) defined a *feature state* vector reflecting the presence or absence of each feature in a student's code at a particular time. A time-based series of feature states can be used to capture a student's progress toward a solution state (where all features are present). For example, the Squiral assignment requires that the code should use a procedure, and should draw something to the screen. Table 13.1 gives further examples of data-driven features for the Squiral assignment as identified by the DDFD algorithm, and an expert description for each. For example, if the algorithm learns four features for a given exercise, and for a given student's code it detects only the first and last features, then the algorithm will output {1, 0, 0, 1} as the code's feature state (Marwan et al., 2020b). Unlike a student's specific code, which is often unique and specific to the student, their feature state is a more abstract state representation, as in prior work on representing programming features (Rivers, 2017; Jin et al., 2012; Price et al., 2017a), which is likely to overlap with others – enabling more effective student modeling (Zhi et al., 2018).

Data-driven features are built using code shapes: common subtrees of correct student Abstract Syntax Trees (ASTs). The presence or absence of these code shapes indicates how close a student is to a correct solution. The DDFD algorithm works as follows. First, the algorithm extracts prior student solutions for Squiral as AST representations that incorporate the abstract syntactic structure of the source code (Baxter et al., 1998). Then, it applies hierarchical code clustering for feature extraction and selection (Zhi et al., 2018). To account for multiple solution strategies for a given programming task, Zhi et al. (2018) introduced *decision shapes,* which detect the presence of only one of a set of code shapes, representing code that may reflect distinct strategy decisions (technical details of decision shapes are described in Zhi et al., 2018). Overall, these data-driven features can be used in practice to provide students

Table 13.1   Data-driven DDFD features derived for the Squiral assignment

Data-driven features	Feature description
F1: "Create" a procedure with one parameter.	Create a procedure to draw Squiral with one parameter.
F2: "Evaluate a procedure" with one parameter in the script area.	Use a procedure with one parameter in the code.
F3: Have a "multiply" block with a variable in a "repeat" block OR two nested "repeat" blocks.	Use loops in the Squiral procedure to rotate the correct number of times; whether using two nested loops or a loop with a multiply operator.
F4: Have a "pen down" block inside a procedure.	Use "pen down" block which is needed for drawing.
F5: Add a variable in a "move" block.	Use a variable in the "move" block to draw each side of the Squiral with a different length.
F6: Have a "move" and "turn_Left" blocks inside a "repeat" block.	Use "move" and "turn_Left" blocks to draw Squiral shape correctly.
F7: Use "Change" a variable block inside a "repeat" block.	Change the value of the side length variable using the "Change" block.

with adaptive feedback that corresponds to their specific feature state. For example, Marwan et al. (2020b) used the DDFD algorithm to adapt iSnap to provide feedback on programming subgoals, where subgoals are expert-labeled clusters of features (Marwan et al., 2020b). The DDFD algorithm facilitates *immediate feedback* since it can detect features regardless of code completion. Since features are derived using data from a specific assignment, DDFD facilitates providing students with *progress feedback*.

The DDFD algorithm suffers two limitations that make it hard to deploy in practice. First, since DDFD learns from data, features are not labeled with meaningful names. Second, DDFD may learn too many features or features that are too specific. To address these limitations, Marwan et al. showed that combining a small amount of expert curation to the DDFD algorithm could improve feature detection accuracy and F1-score compared with supervised learning models (Marwan et al., 2021a). This approach to creating hybrid data-driven and expert features uses a human-interpretable representation of code shapes that can be manually edited by experts to improve their quality. The hybrid approach combines the scalability and flexibility of data-driven features with the reliability and interpretability of expert-authored features (Marwan et al., 2021a). These feature-based approaches show how fully or partially data-driven approaches can be used to create a meaningful representation of student progress on programming problems, without the need for expert-defined skills. As we discuss later, these features can form the basis of effective student models for making early predictions of student learning progressions (Mao et al., 2019, 2020) and can be used to generate adaptive support/hints in ITSs (Marwan et al., 2020).

Machine-Learning Methods

The second group of methods we have explored is based on machine learning, where it typically discovers the representation of skills in a problem in a more implicit way.

Historically in programming, various natural language processing (NLP) techniques have been applied to modeling programming languages (Hindle et al., 2016). Traditional approaches for code representation often treat code fragments as natural language texts and model them based on their tokens (Weimer et al., 2009; Falleri et al., 2014). Despite some similarities, programming languages and natural languages differ in some important aspects (Pane et al., 2001). When models are constructed using tokens, the rich and explicit structural information with programs is not fully utilized.

The use of deep learning models for source code analysis has recently yielded state-of-the-art performance in code functionality classification (Mou et al., 2016), method name prediction (Alon et al., 2019), and code clone detection (Zhang et al., 2019). These successful models usually combine Abstract Syntax Tree (AST) representations with various neural networks to capture structural information from the programming language. For example, TBCNN (Mou et al., 2016) takes the whole AST of code as input and performs convolutional computation over tree structures, outperforming token-based models in program functionality classification and bubble-sort detection. In the educational domain, Piech et al. (2015) proposed NPM-RNN to simultaneously encode preconditions and postconditions into points where a program can be used as a linear mapping between these points, for feedback propagation on student code. Gupta et al. (2019) presented a tree-CNN based method that can localize the bugs in a student program, with respect to a failing test case, without running the program.

More recently, ASTNN (Zhang et al., 2019) and Code2Vec (Alon et al., 2019) have shown great success. Sitting at the root of AST, ASTNN (Zhang et al., 2019) was proposed to handle the long-term dependency problems that arise when taking a large AST as input directly. Similar to long texts in NLPs, large ASTs can make deep learning models vulnerable to gradient-vanishing problems. To address the issue, ASTNN splits the large AST of one code fragment into a set of small AST subtrees within a given statement, and performs code vector embedding. It achieves state-of-the-art performance in both code classification and clone detection. Code2Vec (Alon et al., 2019), on the other hand, utilizes AST-based paths and attention mechanisms to learn a vector representation of code. Instead of a set of AST-trees, it takes a collection of leaf-to-leaf paths as input, and applies an attention layer to average those vectors. As a result, attention weights can help to interpret the importance of paths. Code2Vec has been shown to be very effective at predicting the names for program entities.

Those successful applications of AST-based models led our group to explore a new line of research on skill discovery using machine-learning methods. Shi et al. (2021) used the learned embedding from Code2Vec to cluster incorrect student submissions for misconception discovery. Later, Mao et al. (2021) evaluated ASTNN against Code2Vec on the task of classifying the correctness of student programs across two domains. The results show that AST-based models generally achieve better performance than token-based models, a finding which is consistent with prior research (Mou et al., 2014; Zhang et al., 2019). More importantly, ASTNN consistently outperforms other models including Code2Vec and other token-based baselines in both domains, which is also supported by another work on programming bug detection (Shi & Mao et al., 2021). Based on these findings, Mao et al. (2022) developed a novel ASTNN-based, cross-lingual framework called CrossLing, and showed that it could be effectively used for temporal and non-temporal tasks in programming, by incorporating information from different programming domains (Mao et al., 2022). Wang et al. (2017) used code embeddings to represent student code for the task of knowledge tracing, predicting students' future performance based on their code trace on an earlier problem, achieving 96% accuracy

(Wang et al., 2017). Based on these results, machine-learned representations of student code appear to accurately predict student programming performance, indicating that these models are providing meaningful insights into student knowledge for the classrooms we have studied. However, it can be more challenging to interpret these machine-learned skill models than feature-based approaches.

EFFECTIVE MODELING TO PREDICT STUDENT SUCCESS

In the previous section, we discussed techniques that we have explored for automatically identifying and assessing demonstrated skills in programming problems, defined either explicitly (as in feature-based methods) or implicitly (in machine-learning methods). A student model can incorporate this information in a statistical model to make predictions about a student's future success, for example to inform when to give an intervention like hints or feedback (VanLehn, 2006). For example, BKT (Corbett & Anderson, 1994) and BKT-based models utilize students' performance associated with each skill to make predictions on their future success and have been shown to be effective (Pardos & Heffernan, 2010; Yudelson et al., 2013; Baker et al., 2008; Pardos & Heffernan, 2011; Lin et al., 2016; Mao et al., 2018). Deep learning models, especially Recurrent Neural Network (RNN) or RNN-based models such as LSTM have also been explored in student modeling (Piech et al., 2015; Tang et al., 2016, Khajah et al., 2016; Wilson et al., 2016; Xiong et al., 2016; Lin & Chi, 2017). Some work showed that LSTM has superior performance over BKT-based models (Mao et al., 2018, Piech et al., 2015) or Performance Factors Analysis (Pavlik et al., 2009). However, it has also been shown that RNN and LSTM do not always have better performance when the simple, conventional models incorporated other parameters (Khajah et al., 2016; Wilson et al., 2016).

Traditionally, these statistical models have assumed that students attempt a *discrete* set of problem steps, each of which is either *correct* or *incorrect*. However, in domains like programming, there may not be a discrete definition of a step (is each edit a step? or each line? or each submission?), unless the ITS explicitly breaks the problem down into such steps for the student. Similarly, the skill detectors discussed in the previous section on "Feature-Based Methods" can be applied at any time. A student's progress might therefore be considered *continuous*, and it may be difficult to directly apply traditional student modeling approaches like BKT or DKT. In this section, we discuss how to address this challenge through temporal student modeling that can account for continuous progress. Moreover, student models for programming often suffer from the data scarcity issue since educational datasets are usually relatively small. Therefore, in this section we also discuss how complex statistical models can be more effectively trained on smaller datasets by leveraging semi-supervised learning.

Temporal Modeling

Student modeling has been widely and extensively explored by utilizing student temporal sequences in the domain of programming. For example, Wang et al. (2017) applied a recursive neural network (Piech et al., 2015) as the embedding for student submission sequences, then fed them into a 3-layer LSTM to predict the student's future performance. On the other hand, Emerson et al. (2019) utilized four categories of features: prior performance, hint usage, activity progress, and interface interaction to evaluate the accuracy of Logistic Regression models for multiple block-based programming activities. Furthermore, Dong et al. (2021)

automatically compared timed snapshots of Snap! programs to various solutions and used historical problem-solving time data to label timed trace log data as struggling or making progress. These studies provide strong evidence that syntactic knowledge contributes more to modeling source code and can produce better representations than token-based methods.

Previously, Mao et al. (2019) have explored various temporal models with the expert-designed skills (features) described in the section on "Feature-Based Methods". Specifically, Mao et al. first investigated the prediction power of Recent Temporal Pattern Mining (RTP) (Batal et al., 2012) in the iSnap programming environment (Mao et al., 2019). Temporal Pattern-based approaches are designed to extract interpretable, meaningful temporal patterns directly from irregularly-sampled multivariate time series data. Recently, significant efforts have been made to develop and apply various pattern-based approaches to healthcare, which have been shown to be effective (Batal et al., 2012; Orphanou et al., 2016). The results showed that RTP is able to perform as well as LSTM using the expert-designed skills (Mao et al., 2019). Later on, another study was conducted to investigate whether the performance of LSTM could be further enhanced by taking time-awareness into consideration (Mao et al., 2020). The idea is motivated by previous research, which suggests BKT prediction performance can be improved by leveraging time information (Qiu et al., 2011; Wang & Heffernan, 2012). Mao et al. applied Time-aware LSTM (T-LSTM) (Baytas et al., 2017), which transforms time intervals between successive elements into weights and uses them to adjust the memory passed from previous moments. The intuition behind this method is that incorporating time information may improve performance. The authors compared T-LSTM and other student models in two different domains, each of which focused on a different prediction task: student success prediction in the iSnap programming environment and learning gain prediction in the Pyrenees probability tutoring system. The results revealed that T-LSTM significantly outperforms the other methods on the self-paced iSnap programming environment; while on the tutor-driven Pyrenees, it ties with LSTM and outperforms both BKT and the simple Logistic Regression (LR). In other words, while time-irregularity exists in both datasets, T-LSTM works significantly better than other student models when the pace is driven by students; that is, in the programming environment, students are self-guided, and therefore the amount of time they stay in a state really matters to understand their learning.

As students learn to author code, both their programming code and their understanding of it evolve over time. Therefore, Mao et al. (2022) proposed a general data-driven approach by combining an automatic skill discovery method (ASTNN or CrossLing), which addresses the linguistic structure of the students' artifact, along with T-LSTM, which handles students' learning progressions in continuous time. Researchers compared those proposed models with temporal models embedded with different feature sets including expert-designed skills and token-based features, as well as non-temporal baselines using Logistic Regression. The corresponding findings can be concluded as follows:

1) Temporal models usually outperform non-temporal models;
2) Token-based models can only capture very limited information from student code;
3) CrossLing-based models are the best out of all for the early prediction of student success, especially at the early stage when only the first two minutes of data are available.

These discoveries suggest a path forward in which a fully data-driven model can help us come closer to the truth of student learning progressions within programming. All of these findings indicate the necessity of taking advantage of temporal information in programs, which can be achieved with pattern-based models such as RTPs or deep learning models such as T-LSTM. For more information about this work, see more details and data in Mao et al. (2022).

Semi-Supervised Modeling for Limited Data Size

The usage of deep learning methods (Code2Vec, Alon et al., 2019; ASTNN, Zhang et al., 2019) for modeling student programs has enabled implicit student skills (Mao et al., 2021) and misconceptions discovery (Shi et al., 2021). However, computational-heavy models (often referred to as deep models) are known to be "data-hungry" (Aggarwal, 2018). Previous research has been using large datasets for deep models, for example, localizing student bugs with 270 000 samples (Gupta et al., 2019), or tracing student knowledge with more than 200 000 student answers (Piech et al., 2015). This approach works when a large amount of labeled data is available, but it also causes potential issues for applying these methods more generally, as labeling can be labor intensive (Dutt et al., 2017). Shi and Mao et al. (2021) have addressed this issue by investigating how much labeled data is needed to train a deep learning model. While other researchers used models for educational data analysis, Shi & Mao have investigated specifically how the deep learning models would perform for educational code classification, compared with classical models such as Support Vector Machine (SVM) (Cortes & Vapnik, 1995), and XGBoost (Chen et al., 2015), and whether unlabeled data can be used to help the learning process of models via semi-supervised learning (Zhu & Goldberg, 2009).

In the work of Shi and Mao et al. (2021), the authors have built Code2Vec and ASTNN models to detect student programming bugs from a CS1 Java course at a large public university in the United States. The authors labeled three student bugs in six problems, from ~1 800 submissions, teaching students "if" conditions, and then compared the two models against classical models, and evaluated the performance with a limited number of labels under supervised learning scenarios. The remaining data were then used as unlabeled data for semi-supervised learning. While it is true that simple knowledge engineering methods (e.g. constraint-based methods; Mitrovic et al., 2001) could also work for these three bugs and it may take less effort for ITS authors, some other bugs are not easy to detect and may need lots of manual rules. The authors detect these bugs as examples to explore the use of semi-supervised learning for student bug detection.

Specifically, Shi and Mao et al. (2021) built Code2Vec (Alon et al., 2019), ASTNN (Zhang et al., 2019), SVM (Cortes & Vapnik, 1995), and XGBoost (Chen et al., 2017) models to classify these three student bugs from a CS1 course dataset:

1) Comparison-off-by-one: This bug occurs when students use greater/less-than comparison operators incorrectly. These bugs can be solved by adding or removing "=" in the comparison.
2) Assign-in-conditional: This bug occurs when students use "=" instead of "==" in a conditional expression.
3) And-vs-or: This bug occurs when students use "and" or "or" operators in a logical expression, but the opposite operators are expected to produce correct results.

To enhance the learning of deep models specifically, Shi and Mao et al. (2021) used the Expectation-Maximization (EM) method (Zhu & Goldberg, 2009) to update the trained models. In the experiments, as classical SVM and XGBoost models return binary values in the classification process, the authors implemented both models using regression, assuming a continuous probability output, and used the output for the next Expectation steps.

Semi-Supervised Learning Results

Shi and Mao compared the CodeVec and ASTNN models and evaluated them using F1 Scores with ten resampled runs. While the differences were not statistically significant, their results suggest that:

1) The Code2Vec and ASTNN models can outperform classical machine-learning models, such as SVM and XGBoost, when enough data (~1 800 samples) are available for the bug detection task.
2) The two deep learning models can be successful when data has a limited label size (~50 labels), achieving higher F1 scores than traditional methods.
3) Semi-supervised learning has helped the two deep learning models perform better with less labeled data.

The first result indicates that deep learning models outperform classical models, even with a limited labeled data size. In classifying three bugs, specifically, ASTNN performed better than other models when large label size was available, while Code2Vec performed better than other models when labeled data size was small. Semi-supervised also has the potential to increase the performance of deep learning models. The semi-supervised learning strategy helped both Code2Vec and ASTNN in the learning process, covering differently-sized labeled datasets, especially for ASTNN models. In classifying "Assign-in-conditional" bugs, semi-supervised learning does not help the Code2Vec model when the labeled data size is large. However, on the classification tasks of the other two bugs, semi-supervised learning achieved better results than supervised learning settings, showing that semi-supervised learning has the potential of helping deep learning models when labeled data are not enough. Together, these results suggest that even "data-hungry" deep learning approaches to student modeling are viable for smaller amounts of student programming data, especially when enhanced with semi-supervised learning approaches. However, the results of this study do not suggest that the semi-supervised method might also work on other, or more complex bugs. Nevertheless, future work is needed to make direct comparisons to knowledge engineering methods in terms of effort needed and performance achieved. For more information about semi-supervised strategy in detecting student programming bugs, see more details and data in Shi and Mao et al. (2021).

EVALUATING DATA-DRIVEN SUPPORTS

Our ultimate goal for data-driven student modeling is to build adaptive support systems to promote learning while reducing difficulties and improving students' experience throughout the learning process. In this section, we demonstrate how we used feature-based student modeling to enable adaptive support in iSnap, and the multi-criterion evaluation we have developed to evaluate such systems. Evaluating adaptive supports can be particularly challenging for creative or interactive student programming, where correctness is not straightforward to evaluate. Effectiveness may also be measured using various student outcomes (e.g. learning, persistence, self-efficacy). Furthermore, even state-of-the-art data-driven support systems are not perfect (Rivers et al., 2017; Price et al., 2017b; Toll et al., 2020) and thus, consideration of any inherent limitations of these systems is crucial during evaluation, since it can impact cases where the system is effective and where it is not. Researchers have evaluated data-driven programming support systems based on the capability of generating hints for all programming states (Rivers et al., 2017). To measure learning or students' experience in relationship with using such systems, researchers have used measures including improvement in test scores (Marwan et al., 2019; Rivers, 2017), success in completing more tasks (Zhi et al., 2019), learning efficiency in terms of time (Rivers, 2017) or students' perceptions of such systems derived from interview data (Marwan et al., 2019, 2021b). These evaluations focus on explicit metrics of learning (score, time, task completion rate etc.). However, students' solution approaches, or behaviors in response to the quality of feedback, are also important dimensions to explore for deriving insights on how to design these systems to support problem solving and learning. Thus, we applied a multi-criterion evaluation mechanism (Shabrina et al., 2020, 2022) to evaluate a data-driven adaptive feedback system where we focused on students' behavioral patterns in response to feedback components and accuracy. Such evaluations can be used to guide researchers toward realizing the full potential of data-driven tutoring systems for programming.

A Multi-Criterion Evaluation Mechanism

We designed and evaluated a data-driven support system for the Squiral task (described in the section on "Feature-Based Methods". To build the system, we first built data-driven feature detectors (DDFD) as described in the section on "Feature-Based Methods" and combined the DDFD features into a smaller set of objectives with short textual labels as detailed in Marwan et al. (2020b). In Figure 13.3, the objectives are marked green when they are complete, and red when they are broken, to help guide student problem solving, and assist in metacognitive progress monitoring. We conducted two studies comparing Squiral programs between two semesters of an undergraduate non-major's introductory computer science course, one with 33 students without the system, and one with 27 students using the system. Between the two groups, we compared the amount of time students spent on the task and their level of accuracy. For those using the system, we asked experts to label each code edit where objectives became complete or broken, and compared them to the system detections.

We defined the following evaluation criteria: (1) Accuracy: a quantitative measurement comparing expert and system objective detection; (2) Capability to Imitate Human Support: an estimate of similarity of the system support to expert human tutor support (especially in detecting objective completion); (3) Effectiveness: comparison of student time and performance with and without the system, and how different components of the system helped students; (4) Fallibility: what happened when our system failed to provide reliable feedback; and (5) Students' Response: generalizable patterns in student behavior, for example, student code edits after receiving feedback on a broken objective. The results of our evaluation showed our system to be effective in helping students monitor their progress, stay on track, and complete the given programming task in the absence of human assistance. However, we detected that our system occasionally provides fallible feedback that led to unintended impacts (increased active time, unnecessary work, partial correct submission) when students over-relied on the system, that is, followed system feedback without self-assessment.

Table 13.2   Incorrect feedback types, occurrence count, and percentage of causing an impact

Type of incorrect feedback	Occurrence count	Co-occurrence with an impact	Percent impact (%)	Impact on submission
Incomplete objectives marked complete	14	8	57.1	Two (14%) non-working submissions Six early submissions – need improved instructions
Early detection	29	9	31	Early submissions
Missed detection	12	3	25	Unnecessary work increasing active time
Late detection	9	3	33.3	Unnecessary work increasing active time

Accuracy: how accurate is the data-driven feedback?

We measured accuracy by averaging expert ratings of system feedback as correct or incorrect over all objectives and students. Our system provided correct feedback on complete and incomplete objectives with ~86% accuracy. However, sometimes the objectives were detected early (~35%) or late (~10%) by a few steps. By replaying students' code traces, we determined that our system failed to provide reliable feedback when a student used a new approach not observed in the system's training data, an expected and inherent limitation of data-driven systems. The majority of students (25 of 27) successfully completed the task using our system, demonstrating that they successfully learned to build functions, and how to modify variables within a loop to draw lines of varying length. As shown in Table 13.2, only 23 out of 64 (~35%) cases of early, late, or incorrect detections were observed to co-occur with an unintended impact (submitting incorrect solution, higher working time etc.). We developed two criteria to further investigate system effectiveness and impacts on student behavior.

Effectiveness: how does it help?

We compared time and performance between 33 students in the control group and 27 in the experimental group using the system, as detailed in Marwan et al. (2020b). We found that the system improved students' engagement as measured by the time spent on the programming task, with the experimental group spending significantly longer, an average of 42 minutes, when compared to the control group at 20 minutes. A t-test shows that this difference was significant with a strong effect size ($t_{(40:78)}$ = 3:96; $p < 0:01$; Cohen's $d = 1.08$). The system had a medium effect size on performance (Cohen's $d = 0.45$) with higher scores on the task for the experimental group (mean = 86.4%, SD = 14.5%) than for the control group (mean = 76.9%, SD = 25.5%), but this difference was not significant ($p = 0.19$) (Marwan et al., 2020b).

To further investigate the impacts of the system, we explored trace logs from the 27 students in the experimental group using the system to understand how it promoted more time on task and better performance. Overall, we found that (1) the list of objectives was effective in helping students complete programming tasks, and (2) the visual objective completion feedback served as a guide and a source of motivation for students. We observed that each student closely followed the list of objectives and used the code constructs required to complete the objectives. Although the specific code constructs and organization required to complete an objective were not given to students, the data-driven objective list limited the space of solutions students needed to explore while figuring out a solution for the problem. Thus, the system helped students to focus on *how*, rather than on *what*, to do. Also, students' code traces showed that, whenever a code edit caused a broken objective, in most cases, the students immediately reverted that edit. This behavior potentially indicates the feedback on broken objectives was successful in preventing students from going too far off-track. Finally, we believe that the positive feedback (green highlight) given on completion of an objective was a source of motivation for students and helped them to persist. The code traces showed many students continued to work on the solution as long as the system did not mark all the objectives as completed. This behavior showed the potential of our system to motivate students to continue trying rather than giving up on programming tasks. However, this behavior can also result in unnecessary work in some cases, as we later describe.

A Case Study: Lime

To demonstrate how our system helped a student to complete the Squiral problem, we present here the case of student Lime, who attempted the problem twice, once without and once with the feedback system. Student Lime, when attempting to solve Squiral *without* the system (see Figure 13.2a), gave up while still having three mistakes in their code. The student spent 18 minutes and 18 seconds before giving up, being unable to resolve these issues. Later, when student Lime attempted the Squiral task homework with the system available (see Figure 13.2b), they were observed to resolve the three issues and reach a correct solution. The second objective suggests that there is a correct number of rotations that need to be used within the custom block. With this feedback, Lime used "4 x Rotations" in the "repeat" block instead of using "15" and completed the second objective. The third objective suggests the use of a variable in the "move" statement. Lime used an initialized variable "length" in the "move" statement instead of "length × 2" and the objective was marked green. Finally, Lime incremented "length" within the loop and all objectives were completed and they reached a correct solution. We attributed this success to the list of objectives, since each of the objectives provides hints on the issues. Lime spent 29 minutes and 51 seconds before reaching the correct solution when using our feedback system. Recall that Lime gave up with an incorrect solution after around 18 minutes when no feedback was given.

Our analysis here suggests computational accuracy may reveal limitations of a data-driven support system, but it may not be indicative of the strengths or effectiveness of a system. The source of effectiveness of such systems may depend on other factors, for example, the type of feedback generated, or the presentation of feedback as we believe to be the case for our system. Thus, a complete evaluation should investigate the particulars of how the system impacts students.

Fallibility: what happens when it fails?

Since new programming patterns make our system fallible (state-of-the-art program evaluation techniques are still not 100% accurate), we further investigated how incorrect feedback can impact novice students who were observed to be highly reliant on the system. For the 27 students using the system, we classified incorrect feedback into three major categories: (1) Early Detection: An objective was marked as complete before the student actually completed it; (2) Late Detection: An objective was detected as complete sometime after the student

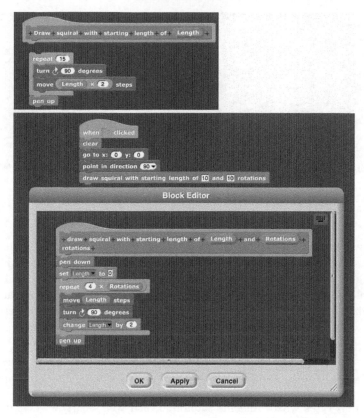

Figure 13.2   *Student Lime's solution (a) without using the Feedback System and (b) using the Feedback System*

actually completed it; and (3) Incorrect Detection: An incomplete objective was detected as complete or a complete objective remained undetected. We investigated each of the instances of incorrect feedback and identified three types of student behaviors that were not intended, that is, had a negative impact (ending up with an incorrect solution leading to rework, spending extra time, and early incorrect submission). In Table 13.2, we show occurrence of different types of detection that co-occurred with an impact and the type of observed impact. Although the impacts seemed to be associated with specific types of detections, those did not occur for all students. We suspect that the impacts potentially occurred only for those who over-relied on the system without performing a self-assessment by running the code, as discussed below.

Unintended impact type 1: marking an incomplete solution fully correct leading toward non-working submissions
We found four attempts where the system incorrectly marked all four objectives as complete, when the code would not draw a Squiral (false positives). As a representative of these cases, student Cyan completed the first three objectives correctly, and the system correctly detected each. However, Cyan then made a code edit to add a new loop that would change the length of each side of the Squiral, but placed this code in the wrong location. The system marked the

Figure 13.3   Incorrect solution initially implemented by student Cyan

related objective 4 as correct, but the code was unable to draw a Squiral (Figure 13.3). Cyan, and two others in this situation where all objectives were incorrectly marked as complete, realized that their attempt was not working, ignored the system's full marks, and worked until their code ran correctly before submission. The one other student in this situation, the only one whose behavior resulted in a negative impact in this situation, failed to self-assess their code, turning in a non-working, partially complete solution that the system had marked as complete.

Unintended impact type 2: incomplete objectives marked complete leading toward early submissions

We discovered six cases where students submitted their work "early," where their code had partially correct output (drawing a Squiral), and the system detected all four objectives, but experts marked objective 2 as incorrect. This represents a student misconception about the instructions/objectives, which indicated that the Squiral block should take a parameter for how many rotations the Squiral should make. Students in this situation did self-assess by running their code, and the all-correct objectives led students to believe that their solutions are correct, but they submitted a solution that is working but is flawed according to experts, a false positive. Student Indigo's attempt (Figure 13.4) shows objectives 1, 3, and 4 correctly completed, according to experts, and the system correctly marked them as complete. However, the rotation count used in the nested loop did not meet the requirements for objective 2, but the system incorrectly marked this as correct. All six students in this situation submitted their attempts that each drew a Squiral, but lacked an inner loop that repeats four times and an outer loop for the correct number of rotations as was intended by the instructions. In these six cases, we conclude that the Squiral instructions need improvement that could lead students and the system to more accurate assessments.

Unintended impact type 3: missed or late detections leading toward unnecessary work increasing active time

Failing to mark a completed objective green (i.e. a False Negative (FN) case: a complete objective remained undetected) led students to think that their solutions were not correct and they unnecessarily spent more time on their already-correct solutions. As a case study, student Azure achieved a correct solution in just 2.4 minutes, but the system marked only objectives

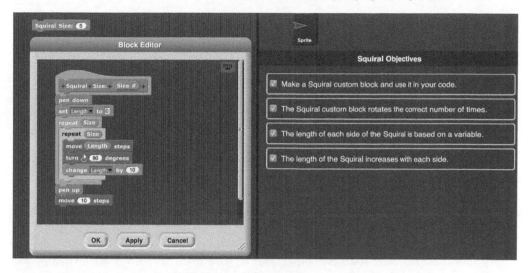

Figure 13.4   Solution submitted by student Indigo

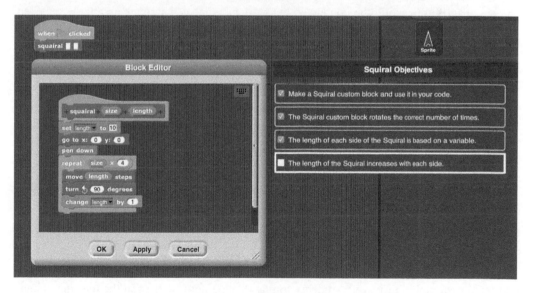

Figure 13.5   Correct solution initially implemented by student Azure

1–3 correct. As shown in Figure 13.5, objective 4 was undetected, because Azure used a "turn left" statement rather than "turn right". Since the fourth objective was not detected by the system, Azure was observed to keep working on their code and spent 12 minutes and 5 seconds more. One other student, Blue, achieved a correct solution in 1 hour, but only three objectives were marked correct, similar to Azure, and Blue continued to work 36 extra minutes. Overall, six of the observed objective detections led to students spending more time after experts marked their code complete.

After investigating the particular instances of fallibility and corresponding student responses, we conducted qualitative analysis to measure the generalizability of the responses. The analysis showed us three generalizable patterns: (1) receiving positive feedback (objective turning green indicating completion) even if inaccurate (early/incorrect) tended to decrease students' idle time in the system; (2) early detection led to partial correct submission within 0.1 to 8 minutes of the detections and students did not modify their implementation of objectives during this time; (3) in case of undetected objectives, student spent more time (12–56 minutes) in the system working on those objectives, even if those were actually complete.

Based on the findings of our multi-criterion evaluation, we recommend that a data-driven support system should be evaluated to make its source of effectiveness, fallibility, and potential impacts (both positive and negative) known to the end-users (teachers and students) to ensure proper usage. The main insights obtained from the evaluation can be summarized as follows:

1. Feature-based student modeling was effective in accommodating adaptive support within ITSs which can guide students in programming tasks in the absence of human assistance.
2. Data-driven adaptive support that provides feedback on correctness or completion of objectives within a programming task or the entire task could be fallible. Thus, an analysis of fallibility should be conducted before deploying such systems on a large scale, so that proper mitigation steps can be infused in the usage plan.
3. Considering the inherent fallibility of such systems and the current state-of-the-art, novice students should be encouraged to self-assess (since they sometimes submitted partially correct solutions when the system (incorrectly) marked all objectives green) and rely on their self-assessment (since students were observed to continue working on complete solutions when the system did not detect an objective) so that they can benefit from the system rather than suffer from any unintended impact due to over-reliance on the system. As suggested by Marwan et al. (2021b), students can be encouraged to self-assess their code and reflect on the feedback by explaining to them how such feedback is generated and how it might be inaccurate, or allowing them to decide themselves whether each objective is complete (such as by checking-off the objective when it is complete) (Marwan et al., 2021b).

Recommended Future Research

The findings from the evaluation of our system motivated research in future ITSs for programming in two different directions. First, we recommend further research on how to communicate system fallibility with students so that they do not lose trust in the tutoring system but exploit its benefits without being over-reliant on it. For example, Marwan et al. (2021b) conducted a study exploring different design strategies to represent feedback and the results of the study showed that being aware of system fallibility motivated the students to override erroneous feedback when needed. Second, we recommend research on the inherent limitations of continuous data-driven supports for programming and methods to overcome those limitations. For example, the primary source of fallibility in our system, as in most data-driven systems, is the common limitation of encountering new student approaches that were not present in our training data. However, adding a few expert constraints, applying semi-supervised learning, or updating the model with new data as it is encountered can mitigate this challenge. Future systems could benefit from more techniques to collect student-intended goals for each part of their programs, and from ways to represent and detect program semantics. Furthermore, future work could also investigate the relationship of the constructed models to pre- to post-test learning gains, or the potential for mapping features into KCs so that the student model could also be used for outer-loop adaptivity (learning activity selection).

SUMMARY

Throughout this chapter, we discussed our research group's work in the domain of programming. This domain poses special challenges to student modeling because student work occurs continuously, and therefore it can be particularly difficult to determine the discrete steps, along with associated skills and performance labels corresponding to those steps. We present our work for automating these student modeling challenges in programming from three different perspectives: (1) skill discovery seeking to address the challenging of missing skill labels; (2) effective modeling including temporal modeling on sequential data and semi-supervised learning when data size is relatively small; and (3) evaluations for data-driven supports, where we seek to align technical and empirical studies. We hope to shed some light on the field for future researchers and provide the basic understanding of student modeling for programming.

Finally, we conclude by aligning our key findings to key design choices one may encounter when designing a student model in the domain of programming, or another domain with continuous student work, rather than discrete, easy-to-assess steps. We discuss implications of our work for how to address these questions.

Finding 1: Data-driven student models can automatically *define* a set of skills to assess, detect *when* they are demonstrated, and *assess them*, leading to accurate predictions of future performance.

Choice 1: Should you model skills explicitly or implicitly?

In the domain of programming, we must assess students' knowledge based on the programs they create, which requires us to somehow translate that program into a set of assessed skills. We presented two techniques for this: *explicit* skill discovery, through data-driven feature detectors that define a discrete set of skills and assess them as correct/ incorrect; and *implicit* skill discovery through machine-learning models that embed students' programs to make accurate predictions about their performance. Explicit models have a number of advantages: they are more interpretable, the model can be made open to the student (Hartley & Mitrovic, 2002), the detected skills can be used for immediate feedback (Marwan et al., 2020a, 2020b), and they can be improved with expert (i.e. human-in-the-loop) effort (see below). Therefore, we recommend an explicit model when you need to interpret the model, or communicate it to students or instructors. Implicit skill discovery with neural networks is fully automated by the model, and can discover new patterns humans may miss, leading to highly accurate predictions of student performance. It is therefore most useful when raw predictive performance is most important.

Finding 2: A small number of expert constraints can greatly improve the accuracy of a data-driven skill detector.

Choice 2: How will you incorporate human expertise into your model?

Our results (Marwan et al., 2021a) suggest that, rather than seeing data-driven and expert-authored skill detectors as mutually exclusive, we should see them as complementary. Importantly, this requires that data-driven skill models be designed in such a way they can be manually adjusted. Additionally, this refinement takes additional expert effort, and without it, purely data-driven features may be difficult to interpret, and detectors may be inaccurate. We recommend planning ahead when designing a data-driven student model to think about how the output can be interpreted, evaluated, and updated by experts.

Finding 3: Temporal information can improve the accuracy of a student model in programming.

Choice 3: How will you model temporal information?

We presented multiple examples of how the student model can leverage temporal information to improve predictive performance. This goes beyond simple sequential information to incorporate specific continuous time intervals (T-LSTM), and temporal patterns (RTP mining). We found such information is more useful in domains like programming, where students' work is continuous, rather than step-by-step, with the price of a higher computational cost. Therefore, you should consider whether, in your domain, the time it takes a student to do a step may be predictive of their success, and if so, how to incorporate that into your student model.

Finding 4: Semi-supervised learning can improve student model performance, but not always.

Choice 4: Will you incorporate semi-supervised learning into your student model?

The answer should depend on: 1) the complexity of your model and 2) how difficult it is to label your data. We found that semi-supervised learning was most useful in deep models, especially the most complex ASTNN model. Additionally, it made sense for misconception detection, when labeling is time intensive and cannot be automated, but not for predicting student success, which is easier to assess.

Finding 5: Evaluations of student models must go beyond technical (i.e. accuracy) to students' experiences in the classroom.

Choice 5: How will you assess the effectiveness of your model?

The real value of a student model is how it is used in a classroom to impact student learning. Therefore, the evaluation of the model must go beyond accuracy on prior datasets to explore how the interventions of the model impact students. This finding is neither new nor specific to the domain of programming, but we hope our examples of evaluation approaches can help readers design their own evaluations that make sense for the models and interventions they develop. We recommend: (1) look at *when* and *why* models are inaccurate, not just how frequently overall; (2) use case studies to highlight affordances and limitations of a model; (3) investigate unintended consequences; and (4) use design choices that allow the system to minimize hard when student models (inevitably) make some incorrect predictions.

REFERENCES

Aggarwal, C. C. (2018). *Neural networks and deep learning*. Springer.

Alon, U., Zilberstein, M., Levy, O., & Yahav, E. (2019). code2vec: Learning distributed representations of code. In *Proceedings of the ACM on Programming Languages*, *3*(POPL), 1–29.

Anderson, J. R., & Reiser, B. J. (1985). The LISP tutor. *Byte*, *10*(4), 159–175.

Baker, R. S., Corbett, A. T., & Aleven, V. (2008). More accurate student modeling through contextual estimation of slip and guess probabilities in Bayesian knowledge tracing. In *International Conference on Intelligent Tutoring Systems* (pp. 406–415). Berlin, Heidelberg: Springer.

Barnes, T. (2005, July). The Q-matrix method: Mining student response data for knowledge. In *American Association for Artificial Intelligence 2005 Educational Data Mining Workshop* (pp. 1–8). Pittsburgh, PA: AAAI Press.

Batal, I., Fradkin, D., Harrison, J., Moerchen, F., & Hauskrecht, M. (2012, August). Mining recent temporal patterns for event detection in multivariate time series data. In *Proceedings of the 18th ACM SIGKDD International Conference on Knowledge Discovery and Data Mining* (pp. 280–288).

Baxter, I. D., Yahin, A., Moura, L., Sant'Anna, M., & Bier, L. (1998). Clone detection using abstract syntax trees. In *Proceedings. International Conference on Software Maintenance* (Cat. No. 98CB36272) (pp. 368–377). IEEE.

Baytas, I. M., Xiao, C., Zhang, X., Wang, F., Jain, A. K., & Zhou, J. (2017, August). Patient subtyping via time-aware LSTM networks. In *Proceedings of the 23rd ACM SIGKDD International Conference on Knowledge Discovery and Data Mining* (pp. 65–74).

Blikstein, P. (2011, February). Using learning analytics to assess students' behavior in open-ended programming tasks. In *Proceedings of the 1st International Conference on Learning Analytics and Knowledge* (pp. 110–116).

Cen, H., Koedinger, K., & Junker, B. (2006, June). Learning factors analysis – A general method for cognitive model evaluation and improvement. In *International Conference on Intelligent Tutoring Systems* (pp. 164–175). Berlin, Heidelberg: Springer.

Chen, T., He, T., Benesty, M., Khotilovich, V., Tang, Y., Cho, H., & Chen, K. (2015). Xgboost: Extreme gradient boosting. *R package version 0.4-2*, *1*(4), 1–4.

Corbett, A. T., & Anderson, J. R. (1994). Knowledge tracing: Modeling the acquisition of procedural knowledge. *User Modeling and User-Adapted Interaction*, *4*(4), 253–278.

Cortes, C., & Vapnik, V. (1995). Support-vector networks. *Machine Learning*, *20*(3), 273–297.

Dong, Y., Marwan, S. Shabrina, P., Price, T. W., & Barnes, T. (2021). Using student trace logs to determine meaningful progress and struggle during programming problem solving. In *Proceedings of the 14th International Conference on Educational Data Mining (EDM'21)*.

Dutt, A., Ismail, M. A., & Herawan, T. (2017). A systematic review on educational data mining. *IEEE Access*, *5*, 15991–16005.

Emerson, A., Rodríguez, F. J., Mott, B., Smith, A., Min, W., Boyer, K. E., ... & Lester, J. (2019). Predicting early and often: Predictive student modeling for block-based programming environments. *International Educational Data Mining Society*.

Falleri, J. R., Morandat, F., Blanc, X., Martinez, M., & Monperrus, M. (2014, September). Fine-grained and accurate source code differencing. In *Proceedings of the 29th ACM/IEEE International Conference on Automated Software Engineering* (pp. 313–324).

Garcia, D., Harvey, B., & Barnes, T. (2015). The beauty and joy of computing. *ACM Inroads*, *6*(4), 71–79.

Gerdes, A., Heeren, B., Jeuring, J., & van Binsbergen, L. T. (2017). Ask-Elle: An adaptable programming tutor for Haskell giving automated feedback. *International Journal of Artificial Intelligence in Education*, *27*(1), 65–100.

Gupta, R., Kanade, A., & Shevade, S. (2019). Neural attribution for semantic bug-localization in student programs. *Advances in Neural Information Processing Systems*, *32*.

Hartley, D., & Mitrovic, A. (2002, June). Supporting learning by opening the student model. In *Proceedings of the 6th International Conference on Intelligent Tutoring Systems* (pp. 453–462). Berlin, Heidelberg: Springer.

Hindle, A., Barr, E. T., Gabel, M., Su, Z., & Devanbu, P. (2016). On the naturalness of software. *Communications of the ACM*, *59*(5), 122–131.

Jin, W., Barnes, T., Stamper, J., Eagle, M., Johnson, M. W., & Lehmann, L. (2012). Program representation for automatic hint generation for a data-driven novice programming tutor. In *Proceedings of the 11th International Conference on Intelligent Tutoring Systems (ITS'12)* (pp. 304–309).

Khajah, M., Lindsey, R. V., & Mozer, M. C. (2016). How deep is knowledge tracing? arXiv preprint arXiv:1604.02416.

Koedinger, K. R., Corbett, A. T., & Perfetti, C. (2010). The knowledge-learning-instruction (KLI) framework: Toward bridging the science-practice chasm to enhance robust student learning. *Cognitive Science*, *36*, 757–798.

Lin, C., & Chi, M. (2017). A comparisons of bkt, rnn and lstm for learning gain prediction. In *International Conference on Artificial Intelligence in Education* (pp. 536–539). Springer, Cham.

Lin, C., Shen, S., & Chi, M. (2016). Incorporating student response time and tutor instructional interventions into student modeling. In *Proceedings of the 2016 Conference on User Modeling Adaptation and Personalization* (pp. 157–161).

Mao, Y., Khoshnevisan, F., Price, T., Barnes, T., & Chi, M. (2022). Cross-lingual adversarial domain adaptation for novice programming. In *Proceedings of AAAI-2022*.

Mao, Y., Lin, C., & Chi, M. (2018). Deep learning vs. Bayesian knowledge tracing: Student models for interventions. *Journal of Educational Data Mining*, *10*(2), 28–54.

Mao, Y., Marwan, S., Price, T. W., Barnes, T., & Chi, M. (2020). What time is it? Student modeling needs to know. In *Proceedings of The 13th International Conference on Educational Data Mining (EDM 2020)* (pp. 171–182).

Mao, Y., Shi, Y., Marwan, S., Price, T., Barnes, T., & Chi, M. (2021). Knowing both when and where: Temporal-ASTNN for early prediction of student success in novice programming tasks. In *Proceedings of the 14th International Conference on Educational Data Mining (EDM'21)* (pp. 172–182).

Mao, Y., Zhi, R., Khoshnevisan, F., Price, T. W., Barnes, T., & Chi, M. (2019). One minute is enough: Early prediction of student success and event-level difficulty during a novice programming task. In *Proceedings of the 12th International Conference on Educational Data Mining (EDM 2019)*. Article 110.

Marwan, S., Gao, G., Fisk, S., Price, T. W., & Barnes, T. (2020a, August). Adaptive immediate feedback can improve novice programming engagement and intention to persist in computer science. In *Proceedings of the 2020 ACM Conference on International Computing Education Research* (pp. 194–203).

Marwan, S., Jay Williams, J., & Price, T. (2019, July). An evaluation of the impact of automated programming hints on performance and learning. In *Proceedings of the 2019 ACM Conference on International Computing Education Research* (pp. 61–70).

Marwan, S., Price, T. W., Chi, M., & Barnes, T. (2020b). Immediate data-driven positive feedback increases engagement on programming homework for novices. In *Proceedings of the 4th Educational Data Mining in Computer Science (CSEDM) Virtual Workshop, in Conjunction With EDM 2020*.

Marwan, S., Shabrina, P., Milliken, A., Menezes, I., Catete, V., Price, T. W., & Barnes, T. (2021b, November). Promoting students' progress-monitoring behavior during block-based programming. In *21st Koli Calling International Conference on Computing Education Research* (pp. 1–10).

Marwan, S., Shi, Y., Menezes, I., Chi, M., Barnes, T., & Price, T. W. (2021a). Just a few expert constraints can help: Humanizing data-driven subgoal detection for novice programming. In *Proceedings of the 14th International Conference on Educational Data Mining (EDM'21)*.

Mitrovic, A. (2003). An intelligent SQL tutor on the web. *International Journal of Artificial Intelligence in Education*, *13*(2–4), 173–197.

Mitrovic, A., Mayo, M., Suraweera, P., & Martin, B. (2001, June). Constraint-based tutors: A success story. In *Proceedings of the 23rd International Conference on Industrial Engineering and Other Applications of Applied Intelligent Systems* (pp. 931–940).

Mou, L., Li, G., Zhang, L., Wang, T., & Jin, Z. (2016, February). Convolutional neural networks over tree structures for programming language processing. In *Proceedings of the 30th AAAI Conference on Artificial Intelligence*.

Orphanou, K., Dagliati, A., Sacchi, L., Stassopoulou, A., Keravnou, E., & Bellazzi, R. (2016, October). Combining naive bayes classifiers with temporal association rules for coronary heart disease diagnosis. In *2016 IEEE International Conference on Healthcare Informatics (ICHI)* (pp. 81–92). IEEE.

Pane, J. F., & Myers, B. A. (2001). Studying the language and structure in non-programmers' solutions to programming problems. *International Journal of Human-Computer Studies*, *54*(2), 237–264.

Pardos, Z. A., & Heffernan, N. T. (2010, June). Modeling individualization in a Bayesian networks implementation of knowledge tracing. In *Proceedings of the 18th International Conference on User Modeling, Adaptation, and Personalization* (pp. 255–266). Berlin, Heidelberg: Springer.

Pardos, Z. A., & Heffernan, N. T. (2011). KT-IDEM: Introducing item difficulty to the knowledge tracing model. In *International Conference on User Modeling, Adaptation, and Personalization* (pp. 243–254). Berlin, Heidelberg: Springer.

Pavlik, P. I., Cen, H., & Koedinger, K. R. (2009, July). Performance factors analysis – A new alternative to knowledge tracing. In *Proceedings of the 2009 Conference on Artificial Intelligence in Education:*

Building Learning Systems That Care: From Knowledge Representation to Affective Modelling (pp. 531–538).

Peddycord, B., III, Hicks, A. & Barnes, T. (2014). Generating hints for programming problems using intermediate output. In *Proceedings of the 7th International Conference on Educational Data Mining (EDM2014)* (pp. 92–98). London, UK.

Piech, C., Bassen, J., Huang, J., Ganguli, S., Sahami, M., Guibas, L., & Sohl-Dickstein, J. (2015, December). Deep knowledge tracing. In *Proceedings of the 28th International Conference on Neural Information Processing Systems-Volume 1* (pp. 505–513).

Price, T. W., & Barnes, T. (2015, June). An exploration of data-driven hint generation in an open-ended programming problem. In *EDM (Workshops)*.

Price, T. W., Dong, Y., & Lipovac, D. (2017a, March). iSnap: Towards intelligent tutoring in novice programming environments. In *Proceedings of the 2017 ACM SIGCSE Technical Symposium on Computer Science Education* (pp. 483–488).

Price, T. W., Zhi, R., & Barnes, T. (2017b, June). Hint generation under uncertainty: The effect of hint quality on help-seeking behavior. In *International Conference on Artificial Intelligence in Education* (pp. 311–322). Cham: Springer.

Price, T., Zhi, R., & Barnes, T. (2017c). Evaluation of a data-driven feedback algorithm for open-ended programming. In *Proceedings of the 10th International Conference on Educational Data Mining* (pp. 192–197).

Qiu, Y., Qi, Y., Lu, H., Pardos, Z. A., & Heffernan, N. T. (2011, July). Does time matter? Modeling the effect of time with Bayesian knowledge tracing. *In EDM* (pp. 139–148).

Rivers, K. (2017). Automated data-driven hint generation for learning programming (*Doctoral Dissertation, Carnegie Mellon University*).

Rivers, K., & Koedinger, K. R. (2017). Data-driven hint generation in vast solution spaces: A self-improving python programming tutor. *International Journal of Artificial Intelligence in Education*, 27(1), 37–64.

Shabrina, P., Marwan, S., Bennison, A., Chi, M., Price, T., & Barnes, T. (2022). A multicriteria evaluation for data-driven programming feedback systems: Accuracy, effectiveness, fallibility, and students' response. arXiv preprint arXiv:2208.05326.

Shabrina, P., Marwan, S., Chi, M., Price, T. W., & Barnes, T. (2020). The impact of data-driven positive programming feedback: When it helps, what happens when it goes wrong, and how students respond. In *Proceedings of the 4th Educational Data Mining in Computer Science (CSEDM) Virtual Workshop, in Conjunction with EDM 2020*.

Shi, Y., Mao, Y., Barnes, T., Chi, M., & Price, T. W. (2021). More with less: Exploring how to use deep learning effectively through semi-supervised learning for automatic bug detection in student code. In *Proceedings of the 14th International Conference on Educational Data Mining (EDM'21)*.

Shi, Y., Shah, K., Wang, W., Marwan, S., Penmetsa, P., & Price, T. (2021, April). Toward semi-automatic misconception discovery using code embeddings. In *Proceedings of LAK21: 11th International Learning Analytics and Knowledge Conference* (pp. 606–612).

Skinner, B. F. (1965). *Science and human behavior* (No. 92904). Simon and Schuster.

Tang, S., Peterson, J. C., & Pardos, Z. A. (2016). Deep neural networks and how they apply to sequential education data. In *Proceedings of the Third ACM Conference on Learning@ Scale* (pp. 321–324).

Toll, D., Wingkvist, A., & Ericsson, M. (2020, October). Current state and next steps on automated hints for students learning to code. In *2020 IEEE Frontiers in Education Conference (FIE)* (pp. 1–5). IEEE.

VanLehn, K. (2006). The behavior of tutoring systems. *International Journal of Artificial Intelligence in Education*, 16(3), 227–265.

Wang, L., Sy, A., Liu, L., & Piech, C. (2017). Learning to represent student knowledge on programming exercises using deep learning. In *Proceedings of the 10th International Conference on Educational Data Mining (EDM'17), International Educational Data Mining Society*.

Wang, Y., & Heffernan, N. T. (2012). Leveraging first response time into the knowledge tracing model. In *Proceedings of the 5th International Conference on Educational Data Mining (EDM'12), International Educational Data Mining Society*.

Weimer, W., Nguyen, T., Le Goues, C., & Forrest, S. (2009, May). Automatically finding patches using genetic programming. In *2009 IEEE 31st International Conference on Software Engineering* (pp. 364–374). IEEE.

Xiong, X., Zhao, S., Van Inwegen, E. G., & Beck, J. E. (2016). Going deeper with deep knowledge tracing. In *International Conference on Educational Data Mining (EDM)*. International Educational Data Mining Society.

Yudelson, M. V., Koedinger, K. R., & Gordon, G. J. (2013). Individualized Bayesian knowledge tracing models. In *International Conference on Artificial Intelligence in Education* (pp. 171–180). Berlin, Heidelberg: Springer.

Zhang, J., Wang, X., Zhang, H., Sun, H., Wang, K., & Liu, X. (2019, May). A novel neural source code representation based on abstract syntax tree. In *2019 IEEE/ACM 41st International Conference on Software Engineering (ICSE)* (pp. 783–794). IEEE.

Zhi, R., Price, T. W., Lytle, N., Dong, Y., & Barnes, T. (2018). Reducing the state space of programming problems through data-driven feature detection. In *Educational Data Mining in Computer Science Education (CSEDM) Workshop@ EDM* (Vol. 18).

Zhi, R., Price, T. W., Marwan, S., Milliken, A., Barnes, T., & Chi, M. (2019, February). Exploring the impact of worked examples in a novice programming environment. In *Proceedings of the 50th ACM Technical Symposium on Computer Science Education* (pp. 98–104).

Zhu, X., & Goldberg, A. B. (2009). Introduction to semi-supervised learning. *Synthesis Lectures on Artificial Intelligence and Machine Learning, 3*(1), 1–130.

14. Human–AI co-orchestration: the role of artificial intelligence in orchestration

Ken Holstein and Jennifer K. Olsen

INTRODUCTION

Artificial intelligence in education (AIEd) has a long history of supporting learning through the use of technology. From the International Artificial Intelligence in Education Society website (2020), the community's focus is on "research and development of interactive and adaptive learning environments for learners of all ages, across all domains". However, this focus on learners does not necessarily attend to how learning technologies fit into broader educational ecosystems. Orchestration provides an additional lens that expands the focus beyond an individual or group of learners to the wider learning environment, such as a classroom (Dillenbourg et al., 2011). In this chapter, we discuss what this lens entails and the active role that artificial intelligence (AI) can play in orchestration, specifically through *human–AI co-orchestration*, which we define later in this chapter. Before addressing co orchestration, we will overview historical trends in orchestration research. This background will allow us to distinguish between traditional orchestration systems, co-orchestration systems, and other types of adaptive support.

Orchestration, as defined broadly, refers to the planning and real-time management of learning that responds to the complexity of the learning scenario, where human instructors are involved in major agentive roles. Often when discussing the conceptual boundaries of "orchestration", two main points emerge. First, the discussion centers around "real-time management" as a central aspect of orchestration. Second, the discussion often centers around the role of the instructor. Rather than directly engage in the debate around whether these two aspects are necessary for work to be considered orchestration research, we propose instead to use orchestration as a *lens* that can be used to develop and study interactive and adaptive learning support. We thus focus on describing what this lens aims to bring into focus. Dillenbourg et al. (2011) proposed that orchestration is the "third circle of usability". When we consider the development of systems, AIEd has often focused on interactions between an *individual* student and an AI system, computer-supported collaborative learning (CSCL) considers focuses on the interactions at the level of *groups* of students, and orchestration considers interactions at the level of a wider *learning ecosystem*, such as a classroom with one or more instructors and groups of learners.

Researchers and designers can choose to *focus* their attention on one or several of these levels. For example, even if a system has been effectively designed to support students working in *groups*, designers might still identify opportunities for the system to better serve *individual* learners within those groups. Similarly, an AIEd system may be well designed to provide adaptive support toward learners' *individual* learning objectives, but, by ignoring the wider learning environment in which it is placed, it may miss out on opportunities to better support *classes* of learners and instructors. Through an orchestration lens, the usability and effectiveness of learning technologies are considered at the level of the whole learning environment;

the focus is not on any one learner but rather on how a network of learners, instructors, and technologies interact. For instance, based on an instructor's goals and the joint learning states of all of the learners in a class, we might consider how a technology can inform the timing of group- or class-wide transitions between activities in order to maximize learning (e.g., when dependencies exist across multiple students or groups) (Faucon et al., 2020). As a second example, we might consider how a technology can guide human instructors in deciding how best to distribute their limited time among multiple learners in need of support (Alavi & Dillenbourg, 2012; Holstein et al., 2018; Martinez-Maldonado et al., 2014; Mavrikis et al., 2019).

This lens is one that instructors naturally take when they write lesson plans and dynamically adjust these plans to what is happening throughout the day. In this chapter, we focus on the intentional design of support for orchestration beyond what an instructor would be able to do independent of that support. These ideas are not new to the AIEd community. For example, the *ASSISTments* system grants instructors a high level of control over how the system adapts to their students, in contrast to many AIEd systems, providing instructors with flexibility to align the system with their classrooms' unique needs and constraints (Baker, 2016; Heffernan & Heffernan, 2014; Holstein et al., 2020). *ASSISTments* also provides instructors with information about their students' performance and common errors, to support instructors' instructional decision making. Orchestration connects naturally with these ideas. For other types of tools developed for instructors, see Chapter 15 by Pozdniakov et al.

In this chapter, we distinguish between different types of research on orchestration based on the extent of involvement from actors beyond the instructor. We first discuss orchestration that instructors engage in without specific technology support in the classroom. We then discuss *orchestration systems* that support instructors in their orchestration tasks, but without taking on a major agentic role in orchestrating the learning scenario. Finally, we discuss *co-orchestration*, in which the orchestration tasks are shared between two or more actors.

Defining Orchestration

Over the years, the definition of orchestration has changed, although without necessarily trending in a single, clear direction (Lawrence & Mercier, 2019). Researchers have debated the meaning of the orchestration metaphor and, through these discussions, what is in scope of orchestration research. A common definition that is cited by researchers comes from Dillenbourg (2013, p. 1), defining orchestration as "how a teacher manages, in real time, multi-layered activities in a multi-constraints context". However, this definition restricts orchestration to only being used with teachers, involving real-time management, and with lessons that span individual, collaborative, and whole class (i.e., different social levels) activities, which does not fully capture the range of orchestration research. In this section, we will explore how the definition of orchestration expands on this seminal definition, and how it has changed over time.

An orchestration lens emphasizes the potential for interactions between instructors and learners, across multiple groups, and between a given technology-supported learning activity and other learning activities that occur outside of the technology. Dillenbourg and Jermann (2010) highlight these points in their 15 design factors to consider for orchestration through which they highlight the role of the instructor, the integration of multiple social levels, time management, and the impact of the physical space. When designing for one-on-one learner–technology experiences, these broader learning environment concerns may not always be at the forefront, in part, because the environment in which the learning technology will be used is not always known ahead of time. It is then crucial to consider how to build orchestrability or adaptability into the system to empower instructors to tailor the technology to their particular contexts.

Prieto et al. (2011a) took a different approach to defining orchestration: rather than focusing on design factors, they summarized the different elements of orchestration that have been referenced in the literature in their theoretical framework, 5+3, which outlined five main aspects of orchestration from the literature on technology-enhanced learning (i.e., adaptation, management, awareness, planning, and roles of the actors). *Planning* relates to the learning design that occurs prior to a learning activity. During an ongoing activity, *adaptation* refers to the on-the-spot tailoring of the plan or design to align with new information emerging during the learning activity. Adaptation goes hand-in-hand with *awareness*: understanding what is occurring in the learning environment and in learners' minds. As with adaptivity and awareness, *management* is another aspect of the real-time nature of orchestration, referring to the continuous, in-the-moment regulation of the many practical aspects of a learning activity. Finally, the *role* of the actors considers the roles that the instructor and learner take on during a learning activity. Although these five aspects have been discussed as part of the orchestration literature, it is not clear whether all five aspects are sufficient or necessary for an orchestration system to address.

In a special section of *Computers and Education* (2013), where the definition by Dillenbourg above was introduced, the discussion of orchestration was broadened from these previous definitions to include dimensional nuances that could help in defining orchestration systems. For example, Tchounikine (2013) discusses the differences between orchestration technology and orchestrable technology to distinguish between technology that supports the process of orchestrating in the former and technology that is flexible and adaptable in the latter. When considering the environment in which a learning technology will be used, both aspects can be important. An instructor may need support from a technology if their load is too high, but they may also need to make changes in real time in response to changing conditions. On the other hand, Kollar and Fischer (2013) pushed the orchestration metaphor further to include and distinguish between *orchestrating*, *arranging*, and *conducting*. They argue for a successful lesson: all of these components are important with a well-designed lesson being created (orchestrated), the lesson being adapted to the relevant situation (arranged), and being carried out (conducted). As a final example, Sharples (2013) proposed that instead of having the technology be only a support for the instructor, the orchestration responsibility could be shared among the instructors, learners, and system. What these conversations have provided for the community is less of an agreed-upon definition of orchestration and rather the level at which the learning environment is being investigated.

Each of these conceptualizations helps us think about how a learning activity fits into the larger environment and the types of actions that are included with orchestration (e.g., activity prep such as grouping of students, administrative tasks including transitioning between activities, or activity feedback tasks related to behavioral, cognitive, and social aspects). They push us to "zoom out" from a focus on learners working alone or in small groups on an isolated set of learning activities. Although these definitions are often applied to formal classrooms – leading to the term *classroom orchestration* – there is nothing inherent to the design factors, elements, and dimensions presented across different definitions that would prevent orchestration from applying to informal environments, which we have in fact seen in the orchestration literature (Tissenbaum et al., 2016; Tissenbaum & Slotta, 2019; Zhang et al., 2017). This focus on the larger, learning environment can apply across learning settings.

INSTRUCTORS AS SOLE ORCHESTRATORS

Although this chapter focuses on AI-based technologies that facilitate the orchestration of learning activities, orchestration systems do not necessarily involve AI. To understand the role of AI in orchestration, it is helpful to first understand how instructors orchestrate learning activities, and how AI can help us to understand these processes, and the orchestration systems developed to support these activities without AI.

Understanding Instructors' Orchestration

A critical part of understanding how to build new orchestration systems is understanding how instructors *currently* orchestrate learning activities without specific technological support. Researchers have studied orchestration by (1) conducting field studies during which they can observe instructors, (2) engaging in user-centered design practices, and (3) adapting prior work from the Learning Sciences focused on understanding of instructor competencies. These three approaches support our understanding of how instructors engage in orchestration and where there may be a need for more support. As much of the work that uses user-centered design methods has focused on developing particular orchestration systems, we will not discuss that work in this section. However, examples of such work are referenced throughout the remainder of this chapter.

Frameworks on instructor competencies capture the same broad classes of activities that are discussed in existing frameworks on orchestration and can help to guide the role that orchestration systems can play during learning activities. Artzt and Armour-Thomas (1998) proposed a framework for instructor practice, including competencies *before*, *during*, and *after* the activity, such as instructor *monitoring* and *regulation* during an ongoing activity. Kaendler et al. (2015) extended this framework for collaborative learning, including *monitoring*, *supporting*, and *consolidating* in the classroom. The language used across these frameworks aligns with ideas presented by Prieto et al. (2011a) to describe aspects of orchestration, such as awareness, adaptation, and management. Although the frameworks mentioned above focus on synchronous classrooms, similar frameworks from informal or asynchronous learning environments could help to define orchestration needs in those contexts.

For a more practice-oriented study of orchestration, we can turn to the observations and measurement of instructors during learning activities. Observations have shown that instructor actions tend to fall into a small set of recurring routines (Prieto et al., 2011b). These routines may be planned in advance or may represent ways of adapting to what is happening in the classroom. During the learning activity, instructors tend to move around the learning space to engage with the learners and provide them with support (Holstein et al., 2019; Shahmoradi et al., 2020). These observations can be used to help guide the design of new orchestration technologies without providing any information to the system about a particular learning session.

As researchers consider how to provide real-time support for orchestration, they need a way to understand what is occurring with instructors that does not rely on observations. Through the use of wearable sensors, researchers have captured sequences of orchestration actions taken by instructors (Martinez-Maldonado et al., 2020; Prieto et al., 2016, 2018) and measured the instructors' orchestration load throughout a session (Prieto et al., 2017). Such measurements can help to identify existing instructor behaviors, routines, and challenges, to inform the design of orchestration technologies that can effectively augment or transform existing practices. These systems are supported through AI to identify the different orchestration tasks. For example, Moodoo uses positional data that is mapped onto different orchestration constructs (Martinez-Maldonado et al., 2020). Many of these systems are currently in their initial stages where they are being used to *identify orchestration* without yet being built into an orchestration system that provides support for the learning activity.

Orchestration Systems without AI

Moving from how instructors orchestrate their learning activities to providing system support for these orchestration activities, it is important to note that not all orchestration systems involve AI. Orchestration systems vary in the degrees of support they provide to instructors, but all aim to support the instructor so that they can help ensure the success of the learning activity. Soller et al. (2005) proposed that systems for collaboration support could provide support as *mirroring* tools, as *meta-cognitive* tools, or as *guiding* tools. A mirroring tool reflects information back to the user of the tool, a meta-cognitive tool provides a comparison between the current state and the desired state, and a guiding tool proposes remedial actions that can be implemented or implements them itself. These same phases of support can be applied to orchestration systems with two additions. Because instructors are the main focus of support rather than learners, the system can go beyond just guiding and can take the action for the instructor, which we will call decision making. On the other side of the spectrum, the system can provide the instructor with no additional information, but can allow for flexibility in the design, which we will call orchestrability (Tchounikine, 2013).

Orchestration systems may serve to make information visible to instructors that would otherwise have been invisible (e.g., an aggregated overview of class engagement), in turn helping instructors to make more informed decisions. These systems may provide information without necessarily changing how instructors take the orchestration actions. Martinez-Maldonado (2016) highlighted that visual learning analytics tools often aim to empower the user of the tool to make their own decisions rather than by taking actions on their behalf. For example, the Lantern project aimed to make the invisible more visible (Alavi & Dillenbourg, 2012). During collaborative group work, students could indicate their current progress through a problem set by adjusting the color of a physical beacon (Lantern), with the intensity of the color indicating how long they had been working on the problem. When needed, the students could request support by pressing the top of the lamp, causing it to blink, with it blinking faster the longer they waited. Lantern made both the progress of students and help queues clearer for the TAs in the room, allowing them to prioritize which groups they visited. The MTDashboard system similarly has a dashboard that shows the instructor each group's progress and participation without making a judgment on these indicators (Martinez-Maldonado et al., 2013). These orchestration systems do not decrease the decisions that the instructor must make. Yet, they can still help to reduce the orchestration load by making this information more readily accessible to instructors.

On the other hand, *orchestrable systems* support the instructor by helping them enact or make adjustments to classroom activities that may otherwise be challenging or impossible without technological support. These tools may embed the orchestration support directly into the learning technologies with which learners interact. For example, researchers developed Tinkerlamp to support the orchestration of logistics lessons in which students developed warehouse simulations and tested their designs (Do-Lenh et al., 2012). To support students in reflecting on their simulation run, the instructor was provided with a paper card that had a QR code that they would have to show before the students could try another simulation. These cards provided the instructor with the ability to adjust the pace at which students were working, where before they had none. Similarly, NumberNet (Mercier, 2016) supports students working in a computer-supported collaborative environment to develop patterns of mathematical expressions. To maintain control over the activity, instructors were provided with orchestration tools within the system. For example, the instructor could pause the activity to gain students' attention, which would not be possible outside of a technology-enhanced environment. Moreover, in real time, the instructor could manipulate if the students saw all or only their correct solutions, which allows the instructor to guide students' attention. These types of tools provide the instructor with more orchestration control that they would not otherwise have over an activity.

Finally, some orchestration technologies focus on supporting synergy and communication across the range of technologies being used in a given learning environment. When a learning activity involves combining or switching between the use of multiple devices or software systems, this can be challenging for an instructor to orchestrate. As with the previous orchestration system examples, in this context, an orchestration system can facilitate the use of multiple technologies to lower the instructor's orchestration load. Many of these systems focus on providing a workbench or architecture for supporting the orchestration process. Phiri et al. (2016) developed an orchestration workbench that allows the instructor to configure their workspace to have all of their relevant documents, tools, and web services in one location. In this case, the orchestration system supports one party orchestrating the use of multiple tools within a lesson. In contrast, Manathunga et al. (2015) designed an architecture that supports the integration of devices in a smart classroom by supporting the communication between these devices, such as a smartTV, smartphones, and wearables. This connection allows the instructor to both send and receive information about the activity. Similarly, GLUEPS-AR (Muñoz-Cristóbal et al., 2013) and GLUE!-PS (Prieto et al., 2014) provide orchestration architectures for across-spaces learning situations and collaborative learning environments, respectively, by integrating a range of learning design tools and learning environments. All of these orchestration systems provide the backend support that allows the instructor to more smoothly orchestrate a learning situation.

CO-ORCHESTRATION WITH AND WITHOUT AI

In any instructional scenario, some actor is responsible for developing the learning objectives and adapting learning activities so that these objectives are met. In a traditional classroom, this actor is the instructor (Dillenbourg & Jermann, 2010). In museum- or library-based learning scenarios, this role may be held by a dedicated facilitator. Conventionally, the agent holding these responsibilities is the direct "user" of an orchestration system. *Co-orchestration* refers to situations where orchestration tasks are *shared* across multiple agents, and thus orchestration systems must be explicitly designed with this task sharing in mind. Orchestration tasks might be distributed between (1) instructors and learners, (2) instructors and AI-based instructional agents, or (3) instructors, learners, and AI agents. We do not include scenarios involving only learners and AI agents in this chapter, as this would go against the lens of orchestration as discussed above. Furthermore, this task distribution may occur via *role splitting,* in which humans and AI agents each take on distinct roles within an instructional scenario, or via *role sharing,* in which humans and AI agents play analogous roles and contribute to the same orchestration tasks. In this section, we discuss instructor–learner and human–AI co-orchestration in turn, illustrating the scope and boundaries of each through examples.

Instructor–Learner Co-Orchestration

In many of the examples of orchestration systems in the last section, learners did not play an active role in the orchestration process. However, under many paradigms – such as during inquiry learning, homework sessions, and when there is support for student self-regulation –instructors share orchestration tasks with students (Sharples, 2013). During inquiry learning, learners are asked to lead their own learning processes, choosing which activities to engage with and which paths to pursue (Urhahne et al., 2010). The instructor still plays an active role in the process as they encourage learners and help to regulate their learning (Molenaar et al., 2019; Urhahne et al., 2010). Similarly, during self-regulated learning, learners are expected to be proactive by setting goals, choosing strategies (and acting on those choices), and monitoring the outcomes (Zimmerman, 2008). Where instructors are present during self-regulated learning, they may still play a role by monitoring students' self-regulation and intervening as needed. Building upon these examples, the sharing of orchestration tasks among instructors and learners can occur in at least two major ways. First, each stakeholder may be given responsibility for certain tasks in a concurrent setting. Second, tasks may be divided across time, such as what happens with homework in formal school settings (Sharples, 2013). During synchronous classroom instruction, the instructor may hold primary responsibility for the orchestration. However, when learning activities are continued at home, learners (and potentially their family members) take on more responsibility for orchestration tasks, such as time management and adapting their learning to their home environment.

One case that may come to mind when considering instructor–learner co-orchestration is when learners engage in peer-tutoring activities during a class session. In peer tutoring, one learner takes on the role of a tutor while the other is in the role of the tutee (King et al., 1998). Although the goal of this paradigm is for learners to learn through teaching, in scope of the activity; one of the learners is taking on the role of an instructor while the tutee is not sharing the orchestration load. However, if you look more broadly at the whole classroom, an instructor may continue taking other orchestration actions in parallel to keep the classroom running smoothly, making this a form of co-orchestration in which responsibility for orchestration is shared between peer tutors (who share in the orchestration of a given small-group activity) and the instructor (who maintains primary responsibility for orchestration across all activities and student groups). The lens through which we examine the activity is again of importance.

Sharing responsibility between instructors and learners may not always lower the orchestration load enough to make it manageable for either party. In fact, sharing the load with learners risks creating *greater* load for the instructor, at least in the early stages when learners are still learning how to share in the orchestration of their learning. In these cases, an orchestration system that is designed to help manage the balance of orchestration tasks between instructors and learners may be beneficial. While researchers have begun to explore this idea (e.g., Holstein et al., 2019; Molenaar et al., 2019; Prieto, 2012), the design of orchestration tools that can support such balancing in practice remains an open area for future research.

Human–AI Co-Orchestration

Unlike our previously discussed orchestration examples, AIEd systems may take on more agentive, decision-making roles, potentially working alongside human instructors. However, this does not mean that all AIEd systems are human–AI co-orchestration systems. Rather, we use this term to describe systems that are explicitly designed to facilitate the sharing of orchestration tasks between human instructors and AI agents.

When AIEd systems are used in real-world educational settings, the human instructors who actually implement these technologies in practice and facilitate their use by learners play critical roles in mediating their effectiveness (Holstein et al., 2018; Kessler et al., 2019; Nye, 2014; Olsen et al., 2020; Ritter et al., 2016; Schofield, 1994). Several technologies have been developed in recent years to support instructors in co-orchestrating AI-supported learning scenarios. One focus of the support has been on guiding instructors' attention to learners who may be most in need of human attention in the moment, during ongoing learning activities, while delegating support for other students to AI agents (Holstein et al., 2018; Martinez-Maldonado et al., 2014; Molenaar et al., 2019; VanLehn et al., 2018). For example, the *Lumilo* instructor smart glasses are used in classrooms where students work individually with AI-based tutoring systems. These glasses are designed to direct classroom instructors' attention, in real time, to situations that the AI tutor may be poorly suited to handle on its own (Holstein et al., 2018). Like *Lumilo*, the *FACT* orchestration system (VanLehn et al., 2018, 2019, 2021) presents classroom instructors with real-time alerts, recommending which students to help, and what to help them with. In addition, *FACT* supports instructors in formulating and enacting instructional responses (e.g., by auto-suggesting prompts that the instructor can broadcast to a particular group of students or to the entire class).

As illustrated through the above examples, human–AI co-orchestration systems can support task sharing between AI systems and human instructors through the adaptive delegation of *instructional support* across different students or student groups. AI systems can also help with more *management-oriented* tasks. For instance, the *SAIL Smart Space (S3)* automates decisions about student grouping, student movement throughout the classroom space, and distribution of learning materials throughout the course of collaborative class activities (Tissenbaum & Slotta, 2019). This support allows instructors to spend more of their time working one-on-one with students. Similar to *FACT* and *Lumilo*, *S3* also supports instructor focus by automatically alerting them to key opportunities for human intervention, which the instructors themselves define before class. As another example, FROG supports complex learning scenarios where students may be grouped based on previous activities, and supported in taking different paths through the activity (Håklev et al., 2019). These instructional support activities would be too time consuming for an instructor to engage in during an activity to make it feasible. With the support of FROG, the decisions can be made quickly to prevent delays in the activity.

AI systems can also support the *transitioning* of learners between activities. Work by Olsen et al. (2020) explores how an AI system and a human instructor may co-orchestrate how learners transition across learning activities. They found that carefully designed co-orchestration support for transitions was critical, so that instructors would not be overwhelmed as they simultaneously focused on providing direct instructional support. This orchestration support allows for more elasticity in the timing between activities, which Manathunga and Hernández-Leo (2019) have shown is beneficial when changing social dynamics. In these systems, although roles are distributed between instructors and AI systems in AI–instructor co-orchestration, instructors still maintain an elevated position above AI systems (Olsen et al., 2020). That is, human instructors still need to have some degree of accountability and control. This can be seen across the system design examples overviewed above, where the AI either provides suggestions to the instructor while the instructor makes the final decisions, or where the scope within which the AI works is defined by the instructor beforehand, as with the *S3* system.

An emerging vision for co-orchestration systems combines the two broad categories discussed above (*instructor–AI* and *instructor–learner* co-orchestration): supporting sharing of orchestration tasks between instructors, learners, and AI agents (Holstein et al., 2019; Molenaar et al., 2019; Prieto, 2012). In *instructor–learner–AI* co-orchestration, a challenge for technology design is to dynamically balance management and regulation tasks between all three of these groups. For example, Molenaar et al. (2019) propose a system for use in technology-enhanced classrooms that dynamically assigns students into different groups based on their current needs for support. For instance, based on students' interaction data within adaptive learning software, at a given point in time they might be recommended for *instructor* regulation, for *instructor–AI* regulation, or for *self*-regulation of learning. In this proposed approach, the goal is ultimately to help students transition to self-regulated learning, but to adaptively provide the level of support they need along the path toward taking greater responsibility of their own learning. In the next section, we briefly discuss future directions within this emerging design space for co-orchestration systems.

DISCUSSION AND FUTURE DIRECTIONS

The design of technologies to support human–AI co-orchestration is a rapidly emerging area of interest in AIEd. As this area grows, it is our hope that the AIEd community uses the lens of co-orchestration to meaningfully expand the kinds of research and design work it conducts, rather than simply assimilating orchestration concepts into the kinds of work the community has already been doing. For instance, the role of human instructors should be emphasized in future work on orchestration in AIEd, and *accountability* and *control* should remain focal aspects of this work. Although we might imagine AI-based systems that automate larger and larger sets of orchestration tasks, through a co-orchestration lens we might ask questions such as: "How *should* tasks be distributed among human instructors, AI agents and learners, in given learning contexts and scenarios?", "Who should ultimately be accountable for particular instructional decisions and design choices?". In addition, the lens of co-orchestration opens up new possibilities for existing areas of AIEd research. For example, moving beyond individual student modeling or even modeling of collaborating groups of students (Olsen et al., 2015), this (relatively) macro-scale lens suggests opportunities to design *class-level models* that capture relevant aspects of a learning environment and the learners and instructors within it. Relatedly, this lens suggests opportunities to explore the design space of *decision policies* for AIEd systems that operate upon such class-level models. Such AIEd systems would make decisions not only based on the modeled learning states of a single learner or group of learners, but instead based on a broader awareness of the learning situation and of the human instructor(s) with whom the system shares control (Holstein et al., 2020).

As research in this area evolves, it will be valuable to move towards a synthesized understanding of relevant design considerations and principles for co-orchestration systems across different learning contexts and learner/instructor characteristics – for example, to understand how co-orchestration systems can best be designed to support instructors with different levels of experience and expertise, or to understand how the distribution of orchestration tasks across instructors, learners, and AI systems should shift based on learner age groups, self-regulated learning skills, or cultural contexts. This kind of synthesis may be accomplished by systematically examining similarities or differences in empirical findings and technology designs across various contexts where co-orchestration systems are designed and tested.

As the research on orchestration moves towards joint human and AI control, it is important to consider how to balance orchestration tasks across the instructors, learners, and AI. Although some initial work has been done in this area (Molenaar et al., 2019), more work is needed to understand how the learning environment impacts these learning supports. As we have mentioned in terms of the design principles, traits of the instructors and learners can influence the balance. For instance, we typically would not expect younger learners to take on as much responsibility as older learners and this may also impact the degree to which orchestration tasks can or should be shared with an AI-based orchestration system. Equally important are the learning objectives that are being targeted. In addition to the domain knowledge being taught, other skills may be targeted, such as self-regulation, learner independence, or group work skills. Some of these skills may overlap with orchestration tasks and can influence the role of each stakeholder. Further research is needed to understand how to balance the orchestration roles under these different conditions.

Finally, as the orchestration research field matures, it is important to develop standards for evaluation. Often the focus of AIEd research has been on improved learning. Although this is an important aspect of orchestration research, is it the only metric that matters? Going back to the lens of orchestration, we are not just focused on the learner but also the instructor. This focus on the instructor should also influence the focus of how we evaluate a successful orchestration system. Some systems are designed not because they will improve the learning of the learners but because they will lower the entry costs for an instructor to engage in that type of activity and to feel more comfortable using it in the classroom. In these cases, conducting a study comparing the learning with the orchestration system to the same activity without may not be a fair comparison. The orchestration system may not have a noticeable impact on the learners. Rather, without the study and support of the researcher, the instructors may not have engaged in the activity. The evaluation then needs to focus at the instructor level. This evaluation may include the time spent on the orchestration activities, a change in the types of activities performed, or qualitative assessments of the system by the instructor. However, focusing on the instructor brings up issues with sample size. It can be difficult to find enough instructors to work with the system to have statistical significance. One solution is to work with student instructors (van Leeuwen et al., 2019), but they may have fundamentally different experiences than established instructors. It is then a discussion for the community as to what a robust evaluation of an orchestration system may entail and what standards should be met.

CONCLUSION

Orchestration provides an additional lens to AIEd researchers, widening the focus beyond learner–technology interactions to consider interactions across the broader learning environment. As the AIEd community increasingly adopts an orchestration lens to inform research and design, we are hopeful that this lens will serve to fundamentally challenge and expand the kinds of work the AIEd community conducts and that work on human–AI co-orchestration will remain in dialog with the broader literature on orchestration technologies.

REFERENCES

Alavi, H. S., & Dillenbourg, P. (2012). An ambient awareness tool for supporting supervised collaborative problem solving. *IEEE Transactions on Learning Technologies*, 5(3), 264–274.

Artzt, A. F., & Armour-Thomas, E. (1998). Mathematics teaching as problem solving: A framework for studying teacher metacognition underlying instructional practice in mathematics. *Instructional Science*, 26(1–2), 5–25.

Baker, R. S. (2016). Stupid tutoring systems, intelligent humans. *International Journal of Artificial Intelligence in Education*, 26(2), 600–614.

Dillenbourg, P. (2013). Design for classroom orchestration. *Computers & Education*, 69, 485–492.

Dillenbourg, P., & Jermann, P. (2010). Technology for classroom orchestration. In *New Science of Learning* (pp. 525–552). Springer, New York, NY.

Dillenbourg, P., Zufferey, G., Alavi, H., Jermann, P., Do-Lenh, S., Bonnard, Q., Cuendet, S., & Kaplan, F. (2011). Classroom orchestration: The third circle of usability. In *Proceedings of the International Conference on Computer-Supported Collaborative Learning* (pp. 510–517). ISLS.

Do-Lenh, S., Jermann, P., Legge, A., Zufferey, G., & Dillenbourg, P. (2012). TinkerLamp 2.0: Designing and evaluating orchestration technologies for the classroom. In *European Conference on Technology Enhanced Learning* (pp. 65–78). Springer, Berlin, Heidelberg.

Faucon, L., Olsen, J. K., Haklev, S., & Dillenbourg, P. (2020). Real-time prediction of students' activity progress and completion rates. *Journal of Learning Analytics*, 7(2), 18–44.

Håklev, S., Faucon, L., Olsen, J., & Dillenbourg, P. (2019). FROG, a tool to author and run orchestration graphs: Affordances and tensions. In K. Lund, G. P. Niccolai, E. Lavoué, C. Hmelo-Silver, G. Gweon, & M. Baker (Eds.), *A Wide Lens: Combining Embodied, Enactive, Extended, and Embedded Learning in Collaborative Settings, 13th International Conference on Computer Supported Collaborative Learning (CSCL) 2019* (Vol. 2, pp. 1013–1016). Lyon, France: International Society of the Learning Sciences.

Heffernan, N. T., & Heffernan, C. L. (2014). The ASSISTments ecosystem: Building a platform that brings scientists and teachers together for minimally invasive research on human learning and teaching. *International Journal of Artificial Intelligence in Education*, 24(4), 470–497.

Holstein, K., Aleven, V., & Rummel, N. (2020). A conceptual framework for human–AI hybrid adaptivity in education. In *International Conference on Artificial Intelligence in Education* (pp. 240–254). Springer, Cham.

Holstein, K., McLaren, B. M., & Aleven, V. (2018). Student learning benefits of a mixed-reality teacher awareness tool in AI-enhanced classrooms. In *International Conference on Artificial Intelligence in Education* (pp. 154–168). Springer, Cham.

Holstein, K., McLaren, B. M., & Aleven, V. (2019). Co-designing a real-time classroom orchestration tool to support teacher–AI complementarity. *Journal of Learning Analytics*, 6(2), 27–52.

International Artificial Intelligence in Education Society (2020). *About*. https://iaied.org/about

Kaendler, C., Wiedmann, M., Rummel, N., & Spada, H. (2015). Teacher competencies for the implementation of collaborative learning in the classroom: A framework and research review. *Educational Psychology Review*, 27(3), 505–536.

Kessler, A., Boston, M., & Stein, M. K. (2019). Exploring how teachers support students' mathematical learning in computer-directed learning environments. *Information and Learning Sciences*, 121(1/2), 52–78.

King, A., Staffieri, A., & Adelgais, A. (1998). Mutual peer tutoring: Effects of structuring tutorial interaction to scaffold peer learning. *Journal of Educational Psychology*, 90, 134–152.

Kollar, I., & Fischer, F. (2013). Orchestration is nothing without conducting–But arranging ties the two together!: A response to Dillenbourg (2011). *Computers & Education*, 69, 507–509.

Lawrence, L., & Mercier, E. (2019). A review of the evolving definition of orchestration: Implications for research and design. In *Proceedings of the International Conference on Computer-Supported Collaborative Learning* (pp. 829–830). ISLS.

Manathunga, K., & Hernández-Leo, D. (2019). Flexible CSCL orchestration technology: Mechanisms for elasticity and dynamism in pyramid script flows. In *Proceedings of the International Conference on Computer-Supported Collaborative Learning* (pp. 248–255). ISLS.

Manathunga, K., Hernández-Leo, D., Caicedo, J., Ibarra, J. J., Martinez-Pabon, F., & Ramirez-Gonzalez, G. (2015). Collaborative learning orchestration using smart displays and personal devices. In *Design for Teaching and Learning in a Networked World* (pp. 596–600). Springer, Cham.

Martinez-Maldonado, R. (2016). Seeing learning analytics tools as orchestration technologies: Towards supporting learning activities across physical and digital spaces. In *Companion Proceedings of the International Learning Analytics and Knowledge Conference*.

Martinez-Maldonado, R., Clayphan, A., Yacef, K., & Kay, J. (2014). MTFeedback: Providing notifications to enhance teacher awareness of small group work in the classroom. *IEEE Transactions on Learning Technologies*, 8(2), 187–200.

Martinez-Maldonado, R., Echeverria, V., Schulte, J., Shibani, A., Mangaroska, K., & Shum, S. B. (2020). Moodoo: Indoor positioning analytics for characterising classroom teaching. In *The Proceedings of the International Conference on Artificial Intelligence in Education* (pp. 360–373). Springer, Cham.

Martinez-Maldonado, R., Kay, J., Yacef, K., Edbauer, M. T., & Dimitriadis, Y. (2013). MTClassroom and MTDashboard: Supporting analysis of teacher attention in an orchestrated multi-tabletop classroom. In *Proceedings of the International Conference on Computer-Supported Collaborative Learning*, (pp. 320–327). ISLS.

Mavrikis, M., Geraniou, E., Gutierrez Santos, S., & Poulovassilis, A. (2019). Intelligent analysis and data visualisation for teacher assistance tools: The case of exploratory learning. *British Journal of Educational Technology*, 50(6), 2920–2942.

Mercier, E. (2016). Teacher orchestration and student learning during mathematics activities in a smart classroom. *International Journal of Smart Technology and Learning*, 1(1), 33–52.

Molenaar, I., Horvers, A., & Baker, R. S. (2019). Towards hybrid human-system regulation: Understanding children's SRL support needs in blended classrooms. In *Proceedings of the International Conference on Learning Analytics & Knowledge* (pp. 471–480).

Muñoz-Cristóbal, J. A., Prieto, L. P., Asensio-Pérez, J. I., Jorrín-Abellán, I. M., Martínez-Monés, A., & Dimitriadis, Y. (2013). GLUEPS-AR: A system for the orchestration of learning situations across spaces using augmented reality. In *Proceedings of the European Conference on Technology Enhanced Learning* (pp. 565–568). Springer, Berlin, Heidelberg.

Nye, B. D. (2014). Barriers to ITS adoption: A systematic mapping study. In *International Conference on Intelligent Tutoring Systems* (pp. 583–590). Springer, Cham.

Olsen, J. K., Aleven, V., & Rummel, N. (2015). Predicting student performance in a collaborative learning environment. In *Proceedings of the Conference on Educational Data Mining*. International Educational Data Mining Society.

Olsen, J. K., Rummel, N., & Aleven, V. (2020). Designing for the co-orchestration of social transitions between individual, small-group and whole-class learning in the classroom. *International Journal of Artificial Intelligence in Education*, 31, 24–56.

Phiri, L., Meinel, C., & Suleman, H. (2016). Streamlined orchestration: An orchestration workbench framework for effective teaching. *Computers & Education*, 95, 231–238.

Prieto, L. P. (2012). Supporting orchestration of blended CSCL scenarios in distributed learning environments. *Unpublished Doctoral Thesis*.

Prieto, L. P., Asensio-Pérez, J. I., Muñoz-Cristóbal, J. A., Jorrín-Abellán, I. M., Dimitriadis, Y., & Gómez-Sánchez, E. (2014). Supporting orchestration of CSCL scenarios in web-based distributed learning environments. *Computers & Education*, 73, 9–25.

Prieto, L. P., Holenko Dlab, M., Gutiérrez, I., Abdulwahed, M., & Balid, W. (2011a). Orchestrating technology enhanced learning: A literature review and a conceptual framework. *International Journal of Technology Enhanced Learning*, 3(6), 583–598.

Prieto, L. P., Sharma, K., Dillenbourg, P., & Rodríguez-Triana, M. (2016). Teaching analytics: Towards automatic extraction of orchestration graphs using wearable sensors. In *Proceedings of the Sixth International Conference on Learning Analytics & Knowledge* (pp. 148–157).

Prieto, L. P., Sharma, K., Kidzinski, Ł., & Dillenbourg, P. (2017). Orchestration load indicators and patterns: In-the-wild studies using mobile eye-tracking. *IEEE Transactions on Learning Technologies*, 11(2), 216–229.

Prieto, L. P., Sharma, K., Kidzinski, Ł., Rodríguez-Triana, M. J., & Dillenbourg, P. (2018). Multimodal teaching analytics: Automated extraction of orchestration graphs from wearable sensor data. *Journal of Computer Assisted Learning*, 34(2), 193–203.

Prieto, L. P., Villagrá-Sobrino, S., Jorrín-Abellán, I. M., Martínez-Monés, A., & Dimitriadis, Y. (2011b). Recurrent routines: Analyzing and supporting orchestration in technology-enhanced primary classrooms. *Computers & Education, 57*(1), 1214–1227.

Ritter, S., Yudelson, M., Fancsali, S. E., & Berman, S. R. (2016). How mastery learning works at scale. In *Proceedings of the Third (2016) ACM Conference on Learning@ Scale* (pp. 71–79). ACM.

Schofield, J. W., Eurich-Fulcer, R., & Britt, C. L. (1994). Teachers, computer tutors, and teaching: The artificially intelligent tutor as an agent for classroom change. *American Educational Research Journal, 31*(3), 579–607.

Shahmoradi, S., Kothiyal, A., Olsen, J. K., Bruno, B., & Dillenbourg, P. (2020). What teachers need for orchestrating robotic classrooms. In *The Proceedings of the European Conference on Technology Enhanced Learning* (pp. 87–101). Springer, Cham.

Sharples, M. (2013). Shared orchestration within and beyond the classroom. *Computers & Education, 69*, 504–506.

Soller, A., Martínez, A., Jermann, P., & Muehlenbrock, M. (2005). From mirroring to guiding: A review of state of the art technology for supporting collaborative learning. *International Journal of Artificial Intelligence in Education, 15*(4), 261–290.

Tchounikine, P. (2013). Clarifying design for orchestration: Orchestration and orchestrable technology, scripting and conducting. *Computers & Education, 69*, 500–503.

Tissenbaum, M., Matuk, C., Berland, M., Lyons, L., Cocco, F., Linn, M., Plass, J. L., Hajny, N., Olsen, A., Schwendimann, B., Boroujeni, M. S., Slotta, J. D., Vitale, J., Gerard, L., & Dillenbourg, P. (2016). Real-time visualization of student activities to support classroom orchestration. In *Proceedings of the 2016 International Conference of the Learning Sciences (ICLS)*. International Society of the Learning Sciences, Singapore.

Tissenbaum, M., & Slotta, J. (2019). Supporting classroom orchestration with real-time feedback: A role for teacher dashboards and real-time agents. *International Journal of Computer-Supported Collaborative Learning, 14*(3), 325–351.

Urhahne, D., Schanze, S., Bell, T., Mansfield, A., & Holmes, J. (2010). Role of the teacher in computer-supported collaborative inquiry learning. *International Journal of Science Education, 32*(2), 221–243.

van Leeuwen, A., Rummel, N., & van Gog, T. (2019). What information should CSCL teacher dashboards provide to help teachers interpret CSCL situations? *International Journal of Computer-Supported Collaborative Learning, 14*(3), 261–289.

VanLehn, K., Burkhardt, H., Cheema, S., Kang, S., Pead, D., Schoenfeld, A., & Wetzel, J. (2018). The effect of digital versus traditional orchestration on collaboration in small groups. In *International Conference on Artificial Intelligence in Education* (pp. 369–373). Springer, Cham.

VanLehn, K., Burkhardt, H., Cheema, S., Kang, S., Pead, D., Schoenfeld, A. H., & Wetzel, J. (2021). Can an orchestration system increase collaborative, productive struggle in teaching-by-eliciting classrooms? *Interactive Learning Environments, 29*(6), 987–1005. DOI: 10.1080/10494820.2019.1616567.

VanLehn, K., Cheema, S., Kang, S., & Wetzel, J. (2019). Auto-sending messages in an intelligent orchestration system: A pilot study. In *International Conference on Artificial Intelligence in Education* (pp. 292–297). Springer, Cham.

Zhang, H., Easterday, M. W., Gerber, E. M., Rees Lewis, D., & Maliakal, L. (2017, February). Agile research studios: Orchestrating communities of practice to advance research training. In *Proceedings of the 2017 ACM Conference on Computer Supported Cooperative Work and Social Computing* (pp. 220–232).

Zimmerman, B. J. (2008). Investigating self-regulation and motivation: Historical background, methodological developments, and future prospects. *American Educational Research Journal, 45*(1), 166–183.

15. Using learning analytics to support teachers

Stanislav Pozdniakov, Roberto Martinez-Maldonado,
Shaveen Singh, Hassan Khosravi and Dragan Gašević

INTRODUCTION

Learning analytics is a relatively new field of research and practice which aims at creating methods and technical infrastructure for the effective collection and analysis of educational data (Lang et al., 2017). However, a distinctive characteristic of this field is that it is aimed at making available curated representations of educational data to various stakeholders (e.g., teachers, students, learning designers, and educational decision makers) for them to gain a deeper understanding of teaching and learning processes, and to take actions accordingly for the purpose of improvement (Knight & Shum, 2017). For example, common applications of learning analytics include reporting the state of learning processes to different educational stakeholders; predicting future student learning performance and retention rates for educators and decision makers to investigate and address potential factors affecting academic achievement; developing infrastructures aimed at facilitating a continuous and automated/ semi-automated feedback loop to support learners; and providing ethical and policy-related recommendations for the sustained implementation of learning analytics initiatives at institutional or regional levels (Gašević et al., 2017). It thus becomes evident that there has been a strong interest in creating analytics systems that provide some sort of user interface for educational stakeholders, who are not necessarily trained in data analysis, to make sense of teaching and learning processes based on curated representations of educational data. This chapter focuses on those learning analytics systems explicitly designed with the purpose of supporting teachers' sensemaking of students' data. We deliberately use the term "learning analytics" instead of "AIED systems" because, to the best of our knowledge, the problem highlighted in this chapter is becoming more prominent in Learning Analytics but discussed less in the AIED community. Learning analytics is a sub-discipline of AIED (see Chapter 2 by McCalla) and learning analytics systems might be AIED systems to the extent to which they use AI.

Teacher-facing learning analytics can enable educators to scrutinise and interact with curated representations of student data with various educational purposes such as identifying students who may need closer attention (Martinez-Maldonado, 2019); providing personalised feedback (Pardo et al., 2018); and assessing the effectiveness of their interventions (Sergis & Sampson, 2017) and learning designs (Mangaroska & Giannakos, 2019) or orchestrating classrooms (see Chapter 14 by Holsten et al.). An original assumption within the learning analytics community was that teachers would come up with interesting questions about their teaching and their students' learning and that a *dashboard* would help them respond to those questions (Li et al., 2021). Indeed, the metaphor of a dashboard is intuitive, since they are commonly used to simplify the assessment of a complex system – at a glance – by providing simple indicators using numbers or visuals (e.g., as in the case of car dashboards).

Recent literature reviews (Bodily & Verbert, 2017; Jivet et al., 2018; Matcha et al., 2020) have questioned the effectiveness of learning analytics dashboards. As a response, some authors are starting to emphasise the need for better understanding of how teachers can effectively interpret results from analytics in order to make sense of students' data (van Leeuwen et al., 2019; Friend Wise & Jung, 2019). Then, the insights gained from teachers' reflection also need to translate into actual actions (Molenaar & Knoop-van Campen, 2019) or improvements to learning design (Ali et al., 2012; Bakharia et al., 2016). In sum, with the increasing complexity of data captured across educational platforms and learning spaces, a more careful consideration of how different types of learning analytics can support sensemaking and pedagogical response should be taken.

This chapter provides an overview of learning analytics systems particularly crafted to support teaching practices. We discuss a number of contemporary teacher-facing learning analytics systems according to the types of analytics they rely upon (i.e., descriptive, predictive and prescriptive analytics). These systems have a visual end-user interface, which allows teachers to interact with them. Such interfaces commonly take the form of either individual visualisations and tables or dashboards consisting of multiple charts and tables. Interfaces allow users to engage with the data and results of analysis performed by the learning analytics systems (for instance, via using filters to limit the analytics results only to a narrow cohort of students). We also introduce a theoretical model that illustrates the sensemaking processes that teachers can ideally engage in while interacting with such learning analytics systems. We next present an in-depth analysis of three illustrative cases of teacher-facing analytics in three distinctive contexts: (i) synchronous online student meetings; (ii) students engaged with learning materials; and (iii) students enrolled in technology-enhanced courses. The chapter concludes with a discussion of potential trends and future challenges in the design of effective learning analytics systems to support teachers.

OVERVIEW OF LEARNING ANALYTICS FOR TEACHERS

This section is divided into two subsections. The first subsection discusses examples of learning analytics systems aimed at supporting teachers according to an existing typology of analytics. The second subsection describes a framework that can serve to explain how teachers commonly make sense of and respond to learning analytics.

Typology

Authors in multiple areas of study have classified analytics systems into three broad categories: descriptive (or diagnostic), predictive or prescriptive (Koh & Tan, 2017; Jørnø & Gynther, 2018). This typology is relevant to learning analytics because it emphasises the kinds of insights that users (e.g., teachers) can gain and the actions that can be performed in consequence. For example, *descriptive* analytics aims at depicting past activity for a user to analyse and act on the evidence made available. By contrast, predictive analytics aims to show what is about to happen given a time frame (forward-looking) for the user to decide on what actions to take. Finally, prescriptive analytics provides recommendations to the user about the kinds of actions that can be performed in order to account for an event that is to happen with a given probability. While some learning analytics systems might simultaneously endorse multiple types of analytics, the next subsections present examples of learning analytics systems that can serve to more clearly illustrate each category in this typology.

Descriptive and diagnostic learning analytics

Descriptive learning analytics (also referred to as comparative analytics) commonly aims to provide an overview of student activity. Learning analytics systems commonly make use of data visualisation techniques and descriptive statistics. Diagnostic learning analytics systems aim at informing teachers (and potentially students) about the underlying reasons for the past and present observed student behaviours. These learning analytics may use both unsupervised and supervised machine learning algorithms, for instance, to group students based on their previous use of learning resources; to infer the emotional state of the learners given the presence of technical devices, like web cameras; and to signal the performance of groups or individual learners with the inferential description of which factors contributed to that level of performance.

One classic example of a learning analytics descriptive system is LOCO-Analyst (Jovanovic et al., 2008). This system uses descriptive statistics for teachers and educational designers, indicating the state of each learning task by aggregating students' performance (e.g., average scores and number of incorrect answers). LOCO-Analyst also provides descriptive analytics depicting to what extent an individual student's performance is deviating from the class average. In addition, LOCO-Analyst enables teachers to see what concerns students might have for a particular learning task (via exploring chat logs). This can additionally help teachers identify potentially problematic tasks that can be re-designed.

Another important mention relates to intelligent tutoring systems designed and built in the ASSISTment project (Heffernan & Heffernan, 2014). Those systems usually have capabilities as both authoring tools (assisting teachers with creation of learning materials) and descriptive learning analytics (see Chapter 12 by Blessing et al.). Those systems use learning analytics in order to aid teachers to automatically assign new learning activities for students who have not successfully completed a particular learning module.

Loop is another descriptive learning analytics system that supports teachers by providing an explicit connection between students' data, learning outcomes and pedagogical aims (Corrin et al., 2015; Bakharia et al., 2016). The capabilities of this tool are focused on presenting the temporal distribution of relevant metrics about student activity (e.g., average session time and the proportion of students who accessed each week's discussion) throughout the course time. The tool enables teachers to filter such metrics according to a set time range and granularity of aggregation (e.g., 1 day, 1 week, etc.).

The previous two examples of descriptive analytics focus on generating summaries of activity fully mediated by digital learning settings. In contrast, *Lumilo* is a descriptive learning analytics tool supporting teachers in physical classrooms (Holstein et al., 2018). *Lumilo* presents real-time indicators of the overall state of students (e.g., who is struggling, who is doing well, who is idle or facing issues) and of the classroom (by flagging exercises for which the number of failed attempts is high), while each student interacts with an intelligent tutoring system using a personal computer. This learning analytics tool supports teachers by describing the most common issues students are facing and visualises this information via a teacher's augmented-reality wearable device.

The Affective class report card is another example of a descriptive learning analytics system (Gupta et al., 2021). In addition to providing information about students' performance, it also provides information about students' affective states. This learning analytics system provides detailed information about the students' performance in the context of mathematical problem solving, for instance, the number of correct responses, how much effort each student dedicated to each task, and the number of total attempts. Yet, the system also automatically recognises the facial expressions of students, allowing for both real-time and historic reports of students' activities for teachers. These data are presented as a dashboard, where cards represent individual students. Each card includes information about the individual effort, last learning activity performed and their corresponding performance and emotional state.

Some learning analytics systems go beyond describing students' past activity by providing a diagnosis of such activity. Van Leeuwen et al. (2019) introduced a teacher-dashboard, with diagnostic capabilities, in order to support online mathematics. The system identifies groups of students which may be experiencing challenges and provides historical information about successful and unsuccessful attempts while solving the task. Analytics in this dashboard incorporates activity indicators for each group, alerts and textual description of the problem a group is experiencing. The activity indicators are given for each group (e.g., number of attempts made or the intensity of verbal activity) and are presented as line and bar charts. Alerts indicate which group is experiencing a problem. The system also presents a textual diagnosis of the issue a group is facing, such as whether the problem is task related or collaboration related.

The MTDashboard (Martinez-Maldonado, 2019) is another example of a diagnostic learning analytics tool aimed at assisting teachers in physical classrooms while students work together using interactive tabletops. This dashboard indicates how similar each group's concept map is to the one predefined by a teacher. This demonstrates the cognitive progress of the group. The tool also generates automated notifications in the form of text narratives that a detector of potential students' misconceptions automatically generates. This algorithm regularly diagnoses student solutions by comparing them to a list of common misconceptions set by the teacher and the teacher's ideal solution. The notifications are sent to the dashboard for the teacher to react if any group is falling behind schedule or experiencing misunderstanding while working on a task.

In sum, both descriptive and diagnostic learning analytics systems make use of varied statistical techniques to extract distilled indicators of past and current student activity while ensuring the agency of teachers in making informed decisions according to their experience and pedagogical intentions. In the next section, we describe learning analytics systems that support teachers by predicting potential activity and learning outcomes of students in the future.

Predictive learning analytics

Predictive learning analytics aims at informing teachers whether the students' behaviour observed in the past can be used to predict any change in behaviour or learning outcomes in a specific time frame in the future. These analytics commonly rely on predictive machine-learning algorithms and provide additional information indicating what factors contribute to a prediction. For instance, predictive learning analytics systems might show what indicators are associated with high or low student engagement or whether a student might be at risk of dropout. It is important to note that some of the machine-learning techniques used in predictive learning analytics might also be used in descriptive or diagnostic systems. For instance, deep learning models might be used in order to recognise the current emotional state of the learner and signal this information to the teacher (descriptive or diagnostic learning analytics), while predicting the future emotional state of the learner. The key difference is that in predictive learning analytics, the outputs of the algorithms are used in order to infer the future state of affairs given the current data instead of classifying previous data points. The common examples of such learning analytics systems include early warning systems, which present information about which students are about to drop out of university or might not pass a unit of study.

One classic example of early warning systems is Course Signals developed at Purdue University (Arnold & Pistilli, 2012). Based on the historic data of previous academic achievements and students' interactions in the Learning Management System, an algorithm predicts students' risk of dropout. The system has a very basic interface, which shows teachers whether a student is at no risk, moderate risk or high risk, using a traffic light colour metaphor. Yet, this system was limited to only flagging at-risk students with no detailed indication of the reasons why students struggled (Tanes et al., 2011). Informed by those predictions, teachers have to plan the intervention strategies by themselves, which might include sending personalised messages or arranging consultations with students.

One of the recent attempts to equip teachers with predictive learning analytics was accomplished through the OUA (Open University Analyse) system (Herodotou et al., 2019). OUA relies on a set of classification algorithms which use both students' demographic and activity data. In contrast to the Course Signals, the current system provides predictions at two more granular levels: whether a student will submit the next assignment and whether the student will pass a course. The system presents a summary of students who are not going to submit an assignment, providing details about previous submissions and the confidence of such predictions. The system also visualises how similar the current student is to other students in terms of demographic and behavioural data. Additionally, it incorporates textual justification for the current prediction in a form of comprehensible rules (for instance, "forum activity > 7" and "online activity is high", "the student will pass").

In sum, predictive learning analytics systems commonly present the outcomes or one or more predictions and, in many cases, the systems also provide the evidence used with the aim of explaining the rationale and enable teachers to make an informed decision.

Prescriptive learning analytics

Prescriptive learning analytics systems commonly present a description of the state of a phenomenon in the past (descriptive learning analytic) or a prediction for the future state (predictive learning analytic) and complements this with a recommendation about general or specific actions that a teacher can perform in order to avoid or change the state of the phenomenon for a given cohort of students or individual students. Prescriptions might be designed manually or provided by rule-based algorithms or heuristics.

Recommender systems used in education can be considered as classic examples of prescriptive analytics (Deschênes, 2020). Yet, not many systems provide direct explanations to teachers on what strategies they may consider based on the analysis of students' data. We can identify only one learning analytics system that falls into this category: the Process Tab (Herder et al., 2018). The Process Tab is designed to be used in the context of internships taken in a virtual learning environment where learners can work on complex tasks emulating a real process (e.g., developing a plan, communicating with stakeholders and writing the final proposal). The Process Tab consists of a teacher's dashboard that includes several views: individual students' networks, advised interventions, high-level overview of students' progress and chat. This system relies on epistemic network diagrams of concepts derived from artifacts produced by students. The tool incorporates a predictive model that learns about students' progression based on students' online chat data. Prescriptive capabilities include direct recommendations to teachers about which student should be scaffolded ("Student A" or "Student B"), the problem description ("a student is discussing stakeholder issues"), and recommendation for the teacher to suggest to help a student (e.g., "focus on fact A because it is important for developing your skills and you have not discussed it yet".) (Herder et al., 2018). Some recent work focused on creating recommender systems for teachers in MOOCs seems to be setting the basis to prescribe to the teacher potential actions based on students' data (Sebbaq et al., 2020).

In sum, prescriptive learning analytics systems enrich the diagnosis of the problem a student or a group of students face with a recommended action a teacher might take to help students' progress with the task.

Teachers' Sensemaking and Pedagogical Actions

Since teachers interact with learning analytics systems via visual interfaces, this subsection discusses how the interfaces of learning analytics systems support teachers. Specifically, we describe what role learning analytics systems can have in supporting teachers' sensemaking, decision making and action. The close inspection of these processes is important in order to overcome limitations of learning analytics systems already reported in the literature (Bodily & Verbert, 2017; Jivet et al., 2018; Matcha et al., 2020).

There is a conceptual difference between descriptive analytics (pointing at what is happening "now") and predictive (pointing at what is about to happen) as described in the previous section. Boland (2008) distinguishes between making sense of past enactments (*sensemaking*) and calculating possible outcomes about the future (*decision making*). In the rest of this section, we provide a consolidated conceptual model of teachers' sensemaking and decision-making processes of learning analytics use, taking into consideration previous models in learning analytics (i.e., Verbert et al., 2013; Wise & Jung, 2019).

The user interface of a learning analytics system can scaffold the sensemaking and decision-making processes of the teacher to different extents. In a learning analytics context, sensemaking is concerned with making past or present learners' activities meaningful to teachers (Boland, 2008) (see Figure 15.1, A). Different authors state that successful interactions

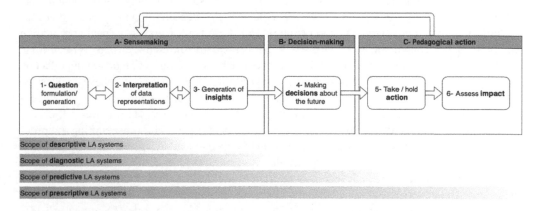

Source: Inspired by Wise & Jung (2019) model

Figure 15.1   *Teachers' sensemaking and decision-making processes of learning analytics use. There is no hierarchy among the types of learning analytics*

between a teacher and a learning analytics system are those motivated by one or more specific educational questions (see Figure 15.1, A1) (Verbert et al., 2013; Sergis & Sampson, 2017; Wise & Jung, 2019). These questions can emerge out of teachers' curiosity (Wise & Jung, 2019) (e.g., how are international students progressing?), based on the pedagogical intentions made explicit in the learning design (Echeverria et al., 2018) (e.g., which students are struggling with Task X, section Y?), or even prompted by the system (Shabaninejad et al., 2020a) (e.g., identifying students' cohorts which deviate from the class average or demonstrating at-risk learning behaviour).

Once teachers know what questions need to or can be addressed (see Figure 15.1, A1), teachers need to "see" previous student activity and make sense of it (Wise & Jung, 2019). However, for this process to occur, the evidence of students' activity needs to be represented in some way. This could be, for example, through a dashboard, information visualisations, a more elaborated data exploration user interface, a report or a text-based notification system. In any case, teachers need to *interpret* such curated information in order to make sense of student activity or algorithmic predictions (see Figure 15.1, A2). This *interpretation* process of the data representations is not a trivial issue. In fact, some authors in the learning analytics literature have suggested that this requires a degree of data literacy or training (Ndukwe & Daniel, 2020), whilst others advocate for designing learning analytics tools that support such interpretation processes (Echeverria et al., 2018). In both cases, the interpretation process involves a great extent of subjectivity (Weick et al., 2005), as teachers give meaning to the data representations put in front of them based on their own mental frameworks. If teachers cannot interpret the data, then it would be impossible for them to make sense of student activity and therefore to use the learning analytics systems to support pedagogical actions.

If the teacher can successfully interpret the results shown in a learning analytics system and make sense of the past or present student activity, ideally, the last step in teachers' sensemaking is gaining insights (Figure 15.1, A3). This would mean that the teacher can effectively get answers to their initial questions. Then, the teacher would need to decide what to do. This process corresponds to decision making (Figure 15.1, B). The process of decision making is concerned with assessing alternative courses of action and making a choice among them (Boland, 2008). The area of consideration in this process is not past student activity but the actions that can be taken in the future. From a teacher's perspective, this decision-making process precedes and culminates in a pedagogical action (Figure 15.1, C). These actions can include providing scaffolding to individual students, to the whole class or revising the course design (Wise & Jung, 2019). Teachers can also decide to gather more evidence before taking action or simply reflect on pedagogical approaches to be revised in the future. Indeed, Wise & Jung (2019) have emphasised that several learning analytics projects provide little clarity about how teachers can take pedagogical action (Figure 15.1, C1) and how the impact of this can be assessed (Figure 15.1, C2).

This process of learning analytics use is by no means linear. The sensemaking subprocesses are cyclical. For example, the interpretation of data can lead to a revision of the teacher's questions. A decision-making process can also lead to a revision of the validity of insights. Teachers can wait and verify if the insights gained are valid before making a decision (for instance, if the pattern observed in visualised student data is recurring after some time). This has been highlighted by some authors as the teacher-inquiry loop (Sergis & Sampson, 2017).

The typology introduced in the previous section is key to understanding how different learning analytics systems can support the teacher's sensemaking process. For example, descriptive and diagnostic learning analytics systems are commonly designed to present evidence about past and present student activity in a way that teachers can easily interpret such data. Descriptive learning analytics tools would not go beyond just showing the data in a distilled way and diagnostic tools would implicitly support the generation of insights to some extent. By contrast, predictive learning analytics tools would provide teachers with a glimpse into the future, contributing to making some sort of decision by considering potential future outcomes or behaviours. Prescriptive analytics would go beyond this and provide support in taking pedagogical action.

ILLUSTRATIVE STUDIES

In this section, we place three recent systems to support teachers, each representing one broader type of learning analytics systems, namely, descriptive, diagnostic and prescriptive. Despite the highlighted importance of predictive learning analytics systems, we have not included an illustrative study for this type. We elaborate on the challenges associated with the design and evaluation of the predictive learning analytics in the later sections of this chapter. We describe their design in relation to how they support teachers' practice.

Case 1: Descriptive Analytics in ZoomSense

ZoomSense is a learning analytics system aimed to support teachers' monitoring students in breakout rooms, using Zoom and Google Documents. ZoomSense belongs to descriptive learning analytics typology and allows for comparing the participation of each group of students. ZoomSense provides support for (a) real-time monitoring of class activities and (b) after-class reflection, where teachers are able to see snapshots of students' cumulative progress within each breakout room session. There is also a possibility to get a snapshot of the classroom at a particular "point of interest". Three data sources are used in ZoomSense, namely traces of students' verbal and textual communications in the main or breakout rooms in Zoom, students' activity in Google Documents, and data about teachers' time spent in breakout rooms. These data sources are used to model discussional dynamics via socio-grams and total discussion level per each group, depict the progress of the group in collaborative documents, indicate teachers' attention distribution over students' groups. This way, teachers are able to monitor groups' progress in multiple collaborative tools, number of inactive students in each group and see how they allocate attention according to each group of students.

The analytics included in ZoomSense explicitly maps teachers' authentic questions to the visual components, each aimed at answering one question. This is achieved by applying data storytelling principles to the interface design (presented in Figure 15.2). Data storytelling elements are intended to aid interpretation of the data. These elements include (a) using semantically meaningful colours to draw the attention of teachers to events which might need their immediate attention (orange is used to draw teachers' attention, while navy and grey are used for the rest of the visual elements); (b) de-cluttering the interface and the charts to minimise distractions and enable easy comparison between the groups; and (c) mapping authentic teachers' questions (i.e., Q1–Q5, elicited during human-centred design sessions) to particular components of the interface, as presented on Figure 15.2. The first component depicts inactivity levels in each group (Q1). Information about students' progress in Google Documents is presented through a dot plot (Q2), where grey, orange and blue indicate that the group has not

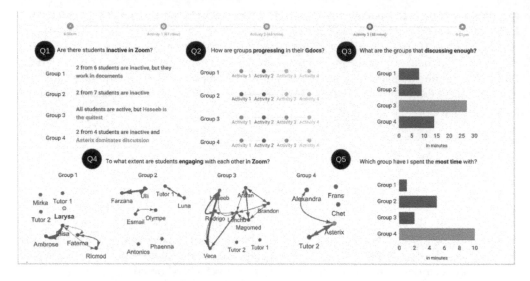

Figure 15.2   *ZoomSense question-driven interface to support teachers during real-time monitoring of breakout rooms in Zoom*

started a section, has started a section or has completed a section, respectively. Horizontal bar charts are used to compare group discussion and the time teacher allocated according to each group (Q3 and Q5). Sociograms enable identifying individual students who are not part of the discussion and get a more in-depth sense of discussion dynamics (Q4). Two nodes are connected if one student has spoken after another one. The sociogram is dynamically weighted, meaning that a connection gets thicker if two or more speakers have consecutively spoken after each other.

Sensemaking

In this illustrative example, explicitly mapping teachers' questions to visual components of the learning analytics interface, and the presence of absolute reference points in charts (see Figure 15.2, e.g., Q1 Q3, Q5) are not only intended to enable quick comparison across groups and charts, but also to support teachers to focus on specific data points instead of exploring the whole visual interface.

In a pilot study conducted in an authentic university unit of study (Pozdniakov et al., 2022), teachers were keen to interpret this interface and externalised diverse interpretations. By seeing students' names, teachers were able to recall additional context about the learning situation and to "triangulate the analytics with additional information about students" (Wise & Jung, 2019). Despite providing a high-level visual representation of how groups are progressing in Google documents, some teachers still highlighted the need to access the actual documents. This indicates that teachers need a more low-level account of how groups work on the writing activities in order to make sense of how the groups are progressing. This is in line with the information visualisation principle of providing details only on-demand (when needed) (Shneiderman, 1996).

Insights

The main insights teachers are able to gain are related to identification of groups, which "are on track" or need assistance. In addition, teachers are able to distinguish two types of inactive groups – those who are not writing or those who are not discussing, based on participation data from Google Docs and Zoom, respectively.

Decision making and pedagogical action

Teachers use ZoomSense to make decisions on which groups to visit next. In this process, teachers mainly relied on components mapped to Q3 ("Are there groups that are not discussing much?"), Q2 ("How are groups progressing in their Gdocs?") and Q1 ("Are there students inactive on Zoom?"). Some teachers make decisions on which group to visit based on how much time they allocated to each group (Q5). This was apparent in the situations when all other charts do not differentiate which group is performing better.

Notably, most of the teachers scaffold the entire group rather than individual students. Teachers indicate that while deciding whether to intervene and ask a group whether they are experiencing any issues, they rely on the overall level of discussion activity (Q3) and whether students are on-track with their writing activity (Q2).

Implications for Practice

Expanding analytics to include previous history

One of the challenges faced during the design of the functionalities of ZoomSense aimed at scaffolding the sensemaking process was that not all of the teachers' needs might have been addressed. For instance, teachers expressed interest to know more about the history of individual students during the course. This is aligned with recent literature (Molenaar & Knoop-van Campen, 2019; Wise & Jung, 2019) that suggests that teachers need to consider changes in a student's engagement over time to make sense of the student's current learning.

Better integration with learning design

While the data storytelling approach was being applied, teachers indicated that for some activities only certain visualisations were appropriate, while others were not useful. Thus, de-cluttering and simplification is not enough and further steps are needed to be taken. This is aligned with recent work that suggests that the data stories about students' work should be closely related to the characteristics of the learning task and the interface should therefore be adapted according to the learning design (Echeverria et al., 2018).

Methodological implication

It has been suggested that carefully identifying the kinds of questions that can be asked and can be addressed with data is key for supporting teachers' sensemaking of learning analytics interfaces (Li et al., 2021). In this illustrative example, we see one of the first attempts to explicitly align the teachers' needs and the components presented in a learning analytics interface. In this case, questions and components are placed according to how they were ranked by teachers. Yet more work is still needed to consider further levels of detail in the data and how teachers can interact with this complexity.

Case 2: Descriptive and Diagnostic Analytics in LearnerFlow

LearnerFlow is an interactive, teacher-facing visual analytics dashboard that supports feedback collection from teaching documents (prescribed reading material, lecture notes, tutorial problem sets and assignment handouts) and assists instructors in interpreting feedback and acting on it in a timely manner. LearnerFlow offers a set of novel visualization designs for presenting the four interleaving aspects of document engagement (i.e., annotations, document traversal path, reading/focus time and student information) in a single consistent interface. In addition, it has an analysis mode which uses automated data analysis and mining techniques to diagnose learning modules and students who deviate from the parameters that can be interactively defined by the course instructor through the interface.

LearnerFlow's interface supports teachers by providing features to assist with data interpretation in the following ways: (a) extensive capabilities to compare use of various learning resources via cross-filtering; (b) scaffolding diagnostics of "notable" learning paths by highlighting statistically significant deviations; and (c) ability to directly access the documents to see interactions (student posts and annotations) within the context (teaching environment) through the linked components.

All the views in LearnerFlow are dynamically coordinated via interactive linking, allowing for seamless exploration of the heterogeneous dataset from multiple levels of perspective (macro-, meso- and micro-levels). The panels within the platform have been grouped and aligned with the needs of the teachers involved in the learning analytics design. The development of LearnerFlow incorporated local instructors' ongoing involvement in the decisions from selecting data sources to organising the interface elements, to foster clearer connections between the analytics data and instructors' teaching concerns.

The data for LearnerFlow is sourced from the logs of students' interactions with the materials in the virtual learning environment, for instance, student annotations on the teaching material, and assessment scores. The data are presented as aggregated at the level of granularity requested by the instructors during the co-design of the system. Additionally, the platform provides the flexibility to expand the data sources to allow analysis of richer user attributes, such as gender, age and education level, and to which teachers they are assigned or any self-reported data collected from instructor-administered questionnaires to gain a deeper understanding of the behaviours and context of these categorisations in the course.

The Filter panel (Figure 15.3a & 15.3b) supports brushing options to select multi-dimensional student and annotation data. The Flow View (Figure 15.3c) represents student pathways and observed deviations while navigating course material. The Minimap View (Figure 15.3d) shows a heatmap of reading time plus annotation locations within syllabi, and the Matrix View (Figure 15.3e) displays a comparison of annotation patterns for different user groups.

Teachers rely on the reference points and make comparisons during interpretation of learning analytics with students' data (Li et al., 2021; Wise & Jung, 2019). In order to ease the load connected with interpretation of the flow patterns, the notion of *intended* (the baseline) and *unintended* pathways (deviations from the baseline) is used. The example of intended path is sequential completion of learning modules in the order they are given (e.g., 1.1->1.2->1.3->2), while sequences which omit this order (e.g. 3.2->1.1 or 1.1->4.5) are considered to be *unintended*. The platform algorithmically computes the stress Index for each module based on the volume of flow to and from the module, factoring in the deviation from the intended path and flow magnitude.

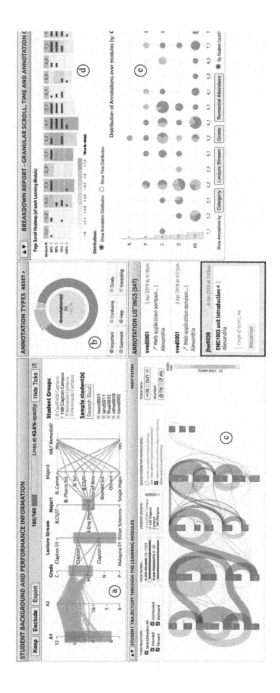

Figure 15.3   LearnerFlow interface showing the five panels acting as interrogation entry points

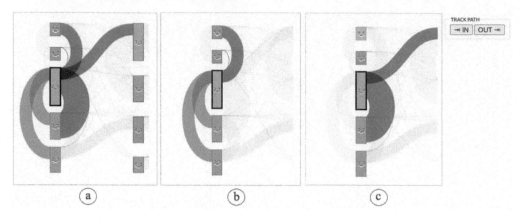

Figure 15.4   *Exploring Stressed Modules: (4a) Tracing flow for a selected module, (4b)*
Tracing inward flow and (4c) Tracing outward flow

A colour gradient is used to flag these modules (see Figure 15.4-c), indicating values of high and low stress. Similarly, students can be ranked based on their deviation from the intended path. LearnerFlow provides real-time support for educators to effectively explore complex multichannel, heterogeneous datasets at macro, meso and micro levels in a single dashboard. Instructors can also use the tool to identify anomalies in their course and explore their own conjectures through the interactive interfaces, as the course progresses during the semester.

Sensemaking

Adopting a human-centred approach in designing LearnFlow fostered clearer connections between analytics data and teaching concerns. The LearnerFlow interface contains five entry points (represented by the corresponding views), allowing the exploration of the document usage data and students' engagement patterns. Those entry points might be characterised as *descriptive* and *diagnostic*. *Descriptive capabilities* are represented by the following views in Figure 15.3: (a) Filter panel supports brushing options to select multi-dimensional data; (b) allows filtering annotations by categories; (d) Minimap View shows a heatmap of reading time plus annotation locations within syllabi; (e) Matrix View displays a comparison of annotation patterns for different user groups. *Diagnostic capabilities* entails (c) the flow view trace-intended student pathways and flags deviations within the course material.

LearnerFlow is designed to target instructors' interpretation towards exploring students' engagement patterns in learning materials and leverages automated data analysis and mining techniques to support deeper exploration and reasoning (e.g. identifying and flagging flaws or unintended execution of learning design). Comparative view scaffolds interpretation by providing multiple contexts for each entity (cohort, group, or individual) the instructor might be interested in. Once the instructor has decided to explore a particular learning module or student group, the tool then synchronises correspondingly multiple data channels and updates all other related views. Diagnostic view scaffolds the instructor's interpretation in a data-driven manner by highlighting "notable" paths which need the instructor's attention, by highlighting paths, modules and annotation activity which are significant. This view exploits data mining techniques, thus partially putting off the load of exploratory interrogation and interpretation of data and/or results from the instructors.

LearnerFlow follows some of the data storytelling techniques. The use of visual metaphors, such as Sankey Diagram (Figure 15.3.c) to represent student navigation paths and Minimaps (Figure 15.3.d) as miniature representations of course pages merged with heatmaps. Hovering over most of the interface components displays detailed related information (such as student achievement/demographic data or module-related information) to assist the sensemaking process. Additionally, clicking on the annotation message opens the exact location in the document where the annotation was made.

Insights

The LearnFlow is primarily designed to provide learning analytics aimed at supporting changes to the learning design. Thus, the user interfaces of LearnerFlow were coordinated accordingly for instructors and educational content authors so that they can easily interrogate their data sources, and thereby formulate insights on how to dynamically adjust learning material and their teaching strategies in classrooms.

Decision making and pedagogical action

Using the insights from LearnerFlow, the instructors can action tangible interventions. For instance, they would be able to find ways to (a) improve the presentation of learning modules or address problems with a structure and sequence of material, and (b) scaffold a subpopulation of learners who experienced difficulty with course materials, and advise supportive materials to the cohort of students.

Initial evaluation

This indicated that teachers were able to make changes to learning sections that are most challenging for students (Singh et al., 2020), by identifying sections or modules aggregating a high number of annotations (tagged as "confusing"), modules having significantly large reading time or with a high number of unintended pathways (looping behaviour/revisits). For such cases, instructors were able to intervene by providing supplementary resources or expanding the reading material with "Hints and Suggestions", which points out which sections to revise in order to better understand the current content (using this evidence of missing, erroneous or superfluous content self-reported by students or their trace data).

Teachers were also able to formulate insights into students' challenges and were able to identify individual struggling students based on their annotation data, reading and navigation behaviour, while the course was in progress.

Implications for Practice

Human-centred design

It is critical to design learning analytics interfaces that incorporate local needs and that ensure productive adaptations between educational practices and the technology (Ahn et al., 2019). The close collaboration with instructors at each stage of co-designing LearnerFlow was reflected in its evaluation (Singh et al., 2020), showing how the alignment of analytics dashboards can be improved to better suit the needs, problems and pedagogical concerns teachers have with their learning design activities, thereby improving actionability and impact of learning analytic.

Integration of multichannel data

Integration of multichannel data (e.g., trace data, demographics and traced self-reports) highlighted how instructors can gain better understanding of the context, learner experience and how it can facilitate sensemaking. The efficacy of incorporating multichannel data has been supported by several studies (Bosch et al., 2016; Bannert et al., 2017; Malmberg et al., 2019) towards improving the recognition of learning episodes and measurement of student engagement.

Exploratory visual analytics approach

Interactive visualisations increase the observation capacity of the teacher, broadening the scope of observable student activities, visibility of learning events and widening the monitoring for reaching scenarios traditionally opaque. Features such on-demand drill-down not only help interpretation and sensemaking but also increase data visibility. Most of the instructors who participated in co-designing LearnerFlow emphasised the importance of being aware of all the used data.

Integrating elements of data-storytelling

As highlighted by Lee et al. (2015), data-storytelling invokes meaning and adds nuance to a visualisation. Thus, including course events (assignment date, etc.) and other data storytelling elements into visualisations can further help in understanding the context, eliminate ambiguity, provoke reflections and explain unexpected patterns detected through use of the system. With the plan to extend LearnerFlow to support other user groups, such as authors and learning designers, more work is needed on this front to cater for these users with diverse analytics skill-sets.

Case 3: Diagnostic and Prescriptive Analytics in Course Insights

Similar to Learnerflow, Course Insights enables instructors to use filters to gain insights and compare performance and behaviour of subpopulations of the class that share some attributes or characteristics (e.g., are studying part-time or are enrolled in a particular tutorial section) to the rest of the class. A key feature of Course Insights is that it recommends filters to instructors that include students whose performance or behaviour deviates from the rest of the class. Given its ability to make recommendations, it has been characterised as a prescriptive learning analytic. Here we provide a brief overview of filter recommendation in Course Insights. A fuller account is available in Khosravi et al. (2021).

Course Insights utilises student data from numerous university data sources, including the university's student information system (i.e., enrolment and demographic information), trace data from interactions with learning management systems used (i.e., Blackboard and edX Edge) and assessment grades. Course Insights is connected to the learning management system at The University of Queensland (UQ) and is accessible to all UQ courses with a Blackboard presence. Employing a number of state-of-the-art approaches from process and data mining, Course Insights enables instructors to explore student data using filters that are manually selected or are recommended by the system, which are discussed below.

An essential element of Course Insights is its comparative analysis functionality, which enables teachers to use a set of filters to drill-down into the available data and explore the behaviour and performance of sub-populations of learners. Figure 15.5 demonstrates the filter builder, which enables teachers to select attributes from demographic, assessment, engagement

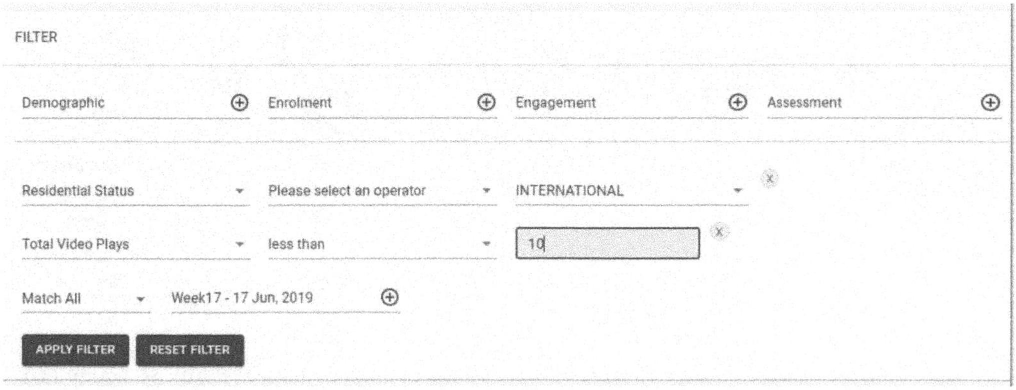

Figure 15.5   The manual filter builder panel used in Course Insights

and enrolment features. The selected set of attributes can be combined using AND (presented by "Match All") or OR (presented by "Match Any").

Inclusion of the filter builder enables teachers to conduct curiosity-driven explorations to answer very specific questions such as "How did students enrolled in the Bachelor of Computer Science who are retaking the course do in the final exam compared with the rest of the class?" Despite their strengths and benefits in support of such specific curiosity-driven exploration, in practice, the use of manual drill-downs to find meaning insights is recognised as being a challenging task (Lee et al., 2019). As reported by Shabaninejad et al. (2020a), the use of manual filters has been under-utilised with the majority of the teachers rarely using drilled-down data with more than one attribute. The combination of student attributes across a growing list of data sources provides a very large search space, making it almost impossible to know what attributes to use. Additionally, the use of manual filters for sensemaking is also associated with another limitation referred to as drill-down fallacy (Lee et al., 2019). Such a fallacy occurs when incorrect reasoning for a deviation found in the dataset is attributed to a smaller subpopulation, while "in fact it is a more general phenomenon" (Lee et al., 2019).

To assist teachers in navigating the filters and avoiding drill-down fallacies, Course Insights employs a suite of state-of-the-art algorithms from data mining and process mining to recommend insightful drill-downs to support teachers who might have not yet decided on what are the areas they want to explore and do not formulate clear questions to ask to analytics. Following the work of Shabaninejad et al. (2020a, 2020b), the notion of an insightful drill-down is defined as a set of filtering rules that identify a subpopulation of students that deviate from the rest of class based on performance- and learning process-based metrics. Figure 15.6 provides a high-level view of how recommendations are produced (for a more detailed description, please see Leemans et al. (2020). Using the event logs as input, main features are identified and are used for building a drill-down tree of all possible subsets of the features. A scoring function is used for approximating the deviance of each subset of features. The subset of features with the highest deviation are recommended to instructors. Unlike predictive models that automatically label students, this approach guides data exploration while still reserving judgement about interpreting student learning to instructors (Khosravi et al., 2021).

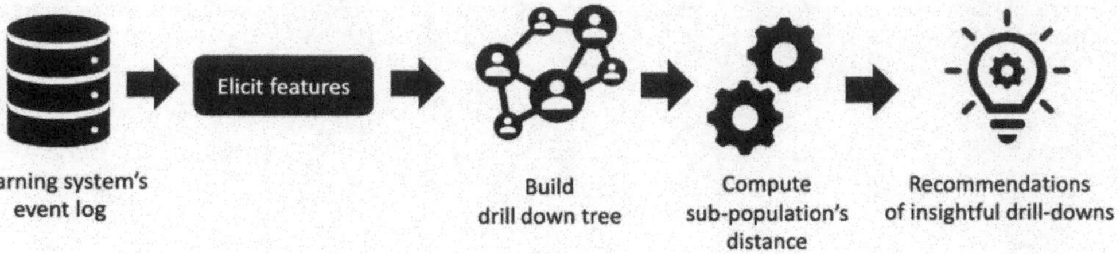

Learning system's event log   Build drill down tree   Compute sub-population's distance   Recommendations of insightful drill-downs

Figure 15.6   An overview of how drill-down recommendations are produced

Figure 15.7 illustrates the filter recommendation interface, which requires teachers to provide: (1) a list of required attributes to be present in the recommended filters; (2) a list of optional attributes that can be present in the recommended filters; (3) the minimum cohort size (in terms of percentage) of a filter being recommended; and (4) the maximum number of attributes that can be included in a recommended filter. Based on the information provided, Course Insights recommends a number of "insightful" filters for the teachers to explore.

Sensemaking

Course Insights incorporates a variety of visualisations to help instructors with sensemaking of students' engagement over time and their detailed account of the learning process.

Engagement over time and absolute and relative points of comparison

Figures 15.8 and 15.9 provide examples of the visualisations achieved once a filter is applied. Figure 15.8 demonstrates a comparison of the results of an assessment item, where statistical information as well as a graph representing the filtered versus unfiltered distribution of the results are presented. Figure 15.9 demonstrates a comparison of engagement of the filtered versus unfiltered distribution.

Learning process

Course Insights incorporates process mining techniques and visualisations to also provide a comprehensive view of students' learning processes in terms of their learning activities, their order and frequencies. Figure 15.10 (left) presents the process map of the low-scoring cohort in which two sequential series of activities stand out. The series which includes formative quiz activities on Chapters 8 to 15 and the series which includes reviewing solutions of summative assessments on Chapters 10 to 16 are highlighted in different colours. It indicates that these students first had a look at the summative answers, after which they took the quizzes. Figure 15.10 (right) presents the high-scoring cohort in which the arrows between different types of activities can be observed to be frequent. It indicates that students attempt a range of different types of activities for most of the chapters. Overall, Figure 15.10 presents an example of how the learning process of high-achieving and low-achieving students can be compared. However, these visualisations show a detailed view of students' learning process, but they are often hard to interpret by teachers. Co-creation and participatory design sessions with teachers are underway to develop appropriate methods of adding process-based visualisations to the platform.

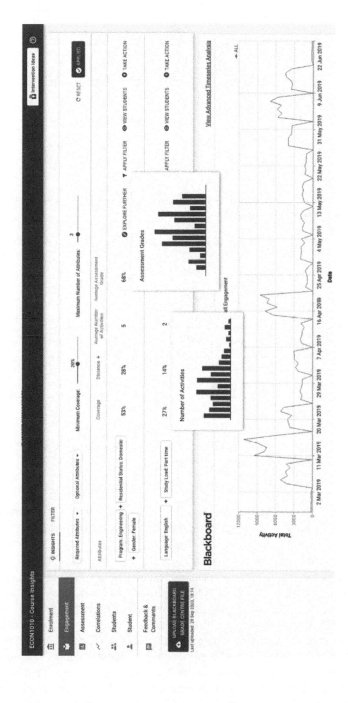

Figure 15.7   An overview of the filter recommendation interface

Figure 15.8   An example visualisation demonstrating the assessment result of the filtered students against the entire class

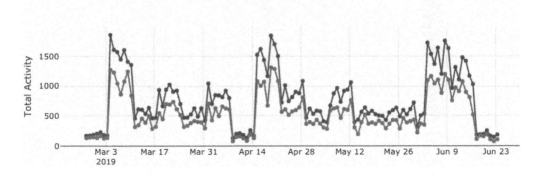

Figure 15.9   An example visualisation demonstrating the engagement pattern of the filtered students against the entire class

Insights

The main insights teachers are able to gain are related to identification of groups which "are on track" or which need assistance based on manual or recommended drill-downs.

Decision making and pedagogical action

Based on the analytics of the students' engagement, teachers might make decisions on whether some students' cohorts are behind schedule and do not cope with studies well. Course Insights enables teachers to reach out to targeted students selected either by a manual or a recommended filter via email. The process of sending out emails based on associated filters is similar to how it is performed in the popular learning analytics tools OnTask (Pardo et al., 2018).

The initial evaluation of drill-down recommendations about students' engagement indicated that teachers were still overwhelmed with the input needed from their side to generate insightful results (see Figure 15.7) and rarely used them. In contrast, teachers found that visualisations of the typical learning pathways, which led to the successful completion of

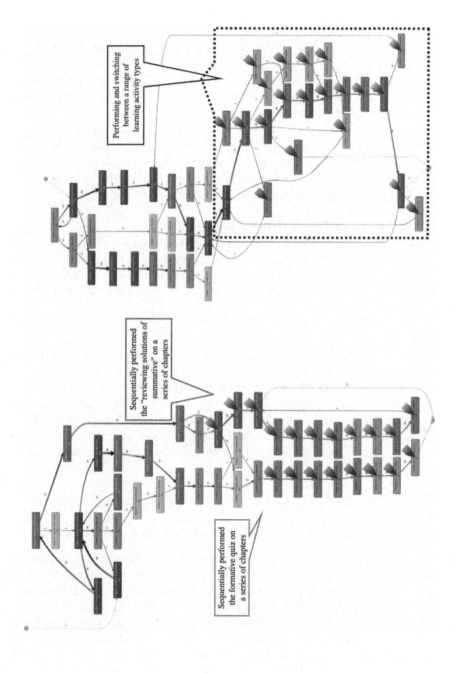

Figure 15.10   *Comparing learning process maps of two recommended cohorts. The process map on the left represents the cohort with a low final exam score. The process map on the right represents the cohort with a high final exam score*

Within the figure:

Sequentially performed the "reviewing solutions of summative" on a series of chapters

Sequentially performed the formative quiz on a series of chapters

Performing and switching between a range of learning activity types

the course, to be useful (see Figure 15.10). In fact, teachers indicated that they would like to show those visualisations to students as a representative example of how one of the learning pathways should look like.

Implications for Practice

Designing learning analytics systems for teachers with a diverse range of digital literacy

Course Insights has been developed in close collaboration with teachers. In particular, design choices about many of the main features or the user interfaces of the platform were made based on suggestions and feedback from over 50 academic or learner designer participants, attending Course Insights workshops. While there were many commonalities in terms of requests for features, there were also some requests for technically advanced features or more complex visualisations that seem to benefit only the more technical users. This raises the challenge of how we can design interfaces that are easy to navigate and use while satisfying the expectations of a technically diverse audience.

Evaluation of prescriptive learning analytics systems

Much of the initial focus in developing Course Insights has been on the development of an approach for generating the recommendations; however, an equally important aspect that needs to be investigated is whether the instructors act upon the provided recommendations. This raises the question of "What are the best research designs or best evaluation approaches for prescriptive learning analytics tools?"

Adoption and engagement

Many steps have been taken towards increasing adoption and engagement with Course Insights including (1) integrating it as an LTI tool in the learning management system, (2) developing extensive self-paced guides and videos, (3) delivering on-campus and online workshops as well as (4) having the tool being centrally supported. While these efforts have led to approximately 20% of the courses engaging with Course Insights, a substantial majority of the courses have not accessed the tool. This raises the question of what other methods and processes can be employed to help with the adoption of teacher-facing learning analytics tools.

OPPORTUNITIES AND FUTURE CHALLENGES

Aligning Teacher-Facing Analytics to Specific or Heterogeneous Learning Designs

The significant role of learning design has been recognised since the early days of the development of learning analytics. This has been demonstrated through the design of relevant teacher-facing analytics tools (Bakharia et al., 2016; Jovanovic et al., 2008) and frameworks that guide creation of learning analytics based on learning design (Lockyer et al., 2013). However, as demonstrated in contrasting Cases 1 and 3, teacher-facing learning analytics tools might be designed to the specific learning design (Case 1) or allow the automated discovery of insights (Case 3) in the courses with heterogeneous learning designs. The benefit of the approach followed in Case 1 is that the analytics provided are tightly coupled with the teachers' questions in order to enable the teachers to monitor the progression of their students according to the learning design. That is, learning design is directly reflected in the design of analytics and user interface of ZoomSense. However, this learning analytics tool design did not use any advanced data analytics algorithm to discover any additional insights that could be of relevance but that teachers might have failed to articulate in the co-design of ZoomSense.

In contrast, Case 3 demonstrated a range of interesting insights that can be obtained by integrating the use of advanced data analysis algorithms with interactive user interfaces as implemented in Course Insights. This approach gives much flexibility to formulate new questions to explore the data about their courses and can potentially lead to novel insights that are not necessarily anticipated through a set of predefined questions. Yet, this approach requires that teachers implicitly map the insights obtained with analytics onto their original pedagogical intent and learning designs. This could be a challenge as the Course Insights may not offer sufficient guidance to the teacher on how to action the insights with respect to the specific needs of a given learning design, as previously noted by teachers while examining LOCO-Analyst (Ali et al., 2012). Therefore, future work is necessary that can bridge further integration of learning design with the use of advanced data analysis techniques in the development of teacher-facing learning analytics tools.

Predictive Modelling and Teacher-Facing Analytics

Limited use of predictive modelling can be observed in all three cases showcased in this chapter. While this may seem somewhat surprising given the early popularity of tools such as Course Signals, this limitation is not uncommon for contemporary teacher-facing learning analytics tools. We attribute the potential reasons for this limitation to two main factors. First, predictive modelling algorithms, although very popular in learning analytics, are often designed and evaluated based on their predictive performance rather than helping with sensemaking or delivery of actionable insights (Akçapınar et al., 2019; Baneres et al., 2019; Marbouti et al., 2016). Consequently, predictive modelling algorithms often do not have an actual teacher-facing analytics tool, but rather just provide a list of the at-risk students. Second, predictive modelling algorithms are implemented at an institutional level to help universities meet key performance indicators related to reducing student drop-out rate rather than at the class-level to enhance learning. In these cases, action taken is often to call students from central student support teams rather than academic or course staff (Dawson et al., 2017).

Further work on integration of predictive modelling and the design of teacher-facing analytics tools is necessary. Some of the early work on teacher-facing analytics tools with predictive modelling demonstrated a positive association with increased student retention. However, follow-up research showed that such tools did not help teachers improve the quality of feedback (Tanes et al., 2011). Instead, such tools helped the teachers mostly increase the frequency of feedback. Gašević et al. (2015) attribute this limitation to the lack of relevant analytics that can support teachers' sensemaking and decision making in order to inform pedagogical action. Therefore, it is an open research challenge to design tools that can effectively integrate predictive modelling into teacher-facing analytics tools.

Applying Theory and Design Practices from Other Fields

If learning analytics dashboards are meant to play a key role in the ecology of tools that teachers can use to better support students, as is being suggested by the learning analytics community (Verbert et al., 2020), it is urgent for educational technology researchers, designers and tool providers to consider the importance of human factors. There is substantial research and development in information visualisation (InfoViz) that can be foundational to creating effective ways to visualise data. For example, Ben Shneiderman's visualisation mantra (Shneiderman, 1996) (i.e., overview first, zoom and filter, then details-on-demand) can be explicitly considered in the design of learning analytics dashboards to avoid delivering cluttered and dense teacher-facing dashboards. Design decisions need to be justified and foundational work in InfoViz and can be key in deciding the type of visualisation that fits the purpose and the audience (Dix, 2012).

Yet a critical question is why choose a teacher's dashboard in the first place? If the goal is to support teachers' awareness, the metaphor of a dashboard is just one of multiple ways in which teaching practice can be supported with data. The provision of evidence to teachers through automated means should ideally be subordinated to the pedagogical values of teachers (Biesta, 2010). At the very least, data should be represented in a way that makes sense to the teacher and that is aligned with the learning intentions of the particular task or the skills that students are developing (Knight et al., 2020). Some authors have considered alternative courses of action by designing visual data stories (Echeverria et al., 2018), combining text and visuals, and automatically written reports (Wiley et al., 2020) that closely match the educator's learning design. Research in human–computer interaction has suggested that using data in educational contexts should be addressed as a meaning making challenge, in which the close consideration of the context of usage and the context in which data were captured should strongly shape the design of the learning analytics tool to effectively support teachers (Martinez-Maldonado et al., 2020). A close consideration of the human factors, and foundational principles in InfoViz and human–computer interaction, may not seem to be a simple task for the already multi-disciplinary learning analytics field. Yet, this is key in designing effective learning analytics to effectively support authentic teaching practices.

Human-Centred Learning Analytics

One way in which human–computer interaction practices are being embraced by learning analytics researchers is by working closely with teachers, students and other stakeholders to co-design learning analytics systems with them. Human-centred design approaches such as co-design (Dollinger et al., 2019), participatory design (Liaqat et al., 2018) and value-sensitive design (Chen & Zhu, 2019) are gaining traction in the creation of learning analytics systems that are closely aligned to the actual teaching and learning practices and the values of the people who will use such systems. Human-centred learning analytics approaches are generally aimed at acknowledging the expertise that stakeholders and users can bring to the design process (Shum et al., 2019). Some approaches, such as co-design and co-creation, even suggest seeing stakeholders as design partners at the same level as researchers, designers and developers (Dollinger & Lodge, 2018). For example, the first and second illustrative cases presented above involved teachers at early stages of the design process rather than considering them as only participants in some evaluation studies. Avoiding this step might contribute to teachers' low engagement with the final learning analytics system, especially if their major needs are not being addressed by the system.

Yet, one important opportunity is not only to account for existing teachers' practices at early stages of the design of learning analytics, but also to consider the ways in which the introduction of data and analytics can influence both teaching and learning practices. For example, if we are able to log previous teachers' interactions and show them visual representations about their practice, it would potentially enable new ways in which to support reflective practices (Molenaar & Knoop-van Campen, 2019) or new ways to educate pre-service teachers by learning from the community of practice.

Other potential directions that are yet to be explored through human-centred design refer to *teacher's agency* – how can teachers decide whether they want to explore the students' data by themselves or consider automatic recommendations; *explainability* – how can parts of the models and the analytics be exposed to or configured by teachers; and *communication of insights* – how to reduce the visual complexity and focus on communicating data that is relevant and meaningful to the teacher.

Fairness, Accountability, Transparency and Ethics

The emergence of predictive learning analytics tools provides potential opportunities for the incorporation of tailored pedagogical actions to support at-risk students. However, there are increasing concerns about fairness, accountability, transparency and ethics (FATE) (Chapter 6 by Kay et al.) and the responsible use of predictive models to support automatic decision making (Hajian et al., 2016). Many known factors, such as dealing with poor quality or imbalanced data, determining the appropriate algorithm and model for the problem at hand, hyperparameter tuning and knowing when to retrain the algorithm with new data, may bias or reduce the accuracy of the results of the model. In addition, as machine-learning techniques learn from historical data, there is a danger of creating a bias towards historically disadvantaged groups. For instance, if students from a particular ethnicity are predicted to have a higher chance of being at-risk, could that be harmful in any way? Could the outcome of the model bias the teacher and lead to further stereotyping? The use of prescriptive models addresses some of these challenges as they rely on teacher judgement to review the recommendations before taking action. However, even in models with the teacher-in-the-loop approach, the risk of inequity still exists. For instance, an overreliance on the recommendations for assisting students may disadvantage students who were not identified by recommendations. While moderate steps have been taken towards measuring fairness in education (Gardner et al., 2019) and developing responsible educational AI systems (Aiken & Epstein, 2000), further investigation is needed to avoid this challenge.

CONCLUDING REMARKS

This chapter offered an overview of the existing approaches to learning analytics for teachers. Despite many promising results, a broad adoption of teacher-facing learning analytics tools is relatively limited. To increase adoption and enhance impact, this chapter highlighted several key points, including that: (i) design of teacher-facing tools requires careful consideration of human-centred design, learning theory and data science to create effective tools for teachers; (ii) the core consideration in the design of tools for teachers should be the processes that can support teachers in sensemaking, decision making and taking pedagogical action based on insights provided in learning analytics; and (iii) future work is needed to create design approaches that can integrate perspective that is underpinned by learning design, advanced data analysis algorithms and predictive modelling. This chapter also provided a description of three cases of teacher-facing learning analytics tools as a means to illustrate techniques and approaches that are used in existing research and practice. The key to take from this chapter is that to create effective teacher-facing analytics tools, data analysis and artificial intelligence techniques should ideally not only be aligned with the existing learning designs but should also account for existing practices and preferences of teachers.

REFERENCES

Ahn, J., Campos, F., Hays, M., & DiGiacombo, D. (2019). Designing in Context: Reaching Beyond Usability in Learning Analytics Dashboard Design. *Journal of Learning Analytics*, 6(2), 70–85. https://doi.org/10.18608/jla.2019.62.5.

Aiken, R. M., & Epstein, R. G. (2000). Ethical guidelines for AI in education: Starting a conversation. *International Journal of Artificial Intelligence in Education*, 11, 163–176.

Akçapınar, G., Altun, A., & Aşkar, P. (2019). Using learning analytics to develop early-warning system for at-risk students. *International Journal of Educational Technology in Higher Education*, 16(1), 1–20.

Ali, L., Hatala, M., Gašević, D., & Jovanović, J. (2012). A qualitative evaluation of evolution of a learning analytics tool. *Computers & Education*, 58(1), 470–489. https://doi.org/10.1016/j.compedu.2011.08.030.

Arnold, K. E., & Pistilli, M. D. (2012). Course signals at Purdue: Using learning analytics to increase student success. In *Proceedings of the 2nd International Conference on Learning Analytics and Knowledge - LAK '12*, 267. Vancouver, British Columbia. Canada: ACM Press. https://doi.org/10.1145/2330601.2330666.

Bakharia, A., Corrin, L., de Barba, P., Kennedy, G., Gašević, D., Mulder, R., … Lockyer, L. (2016). A conceptual framework linking learning design with learning analytics. In *Proceedings of the Sixth International Conference on Learning Analytics & Knowledge - LAK '16*, 329–338. Edinburgh, United Kingdom: ACM Press. https://doi.org/10.1145/2883851.2883944.

Baneres, D., Rodríguez-Gonzalez, M. E., & Serra, M. (2019). An early feedback prediction system for learners at-risk within a first-year higher education course. *IEEE Transactions on Learning Technologies*, 12(2), 249–263.

Bannert, M., Molenaar, I., Azevedo, R., Järvelä, S., & Gašević, D. (2017). Relevance of learning analytics to measure and support students' learning in adaptive educational technologies. In *Proceedings of the Seventh International Learning Analytics & Knowledge Conference*, 568–569.

Biesta, G. J. (2010). Why 'what works' still won't work: From evidence-based education to value-based education. *Studies in Philosophy and Education*, 29(5), 491–503.

Bodily, R., & Verbert, K. (2017). Trends and issues in student-facing learning analytics reporting systems research. In *Proceedings of the Seventh International Learning Analytics & Knowledge Conference*, 309–318. Vancouver, British Columbia, Canada: ACM. https://doi.org/10.1145/3027385.3027403.

Boland, R. J. (2008). Decision making and sensemaking. In F. Burstein & C. W. Holsapple (Eds.), *Handbook on Decision Support Systems* (Vol. 1, pp. 55–63). Berlin, Heidelberg: Springer Berlin Heidelberg. https://doi.org/10.1007/978-3-540-48713-5_3.

Bosch, N., D'Mello, S. K., Baker, R. S., Ocumpaugh, J., Shute, V., Ventura, M., … Zhao, W. (2016). Detecting student emotions in computer-enabled classrooms. *IJCAI*, 4–6, 4125–4129.

Chen, B., & Zhu, H. (2019). Towards value-sensitive learning analytics design. In *Proceedings of the 9th International Conference on Learning Analytics & Knowledge*, 343–352. Tempe, AZ: ACM. https://doi.org/10.1145/3303772.3303798.

Corrin, L., Kennedy, G., De Barba, P., Bakharia, A., Lockyer, L., Gasevic, D., … Copeland, S. (2015). *Loop: A Learning Analytics Tool to Provide Teachers With Useful Data Visualisations*. Perth: ASCILITE.

Dawson, S., Jovanovic, J., Gašević, D., & Pardo, A. (2017). From prediction to impact: Evaluation of a learning analytics retention program. In *Proceedings of the Seventh International Learning Analytics & Knowledge Conference*, 474–478.

Deschênes, M. (2020). Recommender systems to support learners' agency in a learning context: A systematic review. *International Journal of Educational Technology in Higher Education*, *17*(1), 50. https://doi.org/10.1186/s41239-020-00219-w.

Dix, A. (2012). Introduction to information visualisation. In *Proceedings of the 2012 International Conference on Information Retrieval Meets Information Visualization*, 1–27.

Dollinger, M., Liu, D., Arthars, N., & Lodge, J. (2019). Working together in learning analytics towards the co-creation of value. *Journal of Learning Analytics*, *6*(2). https://doi.org/10.18608/jla.2019.62.2.

Dollinger, M., & Lodge, J. M. (2018). Co-creation strategies for learning analytics. In *Proceedings of the 8th International Conference on Learning Analytics and Knowledge*, 97–101. Sydney, NSW, Australia: ACM. https://doi.org/10.1145/3170358.3170372.

Echeverria, V., Martinez-Maldonado, R., Buckingham Shum, S., Chiluiza, K., Granda, R., & Conati, C. (2018). Exploratory versus explanatory visual learning analytics: Driving teachers' attention through educational data storytelling. *Journal of Learning Analytics*, *5*(3), 73–97. https://doi.org/10.18608/jla.2018.53.6.

Echeverria, V., Martinez-Maldonado, R., Granda, R., Chiluiza, K., Conati, C., & Shum, S. B. (2018). Driving data storytelling from learning design. In *Proceedings of the 8th International Conference on Learning Analytics and Knowledge*, 131–140.

Gardner, J., Brooks, C., & Baker, R. (2019). Evaluating the fairness of predictive student models through slicing analysis. In *Proceedings of the 9th International Conference on Learning Analytics & Knowledge*, 225–234.

Gašević, D., Dawson, S., & Siemens, G. (2015). Let's not forget: Learning analytics are about learning. *TechTrends*, *59*(1), 64–71.

Gašević, D., Kovanović, V., & Joksimović, S. (2017). Piecing the learning analytics puzzle: A consolidated model of a field of research and practice. *Learning: Research and Practice*, *3*(1), 63–78. https://doi.org/10.1080/23735082.2017.1286142.

Gupta, A., Menon, N., Lee, W., Rebelsky, W., Allesio, D., Murray, T., … Arroyo, I. (2021). Affective teacher tools: Affective class report card and dashboard. In I. Roll, D. McNamara, S. Sosnovsky, R. Luckin, & V. Dimitrova (Eds.), *Artificial Intelligence in Education* (pp. 178–189). Cham: Springer International Publishing. https://doi.org/10.1007/978-3-030-78292-4_15.

Hajian, S., Bonchi, F., & Castillo, C. (2016). Algorithmic bias: From discrimination discovery to fairness-aware data mining. In *Proceedings of the 22nd ACM SIGKDD International Conference on Knowledge Discovery and Data Mining*, 2125–2126.

Heffernan, N. T., & Heffernan, C. L. (2014). The ASSISTments ecosystem: Building a platform that brings scientists and teachers together for minimally invasive research on human learning and teaching. *International Journal of Artificial Intelligence in Education*, *24*(4), 470–497. https://doi.org/10.1007/s40593-014-0024-x.

Herder, T., Swiecki, Z., Fougt, S. S., Tamborg, A. L., Allsopp, B. B., Shaffer, D. W., & Misfeldt, M. (2018). Supporting teachers' intervention in students' virtual collaboration using a network based model. In *Proceedings of the 8th International Conference on Learning Analytics and Knowledge - LAK '18*, 21–25. Sydney, NSW, Australia: ACM Press. https://doi.org/10.1145/3170358.3170394.

Herodotou, C., Rienties, B., Boroowa, A., Zdrahal, Z., & Hlosta, M. (2019). A large-scale implementation of predictive learning analytics in higher education: The teachers' role and perspective. *Educational Technology Research and Development*, *67*(5), 1273–1306. https://doi.org/10.1007/s11423-019-09685-0.

Holstein, K., McLaren, B. M., & Aleven, V. (2018). Student learning benefits of a mixed-reality teacher awareness tool in AI-enhanced classrooms. In C. Penstein Rosé, R. Martínez-Maldonado, H. U. Hoppe, R. Luckin, M. Mavrikis, K. Porayska-Pomsta, … B. du Boulay (Eds.), *Artificial Intelligence in Education* (Vol. 10947, pp. 154–168). Cham: Springer International Publishing. https://doi.org/10.1007/978-3-319-93843-1_12.

Jivet, I., Scheffel, M., Specht, M., & Drachsler, H. (2018). License to evaluate: Preparing learning analytics dashboards for educational practice. In *Proceedings of the 8th International Conference on Learning Analytics and Knowledge*, 31–40. Sydney, NSW, Australia: ACM. https://doi.org/10.1145/3170358.3170421.

Jørnø, R. L., & Gynther, K. (2018). What constitutes an "actionable insight" in learning analytics? *Journal of Learning Analytics*, *5*(3), 198–221. https://doi.org/10.18608/jla.2018.53.13.

Jovanovic, J., Gasevic, D., Brooks, C., Devedzic, V., Hatala, M., Eap, T., & Richards, G. (2008). LOCO-analyst: Semantic web technologies in learning content usage analysis. *International Journal of Continuing Engineering Education and Life Long Learning*, *18*(1), 54–76.

Khosravi, H., Shabaninejad, S., Bakharia, A., Sadiq, S., Indulska, M., & Gašević, D. (2021). Intelligent learning analytics dashboards: Automated drill-down recommendations to support teacher data exploration. *Journal of Learning Analytics*, *8*(3), 133–154.

Knight, S., Gibson, A., & Shibani, A. (2020). Implementing learning analytics for learning impact: Taking tools to task. *The Internet and Higher Education*, *45*, 100729. https://doi.org/10.1016/j.iheduc.2020.100729.

Knight, S., & Shum, S. B. (2017). Theory and learning analytics. *Handbook of Learning Analytics*, 17–22.

Koh, E., & Tan, J. P.-L. (2017). *Teacher-Actionable Insights in Student Engagement: A Learning Analytics Taxonomy*, 8.

Lang, C., Siemens, G., Wise, A., & Gasevic, D. (2017). *Handbook of Learning Analytics*. New York, NY: SOLAR, Society for Learning Analytics and Research.

Lee, B., Riche, N. H., Isenberg, P., & Carpendale, S. (2015). More than telling a story: Transforming data into visually shared stories. *IEEE Computer Graphics and Applications*, 7.

Lee, D. J.-L., Dev, H., Hu, H., Elmeleegy, H., & Parameswaran, A. (2019). Avoiding drill-down fallacies with *VisPilot*: Assisted exploration of data subsets. In *Proceedings of the 24th International Conference on Intelligent User Interfaces*, 186–196. Marina del Ray California: ACM. https://doi.org/10.1145/3301275.3302307.

Leemans, S. J., Shabaninejad, S., Goel, K., Khosravi, H., Sadiq, S., & Wynn, M. T. (2020). Identifying cohorts: Recommending drill-downs based on differences in behaviour for process mining. In *International Conference on Conceptual Modeling* (pp. 92–102). Cham: Springer.

Li, Q., Jung, Y., & Friend Wise, A. (2021). Beyond first encounters with analytics: Questions, techniques and challenges in instructors' sensemaking. In *LAK21: 11th International Learning Analytics and Knowledge Conference*, 344–353. Irvine, CA: ACM. https://doi.org/10.1145/3448139.3448172.

Liaqat, A., Axtell, B., Munteanu, C., & Epp, C. D. (2018). Contextual inquiry, participatory design, and learning analytics: An example. In *Companion Proceedings 8th International Conference on Learning Analytics & Knowledge*.

Lockyer, L., Heathcote, E., & Dawson, S. (2013). Informing pedagogical action: Aligning learning analytics with learning design. *American Behavioral Scientist*, *57*(10), 1439–1459. https://doi.org/10.1177/0002764213479367.

Malmberg, J., Järvelä, S., Holappa, J., Haataja, E., Huang, X., & Siipo, A. (2019). Going beyond what is visible: What multichannel data can reveal about interaction in the context of collaborative learning? *Computers in Human Behavior*, *96*, 235–245.

Mangaroska, K., & Giannakos, M. (2019). Learning Analytics For Learning Design: A Systematic Literature Review Of Analytics-Driven Design To Enhance Learning. *IEEE Transactions on Learning Technologies*, *12*(4), 516–534. https://doi.org/10.1109/TLT.2018.2868673.

Marbouti, F., Diefes-Dux, H. A., & Madhavan, K. (2016). Models for early prediction of at-risk students in a course using standards-based grading. *Computers & Education*, *103*, 1–15.

Martinez-Maldonado, R. (2019). A handheld classroom dashboard: Teachers' perspectives on the use of real-time collaborative learning analytics. *International Journal of Computer-Supported Collaborative Learning*, *14*(3), 383–411. https://doi.org/10.1007/s11412-019-09308-z.

Martinez-Maldonado, R., Echeverria, V., Fernandez Nieto, G., & Buckingham Shum, S. (2020). From data to insights: A layered storytelling approach for multimodal learning analytics. In *Proceedings of the 2020 CHI Conference on Human Factors in Computing Systems*, 1–15. Honolulu, HI: ACM. https://doi.org/10.1145/3313831.3376148.

Matcha, W., Uzir, N. A., Gasevic, D., & Pardo, A. (2020). A systematic review of empirical studies on learning analytics dashboards: A self-regulated learning perspective. *IEEE Transactions on Learning Technologies*, *13*(2), 226–245. https://doi.org/10.1109/TLT.2019.2916802.

Molenaar, I., & Knoop-van Campen, C. A. N. (2019). How teachers make dashboard information actionable. *IEEE Transactions on Learning Technologies*, *12*(3), 347–355. https://doi.org/10.1109/TLT.2018.2851585.

Ndukwe, I. G., & Daniel, B. K. (2020). Teaching analytics, value and tools for teacher data literacy: A systematic and tripartite approach. *International Journal of Educational Technology in Higher Education*, *17*(1), 1–31.

Pardo, A., Bartimote, K., Shum, S. B., Dawson, S., Gao, J., Gašević, D., ... Mirriahi, N. (2018). OnTask: Delivering data-informed, personalized learning support actions. *Journal of Learning Analytics*, *5*(3), 235–249.

Pozdniakov, S., Martinez-Maldonado, R., Tsai, Y.-S., Cukurova, M., Bartindale, T., Chen, P., ... Gasevic, D. (2022). *The Question-Driven Dashboard: How Can We Design Analytics Interfaces Aligned to Teachers' Inquiry?* 11.

Sebbaq, H., el Faddouli, N., & Bennani, S. (2020). Recommender system to support MOOCs teachers: Framework based on ontology and linked data. In *Proceedings of the 13th International Conference on Intelligent Systems: Theories and Applications*, 1–7. Rabat, Morocco: ACM. https://doi.org/10.1145/3419604.3419619.

Sergis, S., & Sampson, D. G. (2017). Teaching and learning analytics to support teacher inquiry: A systematic literature review. *Learning Analytics: Fundaments, Applications, and Trends*, 25–63.

Shabaninejad, S., Khosravi, H., Indulska, M., Bakharia, A., & Isaias, P. (2020a). *Automated Insightful Drill-Down Recommendations for Learning Analytics Dashboards*, 7.

Shabaninejad, S., Khosravi, H., Leemans, S. J. J., Sadiq, S., & Indulska, M. (2020b). Recommending insightful drill-downs based on learning processes for learning analytics dashboards. In I. I. Bittencourt, M. Cukurova, K. Muldner, R. Luckin, & E. Millán (Eds.), *Artificial Intelligence in Education* (pp. 486–499). Cham: Springer International Publishing. https://doi.org/10.1007/978-3-030-52237-7_39.

Shneiderman, B. (1996). The eyes have it: A task by data type taxonomy for information visualizations. In *Proceedings 1996 IEEE Symposium on Visual Languages*, 336–343. Boulder, CO: IEEE Computer Society Press. https://doi.org/10.1109/VL.1996.545307.

Shum, S., Ferguson, R., & Martinez-Maldonaldo, R. (2019). Human-centred learning analytics. *Journal of Learning Analytics*, *6*(2), 1–9. https://doi.org/10.18608/jla.2019.62.1.

Singh, S., Meyer, B., & Wybrow, M. (2020). UserFlow: A tool for visualizing fine-grained contextual analytics in teaching documents. In *Proceedings of the 2020 ACM Conference on Innovation and Technology in Computer Science Education*, 384–390. Trondheim, Norway: ACM. https://doi.org/10.1145/3341525.3387410.

Tanes, Z., Arnold, K. E., King, A. S., & Remnet, M. A. (2011). Using signals for appropriate feedback: Perceptions and practices. *Computers & Education*, *57*(4), 2414–2422. https://doi.org/10.1016/j.compedu.2011.05.016.

van Leeuwen, A., Rummel, N., & van Gog, T. (2019). What information should CSCL teacher dashboards provide to help teachers interpret CSCL situations? *International Journal of Computer-Supported Collaborative Learning*, *14*(3), 261–289. https://doi.org/10.1007/s11412-019-09299-x.

Verbert, K., Duval, E., Klerkx, J., Govaerts, S., & Santos, J. L. (2013). Learning analytics dashboard applications. *American Behavioral Scientist*, *57*(10), 1500–1509. https://doi.org/10.1177/0002764213479363.

Verbert, K., Ochoa, X., De Croon, R., Dourado, R. A., & De Laet, T. (2020). Learning analytics dashboards: The past, the present and the future. *Proceedings of the Tenth International Conference on Learning Analytics & Knowledge*, 35–40. Frankfurt, Germany: ACM. https://doi.org/10.1145/3375462.3375504.

Weick, K. E., Sutcliffe, K. M., & Obstfeld, D. (2005). Organizing and the process of sensemaking. *Organization Science*, *16*(4), 409–421. https://doi.org/10.1287/orsc.1050.0133.

Wiley, K. J., Dimitriadis, Y., Bradford, A., & Linn, M. C. (2020). From theory to action: Developing and evaluating learning analytics for learning design. In *Proceedings of the Tenth International Conference on Learning Analytics & Knowledge*, 569–578. Frankfurt, Germany: ACM. https://doi.org/10.1145/3375462.3375540.

Wise, A., & Jung, Y. (2019). Teaching with analytics: Towards a situated model of instructional decision-making. *Journal of Learning Analytics*, *6*(2), 53–69. https://doi.org/10.18608/jla.2019.62.4.

16. Predictive modeling of student success

Christopher Brooks, Vitomir Kovanović and Quan Nguyen

INTRODUCTION

While predictive analytics have been used in a wide range of situations, by far the most common use of predictive analytics is to improve student retention and academic performance at a coarse-grained level (Gasevic et al., 2015; Siemens, 2013). In at-risk prediction, the goal is to identify students who are at risk of failing a course or dropping out of the degree program. Slightly more complicated is grade prediction, which involves predicting students' grades for a learning activity or course, either as numerical percentage grades (e.g., 82%) or final letter grades.

While data mining had been used to identify at-risk students since the early 2000s (e.g., Ma et al., 2000), it primarily utilized student demographic or course performance data. The broader adoption of Learning Management Systems (LMS) provided far richer types of data to identify at-risk students, which gave insights into students' learning behavior. One of the earliest examples is by Macfadyen and Dawson (2010), who indicated the strong potential of trace data and asynchronous discussions records to provide early warning about the lack of student progress. Another early system was CourseSignals by Arnold and Pistilli (2012), which utilized simple traffic-light notation to indicate high-risk (red), moderately at-risk (yellow), and not at-risk (green) students. While early evaluations of CourseSignals showed improved retention by 21%, such findings were later disputed due to significant issues in the evaluation analysis (Caulfield, 2013; Feldstein, 2013). Regardless of the controversy, the system was highly influential in bringing broader attention to predictive analytics, especially in the higher education context (Herodotou et al., 2017; Howard et al., 2018; Mahzoon, 2018; Marbouti, 2016; Ming & Ming, 2012; Robinson et al., 2013; Torenbeek et al., 2013; Umer et al., 2017; Van Goidsenhoven et al., 2020; Wolff et al., 2013). The development of Massive Open Online Courses (MOOCs) around the same time proved a new context particularly suitable for the development of at-risk and grade prediction systems (Akhtar, 2015; Brooks et al., 2015b, 2015a; Crossley et al., 2016; Cunningham, 2017; Greene et al., 2015; Jiang et al., 2014; Kennedy et al., 2015; Ramesh et al., 2014; Sinha & Cassell, 2015; Taylor et al., 2014). The driver of the activity around MOOCs was due to a confluence of factors, including larger student cohorts which measured in the tens of thousands instead of hundreds, the high attrition rates than in for-credit courses, and the difference in data availability from the new platforms (Kizilcec et al., 2013).

As predictive modeling techniques in education matured, the focus has expanded to advancing our theoretical understandings of student learning in a particular context (Shmueli, 2010). This includes understanding students' learning strategies and self-regulated learning (Di Mitri et al., 2017; Kizilcec et al., 2017; Maldonado-Mahauad et al., 2018; Moreno-Marcos et al., 2020; Sierens et al., 2009), affect detection (Calvo & D'Mello, 2010; Hussain et al., 2011), reading comprehension (Allen et al., 2015), critical thinking (Barbosa et al., 2020; Kovanović et al., 2014, 2016; Neto et al., 2021, 2018; Waters et al., 2015), reflection (Kovanović et al., 2018), motivation (Sharma et al., 2020; Wen et al., 2014), feedback engagement (Iraj et al., 2020), social interactions (Joksimović et al., 2015; Yoo & Kim, 2012), and team performance (Yoo

& Kim, 2013). In such studies, prediction accuracy is of secondary importance to the understanding of learning processes and the associations between different learning constructs and outcomes. From a theoretical perspective, such studies provide large-scale data-driven evaluations of the relationships between different constructs, showing the potential of predictive analytics to both optimize and understand learning (Macfadyen & Dawson, 2010).

In this chapter, we do not seek to make a hard ontological distinction between this area of *predictive modeling of student success* and the broader field of artificial intelligence in education. Many of the goals, methods, and techniques overlap with those of more focused and clearly defined areas, such as the field of intelligent tutoring systems or personalized learning. However, some of the most significant developments within predictive modeling revolve around (a) using data generated as a *by-product* of student learning interactions (also known as *digital exhaust*, such as Neef, 2014) instead of specifically designed data sources, (b) *large-scale data collection*, both in the number of learners and the time frame across which the data are collected, typically in the thousands of students over a semester or longer and (c) institutionally perceived *student success outcomes*, such as grades or continued enrollment, instead of more fine-grained measures of learning such as knowledge gain.

This chapter aims to characterize some of the current norms of the data and approaches within the scholarly work on predictive modeling of student success while acknowledging both the breadth and the growing depth of the area. Given the rapid adoption of student success technologies, we end the chapter by looking at some of the emerging critical issues that affect further research and development in this area.

COMMON DATA SOURCES

Perhaps the most distinctive trait of student success predictive modeling is that it is based on large-scale data, which is typically a by-product of interactions within educational systems (both in the institutional and technical senses). Indeed, in a Big Data world, it is common for researchers to ask for "all available data" the institution has about learners and their activities. While data collection is only increasing in both amount and scope,[1] there are broadly four different kinds of data used for predictive modeling of students.

Student Information System (SIS)

The most common data sources are demographics, enrollment, and course performance data captured in student information systems (SIS). Being an amalgamation of various data, demographics are generally readily available in most contexts, with analogs in primary, secondary, university, and life-long learning settings. Such data tend to be well formed and mostly complete, generally adhering to institutional schemas and sometimes aligning with national standards (e.g., the Integrated Postsecondary Educational Data System (IPED)[2] maintained by the US Department of Education). For the most part, demographic data is very coarse in terms of temporal granularity, generally on the order of a single academic semester or greater. Given the broad availability of such data, they have been used extensively in building predictive models, and it is not uncommon to find models including more than 50 different SIS measures.

Some data available in the student information system are generated before or after the student learning experience and can be used to predict students' success and outcomes during instruction or beyond. For instance, standardized tests (e.g., SAT by CollegeBoard) are commonly used for admissions into post-secondary education.[3] These tests are often explicitly designed to predict student success in higher education and – in the case of SAT – correlate highly with outcomes such as first-year grade point average or overall retention in programs (Westrick et al., 2019).

Behavioral Interactions within Learning Management Systems

In addition to mostly stable demographic data, another common type of data is student interaction data within institutionally provided Learning Management Systems (LMS). Sometimes referred to as digital exhaust (Neef, 2014), such data are also widely available in most educational institutions, given the broader adoption of LMS technologies. Unlike SIS data, LMS data is much more granular and often used for more fine-grained analysis of students' behavior. Depending on the educational level and context, LMS data is often available in two different forms, either at a state-based system capturing summary information about learners at a given point in time (e.g., individual assessment outcomes, progress through content, and peer discourse), and a finer-grained event log of activities the learner has engaged in (e.g., content access, discussion interactions and contributions, video interactions, or actions within third-party tools integrated into the LMS). The state-based data tend to be high level in nature, providing insights into the general use of the LMS system (e.g., indicating how many messages a learner has not read yet in a discussion forum). In contrast, event-based data – also called *clickstream* or *trace data* – is generally designed by technology vendors to aid system development, debugging, and audit and is often noisy and incomplete. Given its purpose, the format of clickstream data can also often change, requiring significant efforts by researchers to process, prepare, and clean the data. The high-frequency nature of this data, which can be dozens of individual events every minute for a single learner, has led to the use of analysis techniques incorporating both aggregation (e.g., to generate more coarse-grained features of learning activity) and temporal/sequential modeling (e.g., Hidden Markov models or sequential analysis).

While most event-based trace data are inconsistently structured and dependent on the learning platform, there have been significant efforts in developing common standards for representing learning event data and improving the usability and value of such data. A new form of structured event-based behavioral data has emerged through the IMS Caliper[4] and Experience API (xAPI)[5] specifications. These two competing specifications provide a minimal framework for learning platforms to record events according to a predefined schema, leveraging a layer of knowledge engineering and increasing interoperability across different educational technology solutions. These specifications also aim to improve reliability and access expectations by introducing to the learning ecosystem a learner record store (LRS) that could allow interoperability and easier integration of data from different learning platforms. While both Caliper and xAPI have been evolving for more than a decade, it is only recently that these systems are being used for student success prediction. The slow adoption of these systems is mainly due to the significant time required to adopt their respective schemas within the existing tools. With the broader adoption of such standards, we expect to see their more intense use for developing different kinds of predictive models and analytical systems in the future.

Application Level Behavioral Traces

While trace data provides fine-grained data about student interactions, it is important to note that such data are typically limited to critical moments of student interactions, recorded by the server-side of web-based LMS platforms. Within the field of artificial intelligence in education, there has also been significant use of far more granular application-level data of student learning interactions, most prominently from Intelligent Tutoring Systems (ITS).

This application-level data is often used to make moment-by-moment decisions about how to support the student learning process, such as determining when a learner has mastered a competency and should move to the following competency, which particular misconceptions a learner is having, and what should be done to remediate them or how a given interaction between learners in the learning environment might be supported (e.g., triadic dialogue systems). In most of these cases, the time taken to perform a specific action is of critical importance, warranting the use of highly granular and temporal data.

Unlike demographic and interaction data, there is minimal standardization or shared specifications for capturing application-level interaction data. Many applications provide little or no access to external systems (e.g., student success dashboards) for such data. A significant portion of research innovations falls into this category of data, where specific interventions or approaches are being tested and evaluated. Due to the nature of such projects, the software development effort required for wide-scale data sharing has not been prioritized, making it challenging to use and utilize such data outside its initial intended use. However, the advent of institutional learner record stores operating on structured event-based data provides a welcome mechanism to help deal with this problem. For instance, the minimum structure of a Caliper (IMS Global Learning Consortium, Inc., 2020) message is just a few fields, capturing information about the time, user, and event classification, while event-specific data can be packaged without the need to further adhere to any additional schema. The connectors for various programming languages are also readily available, and their integration requires only a modest effort. As a result, we will likely be witnessing their growing adoption in capturing application-specific data, bringing further standardization into how trace data are processed.

Non-Learning Academic Data

A significant amount of data available in academic environments is only indirectly used to describe learner activities, relationships, and physical/mental states. Such data have been increasingly used to predict student success. For instance, residential campus attendance data or room-access data from access cards can be used to capture student physical location and infer purpose or activity (Newland et al., 2015). At a more fine-grained level, wireless access point networks have been used to model relationships between students, showing trends of affiliations which may be helpful for predictive modeling (Nguyen et al., 2020a). There is also growing interest in incorporating data from wearable systems into predictive modeling systems. Early work in this domain highlights the links between physiological measures (e.g., heart rate variability) and student success (Thomas & Viljoen, 2019). However, to this date, the use of such measures is limited to observational research data instead of enterprise-wide predictive models.

RECENT DEVELOPMENTS IN PREDICTIVE MODELING

Machine-learning techniques and practices have changed rapidly over the past two decades, and applied fields, such as artificial intelligence in education, have been impacted by new advances. The once commonplace methods of reporting on technical aspects of predictive modeling in educational research have grown to be more implication oriented, acknowledging the need to understand the pragmatic constraints and opportunities of these models. At a high level, we observe three general changes in how scholarly work has changed when considering predictive modeling, including technical reporting on models, methods for their evaluation, and population choices.

Technical Reporting

In the early days of predictive modeling of student success, a typical output within research work was a "model shootout" table, comparing the performance of various machine-learning techniques on the same data set and with the same target outcome. With little prior work on modeling student success, it was common to include descriptions of numerous different modeling techniques, with decision trees, naive Bayes, support vector machines, neural networks, and logistic regression models being some of the most common (Cui et al., 2019), across typical metrics of evaluation such as accuracy, precision, recall, and f-measures. Such models were (and continue to be) easy to run, thanks to toolkits such as Weka (Frank et al., 2004), providing implementations of numerous methods in a consistent format and lowering the barrier of use for applied researchers. However, such results were rarely accompanied by a deep consideration of how model performance related to the underlying data, measures, or predictive task. The reports of a performance benefit of one model over another, often very slight, did little to move the domain of student success prediction forward. Despite numerous studies comparing the different techniques, the unique nature of each learning setting proved to be a significant factor affecting algorithm performance, with no consensus on the best modeling techniques for particular settings. While shootouts continue to be published, the emphasis has since shifted towards evaluating the value of the best model described, changing contributions from measures of modeling techniques to the value of a model within the domain of education.

One prominent example that contrasts this trend is the comparison of methods for cognitive modeling in intelligent tutoring systems. Historically, the most commonly used methods for cognitive modeling included logistic regression models and Bayesian knowledge tracing (Corbett & Anderson, 1994; Yudelson et al., 2013). The application of deep learning methods, specifically deep knowledge tracing (Piech et al., 2015), caused contention and inspection within the field regarding the limitations and merits of approaches for modeling student knowledge. Such work set out a series of focused investigations across datasets and contexts comparing the performance and interpretability of Bayesian and deep knowledge tracing methods, resulting in several enhancements to the methods and a rigorous evaluation of the performance of these methods (Gervet et al., 2020).

A significant challenge with predictive modeling in education is replicability and comparison of different analyses. While early studies often failed to include information on hyperparameter settings, more recent work has begun to include such information and the source code of the statistical analysis (generally as external auxiliary information). While the maturation of the broader research field is a likely reason for such change, the open science movement has also likely been an important influencing factor, as evidenced by the dedicated statements in the Learning at Scale conference call for papers,[6] the Society for Learning Analytics resolution on openness,[7] and specific practices for enabling openness in educational research (van der Zee & Reich, 2018). Such information would also allow for easier and more accurate replication studies, leading to significant advances in predicting student success and predictive analytics more broadly.

Evaluation of Models

As data became more readily available and educational predictive modeling matured, the norms for robust evaluation of models also evolved. Early work in the area tended towards using cross-validation alone as the primary method for characterizing accuracy and overtraining. Such methods were generally a by-product of data access issues. Most often, one of the researchers on the team was also the instructor for the course and, thus, had the technical ability to access and analyze the data themselves. As the access to data broadened, the evaluation of model quality became more pragmatic, with expectations that model performance would be measured within authentic learning tasks (e.g., a subsequent offering of a course or a future cohort of students). Instead of providing theoretical insights into student learning, many predictive models of student success aim to provide practical results and identify students who are struggling and in need of an intervention. This shift of focus prioritized future model performance, and it is now common to see temporal model evaluation, where predictive models are trained on several semesters of historical data and then evaluated on a hold-out of the most recent year (e.g., Brooks et al., 2015).

The temporal nature of the prediction task also determines when a given prediction is valuable, which has had implications on model evaluation approaches. For instance, the prediction of a student's final grade in a course made just before the final exam is much more accurate than one given in the third week of the course, but the intervention opportunities are minimal given that the course is over. For models based on continually updated data, such as from LMS, it is thus essential to characterize model evaluation over time (Brooks et al., 2015) or at specific times with significant intervention potential (e.g., right before a deadline to withdraw from a course without penalty).

Population Choices

There is a strong interest within educational research to develop predictive models which are fair across different segments of the student population. This issue is nuanced, with a wide range of techniques employed at varying levels of the modeling process, from data acquisition to model deployment. For instance, similar to behavioral psychology, much of educational research is based on typical undergraduate students readily available to be studied. Referred to as WEIRD populations (Henrich et al., 2010), as the samples are drawn from Western, Educated, Industrialized, Rich, and Democratic societies, these groups may not represent the student population more broadly. Does it make sense, then, to build predictive models of student success on just these students and then apply them across other groups of learners?

To support the development of fair and unbiased predictive models in education, the research within Massive Open Online Courses (MOOCs) has been particularly important. Kizilcec and Brooks (2017) suggest one benefit of MOOC data in this process is the breadth of learner backgrounds, especially as it relates to culture and geography. The diverse educational data have the potential to lead to the construction of more generalizable models, where the predictive model incorporates elements of learner demographics from a broader population. Another technique for improving generalization is to measure the sensitivity of a given model for a particular population used to train the model. Such evaluation allows for characterizing whether it is suitable to transfer the developed predictive model to a new population. For example, Ocumpaugh et al. (2014) demonstrated that predictive models in the *ASSISTments* system were sensitive to whether the students were from urban, suburban, or rural communities. The difference in model fit between populations was stark. When measuring and predicting affective states, such as confusion across the three populations, they demonstrated that models trained on one but evaluated on another population had near random (kappa ≤ 0.03 in all cases) predictive power, while the fit on the population from which the model was trained was significantly higher (0.14 ≤ kappa ≤ 0.38). Seeking to understand better how diverse data might affect context-specific modeling choices, the authors revisited these data to see if active machine-learning techniques, which result in data being chosen across context to provide initial model parameters, could be used to create more accurate models. Described more fully in Karumbaiah (2021), the answer is a qualified yes, with evidence to suggest that making a principled choice of data across contexts may be a good technique to create more generalizable models, especially when the cost of collection of data is high (e.g., when it requires human coding).

While measuring bias in student success models is undergoing significant exploration – both through statistical and policy lenses – there have also been significant advances in improving fairness, accountability, and transparency of machine-learning techniques used for student predictive modeling. One example of a bias measurement method specifically focused on education is the Absolute Between-ROC Area (ABROCA) measure (Gardner et al., 2019), which applies slicing analysis methods to quantify the amount of bias between groups across the receiver operating characteristic metric. Developed by Gardner et al. (2019), this technique quantifies the difference in model performance between specific subpopulations, providing insights into model performance for different student groups. However, the critical question of identifying populations of most interest for predictive analytics still remains open, with significant policy implications for the adoption of predictive analytics in education and society more broadly. The answer to this question is still unclear, with a significant challenge of identifying measures that should be protected (as in the legal sense; see Akinwumi, 2019) and how to guide decision making (including deployment and creation of student success models) when predictive models are involved.

CRITICAL ISSUES

Despite the significant potential of predictive modeling for improving student learning, there are still numerous challenges and avenues for future research. Many of these issues are not unique to educational predictive modeling and represent some of the significant challenges within education, psychology, and computer science. In the broadest sense, there is an open question on how to integrate predictive models of student learning with pedagogical and administrative expertise and practice, whether in primary, secondary, tertiary, or lifelong learning settings (Tsai et al., 2021). This section focuses on some of the most significant areas of concern facing the adoption of student success modeling.

Replication, Reproduction, Generalization

One of the critical challenges facing the adoption of educational predictive modeling is to what extent predictive models can be generalized across educational institutions and contexts. While the generalisability and validity of the educational findings represent significant challenges more broadly, they are particularly critical in data-rich contexts such as educational predictive modeling. In such cases, the repeated verification of research findings is of utmost importance to advance our understanding of learning processes and identify effective instructional approaches and interventions (Kirschner & van Merriënboer, 2013). Unfortunately, replication studies represent only a fraction of education research. They are often expensive, time consuming, and require similar study designs and educational contexts.[8] Analyzing articles published in the top 100 educational journals, Makel and Plucker (2014) found that only 0.13% of the studies were replicated, with only 29% of the identified replicated studies being exact replicates rather than conceptual. Fortunately, student success predictive models are well situated for replication since much of the data used in predictive modelings, such as demographic or behavioral engagement data, are reasonably comparable across different institutions and domains. To date, replication and generalization efforts within predictive modeling generally fall within one of the following four categories.

1. *Institutional data-sharing agreements*, where data used for the development of predictive models and their results may be more easily shared between different institutions. One such example is the UNIZIN[9] consortium of thirteen US universities and university systems that produced shared predictive modeling analyses from enrollment data (Matz et al., 2017).
2. *Researcher-led collaborations*, where reproducible data science tools and technologies (Docker, Git) are being used to replicate and validate predictive models on data from other institutions. One such example is the MOOC Replication Framework (MORF) deployed at the University of Pennsylvania and the University of Michigan to evaluate predictive models of student success in MOOC courses. Utilizing open science technologies, the data are not shared between organizations; instead, the analytical infrastructure and data schemas are the same, thus allowing for distributed model creation that preserves learner and institutional data privacy (Kairouz et al., 2019; Gardner et al., 2018b).
3. *Large-scale experimental replications*, where a single large experiment is run in parallel across several contexts. One such example is the ManyClasses project (Fyfe et al., 2021), which focused on evaluating the efficacy of educational interventions. While such approaches significantly increase predictive model validity and rigor, to the best knowledge such approaches have not been used for predictive models of student success but were instead used mainly for fundamental theory confirmation.
4. *Individual researcher replications*, where an individual researcher replicates an already published study. Such studies may or may not involve the authors of the original study, their datasets, analyses, and insights into the design of the original study. Such replications are the least complex to organize, and due to lack of standardization across contexts and familiarity with original studies, they often result in lower rigor of replication.

While each of the four types of replication study designs has its benefits and drawbacks, regardless of the particular study design, several key factors affect the replicability and generalizability of the developed predictive models. The remainder of this section discusses each of these factors and how they affect the replicability and generalisability of predictive models.

Target outcome
There is a wide range of outcomes for predicting "student success" (Gardner & Brooks, 2018): predicting passing or failing a course, predicting final course grade or final exam grade,

predicting the correctness of exam answers, predicting time to degree completion, and predicting whether students drop out of a course or a study program. The choice of target variable in predictive models also depends on the context of the institutions or learning platforms. For example, high-ranked universities often focus more on predicting time to degree completion, having very few students failing courses or dropping out of study programs. In contrast, adult learning, distance learning, and online degree programs emphasize predicting course or degree completion, mainly due to higher student attrition. However, in most studies to date, limited attention has been dedicated to describing and justifying selected outcomes. It is often unclear exactly why a specific outcome has been selected and how and when it has been measured. More work on a diverse set of outcomes to help guide the different adoption and support models of institutions is needed.

Population sample

The demographics, motivations, and cultural contexts of learners are different across degree programs, institutions, and geographic and sociopolitical regions. A predictive model trained using data from a wealthy, white majority student population should be carefully evaluated before applying it to a Black and Hispanic serving institution. Similarly, a model created for urban learners is unlikely to perform well if adopted for rural learners (Ocumpaugh et al., 2014). A predictive model designed for an online degree where most students are adult learners working full-time or part-time seems unlikely to be accurate for a residential university where most students are in their early 20s and studying full-time. There is a need to understand how modeling these populations differ and, importantly, how the developed models might transfer between these populations.

Cold start

While the size of the data sample affects the quality of the developed model, another problem arises when the model is first used to make inferences for new kinds of students or in new circumstances. This problem, commonly known as the cold start problem, can be dealt with in a number of ways, though the most common are either using a form of weak prior with *ad-hoc* reinforcement learning or through model transfer. In the first of these, experts in the domain determine a set of rules to predict student success, and this is used while data are being collected. As data becomes available, predictive models can be trained and either be added to the expert priors (e.g., through ensembling techniques) or to replace those values. While reinforcement learning techniques which continually update predictive models could be used, there is little evidence that this is being done in current student success deployments. Transfer learning, on the other hand, involves taking models developed for similar situations (e.g., with the same task but at a different institution, or with a related task within the same institution) and deploying them either instead of or in addition to models created from new data. It is expected that these transferred models will capture some of the general trends of the data because the context is similar. As the context becomes more dissimilar – for instance taking a model trained on students from one country and applying it to students in a different country or sociopolitical context – the model transfer fitness will decrease.

There is a lack of work in the area of the cold start problem, and more extensive replications may demonstrate which features may transfer among populations, improving the ability of institutions to adopt models instead of building their own predictive models. While the opportunity here is rich, the authors' experience is that institutions tend to identify with "peer universities" of similar stature and selectivity, and that this may reinforce population homogeneity (e.g., prominence, geography, or degree-offering type) and undermine opportunity to develop models which transfer well across contexts. However, many vendor products (e.g., the learning management system or the student information system) do span across diverse institutional contexts, and it may be that vendors have an untapped role to play in diversifying replication efforts to improve model transfer.

Transparency and openness

Despite the increasing focus on the reproduction and replication of published educational research, the actual process of reproducing prediction models of student success is still subject to many barriers. These include lack of access to the training data, differences in data distributions, model underspecification or misspecification, lack of access to the code for building predictive models or underspecification of the metrics used to report results (Pineau et al., 2020). While there are ways to include necessary data and code in research reporting (e.g., supplementary materials for journal articles, through third-party study pre-registrations), the incentive for doing so is minimal. The fear of greater inspection (and potential retraction) often outweighs the perceived benefits for individual researchers, making them less likely to include such information. Supporting openness within research is also a non-trivial activity, going beyond sharing of analysis source code. It requires specifying computing infrastructure, time and cost to run predictive models, details of hyperparameter configurations, details of data distributions, and creating and sharing training data, to name a few. While such details might not be of immediate interest to the reviewers and not relevant to the main contribution of the paper, they are essential to the reproducibility efforts. The need here is multifaceted: more education and better tools are required to reduce the challenges and make studies more replicable. These include workshops to help educational researchers familiarize themselves with reproducible data science tools (e.g., Docker, Git, writing reproducible R/Python code, and checklists such as the Machine Learning Reproducibility Checklist[10]). At the same time, the incentive structure to engage in transparency and openness needs to be strengthened, which can happen both within scholarly societies (e.g., reviewing guidelines, promoting open practices, awards or recognition for particularly open work, replication or generalization challenges) and the academy at large.

Bias and fairness

The wide adoption of predictive analytics and AI in education also calls for careful considerations of algorithmic fairness and bias when designing and engineering such systems. Given the inequality and bias implicit in society and educational systems, machine learning and AI models, if not carefully developed and evaluated, may amplify these biases (Baker & Hawn, 2021). A notable recent example is the use of AI and statistical modeling to predict standardized test results in the UK (Piper, 2020). Rather than administering A-levels and GCSE exams during the COVID-19 pandemic, the UK government decided to use predictive modeling and estimate likely exam scores based on available historical data. However, further analysis revealed that modeling had a disproportionately negative effect on students from low socioeconomic backgrounds. More than one-third of the exam results (39.1%) were downgraded from the teacher-assessed grade with the largest differences seen among students of ethnic minorities and from low socioeconomic backgrounds. In contrast, the proportion of students receiving A or A* grades in private schools was twice as high as in public schools, further amplifying existing class inequality. After a major backlash from the UK public, the predicted scores were disregarded and not used, requiring changes to the existing university admission processes.

Most predictive models are developed to identify patterns from historical data, and the use of such models can perpetuate the existing inequalities in opportunity and outcome in education. For instance, the achievement gap in ethnic minorities in higher education in the United States has been well documented, with 60% of Black students failing to complete a 4-year degree within six years, compared to 36% of white and 26% of Asian students.[11] A large-scale study of 149 672 students enrolled in a distance-learning institution in the UK (Nguyen et al., 2020b) found that given the same amount of time spent on Moodle, Black and ethnic minorities students were between 19% and 79%, respectively, less likely to complete, pass or achieve an excellent grade compared with white students. It is important to reaffirm that the purpose of predictive models in education is to intervene and change learning outcomes. In practice, the ideal predictive model will be paired with interventions which reduce the fit of the model, as the intervention will be targeted to the students who would otherwise not succeed. The pairing of predictive models with interventions is expensive, and often research works will focus on one of these aspects. Larger implementation projects are needed to ground predictive models with interventions in a closed loop, leading to continuous improvement of educational outcomes.

Another important challenge from the standpoint of bias and fairness is the misuse (intentional or accidental) of predictive models. Even when predictive models are developed with an intention of supporting disadvantaged groups, their use can, instead, be used to widen the inequalities of opportunity and outcome. A particularly egregious illustration comes from Mount St. Mary's University in 2016, where models formed to project student attrition were then allegedly used to target such learners for early dismissal such that the three-week retention numbers reported to the government would appear more favorable (Svrluga, 2016). Such examples highlight the critical role of institutional policy to support the appropriate use of predictive models in a given context.

One must also consider the biases within the predictive models themselves, which may arise from training data which may be historically skewed towards underrepresented groups or severely imbalanced with little information about kinds of learners. This bias can come from several different factors and is not yet well accounted for in mainstream student success research. For instance, different minority groups might have vastly different consent rates for the use of their data in predictive analytics models, leading to a population bias, as demonstrated by Li et al. (2021). Such response differences can result in models reflecting an even stronger imbalance with respect to minority classes. As more data generally improve the performance of a given model, such issues can lead to model inaccuracies between classes of learners, and poor deployment of institutional support resources.

Biases can also be introduced through feature engineering and the choice of outcome measures. For instance, the use of behavioral trace data as a proxy of academic engagement in MOOCs assumes a stable and affordable access to the internet and a laptop/tablet for everyone. However, students from low-income countries or rural areas might not have such privileges, which makes their academic engagement artificially lower than their actual workload and their eventual success. While some work has been done to explore diverse-feature generation through crowdsourcing (Smith et al., 2017), this has not yet been widely leveraged in the area of predictive models for student success. We believe that there is more opportunity to reduce bias in models by moving away from naïve use of the data which has historically been made available by systems and toward the collection of data which is rooted in the anticipated determinants (whether formed by theory and prior research or by expert knowledge of the local context) of student success. Within the banking sector, for example, to mitigate negative effects of stereotypes and biases in the historical data, there are strict regulations around the use of predictive models and the kinds of data that can be used to develop predictive models. With the growing use of predictive models in educational contexts, there is a growing need to consider these issues in the education sector to avoid unintended misuse.

Defining and measuring model fairness and bias is one step in which the larger learning analytics and educational data mining communities are engaging. Several fairness metrics have been proposed (e.g., statistical disparities, equalized odds, ABROCA), examined in detail by Kilzicec and Lee's (2020) comprehensive review. There is an increasing body of work in the AIED, EDM, and LAK communities that has started auditing model fairness as well as testing different strategies to mitigate biases in prediction models (Bayer et al., 2021; Gardner et al., 2019; Yu et al., 2020, 2021). For example, Yu et al. (2021) compared the overall performance and fairness of model predictions (N-train = 96,441, N-test = 21,214) with or without four protected attributes (i.e., gender, URM, first-generation student, and high financial need) and found that these attributes did not influence the overall accuracy and marginally improved model fairness. Bayer et al. (2021) demonstrated that the at-risk prediction model (N-train = 35,067, N-test = 32,538) indeed worked more in favor of the majority group than the minority group. The authors also showed that building separate models for each subgroup (e.g., female vs. male) did not improve the accuracy nor the fairness of the model. Taken as first explorations in the space, more work is needed to understand the balance between accuracy and fairness in educational predictive models, especially as the number of observations drop.

Since bias and fairness in student success prediction is more than just an algorithmic and data problem, it is important to consider the broader sociotechnical systems in which a given prediction model was developed. Holstein and Doroudi (2021) proposed several pathways for AI systems to avoid amplifying and to alleviate existing inequities in education. For example, this includes promoting increased transparency and accountability of prediction models, incorporating equity-related outcomes instead of just individual learning outcomes, and enabling wider participation of stakeholders (i.e., students, instructors) in designing and implementing predictive models of student success.

Finally, the question of what to do with biased models of educational success has largely been ignored. Biased models may inaccurately identify the students which need support at differing rates based on demographic characterizations, but little has been said about whether there is a benefit for these models to be put into practice anyway. There is very little translational research showing the effect of predictive models put into practice and measured against human expert systems, and the research on the data science of predictive models and bias far outweighs the educational administration research which is needed to guide successful implementation of student success projects. It is quite possible that a biased model may be better than no model at all.

Adoption, Intervention, and Theory

In the idealized form a predictive model for student success leads to the improvement of student outcomes through targeted interventions which leverage and build up educational theory.

In reality, these three areas are often disconnected from one another, leading to models which either simply measure the impact of existing interventions (e.g., through counterfactual analyses) or never even get deployed to actual student support systems. Writing specifically about assessment models, Ho (2018) elevates the educational intervention and argues that a predictive model is only valid if it is ultimately wrong and under-predicts success due to positive interventions. Ho further cites the work of Perie et al. (2009): "...if the test predicts that a student is on track to perform at the basic level, and then appropriate interventions are used to bring the student to proficient, the statistical analysis of the test's predictive validity should underpredict student performance over time". Such a perspective is a refreshing call to the communities building both predictive models and interventions to carefully consider how they can be paired to improve outcomes.

This pairing of models with interventions has potential to influence how models are created in the first place. For instance, the ABROCA statistic determines the amount of bias between a model for two populations (e.g., male and female), and was built with the notion that the underlying receiver operating characteristic curve (ROC) is a good measure of model evaluation. The ROC curve represents the true-positive-to-false-positive prediction trade-off across a set of parameterizations and is well used within the predictive modeling literature. But are all parameterizations of a model something which warrants consideration by an institution? And how does the capacity of an institution to engage an intervention change which aspects of an ROC curve are prioritized (e.g., does building a more fair models come at the cost of increasing the false positive rate for all, which stretches out the limited resources for intervention)? There is a growing need to engage institutional decision making around how interventions and models (as well as our measurement of said models) are paired in actual implementations.

Not all classification costs are the same, especially in imbalance classification tasks, which are commonly present in education contexts. For example, the cost of misclassifying the minority group of students who failed the course could result in more detrimental effects than misclassifying the majority who passed the course. There is a whole subfield in machine learning, "cost-sensitive learning" (Elkan, 2001), which takes the misclassification costs (i.e., false negative and false positive), as well as other costs, into consideration when building a machine-learning model. For instance, supporting students through an email, telephone call, or dormitory room visit have dramatically different costs to the institution and are likely to elicit a different sense of urgency (and action) by students. Implementing intervention cost parameters, when known, in model training has potential to create models which are *accurate for a given purpose* and improve the actionability and efficacy of such model-intervention pairs.

DISCUSSION

The rapid rise over the last 25 years of machine learning in the areas of computer science and statistics has caused an intense interest in translational application to other domains. One aspect of this in the field of education is the predictive model for "student success", a sometimes nebulous term which includes everything from grade prediction to job placement at the end of an academic career. As the social implications of predictive modeling arise (for instance, fairness and bias in models), the larger field of educational data scientists and learning analytics researchers has been quick to explore how these topics unfold in the field of education.

However, the translation of these models to practice within the field of education has been slow. Researchers in the field are rarely leveraged by their institutions when products are chosen for deployment, and are even less likely to be consulted by vendors when designing new solutions. Most, or all, of the critical issues we have identified require deeper ties and collaborations between administrators, researchers, and solution developers. In addition, there is a rich opportunity to realize predictive model benefits by forming teams of researchers who can tune models for particular interventions and, vice versa, implementing interventions suitable for the fitness and limitations of given models. Thus, we suggest that the largest benefits to society will be gained by engaging in a more holistic investigation of predictive models of student success across the variety of implementation actors in educational settings. Combining predictive modeling expertise with those who have the nuance of the deployment environment will lead to improvements in generalization, help reduce model bias, increase transparency to all involved, and improve both adoption within and theories of education.

NOTES

1. In an increasingly data literate world, the issue of data collection and privacy comes up regularly, and has long been a topic of scholarly interest. An in-depth discussion of this is outside the scope of this chapter, however we suggest readers consider the works of Pardo and Siemens (2014), Tsai et al. (2020), and Sun et al. (2019) as a starting point for further reading.
2. https://nces.ed.gov/ipeds/.
3. There are many different examples of such standardized tests, often formed at the national level for admissions to public universities within a given country. The SAT is one prominent test which has been historically used within the United States; however, the events of COVID-19 made testing difficult, and most institutions waived testing requirements in the 2020/2021 and 2021/2022 academic years. As vaccination has improved, some institutions are reinstating the use of standardized testing for admissions (Cramer & Eduardo, 2022).
4. www.imsglobal.org/activity/caliper.
5. https://xapi.com/.
6. Note the conference is abbreviated to L@S in official calls for papers; see details of the open science statement for the year 2020 at https://learningatscale.acm.org/las2020/call-for-papers/.
7. See the 2021–2022 Society for Learning Analytics Research Strategic Plan (*SoLAR Strategic Plan April 2021–December 2022*, 2021).
8. The growing awareness of the importance of replication studies can be seen in some funding solicitations, such as the IES (Schneider, 2018).
9. "Unizin – Empowering Universities." https://unizin.org/. Accessed 12 July 2021.
10. The Machine Learning Reproducibility Checklist (v2.0, 7 April 2020). Retrieved 8 July 2021, from www.cs.mcgill.ca/~jpineau/ReproducibilityChecklist.pdf.
11. According to NCES IPEDS (Indicator 23).

REFERENCES

Akhtar, S. A. (2015). Developing Predictive Analytics to Enhance Learning and Teaching in Lab Based Courses [Ph.D., University of Surrey (United Kingdom)]. In *PQDT - UK & Ireland* (1827870812). ProQuest Dissertations & Theses Global. https://search.proquest.com/docview/1827870812?account id=14649.

Akinwumi, M. (2019, December 19). The Role of Protected Attributes in AI Fairness. www.trustscience. com/blog/the-role-of-protected-attributes-in-ai-fairness.

Allen, L. K., Snow, E. L., & McNamara, D. S. (2015). Are You Reading My Mind? Modeling Students' Reading Comprehension Skills With Natural Language Processing Techniques. In *Proceedings of the Fifth International Conference on Learning Analytics and Knowledge*, 246–254. https://doi.org/10.1145/2723576.2723617.

Arnold, K. E., & Pistilli, M. D. (2012). Course Signals at Purdue: Using Learning Analytics to Increase Student Success. In *Proceedings of the Second International Conference on Learning Analytics and Knowledge*, 267–270. https://doi.org/10.1145/2330601.2330666.

Baker, R. S., & Hawn, A. (2021). Algorithmic Bias in Education. *International Journal of Artificial Intelligence Education*. Advance online publication. https://doi.org/10.1007/s40593-021-00285-9.

Barbosa, G., Camelo, R., Cavalcanti, A. P., Miranda, P., Mello, R. F., Kovanović, V., & Gašević, D. (2020). Towards Automatic Cross-Language Classification of Cognitive Presence in Online Discussions. In *Proceedings of the Tenth International Conference on Learning Analytics & Knowledge (LAK'20)*, 605–614. https://doi.org/10.1145/3375462.3375496.

Bayer, V., Hlosta, M., & Fernandez, M. (2021). Learning Analytics and Fairness: Do Existing Algorithms Serve Everyone Equally? *Artificial Intelligence in Education*, 71–75.

Brooks, C., Thompson, C., & Teasley, S. (2015a). A Time Series Interaction Analysis Method for Building Predictive Models of Learners Using Log Data. In *Proceedings of the Fifth International Conference on Learning Analytics And Knowledge*, 126–135. https://doi.org/10.1145/2723576.2723581.

Brooks, C., Thompson, C., & Teasley, S. (2015b). Who You Are or What You Do: Comparing the Predictive Power of Demographics Vs. Activity Patterns in Massive Open Online Courses (MOOCs). In *Proceedings of the Second (2015) ACM Conference on Learning @ Scale*, 245–248. https://doi.org/10.1145/2724660.2728668.

Calvo, R. A., & D'Mello, S. (2010). Affect Detection: An Interdisciplinary Review of Models, Methods, and Their Applications. *IEEE Transactions on Affective Computing*, 1(1), 18–37. https://doi.org/10.1109/T-AFFC.2010.1.

Caulfield, M. (2013, September 26). Why the Course Signals Math Does Not Add Up. *Hapgood*. https://hapgood.us/2013/09/26/why-the-course-signals-math-does-not-add-up/.

Corbett, A. T., & Anderson, J. R. (1994). Knowledge Tracing: Modeling the Acquisition of Procedural Knowledge. *User Modeling and User-Adapted Interaction*, 4(4), 253–278.

Cramer, M., & Eduardo M. (2022). "M.I.T. Will Again Require SAT and ACT Scores." *The New York Times*, March 29, 2022. https://www.nytimes.com/2022/03/28/education/mit-sat-act-scores-admission.html.

Crossley, S., Paquette, L., Dascalu, M., McNamara, D. S., & Baker, R. S. (2016). Combining Click-Stream Data With NLP Tools to Better Understand MOOC Completion. In *Proceedings of the Sixth International Conference on Learning Analytics & Knowledge*, 6–14. https://doi.org/10.1145/2883851.2883931.

Cui, Y., Chen, F., Shiri, A., & Fan, Y. (2019). Predictive Analytic Models of Student Success in Higher Education: A Review of Methodology. *Information and Learning Sciences*, 39, 88.

Cunningham, J. A. (2017). Predicting Student Success in a Self-Paced Mathematics MOOC [Ph.D., Arizona State University]. In *ProQuest Dissertations and Theses* (1900990574). ProQuest Dissertations & Theses Global. https://search.proquest.com/docview/1900990574?accountid=14649.

Di Mitri, D., Scheffel, M., Drachsler, H., Börner, D., Ternier, S., & Specht, M. (2017). Learning Pulse: A Machine Learning Approach for Predicting Performance in Self-Regulated Learning Using Multimodal Data. In *Proceedings of the Seventh International Learning Analytics & Knowledge Conference*, 188–197. https://doi.org/10.1145/3027385.3027447.

Elkan, C. (2001). The Foundations of Cost-Sensitive Learning. *International Joint Conference on Artificial Intelligence*, 17, 973–978.

Er, E., Villa-Torrano, C., Dimitriadis, Y., Gasevic, D., Bote-Lorenzo, M. L., Asensio-Pérez, J. I., Gómez-Sánchez, E., & Martínez Monés, A. (2021). Theory-Based Learning Analytics to Explore Student Engagement Patterns in a Peer Review Activity. In *LAK21: 11th International Learning Analytics and Knowledge Conference* (pp. 196–206). Association for Computing Machinery. https://doi.org/10.1145/3448139.3448158.

Feldstein, M. (2013, September 26). Digging into the Purdue Course Signals Results. *eLiterate*. https://eliterate.us/digging-purdue-course-signals-results/.

Frank, E., Hall, M., Trigg, L., Holmes, G., & Witten, I. H. (2004). Data Mining in Bioinformatics Using Weka. *Bioinformatics*, 20(15), 2479–2481.

Fyfe, E. R., de Leeuw, J. R., Carvalho, P. F., Goldstone, R. L., Sherman, J., Admiraal, D., Alford, L. K., Bonner, A., Brassil, C. E., Brooks, C. A., Carbonetto, T., Chang, S. H., Cruz, L., Czymoniewicz-Klippel, M., Daniel, F., Driessen, M., Habashy, N., Hanson-Bradley, C. L., Hirt, E. R., … Motz, B. A. (2021). Many Classes 1: Assessing the Generalizable Effect of Immediate Feedback Versus Delayed Feedback Across Many College Classes. *Advances in Methods and Practices in Psychological Science*, *4*(3), 25152459211027575.

Gardner, J., & Brooks, C. (2018). Student Success Prediction in MOOCs. *User Modeling and User-Adapted Interaction*, *28*(2), 127–203.

Gardner, J., Brooks, C., Andres, J., & Baker, R. (2018a). Replicating MOOC Predictive Models at Scale. In *Proceedings of the Fifth Annual ACM Conference on Learning at Scale*, 1–10.

Gardner, J., Brooks, C., Andres, J., & Baker, R. (2018b) MORF: A Framework for Predictive Modeling and Replication At Scale With Privacy-Restricted MOOC Data. In *2018 IEEE International Conference on Big Data (Big Data)*, 3235–3244. https://doi.org/10.1109/BigData.2018.8621874.

Gardner, J., Brooks, C., & Baker, R. (2019). Evaluating the Fairness of Predictive Student Models Through Slicing Analysis. In *Proceedings of the 9th International Conference on Learning Analytics & Knowledge*. https://doi.org/10.1145/3303772.3303791.

Gasevic, D., Dawson, S., Mirriahi, N., & Long, P. D. (2015). Learning Analytics – A Growing Field and Community Engagement. *Journal of Learning Analytics*, *2*(1), 1–6. https://doi.org/10.18608/jla.2015.21.1.

Gervet, T., Koedinger, K., Schneider, J., & Mitchell, T. (2020). When is Deep Learning the Best Approach to Knowledge Tracing? *Journal of Educational Data Mining*, *12*(3), 31–54.

Greene, J. A., Oswald, C. A., & Pomerantz, J. (2015). Predictors of Retention and Achievement in a Massive Open Online Course. *American Educational Research Journal*, *52*, 925–955. https://doi.org/10.3102/0002831215584621.

Henrich, J., Heine, S. J., & Norenzayan, A. (2010). The Weirdest People in the World? *The Behavioral and Brain Sciences*, *33*(2–3), 61–83; discussion 83–135.

Herodotou, C., Rienties, B., Boroowa, A., Zdrahal, Z., Hlosta, M., & Naydenova, G. (2017). Implementing Predictive Learning Analytics on a Large Scale: The Teacher's Perspective. In *Proceedings of the Seventh International Learning Analytics & Knowledge Conference*, 267–271. https://doi.org/10.1145/3027385.3027397.

Ho, A. (2018, February 14). Made to be Broken: The Paradox of Student Growth Prediction. In *Michigan School Testing Conference*, Ann Arbor, MI.

Holstein, K., & Doroudi, S. (2021). Equity and Artificial Intelligence in Education: Will "AIEd" Amplify or Alleviate Inequities in Education? In *arXiv [cs.HC]*. arXiv. http://arxiv.org/abs/2104.12920.

Howard, E., Meehan, M., & Parnell, A. (2018). Contrasting Prediction Methods for Early Warning Systems at Undergraduate Level. *The Internet and Higher Education*, *37*, 66–75. https://doi.org/10.1016/j.iheduc.2018.02.001.

Hussain, M. S., AlZoubi, O., Calvo, R. A., & D'Mello, S. K. (2011). Affect Detection From Multichannel Physiology During Learning Sessions With AutoTutor. In G. Biswas, S. Bull, J. Kay, & A. Mitrovic (Eds.), *Artificial Intelligence in Education* (pp. 131–138). Springer. https://doi.org/10.1007/978-3-642-21869-9_19.

IMS Global Learning Consortium, Inc. (2020). *Caliper Analytics 1.2 Specification*. https://www.imsglobal.org/spec/caliper/v1p2.

Iraj, H., Fudge, A., Faulkner, M., Pardo, A., & Kovanović, V. (2020). Understanding Students' Engagement With Personalised Feedback Messages. In *Proceedings of the Tenth International Conference on Learning Analytics & Knowledge (LAK'20)*, 438–447. https://doi.org/10.1145/3375462.3375527.

Jiang, S., Warschauer, M., Williams, A. E., O'Dowd, D., & Schenke, K. (2014). Predicting MOOC Performance With Week 1 Behavior. In *Proceedings of the 7th International Conference on Educational Data Mining*, 273–275. http://educationaldatamining.org/EDM2014/uploads/procs2014/short%20papers/273_EDM-2014-Short.pdf.

Joksimović, S., Gašević, D., Kovanović, V., Riecke, B. E., & Hatala, M. (2015). Social Presence in Online Discussions as a Process Predictor of Academic Performance. *Journal of Computer Assisted Learning*, *31*, 638–654. https://doi.org/10.1111/jcal.12107.

Kairouz, P., McMahan, H. B., Avent, B., Bellet, A., Bennis, M., Bhagoji, A. N., Bonawitz, K., Charles, Z., Cormode, G., Cummings, R., D'Oliveira, R. G. L., Eichner, H., Rouayheb, S. E., Evans, D.,

Gardner, J., Garrett, Z., Gascón, A., Ghazi, B., Gibbons, P. B., ... Zhao, S. (2019). *Advances and Open Problems in Federated Learning*. http://arxiv.org/abs/1912.04977.

Karumbaiah, S., Lan, A., Nagpal, S., Baker, R. S., Botelho, A., & Heffernan, N. (2021). Using Past Data to Warm Start Active Machine Learning: Does Context Matter? In *LAK21: 11th International Learning Analytics and Knowledge Conference*, 151–160.

Kennedy, G., Coffrin, C., de Barba, P., & Corrin, L. (2015). Predicting Success: How Learners' Prior Knowledge, Skills and Activities Predict MOOC Performance. In *Proceedings of the Fifth International Conference on Learning Analytics and Knowledge*, 136–140. https://doi.org/10.1145/2723576.2723593.

Kirschner, P. A., & van Merriënboer, J. J. G. (2013). Do Learners Really Know Best? Urban Legends in Education. In *Educational Psychologist* (Vol. 48, Issue 3, pp. 169–183). https://doi.org/10.1080/00461520.2013.804395.

Kizilcec, R. F., & Brooks, C. (2017). Diverse Big Data and Randomized Field Experiments in Massive Open Online Courses: Opportunities for Advancing Learning Research. In George Siemens And (Ed.), *Handbook of Learning Analytics*. Society for Learning Analytics Research.

Kizilcec, R. F., & Lee, H. (2020). Algorithmic Fairness in Education. In *arXiv [cs.CY]*. arXiv. http://arxiv.org/abs/2007.05443.

Kizilcec, R. F., Pérez-Sanagustín, M., & Maldonado, J. J. (2017). Self-Regulated Learning Strategies Predict Learner Behavior and Goal Attainment in Massive Open Online Courses. *Computers & Education*, *104*, 18–33. https://doi.org/10.1016/j.compedu.2016.10.001.

Kizilcec, R. F., Piech, C., & Schneider, E. (2013). Deconstructing Disengagement: Analyzing Learner Subpopulations in Massive Open Online Courses. In *Proceedings of the Third International Conference on Learning Analytics and Knowledge*, 170–179. https://doi.org/10.1145/2460296.2460330.

Kovanović, V., Joksimović, S., Gašević, D., & Hatala, M. (2014). Automated Cognitive Presence Detection in Online Discussion Transcripts. In *Workshop Proceedings of LAK 2014 4th International Conference on Learning Analytics & Knowledge (LAK'14)*, Indianapolis, IN, USA. http://ceur-ws.org/Vol-1137/.

Kovanović, V., Joksimović, S., Mirriahi, N., Blaine, E., Gašević, D., Siemens, G., & Dawson, S. (2018). Understand Students' Self-Reflections Through Learning Analytics. In *Proceedings of the 8th International Conference on Learning Analytics and Knowledge (LAK'18)*, 389–398. https://doi.org/10.1145/3170358.3170374.

Kovanović, V., Joksimović, S., Waters, Z., Gašević, D., Kitto, K., Hatala, M., & Siemens, G. (2016). Towards Automated Content Analysis of Discussion Transcripts: A Cognitive Presence Case. In *Proceedings of the 6th International Conference on Learning Analytics & Knowledge (LAK'16)*, 15–24. https://doi.org/10.1145/2883851.2883950.

Li, W., Sun, K., Schaub, F., & Brooks, C. (2021). Disparities in Students' Propensity to Consent to Learning Analytics. *International Journal of Artificial Intelligence in Education*, 1–45. https://doi.org/10.1007/s40593-021-00254-2.

Ma, Y., Liu, B., Wong, C. K., Yu, P. S., & Lee, S. M. (2000). Targeting the Right Students Using Data Mining. In *Proceedings of the Sixth ACM SIGKDD International Conference on Knowledge Discovery and Data Mining*, 457–464. https://doi.org/10.1145/347090.347184.

Macfadyen, L. P., & Dawson, S. (2010). Mining LMS Data to Develop an "Early Warning System" for Educators: A Proof of Concept. *Computers & Education*, *54*(2), 588–599. https://doi.org/10.1016/j.compedu.2009.09.008.

Mahzoon, M. J. (2018). Student Sequence Model: A Temporal Model for Exploring and Predicting Risk From Heterogeneous Student Data [Ph.D., The University of North Carolina at Charlotte]. In *ProQuest Dissertations and Theses* (2035548390). ProQuest Dissertations & Theses Global. https://search.proquest.com/docview/2035548390?accountid=14649.

Makel, M. C., & Plucker, J. A. (2014). Facts Are More Important Than Novelty: Replication in the Education Sciences. *Educational Researcher*, *43*(6), 304–316.

Maldonado-Mahauad, J., Pérez-Sanagustín, M., Moreno-Marcos, P. M., Alario-Hoyos, C., Muñoz-Merino, P. J., & Delgado-Kloos, C. (2018). Predicting Learners' Success in a Self-Paced MOOC Through Sequence Patterns of Self-Regulated Learning. In V. Pammer-Schindler, M. Pérez-Sanagustín, H. Drachsler, R. Elferink, & M. Scheffel (Eds.), *Lifelong Technology-Enhanced Learning* (pp. 355–369). Springer International Publishing. https://doi.org/10.1007/978-3-319-98572-5_27.

Marbouti, F. (2016). A Standards-Based Grading Model to Predict Students' Success in a First-Year Engineering Course [Ph.D., Purdue University]. In *ProQuest Dissertations and Theses* (1832956412). ProQuest Dissertations & Theses Global. https://search.proquest.com/docview/1832956412 ?accountid=14649.

Matz, R. L., Koester, B. P., Fiorini, S., Grom, G., Shepard, L., Stangor, C. G., Weiner, B., & McKay, T. A. (2017). Patterns of Gendered Performance Differences in Large Introductory Courses at Five Research Universities. *AERA Open*, *3*(4), 2332858417743754.

Ming, N., & Ming, V. (2012). Predicting Student Outcomes from Unstructured Data. In *Proceedings of the 2nd International Workshop on Personalization Approaches in Learning Environments (PALE)*, 11–16.

Moreno-Marcos, P. M., Muñoz-Merino, P. J., Maldonado-Mahauad, J., Pérez-Sanagustín, M., Alario-Hoyos, C., & Delgado Kloos, C. (2020). Temporal Analysis for Dropout Prediction Using Self-Regulated Learning Strategies in Self-Paced MOOCs. *Computers & Education*, *145*, 103728. https:// doi.org/10.1016/j.compedu.2019.103728.

Neef, D. (2014). *Digital Exhaust: What Everyone Should Know About Big Data, Digitization, and Digitally Driven Innovation* (1st edition). FT Press.

Neto, V., Rolim, V., Cavalcanti, A. P., Dueire Lins, R., Gasevic, D., & Ferreiramello, R. (2021). Automatic Content Analysis of Online Discussions for Cognitive Presence: A Study of the Generalizability Across Educational Contexts. *IEEE Transactions on Learning Technologies*. Advance online publication. https://doi.org/10.1109/TLT.2021.3083178.

Neto, V., Rolim, V., Ferreira, R., Kovanović, V., Gašević, D., Dueire Lins, R., & Lins, R. (2018). Automated Analysis of Cognitive Presence in Online Discussions Written in Portuguese. In V. Pammer-Schindler, M. Pérez-Sanagustín, H. Drachsler, R. Elferink, & M. Scheffel (Eds.), *Lifelong Technology-Enhanced Learning* (pp. 245–261). Springer International Publishing. https://doi.org/10 .1007/978-3-319-98572-5_19.

Newland, B., Martin, L., & Ringan, N. (2015). *Learning Analytics in UK HE 2015*. Heads of e-Learning Forum (HeLF). https://cris.brighton.ac.uk/ws/files/413048/HeLFLearningAnalyticsReport2015.pdf.

Nguyen, Q., Poquet, O., Brooks, C., & Li, W. (2020a). Exploring Homophily in Demographics and Academic Performance Using Spatial-Temporal Student Networks. *Educational Data Mining Society*. https://eric.ed.gov/?id=ED607906.

Nguyen, Q., Rienties, B., & Richardson, J. T. E. (2020b). Learning Analytics to Uncover Inequality in Behavioural Engagement and Academic Attainment in a Distance Learning Setting. In *Assessment & Evaluation in Higher Education* (Vol. 45, Issue 4, pp. 594–606). https://doi.org/10.1080/02602938 .2019.1679088.

Ocumpaugh, J., Baker, R., Gowda, S., Heffernan, N., & Heffernan, C. (2014). Population Validity for Educational Data Mining Models: A Case Study in Affect Detection. *British Journal of Educational Technology: Journal of the Council for Educational Technology*, *45*(3), 487–501.

Pardo, A., & Siemens, G. (2014). Ethical and Privacy Principles for Learning Analytics. *British Journal of Educational Technology: Journal of the Council for Educational Technology*, *45*(3), 438–450.

Perie, M., Marion, S., & Gong, B. (2009). Moving Toward a Comprehensive Assessment System: A Framework for Considering Interim Assessments. *Educational Measurement: Issues and Practice*, *28*(3), 5–13.

Piech, C., Spencer, J., Huang, J., Ganguli, S., Sahami, M., Guibas, L., & Sohl-Dickstein, J. (2015). Deep Knowledge Tracing. In *arXiv [cs.AI]*. arXiv. http://arxiv.org/abs/1506.05908.

Pineau, J., Vincent-Lamarre, P., Sinha, K., Larivière, V., Beygelzimer, A., d'Alché-Buc, F., Fox, E., & Larochelle, H. (2020). *Improving Reproducibility in Machine Learning Research (A Report From the NeurIPS 2019 Reproducibility Program)*. http://arxiv.org/abs/2003.12206.

Piper, K. (2020, August 22). The UK Used a Formula to Predict Students' Scores for Canceled Exams. Guess Who Did Well. *Vox*. https://www.vox.com/future-perfect/2020/8/22/21374872/uk-united-kingdom-formula-predict-student-test-scores-exams.

Ramesh, A., Goldwasser, D., Huang, B., Daume, H., III, & Getoor, L. (2014). Uncovering Hidden Engagement Patterns for Predicting Learner Performance in MOOCs. In *Proceedings of the First ACM Conference on Learning @ Scale Conference*, 157–158. https://doi.org/10.1145/2556325.25 67857.

Robinson, R. L., Navea, R., & Ickes, W. (2013). Predicting Final Course Performance From Students' Written Self-Introductions: A LIWC Analysis. *Journal of Language and Social Psychology*, 0261927X13476869. https://doi.org/10.1177/0261927X13476869.

Schneider, M. (2018, December 17). *A More Systematic Approach to Replicating Research*. https://ies. ed.gov/director/remarks/12-17-2018.asp.

Sharma, K., Papamitsiou, Z., Olsen, J. K., & Giannakos, M. (2020). Predicting Learners' Effortful Behaviour in Adaptive Assessment Using Multimodal Data. In *Proceedings of the Tenth International Conference on Learning Analytics & Knowledge*, 480–489. https://doi.org/10.1145/3375462.3375498.

Shmueli, G. (2010). To Explain or to Predict? *Statistical Science*, *25*(3), 289–310. https://doi.org/10.1214/10-STS330.

Siemens, G. (2013). Learning Analytics: The Emergence of a Discipline. *American Behavioral Scientist*, *57*(10), 1380–1400. https://doi.org/10.1177/0002764213498851.

Sierens, E., Vansteenkiste, M., Goossens, L., Soenens, B., & Dochy, F. (2009). The Synergistic Relationship of Perceived Autonomy Support and Structure in the Prediction of Self-Regulated Learning. *British Journal of Educational Psychology*, *79*(1), 57–68. https://doi.org/10.1348/000709908X304398.

Sinha, T., & Cassell, J. (2015). Connecting the Dots: Predicting Student Grade Sequences From Bursty MOOC Interactions Over Time. In *Proceedings of the Second (2015) ACM Conference on Learning @ Scale*, 249–252. https://doi.org/10.1145/2724660.2728669.

Smith, M. J., Wedge, R., & Veeramachaneni, K. (2017). FeatureHub: Towards Collaborative Data Science. In *2017 IEEE International Conference on Data Science and Advanced Analytics (DSAA)*, 590–600.

SoLAR Strategic Plan April 2021 – December 2022. (2021). www.solaresearch.org/wp-content/uploads/2021/06/SoLAR_Strategic-Plan_21-22.pdf.

Sun, K., Mhaidli, A. H., Watel, S., Brooks, C. A., & Schaub, F. (2019). It's My Data! Tensions Among Stakeholders of a Learning Analytics Dashboard. In *Proceedings of the 2019 CHI Conference on Human Factors in Computing Systems*, 1–14.

Svrluga, S. (2016, January 19). University President Allegedly Says Struggling Freshmen Are Bunnies That Should Be Drowned. *The Washington Post*. https://www.washingtonpost.com/news/grade-point/wp/2016/01/19/university-president-allegedly-says-struggling-freshmen-are-bunnies-that-should-be-drowned-that-a-glock-should-be-put-to-their-heads/.

Taylor, C., Veeramachaneni, K., & O'Reilly, U.-M. (2014). Likely to Stop? Predicting Stopout in Massive Open Online Courses. *ArXiv:1408.3382 [Cs]*. http://arxiv.org/abs/1408.3382.

Thomas, B. L., & Viljoen, M. (2019). Heart Rate Variability and Academic Performance of First-Year University Students. *Neuropsychobiology*, *78*(4). https://doi.org/10.1159/000500613.

Torenbeek, M., Jansen, E., & Suhre, C. (2013). Predicting Undergraduates' Academic Achievement: The Role of the Curriculum, Time Investment and Self-Regulated Learning. *Studies in Higher Education*, *38*(9), 1393–1406. https://doi.org/10.1080/03075079.2011.640996.

Tsai, Y.-S., Kovanović, V., & Gašević, D. (2021). Connecting the Dots: An Exploratory Study on Learning Analytics Adoption Factors, Experience, and Priorities. *The Internet and Higher Education*, *50*, 100794.

Tsai, Y.-S., Whitelock-Wainwright, A., & Gašević, D. (2020). The Privacy Paradox and Its Implications for Learning Analytics. In *Proceedings of the Tenth International Conference on Learning Analytics & Knowledge*, 230–239.

Umer, R., Susnjak, T., Mathrani, A., & Suriadi, S. (2017). On Predicting Academic Performance With Process Mining in Learning Analytics. *Journal of Research in Innovative Teaching & Learning*, *10*(2), 160–176. https://doi.org/10.1108/JRIT-09-2017-0022.

van der Zee, T., & Reich, J. (2018). Open Education Science. *AERA Open*, *4*(3), 2332858418787466.

van Goidsenhoven, S., Bogdanova, D., Deeva, G., Broucke, S. vanden, De Weerdt, J., & Snoeck, M. (2020). Predicting Student Success in a Blended Learning Environment. In *Proceedings of the Tenth International Conference on Learning Analytics & Knowledge*, 17–25. https://doi.org/10.1145/3375462.3375494.

Waters, Z., Kovanović, V., Kitto, K., & Gašević, D. (2015). Structure Matters: Adoption of Structured Classification Approach in the Context of Cognitive Presence Classification. In G. Zuccon, S. Geva, H. Joho, F. Scholer, A. Sun, & P. Zhang (Eds.), *2015 Asia Information Retrieval Societies Conference Proceedings* (pp. 227–238). Springer International Publishing. https://doi.org/10.1007/978-3-319-28940-3_18.

Wen, M., Yang, D., & Rose, C. P. (2014). Linguistic Reflections of Student Engagement in Massive Open Online Courses. In *Eighth International AAAI Conference on Weblogs and Social Media*, 525–534. http://www.aaai.org/ocs/index.php/ICWSM/ICWSM14/paper/view/8057.

Westrick, P. A., Marini, J. P., Young, L., Ng, H., Shmueli, D., & Shaw, E. J. (2019). Validity of the SAT® for Predicting First-Year Grades and Retention to the Second Year. *College Board Research Paper*. https://satsuite.collegeboard.org/media/pdf/national-sat-validity-study.pdf.

Wolff, A., Zdrahal, Z., Nikolov, A., & Pantucek, M. (2013). Improving Retention: Predicting At-Risk Students by Analysing Clicking Behaviour in a Virtual Learning Environment. In *Proceedings of the Third International Conference on Learning Analytics and Knowledge*, 145–149. https://doi.org/10.1145/2460296.2460324.

Yoo, J., & Kim, J. (2012). Predicting Learner's Project Performance With Dialogue Features in Online Q&A Discussions. In S. A. Cerri, W. J. Clancey, G. Papadourakis, & K. Panourgia (Eds.), *Intelligent Tutoring Systems* (pp. 570–575). Berlin Heidelberg: Springer. http://link.springer.com/chapter/10.1007/978-3-642-30950-2_74.

Yoo, J., & Kim, J. (2013). Can Online Discussion Participation Predict Group Project Performance? Investigating the Roles of Linguistic Features and Participation Patterns. *International Journal of Artificial Intelligence in Education*, 24(1), 8–32. https://doi.org/10.1007/s40593-013-0010-8.

Yu, R., Lee, H., & Kizilcec, R. F. (2021). Should College Dropout Prediction Models Include Protected Attributes? In *Proceedings of the Eighth ACM Conference on Learning @ Scale*, 91–100.

Yu, R., Li, Q., Fischer, C., Doroudi, S., & Xu, D. (2020). Towards Accurate and Fair Prediction of College Success: Evaluating Different Sources of Student Data. *International Educational Data Mining Society*. http://files.eric.ed.gov/fulltext/ED608066.pdf.

Yudelson, M. V., Koedinger, K. R., & Gordon, G. J. (2013). Individualized Bayesian Knowledge Tracing Models. *Artificial Intelligence in Education*, 171–180.

17. Social analytics to support engagement with learning communities

Carolyn Rosé, Meredith Riggs and Nicole Barbaro

INTRODUCTION

Over the past 30 years, culminating with the recent pandemic, human life has increasingly moved online and the world of learning, including AI-enhanced learning, has been no exception. Because of this movement, we would be remiss not to include a chapter in this volume related to AI in support of learning at a large scale online.

Situating the Topic of Social Analytics in the Field of AI in Education

To enable effective online learning at scale, the authors of this chapter would argue, it would be a lost opportunity not to harness the readily available human resources available in the environment through collaborative learning encounters. To do so, the authors would further argue that AI technologies have demonstrated great potential to catalyze social processes in support of learning. In fact, some of the early work in this space demonstrating the positive impact of conversational tutoring systems triggered by real-time conversation analysis was first published at the AI in Education conference (Kumar et al., 2007). This chapter focuses on one important such AI technology in support of learning through social interaction, namely *social analytics*, which make these catalyst processes visible and usable as triggers of support and as traces for the purpose of assessment and data-driven design and refinement of instructional interventions. Online learning technologies may be embedded in formal learning environments, or more broadly in technology-enriched spaces, and thus the sibling fields to AI in Education, known as Educational Data Mining and Learning Analytics, have been born; within them are research themes closely related to the idea of social analytics, such as discourse analytics (Rosé, 2017a, 2018) and automated collaborative process analysis (Howley et al., 2013; Howley & Rosé, 2016; Borge & Rosé, 2021).

Situating Work in Social Analytics within the History of Online Instruction

Partly in response to economic pressures, the need for learning movements, both formal and informal, to take advantage of online opportunities has grown. These pressures provided the impetus for the rise of the Massive Open Online Courses (MOOCs), a movement that emerged, flourished for a time, and then took its place among multiple contexts for learning at scale. Some of the notable successful MOOCs incorporated intelligent tutoring technologies (Koedinger et al., 2015, 2016) and other artificial intelligence technologies that supported learning (Rosé & Ferschke, 2016). In this chapter, we focus specifically on artificial intelligence technologies that support the social aspects of learning, which has been a growing direction within the AI in Education community, especially since the turn of the century (Chapter 2 by McCalla), and strongly connects with the broader field of Computer-Supported

Collaborative Learning (Chapter 19 by Martinez-Maldonada et al.). This work draws heavily from the field of Natural Language Processing and more broadly from Language Technologies, as covered from a different perspective by Rus, Olney, and Graesser (Chapter 11 by Rus et al.) in connection with natural language interaction in intelligent tutoring systems, and draws from fundamental research in the area of computational sociolinguistics (Nguyen et al., 2016; Rosé, 2017b).

Learning and development are an important part of existing, thriving online communities where social interaction is in abundance. For example, members of online hobby communities such as Ravelry interact in these ways, which would be valuable in online learning contexts designed for formal learning but rarely occur in those contexts (Wang et al., 2015; Wang et al., 2016). Prompted by their common passion, participants in hobby communities work together on ideas, challenging each other to consider problems from multiple angles, and offering necessary advice as they learn together. Though momentum towards informal learning and growth exists in these contexts, it exists in an unguided and potentially unruly way, in the absence of assessment, scaffolding, and sequencing of learning objectives.

With these examples in view, the phenomenon of Massive Open Online Courses (MOOCs) promised to offer educational opportunities to the masses in a form of temporary online community focused on specific curricular goals. Though the material covered by these courses offers promise of great value, so far that value has gone unrealized because, quite unlike successful hobby communities and open-source communities, MOOCs on the whole failed to create an environment that was conducive to the kind of sustained engagement that would be required to take advantage of these resources as well as missing the positive impact on under-represented learners that was originally intended (Healey, 2017).

Analyses of attrition and learning in MOOCs both pointed to the importance of social engagement for motivational support and overcoming difficulties with material and course procedures (Breslow et al., 2013), a finding that provides the inspiration for this chapter. This finding echoes earlier findings that demonstrated the importance of social support for increasing retention of under-represented minorities in STEM majors in brick and mortar institutions (Treisman, 1992). Note that the term *social support* is not limited to interactions aimed to buffer stress or mitigate the effects of crisis situations. Instead, its use in the literature on online communities is broader, and includes exchange of all resources, both instrumental and emotional, that promote all aspects of community well-being, including motivation to stay involved and actively contributing (Kraut & Resnick, 2012).

Despite superficial similarities between MOOCs and other types of online communities, affordances for social interaction included in typical MOOCs were regarded as an afterthought, and the typical experience of MOOC learners remained largely solitary. Results from our own research demonstrate that needed social support may be one of the leading factors explaining patterns of attrition in MOOCs even among the most highly motivated MOOC participants (Yang et al., 2014a) and that despite the efforts of some highly prolific posters (Huang et al., 2014) and teaching staff (Yang et al., 2014b), learners' needs for informational and other types of social support went unanswered in many cases.

Despite demonstrations that social interaction enhances commitment in MOOCs (Ferschke et al., 2013; Tomar et al., 2016), just as it does in other forms of online communities (Wang et al., 2012), and despite early indications that team-based learning in MOOCs can be successful (Wen et al., 2016, 2017), attempts to build ongoing, growing learning communities were not typically successfully realized in this context (McAuley et al., 2010). Some demonstrations of socially focused interventions and designs for intensifying interaction to positive effect were published (Ferschke et al., 2013). Nevertheless, despite that evidence, typical MOOCs remain networked contexts for primarily solitary learning experiences.

A complementary picture can be observed within online universities such as Western Governors University (WGU), where social support is a key part of the benefit of paid tuition, beginning with the provision of a personal mentor (i.e., a "program mentor") for each student. Later in this chapter, as a demonstration of a form of social analytics, we report an analysis of the buffering effect of social support from program mentors during the pandemic that underscores the value of that social support for keeping students focused, productive, and successful, even in the face of unprecedented disruption.

Advance Organizer for the Chapter

As we have argued, a key theoretical insight underlying this chapter is the value of social support in building and sustaining community. In particular, we investigate the impact of social support on engagement in online learning, highlighting in particular work introducing conversational encounters into MOOCs (Rosé et al., 2015; Rosé & Ferschke, 2016) as well as work investigating the impact of those encounters on outcomes in MOOCs, including student retention (Tomar et al., 2016; Wen et al., 2014a, 2014b) and learning (Wang et al., 2015, 2016). Our particular perspective highlights the important potential role of social analytics in addressing issues we will raise. In the remainder of the chapter, we define what we mean by social analytics. Next, we delve into past literature regarding the important role of social support in maintaining engagement in online communities. Then, we offer a survey of the MOOC landscape, highlighting needs and opportunities to bring social analytics and social support together. We then proceed to discuss attempts to do just that and discuss why they were ultimately not enough. We turn our attention then to more recent work in an online university setting, namely Western Governors University based in Salt Lake City in Utah, which offers a more hopeful picture, even during the pandemic. We conclude with implications and a vision for future research.

TECHNICAL FOUNDATIONS: SOCIAL ANALYTICS

In this chapter, we define social analytics very broadly within the area of learning analytics (Rosé, 2022) as any technical approach that accepts as input raw data from a social interaction, which we define as an interaction involving more than one human in which the behavior of one human is contingent in some way on the behavior of another, and returns a measure of some social process manifested within that data. This definition makes a strong connection with the area of collaborative learning process analysis (Howley et al., 2013; Howley & Rosé, 2016; Borge & Rosé, 2021), though it is not limited to activities designed with the intention of participants learning or working together per se (Rosé et al., 2017). We will emphasize conversational interactions in this chapter. However, it is important to note that social interaction may be only a small part of the interaction data (Chaudhary et al., 2020), and the interaction may in fact be largely non-verbal (Nguyen et al., 2021). Social analytics is therefore broader than Discourse Analytics (Rosé, 2017a, 2018; Clarke et al., 2018; Rosé & Tovares, 2015), which focuses explicitly on linguistic data. It also need not involve Artificial Intelligence (AI), per se, though we take this opportunity to highlight areas of AI, in particular Language

Technologies and Computational Linguistics, that have a lot to offer this work (Nguyen et al., 2016; Rosé, 2017b).

Challenges

With an emphasis on conversational interaction, we must acknowledge that automated processing of conversational data comes with challenges over and above that associated with processes of expository text, such as open-ended student answers or essays. Expository text is typically structured top-down and organized around information flow. Conversations, on the other hand, are frequently organized around the task and knowledge of the task structure provides an implicit scaffold for understanding. Thus, speakers feel free to elide or imply important information rather than making it explicit. The challenges have been well documented (Waitzkin, 1989; Lacson et al., 2006). These are challenges that the area of social analytics may be able to address more effectively by leveraging very recent work on what are referred to in the field of Language Technologies as transformer-based conversation models, where a distributed representation of conversational state is constructed as a discussion is processed turn by turn in a way that enables access to some of this implicit information (Khosla et al., 2020; Dutt et al., 2020, 2021). Another challenge is that the clues to the answers to some of the questions we as learning scientists ask may be as needles in a haystack within an interaction, and thus specific techniques to conversation mining that learn to identify not just what these clues look like, but also where to look for them, are also valuable (Mayfield et al., 2013). We must also consider how to identify social constructs above the level of individual turns, such as patterns of role taking (Yang et al., 2015; Maki et al., 2017). When language is explored from a social perspective, we must consider the ways in which cultural symbols are created and used within the social economy of the interaction (Piergallini et al., 2014; Jang et al., 2017). The interplay between social context and social function raises challenges for the generality of models trained in one context and applied in another. Work towards generalizability shows promise but is still an active area of research (Mu et al., 2012; Fiacco et al., 2018).

Successes

Research in the field of Computer-Supported Collaborative Learning (CSCL) has produced technology for automating analysis of collaborative processes in real time (Rosé et al., 2008; Mu et al., 2012; Gweon et al., 2013) and using this analysis to trigger in-process support that increased the effectiveness of collaboration and student learning (Kumar & Rosé, 2011; Dyke et al., 2013; Adamson et al., 2014). Many frameworks have been developed for automated analysis of student discussion, as it has repeatedly been shown to be valuable for assessing student learning processes (McLaren et al., 2007; Joshi & Rosé, 2007; Ai et al., 2010; Gweon et al., 2013; Fiacco & Rosé, 2018), supporting group learning (Kumar et al., 2007), and enabling effective group assignments (Wen et al., 2017). Some work has explicitly addressed the issue of whether these frameworks generalize across domains (Mu et al., 2012; Fiacco & Rosé, 2018), which is critical to enabling educators in a variety of fields to leverage these tools. Consensus building and knowledge integration behaviors, such as what have frequently been referred to as transactive conversational contributions (Berkowitz & Gibbs; 1983; de Lisi & Golbeck, 1999), have been a major focus of work in social analytics. Many of these conversational behaviors involve articulation of mental models and drawing connections between ones thinking and that of others. Successful collaborative learning is broadly believed to be fostered by discourse patterns characterized by the articulation of reasoning and idea co-construction (Chan, 2013; Chin & Clark, 2013; van Alst, 2009), which have theoretical connections with cognitive conflict and learning (de Lisi & Golbeck, 1999).

THEORETICAL FOUNDATIONS: SOCIAL SUPPORT AND ENGAGEMENT

In this chapter, we focus on a specific set of social processes through which social support is exchanged within groups or communities. The human brain requires social connectedness to thrive, grow, and to learn (Dehaene, 2020; Brouwer et al., 2016). Even more so, when faced with stressful events, social support might even be as critical for students to reach their potential as high-quality instructional design. The social support buffering hypothesis (Cohen & Wills, 1985) posits that responsive interpersonal resources can buffer the negative effects of stressful events, perhaps even stressors associated with the recent pandemic. Social support, such as offered by instructors or mentors, appears to be a foundational component to helping students thrive academically during online instruction in the face of limited social interactions between peers, as we will discuss below in connection with the Western Governors University case study.

Work investigating the connection between social support and longevity of participation in online communities began in medical support communities where theories of coping, such as the social cognitive processing model (Lepore, 2001), defined the coping process as one of intense emotional encounters that provide opportunities for confronting and then integrating traumatic experiences in one's psyche, which is referred to as "adaptation". Though its later use in online communities broadly does not specifically focus on coping in the face of extreme stress or trauma, the research in the online community space demonstrates its broader applicability, and highlights its positive impact in the more extreme case of trauma as a sign of its strength. Furthermore, the recent events of COVID speak loudly and clearly that effective education must be resilient to the experience of disruption, extreme stress, and trauma as well.

Of the categories of social support identified as important in this process, two have received the most theoretical and empirical attention – emotional support and informational support (Cutrona & Shur, 1994). Participants in online support groups can receive emotional and informational support either directly through messages or indirectly through comparisons or communication with others who have had similar experiences (Bambina, 2007). Some early work points to the importance of social support for slowing down attrition in online medical support communities (Wang et al., 2012).

Closer to home, social support studies across educational contexts show promising effects on student outcomes, such as positive impacts on college GPA (Mattanah et al., 2012; Lombardi et al., 2016) and reductions of academic stress levels (Rayle & Chung, 2007). Several meta-analyses point to the positive effects of social support on academic outcomes. For instance, students who perceive greater support from their teachers report less academic burnout (Kim et al., 2018) and more positive academic emotions (Lei et al., 2018). Finally, meta-analyses show positive associations between social support and GPA (Richardson et al., 2012) and student retention (Lei et al., 2018).

This literature demonstrates that social support, broadly construed, is positively related to academic outcomes across learning contexts, and thus is not specific to buffering the effects of extreme stress and trauma. These findings raise the question of what role social support might play in supporting successful participation in MOOCs and other online spaces more specifically.

THE MOOC LANDSCAPE

Given the evidence in favor of the importance of social connectedness, which we will argue is a benefit of the experience of social support, we have conjectured that an important hurdle that has prevented MOOCs from reaching their transformative potential is that they have failed to provide the kind of social environment that is conducive to sustained engagement and learning, especially as students typically arrive in waves to these online learning communities (Rosé et al., 2014). In this context, work from the broader AI in Education community has already contributed technologies within the social analytics space, including multimodal sensing technologies and social network analysis (Wong & Zhang, 2018; Labarthe et al., 2016; Anaya et al., 2015). In this section, we explore the impact of social support used to enhance the experience of social connectedness by first analyzing the impact of social interaction on attrition and then discussing a progression of interventions that introduce social support with increasing levels of intensity. We begin with the introduction of collaborative discussions in eXtended MOOCs (xMOOCs), and then discuss team-based MOOCs.

Investigating the Potential for Impact of Social Support in the xMOOC Baseline

The reality of typical content-focused xMOOCs (Kennedy, 2014), such as the typical MOOCs offered through Coursera, edX, and Udacity, is that opportunities for the exchange of ideas, help, and support are limited to threaded discussion forums, which are often not well integrated with instructional activities and, as a result, lack many of the qualities identified as reflecting instructionally beneficial interactions from prior work in the field of CSCL (Rosé et al., 2015). MOOC discussion forums, as they are typically not well integrated into MOOC instruction, frequently engage only a very small percentage of students in a course, and thus lack the critical mass that would enable reliable access to conversation partners for those who do post to them. What stands in the gap is the concept of a connectivistMOOC (cMOOC), an early form of MOOC (Siemens, 2007). cMOOCs are less structured than "traditional" xMOOCs, such as Coursera style MOOCs, and adopt a knowledge generation rather than a knowledge consumption approach to learning (Smith & Eng, 2013). These courses are designed to operate like Communities of Practice, which are loosely structured, allowing participants to find their own individualized path. Nevertheless, even here we fail to find a final solution as these loosely structured MOOCs are known to be confusing for people to get involved in. Another challenge arises around analysis of social networks and content as interaction in a cMOOC does not occur in a central space, such as edX or Coursera.

In order to investigate the impact of social interaction patterns on longevity within MOOCs in our past work, we leveraged a statistical analysis technique referred to as survival analysis to quantify the extent to which the informal relationships between students influenced their dropout (Yang et al., 2014). We operationalized three variables describing important aspects of the experience students have in MOOC social environments, including the number of people with whom they were observed to have a relational bond through frequent interaction, the number of people with whom they had a relational bond who dropped out in the previous week, and the number of people with whom they had a relational bond who dropped out in the current week. We applied this operationalization to three Coursera MOOCs to test the generality of the connection strength we found using the survival modeling technique. We found in three different courses, where we tested this effect, that students are between four and six times more likely to drop out on a time point if significant acquaintances had dropped out on the previous time point than if they had not. Thus, we see that the social support and social comparison provided by a virtual cohort plays an important role in keeping students motivated and involved. This analysis motivates the goal to introduce more social interaction into MOOCs in order to attempt to reduce patterns of attrition that have plagued MOOCs.

Introducing Collaborative Reflection in MOOCs

As a first step towards achieving a positive impact of CSCL technology in MOOCs, we integrated a collaborative chat environment with interactive agent support in a recent 9-week-long MOOC on learning analytics (DALMOOC) that was hosted on the edX platform from October to December 2014 (Rosé et al., 2015). Overall, 21 941 students enrolled in the course. The median age was 31 with 24.8% of the students 25 and under, 50.4% between 26 and 40, and 19.2% being over 40. One hundred and eighty countries were represented in the course with the majority of students from the USA (26%) and India (19%). A self-selected subset of students attempted participation in collaborative reflection activities that were offered each week as enrichment activities subsequent to individual learning activities. Coordinating synchronous social engagement in a MOOC is challenging, however, and the challenges that arise can be frustrating for students. Results of a follow-up study showed positive and negative effects on attrition of a collaborative chat intervention that required students to be matched with exactly one partner prior to beginning the activity (Ferschke et al., 2015b). Negative effects occurred when students had to return multiple times in an attempt to be matched with a partner. That study raised questions about how to provide the benefit of synchronous social engagement without the coordination difficulties.

We then evaluated a revised intervention designed to overcome coordination difficulties by welcoming students into the chat on a rolling basis as they arrive rather than requiring them to be matched with a partner before beginning (Tomar et al., 2016). An earlier study identified positive and negative effects on attrition of a collaborative chat intervention that required students to be matched with exactly one partner prior to beginning the activity (Ferschke et al., 2015b). Negative effects occurred when students had to return multiple times in an attempt to be matched with a partner. That study raised questions about how to provide the benefit of synchronous social engagement without the coordination difficulties. Other follow-up studies showed similar positive effects of collaborative chat on longevity of participation, sometimes as much as a 70% reduction in probability of dropout by the next time point.

Team-Based MOOCs

Though the work introducing collaborative reflection showed some success at slowing down patterns of attrition into MOOCs, it did not substantially increase the number of students who stayed involved long enough to complete the courses. Thus, we sought a method for increasing the dosage, as it were, of the social interaction we provided. In particular, we worked to foster more intensive ongoing social interaction between students in team projects housed within MOOCs

(Wen et al., 2017). Our underlying premise was that if we can foster a sense of community along the lines of a community of practice, we could better leverage available human resources.

Team-based learning is one type of peer learning, where students form small teams to complete a course project together. There has been interest in incorporating a collaborative team-based learning component into MOOCs ever since the beginning (Williams, 2015). Dillahunt et al. showed that learners requested more tangible benefits from MOOCs, such as more project-based experiences and the ability to interact with others (Dillahunt et al., 2016). On the other hand, simply placing online learners in small groups has never guaranteed that collaboration will occur, especially in light of well-known process losses in groups (Kotturi et al., 2015). One reason is that online learners come to courses with a wide range of purposes and levels of motivation (MacNeil et al., 2016). They are typically distributed and do not have existing relationships (Manathunga & Hernández-Leo, 2015). One strategy for team formation occurs through personal messaging early in a course and is typically based on limited learner profiles, such as demographics and prior knowledge (Williams, 2015). After team formation, students mostly interact with their team and lose contact with the larger course community. Many students drop out before engaging in team project collaboration. There has been limited success in self-selected or randomly assigned MOOC teams (Wen et al., 2015; Williams, 2015). The key challenges of forming effective teams in MOOCs include: (1) students depend on their team, though it may become an ineffective source of support due to attrition, and (2) team composition is frequently suboptimal due to scant information regarding which learners will likely work well together.

In our work in this space, we built on a specific construct using social analytics: transactivity (Berkowitz & Gibbs, 1983). Transactivity is a quality of conversational behavior where students explicitly build on ideas and integrate reasoning previously presented during the conversation. The expression of a transact reflects the examination of one's own mental model and possibly another's as well as the connections between them. Engaging in this process offers the opportunity for one to question their own mental model. Thus, this key type of consensus building behavior is theorized to play an important role in collaborative learning discourse. In Piaget's theory, these transactive contributions are most likely to occur within pairs or small groups where the participants are in an equal status relationship. Thus, we expect, and have found (Gweon et al., 2013), a connection between relational factors and the occurrence of transactive contributions. In our own prior work (Joshi & Rosé, 2007) as well as that of others (Azimitia & Montgomery, 1993; Weinberger & Fischer, 2006), we see evidence that prevalence of transactivity in collaborative discussions correlates with learning. Beyond a means for triggering cognitive conflict, transactive conversational contributions are viewed within this community as important steps in a knowledge building or consensus building process (Weinberger & Fischer, 2006). In making connections between newly articulated ideas and material contributed earlier in a conversation, ideas build upon one another, and differing understandings are elaborated, integrated, and possibly transformed. Prevalence of transactivity has also been demonstrated to correlate with successful transfer of expertise in loosely coupled work settings (Gweon et al., 2011). High-quality interactions, characterized by qualities such as transactivity, also foster better team performance (Riedl & Woolley, 2017; Woolley et al., 2008, 2010). Transactive conversational behaviors are believed to develop in groups characterized by a balance of assimilation and accommodation, which is related to power balance, psychological safety, mutual respect, and mutual interest (de Lisi & Golbeck, 1999; Azmitia & Montgomery, 1993).

We developed a technique for effective assignment of students to teams in MOOCs, which was validated in a series of lab studies, and then again in a MOOC. The paradigm was as follows: students first engage in their own individual exploration and learning. At this stage, students may be assigned to different learning foci in order to create a diversity of expertise within the student community. Students then bring their individual work into the community context through a show-and-tell stage. At this stage, they are asked to offer feedback to a small number of other students of their choosing. Based on an automated analysis of the nature of this feedback, in particular measuring pairwise transactivity within the discussion forum (Rosé et al., 2008), an automated assessment of collaboration potential is computed. This measure is then used as the basis for assigning students to collaborative groups where they are matched with the students with whom they have the highest assessed collaboration potential. This is accomplished through an approximate constraint satisfaction algorithm. The students then work together in their teams to share and integrate their individual work, supported by an intelligent facilitator agent. Validation studies conducted both in controlled lab settings as well as in a real MOOC offered through the Smithsonian Institute on the edX platform provide evidence of the success of this paradigm for formation and support of effective collaborative learning groups. In particular, assignment of participants to teams based on transactivity observed in a discussion forum has resulted in significant increases in transactivity within teams and success at knowledge integration in group writing products, but not learning except in connection with other support to explicitly scaffold collaborative processes during interaction (Wen et al., 2017; Wang et al., 2017). Correlational results from a MOOC deployment were consistent, and completion rate for this collaborative project-based MOOC was nearly perfect.

CASE STUDY: MENTOR SUPPORT AT WESTERN GOVERNORS UNIVERSITY

As a counterpoint to the study on MOOCs, we present here a case study on a for-pay online learning platform, namely Western Governors University (WGU), which highlights the value of social support in online instruction more broadly. This research complements the past work on MOOCs by using simple, but ecologically valid indices of social support as a form of social analytics to trace the positive impact of human support in the face of massive disruption.

WGU Students are assigned a program mentor who mentors them, as a continual provision of social support, through their program from enrollment to graduation. On this platform, like in MOOCs, the student experience is largely solitary in the sense that students lack interaction with each other. However, in contrast to the MOOC experience, one important benefit the tuition pays for is the program mentor. As a very contemporary demonstration of the positive impact of social support as highlighted through the use of social analytics, we present a case study. In particular, we offer first evidence that some students within the WGU population experienced substantial COVID-related stress during the pandemic, which influenced their patterns of work on the platform. We then demonstrated that, with the support of their program mentors, these students were ultimately successful at pulling through their courses, though it took them a little more time.

The results of this study underscore the important role of social support in student success. We first discuss the logistics of the mentor–student relationships during the pandemic and establish that overall, regardless of the experience of the pandemic, students maintained a high level of productivity in terms of the number of course units earned. We then investigate evidence of the stressors introduced by the pandemic. Next, we present evidence of the buffering effect of the social support provided by the mentors and then reflect on the implications and questions raised, as just noted.

Student-Mentor Relationships during the Pandemic

WGU program mentors are required to meet with their students at least every two weeks, but students and mentors can interact as often as preferred and needed. Whereas past research on social support and academic outcomes discussed earlier in the chapter is heavily reliant on self-report data, the social analytics methodology used in this research utilizes student behavioral data (i.e., student click-stream data from the online learning platform; recorded program mentor interactions with students) and analysis of qualitative text notes from students' program mentors (i.e., meeting notes and "hashtags" used to tag topics of their meeting notes) to evaluate effects of social support on academic outcomes.

Social support may be particularly beneficial for online university students who, relative to traditional college students, are likely to be older, working full- or part-time, and have families. Social support may therefore be especially beneficial for these students during a crisis when focusing on long-term academic goals may be difficult to prioritize in the face of immediate challenges caused by the pandemic.

The participants in this case study were active students between January 2019 and April 2020 for which we have institutional data on academic outcomes. Program mentors are required to record notes describing each interaction with their student. For each student–mentor pair, we assessed the number of interactions and the nature and substance of those interactions by counting and analyzing the recorded notes. During the time of the pandemic, the university instructed the mentors to use a hashtag system to flag students discussing COVID-related issues. A combination of text mining and structural equation modeling techniques were applied to these data to address our research aims.

We assessed COVID impact using two methods. We first used hashtags to begin assigning students to COVID impact groups. Some mentors, however, did not use the hashtags. For these students, it is not possible to determine whether their program mentors did not comply with the instructions or whether their students did not discuss COVID issues. We therefore assigned students to three groups: students with no hashtags from their program mentor (MissingCOVID); students whose mentors used hashtags with some of their mentees, but not these students, in which we assume these students did not discuss COVID-related issues (LowCOVID); and students with at least one COVID hashtag (HighCOVID) (see Table 17.1). There were no observed differences in Course Units Earned (CUs) between these groups.

Table 17.1   Summary of COVID impact groups by hashtags and mean average course units (CUs) earned per group

Student subset (based on hashtags)	Course units earned: mean (SD)	Number of active weeks: mean (SD)
MissingCOVID (1 000 students)	4.2 (4.4)	20.4 (6.5)
LowCOVID (1 000 students)	4.4 (4.8)	19.9 (6.3)
HighCOVID (80 students)	4.2 (5.1)	19.9 (5.1)

In addition to the hashtags, which not every mentor chose to use, we also applied the Structural Topic Model package (STM) (Roberts et al., 2013) as a very simple form of social analytics to compute a 20-topic model using Latent Dirichlet Allocation over the mentor's qualitative notes in which we compute a percentage of content from each note that the model assigned to each of the 20 topics. We then summed these percentages across the notes written for each student to obtain a measure of how much text written about a student over the term was associated with each topic. Each induced topic is associated in the learned model with a word ranking. The set of highest-ranking words in a topic can be used to identify the theme associated with that topic. Two topics had COVID-related hashtags among the highest ranking words, along with other words related semantically to pandemic themes such as health and childcare issues. Using these topics to assign students to categories allows identification of hard hit students among those whose mentors did not use hashtags. Students in MissingCOVID and LowCOVID had half as much text reported about them related to the two COVID-related topics as those in the HighCOVID group.

Impact of COVID Stress on Patterns of Participation

For the calendar year of 2020, we analyzed the level of activity logged on a per student per week basis in courses and related these data over time to patterns of COVID cases in the United States as tracked by the Centers for Disease Control and Prevention (CDC), using a five-day moving average. We compared these patterns across time for students in the HighCOVID impact group vs. the LowCOVID impact group, as determined based on the prevalence of COVID topic-related terms, as described in the previous section. In this analysis, we use data from nearly one million student-weeks, including data from 38 355 different students. The results are illustrated in Figure 17.1, which demonstrates a very distinctive pattern for HighCOVID students in comparison with LowCOVID students. In particular, the relationship between activity level and overall cases across the country was not linear; students in the LowCOVID category proceeded with their coursework as usual throughout the term,

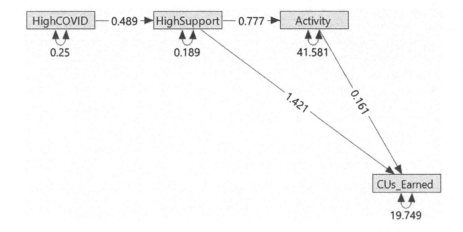

Figure 17.1   *Comparison of number of COVID cases over time in the United States with activity levels per week during the same period of time for HighCOVID vs LowCOVID students*

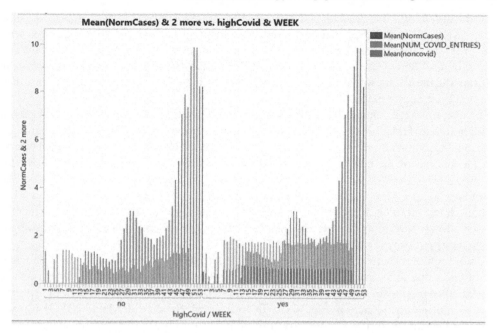

Figure 17.2   *Difference in frequency of mentor notes mentioning COVID terms (indicated in red) vs no COVID terms (indicated in green) for students in the LowCOVID group (HighCOVID = no) vs the HighCOVID group (HIghCOVID = yes) in comparison to frequency of COVID cases across the United States*

including an uptick of activity at the initial part of the term and at the end part of the term. These two upticks were shared between students in the HighCOVID category and LowCOVD category. On the other hand, as cases began to rise, those in the HighCOVID group showed substantial reductions in activity level in comparison with their peers in the LowCOVID group and remained at a consistently low activity level until the end of the term when they showed a major uptick in behavior along with their peers, as they finished out their courses.

We were also interested in how mentors recorded evidence of their interactions with students in these two groups during this time (see Figure 17.2). As we compare across students in the HighCOVID group and the LowCOVID group, we see that despite the consistently low level of activity of students in the HighCOVID group, mentors continued to interact with them and record information about those interactions in their notes. In fact, they wrote substantially more notes regarding those students with low levels of activity while reducing to some extent their interaction with LowCOVID students who were proceeding apace, with a more typical level of activity in their courses.

Effect of Social Support on Outcomes

With an understanding of student activity over time as presented in the previous section, we turn now to evaluating the impact of the COVID19 pandemic on academic outcomes for a random sample of 2 080 students. Our outcome measure of interest is the number of course units earned (CUs). We expected to see that students discussing COVID-related issues with their program mentor would earn fewer CUs than their peers who did not discuss COVID-related issues. As a process variable, we distill an indicator of student effort over time by counting the number of weeks during the term when their click-stream logs indicated that they accessed their course materials.

Because some text related to COVID was present for students in the former two categories, we include a different breakdown of COVID impact among students in Table 17.2 based on topic analysis, rather than hashtags (see Table 17.1). This analysis does show significant effects on CUs, but not on the number of active weeks. Both the contrast between those hardest hit and others ($F_{(1,2078)} = 27.3$, $p < 0.01$), as well as between the hardest-hit half and the rest of the students ($F_{(1,2078)} = 42.3$, $p < 0.001$) were both significant. Unexpectedly, the students hardest hit completed more CUs. Observing online activity trends over time, we see that students showed a lower level of activity during the most intense part of the pandemic, but made up for it with extra intensity in subsequent months.

Assessing the role of social support from the student program mentors as a buffer of negative impacts due to the pandemic, we used structural equation modeling (SEM) (Ullman & Bentler, 2003) to model the interplay between COVID impact, social support from program mentors, online course activity and CUs. In this model, we consider HighCOVID (binary indicator of students in the top 50% from the topic analysis), HighSupport (students whose mentors contacted them at above-median frequency), activity (number of active weeks on the platform) and CUs. Our first SEM included all links from logically prior variables to those logically subsequent. The links from HighCOVID to activity, and from HighCOVID to CUs were not significant, and were thus dropped. We retained the final model (see Figure 17.3), which achieved significantly better fit than the initial model across Akaike information criterion (AIC), Bayesian Information Criterion (BIC), and Root mean square error of approximation (RMSEA). Results show that HighCOVID students received more support from their mentor, which subsequently had a positive impact on students' course activity and ultimately on CUs. But there was also a positive association directly between level of support and outcomes that is not explained by that increase in activity.

Overall, the message of the data from this online university platform is that in this supportive environment, across demographic groups, students are receiving social support in the face of their COVID-related stress, and that support is associated with success across the student population.

Table 17.2   *Summary of COVID impact groups by topic-model analysis and mean average course units (CUs) earned per group and mean average online activity (weeks per group)*

Student subset (based on topic analysis)	Course units earned: mean (SD)	Number of active weeks: mean (SD)
Hardest hit (10th percentile)	5.1 (6.0)	13.0 (6.4)
Upper half	4.7 (5.1)	20.3 (6.1)
Lower half	3.9 (4.0)	19.9 (6.8)

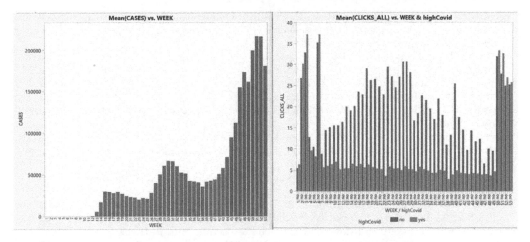

Figure 17.3   *Final structural equation modeling (SEM) results for impact of social support on course units (CUs) earned. Only significant effects shown*

CONCLUSION AND CURRENT DIRECTIONS

This chapter explores the costs and benefits of social support in online communities, including learning communities, and asks the question: Can successful massive open online learning really be free? What have we learned about what works, what can be done with technology, and what questions we still need to answer?

Higher education is facing unprecedented disruption due to the pandemic. Our results provide actionable insights into how higher education institutions can better deliver online education at scale in the coming semesters and beyond to promote positive student outcomes through an infusion of social support. The results specifically highlight the role of personalized social support as a potential buffering mechanism to foster positive student outcomes for diverse learner populations during a crisis.

As we look to the future, we again think about social analytics. Though we may never be able to eliminate the need for human mentoring, we may be able to reduce the cost using social analytics if they can be used to channel resources where they are most needed and draw in student effort to support one another alongside the support of human mentors, in order to increase the pool of available support while bounding the cost allocated to human mentors. These are big questions that must be answered in future research.

ACKNOWLEDGMENTS

This work was funded in part by NSF Grants IIS 1822831 and IIS 1546393.

REFERENCES

Adamson, D., Dyke, G., Jang, H. J., & Rosé, C. P. (2014). Towards an Agile Approach to Adapting Dynamic Collaboration Support to Student Needs. *International Journal of AI in Education*, 24(1), 91–121.

Ai, H., Sionti, M., Wang, Y. C., & Rosé, C. P. (2010). Finding Transactive Contributions in Whole Group Classroom Discussions. In *Proceedings of the 9th International Conference of the Learning Sciences, Volume 1: Full Papers*, 976–983.

Anaya, A. R., Boticario, J. G., Letón, E., & Hernández-del-Olmo, F. (2015). An Approach of Collaboration Analytics in MOOCs Using Social Network Analysis and Influence Diagram. EDM.

Azmitia, M., & Montgomery, R. (1993). Friendship, Transactive Dialogues, and the Development of Scientific Reasoning. *Social Development*, 2, 202–221.

Berkowitz, M., & Gibbs, J. (1983). Measuring the Developmental Features of Moral Discussion. *Merrill-Palmer Quarterly*, 29, 399–410.

Borge, M., & Rosé, C. P. (2021). Quantitative Approaches to Language in CSCL. In R. Cress & W. Oshima (Eds.), *International Handbook of Computer-Supported Collaborative Learning*. Springer.

Breslow, L., Pritchard, D. E., DeBoer, J., Stump, G. S., Ho, A. D., & Seaton, D. T. (2013). Studying Learning in the Worldwide Classroom Research into Edx's First MOOC. *Research & Practice in Assessment*, 8, 13–25.

Brouwer, J., Jansen, E., Flache, A., & Hofman, A. (2016). The Impact of Social Capital on Self-Efficacy and Study Success Among First-Year University Students. *Learning and Individual Differences*, 52, 109–118.

Chan, C. K. (2013). Towards a Knowledge Creation Perspective. In C. E. Hmelo-Silver, C. E. Chinn, C. K. Chan, & A. M. O'Donnell (Eds.), *International Handbook of Collaborative Learning*. Taylor and Francis.

Clarke, S. N., Resnick, L. B., & Rosé, C. P. (2018) Discourse Analytics for Learning. In D. Niemi, R. Pea, C. Dick, & B. Saxberg (Eds.), *Learning Analytics in Education*. Information Age Publishing.

Cohen, S., & Wills, T. A. (1985). Stress, Social Support, and the Buffering Hypothesis. *Psychological Bulletin*, 98, 310–357.

Cutrona, C. E., & Suhr, J. A. (1994). Social Support Communication in the Context of Marriage: An Analysis Session: Health: Games and Online Support Groups, February 11–15, 2012, Seattle, WA, USA.

de Lisi, R., & Golbeck, S. L. (1999). Implications of the Piagetian Theory for Peer Learning. *Cognitive Perspectives on Peer Learning*, 3–37.

Dehaene, S. (2020). *How We Learn: Why Brains Learn Better Than Any Machine ... for Now*. Penguin Publishing Group.

Dillahunt, T., Ng, S., Fiesta, M., & Wang, Z. (2016). Do Massive Open Online Course Platforms Support Employability? In *Proceedings of the 19th ACM Conference on Computer-Supported Cooperative Work & Social Computing*. ACM, 233–244.

Dutt, R., Joshi, R., & Rosé, C. P. (2020). Keeping Up Appearances: Computational Modeling of Face Acts in Persuasion Oriented Discussions. In *Proceedings of the 2020 Conference on Empirical Methods in Natural Language Processing*.

Dutt, R., Sinha, S., Joshi, R., Chakraborty, S., Riggs, M., Yan, X., Bao, H., & Rosé, C. P. (2021). ResPer: Computationally Modelling Resisting Strategies in Persuasive Conversations. In *Proceedings of the 2021 Conference of the European Chapter of the Association for Computational Linguistics*.

Dyke, G., Adamson, A., Howley, I., & Rosé, C. P. (2013). Enhancing Scientific Reasoning and Discussion with Conversational Agents. *IEEE Transactions on Learning Technologies*, 6(3), special issue on Science Teaching, 240–247.

Ferschke, O., Howley, I., Tomar, G., Yang, D., & Rosé, C. P. (2015a). Fostering Discussion Across Communication Media in Massive Open Online Courses. In *Proceedings of Computer Supported Collaborative Learning*, 459–466.

Ferschke, O., Yang, D., Tomar, G., & Rosé, C. P. (2015b). Positive Impact of Collaborative Chat Participation in an edX MOOC. In *Proceedings of AI in Education, Volume 9112 of the Series Lecture Notes in Computer Science*. Springer, 115–124.

Fiacco, J., & Rosé, C. P. (2018). Towards Domain General Detection of Transactive Knowledge Building Behavior. In *Proceedings of Learning at Scale*.

Gweon, G., Jain, M., McDonough, J., Raj, B., & Rosé, C. P. (2013). Measuring Prevalence of Other-Oriented Transactive Contributions Using an Automated Measure of Speech Style Accommodation. *International Journal of Computer-Supported Collaborative Learning*, 8(2), 245–265.

Gweon, G., Kane, A., & Rosé, C. P. (2011, July). Facilitating Knowledge Transfer Between Groups Through Idea Co-Construction Processes. Paper Presented at the Annual Meeting of the Interdisciplinary Network for Group Research (INGRoup), Minneapolis, MN.

Howley, I., Mayfield, E., & Rosé, C. P. (2013). Linguistic Analysis Methods for Studying Small Groups. In Cindy Hmelo-Silver, Angela O'Donnell, Carol Chan, & Clark Chin (Eds.), *International Handbook of Collaborative Learning*. Taylor & Francis, Inc.

Howley, I., & Rosé, C. P. (2016). Towards Careful Practices for Automated Linguistic Analysis of Group Learning. *Journal of Learning Analytics*, 3(3), 239–262. http://dx.doi.org/10.18608/jla.2016.33.12.

Huang, J., Dasgupta, A., Ghosh, A., Manning, J., & Sanders, M. (2014, March). Superposter Behavior in MOOC Forums. In *Proceedings of the First ACM Conference on Learning@ Scale Conference*, 117–126.

Jang, H., Maki, K., Hovy, E., & Rosé, C. P. (2017). Finding Structure in Figurative Language: Metaphor Detection with Topic-Based Frames. In *Proceedings of the 18th Annual SIGdial Meeting on Discourse and Dialogue (SIGDIAL '17)*, Saarbruecken, Germany August 15–17.

Joshi, M., & Rosé, C. P. (2007). Using Transactivity in Conversation Summarization in Educational Dialog. In *Proceedings of the ISCA Special Interest Group on Speech and Language Technology in Education Workshop (SLaTE)*, Farmington, PA.

Kennedy, J. (2014). Characteristics of Massive Open Online Courses (MOOCs): A Research Review, 2009–2012. *Journal of Interactive Online Learning*, 13(1).

Khosla, S., Vashishth, S., Lehman, J., & Rosé, C. P. (2020). Improving Detection and Categorization of Task-Relevant Utterances Through Integration of Discourse Structure and Ontological Knowledge. In *Proceedings of the 2020 Conference on Empirical Methods in Natural Language Processing*.

Kim, B., Jee, S., Lee, J., An, S., & Lee, S. M. (2018). Relationships Between Social Support and Student Burnout: A Meta-Analytic Approach. *Stress and Health*, 34, 127–134.

Koedinger, K. R., Kim, J., Jia, J. Z., McLaughlin, E. A., & Bier, N. L. (2015, March). Learning is Not a Spectator Sport: Doing is Better Than Watching for Learning From a MOOC. In *Proceedings of the Second (2015) ACM Conference on Learning@ Scale*, 111–120.

Koedinger, K. R., McLaughlin, E. A., Jia, J. Z., & Bier, N. L. (2016, April). Is the Doer Effect a Causal Relationship? How Can We Tell and Why It's Important. In *Proceedings of the Sixth International Conference on Learning Analytics & Knowledge*, 388–397.

Kotturi, Y., Kulkarni, C., Bernstein, M., & Klemmer, S. (2015). Structure and Messaging Techniques for Online Peer Learning Systems That Increase Stickiness. In *Proceedings of the Second (2015) ACM Conference on Learning@ Scale*. ACM.

Kraut, R. E., & Resnick, P. (2012). *Building Successful Online Communities: Evidence-Based Social Design*. MIT Press.

Kumar, R., & Rosé, C. P. (2011). Architecture for Building Conversational Agents That Support Collaborative Learning. *IEEE Transactions on Learning Technologies*, 4(1), 21–34.

Kumar, R., Rosé, C. P., Wang, Y. C., Joshi, M., & Robinson, A. (2007). Tutorial Dialogue as Adaptive Collaborative Learning Support. In *Proceedings of the 2007 Conference on Artificial Intelligence in Education: Building Technology Rich Learning Contexts That Work*, 383–390.

Labarthe, Hugues, Bouchet, François, Bachelet, Rémi, & Yacef, Kalina. (2016). Does a Peer Recommender Foster Students' Engagement in MOOCs? In *9th International Conference on Educational Data Mining*, June 2016, Raleigh, 418–423.

Lacson, R., Barzilay, R., & Long, W. (2006). Automatic Analysis of Medical Dialogue in the Home Hemodialysis Domain: Structure Induction and Summarization. *Journal of Biomedical Informatics*, 39(5), 541–555.

Lei, H., Cui, Y., & Chiu, M. M. (2018). The Relationship Between Teacher Support and Students' Academic Emotions: A Meta-Analysis. *Frontiers in Psychology*, 8, 2288.

Lepore, S. J. (2001). A Social–Cognitive Processing Model of Emotional Adjustment to Cancer.

Lombardi, A., Murray, C., & Kowitt, J. (2016). Social Support and Academic Success for College Students With Disabilities: Do Relationship Types Matter? *Journal of Vocational Rehabilitation*, 44, 1–13.

MacNeil, S., Latulipe, C., Long, B., & Yadav, A. (2016). Exploring Lightweight Teams in a Distributed Learning Environment. In *Proceedings of the 47th ACM Technical Symposium on Computing Science Education*. ACM, 193–198.

Maki, K., Yoder, M., Jo, Y., & Rosé, C. P. (2017). Roles and Success in Wikipedia Talk Pages: Identifying Latent Patterns of Behavior. In *Proceedings of the 8th International Joint Conference on Natural Language Processing (IJCNLP '17)*, Taipei, Taiwan.

Manathunga, K., & Hernández-Leo, D. (2015). Has Research on Collaborative Learning Technologies Addressed Massiveness? A Literature Review. *Journal of Educational Technology & Society*, 18(4), 357–370.

Mattanah, J. F., Brooks, L. J., Brand, B. L., Quimby, J. L., & Ayers, J. F. (2012). A Social Support Intervention and Academic Achievement in College: Does Perceived Loneliness Mediate the Relationship? *Journal of College Counseling*, 15, 22–36.

Mayfield, E., Adamson, D., & Rosé, C. P. (2013). Recognizing Rare Social Phenomena in Conversation: Empowerment Detection in Support Group Chatrooms. In *Proceedings of the 51st Annual Meeting of the Association for Computational Linguistics*, Sofia, Bulgaria, August 4–9, 2013, 104–113.

McAuley, A., Stewart, B., Siemens, G., & Cormier, D. (2010). THE MOOC Model for Digital Practice, Created Through Funding Received by the University of Prince Edward Island Through the Social Sciences and Humanities Research Councils.

McLaren, B., Scheuer, O., De Laat, M., Hever, R., de Groot, R., & Rosé, C. P. (2007). Using Machine Learning Techniques to Analyze and Support Mediation of Student E-Discussions. In *Proceedings of the 2007 Conference on Artificial Intelligence in Education: Building Technology Rich Learning Contexts That Work*, 331–338.

Mu, J., Stegmann, K., Mayfield, E., Rosé, C. P., & Fischer, F. (2012). The ACODEA Framework: Developing Segmentation and Classification Schemes for Fully Automatic Analysis of Online Discussions. *International Journal of Computer Supported Collaborative Learning*, 7(2), 285–305.

Nguyen, D., Dogruöz, A. S., Rosé, C. P., & de Jong, F. (2016). Computational Sociolinguistics: A Survey. *Computational Linguistics*, 42(3), 537–593.

Piergallini, M., Gadde, P., Dogruoz, S., & Rosé, C. P. (2014). Modeling the Use of Graffiti Style Features to Signal Social Relations Within a Multi-Domain Learning Paradigm. In *Proceedings of the 14th Conference of the European Chapter of the Association for Computational Linguistics*, Gothenburg, Sweden, April 26–30, 2014, 107–115.

Rayle, A. D., & Chung, K. Y. (2007). Revisiting First-Year College Students' Mattering: Social Support, Academic Stress, and the Mattering Experience. *Journal of College Student Retention: Research, Theory & Practice*, 9, 21–37.

Richardson, M., Abraham, C., & Bond, R. (2012). Psychological Correlates of University Students' Academic Performance: A Systematic Review and Meta-Analysis. *Psychological Bulletin*, 138, 353–387.

Riedl, C., & Woolley, A. W. (2017). Teams vs. Crowds: A Field Test of the Relative Contribution of Incentives, Member Ability, and Emergent Collaboration to Crowd-Based Problem Solving Performance. *Academy of Management Discoveries*, 3(4), 382–403. https://doi.org/10.5465/amd.2015.0097.

Roberts, M. E., Stewart, B. M., Tingley, D., & Airoldi, E. M. (2013, December). The Structural Topic Model and Applied Social Science. In *Advances in Neural Information Processing Systems Workshop on Topic Models: Computation, Application, and Evaluation* (Vol. 4).

Rosé, C. P. (2017a). *Discourse Analytics, Handbook of Data Mining and Learning Analytics*. Wiley.

Rosé, C. P. (2017b). A Social Spin on Language Analysis. *Nature*, 545, 166–167.

Rosé, C. P. (2018). Learning Analytics in the Learning Sciences. In F. Fischer, C. Hmelo-Silver, S. Goldman, & P. Reimann (Eds.), *International Handbook of the Learning Sciences*. Taylor & Francis.

Rosé, C. P. (to appear, 2022). Learning Analytics. In Ian Wilkinson & Judy Parr (section Eds.), *International Encyclopedia of Education, Volume on Learning, Cognition, and Human Development*, 4th edition. Elsevier.

Rosé, C. P., Carlson, R., Yang, D., Wen, M., Resnick, L., Goldman, P., & Sherer, J. (2014, March). Social Factors That Contribute to Attrition in MOOCs. In *Proceedings of the First ACM Conference on Learning@ Scale Conference*, 197–198.

Rosé, C. P., & Ferschke, O. (2016). Technology Support for Discussion Based Learning: From Computer Supported Collaborative Learning to the Future of Massive Open Online Courses. *International Journal of Artificial Intelligence in Education*, 26(2), 660–678.

Rosé, C. P., Ferschke, O., Tomar, G., Yang, D., Howley, I., Aleven, V., Siemens, G., Crosslin, M., & Gasevic, D. (2015). Challenges and Opportunities of Dual-Layer MOOCs: Reflections From an edX Deployment Study. *Interactive Event at CSCL 2015*, 2, 848–851.

Rosé, C. P., Howley, I., Wen, M., Yang, D., & Ferschke, O. (2017). Assessment of Discussion in Learning Contexts. In A. von Davier, M. Zhu, & P. Kyllonon (Eds.), *Innovative Assessment of Collaboration*. New Springer Verlag.

Rosé, C. P., & Tovares, A. (2015). What Sociolinguistics and Machine Learning Have to Say to One Another About Interaction Analysis. In L. Resnick, C. Asterhan, & S. Clarke (Eds.), *Socializing Intelligence Through Academic Talk and Dialogue*. American Educational Research Association.

Rosé, C. P., Wang, Y. C., Cui, Y., Arguello, J., Stegmann, K., Weinberger, A., & Fischer, F. (2008). Analyzing Collaborative Learning Processes Automatically: Exploiting the Advances of Computational Linguistics in Computer-Supported Collaborative Learning. *International Journal of Computer Supported Collaborative Learning*, 3(3), 237–271.

Siemens, G. (2007). Connectivism: Creating a Learning Ecology in Distributed Environments. In *Didactics of Microlearning: Concepts, Discourses and Examples*, 53–68.

Smith, B., & Eng, M. (2013, August). MOOCs: A Learning Journey. In *International Conference on Hybrid Learning and Continuing Education*. 244–255.

Tomar, G., Sankaranaranayan, S., Wang, X., & Rosé, C. P. (2016). Coordinating Collaborative Chat in Massive Open Online Courses. In *Proceedings of the International Conference of the Learning Sciences*.

Treisman, U. (1992). Studying Students Studying Calculus: A Look at the Lives of Minority Mathematics Students in College. *The College Mathematics Journal*, 23(5), 362–372.

Ullman, J. B., & Bentler, P. M. (2003). Structural Equation Modeling. In *Handbook of Psychology*, 607–634.

van Aalst, J. (2009). Distinguishing Between Knowledge Sharing, Knowledge Creating, and Knowledge Construction Discourses. *International Journal of Computer Supported Collaborative Learning*, 4(3), 259–288.

Waitzkin, H. (1989). A Critical Theory of Medical Discourse: Ideology, Social Control, and the Processing of Social Context in Medical Encounters. *Journal of Health and Social Behavior*, 220–239.

Wang, X., Wen, M., & Rosé, C. P. (2016). Towards Triggering Higher-Order Thinking Behaviors in MOOCs. In *Proceedings of Learning, Analytics, and Knowledge*.

Wang, X., Wen, M., & Rosé, C. P. (2017). Contrasting Explicit and Implicit Support for Transactive Exchange in Team Oriented Project Based Learning. In *Proceedings of CSCL*.

Wang, X., Yang, D., Wen, M., Koedinger, K. R., & Rosé, C. P. (2015). Investigating How Student's Cognitive Behavior in MOOC Discussion Forums Affect Learning Gains. In *The 8th International Conference on Educational Data Mining*, 226–233.

Wang, Y., Kraut, R., & Levine, J. (2012). To Stay or to Leave? The Relationship of Emotional and Informational Support to Commitment in Online Health Support Groups. In *CSCW '12 Proceedings of the ACM 2012 Conference on Computer-Supported Cooperative Work*, 833–842.

Weinberger, A., & Fischer, F. (2006). A Framework to Analyze Argumentative Knowledge Construction in Computer-Supported Collaborative Learning. *Computers & Education*, 46, 71–95.

Wen, M., Maki, K., Dow, S., Herbsleb, J. D., & Rose, C. (2017). Supporting Virtual Team Formation Through Community-Wide Deliberation. In *Proceedings of the ACM on Human-Computer Interaction*, 1(CSCW), 1–19.

Wen, M., Maki, K., Wang, X., & Rosé, C. P. (2016). Transactivity as a Predictor of Future Collaborative Knowledge Integration in Team-Based Learning in Online Courses. In *Proceedings of Educational Data Mining (EDM 2016)*.

Wen, M., Yang, D., & Rosé, C. P. (2014a). Sentiment Analysis in MOOC Discussion Forums: What Does It Tell Us? In *Proceedings of the 7th International Conference on Educational Data Mining*, 130–137.

Wen, M., Yang, D., & Rosé, D. (2014b). Linguistic Reflections of Student Engagement in Massive Open Online Courses. In *Proceedings of the Eighth International AAAI Conference on Weblogs and Social Media*, 525–534.

Williams, B. A. (2015). Peers in MOOCs: Lessons Based on the Education Production Function, Collective Action, and an Experiment. In *Proceedings of the Second (2015) ACM Conference on Learning@ Scale*. ACM, 287–292.

Wong, Jian-Syuan, & Zhang, Xiaolong. (2018). MessageLens: A Visual Analytics System to Support Multifaceted Exploration of MOOC Forum Discussions. *Visual Informatics*, 2(1), 37–49.

Yang, D., Piergallinin, M., Howley, I., & Rosé, C. P. (2014b). Forum Thread Recommendation for Massive Open Online Courses. In *Proceedings of the 7th International Conference on Educational Data Mining*, 257–260.

Yang, D., Wen, M., & Rosé, C. P. (2014a). Peer Influence on Attrition in Massively Open Online Courses. In *Proceedings of the 7th International Conference on Educational Data Mining*, 405–406.

Yang, D., Wen, M., & Rosé, C. P. (2015). Weakly Supervised Role Identification in Teamwork Interactions. In *Proceedings of the 53rd Annual Meeting of the Association for Computational Linguistics and the 7th International Joint Conference on Natural Language Processing*, 1671–1680.

PART V

AIED SYSTEMS IN USE

18. Intelligent systems for psychomotor learning: a systematic review and two cases of study

Alberto Casas-Ortiz, Jon Echeverria and Olga C. Santos

INTRODUCTION

Psychomotor learning involves the integration of mental and muscular activity with the purpose of learning a motor skill. The repeated practice of the learned movements over very long periods of time has been proved to improve speed, accuracy, force, and smoothness while executing the motor skill (Gagné et al., 1992). Many types of psychomotor skills can be learned, such as playing musical instruments, dancing, driving, practicing martial arts, performing a medical surgery, or communicating with sign language. Each one has a different set of unique characteristics that can make the learning process even more complex. For instance, playing a musical instrument implies the learning of musical theory, driving a car implies the exact coordination of both legs and arms to properly control the car according to the stimuli on the road, and practicing martial arts implies the coordination of every part of the body to react in advance to the movements of the opponent. To define and categorize the learning process of psychomotor activities, several psychomotor taxonomies have been proposed (Dave, 1970; Ferris and Aziz, 2005; Harrow, 1972; Simpson, 1972; Thomas, 2004). These taxonomies are defined in terms of progressive levels of performance during the learning process, going from observation to the mastery of motor skills. Thus, they all describe a gradual process from a low-performance level (i.e., the learner can hardly recognize the movement) to a high-performance level (i.e., the learner has internalized the movement) (Santos, 2016a).

In this context, artificial intelligence (AI) techniques and concepts (Russel and Norvig, 2010) can be applied to educational (ED) systems conforming the term AIED and involving the following processing steps (Santos, 2016b, 2017; Casas-Ortiz and Santos, 2021a, 2021b):

1) *capture and monitor* the movements of the learner while learning and performing the motor skills in real-time,
2) *compare* the captured movements with predefined patterns to identify problems during the execution and learning of the motor skills, and
3) *correct* the movements when needed by giving feedback to the learner and, when available, also to the instructor.

In this way, it is expected that AIED systems can be useful to enhance the performance of motor skills in a faster and safer way for learners and instructors.

From an educational viewpoint, the educational objectives of psychomotor AIED systems should be clearly defined. Despite educational researchers having studied the domain of psychomotor learning since the work of Bloom and his colleagues (Bloom et al., 1956; Krathwohl et al., 1964) during the second half of the twentieth century, psychomotor AIED systems is a recent research topic (Santos, 2016b). Additionally, embodied learning (Macedonia, 2019), or active learning, is an educational theory that has also gained relevance in the last decade. This theory implies the conjunction between mind and body to learn things in a way that sensori-motor experiences affect and enhance cognitive learning processes by stimulating the brain and improving the affective status of the learner (Yannier et al., 2021). For instance, learners' movements (e.g., hand gestures) can provide a powerful visual indicator that learning is taking place (since thinking and learning are interconnected) and when learners move in ways that are congruent with what is being learned, learning is accelerated (Lane and Santos, 2018). Although the embodied learning theory could be integrated into the psychomotor AIED systems studied in this chapter to learn cognitive skills as shown by Santos and Corbi (2019), this chapter is focused only on the psychomotor aspects of learning while learning motor skills. Nevertheless, we address how embodied cognitive learning could be integrated into psychomotor AIED systems at the end of the chapter.

Given the emergent nature of the field of psychomotor learning supported by AI, this chapter is structured as a systematic review. We decided on this to provide some background on the state-of-the-art of AIED psychomotor systems for teachers, researchers, PhD students, postdoctoral students and even practitioners of psychomotor activities. With these purposes in mind, the chapter starts with a systematic review of psychomotor AIED systems. The systems identified in the review are then analyzed to confirm if they address AIED research. We have then analyzed the information flow of the captured human movements in those systems following the phases defined in the SMDD (Sensing movements, Modeling movements, Designing feedback, and Delivering feedback) framework proposed by Santos (2016b), where the psychomotor domain was identified as a new research field within the AIED research community. To aid in the development of psychomotor AIED systems, we present two cases of study explaining the development of two psychomotor AIED systems called KSAS (Casas-Ortiz, 2020; Casas-Ortiz and Santos, 2021a, 2021b), and KUMITRON (Echeverria and Santos, 2021a, 2021b, 2021c), following the processing steps to build psychomotor AIED systems uncovered in the previous sections. Finally, the chapter presents some challenges and opportunities for psychomotor AIED systems, as well as other directions in which human motion computing can be used for learning purposes.

REVIEW OF PSYCHOMOTOR AIED SYSTEMS

The research on psychomotor learning was introduced to the AIED community in a special issue of the International Journal of AIED entitled "The next 25 years: how advanced interactive learning technologies will change the world".[1] In one of the papers presented, seventeen systems for motor skills learning were reviewed, but the analysis performed showed that they hardly included personalization features, which are specific to AIED systems (Santos, 2016b). Since then, and as far as we know, only two systematic reviews of the field have been published.

The *first systematic review* was conducted in November 2018 by Santos (2019), and it is focused on the AI techniques that can be used to model human motion from inertial sensor data. In the rest of the chapter, we refer to this review as SR-2018. In SR-2018, the search "artificial intelligence" + "psychomotor learning" did not bring any relevant results. Thus, psychomotor learning was changed to a more generic and non-educational specific term: "human movement/motion mode(l)ing". As a result, two relevant papers were found: González-Villanueva et al. (2013) and Yamagiwa et al. (2015).

The *second systematic review* was conducted in November 2019 by Neagu et al. (2020), and it is focused on Intelligent Tutoring Systems (ITS, one of the most typical AIED systems) to train psychomotor abilities. In the rest of the chapter, we refer to it as SR-2019. This review found six relevant works: Almiyad et al. (2017), Goldberg et al. (2018), Hodaie et al. (2018), Lee and Kim (2010), Lieberman and Breazeal (2007), and Skinner et al. (2018). The terms used included "ITS" or other similar concepts to define the educational part, and the combination of terms "psycho(-)motor" or "physical" to define the psychomotor part.

Neither these systematic reviews (SR-2018 nor SR-2019) cover the whole field, since the first one is focused on those AIED psychomotor systems using only inertial sensor data and the second one is focused only on ITS or related systems. Thus, *in this chapter, we have conducted a more integrative systematic review,* referred to as SR-chapter.[2] First, we have created a search query using terms related to the three fields of interest: (i) Artificial Intelligence, (ii) Psychomotor Learning, and (iii) Tutoring Systems. For each one of those terms, several synonyms, and concepts, as well as related terms, have been identified, and a search query has been created using them. To remove irrelevant results that could be overshadowing the systems we are looking for, we have refined this query in two steps. First, we have iteratively reviewed the first hundred results obtained by a given query in the databases. After that, we have removed the terms that biased the search, omitted relevant results, or introduced excessive noise. For instance, including the terms "Neural Networks" and "Machine Learning" in the search query, related to the field of "Artificial Intelligence", was generating results not related to the scope of this systematic review. Thus, these terms have been removed from the final search query and the more general term "Artificial Intelligence" has been kept. The final search query obtained, and the databases consulted can be seen in Table 18.1. Once a refined search query was obtained for each database, the results of this review, plus the results from SR-2018 and SR-2019, have been formed according to the workflow that appears in Figure 18.1. Table 18.1 shows the details of these three systematic reviews regarding psychomotor intelligent systems: SR-2018 (Santos, 2019), SR-2019 (Neagu et al., 2020), and SR-chapter (the review reported in this chapter). Next, we comment on and compare the characteristic of these three systematic reviews.

The *search terms* used to look for publications show how SR-2018 focused on systems using AI techniques to study human motion using inertial sensors, excluding systems using any other kind of sensors. On the other hand, the search terms used by SR-2019 show how their systematic review is focused on ITS for psychomotor activities, leaving other kinds of AIED systems out. To fill the gaps from SR-2018 and SR-2019, SR-chapter is focused on learning and tutoring systems independently of the sensing devices used to capture the movements, encompassing both previous reviews and using more general terms to facilitate finding more results. The only restriction applied to the methods used is that the system must be an AIED system and use AI techniques.

The three reviews have included ScienceDirect,[3] ACM Digital Library,[4] and IEEE Xplore[5] as *databases* to explore. In addition, SR-2018 also included Google Scholar[6] (which has not been included in SR-chapter because of the limit of 256 characters in the search query). On the other hand, SR-2019 also included the Journal of Educational Data Mining[7] (which has not been included in SR-chapter since the search query did not retrieve any relevant results that were not included in another database), Scopus,[8] Web of Science,[9] and Springer.[10] These last three databases have been included in SR-chapter. Finally, we have additionally included the PubMed[11] database, which resulted in some interesting results from the field of health sciences.

Table 18.1   *Details of the three systematic reviews considered in the chapter: SR-2018 (Santos, 2019), SR-2019 (Neagu et al., 2020), and SR-chapter (this chapter)*

	SR-2018 (Santos, 2019)	SR-2019 (Neagu et al., 2020)	SR-chapter (this chapter)
Search terms	Artificial intelligence + [Psychomotor learning OR Human movement/motion OR modeling/modeling OR Inertial sensors OR Accelerometer]	ITS: Intelligent tutoring systems OR Intelligent computer-aided instruction OR intelligent computer-assisted instruction OR knowledge-based tutoring systems OR adaptive tuto·ing systems OR computer-based tutoring system Psychomotor: psycho-motor OR psycho motor OR physical	(Artificial Intelligence OR Expert System) AND (Psychomotor Learning OR Psychomotor Skill OR Psychomotor Domain) AND (Tutoring System OR Intelligent Tutoring OR Intelligent Tutoring System OR Learning System)
Databases	Science Direct IEEE Explore DL ACM DL Google Scholar	Scopus Web of science Science Direct IEEE Explore DL Springer ACM DL Journal of EDM	Scopus Web of Science ScienceDirect IEEE Xplore DL SpringerLink ACM DL PubMed
Inclusion criteria	1. Use of AI techniques to model de performance of complex psychomotor tasks from inertial sensor data	1. Full papers 2. Peer-reviewed papers 3. With empirical research 4. ITS architectures 5. Areas of the psychomotor domain	1. The system must be able to assess the learning of the activity, by personalizing it according to the learner's performance 2. The system assesses learning in humans 3. There is an existing prototype that has been tested 4. The system can give adequate feedback to the learner
Exclusion criteria	None	1. Study protocols 2. Extended abstracts 3. No ITS architectures 4. No psychomotor domain	None
Outcomes	Two papers (González-Villanueva et al., 2013; Yamagiwa et al., 2015)	Seven papers (Almiyad et al., 2017; Goldberg et al., 2018; Hodaie et al., 2018; Lee and Kim, 2010; Lieberman and Breazeal, 2007; Skinner et al., 2018)	Twelve papers Nine papers from this review SR-2021 (Casadio et al., 2009; Chen et al., 2011; Covarrubias et al., 2014; Rajeswaran et al., 2019b; Mirchi et al., 2020; Shire et al., 2016; Shirzad and Van Der Loos, 2012; Stein et al., 2013; Wei et al., 2019) + Three papers from SR-2019 (Almiyad et al., 2017; Lee and Kim, 2010; Lieberman and Breazeal, 2007)

393

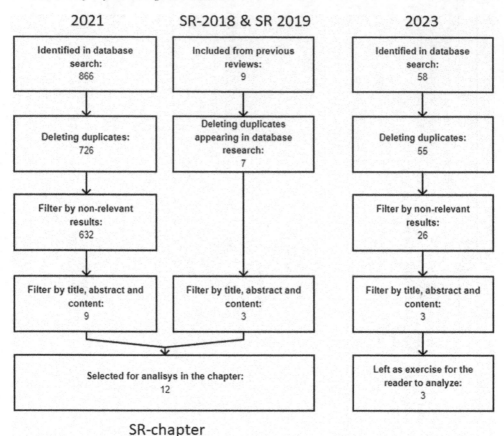

Figure 18.1   *Filtering process applied. For the 2021 analysis (SR-chapter), the workflow at the left corresponds to the filtering process applied to papers identified in our systematic review carried out in March 2021 and the workflow in the middle corresponds to the filtering process applied to papers identified in the two previous systematic reviews (SR-2018 and SR-2019) that were also reviewed in this chapter. The queries were run again in January 2023 (just before the publication of the handbook) to cover the period 2021–2023. The workflow of the right shows this filtering process, which resulted in three relevant papers (Hamadani et al., 2022., Vannaprathip et al., 2022, and Yilmaz et al., 2022) whose analysis is left as exercise for the reader to apply the teachings of this chapter*

The *inclusion and exclusion criteria* of the three systematic reviews vary according to their purpose. The inclusion criteria in SR-2018 focused on systems using AI techniques to model the performance of psychomotor tasks using inertial sensor data, which left out systems using other kinds of sensors. SR-2018 did not introduce any exclusion criteria. In turn, the inclusion criteria in SR-2019 focused on full peer-reviewed papers describing ITS architectures, performing empirical research on areas of the psychomotor domain. SR-2019 also defined exclusion criteria to exclude study protocols, extended abstracts, and systems that are not ITS architectures or do not explore the psychomotor domain. SR-chapter allows any system or architecture if it fits with the following inclusion criteria: (i) it can assess the learning of physical activities, personalizing it according to the learner's performance; (ii) the system assesses learning in humans, and not in animals; (iii) there is an implemented and tested prototype, demonstrating that the system is viable and implementable; and (iv) the system can give feedback to the learner. SR-chapter does not introduce any exclusion criteria.

The *outcomes* of the three systematic reviews are very different. SR-2018 found two papers describing systems that use AI techniques to analyze human motion using inertial sensors. SR-2019 found seven papers that describe ITS architectures for psychomotor learning that comply with the inclusion criteria. Finally, in SR-chapter we have found nine papers that describe systems using AI techniques to teach psychomotor activities. Additionally, we have added to the outcomes of SR-chapter three papers from SR-2019 because they comply with our inclusion criteria. This results in a total of twelve papers that are analyzed in detail in this chapter. The rest of the papers found in SR-2019 and the two papers found in SR-2018 have not been included because they do not meet the inclusion criteria defined in the current systematic review. The three papers included from SR-2019 did not appear in the review presented in this chapter since they did not include terms related to AI. However, they involve AI concepts in their design, so we decided to include them.

AIED ANALYSIS OF THE SELECTED PSYCHOMOTOR SYSTEMS

In this section, we review the characteristics of the twelve systems selected from the previous reviews to analyze if they address AIED research. Note that some of the systems that have been selected for a detailed review in the chapter may be described in more than one paper written by the same authors. When reporting the details of the review in this section, we reference the most updated paper describing the system, and in Table 18.2, we reference all the papers describing it that we have reviewed.

To assess if the twelve papers address AI, we focus on the algorithms implemented. For this, we have analyzed if they are typical algorithms used in the AI field, as well as the intelligent behavior offered by the overall system. To study if the analyzed systems have an intelligent behavior, we follow the ideas of Russell and Norvig (2010), which establish that when a system can act as a human (in our case, a tutor), it is an AI system. Consequently, if the system is also an educational system, then we follow that it is an AIED system (AI system + educational system).

On the other hand, to assess if the twelve papers address an educational perspective, we follow a double analysis. First, we analyze them using Mager's components to describe effective instructional objectives (Mager, 1997) as done in SR-2018 (Santos, 2019):

1) *Performance*: What the learner will do.
2) *Condition*: Under what conditions the performance will occur.
3) *Criterion of Success*: How to assess whether the learner has acquired the skill.

Second, to assess the learning goals and scope of the systems, we have selected Simpson's (1972) psychomotor taxonomy amongst the existing options (Dave, 1970; Ferris and Aziz,

Table 18.2   The psychomotor AIED systems identified in the papers reviewed indicating the AI techniques used, Mager's components of the educational objective, and Simpson's psychomotor categories. This table also includes the systems KSAS and KUMITRON presented in the chapter as case studies

Reference to system	Application field	AI technique	Mager's educational objective			Simpson's psychomotor categories
			Performance	Condition	Criterion of success	
(Winkler-Schwartz et al., 2019; Mirchi et al., 2020)	Laparoscopy	Support Vector Machine (SVM)	Be able to execute a laparoscopy surgery proficiently	Use the NeuroVR simulator in a simulated surgery room	The execution is classified as skilled by obtaining a good score on a trained SVM	Mechanism
(Wei et al., 2018; Wei et al., 2019)	Parkinson disease rehabilitation	Hidden Markov Models (HMM) and SVM	Enhance the execution of movements in people with Parkinson's disease	Use a Kinect or similar hardware for motion capture at home, while a therapist oversights the patient	An expert indicates how well the movement has been executed. The movement modeled by the HMM is classified as well-executed by a trained SVM over the data labeled by the expert	Perception Guided Performance
(Rajeswaran et al., 2018; Rajeswaran et al., 2019a; Rajeswaran et al., 2019b)	Endotracheal intubation	None, but produce intelligent behavior	Be able to execute and understand endotracheal intubation	Use a virtual reality headset with controllers in a simulated surgery room with simulated tools	Complete the tasks (learning objectives) established in the system	Perception Set Guided Performance

(Almiyad et al., 2017)	Laparoscopy and other image-guided procedures	None, but produce intelligent behavior	Be able to execute a laparoscopy surgery proficiently	Use an augmented reality headset and tools with fiducial markers on a flat penetrable surface	Manipulate the tools using the correct angle, position, and depth without harming the patient	Mechanism
(Shire et al., 2016)	Pen-skills	None, but produce intelligent behavior	Enhance pen skills in children with motor difficulties	Use a stylus held by a phantom device	Move the stylus following the correct trajectory (in a 3D space) at a determined speed	Guided Response
(Covarrubias et al., 2014)	Manual activities in people with disabilities	None, but produce intelligent behavior	Enhance manual activities in people with disabilities	Use a stylus held by a phantom device	Move the stylus following the correct trajectory (in a 2D space) at a determined speed	Mechanism
(Stein et al., 2013)	Crane manipulation	PIGEON algorithm (combination of NEAT and PSO)	Be able to manipulate a crane	Use a joystick to manipulate the crane	Obtain less feedback from the PIGEON agent (less feedback means a better execution)	Mechanism Adaptation

(Continued)

Table 18.2   (Continued)

Reference to system	Application field	AI technique	Mager's educational objective			Criterion of success	Simpson's psychomotor categories
			Performance	Condition			
(Shirzad and Van Der Loos, 2012)	Reaching task	None, but produce intelligent behavior	Be able to execute reaching tasks	Use a five-bar robot for executing the reaching task		Obtain less feedback from the system (less feedback means a better execution). Reach the objective following the minimum path correctly	Mechanism Adaptation
(Chen et al., 2011)	Driving without colliding (Toddlers)	Potential fields navigation	Be able to drive without colliding	Use a robotic car inside of an environment with obstacles		Do not collide with obstacles in the environment	Mechanism
(Lee and Kim, 2010)	Ball passing	None, but produce intelligent behavior	Be able to pass a ball to a mate	Use a ball and a robot tutor		Pass the ball to the correct goal at a determined speed and angle	Guided Response
(Casadio et al., 2009)	Stroke rehabilitation	None, but produce intelligent behavior	Enhance manual skills in patients who have suffered a stroke	Use a planar manipulandum		Follow the trajectory and complete the path in a given time	Mechanism
(Lieberman and Breazeal, 2007)	Sports (general)	None, but produce intelligent behavior	Be able to mimic arm movements	Use an optical tracking system and a display for seeing the movements to imitate		Mimic the movement in the correct position of the arm	Perception Set Guided Response

KSAS (Case study in this chapter) (Casas-Ortiz, 2020; Casas-Ortiz and Santos, 2021a, 2021b)	Martial arts	LSTM neural networks	Be able to execute the Blocking Set I of American Kenpo Karate in the correct order	Execute the expected movements in the correct order	The trained LSTM neural network classifies the learner's movement as the expected sequence of movements	Perception Set Guided Response
KUMITRON (Case study in the chapter) (Echeverria and Santos, 2021a, 2021b, 2021c)	Martial arts	Data mining and computer vision	Be able to anticipate an opponent's attack to train anticipatory skills or the strategy to follow in a Karate combat	Anticipate the opponent's movement before it is performed	The data mining classifiers on sensor data and video images processed with computer vision produce information to improve skills required to win the combat	Mechanism

2005; Harrow, 1972; Thomas, 2004) because it can be used to establish the levels of expertise and acquisition of knowledge that each system reaches (Santos, 2016a). Simpson's psychomotor taxonomy defines the following categories:

1) *Perception (Awareness):* This category (the lowest) consists of becoming aware of the objects and qualities of the movement.
2) *Set:* This category is defined as the mental, physical, or emotional readiness or preparatory adjustment to initiate the action.
3) *Guided Response:* This category consists of being able to perform the task under the guidance of the instructor or following instructions or a set.
4) *Mechanism (Basic Proficiency):* This category consists of being able to perform the task without supervision.
5) *Complete Overt Response (Expert):* This category consists of performing a complex pattern of movements and resolving uncertainty.
6) *Adaptation:* This category consists of altering the response to new situations and solving problems.
7) *Origination:* This category (the highest) consists of creating new movements or using the learned movements to fit a particular situation or specific problems. In this category, creativity is an important factor since it means that the concepts and movements are clearly understood.

The AI algorithm used in each paper, our analysis considering Mager's educational objectives, and our analysis considering Simpson's categories are summarized in Table 18.2.[12] The following paragraphs expand the information presented in the table.

For each system reviewed, first, we have identified the *application field*. Nine of the reviewed systems are medical applications. Three systems are rehabilitation systems for patients who have suffered an injury (Casadio et al., 2009; Shirzad and Van Der Loos, 2012; Wei et al., 2019), three are therapy systems for patients with motor difficulties (Chen et al., 2011; Covarrubias et al., 2014; Shire et al., 2016) and three are systems for training medical skills such as laparoscopic surgery or endotracheal intubation (Almiyad et al., 2017; Rajeswaran et al., 2019b; Mirchi et al., 2020). Two systems are sports applications, one of them for learning sports in general and the other one for ball passing (Lee and Kim, 2010; Lieberman and Breazeal, 2007). The remaining system is a job skill training application that teaches how to manipulate a crane (Stein et al., 2013).

After analyzing each paper regarding the *AI perspective*, we concluded that the twelve systems analyzed used either AI algorithms and techniques or produce intelligent behavior (i.e., act as a human). Four of them explicitly use AI techniques or algorithms: (i) one of the systems uses the Support Vector Machine (SVM) algorithm to distinguish well-executed movements from wrongly executed movements and scoring executions (Mirchi et al., 2020); (ii) another system uses Hidden Markov Models (HMMs) to model actions and again SVM to classify them (Wei et al., 2019); (iii) a third system describes an algorithm called PIGEON (Particle Swarm Intelligence and Genetic Programming for the Evolution and Optimization of Neural Networks) that combines Neuroevolution of Augmented Topologies (NEAT) and Particle Swarm Optimization (PSO) to train an agent using experts' data. This software agent is then used to teach a learner (Stein et al., 2013); and (iv) a fourth system uses Potential Fields for navigation, a technique broadly known in reactive robotics (Chen et al., 2011). The rest of the systems do not use a specific AI algorithm or technique, but we have included them in the review because the purpose of those systems is to simulate the acts and thinking of a human tutor by "observing" the movements of a learner, giving feedback as a human tutor would do.

Regarding the educational objectives (following Mager's), the *performance component* for each system depends greatly on the task to learn. When the application field of the system is rehabilitation (Casadio et al., 2009; Shirzad and Van Der Loos, 2012; Wei et al., 2019), the performance objective is to recover the skills that have been lost when a condition is present or after suffering an injury. If the application field of the system is therapy for patients with motor difficulties (Chen et al., 2011; Covarrubias et al., 2014; Shire et al., 2016), the performance objective is to enhance the execution of skills that are compromised by the motor difficulties. If the application of the system is training medical skills (Almiyad et al., 2017; Rajeswaran et al., 2019b; Mirchi et al., 2020) the performance objective is to be able to perform that medical task, for example, laparoscopic surgery or endotracheal intubation. If the application system is training skills for a job (Stein et al., 2013), the performance objective is to be able to perform the motion properly at work. Finally, if the application of the system is to learn or enhance the ability while doing any sport (Lee and Kim, 2010; Lieberman and Breazeal, 2007), the performance objective is to learn the sport and master it.

The *condition component* of Mager's educational objectives depends heavily on the elements used to learn the skill. Here, we need to consider the fact that, in most cases, the elements and conditions used and applied during training are not the same as in a real-life situation. The systems using simulators or assisting elements for training a skill have the condition objective of using the simulator to perform the task and learn the specific skill in a way that can be extrapolated to a real-life situation. This is the case for almost all the analyzed systems (Almiyad et al., 2017; Chen et al., 2011; Covarrubias et al., 2014; Rajeswaran et al., 2019b; Lee and Kim, 2010; Lieberman and Breazeal, 2007; Mirchi et al., 2020; Shire et al., 2016; Stein et al., 2013). The only exceptions are three rehabilitation systems, in which the condition objectives are to enhance the skills executed during the session, with the purpose of recovering the lost psychomotor function (Casadio et al., 2009; Shirzad and Van Der Loos, 2012; Wei et al., 2019).

The *criterion of success component* of Mager's educational objectives depends on the algorithms, sensors, and techniques used to analyze the execution and performance of the movements. In Mirchi et al. (2020), the system used to sense the movements is a NeuroVR simulator, and the algorithm used to analyze the movements is an SVM that classifies the movements into well or badly executed, and gives a score, so the criterion component consists of correctly manipulating the simulator virtual tools, obtaining a good score and a well-executed classification for the movements. In Wei et al. (2019), the movements are captured using an optical depth-sensor (Kinect) and the algorithms used to analyze the movements are an HMM to model the movements and an SVM to classify them, so the criterion component consists of the SVM classifying the movement as well-executed. In Rajeswaran et al. (2019b), a virtual reality (VR) headset (Oculus VR) with controllers is used to simulate a surgery room in a virtual environment with virtual tools. This is a task-based application, so the criterion component consists of completing the tasks (called learning objectives in that paper) established by the system. In Almiyad et al. (2017), an augmented reality (AR) headset and laparoscopic equipment are used to visualize information about the angle, position, and depth of the equipment while the learner is manipulating it on a flat penetrable surface (simulating the body of a patient), so the criterion component consists of manipulating the tools using the correct angle, position, and depth established by the system. Both Shire et al. (2016) and Covarrubias et al. (2014) use a stylus held by a phantom robotic device that can apply force to correct the speed and trajectory of the stylus, so the criterion objectives consist in following a 2D trajectory at a determined speed in the case of Covarrubias and a 3D trajectory at a determined speed in the case of Shire. In Stein et al. (2013), a force joystick can give force feedback, determined by a teaching agent trained using the PIGEON algorithm. In this case, the criterion component consists of obtaining less feedback from the agent, since less feedback means a better execution. Shirzad and Van Der Loos (2012) use a five-bar robot to give feedback while executing a reaching task using the robot, so the criterion component consists of reaching the objective following the minimum path and receiving the minimum feedback from the robot (again, less feedback means a better execution). Chen et al. (2011) use a robotic car controlled by a force joystick, able to correct the feedback if the potential fields algorithm detects an obstacle nearby, so in this case, the criterion component consists in not colliding with obstacles and again, receiving less feedback from the force joystick. Lee and Kim (2010) use a robot that can pass a ball to a learner to teach him/her to pass and receive the ball, so the criterion component consists in passing the ball to the robot at a determined angle and a determined speed. Casadio et al. (2009) use a planar manipulandum that can measure the trajectory and time followed by the patient while executing some reaching tasks, and it can give force feedback to the patient, so the criterion component consists in obtaining less feedback and following the correct trajectory, executing the task within a limited time. Finally, Lieberman and Breazeal (2007) use an optical tracking system with cameras and markers, and it can give vibrotactile feedback to the learner, so, in this case, the criterion component consists of imitating a set of movements correctly, in a way that the feedback given by the system is minimized.

Finally, we analyze each system following the *categories of Simpson's psychomotor taxonomy* (Simpson, 1972). In Mirchi et al. (2020), the category applied is "mechanism" (the learners perform the task). In Wei et al. (2019), the applied categories are "perception" (training videos are shown to teach the movements) and "guided response" (guidance videos are shown to guide the execution of the movements). In Rajeswaran et al. (2019b), the applied categories are "perception" (videos and images showing the task to perform and images of the tools and organs of the patient are shown), "set" (the learner can get ready physically and mentally by selecting the tools he/she wants to use before starting the session) and "guided response" (the task is deconstructed into learning objectives that the learner has to follow). In Almiyad et al. (2017), the category "mechanism" is applied (the learner can use the simulator and receive real-time feedback on the tools' position, depth and angle). In Shire et al. (2016), the applied category is "guided response" (the participants compete against a computer that shows the expected behavior while force haptic feedback is used to correct the execution in real-time). In Covarrubias et al. (2014) the applied category is "mechanism" (haptic feedback is used to guide the execution in real-time, but no guidance is provided). In Stein et al. (2013), the system applies the categories "mechanism" (the system uses an agent that can provide force-feedback when required, but no guidance is provided), and "adaptation" (the boxes are randomly distributed when the simulation starts, and the learner has to adapt his/her abilities to the new distribution). In Shirzad and Van Der Loos (2012), the applied categories are "mechanism" (a target is provided using visual feedback, while force feedback is provided to correct the execution) and "adaptation" (the target appears in random positions and visual distortion is applied). In Chen et al. (2011), the applied category is "mechanism" (the learners start using the system while force feedback is given in real time to correct the trajectory). In Lee and Kim (2010), the "guided response" category is applied (the robot asks the learner to pass the ball and then gives feedback about the execution to correct it in the next iteration). In Casadio et al. (2009), the applied category is "mechanism" (the patients are asked to directly execute the task, while force feedback is provided in real time). In Lieberman and Breazeal (2007), the applied categories are "perception" and "set" (the learners can use the system to get used to how it works and the feedback), and "guided response" (videos showing the expected pose are shown to guide the executions). It can be noted how most of the systems are skipping categories that could be important to enhance the learning process, and how the higher level (origination) is not applied in any of them, probably because it is the most difficult to assess since it entails analyzing creativity.

ANALYSIS OF THE INFORMATION FLOW IN THE SYSTEMS REVIEWED

In this section, we analyze the twelve psychomotor AIED systems regarding the information flow in them to provide the required intelligent support while learning a motor skill. We have classified the flow of information about the captured movements of the selected systems using the SMDD (Sensing-Modeling-Designing-Delivering) framework (see Figure 18.2) defined by Santos (2016b) to build procedural learning environments for personalized learning of motor skills. This framework can be applied along the lifecycle of technology-based educational systems (van Rosmalen et al., 2004), and it is formed by four interconnected phases:

1. *Sensing the learner's corporal movement* as specific skills are acquired within the context in which this movement takes place.
2. *Modeling the physical interactions*, which allows comparing the learner's movements against pre-existing templates of an accurate movement (e.g., a template of how an expert would carry out the movement).
3. *Designing the feedback* to be provided to the learner (i.e., what kind of support and corrections are needed, and when and how to provide them).
4. *Delivering the feedback* in an effective non-intrusive way to advise the learner on how the body and limbs should move to achieve the motor learning goal.

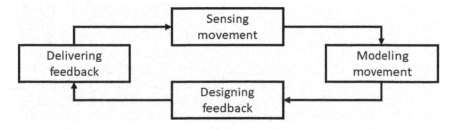

Source: Santos, 2016b

Figure 18.2   *Framework SMDD (Sensing-Modelling-Designing-Delivering) and interaction between the phases involved in the development of AIED psychomotor systems*

As aforementioned, some of the systems selected for analysis do not explicitly employ AI techniques, but they still can be considered AIED systems since they mimic and perform the task that a real human tutor would do. The results of the analysis of the AIED systems using the SMDD framework are compiled in Table 18.3.[13]

After analyzing the systems, we can notice how there is a great variety of methods used to *sense the movements* executed by the learner. Two of the reviewed systems use a joystick to capture the movements (Chen et al., 2011; Stein et al., 2013). Four of the systems use robotic arms, of which two use phantom devices (Covarrubias et al., 2014; Shire et al., 2016), one uses a planar manipulandum (Casadio et al., 2009), and one uses a five-bar robot (Shirzad and Van Der Loos, 2012). One of them uses a VR headset (Oculus VR and HTC Vive) with two hand controllers that capture the movements using optical and inertial sensors (Rajeswaran et al., 2019b). One of the systems uses optical sensors to capture fiducial markers in the tools used during the training (Almiyad et al., 2017). Another system uses a set of cameras with reflective markers in the body (Lieberman and Breazeal, 2007), specifically a Vicon optical tracking system. A depth camera (Kinect) is used in another system to capture 3D poses of the body (Wei et al., 2019). In Lee and Kim (2010), a robot able to capture the angle at which a ball is passed is used as a tutor. Finally, Mirchi et al. (2020) use a body simulator, specifically a NeuroVR, that can obtain information such as the position, rotation, or forces applied to the tools.

The methods used to *model the movement* depend greatly on the method used to sense the motion. Systems using joysticks rely on the representation of the coordinates indicated by the joystick (Chen et al., 2011; Stein et al., 2013). Systems using robotic arms rely on representations of the position of the effector in the space and numerical representations of the inferred speed and characteristics of the movement (Casadio et al., 2009; Covarrubias et al., 2014; Shire et al., 2016; Shirzad and Van Der Loos, 2012). Systems using VR head-mounted displays (HMD) rely on representing the position of the HMD and the controllers in the space (Rajeswaran et al., 2019b). Systems capturing objects using cameras model the position, angle, or depth of those elements using numerical values (Almiyad et al., 2017; Lee and Kim, 2010). Systems capturing portions of the body tend to model the joints of the body using 3D skeletons (Lieberman and Breazeal, 2007; Wei et al., 2019). Finally, systems using body simulators to measure interactions with the simulator tools, like pressure or angle, represent it numerically (Mirchi et al., 2020).

The *design of the feedback*, and how it is given to the learner depends on the objective of each system (what is going to be learned and how), and the methods used for capturing the motion. Some systems base the design of the feedback on following a trajectory or position, and if the learner does not follow it properly, feedback is generated and provided to correct the error (Almiyad et al., 2017; Casadio et al., 2009; Chen et al., 2011; Covarrubias et al., 2014; Rajeswaran et al., 2019b; Lieberman and Breazeal, 2007; Shire et al., 2016; Shirzad and Van Der Loos, 2012). Force fields can be used to calculate the force feedback as seen in Chen et al. (2011). Other systems calculate a score and use it to indicate to the learner the quality of the execution, either mathematically (Lee and Kim, 2010), or by using AI techniques like SVM (Mirchi et al., 2020; Wei et al., 2019), which can also be used to classify correctly or wrongly executed movements. Finally, the design of the feedback can rely on an algorithm that learns the quantity of feedback given to the learner from data collected from real experts (Stein et al., 2013).

Table 18.3   Analysis of the motion information flow in the systems obtained in the review. When used, AI techniques are mentioned. In addition, this table also includes the systems KSAS and KUMITRON presented in the chapter as case studies

Reference to system	Sensing movement	Modeling movement	Designing feedback	Delivering feedback
(Winkler-Schwartz et al., 2019; Mirchi et al., 2020)	NeuroVR simulator obtains information such as tool position, rotation and forces applied.	The obtained measures are normalized, and metrics are generated from raw data.	An SVM is trained for classifying the expertise of participants, giving a score of expertise.	The feedback consists of a score that establishes how good the execution was.
(Wei et al., 2018; Wei et al., 2019)	Optical depth-sensor (Kinect Sensor) captures the patient's movements.	3D-Skeletons are used to model the body poses. HMMs are used to model actions.	An SVM is trained to classify movements between well-executed and badly executed.	Verbal instructions and visual figures are given with information on how to correct the badly executed movements.
(Rajeswaran et al., 2018; Rajeswaran et al., 2019a; Rajeswaran et al., 2019b)	Oculus VR and HTC Vive with hand controllers capture the user movements within the virtual reality environment.	Representation of where the head and hands are (captured by HMD and controllers)	Deconstruct tasks into smaller learning objectives and follow trajectories of hands.	Haptic vibrations are given if the task has not been executed properly. Texts indicate tasks performed and how good was the execution. Auditory feedback indicates how tools work.
(Almiyad et al., 2017)	Optical sensors capture fiducial markers in a needle.	Numbers indicate the angle and depth of the needle.	A protractor indicating the angle of the needle is adjusted to the needle in an augmented reality environment.	Gives visual feedback showing needle position and angle in a protractor background and popups with texts.
(Shire et al., 2016)	A phantom device captures how the stylus is hold and used.	Position of the stylus in 3D coordinates.	Gives feedback proportional to the deviation from the trajectory.	Force feedback is given to guide the execution using the phantom device.

(Continued)

405

Table 18.3 (Continued)

Reference to system	Sensing movement	Modeling movement	Designing feedback	Delivering feedback
(Covarrubias et al., 2014)	A phantom device captures how the stylus is hold and used.	Position of the stylus in 2D coordinates.	Gives feedback proportional to the deviation from the trajectory.	Auditory feedback is given using speakers if the position is incorrect. It also guides execution with force feedback using the phantom device.
(Stein et al., 2013)	Logitech Flight System G940 force-feedback joysticks captures how the user maneuvers the gripper.	The model is learned by a software agent using the PIGEON algorithm.	The trained agent determines the given feedback.	Force haptic feedback is given using the joystick. The current position of the crane and the objects are shown on the display.
(Shirzad and Van Der Loos, 2012)	The encoders of the robot obtain the position of the effector.	A dot represents the position of the effector in a display.	The error and gain for each type of error amplification are used to calculate position and force feedback.	Visual feedback shows the position and trajectory of the robot. Force feedback is used to correct trajectories (adapted to each error amplification).
(Chen et al., 2011)	Force feedback joystick captures how the user moves through obstacles.	Position of the joystick (x-y values). Position of the robot in the maze.	Force feedback is calculated for each maze by using potential fields.	Potential fields are used to give force feedback on the joystick.
(Lee and Kim, 2010)	Robot tutors capture the position of the user and the ball.	The angle, trajectory, and velocity of the ball are calculated.	A score of the execution is calculated mathematically.	Verbal instructions are given on how to enhance the execution.
(Casadio et al., 2009)	A planar manipulandum robot calculates the position of the effector.	2D coordinates of the effector.	If the position is out of the trajectory, gives feedback.	Force feedback is given to the correct position.

(Lieberman and Breazeal, 2007)	Vicon optical tracking system captures the arm pose of the user.	3D representation of the joints of the arm.	If the arm goes beyond the position, the corresponding actuator will vibrate. The higher the error, the higher the vibration.	Tactaid vibrotactile actuators are used to give vibratory feedback.
KSAS (Case study in this chapter) (Casas-Ortiz, 2020; Casas-Ortiz and Santos, 2021a, 2021b)	Sensors of an Android device obtain characteristics of the movement, such as acceleration, orientation, or rotation.	Captures sequences are converted into data series and the EWMA algorithm is used to remove noise and smooth the data series.	An LSTM analyzes the sequences and determines which movement has been executed.	If the executed movement is the expected movement, a victory sound is played, and verbal instructions are given to congratulate the learner and guide the execution of the next movement. If the executed movement is not the expected movement, a buzzing sound is played, the device vibrates, and verbal instructions are given to the learner asking to repeat the movement. KSAS also generates reports after a training session that can be later shared with an instructor or with other learners.

(Continued)

Table 18.3 *(Continued)*

Reference to system	Sensing movement	Modeling movement	Designing feedback	Delivering feedback
KUMITRON (Case study in this chapter) (Echeverria and Santos, 2021a, 2021b, 2021c)	Arduino-based sensors capture inertial information (e.g., acceleration) and the camera of a drone (a static camera can be used, it but cannot follow the learner around the tatami) captures the pose of the user.	Information captured by the inertial sensors is modeled as a diagram of directional vectors. Human poses are modeled as a subtraction between images using OpenCV and OpenPose computer vision algorithms.	Data mining algorithms classify the good and bad performance of the learners, so that personalized support to improve skills required to win the combat can be defined. The Wizard of Oz technique is used to identify rules from the instructor's instructions to design the feedback.	Different metrics and visualizations are shown on a display in real-time to the instructor, and after the combat to the learner. Auditory verbal instructions are also given (currently, by the instructor but in the future with natural language processing techniques). Vibrotactile feedback will also be delivered in the future.

The way *feedback is delivered* to the learner depends on the different elements used by each system. Auditory, haptic, and visual modalities of feedback can be used, as well as a combination of the three modalities (Covarrubias et al., 2014; Rajeswaran et al., 2019b; Shirzad and Van Der Loos, 2012; Stein et al., 2013; Wei et al., 2019), which is known as multimodal feedback. Regarding haptic feedback, the most common type of feedback used is force feedback to correct deviations in trajectories when using joysticks and robotic arms (Casadio et al., 2009; Chen et al., 2011; Covarrubias et al., 2014; Shire et al., 2016; Shirzad and Van Der Loos, 2012; Stein et al., 2013). Vibrotactile actuators are another type of haptic feedback that can also be used to correct poses (Lieberman and Breazeal, 2007) and indicate a wrong execution (Rajeswaran et al., 2019b). Regarding auditory feedback, verbal instructions can be used to give indications and corrections to the learner (Lee and Kim, 2010; Wei et al., 2019), and sounds can be used to notify errors (Covarrubias et al., 2014). Visual feedback techniques often employ displays. In particular, displays and VR/AR techniques (that are based on the use of displays) can be used to show scores (Mirchi et al., 2020), the position of objects, and goals (Shirzad and Van Der Loos, 2012; Stein et al., 2013), measures and metrics like the angle of objects (Almiyad et al., 2017), images and figures of the correct execution (Wei et al., 2019), and texts with indications and information of the execution (Rajeswaran et al., 2019b).

CASE STUDIES ON HOW TO CREATE A PSYCHOMOTOR AIED SYSTEM

In this section, we present two case studies on how to analyze and design a psychomotor AIED system using the SMDD framework, and we have determined that both are psychomotor AIED systems by identifying their AI nature and using Mager´s objectives and Simpson's psychomotor taxonomy categories to identify their educational nature. The two systems presented as case studies are KSAS (Casas-Ortiz, 2020; Casas-Ortiz and Santos, 2021a, 2021b) and KUMITRON (Echeverria and Santos, 2021a, 2021b, 2021c). Both systems have been created as a part of our research line in PhyUM (Physical User Modelling)[14] in the domain of martial arts. However, the two systems have different purposes. The purpose of KSAS is to assist during the learning of the order in which a set of movements (known in martial arts as *katas*, forms, or sets) is performed, and the purpose of KUMITRON is to teach learners how to anticipate the opponent's movement during a martial arts combat (known as *kumite*) to train the combat strategy.

We have selected martial arts for our research because it encompasses many of the characteristics common to other psychomotor activities like the management of strength and speed while executing the movements, visuomotor coordination of different parts of the body to respond to stimuli, participation of different agents during the learning like opponents or instructor, improvisation and anticipation against stimuli or even the use of tools accompanying the movement. In addition, martial arts consist of a set of predefined movements that are structured by levels and their correct execution aligns with the laws of Physics, so there is a clear pattern against which the movements performed by the learners can be compared using human movement computing techniques.

Case Study 1: KSAS System

The first system that we are going to use as a case study is KSAS[15] (Kenpo Set Assisting System) (Casas-Ortiz, 2020; Casas-Ortiz and Santos, 2021a, 2021b). KSAS can assist learners during the learning of a set of defensive movements of the martial art American Kenpo Karate. This set of movements is known as Blocking Set I, and consists of five blocking movements (actually, it consists of six movements, but to ease the data collection and the development of the application, the last movement has been removed). The five poses resulting after executing each movement can be seen in Figure 18.3.

KSAS is a psychomotor AIED system developed for Android[16] devices, and its purpose is to help American Kenpo Karate learners during the learning of the sequence of Blocking Set I. To do this, the system can take advantage of the characteristics of an Android device, like the capacity of performing computations to analyze and model the information, capturing characteristics of the movements using the inertial sensors of the device, delivering feedback using the actuators of the device (display, speakers, and vibrator), or its feasibility to be located in any part of the body as a wearable. The architecture of KSAS can be seen in Figure 18.4.

This application was designed following the framework SMDD (Santos, 2016b). For completeness, a new row has been added in Table 18.3 with the corresponding analysis of the information flow as described in the previous section. First, to sense the movements (*Sensing motion phase*), the sensors of the mobile device are used. Specifically, KSAS uses the inertial and positional sensors of the device to capture characteristics of the movements such as acceleration, orientation, or rotation. The captured movements are modeled to be analyzed in the following phase. In KSAS, the modeling of the movements (*Modelling motion phase*) is done

Figure 18.3   *Five first blocks in American Kenpo Karate's Blocking Set I. This is the set of movements that can be learned using KSAS. From the start position, the learner has to perform an upward block, then an inward block, then an extended outward block, followed by an outward downward block, and finally, a rear elbow block. The photograms shown are performed by the first author (ACO) of this chapter*

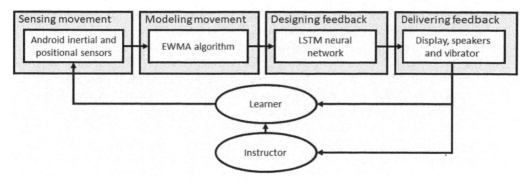

Figure 18.4   *The architecture of KSAS following the SMDD framework. The applica-*
tion starts by giving initial indications to the user (Delivering feedback).
Following those indications, the learner executes the requested movements,
which are captured using the inertial and positional sensors of the Android
device (Sensing movement). The movements are modeled using the EWMA
algorithm (Modeling movement) and analyzed to design the feedback
using an LSTM neural network (Designing feedback). The feedback is then
delivered to the learner using the display, the speakers and the vibrator of
the device (Delivering feedback). Depending on how was the performance
of the movements, the application can give new indications to the learner.
When the training session finishes, the application generates a report of the
session using the feedback generated for each movement (Delivering feed-
back). This report is available to the learner and can be voluntarily shared
with the instructor

by converting the captured sequences into data series and applying the EWMA (Exponentially Weighted Moving Averages) algorithm to remove noise and smooth the curves. Once the movements have been captured and modeled, the next step is to analyze the information to design the feedback that will be given to the learner (*Designing feedback phase*). In KSAS, this is done by classifying the movements using an LSTM (long short-term memory) neural network previously trained using real users' data and then determining if the executed movement is as expected in the sequence of movements of Blocking Set I. Finally, feedback is given to the learner (*Delivering feedback phase*) using verbal instructions (auditory feedback) that asks the learner to execute the next movement or to repeat it if it was wrong. Sounds are also used to tell the learner if the executed movement was as expected (victory sound) or not (buzz sound). Vibrations (haptic feedback) are used to tell the learner when an executed movement is not the expected one. In addition, KSAS generates reports after a training session that can later be shared with an instructor or with other learners.

To be consistent with the rest of the chapter, we now analyze KSAS from an AI and educational perspective and Mager's educational objectives. For completeness, a new row has been added in Table 18.2, with the analysis performed. The application field covered by KSAS is martial arts, and more specifically, American Kenpo Karate's blocking movements performed using the arms. To analyze the movements, LSTM neural networks are used, so it employs an AI technique. Furthermore, the application takes the role of an instructor who guides the learner through the execution of the set and corrects him/her if necessary. Regarding Mager's components, Mager´s performance component for KSAS is: "to be able to execute the Blocking Set I of American Kenpo Karate in the correct order". Mager´s condition component for KSAS is: "to execute the expected movements in the correct order" (since KSAS is used to learn the movements and the order in which they are executed, we do not consider an opponent attacking the learner here). Mager's criterion of success component for KSAS is: "A neural network classifies the learners' movement as the expected movement in the sequence of movements".

Furthermore, KSAS can be encompassed in the first three categories of Simpson's psychomotor taxonomy (Simpson, 1972). Thus, the categories applied in KSAS are perception, set, and guided response. The category "perception" is applied in KSAS by giving a brief introduction and context to the Blocking Set I. The category "set" is applied in KSAS by asking the learner to put in the starting position and take his/her time to push the start button when he/she is ready to start the set. The category "guided response" is applied in KSAS by guiding the execution of the set using verbal instruction and giving adequate feedback. The development of the four remaining categories (Mechanism, Complete Overt Response, Adaptation, and Origination) is planned for future versions of KSAS and other projects deriving from KSAS application.

Case Study 2: KUMITRON System

The second system that we are going to use as a case study in this chapter is KUMITRON[17] (KUMITe and dRON) (Echeverria and Santos, 2021a, 2021b, 2021c). This system is able to anticipate the opponent's movements to give feedback about the combat strategy that the learner can apply in a given situation. For this, the system needs to identify the specific movements performed by the learner during the combat. To detect the movements of an opponent, KUMITRON employs AI techniques, Arduino-based sensors, and a drone equipped with a camera (a conventional camera can also be used, but a drone's camera has the advantage of the mobility offered by drones to follow the learners around the tatami and use the most appropriate point of view to capture the movement). The movements that at this moment can be detected in KUMITRON (see Echeverria and Santos (2021c) for more details) are shown in Figure 18.5 and correspond to specific attack and defense movements in a *kihon kumite*, which is a structured multistep combat in Karate martial art. The architecture of the KUMITRON system is shown in Figure 18.6.

This system was designed following the SMDD framework (Santos, 2016b). For completeness, a new row has been added in Table 18.3 with the corresponding analysis of the information flow as described in the previous section. In KUMITRON, the movements are sensed (*Sensing motion phase*) by collecting information from the Arduino-based sensors and the drone camera. These signals are captured in real-time for multimodal processing of the movements. Physiological signals and audio are also captured. The modeling of the movements (*Modelling motion phase*) captured by the camera is done by applying computer vision techniques (OpenPose algorithm) to model the parts of the captured video that change between frames. The body part that is initiating the attack is also identified using computer vision algorithms such as OpenCV. The information captured from the inertial sensors is modeled as a diagram of directional vectors to show the joint motion interaction of both learners along the combat. To design the feedback (*Designing feedback phase*), data mining algorithms on sensor data and video images processed are used to infer performance indicators by classifying the correct and wrong performance of the learners, so that personalized

Attacker: TORI   Defender: UKE

Kamae   Gedan Barai   Oi Tsuki   Kamae   Soto Uke   Gyaku Tsuki

Figure 18.5   *Movements of kihon kumite currently detected by KUMITRON. Kamae is the initial posture, and both participants start in this position. The attacker performs sequentially the Gedan Barai (a circular downward block) attacks, followed by Oi Tsuki (a horizontal punch with the same leg forwarded). The defender executes the movements of Soto Uke (an outward block) and Gyaku Tsuki (a horizontal punch with the opposite leg forwarded). The photograms shown are performed by the second author (JE) of this chapter*

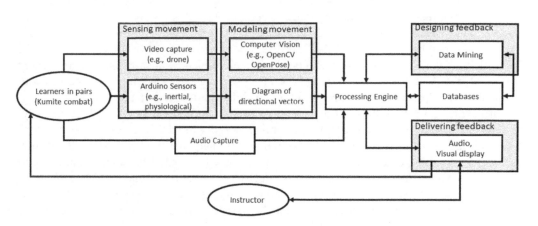

Figure 18.6   *The architecture of the KUMITRON system following the SMDD framework. The movements executed by the learners are captured by collecting information from the Arduino-based sensors and the video capture device (Sensing movement). Subsequently, the movements are modeled using computer vision techniques like OpenCV and OpenPose (Modelling movement), and the information captured from the Arduino-based sensors is modeled as a diagram of directional vectors. Data mining techniques are used to design the feedback by integrating the modeled information from the camera and the Arduino-based sensors (Designing feedback). Finally, auditory feedback is delivered to the learners in the form of verbal instructions, and visual feedback is delivered using a display (Delivering feedback)*

support to improve skills required to win the combat can be defined. In addition, we are using the Wizard of Oz technique to identify rules from the instructions that the Karate instructor tells in the next phase (delivery) so that these can serve to design appropriate feedback. Finally, KUMITRON is able to provide multimodal feedback (*Delivering feedback phase*) in the form of auditory verbal feedback and visual feedback. Currently, the auditory feedback is given by a real Karate instructor during the combat. In the future, the system aims to generate this auditory feedback using natural language processing techniques following a set of rules (if the information sensed and modeled matches a rule, the appropriate feedback is delivered in a specific way). In turn, visual feedback is shown on a display that the martial arts instructor can watch in real time during the combat, and the learners can watch after the combat. The visual feedback consists of the captured video, the analysis performed by the OpenCV and OpenPose algorithms, the data collected by the sensors in real time (e.g., the heartbeat rate), and the movement data represented as a diagram directional vector. Finally, vibrotactile feedback is foreseen in future iterations of KUMITRON.

To be consistent with the rest of the chapter, we now analyze KUMITRON from an AI and educational perspective and Mager's educational objectives. For completeness, a new row has been added in Table 18.2 with the analysis performed. The application field covered by KUMITRON is martial arts, and more specifically, combat strategy in Karate and improving anticipation skills. To analyze the movements, data mining techniques and computer vision are used. Furthermore, the system takes the role of a martial arts instructor that gives verbal feedback during the combat (although as aforementioned, right now the verbal feedback is given by a real instructor). Regarding Mager's components, Mager's performance component for KUMITRON is: "to be able to anticipate an opponent's attack by training anticipatory skills or the combat strategy to follow". Mager's condition component for KUMITRON is: "to anticipate the opponent's movement before it is performed". Mager's criterion component for KUMITRON is: "data mining classifiers on sensor data and video images processed with computer vision produce information to improve skills required to win the combat".

Furthermore, KUMITRON can be encompassed in the first category of Simpson's psychomotor taxonomy (Simpson, 1972). The applied category in KUMITRON is "mechanism", since the learners start fighting and the system starts analyzing the movements. Perception and set, the previous categories, are not applied because the goal of the application is not to teach combat but to identify and teach skills related to the joint performance of movements in pairs, such as anticipatory skills or the subsequent combat strategy, depending on the opponent's movements. The system assumes that the learners already know the rules of *kumite* combat and the movements that can be applied.

CONCLUSIONS

AIED systems for psychomotor learning are a recent research topic. Thus, to produce a body of knowledge that can be of interest to teachers, researchers, PhD students, postdoctoral students, and even practitioners of motor skills, we have carried out a systematic review of the field. As a result, we have selected twelve relevant papers for a deeper analysis, nine from the systematic review performed in this chapter and the other three from two previous systematic reviews that we have also considered. In addition, to show how the theoretical frameworks presented here can be used to develop AIED psychomotor systems, two systems called KSAS and KUMITRON have been described as case studies. These two case studies have been analyzed using the same criteria as the reviewed publications. Thus, the twelve papers selected (plus the case studies KSAS and KUMITRON) have been reviewed in terms of their AI nature and their educational nature, using Mager's objectives and Simpson's psychomotor categories. In addition, we have analyzed the flow of information about the movements of the learners in terms of the SMDD framework (Santos, 2016b) that compiles the different stages in an AIED psychomotor system. The reviewed papers and the two case studies have shown that the SMDD framework, Mager's educational objectives, and Simpson's taxonomy are powerful tools that can be used by the AIED community to design, develop, describe and understand psychomotor AIED systems effectively and efficiently.

Considerations for Further AIED Research

As shown in the systematic review reported in this chapter, the creation of AIED systems to learn psychomotor activities is still in an early stage of research. In addition, human motion computing in education can go beyond learning motor skills. Here we outline other research directions in which human motion computing can be used for learning purposes.

Guidelines for standardization

During the systematic review presented in this chapter, we have identified a major problem in the development of psychomotor AIED systems: the lack of standards and common practices. Five of the reviewed papers (Mirchi et al., 2020; Wei et al., 2019; Almiyad et al., 2017; Lee and Kim, 2010; Lieberman and Breazeal, 2007) follow a framework to develop the proposed system. However, two of those frameworks have been implemented specifically to create systems in their domains (Mirchi et al. (2020) for laparoscopic surgery and Wei et al. (2019) for Parkinson's disease rehabilitation) or their technologies (Almiyad et al. (2017) for AR systems, Lee and Kim (2010) for interactive robot-based tutoring systems and Lieberman and Breazeal (2007) for wearable systems). This is in part because of the high variety of elements, tools, sensors, algorithms, and actuators that can be combined to create a psychomotor AIED system. Moreover, standard visualizations that help to understand the impact of the performance of the psychomotor system regarding the user features and the personalized support provided in the different phases of the interaction lifecycle should be also explored (Santos, 2008).

In our case, to analyze and compare the educational nature of the systems selected from the systematic reviews, we have used Mager´s approach to educational objectives as well as Simpson's categories. And to analyze and compare the AI nature of the systems, we have identified the AI algorithms and AI techniques employed. Finally, to identify the different parts of the system in terms of the information flow used to provide the personalized response, we have used the SMDD framework. The SMDD framework has been especially useful because it allowed to analyze each system independently of the domain or technologies used.

Thus, future research lines could focus on the development and design of new frameworks, theories and visualization approaches that can be applied to standardize the developments of AIED psychomotor systems and are specific to the psychomotor domain. This would ease the development and design of new systems, as well as allow the reuse of components.

Embodied cognition

Another issue that should be considered when studying the psychomotor domain, which is mentioned in the Introduction, is embodied cognition. Embodied cognition is a theory that has gained relevance in the past decade and implies the conjunction between mind and body to learn new things, in a way that sensorimotor experiences can affect and enhance the cognitive learning process and the affective state of learners. For instance, learning Maths is easier when the instructor is gesturing during the lesson (Goldin-Meadow et al., 1999; Goldin-Meadow et al., 2001). Although psychomotor AIED systems can implicitly have embodied cognition – as shown by Santos and Corbi (2019), where Aikido is used to learn physics implicit in Aikido movements – it is still an open research question as to how psychomotor AIED systems can be integrated with the learning of cognitive skills and theories.

Thus, future research in psychomotor AIED systems and embodied cognition theories could be focused on the learning of cognitive skills through the learning of motor skills that have the cognitive skills implicit in their practice.

Affective issues

According to Bloom's taxonomy, there are three domains of learning: psychomotor, cognitive, and affective. However, almost all the reviewed systems only approach the psychomotor domain. Rajeswaran et al. (2019b) is the only work where the cognitive domain is also approached. In turn, none of the analyzed systems approach the affective domain.

As introduced with embodied cognition, the interaction between the three domains of Bloom can bring many advantages for learners, and the integration of the affective domain could bring great benefits to cognitive and psychomotor learning (see Chapter 5 by Arroyo et al.). In this sense, it might be useful to consider knowledge engineering methodologies such as TORMES (Boticario and Santos, 2015) that can define and characterize the emotional support to be provided in educational systems enriched with sensing capabilities (Santos and Boticario, 2012; Santos et al., 2016).

Thus, future research in psychomotor AIED systems could be focused on the integration of psychomotor learning theories into the development of systems to teach and learn motor skills while considering the affective state of the learner, integrating the three domains of learning into a single system.

Online psychomotor learning and learning at home

Situations like the COVID-19 pandemic lockdowns can make learning in person difficult. Also, a busy lifestyle and the lack of time available due to work and personal issues can make it difficult to go to specialized centers to learn and train motor skills.

Psychomotor AIED systems can help in these situations by allowing learners to practice at home, either following a fully online approach, as is done in Wei et al. (2019) where a patient can learn and practice the movements at home using the system while being supervised by an instructor, or following a blended approach in which the movements are taught by an instructor and then practiced at home using the system, as is done in the system KSAS presented as a case study (Casas-Ortiz, 2020; Casas-Ortiz and Santos 2021a). Furthermore, in KSAS, the learner can share the progress of his/her training with the instructor, for a better follow-up of his/her progress.

Thus, future research lines can focus on online psychomotor learning at home as it is done in some of the analyzed systems, where the patient/learner can practice the movements at home with the support of the system, without the need to have the instructor/therapist supervising the practice all the time.

Psychomotor learning in pairs

Learning a motor skill is better when a collaborative approach is followed. This requires that the system monitors the joint interaction of two participants in the psychomotor practice, as for instance it is done in the Karate combat with KUMITRON. However, the psychomotor AIED systems that we identified in the review presented in this chapter focus on teaching only one motor skill individually to one single person.

In addition, collaborative learning of motor skills can also be used to train some capabilities, such as anticipatory skills, which are important in many psychomotor activities, such as martial arts, where the learner must be able to anticipate the opponent's attack to avoid it, block it or counterattack. Psychomotor AIED systems can help in the development of anticipatory skills, as shown with the KUMITRON system presented as a case study, where computer vision algorithms are used to identify the anticipation of the movements of an opponent.

Thus, future lines of research could focus on addressing the gap in collaborative psychomotor activities to enhance the learning of those activities that require the participation of more than just one person, and also support the learning of skills involving another learner, such as movement anticipation. For this, current approaches to collaborative learning (see Chapter 19 by Martinez-Maldonado et al.) could be revised and adapted to support psychomotor collaborative learning.

Psychomotor learning in the open space

Personalized support for learning activities that require moving in an open space, like a classroom or a field, is another future line of research that could be considered. An example of this is nurse training to provide medical treatments to patients (Martinez-Maldonado et al., 2018; Ronda-Carracao et al., 2021).

Thus, future lines of research could explore how to address the psychomotor support in physically situated scenarios and how learners should move around in those scenarios to achieve their learning goals.

Gamification

Gamification techniques are gaining attention in the AIED community because they increase the engagement of learners during the sessions, making them interesting and entertaining (see Chapter 20 by McLaren and Nguyen). In fact, some of the sensors used to capture motion to develop psychomotor AIED systems have their roots in the gaming industry. Moreover, there are multiple stories of success in the exergames (exercise+gaming) field, including Microsoft Kinect, Nintendo Wii Fit, Play Station Eye Toy: Kinetic, Just Dance, or more recently, Virtual Reality games.

Thus, future research on psychomotor AIED systems could learn from gamification experiences so that new ways of engaging physical activities can be developed.

ACKNOWLEDGMENT

The work is partially supported by the project INT^{2}AFF funded under Grant PGC2018-102279-B-I00 (MCIU/AEI/FEDER, UE) from the Spanish Ministry of Science, Innovation, and Universities, the Spanish Agency of Research, and the European Regional Development Fund (ERDF).

NOTES

1. https://link.springer.com/journal/40593/volumes-and-issues/26-2
2. The review reported in this chapter was performed in March 2021. However, in January 2023, just before the publication of the handbok, we ran the queries again on the databases, obtaining three new results: Hamadani et al., 2022., Vannaprathip et al., 2022, and Yilmaz et al., 2022. The analysis of these three works is left to the reader as an exercise to apply the teachings of this chapter.
3. https://www.sciencedirect.com/
4. https://dl.acm.org/
5. https://ieeexplore.ieee.org/
6. https://scholar.google.com/
7. https://jedm.educationaldatamining.org/
8. https://www.scopus.com/
9. https://clarivate.com/webofsciencegroup/solutions/web-of-science/
10. https://link.springer.com/
11. https://pubmed.ncbi.nlm.nih.gov/
12. Note that we have also added in Table 18.2 the KSAS and KUMITRON systems presented later in the chapter as case studies.
13. Note that we have also added in Table 18.3 the KSAS and KUMITRON systems presented later in the chapter as case studies.
14. https://blogs.uned.es/phyum/
15. https://blogs.uned.es/phyum/ksas/
16. https://www.android.com/
17. https://blogs.uned.es/phyum/kumitron/

REFERENCES

Almiyad, M. A., Oakden-Rayner, L., Weerasinghe, A., & Billinghurst, M. (2017). Intelligent augmented reality tutoring for physical tasks with medical professionals. In *Lecture Notes in Computer Science* (pp. 450–454). Cham: Springer International Publishing. doi:10.1007/978-3-319-61425-0_38.

Bloom, B. S., Engelhart, M. D., Furst, E. J., Hill, W. H., & Krathwohl, D. R. (1956). Taxonomy of educational objectives: The classification of educational goals. In *Handbook I: Cognitive Domain.* New York: David McKay Company.

Casadio, M., Giannoni, P., Morasso, P., Sanguineti, V., Squeri, V., & Vergaro, E. (2009). Training stroke patients with continuous tracking movements: Evaluating the improvement of voluntary control. In *Annual International Conference of the IEEE Engineering in Medicine and Biology Society: IEEE Engineering in Medicine and Biology Society,* 5961–5964. doi:10.1109/IEMBS.2009.5334525.

Casas-Ortiz, A. (2020). *Capturing, Modelling, Analyzing and Providing Feedback in Martial Arts With Artificial Intelligence to support Psychomotor Learning Activities* (Universidad Nacional de Educación a Distancia, Escuela Técnica Superior de Ingenieros Informáticos). http://e-spacio.uned.es/fez/view/bibliuned:master-ETSInformatica-IAA-Acasas.

Casas-Ortiz, A., & Santos, O. C. (2021a). KSAS: A Mobile App With Neural Networks to Guide the Learning of Motor Skills. In *Actas de La XIX Conferencia de La Asociación Española Para La Inteligencia Artificial (CAEPIA 20/21),* 997–1000. https://caepia20-21.uma.es/inicio_files/caepia20-21-actas.pdf.

Casas-Ortiz, A., & Santos, O. C. (2021b). KSAS: An AI Application to Learn Martial Arts Movements in Online Settings. *Interactive Events at AIED21 (Artificial Intelligence in Education),* 1–4. https://aied2021.science.uu.nl/wp-content/uploads/2021/05/KSAS-An-AI-Application-to-learn-Martial-Arts-Movements-in-on-line-Settings.pdf.

Chen, X., Ragonesi, C., Galloway, J. C., & Agrawal, S. K. (2011). Training Toddlers Seated on Mobile Robots to Drive Indoors Amidst Obstacles. *IEEE Transactions on Neural Systems and Rehabilitation Engineering: A Publication of the IEEE Engineering in Medicine and Biology Society, 19*(3), 271–279. doi:10.1109/TNSRE.2011.2114370.

Intelligent systems for psychomotor learning   419

Covarrubias, M., Gatti, E., Bordegoni, M., Cugini, U., & Mansutti, A. (2014). Improving manual skills in persons with disabilities (PWD) through a multimodal assistance system. *Disability and Rehabilitation: Assistive Technology, 9*(4), 335–343. doi:10.3109/17483107.2013.799238.

Dave, R. H. (1970). Psychomotor levels. In R. J. Armstrong (Ed.), *Developing and Writing Educational Objectives*. Tucson, AZ: Educational Innovators Press.

Echeverria, J., & Santos, O. C. (2021a). KUMITRON: Artificial intelligence system to monitor karate fights that synchronize aerial images with physiological and inertial signals. In *26th International Conference on Intelligent User Interfaces (IUI 2021)*. doi:10.1145/3397482.3450730.

Echeverria, J., & Santos, O. C. (2021b). Punch anticipation in a karate combat with computer vision. In *Adjunct Proceedings of the 29th ACM Conference on User Modeling, Adaptation and Personalization*. doi:10.1145/3450614.3461688.

Echeverria, J., & Santos, O. C. (2021c). Toward modeling psychomotor performance in Karate combats using computer vision pose estimation. *Sensors (Basel, Switzerland), 21*(24), 8378. doi:10.3390/s21248378.

Ferris, T. L. J., & Aziz, S. M. (2005). A psychomotor skills extension to bloom's taxonomy of education objectives for engineering education. In *Exploring Innovation in Education and Research (ICEER-2005)*. https://www.researchgate.net/publication/228372464_A_Psychomotor_Skills_Extension_to _Bloom's_Taxonomy_of_Education_Objectives_for_Engineering_Education.

Gagne, R. M., Briggs, L. J., & Wager, W. W. (1992). *Principles of Instructional Design* (4th ed.). Fort Worth: Harcourt Brace Jovanovich College Publishers.

Goldberg, B., Amburn, C., Ragusa, C., & Chen, D.-W. (2018). Modeling expert behavior in support of an adaptive psychomotor training environment: A marksmanship use case. *International Journal of Artificial Intelligence in Education, 28*(2), 194–224. doi:10.1007/s40593-017-0155-y.

Goldin-Meadow, S., Kim, S., & Singer, M. (1999). What the teacher's hands tell the student's mind about math. *Journal of Educational Psychology, 91*(4), 720–730. doi:10.1037/0022-0663.91.4.720.

Goldin-Meadow, S., Nusbaum, H., Kelly, S. D., & Wagner, S. (2001). Explaining math: Gesturing lightens the load. *Psychological Science, 12*(6), 516–522. doi:10.1111/1467-9280.00395.

González-Villanueva, L., Alvarez-Alvarez, A., Ascari, L., & Trivino, G. (2013). Computational model of human body motion performing a complex exercise by means of a fuzzy finite state machine. In *Proceedings of the International Conference on Medical Imaging Using Bio-Inspired and Soft Computing (MIBISOC)*, 245–251.

Hamadani, K. M., Jiang, Y., Ahmadinia, A., Hadaegh, A., Moraleja-Garcia, J., Mendez, A., Shaikh, A., Lozano, A., Huang, J., Aquino, A., Palacio, R., & Sheperd, M. (2022). Framework for scalable content development in hands-on virtual and mixed reality science labs. In *2022 8th International Conference of the Immersive Learning Research Network (iLRN)*.

Harrow, A. J. (1972). *A Taxonomy of the Psychomotor Domain*. New York: David McKay Company, Inc.

Hodaie, Z., Haladjian, J., & Bruegge, B. (2018). TUMA: Towards an intelligent tutoring system for manual-procedural activities. In *Intelligent Tutoring Systems* (pp. 326–331). doi:10.1007/978-3-319-91464-0_35.

Krathwohl, D. R., Bloom, B. S., & Masia, B. B. (1964). Taxonomy of educational objectives: The classification of educational goals. In *Handbook II: Affective Domain*. New York: David McKay Company.

Lane, H. C., & Santos, O. C. (2018). Embodied learning and artificial intelligence: Expanding the bandwidth of learning technologies. *Pearson, Ideas Worth Sharing*. https://www.pearson.com/ content/dam/corporate/global/pearson-dot-com/files/innovation/ideas-worth-sharing_embodied-learning-and-artificial-intelligence.pdf.

Lee, D. H., & Kim, J. H. (2010). A framework for an interactive robot-based tutoring system and its application to ball-passing training. In *IEEE International Conference on Robotics and Biomimetics (ROBIO)*. doi:10.1109/robio.2010.5723389.

Lieberman, J., & Breazeal, C. (2007). TIKL: Development of a wearable vibrotactile feedback suit for improved human motor learning. *IEEE Transactions on Robotics: A Publication of the IEEE Robotics and Automation Society, 23*(5), 919–926. doi:10.1109/tro.2007.907481.

Macedonia, M. (2019). Embodied learning: Why at school the mind needs the body. *Frontiers in Psychology, 10*, 2098. doi:10.3389/fpsyg.2019.02098.

Mager, R. F. (1997). *Preparing Instructional Objectives: A Critical Tool in the Development of Effective Instruction* (3rd ed.). Atlanta, GA: Center for Effective Performance.

Martinez-Maldonado, R., Echeverria, V., Santos, O. C., Dias Pereira Dos Santos, A., & Yacef, K. (2018). Physical learning analytics: A multimodal perspective. In *Proceedings of the 8th International Conference on Learning Analytics and Knowledge*. doi:10.1145/3170358.3170379.

Mirchi, N., Bissonnette, V., Yilmaz, R., Ledwos, N., Winkler-Schwartz, A., & Del Maestro, R. F. (2020). The virtual operative assistant: An explainable artificial intelligence tool for simulation-based training in surgery and medicine. *PLoS One, 15*(2). doi:10.1371/journal.pone.0229596.

Neagu, L. M., Rigaud, E., Travadel, S., Dascalu, M., & Rughinis, R. V. (2020). Intelligent tutoring systems for psychomotor training – A systematic literature review. In *Intelligent Tutoring Systems (ITS)* (pp. 335–341). doi:10.1007/978-3-030-49663-0_40.

Rajeswaran, P., Hung, N.-T., Kesavadas, T., Vozenilek, J., & Kumar, P. (2018). AirwayVR: Learning endotracheal intubation in virtual reality. In *25th IEEE Conference on Virtual Reality and 3D User Interfaces (VR)*. doi:10.1109/vr.2018.8446075.

Rajeswaran, P., Kesavadas, T., Jani, P., & Kumar, P. (2019a). AirwayVR: Virtual reality trainer for endotracheal intubation-design considerations and challenges. In *26th IEEE Conference on Virtual Reality and 3D User Interfaces (VR)*. doi:10.1109/vr.2019.8798249.

Rajeswaran, P., Varghese, J., Kumar, P., Vozenilek, J., & Kesavadas, T. (2019b). AirwayVR: Virtual reality trainer for endotracheal intubation. In *26th IEEE Conference on Virtual Reality and 3D User Interfaces (VR)*. doi:10.1109/vr.2019.8797998.

Ronda-Carracao, M. A., Santos, O. C., Fernandez-Nieto, G., & Martinez-Maldonado, R. (2021). Towards exploring stress reactions in teamwork using multimodal physiological data. In *CEUR Workshop Proceedings*, 2902.

Russell, S. J., & Norvig, P. (2010). *Artificial Intelligence: A Modern Approach* (3rd ed.). Upper Saddle River, NJ: Prentice Hall.

Santos, O. C. (2008). A recommender system to provide adaptive and inclusive standard-based support along the elearning life cycle. In *Proceedings of the 2008 ACM Conference on Recommender Systems - RecSys '08*. doi:10.1145/1454008.1454062.

Santos, O. C. (2016a). Beyond cognitive and affective issues: Designing smart learning environments for psychomotor personalized learning. In *Learning, Design, and Technology* (pp. 1–24). Cham: Springer International Publishing. doi:10.1007/978-3-319-17727-4_8-1.

Santos, O. C. (2016b). Training the body: The potential of AIED to support personalized motor skills learning. *International Journal of Artificial Intelligence in Education, 26*(2), 730–755. doi:10.1007/s40593-016-0103-2.

Santos, O. C. (2017). Toward personalized vibrotactile support when learning motor skills. *Algorithms, 10*(1), 15. doi:10.3390/a10010015.

Santos, O. C. (2019). Artificial intelligence in psychomotor learning: Modeling human motion from inertial sensor data. *International Journal of Artificial Intelligence Tools, 28*(4), 1940006. doi:10.1142/s0218213019400062.

Santos, O. C., & Boticario, J. G. (2012). Affective issues in semantic educational recommender systems. In *7th European Conference of Technology Enhanced Learning (EC-TEL 2012)*, 896, 71–82. Workshop RecSysTEL: CEUR Workshop Proceedings. http://ceur-ws.org/Vol-896/paper6.pdf.

Santos, O. C., & Boticario, J. G. (2015). Practical guidelines for designing and evaluating educationally oriented recommendations. *Computers & Education, 81*, 354–374. doi:10.1016/j.compedu.2014.10.008.

Santos, O. C., & Corbi, A. (2019). Can aikido help with the comprehension of physics? A first step towards the design of intelligent psychomotor systems for STEAM kinesthetic learning scenarios. *IEEE Access: Practical Innovations, Open Solutions, 7*, 176458–176469. doi:10.1109/access.2019.2957947.

Santos, O. C., Uria-Rivas, R., Rodriguez-Sanchez, M. C., & Boticario, J. G. (2016). An open sensing and acting platform for context-aware affective support in ambient intelligent educational settings. *IEEE Sensors Journal, 16*(10), 3865–3874. doi:10.1109/jsen.2016.2533266.

Shire, K. A., Hill, L. J. B., Snapp-Childs, W., Bingham, G. P., Kountouriotis, G. K., Barber, S., & Mon-Williams, M. (2016). Robot guided "pen skill" training in children with motor difficulties. *PLoS One, 11*(3). doi:10.1371/journal.pone.0151354.

Shirzad, N., & Van der Loos, H. F. M. (2012). Error amplification to promote motor learning and motivation in therapy robotics. In *Annual International Conference of the IEEE Engineering in Medicine and Biology Society (EMBS)*, 3907–3910. doi:10.1109/EMBC.2012.6346821.

Simpson, E. J. (1972). *The Classification of Educational Objectives in the Psychomotor Domain*. Washington, DC: Gryphon House.

Skinner, A., Diller, D., Kumar, R., Cannon-Bowers, J., Smith, R., Tanaka, A., Julian, D., & Perez, R. (2018). Development and application of a multi-modal task analysis to support intelligent tutoring of complex skills. *International Journal of STEM Education, 5*(1). doi:10.1186/s40594-018-0108-5.

Stein, G., Gonzalez, A. J., & Barham, C. (2013). Machines that learn and teach seamlessly. *IEEE Transactions on Learning Technologies, 6*(4), 389–402. doi:10.1109/tlt.2013.32.

Thomas, K. (2004). *Learning Taxonomies in the Cognitive, Affective, and Psychomotor Domain.* http://www.rockymountainalchemy.com/whitePapers/rma-wp-learning-taxonomies.pdf.

van Rosmalen, P., Boticario, J. G., & Santos, O. C. (2004). The full life cycle of adaptation in aLFanet eLearning environment. *IEEE Learning Technology Newsletter, 4*(4), 59–61. https://tc.computer.org/tclt/wp-content/uploads/sites/5/2016/12/learn_tech_october2004.pdf.

Vannaprathip, N., Haddawy, P., Schultheis, H., & Suebnukarn, S. (2022). Intelligent tutoring for surgical decision making: A planning-based approach. *International Journal of Artificial Intelligence in Education, 32*(2), 350–381. https://doi.org/10.1007/s40593-021-00261-3.

Wei, W., McElroy, C., & Dey, S. (2018). Human action understanding and movement error identification for the treatment of patients with Parkinson's disease. In *2018 IEEE International Conference on Healthcare Informatics (ICHI).* doi:10.1109/ichi.2018.00028.

Wei, W., McElroy, C., & Dey, S. (2019). Towards on-demand virtual physical therapist: Machine learning-based patient action understanding, assessment and task recommendation. *IEEE Transactions on Neural Systems and Rehabilitation Engineering: A Publication of the IEEE Engineering in Medicine and Biology Society, 27*(9), 1824–1835. doi:10.1109/TNSRE.2019.2934097.

Winkler-Schwartz, A., Yilmaz, R., Mirchi, N., Bissonnette, V., Ledwos, N., Siyar, S., Azarnoush, H., Karlik, B., & Del Maestro, R. (2019). Machine learning identification of surgical and operative factors associated with surgical expertise in virtual reality simulation. *JAMA Network Open, 2*(8), e198363. doi:10.1001/jamanetworkopen.2019.8363.

Yamagiwa, S., Kawahara, Y., Tabuchi, N., Watanabe, Y., & Naruo, T. (2015). Skill grouping method: Mining and clustering skill differences from body movement BigData. In *2015 IEEE International Conference on Big Data (IEEE Big Data).* doi:10.1109/bigdata.2015.7364049.

Yannier, N., Hudson, S. E., Koedinger, K. R., Hirsh-Pasek, K., Golinkoff, R. M., Munakata, Y., Doebel, S., Schwartz, D. L., Deslauriers, L., McCarthy, L., Callahgan, K., Theobald, E. J., Freeman, S., Cooper, K. M., & Brownell, S. E. (2021). Active learning: "Hands-on" meets "minds-on." *Science (New York, N.Y.), 374*(6563), 26–30. doi:10.1126/science.abj9957.

Yilmaz, R., Winkler-Schwartz, A., Mirchi, N., Reich, A., Christie, S., Tran, D. H., Ledwos, N., Fazlollahi, A. M., Santaguida, C., Sabbagh, A. J., Bajunaid, K., & Del Maestro, R. (2022). Continuous monitoring of surgical bimanual expertise using deep neural networks in virtual reality simulation. *NPJ Digital Medicine, 5*(1), 54. https://doi.org/10.1038/s41746-022-00596-8.

19. Artificial intelligence techniques for supporting face-to-face and online collaborative learning

Roberto Martinez-Maldonado, Anouschka van Leeuwen and Zachari Swiecki

INTRODUCTION

Collaborative learning is a term that refers to a variety of educational phenomena involving joint intellectual effort by peers interacting with each other and with teachers, for the purpose of learning about a particular topic, or learning to collaborate effectively (Dillenbourg, 1999). Collaborative learning provides particular opportunities for data-intensive, educational innovations (Dönmez et al., 2005; Chi & Wylie, 2014). This is in part because learners need to externalize some of their commonly hidden mental processes in the form of dialogue, drawings, and other representations (Stahl, 2006). Many types of problems may occur during collaborative learning, such as students failing to reach common ground, students engaging in superficial argumentation instead of deep argumentation in which they build on each other's reasoning, or the occurrence of free-riding so that the input from group members is unequal (Kreijns et al., 2003). Digital traces of these automatically captured externalizations can be analyzed using various Artificial Intelligence (AI) and collaboration analytics techniques for the purpose of making collaborative interactions more visible, finding recurrent patterns of behavior, and deepening our understanding of collaborative learning in various contexts and domains. This can further accelerate computer-supported collaborative learning (CSCL) research and the development of more effective tools that support collaborative learning.

Using analytics and AI techniques to support collaborative learning has some history in the field of artificial intelligence in education (AIED). For example, data-intensive techniques have been used to characterize effective collaboration (e.g. Perera et al., 2008), argumentation (e.g. Rosé et al., 2008), and team activity (e.g. Kay et al., 2006) in online collaborative situations. Modeling group interactions has also enabled the creation of mechanisms to adapt the support provided to groups (Kumar et al., 2007), form groups automatically (Amarasinghe et al., 2017), adjust collaboration scripts according to particular group needs (Rummel et al., 2008), and mirror group processes to students (Jermann & Dillenbourg, 2008; Jermann et al., 2005). Moreover, educational data-mining approaches have also been applied to identify patterns of interaction between low- and high-achieving groups in face-to-face situations (Martinez-Maldonado et al., 2013).

Within AIED and other data-intensive educational technology communities, such as ITS (Intelligent Tutoring Systems) and EDM (Educational Data Mining), there has also been a sustained interest in providing "intelligent support to learning in groups" (ISLG). Researchers across these communities organized thematic series of workshops (e.g. ISLG workshop series organized in ITS and AIED conferences between 2012 and 2018, Kim & Kumar, 2012) and special issues in high-impact journals (Isotani, 2011; Kumar & Kim, 2014). The rapidly growing field of Learning Analytics is also focusing on providing techniques for supporting collaborative learning under the new umbrella term Collaboration Analytics (Martinez-Maldonado et al., 2019).

This chapter brings together literature from these communities to describe what we mean by supporting collaborative learning in the second section. The third section discusses techniques currently available for supporting both face-to-face and online collaborative learning situations to: (1) form effective groups, (2) provide direct feedback to students, (3) facilitate adaptive scripting, enhance group (4) and teacher (5) awareness, and (6) perform summative assessments. In this section, we focus on techniques that have been used to *analyze*, rather than *collect*, data from collaborative scenarios. As such, this paper does not address the variety of techniques, challenges, and issues associated with using sensors to automatically collect data of different modalities (e.g. actions, speech, texts, affects) and from different contexts (synchronous vs. asynchronous collaboration.) The fourth section presents potential future trends for research and development in this area. The chapter concludes with some final remarks in the last section.

SUPPORTING COLLABORATIVE LEARNING

Collaborative learning situations involve the interaction between students, teachers, tasks students work on, and (digital and material) tools to support the collaborative processes (Stahl et al., 2006). The success of collaborative learning depends on the quality of this interaction. Therefore, studying collaborative learning does not only include the collaboration as it happens in the classroom or online, but also the preparation for this process and the reflection on the process afterwards. Kaendler et al. (2015) refer to these three phases as the pre-active phase, the inter-active phase, and the post-active phase. Although Kaendler et al.'s framework was originally proposed to describe teachers' competencies for implementing collaborative learning, we use it here to describe the various types of support students may benefit from.

Artificial Intelligence (AI) and analytics techniques may play a supporting role in all three of the phases described above and thereby contribute to the success of collaborative learning in various ways. The ways in which AI and analytics are commonly employed depend on the specific *type of support* for which they are intended. To explain this further, we present Figure 19.1 below. In this figure, the central unit is a group of collaborating students, in this case a triad. From the collaborative process, the captured activity data constitute the input for further analyses (e.g. students' utterances, non-verbal behaviors, and physiological measures). As can be seen by the arrows in Figure 19.1, there are several pathways for offering support, and the specific pathway determines what type of data can be used and what analyses are performed on those data. We will briefly mention these pathways here, and delve deeper into each of them in the next section.

Arrow 1 points at the importance of selecting a strategy for *grouping* students for the collaborative activity, which is often already done as preparation in the pre-active phase (Figure 19.1). Based on student characteristics or data obtained during previous collaborative sessions, AI and analytics techniques can help determine optimal group formations for a specific activity.

Arrows 2–5 point at various types of support during the inter-active phase (Figure 19.1). *Direct feedback* to students (arrow 2) for formative purposes means that the data obtained during the collaborative activity is used immediately and directly to offer support to the students, for example by providing a hint or a prompt. The AI and analytics techniques in this case

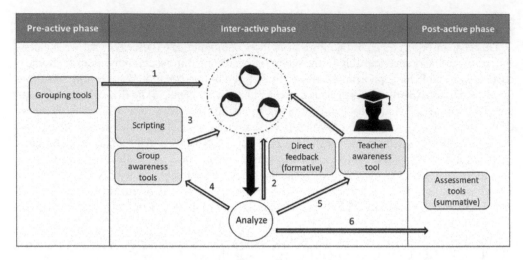

Figure 19.1   *Overview of types of support in pre-active, inter-active, and post-active phases of collaborative learning*

must be granular enough to detect specific occurrences of the event for which the feedback is designed. Arrow 3 represents support in the form of *scripting*, which means that part of the collaboration process is explicitly and dynamically structured so that students engage in the type of activities or processes that may not occur naturally, for example reflecting on the group's progress (Fischer et al., 2013). AI and analytics techniques in this case may help to detect which activities need scripting in the first place, and when scripting is implemented, to detect when each phase of the script needs to be activated.

Arrows 4 and 5 both point to *awareness tools*, the difference being that the awareness tool is either designed for students (arrow 4) or for teachers (arrow 5) (Figure 19.1). In general, these tools are, as their name suggests, designed to enhance the awareness that students or teachers have of the situation. Underlying the idea of student awareness tools is that many problems that may occur during collaboration are caused by a lack of awareness of each other's knowledge and activities within the group (Janssen & Bodemer, 2013). When information about the group's activities is visualized and provided to all group members, understanding and interaction can be enhanced. The idea of providing teachers with awareness tools as well stems from the generally acknowledged importance of teacher guidance during collaboration that may occur in addition to the support that students provide to each other or that technology can provide to students (Van Leeuwen & Janssen, 2019). Rummel (2018) described teacher awareness tools as technological tools that indirectly support collaborating students. By providing an overview of the situation to the teacher, s/he can better attend to the needs of the collaborating students. The role of AI and analytics techniques in the case of awareness tools lies in extracting relevant and actionable information that can be displayed to students and teachers.

Lastly, Arrow 6 points to the use of the data gathered during students' collaboration for purposes of summative assessment (Figure 19.1). In addition to grading the product that students have been working on (such as a collaboratively written text), the interaction process itself may also be assessed, and AI and analytics techniques may aid in this process.

An important issue to remark on is that collaborative learning can take place in various contexts (face-to-face, online, or both) and in various modes (synchronously and asynchronously). For example, computers can connect learners who are separated in time or space, so that all communication occurs online. In this case, communication could be synchronous (i.e. occur in "real time" as in a chat), or asynchronous (i.e. when learners are not necessarily online at the same time, for example in a discussion forum). Another example is when multiple learners share one computer screen and solve tasks together while communicating face-to-face. Each of these combinations has its own potentials and restrictions for the collaborative process (Van Diggelen & Overdijk, 2007), and each combination determines whether certain types of analysis are applicable and whether particular types of data are available. The context also determines whether certain types of support can be delivered or whether the output of the analyses needs to be presented in a certain way. For example, in a face-to-face synchronous setting a teacher awareness tool may take the form of a wearable device and to-the-point information may be preferable, whereas teachers in an asynchronous online context may benefit more from a dashboard with elaborate information.

AI TECHNIQUES TO SUPPORT COLLABORATIVE LEARNING

Group Formation

A key factor influencing group processes and performance is composition. Dillenbourg (1999) described group composition in terms of different *symmetries*: symmetry of action, symmetry of knowledge, and symmetry of status. The first refers to the extent to which members of the group are allowed the same range of actions. For example, groups with well-defined roles exhibit an asymmetrical action structure: leaders can give orders and redistribute workload but other members cannot. Symmetry of knowledge refers to the extent to which team members possess the same knowledge, skills, or expertise. Finally, symmetry of status is the extent to which individuals have similar status in the group.

Much of the early work on collaborative learning explored the effect of different symmetrical structures by varying group heterogeneity. For example, research in the Piagetian paradigm investigated the effects of pairing individuals together at similar developmental levels, but with different viewpoints, in efforts to incite cognitive conflict (Hmelo-Silver et al., 2013). Relatedly, researchers in the social-cultural tradition of Vygotsky often investigated learning that took place between pairs or groups asymmetrical in status, action, and knowledge, for example, by pairing children with older children or adults (Vygotsky, 1978).

Following this work, researchers have continued to argue that group composition can benefit collaborative learning by fostering certain collaborative interactions or hinder it through disproportional participation, demotivation and conflict (Cruz & Isotani, 2014). Consequently, the process of forming groups, and the effects of different formations, have been studied extensively.

In terms of AI, the problem of forming effective groups involves three components and can be generally construed as a constraint satisfaction problem (Amarasinghe et al., 2017) or multi-objective optimization problems (Moreno et al., 2012). First, a set of *characteristics* must be chosen that describe the individuals to be grouped. Researchers have considered a variety of such characteristics including cultural background, interests, knowledge, skills, roles, and gender. Second, a set of *constraints* is chosen to limit the possible number of group formations. Example constraints include the number of groups an individual can be in, homo/heterogeneity of knowledge, background, and gender. Finally, a particular *method* is chosen to form the groups such that they satisfy as many constraints as possible. Of course, one method for forming groups is a manual approach, as is often employed by educators in learning settings. However, given the potential for high numbers of characteristics and constraints, and thus high numbers of possible combinations, manual formation can be difficult and time consuming (Amarasinghe et al., 2017). In response, researchers have developed tools and algorithms for assisting in group formation.

In their systematic literature review of group formation algorithms in collaborative learning contexts, Cruz and Isotani (2014) categorized the kinds of methods that have been used to assist in group formation. They found that the largest portion of methods were probabilistic algorithms—for example, genetic algorithms (Moreno et al., 2012) and swarm intelligence algorithms (Lin et al., 2010), followed by multi-agent formation algorithms (Soh et al., 2008), which model student and teacher decisions. The remaining methods were general data mining approaches, such as k-means clustering (Filho et al., 2010), and finally a set of miscellaneous techniques such as semantic web ontologies (Isotani et al., 2013). The authors suggest that genetic algorithms may be preferable due to their ability to handle large numbers of variables and rapidly generate (semi) optimal solutions automatically.

More recently, researchers have continued to explore data mining approaches to group formation. For example, Lobo et al. (2016) used techniques that included decision trees, naive Bayes, support vector machines, and logistic regression to classify students into groups based on collaborative indicators, social interactions (as measured by social network analysis), peer ratings, and measures of affective states. The authors then suggested effective groupings of learners based on these classifications. Wu et al. (2021) used NLP to create heterogenous and homogenous groupings of learners based on their prior knowledge. By associating a list of "mastered" and "unmastered" topics with each student, they used pre-trained word embeddings to automatically create different groups based on the similarity/dissimilarity of their topic representations in the embedding space.

While the work on AI-based group formation has been insightful, to the present authors' knowledge, systematic comparisons of the different approaches have not been conducted. Thus, it remains an open question as to which algorithms are more effective in which collaborative learning situations.

Direct Formative Feedback to Learners

One of the ultimate aims of data-intensive educational solutions is to provide meaningful feedback to learners on how well they are doing to provoke reflection and improvement (Gašević et al., 2015). This has often been referred to as "*closing the analysis loop*" in which the outputs of the analysis are not only useful to conduct CSCL research, but can be transformed into visual or textual representations that can be understood by learners. This live feedback to groups of learners can affect their behaviors in many ways. However, while the idea of providing direct, formative feedback to students in a live setting has been conceptually proposed, its implementation in authentic settings is uncommon.

There are some notable examples of systems that automatically provide recommendations to groups of learners in synchronous and asynchronous online settings. For example, the AMOEBA system analyzes the collaborative programming work of computer science students and makes recommendations based on the similarity between some students for them to collaborate more closely (Berland et al., 2015). These recommendations contributed to maximizing meaningful student–student interaction and led to improved learning and better programming outputs. Research on intelligent tutoring systems (ITSs) has also focused on providing direct support to learners. Tchounikine et al. (2010) provided a review of ITSs that support collaborative learning tasks. They emphasized different ways in which students can be supported, for example, by providing adaptive intelligent hints (e.g.., detecting problems in the task product or the collaboration, and providing written feedback; Baghaei et al., 2007); or adaptive technological means (such as enabling dynamic communication prompts in the argumentation tool ARGUNAUT; De Groot et al., 2007). The most recent work by Olsen (2017) has also provided foundations for supporting learners while they engage in individual and group tasks while working at an ITS in the context of math learning.

Formative feedback can also be presented to learners in the form of visualizations that invite them to reflect on performance and collaboration, and reach their own conclusions or decide the actions they can take for improvement. These tools have been also known as open learner models like Narcissus (Upton & Kay, 2009). This system displays summaries of activity logs in the context of team software development, in ways that promote reflection on potential issues in team dynamics. The system also allows learners to navigate through their logs from a high-level view to particular instances such as the messages or allocations between two team members. A similar approach has been followed by researchers who have designed more contemporary student-facing dashboards for CSCL (see review by Liu & Nesbit, 2020). Bodily and Verbert (2017) reviewed student-facing dashboard systems, reporting mostly non-collaborative settings. In fact, there is just a growing number of student-facing CSCL dashboard currently available, with some notable exceptions of systems that mostly mirror basic summary statistics from logs captured in forums (May et al., 2011), social networks (Scheffel et al., 2016) and software development systems (Tarmazdi et al., 2015; Upton & Kay, 2009).

Adaptive Scripting

Collaborative learning is typically associated with one or more tasks, such as forming an argument, designing a product, or solving a problem. In educational and professional contexts, tasks are one component of a collaborative *script*. Scripts have been defined broadly as contracts to specify how the collaboration should proceed (Dillenbourg, 2002). More recently, however, scripts have come to be associated with computer-based scenarios that structure collaboration by associating groups with tasks, roles, and resources, and by constraining interactions between individuals (Koller et al., 2006).

Scripts can affect both the overall structure of the collaborative setting (macro-level) and the moment-by-moment collaborative interactions (micro-level). Scripts at the macro-level structure collaboration through task design, group composition, roles, and available resources. At the micro-level, scripts constrain collaborative actions through the mode of communication, by enforcing particular problem-solving steps, or by providing prompts and hints to learners. For example, the PISA 2015 collaborative problem-solving assessment involved scripting at both levels (OECD, 2017). At the macro-level, participants were teamed with automated collaborative agents in a computer-based environment to solve problems in a variety of scenarios. At the micro-level, interactions between the participant and the agent were limited to clicking, dragging, or selecting certain items on the screen. In particular, the participant could only communicate with the agent via a chat window with predefined responses.

Collaborative scripts like those described above were developed with at least two mechanisms for supporting learning in mind (Wise & Schwarz, 2017). First, the script is an external representation of effective collaboration processes. In other words, the script shows learners what good collaboration is. As such, the end goal for the script is to be internalized by the learners so it is no longer needed in the future. Second, research has long focused on the potentially negative effects of collaboration on learning that may arise due to unproductive conflict, unequal participation, and a lack of understanding of how to collaborate effectively. Scripts are meant to mitigate these factors by using constraints such as prompts, modes of interaction, and group composition, to control the setting.

Over time, scripts have evolved from static structures and rules into malleable systems for scaffolding collaboration. In particular, scripts have been designed that are *adaptable*, *adaptive*, or both. Adaptable scripts are those that allow educators or learners to modify the script in some way. For example, researchers have also explored allowing learners and educators to build their own scripts from a pool of components (Prieto et al., 2012).

Adaptive scripts are those that automatically adjust, based on learner actions and interactions. Adaptive collaborative scripting builds on the large body of work on ITSs, which typically use dynamic models to guide automated pedagogical decisions (Graesser et al., 2012). Such systems often rely on *model tracing*, the process by which a model of the problem is compared to the student actions and solutions. If the participant's actions or solutions match those of the model, the automated tutor deems them appropriate; if they do not match or if the participant acts in ways the model associates with struggling, the automated tutor provides prompts, hints, and eventually, solutions. For example, Diziol et al. (2010) implemented an adaptive support system that classified student interactions with the system as they collaborated to solve algebra problems. If interactions were classified as either "hint abuse" or "trial and error"—strategies associated with poor learning outcomes—an adaptive script message was presented to encourage collaboration.

Extending ITSs' features to collaborative situations may involve expanding the kinds of interactions traced by the model. In particular, conversation can be a key component of collaborative interactions. As such, some adaptive collaborative scripts have integrated natural language processing to classify conversational interactions and adapt the script in response. For example, Dowell et al. (2014) proposed integrating the automatic classification of group conversations in online collaborative environments using Coh-metrix (McNamara et al., 2014), a technique that measures features of communication such as cohesion. Similarly, virtual internships, online educational simulations in which students work as teams to solve design problems, use regular expression matching to evaluate collaborative contributions and suggest when groups are ready to change topics in a guided discussion (Saucerman et al., 2017). Research into scripting remains intensive, with a current focus on striking a balance between guiding collaboration and maintaining learner and teacher agency (Wise et al., 2016).

Group Awareness Tools

The central idea of group awareness tools is to make certain aspects of the collaborative process visible to its group members to enhance group members' awareness of these aspects

(Janssen & Bodemer, 2013). Providing group awareness tools is hypothesized to contribute to diminishing these problems by making the process visible, and thereby enabling group members to discuss and regulate the process more adequately (Janssen & Bodemer, 2013).

Many authors have aimed at providing typologies of the type of processes that occur during collaborative learning (and, thus, in what areas potential problems may arise). As group awareness tools can be seen as ways to enhance these processes, their development and empirical investigation can generally be considered in the same typologies. For example, Meier et al. (2007) distinguish between processes concerning: communication, joint information processing, coordination, interpersonal relationships, and motivation. Those processes are thus the aspects of collaboration that are also being analyzed, visualized, and fed back to group members through group awareness tools, making use of a variety of LA and analytics techniques. Some techniques fit better with visualizing certain types of processes, such as using (epistemic) network analysis to focus on communication and interpersonal relationships within a group.

Schnaubert et al. (2020) have recently provided a review for group awareness tools that focus specifically on cognitive aspects of collaboration, meaning tools that provide knowledge-related information. They report that different types of data processing techniques were used, among which aggregating data, categorizing and/or clustering data, and coding and counting data. Interestingly, they also identified studies in which the group awareness tool did not transform the collected data at all. For example, when group members fill in a concept map to display their knowledge over a certain topic, those maps can be provided to the other group members without any changes or transformations. In those cases, all interpretation is left to the user. As Schnaubert et al. (2020) note, in case of tools that use visualizations (such as group awareness tools), one must always consider that "while transformations may be a way of extracting relevant information from complex data or adding relevant information about a domain, they always bear the risk of being incomprehensible (due to complexity or non-transparency) or not acceptable to learners (due to incompatibility with the learners' self-conceptions)". This is also why there is a movement towards human-centered co-design of such tools, in which students are involved in the design and development of the tool to ensure its usability (Sarmiento & Wise, 2022).

A relatively new direction for group awareness tools is reported by, for example, Avry et al. (2020), who developed a tool concerning *emotional* group awareness. As the importance of affective processes during collaboration is increasingly recognized, this is reflected in the development of tools that allow group members more insight into the occurrence of emotions. As Avry et al. (2020) show, the occurrence of emotions indeed relates to specific interaction patterns, and providing emotional group awareness tools indeed influence the type of task-related interactions that occur. The tool described by Avry et al. (2020) relies on group members manually labeling their emotions.

Teacher Awareness Tools

As discussed above, there are a number of similarities between awareness tools aimed at students and those aimed at teachers. Their core goal is the same: to provide information to enhance awareness of the collaborative situation. Teachers generally struggle to monitor student activity in the context of collaborative learning (Kaendler et al., 2016). This is not surprising given that it is a demanding task. Teachers have to pay attention to multiple dimensions (i.e. cognitive versus social aspects of collaboration), and especially in synchronous settings, there are a multitude of activities occurring at the same time. Therefore, the aim of teacher awareness tools is to enhance teachers' overview of the situation (see Chapter 15 by Pozdniakov et al.). Whereas student group awareness tools detail information about one group, teacher awareness tools display information about the whole classroom. This means analyses and visualizations need to be performed not only at a group level, but also at a classroom level, and decisions have to be made about whether and how to aggregate data from individual and group level to classroom level.

Recent reviews (Sergis & Sampson, 2017; Van Leeuwen & Rummel, 2019) show that teacher awareness tools have focused on both cognitive and social aspects of collaboration, using a variety of LA and analytics techniques. For teacher awareness tools to be useful, they need to indicate information that is relevant and actionable. This is a delicate balance; information that is relevant for the collaborative process but hard to interpret for the teacher is not useful, but neither is information that is easy to understand yet can be easily obtained by the teacher through observing students (for example the number of students attending a class). This expresses the same idea as discussed above that involving stakeholders (in this case teachers) in the design process will be beneficial for the usability of the tool. In the sections below, we will discuss two examples of how AI and analytics techniques have been used to extract information from the collaborative process, *and* how this information has been displayed to the teacher.

The first example concerns a teacher awareness tool that visualizes *critical moments*: moments during collaborative learning where the teacher could provide support to enhance learning (Swidan et al., 2019). In a computer-supported, synchronous setting, the teachers received alerts on a dashboard of the following events: idleness; off-topic discourse; technical problems; occurrence of explanation or challenge; confusion; correct solution; and incorrect solution. To analyze these critical moments, several analysis techniques had to be used: textual analysis to detect certain types of discourse between students (such as providing explanations), and comparing student input to canonical solutions (for the correct and incorrect solution alert). Each type of critical moment was given its own color for easy recognition by the teacher. Two aspects are notable about this teacher awareness tool. The first is that the tool not only visualizes when groups do *not* perform expected behavior, but also when they show good progress. Another notable aspect is that the authors of the paper remark that their analyses are based not only on what educational theory describes as important learning events, but also on the boundaries of LA techniques. As the authors put it, they focused on events that are computable. We will reflect on this issue in the next section.

Similar to student group awareness tools, there has been a recent trend in developing and investigating teacher awareness tools that focus on affective measures (e.g. see Chapter 5 by Arroyo et al.). The second example we selected is therefore a teacher awareness tool, Emodash, that displays learners' emotions (Ez-zaouia et al., 2020). In contrast to the previous example, this tool is meant for use *after* learning sessions, so for asynchronous, reflective use by the teacher. The tool is based on facial recognition algorithms (perception-based estimation) in combination with learners' interactions with the learning environment. The resulting visualization was iteratively designed in partnership with teachers and offers several layers of detail: both concerning learners' overall emotions, and the ability to zoom in on emotions occurring during specific learning sessions. This level of detail fits the intended asynchronous use of the tool, when teachers have more time to reflect on the offered visualizations.

Summative Assessment

Finally, there has been interest in providing automated support to the summative assessment of collaboration and teamwork skills (see Chapter 21 by Fang et al.). Two broad goals of the assessment can be identified: (i) assessing communication and collaboration skills; and (ii) assessing the task performance or learning gains. The assessment of the former is critical, given that effectively communicating and working in groups are critical twenty-first-century skills that learners are encouraged to develop for workplace success (Griffin et al., 2012). The assessment of the latter also has an important role in encouraging learners to take responsibility for their participation in the group task and to help them understand the non-competitive nature of a collaborative learning process (Meijer et al., 2020).

Most of the techniques that support the summative assessment of computer-mediated collaborative learning tasks involve some analysis of the content of the conversations between group members. For example, foundational work by Soller (2001) suggested the assessment of collaborative learning conversation skills by mapping conversation skill types (active learning, conversation, and creative conflict) into corresponding sub-skills and actual sentences from learners' conversation. To achieve this, the author provided an interface that allowed learners to scaffold their conversation by explicitly letting them pick short sentence openers. This way, the system could automatically infer the kind of participation of each learner. Currently, with further advancements in text analysis and natural language processing, it is possible to automatically process learners' conversations without forcing them to interact through a constrained interface.

The research agenda led by Carolyn Rosé and her team has been foundational in bringing the advances of computational linguistics to automatically code instances of learners' conversation contributions with various purposes in both synchronous and asynchronous collaborative settings (see Chapter 17 by Rosé et al.). These include the automated classification of text to be mapped to collaborative skill development (e.g. Rosé et al., 2008; Rosé & Ferschke, 2016). Moreover, synchronous conversations have been analyzed to automatically assess participation and collaboration by measuring the semantic cohesion of sentences (Dascalu et al., 2014) and the extent to which the voices of the group members intertwine (Dascalu et al., 2015). Asynchronous team contributions (i.e. in a wiki), have also been modeled to automatically assess the quality of the collaborative writing process by performing regression analysis on linguistic metadiscourse features and features that reflect the depth of cognitive thinking (Hu et al., 2016). In computer science education, progress has also been made in automatically assessing collaborative programming tasks by analyzing the quality of the coding in terms of code writing skills and also problem-solving processes (Staubitz et al., 2015). Techniques for summatively assessing code have a long history (Pettit & Prather, 2017), but more work is needed to articulate various tools to support learners who are expected to work in highly collaborative development environments.

In addition to detecting and assessing what learners are doing while they collaborate, increased attention has been paid to understanding the interdependent nature of collaboration (Swiecki et al., 2019; Swiecki et al., 2020; Swiecki, 2021). For example, researchers have developed coding schemes that attend to *transactivity*, or the ways in which individuals in collaborative situations respond to and build upon one another's contributions (Wang et al., 2017). These coding schemes have been integrated with techniques such as dynamic Bayesian networks to measure the prevalence of transactivity in collaborative discourse (Gweon et al., 2013). Similarly, techniques such as cohesion network analysis (Dascalu et al., 2018), contingency graphs (Suthers, 2017), epistemic network analysis (Shaffer et al., 2016), and group communication analysis (Dowell et al., 2019) have been retrospectively applied to discourse data to create models of collaboration that account for the interdependence between individuals as they work together in terms of the semantic similarity of discourse or the co-presence of automated codes applied to the discourse.

Moving beyond speech- or text-based discourse, there have also been efforts to assess collaborative learning using other relevant data sources. For example, Chua et al. (2019) proposed a multimodal monitoring setting to perform audio and video analysis to extract conversational features, linguistic features, and posture and facial emotions cues to automatically identify the characteristics of team composition and predict the success of learners in the collaborative task. Olsen et al. (2017) also explored the use of dual eye-tracking to identify if features related to joint attention can be used to predict the learning outcomes and assess the level of collaboration of dyads. Moreover, Echeverria et al. (2019) also proposed a multimodal learning analytics ecosystem (based on physiological sensors, microphones, and positioning trackers) to automatically detect errors made by nursing students during a fully immersive healthcare simulation. Although these works point at the recent interest in assessing group work and teamwork in physical spaces, this work is still in its infancy. Particularly, more work is needed both in improving the accuracy of sensors and also the validity of the techniques that can be used to model the multimodal data in educationally meaningful ways.

Table 19.1 provided a summary of some of the AI techniques that have been used to support collaborative learning presented in the previous subsections.

Table 19.1   Summary of techniques for supporting collaborative learning

Type of support	AI techniques used	Contexts explored
Group formation	Genetic algorithms, swarm intelligence algorithms, multi-agent formation algorithms, clustering, semantic web ontologies, social network analysis, word embeddings, decision trees, naive Bayes, logistic regression.	Mostly online
Formative feedback to learners	Recommender systems, intelligent tutoring systems, adaptive intelligent hints, data visualization, dashboards.	Mostly online (some face-to-face cases)
Adaptive scripting	Adaptive scripting, end-user scripting, dynamic modeling, intelligent tutoring systems, classification of group conversations, NLP.	Mostly online
Group awareness	Data aggregation, clustering, basic statistics, data visualization, affective computing (e.g. facial recognition algorithms).	Mostly online (some face-to-face cases)
Teacher awareness	Data aggregation, clustering, basic statistics, data visualization, affective computing (e.g. facial recognition algorithms).	Mostly online (some face-to-face cases)
Summative assessment	NLP, automatic conversation coding, classifiers, multimodal analytics, dynamic Bayesian networks, cohesion networks, contingency graphs, epistemic network analysis, group communication analysis.	Mostly online (some face-to-face cases)

TRENDS AND FUTURE CHALLENGES

In this section we discuss several overarching challenges related to supporting collaborative learning through AI and analytics techniques. We also point at new directions in this field. An overarching issue for all types of support discussed above is that it is of vital importance in evaluating the validity, utility, and interpretability of emerging techniques for modeling and assessing meaningful aspects of collaborative learning (see Chapter 22 by VanLehn). One potential way to address this issue is by considering human-centered approaches when designing a support tool. Taking a human-centered approach is related to ensuring that the user of the support tool—learners or teachers—retains a desired level of agency (e.g. see Chapter 6 by Kay et al.). That is, there should be a balance between the support tool imposing certain actions upon the user, and the support tool acting as a way to inform the user's actions (Wise et al., 2016). Support through scripting (see above) is a clear example of the issue of agency, as the danger of *overscripting* is commonly discussed in the literature (Dillenbourg, 2002). As described in this section, some authors have argued for letting students design (part of) their own scripts, allowing for greater flexibility and agency.

Another dimension of human-centered design concerns the choice for which aspects of the collaborative process are analyzed and visualized by the support tool to facilitate interpretability (Santos & Boticario, 2014, 2015). These aspects should ideally be chosen and visualized in such a way that they are informative yet easy to interpret for the user. However, these two goals are sometimes at odds: what may be easy to visualize is not always informative, whereas complicated yet informative indicators may not be easy to understand. In both cases, the result is that the intended goal of supporting the user may not be reached.

One promising approach to resolving this tension is suggested by the emerging field of Quantitative Ethnography (QE) (Shaffer, 2017). QE provides a conceptual framework for mapping data to constructs in terms of *Codes*—the contextually defined meanings of actions. Critically, Codes may be defined in relation to *etic* concepts—those that are associated with relevant theory—as well as *emic* concepts—those that members of the community being studied use to understand their own actions. Thus, emic coding may help to alleviate the tension between informative and interpretable constructs in the context of collaborative learning support.

Coding alone does not fully address the issue, however. To understand and support collaboration, we need techniques that model and visualize the relationships between Codes that are expressed when learners interact. One such technique, epistemic network analysis (Shaffer et al., 2016), has recently been used to model connections between Codes in collaborative settings and automatically represent these connections to teachers in real time to help them support collaborating learners (Herder et al., 2018). Other promising techniques for modeling the relationships between Codes include dynamic Bayesian Networks (Gweon et al., 2013) and lag sequential analysis (Kapur, 2011). Furthermore, several network techniques exist that have been used to visualize connections between concepts in discourse, such as cohesion, semantic similarity and uptake (Dascalu et al., 2018; Dowell et al., 2019; Suthers, 2017). However, more work is needed to examine these techniques in relation to emic concepts in collaborative learning and, thus, help to address the tension described above.

There is a growing interest in capturing collaborative traces from the increasingly hybrid learning spaces in which group activities span across physical and digital settings. Future research and development of awareness tools could focus on automated detection of emotions, using, for example, physiological indicators (see Chapter 18 by Casas-Ortiz et al.). Multimodal sensors can be used to build more complete models of collaborators to not only consider what can be logged from clicks and keystrokes but also to generate a deeper understanding of the complexity of working in groups, particularly in collocated settings (Martinez-Maldonado et al., 2019). However, more work is still needed to ensure validity in the kind of metrics that can be extracted from sensor data. For example, theory-based dual eye-tracking innovations have been robustly used to predict joint attention as a proxy of effective collaboration (Schneider & Pea, 2013). However, these metrics cannot easily scale to groups of three or more. Metrics from positioning, posture, and affective aspects of group activity are also emerging. For example, Malmberg et al. (2021) used physiological sensors to automatically identify key socially shared regulation constructs. Yet, much work is still needed to fully understand the validity and utility of such metrics to directly support collaborative learning.

Finally, using more sources of evidence about learners' collaborative behaviors can actually lead to building more accurate models (Viswanathan & VanLehn, 2019b). Yet, a key trade-off to consider exists between achieving high accuracy in collaboration detection and the potential privacy and practical challenges that can emerge in authentic settings from collecting richer collaboration data (Viswanathan & VanLehn, 2019a). Bringing AI into authentic collaborative learning settings is already sparking deep discussions around ethics, biases, inequalities, and moral dilemmas (see Chapter 26 by Porayska-Pomsta et al.).

CONCLUDING REMARKS

This chapter presented an overview of AI and analytics techniques to support collaborative learning in face-to-face and online settings. Some of the current techniques have contributed to accelerating CSCL researchers' analysis cycles, but some have also been transformed into tools that support teachers and learners in various ways. This chapter grouped the techniques currently available according to their purpose. We particularly focused on techniques that provide intelligent support to: (i) form effective groups, (ii) provide direct feedback to students, (iii) facilitate adaptive scripting, (iv) enhance group and (v) teacher awareness, and (vi) perform summative assessments. We emphasize that several validity challenges are persisting and more work needs to be done in understanding how low-level group data can be modeled in educational meaningful ways that can serve to inform practice. Validity is a particular challenge for the emerging interest in capturing multiple sources of collaboration data to gain a wider understanding of the group activity. However, the more data is captured, the harder it can be for teachers and learners to understand the relationships between salient aspects highlighted by AI algorithms and this can lead to complex interfaces that are hard to interpret. We propose that human-centered design approaches can enable the creation of AI support tools that serve their purpose in effectively supporting teachers and learners by giving them an active voice in the design decisions of the tools they will end up using. This means there are several future avenues of research in developing techniques for supporting collaborative learning that address authentic educational needs, with integrity.

REFERENCES

Amarasinghe, I., Hernández-Leo, D., & Jonsson, A. (2017). Intelligent group formation in computer supported collaborative learning scripts. In *Proceedings of International Conference on Advanced Learning Technologies* (pp. 201–203). IEEE.

Avry, S., Molinari, G., Bétrancourt, M., & Chanel, G. (2020). Sharing emotions contributes to regulating collaborative intentions in group problem-solving. *Frontiers in Psychology*, *11*, 1160.

Baghaei, N., Mitrovic, A., & Irwin, W. (2007). Supporting collaborative learning and problem-solving in a constraint-based CSCL environment for UML class diagrams. *International Journal of Computer-Supported Collaborative Learning*, *2(2–3)*, 159–190.

Berland, M., Davis, D., & Smith, C. P. (2015). AMOEBA: Designing for collaboration in computer science classrooms through live learning analytics. *International Journal of Computer-Supported Collaborative Learning*, *10*(4), 425–447.

Bodily, R., & Verbert, K. (2017). Trends and issues in student-facing learning analytics reporting systems research. In *Proceedings of International Learning Analytics & Knowledge Conference* (pp. 309–318). ACM.

Chi, M. T., & Wylie, R. (2014). The ICAP framework: Linking cognitive engagement to active learning outcomes. *Educational Psychologist*, *49*(4), 219–243.

Chua, Y. H. V., Rajalingam, P., Tan, S. C., & Dauwels, J. (2019, April). Edubrowser: A multimodal automated monitoring system for co-located collaborative learning. In *International Workshop on Learning Technology for Education in Cloud* (pp. 125–138). Cham: Springer.

Cruz, W. M., & Isotani, S. (2014). Group formation algorithms in collaborative learning contexts: A systematic mapping of the literature. In N. Baloian, F. Burstein, H. Ogata, F. Santoro, & G. Zurita (Eds.), *Collaboration and Technology* (Vol. 8658, pp. 199–214).

Dascalu, M., McNamara, D. S., Trausan-Matu, S., & Allen, L. K. (2018). Cohesion network analysis of CSCL participation. *Behavior Research Methods*, *50*(2), 604–619.

Dascalu, M., Trausan-Matu, Ş., & Dessus, P. (2014, June). Validating the automated assessment of participation and of collaboration in chat conversations. In *Proceedings of International Conference on Intelligent Tutoring Systems* (pp. 230–235). Springer.

Dascalu, M., Trausan-Matu, S., McNamara, D. S., & Dessus, P. (2015). ReaderBench. Automated evaluation of collaboration based on cohesion and dialogism. *International Journal of Computer-Supported Collaborative Learning*, *10*(4), 395–423.

De Groot, R., Drachman, R., Hever, R., Schwarz, B. B., Hoppe, U., Harrer, A., De Laat, M., Wegerif, R., McLaren, B. M., & Baurens, B. (2007). Computer supported moderation of ediscussions: The ARGUNAUT approach. In *Proceedings of International Conference on Computer Supported Collaborative Learning* (pp. 165–167). ISLS.

Dillenbourg, P. (1999). Collaborative learning: Cognitive and computational approaches. In *Advances in Learning and Instruction Series*. NYC: Elsevier Science, Inc.

Dillenbourg, P. (2002). Over-scripting CSCL: The risks of blending collaborative learning with instructional design. In P. A. Kirschner (Ed.), *Three Worlds of CSCL: Can We Support CSCL?* (pp. 61–91). Heerlen: Open Universiteit.

Diziol, D., Walker, E., Rummel, N., & Koedinger, K. R. (2010). Using intelligent tutor technology to implement adaptive support for student collaboration. *Educational Psychology Review*, *22*(1), 89–102.

Dönmez, Pinar, Rosé, C., Stegmann, K., Weinberger, A., & Fischer, F. (2005). Supporting CSCL with automatic corpus analysis technology. In *Proceedings of International Conference on Computer-Supported Collaborative Learning* (pp. 125–134). ISLS.

Dowell, N., Nixon, T., & Graesser, A. (2019). Group communication analysis: A computational linguistics approach for detecting sociocognitive roles in multiparty interactions. *Behavior Research Methods*, *51*(3), 1007–1041.

Dowell, N. M., Cade, W. L., Tausczik, Y., Pennebaker, J., & Graesser, A. C. (2014, June). What works: Creating adaptive and intelligent systems for collaborative learning support. In *Proceeding of International Conference on Intelligent Tutoring Systems* (pp. 124–133). Springer.

Echeverria, V., Martinez-Maldonado, R., & Buckingham Shum, S. (2019, May). Towards collaboration translucence: Giving meaning to multimodal group data. In *Proceedings of CHI Conference on Human Factors in Computing Systems* (pp. 1–16). ACM.

Ez-Zaouia, M., Tabard, A., & Lavoué, E. (2020). EMODASH: A dashboard supporting retrospective awareness of emotions in online learning. *International Journal of Human-Computer Studies*, *139*.

Filho, J. A. B. L., Quarto, C. C., & França, R. M. (2010). Clustering algorithm for the socioaffective groups formation in aid of computer-supported collaborative learning. In *Proceedings of Collaborative Systems II - Simposio Brasileiro de Sistemas Colaborativos* (pp. 24–27).

Fischer, F., Kollar, I., Stegmann, K., & Wecker, C. (2013). Toward a script theory of guidance in computer-supported collaborative learning. *Educational Psychologist*, *48*(1), 56–66.

Gašević, D., Dawson, S., & Siemens, G. (2015). Let's not forget: Learning analytics are about learning. *TechTrends*, *59*(1), 64–71.

Graesser, A. C., Conley, M. W., & Olney, A. (2012). Intelligent tutoring systems. In K. R. Harris, S. Graham, T. Urdan, A. G. Bus, S. Major, & H. L. Swanson (Eds.), *APA Educational Psychology Handbook, Vol. 3: Application to Learning and Teaching* (pp. 451–473).

Griffin, P. E., McGaw, B., & Care, E. (Eds.). (2012). *Assessment and Teaching of 21st Century Skills*. The Netherlands: Springer Science+Business Media Dordrecht.

Gweon, G., Jain, M., McDonough, J., Raj, B., & Rose, C. P. (2013). Measuring prevalence of other-oriented transactive contributions using an automated measure of speech style accommodation. *International Journal of Computer-Supported Collaborative Learning*, *8*(2), 245–265.

Herder, T., Swiecki, Z., Fougt, S. S., Tamborg, A. L., Allsopp, B. B., Shaffer, D. W., & Misfeldt, M. (2018). Supporting teacher's intervention in student's virtual collaboration using a network based model. In *Proceedings of International Conference on Learning Analytics* (pp. 21–25). ISLS.

Hmelo-Silver, C., Chinn, C., Chan, C., & O'Donnell, A. (Eds.). (2013). *The International Handbook of Collaborative Learning* (1st ed.). Abingdon: Routledge.

Hu, X., Ng, T. D. J., Tian, L., & Lei, C. U. (2016, April). Automating assessment of collaborative writing quality in multiple stages: the case of wiki. In *Proceedings of International Conference on Learning Analytics & Knowledge* (pp. 518–519). ACM.

Isotani, Seiji. (2011). Guest editorial: Special issue on intelligent and innovative support systems for CSCL. *IEEE Transactions on Learning Technologies*, *4*(1), 1–4.

Isotani, S., Mizoguchi, R., Capeli, O. M., Isotani, N., de Albuquerque, A. R. P. L., Bittencourt, I. I., & Jaques, P. A. (2013). A semantic web-based authoring tool to facilitate the planning of collaborative learning scenarios compliant with learning theories. *Computers & Education*, *63*, 267–284.

Janssen, J., & Bodemer, D. (2013). Coordinated computer-supported collaborative learning: Awareness and awareness tools. *Educational Psychologist*, *48*(1), 40–55.

Jermann, P., & Dillenbourg, P. (2008). Group mirrors to support interaction regulation in collaborative problem solving. *Computers & Education*, *51*(1), 279–296.

Jermann, P., Soller, A., & Muehlenbrock, M. (2005). From mirroring to guiding: A review of state of the art technology for supporting collaborative learning. *International Journal of Artificial Intelligence in Education*, *15*(4), 261–290.

Kaendler, C., Wiedmann, M., Leuders, T., Rummel, N., & Spada, H. (2016). Monitoring student interaction during collaborative learning: Design and evaluation of a training program for pre-service teachers. *Psychology Learning & Teaching*, *15*(1), 44–64.

Kaendler, C., Wiedmann, M., Rummel, N., & Spada, H. (2015). Teacher competencies for the implementation of collaborative learning in the classroom: A framework and research review. *Educational Psychology Review*, *27*(3), 505–536.

Kapur, M. (2011, March). Temporality matters: Advancing a method for analyzing problem-solving processes in a computer supported collaborative environment. *International Journal of Computer-Supported Collaborative Learning*, *6*(1), 39–56.

Kay, J., Maisonneuve, N., Yacef, K., & Zaïane, O. (2006, June). Mining patterns of events in students' teamwork data. In *Proceedings of Workshop on Educational Data Mining at the 8th International Conference on Intelligent Tutoring Systems (ITS 2006)* (pp. 45–52).

Kim, J., & Kumar, R. (2012). Proceedings of the full-day workshop on intelligent support for learning in groups. In *Held at the 11th International Conference on Intelligent Tutoring Systems (ITS 2012)*, Chania, Greece.

Kollar, Ingo, Fischer, F., & Hesse, F. W. (2006). Collaboration scripts – A conceptual analysis. *Educational Psychology Review*, *18*(2), 159–185.

Kreijns, K., Kirschner, P. A., & Jochems, W. (2003). Identifying the pitfalls for social interaction in computer-supported collaborative learning environments: A review of the research. *Computers in Human Behavior*, *19*(3), 335–353.

Kumar, R., & Kim, J. (2014). Special issue on intelligent support for learning in groups. *International Journal of Artificial Intelligence in Education*, *24*(1), 1–7.

Kumar, R., Rosé, C. P., Wang, Y. C., Joshi, M., & Robinson, A. (2007, June). Tutorial dialogue as adaptive collaborative learning support. In *Proceedings of the 2007 Conference on Artificial Intelligence in Education: Building Technology Rich Learning Contexts That Work* (pp. 383–390).

Lin, Y.-T., Huang, Y.-M., & Cheng, S.-C. (2010) An automatic group composition system for composing collaborative learning groups using enhanced particle swarm optimization. *Computers & Education*, 55(4), 1483–1493.

Liu A. L., & Nesbit J. C. (2020) Dashboards for computer-supported collaborative learning. In M. Virvou, E. Alepis, G. Tsihrintzis, & L. Jain (Eds.), *Machine Learning Paradigms: Intelligent Systems Reference Library* (Vol. 158, pp. 157–182). Cham: Springer.

Lobo, J. L., Santos, O. C., Boticario, J. G., & Del Ser, J. (2016). Identifying recommendation opportunities for computer-supported collaborative environments. *Expert Systems*, 33(5), 463–479.

Malmberg, J., Fincham, O., Pijeira-Díaz, H. J., Järvelä, S., & Gašević, D. (2021). Revealing the hidden structure of physiological states during metacognitive monitoring in collaborative learning. *Journal of Computer Assisted Learning*, 37(3), 861–874.

Martinez-Maldonado, R., Kay, J., Buckingham Shum, S., & Yacef, K. (2019). Collocated collaboration analytics: Principles and dilemmas for mining multimodal interaction data. *Human–Computer Interaction*, 34(1), 1–50.

Martinez-Maldonado, R., Kay, J., & Yacef, K. (2013). An automatic approach for mining patterns of collaboration around an interactive tabletop. In *Proceedings of International Conference on Artificial Intelligence in Education* (pp. 101–110). Springer.

May, M., George, S., & Prévôt, P. (2011). TrAVis to enhance students' self-monitoring in online learning supported by computer-mediated communication tools. *Computer Information Systems and Industrial Management Applications*, 3, 623–634.

McNamara, D. S., Graesser, A. C., McCarthy, P. M., & Cai, Z. (2014). *Automated Evaluation of Text and Discourse With Coh-Metrix*. Cambridge: Cambridge University Press.

Meier, A., Spada, H., & Rummel, N. (2007). A rating scheme for assessing the quality of computer-supported collaboration processes. *International Journal of Computer-Supported Collaborative Learning*, 2(1), 63–86.

Meijer, H., Hoekstra, R., Brouwer, J., & Strijbos, J. W. (2020). Unfolding collaborative learning assessment literacy: A reflection on current assessment methods in higher education. *Assessment & Evaluation in Higher Education*, 1–19.

Moreno, J., Ovalle, D. A., & Vicari, R. M. (2012). A genetic algorithm approach for group formation in collaborative learning considering multiple student characteristics. *Computers & Education*, 58(1), 560–569.

OECD. (2017). *PISA 2015 Assessment and Analytical Framework: Science, Reading, Mathematic, Financial Literacy and Collaborative Problem Solving, Revised Edition*. PISA, OECD Publishing.

Olsen, J. (2017). *Orchestrating Combined Collaborative and Individual Learning in the Classroom* (Doctoral Dissertation, Carnegie Mellon University).

Olsen, J. K., Aleven, V., & Rummel, N. (2017). Exploring dual eye tracking as a tool to assess collaboration. In *Innovative Assessment of Collaboration* (pp. 157–172). Cham: Springer.

Perera, D., Kay, J., Koprinska, I., Yacef, K., & Zaïane, O. R. (2008). Clustering and sequential pattern mining of online collaborative learning data. *IEEE Transactions on Knowledge and Data Engineering*, 21(6), 759–772.

Pettit, R., & Prather, J. (2017). Automated assessment tools: Too many cooks, not enough collaboration. *Journal of Computing Sciences in Colleges*, 32(4), 113–121.

Prieto, L., Muñoz-Cristóbal, J., Asensio-Pérez, J., & Dimitriadis, Y. (2012). Making learning designs happen in distributed learning environments with GLUE!-PS. In A. Ravenscroft, S. Lindstaedt, C. Kloos, & D. Hernández-Leo (Eds.), *21st Century Learning for 21st Century Skills* (pp. 489–494). Berlin/Heidelberg: Springer.

Rosé, C., Wang, Y.-C., Cui, Y., Arguello, J., Stegmann, K., Weinberger, A., & Fischer, F. (2008). Analyzing collaborative learning processes automatically: Exploiting the advances of computational linguistics in computer-supported collaborative learning. *International Journal of Computer-Supported Collaborative Learning*, 3(3), 237–271.

Rosé, C. P., & Ferschke, O. (2016). Technology support for discussion based learning: From computer supported collaborative learning to the future of massive open online courses. *International Journal of Artificial Intelligence in Education*, *26*(2), 660–678.

Rummel, N. (2018). One framework to rule them all? Carrying forward the conversation started by Wise and Schwarz. International *Journal of Computer-Supported Collaborative Learning*, *13*(1), 123–129.

Rummel, N., Weinberger, A., Wecker, C., Fischer, F., Meier, A., Voyiatzaki, E., Kahrimanis, G., Spada, H., Avouris, N., Walker, E., & Koedinger, K. (2008). New challenges in CSCL: Towards adaptive script support. In *Proceedings of International Conference for the Learning Sciences* (pp. 338–345). ISLS.

Santos, O. C., & Boticario, J. G. (2014). Involving users to improve the collaborative logical framework. *The Scientific World Journal*.

Santos, O. C., & Boticario, J. G. (2015). Practical guidelines for designing and evaluating educationally oriented recommendations. *Computers & Education*, *81*, 354–374.

Sarmiento, J. P., & Wise, A. F. (2022, March). Participatory and co-design of learning analytics: An initial review of the literature. In *LAK22: 12th International Learning Analytics and Knowledge Conference* (pp. 535–541).

Saucerman, J., Ruis, A. R., & Shaffer, D. W. (2017). Automating the detection of reflection-on-action. *Journal of Learning Analytics*, *4*(2), 212–239.

Scheffel, M., Drachsler, H., De Kraker, J., Kreijns, K., Slootmaker, A., & Specht, M. (2016). Widget, widget on the wall, am I performing well at all? *IEEE Transactions on Learning Technologies*, *10(1)*, 42–52.

Schnaubert, L., Harbarth, L., & Bodemer, D. (2020). A psychological perspective on data processing in cognitive group awareness tools. In *Proceedings of International Conference of the Learning Sciences* (pp. 951–958). ISLS.

Schneider, B., & Pea, R. (2013). Real-time mutual gaze perception enhances collaborative learning and collaboration quality. *International Journal of Computer-Supported Collaborative Learning*, *8*(4), 375–397.

Sergis, S., & Sampson, D.G. (2017). Teaching and learning analytics to support teacher inquiry: A systematic literature review. In A. Peña-Ayala (Ed.), *Learning Analytics: Fundaments, Applications, and Trends* (pp. 25–63).

Shaffer, D. W. (2017). *Quantitative Ethnography*. Wisconsin: Cathcart Press.

Shaffer, D. W., Collier, W., & Ruis, A. R. (2016). A tutorial on epistemic network analysis: Analyzing the structure of connections in cognitive, social, and interaction data. *Journal of Learning Analytics*, *3*(3), 9–45.

Shaffer, D. W., & Ruis, A. R. (2020). How we code. In *Proceedings of Conference on Advances in Quantitative Ethnography*. Springer.

Soh, L.-K., Khandaker, N., & Jiang, H. (2008). I-MINDS: A multiagent system for intelligent computer-supported collaborative learning and classroom management. *International Journal on Artificial Intelligence in Education*, *18*, 119–151.

Soller, A. (2001). Supporting social interaction in an intelligent collaborative learning system. *International Journal of Artificial Intelligence in Education*, *12*, 40–62.

Stahl, G., Koschmann, T., & Suthers, D. (2006). Computer-supported collaborative learning: An historical perspective. In R. K. Sawyer (Ed.), *Cambridge Handbook of the Learning Sciences* (pp. 409–426). Cambridge, UK: Cambridge University Press.

Stahl, Gerry. (2006). *Group Cognition: Computer Support for Building Collaborative Knowledge*. Cambridge: MIT Press.

Staubitz, T., Klement, H., Renz, J., Teusner, R., & Meinel, C. (2015). Towards practical programming exercises and automated assessment in massive open online courses. In *Proceedings of International Conference on Teaching, Assessment, and Learning for Engineering* (pp. 23–30). IEEE.

Suthers, D. D. (2017). Multilevel analysis of activity and actors in heterogeneous networked learning environments. In Columbia University, USA (Eds.), *Handbook of Learning Analytics* (1st ed., pp. 189–197). SOLAR.

Swidan, O., Prusak, N., Livny, A., Palatnik, A., & Schwarz, B. B. (2019). Fostering teachers' online understanding of progression of multiple groups towards the orchestration of conceptual learning. Un- terrichtswissenschaft.

Swiecki, Z. (2021). Measuring the impact of interdependence on individuals during collaborative-problem solving. *Journal of Learning Analytics*, *8*(1), 75–94.

Swiecki, Z. (a), Lian, Z., Ruis, A. R., & Shaffer, D. W. (2019). Does order matter? Investigating sequential and cotemporal models of collaboration. In *Proceedings of International Conference on Computer-Supported Collaborative Learning* (Vol. 1, pp. 112–120). ISLS.

Swiecki, Z., Ruis, A. R., Farrell, C., & Shaffer, D. W. (2020). Assessing individual contributions to collaborative problem solving: A network analysis approach. *Computers in Human Behavior*, *104*, 105876.

Tarmazdi, H., Vivian, R., Szabo, C., Falkner, K., & Falkner, N. (2015, June). Using learning analytics to visualise computer science teamwork. In *Proceedings of Conference on Innovation and Technology in Computer Science Education* (pp. 165–170). ACM.

Tchounikine, P., Rummel, N., & McLaren, B. M. (2010). Computer supported collaborative learning and intelligent tutoring systems. In R. Nkambou, J. Bourdeau, & R. Mizoguchi (Eds.), *Advances in Intelligent Tutoring Systems: Studies in Computational Intelligence* (Vol. 308). Berlin, Heidelberg: Springer.

Upton, K., & Kay, J. (2009, June). Narcissus: Group and individual models to support small group work. In *Proceedings of International Conference on User Modeling, Adaptation, and Personalization* (pp. 54–65). Springer.

Van Diggelen, W., & Overdijk, M. (2007). Small group face-to-face discussions in the classroom: A new direction of CSCL research. In *Proceedings of Conference on Computer Supported Collaborative Learning* (pp. 726–735). ISLS.

Van Leeuwen, A., & Janssen, J. (2019). A systematic review of teacher guidance during collaborative learning in primary and secondary education. *Educational Research Review*, *27*(July 2018), 71–89.

Van Leeuwen, A., & Rummel, N. (2019). Orchestration tools to support the teacher during student collaboration: A review. *Unterrichtswissenschaft*, *47*(2), 143–158.

Viswanathan, S. A., & VanLehn, K. (2019a). Collaboration detection that preserves privacy of students' speech. In S. Isotani, E. Millán, A. Ogan, P. Hastings, B. McLaren, & R. Luckin (Eds.), *International Conference on Artificial Intelligence in Education: AIED 2019* (pp. 507–517). Berlin: Springer.

Viswanathan, S. A., & VanLehn, K. (2019b). Detection of collaboration: The relationship between log and speech-based classification. In S. Isotani, E. Millán, A. Ogan, P. Hastings, B. McLaren, & R. Luckin (Eds.), *International Conference on Artificial Intelligence in Education* (pp. 327–331). Berlin: Springer.

Vygotsky, L. S. (1978). *Mind in Society: The Development of Higher Psychological Processes*. Massachusetts: Harvard University Press.

Wang, X., Wen, M., & Rosé, C. (2017). Contrasting explicit and implicit scaffolding for transactive exchange in team oriented project based learning. In *Making a Difference: Prioritizing Equity and Access in CSCL, 12th International Conference on Computer Supported Collaborative Learning (CSCL'17)* (pp. 18–22).

Wise, A. F., & Schwarz, B. B. (2017). Visions of CSCL: Eight provocations for the future of the field. *International Journal of Computer-Supported Collaborative Learning*, *12*(4), 423–467.

Wise, A. F., Vytasek, J. M., Hausknecht, S., & Zhao, Y. (2016). Developing learning analytics design knowledge in the "middle space": The student tuning model and align design framework for learning analytics use. *Online Learning*, *20*(2), 155–182.

Wu Y., Nouri J., Li X., Weegar R., Afzaal M., & Zia A. (2021) A word embeddings based clustering approach for collaborative learning group formation. In I. Roll, D. McNamara, S. Sosnovsky, R. Luckin, & V. Dimitrova (Eds.), *Artificial Intelligence in Education. AIED 2021. Lecture Notes in Computer Science* (Vol. 12749). Cham: Springer. https://doi.org/10.1007/978-3-030-78270-2_70.

20. Digital learning games in artificial intelligence in education (AIED): a review

Bruce M. McLaren and Huy A. Nguyen

INTRODUCTION

Digital and computer games have captured the attention and imagination of people around the world. Lobel et al. (2017) report that Dutch children (7 to 12 years old) play digital games for between 4.9 and 5.8 hours per week, while a slightly older age range of children in New York City (10 to 15 years old) has been reported as playing even more: between 30 and 42 hours a week (Homer et al., 2012). Digital gameplay has also been significantly on the rise: According to a 2019 survey by the NPD Group (NPD, 2019), 73 percent of Americans aged 2 and older play digital games, a 6% increase from the prior year. There are reports of more than 2.6 billion people world-wide being video game players, with an expected rise to over 3 billion people by 2023 (Gilbert, 2021).

This general interest in digital games has also transferred to schools and educational use of computer-based games. Digital learning games, also called educational games, began to be designed, developed, and sporadically appeared in classrooms in the late 1990s (Zeng et al., 2020). A flourishing in digital learning games has occurred since 2000, boosted by concurrent advancements in supporting technology, such as computer graphics and faster processors. President Obama helped to push this interest forward by launching the National STEM Game Design Competition in 2010. Today, according to Juraschka (2019), 74% of teachers use digital game-based learning to enhance their lessons and the majority of teachers who use games in the classroom believe games have been helpful in improving their students' learning.

In addition to the increasing interest in and playing of digital learning games, there is also increasing empirical evidence of the effectiveness of games in helping people learn. Academics became interested in the motivational potential of digital learning games some time ago (Castell & Jenson, 2003; Gros, 2007), and an increase in empirical research has followed over the past 15-to-20 years. Meta-analyses over the past five-to-six years have uncovered and discussed the educational benefits of digital learning games (Clark et al., 2016; Crocco et al., 2016; Hussein et al., 2022; Ke, 2016; Mayer, 2019; Tokac et al., 2019; Wouters & van Oostendorp, 2017). Even video games without a specific aim to provide educational benefits have been shown to increase students' skills, for instance perceptual attention (Bediou et al., 2018). The Clark et al. (2016) meta-analysis identified that careful attention to game design – the way in which a game's interface and mechanics supports interaction with the student player – can result in positive learning results. Furthermore, there is strong evidence that designing digital games based on cognitive theories of learning and empirical learning science results can lead to educational benefits. For instance, Parong and colleagues have shown that executive function skills can be trained through a digital learning game designed expressly for that purpose (Parong et al., 2017, 2020). McLaren and colleagues found that designing a game explicitly targeted at mathematics misconceptions and employing self-explanation prompts – a technique that has been shown to lead to learning benefits in a variety of contexts (Chi et al., 1994, 1989; Mayer & Johnson, 2010; Wylie & Chi, 2014) – can lead to learning benefits (McLaren et al., 2017).

While it is clear that game design and attention to what we know about how humans learn have been beneficial to the design and success of digital learning games, what about the use of artificial intelligence (AI) in the design and development of digital learning games? It seems natural to insert AI into digital learning games to make them more realistic, more challenging, and more adaptive to students' skill level and style of play. Yet, a recent meta-analysis of digital learning games notes that over the past 20 years AI has rarely been cited as a component of learning games (Schöbel et al., 2021). Thus, a natural question that arises is has the field of Artificial Intelligence in Education (AIED) actually made an impact on learning with digital games? In this chapter we explore this question by discussing the way that AI has been used in digital learning games until now, as well as how it might provide even more benefit to learning with digital learning games in the future.

FOUNDATIONS OF LEARNING FROM GAMES

Between the mid-1970s and 1990, Czikszentmihalyi developed and described the theory of *flow*, a state of optimal experience, where a person is so engaged in the activity at hand that self-consciousness disappears, a sense of time is lost, and the person engages in complex, goal-directed activity not for external rewards, but simply for the exhilaration of doing (Czikszentmihalyi, 1975, 1990). For over 20 years, Czikszentmihalyi had been studying "states of optimal experience" – times when people, while undertaking an engaging activity, report feelings of concentration and deep enjoyment. Flow induces focused concentration and total absorption in an activity. Everyone experiences flow from time to time and will recognize its characteristics: one feels strong, alert, in effortless control, loses all self-consciousness, and is at the peak of their abilities. Often, the sense of time seems to disappear, and a person in flow experiences a feeling of transcendence.

Digital games often immerse children – and people more generally – in flow and have long been posited to help in the learning process (Gee, 2003). Some very early researchers in the area of cognitive science identified constructs that are often part of games and appear to promote flow. For instance, Malone (1981) identified fantasy, curiosity, and challenge as key to intrinsic motivation and learning with games. Fantasy can serve to connect the player with content that they might otherwise reject as conflicting with their identity (Kaufman & Flanagan, 2015). Curiosity can be promoted when learners have the sense that their knowledge needs to be revised, for example, if it is incomplete or inconsistent. Challenge depends upon activities that involve uncertain outcomes, hidden information, or randomness. While this theoretical work pre-dated most present-day digital learning game research, all of the constructs explored by Malone are clearly relevant and important to learning with games.

While flow and intrinsic motivation appear to be key to learning with digital games, states of human affect, such as determination, confusion, frustration, and boredom, also play an important role (Loderer et al., 2019). For example, even though frustration is a "negative" emotion, it could indicate that a student is highly engaged while playing a challenging learning game (Gee, 2003). Determination and curiosity have also been found to be strongly present during gameplay with learning games (Spann et al., 2019). A line of AIED research that has investigated affect in gameplay has thus emerged, most typically involving data mining of log files of student use of learning games (Baker et al., 2007, 2010; Shute et al., 2015) or using sensors, video, and/or eye trackers to detect affect (Bosch et al., 2016; Conati & Gutica, 2016; Shute et al., 2013).

Given this foundational theoretical (and some empirical) work, a number of researchers and proselytizers have strongly pushed digital learning games as a panacea to the many shortcomings of education in today's world. In the early days, many claims were made about the benefits of learning with digital learning games versus more traditional approaches (Gee, 2007; Prensky, 2006; Squire & Jenkins, 2003). Not long after the claims were made, however, others emphasized the lack of evidence for positive learning outcomes with digital learning games (Honey & Hilton, 2011; Mayer, 2014; Tobias & Fletcher, 2011). Yet, as pointed out above, in recent years evidence has started to accumulate that digital learning games *can* be beneficial to learning (Clark et al., 2016; Mayer, 2019), including substantial evidence from within the AIED community (Arroyo et al., 2013; Easterday et al., 2017; Lee et al., 2011; McLaren et al., 2017; Sawyer et al., 2017; Shute et al., 2015). How the AIED community has explored the space of learning from digital games is discussed in the next section.

DIGITAL LEARNING GAMES RESEARCH IN AIED

For the purposes of this review chapter, it is important to define, first, what a digital learning game is and, second, when a digital learning game is an "AIED" learning game. Given that many digital learning games are arguably not "AIED," two separate definitions are necessary.

Note that many before us have made attempts to define what a "game" is (Rollings & Morris, 2000; Salen & Zimmerman, 2003) and, in turn, what a "digital learning game" is (Mayer, 2014; Prensky, 2004). While it is impossible to precisely define these terms, and any definition is subject to dispute, the following components have typically been part of prior definitions of a digital learning game: (1) an interactive program running on a computer or other electronic device; (2) "gameplay" in the form of an artificial environment in which fun, challenge, and/or fantasy are involved; (3) instructional content or an instructional objective is an integral part of the gameplay; (4) entertainment goals are part of the gameplay (e.g., competition, having fun); and, finally, (5) a set of pre-defined rules guide gameplay. Given this background, our working definition of a *digital learning game* is:

> A digital learning game is an interactive, computer-based system in which (1) users (i.e., players) engage in artificial activities involving fun, challenge, and/or fantasy; (2) instructional and entertainment goals are part of the system; and (3) pre-defined rules guide gameplay.

In turn, our definition of an *AIED digital learning game* is:

> An AIED digital learning game is a digital learning game that (1) employs AI within its operation and interaction with players and/or (2) has been developed and/or extended using AI techniques (e.g., educational data mining, learning analytics, or machine learning).

Note that this definition implies that we include games that may not have been published within the annual AIED conference proceedings or the International Journal of AI in Education. That is, we focus more on how games operate, the extent to which AI is part of their game mechanism or post-use analyses, rather than whether they have been published within the AIED community. That said, we also focus on games that have been subject of some study of their learning efficacy and for which articles have been published. Note further that we include in our review AI learning technology that is "gamified," that is, technology that was not (necessarily) developed originally as a game, but that includes gaming elements such as badges, points, leaderboards, and interactive playful agents (Landers & Landers, 2014; Landers et al., 2017). These elements may alter the game's mechanics, the player's interactions, or aspects of player immersion and emotion, to improve the learner's engagement and experience (Deterding et al., 2011). Such technology falls, we believe, within the above definition of an AIED digital learning game. Key examples of gamified AIED learning technology are *MathSpring* (Arroyo et al., 2013, 2014), *iStart-2* (Jackson & McNamara, 2011; Jacovina et al., 2016), *Gamified Lynnette* (Long & Aleven, 2014, 2018), and *Gamified SQL-Tutor* (Tahir et al., 2020).

In what follows, we explicitly call out the AI aspect of the games we cite and discuss. In the interest of inclusiveness, recency, and broad coverage, we are also somewhat liberal in including games that are nascent, without much (or any) empirical evidence of their instructional effectiveness, especially more recently developed and tested games that may be of interest to the AIED audience (e.g., *Navigo*: Benton et al., 2021; *TurtleTalk*: Jung et al., 2019). On the other hand, we are clear about the games that have been the subject of extensive empirical study (e.g., *MathSpring*: Arroyo et al., 2013, 2014; *Crystal Island*: Lester et al., 2013; *Decimal Point*: McLaren et al., 2017; *Physics Playground*: Shute et al., 2015, 2021).

There are many ways that AIED-based digital learning games can be categorized, for instance, by whether they are pure games or "gamified," by their instructional topic, by the AI techniques used, by the degree of learning impact they've had, and so on. To provide a structure to the review of this chapter, we present AIED games according to the four major ways in which AI has been used in the context of learning games:

1. *AI-Based Adaptation*: Digital learning games that employ AI to perform adaptation in real-time during play. That is, games that provide customized support (e.g., hints and error messages, problems appropriate to a student's current level of understanding, difficulty adjustment) to help students solve problems and learn (Martin et al., 2021).
2. *AI-Based Decision Support*: Digital learning games that feature AI-powered interactive dashboards or recommendations; that is, these are games that don't make decisions for students, such as presenting the next problem or step to take, but instead present options, based on students' on-going performance.
3. *AI Character Interaction*: Games that employ an AI-driven non-player character (or characters) (NPC) to support the learning process with the games. These types of games rely on a "companion" to support students as they learn.
4. *Use of Learning Analytics (LA) and/or Educational Data Mining (EDM) for Game Analysis and Improvement*: These are AIED games that don't explicitly use AI for gameplay or game mechanics, but instead employ AI to do post-game analysis. This analysis is typically done for one of two reasons: to better understand how students interact with the game or to iteratively improve the game.

We also present the games according to their general instructional domain (i.e., math, computer science, natural science, humanities). Table 20.1 summarizes the prominent AIED digital learning games that are reviewed in this chapter. We identified these games by using three

Table 20.1   *Summary of AIED digital learning games*

	AI-based adaptation	AI-based decision support	AI character interaction	Use of learning analytics (LA) and/or educational data mining (EDM) for game analysis and improvement
Math	*Maths Garden* (Klinkenberg et al., 2011) *MathSpring** (Arroyo et al., 2014; 2013) *Prime Climb** (Conati et al., 2013)	*Decimal Point** (Harpstead et al., 2019; Hou et al., 2020, 2021; McLaren et al., 2017) *Gamified Lynnette* (Long & Aleven, 2014, 2018)	*MathSpring** (Arroyo et al., 2013, 2014) *Squares Family* (Pareto, 2009, 2014; Sjödén et al., 2017)	*Battleship Numberline* (Lomas et al., 2013, 2012, 2011) *Decimal Point** (Nguyen et al., 2019, 2020) *Heroes of Math Island* (Conati & Gutica, 2016) *Prime Climb** (Conati & Zhou, 2002) *Refraction* (O'Rourke et al., 2016, 2015; O'Rourke, Ballweber et al., 2014; O'Rourke, Haimovitz, et al., 2014) *Reasoning Mind* (Ocumpaugh et al., 2013) *ST Math* (Peddycord-Liu et al., 2017) *Zombie Division* (Baker et al., 2007; Habgood & Ainsworth, 2011)
Computer Science	*AutoThinking** (Hooshyar et al., 2021) *Gamified SQL-Tutor* (Tahir et al., 2020) *Minerva* (Lindberg et al., 2017, 2018; Lindberg & Laine, 2016)	*TALENT** (Maragos, 2013)	*AutoThinking** (Hooshyar et al., 2021)* *ARIN-561* (Wang et al., 2022) *ELIA* (Kaczmarek & Petroviča, 2018) *TALENT** (Maragos, 2013) *TurtleTalk* (Jung et al., 2019)	*Zoombinis* (Rowe et al., 2020, 2021)
Natural Science	*ELEKTRA* (Peirce et al., 2008) *Physics Playground** (Shute et al., 2021)	*Physics Playground** (Shute et al., 2019; Shute, 2011)	*Betty's Brain** (Biswas et al., 2016) *Crystal Island** (Lester et al., 2013)	*Beanstalk* (Aleven et al., 2013; Harpstead & Aleven, 2015) *Betty's Brain** (Kinnebrew et al., 2017; Munshi et al., 2018; Segedy et al., 2015) *Crystal Island** (Sabourin et al., 2013; Sawyer et al., 2017) *Physics Playground** (Shute et al., 2015)

(Continued)

Table 20.1   (Continued)

	AI-based adaptation	AI-based decision support	AI character interaction	Use of learning analytics (LA) and/or educational data mining (EDM) for game analysis and improvement
Humanities	iStart-2 (Jackson & McNamara, 2011; Jacovina et al., 2016) *Navigo* (Benton et al., 2021) *Policy World* (Easterday et al., 2017)	*Keep Attention* (Hocine, 2019; Hocine et al., 2019) *Tactical Language and Culture Training System** (Johnson, 2010)	*ECHOES* (Bernardini et al. 2014) *Tactical Language and Culture Training System** (Johnson, 2010)	*Downtown: A Subway Adventure* (Cano et al., 2018, 2016) *TC3Sim* (Henderson et al., 2020a, 2020b)

Note: * A digital learning game that is in more than one of the AI categories

prominent databases: Google Scholar, Springer, and Elsevier. In each database, we entered the search query as a combination of three terms: (1) the learning domain, corresponding to a row in Table 20.1 (e.g., "math," "computer science"), the type of AI, corresponding to a column in Table 20.1 (e.g., "adaptation," "interaction"), and (3) the keyword "game." While Table 20.1 provides a substantial number of digital learning games (more than 30), it is likely missing some games that could have been included, that is, it is meant to be a close-to (but perhaps not quite) comprehensive literature review.[1] In addition, as we focus our search dimensions on the learning domain and type of AI, we note that the reviewed games vary broadly in other characteristics, such as maturity, sample sizes of empirical studies, and research findings.

AI-Based Adaptation

Perhaps the most common way that AI is and has been used in AIED digital learning games is by adapting games to individual students and their learning progress. Usually, this means adapting the difficulty of a game, problems within the game, or hints to optimize the game's learning potential (Martin et al., 2021). This approach is derivative of what has long been done with intelligent tutoring systems (VanLehn, 2006, 2011), using approaches such as Bayesian Knowledge Tracing (Corbett & Anderson, 1995) and item response theory (Elo, 1978; Embretson & Reise, 2000).

Perhaps it is unsurprising that adapting instruction for individual students is a key research area of AIED digital learning games, given how much attention this type of computer-based instruction has been given in AIED research since its earliest days (Self, 2016) and until recently (see Chapter 9 by Aleven et al.). As John Self, one of the founders of the AIED research community, reported in his summary of the history of the field:

> AIED systems were, almost by definition, the only ones that carried out a significant, real-time analysis of the interaction with learners, in order to adapt that interaction. Other systems claimed to be adaptive, but they were really only reacting in pre-specified ways to different inputs. AIED systems responded in ways that had not been prespecified or even envisaged. And that, of course, is the essential difference between AI programs and general computer programs. (Self, 2016, p. 9)

In fact, what Self says is essentially the difference between many of the games described in this chapter and, for instance, the games that have come from non-AIED research (Mayer, 2019). On the other hand, it is important that the emphasis is not only on the AI in games, but, like the many games that Mayer (2019) discusses, that AIED digital learning games are proven in well-designed, randomized controlled experiments.

In what follows, we first describe in detail two representative "AI-based adaptation" games from Table 20.1 – one in mathematics (*MathSpring*) and one in humanities (*Policy World*). We also discuss how AI has specifically been used for adaptation in those games, as well as the empirical results that studies with these games have uncovered. Finally, we present and discuss in a more succinct fashion other "AI-based adaptation" games and summarize what we have learned about AI-based adaption games.

MathSpring (Arroyo et al., 2013, 2014) is a single-player online game for fourth- through seventh-grade students to practice math problem solving (Figure 20.1(a)). The game, which was developed as a gamified extension to the tutoring system *Wayang Outpost*, adapts problem difficulty to student performance and offers hints, feedback, worked-out examples, and tutorial videos. The game also provides socio-emotional support from "learning companion" characters (hence this game is also found in the "AI Character Interaction" category). The game supports strategic and problem-solving abilities based on the theory of cognitive apprenticeship (Collins et al., 1989). The software models solutions via worked-out examples with the use of sound and animation and provides practice opportunities on math word problems.

MathSpring uses an AI-based adaptation algorithm to maintain students within their zone of proximal development (Vygotsky, 1978); in particular, the algorithm adapts problem difficulty. The *MathSpring* approach, referred to by the authors as "effort-based tutoring" (EBT), adapts problem selection depending on the effort exerted by a student on a practice activity based on three dimensions of student behavior: attempts to solve a problem, help requested, and time to answer. In addition, student affect is automatically predicted while students play the game. Initially, this was achieved through information from physiological sensors and student behavior within the game. Later, machine-learned detectors were created to predict student emotions. The game also uses AI to drive the learning companion, an animated digital character that speaks to the student (Figure 20.1(b)), deemphasizing the importance of immediate success and instead encouraging effort.

MathSpring has been used in middle schools in the US as part of regular math classes since 2004, in some instances just before students take the Massachusetts statewide-standardized test exams. In a variety of studies involving hundreds of students, the game has led to improved performance in mathematics and on the state standardized tests. It has also led to improved engagement and affective outcomes for groups of students as a whole, as well as for certain subgroups, for example, female students and low-achieving students.

Policy World (Easterday et al., 2017) is a digital learning game targeted at university students in which the player assumes the role of a policy analyst (Figure 20.2(a)) who must defend the public against an unscrupulous corporate lobbyist (Figure 20.2(b)) by persuading a Senator (Figure 20.2(c)) to adopt evidence-based policies that protect the public interest. The game has two modes of operation: game only and game+tutor, the second of which includes a back-end intelligent tutoring system that provides step-level feedback and immediate error correction. The narrative of Policy World emphasizes empowerment: a young policy analyst (i.e., the student playing the game) is recognized as having potential by the head of a policy think-tank. The student is guided by two mentor characters: another young but more senior analyst, and

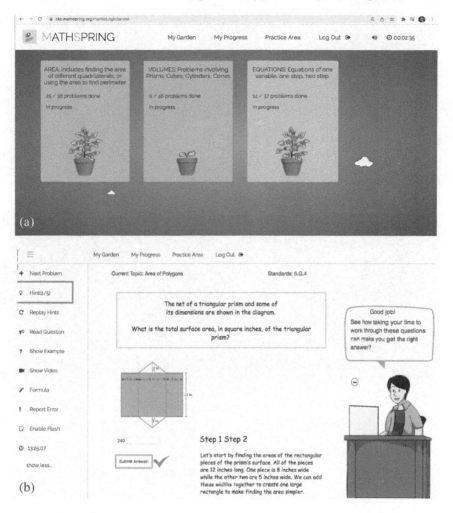

Source: Figures provided by Ivon Arroyo, reproduced by permission

Figure 20.1   *In MathSpring, students use math to grow plants representing progress and effort in the game (a). Plants might bloom and give peppers, or wither if students show disengagement. (b) shows an example of an AI-driven learning companion in MathSpring, used to encourage students' effort*

a sharp-tongued virtual tutor that teaches the student to analyze policies (Figure 20.2(d)). At the end of the game, the player is tested through simulated senate hearings. The player must debate two policies with the corporate lobbyist to save the think-tank's reputation and defend the public against the corrupt agenda.

Policy World provides error flagging, situational feedback, and penalties for errors. The game+tutor version, which is the one that uses AI techniques for adaptation, is the same in all regards except that, as mentioned above, it also includes step-level feedback and immediate error correction (as in most intelligent tutoring systems; see VanLehn, 2006, 2011).

Figure 20.2   Policy World screenshots of the agents involved in the policy debate: (a) the player, (b) the lobbyist, (c) the senator, and (d) the tutor

A total of 105 university students were recruited for a study with *Policy World*. Based on the results of a series of ANOVAs, the game+tutor version resulted in more learning of policy analysis skills and self-reported competence, compared with the game-only version. A path analysis supported the claim that the greater assistance provided by the game+tutor helped students learn analysis better, which increased their feelings of competence, which in turn increased their interest in the game.

As shown in Table 20.1, other AI-based adaptive games include *Maths Garden, Prime Climb, AutoThinking, Minerva,* the *Gamified SQL Tutor, ELEKTRA, iSTART-2, and Navigo.* Mathematics is a key focus area of games in this category, with *Maths Garden* (Klinkenberg et al., 2011) as a prime example. *Maths Garden* is a single-player game used to help K-8 students learn mathematics operations, such as whole number addition, subtraction, multiplication, and division. Students click on different flower beds to try out the different mathematical operations and gain points (coins) by answering prompted questions correctly and lose coins by answering incorrectly. The game reward comes in two forms: first, the flowers in the various flower beds grow as the student makes progress; second, the coins earned from the math tasks can be used to purchase virtual prizes. *Maths Garden* is distinguished as an AIED digital learning game by adapting its problem content within each garden, using an item-response model based on the Elo (1978) rating system. The game has been empirically tested with over 3,500 participants and results indicate that the Elo scoring model is highly correlated with an independent math test and students become highly engaged with the game. Another AI adaptive digital learning game that is targeted at math learning is *Prime Climb* (Conati et al., 2013). *Prime Climb* is a collaborative, two-player learning game in which fifth- and sixth-grade students practice number factorization by climbing a series of "number mountains," composed of numbered hexagons. Players move to numbers in the hexagons that do not share common factors with their partner's number. The two players rely on and cooperate with one another to reach the top of the mountain. Each player can make one or more moves before turning the control to the other player. The game is adaptive through its hints, which are provided to assist the students in climbing the mountain. Using a probabilistic student model, the game predicts when a student doesn't have the factorization skill required for a particular move. The game gives hints at incremental levels of detail. Conati et al.'s most important finding was that students with a positive attitude toward help tend to pay attention to hint content after correct moves, while students with a negative attitude towards help tend to pay attention to hints after incorrect moves, and students with a neutral attitude towards help show limited attention to hints.

A second key focus of AIED digital learning games in this category has been computational thinking and computer programming. For instance, *AutoThinking* (Hooshyar et al., 2021) is a recent adaptive, single-player digital learning game designed to promote elementary-age students' skills and conceptual knowledge in computational thinking (CT). In this game, the player takes the role of a mouse in a maze seeking cheese and evading two cats. Players write "programs" using icons representing program steps to create solutions to evade the cats. One of the two cats is "intelligent," and the other is random. After the player completes a solution, the "intelligent cat" adapts using student log data and a Bayesian Network algorithm that decides which algorithm it should use next to pursue the player and, if necessary, what kind of feedback or hints to provide to the player. In comparison with a more conventional, computer-based approach to learning CT, *AutoThinking* was found to be especially helpful to students with lower prior knowledge. Hooshyar and colleagues also found that *AutoThinking* improved students' attitudes toward CT more than the conventional approach. (Due to the AI-based cat, *AutoThinking* also falls into the "AI Character Interaction" category, which we introduce later in the chapter.) A second CT example is *Minerva* (Lindberg et al., 2018, 2017) a single-player game designed to teach programming to elementary school students, covering five concepts: input, output, math, loop, and condition. In the game, players control a robot to navigate puzzles and repair a damaged ship, while avoiding aliens and other obstacles. The puzzles require players to learn different programming concepts to achieve their task. The adaptation of Minerva is to students' "learning styles" (Lindberg & Laine, 2016), a concept that is controversial, since students having different learning styles has been largely debunked in various learning science literature (Pashler et al., 2008). Despite the perhaps misguided focus of this research, it is another example of "AI-based Adaptation" and a programming focused game. As a final example of games focused on computational thinking and programming, the *Gamified SQL Tutor* (Tahir et al., 2020) includes game elements beyond the well-known, adaptive intelligent tutoring system, *SQL Tutor*, which teaches students the Standard Query Language (SQL). The *SQL Tutor* has been shown in many studies to lead to learning benefits (Mitrovic, 2012). The *Gamified SQL Tutor* was an attempt to gain additional learning benefits by adding "badges" to the tutor related to goals, assessment, and challenges. For instance, if students complete three problems in one session or five problems in one day, they receive goal badges. In a study with 77 undergraduate students, Tahir and colleagues found that while *Gamified SQL Tutor* didn't lead to better learning outcomes than *SQL Tutor*, time on task was found to be a significant mediator between badges and achievement in the gamified condition. This suggests that badges *can* motivate students to spend more time learning with the *SQL Tutor*.

AI-based adaptive games have also been developed to support reading (*iSTART-2*; Jackson & McNamara, 2011; Jacovina et al., 2016; *Navigo*: Benton et al., 2021) and science learning (*ELEKTRA*: Peirce et al., 2008). The highlights of these games include that *iSTART-2* (previously called *iStart-ME*: Jackson & McNamara, 2011) uses AI natural language techniques to assess student self-explanations and adapt gameplay and feedback accordingly; *Navigo* relies on AI-based rules to ensure the learner is at an appropriate reading level within the game, to be sure the language the student encounters is diverse; and that the student generally progresses towards reading fluency. In *ELEKTRA*, which is targeted at 13- to 15-year-old students, AI rules are also used to assess a student's holistic game experience and to execute adaptation that is both pedagogically helpful and non-invasive.

So what have we learned thus far from the research with AI-based adaptation of digital learning games? First, as mentioned above, it is clear that research with intelligent tutoring systems (VanLehn, 2006, 2011) has created a blueprint and paved the way for how adaptation has been implemented, at least thus far, in many digital learning games. The focus on adapting problems and feedback to the level of understanding or skill exhibited by a student is, unsurprisingly, core to most of the games in this category. Some of the most successful work in the "AI-based Adaptation" category of learning games, such as with *MathSpring* and *iStart-2*, essentially started as research with intelligent tutoring systems that later shifted into research with gamified intelligent tutors. Second, it is encouraging to see AI game adaptation be successfully applied in a wide variety of domains, including mathematics (e.g., *MathSpring*, *Maths Garden*), science (e.g., *ELEKTRA*), language learning (e.g., *iStart-2*, *Navigo*), computer science (e.g., *AutoThinking*, *Minerva*) and policy analysis (e.g., *Policy World*). This suggests that adapting instructional content is not constrained to any particular domain or game type. Finally, while adaptive digital learning games appear to be largely focused on elementary to middle-school age students – for instance, with the games *MathSpring*, *Minerva*, *Prime Climb*, and *AutoThinking* – the games within this category show that adaptive games can also be effective with older students, for instance, as shown with *Policy World* and *Gamified SQL Tutor*.

AI-Based Decision Support

AI-based decision support is another relatively common approach found in AIED digital learning games. As opposed to "AI-based Adaptation," these games allow the student to make their own choices of problems to solve and game paths to follow, but with support from an AI recommender system. Often these types of games employ a dashboard or open learner model (OLM: Bull & Kay, 2008; Bull, 2020) to provide the choices to students, as well as data supporting their options. The games in this category are often intended to support and explore self-regulated learning (SRL: Zimmerman & Schunk, 2008), in particular, prompting students to carefully consider their learning trajectories and move thoughtfully forward in the game and in their learning.

As in the previous section, we first describe in detail two representative "AI-based Decision Support" games – one in the domain of mathematics (*Decimal Point*) and one in science (*Physics Playground*). We also discuss how AI has been used for decision support in these games, as well as empirical results from studies with the games. We then summarize and discuss other "AI-based Decision Support" games and, finally, discuss what we have learned thus far from research with "AI-based Decision Support" games.

Decimal Point (Harpstead et al., 2019; Hou et al., 2020, 2021; McLaren et al., 2017; Nguyen et al., 2018; 2022) is a web-based, single-player digital learning game that helps fifth- through seventh-grade students reinforce their knowledge about decimal numbers and decimal operations. The game features an amusement park metaphor with eight theme areas and 24 mini-games (Figure 20.3(a)) that target common decimal misconceptions. The mini-games support playful problem-solving activities (e.g., entering a haunted house, shooting objects in the wild west), each of which connects with one of five decimal exercise types: number line, addition, sequence, bucket, and sorting. As an example, in the mini-game *Whack-A-Gopher* (Figure 20.3(b)), students need to correctly "whack" the gophers, who pop up and retreat at random times, in the order of their number labels. Students receive immediate feedback on their answers and play until they get the correct answer. After each mini-game, students are prompted to answer a self-explanation question to reinforce their understanding (Chi et al., 1994, 1989; Wylie & Chi, 2014). There have been a variety of studies of *Decimal Point* over the years, exploring issues such as student agency (Nguyen et al., 2018), indirect control (Harpstead et al., 2019), instructional context (McLaren et al., 2022a), and adaptive recommendations (Hou et al., 2020, 2021).

One study with *Decimal Point* included an AI-based recommender system that recommends the next mini-game to select from the game map to maximize either learning or enjoyment (Hou et al., 2020, 2021). In the learning-oriented version of *Decimal Point*, the student's mastery of each decimal skill is assessed in real time with Bayesian Knowledge Tracing (BKT: Corbett & Anderson, 1995). Students see their mastery visualized through an open learner model (Bull, 2020) and are recommended to play more mini-games in the two least-mastered skills (Figure 20.3(c)). In the enjoyment-oriented version of the game, the student's rating of each mini-game round is collected after they finish it, and students are recommended to play more mini-games of the type they like the most (Figure 20.3(d)). *Decimal Point* data has also been used in EDM research that uncovers students' learning difficulties (Nguyen et al., 2020), as well as the relationship between in-game learning and post-test / delayed post-test performance (Nguyen et al., 2020). Thus, the *Decimal Point* game is also found in the "Use of Learning Analytics ..." category of AIED digital learning games.

A media comparison study (Mayer, 2019) with the original version of the *Decimal Point* game showed a strong learning benefit over an intelligent tutoring system with the same content (McLaren et al., 2017). For the version that included AI-based recommender discussed above, 196 fifth- and sixth-grade students participated in a study (Hou et al., 2020, 2021). Three game conditions were examined: a learning-focused condition featuring the BKT-based dashboard (Figure 20.3(c)), an enjoyment-focused condition featuring the playful dashboard (Figure 20.3(d)), and a control condition with a neutral dashboard (i.e., a dashboard that does not present either skill mastery or enjoyment scores to the student) (Figure 20.3(e)). Results from the study indicated that the students in the enjoyment-focused group learned more efficiently than the control group, and that females had higher learning gains than males across all conditions. (Subsequent studies have replicated this gender effect – see Nguyen et al., 2022.) *Post hoc* analyses also revealed that the learning-focused group re-practiced the same mini-games, while the enjoyment-focused group explored a wider variety of mini-games. These findings suggest that adaptively emphasizing learning or enjoyment can result in distinctive

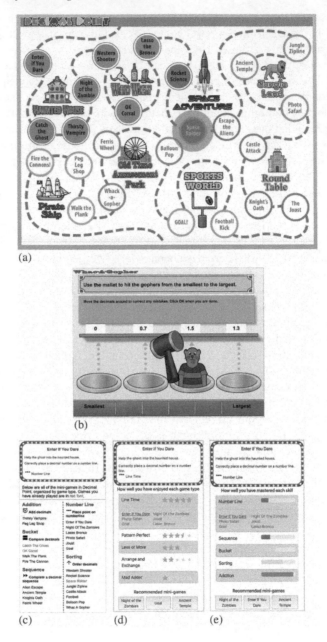

(a)

(b)

(c)   (d)   (e)

Source: Figure from Hou et al. (2021), reproduced by permission from the authors

Figure 20.3   *The main game map on the top left allows students to see the 24 mini-games of Decimal Point (a), an example mini-game on the top right in which the student "whacks" moles in the order of smallest to largest decimal number (b), while the recommender dashboard for the control version of the game (c), the enjoyment-oriented version of the game (d) and the learning-oriented version of the game (e) are shown left to right at the bottom*

gameplay behaviors from students, and that *Decimal Point* can help bridge the gender gap in math education.

Physics Playground (PP: Shute et al., 2019, 2021; Shute, 2011) is a digital learning game designed to enhance the physics understanding of middle to high school students. *PP* was originally designed to be a single-player game but has more recently been converted and also used in a collaborative learning mode (Sun et al., 2020, 2022). The goal of students using *PP* is simple – hit a red balloon using a green ball and various provided tools. In its first version, *PP* included only one type of game level: sketching. Using a mouse or stylus, players could draw objects on the screen, create simple "machines" (i.e., ramp, lever, pendulum, or spring-board), and target the red balloon with the green ball. The second and most recent version of the game incorporates a new task type, manipulation levels, where drawing is disabled with players instead moving the ball to the balloon using new tools, including (1) sliders related to mass, gravity, and air resistance, (2) the ability to make the ball bounce by clicking the boun-ciness checkbox, and (3) new sources of external force (e.g., a puffer, and static and dynamic blowers). *PP* includes *stealth assessment*, in which real-time assessment is embedded in the learning environment, invisible to the learner (Shute, 2011). The idea behind stealth assess-ment is to assess student skills, and how students are dynamically advancing in those skills, without incurring the usual anxiety and time commitment that comes from standard testing.

To engage and enhance student performance, Shute et al. (2019) recently added AI-based learning supports and, in particular, an incentive and recommendation system called *My Backpack*. When clicked, *My Backpack* provides information about the player's progress and physics understanding, as well as a space to customize gameplay (e.g., the type of ball they use). More specifically, the "Physics" tab shows the estimated competency level for each targeted physics concept – essentially an open learner model, based on real-time stealth assessment. Because stealth assessment is used to personalize content and adapt feedback (Shute et al., 2021), the *Physics Playground* is also in the "AI-Based Adaptation" category discussed previ-ously. In addition, Shute et al. (2015) have performed post-gameplay analyses of student log data to investigate student affect and predictors of learning outcomes while game playing; thus, *PP* is also in the "Use of Learning-Analytics ..." category of AIED digital learning games.

Shute and colleagues have conducted many studies with *PP* since its initial creation as "Newton's Playground" (Shute & Ventura, 2013). For example, Shute et al. (2015) reports a study with 137 eighth- and ninth-grade students who played *PP* for 2.5 hours. The students had a significant increase in scores from pre-test to post-test, thus indicating that *PP* does indeed lead to physics learning. In post-gameplay analyses, they also found evidence that (1) both the pre-test and the in-game measure of student performance significantly predicted learning outcomes and (2) a detector of frustration, a detector of engaged concentration, and the pre-test predicted the in-game measure of performance. Finally, they found evidence for pathways from engaged concentration and frustration to learning, via the in-game pro-gress measure. More recently, Shute et al. (2021) conducted a study to explore the benefits of the *PP* learning supports, such as *My Backpack*, a glossary, and animations of physics concepts. The study included 263 ninth-to-eleventh graders who played *PP* for 4 hours. In this study, students were randomly assigned to one of four conditions: an adaptive version of *PP*, in which a Bayesian algorithm was used to present game levels to students according to their physics competencies; a linear version, in which students followed a predetermined sequence of game levels; a free-choice version, in which the students were presented the lin-ear sequence of levels, but could skip levels, and a no-treatment control. Surprisingly, there were no significant differences in learning between the four conditions. However, Shute and colleagues found that stealth assessment was an accurate estimate of students' physics understanding (i.e., stealth assessment was highly correlated with external physics scores), and physics animations were the most effective of eight supports in predicting both learning and in-game performance. Like the *Decimal Point* study discussed previously, this study is an excellent example of how digital learning games are becoming tremendous platforms for pursuing various research questions, such as whether self-regulated learning can be productive in a game context and what the effects of various types of support are in game-based learning.

There are fewer learning games in the "AI-based Decision Support" category than in any of the other learning games categories, but the few games that include decision support, typically in the form of an open learner model, include *Gamified Lynnette, TALENT, Keep Attention*, and the *Tactical Language and Cultural Training System (TLCTS)*. *Gamified Lynnette* (Long & Aleven, 2014) is an example of a gamified intelligent tutoring system, based on the linear equation tutor *Lynnette* (Waalkens et al., 2013). To extend *Lynette* with game features – creating what we (but not the authors) call *Gamified Lynnette* – Long and Aleven added two key features: (1) the possibility to re-practice problems, under student control, and (2) rewards given to students based on their performance on individual problems. The two features are connected (at least loosely) as students are encouraged to re-practice by earning rewards. The core AI technique of *Gamified Lynnette* is its use of BKT (Corbett & Anderson, 1995) to assess students' skills and to support problem selection, either by the system (implementing mastery learning) or student (through an OLM dashboard, thus, its inclusion in the "AI-based Decision Support" category). *Gamified Lynnette*'s dashboard shows the student their rewards (i.e., badges) and allows students to select the BKT-assessed problem to tackle next. In their first experiment with *Gamified Lynnette*, Long and Aleven compared four versions of *Gamified Lynnette*, with and without re-practice enabled and with and without rewards, as well as to standard *Lynnette* (i.e., with problems all system selected and no dashboard) and *DragonBox* (www.dragonboxapp.com), a highly acclaimed and popular commercial digital learning game that covers the same mathematics content as *Gamified Lynnette*. A total of 267 seventh- and eighth-grade students were randomly assigned to the six conditions, with 190 of those students finishing all activities and thus being subject to analyses. Long and Aleven did not find a significant difference between the different versions of *Gamified Lynnette* and the *Lynnette* control with respect to enjoyment or learning. However, *Gamified Lynnette* students who had the freedom to re-practice problems, but were not given rewards, performed significantly better on the post-tests than their counterparts who received rewards. This suggests that adding game features – in this case rewards – does not always enhance learning. Of particular note is that each of the *Gamified Lynnette* conditions led to more learning than the *DragonBox* condition, indicating that just a small dose of game features added to more traditional learning technology may be enough to lead to more learning versus a game. Long and Aleven (2018) later re-analyzed the 190 students of the Long and Aleven (2014) study, comparing the combined results of the five versions of *Lynnette* (i.e., the four gamified and the original, non-gamified versions of *Lynnette*) with *DragonBox*. They found that while students solved more problems and enjoyed playing *DragonBox* more, they learned more using *Lynnette* and *Gamified Lynnette*. This is an important additional finding to that of Long and Aleven (2014), as it shows that full-scale digital learning games, such as *DragonBox*, while often more engaging, may not always lead to better learning outcomes than more traditional and/or gamified technology. This finding further emphasizes the importance of conducting empirical studies of learning

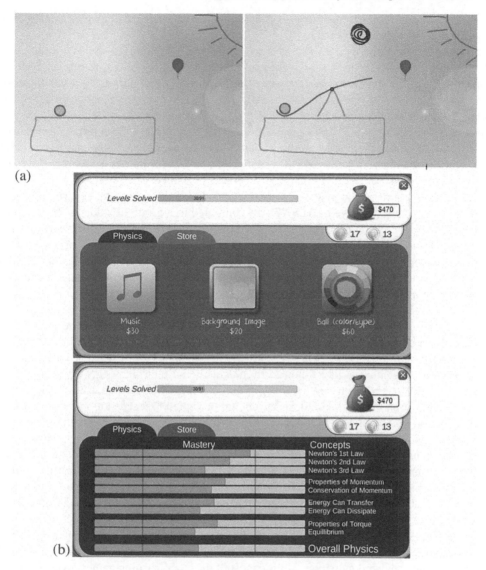

Figure 20.4   *The figure at the top (a) is an example of a student solving a Physics Playground problem by drawing a lever with a weight on one side of the lever to hit the balloon. At the bottom (b) is the My Backpack view, which provides estimates of student progress, physics skill, and concept understanding*

games (something that had not been done previously with *DragonBox*) before setting them loose with students in classrooms.

Another representative game in this category is *TALENT* (Maragos, 2013), a multiplayer adventure game that helps high school students learn introductory programming. To play and learn with *TALENT* students explore a game world, solving programming tasks as they proceed. They can chat with one another to discuss their game progress or exchange programming advice. *TALENT* has an open learner model based on information about the student's in-game activities, such as navigation, tool usage, and learning progress. Furthermore, it proposes the next mission to undertake, based on the student's current level of game-assessed knowledge. The game also features a pedagogical agent whose role is to provide real-time hints (and thus *TALENT* is also in the "AI Character Interaction" category). A study of *TALENT* was conducted with 65 high school students, over a period of eight weeks. An experimental condition in which students played *TALENT* was compared to a group of students that attended traditional lectures. While both groups improved from pre-test to post-test, the experimental group had significantly higher post-test scores. However, given the stark comparison of traditional classroom instruction with the *TALENT* game, including collaboration and an OLM, it is not clear which feature, or combination of features, led to the better learning outcomes of the game-playing group.

Two other games in the "AI-based Decision Support" category are *Keep Attention* and *TLCTS*. *Keep Attention* (Hocine, 2019; Hocine et al., 2019) is a learning game for children with attention deficit disorders and trains attention skills (Hocine et al., 2019), as well as self-regulation skills (Hocine, 2019). The base game operates by first using basic tasks to assess students' attention skills, followed by personalizing their gameplay training – using the assessed skills as a guide – in a variety of game contexts (e.g., a zoo, card playing, outer space). For instance, in the zoo context players are prompted to rescue animals, while avoiding insects and monsters. The basic assessment is composed of selective attention tasks that prompt players, under time pressure, to select given targets in different contexts, while avoiding obstacles (distractors). In one version of the game, an open learner model (OLM) was developed to explore self-regulated learning by allowing users to reflect upon their actions during assessment and make decisions about their subsequent gameplay. The OLM uses a visual presentation of the player's performance, analyzed using AI techniques. To gamify the player's interaction with the OLM, *Keep Attention* prompts the player to predict their performance in the assessment exercises and levels based on an interactive questionnaire that provides feedback. Through the OLM, players can decide whether to accept or not the system's decisions on personalized gameplay. Unlike most of the other learning games reviewed in this chapter, no large-scale empirical studies have been conducted with *Keep Attention*. However, in a pilot study of the open learner model with 16 middle school students (Hocine, 2019) it was found that without the OLM, subjects found it difficult to assess their attention level, and consequently to choose the appropriate level of difficulty in the game context. Conversely, it appeared that what students learned about their attention from the OLM helped them during subsequent gameplay. While the *TLCTS* game is more representative of the "AI Character Interaction" category, given its extensive use of interactive NPCs to support language and culture learning, it also uses an AI recommender system to give learners advice on which lessons and game episodes to tackle next. *TLCTS* is described in more detail in the next section,

As with other forms of educational technology, open learner models and recommender systems in digital learning games are designed to support and enhance students' self-regulated learning skills, ultimately leading, it is hoped, to better learning outcomes. OLMs seem especially appropriate for digital game contexts, given that computer-based games often allow players to make their own decisions about the next game level, challenge, or pathway to pursue during play. The difference in digital learning games is that player choices are not only about engagement and enjoyment but also about optimizing learning outcomes. So far, the results have been inconclusive regarding the benefits of OLMs in digital learning games. For instance, the learning-focused OLM in *Decimal Point* did not lead to clear learning benefits over the enjoyment-focused OLM; in fact, the enjoyment-focused OLM led to more efficient learning than for the students in the control group. Also, the *Physics Playground* OLM (i.e., *My Backpack*) may have helped students but did not lead conclusively to better learning. There is at least a hint that the dashboard of *Gamified Lynnette* may have been responsible for better learning outcomes, given the better learning outcomes of the *Gamified Lynnette* with a dashboard but without rewards over *Gamified Lynnette* with rewards. Even so, further study, focused on testing the dashboard, would be necessary to confirm the benefits of a dashboard. In short, the jury is still out on the impact and benefits of AI-supported OLMs and recommender systems in the context of digital learning games. Testing OLMs and recommender systems with digital learning games is perhaps more challenging and complicated than with other learning technologies, given the trade-offs and tension between engagement and learning inherent in digital learning games.

AI Character Interaction

AI-based character interaction involves the use of Non-Player Characters, commonly called NPCs, engaging and interacting with students as they play a digital learning game. In the context of digital learning systems and games, these characters are also sometimes called "pedagogical agents" (Johnson & Lester, 2018): virtual characters that are part of learning scenarios and engage in rich interactions with students. Some games that have already been discussed in this chapter also fall into this category, including *MathSpring* (Arroyo et al., 2013, 2014), which uses NPCs to provide socio-emotional support to students, and the *Tactical Language and Culture Training System* (Johnson, 2010), which was briefly discussed in the previous section, and which uses NPCs to help adult trainees understand foreign language and culture. "AI Character Interaction" games often employ AI in the form of Natural Language Processing (NLP), as well as machine learning to develop the language capabilities and affect of such characters.

In this section we describe in detail three highly representative "AI Character Interaction" games, across the disparate domains of microbiology (*Crystal Island*), language and cultural instruction (the *Tactical Language and Culture Training System*, TLCTS), and programming (*TurtleTalk*). We describe the NPCs that have been implemented in those games and how AI has been used to bring the NPCs to life as interactive pedagogical agents with human learners. In some cases, in particular with *Crystal Island*, we also discuss other ways that AI has been employed in the game. We also summarize the results attained from experimenting with these three games, ranging from extensive and substantial in the case of *Crystal Island* to very preliminary in the case of *TurtleTalk*. We also briefly discuss other games that fall within the category of "AI Character Interaction" games and conclude by discussing what has been learned thus far from "AI Character Interaction" game research.

Crystal Island (Lester et al., 2013) is a single-player narrative learning game designed for the domain of microbiology, typically targeted at late-middle-school students (but even university students have been a target population). The game features a science mystery situated on a remote tropical island (Figure 20.5(a)). Within the narrative of *Crystal Island*, the student plays the role of a medical field agent attempting to discover the identity of an infectious disease plaguing the island inhabitants. To solve the mystery, the student collects data and symptoms, forms hypotheses, and tests those hypotheses by interviewing a number of NPCs on the island, including a camp nurse, the camp cook, and virus and bacterial scientists. The student's learning is scaffolded by interaction with the NPCs (Figure 20.5(b)) and a diagnosis worksheet (Figure 20.5(c)). When the student makes an incorrect diagnosis, the camp nurse identifies the error and provides feedback. The student successfully completes the game when they correctly identify the illness and specify an appropriate treatment.

A variety of AI techniques have been employed and tested with *Crystal Island*, including narrative-centered tutorial planning (Lee et al., 2011, 2012), student knowledge modeling (Rowe & Lester, 2010), and student goal recognition and affect recognition models (Sabourin et al., 2011). Most of these AI directions have been aimed at making the camp nurse smarter and more adaptable to and supportive of students playing the game. For instance, the narrative-centered tutorial planning uses a dynamic decision network (Dean & Kanazawa, 1989) to update the beliefs of the NPCs and to select actions that maximize expected tutorial utility. For student modeling and affect recognition, Lester and colleagues developed a dynamic Bayesian network that connects student goals (e.g., mastery or performance) with emotions (e.g., boredom, confusion) and actions (e.g., notes taken, tests run) (Rowe & Lester, 2010). The game's data have also recently been analyzed with deep learning techniques to build student models from log data and reflection texts (Geden et al., 2021), to recognize student goals from game events and eye tracking (Min et al., 2017), and to enable data-driven and interactive narrative personalization (Wang et al., 2017). These data mining studies also place *Crystal Island* in the "Use of Learning Analytics ..." game category, still to be discussed.

Crystal Island is one of the earliest developed and most prolific AIED learning games; it has been the subject of many empirical studies, exploring a variety of issues – like *Decimal Point* and *Physics Playground*, it has proven to be an excellent research platform. Here, we cite and summarize just four studies. An early observational study conducted by Rowe et al. (2011), in which the goal was to investigate the synergistic impact of engagement and learning, 150 students played *Crystal Island*. Students achieved significant learning gains from pre- to post-test, providing evidence that the game is effective in engaging learners and supporting learning. In an experiment comparing three narrative-centered tutorial planning models, 150 eighth-grade students used *Crystal Island*, completing a pre- and post-test (Lee et al., 2012). While it was found that all students learned, only students in the "full guidance" condition (compared with intermediate and minimal guidance conditions) achieved significant learning gains. A study that did not yield positive learning outcomes for *Crystal Island* was conducted by Adams et al. (2012) in which students using *Crystal Island* were compared with students viewing a slideshow with the same microbiology materials. The *Crystal Island* group performed much worse than the slideshow group on a subsequent test of infectious disease with an effect size of −0.31. Finally, in Sawyer et al. (2017), Lester's lab explored the concept of *agency*, that is, student (versus system) control within a game. In this study, 105 college-age students were randomly assigned to one of three agency conditions: high agency, which allowed students to navigate to island locations in any order; low agency, which restricted students to a prescribed order of navigation; and no agency, in which students simply watched a video of an expert playing *Crystal Island*. They found that students in the low agency condition attempted more incorrect submissions but also attained significantly higher learning

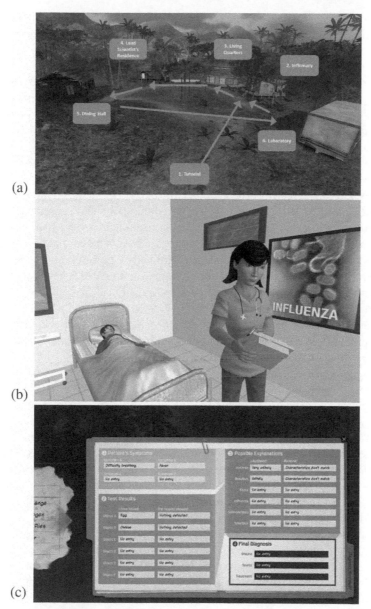

Source: Figures from Taub et al. (2020) and Lester et al. (2013), reproduced by permission from the authors

Figure 20.5   *The locations on Crystal Island where the student can visit to solve the infectious disease mystery (a). The student interacts with AI-infused NPCs, such as the camp nurse and patients (b). A diagnosis worksheet scaffolds students learning; they can record their findings in the worksheet (c)*

gains. Their results suggest that limiting agency in their game (and possibly in other games, as well) can improve learning performance but at the potential cost of undesirable student behaviors, such as a propensity for guessing.

The *Tactical Language and Culture Training System* (*TLCTS*: Johnson, 2010) is a virtual learning environment that helps learners acquire basic communication skills and cultural understanding of foreign countries. This is done through interactive and practical lessons. *TLCTS* modules have been deployed to teach Arabic, Chinese and French, among other languages and cultures. Each module includes three major components: Skill Builder, Arcade Game, and Mission Game. In the Skill Builder, learners practice vocabulary and phrases, and complete assessment quizzes that require mastery of spoken language. In the Arcade Game, learners give voice commands in the target language to control the behaviors of game characters. In the Mission Game, learners speak on behalf of their characters to interact with in-game NPCs. All *TLCTS* content is highly task-based and promotes hands-on practice, while leveraging game elements to help learners overcome the motivational barrier of language learning.

TLCTS incorporates AI dialog models to support robust, spoken dialog with NPCs; these models can interpret the learner's verbal and non-verbal gestures and control the NPCs' responses accordingly. More specifically, the game uses automated speech recognition to provide immediate feedback, both on simple repeat-and-recall tasks and on more complex dialog exercises. The speech recognition is enabled through an underlying acoustic model, trained on a combination of native speech and learner speech to ensure an acceptable recognition rate. *TLCTS* also uses AI to maintain student models to track students' mastery of targeted language skills throughout gameplay; these models provide learners with recommendations on the lessons and game episodes to undertake next (thus, this game is also in the "AI-based Decision Support" category).

Three evaluations have been conducted on *TLCTS*, all of Iraqi Arabic language and culture. The first study involved 89 marines, each of whom underwent four hours of self-paced computer-based training each week over three months. The second study recruited eight military personnel who spent eight hours of *TLCTS* training per day, over five days. The third study had 268 participants, who had 28 hours of training with *TLCTS*. All three studies yielded significant increases in knowledge of Iraqi Arabic language, as measured by an independently constructed post-test; in two of the studies, participants also reported significant increases in speaking and listening self-efficacy.

The final game we'll discuss in detail in the "AI Character Interaction" category is *TurtleTalk* (Jung et al., 2019), a single-player web-based programming game that interacts with learners through voice recognition and speakers (see Figure 20.7). The children's utterances are converted directly into code. The game focuses on the programming topics of sequencing and iteration, both of which are fundamental programming constructs. In the case of sequencing, child users learn that a program runs in a sequence of steps, where an action, or step, leads to the next ordered action. In the case of iteration, children learn that programs often contain loops of steps that are executed repeatedly. The child and *TurtleTalk* communicate with one another in a turn taking manner to control the conversation and help the child focus on their given tasks. *TurtleTalk* provides hints to help the child decide what to do, but it does not appear that, as of this writing, the authors have grounded the pedagogical model underlying the game in established learning science.

Although there have been other computer gamified environments for learning programming, such as *Scratch* (Resnick et al., 2009) and *Blockly* (Fraser et al., 2013), *TurtleTalk* brings a new twist: an AI-infused NPC – the turtle – that guides and helps children through its voice

Figure 20.6   *An active dialog in TLCTS. Trainees learn how to use language and act culturally appropriate when interviewing Iraqi civilians*

and voice understanding. The Turtle appears on the screen and moves onto blocks according to voice commands, which are converted into programming code by a neural network.

Thus far, however, only a small pilot study of *TurtleTalk* has been conducted. Eight participants, 6 to 9 years of age, were recruited for the study. Players were surveyed after playing the game to learn about their playing experience (there was no pre-test or post-test). The general results (which are, of course, very preliminary and based on minimal data) are: (1) Children appear to learn programming easily, enjoyably, and confidently with *TurtleTalk*; (2) Children understand the key constructs of programming through *TurtleTalk*; and (3) Voice interaction allows children to become more immersed in the game.

Other digital learning games in the "AI Character Interaction" category include *ARIN-561, ELIA, ECHOES, Squares Family, TALENT* (already discussed), and *Betty's Brain. ARIN-561* is a single-player role-playing game that helps K-12 students learn about concepts in Artificial Intelligence. The player is a scientist who is lost on an alien planet, *ARIN-561*, and must solve AI problems to uncover the planet's mystery and survive. The problems in the game are related to three classical AI search algorithms – breadth-first, depth-first, and greedy search – embedded in the in-game tasks that involve searching for lost parts or cracking passwords. The game also features a pedagogical agent, in the form of a friendly robot that follows the player and conducts dialogues that either advance the game's narrative or prompt students to reflect on their mental process. A study with 125 students found that their AI knowledge increased significantly and correlated with time spent in the game, but not with gender identity, grade level, or math confidence measures. *ELIA* (*E*motions for *L*earning and *I*ntelligent *A*ssessment: Kaczmarek & Petroviča, 2018) is a single-player game targeted at university students for learning about artificial intelligence. The game is patterned after the famous "*Who wants to be a Millionaire*" television game show in which students try to win

Source: Figure from Jung et al. (2019), reproduced by permission from the authors

*Figure 20.7   A child listening to TurtleTalk's questions and then commanding the turtle
NPC to act through voice command*

a "million-dollar prize" by correctly answering a series of questions. *ELIA* integrates game
mechanics, most importantly an on-screen NPC that supports the student, with an underlying intelligent tutor. The game uses facial expression recognition software, supported by a
neural network, to help in identifying student emotions and deciding on a tutoring approach.
ELIA analyzes and classifies students through a pre-game questionnaire, subsequently selecting an appropriate supporting NPC (friend, expert, coach, or evaluator) and teaching strategy
(mastery or performance). During gameplay questions to the student are adapted with the aid
of the *Emotion API*, a commercially available API from Affectiva,[2] which is based on more
than 6 million face videos collected from 87 countries. Each of the supporting NPCs has their
own (different) rules for tutoring based on different perceived emotions and student progress.
In a study with 240 university students, a game-based condition in which 87 students used
ELIA, compared to a paper-based, business-as-usual condition with the same content, showed
that the game led to lower post-test scores. However, the game also led to increased motivation and engagement for lower-performing students, prompting the authors to suggest that the
game still could be beneficial for that class of students. *ECHOES* (Bernardini et al., 2014) is
a digital learning game designed to train young children with Autism Spectrum Conditions
(ASCs) to acquire social communication skills. An intelligent virtual character, Andy, guides
and teaches children, by playing the role of both a peer and a tutor, through a multi-touch LCD
display with eye tracking. All activities take place in a sensory garden populated by Andy
with interactive magic objects that react in unusual ways when touched by either the children
or the agent. Children practice two forms of activities: *goal-oriented*, where they follow steps
with an identifiable end-goal, and *cooperative turn-taking*, where they take turns exploring
the garden with Andy to promote social reciprocity. Andy is also responsible for fostering the

children's initiative and exposing them to positive peer interactions. Andy employs a domain-independent architecture FAtiMA (Dias & Paiva, 2005) to display one of 22 emotions, based on its assessment of the current events. The agent's back-end has a pedagogical component that monitors its interaction with the child, and a "child model," which assesses in real time the child's cognitive and emotional state. *ECHOES* was tested in a small study of twenty-nine (29) children 4 to 14 years old from the UK with ASC and/or other disabilities. While no significant transfer of increased social responsiveness or initiations to real-world contexts was observed across all children, the experimental results showed that the number of initiations made by the children when first using *ECHOES* was significantly less than the number of initiations made during the final session.

The last two games in the "AI Character Interaction" category, *Squares Family* and *Betty's Brain*, employ an instructional paradigm known as "teachable agents" (TA: Brophy et al., 1999; Chase et al., 2009; Leelawong & Biswas, 2008). Teachable agent technology draws on the social metaphor of a student teaching a computer agent, which in turn can help the student themselves learn. TA is based on the theories of learning-by-teaching (Bargh & Schul, 1980; Palthepu et al., 1991) and the protégé effect (Chase et al., 2009), in which students are coaxed to work harder to learn for their TAs than on their own. *Squares Family* (Pareto, 2009, 2014; Sjödén et al., 2017) is a two-player math card game (either two humans or a human and computer player) designed to teach elementary school students a conceptual understanding of mathematics and mathematical reasoning, in particular of positive and negative integer operations. The game prompts discussion between pairs, using a graphical metaphor of colored squares that denote 100s, 10s, and 1s and collected squares that go into virtual boxes. A key feature of the game is that students train an on-screen teachable agent (TA) as they play the game (e.g., Pareto, 2014; Sjödén et al., 2017). The AI component of *Squares Family* lies in how the TA "learns" as the game is played. Just as a human learner, the teachable agent asks questions of the student during gameplay to complement and build its knowledge. The TA will only ask questions that are, according to its understanding, within the student's *zone of proximal development* (Vygotsky, 1978). Pareto (2014) reports a three-month study in which 314 students played *Squares Family* and taught their teachable agents, while 129 took a standard math class without the game (i.e., the control). Results showed that there was a significant learning advantage in playing *Squares Family* compared with the control, also suggesting that young students can act as successful tutors. In another study, Sjödén et al. (2017) analyzed the anonymous log data of 163 fourth-graders playing *Squares Family* competitively against the computer from nine classes in a school in Sweden (age 10–11, total of 3,983 games). Results showed that students who tutored a TA had higher performance than students who played without a TA.

We note that the final game in the "AI Character Interaction" category, *Betty's Brain* (Biswas et al., 2016), unlike *Squares Family*, is more purely a TA learning technology than a game. However, because of the rich interaction between students and agents, as well as the goals of *Betty's Brain*, which arguably fit our earlier definition of digital learning games, for the purposes of this chapter, we include it as a learning game.[3] *Betty's Brain* trains students in modeling chains of cause-and-effect relationships, using a concept map that students develop. Students actively engage with an agent named Betty in three activities: teaching Betty to answer hypothetical questions about their concept maps, Betty reasons in real time visually in the concept map (which helps to remediate student knowledge), and Betty is quizzed by a mentor NPC at the end of a session. By interacting with and guiding Betty, the idea is for students to update their concept maps and, along the way, learn more about cause and effect. Betty's use of AI includes a breadth-first search of the concept map to deduce relationships in the student's concept map (Leelawong & Biswas, 2008). Betty also displays AI-controlled affect – for example, happiness, disappointment – as she solves problems. Other uses of AI with Betty's Brain include the application of learning analytics to improve the game (Segedy et al., 2014; Kinnebrew et al., 2014) – hence, *Betty's Brain*'s inclusion in the fourth and final category of AI in digital learning games, "Use of Learning-Analytics (LA) ..." *Betty's Brain* has been subject to a variety of studies including one by Segedy et al. (2015) in which 98 sixth-grade students used *Betty's Brain* to learn about two topics: climate change and human thermoregulation. Results demonstrated learning gains by students in multiple-choice and short-answer item questions, but not on causal reasoning, causal link extraction, or quiz evaluation items.

It can be concluded that AI Character Interaction research has had some clear successes (Johnson, 2010; Pareto, 2014; Sawyer et al., 2017) in making games more realistic, engaging, and motivating, as well as leading to better learning outcomes. However, AI-supported characters in a game context have not always led to better learning outcomes. For instance, as earlier mentioned, in one *Crystal Island* study students playing the game did not learn more than from a slideshow of the same material (Adams et al., 2012). As another example, *ELIA* motivated students more than a business-as-usual condition with the same content but led to worse learning outcomes (Kaczmarek & Petroviča, 2018). The challenge in creating interactive, engaging, and helpful NPCs that lead to learning is clearly very high – perhaps higher than any other challenge in AIED digital learning games – thus leading to mixed results so far. We'll return to this issue, and how it might be addressed, in the "Future Directions" section of this chapter. Another interesting and unique aspect of research in this area is how it can support the investigation of affect during instruction, both the affect of NPCs and that of students interacting with the game. For instance, some of the work with *Crystal Island* has been aimed, at least in part, at assessing student affect while game playing (Sabourin et al., 2011). Arroyo et al. (2013, 2014) have shown that an NPC can promote positive affect in students. In short, AI Character Interaction research is likely to continue to be a very interesting and fruitful direction for AIED digital learning game research.

Use of Learning Analytics (LA) and/or Educational Data Mining (EDM) for Game Analysis and Improvement

Learning analytics and educational data mining have led to important insights into learner behavior and affect while playing games (Alonso-Fernandez et al., 2019; Baker et al., 2007; Nguyen et al., 2020, 2019; O'Rourke, Haimovitz et al., 2014; Wang et al., 2019). For instance, in the learning game *Decimal Point*, EDM has helped in identifying students' learning difficulties (Nguyen et al., 2020), as well as the relationship between in-game learning and post-test/delayed post-test performance (Nguyen et al., 2019). An example finding is that while problems involving a number line tend to be the most difficult to master, performance on these problems is predictive of performance on the delayed post-test. Engagement and affect have also been a focus of AIED analyses in the use of digital learning games, given the hypothesis that these constructs are mediators to learning with games. As students interact with games, they typically display a variety of affective responses, including delight, engaged concentration, happiness, boredom, confusion, and frustration (Graesser et al., 2014; D'Mello, 2013), and learners' affective state has often been shown to be correlated with their learning processes (e.g., D'Mello, 2013; Shute et al., 2015).

Learning analytics and educational data mining have also helped in designing, redesigning, and extending digital learning games. Often, this involves using machine learning as a means of analyzing and improving games (Shute et al., 2015; Harpstead & Aleven, 2015). Many of the techniques used for player modeling, analysis, and game improvement in AIED digital learning games are derived from research on intelligent tutoring systems (Mousavinasab et al., 2021). For example, learning curve analysis, which is based on the power law of practice (Card et al., 1983) and is often used in intelligent tutoring system research (Martin et al, 2005), has been used to model the acquisition of fluent skills in the game *Zombie Division*. This analysis provided insights into student skills that suggests (re)design of the game and its content (Baker et al., 2007). Likewise, Harpstead and Aleven (2015) used learning curves to help in analyzing student strategies and guiding redesign of the *Beanstalk* game.

In what follows, we describe in detail two games – *Refraction* and *Zombie Division* – for which post-gameplay learning analytics and/or data mining help us both better understand student behavior and learning in gameplay and suggest ideas on how to revise, improve, and/ or extend the games. We also discuss the specific way learning analytics and data mining was applied to data collected from those games. We then summarize and briefly discuss other games in the "Use of Learning Analytics (LA) …" category. Finally, we discuss what learning analytics and data mining have revealed to us more generally about learning from digital games. Note that some digital learning games for which learning analytics and/or EDM have been applied – namely, *Betty's Brain*, *Crystal Island*, and *Decimal Point* – are not further discussed here; information about how learning analytics or data mining was used in analyzing these games is provided in earlier sections.

The first game we describe in detail is *Refraction* (O'Rourke et al., 2015, 2016; O'Rourke, Ballweber, et al., 2014; O'Rourke, Haimovitz, et al., 2014), a single-player puzzle game designed to teach fraction concepts to elementary school students. To play, a child interacts with a grid that contains laser sources, target spaceships, and asteroids (see Figure 20.8). The goal of the game is to split a laser shooter into correct fractional amounts to shoot target spaceships. The student must, at the same time, avoid moving asteroids. To win, a player must accurately shoot all the target spaceships at the same time (i.e., correctly satisfy the fractions). Since its release in 2012, *Refraction* has been played hundreds of thousands of times on the educational website Brainpop.com. O'Rourke and colleagues modified the game to experiment with the concept of a *growth mindset*, the theory that intelligence is malleable and can be improved with effort (Dweck, 2006; Heyman & Dweck, 1998). A "fixed mindset," on the other hand, is a theory stating that intelligence is set and unchangeable.

O'Rourke and colleagues extended *Refraction* to reward players with "brain points" when they exhibited growth mindset behavior, such as effort, use of strategy, and incremental progress (O'Rourke, Haimovitz, et al., 2014). Heuristics were used in real-time play to detect and reward positive, behavioral patterns. The heuristics were developed by first observing various patterns in student play. O'Rourke and colleagues then developed heuristic rules to identify those patterns during actual gameplay. For example, one rule identifies when a player solves a math sub-problem (incremental progress). Developing hand-authored rules – versus machine-learned or statistical rules – was key, because the rules needed to be semantically meaningful, providing feedback to students. The work of O'Rourke, Bellweber et al. (2014) also developed different "hints" versions of *Refraction*, in the intelligent tutoring tradition (VanLehn, 2006, 2011). (Surprisingly, in an experiment involving over 50,000 students, they found that students who used a no-hint version of the game learned more than students in four hint conditions – hint content (concrete versus abstract) and hint presentation (by level versus reward).)

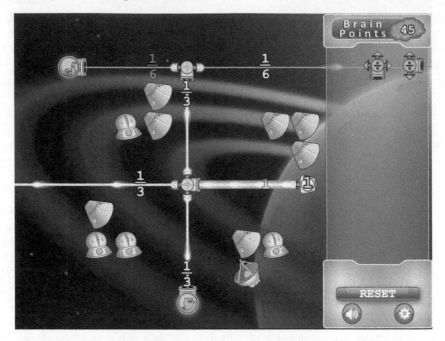

Source: Figure from O'Rourke et al. (2014), reproduced by permission from the first author

Figure 20.8   *A level of Refraction. The goal of the game is to use the elements on the*
right to split lasers into fractional pieces and redirect them to satisfy the
target spaceships. All spaceships must be satisfied at the same time to win

The critical way that *Refraction* uses AI, however, is in its post-game quantitative analyses of student behavior. Use of *Refraction* was evaluated through an iterative series of studies. First, the "brain points" version of *Refraction* was compared to a control version that awarded "level points" for each completed level (performance). Using educational data mining techniques, this study showed that players in the "brain points" version persisted longer and exhibited more productive learning behaviors than those in the control (O'Rourke, Haimovitz, et al. 2014). A second study, again comparing the "brain points" and "level points" versions of *Refraction*, showed, again applying data mining, that students who were younger, male, and of higher income were more engaged in the game (O'Rourke et al., 2015). In a third study, five different versions of "brain points" *Refraction* were compared, each of which removed features to isolate the impact of a particular aspect of the intervention (e.g., the brain points, growth mindset animation, a summary screen). The results of this study showed that brain points are not effective when awarded randomly, demonstrating that brain points are successful precisely because they are given to students in response to productive learning behaviors (O'Rourke et al., 2016). In short, this series of studies shows how quantitative and data mining analyses can be used to better understand how game features impact an educational game's effectiveness – and, in turn, point to how to improve the game.

Zombie Division (Habgood & Ainsworth, 2011) is a single-player 3D adventure game developed to help children from seven to eleven years old learn division and number patterns.

Source: Figure provided by M. P. Jacob Habgood, reproduced by permission

Figure 20.9   *This is a screenshot of the intrinsic version of the Zombie Division game. The player's avatar is in the foreground and chooses weapons from the top of the screen to attack zombies as they appear. The goal is to choose weapons that are equal divisors of the zombies, which have numbers on their chests. The "magical book of times tables" is shown in the upper right. The hearts indicate the health of the player, the skull on the bottom right shows how many zombies are yet to appear in this level*

The player in the game uses different weapons to kill attacking zombies by mathematically dividing into whole parts the numbers displayed on the zombies (see Figure 20.9). The game has different levels, as in many games, with approximately 20 attacking zombies per level. The game also includes game mechanics in which players explore a dungeon and collect keys; however, these are not integrated with the mathematical content of the game. Players can get two types of in-game help: a magical book of times tables (the multiplication grid) and an NPC that provides helpful feedback.

Habgood and Ainsworth (2011) report two studies that explore whether intrinsic or extrinsic integration of academic content into a digital learning game leads to better learning and which version of the game students prefer. In the *intrinsic* version of the game (Figure 20.9), the player attacks zombies through the game mechanic of whole number division, as described above. In an *extrinsic* version of the game, the game is played *without* the numbered weapons and zombies. Instead, the same division problems are presented to students to solve *between* levels (i.e., completely outside of the game). A control condition was also included in which students played *Zombie Division* without the numbered weapons and numbered zombies or division problems presented between levels. In study 1, a total of 58 kids, seven to 11 years old, participated, 20 in the extrinsic, 20 in the intrinsic, and 18 in the control condition. The intrinsic condition led to significantly better learning outcomes on both a post-test and delayed post-test than both the extrinsic and control conditions. In study 2, 16 children had the free choice to play either the intrinsic or extrinsic version of *Zombie*

Division and for as long as they desired. This study demonstrated an overwhelming preference for the intrinsic version of the game; the kids in the intrinsic version spent on average more than seven times longer playing than the extrinsic version. Essentially, the Habgood and Ainsworth results demonstrate that integrating math content directly into a game leads to both better enjoyment and learning outcomes than playing the same game, yet doing math separately.

While the *Zombie Division* game itself has no AI functionality, a learning curve analysis by Baker et al. (2007) was used to model skill fluency in the game and to suggest useful modifications. In particular, this analysis found, among other things, that students quickly and successfully gained fluency in divisibility by 2, 4, and 5, but not by 3, implying that future versions of the game should include extra support for the division-by-3 skill. In short, this is a stereotypical example of using EDM as a means for both assessing student behavior *and* subsequently suggesting changes to the game.

In general, a wide variety of AI, data mining, and statistical techniques have been used to investigate and model students' engagement and affective states. For example, Shute et al. (2015) used structural equation modeling to discover that in-game performance playing the *Physics Playground* (discussed earlier) can be predicted by pre-test data, frustration, and engaged concentration. In the game *Prime Climb* (also discussed earlier), Conati and Zhou (2002) experimented with using a Dynamic Decision Network to model students' emotional reactions during their interaction with the game, based on a cognitive theory of emotion. Data from the BROMP protocol – in which observational data are used to build machine-learned models of affect (Ocumpaugh et al., 2015) – has been used to develop affect detectors for several digital learning games or game-like instructional systems, including *TC3Sim* (Henderson et al., 2020a, 2020b), *Physics Playground* (Shute et al., 2015), and *Reasoning Mind* (Ocumpaugh et al., 2013). Eye-tracking and other sensor technologies have been used to capture students' physiological data (e.g., in *Prime Climb*: Conati et al., 2013), which are increasingly used to create deep-learning models that can infer students' affective states (Henderson et al., 2020a, 2020b; Loderer et al., 2019; Wiggins et al., 2018a, 2018b).

Other learning games for which learning analytics and data mining have been used for analyzing game behavior and/or game improvement include *Battleship Numberline, Heroes of Math Island, ST Math, Zoombinis, Beanstalk,* and *Downtown: A Subway Adventure. Battleship Numberline* (Lomas et al., 2011, 2012, 2013), a single-player game that gives players practice in estimating where whole numbers, fractions, and decimals fall on a number line, has been, for instance, used to examine student engagement. A large-scale study with the game, involving approximately 70,000 players, found that players were more engaged and played longer when the game was easier, contradicting the common assumption that maximum engagement occurs at a moderate difficulty level (Lomas et al., 2013). Conati and Gutica (2016) developed a variety of machine learned detectors of affect for players of the game *Heroes of Math Island*, a narrative math game for middle-school students targeted at learning about divisibility, prime numbers, and number decomposition. Their ultimate aim was to detect student affect while playing the game, using a camera, and then to adjust the affect of a supporting NPC (a monkey) to help students while learning. Based on a small study of 15 students, Conati and Gutica were able to identify the frequencies of a wide range of emotions, but also noted the steep challenges of labeling game data to identify emotions. In the area of using EDM and statistical analysis for helping to improve a game and its content, Peddycord-Liu et al. (2017, 2019) experimented with *ST Math*, a single-player learning game that uses spatial puzzles to teach mathematical concepts. They uncovered predictive relationships between different objectives and math concepts. For instance, they used linear regression to identify the most predictive prior objectives. In a study of 1,565 third-grade students, Peddycord-Liu et al were able to use their techniques to identify the skills that students needed more practice on, a redesign of lessons within the game, and clusters of difficult problems that should be separated to balance students' pacing through the game. Rowe et al. (2020, 2021) conducted EDM analyses of *Zoombinis* (Hancock & Osterweil, 1996), a single-player game designed to help students learn computational thinking (CT), to better understand student behaviors in playing the game. For instance, Rowe et al. (2021) investigated the frequency of systematic testing and trial and error, common CT constructs, by hand labeling the data of 194 students, building machine-learned detectors, and then validating the detectors with 54 additional students. Harpstead and Aleven (2015) applied learning analytics to learn more about and to modify *Beanstalk*, a single-person learning game for five- to eight-year-olds based on the folktale of Jack and the Beanstalk and designed to teach the physical properties of a balance beam. They used learning curves to analyze the in-game behavior of 177 students playing *Beanstalk*. Their analysis suggested a game redesign related to a previously unidentified shallow game strategy that "wins" but does not reflect an understanding of the underlying balance beam principle. Finally, Cano et al. (2016, 2018) used learning analytics to investigate *Downtown: A Subway Adventure*, a spy game where a single player must discover the location and time of their enemy's gathering by navigating the Madrid subway and collecting clues along the way. The goal of the game is to train students with intellectual disabilities to use the public subway system. In a study of 51 adults with varying intellectual disabilities, they found, for instance, that students' prior experience with transportation training did not have an impact on their game performance, but those who played video games regularly performed better than their counterparts. In summary, a wide variety of techniques have been used to analyze student gameplay and affect in the use of AIED digital learning games, including machine-learned detectors, learning curve analysis, BKT analysis, deep learning, eye-tracking, video, and linear regression. All of these tools in the AIED "toolbox" have uncovered important findings about how students interact with learning games, as well as how we could make the games better, both in game mechanics and content. Note also that this category of AIED digital learning games is the most active, with the largest number of games having been analyzed (15).

SUMMARY OF WHAT HAVE WE LEARNED FROM RESEARCH WITH AIED DIGITAL LEARNING GAMES

This chapter has presented a variety of AIED digital learning games that employ AI in various ways and that have been applied to many different topic areas, from math to science, computer science, cultural understanding, language learning, and social communication. Many of the games that have been presented in this chapter use AI to adapt gameplay, content, and help in a manner similar to what is often seen in intelligent tutoring systems (e.g., *iStart-2, MathSpring, Policy World, Prime Climb*). Other learning games use AI to provide useful real-time information, in the form of learning analytics, to help students make their *own* instructional decisions (e.g., *Decimal Point, Physics Playground, TALENT*) and to explore self-regulated learning. Still others include AI-supported non-player characters (NPCs) to guide and motivate students in their learning and social well-being (e.g., *Crystal Island, MathSpring, TLCTS, Turtle Talk*). Finally, perhaps the most important and prolific area of AI applied to digital learning games has been that of using learning analytics, data mining, and statistics to analyze student behavior and affect to help in better understanding student use of games and in redesigning the games (e.g., *Battleship Numberline*, *Beanstalk*, *Crystal Island*, *Physics Playground*, *Prime Climb*, *Refraction*, *Zombie Division*, *Zoombinis*).

AIED digital learning games have also demonstrated a considerable amount of success in a variety of studies, uncovering various aspects of learning from games that were not previously known. For instance, *Decimal Point* has been shown to be more effective and engaging in helping kids reinforce their understanding of decimals than a comparable decimal tutoring system (McLaren et al., 2017). *Decimal Point* has also been shown to be more effective in helping females learn (Hou et al., 2020; McLaren, Farzan, et al., 2017; McLaren et al., 2022b; Nguyen et al., 2022). *AutoThinking* (Hooshyar et al., 2021) and *Zoombinis* (Rowe et al., 2021), through well-designed and reasonably sized studies, have shown that computational thinking can be learned through gameplay. *Crystal Island*, a narrative game that is perhaps the longest standing and most studied of any AIED learning game, has shown in a variety of studies that students can learn microbiology from an NPC and a narrative-driven game (Lee et al., 2012; Sawyer et al., 2017). A variety of studies have shown that students can "learn by teaching" an NPC, through interaction with *Betty's Brain* (Biswas et al., 2016) and *Squares Family* (Pareto, 2014; Sjödén et al., 2017). A classroom study of *Zombie Division* demonstrated an important and previously unknown aspect of digital learning games: that tightly integrating academic content and gameplay is more effective for learning than separating the two (Habgood & Ainsworth, 2011).

A critical realization of the AIED digital learning game community has been the need for AIED researchers, who are predominantly learning scientists and educational technologists, to collaborate with game designers to be successful. The development of games with AI is inherently a multi-disciplinary undertaking; it requires not only the usual experts in learning science, educational technology, and human–computer interaction, but also those versed in the intricacies of game mechanics and game design. An indication of this movement was the convening of a CHI 2018 workshop, "CHI 2018 Workshop: Data-Driven Educational Game Design" (McLaren et al., 2018), in which game designers, learning scientists and educational data miners met to discuss the various disciplines and issues that need to be addressed in order to create AIED digital learning games. More such workshops and events, with participation across a variety of disciplines, will benefit the further development of AIED learning games.

FUTURE DIRECTIONS

While there has been much work done in the area of AIED digital learning games, with much success as outlined in the prior section, there are also several areas of potential work with digital learning games that have been under-explored.

For instance, AI could play a more prominent role in providing more realistic and compelling non-player characters and/or pedagogical agents within digital learning games. While games such as *Crystal Island* (Lester et al., 2013; Sawyer et al., 2017), *MathSpring* (Arroyo et al., 2014, 2013), and *TLCTS* (Johnson, 2010) have shown that even relatively primitive AI-infused non-player characters can make a significant difference to learning, there have been more recent developments in man–machine communication that could lead to an even greater impact. For instance, the emergence of relatively sophisticated virtual assistants, such as Alexa (Lopatovska et al., 2019), has demonstrated the possibilities of more natural and effective communication between humans and technology. AI, and in particular natural language processing (NLP), could have a much bigger and direct impact on students' learning experience when incorporated into pedagogical agents that accompany the student, either as learning companions or competitors (see, for instance, Chapter 11 by Rus et al. in this handbook). There is ample opportunity to apply state-of-the-art methods in NLP (Crossley et al., 2017; Howard & Ruder, 2018; Ruseti et al., 2018; Young et al., 2018) to this area. Of course, a challenge with many of the natural language machine-learning techniques is their need for a large amount of in-domain training data, often thousands or more examples. This requirement is difficult for many AIED digital learning games, which have typically been tested in traditional randomized controlled experiments in labs or classrooms with, at most, a few hundred students (with a couple of notable exceptions: *Battleship Numberline* (Lomas et al., 2013) and *Refraction* (O'Rourke, Bellweber, et al., 2014), both of which managed to reach more than 50,000 players through internet presence). Yet, with the pandemic of 2020–2022 and the sudden and significant move to online learning, more AIED games may be positioned to reach much larger, out-of-school audiences. Working with organizations like Brainpop.com is perhaps a wise move for more AIED game researchers.

Equity and inclusiveness have rarely been considered in digital learning games (Buffum et al., 2016). Most prior work with AIED learning games – and in fact in AI instructional systems more generally – has treated student populations as though all individual learners are the same, or very similar. However, it is likely that different sub-populations learn and play in different ways. For instance, Ogan et al. (2015) found that the help-seeking behavior of students using intelligent tutors can vary considerably across different cultures; they specifically found differences between Costa Rican students and students from the United States and the Philippines. In digital learning game research more specifically, McLaren and colleagues have consistently found that female students learn better than males with *Decimal Point* (Hou et al., 2020; McLaren, Farzan, et al., 2017; McLaren et al., 2022b; Nguyen et al., 2022). Likewise, Arroyo and colleagues found that *MathSpring* improved mathematics learning, engagement, and other affective outcomes for both female and low-achieving students (Arroyo et al., 2013, 2014). As another example, the collaborative game *Engage* was explicitly designed to support females and students with less prior game experience in learning computing science (Buffum et al., 2016). A couple of the games reviewed in this chapter have reached under-served populations, such as people with disabilities (*ECHOES*: Bernardini et al., 2014; *Downtown: A Subway Adventure*: Cano et al., 2016, 2018). Identifying and reacting to these learner differences is an important step towards more equity, better personalization, and, presumably, the increased effectiveness of games. AI could certainly play a role in better adapting games for these different and diverse populations. On the other hand, just as with AI research more generally, designers of AIED digital learning games must be extremely careful to avoid AI bias (Manyika et al., 2019; Prates et al., 2019). On this issue, the AIED community should engage with the larger AI community, following breakthroughs that might occur in machine-learning algorithms and approaches, to help in eradicating AI bias in AIED digital learning games (and other AIED systems).

Another way that digital learning games could better employ AI is in the use of more sophisticated student models and adaptation approaches, for instance, to track enjoyment in addition to domain understanding and skills. While various adaptive algorithms have been used to modify gameplay to support increasing difficulty and help students reach mastery (Arroyo et al.,

2013, 2014; Conati et al., 2013; Hooshyar et al., 2021), these algorithms have only been used in a relatively small number of learning games and have almost exclusively focused on learning objectives and domain skills. However, such models could also be used to modify gameplay to maximize fun and/or engagement for students, as has been implemented using dynamic difficulty adjustment in digital game research (i.e., video game research that is not focused on instruction: Ang & Mitchell, 2019; Baldwin et al., 2016; Frommel et al., 2018; Zohaib, 2018). There have been some steps in this direction, most notably, the research with *Decimal Point* in which students self-reported their enjoyment in playing specific mini-games within *Decimal Point*, a student model of that enjoyment was displayed to them on a dashboard and was used by students to select further mini-games to play (Hou et al., 2020; 2021). While this research is a step in the direction of an "enjoyment" or "engagement" student model, there are still a lot of interesting and related research questions that may involve the support of AI. For instance, how do students react to different representations of their enjoyment? Is enjoyment more about encouraging what has already been enjoyed or seeking new and unknown opportunities?

An exciting new direction that a few AIED researchers have started to pursue, but is still at an embryonic stage, is supporting tangible game-based learning. These types of games involve a synergy of real-world physical play with computer-based instruction. For instance, Arroyo et al. (2017) have developed a game environment for learning mathematics that involves the use of "wearable tutors" in the form of smartphones and smartwatches. The wearable devices act as mobile tutors, while students are given real-world tasks – e.g., a scavenger hunt where students search for physical objects – and provide input to the devices on what they have done, while the tutors provide hints to help them in the physical environment. Students manipulate, measure, estimate, and find mathematical objects that satisfy certain constraints to help in playing the games. Another example is Yannier et al. (2016, 2020, 2021) who added the manipulation of physical objects, such as blocks and towers, to an AI-based mixed-reality game to help 4- to 8-year-old children learn basic physics (see Figure 20.10).

A specialized AI computer vision algorithm is used to track what children do in the physical environment and then to provide personalized feedback in the form of an on-screen character (Yannier et al., 2020, 2022). They were able to show that adding physical objects to the game – in essence, bridging the physical and virtual worlds in a mixed-reality setting – can lead to more learning compared with an equivalent solely screen-based game. There are a number of exciting questions that AIED could tackle in this space, such as: How can actions taken in the physical world be input to adaptive AI algorithms that provide pedagogical advice on what to do in the physical world? Can the physical objects themselves – for instance, an item being searched for in a scavenger hunt – be imbued with AI to add to the "smarts" and engagement of the games?

It should be noted that most of the games reviewed in this chapter are single-player games, with just a few exceptions (*TALENT*: Maragos, 2013; *Prime Climb*: Conati et al., 2013; *Squares Family*: Pareto, 2009; 2014; *Physics Playground*: Sun et al., 2020, 2022). Thus, there may be learning opportunities that are being missed by not developing more collaborative AIED learning games. Working collaboratively could help students help one another by bringing their strengths, weaknesses, knowledge, and misconceptions to the game, thus complementing one another so that together group members can solve the problem at hand and learn (Housh et al., 2021; see also Chapter 19 by Martinez-Maldonado et al. in this handbook). As previously mentioned, Buffum et al. (2016) explicitly designed for and found that their collaborative game, *Engage*, better supported female and less-experienced students in collaborative

Source: Figure provided by Nesra Yannier and Trinity Area School District, reproduced by permission

Figure 20.10   Students playing with the Intelligent Science Station (norilla.org)

play versus single-player use of the game. Feedback from students in their study revealed potential benefits to collaboration, such as how a partner in gameplay can be a "sounding board" for what to try next or when one player is stuck in gameplay they can rely on their partner to take over. Perhaps AI could be supportive in such circumstances by having an AI agent that explicitly prompts the collaborating students to help one another in these, and other ways. As with *Squares Family* (Pareto, 2009) and AI programs in general, such as AI chess-playing programs (Warwick, 2017), having students alternately play with or against an AI or a human might provide instructional opportunities not otherwise possible. For instance, the concept of learning by teaching (Biswas et al., 2005; Brophy et al., 1999; Palthepu et al., 1991) could be exercised in such collaborative gameplay circumstances, prompting students to teach *both* human and AI confederates in a game context.

Finally, the ultimate goal of research on AIED digital learning games should be to transfer more of the evidence-based learning games to the real world. In this way, we not only *study* AI in learning games at schools and with students, but also provide those schools and students with substantial, ongoing use of games that have been proven in rigorous empirical tests. Leading the way – and potentially providing a blueprint for others to follow – are games such as *Zoombinis* and *TLCTS*. TERC has sold almost 40,000 copies of the non-web version of *Zoombinis* and last year sold approximately 13,000 new licenses to the internet version of the game.[4] Lewis Johnson has spun off a company, Alelo, that sells an updated version of TLTS to the US military.[5] Hundreds of thousands of trainees have used Alelo's cultural games and tools to get cultural training. The military has required this training for people deployed in over 80 countries. While there are these glimmers of success in the real world, there need to be more efforts made to transfer thoroughly tested learning games to real and widespread use in education and training contexts. To learn more about real-world transfer and commercialization of AI-based learning technology, see Chapter 23 by Ritter and Koedinger in this handbook.

In conclusion, while there has already been a lot of impressive research done with AIED digital learning games, the future is bright with exciting new directions before us. By creating multi-disciplinary teams of learning scientists, educational technologists, game designers, and AI experts, we foresee a future in which AIED digital learning games will become an ever-increasing and important component of education.

ACKNOWLEDGMENTS

This work has been influenced by conversations and collaborations with many of our colleagues, including Ryan Baker, Rosta Farzan, Jodi Forlizzi, Jessica Hammer, Richard Mayer, Michael Mogessie, Eleanor O'Rourke, and Liz Richey.

NOTES

1. The authors apologize for any AIED digital learning games that may have been overlooked in this review.
2. www.affectiva.com/
3. We contacted Gautam Biswas, the leader of the group that developed *Betty's Brain*, and he also noted anecdotally that during talks he has given, audiences have suggested that *Betty's Brain* could be viewed as a game.
4. From personal correspondence with Elizabeth Rowe of TERC.
5. From personal correspondence with Lewis Johnson of Alelo.

REFERENCES

Adams, D. M., Mayer, R. E., MacNamara, A., Koenig, A., & Wainess, R. (2012). Narrative games for learning: Testing the discovery and narrative hypotheses. *Journal of Educational Psychology, 104*(1), 235–249. https://psycnet.apa.org/doi/10.1037/a0025595.

Aleven, V., Dow, S., Christel, M., Stevens, S., Rosé, C., Koedinger, K., Myers, B., Flynn, J. B., Hintzman, Z., Harpstead, E., & Hwang, S. (2013). Supporting social-emotional development in collaborative inquiry games for K-3 science learning. In *Proceedings of Games+Learning+Society Conference (GLS 9.0)*. ETC Press, 53–60.

Alonso-Fernandez, C., Martínez-Ortiz, I., Caballero, R., Freire, M., & Fernández-Manjón, B. (2019). Predicting students' knowledge after playing a serious game based on learning analytics data: A case study. *Journal of Computer Assisted Learning.* Advance online publication. https://doi.org/10.1111/jcal.12405.

Ang, D., & Mitchell, A. (2019). Representation and frequency of player choice in player-oriented dynamic difficulty adjustment systems. In *Proceedings of the Annual Symposium on Computer-Human Interaction in Play - CHI PLAY '19*, 589–600. https://doi.org/10.1145/3311350.3347165.

Arroyo, I., Burleson, W., Tai, M., Muldner, K., & Woolf, B. P. (2013). Gender differences in the use and benefit of advanced learning technologies for mathematics. *Journal of Educational Psychology*, *105*(4), 957–969. https://psycnet.apa.org/doi/10.1037/a0032748.

Arroyo, I., Micciollo, M., Casano, J., Ottmar, E., Hulse, T., & Rodrigo, M. (2017). Wearable learning: Multiplayer embodied games for math. In *Proceedings of the ACM SIGCHI Annual Symposium on Computer-Human Interaction in Play (CHI PLAY 2017)*, Amsterdam, Netherlands. https://doi.org /10.1145/3116595.3116637.

Arroyo, I., Woolf, B. P., Burleson, W., Muldner, K., Rai, D., & Tai, M. (2014). A multimedia adaptive tutoring system for mathematics that addresses cognition, metacognition and affect. *International Journal of Artificial Intelligence in Education*, *24*(4), 387–426. https://doi.org/10.1007/s40593-014-0023-y.

Baker, R. S. J. D., D'Mello, S. K., Rodrigo, M. M. T., & Graesser, A. C. (2010). Better to be frustrated than bored: The incidence, persistence, and impact of learners' cognitive-affective states during interactions with three different computer-based learning environments. *International Journal of Human-Computer Studies*, *68*(4), 223–241. https://doi.org/10.1016/j.ijhcs.2009.12.003.

Baker, R. S. J. D., Habgood, M. P. J., Ainsworth, S. E., & Corbett, A. T. (2007). Modeling the acquisition of fluent skill in educational action games. In C. Conati, K. McCoy, & G. Paliouras (Eds.), *User Modeling 2007 (UM 2007)*. Lecture Notes in Computer Science, Vol. 4511. Berlin, Heidelberg: Springer. https://doi.org/10.1007/978-3-540-73078-1_5.

Baldwin, A., Johnson, D., & Wyeth, P. (2016). Crowd-pleaser: Player perspectives of multiplayer dynamic difficulty adjustment in video games. In *Proceedings of the 2016 Annual Symposium on Computer-Human Interaction in Play - CHI PLAY '16*, 326–337. https://doi.org/10.1145/2967934.2968100.

Bargh, J., & Schul, Y. (1980). On the cognitive benefits of teaching. *Journal of Educational Psychology*, *72*(5), 593–604. https://psycnet.apa.org/doi/10.1037/0022-0663.72.5.593.

Bediou, B., Adams, D. M., Mayer, R. E., Tipton, E., Green, C. S., & Bavelier, D. (2018). Meta-analysis of action video game impact on perceptual, attentional, and cognitive skills. *Psychological Bulletin*, *144*(1), 77–110. https://psycnet.apa.org/doi/10.1037/bul0000130

Benton, L., Mavrikis, M., Vasalou, M., Joye, N., Sumner, E., Herbert, E., Revesz, A., Symvonis, A., & Raftopoulou, C. (2021). Designing for "challenge" in a large-scale adaptive literacy game for primary school children. *British Journal of Educational Technology*, *52*(5), 1862–1880. Wiley. https://doi.org /10.1111/bjet.13146.

Bernardini, S., Porayska-Pomsta, K., & Smith, T. J. (2014). ECHOES: An intelligent serious game for fostering social communication in children with autism. *Information Sciences*, *264*, 41–60. https:// doi.org/10.1016/j.ins.2013.10.027.

Biswas, G., Leelawong, K., Belynne, K., & Adebiyi, B. (2005). Case studies in learning by teaching behavioral differences in directed versus guided learning. In *Proceedings of the 27th Annual Conference of the Cognitive Science Society*, 828–833.

Biswas, G., Segedy, J. R., & Bunchongchit, K. (2016). From design to implementation to practice – A learning by teaching system: Betty's brain. *International Journal of Artificial Intelligence in Education*, *26*(1), 350–364. https://doi.org/10.1007/s40593-015-0057-9.

Bosch, N., D'Mello, S., Baker, R., Ocumpaugh, J., & Shute, V. (2016). Using video to automatically detect learner affect in computer-enabled classrooms. *ACM Transactions on Interactive Intelligent Systems*, *6*(2), 17.11–17.31. https://doi.org/10.1145/2946837.

Brophy, S., Biswas, G., Katzlberger, T., Bransford, J., & Schwartz, D. (1999). Teachable agents: Combining insights from learning theory and computer science. In S. P. Lajoie & M. Vivet (Eds.), *Proceedings of Artificial Intelligence in Education* (pp. 21–28). Amsterdam: IOS Press.

Buffum, P. S., Frankosky, M., Boyer, K. E., Wiebe, E. N., Mott, B. W., & Lester, J. C. (2016). Collaboration and gender equity in game-based learning for middle school computer science. *Computing in Science & Engineering*, *18*(2), 18–28. https://doi.org/10.1109/MCSE.2016.37.

Bull, S. (2020). There are open learner models about! *IEEE Transactions on Learning Technologies*, *13*(2), 425–448. https://doi.org/10.1109/TLT.2020.2978473.

Bull, S., & Kay, J. (2008). Metacognition and open learner models. In *The 3rd Workshop on Meta-Cognition and Self-Regulated Learning in Educational Technologies, at ITS2008*, 7–20.

Cano, A. R., Fernández-Manjón, B., & García-Tejedor, Á. J. (2016). Downtown, a subway adventure: Using learning analytics to improve the development of a learning game for people with intellectual disabilities. In *2016 IEEE 16th International Conference on Advanced Learning Technologies (ICALT)* (pp. 125–129). IEEE. https://doi.org/10.1109/ICALT.2016.46.

Cano, A. R., Fernández-Manjón, B., & García-Tejedor, Á. J. (2018). Using game learning analytics for validating the design of a learning game for adults with intellectual disabilities. *British Journal of Educational Technology, 49*(4), 659–672. https://doi.org/10.1111/bjet.12632.

Card, S. K., Moran, T. P., & Newell, A. (1983). *The Psychology of Human-Computer Interaction.* Hillsdale, NJ: Lawrence Erlbaum Associates.

Castell, S. D., & Jenson, J. (2003). Serious play: Curriculum for a post-talk era. *Journal of the Canadian Association for Curriculum Studies, 1*(1).

Chase, C., Chin, D. B., Oppezzo, M., & Schwartz, D. L. (2009). Teachable agents and the protégé effect: Increasing the effort towards learning. *Journal of Science Education and Technology, 18*(4), 334–352. https://doi.org/10.1007/s10956-009-9180-4.

Chi, M. T., Bassok, M., Lewis, M. W., Reimann, P., & Glaser, R. (1989). Self-explanations: How students study and use examples in learning to solve problems. *Cognitive Science, 13*(2), 145–182. https://doi.org/10.1207/s15516709cog1302_1.

Chi, M. T., De Leeuw, N., Chiu, M. H., & LaVancher, C. (1994). Eliciting self-explanations improves understanding. *Cognitive Science, 18*(3), 439–477. https://doi.org/10.1207/s15516709cog1803_3.

Clark, D. B., Tanner-Smith, E., & Killingsworth, S. (2016). Digital games, design, and learning: A systematic review and meta-analysis. *Review of Educational Research, 86*(1), 79–122. https://doi.org/10.3102/0034654315582065.

Collins, A., Brown, J. S., & Newman, S. E. (1989). Cognitive apprenticeship: Teaching the crafts of reading, writing, and mathematics. In L. B. Resnick (Ed.), *Knowing, Learning, and Instruction: Essays in Honor of Robert Glaser* (pp. 453–494). Hillsdale: Lawrence Erlbaum Associates.

Conati, C., & Gutica, M. (2016). Interaction with an edu-game: A detailed analysis of student emotions and judges' perceptions. *International Journal of Artificial Intelligence in Education, 26,* 975–1010. https://doi.org/10.1007/s40593-015-0081-9.

Conati, C., Jaques, N., & Muir, M. (2013). Understanding attention to adaptive hints in educational games: An eye-tracking study. *International Journal of Artificial Intelligence in Education, 23,* 131–161. https://doi.org/10.1007/s40593-013-0002-8.

Conati, C., & Zhou, X. (2002). Modeling students' emotions from cognitive appraisal in educational games. In *Proceedings of the International Conference on Intelligent Tutoring Systems (ITS 2002),* 944–954. http://dx.doi.org/10.1007/3-540-47987-2_94.

Corbett, A. T., & Anderson, J. R. (1995). Knowledge tracing: Modeling the acquisition of procedural knowledge. *User Modeling and User-Adapted Interaction, 4*(4), 253–278. https://psycnet.apa.org/record/1996-29060-001.

Crocco, F., Offenholley, K., & Hernandez, C. (2016). A proof-of-concept study of game-based learning in higher education. *Simulation & Gaming, 47*(4), 403–422. https://doi.org/10.1177/%2F1046878116632484.

Crossley, S., Liu, R., & McNamara, D. (2017). Predicting math performance using natural language processing tools. In *Proceedings of the Seventh International Learning Analytics & Knowledge Conference* (pp. 339–347). ACM. https://doi.org/10.1145/3027385.3027399.

Czikszentmihalyi, M. (1975). *Beyond Boredom and Anxiety.* San Francisco: Jossey Bass.

Czikszentmihalyi, M. (1990). *Flow: The Psychology of Optimal Experience.* New York: Harper & Row.

Dean, T., & Kanazawa, K. (1989). A model for reasoning about persistence and causation. *Computational Intelligence, 5*(3), 142–150. https://doi.org/10.1111/j.1467-8640.1989.tb00324.x.

Deterding, S., Dixon, D., Khaled, R., & Nacke, L. (2011). From game design elements to gamefulness: Defining "gamification." In *Proceedings of the 15th International Academic MindTrek Conference: Envisioning Future Media Environments* (pp. 9–15), Tampere, Finland: ACM. https://doi.org/10.1145/2181037.2181040.

D'Mello, S. (2013). A selective meta-analysis on the relative incidence of discrete affective states during learning with technology. *Journal of Educational Psychology, 105*(4), 1082–1099. https://psycnet.apa.org/doi/10.1037/a0032674.

Dias, J., & Paiva, A. (2005). Feeling and reasoning: A computational model for emotional characters. In *Proceedings of the Portuguese Conference on Artificial Intelligence* (pp. 127–140). Berlin, Heidelberg: Springer. https://doi.org/10.1007/11595014_13.

Dweck, C. S. (2006). *Mindset: The New Psychology of Success.* New York: Random House.

Easterday, M. W., Aleven, V., Scheines, R., & Carver, S. M. (2017). Using tutors to improve educational games: A cognitive game for policy argument, *Journal of the Learning Sciences, 26*(2), 226–276. https://doi.org/10.1080/10508406.2016.126928.

Elo, A. (1978). *The Rating of Chess Players, Past and Present.* New York: Arco Publishers.

Embretson, S. E., & Reise, S. P. (2000). *Item Response Theory for Psychologists.* Psychology Press. ISBN 9780805828191.

Fraser, N., et al. (2013). Blockly: A visual programming editor. https://blockly-games.appspot.com.

Frommel, J., Fischbach, F., Rogers, K., & Weber, M. (2018). Emotion-based dynamic difficulty adjustment using parameterized difficulty and self-reports of emotion. In *Proceedings of the Annual Symposium on Computer-Human Interaction in Play Extended Abstracts - CHI PLAY '18*, 163–171. https://doi.org/10.1145/3242671.3242682.

Geden, M., Emerson, A., Carpenter, D., Rowe, J., Azevedo, R., & Lester, J. (2021). Predictive student modeling in game-based learning environments with word embedding representations of reflection. *International Journal of Artificial Intelligence in Education, 31*(1), 1–23. https://doi.org/10.1007/s40593-020-00220-4.

Gee, J. P. (2003). *What Video Games Have to Teach Us About Learning and Literacy.* New York: Palgrave/Macmillian.

Gee, J. P. (2007). *Good Video Games and Good Learning Collected Essays on Video Games, Learning and Literacy,* 2nd Edition. Peter Lang International Academic Publishers. https://doi.org/https://doi.org/10.3726/978-1-4539-1162-4.

Gilbert, N. (2021). *Number of Gamers Worldwide 2021/2022: Demographics, Statistics, and Predictions.* FinancesOnline-Reviews for Business. https://financesonline.com/number-of-gamers-worldwide/.

Graesser, A. C., D'Mello, S. K., & Strain, A. C. (2014). Emotions in advanced learning technologies. In R. Pekrun & L. Linnenbrink-Garcia (Eds.), *Educational Psychology Handbook Series: International Handbook of Emotions in Education* (pp. 473–493). Routledge/Taylor & Francis Group.

Gros, B. (2007). Digital games in education: The design of games-based learning environments. *Journal of Research on Technology in Education, 40*, 1–23.

Habgood, M. P. J., & Ainsworth, S. (2011). Motivating children to learn effectively: Exploring the value of intrinsic integration in educational games. *Journal of the Learning Sciences, 20*(2), 169–206. https://doi.org/10.1080/10508406.2010.50802.

Hancock, C., & Osterweil, S. (1996). *Zoombinis* and the art of mathematical play. *Hands On! 19*(1), 17–19.

Harpstead, E., & Aleven, V. (2015). Using empirical learning curve analysis to inform design in an educational game. In *Proceedings of CHI Play 2015.* https://doi.org/10.1145/2793107.2793128.

Harpstead, E., Richey, J. E., Nguyen, H., & McLaren, B. M. (2019). Exploring the subtleties of agency and indirect control in digital learning games. In *Proceedings of the 9th International Conference on Learning Analytics & Knowledge (LAK'19).* (pp. 121–129). ACM. https://doi.org/10.1145/3303772.3303797.

Henderson, N., Min, W., Rowe, J., & Lester, J. (2020a). Enhancing affect detection in game-based learning environments with multimodal conditional generative modeling. In *Proceedings of the 2020 International Conference on Multimodal Interaction* (pp. 134–143).

Henderson, N., Min, W., Rowe, J., & Lester, J. (2020b). Multimodal player affect modeling with auxiliary classifier generative adversarial networks. In *Proceedings of the AAAI Conference on Artificial Intelligence and Interactive Digital Entertainment* (Vol. 16, No. 1, pp. 224–230).

Heyman, G. D., & Dweck, C. S. (1998). Children's thinking about traits: Implications for judgments of the self and others. *Child Development, 64*(2), 391–403.

Hocine, N. (2019). Personalized serious games for self-regulated attention training. In *Proceedings of the 27th Conference on User Modeling, Adaptation and Personalization (UMAP '19).* https://doi.org/10.1145/3314183.3323458.

Hocine, N., Ameur, M., & Ziani, W. (2019). Keep Attention: A personalized serious game for attention training. In *Proceedings of the 3rd International Symposium on Gamification and Games for Learning (GamiLearn '19).*

Homer, B. D., Hayward, E. O., Frye, J., & Plass, J. L. (2012). Gender and player characteristics in video game play of preadolescents. *Computers in Human Behavior, 25*(5), 1782–1789.

Honey, M. A., & Hilton, M. L. (2011). *Learning Science Through Computer Games and Simulations.* The National Academies Press. http://www.nap.edu/openbook.php?record_id=13078&page=R1.

Hooshyar, D., Malva, L., Yang, Y., Pedaste, M., Wang, M., & Lim, H. (2021). An adaptive educational computer game: Effects on students' knowledge and learning attitude in computational thinking. *Computers in Human Behavior, 114.*

Hou, X., Nguyen, H. A., Richey, J. E., Harpstead, E., Hammer, J., & McLaren, B. M. (2021). Assessing the effects of open models of learning and enjoyment in a digital learning game. *International Journal of Artificial Intelligence in Education*, 1–31. https://doi.org/10.1007/s40593-021-00250-6.

Hou, X., Nguyen, H. A., Richey, J. E., & McLaren, B. M. (2020). Exploring how gender and enjoyment impact learning in a digital learning game. In I. Bittencourt, M. Cukurova, K. Muldner, R. Luckin, & E. Millán (Eds.), *Proceedings of the 21st International Conference on Artificial Intelligence in Education: AIED 2020.* Lecture Notes in Computer Science (LNCS, Vol. 12163). Cham: Springer. https://doi.org/10.1007/978-3-030-52237-7_21.

Housh, K., Saleh, A., Phillips, T., Hmelo-Silver, C. E., Glazewski, K., Lee, S., Mott, B., & Lester, J. (2021). Designing for equitable participation in collaborative game-based learning environments. In *Proceedings of the International Conference of the Learning Sciences (ICLS 2021).*

Howard, J., & Ruder, S. (2018). Universal language model fine-tuning for text classification. In *Proceedings of the 56th Annual Meeting of the Association for Computational Linguistics* (Volume 1: Long Papers) (Vol. 1, pp. 328–339).

Hussein, M. H., Ow, S. H., Elaish, M. M., & Jensen, E. O. (2022). Digital game-based learning in K-12 mathematics education: A systematic literature review. *Education and Information Technologies, 27*, 2859–2891. https://doi.org/10.1007/s10639-021-10721-x.

Jackson, G. T., & McNamara, D. S. (2011). Motivational impacts of a game-based intelligent tutoring system. In *Proceedings of the Twenty-Fourth International Florida Artificial Intelligence Research Society Conference.*

Jacovina, M. E., Jackson, G. T., Snow, E. L., & McNamara, D. S. (2016). Timing game-based practice in a reading comprehension strategy tutor. In *Proceedings of the International Conference on Intelligent Tutoring Systems* (pp. 59–68). Cham: Springer.

Johnson, W. L. (2010). Serious use of a serious game for language learning. *International Journal of Artificial Intelligence in Education, 20*(2), 175–195.

Johnson, W. L., & Lester, J. (2018). Pedagogical agents: Back to the future. *AI Magazine, 39.* https://doi.org/10.1609/aimag.v39i2.2793.

Jung, H., Kim, H. J., So, S., Kim, J., & Oh, C. (2019) TurtleTalk: An educational programming game for children with voice user interface. In *CHI Conference on Human Factors in Computing Systems Extended Abstracts (CHI'19 Extended Abstracts)*, May 4–9, 2019, Glasgow, Scotland UK. ACM, New York, NY, 6 pages. https://doi.org/10.1145/3290607.3312773.

Juraschka, R. (2019, September 29). *How Digital Game-Based Learning Improves Student Success.* Prodigy Math Blog. https://www.prodigygame.com/main-en/blog/digital-game-based-learning/.

Kaczmarek, S., & Petroviča, S. (2018). Promotion of learning motivation through individualization of learner-game interaction. In *Proceedings of the 2018 IEEE Conference on Computational Intelligence and Games (CIG 2018).* https://ieeexplore.ieee.org/document/8490371.

Kaufman, G., & Flanagan, M. (2015). A psychologically "embedded" approach to designing games for prosocial causes. *Cyberpsychology: Journal of Psychosocial Research on Cyberspace, 9*(3). https://doi.org/10.5817/CP2015-3-5

Ke, F. (2016). Designing and integrating purposeful learning in game play: A systematic review. *Educational Technology Research and Development, 64*(2), 219–244. https://eric.ed.gov/?id=EJ1094502.

Kinnebrew, J. S., Segedy, J. R., & Biswas, G. (2014). Analyzing the temporal evolution of students' behaviors in open-ended learning environments. *Metacognition and Learning, 9*(2), 187–215.

Kinnebrew, J. S., Segedy, J. R., & Biswas, G. (2017). Integrating model-driven and data-driven techniques for analyzing learning behaviors in open-ended learning environments. *IEEE Transactions on Learning Technologies, 10*(2), 140–153. https://eric.ed.gov/?id=EJ1146025.

Klinkenberg, S., Straatemeier, M., & van der Maas, H. L. J. (2011). Computer adaptive practice of Maths ability using a new item response model for on-the-fly ability and difficulty assessment. *Computers & Education, 57*, 1813–1824. https://doi.org/10.1016/j.compedu.2011.02.003.

Landers, R., Armstrong, M., & Collmus, A. (2017). How to use game elements to enhance learning: Applications of the theory of gamified learning. *Serious Games and Edutainment Applications*, 457–483. https://doi.org/10.1177/1046878114563660.

Landers, R., & Landers, A. (2014). An empirical test of the theory of gamified learning: The effect of leaderboards on time-on-task and academic performance. *Simulation & Gaming, 45*(6), 769–785. https://doi.org/10.1177/1046878114563662.

Lee, S. Y., Mott, B. W., & Lester, J. C. (2011). Modeling narrative-centered tutorial decision making in guided discovery learning. In *Proceedings of the Fifteenth International Conference on Artificial Intelligence and Education*, 163–170. Berlin: Springer.

Lee, S. Y., Mott, B. W., & Lester, J. C. (2012). Real-time narrative-centered tutorial planning for story-based learning. In *Proceedings of the Eleventh International Conference on Intelligent Tutoring Systems*, 476–481. Berlin: Springer. https://dl.acm.org/doi/10.1007/978-3-642-30950-2_61.

Leelawong, K., & Biswas, G. (2008). Designing learning by teaching agents: The Betty's Brain system. *International Journal of Artificial Intelligence in Education, 18*(3), 181–208. https://psycnet.apa.org /record/2008-15202-002.

Lester, J. C., Ha, E. Y., Lee, S. Y., Mott, B. W., Rowe, J. P., & Sabourin, J. L. (2013). Serious games get smart: Intelligent game-based learning environments. *AI Magazine, 34*(4), 31–45. https://doi.org/10 .1609/aimag.v34i4.2488.

Lindberg, R. S., Hasanov, A., & Laine, T. H. (2017). Improving play and learning style adaptation in a programming education game. In *Proceedings of the International Conference on Computer Supported Education (CSEDU 2017)* (pp. 450–457).

Lindberg, R. S., & Laine, T. H. (2016). Detecting play and learning styles for adaptive educational games. In *Proceedings of the International Conference on Computer Supported Education (CSEDU 2016)* (pp. 181–189).

Lindberg, R. S., & Laine, T. H. (2018). Formative evaluation of an adaptive game for engaging learners of programming concepts in K-12. *International Journal of Serious Games, 5*(2), 3–24. https://doi .org/10.17083/ijsg.v5i2.220.

Lobel, A., Engels, R. C. M. E., Stone, L. L., Burk, W. J., & Granic, I. (2017). Video gaming and children's psychosocial well-being: A longitudinal study. *Journal of Youth and Adolescence, 46*(4), 884–897. https://doi.org/10.1007/s10964-017-0646-z.

Loderer, K., Pekrun, R., & Plass, J. (2019). Emotional foundations of game-based learning. In J. L. Plass, R. E. Mayer, & B. D. Homer (Eds.), *Handbook of Game-Based Learning* (pp. 111–151). Cambridge, MA: MIT Press.

Lomas, D., Ching, D., Stampfer, E., Sandoval, M., & Koedinger, K. (2011). Battleship numberline: A digital game for improving estimation accuracy on fraction number lines. *Society for Research on Educational Effectiveness*. https://eric.ed.gov/?id=ED528880.

Lomas, D., Patel, K., Forlizzi, J. L., & Koedinger, K. R. (2013). Optimizing challenge in an educational game using large-scale design experiments. In *Proceedings of the SIGCHI Conference on Human Factors in Computing Systems* (pp. 89–98). ACM. https://doi.org/10.1145/2470654.2470668.

Lomas, D., Stamper, J., Muller, R., Patel, K., & Koedinger, K. R. (2012). The effects of adaptive sequencing algorithms on player engagement within an online game. In *Proceedings of the International Conference on Intelligent Tutoring Systems* (pp. 588–590). Berlin, Heidelberg: Springer. https://citeseerx.ist.psu.edu/viewdoc/download?doi=10.1.1.353.186&rep=rep1&type=pdf.

Long, Y., & Aleven, V. (2014). Gamification of joint student/system control over problem selection in a linear equation tutor. In S. Trausan-Matu, K. E. Boyer, M. Crosby, & K. Panourgia (Eds.), *Proceedings of the 12th International Conference on Intelligent Tutoring Systems (ITS 2014)* (pp. 378–387). New York: Springer. https://doi.org/10.1007/978-3-319-07221-0_47.

Long, Y., & Aleven, V. (2018). Educational game and intelligent tutoring system: A classroom study and comparative design analysis. In *Proceedings of CHI 2018*. https://doi.org/10.1145/3057889.

Lopatovska, I., Rink, K., Knight, I., Raines, I., Cosenza, K., Williams, H., Sorsche, P., Hirsch, D., Li, Q., & Martinez, A. (2019). Talk to me: Exploring user interactions with the Amazon Alexa. *Journal of Librarianship and Information Science, 51*(4). https://doi.org/10.1177/0961000618759414.

Malone, T. W. (1981). Toward a theory of intrinsically motivating instruction. *Cognitive Science, 5*, 333–369. https://doi.org/10.1207/s15516709cog0504_2.

Manyika, J., Silberg, J., & Presten, B. (2019). What do we do about the biases in AI? *Harvard Business Review*. https://hbr.org/2019/10/what-do-we-do-about-the-biases-in-ai.

Maragos, K. (2013). Web-based adaptive educational games-Exploitation in computer science education. *The Committee of Research and Development*, University of Athens, 81, 2013.

Martin, B., Koedinger, K. R., Mitrovic, A., & Mathan, S. (2005). On using learning curves to evaluate ITS. In *Proceedings of the 12th International Conference on Artificial Intelligence in Education, AIED 2005*, 419–426. ISBN 978-1-58603-530-3.

Martin, S. M., Casey, J. R., & Kane, S. (2021). *Serious Games in Personalized Learning: New Models for Design and Performance*. Routledge. ISBN 9780367487508.

Mayer, R. E. (2014). *Computer Games for Learning: An Evidence-Based Approach*. Cambridge, MA: MIT Press. ISBN 9780262027571.

Mayer, R. E. (2019). Computer games in education. *Annual Review of Psychology*, 70, 531–549. https://doi.org/10.1146/annurev-psych-010418-102744.

Mayer, R. E., & Johnson, C. I. (2010). Adding instructional features that promote learning in a game-like environment. *Journal of Educational Computing Research*, 42(3), 241–265. https://journals.sagepub.com/doi/10.2190/EC.42.3.a.

McLaren, B. M., Adams, D. M., Mayer, R. E., & Forlizzi, J. (2017). A computer-based game that promotes mathematics learning more than a conventional approach. *International Journal of Game-Based Learning (IJGBL)*, 7(1), 36–56. https://doi.org/10.4018/IJGBL.2017010103.

McLaren, B. M., Asbell-Clarke, J., & Hammer, J. (2018). CHI 2018 workshop: Data-driven educational game design. In *CHI 2018 Workshop at the CHI Conference in Montreal*, Quebec, Canada.

McLaren, B. M., Farzan, R., Adams, D. M., Mayer, R. E., & Forlizzi, J. (2017). Uncovering gender and problem difficulty effects in learning with an educational game. In E. André, R. Baker, X. Hu, M. M. T. Rodrigo, & B. du Boulay (Eds.), *Proceedings of the 18th International Conference on Artificial Intelligence in Education (AIED 2017)*. LNAI 10331 (pp. 540–543). Springer: Berlin.

McLaren, B. M., Richey, J. E., Nguyen, H., & Hou, X. (2022a). How instructional context can impact learning with educational technology: Lessons from a study with a digital learning game. *Computers & Education*, 178. https://doi.org/10.1016/j.compedu.2021.104366

McLaren, B. M., Richey, J. E., Nguyen, H. A., & Mogessie, M. (2022b). A digital learning game for mathematics that leads to better learning outcomes for female students: Further evidence. In *Proceedings of the 16th European Conference on Game Based Learning (ECGBL 2022)* (pp. 339–348).

Min, W., Mott, B., Rowe, J., Taylor, R., Wiebe, E., Boyer, K., & Lester, J. (2017). Multimodal goal recognition in open-world digital games. In *Proceedings of the AAAI Conference on Artificial Intelligence and Interactive Digital Entertainment* (Vol. 13, No. 1).

Mitrovic, A. (2012). Fifteen years of constraint-based tutors: what we have achieved and where we are going. *User Modeling and User-Adapted Interaction*, 22(1–2), 39–72. https://doi.org/10.1007/s11257-011-9105-9.

Mousavinasab, E., Zarifsanajey, N., Niakan Kalhori, S. R., Rakhshan, M., Keikha, L., & Ghazi Saeedi, M. (2021). Intelligent tutoring systems: A systematic review of characteristics, applications, and evaluation methods. *Interactive Learning Environments*. https://doi.org/10.1080/10494820.2018.1558257.

Munshi, A., Rajendran, R., Ocumpaugh, J., Biswas, G., Baker, R. S., & Paquette, L. (2018). Modeling learners' cognitive and affective states to scaffold SRL in open ended learning environments. In *Proceedings of the International Conference on User Modelling, Adaptation and Personalization (UMAP)*, Singapore, pp. 131–138. https://doi.org/10.1145/3209219.3209241.

Nguyen, H., Harpstead, E., Wang, Y., & McLaren, B. M. (2018). Student agency and game-based learning: A study comparing low and high agency. In C. Rosé, R. Martínez-Maldonado, H. U. Hoppe, R. Luckin, M. Mavrikis, K. Porayska-Pomsta, B. McLaren, & B. du Boulay (Eds.), *Proceedings of the 19th International Conference on Artificial Intelligence in Education (AIED 2018)*. LNAI 10947 (pp. 338–351). Springer: Berlin.

Nguyen, H. A., Hou, X., Stamper, J., & McLaren, B. M. (2020). Moving beyond test scores: Analyzing the effectiveness of a digital learning game through learning analytics. In *Proceedings of the 13th International Conference on Educational Data Mining (EDM 2020)* (pp. 487–495).

Nguyen, H., Wang, Y., Stamper, J., & McLaren, B. M. (2019). Using knowledge component modeling to increase domain understanding in a digital learning game. In *Proceedings of the 12th International Conference on Educational Data Mining (EDM 2019)* (pp. 139–148). https://eric.ed.gov/?id=ED599221.

Nguyen, H., Hou, X., Richey, J. E., & McLaren, B. M. (2022). The impact of gender in learning with games: A consistent effect in a math learning game. *International Journal of Game-Based Learning (IJGBL), 12*(1), 1–29. http://doi.org/10.4018/IJGBL.309128.

Ocumpaugh, J., Baker, R. S., Gaudino, S., Labrum, M. J., & Dezendorf, T. (2013). Field observations of engagement in reasoning mind. In *Proceedings of the International Conference on Artificial Intelligence in Education* (pp. 624–627). Berlin, Heidelberg: Springer.

Ocumpaugh, J., Baker, R. S., & Rodrigo, M. T. (2015). *Baker Rodrigo Ocumpaugh Monitoring Protocol (BROMP) 2.0 Technical and Training Manual.*

Ogan, A., Walker, E., Baker, R., Rodrigo, M. M. T., Soriano, J. C., & Castro, M. J. (2015). Towards understanding how to assess help-seeking behavior across cultures. *International Journal of Artificial Intelligence in Education, 25*, 229–248. https://doi.org/10.1007/s40593-014-0034-8.

O'Rourke, E., Ballweber, C., & Popović, Z. (2014a). Hint systems may negatively impact performance in educational games. In *Proceedings of the First Annual ACM Conference on Learning @ Scale (L@S '14)* (pp. 51–60). https://doi.org/10.1145/2556325.2566248.

O'Rourke, E., Chen, Y., Haimovitz, K., Dweck, C. S., & Popović, Z. (2015). Demographic differences in a growth mindset incentive structure for educational games. In *Proceedings of the Second Annual ACM Conference on Learning at Scale Works in Progress (L@S WIP 2015).*

O'Rourke, E., Haimovitz, K., Ballweber, C., Dweck, C. S., & Popović, Z. (2014b). Brain points: A growth mindset structure boosts persistence in an educational game. In *Proceedings of the ACM Conference on Human Factors in Computing Systems (CHI 2014).* https://doi.org/10.1145/2556288.2557157.

O'Rourke, E., Peach, E., Dweck, C. S., & Popović, Z. (2016). Brain points: A deeper look at a growth mind-set incentive structure for an educational game. In *Proceedings of the ACM Conference on Learning at Scale (L@S 2016).* https://doi.org/10.1145/2876034.2876040.

Palthepu, S., Greer, J., & McCalla, G. (1991). Learning by teaching. In *Proceedings of the International Conference on the Learning Sciences, AACE* (pp. 357 363).

Pareto, L. (2009). Teachable agents that learn by observing game playing behaviour. In *Proceedings of the Workshop on Intelligent Educational Games at the 14th International Conference on Artificial Intelligence in Education* (pp. 31–40).

Pareto, L. (2014). A teachable agent game engaging primary school children to learn arithmetic concepts and reasoning. *International Journal of AI in Education, 24*, 251–283. https://doi.org/10.1007/s40593-014-0018-8.

Parong, J., Mayer, R. E., Fiorella, L., MacNamara, A., Homer, B. D., & Plass, J. L. (2017). Learning executive function skills by playing focused video games. *Contemporary Educational Psychology, 51*, 141–151. https://doi.org/10.1016/j.cedpsych.2017.07.002.

Parong, J., Wells, A., & Mayer, R. E. (2020). Replicated evidence towards a cognitive theory of game-based training. *Journal of Educational Psychology, 112*(5), 922–937. https://doi.org/10.1037/edu0000413.

Pashler, H., McDaniel, M., Rohrer, D., & Bjork, R. (2008). Learning styles: Concepts and evidence. *Psychological Science in the Public Interest, 9*(3), 105–119. https://doi.org/10.1111/j.1539-6053.2009.01038.x.

Peddycord-Liu, Z., Catete, V., Vandenberg, Barnes, J. T., Lynch, C., & Rutherford, T. (2019). A field study of teachers using a curriculum-integrated digital game. In *Proceedings of CHI Conference on Human Factors in Computing Systems (CHI '19)*, May 4–9, 2019, Glasgow, Scotland UK. ACM, New York, NY, 12 pages. https://doi.org/10.1145/3290605.3300658.

Peddycord-Liu, Z., Cody, C., Kessler, S., Barnes, J. T., & Lynch, C. F. (2017). Using serious game analytics to inform digital curricular sequencing: What math objective should students play next? In *CHI Play '17: Proceedings of the Annual Symposium on Computer-Human Interaction in Play* (pp. 195–204). https://doi.org/10.1145/3116595.3116620.

Peirce, N., Conlan, O., & Wade, V. (2008). Adaptive educational games: Providing non-invasive personalised learning experiences. In *Proceedings of the 2008 Second IEEE International Conference on Digital Game and Intelligent Toy Enhanced Learning* (pp. 28–35). IEEE.

Prates, M. O. R., Avelar, P. H. C., & Lamb, L. (2019). Assessing gender bias in machine translation – A case study with Google Translate. *Computers and Society.* https://doi.org/10.1007/s00521-019-04144-6.

Prensky, M. (2004). *Digital Game-Based Learning.* McGraw-Hill. ISBN 0071454004; ISBN13 9780071454001.

Prensky, M. (2006). *Don't Bother Me, Mom, I'm Learning! How Computer and Video Games Are Preparing Your Kids for 21st Century Success and How You Can Help.* St. Paul: Paragon House.

Resnick, M., Maloney, J., Monroy-Hernández, A., Rusk, N., Eastmond, E., Brennan, K., Millner, A., Rosenbaum, E., Silver, J., Silverman, B., et al. (2009). Scratch: Programming for all. *Communications of the ACM*, *52*(11), 60–67. https://doi.org/10.1145/1592761.1592779.

Rollings, A., & Morris, D. (2000). *Game Architecture and Design: Learn the Best Practices for Game Design and Programming.* Coriolis. ISBN-13 978-1576104255; ISBN-10 1576104257.

Rowe, E., Almeda, M. V., Asbell-Clarke, J., Scruggs, R., Baker, R., Bardar, E., & Gasca, S. (2021). Assessing implicit computational thinking in Zoombinis puzzle gameplay. *Computers in Human Behavior*, *120*. Special Issue on "Towards Strengthening Links between Learning Analytics and Assessment: Challenges and Potentials of a Promising New Bond." https://doi.org/10.1016/j.chb.2021.106707.

Rowe, E., Asbell-Clarke, J., Bardar, E., Almeda, M. V., Baker, R. S., Scruggs, R., & Gasca, S. (2020). Advancing research in game-based learning assessment: Tools and methods for measuring implicit learning. In *Advancing Educational Research With Emerging Technology*. https://doi.org/10.4018/978-1-7998-1173-2.ch006.

Rowe, J. P., & Lester, J. C. (2010). Modeling user knowledge with dynamic Bayesian Networks in interactive narrative environments. In *Proceedings of the Sixth Annual Artificial Intelligence and Interactive Digital Entertainment Conference*, 57–62. Palo Alto, CA: AAAI Press.

Rowe, J. P., Shores, L. R., Mott, B. W., & Lester, J. C. (2011). Integrating learning, problem solving, and engagement in narrative-centered learning environments. *International Journal of Artificial Intelligence in Education*, *21*(2), 115–133. http://dx.doi.org/10.3233/JAI-2011-019.

Ruseti, S., Dascalu, M., Johnson, A. M., Balyan, R., Kopp, K. J., McNamara, D. S., Crossley, S. A., & Trausan-Matu, S. (2018). Predicting question quality using recurrent neural networks. In *Proceedings of the International Conference on Artificial Intelligence in Education (AIED 2018)* (pp. 491–502). Cham: Springer. https://doi.org/10.1007/978-3-319-93843-1_36.

Sabourin, J. L., Mott, B. W., & Lester, J. C. (2011). Modeling learner affect with theoretically grounded dynamic Bayesian Networks. In *Proceedings of the Fourth International Conference on Affective Computing and Intelligent Interaction*, 286–295. Berlin: Springer. https://doi.org/10.1007/978-3-642-24600-5_32.

Sabourin, J. L., Shores, L. R., Mott, B. W., & Lester, J. C. (2013). Understanding and predicting student self-regulated learning strategies in game-based learning environments. *International Journal of Artificial Intelligence in Education*, *23*, 94–114. https://doi.org/10.1007/s40593-013-0004-6.

Salen, K., & Zimmerman, E. (2003). *Rules of Play: Game Design Fundamentals.* Cambridge, MA: MIT Press. ISBN 9780262240451.

Sawyer, R., Smith, A., Rowe, J., Azevedo, R., & Lester, J. (2017). Is more agency better? The impact of student agency on game-based learning. In E. Andfe, R. Baker, X. Hu, M. Rodrigo, & B. du Boulay (Eds.), *Proceedings of the International Conference on AI in Education (AIED 2017) LNCS* (Vol. 10331, pp. 335–346). Cham: Springer. https://doi.org/10.1007/978-3-319-61425-0_28.

Schöbel, S., Saqr, M., & Janson, A. (2021). Two decades of game concepts in digital learning environments–A bibliometric study and research agenda. *Computers & Education*, *173*, 104296. https://doi.org/10.1016/j.compedu.2021.104296.

Segedy, J. R., Biswas, G., & Sulcer, B. (2014). A model-based behavior analysis approach for open-ended environments. *Journal of Educational Technology & Society*, *17*(1), 272–282.

Segedy, J. R., Kinnebrew, J. S., & Biswas, G. (2015). Using coherence analysis to characterize self-regulated learning behaviors in open-ended learning environments. *Journal of Learning Analytics*, *2*(1), 13–48. https://doi.org/10.18608/jla.2015.21.3.

Self, J. (2016). The birth of IJAIED. *International Journal of Artificial Intelligence in Education*, *26*, 4–12. https://doi.org/10.1007/s40593-015-0040-5; https://link.springer.com/article/10.1007/s40593-015-0040-5.

Shute, V. J. (2011). Stealth assessment in computer-based games to support learning. *Computer Games and Instruction*, *55*(2), 503–524.

Shute, V. J., D'Mello, S., Baker, R., Cho, K., Bosch, N., Ocumpaugh, J., Ventura, M., & Almeda, V. (2015). Modeling how incoming knowledge, persistence, affective states, and in-game progress influence student learning from an educational game. *Computers & Education*, *86*, 224–235. https://psycnet.apa.org/doi/10.1016/j.compedu.2015.08.001.

Shute, V. J., Rahimi, S., & Smith, G. (2019). Chapter 4: Game-based learning analytics in physics playground. In A. Tlili & M. Chang (Eds.), *Data Analytics Approaches in Educational Games and Gamification Systems*, Smart Computing and Intelligence. https://doi.org/10.1007/978-981-32-9335-9_4.

Shute, V. J., Rahimi, S., Smith, G., Ke, F., Almond, R., Dai, C.-P., Kuba, R., Liu, Z., Yang, X., & Sun, C. (2021). Maximizing learning without sacrificing the fun: Stealth assessment, adaptivity and learning supports in educational games. *Journal of Computer Assisted Learning*, 127–141. https://doi.org/10.1111/jcal.12473.

Shute, V. J., & Ventura, M. (2013). *Measuring and Supporting Learning in Games: Stealth Assessment*. Cambridge, MA: The MIT Press.

Shute, V. J., Ventura, M., & Kim, Y. J. (2013). Assessment and learning of qualitative physics in Newton's playground. *The Journal of Educational Research*, *106*(6), 423–430. https://doi.org/10.1080/00220671.2013.832970.

Sjödén, B., Lind, M., & Silvervarg, A. (2017). Can a teachable agent influence how students respond to competition in an educational game? In *Proceedings of the 18th International Conference on Artificial Intelligence in Education (AIED 2017)*. https://doi.org/10.1007/978-3-319-61425-0_29.

Spann, C. A., Shute, V. J., Rahimi, S., & D'Mello, S. K. (2019). The productive role of cognitive reappraisal in regulating affect during game-based learning. *Computers in Human Behavior*, *100*, 358–369. https://doi.org/10.1016/j.chb.2019.03.002.

Squire, K., & Jenkins, H. (2003). Harnessing the power of games in education. *Insight*, *3*(7), 5–33.

Sun, C., Shute, V. J., Stewart, A. E. B., Beck-White, Q., Reinhardt, C. R., Zhou, G., Duran, N., & D'Mello, S. K. (2022). The relationship between collaborative problem solving behaviors and solution outcomes in a game-based learning environment. *Computers in Human Behavior*, *128*, 107120. https://doi.org/10.1016/j.chb.2021.107120.

Sun, C., Shute, V. J., Stewart, A., Yonehiro, J., Duran, N., & D'Mello, S. (2020). Towards a generalized competency model of collaborative problem solving. *Computers & Education*, *143*, 103672. https://doi.org/10.1016/j.compedu.2019.103672.

Tahir, F., Mitrovic, A., & Sotardi, V. (2020). Investigating the effects of gamifying SQL-tutor. In H. J. So (Eds.), *Proceedings of the 28th International Conference on Computers in Education* (pp. 416–425). Asia-Pacific Society for Computers in Education. ISBN 978-986-97214-5-5.

Taub, M., Sawyer, R., Smith, A., Rowe, J., Azevedo, R., & Lester, J. (2020). The agency effect: The impact of student agency on learning, emotions, and problem-solving behaviors in a game-based learning environment. *Computers & Education*, *147*, 1–19. https://doi.org/10.1016/j.compedu.2019.103781.

The NPD Group. (2019). Retail Tracking Service, 2019 Entertainment Survey. https://igda-website.s3.us-east-2.amazonaws.com/wp-content/uploads/2019/10/16161928/NPD-2019-Evolution-of-Entertainment-Whitepaper.pdf.

Tobias, S., & Fletcher, J. D. (2011). *Computer Games and Instruction*. Charlotte, NC: Information Age. https://eric.ed.gov/?id=ED529495.

Tokac, U., Novak, E., & Thompson, C. G. (2019). Effects of game-based learning on students' mathematics achievement: A meta-analysis. *Journal of Computer Assisted Learning*, *35*(3), 407–420. https://doi.org/10.1111/jcal.12347.

VanLehn, K. (2006). The behavior of tutoring systems. *International Journal of Artificial Intelligence in Education*, *16*(3), 227–265. https://psycnet.apa.org/record/2007-08276-002.

VanLehn, K. (2011). The relative effectiveness of human tutoring, intelligent tutoring systems, and other tutoring systems. *Educational Psychologist*, *46*(4), 197–221. https://doi.org/10.1080/00461520.2011.611369.

Vygotsky, L. S. (1978). In: M. Cole, V. John-Steiner, S. Scribner, & E. Souberman (Eds.), *Mind in Society: The Development of Higher Psychological Processes*. Cambridge: Harvard University Press. ISBN 9780674576292.

Waalkens, M., Aleven, V., & Taatgen, N. (2013). Does supporting multiple student strategies lead to greater learning and motivation? Investigating a source of complexity in the architecture of intelligent tutoring systems. *Computers & Education*, *60*, 159–171. https://doi.org/10.1016/j.compedu.2012.07.016.

Wang, N., Greenwald, E., Montgomery, R., & Leitner, M. (2022). ARIN-561: An educational game for learning artificial intelligence for high-school students. In *International Conference on Artificial Intelligence in Education* (pp. 528–531). Springer, Cham.

Wang, P., Rowe, J. P., Min, W., Mott, B. W., & Lester, J. C. (2017). Interactive narrative personalization with deep reinforcement learning. In *Proceedings of the Twenty-Sixth International Joint Conference on Artificial Intelligence* (pp. 3852–3858). https://doi.org/10.24963/ijcai.2017/538.

Wang, Y., Nguyen, H., Harpstead, E., Stamper, J., & McLaren, B. M. (2019). How does order of gameplay impact learning and enjoyment in a digital learning game? In S. Isotani, E. Millán, A. Ogan, P. Hastings, B. McLaren, & R. Luckin (Eds.), *Proceedings of the 20th International Conference on Artificial Intelligence in Education (AIED 2019)*. LNAI 11625 (pp. 518–531). Cham: Springer. https://doi.org/10.1007/978-3-030-23204-7_43.

Warwick, K. (2017). A Brief History of Deep Blue, IBM's Chess Computer. *Mental Floss*. From July 29, 2017. Retrieved November 9, 2020, from https://www.mentalfloss.com/article/503178/brief-history-deep-blue-ibms-chess-computer.

Wiggins, J., Kulkarni, M., Min, W., Mott, B., Boyer, K., Wiebe, E., & Lester, J. (2018a). Affect-based early prediction of player mental demand and engagement for educational games. In *Proceedings of the AAAI Conference on Artificial Intelligence and Interactive Digital Entertainment* (Vol. 14, No. 1). https://ojs.aaai.org/index.php/AIIDE/article/view/13047.

Wiggins, J. B., Kulkarni, M., Min, W., Boyer, K. E., Mott, B., Wiebe, E., & Lester, J. (2018b). User affect and no-match dialogue scenarios: An analysis of facial expression. In *Proceedings of the 4th International Workshop on Multimodal Analyses Enabling Artificial Agents in Human-Machine Interaction* (pp. 6–14). https://doi.org/10.1145/3279972.3279979.

Wouters, P., & van Oostendorp, H. (Eds.). (2017). *Instructional Techniques to Facilitate Learning and Motivation of Serious Games*. New York: Springer.

Wylie, R., & Chi, M. T. H. (2014). The self-explanation principle in multimedia learning. In R. E. Mayer (Ed.), *Cambridge Handbooks in Psychology: The Cambridge Handbook of Multimedia Learning* (pp. 413–432). Cambridge: Cambridge University Press. https://doi.org/10.1017/CBO9781139547369.021.

Yannier, N., Crowley, K., Do, Y., Hudson, S. E., & Koedinger, K. R. (2022). Intelligent science exhibits: Transforming hands-on exhibits into mixed-reality learning experiences. *Journal of the Learning Sciences*, *31*(3), 335–368. 10.1080/10508406.2022.2032071.

Yannier, N., Hudson, S. E., & Koedinger, K. R. (2020). Active learning is about more than hands-on: Mixed-reality AI system to support STEM education. *International Journal of Artificial Intelligence in Education*, *30*, 74–96. https://doi.org/10.1007/s40593-020-00194-3.

Yannier, N., Hudson, S. E., Koedinger, K. R., Hirsh-Pasek, K., Golinkoff, R. M., Munakata, Y., ... Brownell, S. E. (2021). Active learning: "Hands-on" meets "minds-on." *Science*, *374*(6563), 26–30. https://doi.org/10.1126/science.abj99.

Yannier, N., Hudson, S. E., Stampfer Wiese, E., & Koedinger, K. R. (2016). Adding physical objects to an interactive game improves learning and enjoyment: Evidence from earthshake. *ACM Transactions Computer-Human Interaction*, *23*(4), Article 26 (September 2016), 31 pages. https://doi.org/10.1145/2934668.

Young, T., Hazarika, D., Poria, S., & Cambria, E. (2018). Recent trends in deep learning based natural language processing. *IEEE Computational Intelligence Magazine*, *13*(3), 55–75. http://dx.doi.org/10.1109/MCI.2018.2840738.

Zeng, J., Parks, S., & Shang, J. (2020). To learn scientifically, effectively, and enjoyably: A review of educational games. *Human Behavior and Emerging Technologies*, *2*(2), 186–195. https://doi.org/10.1002/hbe2.188.

Zimmerman, B. J., & Schunk, D. J. (2008). *Self-Regulated Learning and Academic Achievement: Theoretical Perspectives* (2nd ed.). Lawrence Erlbaum Associates. ISBN 978-1-4612-8180-1.

Zohaib, M. (2018). Dynamic difficulty adjustment (DDA) in computer games: A review. *Advances in Human-Computer Interaction*, 2018, 1–12. https://doi.org/10.1155/2018/5681652.

21. Artificial intelligence-based assessment in education

Ying Fang, Rod D. Roscoe and Danielle S. McNamara

Artificial intelligence (AI) refers to the ability of machines to adapt to new situations, deal with emerging situations, solve problems, answer questions, devise plans, and perform other functions that require some level of intelligence typically evident in human beings (Coppin, 2004). AI methods have been increasingly used in a variety of settings such as employment, healthcare, policing, and education to assess human behaviors and influence decision making. For example, AI tools are used in today's recruitment to screen résumés, conduct interviews and analyze candidates' personality traits and skills (Upadhyay & Khandelwal, 2018; Van Esch et al., 2019). AI techniques are also widely used in healthcare to collect patients' information, process and analyze the information, help decision making, and improve resource utilization (Jiang et al., 2017; Yu et al., 2018). In the field of policing, facial recognition technology is used by police officers to identify suspects from the image data captured by cameras (Aricl, 2019; Robertson et al., 2016). Additionally, AI methods enable predictive policing, which purports to anticipate where crimes may occur, who might commit the crimes, and potential victims based on historical crime records (Ariel, 2019; Perrot, 2017). AI methods and techniques are also applied in manufacturing to facilitate planning and control, such as detecting defective products, optimizing manufacturing supply chains, and designing products (Hayhoe et al., 2019; Li et al., 2017, Singh & Gu, 2012).

With respect to education, AI techniques undergird diverse tools used to evaluate students and in turn guide learning and instruction (Corbett et al.,1997; Mousavinasab et al., 2021). One class of widely used educational technology is intelligent tutoring systems (ITSs), which provide immediate feedback and customized instruction to learners (Graesser et al., 2012; Psotka et al., 1988; Shute & Psotka, 1996; VanLehn, 2011). For such systems to be "intelligent," AI tools and techniques are used to communicate with students, collect data, conduct analyses, and make instructional decisions. In digital learning games and simulations, AI methods have also been used to provide personalized and engaging experiences to learners. AI methods are implemented in these learning environments to assess students dynamically, adjust task difficulty and learning paths, and provide cognitive feedback and motivational support (Conati et al., 2013; Hooshyar et al., 2021; Peirce et al., 2008; see Chapter 20 by McLaren and Nguyen and Chapter 9 by Aleven et al.). In the field of educational assessment, such as automated writing evaluation (AWE), AI technology is used to grade essays and provide qualitative and quantitative feedback during or after essay drafts (Burstein et al., 2013; Foltz et al., 2013; Warschauer & Ware, 2006). The common features across these educational technologies are the automated and personalized feedback, instruction, or experiences provided to students that are enabled by assessments using AI techniques.

There are many approaches for AI-based assessments in educational technologies, and some technologies use multiple approaches as means of assessments. For example, machine learning and natural language processing are used together by some technologies to analyze language data and evaluate students' performance. Meanwhile, different approaches (e.g., collecting diverse data sources or applying different computational methods) may be used to assess the same constructs (e.g., performance or knowledge). To develop effective educational technologies, developers and educators need to make decisions about how AI-based assessments will be implemented to meet the educational goals. In turn, these decisions introduce dependencies and constraints on other assessment components. For instance, the type of data that are collected may be constrained by the student traits targeted for evaluation. Additionally, the data type may restrict the computational methods. To describe and facilitate some of these considerations, this chapter will provide a framework for AI-based assessment (AIBA) in educational technology and design.

The framework comprises five interrelated dimensions that broadly address the "purposes" and "procedures" of AIBA for educational technologies: goals, target constructs, data sources, computational methods, and visibility. Purposes broadly refer to the overarching aims of the assessment, which include two dimensions: *goals* of AIBA and *constructs* to be assessed in support of those goals. Procedures primarily refer to the means for achieving the purposes, which involve data sources, computational methods, and visibility of assessments. *Data sources* refer to the data collected to measure the constructs in a robust, valid, and reliable way. *Computational methods* are the methods used in AIBA to process, transform, and analyze the data to make inferences. Assessment *visibility* refers to whether assessments are overt and obvious to the learner or if they are covert or unobtrusive (i.e., stealth assessment).

The remainder of this chapter will further describe each of the five dimensions within the contexts of purposes and goals while using educational systems and software as examples to illustrate each dimension. We anticipate this framework to be useful to researchers, educators, and designers who value a common language for discussing AIBAs for educational technology. We also anticipate that this framework will help researchers, educators, and designers to begin thinking about the complex decisions related to implementing AIBAs in educational technologies.

THE AIBA FRAMEWORK

As shown in Figure 21.1, the framework comprises five dimensions that are nested within two overarching themes: (1) purposes, including the *goals* of assessments and the *constructs* to be assessed, and (2) procedures for achieving purposes, including *data sources*, *computational*

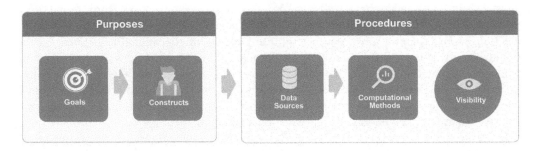

Figure 21.1   AI-based assessment (AIBA) framework

methods, and *visibility*. Purposes will be described first, followed by procedures, because the decisions about goals and constructs of assessments often influence decisions concerning procedures. Nevertheless, methodological innovations can inspire new purposes by making it possible for educational technologies to implement assessments (e.g., natural language processing innovations render it possible for technologies to provide feedback on certain aspects of writing). Therefore, the relationship between purposes and procedures is often reciprocal.

Purposes of AIBA

Goals

Educational technology developers, educators, and learners use AI-based assessments to support a variety of needs (see Chapter 9 by Aleven et al., Chapter 15 by Pozdniakov et al., and Chapter 23 by Ritter and Koedinger). Perhaps the most prominent or commonplace of these goals are personalized instruction and feedback (see Chapter 9 by Aleven et al.). Educational technologies can help students develop their declarative knowledge of the subject or acquire essential procedural knowledge and skills, and technologies can facilitate learners' awareness of their performance and progress (see Chapter 18 by Casas-Ortiz et al. and Chapter 19 by Martinez-Maldonado et al.).

One goal of AIBAs is to guide *personalized instruction* or *training* offered via educational technologies (e.g., to teach physics knowledge or train reading strategies). AI-based assessments can use learners' inputs, behaviors, performance, and related metrics to deliver or recommend appropriate learning materials or practice opportunities needed by individual learners. Technologies that incorporate such personalization features have been shown to be more effective in facilitating student learning than traditional instruction or computer-based tools without such features (see Kulik & Fletcher, 2016; Ma et al., 2014; Steenbergen-Hu & Cooper, 2013; VanLehn, 2011).

Personalization is a ubiquitous and defining goal for many educational technologies (see Chapter 23 by Ritter and Koedinger). Two examples are *AutoTutor for CSAL* (Center for the Study of Adult Literacy) and *Assessment and LEarning in Knowledge Spaces* (ALEKS). AutoTutor for CSAL is a web-based ITS that delivers comprehension instruction (Graesser et al., 2016; Fang et. al., 2021). A typical lesson in the system consists of a video reviewing a comprehension strategy and practices scaffolded by conversational agents. When students practice the reading strategy within a lesson, they usually begin with medium-level materials. The system subsequently branches students into different conditions where the learning materials are of different difficulty based on the assessment of their performance. ALEKS is an ITS that provides math skill training. This system tracks the knowledge states of students (e.g., the topics students know and the topics students are ready to learn) and adaptively responds with assignments that are sensitive to these knowledge states (Craig et al., 2013).

Another important goal of AIBAs is to provide *feedback* to facilitate or inform students regarding their progress. Feedback in the context of education is essential for knowledge and skill acquisition, and is thus an important element of the instruction in educational technologies (Epstein et al., 2002; VanLehn, 2011; see Chapter 9 by Aleven et al.). AI affords rapid or real-time assessments in educational technologies, which in turn enable automated, immediate, and personalized feedback. Educational assessment is typically categorized into summative assessment, which evaluates how much students learn, and formative assessment, which assesses how students learn. The feedback generated from these two types of assessments is referred to as summative and formative feedback, respectively.

Summative feedback provides information regarding learners' current performance or performance relative to others (e.g., scores, skill bars, rankings, and completion reports). For example, Criterion is an automated writing evaluation tool developed by Educational Testing Service (Burstein et al., 2013) that generates summative feedback immediately after a student submits an essay. The feedback includes a holistic score and diagnostic feedback about grammar, vocabulary usage, mechanics, style and organization, and development.

In contrast, formative feedback includes information that helps learners appreciate current states, desired states, and ways to improve or grow (e.g., hints, prompts, and motivating messages). Durlach and Spain (2014) summarized formative feedback generated during the instruction of intelligent tutoring systems into two types: corrective feedback and supportive feedback. Additionally, within each type, there are five levels according to the purpose of feedback, the amount of information within the feedback, and the techniques used to trigger and deliver feedback. Corrective feedback includes feedback with only summary score (level 0), minimal feedback with item accuracy information (level 1), correct answers or explanation of correct answers (level 2), error-sensitive feedback (level 3), and context-aware feedback (level 4). Supportive feedback includes no support (level 0), fixed hints on request (level 1), locally adaptive hints on request or triggered (level 2), context-aware hints on request or triggered (level 3), and context-aware hints on request or triggered together with interactive dialogue (level 4).

Many systems provide both corrective and supportive feedback, but to different levels. For example, *AutoTutor* is a conversation-based learning environment that has been used to teach a wide range of topics such as computer literacy, physics, scientific reasoning, and comprehension strategies (Graesser et al., 2020; Nye et al., 2014; see Chapter 11 by Rus et al.). *AutoTutor* provides formative feedback to scaffold student learning through conversations between students and computer agents. After students answer a question, the computer agents typically provide formative feedback including whether the student's answer is positive or negative, pumps that ask students to say more or take some action, hints that guide students toward a particular answer, and prompts that get students to use a particular word or phrase (Graesser et al., 2020).

Some systems provide both summative and formative feedback. For example, *Writing Pal* is an ITS for writing that can provide formative feedback to students during their writing practice (McNamara et al., 2012; Roscoe & McNamara, 2013). After a student submits an essay, the system provides immediate formative feedback, including a holistic rating from poor to great (6-point scale), a message addressing particular writing goals and strategy-based solutions, and prompts toward relevant lessons or practice games for just-in-time strategy instruction or practice (Roscoe & McNamara, 2013; Roscoe et al., 2014). *Betty's Brain* is a computer-based learning environment built upon the "learning-by-teaching" paradigm in which students teach a virtual agent, Betty, scientific topics (e.g., ecology) (Biswas et al., 2016; see Chapter 20 by McLaren and Nguyen). The feedback generated by the system includes summative feedback such as Betty's performance on the quizzes, and formative feedback including Betty's explanations for her answers and learning strategies provided by the mentor agent (Biswas et al., 2016; see Chapter 4 by Azevedo and Wiedbusch).

Importantly, these goals (i.e., guiding personalized instruction and providing feedback) are not mutually exclusive, and many modern systems address both. For example, *Cognitive Tutor* is a math ITS that provides step-by-step feedback to students as they work through problems (Koedinger & Corbett, 2006; Pane et al., 2014; Ritter et al., 2007). The system also evaluates students during their problem solving and reconstructs what knowledge students have already mastered versus what they have yet to learn. The system then decides the learning path (e.g., selects the problem targeting the knowledge components that are missing or in error) for each individual student (Anderson & Gluck, 2001; Koedinger & Corbett, 2006). VanLehn (2006) considered two loops while describing ITS behaviors: an outer loop at the task level (e.g., solving a mathematics problem) and an inner loop at the step level (e.g., a solution step in a mathematics problem). The outer loop involves customizing the learning paths (e.g., problem selection), and the inner loop is usually where the detailed step-by-step feedback is provided to students. Many ITSs include both loops to achieve their educational goals. It should be noted that achieving the specific goals may require different data sources, or computational methods, which foreshadows later elements of the framework.

Constructs

Constructs refer to the variables, states, or phenomena that will be assessed or measured. As alluded to earlier, the constructs are partly specified by the AIBA goals. That is, the constructs are typically important learner characteristics that potentially influence the efficacy of instruction and training (e.g., prior knowledge or skill mastery) or require feedback (e.g., on the accuracy of a solution or appropriate use of a strategy). For example, if the goal of an educational system is to provide customized math instruction and formative feedback, measuring students' math competencies is the basis for the system to time the delivery of appropriate learning materials and just-in-time feedback. Similarly, students' affect (e.g., boredom or confusion) may affect their level of engagement and efficacy of the instruction. As such, the system may also embed assessments to measure students' affective states for further motivational intervention. Constructs that are commonly measured in AIBAs include knowledge, skills, learning strategies, and learners' cognitive and affective states.

Knowledge and *skills* are perhaps the most common constructs assessed in many educational technologies. Knowledge refers to familiarity with factual information and theoretical concepts. Skill refers to the ability to apply knowledge to specific situations. Knowledge and skills are typically evaluated to determine what instruction or training to provide, what feedback to offer, and to understand whether the instruction or training provided by the technologies is effective. For example, *Why2/AutoTutor* (Nye et al., 2014) is an ITS designed to teach physics. The system dynamically assesses students' physics knowledge to provide feedback and customize instruction. *Physics Playground* is a 2-dimensional computer game helping students learn Newtonian physics (Shute et al., 2020). The assessments embedded in the game evaluate students' physics knowledge to guide the game level selection and learning support (e.g., hints and worked examples) provided by the system. *Cognitive Tutor* and *Wayang Outpost* (Arroyo et al., 2014) are ITSs to improve mathematics skills. When students interact with these systems, their mathematics problem-solving skills are continuously assessed to guide which feedback and instructional materials to provide. *AutoThinking* is an adaptive digital game designed to promote students' skills and conceptual knowledge in computational thinking (Hooshyar et al., 2021; see Chapter 20 by McLaren and Nguyen). The player takes the role of a mouse that solves programming problems to collect cheese pieces in a maze while also escaping from two cats. Students' skills and knowledge are assessed during the game, and the system adaptively adjusts the performance of the cats based on student performance.

The game also provides different types of feedback (i.e., textual, graphical, and video) to players based on the assessment of the current state of the maze and students' skill levels.

Strategies refer to intentional procedures that students know and use to improve their performance, which are also commonly assessed constructs. Strategies include domain-specific and domain-general strategies, and adaptive and maladaptive strategies. The assessment of students' learning strategies is to provide feedback, facilitate instruction or training and help improve the effectiveness of educational technologies. For instance, *MetaTutor* is an ITS designed to foster students' self-regulated learning (Azevedo et al., 2019; see Chapter 4 by Azevedo and Wiedbusch). It evaluates domain-general learning strategies such as planning, monitoring, and note-taking when students work on biology problems, and provides feedback to help students enhance self-regulated learning. *Interactive Strategy Training for Active Reading and Thinking* (*iSTART*, Boonthum et al., 2011; McNamara, 2021; McCarthy et al., 2020b) is an ITS that provides reading strategy training. *iSTART* evaluates students' comprehension strategies such as monitoring, paraphrasing, bridging, and elaboration while they read challenging texts.

Learner states such as cognitive states (e.g., cognitive load and confusion) and affective states (e.g., emotions and boredom) are more frequently assessed during the initial development of AIBAs, often to assess students' attitudes toward the instruction, training, or feedback (i.e., user experience) (Taub et al., 2021; see Chapter 4 by Azevedo and Wiedbusch and Chapter 20 by McLaren and Nguyen). These states are the signals of success and struggles and may mediate or moderate how students approach learning and assessment tasks (Jackson & McNamara, 2013). Some ITSs further incorporate algorithms to assess learner states to guide adaptive instruction. For example, *Cognitive Tutor* implements multiple algorithms to assess students' engagement by detecting their gaming behavior (e.g., repeatedly asking for help until the system reveals the correct answer, or inputting answers quickly and systematically) and off-task behavior (Baker, 2007; Baker et al., 2008a, 2008b). Similarly, *Affective AutoTutor* is a version of *AutoTutor* that detects students' affective states such as boredom, confusion, and frustration. When negative emotions are detected, the system provides empathetic and motivational statements with the goal of reengaging students (D'Mello et al., 2009; D'Mello & Graesser, 2013).

Procedures of AIBA

Procedures refer to the means of achieving AIBA purposes and goals, which involve data sources, computational methods, and visibility of assessments. Data sources refer to the data collected to measure constructs in a robust, valid, and reliable manner. Computational methods are employed to process, transform, and analyze the data to make inferences. Assessment visibility refers to whether assessments are overt and obvious to the learner, or if they are covert (i.e., explicit) or unobtrusive (i.e., implicit or stealth assessment). In short, these design dimensions broadly describe the methods and approaches used to operationalize the assessments.

Data sources

Data sources refer to information, input, or output from students that inform assessments such as knowledge, skills, strategies, and emotions. Commonly collected data sources include performance, behavior, language, and biometric data.

Performance data are commonly collected to assess student work and outcomes (e.g., completeness, accuracy, and quality), and in turn, make inferences about students' knowledge or skills. The specific form of performance data can vary between tasks. For example, *iSTART* embeds two types of tasks. One type requires students to generate constructed responses (e.g., writing self-explanations) in sentences or paragraphs. The other type asks students to select correct answers from the provided choices. The performance data for the two types of tasks are the quality of constructed responses and correctness of the answers, respectively (McCarthy et al., 2020b). In the domain of computer science, student submission sequences on programming tasks can be collected as a type of performance data (see Chapter 13 by Mao et al.).

Another frequently collected data source are students' *behaviors*, which contain information about student actions and interactions. Behavior data include students' actions such as their keystrokes, button clicks, mouse movements, and navigation through the system as well as how they implement the actions (e.g., time interval between actions; see Chapter 15 by Pozdniakov et al.). Behavior data have often been used to infer students' learning strategies, cognitive states, or affective states in many educational systems (Aleven et al., 2016; Paquette & Baker, 2019; Snow et al., 2014, 2015, 2016; see Chapter 4 by Azevedo and Wiedbusch).

Language is a data source containing information about what and how students communicate verbally (e.g., via spoken or written input). Language products can be revealing of performance (e.g., knowledge and skills). For example, one type of *iSTART* practice requires students to generate constructed responses (e.g., self-explanations) in sentences or paragraphs. From this practice, students' reading skills can be assessed using features of these student-generated texts; the quality of the constructed responses is a performance metric (Allen & McNamara, 2015; McCarthy et al., 2020a).

Biometric data refers to the information about students' physiology, gaze, posture, and facial expressions (e.g., electroencephalogram (EEG), galvanic skin response (GSR), and eye-tracking), which is usually collected to assess learner states (Azevedo & Gašević, 2019; Cabada et. al., 2020; Pham & Wang, 2018).

Finally, when multiple data sources are used together, they are often referred to as *multimodal data* (Blikstein & Worsley, 2016; Worsley, 2018; Worsley & Blikstein, 2018; see Chapter 10 by Lajoie and Li). It is a common practice for researchers and designers to use multimodal data sources to evaluate students and provide instruction and feedback accordingly. For example, biometric data are often used together with performance data to infer students' affective states (Azevedo & Gašević, 2019; D'Mello & Graesser, 2013; Sharma et al., 2020; Wang & Lin, 2018).

Computational methods

Computational methods refer to statistical analyses, AI, machine learning, and other methods used to process and analyze data, make inferences, and automate responses to students. These methods may depend on or be influenced by data sources because some data sources demand specific methods for data processing or transformation. For example, natural language processing (NLP) methods are required to process and analyze language data. Computational methods may also be influenced by purposes. Different methods may provide output that is more or less useful depending on the types of feedback provided to students or adaptivity adopted by the educational technologies. In this section, we discuss how three categories of computational methods of AIBAs (i.e., Bayesian methods, NLP methods, and machine-learning methods) are implemented in various systems to assess the target constructs and achieve educational goals.

Bayesian methods

Bayesian methods refer to the statistical methods that use probability to represent uncertainty; they have been adopted by a wide range of educational technologies. One frequently used Bayesian method is Bayesian network analysis, which graphically represents a set of variables and their conditional independencies, and then exploits this information to reduce the complexity of probabilistic inference (Culbertson, 2016; Pearl, 1988).

Bayesian network analysis is often used to assess the mastery of a skill or a knowledge component. In the design of several ITSs, domain knowledge is decomposed by researchers into smaller units referred to as knowledge components (Conati & Zhou, 2002; Conati et al., 2018; VanLehn et al., 2005). A complex cognitive task usually involves numerous knowledge components (Anderson, 2014). For example, *Andes* (VanLehn et al., 2005) is an ITS developed to assist physics problem solving, covering about 75% of the AP Physics B curriculum. The *Andes* developers decomposed relevant content into 308 knowledge components addressing well-known principles, such as Newton's Second Law or Ohm's Law. Solving a problem in *Andes* typically involves multiple knowledge components and requires several steps. To assess a student's mastery of a knowledge component (e.g., a physics rule), the system evaluates the probability of mastery of the prerequisite knowledge and students' performance on each step while solving a problem. Specifically, *Andes* builds a Bayesian network whose nodes and links represent how the steps in a problem solution derive from previous steps and physics rules for each problem or task solved by a student. When a problem-solving step is entered in the *Andes* interface, *Andes* retrieves the corresponding node in the Bayesian network, sets its value to "true" and computes the posterior probability of other nodes in the network given this new evidence. The posterior probabilities become the prior probabilities of the nodes in the network for the next problem that uses the previous rule (Conati, 2010). As such, *Andes* dynamically assesses students' knowledge and updates the student model.

Cognitive Tutor is an ITS developed to teach math, and it also implements Bayesian methods for real-time diagnosis of students' math knowledge and skills. Referred to as *Bayesian Knowledge Tracing* (BKT; Corbett & Anderson, 1995), it is equivalent to the two-node Bayesian network (Baker et al., 2008a). BKT algorithms compute the probability of a student mastering a rule at time T_{i+1} as a function of the probability of knowing the rule at time T_i and observations of the student's performance on steps pertaining to that rule at T_{i+1}. With BKT, *Cognitive Tutor* diagnoses students' knowledge while they interact with the system, and provides individualized feedback and instruction based on the diagnosis. In addition to assessing knowledge and skills, Bayesian network analysis has also been used to estimate learner states. For example, *Prime Climb* is an educational game designed to help students learn number factorization. Bayesian networks were used to model students' affective states (e.g., joy, distress, shame) when they play the game (Conati & Zhou, 2002; Conati, 2011). *Wayang Outpost* is an ITS designed to teach high-school mathematics, and a Bayesian network was applied to infer students' attitudes toward learning (Arroyo & Woolf, 2005; Arroyo et al., 2014).

Natural language processing (NLP) methods

NLP is a broad category of methods used for different levels of natural language processing, such as speech recognition, syntactic analysis, semantic analysis, and discourse analysis (Burstein et al., 2013; Elliot et al., 2003; D'Mello et al., 2011; Litman et al., 2006; McNamara et al., 2007, 2013). Speech recognition focuses on diagramming a continuous speech signal into a sequence of known words. Syntactic analysis analyzes groups of words conforming to the rules of formal grammar. For example, it determines the ways words are clustered into components such as noun and verb phrases. Semantic analysis focuses on understanding the meaning and interpretation of words, signs and sentence structure. It involves diagramming a sentence to a type of meaning representation such as a logical expression. Discourse analysis focuses on the nature of the discourse relationships between sentences and how context impacts sentential interpretations. NLP methods are widely used in ITSs designed for language and literacy training (e.g., reading, comprehension, and writing), and conversation-based ITSs that require students' input to be in the form of language (Dascalu et al., 2017, 2018; McNamara et al., 2018).

In addition to ITSs, NLP methods are also widely used in AWE systems to assign scores and provide diagnostic feedback. For example, the *Intelligent Essay Assessor* (IEA) developed by Pearson Education is an AWE system that can analyze students' writing and provide automated feedback (Foltz et al., 2013). The feedback generated by IEA includes a holistic score and analytic feedback on six traits: ideas (i.e., developing a main idea with supporting ideas), organization (using organization to highlight the main idea and move to the conclusion), conventions (using conventions such as spelling, punctuation, and grammar correctly), sentence fluency (using a variety of sentence lengths and structures correctly), word choice (using a variety of specific, descriptive, and appropriate words), and voice (using a consistent and effective tone). The NLP method embedded in IEA is Latent Semantic Analysis (LSA), which uses statistical computations to extract and represent the meaning of words. Specifically, given a large corpus of text with millions of words and thousands of documents, a matrix is created that indicates the context in which each word occurs. The context of a word is the document in which it occurs, which may be the sentence, paragraph, or entire text. This is a sparse matrix because most terms occur in few documents, and it is a large matrix because there are many terms across many documents. The matrix is then reduced to discover its latent properties using singular value decomposition (SVD). This process creates a multidimensional LSA space, wherein a word is represented by a fixed-size vector of real numbers. A sentence or document is also represented by a fixed-size vector, made by summing component word vectors. Words, sentences, and documents can be compared with each other by comparing their vectors. To assess the quality of essays, IEA compares the LSA vectors representing student essays with the vectors of pre-scored essays on the same topic to assess the semantic similarity. The similarity between a target essay and a pre-scored essay is measured by the cosine between the two vectors. As such, the semantic content of two essays can be compared and a score derived based on their similarity (Foltz et al., 1999; Landauer et al., 2007, 2013; McNamara, 2011).

Another example of using NLP methods for data processing and analysis is *AutoTutor*, in which conversational agents hold conversations with students in natural language and provide feedback (Graesser et al., 2004, 2020); therefore, one key data source is language. For a typical *AutoTutor* task, there are multiple conversational turns between students and computer agents. The conversations in the system are designed according to a conversational framework referred to as expectation and misconception tailored (EMT) dialogue. Specifically, for each main question there is a list of expectations (e.g., anticipated good answers and steps in a procedure) and a list of anticipated misconceptions (e.g., bad answers, incorrect beliefs, errors, and bugs) created by domain experts. As students articulate their answers over multiple conversational turns, their answers are compared with the expectations and misconceptions using LSA. *AutoTutor* compares the LSA vector of students' answers to the vectors of the expectations and misconceptions (Graesser et al., 2020). The assessment results indicate whether an expectation is covered or a misconception exists, and also affect the next dialog move to present to students (e.g., pumps, hints, and prompts).

Machine-learning methods

Machine learning (ML) had been defined as a "field of study that gives computers the ability to learn without being explicitly programmed" (Samuel, 1959). Machine-learning methods refer to the computer algorithms that improve automatically through experience and data. Machine-learning methods are frequently used in AIBAs to analyze different types of data, such as language, performance, behavioral and multimodal data. Machine-learning algorithms usually build models based on sample data, known as "training data," in order to make predictions or decisions.

Machine-learning methods have been combined with NLP in many AWE systems to grade essays and provide automated feedback. The implementation of automatic essay scoring usually consists of a training stage and a scoring stage. During the training stage, NLP tools are used to identify and extract linguistic features that can predict the scores of the sample essays (i.e., training data) rated by human experts. Weighted statistical models are then trained to predict the score using the features. The linguistic features identified for the scoring are usually related to the rubrics which define how the essays should be scored. For example, *Criterion* is an AWE designed to help students develop their writing skills by providing automated and constructive feedback. *Criterion* uses the e-rater scoring engine to identify linguistic features and score essays (Burstein, 2003; Burstein et al., 2013). The linguistic features e-rater extracts consist of three modules: syntax, discourse, and topic. The features in the syntax module (e.g., subjunctive auxiliary verbs, subordinate clauses) capture syntactic variety in an essay, and they are identified by a parser. The discourse module features capture discourse-based relationships and organization in essays, and are identified using a conceptual framework of conjunctive relations including cue words (e.g., using words like "perhaps" or "possibly" to express a belief), terms (e.g., using conjuncts such as "in summary" and "in conclusion" for summarizing), and syntactic structures (e.g., using complement clauses to identify the beginning of a new argument). The topic module features capture the vocabulary usage and topical content. A vector–space model is used to convert the training essays into weight vectors which populate the training space.

Similar to *Criterion*, *My Access!* is an AWE system developed by Vantage Learning, and it uses the IntelliMetric scoring system to evaluate over 400 syntactic, discourse, and semantic features. Those features are described in five dimensions: focus and coherence, organization, development and elaboration, sentence structure, and mechanics and conventions. The features in focus and coherence dimension capture a single point of view, cohesiveness and consistency of purpose, and main ideas in an essay. The features on organization focus on an essay's transitional fluency and logic of discourse, such as the introduction and conclusion, logical structure, logical transitions, and the sequence of ideas. The features in development and elaboration dimension analyze the breadth of the content and the supporting ideas in an essay. The sentence structure category features examine sentence complexity and variety such as syntactic variety, sentence complexity, usage, readability, and subject-verb agreement. The features about mechanics and conventions describe whether the essay includes the conventions of standard English such as grammar, spelling, capitalization, sentence completeness, and punctuation (Elliott et al., 2003; Schultz, 2013).

Although the systems differ in the approach of extracting linguistic features, the goal of training the statistical models is to accurately predict the expert-rated scores with the selected features. Next, the statistical models including selected linguistic features and their weights are fitted into the new data (i.e., essays) to assign scores and provide diagnostic feedback on a set of dimensions. For instance, e-rater provides a holistic score and diagnostic feedback about grammar, vocabulary usage, mechanics, style and organization, and development (Burstein, 2013). Similar to e-rater, IntelliMetric generates a score reflecting overall performance as well as diagnostic feedback on five rhetorical and analytical dimensions such as conventions and organization (Elliott et al., 2003; Schultz, 2013).

Some ITSs designed to help students improve their literacy skills (e.g., reading and writing) also use machine-learning and NLP methods to estimate the performance in the form of language. For example, *iSTART* implements NLP and machine-learning methods to assess self-explanations generated by students and provide formative feedback. To evaluate a self-explanation, *iSTART* compares its LSA vector with the vector of four benchmarks separately. The four benchmarks are (1) the words in the title of the passage, (2) the words in the target sentence, (3) prior words or sentences in the prior text that are causally related to the target sentence, and (4) the words that appear more than once in the previously collected explanations and do not appear in the other benchmarks. The final rating of the self-explanation is based on a weighted sum of the four LSA cosines between the explanation and the four benchmarks (McNamara et al., 2007). In addition, *iSTART* combines LSA and word-based algorithms using machine-learning methods (i.e., discriminant function analysis) to generate formative feedback that prompts the readers to improve their self-explanations (McNamara, 2021). *Writing Pal* also implements NLP and machine-learning methods to assess essays and guide the feedback and individualized training (McNamara et al., 2012; Roscoe & McNamara, 2013; Roscoe et al., 2014).

In addition to analyzing language, machine-learning methods are used for the analysis of other data sources. For example, *Affective AutoTutor* is a version of *AutoTutor* that can detect students' affective states and provide supportive feedback based on students' emotions (D'Mello et al., 2009; D'Mello & Graesser, 2013). In addition to recording students' inputs when they have conversations with the computer agents in the system log files, *Affective AutoTutor* also records students' facial features and body languages with cameras and the body posture measurement system (BPMS). The multimodal data, including conversational cues (i.e., dialogue features), facial expressions, and body language, are analyzed with machine-learning methods (e.g., Naive Bayes logistic regression and support vector machines) to classify students' emotions such as confusion, boredom, flow, frustration, and neutral emotion (D'Mello & Graesser, 2013). Similar to *Affective AutoTutor*, *MetaTutor* applies machine-learning algorithms such as Random Forests, Naive Bayes, Logistic Regression, and Support Vector Machines to analyze eye-tracking data (i.e., gaze data) and classify students' emotions (e.g., boredom and curiosity) during learning (Jaques et al., 2014).

Machine-learning methods are also used to analyze performance and behavioral data. For example, *LP-ITS Tutor* is an ITS teaching students linear programming. It adopts machine-learning methods to assess students' performance so that the system can provide individualized instruction (Abu Naser, 2012). Specifically, the log files recorded by the system contain rich information about students and their learning details, such as performance, actions, time on task, and problem details. The log files are analyzed with the machine-learning algorithm (i.e., Artificial Neural Networks) to predict students' performance and decide what learning materials to provide to each individual student. *Cognitive Tutor* embeds machine-learning algorithms to detect students' off-task behavior and gaming behavior using performance and behavioral data such as actions and action times (Baker, 2007; Baker et al., 2008b). *iSnap* is a computer-based learning environment designed to teach a computer science course for non-majors (Price et al., 2017). This system implemented deep-learning algorithms to model student learning progression (e.g., temporal sequences in log files) and predict student success or failure to provide adaptive intervention (see Chapter 13 by Mao et al.).

Bayesian, NLP, and machine learning are widely used methods in educational technologies. However, other methods are also viable. For example, several ITSs use constraint-based modeling, such as *SQL-Tutor*, which teaches SQL database language (Mitrovic, 2003), *EER-Tutor*, which teaches conceptual database design (Mitrovic & Suraweera, 2016), and *J-LATTE*, a tutor for learning Java (Holland et al., 2009). The fundamental idea behind constraint-based modeling is that all correct solutions to a problem are similar in that they do not violate any domain principles. The constraint-based systems store a set of domain-specific constraints representing the characteristics of correct solutions. A constraint is usually in the form of "If is <relevant condition> is true, then <satisfaction condition> had better also be true." A solution is incorrect if it violates one or more constraints. As such, constraint-based modeling is primarily the match between students' solutions and constraints.

Visibility

Assessment visibility refers to whether the AIBAs implemented in educational technologies are overt and obvious to the learner, or if they are covert or unobtrusive. In most current educational technologies, students' task performances are explicitly evaluated: students usually know that the feedback they receive is based on performance assessment. For example, when students submit an essay in an AWE system and receive the score and analytical feedback immediately, it is evident that the essay is assessed by the system, and the feedback is based on the assessment. Similarly, when a computer agent tells a student whether an answer is correct, and gives some hints, students usually understand the feedback is based on an underlying evaluation.

By contrast, *stealth assessment* is a type of assessment that evaluates students covertly and unobtrusively. Stealth assessment refers to the evidence-based assessments woven directly and invisibly into gaming environments (Shute, 2011; Shute & Ventura, 2013). The data needed to assess students (i.e., players) are generated when students interact with the game, and can be used to infer students' skills or knowledge. In a well-designed game assessment scenario, students may not be aware of being assessed during the gameplay. Stealth assessment was initially proposed and explored because some competencies such as persistence, creativity, self-efficacy, openness, and teamwork were revealed to substantially impact student academic achievement (O'Connor & Paunonen, 2007; Poropat, 2009; Sternberg, 2006). However, those competencies were not assessed in the educational technologies. Researchers then proposed using performance-based assessments to assess those competencies by analyzing how students use knowledge and skills in the real world. One approach to assessing those competencies is via game-based learning environments, which can provide students with diverse scenarios requiring the application of differing competencies. When students play games, their performance, behavior and other types of data are collected, and analyzed to infer their competencies. As such, students are being assessed unobtrusively during the gameplay.

For example, in *Physics Playground* stealth assessments have been implemented to evaluate students' competencies including physics knowledge, persistence, and creativity (Shute & Rahimi, 2021; Ventura & Shute, 2013; Wang et al., 2015). Specifically, a student produces a dense stream of performance data during the gameplay. The data is recorded by the game system in a log file, which is analyzed using Bayesian methods (i.e., Bayesian networks) to infer students' competencies. The system then provides formative feedback and other forms of learning support to students during gameplay based on the assessment. Stealth assessments for performance-based measures and domain-general competencies (e.g., persistence) have been found to be valid across a variety of game environments (Ventura & Shute, 2013; Ventura et al., 2013).

Another example of stealth assessment is embedded in a game called *Use Your Brainz*, which is a slightly modified version of a popular commercial game *Plants vs. Zombies 2* (Shute et al., 2016). The stealth assessment also uses players' performance data, which are the log files recording in-game behaviors. The performance is analyzed with Bayesian methods to infer students' problem-solving skills. The stealth assessment measures based on performance data have also been validated against external measures.

In addition to assessing general competencies independent of domain, stealth assessments can also be used to assess domain knowledge and skills that are not explicitly evaluated by the intelligent systems. For example, during the self-explanation practice in *iSTART*, students receive immediate feedback on the quality of their self-explanations which is based on the NLP analysis of the self-explanations. The linguistic and semantic features of those explanations are not just signatures of self-explanation quality, they also provide windows into students' underlying comprehension skills and knowledge. Features of language provide information about individual differences in vocabulary, domain, and world knowledge as well as literacy skills. For example, rare words, complex syntax, and language that is cohesive are signatures of stronger reading skills (Allen et al., 2015, 2016a, 2016b; Allen & McNamara, 2015; McCarthy et al., 2020a). NLP provides a means to understand and evaluate language skills and knowledge because features of language (e.g., syntax, concreteness, meaningfulness, cohesion) provide proxies aligned with how students are processing, can process, are producing, and can produce language (McNamara, 2021). Stealth assessment of literacy skills has strong potential to enhance the adaptivity of systems in which students generate natural language input.

DISCUSSION

This chapter introduces the AI-based assessment (AIBA) framework, which categorizes the purposes and procedures of AIBA using five interrelated dimensions in educational technologies: goals, constructs, data sources, computational methods, and visibility.

The overarching purposes are described from two dimensions (see Figure 21.1), which are goals of AIBA, and constructs to be assessed in support of those goals. The broad goals of AIBA comprise the provision of summative and/or formative feedback to students, and guidance of personalized instruction or training. These goals are not mutually exclusive as many educational technologies address both. Constructs refer to the variables that are assessed by AIBA, which are heavily influenced by the goals. Specifically, constructs are typically important learner characteristics that potentially influence the efficacy of instruction, training, and feedback. The commonly measured constructs include knowledge, skills, learning strategies, and learners' cognitive states and emotions.

The procedures of AIBAs refer to how the purposes are achieved in educational technologies, which involve three dimensions: data sources, computational methods, and visibility of assessments. Data sources refer to data collected in order to reliably and accurately measure the constructs. The commonly collected data sources in modern educational technologies include performance data, language, behavior, and biometric data (e.g., physiology, gaze, body language, and facial expressions). Multiple data sources are sometimes used together in the assessments, referred to as multimodal data. The access to rich data enables the assessment of some constructs that can be challenging to evaluate. Data collected within the AIBAs are processed and analyzed using appropriate computational methods to infer the target learner traits. The commonly used methods in current educational technologies include Bayesian methods, NLP, and machine-learning methods. Each category includes a variety of specific techniques for data processing and analysis. Different methods and techniques are often used together in educational tools to evaluate the target constructs and achieve their goals. Finally, visibility refers to whether the AIBAs implemented in educational technologies are obvious or unobtrusive to learners. The latter dimension includes stealth assessments, which are usually implemented in game-based learning environments seamlessly to evaluate students unobtrusively during their gameplay.

Regarding recent AIBA advances, learning analytics is a research area that has played an important role. Learning analytics researchers have collected data generated in various AI systems and explored diverse methods, particularly machine-learning methods, to analyze the data, which helps achieve the goals of AIBAs. For example, learning analytics research examined the data from digital games to better understand how students interacted with games and help improve game design (see Chapter 20 by McLaren and Nguyen). Learning analytics researchers also analyzed data collected from Massive Open Online Courses (MOOCs) to help improve the instructional design (Doleck et al., 2021; Er et al., 2019; Shukor & Abdullah, 2019). Importantly, although we can collect rich data from many sources, it is not the case that more data is always better. We should make evaluations based on the goals of AIBAs and the characteristics of learning environments to decide what data are necessary for valid and reliable assessments.

AIBAs undergird diverse educational technologies to guide students' learning and teachers' instruction during their use of the educational technologies. Designers and educators make multiple, intertwined decisions regarding the design of the instructional technologies. Each decision and design choice can impact others as they often introduce constraints in the assessments. System designers often consider these dimensions prior to developing an educational system. The AIBA framework is designed to facilitate and guide that process such that researchers and developers can discern a clearer picture of the AI-based technology prior to development. As the five dimensions of AIBA are interrelated and intertwined, we recommend that they are considered as a whole during the design and implementation of AI-based educational technologies.

REFERENCES

Abu Naser, S. S. (2012). Predicting learners' performance using artificial neural networks in linear programming intelligent tutoring system. *International Journal of Artificial Intelligence & Applications, 3*(2), 65–73.

Aleven, V., Roll, I., McLaren, B. M., & Koedinger, K. R. (2016). Help helps, but only so much: Research on help seeking with intelligent tutoring systems. *International Journal of Artificial Intelligence in Education, 26*(1), 205–223.

Allen, L. K., Dascalu, M., McNamara, D. S., Crossley, S. A., & Trausan-Matu, S. (2016a). Modeling individual differences among writers using ReaderBench. In *EduLearn* (pp. 5269–5279). Barcelona, Spain: IATED.

Allen, L. K., & McNamara, D. S. (2015). You are your words: Modeling students' vocabulary knowledge with natural language processing. In O. C. Santos, J. G. Boticario, C. Romero, M. Pechenizkiy, A. Merceron, P. Mitros, J. M. Luna, C. Mihaescu, P. Moreno, A. Hershkovitz, S. Ventura, & M. Desmarais (Eds.), *Proceedings of the 8th International Conference on Educational Data Mining (EDM 2015)* (pp. 258–265). Madrid, Spain: International Educational Data Mining Society.

Allen, L. K., Perret, C. A., & McNamara, D. S. (2016b). Linguistic signatures of cognitive processes during writing. In J. Trueswell, A. Papafragou, D. Grodner, & D. Mirman (Eds.), *Proceedings of the 38th Annual Meeting of the Cognitive Science Society in Philadelphia, PA* (pp. 2483–2488). Austin, TX: Cognitive Science Society.

Allen, L. K., Snow, E. L., & McNamara, D. S. (2015). Are you reading my mind? Modeling students' reading comprehension skills with natural language processing techniques. In J. Baron, G. Lynch, N. Maziarz, P. Blikstein, A. Merceron, & G. Siemens (Eds.), *Proceedings of the 5th International Learning Analytics & Knowledge Conference* (pp. 246–254). Poughkeepsie: ACM.

Anderson, J. R. (2014). *Rules of the Mind*. Psychology Press.

Anderson, J. R., & Gluck, K. (2001). What role do cognitive architectures play in intelligent tutoring systems. *Cognition & Instruction: Twenty-Five Years of Progress*, 227–262.

Ariel, B. (2019). Technology in policing. In D. L. Weisburd & A. A. Braga (Eds.), *Innovations in Policing: Contrasting Perspectives* (2nd ed., pp. 521–516). Cambridge, England: Cambridge University Press.

Arroyo, I., & Woolf, B. (2005). Inferring learning and attitudes from a Bayesian network of log file data. In C. K. Looi, G. McCalla, B. Bredeweg, & J. Breuker (Eds.), *Twelfth International Conference on Artificial Intelligence in Education* (pp. 33–40). Amsterdam: IOS Press.

Arroyo, I., Woolf, B. P., Burelson, W., Muldner, K., Rai, D., & Tai, M. (2014). A multimedia adaptive tutoring system for mathematics that addresses cognition, metacognition and affect. *International Journal of Artificial Intelligence in Education, 24*(4), 387–426.

Azevedo, R., & Gašević, D. (2019). Analyzing multimodal multichannel data about self-regulated learning with advanced learning technologies: Issues and challenges. *Computers in Human Behavior, 96*, 207–210.

Azevedo, R., Mudrick, N. V., Taub, M., & Bradbury, A. (2019). Self-regulation in computer assisted learning systems. In J. Dunlosky & K. Rawson (Eds.), *Handbook of Cognition and Education* (pp. 587–618). Cambridge, MA: Cambridge University Press.

Baker, R. S. (2007). Modeling and understanding students' off-task behavior in intelligent tutoring systems. In *CHI '07: Proceedings of the SIGCHI Conference on Human Factors in Computing Systems*, ACM, 1059–1068.

Baker, R. S., Corbett, A. T., & Aleven, V. (2008a). More accurate student modeling through contextual estimation of slip and guess probabilities in Bayesian knowledge tracing. In *International Conference on intelligent Tutoring Systems* (pp. 406–415). Heidelberg, Berlin: Springer.

Baker, R. S., Corbett, A. T., Roll, I., & Koedinger, K. R. (2008b). Developing a generalizable detector of when students game the system. *User Modeling and User-Adapted Interaction, 18*(3), 287–314.

Biswas, G., Segedy, J. R., & Bunchongchit, K. (2016). From design to implementation to practice a learning by teaching system: Betty's Brain. *International Journal of Artificial Intelligence in Education, 26*(1), 350–364.

Blikstein, P., & Worsley, M. (2016). Multimodal learning analytics and education data mining: Using computational technologies to measure complex learning tasks. *Journal of Learning Analytics, 3*(2), 220–238.

Boonthum, C., McCarthy, P. M., Lamkin, T., Jackson, G. T., Magliano, J., & McNamara, D. S. (2011). Automatic natural language processing and the detection of reading skills and reading comprehension. In R. C. Murray & P. M. McCarthy (Eds.), *Proceedings of the 24th International Florida Artificial Intelligence Research Society (FLAIRS) Conference* (pp. 234–239). Menlo Park, CA: AAAI Press.

Burstein, J. (2003). The e-rater scoring engine: Automated essay scoring with natural language processing. In M. D. Shermis & J. C. Burstein (Eds.), *Automated Essay Scoring: A cross Disciplinary Approach* (pp. 113–121). Mahwah, NJ: Lawrence Erlbaum Associates.

Burstein, J., Tetreault, J., & Madnani, N. (2013). The e-rater automated essay scoring system. In M. D. Shermis & J. Burstein (Eds.), *Handbook of Automated Essay Evaluation: Current Applications and New Directions* (pp. 55–67). New York: Routledge.

Cabada, R. Z., Rangel, H. R., Estrada, M. L. B., & Lopez, H. M. C. (2020). Hyperparameter optimization in CNN for learning-centered emotion recognition for intelligent tutoring systems. *Soft Computing, 24*(10), 7593–7602.

Conati, C. (2010). Bayesian student modeling. In *Advances in Intelligent Tutoring Systems* (pp. 281–299). Berlin, Heidelberg: Springer.

Conati, C. (2011). Combining cognitive appraisal and sensors for affect detection in a framework for modeling user affect. In *New Perspectives on Affect and Learning Technologies* (pp. 71–84). New York, NY: Springer.

Conati, C., Jaques, N., & Muir, M. (2013). Understanding attention to adaptive hints in educational games: An eye-tracking study. *International Journal of Artificial Intelligence in Education, 23*(1), 136–161.

Conati, C., Porayska-Pomsta, K., & Mavrikis, M. (2018). AI in education needs interpretable machine learning: Lessons from open learner modelling. *arXiv preprint.* https://arxi.org/1807.00154.

Conati, C., & Zhou, X. (2002). Modeling students' emotions from cognitive appraisal in educational games. In *International Conference on Intelligent Tutoring Systems* (pp. 944–954). Heidelberg, Berlin: Springer.

Coppin, B. (2004). *Artificial Intelligence Illuminated*. Boston, MA: Jones & Bartlett Learning.

Corbett, A. T., & Anderson, J. R. (1995) Knowledge tracing: Modeling the acquisition of procedural knowledge. *User Modeling and User-Adapted Interaction, 4*, 253–278.

Corbett, A. T., Koedinger, K. R., & Anderson, J. R. (1997). Intelligent tutoring systems. In *Handbook of Human-Computer Interaction* (pp. 849–874). North-Holland.

Craig, S. D., Hu, X., Graesser, A. C., Bargagliotti, A. E., Sterbinsky, A., Cheney, K. R., & Okwumabua, T. (2013). The impact of a technology-based mathematics after-school program using ALEKS on student's knowledge and behaviors. *Computers & Education, 68*, 495–504.

Culbertson, M. J. (2016). Bayesian networks in educational assessment: The state of the field. *Applied Psychological Measurement, 40*(1), 3–21.

Dascalu, M., Allen, K. A., McNamara, D. S., Trausan-Matu, S., & Crossley, S. A. (2017). Modeling comprehension processes via automated analyses of dialogism. In G. Gunzelmann, A. Howes, T. Tenbrink, & E. Davelaar (Eds.), *Proceedings of the 39th Annual Meeting of the Cognitive Science Society* (pp. 1884–1889). London, UK: Cognitive Science Society.

Dascalu, M., Crossley, S. A., McNamara, D. S., Dessus, P., & Trausan-Matu, S. (2018). Please Readerbench this text: A multi-dimensional textual complexity assessment framework. In S. Craig (Ed.), *Tutoring and Intelligent Tutoring Systems* (pp. 251–271). Hauppauge, NY: Nova Science Publishers.

D'Mello, S., Craig, S., Fike, K., & Graesser, A. (2009). Responding to learners' cognitive-affective states with supportive and shakeup dialogues. In *International Conference on Human-Computer Interaction* (pp. 595–604). Heidelberg, Berlin: Springer.

D'Mello, S., & Graesser, A. (2013). AutoTutor and affective AutoTutor: Learning by talking with cognitively and emotionally intelligent computers that talk back. *ACM Transactions on Interactive Intelligent Systems (TiiS), 2*(4), 1–39.

D'Mello, S. K., Dowell, N., & Graesser, A. (2011). Does it really matter whether students' contributions are spoken versus typed in an intelligent tutoring system with natural language? *Journal of Experimental Psychology: Applied, 17*(1), 1.

Doleck, T., Lemay, D. J., & Brinton, C. G. (2021). Evaluating the efficiency of social learning networks: Perspectives for harnessing learning analytics to improve discussions. *Computers & Education, 164*, 104124.

Durlach, P. J., & Spain, R. D. (2014). *Framework for Instructional Technology: Methods of Implementing Adaptive Training and Education*. Fort Belvoir, VA: Army Research for the Behavioral and Social Sciences.

Elliott, S., Shermis, M. D., & Burstein, J. (2003). Overview of intelliMetric. In *Automated Essay Scoring: A Cross-Disciplinary Perspective* (pp. 67–70). Elbaum.

Epstein, M. L., Lazarus, A. D., Calvano, T. B., Matthews, K. A., Hendel, R. A., Epstein, B. B., et al. (2002). Immediate feedback assessment technique promotes learning and corrects inaccurate first responses. *The Psychological Record, 52*, 187–201.

Er, E., Gómez-Sánchez, E., Dimitriadis, Y., Bote-Lorenzo, M. L., Asensio-Pérez, J. I., & Álvarez-Álvarez, S. (2019). Aligning learning design and learning analytics through instructor involvement: A MOOC case study. *Interactive Learning Environments, 27*(5–6), 685–698.

Fang, Y., Lippert, C. Z., Chen, S., Frijters, J. C., Greenberg, D., & Graesser, A. C. (2021). Patterns of adults with low literacy skills interacting with an intelligent tutoring system. *International Journal of Artificial Intelligence in Education.* Advance online publication. DOI: 10.1007/s40593-021-00266-y.

Foltz, P. W., Laham, D., & Landauer, T. K. (1999). The intelligent essay assessor: Applications to educational technology. *Interactive Multimedia Electronic Journal of Computer-Enhanced Learning, 1*(2), 939–944.

Foltz, P. W., Streeter, L. A., Lochbaum, K. E., & Landauer, T. K. (2013). Implementation and applications of the intelligent essay assessor. In *Handbook of Automated Essay Evaluation* (pp. 68–88).

Graesser, A. C., Cai, Z., Baer, W. O., Olney, A. M., Hu, X., Reed, M., & Greenberg, D. (2016). Reading comprehension lessons in AutoTutor for the center for the study of adult literacy. In *Adaptive Educational Technologies for Literacy Instruction* (pp. 288–293).

Graesser, A. C., Conley, M. W., & Olney, A. (2012). Intelligent tutoring systems. In K. R. Harris, S. Graham, & T. Urdan (Eds.), *APA Educational Psychology Handbook, Vol 3: Application to Learning and Teaching* (pp. 451–473). Washington, DC: American Psychological Association.

Graesser, A. C., Hu, X., Rus, V., & Cai, Z. (2020). AutoTutor and other conversation-based learning and assessment environments. In A. Rupp, D. Yan, & P. Foltz (Eds.), *Handbook of Automated Scoring: Theory into Practice* (pp. 383–402). New York: CRC Press/Taylor and Francis.

Graesser, A. C., Lu, S., Jackson, G. T., Mitchell, H. H., Ventura, M., Olney, A., & Louwerse, M. M. (2004). AutoTutor: A tutor with dialogue in natural language. *Behavior Research Methods, Instruments, & Computers, 36*(2), 180–192.

Hayhoe, T., Podhorska, I., Siekelova, A., & Stehel, V. (2019). Sustainable manufacturing in Industry 4.0: Cross-sector networks of multiple supply chains, cyber-physical production systems, and AI-driven decision-making. *Journal of Self-Governance and Management Economics, 7*(2), 31–36.

Holland, J., Mitrovic, A., & Martin, B (2009). J-LATTE: A constraint-based tutor for java. In S. C. Kong, H. Ogata, H. C. Arnseth, C. K. K. Chan, T. Hirashima, F. Klett, J. H. M. Lee, C. C. Liu, & C. K. Looi (Eds.), *Proceedings of 17th International Conference on Computers in Education ICCE 2009* (pp. 142–146). Hong Kong: Asia-Pacific Society for Computers in Education.

Hooshyar, D., Malva, L., Yang, Y., Pedaste, M., Wang, M., & Lim, H. (2021). An adaptive educational computer game: Effects on students' knowledge and learning attitude in computational thinking. *Computers in Human Behavior, 114*, 106575.

Jackson, G. T., & McNamara, D. S. (2013). Motivation and performance in a game-based intelligent tutoring system. *Journal of Educational Psychology, 105*, 1036–1049.

Jaques, N., Conati, C., Harley, J. M., & Azevedo, R. (2014). Predicting affect from gaze data during interaction with an intelligent tutoring system. In *International Conference on Intelligent Tutoring Systems* (pp. 29–38). Cham: Springer.

Jiang, F., Jiang, Y., Zhi, H., Dong, Y., Li, H., Ma, S., ... Wang, Y. (2017). Artificial intelligence in healthcare: Past, present and future. *Stroke and Vascular Neurology, 2*(4), 230–243.

Koedinger, K. R., & Corbett, A. (2006). *Cognitive Tutors: Technology Bringing Learning Sciences to the Classroom.* The Cambridge Handbook of the Learning Sciences. New York, NY: Cambridge University Press.

Kulik, J. A., & Fletcher, J. D. (2016). Effectiveness of intelligent tutoring systems: A meta-analytic review. *Review of Educational Research, 86*(1), 42–78.

Landauer, T. K., McNamara, D. S., Dennis, S., & Kintsch, W. (Eds.). (2007). *Handbook of latent Semantic Analysis.* Mahwah, NJ: Erlbaum.

Landauer, T. K., McNamara, D. S., Dennis, S., & Kintsch, W. (Eds.). (2013). *Handbook of latent Semantic Analysis.* Psychology Press.

Li, B. H., Hou, B. C., Yu, W. T., Lu, X. B., & Yang, C. W. (2017). Applications of artificial intelligence in intelligent manufacturing: A review. *Frontiers of Information Technology & Electronic Engineering, 18*(1), 86–96.

Litman, D. J., Rosé, C. P., Forbes-Riley, K., VanLehn, K., Bhembe, D., & Silliman, S. (2006). Spoken versus typed human and computer dialogue tutoring. *International Journal of Artificial Intelligence in Education, 16*(2), 145–170.

Ma, W., Adesope, O. O., Nesbit, J. C., & Liu, Q. (2014). Intelligent tutoring systems and learning outcomes: A meta-analysis. *Journal of Educational Psychology, 106*(4), 901.

McCarthy, K. S., Allen, L. K., & Hinze, S. R. (2020a). Predicting reading comprehension from constructed responses: Explanatory retrievals as stealth assessment. In *International Conference on Artificial Intelligence in Education* (pp. 197–202). Cham: Springer.

McCarthy, K. S., Watanabe, M., Dai, J., & McNamara, D. S. (2020b). Personalized learning in iSTART: Past modifications and future design. *Journal of Research on Technology in Education, 52*(3), 301–321.

McNamara, D., Allen, L. K., McCarthy, S., & Balyan, R. (2018). NLP: Getting computers to understand discourse. In K. Millis, D. Long, J. Magliano, & K. Wiemer (Eds.), *Deep Learning: Multi-Disciplinary Approaches.* Routledge.

McNamara, D. S. (2011). Computational methods to extract meaning from text and advance theories of human cognition. *Topics in Cognitive Science, 2,* 1–15.

McNamara, D. S. (2021). Chasing theory with technology: A quest to understand understanding [Manuscript submitted for publication]. Department of Psychology, Arizona State University.

McNamara, D. S., Boonthum, C., Levinstein, I. B., & Millis, K. (2007). Evaluating self-explanations in iSTART: Comparing word-based and LSA algorithms. In *Handbook of latent Semantic Analysis* (pp. 227–241).

McNamara, D. S., Crossley, S. A., & Roscoe, R. (2013). Natural language processing in an intelligent writing strategy tutoring system. *Behavior Research Methods, 45*(2), 499–515.

McNamara, D. S., Raine, R., Roscoe, R., Crossley, S., Jackson, G. T., ... Graesser, A. C. (2012). The Writing-Pal: Natural language algorithms to support intelligent tutoring on writing strategies. In P. M. McCarthy & C. Boonthum-Denecke (Eds.), *Applied Natural Language Processing and Content Analysis: Identification, Investigation, and Resolution* (pp. 298–311). Hershey, PA: IGI Global.

Mitrovic, A. (2003). An intelligent SQL tutor on the web. *International Journal of Artificial Intelligence in Education, 13*(2–4), 173–197.

Mitrovic, A., & Suraweera, P. (2016). Teaching database design with constraint-based tutors. *International Journal of Artificial Intelligence in Education, 26*(1), 448–456.

Mousavinasab, E., Zarifsanaiey, N., Niakan Kalhori, S., Rakhshan, M., Keikha, L., & Ghazi Saeedi, M. (2021). Intelligent tutoring systems: A systematic review of characteristics, applications, and evaluation methods. *Interactive Learning Environments, 29*(1), 142–163.

Nye, B. D., Graesser, A. C., & Hu, X. (2014). AutoTutor and family: A review of 17 years of natural language tutoring. *International Journal of Artificial Intelligence in Education, 24*(4), 427–469.

O'Connor, M. C., & Paunonen, S. V. (2007). Big Five personality predictors of post-secondary academic performance. *Personality and Individual Differences, 43*(5), 971–990.

Pane, J. F., Griffin, B. A., McCaffrey, D. F., & Karam, R. (2014). Effectiveness of cognitive tutor algebra I at scale. *Educational Evaluation and Policy Analysis, 36*(2), 127–144.

Paquette, L., & Baker, R. S. (2019). Comparing machine learning to knowledge engineering for student behavior modeling: A case study in gaming the system. *Interactive Learning Environments, 27*(5–6), 585–597.

Pearl, J. (1988). *Probabilistic Reasoning in Intelligent Systems.* San Francisco, CA: Morgan Kaufmann.

Peirce, N., Conlan, O., & Wade, V. (2008). Adaptive educational games: Providing non-invasive personalised learning experiences. In *2008 Second IEEE International Conference on Digital Game and Intelligent Toy Enhanced Learning* (pp. 28–35). Banff, Canada: IEEE.

Perrot, P. (2017). What about AI in criminal intelligence: From predictive policing to AI perspectives. *European Police Science and Research Bulletin, 16,* 65–76.

Pham, P., & Wang, J. (2018). Adaptive review for mobile MOOC learning via multimodal physiological signal sensing-a longitudinal study. In *Proceedings of the 20th ACM International Conference on Multimodal Interaction* (pp. 63–72). https://doi.org/10.1145/3242969.3243002.

Poropat, A. E. (2009). A meta-analysis of the five-factor model of personality and academic performance. *Psychological Bulletin, 135*(2), 322.

Price, T. W., Dong, Y., & Lipovac, D. (2017). iSnap: Towards intelligent tutoring in novice programming environments. In *Proceedings of the 2017 ACM SIGCSE Technical Symposium on Computer Science Education* (pp. 483–488). New York, NY: ACM.

Psotka, J., Massey, L. D., & Mutter, S. A. (1988). *Intelligent Tutoring Systems: Lessons Learned.* Hillsdale: Lawrence Erlbaum Associates.

Ritter, S., Anderson, J. R., Koedinger, K. R., & Corbett, A. (2007). Cognitive tutor: Applied research in mathematics education. *Psychonomic Bulletin & Review, 14*(2), 249–255.

Robertson, D. J., Noyes, E., Dowsett, A., Jenkins, R., & Burton, A. M. (2016). Face recognition by metropolitan police super-recognisers. *PLoS One, 11*(2), e0150036.

Roscoe, R. D., Allen, L. K., Weston, J. L., Crossley, S. A., & McNamara, D. S. (2014). The Writing Pal intelligent tutoring system: Usability testing and development. *Computers and Composition, 34,* 39–59.

Roscoe, R. D., & McNamara, D. S. (2013). Writing Pal: Feasibility of an intelligent writing strategy tutor in the high school classroom. *Journal of Educational Psychology, 105*(4), 1010.

Rus, V., D'Mello, S., Hu, X., & Graesser, A. C. (2013). Recent advances in intelligent systems with conversational dialogue. *AI Magazine, 34,* 42–54.

Samuel, A. L. (1959). Some studies in machine learning using the game of checkers. *IBM Journal of Research and Development, 3*(3), 210–229.

Schultz, M. T. (2013). The intellimetric automated essay scoring engine-a review and an application to Chinese essay scoring. In M. D. Shermis & J. Burstein (Eds.), *Handbook of Automated Essay Scoring: Current Applications and Future Directions* (pp. 89–98). New York, NY: Routledge.

Sharma, K., Papamitsiou, Z., Olsen, J. K., & Giannakos, M. (2020). Predicting learners' effortful behaviour in adaptive assessment using multimodal data. In *Proceedings of the Tenth International Conference on Learning Analytics & Knowledge* (pp. 480–489).

Shukor, N. A., & Abdullah, Z. (2019). Using learning analytics to improve MOOC instructional design. *International Journal of Emerging Technologies in Learning (iJET), 14*(24), 6–17.

Shute, V. J. (2011). Stealth assessment in computer-based games to support learning. *Computer Games and Instruction, 55*(2), 503–524.

Shute, V. J., & Psotka, J. (1996). Intelligent tutoring systems: Past, present and future. In D. Jonassen (Ed.), *Handbook of Research on Educational Communications and Technology.* Scholastic Publications.

Shute, V. J., & Rahimi, S. (2021). Stealth assessment of creativity in a physics video game. *Computers in Human Behavior, 116,* 106647. https://doi.org/10.1016/j.chb.2020.106647.

Shute, V., & Ventura, M. (2013). *Stealth Assessment: Measuring and Supporting Learning in Video Games.* Cambridge, MA: MIT Press.

Shute, V. J., Smith, G., Kuba, R., Dai, C. P., Rahimi, S., Liu, Z., & Almond, R. (2020). The design, development, and testing of learning supports for the physics playground game. *International Journal of Artificial Intelligence in Education,* 1–23.

Shute, V. J., Wang, L., Greiff, S., Zhao, W., & Moore, G. (2016). Measuring problem solving skills via stealth assessment in an engaging video game. *Computers in Human Behavior, 63,* 106–117.

Singh, V., & Gu, N. (2012). Towards an integrated generative design framework. *Design Studies, 33*(2), 185–207.

Snow, E. L., Allen, L. K., Jacovina, M. E., & McNamara, D. S. (2015). Does agency matter?: Exploring the impact of controlled behaviors within a game-based environment. *Computers & Education, 26,* 378–392.

Snow, E. L., Jackson, G. T., & McNamara, D. S. (2014). Emergent behaviors in computer-based learning environments: Computational signals of catching up. *Computers in Human Behavior, 41,* 62–70.

Snow, E. L., Likens, A. D., Allen, L. K., & McNamara, D. S. (2016). Taking control: Stealth assessment of deterministic behaviors within a game-based system. *International Journal of Artificial Intelligence in Education, 26,* 1011–1032.

Steenbergen-Hu, S., & Cooper, H. (2013). A meta-analysis of the effectiveness of intelligent tutoring systems on K–12 students' mathematical learning. *Journal of Educational Psychology, 105*(4), 970–987.

Sternberg, R. J. (2006). The nature of creativity. *Creativity Research Journal, 18*(1), 87.

Taub, M., Azevedo, R., Rajendran, R., Cloude, E. B., Biswas, G., & Price, M. J. (2021). How are students' emotions related to the accuracy of cognitive and metacognitive processes during learning with an intelligent tutoring system? *Learning and Instruction, 72*, 101200.

Upadhyay, A. K., & Khandelwal, K. (2018). Applying artificial intelligence: Implications for recruitment. *Strategic HR Review, 17*(5), 255–258.

Van Esch, P., Black, J. S., & Ferolie, J. (2019). Marketing AI recruitment: The next phase in job application and selection. *Computers in Human Behavior, 90*, 215–222.

VanLehn, K. (2006). The behavior of tutoring systems. *International Journal of Artificial Intelligence in Education, 16*, 227–265.

VanLehn, K. (2011). The relative effectiveness of human tutoring, intelligent tutoring systems, and other tutoring systems. *Educational Psychologist, 46*(4), 197–221.

VanLehn, K., Lynch, C., Schulze, K., Shapiro, J. A., Shelby, R., Taylor, L., … Wintersgill, M. (2005). The Andes physics tutoring system: Lessons learned. *International Journal of Artificial Intelligence in Education, 15*(3), 147–204.

Ventura, M., & Shute, V. (2013). The validity of a game-based assessment of persistence. *Computers in Human Behavior, 29*(6), 2568–2572.

Ventura, M., Shute, V., & Zhao, W. (2013). The relationship between video game use and a performance-based measure of persistence. *Computers & Education, 60*(1), 52–58.

Wang, C. H., & Lin, H. C. K. (2018). Emotional design tutoring system based on multimodal affective computing techniques. *International Journal of Distance Education Technologies, 16*(1), 103–117.

Wang, L., Shute, V., & Moore, G. R. (2015). Lessons learned and best practices of stealth assessment. *International Journal of Gaming and Computer-Mediated Simulations, 7*(4), 66–87.

Warschauer, M., & Ware, P. (2006). Automated writing evaluation: Defining the classroom research agenda. *Language Teaching Research, 10*, 1–24.

Worsley, M. (2018). Multimodal learning analytics: Past, present and potential futures. In *Proceedings of 8th International Conference on Learning Analytics & Knowledge*, Sydney, Australia.

Worsley, M., & Blikstein, P. (2018). A multimodal analysis of making. *International Journal of Artificial Intelligence in Education, 28*(3), 385–419.

Yu, K. H., Beam, A. L., & Kohane, I. S. (2018). Artificial intelligence in healthcare. *Nature Biomedical Engineering, 2*(10), 719–731.

22. Evaluations with AIEd systems

Kurt VanLehn

This chapter is aimed at those just entering the field of Artificial Intelligence in Education (AIEd). It is an introduction to options for designing evaluations of AIEd projects. It focuses on non-statistical design choices, such as what to compare one's system to. Although it describes options for what kind of data to collect, it does not discuss what kinds of data analysis to do. Once the study and data collection have been designed, there are experimental methods textbooks, machine-learning textbooks, and other resources that prescribe data analytic methods. This chapter will also not cover protection of human participants, because anyone doing studies with human participants will be required by their Institutional Review Board to pass a course on this important topic.

A typical methodological review would simply describe each of the major methods. To avoid such a dry approach, this chapter also tries to give the reader a sense of which types of evaluations are common and which are rare in the recent literature. The chapter mentions how many evaluations of each type occur in a sample of AIEd publications. The sample is small. It includes all 48 full-length papers in one of the annual conferences, *Artificial Intelligence in Education 2020*, and all 35 articles in two recent volumes (29 and 30) of *International Journal of Artificial Intelligence in Education*. These venues are arguably close to the "center of mass" of the field, if there is such a thing.

Because the focus of this chapter is on evaluation designs and not on their popularity, counts of publications within a category are not followed by citations to the publications themselves. The intent is merely to convey a general impression of category popularity without making disputable claims about any single publication's classification. A proper census would require many more publications, multiple experts doing the classification, and measures of inter-rater reliability.

AIEd has always been a bit ill-defined, but one feature of most AIEd publications is that they describe a non-trivial computer system. Of the 83 publications in the sample, 74 described a non-trivial computer system. Of the remaining nine publications, three were reviews, two were methodological, one was a conceptual framework, one reported user preferences for gamification features, one developed a mapping between job ad competencies and *curriculum vitae* competencies, and one reported the impact of framing results as AIEd compared to framing the same results as neuroscience or educational psychology. This chapter concerns evaluations used in the 74 publications that described computer systems.

In the early days, describing a system was all that most AIEd publications did (Mark & Greer, 1993). Nowadays, most AIEd publications include an evaluation as well as a description. All 74 publications that described a system also presented an evaluation. This is a welcome advance in the scientific maturity of the field.

The evaluations can be divided according to the type of system that they target. There were three clear types of systems in the 74-publication sample. (1) *Instructional systems* are used by students. Their function was usually to help the students learn. Instructional systems are the topic of 29 publications in the sample. (2) *Assessment systems* are also used by students.

Unlike instructional systems, which take actions intended to help students learn, assessment systems only collect and analyze data on student performance. Although sometimes the assessment system is part of an instructional system, in all 31 publications that address assessment systems, the system's analyses are intended to be viewed by teachers, students, researchers, administrators, or parents. These people may make decisions and take actions based on the assessments they see, but the evaluated system does not. (3) *Teacher and developer aids* are used by instructors and developers outside of class to author or analyze instruction, or by instructors during class to help with conducting the class. Such systems are the topic of 14 publications in the sample.

Of the 29 instructional systems and 31 assessment systems in the sample, most were used by students working alone. Only one instructional system was used by students working in pairs. Teams were completely absent. This is typical of the AIEd literature. Systems for instructing and assessing small groups and teams are typically reported in other venues, such as the *International Journal of Computer Supported Collaborative Learning* (www.springer.com/journal/11412), but see Chapter 19 by Martinez-Maldonado et al..

Let us begin with the most popular category, assessment systems.

EVALUATION OF ASSESSMENT SYSTEMS

A student assessment system inputs data from a student and outputs some classification, score or other characterization of the student (see Chapter 21 by Fang et al., Chapter 16 by Brooks et al., and Chapter 15 by Pozdniakov et al.). Sometimes the output is complex, such as the probability of mastery of each of several hundred knowledge components, where a *knowledge component* is a small piece of knowledge that the student is expected to learn. When the outputs are complex, the systems are often referred to as *student modeling systems* or *learner modeling systems* (see Chapter 8 by Conati and Lallé). (NB: technical terms are italicized when first mentioned.)

Although assessment systems often focus on measuring the students' knowledge or skill, they sometimes focus on measuring the students' *self-efficacy* (their confidence in their abilities; see Chapter 4 by Azevedo & Wiedbusch), their *affect* (e.g., boredom, engagement, or frustration; see Chapter 5 by Arroyo et al.) or other constructs. Similarly, instructional systems can focus on improving not only the students' knowledge and skill, but also their self-efficacy, affect, and so on. There is no widely used term that covers all these things that an assessment system can assess or an instructional system can improve, so this chapter will use *knowledge* with the understanding that it encompasses many other things than knowledge per se.

There are two types of evaluation for assessment systems, which in psychometrics are called *reliability* and *validity*. Reliability just means that when a measurement instrument measures the same thing twice, it outputs the same value. If you get on your bathroom scale twice a few seconds apart, then it should report the same weight. If it does not, it is unreliable. Similarly, if you take the SAT test twice in the same month, you should get very similar scores. The other main type of evaluation, validity, is complex and multifaceted (Messick, 1989). For example, if a student's Math SAT score is 750, is that score valid, in other words, "true"? Does the score have the same meaning for all races and all genders? What if the examinee's first language is not English? What impact does this assessment have on the educational systems that use it?

Of the 31 publications evaluating assessment systems, three measured the reliability of their systems (Alexandron et al., 2019; Double et al., 2019; Filighera et al., 2020). They did not input the same student data twice, because these assessment systems produce the same output when given the same input. Instead, they introduced variations in the student data that shouldn't make any difference in the output. For example, one assessment system classified student essays according to their correctness (Double et al., 2019). To evaluate reliability, researchers prepended a few words to each essay. This caused the system to change its classification of the essays significantly, so the researchers concluded that the assessment system was unreliable.

All the remaining publications measured the validity of their systems. They compared their systems' classification to either existing standard assessments, the judgment of experts, or objective data. These comparison data were treated as a gold standard whose validity was assumed to be acceptable. That is, when the system's classification disagreed with the comparison data's classification, the system's classification was considered to be incorrect. Thus, this measure was called *accuracy*. Let's consider examples of each type of accuracy evaluation.

Two of the publications compared their judgments about students with the results from standard assessments (Munshi et al., 2020; Wu et al., 2019). For example, one publication had students take a standard clinical questionnaire that assigned them a value for each of the Big Five personality traits (Wu et al., 2019). The assessment system also assigned them five values based on their chat and forum posting during a web-based course. The system's accuracy was computed by comparing its values to the questionnaire's values.

The judgment of expert humans was often used as the gold standard. Judgments included scores on essays, observation of gaming or off-task behavior when using a tutoring system in a classroom, and judgments of *wheel-spinning* (repeated unsuccessful tries). Ten of the publications compared their systems' judgments to human judgments.

Lastly, 15 publications evaluated their systems against objective data. For example, one system predicted whether students would pass a course based on the texts they wrote during it and their gender (Lin et al., 2020). Another system predicted whether students would log into an instructional system next week based on their performance up until now (Chatterjee et al., 2020). This latter example illustrates that the output of an assessment system doesn't have to be a score, letter grade, or some other conventional measure. It can be any information valuable to a decision maker. In this case, teachers could use the assessment system's output to decide which students to proactively encourage to attend next week's class.

These days, almost all assessment systems are machine learned in whole or in part. Just as there has been an explosion of machine-learning methods, there has also been an explosion of methods for measuring accuracy. The accuracy measures often do not completely agree. One of the methodological papers in the sample demonstrates the importance of this complex consideration (Effenberger & Pelanek, 2019).

EVALUATION OF INSTRUCTIONAL SYSTEMS

AIEd is concerned not only with building effective educational technology, but also with understanding how students learn from such technology. Although an evaluation might involve measuring the effectiveness of a system, it also might involve testing a hypothesis such as "Does A cause B?" or "Do A and B tend to co-occur?" Often a study addresses several research questions.

Despite the wide variety of systems and research questions, the studies often tend to use the same variables, albeit in different contexts. Here, *variable* means a measure of student performance. The literature often assumes that the reader is familiar with the common variables, so this section will introduce them. Subsequent sections will discuss types of evaluations, referring as necessary to these common student performance variables.

Common Variables

Post-test score: Many instructional systems teach knowledge that is well-defined enough that it is possible to classify some student performances as errors. A post-test is typically scored by counting errors. Sometimes speed matters, too.

Pre-test score: While post-tests are given after the instruction, pre-tests are given before the instruction. Pre-tests are typically designed and interpreted as a measure of the student's *prior knowledge*, that is, knowledge that is helpful for learning the taught knowledge.

Transfer test score: A transfer test is a kind of post-test where the knowledge assessed by the test is not exactly the knowledge taught by the system. Instead, students must extend, adapt or transfer the taught knowledge in order to perform the transfer test tasks successfully. However, the distinction between post-tests, *near transfer* tests and *far transfer* tests is rather fuzzy.

Gain score: When a student takes both a pre-test and a post-test, then the student's gain score is PostTestScore – PreTestScore. Using a gain score assumes that the two tests measure approximately the same knowledge and that they are scored on the same scale (e.g., both are scored as percent-correct).

Normalized gain score: If a student's pre-test score is high, then they don't have much room to improve. For example, if the student scores 90 percent on the pre-test, then they must do very well on the post-test in order to have a positive gain score. Thus, when pre-test scores vary widely, and the researchers want to treat the high pre-test students "the same" as those with low pre-test scores, then they use the normalized gain score, which is the gain score divided by MaxScore – PreTestScore, where MaxScore is 100 percent or whatever is the highest possible score on the post-test. For instance, suppose one student scores 90 percent on the pre-test and the other scores 0 percent. Suppose their gain scores are the same. Then using normalized gain scores, the student with the high pretest would have a ten times larger impact on the average score of the class than the student with the low pretest score. Sometimes, a study that has a null result using gain scores will have a non-null result when using normalized gain scores, and vice versa.

Errors during instruction: When the instruction involves a sequence of tasks or steps where the student's performance on each can be judged as correct or incorrect, then their error rate during the instruction can be calculated. Error rate is the number of errors per unit of time or per unit of work. However, interpreting error rates is tricky. Different students may tolerate different error rates, or they may trade off speed and errors differently. Even if error rates are compared across a single student's performance (e.g., comparing the student's error rate early in the instruction to the student's error rate late in the instruction), students can change their error-tolerance policies in the middle. For example, they might move faster and get sloppier as they near the end of the instruction.

Learning curves: When the instruction involves a sequence of tasks or steps that are either identical or very similar, then one can calculate a learning curve. The vertical axis of the plot is a numerical measure of student knowledge, such as their speed at responding to the task or the frequency of errors in a group of students. The horizontal axis is the ordinal position of the task in the sequence. For example, if there are 100 students in the group, and 80 make an error on the first task, then the first point on the curve is at [1, 0.80]. If 55 students make an error on the second task, then the second point of the curve is at [2, 0.55], and so on.

Game score: Game score is often used when the instruction is a game or part of a game. However, game scores blur the distinction between aiding learning and aiding performance during the game. Moreover, some students may focus exclusively on raising their game score while other students may play for enjoyment or play to learn.

Grades: If the instruction is part of a course, then the course grade is sometimes used as a variable.

Attrition: If the instruction is part of a course, then the number of students who quit before finishing the course (attrition) is sometimes used as a variable.

Retention tests. A retention test is a post-test that is given a significant time after the instruction. Sometimes the gap is an hour or sometimes it is several months or longer.

Preparation for future learning: This measure, pioneered by Bransford & Schwartz (1999), gives the students a post-test that includes an ordinary lesson: the lesson might introduce a new concept, give some examples, and then have students do some exercises. The students' learning of the new concept is measured somehow, typically by counting the errors made during the exercise phase. Students' learning of the new concept is used as a dependent variable for the main instruction, which could, for example, have taught them a learning strategy or studying skill such as self-explanation (Chi, 2000) or how to properly use feedback and hints (Roll et al., 2011).

Acceleration of future learning: Another way to measure the impact of learning strategies is to teach two topics that share few or no knowledge components, and treat learning gains on the second topic as a measure of success for learning strategy instruction on the first topic. For example, (Chi & VanLehn, 2007) used probability problem solving and physics problem solving. Half the students studied one topic first, and the other half got them in reverse order. All students were taught a learning strategy when learning the first topic. They were free to use it or not during the second. The learning strategy instruction was considered a success because students both chose to use the learning strategy when taught the second topic and it sped up their learning of the second topic.

Both Preparation for Future Learning (PFL) and Acceleration of Future Learning (AFL) can be viewed as transfer measures. However, they measure improvements in learning whereas a typical transfer test measures improvements in problem solving. That is, a transfer test doesn't have any instruction embedded in it, whereas the tests of both PFL and AFL do.

Eye fixations or *gaze*: There are a variety of eye-tracking devices that can determine what a student's eyes are looking at.

Physiological measures: There are a variety of devices for measuring galvanic skin resistance, heart rate, posture, eye dilation, brain activity (e.g., EEG, PET, FMRI), and other physiological measures. In the instruction literature, these are often automatically interpreted by *affect detectors* (D'Mello & Kory, 2015) which can indicate whether a student is bored, engaged, frustrated, and so on.

Questionnaire measures: There are a variety of standard student questionnaires for measuring self-efficacy (i.e., confidence in one's ability to do a task), *cognitive load* (i.e., how hard a task is), engagement, affect, and other constructs. These should always be interpreted as the students' opinion. For example, if one asks students whether they learned what they were taught, their responses are often at odds with objective measures of learning.

Observation rubrics: When students are either in a classroom or engaged in a physical activity (e.g., applying a tourniquet), then human observers often use rubrics to convert their observations to numbers. A rubric is a set of rules, guidelines, and examples, often accompanied by a paper or online form for data collection. For example, BROMP (Ocumpaugh et al., 2015) is a rubric-based method for measuring students' affect in the classroom.

Log data measures: AIEd systems often generate a stream of interpreted user interface actions, called log data. Errors during instruction can be extracted from log data. So can many other measures. For example, log data can measure help abuse (Roll et al., 2011), wheel-spinning (Beck & Gong, 2013), and how long students pause after receiving negative feedback (Shih et al., 2008).

The preceding list includes common measures used in AIEd studies, but of course there are many others. For example, one study in the sample measured how often students asked for critical, specific feedback rather than right/wrong feedback (Ternblad & Tarning, 2020). A second study measured students' willingness to communicate during second-language instruction (Ayedoun et al., 2019).

Outcome Variables and Moderators

Instructional systems generally have the goal of improving the students' knowledge, which we have defined to include knowledge per se, skill, attitude, identity, practices, habits, or some other relatively stable attribute of the student. A measure of an attribute that is both valued and relatively stable but *malleable* (i.e., can be changed by instruction) is often called an *outcome variable*, because it measures the desired outcome or result of the instruction. Among the 29 publications, gain score was clearly the most common outcome variable (11 publications), followed by errors during instruction (seven publications) and post-test scores (four publications).

Many evaluations use multiple outcome variables. For example, Chase et al. (2019) used not only errors during the instruction, but also a transfer test, a measure of cognitive load, and a measure specific to their activity (efficiency in exploring the problem space).

Evaluations that use multiple variables often treat some of the variables as *moderators*. A moderator is a factor which can strengthen, weaken, or otherwise change the relationship between the instruction and the outcome variable(s). For example, suppose that a study compares two versions of the system, A and B, and both versions allow students to choose how many problems they do. Suppose it turns out that students who do few problems do equally well in both A and B whereas students who do many problems do much better with A than B. In this case, the factor "number of problems done" is moderating the difference in outcomes.

A particularly common hypothesis asks whether the instruction is differentially effective for high-prior-knowledge students versus low-prior-knowledge students. That is, it tests whether prior knowledge is a moderator. This particular moderator analysis is often referred to as *aptitude–treatment interaction* (ATI). Because a common goal of instruction is to reduce inequality, an ATI is "good" if the target instruction is especially effective with low prior knowledge students. For example, if the high-prior knowledge students in the experimental condition tie with those in the control condition, and yet the low-prior-knowledge students learn much more in the experimental condition than in the control condition, then the experimental condition is reducing inequality. That's why this is sometimes called a "good" ATI.

Novice researchers often do few moderator analyses. This is unfortunate, because sometimes the moderators are more interesting than the main effect. For example, the main analysis of one study in the sample revealed a protégé effect (Ternblad & Tarning, 2020). That is, when students have their teachable agent submit answers and get feedback, they do better than students who submit their own answers and get feedback. That's the main effect, repeating an effect found earlier (Chase et al., 2009). A moderator analysis showed that the protégé effect was stronger with lower-achieving students (a new result; a good ATI) but only when the feedback was only mildly negative (another moderator). In this publication, the moderators were more novel than the main results, which was reflected in the authors' choice of a title.

A common mistake is to get a null result, give up and perhaps not even publish the study. However, null results can sometimes mask interesting trends that can be uncovered with moderator analyses. For example, suppose that the experimental instruction is better than the control instruction for students with good reading skills, whereas the experimental instruction is worse for those with poor reading skills. These two trends might cancel each other out, creating a null result overall. A moderator analysis might uncover this situation.

As the list presented earlier suggests, many moderators could be used. However, only a few can be measured in a feasible study. Although researchers can use their own intuition about which moderators to include, it may be better to use theory, teachers' intuitions, or interviews with pilot students.

Study Design: Single Condition Studies

Now we come to the issue of how to design the study. Several sections will be needed to cover this complicated issue. This section discusses studies that have only one condition.

Although most of the 29 publications used multiple conditions, where the students in different conditions used different instruction, ten publications used a single condition where all students used the instructional system and none used other forms of instruction. Of these ten studies, six used a correlation design. That is, they tested whether two (or more) variables were statistically associated with each other. For example, Taub et al. (2020) showed that students' emotions at certain points during an educational game correlated with their game score. This is an example of behavior during the instruction being correlated with outcomes. Other studies included prior attributes in the correlations. For example, one study showed that the eye fixations of students with high prior knowledge were different from the eye fixations of students with low prior knowledge (Taub & Azevedo, 2019).

The remaining four single-condition studies did not look for correlations, but instead reported outcome variables: gain scores, post-test scores, or errors during instruction. Researchers often deprecate single-condition studies of instruction that only report outcomes on the assumption that even weak instruction usually produces some positive outcome, so single-condition outcome-only studies don't add much information (in the Shannon sense, where information is the size of the change from prior probability to posterior probability) to the literature nor do they advocate well for the system's effectiveness. However, AIEd systems are often based on emerging technology such as speech recognition, gaze tracking, indoor position sensing, gesture recognition, and so on. When the technology has a high error rate, it seems likely that students will disengage from the instruction and/or fail to learn from it. Thus, evidence that the instruction is acceptable and fosters gains is information: it is surprising given the current crude state of the technology. Of the four single-condition studies that used outcomes only, three evaluated systems that taught spoken language skills, and their value to the literature was measuring whether tutoring was acceptable and even successful given the current high error rates of speech recognition technology (Johnson, 2019; Lehman et al., 2020; Lothian et al., 2020). The fourth publication (Di Mitri et al., 2020) evaluated whether brief audio feedback in the midst of a high-pressure task (administering CPR) improved performance despite the risk of distracting the participants. To put it bluntly, a single-condition study can be acceptable if the authors argue convincingly that the results are surprising, that is, that they add information to the literature.

Comparing Multiple Versions of the System

Of the 29 publications about instructional systems, 19 publications had evaluations with multiple conditions. Of these, 17 compared multiple versions of the system. This kind of evaluation is often called an A/B test, because it compares version A to version B (and possibly C, etc.). The remaining two publications compared the instructional system to *baseline instruction*, which refers to existing, typical instruction used for teaching what the instructional system teaches.

This section covers issues common to both kinds of multi-condition studies. The next section covers issues relevant to baseline comparisons only.

All the multi-condition studies used a *between-subjects* design. That is, different instruction is assigned to different students. For example, Ausin et al. (2020) conducted an A/B study where all the students used the same tutoring system. However, half the students were assigned to use a version of the system that utilized a machine-learned policy for task selection (condition A) and the other students used an expert-authored policy for task selection (condition B).

The alternative to a between-subjects design is a *within-subjects* design, where every student experiences every instruction, albeit at different times. A typical design is to have half the students use instruction A first followed by instruction B, and the other students use B first followed by A. As well as the usual pre-test and post-test, all students take a mid-test that occurs between A and B. The research hypothesis is that A is more effective than B (or vice versa), regardless of which came first. The within-subjects design may require longer sessions than the between-subjects design, because students must use both A and B. However, because each student generates two data points (one for A and one for B), it may take fewer students to achieve adequate statistical power (power is discussed later). Unfortunately, if both A and B teach the same knowledge or skill, then students' learning during the first instruction can't be compared to their learning during the second, because they will be starting with more knowledge when they start the second instruction. Thus, a within-subjects design typically uses topics that don't overlap much, such as physics and probability. One is taught first, and the other is taught second. For instance, half the students would use A to learn physics and then B to learn probability, and the other students would use B to learn physics and then A to learn probability.

For both between-subjects and within-subjects designs, students are assigned to conditions. Perhaps the best way to do this is *stratified assignment*. The basic idea is to somehow determine each student's relevant prior knowledge, typically by administering a pre-test before assigning students to conditions. Students are then rank-ordered by their pre-test score. Even-numbered students are then assigned to one condition and odd-numbered students are assigned to the other. For example, suppose students are identified by numbers, and the ranking is S25, S36, S5, S22... Then S25, S5... would be assigned to one condition and S36, S22... would be assigned to the other. Stratified assignment virtually guarantees that the two conditions have the same average pre-test score.

The next best method for assigning participants to conditions is to assign them randomly. In this case, it is wise to give students a pre-test and check that the average pre-test scores are the same across conditions. If they are not, there are statistical methods (e.g., ANCOVA) for compensating for the bad luck assignment. If students cannot be assigned randomly, then these same statistical methods can be used to partially compensate for differences across conditions.

Comparisons to Baseline Instruction

Whereas A/B studies compare two versions of the same instructional system, a second kind of multi-condition study compares the instructional system to the instruction that it is intended to replace, which is called the baseline instruction. Typically, the baseline instruction is either classroom instruction, unsupervised homework, human tutoring, or a combination of them. For example, several evaluations compared a *Cognitive Tutor* used in the classroom to doing similar in-class problem solving on paper, where, in both conditions, teachers circulated among students, providing help (Koedinger et al., 1997; Pane et al., 2014; Pane et al., 2015). The *Andes* physics tutor was evaluated by comparing homework done on paper to homework done on the tutor, with instructors in both conditions holding the same lectures, discussions, exams, and office hours (VanLehn et al., 2005). The *Why2-Atlas* tutor was compared with human tutors coaching students on the same physics problems as *Why2-Atlas* (VanLehn et al., 2007).

If the study reports that the mean of the outcome variable(s) is larger for the instructional system than the baseline instruction, then policy makers will want to know two things in order to decide whether to move toward replacing the baseline instruction with the instructional system: (1) Is the positive result statistically reliable? That is, is $p<0.05$? and (2) How large is the difference between outcomes? This is reported as the *effect size* of the comparison. There are several methods for computing effect sizes. A popular one in the AIEd literature is Cohen's d, which is (M1–M2)/SD where M1 is the mean of the instructional system's outcome, M2 is the mean of the baseline instruction, and SD is pooled standard deviation.

In order to evaluate a set of instructional systems that all use the same general technology, policy makers and researchers conduct a *meta-analysis*. This is a rigorous review of the publications that compare such instructional systems to baselines. The hallmark of such reviews is the effect size averaged over all the studies in the publications. For example, (Kulik & Fletcher, 2016) conducted a meta-analysis of 50 studies of intelligent tutoring systems, and found that the average effect size was 0.66. If you intend that your evaluation be included in such meta-analyses, then it is wise to report effect size and other data used by meta-analyses.

Perhaps now would be an appropriate place to discuss a confusing terminological issue. Researchers often characterize their evaluations as either *formative* or *summative*. The basic idea is that a formative evaluation provides diagnostic information, whereas a summative evaluation provides only an outcome. However, the terms are used in two ways. Sometimes the focus is students, so a formative evaluation provides rich information on the student that can be used for diagnosis, remediation, and so on. A summative evaluation of a student is like a grade or class ranking. It doesn't provide much diagnostic information. On the other hand, the terms can focus on the instructional system. A formative evaluation of a system provides rich diagnostic information on how to make the system better or on how students learn when using the system. A summative evaluation of a system compares the system to baseline instruction; it reports the statistical reliability, effect size, and little else. Thus, the studies in this section are summative evaluations, in this second use of the term.

Many published evaluations are both formative and summative evaluations of an instructional system. That is, they compare the system to baseline, but they also include moderator analyses that help understanding why the system worked well or failed to work well.

When a between-subjects design is used for summative evaluation of a system, ethical issues can arise. Typically, a summative evaluation is launched only after the instructional system has already shown benefits in A/B studies or pilot studies. If there is reliable evidence that the instructional system is more effective than the baseline condition, it may be unethical to withhold it from some of the students, as a between-subjects design requires. To avoid this ethical issue, studies in real classes sometimes use more elaborate designs than between-subjects. One has been mentioned already: within-subjects. Several others are mentioned next.

One ethical assignment policy does not require students to use the target system but does let them use it voluntarily. That is, if they choose to use the instructional system, they are in the experimental condition, and otherwise they are in the baseline condition. To overcome the self-selection bias that this procedure creates, *propensity score matching* is used. The basic idea of propensity score matching is to construct a control condition that is a subset of the students who chose not to use the system. For each student in the experimental condition, one adds a matching student to the control condition. To match students, one must have information about student features that could conceivably affect the success of the instruction, such as prior test scores, attendance in class, reading ability, socioeconomic status, and so on. Various algorithms are used to compute similarity in this features space and select the most similar control student for a given experimental student. Interestingly, one of the methodological publications in the sample compared propensity score matching with a new technique, which uses machine learning to build models of the outcomes based on features of students in both conditions (Smith et al., 2020).

When students select which condition they are in, too few or too many students may volunteer to use the instructional system that is the target of the evaluation. Either way would result in low statistical power. An alternative assignment policy is to assign the more effective instruction, which is presumably the experimental one, to the students who need it the most. This is called a *regression discontinuity* design, and it was used in one of the publications in the sample (Vanlehn et al., 2020). This design can be used when students' post-test scores are strongly correlated with their pre-test scores, which is often the case. The procedure is to give all the students a pre-test, and then assign students who score below the pre-test median (or some other threshold) to the experimental condition and students who are above the threshold to the control condition. This makes sense ethically when the experimental condition is thought to be more effective than the control condition. If the experimental condition is in fact more effective, then the post-test scores of the experimental students will be higher than they would have been had they taken the control instruction, creating a discontinuity in the regression line, as shown in Figure 22.1.

Whereas propensity score matching constructs a control condition, another method constructs both the experimental and control conditions. One of the publications in the sample (Damacharla et al., 2019) used this design. The authors hypothesized that when gamification

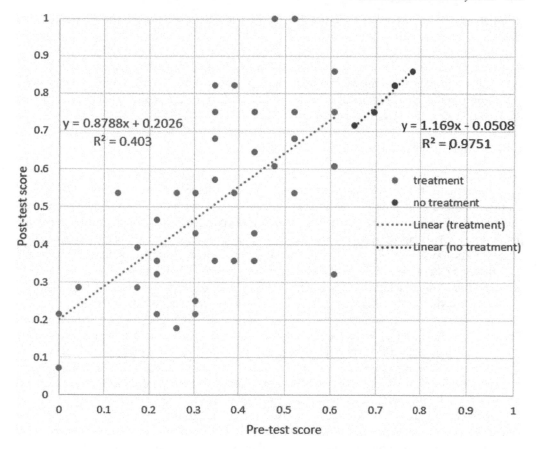

Source: VanLehn et al. (2020)

Figure 22.1 *A regression discontinuity. There were only five students above the pre-test threshold and thus in the no-treatment condition. Two of them had identical pre- and post-test scores, so they show as one point in the plot above*

elements (e.g., leaderboards, avatars, points, timers) matched the student's attributes, then the student would be more engaged, perform better and have more motivation. They had three different policies for how to match gamification elements to students. A conventional experimental design would implement the three policies, and use an A/B/C between-subjects design to compare them. Instead, the researchers assigned gamification elements to all students *randomly*. After the data were collected, they constructed three pairs of groups, one pair for each policy. The pair for a policy consisted of students who did and did not receive gamification elements that matched their profile according to that policy. The authors then tested each policy by comparing outcomes across the two groups that comprised the policy's pair. This design could be used by anyone studying adaptation of treatments to attributes of student.

Lastly, we come to *Randomized Controlled Trials* or RCTs. Although this term is sometimes applied to a summative evaluation with a modest number of students, it is usually reserved for summative evaluations involving multiple schools, multiple teachers per school, and multiple classes per teacher. All these factors can influence outcomes dramatically. For instance, the impact of the instructional system vs. baseline instruction may be quite small compared with the impact of an expert teacher vs. a novice. Although there are statistical methods that can help find the impact of the instructional manipulation amidst the "noise" of other factors, even using these tools it has historically been difficult to find a statistically reliable effect in an RCT, and large effect sizes are even rarer.

How Many Students to Run?

When designing an experiment, a vexing question is how many students to run. The more students you run, the more likely that your results will represent the underlying reality. For example, suppose you are evaluating an instructional system by comparing the mean learning gains of students in two versions of the system, A and B. Your hypothesis is that A is more effective. Your plan is to use a two-tailed *t*-test. If the test reports $p<0.05$, you will conclude that A is indeed more effective. As you know, the chances of such a positive result (under the assumption that your main hypothesis is true) are small if you run 10 students per condition, but large if you run 100 students per condition. You decide that you want the probability of reporting success to be high, like 0.8, assuming that the positive effect actually exists. How many students should you run?

The *power* of the experiment is the probability that you can report a non-null effect given that one actually exists. Power depends on sample size, the particular test you run (two-tailed *t*-test, in this example), the level of acceptance ($p<0.05$ is the typical choice), and on how far apart the actual results really are, which is called the population *effect size*. There are many measures of effect size. When comparing means, most AIEd publications measure effect size with Cohen's d, which is the difference in the means divided by the standard deviation pooled over both conditions. When designing an experiment, you usually don't have data that allows you to calculate the population effect size, so it is good practice to somehow estimate it, typically by considering the effect sizes of similar evaluations. You then use *G-Power* (www .psychologie.hhu.de/arbeitsgruppen/allgemeine-psychologie-und-arbeitspsychologie/gpower) to calculate the number of students you need to run. *G-Power* can also draw graphs like the one in Figure 22.2, which shows how power varies with both the number of students and the population effect size. You will undoubtedly be discouraged. It always takes more students than you would like to reach a power of 0.8, which is often considered the minimal adequate power. For example, even if you expect an effect size of 0.5, which is considered a good result for an instructional system (VanLehn, 2011), you will need about 125 students per condition to have an 80 percent chance of detecting such an effect. Note that, even with 125 students per condition, there is a 20 percent chance of getting a null result, even though your experiment doesn't "deserve" it. If you can only run 50 students, then Figure 22.2 indicates that your experiment will have a good 80 percent chance of detecting a really large, underlying difference (effect size $d=0.8$), a moderate 40 percent chance of detecting a moderate effect ($d=0.5$), and almost no chance (10 percent) of detecting a small effect ($d=0.2$).

Even if you are willing to accept the risk of a low-powered study, others might not be. Funding agencies often require you to report the power of experiments that you propose to do. If your experiment has any possibility of harming the students, even a small one, then your Institutional Review Board may also require a high probability of scientific benefit in order to justify the risk to the participants. Thesis committees sometimes require power calculations.

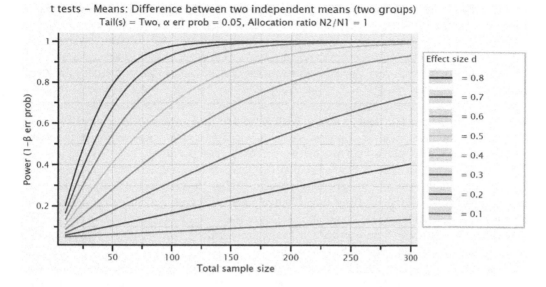

Figure 22.2   *G-power's graph of the power of a specific statistical test and acceptance level*

EVALUATION OF SYSTEMS THAT INSTRUCTORS AND DEVELOPERS USE

This subset of the sample includes systems used either by instructors during class or by instructors or developers outside of class. They use the systems to analyze student performance and/or design instruction. Because the systems are quite different, so are the evaluations. Thus, this section is just a list of the types of systems and their corresponding evaluations.

Of the 13 publications in this subset, two addressed generation of questions (Leo et al., 2019; Steuer et al., 2020). The main evaluation in both publications involved experts judging whether the questions generated were usable in their exams or courses. Secondary analyses evaluated the grammaticality of the questions and other features. One of the review articles in the sample also addressed question generation (Kurki et al., 2020). It contains a more thorough discussion of evaluation methods than this one.

One publication evaluated a system that answered questions that students sent to the teaching staff of a large course (Zylich et al., 2020). Students often ask questions about the class itself (e.g., is the next exam open book?) as well as questions about the knowledge it teaches (e.g., what's the difference between a Java class and a Java object?). The system's job is to answer some questions and direct the others to the teaching staff. The evaluation simply measured the proportion of questions it answered and of those, the proportion where its answer was appropriate.

Two publications addressed the usability of learning analytics dashboards (Al-Doulat et al., 2020; Shabaninejad et al., 2020). Although many other publications in the sample evaluated the accuracy of a learning analytic system that has a dashboard, they did not evaluate the way the dashboard communicated findings to the user nor the overall utility of the dashboard. These two publications did. Their systems were designed to be used outside the classroom to help instructors give students advice or customize instruction. The two publications evaluated their dashboards by presenting them to potential users and collecting the users' comments.

Users' comments are often viewed with suspicion. For example, users sometimes don't use the features that they request. Thus, one study not only collected users' opinions, but also evaluated the decisions that the users made (Paiva & Bittencourt, 2020). The users were given scenarios. They analyzed them with the dashboard and then made a pedagogical decision. They were scored on whether or not the decision was appropriate. One version of the dashboard fostered higher scores than another version of the dashboard.

Dashboards that are designed to be used during class are often called *classroom orchestration systems* (Dillenbourg et al., 2018) (see Chapter 14 by Holstein and Olsen) because their goal is to help instructors smoothly and effectively conduct on-ground classes or online, synchronous classes. Although no classroom orchestration systems were included in the sample of publications, it is worth reviewing their evaluation methods, which can be applied equally well to dashboards used outside the classroom.

Although there can be complex relationships between dashboards, instructors, students, and others (Dillenbourg & Jermann, 2010; Holstein et al., 2018a), a simplified perspective (Dillenbourg et al., 2011) focuses on a three-step cycle: (1) the dashboard increases the instructor's awareness of the states of the students in the classroom and the topics that they are having difficulty with; (2) this increased awareness modifies the teacher's behavior, and in particular, the teacher's choice of students or topics to focus on; and (3) because the dashboard enables teachers to focus their attention on students or topics that most need the teachers' attention, the class proceeds more smoothly and the students learn more. An evaluation of dashboard usage can examine any or all steps in this cycle as it occurs in actual practice. Evaluations have measured (1) instructor awareness (van Leeuwen et al., 2015), (2) instructor allocation of attention (Molenaar & Knoop-van Campen, 2017), and (3) outcomes such as increased learning gains (Holstein et al., 2018b) or reduction in wasted class time (Wetzel et al., 2018).

Whereas a *classroom orchestration* system is intended to help instructors in real time as they conduct their class, an *instructor assessment* system collects data on instructor activities during class so that they could review the findings after class and determine how to improve their teaching. Three systems in the sample were instructor assessment systems. One system identified four types of questions in the speech of teachers in online classrooms, and it was evaluated by comparing its classifications to the classifications of human judges (Huang et al., 2020). The second system classified instructors' speech according to the number of students whose minds were wandering as they listened to it (Gliser et al., 2020). The third system used an indoor positioning system to count how many times the teacher stopped to visit with students, how long they spent at the lectern, and how long they spent at the whiteboard (Martinez-Maldonado et al., 2020). The evaluation showed that these classifications varied in sensible ways across three lesson plans, but it did not measure the system's accuracy in comparison with human judgments. For all three systems, none of the evaluations involved using the system with teachers to provide them with feedback and help them improve.

The remaining systems in this subset are intended to be used by the developers of AIEd systems (see Chapter 12 by Blessing et al.). One system measured the quality of hints given by tutoring systems, so its evaluation was against hint ratings given by humans (Price et al., 2019). A second system generated *knowledge components* (Moore et al., 2020). Knowledge components are small pieces of domain knowledge that need to be learned by students. The system was evaluated by seeing which of the knowledge components it generated were also generated by human experts. A third system simulated human learners, so it could, in principle, be used to vet instruction prior to giving that instruction to human students (Weitekamp et al., 2020). It was evaluated by comparing its learning curves and error types to those of human students. A fourth system compared the predicted difficulty of a question to its actual difficulty (Pandarova et al., 2019). The actual difficulty was measured by giving the question to a large number of students and measuring the frequency of incorrect answers. The predicted difficulty was calculated from the text of the question itself. A fifth system gave surgeons feedback as they operated on virtual temporal bones (Lamtara et al., 2020). It gave the same feedback on all bones, even though the feedback was originally developed for just one of the bones. Human judges evaluated the feedback given during several students' usage of the system. There was no difference in their ratings for feedback on the original bone versus all the other bones. Notice that the first four systems automate a development process normally done by humans, so their evaluations simply compared their performance to the performance of humans.

SOME PARTING ADVICE

As promised, this review has stayed away from addressing statistical and analytical methods. Of course, these methods cannot be ignored. The statistical procedures used in the sample include t-tests, ANOVA, ANCOVA, linear regression, logistic regression, Chi-squared test, Mann-Whitney U-test, and Wilcoxon's rank-sum test. Measures of accuracy used in the sample include RMSE, AUC, MAE, Kappa, accuracy, F1, precision, recall, and linear regression. Measures of effect size include Cohen's d, eta, and Hedge's g. These are just some of the available tests and measures. Although the algorithms are included in R, SPSS, MatLab, SciPy, Excel, and other sources, the AIEd researcher needs to know which ones are appropriate and how to avoid known problems, such as failing to use a Bonferroni correction. Although graduate training often introduces the basic concepts, one should get in the habit of looking up unfamiliar tests or measures as soon as one sees them in a relevant publication. Although self-taught methodological knowledge probably suffices for reading the literature and deciding whether to believe the results, it can be dangerous when used to write grant proposals or to design high-stakes or high-cost studies. It is much better to consult an expert methodologist.

Many AIEd researchers and observers wonder why AIEd systems are not scaled up or even adopted in their current state. For a teacher, company, or educational institution to decide to adopt an AIEd system, they need evidence that using it is better than not using it. That is, if the system is used to replace or supplement baseline instruction, outcomes are better than if students use only the baseline instruction. Only a few papers in this sample presented such evidence. If your instructional system is mature and showing good benefits, then you can increase the societal impact of AIEd by doing a rigorous comparison of your system to baseline practices.

ACKNOWLEDGMENTS

This work was supported by NSF 1840051 and NSF 1628782. I thank Vincent Aleven, whose astute comments on an early draft significantly improved it.

REFERENCES

Al-Doulat, A., Nur, N., Karduni, A., Benedict, A., Al-Hossami, E., Maher, M. L., ... Niu, X. (2020). Making sense of student success and risk through unsupervised machine learning and interactive storytelling. In I. I. Bittencourt, M. Cukurova, & K. Mulder (Eds.), *Artificial Intelligence in Education, 21st International Conference, AIED 2020* (pp. 3–15). Switzerland: Springer Nature.

Alexandron, G., Yoo, L. Y., Reiperez-Valiente, J. A., Lee, S., & Pritchard, D. E. (2019). Are MOOC learning analytics results trustworthy? With fake learners, they might not be! *International Journal of Artificial Intelligence in Education, 29*(4), 484–506.

Ausin, M. S., Maniktala, M., Barnes, T., & Chi, M. (2020). Exploring the impact of simple explanations and agency on batch deep reinforcement learning induced pedagogical policies. In I. I. Bittencourt (Ed.), *Proceedings of the 2020 Conference on Artificial Intelligence in Education (AIED 2020)* (pp. 472–485). Switzerland: Springer Nature.

Ayedoun, E., Hayashi, Y., & Seta, K. (2019). Adding communicative and affective strategies to an embodied conversational agent to enhance second language learners' willingness to communicate. *International Journal of Artificial Intelligence in Education, 29*(1), 29–57.

Beck, J., & Gong, Y. (2013). *Wheel-Spinning: Students Who Fail to Master a Skill*. Paper Presented at the AIED 2013, Memphis, TN.

Bransford, J. D., & Schwartz, D. L. (1999). Rethinking transfer: A simple proposal with multiple implications. In A. Iran-Nejad & P. D. Pearson (Eds.), *Review of Research in Education* (Vol. 24, pp. 61–100). Washington, DC: American Educational Research Association.

Chase, C. C., Chin, D. B., Oppenzzo, M., & Schwartz, D. L. (2009). Teachable agents and the Protégé effect: Increasing the effort towards learning. *Journal of Science Education and Technology, 18*(4), 334–352.

Chase, C. C., Connolly, H., Lamnina, M., & Aleven, V. (2019). Problematizing helps! A classroom study of computer-based guidance for invention activities. *International Journal of Artificial Intelligence in Education, 29*(2), 283–316.

Chatterjee, R., Madaio, M., & Ogan, A. (2020). Predicting gaps in usage in a phone-based literacy intervention system. In I. I. Bittencourt, M. Cukurova, K. Mulder, R. Luckin, & E. Millan (Eds.), *Artificial Intelligence in Education, 21st International Conference, AIED 2020* (pp. 92–105). Switzerland: Springer Nature.

Chi, M., & VanLehn, K. (2007). Accelerated future learning via explicit instruction of a problem solving strategy. In K. R. Koedinger, R. Luckin, & J. Greer (Eds.), *Artificial Intelligence in Education* (pp. 409–416). Berlin: Springer.

Chi, M. T. H. (2000). Self-explaining: The dual processes of generating and repairing mental models. In R. Glaser (Ed.), *Advances in Instructional Psychology* (pp. 161–238). Mahwah, NJ: Erlbaum.

Damacharla, P., Dhakal, P., Stumbo, S., Javaid, A. Y., Ganapathy, S., Malek, D. A., ... Devabhaktuni, V. (2019). Effects of voice-based synthetic assistant on performance of emergency care provider in training. *International Journal of Artificial Intelligence in Education, 29*(1), 122–143.

Di Mitri, D., Schneider, J., Trebing, K., Sopka, S., Specht, M., & Drachsler, H. (2020). Real-time multimodal feedback with the CPR Tutor. In I. I. Bittencourt, M. Cukurova, K. Muldner, R. Luckin, & E. Millan (Eds.), *Artificial Intelligence in Education, 21st International Conference, AIED 2020* (pp. 141–152). Switzerland: Springer Nature.

Dillenbourg, P., & Jermann, P. (2010). Technology for classroom orchestration. In M. S. Khine & I. M. Saleh (Eds.), *New Science of Learning: Cognition, Computers and Collaboration in Education* (pp. 525–552). New York: Springer.

Dillenbourg, P., Prieto, L. P., & Olsen, J. (2018). Classroom orchestration. In F. Fischer, C. Hmelo-Silver, S. Goldman, & P. Reimann (Eds.), *International Handbook of the Learning Sciences* (pp. 180–190). New York, NY: Routledge.

Dillenbourg, P., Zuffery, G., Alavi, H., Jermann, P., Do-Lenh, S., Bonnard, Q., ... Kaplan, F. (2011). Classroom orchestration: The third circle of usability. In H. Spada, G. Stahl, N. Miyake, & N. Law (Eds.), *Computer Supported Collaborative Learning: CSCL 2011 Proceedings Volume 1* (pp. 510–517).

D'Mello, S. K., & Kory, J. (2015). A review and meta-analysis of multimodal affect detection systems. *ACM Computing Surveys, 47*(3), 43.

Double, C., Matayoshi, J., Cosyn, E., Uzun, H., & Karami, A. (2019). A data-based simulation study of reliability for an adaptive assessment based on knowledge space theory. *International Journal of Artificial Intelligence in Education, 29*(2), 258–282.

Effenberger, T., & Pelanek, R. (2019). Impact of methodological choices on the evaluation of student models. In I. I. Bittencourt, M. Cukurova, K. Mulder, R. Luckin, & E. Millan (Eds.), *Artificial Intelligence in Education, 21st International Conference, AIED 2020* (pp. 153–164). Switzerland: Springer Nature.

Filighera, A., Steuer, T., & Rensing, C. (2020). Fooling automatic short answer grading systems. In I. I. Bittencourt, M. Cukurova, K. Mulder, R. Luckin, & E. Millan (Eds.), *Artificial Intelligence in Education, 21st International Conference, AIED 2020* (pp. 177–190). Switzerland: Springer.

Gliser, I., Mills, C., Bosch, N., Smith, S., Smilek, D., & Wammes, J. D. (2020). The sound of inattention: Predicting mind wandering with automatically derived features of instructor speech. In I. I. Bittencourt, M. Cukurova, K. Muldner, R. Luckin, & E. Millan (Eds.), *Artificial Intelligence in Education, 21st International Conference, AIED 2020* (pp. 204–215). Switzerland: Springer Nature.

Holstein, K., McLaren, B., & Aleven, V. (2018a). Informing the design of teacher awareness tools through causal alignment analysis. In *Proceedings of the International Conference on the Learning Sciences (ICLS 2018)*.

Holstein, K., McLaren, B., & Aleven, V. (2018b). Student learning benefits of a mixed-reality teacher awareness tool in AI-enhanced classrooms. In *International Conference on Artificial Intelligence in Education* (pp. 154–168). London: Springer.

Huang, G. Y., Chen, J., Liu, H., Fu, W., Ding, W., Tang, J., … Liu, Z. (2020). Neural multi-task learning for teacher question detection in online classrooms. In I. I. Bittencourt, M. Cukurova, K. Muldner, R. Luckin, & E. Millan (Eds.), *Artificial Intelligence in Education, 21st International Conference, AIED 2020* (pp. 269–281). Switzerland: Springer Nature.

Johnson, W. L. (2019). Data-driven development and evaluation of Enskill English. *International Journal of Artificial Intelligence in Education, 29*(32), 425–457.

Koedinger, K. R., Anderson, J. R., Hadley, W. H., & Mark, M. A. (1997). Intelligent tutoring goes to school in the big city. *International Journal of Artificial Intelligence in Education, 8*(1), 30–43.

Kulik, J. A., & Fletcher, J. D. (2016). Effectiveness of intelligent tutoring systems: A meta-analytic review. *Review of Educational Research, 86*(1), 42–78.

Kurki, G., Leo, J., Parsi, B., Sattler, U., & Al-Emari, S. (2020). A systematic review of automatic question generation for educational purposes. *International Journal of Artificial Intelligence in Education, 30*(1), 121–204.

Lamtara, J., Hanegbi, N., Talks, B., Wijewickrema, S., Ma, X., Piromchai, P., … O'Leary, S. (2020). Transfer of automated performance feedback models to different specimens in virtual reality temporal bone surgery. In I. I. Bittencourt, M. Cukurova, K. Muldner, R. Luckin, & E. Millan (Eds.), *Artificial Intelligence in Education, 21st International Conference, AIED 2020* (pp. 296–308). Switzerland: Springer Nature.

Lehman, B., Gu, L., Zhao, J., Tsuprun, E., Kurzum, C., Schiano, M., … Jackson, G. T. (2020). Use of adaptive feedback in an app for English language spontaneous speech. In I. I. Bittencourt, M. Cukurova, K. Muldner, R. Luckin, & E. Millan (Eds.), *Artificial Intelligence in Education, 21st International Conference, AIED 2020* (pp. 309–320). Switzerland: Springer Nature.

Leo, J., Kurdi, G., Matentzoglu, N., Parsia, B., Sattler, U., Forge, S., … Dowling, W. (2019). Ontology-based generation of medical, multi-term MCQs. *International Journal of Artificial Intelligence in Education, 29*(2), 145–188.

Lin, Y., Yu, R., & Dowel, N. (2020). LIWCs the same, not the same: Gendered linguistic signals of performance and experience in online STEM courses. In I. I. Bittencourt, M. Cukurova, K. Mulder, R. Luckin, & E. Millan (Eds.), *Artificial Intelligence in Education, 21st International Conference, AIED 2020* (pp. 333–345). Switzerland: Springer Nature.

Lothian, D., Akcayier, G., Sparrow, A., Mcleod, O., & Epp, C. D. (2020). SoundHunters: Increasing learning phonological awareness in Plains Cree. In I. I. Bittencourt, M. Cukurova, K. Muldner, R. Luckin, & E. Millan (Eds.), *Artificial Intelligence in Education, 21st International Conference, AIED 2020* (pp. 346–359). Switzerland: Springer Nature.

Mark, M. A., & Greer, J. (1993). Evaluation methodologies for intelligent tutoring systems. *International Journal of Artificial Intelligence in Education, 4*(2/3), 129–153.

Martinez-Maldonado, R., Echeverria, V., Schulte, J., Shibani, A., Mangaroska, K., & Shum, S. B. (2020). Moodoo: Indoor positioning analytics for characterizing classroom teaching. In I. I. Bittencourt, M. Cukurova, K. Muldner, R. Luckin, & E. Millan (Eds.), *Artificial Intelligence in Education, 21st International Conference, AIED 2020* (pp. 350–373). Switzerland: Springer Nature.

Messick, S. (1989). Validity. In R. L. Linn (Ed.), *Educational Measurement* (3rd ed., pp. 13–103). New York: Macmillan.

Molenaar, I., & Knoop-van Campen, C. A. (2017). *Teacher Dashboards in Practice: Usage and Impact.* Paper presented at the European Conference on Technology Enhanced Learning: EC-TEL.

Moore, S., Nguyen, H. A., & Stamper, J. (2020). Evaluating crowdsourcing and topic modeling in generating knowledge components from explanations. In I. I. Bittencourt, M. Cukurova, K. Muldner, R. Luckin, & E. Millan (Eds.), *Artificial Intelligence in Education, 21st International Conference, AIED 2020* (pp. 398–410). Switzerland: Springer Nature.

Munshi, A., Mishra, S., Zhang, N., Paquette, L., Ocumpaugh, J., Baker, R., & Biswas, G. (2020). Modeling the relationships between basic and achievement emotions in computer-based learning environments. In I. I. Bittencourt, M. Cukurova, K. Mulder, R. Luckin, & E. Millan (Eds.), *Artificial Intelligence in Education, 21st International Conference, AIED 2020* (pp. 411–422). Switzerland: Springer Nature.

Ocumpaugh, J., Baker, R. S., & Rodrigo, M. M. T. (2015). *Baker Rodrigo Ocumpaugh Monitoring Protocol (BROMP) 2.0 Technical and Training Manual.* New York, NY. https://www.upenn.edu/learninganalytics/ryanbaker/BROMP.pdf.

Paiva, R., & Bittencourt, I. I. (2020). Helping teachers help their students: A human-AI hybrid approach. In I. I. Bittencourt, M. Cukurova, K. Mulder, R. Luckin, & E. Millan (Eds.), *Artificial Intelligence in Education, 21st International Conference, AIED 2020* (pp. 448–459). Switzerland: Springer Nature.

Pandarova, I., Schmidt, T., Hartig, J., Boubekki, A., Jones, R. D., & Brefeld, U. (2019). Predicting the difficulty of exercise items for dynamic difficulty adaptation in adaptive language tutoring. *International Journal of Artificial Intelligence in Education, 29*(3), 342–367.

Pane, J. F., Griffin, B. A., McCaffrey, D. F., & Karam, R. (2014). Effectiveness of cognitive tutor algebra I at scale. *Educational Evaluation and Policy Analysis, 36*(2), 127–144.

Pane, J. F., Steiner, E. D., Baird, M. D., & Hamilton, L. S. (2015). *Continued Progress: Promising Evidence on Personalized Learning* (RR-1365-BMGF). https://www.rand.org/pubs/research_reports/RR1365.html.

Price, T. W., Dong, Y., Zhi, R., Paaßen, B., Lytle, N., Cateté, V., & Barnes, T. (2019). A comparison of the quality of data-driven programming hint generation algorithms. *International Journal of Artificial Intelligence in Education, 29*(3), 368–395.

Roll, I., Aleven, V., McLaren, B., & Koedinger, K. R. (2011). Improving students' help-seeking skills using metacognitive feedback in an intelligent tutoring system. *Learning and Instruction, 21*, 267–280.

Shabaninejad, S., Khosravi, H., Leemans, S. J. J., Sqdiq, S., & Indulska, M. (2020). Recommending insightful drill-downs based on learning processes for learning analytics dashboards. In I. I. Bittencourt, M. Cukurova, H. Maldonado, R. Luckin, & E. Millan (Eds.), *Artificial Intelligence in Education, 21st International Conference, AIED 2020* (pp. 486–499). Switzerland: Springer Nature.

Shih, B., Koedinger, K. R., & Scheines, R. (2008). A response time model for bottom-out hints as worked examples. In C. Romero, S. Ventura, M. Pechenizkiy, & R. S. J. d. Baker (Eds.), *Handbook of Educational Data Mining* (pp. 201–211). Boca Raton, FL: Taylor & Francis.

Smith, B. I., Chimedza, C., & Buhrmann, J. H. (2020). Global and individual treatment effects using machine learning methods. *International Journal of Artificial Intelligence in Education, 30*(3), 431–458.

Steuer, T., Filighera, A., & Rensing, C. (2020). Remember the facts? Investigating answer-aware neural question generation for text comprehension. In I. I. Bittencourt, M. Cukurova, K. Muldner, R. Luckin, & E. Millan (Eds.), *Artificial Intelligence in Education, 21st International Conference, AIED 2020* (pp. 512–523). Switzerland: Springer Nature.

Taub, M., & Azevedo, R. (2019). How does prior knowledge influence eye fixations and sequences of cognitive and metacognitive SRL processes during learning with an intelligent tutoring system? *International Journal of Artificial Intelligence in Education, 29*(1), 1–28.

Taub, M., Sawyer, R., Lester, J., & Azevedo, R. (2020). The impact of contextualized emotions on self-regulated learning and scientific reasoning during learning with a game-based learning environment. *International Journal of Artificial Intelligence in Education, 30*(1), 97–120.

Ternblad, E.-M., & Tarning, B. (2020). Far from success – Far from feedback acceptance? The influence of game performance on young students' willingness to accept critical constructive feedback during play. In I. I. Bittencourt, M. Cukurova, K. Muldner, R. Luckin, & E. Millan (Eds.), *Artificial Intelligence in Education, 21st International Conference, AIED 2020* (pp. 537–548). Switzerland: Springer Nature.

van Leeuwen, A., Janssen, J., Erkens, G., & Brekelmans, M. (2015). Teacher regulation of cognitive activities during student collaboration: Effects of learning analytics. *Computer and Education, 90*, 80–94.

VanLehn, K. (2011). The relative effectiveness of human tutoring, intelligent tutoring systems and other tutoring systems. *Educational Psychologist, 46*(4), 197–221.

Vanlehn, K., Banerjee, C., Milner, F., & Wetzel, J. (2020). Teaching algebraic model construction: A tutoring system, lessons learned and an evaluation. *International Journal of Artificial Intelligence in Education, 30*(3), 459–480. doi:10.1007/s40593-020-00205-3.

VanLehn, K., Graesser, A. C., Jackson, G. T., Jordan, P., Olney, A., & Rose, C. P. (2007). When are tutorial dialogues more effective than reading? *Cognitive Science, 31*(1), 3–62.

VanLehn, K., Lynch, C., Schultz, K., Shapiro, J. A., Shelby, R. H., Taylor, L., … Wintersgill, M. C. (2005). The Andes physics tutoring system: Lessons learned. *International Journal of Artificial Intelligence and Education, 15*(3), 147–204.

Weitekamp, D., Ye, Z., Rachatasumrit, N., Harpstead, E., & Koedinger, K. R. (2020). Investigating differential error types between human and simulated learners. In I. I. Bittencourt, M. Cukurova, K. Muldner, R. Luckin, & E. Millan (Eds.), *Artificial Intelligence in Education, 21st International Conference, AIED 2020* (pp. 586–597). Switzerland: Springer Nature.

Wetzel, J., Burkhardt, H., Cheema, S., Kang, S., Pead, D., Schoenfeld, A. H., & VanLehn, K. (2018). A preliminary evaluation of the usability of an AI-infused orchestration system. In C. Rosé, R. Martínez-Maldonado, U. Hoppe, R. Luckin, M. Mavrikis, K. Porayska-Pomsta, B. McLaren, & B. du Boulay (Eds.), *Artificial Intelligence in Education: Proceedings of the 19th International Conference* (pp. 378–383). Berlin: Springer.

Wu, W., Chen, L., Yang, Q., & Li, Y. (2019). Inferring students' personality from their communication behavior in web-based learning systems. *International Journal of Artificial Intelligence in Education, 29*(2), 189–216.

Zylich, B., Viola, A., Toggerson, B., Al-Hariri, L., & Lan, A. S. (2020). Exploring automated question answering methods for teaching assistance. In I. I. Bittencourt, M. Cukurova, K. Mulder, R. Luckin, & E. Millan (Eds.), *Artificial Intelligence in Education, 21st International Conference, AIED 2020* (pp. 620–622). Switzerland: Springer Nature.

23. Large-scale commercialization of AI in school-based environments

Steven Ritter and Kenneth R. Koedinger

INTRODUCTION

In the not-so-distant past, the barriers to implementing AI-based tools in educational environments had to do with the limited availability of technology and an inability to aggregate and make decisions based on large amounts of data. Drops in the cost of technology and the ubiquity of the internet have not yet eliminated these barriers, but they are very much reduced. Many AI-based educational tools have been developed and tested and so, with the reduction of technological barriers, we might expect the use of artificial intelligence in schools to explode. That has not yet happened. Instead, the adoption of AI technologies in schools has been slow and piecemeal, despite demonstrations of effectiveness for these technologies and the potential for AI-based technologies to do things that schools say they want: personalize instruction, automate assessment, and provide data to teachers and administrators. Given their advantages, the fundamental question addressed in this chapter is why have AI-based technologies not yet taken the place of more traditional approaches on a large scale?

We may be on the cusp of widespread adoption of AI-based educational tools, but, to transition from successful small-scale pilots to large-scale adoption in schools, the developers of such tools need to find a way to fit into the school environment. As in any complex field, those who want to make an impact on education need to consider whether they will work within the system or try to disrupt the system in a way that forces radical change (Christenson et al., 2008; Reich, 2020). Although AI-based systems tend to be visionary and thus philosophically aligned with the disruptive technology view, our review of the AI systems that have gained widespread acceptance in schools is that they tend to be those that have focused on working within the system. While this may change, it appears that the current path to large-scale adoption for most AI-based educational tools is to find a way to work with schools as they are currently constituted. Doing so does not prevent innovation; it simply means that innovations must address existing needs as school professionals perceive them, while, at the same time, they inspire and address new needs that stretch the current school mold.

Our review of large-scale commercialization of AI-based tools in education focuses primarily on K-12 schools in the United States. Within this scope, we consider, in turn, three goals that AI-based applications offer to schools: (1) personalized instruction, (2) automated assessment, and (3) partnering with teachers and administrators by providing useful data and data-derived insights.

PERSONALIZATION

One of the great promises of AI in education is for systems to be able to adapt to student characteristics and provide each student with the personalized attention and approach that they need (Aleven et al., 2016). It is easy for developers of educational resources to focus on the student experience without considering the full environment in which this experience takes place. Educational experiences, at least within schools, are influenced and constrained by requirements that may be only tangentially related to learning. For example, the teacher (particularly in lower grades) needs to behaviorally monitor students to ensure that they don't disrupt other students. The school's principal has an interest in ensuring that the teacher is following a curriculum that is intended to satisfy the school's educational goals (for example, matching state and/or national standards for the subject and grade level). Administrators at the school district level have an interest in ensuring that students are making adequate progress toward educational goals, so that they can better train and assign teachers and allocate resources to schools, classes, and students. All of these institutional requirements affect the adoption of educational resources, and, at every level, they tend to favor approaches that emphasize consistency in the way that students are provided resources and assessed. A teacher wishing to understand if students are behaving appropriately has an easier time monitoring this if she has a standard model of appropriate behavior for all students. The principal has an easier time if all classes in the school (within a subject and grade level) follow the same curriculum. Administrators have an easier time when all schools report common metrics regarding student learning and other factors. In short, these institutional factors favor standardization.

Although adapting the educational approach to match the needs, abilities, and interests of each student, it is important to recognize that such personalization may conflict with institutional preferences that favor standardization (Rose, 2016). This does not mean that personalized approaches to instruction are doomed to fail. Rather, it means that systems using AI-driven personalization need to be aware of and respond to the needs that are currently being satisfied by consistency. To do that, we first consider three ways that AI-based systems personalize instruction for students and some considerations for how those forms of personalization fit into schools' institutional models.

Our discussion focused on personalization related to student knowledge, since commercial systems have advanced the most with respect to personalization of academic content. For a discussion of the potential for AI-based systems to personalize instruction with respect to affect and metacognitive behaviors (see Chapter 8 by Conati et al. and Chapter 17 by Rosé et al.).

Personalization of Student Progression within the Curriculum

The most common form of personalization adjusts the amount of time that each student spends learning each course objective (Enyedy, 2014). The need for personalization is driven by the fact that students start with differing levels of knowledge and that they learn at different rates. It follows from this premise that students will take differing amounts of time to learn the educational objectives. In traditional teacher-led instruction, the class as a whole progresses through the curriculum at a pace set by the teacher (which may or may not be responsive to the class's ability to learn the material at the pace set by the teacher). Many AI systems incorporate some form of formative assessment capability that is evaluating the student's knowledge and deciding which activity or activities the student is ready to learn (Koedinger et al., 1997). In this way, students can progress through the curriculum at their own pace, guided by activities recommended for them based on their abilities.

Mastery learning (Bloom, 1968) is a form of this approach in which the policy for recommending activities to students is that the student demonstrates mastery of each topic before progressing to the next. Many studies have shown mastery learning to be educationally effective (Kulik et al., 1990). While some early forms of mastery learning involved class-based progression, computer-based systems have focused on allowing students to progress at their own pace. One advantage of AI underlying mastery learning is that the notion of "mastery" can be driven to the level of knowledge components (KCs) – the individual cognitive steps that represent units of knowledge – and that activities within a topic can be selected based on a match between the KCs required to master the topic as a whole and an estimate of the student's level of knowledge on each of these components (Koedinger et al., 2012). Large-scale implementations allow the KCs themselves and the parameters which control the system's estimate of students' mastery of these KCs to be discovered from data.

Such an approach is often termed "competency-based progression" (Pane et al., 2015), particularly when referring to the progression across grade levels or courses. At this high level, competency-based progression might lead to eliminating grade levels, allowing students to progress through courses at their own pace, regardless of the usual grade level for each course. Indeed, some innovative schools have used competency-based progression in this way, but the institutional barriers are such that few schools operate in this way. Thus, AI-based systems that contemplate implementing mastery learning across courses might currently find a limited audience.

Within a course, mastery learning might enable students to spend more time on topics that they find difficult to learn and less time on those topics that they already know or that they find easy to learn. As a consequence, in contrast to a teacher-led class, students within a self-paced, mastery learning class may be working on different topics at the same time. From the teacher perspective, this may introduce difficulties, despite the educational effectiveness of the approach (Ritter et al., 2016). For example, in a teacher-led class, if an upcoming class is to address a topic with which the teacher feels insecure, she could refresh her knowledge about the topic the evening before the class. In a student-paced class, the teacher might be asked about a wide range of topics on any given day, based on the topics that students are addressing. In practice, fielded systems typically provide teachers a way to override the system's mastery judgment and assign students to work on particular topics. While intended as a feature to use under exceptional circumstances, some teachers use this facility as a way to transform a student-paced class into a teacher-paced one. The most common form of this is to periodically move the slower students to the topic being addressed by the whole class, regardless of whether this movement deprives these slower students of the opportunity to master prerequisites required for the current topic. Several studies (Ritter et al., 2016; Sales & Pane, 2020) have shown that students whose teachers move them in this way make more errors and perform worse on standardized tests.

In light of the institutional barriers to implementing competency-based progression, implementation of systems that personalize instruction by allowing students to progress at their own pace may need to provide ways for teachers and students to balance the educational benefits of student-based progression with the institutional constraints that favor teacher-paced classes. Since in-school class time is fixed, an AI-based mastery learning system might recommend that, for students who need it, work be done outside of class time. This approach accommodates students who need longer to master a topic, while keeping the whole class relatively in sync. Implementers may want to consider the appropriate timeframe for this synchronization to take place. Depending on the environment, this kind of synchronization could take place daily, weekly, or monthly in order to strike the right compromise between class and personal progress. Systems might also provide agency to students in making such decisions, which might support development of appropriate metacognitive behaviors (see Chapter 4 by Azevedo and Wiedbusch).

Personalization of Activities and Curricular Content

In contrast to some AI-based Tutors that personalize student progress within particular curriculum units (e.g., on adding fractions or solving two-step linear equations), some commercial systems personalize at the broader level of selecting which curricular unit(s) students should work on next. A typical approach here is to start by giving students a diagnostic placement test and use the results to select the specific curricular units (or the placement within a curriculum sequence) adapted to specific student capabilities and needs. Thus, for example, some students may be given units on fractions whereas others will be advanced to units on equation solving. This more "macro-adaptive" approach (Shute, 1993) makes larger-grained adjustments than the more "micro-adaptive" approach discussed above.

One approach to macro-adaptation is to use the results of a diagnostic exam to determine the units of instruction to be presented to the student and then (potentially) use micro-adaptation within that topic. For example, the *ESpark* system (www.esparklearning.com) and Khan Academy (www.khanacademy.org/math/mappers) can use the results of NWEA's MAP exam (www.nwea.org/map-growth/) to recommend personalized sequences for students (called "quests" in *ESpark*). ALEKS (www.aleks.com) incorporates Knowledge Checks, which are 20–30 item quizzes that help to set the learning path in a similar way. While these approaches have a clearly defined diagnostic that is distinguishable from the micro-adaptation, other systems like *MATHia* (www.carnegielearning.com/solutions/math/mathia/; Ritter et al., 2007) use the continuous formative assessment incorporated into the standard instruction to substitute for a defined diagnostic component. As discussed later, this model introduces the possibility of formative assessment becoming summative and reducing or eliminating the need for external exams.

Systems like *Kidaptive* (www.kidaptive.com) and *Gooru* (https://gooru.org) implement macro-adaptation by selecting instructional approaches delivered by other instructional systems. They aim to direct students to activity types that are best suited to individual students, based on the data they have collected from the students themselves. Instead of adapting within a set of content that they develop, they curate content from a wide variety of providers. This provides maximum flexibility and range in educational experiences, at the potential risk of providing students with a less coherent trajectory through the content than would be provided by a human-designed sequence.

As with other forms of personalization, macro-adaptation is disruptive and, as such, may get rejected by schools or teachers. Having students working on different curricular units is challenging for many teachers who want to keep the class together and have whole-group activities on a particular unit. For teachers or administrators who place high value on whole-group instruction (e.g., lectures on the same topic or the same homework for everyone), systems that provide macro-adaptation capabilities are less likely to be adopted or, when adopted, may not get used by teachers as developers intend.

At the same time, there are many organizations providing out-of-school learning support. These organizations often serve students in low-income or minoritized communities, and students receiving this support typically vary widely in their needs and not just because they serve students of many ages. Students in the same grade in school (e.g., sixth grade) may nevertheless be three grade levels different in their achievement (e.g., some at a fourth-grade level in literacy or math and others at a seventh-grade level). Such students may benefit from larger-grained macro-adaptation.

Personalization of Content

As described above, mastery learning systems typically incorporate a kind of recommendation system that includes specialized algorithms to recommend tasks based on its estimate of student knowledge. Given the prevalence of AI-based recommendation systems based on catering to user interests, a different use of AI in personalized learning could be to recommend educational resources based on student preferences and interests, rather than (or in addition to) those based on the academic and cognitive requirements of the task. There is evidence that selecting content to match student interests can improve learning outcomes (Walkington, 2013; Walkington et al., 2015).

There is a strong interest in educational resources that are more culturally responsive (Ladson-Billings, 1995), which suggests a demand for materials that could adapt to interests that more closely reflect student interests and concerns. Although this is a promising direction for AI in deployed systems, it is rare in practice. Perhaps companies have privacy concerns related to collecting and responding to student interests, which could be seen as being peripheral to educational goals. Perhaps the resulting personalized recommendations create logistical difficulties for teachers, who need to support students receiving different content (Sleeter, 2012). We are starting to see recommendation systems that incorporate student interests in widely deployed systems, particularly focusing on student reading. For example, Age of Learning's *ReadingIQ* system takes student interests into account in recommending books to students (Rothschild et al., 2019).

ASSESSMENT

One approach to scaling up the use of AI in school districts is for AI to take over tasks and responsibilities where districts see a need for change. Assessment is one such area. At the classroom level, teachers view grading quizzes and homework as a necessary burden. At the state level, assessments are used for accountability – to ensure that schools, administrators, and teachers are helping students make adequate progress with respect to educational goals. The need for administrators to understand progress relative to a common standard and to ensure that performance is measured similarly for all students has led to using standardized tests to accomplish this purpose. These tests are formal exams with well-validated questions that are taken by students under controlled conditions. However, there is great resistance to the use of these kinds of exams. The tests are highly stressful for students and teachers. The types of questions asked on such exams are often limited by the ability to develop and grade questions cheaply and efficiently, meaning that the tests rely heavily on multiple-choice questions. During the COVID-19 pandemic in 2020, most end-of-year assessments were canceled, leaving districts with little insight into how well students met course goals. See Chapter 21 by Fang et al. for more information on the use of AI for assessment.

Stealth Assessment

Instructional systems based on AI adapt to student needs through a type of assessment. That assessment is internal to the operation of the instructional system, typically only appearing through reports that indicate student progress. However, if the system is truly gaining insight into the student's abilities, then why couldn't that assessment substitute for the kinds of standardized tests we currently use for accountability purposes? The use of assessments embedded in activities is often termed "stealth assessment" (Shute & Ventura, 2013; see also Chapter 20 by McLaren & Nguyen). Much of the work on stealth assessment has taken place in the context of game environments, taking advantage of the observation that video games incorporate this kind of assessment, as players "level up" when they demonstrate mastery.

AI-based instructional systems, through the use of stealth assessment, hold the potential for changing both the form and content of accountability assessments. Their ability to assess students who are completing complex and authentic tasks can be a way to focus assessments on higher-level skills than are typically addressed by simpler item types. Embedding these assessments within instruction enables students to, potentially, certify their knowledge at any point in the school year, which could lead to true competency-based progression.

Apprendis's *Inq-ITS* (www.inqits.com) is a good example of a system focused on changing the form of assessments (Dickler et al., 2019). *Inq-ITS* provides virtual science lab environments and is focused on the kind of inquiry-based science that is the focus of the new US Next-Generation Science Standards. As students work through these lab activities, the system is able to associate the student's activity with the academic objectives of the activity, providing the teacher with insight into both student and class performance on these objectives. *Inq-ITS* also incorporates evaluation of natural language laboratory reports, in a manner similar to essay grading approaches. While *Inq ITS* is currently used at the classroom level, it is not hard to imagine that such approaches might be extended to be used in large-scale summative assessments, allowing those assessments to be incorporated into authentic scientific reasoning tasks, as opposed to solely relying on simpler question types that emphasize easier-to-grade fact-based questions.

Formative assessments like *Inq-ITS* are used instructionally, but, to the extent that they are able to address the full set of course objectives, there is no reason why they could not also be used for accountability purposes. The first step in this process must be to demonstrate that the assessment of student knowledge used within the system is, in some sense, as valid an assessment of student accomplishment with respect to course objectives as the standardized tests currently used. Such demonstrations have been performed with two widely deployed instructional systems. Pardos et al. (2014) demonstrated that student process data from the *ASSISTments* system, including inferred affect data, was able to predict outcomes on the end-of-year MCAS standardized tests used in Massachusetts. Similarly, Zheng et al. (2019) were able to predict student end-of-year test scores on the FSA standardized exam used in Florida. Work on validating adaptive AI systems as equivalent to standardized tests has the potential to dramatically expand the use of such systems, since it would incorporate assessment for accountability purposes into everyday instructional practice, reducing the amount of instructional time spent preparing for end-of-year exams.

Automated Essay Scoring

Standardized tests favor content that is easy to develop and grade, which has typically meant that such tests include large numbers of multiple-choice questions. One important exception to this trend has been the great progress made toward automatically grading essays and shorter, constructed-response questions. Products like ETS's *e-rater* and related products (Attali & Burstein, 2006), Pearson/Saavas's *Intelligent Essay Assessor* (Foltz et al., 1999), and

Cambium's *Autoscore* (Lottridge et al., n.d.) have been used in a variety of contexts to automatically score free response answers within tests. Automated essay scoring has shown great success in terms of providing grades for essays that correlate with grades given by human scorers (Liu et al., 2016) and are widely used for standardized testing, but the field has drawn back from the goal of using such systems as a substitute for human grading. Instead, the trend is for such systems to be used either in low-stakes situations (like formative assessments) or in standardized tests where there are multiple graders, some of which are human and some of which are AI-based. There appear to be two persistent issues driving this trend. First, the statistical techniques underlying these systems can be fooled by "unusual responses" (Zhang et al., 2016). Such responses might include highly creative responses (such as poetry and metaphors) that humans but not AI graders recognize as responsive, but they also include responses in which students are deliberately "gaming the system" by attempting to gain high scores through responses which are deliberately intended to fool the algorithm without addressing the prompt (Higgins and Heilman, 2014). Such gaming techniques include increasing essay length through repetition, increasing syntactic complexity, including relevant vocabulary in sentences that are non-responsive or nonsensical, and providing prepared "shell text" – responses in the appropriate domain that were not specifically written in response to the prompt. More recent automated essay-scoring algorithms are more robust against such gaming techniques (Bejar et al., 2014) and it is unclear how often such responses occur in realistic conditions, but public demonstrations of failures along these lines and reports in the popular media (Winerip, 2012; Feathers, 2019) have undermined confidence in fully automated scoring.

A second issue leading to the use of human scorers in addition to automated essay scoring is concern about bias (Ramineni & Williamson, 2018), reflected in findings that discrepancies in ratings between humans and automated scoring systems are sometimes found to be greater for test-takers in specific demographic groups. As in other areas of AI, algorithms are sensitive to training data, which might not fully reflect the demographics of the populations which are actually using automated scoring. There is also the possibility that humans and automated scoring algorithms are differentially sensitive to essay characteristics that are correlated with demographic characteristics of the test-takers. For example, Ramieni and Williamson found that shell text content was more prevalent in essays submitted by test-takers in China and also that human raters tended to provide lower grades to essays with more shell content than the automated scorers. For additional discussion about potential biases in the use of artificial intelligence in educational contexts, see Chapter 15 by Pozdniakov et al. and Chapter 26 by Porayska-Pomsta et al.

Formative Assessment of Language-Based Activities

Automated essay scoring has been enabled by recent advances in the ability of artificial intelligence to understand natural languages. Indeed, some of the greatest successes for Artificial Intelligence in recent years have been in the area of natural language processing, both in text and speech. These advances have led to several applications to education. See Chapter 11 by Rus et al. for a more complete discussion of language technologies used in educational AI.

While essay scoring addressed in the previous section focuses on the use of language understanding in a summative assessment context, the ability to use AI to provide formative assessment as part of language-based instruction has also made many recent advances.

TurnItIn's *Revision Assistant* (www.revisionassistant.com) is focused on providing support to student writing through natural language. It provides an example of transition from a pure essay-grading tool to a learning environment to support students in learning to become better writers. Revision Assistant began through research efforts in developing a free and open software tool for text mining, called *LightSIDE* (Mayfield & Rose, 2013). The team used *LightSIDE* to perform well in a Hewlett Foundation-sponsored automated grading essay competition (EdSurge, 2013). The success drew attention and led to a spin-off company, LightSIDE Labs, which was later acquired by TurnItIn. *Revision Assistant* emerged from a deliberate effort to build learning support for writing around the AI capabilities provided by sophisticated AI for text mining. Writing tasks were created and organized into a writing curriculum. We suspect that these tasks and the associated curriculum have been a key feature in the product's commercial success. TurnItIn hired User Experience Designers and sponsored a team of Human–Computer Interaction (HCI) Master's students to drive the development, paying particular attention to what teachers want and what would be useful and be adopted in schools. In addition, the use of HCI-based design of tasks had an important influence on making the AI work better. For example, one topic in the curriculum is use of source material in writing, with specific learning goals of quoting source content when it is used *verbatim* and of drawing from multiple sources. AI for detecting whether these goals are achieved in an unconstrained student writing submission is quite difficult. The *Revision Assistant* designers cleverly created tasks within this curricular unit whereby students were given the text of three sources and were asked to write an essay using these sources. Because the AI now knows what the source texts are, AI detection of whether students are appropriately quoting and using multiple sources is much more feasible and accurate.

The *Amira* reading tutor (www.amiralearning.com) provides a good example of a technology that transitioned, after more than 20 years of research, from an academic project to a well-funded commercial endeavor. Amira is based on Project LISTEN's *Reading Tutor* (Mostow, 2016), which was developed to support students learning to read. The Reading Tutor listens as students read out loud. The research behind the reading tutor focused on three broad areas: the speech recognition engine, which has the responsibility to interpret whether the student's pronunciation corresponded to the text; the domain model, which encoded the essential elements of reading that are the target of instruction; and the feedback and instructional model, which is responsible for communicating errors and suggesting remediation to students. The feedback model is a particularly interesting element because it involves tradeoffs between the capabilities of the technology and the practical requirements of instruction. There is always some uncertainty in the speech engine's interpretation of the student's utterances, and that uncertainty needs to be reflected in the feedback given to students (Li & Mostow, 2012). Even if speech recognition were perfect, however, practical considerations may dictate the form, timing, and frequency of feedback. For example, in the domain of reading, encouraging fluency is essential, so interrupting a student to correct a minor pronunciation error may do more harm than good (Sitaram et al., 2011). It is in keeping with the theme of this chapter that many of the modifications to the *Reading Tutor* that took place to commercialize it as *Amira* were focused on more fully integrating the tutor into the standard routine of the classroom, including ensuring that schools understand that *Amira* is intended to be a tool used to support teachers and teaching.

Spoken language instruction can be especially difficult in school environments because developing such skill relies, in part, on dialog, and a teacher's opportunity to speak with individual students is particularly limited. Alelo's *Enskill* (www.alelo.com) is intended to fill this role by using AI to scaffold a dialog with a student, including both language moves and pedagogical agents (Johnson & Lester, 2015). The focus is primarily on learning English, with a secondary focus on students learning Spanish. *Enskill* addresses language instruction by immersing students in a realistic environment with a well-defined task. For example, the student may be asked to go to a (virtual) train ticket office and buy a round-trip ticket to Paris, spending under €200. In completing this task, the student may need to hear and produce speech relating to time, locations, and money. *Enskill* uses speech processing technology to understand student utterances and is able to provide feedback either verbally or in text and in either the student's native or target language. The combination of visuals through both the avatar and on-screen text and auditory speech scaffolds students in completing the task. The system also provides analytics that enable teachers to track students' progress. While the most impressive features of the system involve the immersive simulations, *Enskill* also provides individual skill-building activities for students. Such activities may be recommended based on student performance in the immersive exercises.

TEACHER SUPPORT

Some of the most complex decisions with respect to how AI systems are widely deployed in schools revolve around how the system relates to teachers. Instructional AI systems developed independently of school deployment often take an *intervene-on-failure* model, in which the system takes primary responsibility for instruction (or, at least, for the component of instruction addressed by the system), and the teacher intervenes only when the AI system hits its limit. An alternative approach is to design the AI system around the expectation that the AI and the teacher are each instructional resources with particular roles to play in the student's instructional experience. The challenge for the overall instructional approach, then, is to determine what aspects of instruction are best suited to AI, which to teachers, and how the AI and the teacher communicate to optimize "handoffs" between these two components of the system (Fancsali et al., 2018). Within any system, professional development and support tools must focus on helping teachers to understand their role and abilities within the system as well as providing guidance on appropriate and effective implementation.

Work in this area acknowledges that AI and teachers are both instructional resources, but they are not equivalent instructional resources. In particular, the teacher is a scarce resource and so focusing on how to best use the teacher's limited time is paramount. Work in this area often falls into the category of teacher "orchestration," since it is concerned with guiding the teacher's role based on data and insights provided by the instructional systems working with students. For a more complete discussion of the forms of orchestration and the ways in which AI is being used to support teachers, see Chapter 14 by Holstein and Olsen.

Carnegie Learning's *MATHia* intelligent tutoring system includes a dashboard system called *LiveLab*, which is focused on teacher orchestration. *LiveLab* uses a machine-learned model to classify students according to whether they are progressing toward mastery within each mathematics topic (Fancsali et al., 2020). This classification task can be difficult, since students are expected to make errors and ask for hints as they learn, so an approach that focuses solely on the frequency of hints and errors would fail to distinguish between students who are productively struggling (and learning from their errors) and those who are unproductively struggling.

However, in many cases, machine learning is able to identify "indicator skills," which distinguish unproductive from productive struggle. The *LiveLab* algorithm is also tuned to direct teachers to help students when they can have the greatest impact: that is, not only after there is sufficient evidence that students are not on a trajectory towards mastery but also early enough that the teacher's intervention is likely to be able to get the student back on track before *MATHia* concludes that the student has failed to master the content.

One particularly promising extension to this kind of orchestration approach considers the form that information is given to teachers. *Lumilo* (Holstein et al., 2018) uses augmented reality to present information to teachers in a way that does not distract them from direct interaction with students. The teacher can gaze at the classroom and see indicators floating above students' heads. These indicators include signals that particular students are struggling or are off task. As the teacher walks to a student's desk, she can dig deeper into the reasons for the student's struggle, using that time to prepare for a productive conversation with the student.

In response to the COVID-19 pandemic, teachers and students have become used to virtual instruction via video conferencing. For AI-based instructional systems, growing acceptance of this kind of remote instruction could lead to a need to prepare human tutors to better interact with students who periodically require help from a human tutor. One model is that, while a student uses an AI-based instructional system like *MATHia*, the system is monitoring for conditions that indicate that the student might be unproductively struggling. As described above, the detection of this state might indicate to the teacher, through an application like *LiveLab*, that the teacher should help the student. But what if the teacher is busy or the student is working independently at home? Depending on the context of use, *MATHia* might direct the student to an online video conference with a human tutor. In addition to the AI system being able to detect unproductive struggle, success in this use case depends on the system's ability to communicate to the human tutor some background information about the kinds of difficulties that led the system to recommend tutoring and, perhaps, suggestions for remediation. The use of remote instruction in this way breaks down the distinction between schoolwork and out-of-school work and flexibly guides the student through using educational resources that might include an intelligent tutoring system, the student's regular teacher, or a human tutor. Such systems point towards ways in which AI-based systems might disrupt educational practice in a more fundamental way. Further discussion of the ways in which data are used to help guide instruction can be found in Chapter 15 by Pozdniakov et al.

CONCLUSION

Our review of AI-based instructional technologies that have made the transition from academic pilots to large-scale use in schools focuses on the ways that developers have positioned such technologies to fit into the institutional requirements imposed by school systems. Personalized learning systems like *MATHia*, *ALEKS*, and *eSpark* position themselves as core or supplemental curricula that fit into schools' standard course structure and objectives. They focus on supporting schools in accommodating personalization within this structure and emphasize their ability to more effectively and efficiently instruct students. Macro-adaptive systems, like *Kidaptive* and *Gooru*, focus on flexibility and the availability of a wide range of instructional activities but also fit within schools' course structure and academic standards.

AI systems following the "golden triangle" model presented in Chapter 24 by Luckin and Cukurova may be successful in making the transition to large-scale use.

AI systems that focus on assessment have a natural way to fit into school systems, which are actively seeking ways to reform their approach to assessment. Stealth assessment systems like *Inq-ITS* position themselves as formative assessments that allow teachers to gain insights into students' abilities in areas that are not typically addressed by traditional assessments, such as science inquiry. Automated essay-scoring systems have proven to be useful, particularly in large-scale, high-stakes assessments, but they still struggle with gaining trust from the public.

Technologies that take advantage of natural language processing to deliver instructional experiences that would normally require the attention of a teacher have the potential to expand widely as they figure out how to integrate better into school-based instruction. *Revision Assistant* as a support for writing, *Amira* as a support for reading, and *Alelo* as a support for culturally embedded language instruction hold promise in this area and are poised to expand in the future.

Technologies, like Carnegie Learning's *MATHia*, that support teachers by helping to orchestrate instruction, are not a primary reason to bring AI into the classroom; they gain support because an AI-based tool, through regular use by students, is able to provide insight to teachers that can help them do their job better. We expect systems focused on helping teachers to expand rapidly in concert with AI-based instructional systems. Focusing on helping teachers not only aids in countering the incorrect perception that the role of AI systems is to take autonomy away from teachers, but also, and more importantly, designing for a partnership with teachers is a critical element in making these systems as effective as they can be. To the extent that such tools encourage teachers to welcome AI technologies into their classrooms, instead of fearing them, we expect that the ability of AI systems to provide teachers with insights will be an essential support for continued large-scale adoption of AI systems in schools.

REFERENCES

Aleven, V., McLaughlin, E. A., Glenn, R. A., & Koedinger, K. R. (2016). Instruction based on adaptive learning technologies. In Mayer, R. E., & Alexander, P. (Eds.), *Handbook of research on learning and instruction* (pp. 522–560). New York: Routledge.

Attali, Y. & Burstein, J. (2006). Automated essay scoring with e-rater® V.2. *Journal of Technology, Learning, and Assessment, 4*(3). http://www.jtla.org.

Bejar, I., Flor, M., Futagi, Y., & Ramineni, C. (2014). On the vulnerability of automated scoring to construct-irrelevant response strategies (CIRS): An illustration. *Assessing Writing, 22*, 48–59.

Bloom, B. S. (1968, May). Mastery learning. In *Evaluation comment* (Vol. 1, No. 2). Los Angeles: University of California at Los Angeles, Center for the Study of Evaluation of Instructional Programs.

Christensen, C. M., Horn, M., & Johnson, C. W. (2008). *Disrupting class: How disruptive innovation will change the way the world learns*. New York: McGraw-Hill.

Dickler, R., Li, H., & Gobert, J. (2019). A data-driven approach for automated assessment of scientific explanations in science inquiry. In *Proceedings of the Twelfth International Conference on Educational Data Mining* (pp. 536–539).

EdSurge (2013). Breaking down myths behind automated essay graders. www.edsurge.com/news/2013 -04-08-breaking-down-myths-behind-automated-essay-graders.

Enyedy, N. (2014). *Personalized instruction: New interest, old rhetoric, limited results, and the need for a new direction for computer-mediated learning*. Boulder, CO: National Education Policy Center. Retrieved 10/29/2015 from http://nepc.colorado.edu/publication/personalized-instruction.

Fancsali, S. E., Holstein, K., Sandbothe, M., Ritter, S., McLaren, B. M., & Aleven, V. (2020) Towards practical detection of unproductive struggle. In I. Bittencourt, M. Cukurova, K. Muldner, R. Luckin, & E. Millán (Eds.), *Artificial intelligence in education. AIED 2020. Lecture notes in computer science*, Vol. 12164. Cham: Springer. https://doi.org/10.1007/978-3-030-52240-7_17.

Fancsali, S. E., Yudelson, M. V., Berman, S. R., & Ritter, S. (2018). Intelligent instructional hand offs. In *Proceedings of the 11th International Conference on Educational Data Mining* (pp. 198–207).

Feathers, T. (2019, August 20). Flawed algorithms are grading millions of students' essays. *Vice*. www.vice.com/en/article/pa7dj9/flawed-algorithms-are-grading-millions-of-students-essays.

Foltz, P. W., Laham, D., & Landauer, T. K. (1999). The intelligent essay assessor: Applications to educational technology. *Interactive Multimedia Electronic Journal of Computer-Enhanced Learning, 1*, 2, http://imej.wfu.edu/articles/1999/2/04/ index.asp.

Higgins, D., & Heilman, M. (2014). Managing what we can measure: Quantifying the susceptibility of automated scoring systems to gaming behavior. *Educational Measurement: Issues and Practice, 33*.

Holstein, K., Hong, G., Tegene, M., McLaren, B., & Aleven, V. (2018). The classroom as a dashboard: Co-designing wearable cognitive augmentation for K-12 teachers. In *Proceedings of the International Conference on Learning Analytics and Knowledge*.

Johnson, W. L., & Lester, J. C. (2016). Face-to-face interaction with pedagogical agents, twenty years later. *International Journal of Artificial Intelligence in Education, 26*, 25–36.

Koedinger, K. R., Anderson, J. R., Hadley, W. H., & Mark, M. A. (1997). Intelligent tutoring goes to school in the big city. *International Journal of Artificial Intelligence in Education (IJAIED), 8*, 30–43.

Koedinger, K. R., Corbett, A. C., & Perfetti, C. (2012). The Knowledge-Learning-Instruction (KLI) framework: Bridging the science-practice chasm to enhance robust student learning. *Cognitive Science, 36*(5), 757–798.

Kulik, C. L., Kulik, J. A., & Bangert-Drowns, R. L. (1990). Effectiveness of mastery learning programs: A meta-analysis. *Review of Educational Research, 60*, 265–299.

Ladson-Billings, G. (1995). Toward a theory of culturally relevant pedagogy. *American Educational Research Journal, 47*, 465–491.

Li, Y., & Mostow, J. (2012). Evaluating and improving real-time tracking of children's oral reading. In *Proceedings of the 25th Florida Artificial Intelligence Research Society Conference (FLAIRS-25)* (pp. 488–491). Marco Island, Florida.

Liu, O. L., Rios, J., Heilman, M., Gerard, L., & Linn, M. C. (2016). Validation of automated scoring of science assessments. *Journal of Research in Science Teaching, 53*(2), 215–233. https://doi.org/10.1002/tea.21299.

Lottridge, S., Godek, J., & Patel (n.d.) Comparing the robustness of deep learning and classical automated scoring approaches to gaming strategies. https://cambiumassessment.com/-/media/project/cambium/corporate/pdfs/cai-comparing-robustness-of-dl-and-cas_white-paper.pdf.

Mayfield, E., & Rose, C. P. (2013), LightSIDE: Open source machine learning for text. In M. D. Shermis & J. C. Burstein (Eds.), *Handbook of automated essay evaluation: Current application and new directions* (pp. 124–135). New York: Psychology Press.

Mostow, J. (2016). Project LISTEN's reading tutor. In S. A. Crossley & D. S. McNamara (Eds.), *Adaptive educational technologies for literacy instruction* (pp. 263–267). New York: Taylor & Francis, Routledge.

Pane, J., Steiner, E., Baird, M., & Hamilton, L. (2015). Continued progress executive summary. In *Continued Progress: Promising Evidence on Personalized Learning: Executive Summary* (pp. 1–8). RAND Corporation. Retrieved April 16, 2021, from http://www.jstor.org/stable/10.7249/j.ctt19w724m.1.

Pardos, Z. A., Baker, R. S., San Pedro, M., Gowda, S. M., & Gowda, S. M. (2014). Affective states and state tests: Investigating how affect and engagement during the school year predict end-of-year learning outcomes. *Journal of Learning Analytics, 1*(1), 107–128. https://doi.org/10.18608/jla.2014.11.6.

Ramineni, C., & Williamson, D. (2018). Understanding mean score differences between the e-rater® automated scoring engine and humans for demographically based groups in the GRE® general test. *ETS Research Report Series, 2018*, 1–31.

Reich, J. (2020). *Failure to disrupt: Why technology alone can't transform education*. Cambridge, MA: Harvard University Press.

Ritter, S., Anderson, J. R., Koedinger, K. R., & Corbett, A. (2007). Cognitive tutor: Applied research in mathematics education. *Psychonomic Bulletin & Review, 14*(2), 249–255.

Ritter, S., Yudelson, M., Fancsali, S. E., & Berman, S. R. (2016). How mastery learning works at scale. In *L@S*, 2016, 71–79. ACM.

Rose, T. (2016). *The end of average: How we succeed in a world that values sameness*. San Francisco, CA, HarperOne.

Rothschild, M., Horiuchi, T., & Maxey, M. (2019) Evaluating "just right" in edtech recommendation. In *3rd KidRec Workshop Co-Located With ACM IDC 2019*. https://kidrec.github.io/papers/KidRec _2019_paper_6.pdf.

Sales, A. C., & Pane, J. (2020). The effect of teachers reassigning students to new cognitive tutor sections. In *Proceedings of the 13th International Conference on Educational Data Mining (EDM 2020)*, pp. 202–211.

Shute, V. (1993). A macroadaptive approach to tutoring. *Journal of Artificial Intelligence in Education, 4*, 61–93.

Shute, V., & Ventura, M. (2013). *Stealth assessment: Measuring and supporting learning in video games*. Cambridge, MA: MIT Press.

Sitaram, S., Mostow, J., Li, Y., Weinstein, A., Yen, D., & Valeri, J. (2011). What visual feedback should a reading tutor give children on their oral reading prosody? In *SLaTE: ISCA (International Speech Communication Association) Special Interest Group (SIG) Workshop on Speech and Language Technology in Education*, Venice, Italy.

Sleeter, C. E. (2012). Confronting the marginalization of culturally responsive pedagogy. *Urban Education, 47*(3), 562–584. https://doi.org/10.1177/0042085911431472.

Walkington, C. (2013). Using learning technologies to personalize instruction to student interests: The impact of relevant contexts on performance and learning outcomes. *Journal of Educational Psychology, 105*, 932–945. http://dx.doi.org/10.1037/a0031882.

Walkington, C., Clinton, V., Ritter, S., & Nathan, M. J. (2015). How readability and topic incidence relate to performance on mathematics story problems in computer-based curricula. *Journal of Educational Psychology, 107*(4), 1051–1074.

Winerip, M. (2012, April 22). Facing a Robo-grader? Just keep obfuscating mellifluously. *The New York Times*. www.nytimes.com.

Zheng, G., Fancsali, S. E., Ritter, S., & Berman, S. (2019). Using instruction-embedded formative assessment to predict state summative test scores and achievement levels in mathematics. *Journal of Learning Analytics, 6*(2), 153–174. https://doi.org/10.18608/jla.2019.62.11.

Zhang, M., Chen, J., & Ruan, C. (2016). Evaluating the advisory flags and machine scoring difficulty in the e-rater® automated scoring engine. *ETS Research Report Series, 2016*, 1–14.

24. Small-scale commercialisation: the golden triangle of AI EdTech

Rosemary Luckin and Mutlu Cukurova

INTRODUCTION AND CONTEXT

There is a growing body of educational research on the importance of connecting research with practice, research with design and the difficulty of making these connections. In addition, the importance of connecting research with educational practice is argued in various policymaking reports. For example, Cooper (2010) demonstrated that successful schools were shown to have facilitated the use of external research and the navigation of the world of academia. Similarly, Bell et al. (2010) conducted a systematic review into educational practitioners' engagement in or with research and the impact that this engagement had on learners. Their report showed that there was a relationship between "strong evidence of links between teacher engagement in and with research and significant changes in practice with a positive impact on student outcomes" (p. 81). Evidence of the potential for research-informed EdTech applications to positively impact learning interventions is also starting to appear. For example, an OECD report indicated that teachers who participated in professional development that involved research were more likely to report using active teaching strategies, including the use of EdTech. In turn, such active teaching strategies are observed to have positive effects on learners (OECD TALIS, 2013).

Furthermore, the "Decoding Learning: The Proof, Promise and Potential of Digital Education Report" (Luckin et al., 2012) critically examined the evidence about whether EdTech supported learning and teaching, and asked how such technology might be better exploited to support learning. The title of the report emphasizes that its intention was to investigate the Proof, putting learning first; the Promise, for technology to help learning in new ways; and the Potential, to make better use of technologies already in use. The report examined over 1,300 publications that described EdTech innovations and looked for evidence of their effectiveness. It makes clear that, as stressed in many other papers and reports, no technology has an impact on learning in its own right. Any impact is a consequence of many factors, including how the technology is used, where it is used, by whom and with whom. In addition, the report also highlighted further activities and practical advice to guide the use of EdTech. Of particular relevance to this chapter is the suggestion in the report for Collaborative Evidence-Based Product Design. This approach argues for the value of co-designing EdTech that is designed and implemented through the conscientious, explicit and astute use of four sources of information: a critical evaluation of the best available research evidence, practitioner expertise and judgement, evidence from the local context and the perspectives and values of those people who are directly or indirectly affected by the EdTech (Cukurova et al., 2019).

The report highlighted the significant disconnect between the key educational technology stakeholders: EdTech companies, researchers, educators and learners. The barriers to changing this disconnect were acknowledged and ways to address these barriers were seen as vital next steps. The key to success would be demonstrating the benefits of collaborative evidence-based product design to show teachers how it could help them improve their classroom practice, and to show developers how it could improve their products or services. This would also require that misunderstandings about what constitutes research and evidence would need to be corrected. For example, the belief amongst many EdTech companies is that the only research they need is market research.

With this broad overview, in this chapter, we discuss the Educate research accelerator programme which aimed to address the challenge of connecting research with practice and design of educational technology. The Educate Accelerator was originally set up as a 3-year project hosted by University College London (2017–2019) and funded by the European Regional Development Fund. The accelerator aimed to develop better evidence-informed educational technology by connecting EdTech development with research methodologies and evidence. In the programme, EdTech was considered broadly, including digital instructional technology systems, networks, tools and resources. There was also no particular focus on the education levels in which the digital technology was used, including from early years through to higher, technical and vocational education, professional development and training. This allowed a broad range of small-scale companies to be part of the programme. Educate brought together researchers, such as those within the UCL Institute of Education and the wider University College London organisation, and educators with EdTech entrepreneurs in start-ups and small businesses. During the three-year project, Educate supported over 260 EdTech businesses with research and business training to enable them to better develop effective EdTech with solid evidence about the efficacy of their product or service. A parallel programme for educators was also developed and piloted to help them apply EdTech effectively and to generate and share data and evidence to demonstrate what EdTech worked for them, thus building capacity and demand in the EdTech marketplace into which EdTech businesses sell.

The approach adopted by the Educate Accelerator is grounded in collaborative evidence-based product development and is expressed in the *Educate Golden Triangle*™ (Luckin, 2015). This is illustrated in Figure 24.1, which shows how the three corners of the triangle represent the three communities that need to be connected for the development and application of effective EdTech products and services. The three communities are:

• Educators, students and parents, who want to know what works when using technology to support learning;
• Researchers, who need to know how better to communicate their research to teachers and EdTech developers to demonstrate that it has an impact in the real world; and
• EdTech developers, who need to understand how research evidence is relevant to them and how they can find out about educators', parents' and learners' experiences with their product or service.

The premise of the *Educate Golden Triangle*™ is that by connecting these three communities within the context of seeking evidence about whether EdTech products and services meet the needs of their customers, the following benefits would also be reaped:

1. Improved learning by those benefitting from the evidence-informed EdTech;
2. Improved and more effective application of technology by educators;

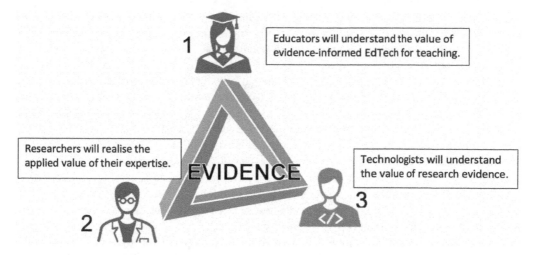

Source: Cukurova et al., 2019

Figure 24.1   *The Educate Golden Triangle*

3. Increased sales for the EdTech companies who are better able to show and provide evidence for the effectiveness of their products;
4. Improved communication of research to non-academic audiences; and
5. Increased relevance of research to real-world needs.

The Educate triangle represents the connection between these communities, the thread that brings them together is the gold of data and evidence.

EdTech companies attended the Educate training programme in cohorts of about 30 companies and their stay with Educate lasted for six months, after which time the companies joined the Educate Alumni community. Participants were explicitly taught research methods, both how to access existing research evidence and about the basic tools and methodologies that can be implemented in research. They were also allocated a personal research mentor who guided them through the application of these research tools and methods to their own business context. The training helped participants to use existing research findings and it offered them guidance about conducting their own research project to generate evidence about how (and if) their product or service met the needs of learners or educators. Alongside the research training, the programme also offered business and product development training support, a co-working space to enable them to work alongside researchers and educators, and an online tool called "Lean" for integrated business and research planning. For more information about the research training materials, see Luckin and Cukurova (2019).

A CASE STUDY WITH AN AI EDTECH EDUCATE PARTICIPANT

Interdisciplinarity is fundamental to the Educate methodology. When working with EdTech companies who are considering how AI might be used in their business, for example, we work across educational, technical and research stakeholders. Collaboration between technology developers and educators is essential to ensure that there is a two-way knowledge exchange that enables developers to understand more about teaching and learning and educators to understand more about the process of developing AI technology for use in education and training.

In this case study, the collaboration was between researchers who were part of the Educate programme and a company called DebateMate (see https://debatemate.com for more information) that provides programmes and competitions to participating secondary-level schools in some of the most deprived communities in the UK and in other parts of the world. For example, the company recruits and trains university students to run face-to-face debate workshops as extra-curricular activities in secondary-level schools. However, they were keen to understand how AI might best be used to leverage their new online business. Through collaboration between Educate researchers and educators at DebateMate, the process of interviewing and selecting young people to run the after-school debate clubs was identified as an area where AI might be able to offer assistance in the first instance.

The Educate programme's research training encourages participants to explore existing literature as part of the process of developing their own research proposals. In particular, we, as the research team, explained to the DebateMate educators the relevance of the recent progress made in multimodal analytics to help better analyse and interpret complex learning processes and tasks in social contexts (see Baltrušaitis et al., 2019). In particular, we stressed the value of using AI to augment human intelligence (Luckin, 2018; Malone, 2018) and suggested that this might be an approach that could benefit DebateMate. We also explored and discussed what could be learnt from the research literature about decision-making processes and the array of different mechanisms involved (Evans, 2008). This is precisely the process that the Educate Research training proposed.

We identified two categories of the decision-making process involved in the process of interviewing and selecting young people to run the after-school debate clubs: heuristic processes for intuitive decision making that operates autonomously and automatically (Kahneman & Frederick, 2002) and analytic processes performed step-by-step with conscious awareness and deliberation. It was likely that the recruitment process being used by DebateMate was a mix of the two types of the decision-making process. However, it was also the case that whilst the goal of those evaluating the candidate debate tutors may well be to make an analytical decision, the reality is that the complexity and non-routine and dynamic nature of the situation make it more likely that an intuitive approach is inevitable. It was therefore deemed appropriate to consider how data and AI can be used to support this intuitive process by providing transparent models that are analytical and that can complement the intuitive human decision-making processes the educators were using. We worked with DebateMate to explore the way in which AI could support their intuitive decision-making processes when they were evaluating candidate tutor trainees. In particular, we introduced the educators at DebateMate to how multimodal data, about which they had learnt in their training, can be used to develop analytical classification models that are transparent and that can support their decision making.

Research Literature about Debate Tutoring

We also explored the literature about debating and tutoring to identify relevant psychometric measures, including personal characteristics, such as emotional intelligence and temperament, and personality traits such as extraversion/introversion and neuroticism/emotional stability. We explored existing research tools, including the Adult Temperament Questionnaire (ATQ;

Evans & Rothbart, 2007), the Trait Emotional Intelligence Questionnaire (TEIQue- SF; Petrides, 2009), the General Charisma Inventory (GCI; Tskhay et al., 2018) and the Big Five Inventory (BFI; John & Srivastava, 1999).

We also briefly reviewed the literature about multimodality in AI, education and analytics. Research in these areas has been growing quickly, with increasing numbers of researchers trying to build AI models that can process information from multiple modalities (Vinciarelli et al., 2009; Zhou & De la Torre, 2012; Atrey et al., 2010; Grawemayer et al., 2017). Importantly, work within the AI community has demonstrated how multimodal AI models can help humans make better-informed decisions with the support of analytics (Blikstein, 2013, Ochoa et al., 2018; Martinez-Maldonado et al., 2013; Cukurova et al., 2020), as compared with purely machine-learning approaches that aim to automate the decision-making process (see, for example, Baltrušaitis et al., 2019; Spikol et al., 2018). In educational contexts, such automation is rarely the most appropriate approach.

Data Sources Identified and Collected

We collected data from both the candidates who had applied to become debate tutors and from the DebateMate educators who were conducting the evaluations of these candidates.

Over a three-month period, we observed the educators at work, analysed the notes they took during evaluations and conducted interviews.

When university students apply to become debate tutors in schools, their CV is assessed to ensure their academic achievements are sound. They then take part in a live debating evaluation and are observed by expert educators. Following our survey of the literature with DebateMate educators, we conducted a knowledge elicitation activity with some of their expert debate tutors who were involved in the evaluation of applicants.

Two essential domains of evaluation were found:

1. Candidates' social and emotional skills, such as social interactivity, engagement, emotional intelligence and appropriate encouragement/praise of others;
2. Candidates' tutoring skills, such as the use of contingent tutoring techniques, appropriate pitching and management of the students.

These expert educators also identified the 'style', professionalism, content and strategy as essential elements of debating for which they would also be looking. Three different expert educators would use these criteria to give each candidate a score ranging from 1 to 5, where 1 and 2 described excellent debate tutors, who can be placed at any school, 3 is used for those who are acceptable but might need some further training and 4 and 5 are used for candidates who are not suitable to be debate tutors. Any discrepancies among the educators were negotiated to reach a consensus. However, in reality, it was clear that whilst educators did adhere to this protocol, they also took into account a range of other skills through an intuitive decision-making process that tapped into their experience. The educators accepted that this was the case and openly admitted that sometimes they just knew instinctively that someone would be great at tutoring in the debate clubs. The evidence from our analysis of the notes taken by educators also showed the consideration of a much wider set of skills, for example: 'nice and fun', 'cool vibes', 'Sweet'.

Balancing the additional value of adding a new modality for the accuracy of models built and the practical and ethical challenges of collecting data from a new modality, we proposed the use of two modalities: (i) Information collected through a personality traits question-naire and (ii) audio recordings of candidate debate tutors. Based on the instruments that our literature review had identified, we selected appropriate questions and added two items about candidates' previous experience in debating and tutoring. The questionnaire was completed by 127 candidates and we collected audio recordings from 47 candidates.

Data Analysis

For the questionnaire data, we used principal components analysis (PCA) to reduce the large set of variables that would account for most of the variance. The combination of PCA and a visual inspection of the scree plot it produced showed that four components explained 57.193% of the total variance:

1. The extrovert leader factor: Extraversion, outgoingness and leadership;
2. The charismatic factor: Charisma, enthusiasm and the tendency to make people comfort-able items;
3. The assertive organized factor: Assertiveness, organisation and the tendency of being influential; and
4. The neurotic factor: Neuroticism and non-assertiveness.

Figure 24.2 shows a radar chart of the median value of each of these four factors, for the score categories used by the DebateMate educators.

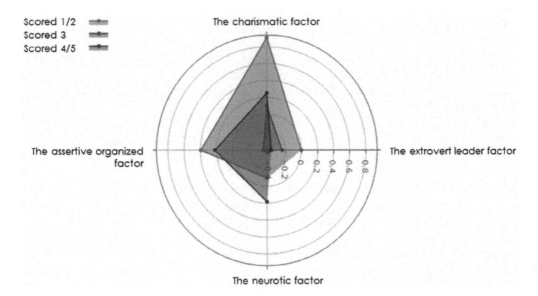

Source: Cukurova et al., 2019

Figure 24.2   *Significant components accounting for most of the variance in the question-naire data*

Analysis of the audio data was conducted using an open-source software application called OpenSMILE that automatically extracts features, such as loudness, from audio signals and classifies them to interpret the speaker's emotional and affective states and traits. For the research reported in this paper, we used 16 voice-based emotion features: the seven classes of basic emotion, combined with six affections and three levels of interest (for more information, see Burkhardt et al., 2005; Schuller et al., 2007, 2009). The total feature set was as follows: *Anger, Fear, Happiness, Disgust, Boredom, Sadness, Neutral, Aggressive, Cheerful, Intoxicated, Nervous, Neutral, Tired, Passive interest levels, Neutral interest levels* and *Strong interest levels*.

A correlation matrix of all the variables investigated across both the questionnaire and audio data illustrated that there were very few inter-modal correlations, suggesting that the different modalities of data we had collected contributed different input to the classification model built.

The evaluation scores awarded to candidate tutors were the comparison of our data-driven analytics and the human educators' intuitive scores.

Multinomial logistic regression was used to classify the scores of the tutor candidates. The results presented in Table 24.1 show the results of classification results of performance based only on the audio variables (unimodal model). The model's goodness of fit analysis shows that the model fits the data well (Pearson's chi-square (df=56) = 61.63, p=0.282). The results when multimodal data are used for the same classification task are presented in Table 24.2. When classifying the candidates' data by including the survey variables, the two experience variables and two of the significant audio variables, the affect 'nervous' and emotion 'arousal' variables, the model's goodness of fit analysis shows that the model fits the data well (Pearson's chi-square (df=52) = 48.56, p=0.610). Moreover, the model's fitting information shows that the full model predicts the score significantly better than the intercept-only model alone (Pearson's chi-square (df=28) = 47.05, p=0.014) and better than the unimodal model presented in Table 24.1.

DISCUSSION OF THE DEBATEMATE CASE STUDY

The work we conducted with DebateMate showed them that transparent classification models constructed from multimodal data could assist expert educators to reflect upon their

Table 24.1   *Unimodal classification of debate tutors' performance based on only the audio variables*

Observed score	Estimated score			Per cent correct
	1/2	3	4/5	
1/2	8	1	0	88.9%
3	2	15	5	68.2%
4/5	0	3	7	70.0%
Overall	24.4%	46.3%	29.3%	73.2%

Source: Cukurova et al., 2019

Table 24.2   *Multimodal classification of debate tutors' performance, based on the experi-*
                  ence, survey and two of the strong predictive audio variables

Observed score	Estimated score			Per cent correct
	1/2	3	4/5	
1/2	8	1	0	88.9%
3	1	19	2	86.4%
4/5	0	4	6	60.0%
Overall	22.0%	58.5%	19.5%	80.5%

Source: Cukurova et al., 2019

decision-making processes and they could provide candidate tutors with some feedback on what aspects need to be developed to help them become better debate tutors. Educators can complement the data from the classification model with the information from the notes they take during the evaluation, which is particularly helpful when the scores from the educators differ from those suggested by the model. The detail from the model could also be used to be more specific about what some of the educators' notes meant.

It is important to note that we, as researchers, were not trying to show the DebateMate educators how AI techniques could automatically classify tutor candidates. Rather, we wanted to show them how AI could be applied to multimodal data to provide more information about the decision-making process and in this way to better support their human decision-making processes, by providing transparency rather than black-box models. The point here is not to say that black-box machine learning does not have a role in education, but rather to illustrate the value of using a range of approaches to modelling that are selected in accordance with their appropriateness for the purpose of using AI.

Through working together, the educators at DebateMate and the researchers who were part of the Educate accelerator team were able to collaborate and exchange expertise as they developed an approach to the use of AI to support intuitive decision making when evaluating candidate debate tutors. This collaboration was also an opportunity to confirm and apply the training that the DebateMate team had received through the Educate Research Accelerator, such as the training content about multimodal data collection, analysis and application.

The Importance of Cross-Stakeholder Collaboration for Future AI in Education Development and Research Commercialisation

The importance of collaboration between AI developers, researchers and educators is key to engendering the bi-directional knowledge exchange that is vital for AI developers to understand what they need to know about teaching and learning and for educators to be able to understand the process of developing AI. This is the philosophy at the heart of the *Golden Triangle* upon which the *Educate Accelerator* is built. In the case of the accelerator, the technology being developed does not necessarily have to involve AI. However, the cross-stakeholder collaborative approach is even more important when it comes to AI technology, because AI is steeped in mystery, is a far less familiar technology to educators than much other EdTech and might bring far greater fear and risks in its use in education (see Cukurova et al., 2020).

In Luckin et al. (2019), we proposed a framework for the development of AI within education based on the *Golden Triangle* philosophy, which is illustrated in Figure 24.3. AI

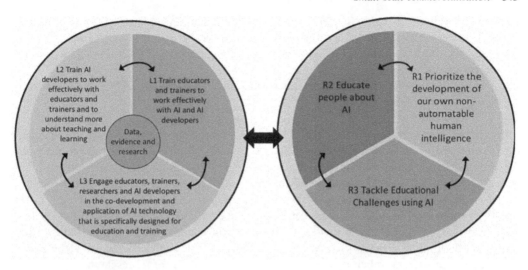

Source: Luckin & Cukurova, 2019

Figure 24.3   *The Golden Triangle Framework for multi-stakeholder collaboration in AI*
              for education

has much to offer education, both teachers and learners, but to reap the benefits of AI, we need to ensure that educators, students, parents and policymakers all know enough about AI to apply it effectively. In particular, educators will have a key role in helping others to understand AI. We, therefore, need to build capacity within education to ensure that teachers are able to communicate the key factors of importance about AI. The cross-stakeholder collaborative development framework that we created also aims to improve the quality of the AI that is made available in education. It is essential that we build an educational AI ecosystem that supports the development and application of AI and that is founded on co-design principles.

Figure 24.3 depicts two concentric elements that are interconnected and interdependent. Data are at the core of the left-hand circle, because data power AI, and because data also underpin evidence that can be about the effectiveness of an AI application. Three interconnected partnership activities need to take place between stakeholders surrounding the central data core:

1. Training educators to understand AI;
2. Training AI developers to understand teaching and learning, and the context in which it takes place;
3. Creating opportunities for AI developers, researchers and educators to work together, through which their training needs can start to be met and more appropriate AI can be developed.

These three activities are interconnected and progress in one activity area will support progress in the other two areas of activity, and vice versa.

Similarly, the right-hand circular element also has three interconnected and mutually beneficial activities that need to happen for society to get the greatest benefits from AI:

1. Give a higher priority to the elements of our human intelligence that we cannot automate with AI, such as emotional and subjective intelligence;
2. Prioritise educating everybody to understand enough about AI to enable them to use it safely and effectively;
3. Develop and apply AI to solve big educational challenges, informed by the interdisciplinary Learning Sciences.

Through working with companies such as DebateMate, the value of the framework is becoming clearer and its consistency with the *Educate Golden Triangle* underpins the connections between and the training of both educators and technology developers. Additionally, with a new cycle of the Educate Accelerator starting in June 2021, we have added some new features to the training programme that we offer. In particular, we have developed a course in AI Readiness that will be taken by all accelerator participants. This course aims to provide a first step towards increasing the number of entrepreneurs who engage with AI and building a pipeline for collaborations, such as that described in this paper between Educate and DebateMate to foster an increased number of small-scale commercialisations of AI research.

AI READINESS: A TOOL TO INITIATE SMALL-SCALE COMMERCIALISATION

Everyone will likely need to build an AI Mindset to safely reap the benefits of AI. Within the education and training sector, the need is, if anything, more urgent. Those involved in education and training others need to develop an AI Mindset so that they understand enough to teach the basics and use AI to benefit teaching and learning in a safe and risk-reduced manner. The concept of AI Readiness™ was developed in order to help people develop an AI Mindset. The AI Readiness™ concept has been developed into a training programme of seven steps. This programme is initially aimed at educational and training organisations and institutions: schools, colleges, universities, training providers and educational technology developers and businesses. The initial focus of the training programme on organisations, rather than individuals, embraces the need for whole workforces to be engaged in developing their AI Mindset, and the fact that employers not only have a responsibility for upskilling their employees but that organisations can benefit to a much greater extent if they tackle the challenges of integrating data and AI into their work through engaging their entire workforce, at least to some extent.

AI Readiness™ is what educational businesses, schools, colleges or universities need to achieve in order to ensure that they are ready to leverage the power of AI and data to deliver its products or services more effectively. The need for AI Readiness may extend beyond the Education and Training sector, but the initial focus of the work reported here is on organisations within the Education and Training sector.

Once an organization is *AI ready*, they will be *able to identify*:

- *What* challenge or activity within their organization could best be augmented by leveraging the power of data and AI. The AI Readiness™ programme includes tasks to identify the type of human Intelligence that the organisation wants to develop within their students, pupils or customers as well. For example, perhaps the data they have collected has demonstrated that a particular profile of student will need more support with a course that has an essay as part of its assessment. The organisation might therefore identify that the provision of a writing mentor for such students would be a good challenge for AI and the human expert mentor to work together to provide.

- *Where* AI would best be applied. For example, the AI readiness training may show that an organization is recruiting some staff who are not likely to be effective without a significant amount of professional development. This knowledge allows the organisation to decide whether or not to invest in an AI-enhanced support service for staff that is particularly suitable for the type of staff identified through the data analysis or the organisation might decide that it is at the recruitment stage that they need to change the type of staff they appoint – again, AI may help here too.

- *Why* AI? This is the imperative of any AI the organisation intends to apply. The most important aspect of any Machine-Learning (ML) AI algorithm is the imperative for its design – the unique contribution that the ML is going to provide for the organization. The same data can be used to achieve very different outcomes, depending on the imperative of the ML algorithm. For example, facial expressions and spoken audio data from learners could be used to identify their emotional state in order to provide some targeted support when they look disappointed with their performance. The same data and algorithm could also be used to provide punitive feedback when they look disappointed. The data and algorithm are essentially the same, the imperative is not.

- *Who* will be involved? This will be staff and it could also be learners, customers, parents, broader stakeholders and partners. This is about identifying the people in the organization who will be working with the AI or working to provide the resources the AI needs, such as data, to ensure that the organisation has involved them in the next steps of the design process of the way that AI is going to be used. It is also the point at which looking for other partners to work with the organisation is important.

AI readiness of an organisation can be structured through the 7 Step EThICAL AI Readiness™ programme, the design of which is informed by the Organizational Readiness CRISP-DM iterative cycle process – knowledge elicitation, data understanding, network preparation, analysis of readiness evaluation and recommendation (Wirth & Hipp, 2000):

Step 1 – what is AI and how can each organisation and their workforce develop an AI mindset? This step is very much about helping the *organisation* to engage their staff with the idea of becoming AI Ready.

Step 2 – what is the particular challenge the organisation wants to focus on? This part of the process involves exploring the types of challenges faced by the organisation and selecting between one and three challenges that are to be the focus of the rest of the AI Readiness™ activity.

Step 3 – what data do the organisation have access to and how can the organisation collate it? At this stage, attention turns to the data that are currently available to the organisation. Data appropriate to the challenges selected must be collated, cleaned and prepared for analysis.

Step 4 – what new data do the organisation need to collect in order to address the challenge the organisation identified in STEP 2? The training explains different data collection methods and the practicalities of each of these.

Step 5 – what AI techniques are relevant for the data the organisation has and intends to collect? A range of analytical and AI techniques are explained along with the criteria for the selection of those techniques most appropriate for their particular context.

Step 6 – what can the organisation learn from the AI applied in STEP 5? The training programme helps illustrate how the results of the analysis and AI modelling that STEP 6 has applied to the data can be completed and it will help the organisation interpret this analysis and modelling to identify where AI could best be applied within their organisation, the type of AI and its main purpose.

Step 7 and iteration – do the organisation need to go back to STEP 1? How is the organisation conducting the approach to AI – is it ethical? This is the point at which discussion about the extent to which the iteration of the EThICAL AI Readiness™ programme just completed has produced AI Readiness™ within them and their workforce. If AI Readiness™ has not yet been achieved, then another iteration through the programme is recommended. If AI Readiness™ has been achieved, the customer is ready to select and apply the AI that is best for them or to develop their own AI, if appropriate.

One of the many challenges facing those wishing to implement AI Readiness™ as a process within an organisation is being able to both benchmark where the organisation and its workforce are when they start the training programme and to demonstrate the progress the organisation and its workforce make over time through clear outcome measures, criteria or descriptions. The concept of *Latent AI readiness* could be useful for both these evaluation tasks, at the outset and throughout the programme. In turn, such evaluations could prove extremely valuable for developing the most appropriate training programmes for any particular organisation at a specific point in time.

The AI Readiness™ course that will be taken by the Educate accelerator participants includes an initial set of assessments that are embedded throughout the seven-step process described above. These are merely a starting point and require further development to include reflective self-evaluations and organization-wide criteria. They are, however, a useful starting point.

To clarify: the concept of AI Readiness™ is concerned with the development of specified skills, knowledge, behaviours and attitudes associated with being *ready* to leverage the power of AI safely and ethically. In practical terms, at the outset of an organisation's journey through the AI Readiness™ training, the ability to quantify the existing skills, attitudes, knowledge and behaviours within a management team and workforce could be, at least partly, addressed through identifying existing workforce skills and knowledge and mapping them against the skills identified as being required within the AI Readiness™ course assessments. This mapping would produce information about the Latent AI Readiness™ within an organisation. In a similar manner, throughout the course, the existing assessments and evaluations could be complemented by consideration of the extent to which the initial Latent AI Readiness™ evaluation is gradually increasing in its alignment with the desired AI Readiness™ skills and knowledge sets associated with the AI Readiness™ evaluation.

THE FUTURE GLOBAL LANDSCAPE FOR AI IN EDUCATION

The work to take the use of AI within education and training beyond the early days of Intelligent Tutoring Systems, which were very much academic research tools, was initially slow (VanLehn et al., 2005; Brown & Burton, 1978; Carbonell, 1970). However, in recent years AI research tools have scaled up to successful commercial products (see, for example, www.alelo.com; www.aleks.com and www.carnegielearning.com). A detailed discussion of this relatively large-scale commercialisation of AI in Education, particularly in the USA context, can be found in this handbook (see Chapter 23 by Ritter & Koedinger). Beyond this, most of the AI that has been used at scale in education has been in the form of AI tools developed by large technology companies, such as Google and Microsoft.

However, the situation is now changing and there are great opportunities for the types of companies that come through the EDUCATE research accelerator programme, and for any academics who are savvy enough to link up to the best of these. An increasing number of entrepreneurs are forming EdTech businesses that are developing AI-based systems or intend to develop and/or apply AI (see, for example, www.century.tech; http://squirrelai.com; and www.riiidlabs.com/home). It is important to contextualise these start-up and small business activities in the larger EdTech and AI landscape to appreciate the real possibilities for AI corporate and academic partnerships and likewise the increasing, and now urgent, need for AI readiness education for teachers and trainers across the globe.

A recent paper by Deloitte (2019) charts the global development of AI and notes that, in 2019, the number of mainstream AI adaptive-learning companies exceeded 100. The largest number of these was located in the United States (52), and investment obtained by US companies to this date exceeded USD 2.3 billion. China was also starting to invest heavily in AI and their share of the landscape is still growing. Other regions identified by Deloitte as supporting AI companies were located in areas where there was advanced AI technology development, for example, Ireland, Canada, Australia, Israel and India.

It is interesting to note that it is not the Googles or Microsofts of the world who are gaining ground in China, it is homegrown companies who understand what the Chinese population and government want from this educational technology. Some of these companies are traditional education groups, such as New Oriental, but others are start-ups, such as Squirrel AI. Of the 24 EdTech unicorns listed by HolonIQ in June 2021 (www.holoniq.com/edtech-unicorns/) who represent a collective value of over USD 72 billion, eight of them are located in China and their total value, at over USD 35 billion, is just under 50% of the collective value of all 24 unicorns (Deloitte, 2019). (A unicorn is a private start-up company with a valuation of over USD 1 billion; only EdTech companies located in China, North America and India have achieved this status to date). The three unicorns who account for USD 30 billion of the USD 72 billion collective value of those 24 unicorns (VIPKid, Zuoyebang and Yuanfudao) are all Chinese and they all use AI to deliver learning that adapts to the needs of each child and helps them to progress. The trend in China, and many other parts of the world, has been towards addressing the needs of the parent market. For example, in 2018, the revenue of Squirrel AI, a start-up that supplies adaptive-learning platforms that parents pay for through after-school clubs exceeded renminbi (RMB) 500 million (Deloitte, 2019).

Perhaps one of the reasons that start-ups in China are growing at a great pace to become unicorns is not down solely to government investment, but also the investment from educational companies. For example, in 2017, New Oriental invested in 12 companies to produce an AI-based education product, called *RealSkill*, and also entered into a joint venture with AI start-up unicorn iFLYTEK to produce *Oriental iFly*, which helps students prepare for TOEFL and IELTS English language assessments. Of particular interest to the subject of this chapter is the fact that TAL, a large Chinese education company, was an early investor in Squirrel AI. Squirrel AI has a close collaborative relationship with academics at Carnegie Mellon University, where Carnegie Learning originated (www.cs.cmu.edu/news/cmu-yixue-education-inc-announce-ai-research-project-adaptive-k-12-education). This corporate and academic collaboration is encouraging for the spread of the *Golden Triangle Framework* beyond the UK. However, there is little, if any, evidence that any of the growing number of AI EdTech companies are collaborating closely with educators, as our framework suggests needs to be the case. They certainly look to educators to produce content for their platforms and may even consult with teachers. They do not, however, design with educators in a participatory manner as is a key part of the *Golden Triangle Framework* approach.

AI EdTech is on a fast-growing trajectory at the moment. It is also clear that there are hungry investors, and that start-ups and small companies can scale up quickly and become extremely successful. The centre of gravity is certainly shifting eastwards, but the US is still an important force (See Chapter 23 by Ritter & Koedinger) and other countries with AI capability should be able to compete. However, it is not all good news for the EdTech start-up ecosystem. There have been a growing number of acquisitions of start-ups by large companies. For example, Carnegie Learning was acquired by CIP capital in 2018, and Gradescope was acquired by Turnitin that same year (Deloitte, 2019). These acquisitions may be good news for the founders of the start-ups, but it is not so good for the health of the ecosystem, nor perhaps for the collaboration between corporate and academic AI that was at the heart of the creation of Carnegie Learning.

CONCLUSION

The start-up of the 2021 EDUCATE research accelerator programme presents an exciting opportunity to help a new set of EdTech entrepreneurs appreciate the importance of cross-stakeholder collaboration and learning at the heart of the *Golden Triangle*. However, the challenge of scaling the take-up of this approach is significant. As the data about AI EdTech from across the world illustrates, there is a great deal of work for the EDUCATE-like programmes to achieve within EdTech and AI EdTech, in particular.

During the 2017 to 2020 EDUCATE programme, of the 260-plus companies who completed the programme, some 10% were applying AI in their product or service. At that time, the companies completing the EDUCATE programme represented some 25% of the UK EdTech ecosystem. It will be interesting to see how many of the companies who complete the 2021 EDUCATE programme will be applying AI, but it would be reasonable to predict that it will be an increase on the first EDUCATE programme. The EDUCATE programme will support the collaboration at the heart of its *Golden Triangle* foundation and will apply the Golden Triangle Framework for Multistakeholder Collaboration in AI for Education (Luckin et al., 2019). Additionally, all companies who take the EDUCATE programme will receive AI readiness training to help them appreciate the need for them to leverage AI within their organisations. The same will be true of the educators who complete the Educate 4 Schools programme that we plan to launch in 2022.

The Golden Triangle Framework for Multistakeholder Collaboration in AI for Education we have described in this chapter and exemplified through the DebateMate case study is core to the Educate Research Acceleration process, and it is core to the expansion of the small-scale commercialisation we have seen to date. We certainly plan to help many more EdTech companies to leverage the power of AI within their businesses. Additionally, through the data strategy adopted for the second phase of the Research Accelerator, we plan to develop Educate as a data-driven AI engine for the EdTech ecosystem itself, through which we can analyse examples of successful scaling of AI in education, effective implementations of AI in education and training, the decisive conditions and contextual factors that impact on scaling and effectiveness and the overall market trends.

REFERENCES

Atrey, P. K., Hossain, M. A., El Saddik, A., & Kankanhalli, M. S. (2010). Multimodal fusion for multimedia analysis: A survey. *Multimedia Systems*, 16(6), 345–379.

Baltrušaitis, T., Ahuja, C., & Morency, L. P. (2019). Multimodal machine learning: A survey and taxonomy. *IEEE Transactions on Pattern Analysis and Machine Intelligence*, 41(2), 423–443.

Bell, M., Cordingley, P., Isham, C., & Davis, R. (2010). *Report of professional practitioner use of research review: Practitioner engagement in and/or with research*. Coventry, UK: CUREE, GTCE, LSIS & NTRP. www.curee-paccts.com/node/2303.

Blikstein, P. (2013). Multimodal learning analytics. In *Proceedings of the third international conference on learning analytics and knowledge* (pp. 102–106). ACM.

Brown, J. S., & Burton, R. R. (1978). Diagnostic models for procedural bugs in basic mathematical skills. *Cognitive Science*, 2, 155–191.

Burkhardt, F., Paeschke, A., Rolfes, M., Sendlmeier, W. F., & Weiss, B. (2005). A database of German emotional speech. In *Ninth European conference on speech communication and technology*.

Carbonell, J. (1970). AI in CAI: An artificial intelligence approach to computer-aided instruction. *Science*, 167, 190–202.

Cooper, A. (2010). Knowledge mobilization intermediaries in education. www.oise.utoronto.ca/rspe/UserFiles/File/CSSE2010KMIntermediariesFinal.doc.

Cukurova, M., & Luckin, R. (2018). Measuring the impact of emerging technologies in education: A pragmatic approach. In *Second handbook of information technology in primary and SECONDARY education* (pp. 1–19).

Cukurova, M., Luckin, R., & Baines, E. (2018). The significance of context for the emergence and implementation of research evidence: The case of collaborative problem-solving. *Oxford Review of Education*, 44(3), 322–337.

Cukurova, M., Luckin, R., & Kent, C. (2019). Creating the golden triangle of evidence-informed EdTech with EDUCATE. *British Journal of Educational Technology*, 50(2), 490–512. doi:10.1111/bjet.12727.

Cukurova, M., Kent, C., & Luckin, R. (2019). Artificial intelligence and multimodal data in the service of human decision-making: A case study in debate tutoring. *British Journal of Educational Technology*, 50(6), 3032–3046. https://doi.org/10.1111/bjet.12829.

Cukurova, M., Luckin, R., & Kent, C. (2020). Impact of an artificial intelligence research frame on the perceived credibility of educational research evidence. *International Journal of Artificial Intelligence in Education*, 30(2), 205–235. doi:10.1007/s40593-019-00188-w.

Cukurova, M., Luckin, R., Millan, E., & Mavrikis, M. (2018). The NISPI framework: Analysing collaborative problem-solving from students' physical interactions. *Computers & Education*, 116, 93–109.

Cukurova, M., Martinez-Maldonado, R., & Giannakos, M., (2020). The promise and challenges of multimodal learning analytics. *British Journal of Educational Technology*, 50(2), 1–22.

Deloitte. (2019). www2.deloitte.com/content/dam/Deloitte/cn/Documents/technologymedia-telecommunications/deloitte-cn-tmt-global-development-of-ai-based-education-en-191108.pdf.

Evans, D. E., & Rothbart, M. K. (2007). Developing a model for adult temperament. *Journal of Research in Personality*, 41(4), 868–888.

Evans, J. S. B. T. (2008). Dual-processing accounts of reasoning, judgment, and social cognition. *Annual Review of Psychology*, 59, 255–278.

Grawemeyer, B., Mavrikis, M., Holmes, W., Gutiérrez-Santos, S., Wiedmann, M., & Rummel, N. (2017). Affective learning: Improving engagement and enhancing learning with affect-aware feedback. *User Modeling and User-Adapted Interaction*, 27(1), 119–158.

John, O. P., & Srivastava, S. (1999). The Big Five trait taxonomy: History, measurement, and theoretical perspectives. *Handbook of Personality: Theory and Research*, 2, 102–138.

Kahneman, D., & Frederick, S. (2002). Representativeness revisited: Attribute substitution in intuitive judgment. *Heuristics and Biases: The Psychology of Intuitive Judgment*, 49, 81.

Luckin, R. (2015) Mainstreaming innovation in educational technology. *Advances in Scholarship of Teaching and Learning*, 3(1), 2015.

Luckin, R. (2018). *Machine learning and human intelligence*. London: IOE Press.

Luckin, R., Bligh, B., Manches, A., Ainsworth, S., Crook, C., & Noss, R. (2012). *Decoding learning: The proof, promise and potential of digital education*. London, UK: Nesta. www.nesta.org.uk/ publications/decoding-learning.

Luckin, R., & Cukurova, M. (2019). Designing educational technologies in the age of AI: A learning sciences-driven approach. *British Journal of Educational Technology*. Advance online publication. doi:10.1111/bjet.12861.

Malone, T. W. (2018). How human-computer 'superminds' are redefining the future of work. *MIT Sloan Management Review*, 59(4), 34–41.

Martinez-Maldonado, R., Dimitriadis, Y., Martinez-Mon, S. A., Kay, J., & Yacef, K. (2013). Capturing and analyzing verbal and physical collaborative learning interactions at an enriched interactive tabletop. *International Journal of Computer-Supported Collaborative Learning*, 8(4), 455–485.

Ochoa, X., Dominguez, F., Guaman, B., Maya, R., Falcones, G., & Castells, J. (2018). The rap system: Automatic feedback of oral presentation skills using multimodal analysis and low-cost sensors. In *Proceedings of the 8th international conference on learning analytics and knowledge*, 360–364.

OECD TALIS. (2013). TALIS 2013 results: An international perspective on teaching and learning. www.keepeek.com/Digital-Asset-Management/oecd/education/talis-2013-results_9789264196261-en#page1.

Petrides, K. V. (2009). Psychometric properties of the trait emotional intelligence questionnaire (TEIQue). In *Assessing emotional intelligence* (pp. 85–101). Boston, MA: Springer.

Schuller, B., Arsic, D., Rigoll, G., Wimmer, M., & Radig, B. (2007). Audiovisual behavior modeling by combined feature spaces. In 2007 *IEEE international conference on acoustics, speech and signal processing*-ICASSP'07 (Vol. 2, pp. II–733). IEEE.

Schuller, B., Steidl, S., & Batliner, A. (2009). The interspeech 2009 emotion challenge. In *Tenth annual conference of the international speech communication association*.

Spikol, D., Ruffaldi, E., Dabisias, G., & Cukurova, M. (2018). Supervised machine learning in multimodal learning analytics for estimating success in project-based learning. *Journal of Computer Assisted Learning*. doi:10.1111/jcal.12263.

Tskhay, K. O., Zhu, R., Zou, C., & Rule, N. O. (2018). Charisma in everyday life: Conceptualization and validation of the General Charisma Inventory. *Journal of Personality and Social Psychology*, 114(1), 131.

Vanlehn, K., Lynch, C., Schulze, K., Shapiro, J. A., Shelby, R., Taylor, L., ... & Wintersgill, M. (2005). The Andes physics tutoring system: Lessons learned. *International Journal of Artificial Intelligence in Education*, 15(3), 147–204.

Vinciarelli, A., Pantic, M., & Bourlard, H. (2009). Social signal processing: Survey of an emerging domain. *Image and Vision Computing*, 27(12), 1743–1759.

Wirth, R., & Hipp, J. (2000). Crisp-dm: Towards a standard process model for data mining. In *Proceedings of the 4th international conference on the practical applications of knowledge discovery and data mining* (Vol. 1, pp. 29–40).

Zhou, F., & De la Torre, F. (2012). Generalized time warping for multi-modal alignment of human motion. In *2012 IEEE conference on computer vision and pattern recognition* (pp. 1282–1289). IEEE.

25. Critical perspectives on AI in education: political economy, discrimination, commercialization, governance and ethics

Ben Williamson, Rebecca Eynon, Jeremy Knox and Huw Davies

INTRODUCTION

As Artificial Intelligence (AI) has penetrated into human lives, social practices, cultural experiences and political and economic processes, it has become the focus of significant critical attention (Whittaker et al., 2018; Broussard, 2019). The development and uses of AI in educational practice, policy and research are also becoming the subjects in a growing body of critical social scientific analysis (Davies et al., 2020; Knox et al., 2020; Williamson, 2020; Gulson et al., 2021). This chapter provides an overview of critical perspectives on AI in education (AIED), highlighting the interdisciplinary and multisector historical development of AIED as a research field; the particular political economy of AI in education; the emergence of ethical issues of bias and discrimination; the expansion of commercial 'edu-businesses' and 'Big Tech' companies promising AI solutions in education; the role of AI in educational policy and governance; and the recent emergence of AIED ethics proposals and frameworks.

Although AI has become part of popular discourse, used generally in efforts 'to make computers do the sorts of things that minds can do' (Boden, 2016, 1), it encompasses diverse technological approaches and aspirations. Our approach, as social scientific 'outsiders' rather than 'internal' participants in AIED research or application, treats AI as a complex social, cultural and material artifact that is understood and constructed by different stakeholders in various ways, each with significant social and educational implications (Eynon & Young, 2020). We also recognize AIED is an extremely complex area of technical development and educational thought, practised by highly diverse experts from across fields such as computer science, psychology and education, which makes its objectives challenging to operationalize while its tangible impacts and long-term consequences remain difficult to anticipate. Following this approach, we do not view AIED simply as a coherent field of research or as a singular set of technologies with clearly identifiable features or demarcated boundaries. Instead, we see AIED as the products of diverse understandings, perceptions and practices that are contextually situated, historically evolving and involving a variety of actors and organizations that cut across domains of research, commerce, civil society and governance (Williamson & Eynon, 2020). By bringing a critical perspective to AI in education, the intention of the chapter is to highlight potentially productive interdisciplinary approaches to AI in education that would involve the expertise of learning scientists, computer scientists and social scientists working together to design and assess the results and implications of AIED.

HISTORICAL DEVELOPMENTS OF AIED

Importantly, AIED needs to be situated in the longer history and contexts of artificial intelligence development. The history of AI stretches back at least as far as the birth of computer science and cybernetics in the 1940s and 1950s. From the 1960s to the 1990s, AI research and development focused first on encoding principles of human reasoning to simulate human intelligence, processing human language and then on 'expert systems' that emulated the procedural decision-making processes of experts based on defined knowledge bases. AI gradually returned under a new data-scientific paradigm in the twenty-first century as data-processing software and algorithms that can learn and make predictions from classifying and correlating huge quantities of 'big data' (Alpaydin, 2016). Computational processes including data analytics, machine learning, neural networks, deep learning and reinforcement learning underpin most contemporary forms of AI: machines that can learn from their own experience, adapt to their contexts and uses, improve their own functioning, craft their own rules, construct new algorithms, make predictions and carry out automated tasks without requiring control or oversight by human operatives (Mackenzie, 2017).

The application of AI to education also has a long history, and has similarly evolved from reasoning applications to machine learning and big data. 'AI in education' has existed as a coherent academic research field since at least the 1980s, as signalled by a series of AIED conferences in Europe, the US and Japan in the 1980s and 1990s, the first publication of the *Journal of Artificial Intelligence in Education* in 1989, the 1996 launch of the *International Journal of Artificial Intelligence in Education*, and the formation of the International AI in Education Society in 1993, although these early days were marked by significant disciplinary and organizational conflicts (Self, 2016). The emergence of AIED in the 1980s, however, was preceded by the development of Intelligent Tutoring Systems and Computer Assisted Instruction systems in the 1960s and 1970s (du Boulay, 2016; Alkhatlan & Kalita, 2018). It was also anticipated by a much longer history of 'teaching machines' which blended psychological theories of learning and behaviour with mechanical forms of automated technology (see Chapter 2 by McCalla; Watters, 2021).

The early days of AIED in the 1980s and 1990s were marked by both innovation and attempts to define the field and its objectives. In the second issue of the *Journal of Artificial Intelligence in Education*, published in 1989, Schank and Edelson (1989, 3–4) claimed that AI is 'intimately bound up with education':

> AI concerns itself with getting machines to read, to reason, to express themselves, to make generalizations, and to learn. These issues are the stuff of education after all. … AI people are in a unique position to improve education … . [W]e can couple our expertise in computer technology with our theories of learning and understanding to build computer-based instructional systems that will have a positive impact on education.

For the 'AI people', such technological innovations promised to bring far-reaching changes to the ways that teaching and learning were understood and practised. Definitions of AI in education have continued to evolve in the decades since. The aims and scope of the *International Journal of Artificial Intelligence in Education* include a list of 50 relevant topics, including adaptive systems, statistical methods, cognitive models, robotics, intelligent agents, tutoring systems, neural models, student modelling and cognitive diagnosis, and theories of learning (https://www.springer.com/journal/40593/aims-and-scope). The launch of a new journal, *Computers and Education: Artificial Intelligence*, in 2020, set out a further list of ten topics and research priorities for AIED emerging from the development of machine learning and deep learning (Hwang et al., 2020).

Despite an expansion of its topics and evolution of its technological underpinnings, as a field AIED has continued to develop along two complementary strands of activity for several decades: the development of AI-based tools for classrooms and the use of AI to understand, measure and improve learning (Holmes et al., 2019). Particularly as basic research on learning, AIED is also closely related to the learning sciences and cognitive science – the 'cognition, technology and education nexus' (Pea, 2016, 51) – as reflected in the International AIED Society's continuing emphasis on 'interdisciplinary' research at 'the frontiers of the fields of computer science, education, and psychology' (https://iAIED.org/about).

However, AIED has never been a purely academic, interdisciplinary endeavour. It is also characterized by multisectoral relations between research and commercial application. In a 1995 review of applications of AI in education completed for the RAND Corporation, McArthur et al. (1995, 42–43) argued that building AI applications 'to improve the speed and quality of students' learning' would require bringing 'high-tech companies into better cooperation with educational technology research and classroom practice'. As such, since the 1990s, AIED basic research has been closely mirrored by commercial interests in the application of technology to teaching and learning (Selwyn, 2019).

Decades later, many of the transformative aims of the 'AI people' in education (both from academic research and commercial development contexts) remain similar, even if the underlying computational logics of AI have shifted from programmable expert systems to big data analytics, machine learning, neural networks and deep learning (Knox et al., 2020). Intelligent tutoring systems have continued to evolve in AIED research labs and commercial settings for 40 years (du Boulay, 2019), while new research fields of educational data mining and learning analytics have appeared at the confluence of the learning and computer sciences, opening up new professional positions for 'education data scientists' and other analytics experts (Fischer et al., 2020). Learning analytics and educational data mining are increasingly intertwined and related with AIED, particularly in the commercial education technology (edtech) industry (Buckingham Shum & Luckin, 2019). In edtech, AI has become synonymous with the ideal of 'personalized' learning, a model in which an individual student's data is mined from their learning activities and experiences and then used by AI as the basis for adapting and modifying the content to meet the individual's predicted needs (Watters, 2021).

As such, AIED continues to expand as an academic field, consolidating its disciplinary influence as a distinctive field of knowledge production and evolving into an increasingly commercialized part of the edtech industry. In this respect, AIED mirrors the wider AI domain, in which academic research and commercial development have become increasingly porous, leading to significant power struggles between the values of academic inquiry and business imperatives or even the capture of independent research by industrial power (Whittaker, 2021).

These brief historical notes importantly highlight how AIED has developed genealogically with the wider field of AI R&D and the commercial application of AI across various industries. AIED is specifically located in a longer history of knowledge production, theory generation and the development of epistemic expertise in the learning sciences and educational data science that is related to political and economic interests.

THE POLITICAL ECONOMY OF AIED

Research under the banner of political economy examines the relationships between states and markets and has in recent years become increasingly central to understanding the role of advanced technologies such as AI in the work of governments and economies (Beer, 2016). AI-based technologies used in education are significant from a political economy perspective because they can amplify existing governmental rationalities of 'marketization', for example by measuring the 'performance' of students, staff and institutions, comparing them in terms of a 'market competition', and (in some cases) providing automated prompts and adaptive 'nudges' towards measurable performance improvement (Williamson et al., 2020).

The extent to which the field of AIED has been shaped by the wider political and economic environment appears to have been a minor concern for associated researchers and practitioners (Knox, 2020; Selwyn, 2019; Witzenberger & Gulson, 2021). The scope has tended to focus AIED interests on the inner workings of cognitive science, lab studies assessing learning outcomes and the orderly arrangement of classroom experiments, as well as on more fundamental computer science developments, rather than the broader political and economic circumstances that have enabled and constrained AI research and development.

This is not to suggest that the field of AIED has been necessarily or problematically narrow in scope (Morrison & Miller, 2018). Nevertheless, the idea that AIED might be considered itself political seems to have been beyond the boundaries of interest – political in the sense not only that its fate as a field of research might be necessarily tied to the strategies and preferences of successive government administrations, but also that its encoding of various educational decisions might itself be considered a matter of inherent contestation, involving latent tensions between differing perspectives and assumptions. In this sense, AIED needs to be understood as being intertwined with the political and economic conditions in which statistics, big data and digital infrastructures have become integral to the operations and functioning of education systems and institutions (Williamson, 2017; Wyatt-Smith et al., 2021).

In a recent examination of how the field of AIED might respond to the contemporary 'mainstreaming' of the technology, Nye (2016, 767) suggests that 'in the distant future, such questions may even reach the political realm, where legislative debates consider the appropriate reward metrics that educational technology should target'. The political domain appears to be framed rather firmly here as something quite separate from the field of research and development. Nevertheless, the idea that AIED might be shaped through discordant relationships with the political realm is often suggested by the concern for privacy legislation. For example, Pinkwart (2016, 780) asks: '[h]ow can commercial AIED systems be profitable under strict privacy policies that, for instance, prohibit giving student data away to anyone?' Further, the discourse around AIED has not necessarily been blind to the idea of internal conflict and contestation either. Pinkwart suggests 'avoiding too much fragmentation' (782) across the various subfields of related education technology research, revealing some of the inner struggles of focus and legitimacy within the research community.

A more direct political economy analysis of AIED would, first and foremost, examine relationships between government policy and the sway of economic markets. This constitutes a shift of analytic focus, away from inward-looking debates about the quality of AI engineering or the extent to which learning has been 'enhanced' by it, towards wider considerations of the contexts in which technology is produced and consumed in a global educational marketplace. The purpose of a political economy analysis is to demonstrate that such broader dynamics are structural characteristics of the field of AIED itself, circumscribing the ways in which it can exercise influence, and, ultimately, actively shaping the project of education into which it is situated. Critical studies of the wider field of education technology have sought to highlight precisely this formative dimension. For example, Mirrlees and Alvi (2019, 14) suggest 'EdTech is not an island but part and product of society; it is shaped by and shapes the capitalist mode of production (the economic sphere), the State and civil society (the political sphere) and culture (the sphere of discourses, ideas and meanings).'

Importantly, a political economy analysis is concerned with tracing such entangled relationships in order to 'make explicit issues of power in society' (Selwyn, 2013, 30). For example, recent work in the context of the US has exposed the ways in which the liberalization of the education technology sector has led to the growing privatization of the public education system, as for-profit companies view schools, classrooms, and lecture halls as increasingly valuable markets for their products (Poritz & Rees, 2017). Such perspectives motivate important questions about how this technology comes to be developed, which organizations and entities have the capacity to define its trajectories, and whose interests and values are ultimately served. If AIED is indeed currently experiencing a 'mainstreaming' of its work, such questions would be essential for understanding its broad impact on society.

Drawing on political economy analysis perspectives that emphasize power (e.g. Mosco, 1995), we suggest three useful directions for AIED research: firstly, examining the extent to which AIED is shaped by a wide range of actors, and in particular, national policy and geopolitical competition, not just the technical designers and educational practitioners involved directly in the research and implementation; secondly, surfacing and analyzing the inherent conflict and contingency that characterizes the field of AIED, rather than relying on neat explanations of 'technical progress'; and finally, acknowledging the already-existing contexts within which AIED is embedded and shaped, instead of maintaining the habitual discourses of technological 'disruption' and 'innovation' that tend to accompany the promotion of education technology in general. These three directions are concerned with adopting a broader view of the AIED field and its constituent influences and offer the means to develop critical perspectives that move beyond the instrumentalist and solutionist discourses that limit our understanding of its role in society.

A recent illustrative example is Knox's (2020) study of the relationships between AI and education in China, which examines the ways in which high-profile government policy, overtly positioned to assert China's ambitions for geopolitical dominance through technology, has created favourable conditions for a thriving Chinese AIED industry. However, as Knox demonstrates, this context leads directly to the 'pursuit of marketable products … rather than any underlying educational rationale for the design and development of AI applications' (2020, 308). Countering common-place views of China's uniform, hierarchical governance, Knox also shows how the rapid rise of Chinese AI is better understood in terms of regional disparities and internal conflict, which directly shape how AIED products are designed and deployed. Further, AIED, rather than being framed as simply a novel intervention in education, is shown to be rooted in historical science and technology development, and a long-standing education system characterized by competition and high-stakes assessment.

More recently, the imposition of state regulation on the domestic industry of online tutoring providers, which includes many companies dedicated to AI-based instruction and resulted in the outright prohibition of profit-making or raising investor capital for some firms, demonstrates intense conflict between Chinese state government and capitalist technology markets

(Kologriyava & Shleifer, 2021). One major catalyst for this regulation was the communist anxiety about unequal access to technology and the role of the education technology industry and market in widening social inequalities, with the likely result being intensification of AI use within the public education system rather than the private online tutoring market (Knox, 2021). This example highlights the importance of political economy analyses of AIED, particularly in light of recent controversies over the impact of AI systems on societies more generally.

ALGORITHMIC DISCRIMINATION

Across a range of areas of public life, there has been a growing concern that the use of AI systems risks maintaining, and exacerbating, existing inequalities in society. Automated systems used to help make decisions about who to employ, who to send to prison, who to offer a mortgage to and so on are clearly biased across intersections of gender, race and class (Eubanks, 2018; O'Neil, 2016). Relatedly, our everyday experiences of AI, such as when searching for information or interacting with a digital assistant, also tend to reinforce existing power structures in society, where the experiences of white, well-off, well-educated males are typically privileged (Noble, 2018).

Similar tensions are emerging in schools and other educational settings, with a number of authors raising concerns that the use of AI risks inequitable outcomes. Systems designed to facilitate school choice and integration, evaluate essay writing, detect concentration and emotion in the classroom, evaluate the effectiveness of teachers, assess students, check for cheating and map attendance are just some of a growing number of examples of systems that can favour certain groups of students over others through 'discriminatory designs' (Benjamin, 2019). The particular harms caused by the use of these systems can emerge from a misallocation of opportunities and resources of various kinds or from representational harms where certain groups are portrayed in ways that diminish their identity (Mayfield et al., 2019).

Many systems could cause both kinds of harm. For example, automated essay-scoring systems may encode biases along racialized lines (Dixon-Román et al., 2019). AI systems that predict future trajectories and/or recommend particular learning paths may lead to a reduced learning experience for some students (Davies & Eynon, 2018) or create self-fulfilling prophesies that unfairly limit future opportunities for others (Zeide, 2017). Forms of educational red-lining are also emerging (e.g., the differential use of AI bots in MOOCs) with those able to pay provided with a more sophisticated human-mediated experience (Winters, et al., 2020). As a final example, dubious systems that use facial recognition to check for cheating in an online exam risk disadvantaging those students with disabilities as they may not behave in ways such models assume to be 'correct' (Watters, 2020).

Suresh and Guttag (2020) identify six sources of bias across the machine-learning 'pipeline' of collecting, modelling and using data-driven AI models that can cause these issues. These are: historical biases due to existing inequalities in society that are already present in the data; representational biases arising from underrepresentation in the data and/or underrepresentation in society; measurement biases due, for example, to the use of poor or limited proxies for complex entities such as knowledge of a topic or poorer quality measures for particular groups; aggregation biases as a result of the use of one-size-fits-all models which do not apply well to certain sub-groups; biases in evaluation when benchmark data are not representative of the target population; and bias in deployment when models are used in different contexts in ways different from those intended by the modellers. When trying to ensure a system is fair, experts in machine learning select a mathematical model of fairness (e.g. that predictions are not conditional on group membership, or where the accuracy/performance of the model is equivalent across different groups) and then the ML pipeline is adjusted to ensure a fair outcome under these conditions (Barocas et al., 2019).

These risks of bias are similarly reflected in the AIED literature and related fields, where concerns about representational, measurement, evaluation and deployment biases and how best to mitigate them are clearly articulated (Fischer et al., 2020). However, discussion within the AIED community about what fairness, even concepts of statistical fairness, should look like have been slower to surface. A recent topical collection of the *International Journal of AI in Education* has begun exploring issues regarding the fairness, accountability, transparency and ethics of AIED systems (*IJAIED*, 2021). Although FATE frameworks enable a more transparent approach to tackling bias, data-centric and statistical notions of fairness can only go so far. One central challenge is that such approaches do not offer us a way to fully conceptualize how 'humans and technology co-conspire to not just passively reproduce but actively uphold and reproduce discriminatory social structures' (Hoffmann, 2019, 905). Nor does it offer us a way to think about precisely what we mean by fair educational experiences and systems. Relatedly, such a statistical frame tends towards a focus on allocation issues as the primary focus of inequality and ignores other ways that injustices arise within our education system including representational harms, culturally relevant pedagogy and surveillance capitalism (Regan and Jesse, 2019).

However, critics argue that the importance of exploring bias within education models in terms of its possible wider educational and social impacts has attracted insufficient attention (Paquette et al., 2020). This current context is somewhat surprising as it is in direct contradiction with the social values of many researchers in this space who wish to address inequalities in our education systems and improve the educational offer to many young people. What is central to future developments in this space is to change data science curricula in order to bring into focus the highly political nature of data science in education, to facilitate more meaningful links between sociologists of education and educational philosophers with the AIED community to develop better conceptual framings on inequalities and to promote the use of more participatory, emancipatory and inclusive approaches to design where teachers, students and other stakeholders are meaningfully included (D'Ignazio & Klein, 2019; Winters et al., 2020). It is also perhaps important to note that many of the current 'worst offenders' in terms of bias primarily emerge from the commercial sector.

COMMERCIALIZATION OF AIED

Artificial intelligence has become integral to the business objectives of major technology companies in the 2020s (Broussard, 2019), and also a central preoccupation of the commercial education technology industry (Gulson & Witzenberger, 2020). The commercial sector is involved in AI in education in two ways: international education companies developing AIED applications to sell directly to institutions and students, and global technology corporations developing AI infrastructure to enable enhanced data analysis in educational institutions (Witzenberger & Gulson, 2021).

These commercialization developments raise the critical issue of how public educational institutions may become dependent upon private educational platforms and data-extractive infrastructures for many key functions, processes and operations. The global education business Pearson, for example, has supported AI in education enthusiastically for more than a decade, first through support for big data and learning analytics, and later explicitly by advocating and producing AI-based intelligent tutors and other 'adaptive and personalized learning' applications (Luckin et al., 2016). The Google suite of educational platforms and apps is already used by schools around the world, reaching an estimated 150 million students globally, with Google increasingly introducing advanced analytics features and other AI-based add-ons (Perrotta et al., 2020). Commercial companies that operate within the education industry, and outside of it, are therefore equally promoting AI in education and actively pushing products into schools, universities, and informal educational settings and practices.

Such endeavours are also supported by highly influential technology philanthropists and investors. In the US context, major supporters and funders of AI-based education include the Bill and Melinda Gates Foundation, Schmidt Futures and the Chan Zuckerberg Initiative, these being the funding and investment vehicles of Microsoft founder Bill Gates, ex-Google chair Eric Schmidt and Facebook founder Mark Zuckerberg, respectively. These organizations make significant claims for the effectiveness of AI and 'personalized learning' in raising student achievement, enabling students to develop 'mastery' over knowledge domains and in reducing inequalities by distributing support to underserved students, although, despite the millions of dollars they lavish on such efforts, their claims that AI improves outcomes or reduces inequalities remain highly contested (Boninger et al., 2020). At the same time, a 'startup' scene of AIED developers has emerged, supported by 'accelerator' programmes and financial investors (see Chapter 24 by Luckin and Cukurova), and investment in edtech has grown rapidly as investors anticipate great earnings power from AI-enabled products (Regan & Khwaja, 2019; Komljenovic, 2021).

Global technology companies have begun inserting AI infrastructure into educational institutions and practices too. Companies including Amazon, Google, Microsoft, Salesforce and IBM are increasingly present in education through the back-end 'AI-as-a-service' systems that educational institutions require to collect and analyse data. Amazon, for example, claims that the AWS Cloud enables schools, universities and districts to track student performance, use machine-learning analytics to predict student outcomes, mobilize AI-enabled teaching assistants and tutors and develop personalized learning experiences (AWS, 2020). Its competitor for cloud computing services, Salesforce, offers both an Education Data Architecture and an AI application called Einstein for Education Cloud, with Microsoft also promoting the 'transformative' prospects of AI in education (Microsoft Education Team, 2020). These examples indicate how huge global technology companies are in competition for structural dominance over the digital infrastructures of education, providing cloud, data and AI systems that are capable of integrating various platforms for seamless and frictionless data flow, aggregation and analysis (Perrotta, 2021).

The insertion of 'AI-as-a-service' into educational institutions is not solely commercially driven, but the result of emerging public–private partnership agreements that cut across businesses, education policy centres and institutions (Williamson, 2017). The Learning and Teaching Reimagined Initiative, launched to support the 'digital transformation' of the UK higher education sector in 2020, for example, is a multisector programme of HE reconstruction involving the organizations Jisc (UK's digital learning agency for HE), Universities UK (the sector's representative body), Emerge Education (an edtech startup investment company) and the cloud company Salesforce. In the joint report 'Digital at the Core', this group presents a strategy for 'digital transformation':

> The technology now exists to connect the variety of applications used within the university, where the IT landscape tends to be more fragmented than in the enterprise. Replacing these siloed 'information systems' with intelligent information networks will enable highly personalised engagement with students and staff, individualised experiences, and actionable strategic intelligence. … Now, advanced analytics with augmented intelligence have the capacity to predict what will happen and prescribe actions which can be taken to cause an outcome. (Iosad, 2020, 32)

Part of the programme is a 'new national Centre for AI in tertiary education that will deliver real AI solutions' (Feldman, 2020). At the core of this vision is enhanced partnership between universities and technology providers, with Silicon Valley companies such as Salesforce, Amazon and Netflix as named influences.

These 'AI-out-of-the-box' partnerships stand to make public education institutions dependent upon commercial cloud and data infrastructures for key functions of digital service hosting and data storage, analysis and reporting (Fiebig et al., 2021). They are also part of the history of how Amazon, Google, Microsoft and IBM have sought and competed for structural dominance over the infrastructure services used across myriad sectors and services. Global tech companies are expanding into education through the provision of infrastructure and platform services, potentially engendering new long-term dependencies and lock-ins to corporate AI. This brings new risks, as educational institutions are integrated into sprawling global AI and data processing operations in order to deliver their core educational services, although it is an increasingly attractive prospect to government centres wishing to find new ways of measuring system performance.

AI IN EDUCATIONAL POLICY AND GOVERNANCE

AI has become a recent educational policy preoccupation, as part of a longer history of the use of large-scale statistics and big data in education policy (Piattoeva & Boden, 2020). Over the last few decades, large-scale data infrastructures for collecting, processing and disseminating educational data have become key to enacting policies concerned with performance measurement and accountability (Anagnostopoulos et al., 2013; Grek et al., 2021). These key changes in the technologies of policy enactment, reflected worldwide, have since catalysed policy interest in analytics packages and data dashboards for analysing, interpreting and displaying up-to-date data for data-driven decision making (Williamson, 2017), culminating in the embedding of complex AI-based technologies and automated processes in many policy centres and operations (Gulson et al., 2021).

Policy-influencing organizations including the OECD have begun to firmly advocate for 'the use of Big Data, Artificial Intelligence algorithms, education data mining and learning analytics' in 'real-world education practice and policy' (Kuhl et al., 2019, 13–14). Indeed, the OECD launched a major report on the frontiers of AI for education in 2021 (OECD, 2021). In this context, processes of educational governance have become increasingly reliant upon data stored in student information systems and learning management systems, and by the proliferation of analytics and AI-based packages for generating historical and predictive insights into institutional and individual-level performance (Hartong, 2016).

AI technologies can extend the capacity of these data systems to perform predictive analytics and automated decision making (Sellar & Gulson, 2019). As Webb, Sellar, and Gulson (2020) argue, data-led forms of governance have now begun mutating into 'anticipatory' forms of AI-enhanced governance. AI and learning analytics platforms create new conceptions of temporality in education, where past actions captured in huge comparative datasets can be used to make predictions at the level of the individual student in 'real time'. This involves the modelling of probable futures from continuously generated and analysed data streams, providing synchronous diagnoses and interventions which model multiple temporal trajectories in order to anticipate student futures. In these ways, the influence of AI on education policy has been to inspire ideas about real-time, predictive and even pre-emptive forms of 'automated governance' (Gulson & Witzenberger, 2020).

AI-enabled learning and the preparation of AI workforces are also new parts of different nations' educational policies. In India, for example, the National Education Policy 2020 framework states that 'New technologies involving artificial intelligence, machine learning, block chains, smart boards, handheld computing devices, adaptive computer testing for student development, and other forms of educational software and hardware will not just change what students learn in the classroom but how they learn' (Government of India, 2020, 54). It also highlights the need for AI education to enable India to become a 'digital superpower'. Likewise, the European Parliament has begun considering a resolution on AI in education, highlighting how 'AI is transforming learning, teaching, and education radically', most notably through the potential of 'personalised learning experience' made possible by the collection, analysis and use of 'large amounts of personal data' (European Parliament, 2020, 7). The OECD, again, has begun producing intelligence about the effects of AI on economies and societies, and producing policy guidance on the kinds of human skills that need to be taught in education systems to ensure seamless human–machine economic productivity in the so-called 'Fourth Industrial Revolution' (Williamson, 2021).

These initiatives exemplify the emergence of AIED as an object of global education policy. As such, we see AI operating in two distinctive ways within education policy. It is being deployed as a specific instrument of policy, with the aim of speeding up policy implementation and feedback, or even enacting anticipatory and pre-emptive forms of intervention based on constant digital tracings of students, staff and settings. At the same time, AI has become a major focus of education policy, and is being included in major policy documents that aim to introduce AIED applications into classrooms as a way of 'upskilling' students as 'human capital' for productive participation and performance in digital economies.

A key emphasis in such policy documents is on AI enabling 'personalized learning' to achieve both of these aims. This idea generally refers to the use of digital technologies that can learn from and adapt to individual students, although pedagogic ideals of personalization have much longer histories in philosophical and psychological accounts of education (Watters, 2021). Nonetheless, personalization has become a global policy discourse and an enabler of AI approaches in education (Davies et al., 2020). For example, Jisc (the body that advises UK universities on digital policy) claims that 'personalised adaptive learning' will fix the 'factory system' of education (THE, 2018). It is, however, difficult to validate any claims about AI-enabled personalization because there is little clear and agreed definition of what personalization means, either pedagogically or technically (Bulger, 2016). It is largely left to vendors to establish within their company what personalization is and how to operationalize it within schools, with few legal or ethical obligations.

Moreover, Perrotta and Selwyn (2020) highlight how AIED methods of predictive analytics employed for personalized learning superimpose algorithmic complexity on reductionist and contested understandings of human learning. They note that applied AI techniques of 'automated knowledge discovery' such as pattern recognition and correlational analysis used in personalized learning are based on a mechanical, inductivist epistemology that assumes all patterns are interpretable in the same standardized ways across all cultures and contexts. They highlight instead how AI-generated patterns reflect the specific situations from which they are gathered and are imprinted with the professional, disciplinary and economic contingencies of their own production. The knowledge of learning generated by AI is at least partly an artefact of the very apparatus of technologies, funding and epistemic expertise that brought it into being, rather than an objective discovery (Williamson, 2020). As such, concepts of personalized learning that are being taken up in various policy concepts are rooted in computational theories of learning and pedagogy that assume a mechanical, behaviourist process of automated observation and intervention (Knox et al., 2020).

This matters because AIED is emerging from a wider policy context in which public education is being transformed into something that can be quantified, graded, compared, audited, translated into league tables and made accountable to managerial decisions (Grek et al., 2021). Increasingly, education is about providing a productive workforce that has been 'upskilled' in STEM subjects to meet the calculated and urgent needs of the economy: 'a pipeline to prosperity' lubricated by personalized learning policies (Davies & Eynon, 2018). There is a danger that personalization via AI becomes the latest phase in the marketization of education and a new factory model that standardizes and automates the functions of pedagogy, curriculum and assessment (Davies et al., 2020). Equally, if there are unequivocal benefits to personalization augmented through AI, only schools with the infrastructure and financial resources to buy the technology, support its implementation and upkeep, renew licences, train staff and use it to complement specialized qualified teachers will be able to reap its rewards, rather than the significantly under-resourced or poorly managed schools in most need of positive interventions. In other words, AIED and its correlate of personalized learning raise a host of deeply ethical challenges.

ETHICAL FRAMEWORKS FOR AIED

A plethora of ethical frameworks have been developed to control and regulate the potential deleterious effects of AI on society (Greene et al., 2018; Jobin et al., 2019). Recent controversies, such as Google firing one of its own AI ethics researchers over claims the company was failing to address biases in machine-learning training datasets, illuminate the increasingly complex intersections of commercial objectives around AI and AI ethics, as 'properly probing the societal effects of AI is fundamentally incompatible with corporate labs' (Simonite, 2020). In this context, the ethical implications of AIED are also a growing area of focus (Kitto & Knight, 2019; Röhl, 2021), with concerted efforts being made to develop ethical approaches to the use of AI in schools and research settings (Selinger & Vance, 2020; Holmes et al., 2021; also see Chapter 26 by Porayska-Pomsta et al.). In thinking about some of these, it is useful to focus on the important interactions between digital ethics, digital governance and digital regulation in understanding how we are navigating the use of AI in society (Floridi, 2018).

At the heart of debates around the ethics of AI are the differing schools of ethical thought which serve as alternate lenses with which to view specific contexts, individuals and social relationships (Gray & Boling, 2016). A large body of work within AI tends towards a consequentialist (particularly utilitarian) ethics, as has similar related fields such as learning analytics (Willis, 2014; Hakimi et al., 2021), where it is taken as a given that AIED is a 'good thing'. Therefore, collecting student data is acceptable as more data leads to better models, and this will lead to AI in Education doing the best for the most students. Within such a frame, discussions move quickly to the legal basis to protect individuals' information (Willis, 2014). Thus, the ethics of AIED becomes a debate about legal and practical requirements rather than wider questions of morals and values within education (Eynon, 2013). However, as we have seen above, AI is not straightforwardly 'a good thing' and often there are many unanticipated effects.

Not all those working in AIED take such a utilitarian view. For example, ideas around the ethics of care are also becoming more common in some circles (Prinsloo & Slade, 2016). However, a significant problem is that few debates about ethics in AI make explicit the schools of ethical thought that their debates relate to (West et al., 2016). In practice, the values underpinning ethical practice are rarely set out clearly, justified, interrogated or consistent from country to country, from institution to institution or even from classroom to classroom (Ferguson et al., 2016). A recent review of the academic work in this domain concluded that 'ethics' in many of the papers was presented as a given, as if all authors and readers have a shared understanding, and explicit discussions of the theoretical/epistemological underpinnings of their work tended to be missing (Hakimi et al., 2021). Indeed, some writing about the moral questions around AIED may not use the term 'ethics' at all, thus reducing the much needed ability for such work to shape governance and regulation.

This is particularly important given current governance structures within AIED. Digital governance is the practice of establishing and implementing procedures, policies and standards for the use and management of data (Floridi, 2018) and can be seen in the numerous ethical frameworks and codes of practice that have been developed within individual higher education institutions in relation to learning analytics that tend to focus on security, transparency, accountability and reliability (Sclater, 2016). Although the sheer number of such frameworks perhaps gives a sense that ethical governance is 'working', critical scholars have expressed concerns, particularly around the increasing power of the private sector in this space (Sahlgren, 2021). These concerns are multiple but relate both to the ways that AIED is changing educational practice and policy, as well as the power of non-state actors to make decisions in this space. As MacGilchrist (2019, 83) notes,

> no matter how good the motives, and how pedagogically well-founded the decisions, it is a post-democratic moment when the ability to make these decisions has shifted from publicly accountable government officials, policy-makers or educators, to developers, programmers, designers and other staff in private edtech organisations.

The ethical domain is one in which power is contested: who gets to decide what ethics are will determine much about what kinds of interventions technology can make in all of our lives, including who benefits, who is protected and who is made vulnerable (Moss & Metcalf, 2020). In AI and AIED, many companies are setting up governance structures. Yet, there are concerns that these governance structures operate as self-regulatory 'checklists' that substitute for independent legal or regulatory oversight (Greene et al., 2019). Many of these governance structures are increasingly contested, including concerns about practices of 'ethics washing', where companies promote an image of concern about ethics, while fundamental practices remain unperturbed by these public-facing activities (Wagner, 2018). Relatedly, there are growing concerns that the commercial sector has too much power in determining ethical governance and regulation of AI across all areas of social life (Benkler, 2019).

For ethical approaches to AIED then, digital regulation is a vital consideration. However, there are challenges here too. In general, legal frameworks tend not to keep up with technical advances effectively (Eynon et al., 2017). Legal analysis of US policy shows a focus on information practice principles, which means that the kinds of concerns raised about student agency, about discrimination with education are not dealt with in legal policy making (Boninger et al., 2017; Regan & Jesse, 2019). Similarly, while there has been significant progress in relation to privacy and data protection, such frameworks do not fully account for the ways that AIED has implications for human rights (Berendt et al., 2020). Moreover, it may be difficult to regulate AI in education as it operates across geographical (and thus different regulatory) borders, includes multinational corporations that can escape regulatory jurisdictions and is becoming so complex and networked that it may exceed human control (Gulson et al., 2021). Recently, some have begun to suggest that energy-intensive technologies used in education, such as AI, are also implicated in environmental planetary destruction, and have called for suitable responses informed by ecological commitments (Macgilchrist, 2021).

It is clear then, that there is far more to do in terms of conceptualizing, governing and regulating ethical AIED. At present, different communities are focused on different parts of ethical questions and need to be brought together, in ways that take account of the complexity of global, national and local contexts. One way to achieve this may be to take an 'ethics by design' approach where ethical considerations and their renegotiation are at the heart of AIED initiatives and involve key stakeholders at all stages (Gray & Boling, 2016; Hakimi et al., 2021). An important part of this will be for those from more critical approaches to AIED, those more engaged in the practicalities of designing and implementing AIED and practitioners tasked with teaching with or about AI to find ways to collaborate productively (Selinger & Vance, 2020).

CONCLUSION

The critical perspectives offered in this chapter open up artificial intelligence in education to specifically social scientific, philosophical and ethical interrogation. We have located AIED in relation to wider historical developments in AI, political economy and geopolitical contexts, identified significant issues of algorithmic discrimination and bias, highlighted the ways global edu-businesses and Big Tech corporations are mobilizing AI in education, identified the uses of AI in policy and governance and flagged some pressing and unresolved ethical tensions and issues. Our aim in presenting these critical perspectives is to call for stronger interdisciplinary collaboration across the learning, computing and social sciences in relation to AIED. Developing a broader academic community which could both use and critique the development of AI is an important aspect for future work, enabling AIED researchers and developers to design products based on the needs of those likely to be most affected, informed by strong ethical principles and receiving feedback on their contexts of use.

Expanding methodologies and approaches to research may be an important strategy to protect against the current pattern of events where, despite the complexity of AIED we have shown above, it seems often to fail to acknowledge the growing social, political and ethical problems, as well as promises, that are associated with artificial intelligence in society. Depoliticized, ahistorical and asocial approaches are a continued problem in many studies of edtech, and enable those with limited expertise but significant (often commercial, economic or political) power to take centre stage in shaping and investing in educational futures.

REFERENCES

Alkhatlan, A., & Kalita, J. (2018). Intelligent tutoring systems: A comprehensive historical survey with recent developments. *arXiv*. http://arxiv.org/abs/1812.09628.

Alpaydin, E. (2016). *Machine Learning*. London: MIT Press.

Anagnostopoulos, D., Rutledge, S., & Jacobsen, R. (Eds.). (2013). *The Infrastructure of Accountability: Data Use and the Transformation of American Education*. Cambridge, MA: Harvard Education Press.

AWS (Amazon Web Services). (2020). Machine learning in education. *Amazon*. https://aws.amazon .com/education/ml-in-education/.

Barocas, S., Hardt, M., & Narayanan, A. (2019). Fairness and machine learning: Limitations and opportunities. https://fairmlbook.org.

Beer, D. (2016). *Metric Power*. London: Palgrave Macmillan.

Benjamin, R. (2019). Discriminatory design, liberating imagination. In R. Benjamin (Ed.), *Captivating Technology: Race, Carceral Technoscience, and Liberatory Imagination in Everyday Life* (pp. 1–22). Durham, NC: Duke University Press.

Benkler, Y. (2019). Don't let industry write the rules for AI. *Nature*, 569(7754), 161–162.

Berendt, B., Littlejohn, A., & Blakemore, M. (2020). AI in education: Learner choice and fundamental rights. *Learning, Media and Technology*, 45(3), 312–324.

Boden, M. A. (2016). *AI: Its Nature and Future*. Oxford: Oxford University Press.

Boninger, F., Molnar, A., & Murray, K. (2017). *Asleep at the Switch: Schoolhouse Commercialism, Student Privacy, and the Failure of Policymaking*. Boulder, CO: National Education Policy Center.

Boninger, F., Molnar, A., & Saldaña, C. (2020). *Big Claims, Little Evidence, Lots of Money: The Reality Behind the Summit Learning Program and the Push to Adopt Digital Personalized Learning Platforms*. Boulder, CO: National Education Policy Center. https://nepc.colorado.edu/publication/ summit-2020.

Broussard, M. (2019). *Artificial Unintelligence: How Computers Misunderstand the World*. London: MIT Press.

Buckingham Shum, S., & Luckin, R. (2019). Learning analytics and AI: Politics, pedagogy and practices. *British Journal of Educational Technology*, 50(6), 2785–2793.

Bulger, M. (2016). Personalized learning: The conversations we're not having. *Data and Society*. https:// datasociety.net/pubs/ecl/PersonalizedLearning_primer_2016.pdf.

Davies, H. C., & Eynon, R. (2018). Is digital upskilling the next generation our 'pipeline to prosperity'? *New Media and Society*, 20(11), 3961–3979.

Davies, H. C., Eynon, R., & Salveson, C. (2020). The mobilisation of AI in education: A Bourdieusean field analysis. *Sociology*. Advance online publication. doi:10.1177/0038038520967888.

D'Ignazio, C., & Klein, L. (2019). *Data Feminism*. London: MIT Press.

Dixon-Román, E., Nichols, T. P., & Nyame-Mensah, A. (2019). The racializing forces of/in AI educational technologies. *Learning, Media and Technology*, pp. 1–15.

du Boulay, B. (2016). Recent meta-reviews and meta-analyses of AIED systems. *International Journal of Artificial Intelligence in Education*, 26(1), 536–537.

du Boulay, B. (2019). Escape from the skinner box: The case for contemporary intelligent learning environments. *British Journal of Educational Technology*, 50(6), 2902–2919.

Eubanks, V. (2018). *Automating Inequality: How High-Tech Tools Profile, Police, and Punish the Poor*. St. Martin's Press.

European Parliament. (2020). Draft report on artificial intelligence in education, culture and the audiovisual sector. https://www.europarl.europa.eu/doceo/document/CULT-PR-655862_EN.pdf.

Eynon, R. (2013). The rise of Big Data: What does it mean for education, technology, and media research? *Learning, Media and Technology*, 38(3), 237–240.

Eynon, R., Fry, J., & Schroeder, R. (2017). The ethics of online research. In *The SAGE Handbook of Online Research Methods* (pp. 19–37). London: Sage.

Eynon, R., & Young, E. (2020). Methodology, legend, and rhetoric: The constructions of AI by academia, industry, and policy groups for lifelong learning. *Science, Technology, and Human Values*. Advance online publication. doi:10.1177/0162243920906475.

Feldman, P. (2020). Let's 'build back better' on post-Covid digital transformation. *Fe News*, 26 November. https://www.fenews.co.uk/fevoices/59337-let-s-build-back-better-on-post-covid-digital-transformation.

Ferguson, R., Hoel, T., Scheffel, M., & Drachsler, H. (2016). Guest editorial: Ethics and privacy in learning analytics. *Journal of Learning Analytics*, 3, 5–15.

Fiebig, T., Gürses, S., Gañán, C. H., Kotkamp, E., Kuipers, F., Lindorfer, M., Prisse, M., & Sari, T. (2021). Heads in the clouds: Measuring the implications of universities migrating to public clouds. arXiv preprint: arXiv:2104.09462.

Fischer, C., Pardos, Z. A., Baker, R. S., Williams, J. J., Smyth, P., Yu, R., Slater, S., Baker, R., & Warschauer, M. (2020). Mining big data in education: Affordances and challenges. *Review of Research in Education*, 44(1), 130–160.

Floridi, L. (2018). Soft ethics and the governance of the digital. *Philosophy and Technology*, 31(1), 1–8.

Government of India. (2020). National education policy 2020. https://nenow.in/wp-content/uploads/2020/07/NEP-final-for-circulation.pdf.

Gray, C. M., & Boling, E. (2016). Inscribing ethics and values in designs for learning: A problematic. *Education Technology and Research Development*, 64, 969–1001.

Greene, D., Hoffman, A. L., & Stark, L. (2019). Better, nicer, clearer, fairer: A critical assessment of the movement for ethical artificial intelligence and machine learning. In *Proceedings of the 52nd Hawaii International Conference on System Sciences*. https://scholarspace.manoa.hawaii.edu/bitstream/10125/59651/0211.pdf.

Grek, S., Maroy, C., & Verger, A. (Eds.). (2021). *Accountability and Datafication in the Governance of Education*. London: Routledge.

Gulson, K. N., Sellar, S., & Webb, P. T. (2021). Synthetic governance: On the impossibility of taming Artificial Intelligence in education. *On Education Journal for Research and Debate*, 4(12). doi:10.17899/on_ed.2021.12.1.

Gulson, K. N., & Witzenberger, K. (2020). Repackaging authority: Artificial intelligence, automated governance and education trade shows. *Journal of Education Policy*. doi:10.1080/02680939.2020.1785552.

Hakimi, L., Eynon, R., & Murphy, V. (2021). The ethics of using digital trace data in education: A thematic review of the research landscape. *Review of Educational Research*, 91(5), 671–717.

Hartong, S. (2016). Between assessments, digital technologies and big data: The growing influence of 'hidden' data mediators in education. *European Educational Research Journal*, 15(5), 523–536.

Hoffmann, A. L. (2019). Where fairness fails: Data, algorithms, and the limits of antidiscrimination discourse. *Information, Communication and Society*, 22(7), 900–915.

Holmes, W., Bialik, M., & Fadel, C. (2019). *Artificial Intelligence in Education: Promises and Implications for Teaching and Learning*. Boston: Centre for Curriculum Redesign.

Holmes, W., Porayska-Pomsta, K., Holstein, K., et al. (2021). Ethics of AI in education: Towards a community-wide framework. *International Journal of Artificial Intelligence in Education*. doi:10.1007/s40593-021-00239-1.

Hwang, G.-J., Xie, H., Wah, B. W., & Gašević, D. (2020). Vision, challenges, roles and research issues of Artificial Intelligence in Education. *Computers and Education: Artificial Intelligence*, 1. doi:10.1016/j.caeai.2020.100001.

International Journal of AI in Education. (2021). The FATE of AIED. IJAIED topical collections. https://link.springer.com/journal/40593/topicalCollection/AC_dcac58fbbf2e68a27dd420b8fa69ba47/page/1.

Iosad, A. (2020). *Digital at the Core: A 2030 Strategy Framework for University Leaders*. Bristol: Jisc.

Jobin, A., Ienca, M., & Vayena, E. (2019). The global landscape of AI ethics guidelines. *Nature Machine Intelligence*, 1(9), 389–399.

Kitto, K., & Knight, S. (2019). Practical ethics for building learning analytics. *British Journal of Educational Technology*, 50(6), 2855–2870.

Knox, J. (2020). Artificial intelligence and education in China. *Learning, Media and Technology*. doi:10.1080/17439884.2020.1754236.

Knox, J. (2021). How the 'taming' of private education in China is impacting AI. *On Education: Journal for Research and Debate*, 4(12). doi:10.17899/on_ed.2021.12.6.

Knox, J., Williamson, B., & Bayne, S. (2020). Machine behaviourism: Future visions of 'learnification' and 'datafication' across humans and digital technologies. *Learning, Media and Technology*, 45(1), 31–45.

Kologriyava, K., & Shleifer, E. (2021). After government crackdown, what's next for China's edtech firms? *The Diplomat*, 3 September. https://thediplomat.com/2021/09/after-government-crackdown -whats-next-for-chinas-edtech-firms/.

Komljenovic, J. (2021). The rise of education rentiers: Digital platforms, digital data and rents. *Learning, Media and Technology*. doi:10.1080/17439884.2021.1891422.

Kuhl, P. K., Limii, S. S., Guerrieroiii, S., & van Damme, D. (2019). *Developing Minds in the Digital Age: Towards a Science of Learning for 21st Century Education, Educational Research and Innovation*. Paris: OECD Publishing.

Luckin, R., Holmes, W., Griffiths, M., & Forcier, L. B. (2016). *Intelligence Unleashed: An Argument for AI in Education*. London: Pearson Education.

Macgilchrist, F. (2019). Cruel optimism in edtech: When the digital data practices of educational technology providers inadvertently hinder educational equity. *Learning, Media and Technology*, 44(1), 77–86.

Macgilchrist, F. (2021). Rewilding technology. *On Education. Journal for Research and Debate*, 4(12). doi:10.17899/on_ed.2021.12.2.

Mackenzie, A. (2017). *Machine Learners: Archaeology of a Data Practice*. Cambridge, MA: MIT Press.

Mayfield, E., Madaio, M., Prabhumoye, S., Gerritsen, D., McLaughlin, B., Dixon-Román, E., & Black, A. W. (2019). Equity beyond bias in language technologies for education. In *Proceedings of the Fourteenth Workshop on Innovative Use of NLP for Building Educational Applications* (pp. 444–460).

McArthur, D., Lewis, M., & Bishay, M. (1995). The roles of artificial intelligence in education: Current progress and future prospects. *i-manager's Journal of Educational Technology*, 1(4), 42–80.

Microsoft Education Team. (2020). New IDC report shows big opportunities to transform higher education through AI. *Microsoft Education Blog*, March 3. https://educationblog.microsoft.com/en-us/2020/03/new-report-shows-big-opportunities-to-transform-higher-education-through-ai/.

Mirrlees, T., & Alvi, S. (2019). *EdTech Inc.: Selling, Automating and Globalizing Higher Education in the Digital Age*. Abingdon: Routledge.

Morrison, D. M., & Miller, K. B. (2018). Teaching and learning in the pleistocene: A biocultural account of human pedagogy and its implications for AIED. *International Journal of Artificial Intelligence in Education*, 28, 439–469. doi:10.1007/s40593-017-0153-0.

Mosco, V. (1995). *The Political Economy of Communication*. London: Sage.

Moss, E., & Metcalf, J. (2020). Too big a word? What does it mean to do ethics in the technology industry? We found four overlapping meanings. *Data and Society*. https://points.datasociety.net/too -big-a-word-13e66e62a5bf.

Noble, S. U. (2018). *Algorithms of Oppression: How Search Engines Reinforce Racism*. New York: NYU Press.

Nye, B. D. (2016). ITS, the end of the world as we know it: Transitioning AIED into a service-oriented ecosystem. *International Journal of Artificial Intelligence in Education*, 26, 756–770.

OECD (2021). *OECD Digital Education Outlook 2021: Pushing the Frontiers With Artificial Intelligence, Blockchain and Robots*. Paris: OECD Publishing. doi:10.1787/589b283f-en.

O'Neil, C. (2016). *Weapons of Math Destruction: How Big Data Increases Inequality and threatens Democracy*. Broadway Books.

Paquette, L., Ocumpaugh, J., Li, Z., Andres, A., & Baker, R., (2020). Who's learning? Using demographics in EDM research. *Journal of Educational Data Mining*, 12(3), 1–30.

Perrotta, C. (2021). Programming the platform university: Learning analytics and predictive infrastructures in higher education. *Research in Education*, 109(1), 53–71.

Perrotta, C., Gulson, K. N., Williamson, B., & Witzenberger, K. (2021). Automation, APIs and the distributed labour of platform pedagogies in Google Classroom. *Critical Studies in Education*, 62(1), 97–113.

Perrotta, C., & Selwyn, N. (2020). Deep learning goes to school: Toward a relational understanding of AI in education. *Learning, Media and Technology*. doi:10.1080/17439884.2020.1686017.

Piattoeva, N., & Boden, R. (2020). Escaping numbers? The ambiguities of the governance of education through data. *International Studies in Sociology of Education*, 29(1–2), 1–18.

Pinkwart, N. (2016). Another 25 years of AIED? Challenges and opportunities for intelligent educational technologies of the future. *International Journal of Artificial Intelligence in Education*, 26, 771–783.

Poritz, J., & Rees, J. (2017). *Education is Not an App: The Future of University Teaching in the Internet Age*. Abingdon: Routledge.

Prinsloo, P., & Slade, S. (2016). Student vulnerability, agency, and learning analytics: An exploration. *Journal of Learning Analytics*, 3(1), 159–182.

Regan, P. M., & Jesse, J. (2019). Ethical challenges of edtech, big data and personalized learning: twenty-first century student sorting and tracking. *Ethics and Information Technology*, 21(3), 167–179.

Regan, P. M., & Khwaja, E. T. (2019). Mapping the political economy of education technology: A networks perspective. *Policy Futures in Education*, 17(8), 1000–1023.

Röhl, T. (2021). Taming algorithms. *On Education. Journal for Research and Debate*, 4(12). doi:10.17899/on_ed.2021.12.3.

Sahlgren, O. (2021). The politics and reciprocal (re)configuration of accountability and fairness in data-driven education. *Learning, Media and Technology*. doi:10.1080/17439884.2021.1986065.

Schank, R. C., & Edelson, D. J. (1989). A role for AI in education: Using technology to reshape education. *International Journal of Artificial Intelligence in Education*,1(2), 3–20.

Sclater, N. (2016). Developing a code of practice for learning analytics. *Journal of Learning Analytics*, 3(1), 16–42.

Self, J. (2016). The birth of IJAIED. *International Journal of Artificial Intelligence in Education*, 26(1), 4–12.

Selinger, E., & Vance, A. (2020). Teaching privacy and ethical guardrails for the AI imperative in education. *Future Edge*, 3 December, 30–53.

Sellar, S., & Gulson, K. N. (2019). Becoming information centric: The emergence of new cognitive infrastructures in education policy. *Journal of Education Policy*. doi:10.1080/02680939.2019.1678766.

Selwyn, N. (2013). *Education in a Digital World: Global Perspectives on Technology and Education*. New York: Routledge.

Selwyn, N. (2019). *Should Robots Replace Teachers?* Cambridge: Polity.

Simonite, T. (2020). The dark side of big tech's funding for AI research. *Wired*, 10 December. https://www.wired.com/story/dark-side-big-tech-funding-ai-research/.

Suresh, H., & Guttag, J. V. (2020). A framework for understanding unintended consequences of machine learning. arXiv preprint arXiv:1901.10002.

THE (Times Higher Education). (2018). Preparing for education 4.0. *THE*. https://www.timeshighereducation.com/hub/jisc/p/preparing-education-40.

Wagner, B. (2018). Ethics as an escape from regulation: From ethics-washing to ethics-shopping. In *Being Profiling: Cogitas Ergo Sum*, pp. 1–7.

Watters, A. (2020). Cheating, policing, and school surveillance. National Education Policy Center Blog. https://nepc.colorado.edu/blog/cheating-policing.

Watters, A. (2021). *Teaching Machines: The History of Personalized Learning*. London: MIT Press.

Webb, P. T., Sellar, S., & Gulson, K. N. (2020). Anticipating education: Governing habits, memories and policy-futures. *Learning, Media and Technology*. doi:10.1080/17439884.2020.1686015.

West, D., Huijser, H., & Heath, D. (2016). Putting an ethical lens on learning analytics. *Educational Technology Research and Development*, 64(5), 903–922.

Whittaker, M. (2021). The steep cost of capture. *Interactions*, 28(6), 50–55.

Whittaker, M., Crawford, K., Dobbe, R., Fried, G., Kaziunas, E., Mathur, V., West, S. M., Richardson, R., Schultz, J., & Schwartz, O. (2018). *AI Now Report 2018*. New York: AI Now Institute/New York University. https://ainowinstitute.org/AI_Now_2018_Report.pdf.

Williamson, B. (2017). *Big Data in Education: The Digital Future of Learning, Policy and Practice*. London: Sage.

Williamson, B. (2020). New digital laboratories of experimental knowledge production: Artificial intelligence and education research. *London Review of Education*, 18(2), 209–220.

Williamson, B. (2021). PISA for machine learners. *Code Acts in Education*, 25 November. https://codeactsineducation.wordpress.com/2021/11/25/pisa-for-machine-learners/.

Williamson, B., Bayne, S., & Shay, S. 2020. The datafication of teaching in higher education: critical issues and perspectives. *Teaching in Higher Education*, 25(4), 351–365. doi:10.1080/13562517.2020. 1748811.

Williamson, B., & Eynon, R. (2020). Historical threads, missing links, and future trajectories in AI in education. *Learning, Media and Technology*, 45(3), 223–235.

Willis, J. E., III. (2014). Learning analytics and ethics: A framework beyond utilitarianism. *EDUCAUSE Review*, August 2014.

Winters, N., Eynon, R., Geniets, A., Robson, J., & Kahn, K. (2020). Can we avoid digital structural violence in future learning systems? *Learning, Media and Technology*, 45(1), 17–30.

Witzenberger, K., & Gulson, K. N. (2021). Why EdTech is always right: Students, data and machines in pre-emptive configurations. *Learning, Media and Technology*. doi:10.1080/17439884.2021.1913181.

Wyatt-Smith, C., Lingard, B., & Heck, E. (Eds.). (2021). *Digital Disruption in Teaching and Testing: Assessments, Big Data, and the Transformation of Schooling*. Abingdon: Routledge.

Zeide, E. (2017). The structural consequences of big data-driven education. *Big Data*, 5(2), 164–172.

26. The ethics of AI in education

Kaśka Porayska-Pomsta, Wayne Holmes and
Selena Nemorin

INTRODUCTION

The advent of big data, and of Artificial Intelligence (AI) applications that collect and consume such data, has led to fundamental questions about the ethics of AI designs and to efforts aimed to highlight and safeguard against any potential harms caused by the deployment of AI across diverse domains of applications. Typically, questions raised relate to the *trustworthiness* of AI as agent technologies that autonomously or semi-autonomously operate in human environments and that have the ability to alter human behaviour. Other questions concern the role that AI may play now and in the future in either resolving or amplifying pre-existing social biases and any resulting harms. Specifically, *Ethical AI* as an emergent area of AI research and policy, has been spurred by the revelations of AI applications (usually unintentionally) promoting and amplifying many of the discriminatory and oppressive practices and assumptions that underpin pre-existing social and institutional systems, such as historical biases against non-dominant populations, against users characterised by some divergence from the so-called cognitive or physical 'norm', or those who are socio-economically disadvantaged (Crawford, 2017a; Madaio et al., 2022; Porayska-Pomsta & Rajendran, 2019; Chapter 25 by Williamson et al. in this handbook). Numerous examples of AI bias are both well documented and rehearsed throughout the emergent ethics of AI literature, in hundreds of policy reports about AI ethics and governance that have been published to date (c.f. Jobin et al., 2019; Hargendorff, 2020) and in the media. Despite this, our understanding of the ethics for AI in Education (AIED) is still at a fledgling stage (Holmes et al., 2021).

One reason why the ethics of AIED have received little attention to date may be because the field has traditionally adopted a self-image of being inherently 'good' in its intentions and as such it has implicitly assumed that these good intentions are automatically encoded in the AIED technologies (Holmes et al., 2021). This positive self-image stems from two further face-value assumptions tacitly adopted by AIED researchers, namely that: (a) AIED is, by default, simultaneously guided by and guarded against any potential pitfalls and unintended consequences by the intentions and practices of the broader education system; and (b) AI technology can serve to promote social justice and inclusive high-quality education for all. However, neither assumption has so far received much critical attention from the community and few attempts have been made to examine the ethical value, safety and trustworthiness of AIED systems, approaches and methods in the broader socio-technical context.

The first assumption reflects AIED researchers' historic surrender of the responsibility for reflecting on and addressing the questions about the ethical implications of their AIED intervention designs and use to the decision makers within the broader education system which they intend to fit and serve. The second assumption derives from a particular approach in formal education, which proved convenient for the early computer-assisted learning technologies, namely the drill-and-practice mastery learning-focused pedagogies. This approach is deeply ingrained in traditional educational practices focused on school-based subject-domain teaching, which was further boosted by Bloom's influential '2-sigma effect' studies (Bloom, 1984). These studies have served as the foundation for much AIED work, with the mastery learning model of education and the perceived benefits of one-to-one individualised, adaptive teaching support providing the ultimate ambition for the AIED technologies to strive for, and against which to measure their success. However, as in other domains of AI applications such as healthcare, just because AIED explicitly aims to fit into a pre-existent system does not *de facto* guarantee that the practices that it promotes are ethical. Similar to other domains, both the possible systemic biases and the domain-dependent definitional idiosyncrasies related to concepts such as fairness, equity or human autonomy need to be determined and examined in the context of AI applications for education, to allow the AIED engineers and diverse users of AIED technologies to develop an understanding of the ethics of AIED systems' designs, and to guide those designs and their deployments accordingly.

In this chapter, we discuss concepts that have emerged in the broader AI applications' contexts as key to the ethics of AI, and we contextualise them in the discussions of and directions taken in the ethics of AIED research. First, we consider briefly what might count as an 'ethical approach', in order to ground and examine these concepts specifically within AI and AIED. We recognise that AIED provides a unique domain in which to study the ethics of AI, not least because of its central focus on supporting the interaction with human cognition and on delivering pedagogies that nudge learners towards long-term learning behaviour changes. As such the examination of the assumptions, approaches and methods employed within the discipline of AIED has the potential to lead to a greater understanding of whether and how AIED systems are ethical, of the blind spots and areas for improvement for the field with respect to ethics, and to insights from the AIED of potential importance to other areas of AI that intend to influence or enhance human cognition, decision making and behaviour. We review key Ethical AI concepts, which provide the foundations for the study of Ethical AIED. Next, the broad Ethical AI concepts are contextualised within AIED, and the unique aspects of the AIED domain are highlighted. The penultimate section provides an outline of an Ethics of AIED framework and offers detailed initial mapping between different forms of bias in AI, AIED and broader socio-technical context (Table 26.2). We conclude the chapter with a brief examination of the gaps and the future directions for Ethical AIED.

WHAT COUNTS AS AN ETHICAL APPROACH?

AIED's self-image of being inherently good, for the assumptions outlined above, begs the question: what does 'being good' actually mean? Are there immutable, universal ethical principles that should guide individual and collective behaviour; or does what constitutes being good depend on one's individual socio-political perspective? Such questions are inevitably complex and remain open despite more than two thousand years of ethics discourse. The emergent research on Ethical AI provides a starting point for considering the necessary, even if not sufficient, principles of Ethical AIED. Specifically, within the broader context of AI, a consensus has emerged that any attempt to develop robust and actionable principles that ensure AI research and practices are 'good' ought to be grounded in core concepts from moral philosophy, with special emphasis on universal human rights and obligations (Kant, 1785; Ross, 1930). Such obligations have been recently re-conceptualised specifically in the context of AI by Floridi and

Cowls (2019) as: (i) *beneficence* ('do good' for human wellbeing, dignity and for the planet); (ii) *non-maleficence* ('do no harm' by avoiding over-reliance, over-use or misuse of AI technologies, in order to preserve personal privacy of users, and to prevent use for harmful purposes); (iii) *autonomy* (promote human autonomy, do not impair human freedom of choice and decision making, by delegating decisions to AI); (iv) *justice* (seek and preserve justice, prevent any forms of discrimination, foster diversity, including the way in which AI is used to enhance human decision making); and (v) *explicability*, that is, *transparency* with respect to how AI works, and *accountability* relating to who is responsible for how AI works. The explicability principle is considered an enabler for applying the first four principles, insofar as it gives access to how a given AI technology allows the user to exercise their autonomy and to be audited with respect to any potential benefits and harms. All five principles are considered necessary to support trustworthy and responsible AI designs and deployment. Floridi and Cowls' principles aim for universality, domain-independence and to serve as a basis for a dialogue between engineering and social scientific perspectives on AI. However, this comes at the price of a lack of concreteness. In short, there remains a paucity of guidelines for how those principles might be actioned in specific AI designs and application contexts. A substantial part of the problem lies in the relativistic nature of the concepts involved which tend to depend on: (a) socio-cultural norms, which are in themselves subject to change over time (e.g., the concept of justice is perpetually evolving), (b) circumstances and needs of individuals (e.g., the concept of individual fairness is deeply rooted in the situational and subjective realities of individuals) and (c) context (e.g., the tension between multiple conflicting interests, expectations and needs of different stakeholders, which may lead to different interpretations of the beneficent nature of AI).

ETHICS OF AI: KEY DIMENSIONS AND CONCERNS

One way in which researchers are trying to understand how the overarching ethics principles might be considered in AI systems' designs and their deployment is by exploring the exact sources and the potential consequences of the AI principles being violated. This allows for the specific related harms to be considered and articulated, and to highlight the complex relationships between data that encode historical inequalities and the socio-cultural biases in the decisions affecting different groups. Although the related work so far has improved our understanding of the different forms of societal and systemic biases and of how such biases may be both reinforced through and mitigated within AI algorithms, researchers in this area are still faced with substantial challenges arising from different disciplinary perspectives involved (e.g., moral philosophy vs. law, vs. social justice, vs. AI engineering, and so on) bringing varying definitions of the key terms (e.g., sociological vs. statistical understanding of bias). Bias in AI has long been the subject of research, revealing overlapping definitions and different points at which it may enter the AI development and deployment pipeline (Crawford, 2017a; Blodgett et al., 2020; Baker et al., 2021). In this context, it remains critical for AI practitioners to question when and how bias may enter into AI systems that they build, and how to mitigate or eliminate it.

General Forms of Bias

Bias has emerged as a concept that underpins key ethical concerns in AI. There are many different conceptions of bias available through diverse science disciplines and schools of thought. Fundamentally, bias usually refers to people's tendency to stereotype situations, groups or individuals (Cardwell, 1999), and this ultimately leads to people's tendency to favour certain things or people over others. One common feature of the different definitions of bias is their reference to some form of *discrimination* that creates a disparity in the treatment of different groups of people or individuals. Danks and London (2017) distinguish between: (a) *moral bias*, that is, a deviation from certain moral principles related to equity, autonomy and human rights; (b) *legal bias*, that is, undue prejudice, such as judgements based on preconceived notions of particular groups, which violates written legal norms prohibiting discrimination, and (c) *statistical bias*, that is, a flaw in the data, in the data collection process, or in the experimental design, which generates results that do not represent accurately the population at large, either because of *under-* or *over*-representation. These different types of bias do not always align and thus, addressing one type of bias may not render a system ethically 'better'. For example, it is possible for data collection to be statistically unbiased and to generalise well to new data. Nevertheless, if the data collection takes place in the context where there is historical bias, these training data could lead to biased decisions in the legal and moral sense, due to structural inequalities encoded into these data. An algorithm might also not be statistically or legally biased, but it might be morally deviant insofar as it (re)produces structural inequalities or reinforces stereotypes that violate commonly held ideals of equity, such as use of gendered language-models that accurately reflect how language is used in society, but that also reinforce historically ingrained gender stereotypes.

Algorithmic Bias and Sources of Bias in AI Systems

Much has been said to date about bias that is encoded in data and that is inherited from people's attitudes and beliefs (Crawford, 2017b). Recently, with the greater use of AI systems in diverse mainstream application contexts, increased attention has been dedicated to the AI systems' development process during which different forms of bias can be introduced. In this broader context, bias is referred to as *algorithmic bias*.

Algorithmic bias is predominantly studied in the context of the AI subdomain of machine learning, with the machine-learning system development process, from task definition to deployment of an AI system, being referred to as the *machine-learning pipeline*. Given that machine learning is a statistical inference method, algorithmic bias is typically understood as statistical bias. In this subsection we synthesise the key considerations with respect to algorithmic bias, as studied within the context of machine learning, looking specifically at the sources of bias and the steps in the AI systems' development at which bias may be introduced. We also provide some specific recommendations made in the literature for best practices aimed to mitigate or reduce bias in AI systems. However, many considerations presented here also apply to AI rule-/knowledge-based approaches, including to the knowledge representation models and the types of heuristics that are used to drive inference in such systems.

Cramer et al. (2019) propose a seven-step machine learning pipeline, involving (a) *task definition*, concerned with identifying and specifying the problem an AI system is designed to address, such as to help predict student attainment; (b) *data construction*, which involves selecting a data source, acquiring data, pre-processing and labelling data; (c) *model definition*, which involves the selection of a specific AI approach and of the objective function; (d) *training process*, when the model is trained on data; (v) *evaluation process*, when the model is validated on additional data and where there is an opportunity to check for biases in the entire system; (e) *deployment*, when the system leaves the lab and where any mismatches between training data and target populations become apparent; and (f) *feedback* on how the system fares in the wild, based on the way that it is being used. Bias can enter, or it can be reinforced, at any step in this pipeline, with decisions made during earlier steps also affecting the ethical quality of the steps downstream. For example, the choice of a task (part of step 1) may affect whether an entire system is ethical, as demonstrated by the infamous case of the Wu and Zhang (2016) classification system designed to predict people's criminality based on their facial features.

Nonetheless, data are considered the main source of algorithmic bias. Data bias may be introduced: (a) *at the source*, such as during sampling, (b) *during pre-processing of data*, such as during data cleaning or labelling, or (c) *through the data collection method*, including the specific data collection software, sampling strategy or human interpretation of responses (e.g., when qualitative methods such as semi-structured interviews are used). At each point in the process, there is a need for AI researchers and designers to assess their decisions for their ethical value, by carefully considering the provenance of the data, how the data has been acquired and whether the handling of the data (pre-processing and labelling) is trustworthy and ethically sound (Cramer et al., 2019). Researchers have also identified different forms of data bias. For example, Suresh and Guttag (2020) discuss seven categories (listed in Table 26.1 along with their potential sources and harmful consequences):

Historic bias, which typically occurs at the point at which data is being generated, refers to bias that is deeply embedded in historic, cultural and social stereotypes that discriminate against particular groups (e.g., word embeddings and gendering of nouns describing professions such as female nurse vs. male doctor).

Representational bias refers to lack of generalisability of the sample data to different populations due to certain populations being under-represented, over-represented, or due to sampling methods that are uneven or limited. For example, this form of bias can be found in systems such as ImageNet (a dataset of labelled images), which are based on data collected predominantly in specific socio-geographical settings (e.g., North America), with limited data from the rest of the world.

Measurement bias typically occurs during decisions related to what features and labels should be used in a model and how such features should be collected and computed. Since labels are proxies for often complex and abstract constructs (e.g., creditworthiness or student engagement), they are inevitably oversimplifications of the real things. Furthermore, measurement bias may occur when the measurement method, or when the accuracy of measurement, varies between groups, for example, when more stringent assessment of students is applied in one school district than in another.

Aggregation bias happens when a model cannot account for the data that should be considered differently from the data on which the model was trained (e.g., when a model derived from data of neurotypical learners is used for neurodivergent students). This type of bias results from an assumption that the mappings between inputs and the labels are consistent across different subsets of data. A model harbouring aggregation bias may either fit only a dominant population, or it may not be optimal for any group.

Learning bias is introduced when modelling choices, such as the choice of an objective function in machine learning, lead to performance differences across different data. An objective function encodes the goals of an agent and a measure of accuracy of a model (according to assumptions that may in themselves be biased), so prioritising one objective over another may lead to inaccurate classification and even dangerous outcomes. For

Table 26.1   Main types of AI bias, their potential sources and related harms

AI bias		
Type	Sources	Harms
Historic *(Diffused through time, cultures and society)*	Moral, legal and socio-cultural biases	Representational (especially recognition, denigration and exnomination); allocative; outcome, process, individual and group fairness; human autonomy
Representation *(Over-/under-representation of some populations; methodological biases)*	Moral, legal, historic; assumptions and methodological biases	Representational; allocative; outcome, process, individual and group fairness
Measurement *(Choices of features and labels and how these should be composed)*	Inconsistencies between measurement methods, including accuracy of measurements, used for different groups	Representational; allocative; individual and group fairness
Aggregation *(Assumptions of mapping consistency between inputs and labels)*	Model's inability to account for data other than the data that it was trained on; untested assumptions of mapping consistency	Representational (especially recognition and exnomination); outcome; individual and group fairness
Learning *(Performance differences resulting from different choices of modelling and model evaluation/objective functions)*	Assumptions and methodological biases; mal-informed/unverified goal satisfaction priorities	Representational; outcome, process, individual and group fairness
Evaluation *(Failure of the benchmark data to match the use population data; lack of generalisability; overclaimed quality of models)*	Historic, context; representation; benchmark data bias	Representational; allocative; outcome, process, individual and group fairness
Deployment *(Mismatch between the task the model is designed to solve and the task for which it is being used)*	Assumptions bias; mal-informed/unverified definition of deployment context; technocentric methods and focus	Representational; allocative; outcome, process, individual and group fairness

example, the infamous case of the Microsoft Tay twitter chatbot illustrates how the objective of increasing user engagement at all costs may lead to the system's morally deviant behaviours, such as racist abuse.

Evaluation bias occurs when the so-called benchmark data fails to match the user population data. This is a known issue with respect to models that are optimised for training data, but which fail to generalise to new data. The issue is exacerbated by the fact that models are frequently evaluated against each other, which can lead to unsubstantiated generalisations about how good the specific models actually are in real-world contexts. A key question here relates to whether the benchmark data harbours historical, representation or benchmark biases that may be obscured by lack of evaluations against real-world scenarios.

Deployment bias refers to a mismatch between the task that the model is supposed to solve and the task for which it is being used. This form of bias can be hard to control, since users can and often do appropriate technologies in ways that may not have been intended by their designers. This may introduce bias and unintended harms, for example when users interfere with or override system decisions, or when a system is presented as fully autonomous when in fact it requires human intervention to reach its goals. Risk assessment tools used in the criminal justice context offer examples of this form of bias, providing a warning of potential similar dangers in the context of learning analytics.

Cramer et al. (2019) offer important recommendations for what AI designers need to consider in order to address different sources of data bias. For example, with respect to examining the data source, it is important to consider the possibility of any potential societal or cultural basis for data bias such as a tendency to use gendered language to describe professions (again, female nurses vs. male doctors), and to consider carefully whether and how exactly data sources match the system's intended deployment contexts. Regarding bias that results from pre-processing and labelling of data, Cramer et al. (2019) recommend examining data for any biases that may be the result of *discarding data* (e.g., when someone may not want to declare their gender or ethnicity), *bucketing values* (e.g., if someone identifies with more than one race), *using pre-processing and labelling software* which may already harbour bias (e.g., Google Translate assigning gender to profession nouns), and *human labellers* who make inherently subjective judgements.

With respect to the data collection methods, it is critical to audit carefully the pre-processing tools for bias and to develop and employ techniques to quantify and reduce bias introduced by human labellers. It is also key to ensure that data is representative of target users and to be transparent about any known representational limitations in data. Finally, it is also important to question whether the data collection process is ethical in itself. For example, efforts to limit representational bias may also lead to overburdening under-represented groups. Considering what methods (if any) may help reduce or eliminate such a 'participation tax' should be integral to any ethical data collection practices.

Harm

Bias is considered to be the root cause of diverse forms of *harms*. The different forms of bias have been linked to specific forms of harmful consequences for those individuals and groups against whom the bias is tilted. Barocas et al. (2017) identify two overarching categories of harms: (a) harms of allocation, i.e., harms that relate to certain opportunities or resources being withheld from some groups or individuals and (b) harms of representation, i.e., usually stereotypical and negative ways in which certain groups may be represented or in which they may not be represented in a positive light.

Harms of allocation have been studied in greater depth than harms of representation, since they are also often considered from an economic perspective. Examples of allocative bias and harms include restrictions imposed on young people below a certain age on getting mortgages or high-achieving students in schools in poor socio-economic communities being graded as lower achieving, based on a grade average for the schools. Allocative harms are transactional in nature. They are immediate, easily quantifiable, and time-bound. Thus, harms of allocation raise questions of fairness and justice that can be examined with respect to precise and discrete transactions or decision incidents.

By contrast **harms of representation** refer to a relatively neglected area of study within computer science and AI, mainly because such harms are not discrete and they do not occur in single transactions, instead being ingrained within cultural and institutional contexts. As such, representational harms are long-term processes that impact people's beliefs and attitudes. They are diffused across time, diverse historical and socio-cultural contexts. They often lie at the root of allocative harms (Crawford, 2017b).

Barocas et al. (2017) specify five sub-types of harms of representation that need to be considered in the context of algorithmic bias: (a) *stereotyping*, for example, gender stereotyping used in translation algorithms (Boloukbasi et al., 2016); (b) *recognition*, which involves certain groups being erased or made invisible to the algorithm (Sweeney, 2013), such as AI technologies not being able to recognise users of colour (Buolamwini & Gebru, 2018); (c) *denigration*, which involves users' dignity being violated by an algorithmic bias, with the infamous example of black people not being recognised as humans by the Google picture classification algorithm (Alciné, 2015); (d) *under-representation*, which refers to certain groups being systematically ignored as representative of, for example, certain professions, such as women as CEOs; (e) *ex-nomination*, where the majority demographic becomes accepted as the norm, thereby amplifying any difference as an undesirable deviation, e.g., neurodiversity in a mainstream education system that is geared towards neurotypicality.

The two overarching types of harms (of allocation and representation) and the subtypes of representational harms are not only interrelated, but multiple types of harms may also be embedded in any given system design, in the way that it is deployed and in the impact that it might have on different users. Such impact, and bias more broadly, is inextricably linked to questions of *fairness* and *justice* and of how technology contributes to mitigating or exacerbating social inequalities.

Fairness

The questions about algorithmic bias cannot be separated from the questions about what constitutes *fairness* (Kizilcec & Lee, 2022; Narayanan, 2018). Fairness in the context of technology concerns what and whose values are embedded into the technology, who is excluded as a result, and whether this is justified in the eyes of the law, in the light of moral principles and in the eyes of the individuals who may be affected by the way in which a given technology operates. The notion of fairness has been studied within moral and political philosophy for centuries (see, e.g., Rawls' (1958) justice as fairness). Recently, the notion of fairness has also become a subject of particular interest in AI research and engineering. In the AI engineering context, one aim is to furnish algorithms with *fairness metrics*, through quantifying the notion of fairness, to enable appropriate mitigation of any biases and related harms. In this context, there is an inevitable tension between the social and computational sciences conceptions of fairness. Attempting to mathematically quantify a context- and perspective-dependent notion of fairness is considered non-trivial, if not doomed to failure. To paraphrase Narayanan, fairness cannot be equated with the number 0.78 (or any other number for that matter), however hard computer scientists might try, because of the definitional multiplicity of the construct of fairness, which is socio-culturally, institutionally, situationally and subjectively determined (Barocas et al., 2021; Narayanan, 2018).

To illustrate his point, Narayanan identifies at least 21 different definitions of fairness within computer science alone, depending on whose perspective one assumes: (a) the perspective of the designer, in which the fairness-related questions asked of an algorithm will concern its *predictive value*, such as the algorithm's ability to classify data correctly with respect to some feature of interest, (b) the perspective of the person affected (who may or may not agree with the given decision) or (c) the perspective of society, in which the question of fairness is considered in terms of its benefits for a wider group and where the interests of any given individual may be overridden. With respect to society's perspective, any evaluation of what is and is not fair will be made based on what is considered socio-culturally acceptable within any given socio-historical context. In particular, if specific biases form part of a given culture or society's habitual perceptions (e.g., the perception of inferiority of some social groups as in racial discrimination or deviation from some culturally established notion of the norm as is routinely experienced by neurodivergent groups), then these biases will inevitably infiltrate any local interpretation of fairness and the related actions. Thus, fairness is by no means a neutral notion. Hence, the questions we ask about fairness and the way in which we approach algorithmic fairness cannot simply be about mathematical neutrality, but rather about people's preferences, judgements, beliefs, desires and needs – with an accompanying explicit acknowledgement that, when it comes to different perspectives, neutrality is virtually impossible.

The challenges of furnishing AI systems with fairness are highlighted when we consider the different types of fairness at play. Discussions about AI fairness centre on two dimensions: (a) *individual fairness* (judged in terms of the outcomes for individuals) vs. *group fairness* (judged in terms of outcomes for groups of individuals defined along some common identity criteria), and (b) *outcome fairness* (i.e., *equality of the results* of certain processes for groups or individuals) vs. *process fairness* (i.e., *equality of treatment* defined by the factors that bear on how the specific processes come about and are undertaken). Friedler et al. (2016) demonstrate that reconciling these dimensions is effectively impossible, since the different perspectives often lead to conflicting interpretations of what is and what is not fair: what may seem fair for one group may be deemed unfair for another group or it may seem completely unfair to specific individuals. Hence, there is an acute need in AI engineering to make explicit the diverse and often conflicting assumptions that underpin the particular conceptions of fairness embedded in the system. The nature of the goals of any given system, its efficacy in achieving those goals, the target users, the context for which a system is being designed and in which it is being deployed and evaluated, all need to be made *transparent*. Simultaneously, the system's operation needs to be made *explainable* for the users for the systems to be rendered trustworthy and their designers and decision-makers to be made accountable for the outcomes resulting from their systems' use.

ETHICAL CONSIDERATIONS FOR AI IN EDUCATION

The key ethical considerations reviewed, including the specific issues related to algorithmic bias, the associated harm and fairness are of direct pertinence to AIED (see also Chapter 25 by Williamson et al. and Chapter 16 by Brooks et al.). As an academic field, AIED inherently aims to contribute to a fairer, more equitable, more accountable and more educated global society either by helping to reduce attainment gaps (O'Shea, 1979; Reich & Ito, 2017; VanLehn, 2011), or by addressing specific gaps in existing education systems (Saxena et al., 2018; Uchiduino et al., 2018; Madaio et al., 2020; Holstein & Doroudi, 2022). Driven by those aspirations and shaped by its central focus on supporting and enhancing human learning, the field has invested in design, usage and evaluation practices (some decades ahead of other AI subfields), that are explicitly aimed to generate evidence of the efficacy and safety of the AIED systems for human learners, for example, through methods adopted from the psychological and learning sciences. As a design discipline, the field has also invested in increasing the relevance of the AIED technologies to diverse users, such as through the application of user-centred and participatory design methods (Porayska-Pomsta et al., 2013; Porayska-Pomsta & Rajendran, 2018) and in improving the accuracy, transparency and explainability of the underlying models, notably through *glass box* approaches such as the open learner models (Bull & Kay, 2016; Conati et al., 2018; see also Chapter 6 by Kay et al.). AIED, therefore, has an important contribution to offer to the wider AI community with respect to the methods, practices and examples of rigorous research that respond to many Ethical AI research recommendations and concerns (Conati et al., 2018). However, the *a priori* intended beneficence of the AIED has also led to a certain level of complacency with respect to identifying and addressing any real and potential ethical blind spots for the field (Holmes et al., 2021), which are now increasingly being identified and examined by the AIED community (Holmes & Porayska-Pomsta, 2022).

In their overview of the key issues surrounding the ethics of AI for education, Holstein and Doroudi (2022) identify two overarching levels at which questions about the ethics of AIED need to be addressed: (a) the *socio-technical level*, including the questions about equity of access to and benefits from using technology, and about the mutual influence that the socio-technical system and AI exert on each other; and (b) the *AIED Interface level*, where the underlying data and AI algorithms, as also considered for AI more broadly, need to be examined. A key tenet of their account is that developing a deep understanding of the ethical quality of AIED systems requires one to examine AIED through multiple lenses at those two levels. It is only by adopting such multiple lenses that a balanced understanding of the ethics of AIED approaches and systems can be achieved. We now briefly review the key factors pertaining to the two levels identified by Holstein and Doroudi, and, through illustrative examples from AIED, we elaborate on how this overarching framing of AIED's ethics aligns with the broader Ethical AI considerations reviewed in the earlier sections. As well as allowing to situate the ethics of AIED within the broader ethical AI debates, such an alignment is needed to identify specific areas where AIED can help advance those debates.

Equity of Access to Advanced Technologies in AIED

The *digital divide*, between those who have access to suitable technologies and those who do not, has been the subject of research in education and of ongoing discussions within policy and media since the first wave of ICT in Education in the early 2000s. The digital divide has been formally defined as 'the gap between individuals, households, businesses and geographic areas at different socioeconomic levels with regard both to their opportunities to access ICT and to their use of the Internet for a wide variety of activities' (OECD, 2001, p. 4). In other words, certain groups do not have suitable access to ICT – a prerequisite for being able to use AI applications. This is a disparity which holds implications for people's quality of life and the opportunities that are available to them. In this context, cautious observers of the recent drive to introduce and promote AI for Education have reasoned that in the best interests of students and teachers, before determining whether AI is of benefit to schools, it is necessary first to obtain rigorous evidence of both qualitative and quantitative dimensions of AIED (Facer &

Selwyn, 2021; Holmes et al., 2019; Nemorin, 2021). Central to these discussions is the question of how AI might exacerbate the digital divide and social inequities, rather than close the gaps, with some suggesting that AI in education may potentially result in amplified advantages for the individuals and organisations that have the ability to capitalise on it, while it disadvantages those who do not possess the requisite skills to use AI effectively (Carter et al., 2020). The digital divide is typically determined by socio-economic factors, deriving from a combination of representational and allocative biases. In the context of education, where technology is increasingly incorporated as an essential tool for learning, and with education being a compulsory component of people's lives from early years to adulthood, the harms that might result from such biases being reinforced through AIED are likely to be profound and long term.

The challenges related to equity of access to education are not limited solely to socio-economic factors or even to specific countries or world regions. This was put in sharp focus during the COVID-19 pandemic, when in many contexts online learning became the norm and where many students were periodically excluded from education because they lacked adequate equipment or access to the internet at home, even in technologically enabled countries. Lack of up-to-date or sufficient quantity of equipment is also a known issue in many schools in many countries (Baker, 2019). This leads to some schools being disadvantaged not only in terms of whether their pupils can access diverse technologies, but also whether their student populations are represented in research that powers 'computerised' or 'AI interventions' designs.

The unLOCKE project (Gauthier, 2021; Gauthier et al., 2022; Wilkinson et al., 2019) offers a recent and quite common example. This project aimed to ascertain the efficacy of a computerised neuroscience intervention to support primary school children in learning how to inhibit impulsive and incorrect responses to counterintuitive maths and science problems. Substantial intervention and deployment challenges were experienced by the researchers owing to a large proportion of schools, mainly in rural areas, not having adequate equipment or reliable internet access. This determined how the intervention was delivered, and limited what kind of data could be collected, which prevented the researchers from gaining valuable access to the diversity of children's experiences and interaction patterns necessary to inform adaptive components of the system. While justifiable, this raises questions regarding the representational quality of the data collected and illustrates how representation bias often arises and persists in AIED research. Other studies related to the impact of children's access to technology suggest that children with access to desktop or laptop computers are more likely (52%) to use technology for learning than those who have mobile-only access (35% of children) (Holstein & Doroudi, 2022; Rideout & Katz, 2016). Furthermore, stakeholders' (teachers, parents, school administrators) familiarity with and access to diverse ICT also impacts on whether there is the skill, the daring and the appetite for innovative technology-mediated pedagogies.

Equity of Accessibility of AIED Systems

Access to prerequisite equipment is not the only source of ethical concerns in this context. Holstein and Doroudi highlight an important point related to linguistic and cultural *accessibility* of technology. In their examples of the under-explored barriers to equity of educational outcomes, they highlight the dominance of the mainstream language communication models and cultural references in the content (usually American or British English) of many AIED systems. Such models and references, when used with learners from non-dominant backgrounds, non-native speakers or vernacular language speakers (e.g., African American Vernacular English speakers: AAVE) likely hinder the accessibility of such technologies and reduce any resulting benefits. Indeed, Finklestein (2013) demonstrated that students using AAVE as their main language are likely to show greater scientific reasoning when interacting with technology that communicates with them in AAVE than in mainstream American English, suggesting that an investment in environments that are culturally and linguistically aligned with the learners may be essential to removing certain barriers to learning and academic achievement.

A broader point that relates to the culturally and linguistically inflexible designs of AIED is how learners' familiarity with the content presented affects their learning (e.g., maths problems situated in contexts familiar to students), the way in which such content might be delivered (e.g., through linguistically heavy word problems in maths vs. abstract equations), and specific learning methods (e.g., individual vs. collaborative learning methods). Culture-comparative neuroscience in education research (Ngan Ng & Rao, 2010; Tang & Liu, 2009) suggests that how we learn is not just related superficially to our specific cultural and linguistic traditions, but that it is also reflected in how we engage with learning content at a deep neurocognitive level. For example, functional magenetic resonance imaging (fMRI) studies provide emerging evidence of the differences between Western (sic American) and Eastern (sic Chinese) students' mathematical problem solving. These differences are often conditioned by culturally determined ways of teaching mathematics in the USA vs. China and by the influence of language (in particular, number words in Chinese vs. English) on student number conceptualisation. In turn, how students conceptualise numbers has a knock-on effect on the efficacy of their mathematical problem solving. Bearing this emerging knowledge and culture comparative evidence in mind, it is important to interrogate the questions about what exactly AIED systems ought to adapt, to whom they should adapt and how they might create environments aligned with students' cultural and linguistic backgrounds.

Related to questions about how AIED adaptive support might contribute to more culturally inclusive education are questions about AIED inclusive practices in the context of physically disabled and neurodiverse learners (or more generally – *differently abled* learners). There is a notable paucity of effort within AIED in this context, with a vast majority of AIED systems being geared towards mainstream education. This not only constitutes a pronounced representational bias in the field, but it also occludes important opportunities for innovation. For example, looking through the perspective of human–computer interaction design, Treviranus (2022) observes that research focused on the 'norm' rarely can be transferred to those outside the so-called 'norm', whereas going in the opposite direction is relatively straightforward. The emphasis on the so-called norm, in turn, proliferates exclusive practices within education and representational harms of recognition, under-representation and ex-nomination (see earlier sections). The few examples of AIED systems that focus on neurodiversity (Rashedi et al., 2020; Porayska-Pomsta et al., 2018; Benton et al., 2021) suggest that AIED's relative lack of emphasis on non-mainstream education is a missed opportunity not only with respect to enhancing AIED's inclusive practices, but also for leveraging the affordances of digital technologies and insights from special needs education to enhance the adaptive capabilities of AIED systems. This is particularly important for the deployment of AIED systems in a way that is relevant to users in specific contexts, and to making a real and positive difference for a diversity of learners (Porayska-Pomsta & Rajendran, 2019). For example, based on the ECHOES project (Porayska-Pomsta et al., 2018), which focused on developing AIED support for autistic children's social communication skills acquisition via an adaptive virtual peer, the SHARE-IT project (Porayska-Pomsta et al., 2013) investigated how the AIED system's interaction and pedagogy may be enhanced by allowing parents and teachers to modify user and communication models of the ECHOES AIED system. The findings suggest an acute need for technologies that are not pedagogically prescriptive, which give educational practitioners the flexibility to change diverse parameters such as timings and types of feedback given by the system and which allow for *shareability* of the models between stakeholders to enable adaptation that is bespoke to individual learners.

The idea of modifiable models, as discussed above, is aligned with the ethos of editable and negotiable open learner models (OLMs; see Bull & Kay, 2016), with the difference being that the users doing the editing are educators and caregivers. The insights here, which may be easily missed in mainstream contexts of education, are two-fold. The first insight relates to the role that AIED systems can play in fostering the development of shared support mechanisms for individual learners that rely on in-depth negotiation between different environments inhabited by the learners, such as between home and school. Through negotiation, facilitated by the specialised AIED approaches such as OLMs, educators and caregivers are better enabled to understand learners' needs across diverse contexts and to deliver holistic support. In extreme cases, this can lead to a complete overhaul of the approaches adopted with the individual learners, since the behaviours manifested at home may be sometimes or completely absent in classroom environments (e.g., the willingness of a child to communicate; Bernardini et al., 2012). Thus, understanding learners in diverse contexts is often necessary for creating entirely new support environments (physical and pedagogical) in which they can build on their strengths rather than be identified by their deficits (Guldberg et al., 2017). The second, related insight spotlights the need for flexible designs and open models that can be modified by education experts and caretakers *on demand* and according to the changing circumstances and needs of the students. Such changing needs and circumstances may be inaccessible to even the most sophisticated AIED systems. Naturally, creating such flexible designs does present substantial technical challenges, but it also raises a possibility of creating AIED systems that are more attuned to their users, that inspire and aid improvements in the wider system of education and that more readily reflect the field's aspirations to improve educational and life outcomes for all. Indeed, such flexible designs also align with an emergent vision of responsible AI more broadly – a vision that challenges the ethical and societal value of the standard model on which AI systems are presently based (Russell, 2019; Porayska-Pomsta & Holmes, 2022).

Equity of AIED's Pedagogies

Linked to the learning support innovations that may be missed because of representational biases in AIED's research is the issue of the dominant pedagogies that are promoted through AIED's systems. Driven by the ambition to achieve the 2-sigma effect identified by Bloom and his colleagues in the context of one-to-one mastery learning, AIED as a field has disproportionately concentrated its efforts on drill-and-practice type of pedagogies, and exam-type assessments. This, combined with the relatively easy-to-model and assess well-defined science subjects, gives rise to forms of bias that are very specific to the context of education. We propose to call these biases the *domain-value bias* and the *learning-culture bias*, respectively. The *domain-value bias* refers to society valuing some subject domains more than others. Arguably, mathematical and biological sciences are presently considered more valuable than arts subjects. This is acutely visible in the national curricula across much of the world, where subjects such as history or arts are no longer obligatory, while other subjects, such as philosophy, are poorly subscribed to at universities.

We use the term *learning-culture bias* to refer to some modes of learning tending to be more dominant and more *bankable* in mainstream educational contexts than others. For example, drill-and-practice, exam-oriented type of learning tends to dominate in many mainstream educational contexts across the world as it forms part of a wider educational machinery that requires educational institutions' administrators and politicians to quantify (usually in monetary terms) people's intellectual and societal worth. However, while in some circumstances, the mastery-learning and exam-based pedagogies are of value to the development of people's skills and erudition, they often leave little room for curiosity-driven enquiry, exploration, discovery, collaboration or for productive failure. In this, they contribute to the proliferation and entrenchment of an oppressive educational system, where increasingly, one can only be either an A* genius or an academic failure (e.g., see typical university entry requirements in the UK). While systems that employ OLMs or those that promote self-regulation and metacognitive skills in their pedagogies (Bull & Kay, 2016; Blair et al., 2007; Chapter 9 by Aleven et al.) implicitly mitigate some of this bias, it is important to interrogate whether AIED's ethical value might be enhanced by the field's greater investment in going against the established grain within a broader educational system to offer more diverse and daring forms of learning supports.

Both the domain-value and learning-culture biases within the broader education systems are exploited and reinforced by the EdTech industry, much of which has seized on the current AI hype. While the extent to which many of the EdTech companies actually offer AIED-driven systems is debatable, it is hard to overlook the EdTech industry's efforts, encouraged by policy makers, to bank on the exam-driven, hard sciences favouring education system. In this context, Blikstein (2018) spotlighted a number of disturbing EdTech trends of pertinence to the ethics of AIED, which proliferate and reinforce questionable pedagogical practices. Specifically, he highlighted the persistent rhetoric surrounding EdTech and the policy's push towards embedding technologies in classrooms and the related funding in and out of academia (see also Madaio, 2022; Chapter 23 by Ritter & Koedinger). This rhetoric focuses on persistent, but broadly unevidenced claims of technologies' ability to rescue teachers from boring and repetitive tasks by making learning management information systems more efficient in order to allow teachers and administrators to allocate their time more efficiently to less mundane tasks (Miao & Holmes, 2021; Watters, 2021), and on technologies' ability to offer endless explanations to students, along with opportunities for repetition, drill-and-practice and breaking content into tiny pieces of information. He spotlighted the ethical risks associated with adopting this rhetoric, which stands in stark contrast with evidence-based educational practices that have debunked the transmitter model of education as both inefficient and oppressive (Blikstein, 2018). Ultimately, not only the rhetoric behind the educational technologies' industry fails to align with the best educational practices, but the industry's practices are also notorious for lack of any auditing procedures (du Boulay, 2022) that would ensure the safety of the systems for the learners, some as young as toddlers. Here, a key question for AIED as a field relates to its potential role in guiding the best EdTech practices and highlighting both the opportunities for educational innovation and identifying and addressing related ethical challenges.

Interaction between Human and Machine Autonomy

Important ethical considerations also arise because of context-specific interactions between humans and the AI artefacts. Holstein and Doroudi (2022) highlight the importance of appreciating the complexity of the socio-technological ecosystem, including the AI systems (the artefacts), the designers of the technology and the users (decision makers, teachers, school, administrators and learners). They emphasise the need to design carefully for the interplay between the different elements within this ecosystem to ensure more equitable futures for AI in Education. They observe that even if AIED or Learning Analytics do not contain harmful biases in their underlying algorithms or data, the way in which they are mediated at the user interface level may still lead to potentially undesirable or harmful effects, through the systems' interaction with the users' pre-existing beliefs and habits. They suggest that it is critical to consider the intent with which a tool is built, and the human–AI interaction that is facilitated. They focus specifically on the example of teachers as users and propose that if a tool has the capacity to challenge users' *a priori* beliefs and ways of thinking, then it may help them develop and/or adopt more equitable practices. If a tool does not possess such capabilities, then it may only serve to reinforce pre-existing beliefs and associated biases. Ultimately, while humans shape the technology to their needs and aspirations, the technology inevitably also shapes the humans. A key conclusion delivered by Holstein and Doroudi is that to address any ethical challenges in AIED, the field ought to be centrally concerned with understanding and designing for such human–AI feedback loops.

The idea that we shape our technologies and are shaped by them in return is well rehearsed within the philosophy of technology and AI: from Kelly's concept of *technium* – a self-reinforcing system of technological inventions and reinventions (Kelly, 2010), through Kurzweil's ideas around technological singularity arising from ever-accelerating technological inventions (Kurzweil, 2014), to more recent discussions by Russell of the fundamental ways in which technology changes us (Russell, 2020), and Harrari's historically situated examination of the rise of biotech as means for human enhancement (Harrari, 2019). Although these perspectives may seem far away from the AIED work and focus, we argue that they in fact raise fundamental questions for the field and demand new lines of investigation that pertain to the impact of the AIED technologies on users' cognition, perception of their environment and decision-making capacities that go beyond subject-based assessment of knowledge. They put in sharp relief the possibility of trade-offs related to technological enhancements, such as scheduling systems that allow us to be more organised at the cost of lost opportunities for exercising working memory (The Royal Society, 2019); or use of learning analytics to aid assessment of students in quantifiable curricula, potentially at the cost of lost opportunities for teachers to rehearse and critically appraise their students' journeys as developing humans who inhabit complex socio-emotional environments (see also Chapter 5 by Arroyo et al. in this volume). Here the questions for the field go beyond the specific AIED systems that we build. They extend to the need to interrogate what role AIED as a field that is concerned with the interaction between AI and human cognition wants to and can play in influencing and shaping education of the future. These questions spotlight that the ethics of AIED are not only about addressing biases and harms within the systems we build, but they are also fundamentally about how the field contributes (actively or through complacency) to entrenching education as an exam-passing machine and also potentially to de-skilling and de-professionalisation of teachers by virtue of automating some of the most important of their tasks such as assessment of students – a task, demanding and time consuming as it is, that allows teachers to connect with their students as living, breathing, developing humans.

The Ethics of Datasets, Algorithms and Methods in AIED

Many of the ethical considerations related to data, algorithmic bias and methods used in AI apply more generally in the context of AIED. Specifically, many of the same ethical challenges and questions that arise during the machine-learning pipeline discussed in earlier sections, are of relevance to educational contexts. Issues of allocative and representational bias can be observed across AIED work, with substantial gaps related to the diversity of demographic categories also being apparent. Earlier in this chapter, we offered some examples of how representational bias may arise, such as limited access to schools with adequate equipment. Baker and Hawn (2021) provide a detailed inventory of groups of learners (categorised by demographics and protected characteristics) for whom there is little data in AIED research. Specifically, AIED datasets lack in diversity with respect to students' different ethnicities, nationalities, different-*ableness* (physical and neurocognitive), urbanicity, parental education, socio-economic status, international students and military-connected status. Inclusion or exclusion of any of these categories in the AIED designs may lead to disparities in the fairness of treatment by and outcomes from using an AIED system. In previous subsections, we discussed some of the representational biases in and out of the context of education. For a detailed inventory and analysis of the representational gaps in AIED research, we refer the interested reader to Baker and Hawn (2021). In this section, we instead focus briefly on the challenges related to algorithmic fairness in AIED and the methods that are available or that we should be developing to mitigate bias in AIED systems. Understanding these challenges is important for formulating ethics-related questions that AIED researchers need to consider before, during, and after the design and deployment of their systems.

Algorithmic fairness in AIED

Kizilcec and Lee (2022) and Baker and Hawn (2021) offer two of the most recent overviews of issues pertaining to algorithmic fairness and related data collection methods in the context of AIED, drawing attention to the types of assumptions and methodologies that impact on the quality of data and algorithms in AI applications for education. Kizilcec and Lee elaborate on the challenges identified in the broader AI context with respect to defining fairness and building fairness into AIED algorithms. They highlight equity and equality as two somewhat contradictory central notions related to fairness in education, and they link those notions to questions about disparities between how AIED's diverse users are treated vs. how they are impacted by an algorithmic intervention. Specifically, while equality may be achieved through innovation if all individuals benefit the same amount regardless of their pre-existing capabilities, to achieve equity (i.e., closing the achievement gaps) the impact of innovation must be positively greater for those who start from behind. This positioning presents a set of questions, likely some dilemmas, and the obligation of transparency for AIED designers with respect to both what form of algorithmic fairness they choose to furnish their systems with and what claims they can make about the generalisability of their applications to diverse users and contexts.

Three representative notions of fairness are discussed by Kizilcec and Lee, each highlighting different and not necessarily compatible ways in which fairness may be considered. The first notion of fairness is *statistical fairness*, which relies on three fairness criteria: (a) *independence*, which is satisfied if an algorithm's decisions are independent of group membership; (b) *separation*, which is satisfied if the algorithm makes correct or incorrect predictions independently of a group membership; and (c) *sufficiency*, which is satisfied if an algorithm's decisions are equally significant for all groups. All three criteria can be useful in enhancing algorithmic fairness, but all three can also lead to unpredictable outcomes, depending on the context and purpose of the algorithm's application (see also Baker and Hawn (2021) for a discussion of the trade-offs between these different fairness metrics and fairness of outcomes).

Approaches to the second notion of fairness, *similarity-based*, are known as group measures of fairness, because they ignore individual features of and differences between cases. Typically, fairness criteria for similarity-based approaches include *fairness through unawareness*, that is, achieved by ignoring any protected attributes in the data during model training; and *individual fairness*, which involves constructing similarity metrics between individuals for specific prediction tasks. While evaluations of the fairness through unawareness approach suggest improvements in accuracy in some decision-making contexts such as algorithmic admissions systems (Kleinberg et al., 2018; Yu et al., 2020), they also carry a danger of a model inadvertently reconstructing the protected attributes from features which may seem unrelated. The individual fairness metric addresses this issue, but its specific weakness relates to its reliance on distance metrics (which may also contain fairness imbalances) and on the assumption that treating similar individuals similarly will lead to the same outcomes.

The final notion of fairness discussed by Kizilcec and Lee is the *causal notion of fairness*, whereby an algorithm can be considered fair if it produces the same predictions under different counterfactual scenarios, for example, predicting the same outcome for an individual by varying a specific feature, such as gender, while keeping all other known features constant. The idea behind this approach derives from the observation that understanding how different predictions might change for different group memberships relies on causal inference. While offering a way to evaluate equality of predictions, the causal notion of fairness relies on the validity of a causal model, which needs to make predictions based largely on observational data. Therefore, this approach is itself open to incorporating diverse biases.

While the above three notions of fairness and the corresponding approaches represent only a subset of existing conceptualisations of algorithmic fairness, they demonstrate the difficulty of finding a principled way of selecting metrics of fairness and indeed, of measuring fairness in a way that satisfies all possible scenarios of AIED applications. In this context, Kizilcec and Lee suggest that more than one approach may be needed to evaluate fairness for each AIED scenario. Such an approach would promote concrete discussions about the ethical value of any specific AIED system. However, facilitating such discussions demands from the AIED designers clarity and transparency of goals related to equity and equality that their specific systems aim to deliver.

Methodological considerations for ethical AIED

Fundamental to the choices of fairness metrics are also questions about data collection methods used in AIED. Baker and Hawn (2021) draw attention to the critical role of data collection choices in mitigating diverse forms of algorithmic bias downstream in system development and deployment. Specifically, they focus on two key forms of data bias in AIED, namely representational bias and measurement bias, and on the corresponding methods that may lead to or mitigate against those biases. Addressing representational bias in data is fundamental to developing AIED systems that cater for diverse learners and contexts of use. Achieving representationally balanced data is not trivial and cannot be guaranteed by simply adopting a proportional sampling method. Although Baker and Hawn recommend that over-sampling is better than under-sampling, they also highlight real-world obstacles in this context, such as the tendency of only certain groups of participants (e.g., learners in privileged socio-economic urban areas) to be available to take part in data collection efforts, of the lack of appropriate infrastructure in schools or of access to technology at home, as well as research-readiness of institutions and individual decision makers responsible for promoting or facilitating links between institutions and academic research.

Following Suresh and Guttag (2020), earlier in this chapter, we defined measurement bias as potentially arising in training labels and predictor variables. Baker and Hawn contextualise this for some of the most common methods employed in AIED research. They are mainly concerned with the measurement bias that arises in training labels and they provide a number of indicative examples that are pertinent to AIED. They include in their list labelling bias that arises from (a) historical prejudices such as racism which might discriminate against specific populations (e.g., students of colour); (b) mismatch between the culture of the coders and the culture of the learners whose data is being encoded (e.g., when coding emotions based on facial expressions), and (c) self-reporting (in which learners may carry a bias towards self, due to diverse possible factors such as lack of confidence, cultural factors or fear of being stereotyped or judged).

While Baker and Hawn are less clear on the subject of predictor bias, it is also important to consider how such bias may influence the ethical value of an AIED system, in particular whether it offers a reasonable proxy for the kind of thing that the system is trying to predict. This is particularly important in the context of student modelling where interaction data with the system is often used to predict things such as student understanding of a topic, based on their performance on specific problems or level of interaction with the system. In this context, the appropriateness and validity of the predictors chosen have to be examined in the context of the pedagogies that an AIED aims to encapsulate. For example, if an AIED system's purpose is to train students to perform well on particular types of problems, then while the students may do well on such problems, they may still not have a good knowledge of the other related elements of the domain within which these problems exist.

It is important to acknowledge that, while many ethics-related questions need to be considered at every step in an AIED system development, in many ways, as a design science, AIED has been ahead of other subfields of AI in the adoption of methods that connect AIED systems and algorithms with the humans who use them. There are many exemplars of user-centred and participatory design approaches across different AIED projects (see Grawemayer et al., 2017; Porayska-Pomsta et al., 2018), with knowledge elicitation methodologies and contextualised interaction data forming the backbone of many AIED models and decision-making processes. In this, AIED has always aimed to be not only relevant to the users, but also educationally efficacious, and AIED researchers have long understood the importance of the contextual and representational validity of data, and of the methods used to generate such data (Porayska-Pomsta et al., 2013). Open Learner Models (OLMs) are in many ways unique to AIED insofar as they offer the users a degree of ownership over their data, explicitly acknowledging that AI models are not accurate and that AI *transparency* and *explainability* plays a pivotal role in supporting human learning and criticality (Bull & Kay, 2016; Chapter 6 by Kay et al. in this volume; Conati et al., 2019). In a number of ways, OLMs may represent the future for AIED – for increasing the field's ethical value in its practices and solutions – a future which also aligns with the recommendations of Holstein et al. (2019) for how to address the challenges of bias and how to improve on the fairness of AIED by allowing the educational practitioners to collect data themselves.

TOWARDS A FRAMEWORK OF ETHICS OF AIED

In this chapter, we have emphasised the need for any effective ethics of AIED to be robustly grounded in broader ethical debates – specifically, the ethics of AI in general, in moral philosophy, and in the ethics of educational practice. Yet, as we have noted, while a large number of ethical principles are frequently invoked for AI in general, it is not always clear how those principles are best enacted in the particular domain in which the AI is being applied. While issues such as the ethics of data use (e.g., consent and data privacy) and the ethics of models and algorithmic computations (e.g., transparency and fairness) are transversal – they have relevance for all domains in which AI is applied – the AI domains of healthcare, transport, ecology, education, and others self-evidently all have domain-specific ethical issues that also need to be properly considered and addressed (Holmes et al., 2021). Ethical challenges in education that need to be thoroughly considered include the accuracy and validity of assessments, what constitutes useful knowledge, educators' roles and agency in selecting pedagogies that suit their learners' needs best, and particular approaches to pedagogy.

To help AIED practitioners conceptualise and address the ethics of AIED in their work, elsewhere we hypothesised a 'strawman' draft framework (Holmes et al., 2021) (Figure 26.1). This framework, which begins with the three ethics foci identified (data, models and education) was designed for the purpose of stimulating discussion. In this framework, data, models and education constitute the foundational level; while at the overlaps is a second level: the ethics of data in AI (Floridi & Cowls, 2019), the ethics of data in education (Ferguson et al., 2016) and the ethics of models and algorithms applied in educational contexts, the last of which remains the least developed area of research. There is also the central intersection: the specific interaction between AI systems and human cognition at the individual level (indicated by the question mark in Figure 26.1).

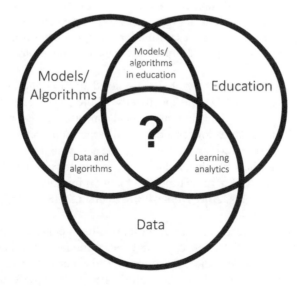

Source: Based on Holmes et al. (2021)

Figure 26.1   *'Strawman' framework for the ethics of AIED*

This framework was proposed as a first step in the necessary conversation and, as such, it is open to refinements by insights from all the emergent work in this area. Here, we propose a second step, by recognising and disambiguating two fundamental dimensions of the broader concept of education: (1) pedagogy, or educational practices and (2) the socio-technical context within which education happens. In Table 26.2, we explore this amended framework (comprising four foci: 'Data', 'Models/Algorithms', 'Pedagogy' and the 'Socio-technical context') in terms of the different biases identified throughout this chapter. For each, we offer an example problem and a necessary (but by no means exhaustive) set of questions that AIED practitioners may need to consider and address. How we as a community formulate and address such questions may have profound existential implications for how our societies and our cultures progress and develop, and our individual social, cognitive and physical functioning changes. Accordingly, for each set of problems and questions, we also offer an indicative set of consequences or risks associated with the diverse biases. This approach aims to avoid the framework becoming or being seen as only generating a list of prohibitions to stop 'unethical' AI in education activities. Instead, the aim is to provide a foundation to facilitate forward thinking and *ethics-conscious AIED research and development by design.*

CONCLUSIONS

AI has been and continues to be presented as an opportunity for successfully tackling global education challenges. Given the COVID-19 pandemic, recent discussions have focused on how AI might progress education by enabling teaching and learning online. Companies have scrambled to gain entry into a lucrative educational technology market, spurring calls and demands for EdTech as the foundational infrastructure for accessible remote learning (Williamson, 2021). Popular media and online/offline spaces representing AIED stakeholders (individuals, groups and organisations, for example) suggest general acceptance that AI *is* the future of education and AI *will* provide a solution for achieving the Sustainable Development Goal 4: 'Ensure inclusive and equitable quality education and promote lifelong learning opportunities for all'.

However, throughout this chapter, we have discussed diverse questions and challenges related to the ethics of AI and AIED more specifically. While AI can certainly be of benefit to education, there are social, environmental and ethical concerns that cannot be ignored when weighing the value of AI *for* education, especially when the implementation of AI can result in unfair practices that centre on who has access to these new technologies, or who has access to education at all. These kinds of ethical challenges, if left unexamined by the AIED community, can potentially result in perpetuating and maintaining forms of bias against historically oppressed bodies (Eubanks, 2018; Noble, 2018; Reuters, 2018; O'Neil, 2017; ProPublica, 2016).

In this chapter, we have focused only on a subset of ethical considerations of relevance to AIED. There are further ethical challenges related to data management, liability, data ownership, data privacy and to who sets the educational agenda. For example, related to liability issues, if students' personal data were sold to a third party without the knowledge of the student, it is not clear who should be accountable: Is it the system's commercial developer? Is it the teacher? Or is it the school? The pandemic has also rendered in stark relief that educational technologies for remote learning have been largely concentrated in a handful of transnational

Table 26.2   *Key considerations and questions for AIED designers and users*

| | Dimensions of AIED design and deployment | | | |
	AIED data	AIED models/algorithms	AIED pedagogy	Socio-technical context
Historic	**Problem:**			
	• Historic datasets harbouring prejudices or stereotypes (e.g., boys are good at sciences, girls are good at arts)	• Pre-existent prejudices or inflexible pedagogies encoded in the choice of an objective function or heuristics (e.g., language models based on mainstream language forms such as mainstream American or British English for learners who speak vernacular English)	• Inflexible or limited or outdated pedagogies such as knowledge transmission, drill-and-practice approaches	• Students from lower socioeconomic backgrounds or minorities having lower access to resources • Education as a mechanism for transmitting information, and training students to pass exams • Devaluation of soft skills and subject domains
	Questions:			
	• How old is your data? • Where does it come from? • Have you checked for prejudices and stereotypes therein?	• Who are your target learners and contexts of use? • Have you checked that your assumptions are adequate for those learners and contexts?	• Is the choice of pedagogy adequate for the educational goals you aim to achieve? • How flexible is your system in allowing users to modify the pedagogical model?	• Is your system affordable and usable across contexts? • Have you accounted for the infrastructure available in the target context? • Is your system reinforcing or innovating existing educational practices?
	Consequences/Risks:			
	• Harm of representation • Outcome fairness • Equity of access	• Harm of representation • Outcome fairness • Equity of accessibility	• Harm of representation • Equity of accessibility • Outcome fairness • Process Fairness • Human autonomy	• Harm of allocation • Harm of representation • Outcome fairness • Equity of Access • Equity of Accessibility

(Continued)

Table 26.2   (*Continued*)

Dimensions of AIED design and deployment			
AIED data	AIED models/algorithms	AIED pedagogy	Socio-technical context

Representational

Problem:

AIED data	AIED models/algorithms	AIED pedagogy	Socio-technical context
• Sampling is not representative of student populations (e.g., data contains gender, race, urbanicity bias etc.).	• Models that generalise assumptions (objective function, or inference) reflecting limited population subsets or designers/software developers' pre-conceptions.	• Prescriptive pedagogies which accommodate and enforce limited learning cultures (e.g., exam-oriented drill and practice).	• AIED aims not being representative of educators' aims or diverse learners' needs.

Questions:

AIED data	AIED models/algorithms	AIED pedagogy	Socio-technical context
• Who are the target populations for your system? • Is your data representative of all students and contexts in which you envisage your AIED, some, or only one specific context?	• How are your models' assumptions validated? • Do your choices of objective function/inference align with diverse learners' behaviours, cultures, and forms of communication?	• Is your AIED able to accommodate different learning cultures and needs of the users? • How flexible are your pedagogical and communication models?	• Does your system respond to a diversity of needs of educators and/or learners? • How did you establish those needs (e.g., through literature, by working with diverse stakeholders, etc.)?

Consequences/risks:

AIED data	AIED models/algorithms	AIED pedagogy	Socio-technical context
• Harm of representation • Equity of accessibility • Outcome fairness	• Harm of representation • Equity of accessibility • Outcome fairness • Process fairness	• Harm of representation • Equity of accessibility • Outcome fairness • Process fairness • Human autonomy	• Harm of representation • Equity of accessibility

Measurement	Problem:		Questions:	
	• Sampling is not representative of student populations (e.g., data contains gender, race, urbanicity bias etc.). • Sampling is inconsistent between contexts • Mismatch between data coders' and data donors' cultures (e.g., Americans coding emotional states of Turkish students). • Inappropriate choice of a predictor variable (e.g., conflating login/logoff duration with engagement or clicking a document download link with reading the document). • Objective function or inference mechanism based on.	• Mismatch between learners' needs and the support they receive (e.g., neuro-divergent learners receiving support designed for neuro-typical learners including inappropriately timed or volume of feedback, over-reliance on reading instructions, etc.). • Misinterpretation of learner behaviours, leading to inaccurate or unfair assessments. • Reliance on data from dominant groups to devise pedagogies and school/district/national educational policies. • Entrenchment of limited forms of assessment. • De-skilling educators by introducing process and outcome measures (e.g., through LMSs, which may be inaccurate, inadequate, or meaningless to educators (click data as a measure of engagement, response on specific test problems as a measure of student knowledge).	• Have you checked for proportionality in your sample vis-à-vis the target population? • Have you controlled for the consistency of application of methods and procedures across contexts (e.g., by training and auditing researchers collecting data in different schools)? • Is there cultural alignment between data coders and data donors? • Did you verify the pedagogical and cultural validity of your predictors (e.g., using student click data to predict engagement, or norms of one culture to predict student emotions of another culture)? • How did you verify the validity of your predictors (e.g., by following other researchers, by exploring with and eliciting from experts)? • Can users negotiate with/ change your models (e.g., through OLM; adjusting/ choosing communication model, etc.)?	• Is your system's pedagogical approach appropriate for the target group? • Does/should your system allow for any adjustments to be made (either a priori or in real time) by human practitioners (e.g., to improve the idiosyncrasy in your system's diagnoses) of diverse learners? • Is your system reinforcing or challenging the dominant group's education culture? • Is your system challenging, enhancing, or confirming educators' prior beliefs and assessments? • Does your system enhance or undermines human educators' skills and practices by offering insights that meaningful to them (e.g., by reference to process and outcome measures that are familiar to teachers /grounded in best educational practices)

(*Continued*)

Table 26.2 (Continued)

	Dimensions of AIED design and deployment			
	AIED data	AIED models/algorithms	AIED pedagogy	Socio-technical context
	Consequences/risks:			
	• Harm of representation • Outcome fairness • Process fairness	• Outcome fairness • Process fairness • Human autonomy	• Harm of representation • Equity of accessibility • Outcome fairness • Individual fairness • Human autonomy	• Harm of representation • Equity of accessibility • Outcome fairness • Process fairness • Human autonomy
Aggregation	Problem:			
	• Erasure of some groups or individuals from data (e.g., because of insufficient numbers). • Demographic and protected categories blindness.	• Reduced adaptivity and relevance of systems to 'outlier' students due to models operating on dominant behavioural patterns.	• Inappropriate, discriminatory, or ineffective support for the target group (e.g., pedagogies for non-dyslexic used for dyslexic students).	• Reliance on aggregated/historic data to derive assessments for individuals (e.g., 2020 A-level fiasco in the UK). • Lack of educationally inclusive practices; practices that are blind to non-typical, non-dominant groups (e.g., neurodivergent, low SES, or protected categories students).
	Questions:			
	• Have you assessed the risks of aggregating data to your systems' ability to adapt to your target population? • Have you assessed pros and cons of data aggregation vis-à-vis the goals of your system (e.g., university admission vs. adaptive support).	• What is the necessary and sufficient level of the representational granularity of data for your system to model and adapt effectively to individual or groups of learners?	• Are the pedagogies encoded in your system based on best practices available for the target population? • Can your system's pedagogy be adapted by human educators or through negotiation with learners?	• Does/can your system actively contribute to increasing individual fairness? • Does your system encode inclusive educational practices and if so, how?

		Consequences/risks:			
		• Harm of representation • Harm of allocation • Outcome fairness • Process fairness • Individual fairness • Group fairness	• Harm of representation • Harm of allocation • Outcome fairness • Process fairness • Individual fairness • Group fairness	• Harm of representation • Harm of allocation • Outcome fairness • Process fairness • Individual fairness • Group fairness • Human autonomy	• Harm of representation • Outcome fairness • Individual fairness • Group fairness
Model Learning	Problem:				
		• Data which is too small and/or not representative enough of the target population or problem to facilitate model learning or learning of model that generalises across contexts. • Relying on inadequate predictor variable (e.g., click data as predictor of underlying intentions behind a particular search term).	• Choice of an objective function, heuristics or inference mechanism that leads to performance differences across different data. • Prioritising one objective over another may limit the applicability of the model to different learner populations and contexts of use.	• Pedagogical choices based on the model may not transfer across different contexts (e.g., the same help-seeking behaviours may be explained differently depending on the target population, their learning culture, neurodivergent status, etc.). • Users' decisions and actions may be adversely affected by predictions/inferences or recommendations that are incorrect, irrelevant, or based on incomplete information.	• A model that does not generalise across contexts may reinforce/introduce exclusive or harmful practices in education. • A model that makes incorrect, inaccurate, or irrelevant predictions or recommendations may influence users' behaviours in undesirable ways (e.g., it may compromise the quality and fairness of educators' pedagogical decisions).
	Questions:				
		• Do the volume and representational quality of your data sufficient to cater for diversity of contexts? • What evidence have you chosen your predictor variables based?	• To what extent does your chosen objective function/heuristics/inference mechanism allow your model to make meaningful and pedagogically appropriate predictions/recommendations/action?	• To what extent does your objective function/heuristics/inference allow your model to account for users' idiosyncratic behaviours and needs? • Does your model promote users' critical thinking (e.g., by inviting them to challenge the models' predictions/recommendations), or does it dictate the 'answers'? • Is your model explainable to all/some of the users?	• What contexts, what users and what educational tasks does your model support? • How well does it generalise to new contexts, users, and tasks? • Does your model dictate a particular way of analysing the users or support a specific mode of learning and teaching, or is it open to being critiqued and modified?

(Continued)

Table 26.2   (Continued)

	Dimensions of AIED design and deployment			
	AIED data	AIED models/algorithms	AIED pedagogy	Socio-technical context
	Consequences/risks:			
	• Harm of representation • Harm of allocation • Outcome fairness • Process fairness	• Harm of representation • Harm of allocation • Outcome fairness • Process fairness • Individual fairness • Group fairness	• Harm of representation • Harm of allocation • Outcome fairness • Process fairness • Individual fairness • Human autonomy	• Harm of representation • Harm of allocation • Outcome fairness • Process fairness • Individual fairness • Human autonomy
Evaluation	Problem:			
	• Benchmark data may fail to match the user population data.	• Model performance might be evaluated using different performance metrics, each metric presenting its own challenges (e.g., aggregate measures can hide subgroup underperformance). • Overfitting of a model performance based on comparison with other models against the benchmark data.	• Pedagogical decisions/ recommendations which are ineffective, irrelevant, or even harmful.	• Overgeneralised claims about the efficacy and relevance of a given technology. • Choice of model performance metrics may cater for the needs and interests of some stakeholders (e.g., businesses, policy decision makers), but not others (e.g., students, front-line practitioners). • Investment in pedagogically limited, prescriptive, or potentially harmful technologies.
	Questions:			
	• How representative is your benchmark data of the user population?	• What performance metrics are needed to ensure educational efficacy, relevance, and safety of your models? • What have you compared your model's performance to?	• Are your system's models representative of all target users in all target contexts? • In what way exactly are your system's pedagogies efficacious? • What are the pedagogical limitations of your system? • How transparent are the limitations of your system to the users?	• Who is the evaluation for (e.g., engineers, educators, educational administrators, investors, policy decision-makers)? • How transparent are the limitations of your system to different stakeholders?

	Consequences/Risks: • Harm of representation • Harm of allocation • Outcome fairness • Process fairness	• Harm of representation • Harm of allocation • Outcome fairness • Process fairness • Individual fairness • Group fairness	• Harm of representation • Harm of allocation • Outcome fairness • Process fairness • Individual fairness • Group fairness • Human autonomy	• Harm of representation • Harm of allocation • Outcome fairness • Human autonomy
Deployment	**Problem:** • Data (learning, test, or benchmark) is not collected in deployment context(s)	• Decontextualised model designs and evaluations. • Inflexible model designs that exclude the users from calibrating them *in situ*.	• Learning designs for homogenous group and mainstream contexts do not transfer to non-typical groups (e.g., pedagogies used for neurodivergent students usually transfer to neurotypical students, but not the reverse).	• Socio-technical context ignored in the evaluation of your system leading to mismatch between the problem your system trying to solve and the way it is used.
	Questions: • Does the design context match the context of deployment? • Is your data collected in representative contexts of use? • Can the context in which the system is deployed change?	• Do your system's models encode the contextual information needed for their performance efficacy and relevance to those contexts?	• Can your system's pedagogy be changed, adjusted, or 'sabotaged' by human practitioners should they need to calibrate it to their specific needs (e.g., through adjusting when and how to deliver feedback to specific learners)?	• In what context is your technology deployed? • Does your system design context match the context(s) it claims it will work in? • Is your system transparent about its strengths and weaknesses? • Can your system's use be modified by front-line users?
	Consequences/Risks: • Harm of representation • Outcome fairness • Process fairness	• Harm of representation • Harm of allocation • Outcome fairness • Process fairness • Individual fairness • Group fairness • Human autonomy	• Harm of representation • Harm of allocation • Outcome fairness • Process fairness • Individual fairness • Group fairness • Human autonomy	• Harm of representation • Harm of allocation • Outcome fairness • Process fairness • Individual fairness • Group fairness • Human autonomy

(Continued)

Table 26.2   (Continued)

	Dimensions of AIED design and deployment			
	AIED data	AIED models/algorithms	AIED pedagogy	Socio-technical context
Domain-value	**Problem:** • Datasets available in limited types of subject domains (e.g., sciences), with sparse data being available in other domains • Subject domain may interact with performance of students belonging to different demographic groups, proliferating historic and representational biases and harms.	• Models specialised for limited types of subject domains. • Models for less favoured domains built on the assumptions (objective function etc.) derived from research in favoured domains (e.g.m student emotion modelling in maths applied in history learning context).	• Unequal access to AIED resources for educators in different domains (e.g., maths vs. history) • Danger of segregation of skills (e.g., problems solving on specific tasks vs. creative and critical thinking). • Limited pedagogical innovation.	• Investment in AIED supports the more valued domains (e.g., maths and sciences) • Generalisation of claims made for a limited set of AIED models and technologies to the whole of education.
	Questions: • Are sufficient and representative datasets available in your target domain?	• Do your system's models differentiate between subject-domain specific and subject-independent assumptions that drive the selection/definition of its objective function/inference?	• Is your system designed for a currently favoured or less favoured domain? • Does your system's pedagogy draw from other domains explicitly to promote and build on diversity of students' skills (e.g., problem solving, creative and critical thinking)?	• Is your system addressing a gap in AIED support provision or fitting into/exploiting a trend?
	Consequences/Risks: • Harm of representation • Harm of allocation • Outcome fairness	• Harm of representation • Outcome fairness • Process fairness	• Harm of representation • Harm of allocation • Outcome fairness	• Harm of representation • Harm of allocation • Outcome fairness

Learning-culture

	Problem:			
Problem:	• Datasets available in limited cultures of learning (e.g., drill-and-practice, collaborative, enquiry, or project driven). • Learning culture may interact with performance/outcomes of student demographic, cultural and neuroability groups, proliferating historic and representational biases and harms.	• System models specialised to specific forms of learning may be misaligned with the strengths and moment to moment needs of the students (e.g., a student may underperform in drill-and-practice context but thrive in an enquiry one).	• AIED's support of learners and teachers may be limited and/or limiting to them. • AIED may contribute to entrenching modes of learning (e.g., exam-driven drill-and-practice) as dominant.	• Pedagogies that lead to examinable outcomes dominate the education system. • AIED is expected to support the current policies and modes of learning dominant within the current education system.
Questions:	• Are sufficient and representative datasets available in your system's target learning mode? • Have you assessed for strengths of target learners in the target learning mode (e.g., some neurodivergent students may perform better in an exploratory or collaborative mode than in drill-and-practice)?	• Do your system's models encode a single/specific mode of learning (e.g., drill-and-practice) or multiple forms of learning (e.g., collaborative, exploratory)? • Are your models open to exploration and calibration by users with respect to learning modes?	• Is your system's pedagogy appropriate for the target group (e.g., does it detect, adapt to, and build on students' strengths rather than speaking to their weaknesses)? • Is your system pedagogy open to calibration and authoring by practitioners?	• Is your system addressing a gap in AIED support provision or fitting into/exploiting a trend?
Consequences/risks:	• Harm of representation • Harm of allocation • Outcome fairness	• Harm of representation • Harm of allocation • Outcome fairness • Process fairness	• Harm of representation • Harm of allocation • Outcome fairness • Human autonomy	• Outcome fairness • Process fairness

technology companies such as Microsoft, Facebook, Boxlight and Amazon. Two primary concerns arise here: (i) the concentration of personal (student and teacher) information might create a privacy risk (e.g., attracting malicious parties); and (ii) these dominant platforms could form a monopoly to dominate the market on research and development of algorithms (UNESCO, 2019), ultimately having the power to dictate, or at least strongly influence, educational policies and practices. Related to this are the distributed service architectures used as foundational for algorithms being integrated and deployed across education. These architectures comprise feedback in real time from users and third-party service providers, which is used for a range of optimisation activities designed to extract value through the system. While optimisation tends to be used for technical performance and reduction of costs, it has also become a part of the allocation of continuous development to build adaptive systems. The issue is that such optimisations are designed to capture detailed information about individuals and groups and to manipulate behaviours. In this capacity, such systems introduce to education risks and harms that extend beyond bias and discrimination. As also discussed by Williamson et al. (Chapter 25 in this volume), focusing only on algorithms misses the results of optimising all aspects of a broader socio-technical system, with discrimination becoming one of the injustices that emerge when these systems are designed and developed to maximise profits. Failing to attend to incentives of service providers and their ability to enforce solutions constrains our understanding of how they operate and fixes in certain actors the power to shape decisions and behaviours which have significant impacts on society at large (Kulynych et al., 2018).

Many of the issues related to optimisation are beyond the scope of this chapter. Nevertheless, it is critical for the AIED community to be cognisant of the context in which its technologies are being developed, deployed and exploited. Trying to understand this context is critical to the community and individual designers being able to appraise the role of their work in the broader socio-technological context and to being able to question the ethical value of the methods they use and the systems they create beyond the declared good intentions. A comprehensive understanding of the ethics of AIED needs to involve horizon scanning and interdisciplinary conversations, explicitly taking into account insights from the learning sciences, cognitive and educational neuroscience, the sociology of education and philosophical introspection. It also calls for the community to consider fundamental questions about what education is for, what kind of educational systems does AIED as field support (and whether that in itself is ethical) and how the community might be able to shape, through engaging in ethics by design, the beneficence of education for all. All of these are necessary to help us identify and explore the *unknown unknowns* of the ethics of AIED, in order to establish a balanced, self-aware and – above all – actionable approach to *Ethical AIED* practices that are able to bridge between the ethical implications of AIED systems' design decisions at the algorithmic micro level and the key considerations at the socio-technological macro level.

REFERENCES

Alciné, J. [@jackyalcine]. (2015). Google Photos, y'all f– up. My friend's not a gorilla. [Tweet]. https://twitter.com/jackyalcine/status/615329515909156865 (accessed 1 September 2021).

Angwin, J., Larson, J., Mattu, S., & Kirchner, L. (2016). Machine Bias There's software used across the country to predict future criminals. And it's biased against blacks. https://www.propublica.org/article/machine-bias-risk-assessments-in-criminal-sentencing (accessed 1 September 2021).

Asilomar AI Principles (2017). https://futureoflife.org/ai-principles (accessed 1 September 2021).

Baker, R. S. (2019). Challenges for the future of educational data mining: The baker learning analytics prizes. *Journal of Educational Data Mining*, 11(1), 1–17. https://doi.org/10.5281/zenodo.3554745.

Baker, R. S., & Hawn, A. (2021). Algorithmic bias in education. *International Journal of Artificial Intelligence in Education*. Advance online publication. https://doi.org./10.1007/s40593-021-00285-9

Baker, R. S., Ocumpaugh, J. L., & Andres, J. M. A. L. (2011). BROMP quantitative field observations: A review. In R. Feldman (Ed.), *Learning Science: Theory, Research, and Practice*. McGraw-Hill. http://radix.www.upenn.edu/learninganalytics/ryanbaker/BROMPbookchapter.pdf (accessed 1 September 2021).

Barocas, S., Crawford, K., Shapiro, A., & Wallach, H. (2017). The problem with bias: Allocative versus representational harms in machine learning. In *SIGCIS Conference*. http://meetings.sigcis.org/uploads/6/3/6/8/6368912/program.pdf (accessed 1 September 2021).

Benton, L., Mavrikis, M., Vasalou, A., Joye, N., Sumner, E., Herbert, E., Symvonis, A., & Raftopolou, C. (2021). Designing for 'challenge' in a large-scale adaptive literacy game for primary school children. *British Journal of Educational Technology*, 52(5), 1862–1880. Wiley.

Bernardini, S., Porayska-Pomsta, K., Smith, T., & Avramides, K. (2012). Building autonomous social partners for autistic children. In *International Conference on Intelligent Virtual Agents*, 46–52. Springer.

Blair, K., Schwartz, D. L., Biswas, G., & Leelawong, K. (2007). Pedagogical agents for learning by teaching: Teachable agents. *Educational Technology*, 56–61.

Blikstein, P. (2018). Time to make hard choices for AI in education. In *Keynote at the 19th International Conference on Artificial Intelligence in Education*, London.

Blodgett, S. L., Barocas, S., Daumé, H., III, & Wallach, H. (2020). Language (technology) is power: A critical survey of 'bias' in nlp. *arXiv preprint* arXiv:2005.14050. https://arxiv.org/abs/2005.14050.

Bloom, B. S. (1984). The 2 sigma problem: The search for methods of group instruction as effective as one-to-one tutoring. *Educational Researcher*, 13(6), 4–16.

Bogdan, K., Overdorf, R., Troncoso, C., & Gürses, S. (2018). POTs: Protective optimization technologies. *arXiv.org*. https://arxiv.org/abs/1806.02711.

Bolukbasi, T., Chang, K.-W., Zou, J. Y., Saligrama, V., & Kalai, A. T. (2016). Man is to computer programmer as woman is to homemaker? Debiasing word embeddings. In D. D. Lee, M. Sugiyama, U. V. Luxburg, I. Guyon, & R. Garnett (Eds.), *Advances in Neural Information Processing Systems* (Vol. 29, pp. 4349–4357). Curran Associates, Inc.

Brooks, C., Kovanovic, V., & Nguyen, Q. (*in this volume*). Predictive modelling of student success.

Bull, S., & Kay, J. (2016). SMILI☺: a framework for interfaces to learning data in open learner models, learning analytics and related fields. *International Journal of Artificial Intelligence in Education*, 26(1), 293–331. https://doi.org/10.1007/s40593-015-0090-8.

Buolamwini, J., & Gebru, T. (2018). *Gender Shades: Intersectional Accuracy Disparities in Commercial Gender Classification* (Vol. 15).

Cardwell, M. (1999). *The Dictionary of Psychology*. Taylor & Francis.

Carter, L., Liu, D., & Cantrell, C. (2020). Exploring the intersection of the digital divide and artificial intelligence: A hermeneutic literature review. *AIS Transactions on Human-Computer Interaction*, 12(4), 253–275.

Conati, C., Porayska-Pomsta, K., & Mavrikis, M. (2018). AI in education needs interpretable machine learning: Lessons from open learner modelling. *Arxiv:1807.00154 [Cs]*. http://arxiv.org/abs/1807.00154.

Cramer, H., Vaughan, W. J., & Holstein, K. (2019). Challenges of incorporating algorithmic 'fairness' into practice. In *Tutorial at the ACM Conference on Fairness, Accountability, and Transparency (FAT* 2019)* (accessed 1 September 2021).

Crawford, K. (2013). The hidden biases in big data. *Harvard Business Review*. https://hbr.org/2013/04/the-hidden-biases-in-big-data (accessed 1 September 2021).

Crawford, K. (2017a). Hidden biases in big data, in analytics and data science. *Harvard Business Review*. https://hbr.org/2013/04/the-hidden-biases-in-big-data (accessed 1 September 2021).

Crawford, K. (2017b). Artificial intelligence—With very real biases. *The Wall Street Journal*. https://www.wsj.com/articles/artificial-intelligencewith-very-real-biases-1508252717?mod=e2fb (accessed 1 September 2021).

Danks, D., & London, A. J. (2017). Algorithmic bias in autonomous systems. *IJCAI*, 17, 4691–4697.

du Boulay, B. (2022). Artificial intelligence in education: A brief discussion about ethics. In W. Holmes & K. Porayska-Pomsta (Eds.), *The Ethics of Artificial Intelligence in Education: Practices, Challenges, and Debates*. Routledge.

EGE Principles for Ethical AI (2018). https://op.europa.eu/en/publication-detail/-/publication/dfebe62e -4ce9-11e8-be1d-01aa75ed71a1/language-en/format-PDF/source-78120382 (accessed 1 September 2021).

Eubanks, V. (2018). *Automating Inequality: How High-Tech Tools Profile, Police, and Punish the Poor*. St Martin's Press.

Facer, K., & Selwyn, N. (2021). *Digital Technology and the Futures of Education – Towards 'Non-Stupid' Optimism*. UNESCO. https://unesdoc.unesco.org/ark:/48223/pf0000377071 (accessed 1 September 2021).

Ferguson, R., Brasher, A., Clow, D., Cooper, A., Hillaire, G., Mittelmeier, J., Rienties, B., Ullmann, T., & Vuorikari, R. (2016). Research evidence on the use of learning analytics: Implications for education policy. http://oro.open.ac.uk/48173/ (accessed 1 September 2021).

Finkelstein, S., Yarzebinski, E., Vaughn, C., Ogan, A., & Cassell, J. (2013). The effects of culturally congruent educational technologies on student achievement. In *International Conference on Artificial Intelligence in Education* (pp. 493–502). Springer.

Floridi, L. (2013). *The Ethics of Information*. Oxford: Oxford University Press.

Floridi, L., & Cowls, J. (2019). A unified framework of five principles for AI in society. *Harvard Data Science Review*, 1(1). https://doi.org/10.1162/99608f92.8cd550d1 (accessed 1 September 2021).

Friedler, S. A., Scheidegger, C., & Venkatasubramanian, S. (2016). On the (im)possibility of fairness. *arXiv preprint* arXiv:1609.07236.

Gauthier, A., Porayska-Pomsta, K., Dumontheil, I., Mayer, S., & Mareschal, D. (2022). Manipulating interface design features affects children's stop-and-think behaviours in counterintuitive-problem game. *ACM Transactions on Computer-Human Interaction*, 29(2), 1–22. ACM.

Gauthier, A., Porayska-Pomsta, K., & Mareschal, D. (2020). Using eye-tracking and click-stream data to design adaptive training of children's inhibitory control in a maths and science game. In I. I. Bittencourt, M. Cukurova, K. Muldner, R. Luckin, & E. Millán (Eds.), *Artificial Intelligence in Education* (pp. 103–108). Springer International Publishing. https://doi.org/10.1007/978-3-030 -52240-7_19.

Grawemayer, B., Mavrikis, M., Holmes, W., Gutierrez-Santos, S., Wiedmann, M., & Rummel, N. (2017). Affective learning: Improving engagement and enhancing learning with affect-aware feedback. *User Modelling and User-Adapted Interaction*, 27(1), 119–158.

Guldberg, K., Parsons, S., Keay-Bright, W., & Porayska-Pomsta, K. (2017). Challenging the knowledge transfer orthodoxy: Knowledge co-construction in technology-enhanced learning for children with autism. *British Educational Journal*, 42(2), 394–413.

Hagendorff, T. (2020). The ethics of AI ethics: An evaluation of guidelines. *Minds and Machines*, 30(1), 99–120. https://doi.org/10.1007/s11023-020-09517-8.

Harrari, Y. (2019). *21 Lessons From the 21st Century*. Vintage.

Heaven, W. D. (2020). Predictive policing algorithms are racist. They need to be dismantled. *MIT Technology Review*, July 17, 2020 (accessed 1 September 2021).

Holmes, W., Bialik, M., & Fadel, C. (2019). *Artificial Intelligence in Education: Promises and Implications for Teaching and Learning*. Center for Curriculum Redesign.

Holmes, W., & Porayska-Pomsta, K. (2022). *The Ethics of Artificial Intelligence in Education: Practices, Challenges, and Debates*. Routledge.

Holmes, W., Porayska-Pomsta, K., Holstein, K., Sutherland, E., Baker, T., Shum, S. B., Santos, O. C., Rodrigo, M. T., Cukurova, M., Bittencourt, I. I., & Koedinger, K. R. (2021). Ethics of AI in education: Towards a community-wide framework. *International Journal of Artificial Intelligence in Education*. Advance online publication. https://doi.org/10.1007/s40593-021-00239-1.

Holstein, K., & Doroudi, S. (2022). In W. Holmes & K. Porayska-Pomsta (Eds.), *The Ethics of Artificial Intelligence in Education: Practices, Challenges, and Debates*. Routledge.

Holstein, K., Wortman Vaughan, J., Daumé, H., III, Dudik, M., & Wallach, H. (2019). Improving fairness in machine learning systems: What do industry practitioners need? In *Proceedings of the 2019 CHI Conference on Human Factors in Computing Systems* (pp. 1–16) (accessed 1 September 2021).

IEEE General Principles. (2017). https://standards.ieee.org/content/dam/ieee-standards/standards/web/documents/other/ead1e_general_principles.pdf.

Jobin, A., Ienca, M., & Vayena, E. (2019). Artificial intelligence: The global landscape of ethics guidelines. *Nature Machine Intelligence*, 1(9), 389–399. https://doi.org/10.1038/s42256-019-0088-2Kant, 1785.

Kant, I. (1785). *Grundlegung zur Metaphysik der Sitten (Groundwork of the Metaphysic of Morals)*. Hartknoch.

Kay, J., Kummerfeld, B., Conati, C., Holstein, K., & Porayska-Pomsta, K. (*this volume*). Scrutability and learner control: A learner-centred approach to learning data, learner models, and their uses.

Kelly, K. (2010). *What Technology Wants*. Penguin Books.

Kleinberg, J., Ludwig, J., Mullainathan, S., & Sunstein, C. R. (2018). Discrimination in the age of algorithms. *Journal of Legal Analysis*, 10, 113–174.

Kurzweil, R. (2014). The singularity is near. In *Ethics and Emerging Technologies* (pp. 393–406). Palgrave Macmillan.

Lee, H., & Kizilcec, R. F. (2020). Evaluation of fairness trade-offs in predicting student success. In *Proceedings of the Conference on Educational Data Mining (EDM) Fairness, Accountability, and Transparency in Educational Data (FATED) Workshop*. https://arxiv.org/abs/2007.00088 (accessed 1 September 2021).

Madaio, M., Blodgett, S. L., Mayfield, E., & Dixon-Román, E. (2020). Beyond 'fairness': Structural (in)justice lenses on AI for education. In W. Holmes & K. Porayska-Pomsta (Eds.), *The Ethics of Artificial Intelligence in Education: Practices, Challenges, and Debates*. Routledge.

Madaio, M., Yarzebinski, E., Zinszer, B., Kamath, V., Akpe, H., Seri, A. B., Tanoh, F., Hannon-Cropp, J., Cassell, J., Jasinska, K., & Ogam, A. (2020). Motivations and barriers for family engagement with home literacy technology in rural communities. In *CHI Conference on Human Factors in Computing Systems*. ACM.

Miao, F., & Holmes, W. (2021). AI and education: Guidance for policy-makers. UNESCO. https://unesdoc.unesco.org/ark:/48223/pf0000376709 (accessed 1 September 2021).

Narayanan, A. (2018). 21 fairness definitions and their politics. In *Tutorial at the FACCT Conference*, 2018. Video available at https://www.youtube.com/watch?v=jIXIuYdnyyk (accessed 1 September 2021).

Nemorin, S. (2021). Fair AIED. www.fair-ai.com (accessed 1 September 2021).

Ngang Ng, S., & Rao, N. (2010). Chinese number words, culture and mathematics learning. *Review of Educational Research*, 80(2), 180–206.

Noble, S. (2018). *Algorithms of Oppression*. NYU Press.

OECD. (2001). Understanding the digital divide. https://stats.oecd.org/glossary/detail.asp?ID=4719 (accessed 1 September 2021).

O'Shea, T. (1979). An implementation of a self-improving teaching program. In *Self-Improving Teaching Systems* (pp. 85–111). Birkhäuser.

Porayska-Pomsta, K., Alcorn, A. M., Avramides, K., Beale, S., Bernardini, S., Foster, M.-E., Frauenberger, C., Good, J., Guldberg, K., Keay-Bright, W., Kossyvaki, L., Lemon, O., Mademtzi, M., Menzies, R., Pain, H., Rajendran, G., Waller, A., Sam Wass, Smith, T. J. (2018). Blending human and artificial intelligence to support autistic children of social communication skills. *TOCHI*, 25(6), 1–35. ACM.

Porayska-Pomsta, K., Anderson, K., Bernardini, S., Guldberg, K., Smith T., Kossivaki, L., Hodgins, S., & Lowe, I. (2013). Building an intelligent, authorable serious game for autistic children and their carers. In *International Conference on Advances in Computer Entertainment Technology* (pp. 456–475). Springer.

Porayska-Pomsta, K., & Holmes, W. (2022). Towards ethical AIED, conclusions of the edited volume: The ethics of artificial intelligence in education: Practices, challenges and debates (to appear in August 2022, Routledge).

Porayska-Pomsta, K., & Rajendran, G. (2019). Accountability in human and artificial intelligence decision-making as the basis for diversity and educational inclusion. In *Artificial Intelligence and Inclusive Education* (pp. 39–59). Springer.

Rashedi, R., Bonnet, K., Schulte, R., Schlundt, D., Swanson, A., Kinsman, A., Bardett, N., Warren, Z., Juárez, P., Biswas, G., & Kunda, M. (2020). Opportunities and challenges in developing technology-based social skills interventions for youth with autism spectrum disorder: A qualitative analysis of parent perspectives. In M. Gresalfi & I. S. Horn (Eds.), *The Interdisciplinarity of the Learning Sciences*.

Rawls, J. (1958). Justice as fairness. *The Philosophical Review*, 67(2), 164–194.

Reich, J., & Ito, M. (2017). *From Good Intentions to Real Outcomes: Equity by Design in Learning Technologies*. Digital Media and Learning Research Hub.

Rideout, V., & Katz, V. S. (2016). Opportunity for all? Technology and learning in lower-income families. In Joan Ganz Cooney Center at Sesame Workshop. Joan Ganz Cooney Center at Sesame Workshop, New York, NY. https://eric.ed.gov/?id=ED574416.

Ritter, S., & Koedinger, K. R. (*in this volume*). *Large Scale Commercialization of AI in Education Systems*.

Ross, W. D. (1930). *The Right and the Good*. Clarendon Press, The Royal Society.

Russell, S. (2019). *Human Compatible: Artificial Intelligence and the Problem of Control*. Penguin.

Sandberg, A., & Bostrom, N. (2008). The wisdom of nature: An evolutionary heuristic for human enhancement. In J. Savulescu & N. Bostrom (Ed.), *Human Enhancement* (pp. 375–416). Oxford University Press.

Saxena, M., Pillai, R. K., & Mostow, J. (2018). Relating children's automatically detected facial expressions to their behaviour in RoboTutor. In *32nd AAAI Conference on Artificial Intelligence*.

Suresh, H., & Guttag, J. (2021). Understanding potential sources of harm throughout the machine learning life cycle. https://mit-serc.pubpub.org/pub/potential-sources-of-harm-throughout-the-machine-learning-life-cycle/release/2?readingCollection=872d7145.

Sweeney, L. (2013). Discrimination in online ad delivery. *Communications of ACM*, 56(5), 44–54. https://doi.org/10.1145/2447976.2447990.

Sweeney, Latanya. (May 1, 2013). Discrimination in online Ad delivery. *ACM*, 56(5), 44–54.

Tang, Y.-Y., & Liu, Y. (2009). Numbers in the cultural brain. *Progress in Brain Research*, 178, 151–157.

The Royal Society Workshop Report. (2019). Digital technology and human transformation, November 2019 DES6259. https://royalsociety.org/-/media/policy/Publications/2020/human-transformation-summary.pdf.

Treviranus, J. (in press). Learning to learn differently. In W. Holmes & K. Porayska-Pomsta (Eds.), *The Ethics of Artificial Intelligence in Education: Practices, Challenges, and Debates*. Routledge.

Uchidiuno, J., Yarzebinski, E., Madaio, M., Maheshwari, N., Koedinger, K., & Ogan, A. (2018). Designing appropriate learning technologies for school vs home settings in Tanzanian rural villages. In *Proceedings of the 1st ACM SIGCAS Conference on Computing and Sustainable Societies* (pp. 1–11).

VanLehn, K. (2011). The relative effectiveness of human tutoring, intelligent tutoring systems, and other tutoring systems. *Educational Psychologist*, 46(4), 197–221. https://doi.org/10.1080/00461520.2011.611369.

Watters, A. (2021). *Teaching Machines: The History of Personalized Learning*. MIT Press.

Wilkinson, H. R., Smid, C., Morris, S., Farran, E. K., Dumontheil, I., Mayer, S., Tolmie, A., Bell, D., Porayska-Pomsta, K., Holmes, W., Mareschal, D., Thomas, M. S. C., & The UnLocke Team. (2019). Domain-specific inhibitory control training to improve children's learning of counterintuitive concepts in mathematics and science. *Journal of Cognitive Enhancement*. Advance online publication. https://doi.org/10.1007/s41465-019-00161-4.

Williamson, B., Eynon, R., Knox, J., & Davies, H. (in this volume). Critical perspectives on AI in education: Political economy, discrimination, commercialization, governance and ethics.

Wu, X., & Zhang, X. (2016). Responses to critiques on machine learning of criminality perceptions. *ArXiv*:1611.04135 [Cs.CV]. http://arxiv.org/abs/1611.04135v1.

Yu, R., Li, Q., & Wu, X. (2020). Towards accurate and fair prediction of college success: Evaluating different sources of student data. In *Proceedings of the 13th International Conference on Educational Data Mining (EDM' 20)*.

PART VI

THE FUTURE

27. The great challenges and opportunities of the next 20 years

Each section of this chapter is written by a different author focusing on a particular challenge or opportunity for the future of their own choosing. There are various ways in which the sections could have been organised but in the end, we left them in the order that they were originally submitted. Note however that Sections 1, 3, 7 and 9 all deal with issues around *access and equity*, Sections 4, 5, 8, 10 and 11 cover different kinds of *learning and enabling technology* and Sections 2 and 6 offer two aspects of the same issue, namely *ubiquity and information overload*.

1. AIED AND EQUITY

Maria Mercedes T. Rodrigo

The United Nations Sustainable Development Goal #4 aims to "ensure inclusive and equitable quality education and promote lifelong opportunities for all" (UNESCO, 2021). The problem this goal seeks to address, though, is massive and dire: 262 million children are out of school, two-thirds of children do not acquire basic literacy and numeracy skills despite several years in school, and 750 million adults are illiterate.

AI-based learning technologies offer a partial solution. Intelligent tutoring systems (ITSs), adaptive instructional systems and other similar technologies have been shown to improve learning outcomes, outperforming other instructional methods such as traditional classroom instruction, reading printed or computer-based texts and laboratory and homework assignments (Streenbergen-Hu & Cooper, 2014). Indeed, the effect sizes of computer-based intelligent tutors approach those of human one-on-one tutoring (VanLehn, 2011).

AI-based technologies are particularly promising for low-prior-knowledge (LPK) learners. A meta-analysis from Ma and colleagues (Ma et al., 2014) showed that, regardless of prior knowledge, learners achieve comparable learning gains from ITS use. Indeed, ITSs offer LPK learners the opportunity to catch up with their high-prior-knowledge (HPK) peers (Jackson et al., 2010). LPK learners benefit more than HPK learners from immediate feedback (Razzaq et al., 2020) and from polite rather than direct intelligent tutors (McLaren et al., 2011). As the technology matures even further, some researchers speculate that we could design AI-based educational interventions to make use of eye trackers, brain signals, cameras and microphones to monitor student attention and dynamically redirect it in order to make better use of sparse attention resources (D'Mello, 2016). Some researchers are already integrating intelligent learning technologies with Massive Open Online Courses (MOOCs) in order to make adaptive learning systems available at scale (Aleven et al., 2018).

Under-resourced classrooms, whether in the Global North or South, seem like the environment in which AI-based educational systems can achieve the most impact. These technologies offer learners who are lagging behind a chance to raise their levels of achievement and potentially their life outcomes. However, many factors prevent this from taking place. Of these, we discuss three: accessibility, cultural bias and teacher preparedness.

Lack of access to hardware and the internet is the most obvious impediment to use of ITSs and other AI-based learning systems. Five percent of US families with children in the United States do not have computers and 15% have no internet subscriptions (Holstein & Doroudi, 2021). Many low- to middle-income families are under-connected, that is, they have slow or mobile-only internet access, or family members have to share devices. Some researchers have suggested that educational interventions be designed specifically for use on mobile phones, the primary computing platform of the Global South (Nye, 2015). However, people from lower-income groups tend to use low-cost internet access, buying internet time and bandwidth as needed and using it conservatively (Uy-Tioco, 2019). Telecommunication companies provide zero-rated internet that allows users access to certain news and social media sites. These plans, though, limit the types of content and media that subscribers can access. AI-based interventions, even when deployed on mobile technologies, are unlikely to be part of these zero-rated plans and will tend to be beyond reach as these technologies are often built to run on 5G networks (Gallagher, 2019).

A second impediment is cultural bias. Most ITS and AI in education research takes place in Western, educated, industrialized, rich and democratic (WEIRD) countries (Blanchard, 2012). In terms of language alone, many AI-based materials are made for English speakers, hence adoption in non-English-speaking countries requires extensive translation (Holstein & Doroudi, 2021). Beneath these surface features, the models themselves on which these systems base their intelligence are created using data from WEIRD populations and do not reliably transfer to other cultures. Ignoring cultural and contextual factors can decrease a technology intervention's effectiveness on a target group (Baker et al., 2019). The study by Ogan et al. (2015), for example, illustrates how most ITSs are designed for one-on-one instruction and do not work as intended when used in Chilean classrooms where students often work collaboratively.

A third impediment is teacher preparedness and support. Many teachers, especially those in the Global South, lack the training and exposure that they need to effectively integrate AI-based interventions in their classes (Rodrigo, 2021). Many have experience with productivity tools such as word processors and spreadsheets, but they do not have the skills to make use of these and other resources in innovative ways. Teachers lack in-service training opportunities to improve on their skills. They also lack curriculum support: often, there is no premade curriculum that integrates an ITS's use. Teachers do not have a lesson plan that guides their use of an innovation in a class or even an articulation of the alignment between the ITS's learning objectives and curriculum goals (Nye, 2014).

The result of these and other impediments is a "Matthew Effect", also known as an accumulated advantage phenomenon: those who already have access to sophisticated educational systems will continue to improve their knowledge, skills and life opportunities (Gallagher, 2019). This pattern is already evident in studies regarding the use of MOOCs. MOOCs were seen as democratizing technologies because they could provide quality education at little to no cost, therefore increasing the number of people with post-secondary education (Ebben & Murphy, 2014; Veletsianos & Shepherdson, 2016). Summaries of MOOC learner demographics, however, show the opposite: those who benefit are those who are already privileged, that is, people aged between 20 and 40 who already have a post-secondary degree (Ebben & Murphy, 2014; Gynther, 2016). Those who are less privileged will lag behind even further, unless course-corrected by other social, political or economic forces. Good education and good educational technologies are among these forces.

How, then, can ITSs and other AI-based interventions contribute to greater equity? We ask a few questions that might point to ways forward, in relation to the impediments cited earlier. In terms of access: How can researchers and developers design AI-based interventions for lower technology platforms? Instead of assuming high-end computers or mobile devices and high-speed internet access, can we capitalize on more broadly available but less sophisticated devices and platforms? In terms of cultural bias: How can we work with stakeholders from the Global South to create systems that address their cultures and contexts? How do we adopt pedagogies, content and teaching/learning strategies so that they embrace a greater diversity of learners and their circumstances? Finally, in terms of teacher preparedness: How can we create mappings between our systems and curricula? Can we build in teacher training, monitoring and support as part and parcel of our research undertakings? If we have constructive answers to these questions, we stand to increase the adoption and impact of the technologies we create and move all our learners towards the realization of universal, inclusive, equitable and high-quality education.

2. ENGAGING LEARNERS IN THE AGE OF INFORMATION OVERLOAD

Julita Vassileva

AI-powered tools free us from unpleasant, annoying, or boring tasks and make our lives more comfortable and easier. Yet intelligent technologies also make us lazier, both physically and cognitively. The abundance of information, including online learning sites and applications, that are available at the tip of our fingers is both a blessing and a curse. We register the new information, but do not have time to make sense of it, to see how it can be integrated with what we already know; we live in a constant "cognitive dissonance". Thinking, understanding and aligning knowledge structures requires time and focused attention – a resource we lack, due to our fear of missing out on something new in the meanwhile. We keep scrolling down to find information that we already know and that confirms our current beliefs and prejudices; this makes us feel comfortable and safe, more in control of the information barrage. How to know which information or authority (source) to trust in an age when old authorities are questioned, old monuments are falling to the ground, and political corruption is exposed on a massive scale around the world? We are paralyzed by hesitation – what is worth remembering or learning?

Nevertheless, humanity does adapt to the technologies it creates. An increasing proportion of human skills are automated and we lose them. Do we even need to be literate? Do we need typing or handwriting skills? We now dictate text to the computer, smartphone, smartwatch or laptop, and they produce text that can be easily processed. Who needs spelling or grammar skills? There are excellent spellcheckers, and decent grammar- and style-proofing tools. Duolingo has revolutionized learning languages and made it available to everyone everywhere, in an engaging, playful way. But why even bother to learn a new language? Computer translations are already quite good, at least between the most common languages. Google translates for free even specialized legal documents, which normally require an experienced professional translator in the area.

Professions and entire categories of work are transforming or even disappearing at an unprecedented rate; the profession "translator" (at least from languages such as English, French, Spanish and German) will almost certainly employ very few people in the future. Similarly, many professions requiring high-level training, e.g., family doctors, lawyers, financial advisors, possibly civil engineers and architects will likely be significantly reduced in numbers. It could happen to teachers as well. We have already experienced telemedicine and telelearning on a massive scale during the pandemic and it seems to work relatively well, while yielding massive efficiencies. All these jobs require skills and knowledge developed after years of systematic training, and they are likely to disappear or become extremely competitive. For what jobs should we prepare our children? What skills should we learn to be able to requalify ourselves after losing our jobs, when big changes happen in such a short time? Is human learning becoming obsolete? Is there a place for education, training, and mentoring in the future?

I believe that we need to commit a lot more attention to human learning, just as we do now to climate change, and support it with technology to meet the new challenges. It seems that basic literacy, numeracy, and language skills are important "Lego blocks" needed to build higher-order (meta-) skills for abstract thinking, categorization, and organization, as well as discipline, grit, and ability to focus attention on a problem and not give up. It is hard to learn high-level skills directly. Skills for problem solving, discovery, creativity, planning, and decision making are best learned in the context of specific domains, and learners generalize their experiences through a lot of practice and failures. New meta-skills will be needed by the lifelong learner in the age of information glut: skills for searching and evaluating the credibility of information sources, communication and collaboration skills, skills of meditation to focus the mind, fight procrastination, and the patience and determination required to study and practice challenging concepts and skills.

Young people now communicate less face-to-face and more online. This is not only due to the pandemic waves with the recurring school closures and masking regulations, but also because young people are growing up being baby-sat by smart phones and tablets, and social networks entice them early on into non-stop communication with their peers through screens. Yet it is not clear that this communication leads to learning social and collaboration skills, or how to empathize with others. On the contrary, we see an increase in mental health issues at increasingly younger ages. It becomes important also to learn "hygge" or how to "switch off" technology, to keep peace of mind, to appreciate poetry and deep friendships. With all of these categories of knowledge that seem necessary (basic skills, higher-level thinking skills, information-handling skills and mental health skills), what is the minimal basic common knowledge and skills that young people need to learn to be able to function in a society?

These are hard problems that cannot be solved by intelligent computers; they need to be solved by society, by humans. Yet, AI-powered technologies can provide educational tools that help to learn some of the skills listed above. Many AI-powered educational tools and apps are already freely available online and their number will grow constantly. They offer personalized learning paths to acquire specialized knowledge in many domains, for example, astronomy, biology, a language, or food chemistry. Learners will use these tools to develop domain-specific skills in areas of their choice, so that they can build upon them and practice their higher-order (meta-)skills: discovery, critical thinking, problem solving, and decision making. Can we use AI-powered technology to teach meta-skills? As the recent misinformation epidemic shows, we really need intelligent tutors to teach skills in critical and selective information consumption, problem solving with basic probability and statistics. We need tutors using Socratic dialogues challenging learners' existing beliefs and stereotypes, and helping them expand their knowledge, views, and online social circles. There are already persuasive technology apps that advise people on how to maintain their physical and mental health, and AI-based systems that mentor users on how to work effectively together with others, respecting others' autonomy, views, and cultural background (Dimitrova & Mitrovic, 2021). Further research should explore how to better personalize these systems using holistic learner models and to use data mining with different data modalities: not just text, but also voice, motion and gesture, facial expressions, and various context features to uncover the cognitive, affective, and motivational states, and the current goals of the learner.

While the big unsolved problems described above are related to the question "What to teach?", many new problems also arise around the question "How to teach?". The advances in learner modelling need to be matched by advances in the pedagogy for personalized instruction and guidance. For example, how to use the insights into the learner's mental state to select the best teaching or motivational action? Machine learning can help discover successful pedagogical interventions for identified learner states, if there is a lot of training data available. This leads to the need to share learner data widely and openly among developers of AI-based educational systems. Balancing the need for sharing data with privacy legislation and security constraints will be challenging. Using anonymized data-sets and synthetic data to pre-train models can alleviate privacy concerns, but may increase bias and inequality, if not done carefully.

One problem that will be gaining importance is how to maintain the learner in a favourable motivation state for learning. This is especially important when they are trying to acquire conceptually difficult knowledge or to practice skills that require a lot of mundane and repetitive training. While there has been significant progress in detecting learner attention and affect using eye-gaze and various sensors, discovering motivation states is not straightforward. How to influence a deteriorating level of motivation with appropriate actions? A human teacher may choose to address the student's decreasing motivation by many means, for example, by letting the learner try a simpler problem to boost their self-efficacy, by cracking a joke, by emphasizing the importance of a particular concept or skill relative to the overall learning, by reminding and reinforcing the learner's commitment to their learning goal, or by suggesting to take a break. But how to discover whether the decreasing motivation is the short-term result of negative affect, such as a temporary distraction, fatigue, or because of a long-term change in goals, interests, and priorities? How to proactively engage the student in a dialogue to disambiguate the diagnosis, without becoming obtrusive? A lot of relevant research on conversational agents has been done over the last 25 years in specific domains and learning contexts; as natural language generation technology and conversational agents are becoming ubiquitous (Alexa, Google Assistant, Siri), the education field is ripe for applying these technologies widely and developing new ones.

In addition to maintaining learner motivation during a particular learning experience, an important problem is getting learners motivated to embark on learning something. As technologies evolve and take over tasks that were done by humans, we all need to be life-long learners. How to keep motivated to invest the time and effort to learn a new domain of knowledge and skills, when it is not certain how long before computers take over and the knowledge/skill also becomes obsolete? The optimistic view is that people will always want to learn new things, because they are naturally curious. The pessimistic view is that people will "give up" and resign themselves to the state of passive consumers, sustained by universal income, seeking satisfaction in a meta-world, playing games or taking drugs that make them feel happy and fulfilled.

Educational games and gamification of learning systems are ways to make learning more engaging and attractive. There has been a lot of research in this area over the last ten years which has shown strong positive results, and yet still relatively few approaches use personalization and adapt the game mechanics to the learner's engagement, motivation and knowledge levels (Rodrigues et al., 2021). There is untapped potential in using machine learning and data mining in the context of educational games and gamification. Dynamic personalization of gamified educational systems and educational games is an open research area that is likely to attract a lot more attention in the future.

Persuasive technology is an area of research that can offer useful strategies and insights into increasing user motivation and engagement. There is a large set of persuasive strategies that can be used to influence user behaviour without coercion, for goals that benefit the user and society. Until recently this area has developed applications mostly to stimulate behaviour change in e-commerce or in health-related apps, helping users to eat properly and exercise regularly. There is an active research stream in personalizing persuasive strategies considering psychological types, culture, and demographic factors (Oyibo et al., 2017), personality features, goals, and context. Attempts to incorporate dynamic personalization by learning from user response to persuasion are ongoing. Applications of personalized persuasive technologies are now also appearing in educational systems (Orji, 2021; Orji & Vassileva, 2021), and mental health (Adib et al., 2021; MacLeod et al., 2021) and this is a promising direction of research to address learner engagement, and, more generally, to promote behaviours that are conductive to acquiring higher-level personal and interpersonal skills.

To summarize, the ongoing information revolution raises many new problems for education. Some of them relate to the question "how to teach and engage" and they can be foreseeably addressed with solutions relying on rapidly developing AI technologies, such as data mining, advanced learner modelling of affect with personalized games and persuasive technologies. However, there are many important problems that society needs to tackle and define, before technological optimizations can be found. They are related to the question "what to teach" and generally, how to make human learning socially rewarding again.

3. PEDAGOGICAL AGENTS FOR ALL: DESIGNING VIRTUAL CHARACTERS FOR INCLUSION AND DIVERSITY IN STEM

H. Chad Lane

Introduction

A pedagogical agent (PA) can be defined as a virtual character or physical robot that seeks to promote learning, enhance motivation, and provide support to engage in an educational activity. PAs can be non-interactive or interactive, and typically seek to emulate naturalistic communication with learners through speech, gesture, emotions, and action. In AIED systems, PAs are typically considered as part of the user interface and designed in the context of system features intended to support learning, such as for problem solving and with natural interaction (see Chapter 10 by Lajoie & Li, Chapter 11 by Rus et al.).

There are many reasons to think that PAs can be beneficial. Given that much learning is fundamentally social and occurs with other people, such as in classrooms (Kumpulainen &

Wray, 2003) and museums (Leinhardt et al., 2003), it is intuitive to extend AIED systems to include naturalistic interactions including questions, dialogue, smiling, pointing, and more. It is established that people are prone to adopt social frames when interacting with computers (Reeves & Nass, 1996) and so including an embodied PA may activate an even deeper social frame for learners as they gain new skills or knowledge.

Over the last three decades, substantial effort has gone into investigating the designs, roles and impacts of pedagogical agents (Heidig & Clarebout, 2011; Johnson & Lester, 2018; Lane & Schroeder, 2022; Moreno et al., 2000). The field has worked diligently to identify evidence-based design principles (Baylor, 2011; Craig & Schroeder, 2018) and to conduct wide-ranging efficacy studies (Schroeder et al., 2013). So the challenge now lies in how best to leverage this important technology as it inches closer to becoming more mainstream and having the potential for greater societal impact. In this contribution, I argue that the next phase of research should focus on the power of PAs to promote more inclusive and welcoming learning environments. Specifically, I describe a roadmap that positions PAs as *ambassadors of STEM education* and that focus on improving learner feelings about domain content. We should view PAs as tools in an ongoing battle to bring equity and diversity to STEM (Ferrini-Mundy, 2013). Operationally, I advocate for investigation of identifying strategies that seek to invite learners to participate, engage, and persist in STEM such that their learning experiences have longer-lasting effects that sustain the goal of the acquisition of knowledge as essential, but also produce meaningful impacts on noncognitive outcomes, such as interest, persistence, academic resilience, and motivation.

The Critical Influences of Appearance and Social Interaction

A long list of factors influence the relationship children have with STEM. First, children are bombarded with depictions of STEM professionals on television, in advertisements, and even in the video games they play. Decades of research has demonstrated that these (often subtle) messages shape attitudes and beliefs about their own self-concept and identity (Dill-Shackleford et al., 2017). Second, a child's relationship with STEM is highly influenced by the social STEM experiences in their lives. For example, the presence of "everyday science talk" around friends and family (Cian et al., 2021), access to early, informal STEM learning experiences (Dou et al., 2019), and classroom activities with teachers and peers (Hachey, 2020) are all known to play important roles.

PAs can be considered to address both of these aspects directly. For example, the decision to use a PA is an implicit agreement to also design a representative of the topic being taught.[1] Early research indeed confirmed that PA designs could invoke stereotypes by the learner (Moreno et al., 2002). Baylor and Kim (2004) explored some of the design space of agents, such as ethnicity and gender, concluding (among other findings) that agents that challenged stereotypes lead to greater transfer of learning. However, this finding has proven difficult to replicate. For example, Schroeder and Adesope (2015) found that gender had no impact on cognitive or affective outcomes in their studies. Continued investigation into the subtle consequences of PA design is much needed.

Perhaps more importantly, however, PAs that engage in natural interaction with the learner (e.g, spoken or typed input, natural language output, or nonverbal signals) are aligned with the second key influencer of STEM identity: social experiences. Some PA research is suggestive that fine-tuning social behaviors can fundamentally change a learning experience. For example, Finkelstein et al. (2013) found that a peer agent that used a *culturally congruent* dialect (i.e., the same dialect as the learner) produced improved science communication and science reasoning by learners. This study suggests that, for younger learners, PAs should seek to communicate in familiar ways that enable learners to focus on expressing STEM understanding and less on whether or not they are speaking "correctly". A different study on agent behaviors showed that a PA in an informal learning environment who conveyed excitement and high levels of interest in the topic produced fewer non-productive learning behaviors and greater feelings of self-efficacy in learners (Lane et al., 2013). Many more studies support the idea that agent behaviors can influence both cognitive and affective outcomes (Schroeder & Adesope, 2014), an essential point if we adopt the goal to position PAs in more prominent roles in the future.

Roadmap for Leveraging Pedagogical Agents for STEM Inclusion

Although the design of PAs for more "traditional" learning environments is far from solved, there are reasons to assume PAs can achieve much more and have more lasting impacts. In this final section, I outline three goals for future research that emphasize their potential roles in addressing challenges associated with broadening participation in STEM (NSF INCLUDES Coordination Hub, 2020).

Support for social and emotional learning (SEL)
A key barrier for participation in STEM is that learners from historically underrepresented and underserved groups often face stress and anxiety from numerous sources. These can be related to legacy inequalities, such as lack of access to needed resources (e.g., internet), or to factors related to poverty. While a PA is not likely to solve such systemic problems, awareness of such factors and the ability to convey empathy could be part of a coordinated effort (say with educators or counselors) to promote the emotional self-regulatory skills, like academic resilience and persistence, that would enable a young disadvantaged learner to become more engaged with STEM. Arming PAs with knowledge about how to bolster SEL skills holds incredible promise to lead to downstream success in STEM (Garner et al., 2018).

Entry points to STEM and support for interest development
Early learning experiences are critical in the development of STEM learning (McClure et al., 2017) and for long-term interest development in STEM (Renninger & Hidi, 2016). For example, young learners in early stages of interest typically need to experience more positive emotions and require high levels of support to receive positive feedback and encouragement (Renninger et al., 2019). While ideally such support would come naturally through peers and adults, it doesn't always happen. A PA that is specifically designed to gently introduce a topic to a learner, use personalized motivational techniques (e.g., that reflect personal relevance), and offer ongoing encouragement could have a positive effect on a child (just as their television and media consumption do).

Identify learner assets and broaden adaptivity of PAs
Finally, I propose that AIED researchers seek a new breed of PAs that are able to exercise a new level of adaptivity. While beyond the scope of current technologies, it is certainly not

unreasonable to imagine a PA being able to infer and elicit more about the learners they interact with. Specifically, *asset-based* approaches to STEM education suggest that deficit-based approaches (i.e., correcting what is "wrong" about learners who are not in STEM) can be equally as damaging as systematic societal biases. Such a PA would be more driven to learn about the learner, their interests, their strengths, and their possible goals. This would then directly influence the pedagogical choices that are made, such as what content to present and feedback policies.

An example content area for such an approach can be found in the (now numerous) STEM programs in the US that build on Black youth interest in Hip-hop (Emdin et al., 2016). It is possible to imagine a PA adopting the goal of "bringing out the STEM" in such domains and building learner confidence to learn and achieve self-selected goals. Highlighting connections to STEM, such as between computational thinking and music, or digital skills for music production, would be essential. The design of a knowledge base for culturally aligned learning activities would be needed, but strengthened with the capability for dynamic retrieval of content from the web to improve relevance and timeliness (Zhai & Massung, 2016).

Conclusion

Substantial progress has been made in PA research over the last 30 years, demonstrating their efficacy to both enhance learning and define fundamental design principles. The trajectory of this broad body of work along with rapid advances in relevant areas of AI suggests that a new wave of PAs is coming. It is not clear whether current PAs tap fully into their full potential power to create social learning experiences, and so a new generation of PAs that specifically address goals related to inclusion and cultural adaptivity could have profound impacts on how learners view their own learning experiences. I have proposed that this new generation of PAs should include techniques to support the social and emotional learning needs of children, focus on "ambassador"-like skills such as introducing STEM domains and promoting interest, and gaining a new level of adaptivity to support learning in ways that adapt to emergent learner goals. Together, these goals could position PAs as an important tool in creating AIED systems that are more inclusive and which catalyze other related efforts to broaden participation in STEM.

4. INTELLIGENT TEXTBOOKS

Peter Brusilovsky and Sergey Sosnovsky

Textbooks are one of the most popular tools for learning. Traditional textbooks are a product of many decades of refinement and improvement. Page numbers, table of contents, index, and glossary are examples of important empowering functionalities that were added over the years and are now expected by every reader. However, a quiet revolution in the area of textbooks that we are witnessing now is going far beyond past attempts on improving textbooks. Starting in the early days of multimedia with the first interactive textbooks on CD-ROM, every new technology wave encouraged publishers and authors to explore new opportunities for textbook production and distribution. With their popularity and support growing year by year, digital textbooks are gradually replacing their printed counterparts. In turn, it encourages researchers from several fields to explore digital textbooks as an application area for advanced technologies. Over the last 25 years, the research on *intelligent textbooks*, that is, the use of AI to

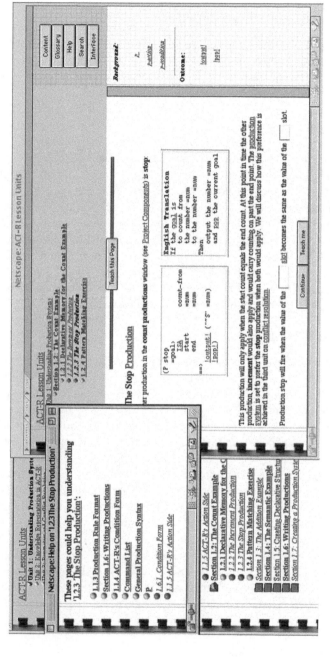

Source: Brusilovsky, 1998

Figure 27.1   *Adaptive navigation support and content recommendation in an adaptive textbook developed with InterBook*

enrich textbooks, has gradually become one of the main directions of textbook innovation. Below, we review the research on intelligent textbooks by examining opportunities provided by several popular AI technologies.

Crafting Textbooks Augmented with Intelligence

The first wave of intelligent textbooks was developed by researchers on *adaptive hypermedia* within the traditional stream of AI research focused on knowledge elicitation and representation (Hohl, 1996; Brusilovsky, 1998; Weber, 2001). The goal of adaptive hypermedia textbooks was to guide different readers to the most relevant sections of hypermedia-based textbooks using *adaptive navigation support* or to choose the most relevant content to present through *adaptive presentation*. The intelligence and personalization in these books were based on augmenting textbook sections with domain knowledge elicited from domain experts. For every textbook, domain experts were expected to create a *domain model* (a set of key concepts presented in the book) and use it to create a *content model* for every book section (i.e., a set of concepts covered by the section). Most advanced adaptive textbooks used domain models in a form of semantic network and distinguished prerequisite/outcome concepts for each section (Brusilovsky, 1998). The knowledge of individual learners was represented as a traditional *overlay student model* which maintained an estimation of student knowledge for each domain concept. Early adaptive textbooks demonstrated that these knowledge models could support a number of intelligent functionalities – such as various kinds of adaptive link annotation (Brusilovsky, 1998; Weber, 2001), adaptive presentation (Hohl, 1996), content recommendation (Kavcic, 2004), concept-based navigation (Brusilovsky, 1998) and textbook assembly (Melis, 2001).

Enriching Textbooks with Intelligence

One of the classic problems of early intelligent textbooks was that they followed a closed-box approach. Once implemented, it was impossible to modify them or enrich them with additional content or knowledge. The development of Semantic Web technologies offered new standardization formats and modeling languages for shareable and expressive knowledge representation along with new architectural solutions for intelligent software. This allowed intelligent textbook researchers to implement knowledge models as ontologies and educational material as interlinked and annotated learning objects, facilitating integration of external content. Initial projects developing these ideas focused on proposing new fully ontological architectures that allowed manual extension of adaptive textbooks with external learning objects (Dolog et al., 2004). Later, successful attempts were also made to automate semantic integration of external content into adaptive textbooks (Sosnovsky, 2012) and to adaptively assemble textbooks from large repositories of interlinked learning objects (see Figure 27.2). Semantic Web has also supplied intelligent textbook researchers with the expressive power of description logic. When combined with symbolic natural language processing (NLP), it supported development of semantically annotated textbook prototypes that can "understand" their content and engage in rich interactions with students, such as meaningful question answering and concept mapping exercises (Chadhuri, 2013).

Extracting Intelligence from Textbook Content

Over the last decade, a few projects started investigating textbooks from a very different perspective. They looked at the textbooks not as an object to add value to, but rather as a source

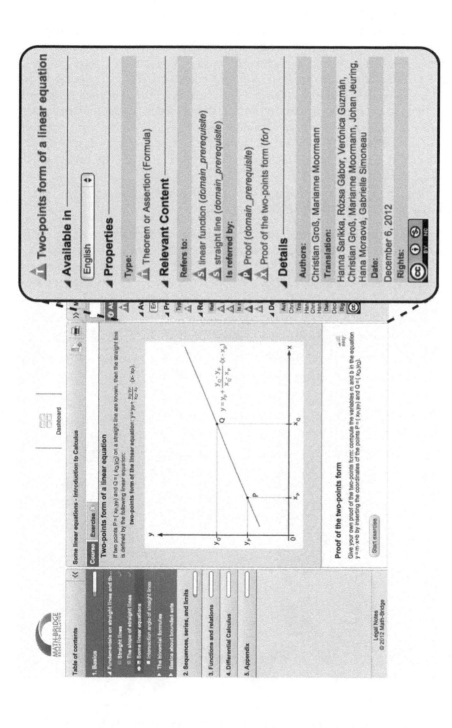

Source: Sosnovsky, 2014

Figure 27.2 Interface of the Math-Bridge system: an adaptively assembled textbook with links between different learning objects displayed in the right-hand panel

617

of value. This new generation of research has been enabled by advances in the fields of NLP and machine learning (ML). The content, the structure, and the formatting elements of text-books have been utilized to extract domain knowledge and different types of learning objects. A number of papers explored approaches for automatic extraction of topics and concepts from textbooks (Wang et al., 2016), as well as harvesting relationships between them (Adorni, 2019). Ultimately, this line of research leads to automatic construction of full concept-based domain models "behind pages" (Alpizar-Chacon, 2021). These models can be used to support intelligent and adaptive services pioneered by the early textbooks (such as concept-based navigation or integration of external content), yet without expensive manual knowledge engineering. Another application of NLP technologies that has gained prominence in the last few years is the use of textbooks to generate additional learning content, such as assessment questions (Kumar, 2015) or definitions (Yarbro, 2021).

Extracting Intelligence from Textbook Interaction Data

Several interesting directions of research on intelligent textbooks have been motivated by rapidly increased volume of data capturing user interactions with online textbooks. Existing research leverages these data in several ways. Most importantly, large volumes of learner data enabled researchers to better understand reading behavior and connect it to learning progress. On a coarse-grained level, understanding patterns in textbook navigation and annotation

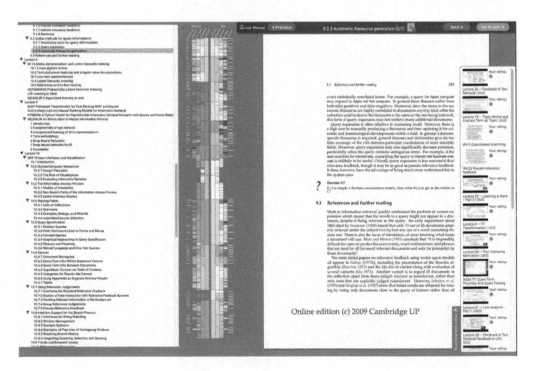

Source: Barria-Pineda, 2019

Figure 27.3   *Social comparison and external content recommendation in ReadingMirror*

behavior could be used to predict learner success or failure, which could be used for early intervention (Winchell, 2018; Yin, 2019). On a fine-grained level, student interaction with a textbook could be used to model student knowledge for different textbook concepts. These fine-grained models could be used to recommend most relevant internal (Thaker, 2020) or external (see Figure 27.3) content to read.

User interaction data could be also used to improve the textbook organization or representation. For example, in combination with content data, log data could be used for a more reliable elicitation of prerequisite relationships (Liu, 2016). Finally, in the spirit of transparency, interaction data could be released directly to the readers through the textbook interface. This approach could be used to support open learner modeling and social awareness. Figure 27.3 shows an example of a socially transparent textbook interface ReadingMirror (Barria-Pineda, 2019) where a combination of personal and social reading data offers social navigation and social comparison.

5. AI-EMPOWERED OPEN-ENDED LEARNING ENVIRONMENTS IN STEM DOMAINS
Gautam Biswas

Introduction

The last twenty years have produced significant developments in AI, machine learning and technologies that support data collection and analyses in computer-based learning environments. New directions have evolved in the field of AI in Education, one primarily being the development of Open-Ended Learning Environments (OELEs) that adopt a constructivist epistemology to support the acquisition of domain knowledge along with critical thinking and problem-solving skills (Biswas et al., 2016). Students working in these environments have a specified learning goal, such as constructing a model of a scientific process. To facilitate learning with understanding and to help students develop problem-solving skills (Bransford et al., 2000), we have adopted AI and machine-learning methods that provide students with tools and resources that support hypothesis generation, solution construction and hypothesis verification and refinement in different phases of learning. Betty's Brain (Biswas et al., 2016), C2STEM (Hutchins et al., 2020a) and SPICE (Zhang et al., 2019) are examples of OELEs developed by our group. In addition, we have developed machine-learning methods and learning analytics to analyze students' learning behaviors and performance from their activity logs in our OELEs.

AI Representations to Support STEM Learning

In all of our systems, we adopt AI-driven modeling representations (e.g., causal maps, block-structured programming languages) that are intuitive, visual, and executable. The ability to execute their evolving models helps students develop important reasoning, explanation, and debugging strategies (Biswas et al., 2016; Zhang et al., 2021). In recent work, we have exemplified the importance of AI representations in developing domain-specific modeling languages (DSMLs) to scaffold students' computational modeling of scientific phenomena (Hutchins et al., 2020b). We illustrate the use of AI representations in two example systems below.

The *Betty's Brain* learning environment (Biswas et al., 2016) presents students with the task of teaching a virtual agent generically named Betty, about a scientific process by constructing a visual causal map. The DSML representation of the causal map provides a set of concepts relevant to the science topic and directed links that students can use to model causal relations between concepts. Betty uses a simple qualitative reasoning mechanism with the map she has been taught (Leelawong & Biswas, 2008) to answer questions and explain her answers. The student's goal in this OELE is to teach Betty a causal map that matches a hidden, expert model of the domain. The students' learning and teaching tasks are organized around three primary activities: (1) reading hypertext resources, (2) building the map, and (3) assessing the correctness of the map. The hypertext resources describe the science topic under study. As students read the resources, they need to identify causal relations and then explicitly teach those relations to Betty in the form of the causal map. To check the correctness of their current map, students can ask Betty to take a quiz. The quiz results help students determine the correctness and completeness of their current map. Figure 27.4 illustrates the Betty's Brain system quiz interface.

SPICE (Science Projects Integrating Computing and Engineering) implements a novel middle- school three-week NGSS-aligned water runoff curriculum (WRC) (McElhaney et al., 2020; Zhang et al., 2021). Students take on an engineering design challenge to redesign their schoolyard and overcome flooding problems during periods of heavy rainfall. The challenge is to minimize surface water runoff during a storm, while adhering to constraints on the total cost, accessibility of the schoolyard, and the need to accommodate different play activities (e.g., soccer field and basketball court). The science investigation involves hands-on activities and developing a conceptual model that focuses on the *conservation of matter*, that is, the amount of water runoff is the difference between the total rainfall and water absorbed by surface materials. Students are then introduced to

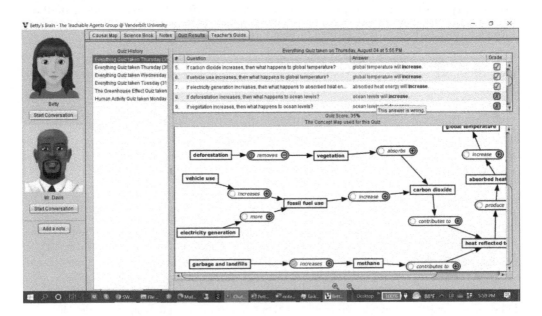

Figure 27.4   Quiz interface in the Betty's Brain system

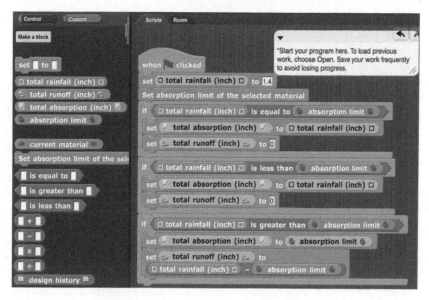

Figure 27.5   Computational Modeling Interface in the SPICE environment

the computational concepts of variables, expressions and conditionals, which they apply to develop a computational water runoff model. Like before, this model is executable and supports testing and debugging activities to help students refine their models. Figure 27.5 shows the DSML created for the computational modeling activity (left) and a correct implementation of the runoff model (right). Students then use their runoff model code in an environment comprising 4×4 squares representing the playground layout for the engineering design task. Students select appropriate materials for the different parts of the schoolyard. The model, when executed, computes the total run off and cost for the current design solution.

These examples illustrate the use of AI representational and reasoning mechanisms in our OELEs:

- The use of domain-specific, intuitive, visual representations mechanisms that make explicit the concepts and reasoning mechanisms of the science domain (Hutchins et al., 2020b);
- Providing students with a sequence of linked domain representations (e.g., conceptual, computational, and engineering design models in SPICE (Hutchins et al., 2021) that facilitate learning with multiple representations;
- An exploratory, inquiry-based approach to learning of scientific processes using executable models, so students can formulate and test hypotheses, and learn to verify (debug) their models, thus developing critical thinking skills.

Analyzing Students' Learning Behaviors

When working in OELEs, novice learners often have difficulties in keeping track of the tools provided in the learning environment and combining the use of these tools in an effective manner to accomplish their goals (Basu et al., 2016). These problems are exacerbated by the students' lack of self-judgment and strategic thinking abilities. To understand students' challenges and help them make progress in their learning tasks, we have developed machine-learning methods to track students' performance and learning behaviors as they progress through a sequence of curricular units (Kinnebrew et al., 2017; Hutchins et al., 2021). Our approaches combine model-driven learning analytics and data-driven sequence mining methods in machine learning to understand students' difficulties (Kinnebrew et al., 2017).

For example, we have developed sequence mining methods (Kinnebrew et al., 2013) to analyze students' activity data capture in log files to extract their frequent activity patterns and associate them with learning behaviors and strategies (Kinnebrew et al., 2017). In addition, we have developed analytic measures based on the concept of coherence analysis (Segedy et al., 2015) to understand the relations between their consecutive actions in the context of their associated tasks. In studies with Betty's Brain conducted in middle-school classrooms, a frequent pattern we have observed students performing is: *Add Incorrect Link* (AIL) → *Take Quiz* (Quiz) → *Remove Incorrect Link* (RIL). Students add an incorrect link to their map, follow that by taking a quiz, and then make the deduction that the link added was incorrect and remove it from their map. A first reaction is that this pattern represents a *Guess and check strategy* used by the students. However, a deeper analysis reveals that *high-performing students*, that is, those who succeed in building a correct causal model, tend to use this activity pattern mainly toward the end of their map building tasks. On the other hand, students who had difficulty in building correct models use this pattern frequently when they commence their map-building tasks.

This indicates differences in the use of the pattern by the two groups of students. To investigate further, we computed two analytic measures: (1) *pattern coherence*, implying the link added was the link removed; and (2) *pattern support*, implying the quiz results provided evidence that the link removed was incorrect. These results show that the high performers were more likely (3:1) to use this pattern for systematically checking the link they had just added (pattern was coherent and supported), whereas the low performers were much more likely (10:1) to use this pattern as an uninformed guess and check strategy (their use of the pattern was not coherent and not supported).

As a second example, we investigate how students' performance in each one of the curricular activities in SPICE influenced performance in subsequent activities. We developed a number of measures that included pre- and post-tests that covered science, engineering, and CT to quantify students' prior knowledge and knowledge gained through the intervention, respectively; formative assessments to scaffold student learning, students' performance in building their computational models, and the quality of their engineering design solutions generated.

We used a machine-learning approach, *Path Analysis* (Ahn, 2002), to study the relative importance of effects among the measured performance values for the sequence from pre-test to formative assessment to computational modeling to engineering design to post-test scores in the WRC curriculum. Path analysis represents a form of structured equation modeling (Kline, 2015), and may be considered as a simplified form of learning a Bayesian network (Pearl & Mackenzie, 2018). Figure 27.6 shows the derived path model.

The figure points to a number of informative pathways that form the basis of understanding students' progress through the curriculum. For example, higher prior knowledge in computational thinking led to better performance in the formative assessments, then better

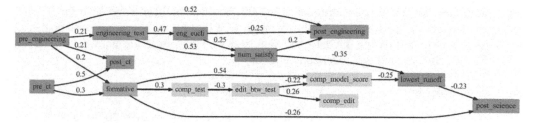

Figure 27.6   Causal paths discovered with statistically significant direct effects

computational model-building strategies (e.g., building the model in parts, testing the model for correctness), which in turn led to the building of more correct computational models of the science phenomenon. Further, this path showed that these students also generated the best design solutions, that is, solutions that met the cost and accessibility constraints and minimized runoff. Last, they had higher scores in their science and CT post-tests. Similarly, higher prior knowledge in engineering led to using more effective search methods and testing to generate design solutions, resulting in more optimal design solutions as well as higher science and engineering post-test scores.

In summary, the two examples above, demonstrate the use of machine-learning techniques that we have employed to analyze logs of students' activities in our systems to gain a deeper understanding of their learning behaviors and their performance in learning STEM concepts and practices.

The Future: From Log File Analysis to Multimodal Analytics to Understand Students' SRL Behaviors

Researchers have established comprehensive frameworks for studying self-regulated learning (SRL) as a dynamic, interacting collection of students' cognitive, affective, metacognitive, and motivational (CAMM) processes (Azevedo et al., 2017; Panadero, 2017). Our prior work primarily focused on understanding students' cognitive and metacognitive processes and strategies. However, recent work has used additional sensors to better understand students' learning behaviors. For example, we have used:

- *Microphones* and *natural language processing* techniques to capture and interpret students' conversations and understand the difficulties they face in their computational modeling tasks when they work in pairs in the C2STEM environment (e.g., Snyder et al., 2019);
- *Eye-tracking devices* and machine-learning *classifiers* to predict how students' gaze patterns during reading resources are predictive of their abilities to construct correct causal maps in Betty's Brain (Rajendran et al., 2018); and
- *Face-tracking devices* and *deep-learning* algorithms to understand the relations between students' affective states and their cognitive and metacognitive behaviors (Munshi et al., 2018; Taub et al., 2021).

Currently, we are developing *multimodal analysis frameworks* that combine data from multiple sensors, such as students' activity logs, microphones, videos, eye-tracking, and face-tracking devices, along with advanced machine-learning algorithms to build comprehensive models of learner behaviors and performance as they work in OELEs. Our long-term research goals are to design adaptive scaffolding in OELEs to help students overcome their learning difficulties and become self-regulated and independent learners.

Acknowledgments

This research is partially supported by NSF (IIS) Cyberlearning award # 2017000 and a previous NSF STEM+C award DRL-1742195. The author would also like to support a long list of graduate students and collaborators who have worked with him on a variety of research projects in the area of AI in Education.

6. UBIQUITOUS-AIED: PERVASIVE AI LEARNING TECHNOLOGIES

James C. Lester

AI has emerged as a powerful family of technologies that promise to reshape every facet of society. AI systems are rapidly becoming more accurate, training times for machine learning are falling dramatically, and the range of AI-driven applications is expanding at an unprecedented rate. Through "edge AI," natural language processing, computer vision, and machine learning are being deployed on a broad array of platforms that operate in the field, not just in the cloud. Perhaps the most striking development in the emergence of AI is its ubiquity. With the proliferation of ever more powerful computing devices, sensors, and networks that support extraordinary volumes of data, AI is quickly becoming deeply enmeshed in our everyday lives.

Just as AI is rapidly becoming ubiquitous, so will AI learning technologies. This development introduces both the opportunity and the need to re-envision how learners will interact with AI-empowered learning environments. A significant departure from how the pioneers of AIED imagined the systems they were designing would be used, *ubiquitous-AIED* calls for a research program that fundamentally changes how we envision the field. It pushes to the forefront issues of the learner operating in a wide range of naturalistic learning contexts.

Assumptions of Ubiquitous AIED

AI capabilities are becoming increasingly commoditized with core AI technologies quickly becoming exceptionally accurate, fast, and inexpensive. Because AI-driven learning environments directly leverage AI technologies, hardware and software barriers to widescale usage of AIED are rapidly falling. In a very few years, it seems all but certain that AI-driven learning environments could be physically distributed throughout schools, informal learning contexts (e.g., museums, after-school programs), homes, and workplaces, and running on devices with a range of form factors from the large (e.g., wall-sized displays) to the mid-sized (e.g., laptops) to the small (e.g., phones, watches). They could also be delivered through increasingly powerful media that include virtual reality, augmented reality, and mixed-reality media. With the proliferation of increasingly powerful and inexpensive sensors, they could have access to many modalities of learner data spanning auditory (speech) and visual (learner facial expression, gaze, gesture, posture) data streams, as well as locational and physiological data streams.

In addition, they could readily have access to temporal data about learners spanning windows of milliseconds, minutes, hours, weeks, months, and even years. Whether they *should* have access to these data is a deeply important question.

Ubiquitous-AIED Opportunities

When AI becomes a utility, AIED can become pervasive, and the prospect of ubiquitous AIED opens up a wide vista of AI-empowered learning. Learner models will become unimaginably powerful. In addition to the high-volume streams of multimodal data for an individual learner, learner models will be trained on data from a multitude of learner populations in myriad learning contexts for countless subject matters and skills. They will achieve levels of accuracy never previously imagined. Their capabilities for recognizing learners' goals and plans will grow rapidly, and the range of the competencies they model will dramatically expand. In addition to cognitive and disciplinary competencies typically associated with traditional curricula, they will be able to accurately model metacognitive and social skills, complemented by highly accurate affective models. Significant increases in diagnostic power will shape individualization of learning experiences in ways that we cannot currently envision. They will be able to generate problem-solving scenarios, scaffold learning, and create extraordinarily motivating experiences that are deftly crafted for individual learners in very specific learning contexts. Furthermore, because the contexts of AIED deployments will be represented at high levels of granularity, they will enable group learner modeling that supports rich collaborative learning interactions.

Ubiquitous-AIED will profoundly reshape AI-empowered learning experiences. Consider the case of pedagogical agents. Learners will engage with ubiquitous-AIED pedagogical agents that are unfettered by current-day computational constraints. Learners will converse with their agents in rich spoken dialogue, regardless of whether the agent is on their laptop, phone, or watch. Agents will be able to reason about learners' non-verbal signals as learners express delight, furrow their brow, use a gesture to convey nuance, or walk with a quickened gait.

Agents will tailor problem-solving advice not only to the learner herself but also to the physical context in which she is situated. And because agents will be able to draw on potentially years of experience interacting with the learner in many contexts, they will be able to create motivating learning experiences and provide guidance that are extraordinarily attuned to the needs and interests of that particular learner.

Ubiquitous-AIED will manifest in many ways. In addition to personified pedagogical agents with visual personae, it will drive speech-only pedagogical agents. It will unobtrusively shape learning experiences in text (e.g., learner-unique textbooks), audio (e.g., learner-unique podcasts) and video (learner-unique animations and documentaries). It will create educational gameplay experiences in which the levels and non-player character interactions are specifically tailored to that learner and learning context (including the platform). It will support multi-context learning in which learners move from one context, such as their elementary school classroom, to another, such as a museum or their home. It will seamlessly shift from coaching traditional subject matters to coaching sports to coaching health behaviors (e.g., nutrition) for wellbeing.

Ubiquitous-AIED will play a prominent role in the workplace. It will soon be hard to conceive of a worker performing a job in the absence of AIED technologies. Workers in sectors ranging from science and technology to finance, transportation, retail, media, agriculture, and healthcare will experience continuous learning with AIED technologies. The education workforce will experience a seismic shift: with the appearance of omnipresent AIED teaching assistants, K-12 teachers and university faculty will soon have at their disposal the means to create learning experiences that fundamentally change how instructors perform their jobs. And rather than experiencing artificially separated phases of working and training, workers will access their AIED technologies to acquire new competencies on demand. Furthermore, as AI–human "teaming," in which job responsibilities are shared between workers and their AI tools, emerges as the dominant paradigm, AIED technologies will take on a new role of scaffolding "teaming" competencies.

The arrival of ubiquitous-AIED will spawn a new era of learning analytics and assessment. The enormous volumes of learner interaction data noted above will yield learning analytics that provide deep insight into learning for researchers and educators. These in turn will give rise to a new generation of powerful assessment technologies for both formative and summative (including high-stakes) assessment. Ubiquitous-AIED-based assessment will be psychometrically grounded and achieve levels of reliability and validity never seen before. Notably, it will support measurement for a broad range of competencies and will be conducted in naturalistic contexts.

Design and Policy Implications for Ubiquitous-AIED

Emerging AI capabilities point toward design and policy implications for ubiquitous-AIED learning technologies. First, considerations of context become increasingly important. Because learners will interact with ubiquitous-AIED learning technologies in specific contexts, these technologies should be designed to reason about the cultural, social, and physical contexts in which they will be deployed. Thus, rather than the comparatively impoverished sense of context that AIED as a field has typically explored, it will be important to give primacy to considerations of the cultural, social, and physical contexts in which learning will occur, as well as their affordances for different aspects of learning. For example, free-choice learning environments such as museums suggest that AI learning environments should be designed to support short dwell times with large groups of learners interacting collaboratively, while home-based learning environments might be designed for much longer learning scenarios.

Second, it is imperative that we consider issues of AI ethics in the design of ubiquitous-AIED learning environments. Fairness, accountability, and transparency all emerge as matters of great importance because of the dramatically increased ability to affect learners' lives. Privacy concerns loom large. With rapidly rising capabilities for reasoning about individual learners, it is paramount that national and international policy be developed around considerations for creating ubiquitous-AIED environments that foreground diversity, equity and inclusion and have a firm ethical foundation that supports and protects all learners.

Third, AIED designers will need to imaginatively lift their sights to most effectively leverage powerful new AI capabilities. For example, with the new reality of natural language processing (NLP), computer vision (CV), and machine learning (ML) models growing nonlinearly in speed and accuracy, it will be important to investigate ubiquitous-AIED frameworks for pedagogical planners, learner modeling, and natural language tutorial dialogue that draw on underlying NLP, CV, and ML methods that support much more robust learning interactions than we have previously considered. And given the rate at which AI capabilities are increasing, we will need to design for multiple generations of AI beyond the current one, which introduces the opportunity to explore new learning technology paradigms supporting qualitatively new forms of learning.

Acknowledgments

This research is supported by the National Science Foundation under Cooperative Agreement DRL-2112635. Any opinions, findings, and conclusions or recommendations expressed in this material are those of the authors and do not necessarily reflect the views of the National Science Foundation.

7. CULTURE, ONTOLOGY AND LEARNER MODELING

Riichiro Mizoguchi

In this essay, I briefly discuss cultural, ontological, and learner modeling issues which I have been investigating recently, and then their implications for future research are discussed.

Cultural Aspects

Millions of different species exist depending on each other to enable sustainable development. Even at the individual level, people are so different in many respects that the differences sometimes cause misunderstandings or struggles. Nevertheless, we should be in a harmony with people. It is the reason why diversity has gained considerable attraction these days. The difference is caused not only by personal factors but by cultural factors. In the Asian culture, in the context of education, teachers are highly respected and have a rather strong initiative in the classroom, which contrasts with Western culture. The belief that what a teacher says is right so that students should accept it is not an extreme case in Asian culture. It is along the line that seniority is respected in Asian culture. At a concrete level, the meaning or connotation of color is different from culture to culture. Although red means danger in many cultures, it means happiness in China, and vermilion is a symbol of long life or a talisman in China and Japan, so shrines in China and Japan are painted in vermilion. This suggests that color coordination at the interface of learning systems needs careful consideration of such cultural differences.

Frankly speaking, these observations are not new but have been discussed in the papers presented at CATS (Culturally Aware Tutoring System) (CATS, 2015) workshops. Although culture has been investigated in sociology, anthropology and related fields extensively to date (Hofstede, 2022; Sociology Group, 2022), there exists a gap between the achievements and educational systems. In order to contribute to bridging the gap, I have built two ontologies of culture with my collaborators, Blanchard (2014) and Savard (2019). The former is designed based on the so-called declarative perspective and the latter is on the procedural perspective, the two being mutually complementary. These ontologies would be useful for the future design of culturally aware tutoring systems that have been discussed in CATS.

Ontological Aspects

The utility of ontology includes making the fundamental conceptual structure of complex entities explicit so that application systems can select necessary concepts from them and consistently exploit them. The above ontologies should evolve through intensive use and feedback.

It would be beneficial to mention another kind of utility of ontology application. What we have seen to date includes an ontology of some entities followed by its use in applications. I would like to introduce a completely different way of the use of ontology in which no ontology is built. It utilizes ontological thinking itself and is applied to English teaching (Alard & Mizoguchi, 2021).

Most of the conventional technology-supported learning systems employ technology for facilitating the learning/instructional process. On the other hand, the system we are talking about uses ontological theories in reorganizing the teaching material, in particular, that of the English grammar of tense and aspects that are notorious for the *ad-hoc* rules. Learners taught using conventional textbooks are often forced to memorize those rules without convincing reasons or justifications. To avoid such a memory-oriented instruction, Danielle Alard and I have tried to reorganize those rules by employing ontological thinking/theories about events. We eventually came up with the following ontological findings:

(1) An event is necessarily a past or future happening, and it cannot be a present happening because the present is an instant and an event needs a non-zero interval,
(2) A process is ongoing so that it is expressed according to the present progressive aspect, and
(3) There exists no event expressed by the simple present tense in the real world.

The third fact derives a very powerful rule that the simple present tense should be used to express what we call *floating* happenings by which we mean events that are not anchored at any definite time in the real world. Typical examples include "I go to school", "The sun rises from the East", and "Go down this street about 100 m, then turn to the right…" which are organized in rules for the use of the simple present tense such as the expression about *custom*, *general truth*, and *instruction* in the conventional textbooks. About ten rules are successfully reduced to just one rule that "Use the simple present tense to express floating happenings".

We went through all the rules about the tense and aspects extracted from several popular textbooks and investigated them in the way described above to come up with new rules whose number is about one-third of the current ones. What is good is not only the drastic reduction in the number of rules but also that most of them are comprehensible to students, which frees them from memorization of *ad-hoc* rules. Although some exceptional rules remain, the majority of the new rules are derived from the ontological nature of events and time so that students can comprehend them independently of their cultural background. Danielle Alard, who is also a teacher of English, has deployed our new rules in her class for more than three years and confirmed a remarkable improvement with surprisingly high satisfaction from the students. I can say this is a great success both for the learning of the English tense and aspects and the innovative use of ontology.

Learner Modeling Aspects

Learner modeling has been a dominant research topic in the AIED community for years because it is key to the adaptive behavior of the learning support systems (see Chapter 7 by Aleven et al. on domain and student modelling) (Nkambou, et al., 2010). Theoretically put, model-building of the learner's understanding of the learning material has been the main focus of the research of learner modeling, which has led to the research on how to represent the state of understanding of a learner supported by an academic interest in what understanding is. This is the reason why all the existing learner modeling methods are about representing how students *understand* the subject. People might have an objection that the bug model does not fit this observation. Although such an objection seems to make sense at first glance, it is not the case. The bug model takes care of misunderstanding which is still in the same realm as the modeling of understanding because it is another "understanding", just one which is incorrect. What we want to explore here is the modeling of *"not understanding"*. Imagine a situation where a student is completely at a loss. She has no idea about what she should do next.

Note here that we do not intend to tackle an intractable task such as modeling how learners misunderstand or uncovering what kind of incorrect knowledge learners would have. The idea of modeling "not understanding" does not deal with learners' knowledge nor its use but deals with the search space in which knowledge is applied.

Let's employ the notion of the search space in GPS (General Problem Solver). Conventional learner modeling methods deal explicitly with knowledge (operators) and its applications to problem solving. They implicitly assume the existence of a search space within which learners perform problem-solving activities (searching for a solution) by applying the knowledge (operators). To represent the "not understanding" state of a learner, we explicitly deal with the search space itself rather than knowledge and its application. Such a student who is completely at a loss is represented as having no search space and a student who fails to find a solution despite her continuous effort might be because of her incomplete search space caused by a failure of establishing a correct search space rather than the lack of knowledge to apply. In particular, for helping low-performance learners who are often at a loss and need effective help to get themselves out of such a state, suggestions to establish an appropriate search space for the problem solving at hand might be more effective than the explanation of necessary knowledge to apply (Mizoguchi, 2020).

Implications for Future Research

Here, I summarize some implications derived from what has been discussed above.

Culturally aware systems

The reformulation of the achievements about culture and cultural differences in sociology and anthropology for its applications to education/learning would be beneficial for building culturally aware tutoring systems. Ontologies of culture or cultural differences would contribute to this enterprise in many ways because they provide the underlying conceptual structure of culture in a computer-understandable manner. Teaching cultural differences would be also a promising topic in which ontologies are useful for producing convincing teaching materials supported by an in-depth understanding of culture as well as cultural differences.

New way of the use of ontology engineering

The success of the new way of ontology use in the reformulation of the teaching materials themselves would open up an innovative way of applying ontology engineering to building learning support systems. The research of OMNIBUS/SMARTIES is viewed as cognate (Mizoguchi & Bourdeau, 2016). The OMNIBUS ontology is built to operationalize learning/ instructional theories to build a theory-aware authoring system named SMARTIES. Those theories are descriptive and have to be interpreted by researchers to use them for building theory-justified learning support systems. OMNIBUS enables such manual interpretation to be skipped by providing operationalized theories that can be interpreted by the SMARTIES authoring system. The reorganization of the rules for the use of English language tense and aspects together with such operationalization of theories by the use of ontology should develop further in the future.

LM of "not understanding"

Although there remains much room for refinement of the method, it is a first step toward establishing a new paradigm of modeling the search space that has been ignored to date. In an extreme case, the notion of the search space itself can be a subject to learn. Not only students but ordinary people rarely have a clear notion of the search space. They tend to think or solve problems simply by applying the knowledge at hand without noticing that they cannot explore outside of the search space implicitly specified (limited) by the knowledge at hand, and hence they are sometimes at a loss when they fail to find a solution in a given time. In such a case, they should pay attention to the search space that has been implicitly assumed/specified and examine its possible limitations to extend or improve it by assessing the potential capacity of the search space. Note here that it is not the problem of whether or not learners possess relevant operators (knowledge), but rather the problem is of noticing relevant kinds of knowledge out of many they already possess to successfully extend the current search space.

8. CROWDSOURCING PAVES THE WAY FOR PERSONALIZED LEARNING

Ethan Prihar and Neil Heffernan

The desire for personalized learning comes from the idea that giving students instruction and support tailored to their specific needs or traits can lead to higher learning gains (Bulger, 2016). In the past, there have been statistically significant positive attempts to personalize learning, such as providing students with different instructional material based on their competency (Kulik & Kulik, 1982; Razzaq & Heffernan, 2009), and statistically insignificant attempts, such as giving students different material based on their assumed learning style (Pashler et al., 2008). Recently, the increased adoption of online learning platforms has enabled methods for personalizing students' learning to be incorporated into students' curricula at a much larger scale than what was previously possible in classroom settings, but while many online learning platforms purport to implement personalized learning, very few have evidence to support the efficacy of their methods (Bulger, 2016). The growing integration of online learning into students' curricula has provided online learning platforms with an unprecedented opportunity to improve their design by engaging with users to create and validate their content, as well as explore for further opportunities for personalization. Educators and researchers using these platforms can be solicited to create content for students, and the impact of this new content on students' learning can be evaluated empirically with data collected from students using the platforms.

ASSISTments, an online learning platform that has been running since 2006, not only has evidence that the platform is effective at increasing students' learning gains (Roschelle et al., 2016), but has also been engaging with educators and researchers to create tutoring for struggling students (Ostrow et al., 2017; Patikorn & Heffernan, 2020). Within *ASSISTments*, students are assigned mathematics problem sets from one of multiple open access curricula, which they complete online through the *ASSISTments Tutor*. The *ASSISTments Tutor* displays each mathematics problem for the students and offers on-demand tutoring if the student is struggling (Heffernan & Heffernan, 2014). Tutoring can come in the form of a complete explanation of how to solve the problem, individual steps that explain how to solve one part of the problem at a time, a series of simpler problems that walk the student through how to solve the more complicated problem, an explanation of how to solve a similar problem or feedback on the specific error a student made. Using the same terminology found in Chapter 9 by Aleven et al. on instructional approaches, *ASSISTments* implements the tutored problem-solving approach through *ASSISTments Tutor*, in which students are provided with step-level formative feedback. An example of the *ASSISTments Tutor* displaying a problem along with a text-based explanation is shown in Figure 27.7.

One way in which *ASSISTments* has leveraged its users to discover opportunities for personalization is by allowing external researchers to create and evaluate different tutoring strategies. Since 2015, more than 100 teams of researchers have been able to run randomized controlled experiments in *ASSISTments*. These experiments have compared video-based tutoring to text-based tutoring, examples of how to solve similar problems to examples of how to solve the problem the student is struggling with, language with positive sentiment to neutral sentiment, and more. By allowing these researchers to create experiments and evaluate different hypotheses, *ASSISTments* has collected over 50 000 instances of a student participating in an experiment. These data can be used to understand the relationships between traits of the students and the effectiveness of different tutoring. For example, one study in *ASSISTments* found that students with below-average prior knowledge benefited more from tutoring that broke the problem down into individual steps while students with

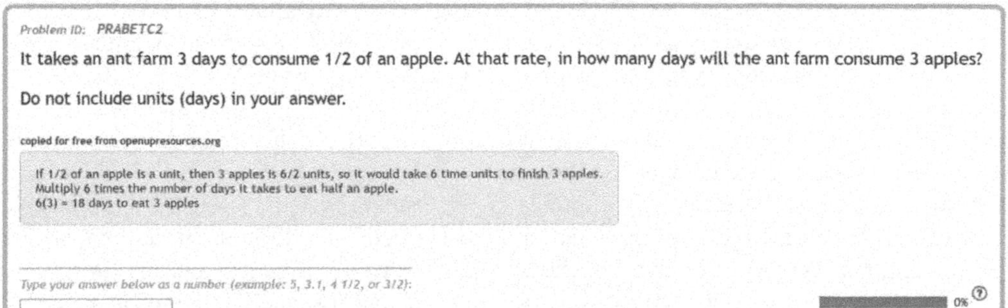

Problem ID: PRABETC2

It takes an ant farm 3 days to consume 1/2 of an apple. At that rate, in how many days will the ant farm consume 3 apples?

Do not include units (days) in your answer.

copied for free from openupresources.org

If 1/2 of an apple is a unit, then 3 apples is 6/2 units, so it would take 6 time units to finish 3 apples.
Multiply 6 times the number of days it takes to eat half an apple.
6(3) = 18 days to eat 3 apples

Type your answer below as a number (example: 5, 3.1, 4 1/2, or 3/2):

0% ⑦

Submit Answer   Show Answer

Figure 27.7   *A problem in the ASSISTments Tutor with a text-based explanation*

above-average prior knowledge benefited more from tutoring that gave them a full explanation of the solution all at once (Razzaq & Heffernan, 2009). By allowing external researchers to use *ASSISTments* as a tool for performing randomized controlled experiments, the insight gained from these experiments can be used to personalize content for students using the platform.

ASSISTments has also crowdsourced tutoring directly from teachers using the platform. Through *TeacherASSIST*, a program started in 2018, teachers in good standing that had created tutoring for their own students could agree to allow their content to be given to struggling students outside their class. A randomized controlled trial was conducted within the platform in which students that were struggling were given either just the answer or crowdsourced tutoring relevant to the problem they were struggling with. In 2020, the results of this study showed that the crowdsourced tutoring collected from teachers had a statistically significant benefit on students' learning gains (Patikorn & Heffernan, 2020). In 2021 this study was repeated and again the crowdsourced content was shown to have a statistically significant benefit on students' learning gains (Prihar et al., 2021). In addition to being able to determine the overall effectiveness of crowdsourced tutoring, the dataset collected on the effectiveness of *TeacherASSIST* was used to evaluate the individual effects of specific content creators' tutoring. It was discovered that while most content creators' tutoring was better than receiving just the answer, many of the content creators' tutoring was not statistically significantly better, and some content creators had content which was statistically significantly worse than just receiving the answer (Prihar et al., 2021).

Using crowdsourcing to collect tutoring not only helps struggling students but can also enable the exploration for opportunities to personalize students' learning. The *TeacherASSIST* project created an average of about three tutoring messages each for 6 044 problems in *ASSISTments*. For these problems where multiple tutoring messages are available, it is possible that one type of tutoring could be more beneficial to one group of students, and another type of tutoring could be better for a different group of students. This type of interaction, referred to as a qualitative interaction, is the ideal case for personalized learning because different content is more effective for different students. Using the crowdsourced tutoring and statistics collected on students and problems from prior usage data, it is possible to investigate qualitative interactions within the data collected through *TeacherASSIST*. However, with so much data available and so many potential interactions, using a statistical approach to test for qualitative interactions between the different tutoring messages available for each problem for every piece of information on students and problems would result in so many hypotheses that the correction for multiple hypothesis testing would take away any significance in the results. Therefore, to investigate qualitative interactions between students and crowdsourced content, *ASSISTments* has begun to use reinforcement learning to both provide the best content available to students and explore for opportunities to personalize students' tutoring. A reinforcement learning approach to search for opportunities to personalize students' learning would be able to learn over time which tutoring strategies are most effective for different groups of students and recommend the most effective content to students when they request tutoring. In simulations conducted on the *TeacherASSIST* data, even a simple Bernoulli Thompson sampling multi-armed bandit (Agrawal & Goyal, 2012) can increase students' next problem correctness by about 2.5% when selecting the tutoring the student will receive, and that doesn't even take into account specific traits of the student, problem, or tutoring. To explore the potential of reinforcement learning for personalization within ASSISTments, an algorithm, Decision Tree

Based Thompson Sampling, was designed to both personalize students' tutoring and identify qualitative interactions. This algorithm, by taking into account qualities of the students, problems, and tutoring strategies available, was able to increase students' next problem correctness by about 8.4%. In addition to increasing students' next problem correctness, Decision Tree Based Thompson Sampling was able to identify two qualitative interactions within the *TeacherASSIST* data. The first was that students benefited more from tutoring with images when the problem was more difficult than average, and from tutoring without images when the problem was easier than average. The second was that students benefited more from tutoring from a particular content creator when the problem was easier than average, and from tutoring from other content creators when the problem was more difficult than average. By crowdsourcing content from *ASSISTments* users, *ASSISTments* has been able to identify qualitative interactions and design algorithms that are key in ensuring that each student using the platform is given the content most helpful to them.

Crowdsourcing has paved the way for personalized learning within *ASSISTments* through the aggregation of step-level formative feedback (see Chapter 9 by Aleven et al. on instructional approaches), and can do so in other platforms as well. By encouraging users to create a variety of content, new algorithms capable of identifying interpretable qualitative interactions can be rapidly developed, tested, and deployed to discover new opportunities for personalization. Moving forward, platforms can even integrate public content as well as user-created content into the platform. By crowdsourcing opinions from teachers on publicly available educational videos, these videos could be offered to students when they are struggling with particular mathematics concepts, in addition to the tutoring already provided to them on the specific problem they are struggling with. Reinforcement learning algorithms can recommend what publicly available content and tutoring strategies the students should receive based on features of the student, the problem they are solving and the educational material available to them. These algorithms will not only determine the most effective tutoring for each student, but will also identify qualitative interactions that will provide insight into how to effectively personalize content for students, which can improve educational pedagogue and the design of future curricula.

Acknowledgments

We would like to thank NSF (e.g., 2118725, 2118904, 1950683, 1917808, 1931523, 1940236, 1917713, 1903304, 1822830, 1759229, 1724889, 1636782, & 1535428), IES (e.g., R305N210049, R305D210031, R305A170137, R305A170243, R305A180401, & R305A120125), GAANN (e.g., P200A180088 & P200A150306), EIR (U411B190024), ONR (N00014-18-1-2768) and Schmidt Futures for grant funding.

9. AIED IN DEVELOPING COUNTRIES: BREAKING SEVEN WEIRD ASSUMPTIONS IN THE GLOBAL LEARNING XPRIZE FIELD STUDY

Jack Mostow

Advances in education technology are enabling tremendous advances in learning at scale. However, modern educational software is typically developed in, by, and for WEIRD (Western,

Educated, Industrialized, Rich, Democratic) countries, and therefore assumes resources taken for granted in such countries, including:

1) Reliable electricity,
2) Powerful computers,
3) High-bandwidth internet access,
4) Fast WiFi,
5) Accurate data collection,
6) Sophisticated sensors, and
7) Expert technical and instructional support to keep it all working.

Research to evaluate such software relies even more heavily on these assumptions due to the additional instrumentation and data collection involved. Though common in AIED, these assumptions are often violated in developing countries. This section discusses them in the context of the Global Learning XPRIZE (XPRIZE, 2019), a US$15 M worldwide competition to develop an open-source Android tablet app to teach basic reading, writing, and numeracy to children with little or no access to schools. XPRIZE tested the five finalists' Swahili apps in a 15-month-long independent controlled field study with over 2,000 children in 168 villages in Tanzania. An analysis of their learning gains appears elsewhere (McReynolds et al., 2020). This section examines how XPRIZE and some of the apps addressed each of the seven assumptions, whether by enabling it or by working around it.

Electrical Power

Educational apps typically assume reliable electricity. In developing countries, the reality tends to be quite different, with limited availability and fluctuating voltage.

The obvious and widespread workaround is to use batteries, but batteries must be replaced or recharged. XPRIZE worked around this limitation by providing a solar-powered station for each village with recharger cables, WiFi router, and ftp server. Another solution is to include a small solar recharger in or with each tablet.

Computers

Educational software in WEIRD countries can assume that computers are plentiful, powerful, and personal. XPRIZE enabled this assumption by providing a high-end tablet for every child at its study sites and replacing it if lost, stolen, or broken. Google donated 8,000 Pixel C tablets for the study. However, the reality is that computers in developing countries are typically scarce, low-end, and shared. Tablet sharing is not an issue for non-adaptive apps, but it is a problem for apps that depend on tracking individual progress to adapt to the student.

The *RoboTutor* team (Mostow, 2019; RoboTutorLLC, 2019) user-tested successive versions at several beta sites in Tanzania but could not afford to provide a separate tablet for each child. As a workaround, we supported tablet sharing by developing a self-enrollment and login mechanism that children could operate without being able to read, write, or require help from anyone who could. An alternative workaround developed by another team used continual assessment in its app to adapt quickly when the tablet changed hands. This approach eliminated enrollment but required adaptation based on scant data from the student.

Internet

Many educational apps assume reliable, wide-coverage, high-bandwidth internet access. The reality in developing countries is that internet access is limited, slow, or non-existent.

The obvious and necessary workaround was for apps to run without relying on an internet connection. Remote villages in the XPRIZE study had no internet connection. Cell phone service was sometimes available, but with bandwidth too low to transmit large quantities of data. XPRIZE's workaround was for its field staff to collect log data on portable devices and send it back via motorcycle to a location with a good internet connection. From there, XPRIZE staff uploaded each team's data to the Box cloud server for the team to download.

WiFi

Similarly, many apps assume reliable, wide-coverage, high-bandwidth WiFi. The reality in developing countries is that WiFi, when available at all, has frequent outages, limited coverage, and low bandwidth.

XPRIZE's workaround let tablets transfer files to and from the ftp server while within WiFi range, typically while recharging. The finalists' apps worked around limited WiFi access by running client-side without relying on the server, but took advantage of WiFi when available to transfer data, in particular log files.

Data Collection

AIED research in WEIRD countries can often rely on automated collection of comprehensive, accurate data. However, the reality in XPRIZE is that manual and automated data collection led to some incompleteness and incorrectness.

For example, whenever the Pixel C tablet battery ran out of power, recharging it reset the tablet clock to 12/31/1999, rendering logged timestamps invalid and wreaking havoc on analysis of log data. The *RoboTutor* team's workaround was to deduce lower and upper bounds on when they were actually created, based on the week that XPRIZE staff uploaded the log files. Another team's workaround to this problem was to advance the clock after each clock reset by a large, increasing time interval.

Fluctuating WiFi access apparently prevented transfer of an unknown number of files. A partial workaround for unknown data loss was to number log files sequentially and include their sequence numbers in their filenames. This remedy did not eliminate the data loss, but at least the sequence numbers made it possible to order log files chronologically and infer the number of missing logs from gaps in the log numbering sequence.

Field staff manually recorded a "tablet tracker table" listing the three-digit site ID assigned to each village, the six-character anonymized ID assigned to each child when pretested, the ten-character tablet IDs assigned to that child, and the dates assigned. The typos inevitable in manual data entry caused discrepancies in the form of "phantom tablet IDs" logged by the app but missing from the table. The *RoboTutor* team worked around such errors by finding whichever logged ID matched the table entry most closely.

Each week, field staff uploaded data to a folder named by the upload date, for example, 2018-12-22, with the subfolder for each site named by its site ID, such as 131. This process was manual and therefore vulnerable to "phantom village" errors. For example, we determined that the data in subfolder 131 of the 2018-12-22 upload folder actually came from site 139, based on the tablet IDs located there according to the tablet tracker table.

The lesson from these problems is that both manual errors (e.g. typos) and automated errors (e.g. clock resets) are inevitable, so redundancy in data collection is essential to work around them.

Sensors

Advanced educational software typically assumes that sensors are reliable, accurate, and many-modal, that is, exist for diverse forms of input (audio, vision, touch) and are used in a controlled environment. The reality in developing countries is that sensors are typically unreliable, inaccurate, few in number and used in noisy environments.

Various workarounds can help, for example:

1) Apply the sensor selectively, that is, only in situations where it can work. For instance, *RoboTutor* uses speech recognition only for highly predictable speech, such as listening to oral reading of a known text or listening for an expected answer to a problem.
2) Degrade gracefully. For instance, read a word aloud to the child after two attempts by the child to read it.
3) Provide a fallback. For instance, let the child tap to make *RoboTutor* read the next word.

Support

Educational software is typically used in environments where expert assistance and assessment – both technical and instructional – are available when needed. For example, a teacher or parent can help a student who has difficulty understanding the content or operating the software and assess whether it is at an appropriate level for the student. In developing countries, such expertise is often scarce or absent. Available adults are inexpert or even illiterate. Teachers are over-burdened, under-trained, absent, or non-existent.

Workarounds used by finalists' apps included verbally prompting the student what to do and pointing with an animated hand to indicate a target to look at or tap, because just highlighting it is not self-explanatory to users unfamiliar with touchscreens – the sort of cultural difference revealed by in-person study of the context of use. Such animations are useful within the context of an app, but video provides a useful workaround for unavailable human assistance by displaying external context. For instance, *RoboTutor* plays short video tutorials of humans demonstrating how to hold the tablet and operate various activities in order to work around the lack of someone to do it in person.

Finalists' apps used various workarounds to assess student knowledge in the absence of a human teacher. One simplistic workaround is to advance through the curriculum in a fixed order starting from the easiest lesson. This workaround relies on the unrealistic simplifying assumption that the resulting sequence will fit every student's rate of learning. Another workaround is to let students choose what to do. This "learner control" makes the unrealistic assumption that children's goal is to optimize their learning, and that they know which choice will do so. This assumption can be mitigated somewhat by restricting the choices to activities whose prerequisites the student has completed. A more sophisticated workaround is to automate assessment. Automated placement determines where in the curriculum the student should start. Automated promotion determines when the student has made sufficient progress to advance. Automated assessment uses and updates a student model.

Conclusion

The Global Learning XPRIZE was a landmark experiment in education technology. We hope that this discussion of AIED assumptions violated in developing countries may help AIED scale toward a world-class education for every child on the planet.

Acknowledgments

The Global Learning XPRIZE created the opportunity for this project. A large, dedicated, almost entirely volunteer team developed *RoboTutor*, with funding from generous donors and the $1M Finalist Award, and enthusiastic support from the Simon Initiative at Carnegie Mellon University.

10. THE FUTURE OF LEARNING ASSESSMENT

Claude Frasson

Traditional Assessment of Learning

Since Plato, Archimedes, and Pythagoras, assessment of learning has been the subject of many theories, methods, and practices. Thus, faced with behaviorism (Skinner), which considered learning as the association of a response to a stimulus, Piaget was able to develop constructivist approaches based on the idea that knowledge is constructed by the learner based on the mental activity. The learner is active and will seek to make sense of what he perceives from his experiences.

For Vygotsky, the learner builds his knowledge by socializing himself with fundamental tools such as language. Cognitivism aims to study observable behavior by ignoring mental representations that are not observable. This notion of the observable joins that known in quantum mechanics of an observable physical quantity (position, momentum, energy) capable of being broken down into quantifiable and deductible states. But how do you know if the learner has learned? Traditionally, pedagogical, psychological, or statistical theories are used to explain or deduce the knowledge that has been mastered and that which is not, from the performances obtained. But this constitutes an indirect assessment of the learner by his results and does not consider his mental state at the time. It is totally unknown whether the learner is tired, distracted, or not engaged in the learning process. Sometimes, the lack of interest in a teacher can cause difficulties in acquiring the subject. Educational approaches, involving the notion of learning style, have tried to provide solutions by taking more account of the individual. Thus, the "big five" theory (Golberg, 1981) made it possible to consider five types of learning relating to the personality traits of learners. There is therefore a progression of approaches tending towards a deeper knowledge of the individual, but this will remain insufficient until emotions are considered (Picard, 1997; Chapter 5 by Arroyo et al.) in learning.

Importance of Emotions in Learning

To come back to Archimedes, how did he discover the law of the principle of flotation? He was in his bath, in the ideal emotional conditions of relaxation and concentration to watch his leg float and suddenly he understood (Eureka!). The same is true of many fortuitous discoveries (Fleming, Pasteur) which have drawn conclusions from an observation, a high state of concentration and chance (phenomenon of serendipity). Indeed, emotions are narrowly linked to the cognitive process (Frasson & Heraz, 2011). Without emotions, we are unable to make even the simplest decision. Moreover, some strong emotions, like anger or anxiety, can prevent us from concentrating on our everyday tasks and particularly on learning (Goleman, 2006). People who have positive emotions will think in a more creative, expansive, and motivated way. On the other hand, negative emotions (stress, fear, disgust, boredom), can result in sleeping trouble, lack of concentration or hyperactivity and reduction of cognitive and memory functions.

Cognitive processes, such as problem solving and decision making, not only depend on the individual's emotional state, but are greatly intertwined with it (Chaouachi et al., 2010). Some emotions or combinations of emotions lead to a mental state which is in fact the condition of cognitive receptivity of the brain. Among these mental states, engagement and mental workload are fundamental. A series of failures can lead to a decrease in engagement but a series of successes will lower attention.

It has been found (Chaouachi et al., 2010) that for some learners, a consecutive series of wrong answers lowered their mental engagement. For others, the same effect was observed for a consecutive series of good answers. Indeed, learners tend to relax after getting a few good answers and consequently become less engaged. This is where the contribution of the emotional factor is crucial and must be assessed permanently to adopt adequate pedagogical strategies. Experiments have shown that emotions impact the engagement index, that the engagement index is more correlated with arousal than valence, that it represents a valid indicator of learners' performance, and construction of a personalized model to predict the variation of that engagement index is not only possible but highly recommended.

Mental workload is an indicator of acceptability, of the availability of the learner's mental resources (Berka, 2007). It is useless to explain anything to them if their mental workload is high (saturated); they will not be able to understand, hence the importance of being able to measure it. An experiment (Chaouachi et al., 2011) showed real-time monitoring of engagement and mental load. Faced with the impossibility of understanding a problem (too much workload), simple advice was enough to lower this workload and suddenly allow the problem to be understood.

Contribution of Neurosciences

Often researchers stick to their usual discipline to analyze or build experiments. However, the richness of different disciplines (and particularly the neurosciences) is that they constitute different points of view making it possible to find complementary solutions and original methods of investigation. Thus, the study of the components of the brain allows us to better understand the fundamental role of the cortex, the thalamus and especially the limbic system in the acquisition of knowledge. The latter regulates both the acquisition and the deployment of knowledge with the amygdala (center of emotions and implicit memory), the hippocampus (explicit contextual memory) and areas of short-term and long-term memory. Understanding this architecture of the brain is very important not only to understand the process of acquisition, memorization, but also to measure them. This time, we no longer consider indirect performance measures but take direct measures of the mental state of the learner by picking up brain signals. The most reliable and accurate physiological signal for monitoring cognitive state changes remains the electroencephalogram (EEG). The EEG data has a high level of time resolution and precision resulting from electrical neural activity in the brain. They measure four EEG bands: *Theta* (4–8 Hz), *Alpha* (8–13 Hz), *Beta* (13–32 Hz) and *Gamma* (32-40 Hz), which, by combination, allow assessment of various mental states.

In addition, neuroscience measures provide access to the distinction of brain areas involved in information processing. This is important for understanding how the reasoning is triggered. It is thus possible to distinguish processing by the conscious (left part, with the language area) and by the subconscious (right part, with the image processing area). We can follow the forms of reasoning which can switch from the deductive mode to the inductive mode which represents a great progress compared to the studies which sought to know by tests of approximations, the famous path of knowledge. A surprising experiment was made by Heraz et al. (2009), using the P-300 (positive) and N-300 (negative) brain waves: a learner had to choose a correct answer from three questions. When he chose the right answer, a P-300 brain wave was generated, but when he chose a false one it was an N-300 wave which manifested, which means that the subconscious part of the brain could guess that the answer was wrong.

Brain Assessment Parameters and Tools

As we have seen, the most important aspect of future learning assessment is to allow a direct assessment of the cognitive processing brain conditions of the learner and no longer a probable estimation of the reasons for their performance. EEG-based brain–computer interfaces use sensors placed on the head to detect brainwaves and allow mental states of fatigue, engagement, workload, stress, anxiety, concentration, or distraction to be distinguished. Great progress has been made in the precision and ease of use of these devices.

However, if you explain something to a learner while they are looking in another direction of the demonstration, they will not grasp it. This is why eye-tracking is useful.

Eye-tracking systems have flourished in the past few years due to their ease of use, high sensitivity, and especially their non-intrusiveness. It is a very useful tool in many research domains, including visualization, activity recognition, affect detection, and especially learning, to understand how students evolve and progress while learning. In fact, how students are reasoning while solving problems is a fundamental issue, regarding the technical and methodological challenges, due to the complexity of the reasoning process. Research has demonstrated that a relationship exists between *eye movements* and *cognitive processes* (Hunter et al., 2010). As a result, the use of eye-tracking can be beneficial as a means to identify the link between the task-relevant information and the learner's knowledge state (BenKheder et al., 2019).

Combining EEG and eye-tracking through neurofeedback methods should be a challenge for future methods of learning assessment. Neurofeedback can be used to enable people to learn to manage specific aspects of their neuronal activity and develop skills for self-regulation of brain activity, through a brain–computer interface.

In the same way that the evolution of theories has gradually converged towards the individual, the present and the future of the evaluation of learning will pass by measurements of the cerebral activities and eye-tracking which are more and more refined thanks to technological means under development. A vast field of research is opening on new learning strategies.

11. INTELLIGENT MENTORING SYSTEMS: TAPPING INTO AI TO DELIVER THE NEXT GENERATION OF DIGITAL LEARNING
Vania Dimitrova

In the past decades, the successful and deployable solutions of intelligent learning environments have predominantly been in formal education, usually school or university settings. In the next decades, I believe that AI in Education (AIED) will be established strongly in the broader educational landscape, with regard to a range of learning contexts, such as informal learning, adult education, professional learning, to name but a few. I argue that this calls for a change in the way we envisage the role of AIED and the way we design AIED systems. I believe that this will lead to a new family of AIED systems that provide support for coaching and mentoring.

Changing the Learning Landscape

Changes in a field, which can lead to new paradigms, often come from external drivers linked to socioeconomic and technological developments. A key driver calling for a change in our view of intelligent learning environments is the new learning landscape. There are strong voices for education to prepare for the rapidly changing skills demand. For example, the World Economic Forum lists key skills needed for jobs, such as analytical thinking and innovation, active learning and learning strategies, complex problem solving, critical thinking, and creativity. The Council of Europe's key competences for living in democratic societies and participating in democratic culture include: values (e.g. valuing human dignity and human rights, cultural diversity, democracy, and fairness), attitudes (e.g. openness to cultural otherness and to other beliefs, respect, civic-mindedness and self-efficacy), skills (e.g. autonomous learning skills, listening and observing, empathy, flexibility and adaptability, cooperation, and conflict-resolution), knowledge and critical understanding (e.g. critical understanding of the self, of language and communication, and of the world, human rights, culture, environment, and sustainability). This broadens the education scope to address soft (transferable) skills and to include lifelong learning in real contexts and everyday life experiences. At the same time, there is a growing demand for re-skilling, as stated by the futurist Alvin Toffler: "The illiterate of the 21st century will not be those who cannot read and write, but those who cannot learn, unlearn, and relearn." Hence, stronger emphasis is being put on lifelong learning, self-regulation, and developing growth mindset. Professional learning models aimed at developing reflexive practitioners who can make meaning of their practical experience and become lifelong learners, are becoming endorsed in workplace-based learning.

Mentoring

Mentoring is seen as a highly effective method to support the development of transferable skills, to increase motivation and confidence, and to develop self-regulation and self-determination. Because of insufficient space, I will not review the various definitions of mentoring and coaching and the nuances of differences between them. Hereinafter, I will use the term *mentor* as a generic term for the various interactions one can have with a more experienced person or with peers helping us to make meaning from our experience, develop self-awareness, become more engaged and motivated, set goals and reflect on their achievement, develop confidence and self-esteem, and thus realise one's full potential. Mentoring support can be offered by tutors, supervisors, friendsand particularly dedicated mentors and coaches. Mentoring can take different forms: 1:1 (the traditional model of mentor and mentee), 1:M (one mentor for a group of mentees), M:M (peer mentoring, usually in collaborative settings), M:1 (experience shared by many people in helping a mentee). Technology can play a key role by providing scalable and cost-effective support, tailored to the different mentoring models and adapted to individual needs and contexts.

Diversity-Aware Intelligent Mentoring Systems

Today, a vast number of learners use technology for educational purposes; and this will apply for future uses of technology to support mentoring. Consequently, technology support for mentoring would need to consider learner diversity, including demographic diversity (gender, age, culture), functional diversity (different experiences, different knowledge), and subjective diversity (personality characteristics, traits, values, motivations, beliefs). Educators and technologies supporting the education process would need to think about a wider scope of learner characteristics beyond knowledge and experience. A key challenge then would be how to understand diversity at scale. Digital transformation of education enables the capturing of digital traces which can be analysed to understand the learners, their behaviour, and the overall learning process. Hence, learning analytics approaches can provide "sensors" about aspects of the learners and the learning context.

This can then indicate situations in which we can provide nudges to foster behaviour change and facilitate learning. Nudges are widely used in behaviour change interventions (e.g. health, driving, green living) to influence choice without restricting any options. In mentoring systems, nudges can direct the learner to aspects that are beneficial for learning (e.g. to promote reflection, to improve engagement), yet preserve the freedom of exploration and the notion of self-control. Learning analytics combined with nudges can augment the mentoring models.

1:1 mentoring

We can provide intelligent personal mentors that act as conversational agents capable of "sensing" relevant situations about the learner (e.g. disengagement, lack of confidence, lack of motivation, boredom, procrastination, frustration) and offer interactive nudges (e.g. prompts, hints, questions, tips, suggestions) to help the learner become self-aware of their behaviour and identify what and how they may change. Another direction for using intelligent personal mentors is learning from experience – an effective approach for soft skills learning and for professional learning. Through the new technologies, such as speech, sensing devices, information about real-world experience can be captured. The personal mentor can then detect relevant situations in the digital traces with learners' experience and help them set goals and devise ways to achieve these goals.

1:M mentoring

These are group mentoring contexts done by one mentor, which refers to group-based interactive systems or collaborative spaces. Intelligent support can be offered to both the mentor and the mentees. We can envisage "sensors", in the form of group behaviour analytics, to understand individual differences and group dynamics. This can then inform nudges to be sent to individual members or to the group as a whole. Nudges can be offered automatically to the learners or can be suggested to a human mentor to help them moderate the group discussions.

M:M mentoring

Consider diversity-aware social interaction spaces where learners share experiences, knowledge, tips. As with 1:M, we can envisage "sensors" of group behaviour to detect interesting situations and nudges to offer direction that can change behaviour to benefit learning. Different contexts – soft skills learning, professional learning, informal learning – can utilise this approach. One of the main challenges in group contexts with diverse learners (e.g. cross-generational, cultural differences) is to ensure that the virtual social spaces are inclusive, that is, that everyone can benefit from their social experience. Analysis of the group interaction data can identify critical moments where members are ignored, may be confused, or become disengaged. The system can interfere to make the collective experience beneficial for the individual (e.g. raise group awareness, foster links, promote knowledge exchange of knowledge and experience).

M:1 mentoring

This refers to learning from collective intelligence. We can envisage nudging for informal learning where the learner freely explores a large information space with contributions from other people (e.g. comments, tips, stories, shared resources). In this case, domain models (ontologies) can help to map content to concepts from the domain, in order to design navigation nudges that direct the learner (offering signposts or recommendations) to content that can expand their knowledge and help them learn from others' experience. Learning through information exploration is being explored by the information retrieval community. In the future, closer links with the AIED community will enable more robust models that turn exploratory search tasks into effective informal learning scenarios.

Research Directions

To realise the intelligent mentoring system vision, we will need interdisciplinary partnerships that link researchers from computer scientists, professional learning, cognitive science, social science, and management. Possible research questions that these partnerships can consider include:

- **Learner needs:** What are the key lifelong learning challenges which require mentoring? What digital technologies do learners and tutors use to tackle these challenges? What are the main barriers (e.g. ethics, security, reliability)?
- **Technology:** What are the potential platforms/technologies that can be utilised for mentoring? What are the strengths and limitations of these platforms? What mentor-like features can we add to existing systems and how?
- **Learner/group sensing:** What individual differences should be considered; and how can they be captured/utilised in a holistic contextual model? What digital traces about the learner experience can be collected? What intelligent data analytics methods can be used to derive high-level behaviour models from low-level interaction data?
- **Domain modelling:** What "critical" situations do human mentors recognise when advising mentees? What contextual factors do human mentors take into account? What "nudging interventions" do human mentors use?
- **Intelligent nudges:** Can we shape a generic nudging framework (e.g. aspects which may include "sensors" to detect problem behaviour, interaction and navigation nudges to foster target behaviour)? What individual differences shall we consider for effective nudges?

- **Validation:** How reliable are the computational models? What are the pedagogical benefits of intelligent mentors, for example, evidence of reflection and self-awareness, improved confidence and self-esteem, better self-regulated learning, improved motivation? Who benefits and who does not?
- **Impact:** What findings can inform adopting mentor-like features in intelligent systems? How to turn proof-of-concept prototypes into deployable intelligent mentoring systems?

NOTE

1. For the purposes of this chapter, we consider the default role for a PA to be as a tutor, coach, or teacher. In other situations, such as role playing or peer learning, other factors may play a more important role in their design (e.g., in language training, agents would be designed to accurately represent a foreign country).

REFERENCES

Adib, A., Norman, A., & Orji, R. (2021). Persuasive application for discouraging unhealthy gaming behaviour. In *2021 IEEE 9th International Conference on Serious Games and Applications for Health (SeGAH)* (pp. 1–9). https://ieeexplore.ieee.org/abstract/document/9551891/.

Adorni, G., Alzetta, C., Koceva, F., Passalacqua, S., & Torre, I. (2019). Towards the identification of propaedeutic relations in textbooks. In *International Conference on Artificial Intelligence in Education* (pp. 1–13).

Agrawal, S., & Goyal, N. (2012, June). Analysis of Thompson sampling for the multi-armed bandit problem. In *Conference on Learning Theory* (p. 39). JMLR Workshop and Conference Proceedings.

Ahn, J. (2002). Beyond single equation regression analysis: Path analysis and multi-stage regression analysis. *The American Journal of Pharmaceutical Education*, 66(1), 37–41.

Aleven, V., Sewall, J., Andres, J. M., Sottilare, R., Long, R., & Baker, R. (2018, June). Towards adapting to learners at scale: Integrating MOOC and intelligent tutoring frameworks. In *Proceedings of the Fifth Annual ACM Conference on Learning at Scale* (pp. 1–4).

Allard, D., & Mizoguchi, R. (2021). Dr. Mosaik: A holistic framework for understanding the English tense-aspect system based on ontology engineering. *Research and Practice in Technology Enhanced Learning*, 16(1), 1–38.

Alpizar-Chacon, I., & Sosnovsky, S. (2021). Knowledge models from PDF textbooks. In *New Review of Hypermedia and Multimedia* (pp. 1–49).

Azevedo, R., Taub, M., & Mudrick, N. V. (2017). Understanding and reasoning about real-time cognitive, affective, and metacognitive processes to foster self-regulation with advanced learning technologies. In *Handbook of Self-Regulation of Learning and Performance* (pp. 254–270). Routledge.

Baker, R. S., Ogan, A. E., Madaio, M., & Walker, E. (2019). Culture in computer-based learning systems: Challenges and opportunities. *Computer-Based Learning in Context*, 1(1), 1–13. https://doi.org/10.5281/zenodo.4057223.

Barria-Pineda, J., Brusilovsky, P., & He, D. (2019). Reading mirror: Social navigation and social comparison for electronic textbooks. In *First Workshop on Intelligent Textbooks at 20th International Conference on Artificial Intelligence in Education* (pp. 30–37). http://ceur-ws.org/Vol-2384/paper03.pdf.

Basu, S., Biswas, G., Sengupta, P., Dickes, A., Kinnebrew, J. S., & Clark, D. (2016). Identifying middle school students' challenges in computational thinking-based science learning. *Research and Practice in Technology Enhanced Learning*, 11(1), 1–35.

Baylor, A. L. (2011). The design of motivational agents and avatars. *Educational Technology Research and Development*, 59(2), 291–300. https://doi.org/10.1007/s11423-011-9196-3.

Baylor, A. L., & Kim, Y. (2004). Pedagogical agent design: The impact of agent realism, gender, ethnicity, and instructional role. In J. C. Lester, R. M. Vicari, & F. Paraguaçu (Eds.), *Intelligent Tutoring Systems*. Heidelberg.

Ben Khedher, A., Jraidi, I., & Frasson, C. (2019). Predicting learners' performance using EEG and eye tracking features. In *The 32nd International FLAIRS Conference*, May 19–22, 2019, Florida, USA.

Berka, C., Levendowski, D. J., Lumicao, M. N., et al. (2007). EEG correlates of task engagement and mental workload in vigilance, learning, and memory tasks. *Aviation, Space, and Environmental Medicine*, 78, B231–B244.

Biswas, G., Segedy, J. R., & Bunchongchit, K. (2016). From design to implementation to practice – A learning by teaching system: Betty's brain. *International Journal of Artificial Intelligence in Education*, 26(1), 350–364.

Blanchard, E., & Mizoguchi, R. (2014). Designing culturally-aware tutoring systems with MAUOC, the more advanced upper ontology of culture. *Research and Practice in Technology Enhanced Learning*, 9(1), 41–69.

Blanchard, E. G. (2012, June). On the WEIRD nature of ITS/AIED conferences. In *International Conference on Intelligent Tutoring Systems* (pp. 280–285). Berlin, Heidelberg: Springer.

Bransford, J. D., Brown, A. L., & Cocking, R. R. (2000). *How People Learn* (Vol. 11). National Academy Press.

Brusilovsky, P., Eklund, J., & Schwarz, E. (1998). Web-based education for all: A tool for developing adaptive courseware. In H. Ashman & P. Thistewaite (Eds.), *Seventh International World Wide Web Conference* (pp. 291–300).

Bulger, M. (2016). Personalized learning: The conversations we're not having. *Data and Society,* 22(1), 1–29.

CATS. (2015). Sixth international workshop on culturally-aware tutoring systems. https://archium .ateneo.edu/discs-faculty-pubs/175/.

Chaouachi, M., & Frasson, C. (2010). Exploring the relationship between learners EEG mental engagement and affect, short paper. In *ITS 2010: 10th International Conference on Intelligent Tutoring Systems*. Pittsburgh, Pennsylvania: Springer Verlag, June 14–18, 2010.

Chaouachi, M., Jraidi, I., & Frasson, C. (2011). Modeling mental workload using EEG features for intelligent systems. In *User Modeling, Adaptation and Personalization, UMAP 2011*, Girona, Spain, July 2011.

Chaudhri, V. K., Cheng, B., Overholtzer, A., Roschelle, J., Spaulding, A., Clark, P., Greaves, M., & Gunning, D. (2013). Inquire biology: A textbook that answers questions. *AI Magazine*, 34(3), 55–72.

Cian, H., Dou, R., Castro, S., Palma-D'souza, E., & Martinez, A. (2021). Facilitating marginalized youths' identification with STEM through everyday science talk: The critical role of parental caregivers. *Science Education*. Advance online publication. https://doi.org/10.1002/sce.21688.

Craig, S. D., & Schroeder, N. L. (2018). Design principles for virtual humans in educational technology environments. In *Deep Comprehension* (pp. 128–139). Routledge.

Dill-Shackleford, K. E., Ramasubramanian, S., Behm-Morawitz, E., Scharrer, E., Burgess, M. C., & Lemish, D. (2017). Social group stories in the media and child development. *Pediatrics*, 140(Supplement 2), S157–S161.

Dimitrova, V., & Mitrovic, A. (2021). Choice architecture for nudges to support constructive learning in active video watching. *International Journal of Artificial Intelligence in Education*. Advance online publication. https://doi.org/10.1007/s40593-021-00263-1.

D'Mello, S. K. (2016). Giving eyesight to the blind: Towards attention-aware AIED. *International Journal of Artificial Intelligence in Education*, 26(2), 645–659.

Dolog, P., Henze, N., Nejdl, W., & Sintek, M. (2004). The personal reader: Personalizing and enriching learning resources using semantic web technologies. In P. M. E. Bra & W. Nejdl (Eds.), *Third International Conference on Adaptive Hypermedia and Adaptive Web-Based Systems* (pp. 85–94). Lecture Notes in Computer Science. Springer-Verlag.

Dou, R., Hazari, Z., Dabney, K., Sonnert, G., & Sadler, P. (2019). Early informal STEM experiences and STEM identity: The importance of talking science. *Science Education*, 103(3), 623–637.

Ebben, M., & Murphy, J. S. (2014). Unpacking MOOC scholarly discourse: A review of nascent MOOC scholarship. *Learning, Media and Technology*, 39(3), 328–345.

Emdin, C., Adjapong, E., & Levy, I. (2016). Hip-hop based interventions as pedagogy/therapy in STEM: A model from urban science education. *Journal for Multicultural Education*, 10(3), 307–321.

Ferrini-Mundy, J. (2013). Driven by diversity. *Science*, 340(6130), 278.

Finkelstein, S., Yarzebinski, E., Vaughn, C., Ogan, A., & Cassell, J. (2013). The effects of culturally congruent educational technologies on student achievement. *International Conference on Artificial Intelligence in Education.*

Frasson, C., & Heraz, A. (2011). Emotional learning. In *Encyclopedia of the Sciences of Learning.* Springer Verlag.

Gallagher, M. (2019). Artificial intelligence and the mobilities of inclusion: The accumulated advantages of 5G networks and surfacing outliers. In *Artificial Intelligence and Inclusive Education* (pp. 179–194). Springer.

Garner, P. W., Gabitova, N., Gupta, A., & Wood, T. (2018). Innovations in science education: Infusing social emotional principles into early STEM learning. *Cultural Studies of Science Education*, 13(4), 889–903.

Goldberg, L. R. (1981). Language and individual differences: The search for universals in personality lexicons. In Wheeler (Ed.), *Review of Personality and Social Psychology* (Vol. 1, pp. 141–165). Sage.

Goleman, D. (Ed.). (2006). *Emotional Intelligence, Why It Can Matter More Than IQ.* Bentam. ISBN-13 9780553804911.

Gynther, K. (2016). Design framework for an adaptive MOOC enhanced by blended learning: Supplementary training and personalized learning for teacher professional development. *Electronic Journal of e-Learning*, 14(1), 15–30.

Hachey, A. C. (2020). Success for all: Fostering early childhood STEM identity. *Journal of Research in Innovative Teaching & Learning*, 13(1), 135–139. https://doi.org/10.1108/JRIT-01-2020-0001.

Heffernan, N. T., & Heffernan, C. L. (2014). The ASSISTments ecosystem: Building a platform that brings scientists and teachers together for minimally invasive research on human learning and teaching. *International Journal of Artificial Intelligence in Education*, 24(4), 470–497.

Heidig, S., & Clarebout, G. (2011). Do pedagogical agents make a difference to student motivation and learning? *Educational Research Review*, 6(1), 27–54.

Heraz, A., & Frasson, C. (2009). Predicting learner answers correctness through brainwaves assessment and emotional dimensions. In *AIED'2009: 14th International Conference on Artificial Intelligence in Education.* IOS Press.

Hofstede, G. (2022). Hofstede's cultural dimensions theory. https://en.wikipedia.org/wiki/Hofstede %27s_cultural_dimensions_theory.

Hohl, H., Böcker, H.-D., & Gunzenhäuser, R. (1996). Hypadapter: An adaptive hypertext system for exploratory learning and programming. *User Modeling and User-Adapted Interaction*, 6(2–3), 131–156.

Holstein, K., & Doroudi, S. (2021). Equity and artificial intelligence in education: Will "AIEd" amplify or alleviate inequities in education? *arXiv preprint arXiv:2104.12920.*

Hunter, M., Mach, Q. H., & Grewal, R. S. (2010). The relationship between scan path direction and cognitive processing. In *Proceedings of the Third C* Conference on Computer Science and Software Engineering* (pp. 97–100).

Hutchins, N. M., Biswas, G., Maróti, M., Lédeczi, Á., Grover, S., Wolf, R., … McElhaney, K. (2020a). C2STEM: A system for synergistic learning of physics and computational thinking. *Journal of Science Education and Technology*, 29(1), 83–100.

Hutchins, N. M., Biswas, G., Zhang, N., Snyder, C., Lédeczi, Á., & Maróti, M. (2020b). Domain-specific modeling languages in computer-based learning environments: A systematic approach to support science learning through computational modeling. *International Journal of Artificial Intelligence in Education*, 30, 537–580.

Hutchins, N. M., Snyder, C., Emara, M., Grover, S., & Biswas, G. (2021). Analyzing debugging processes during collaborative, computational modeling in science. In C. Hmelo-Silver, B. de Wever, & J. Oshima (Eds.), *14th International Conference on Computer-Supported Collaborative Learning – CSCL 2021* (pp. 221–224). International Society of the Learning Sciences.

Jackson, G. T., Boonthum, C., & McNamara, D. S. (2010, June). The efficacy of iSTART extended practice: Low ability students catch up. In *International Conference on Intelligent Tutoring Systems* (pp. 349–351). Berlin, Heidelberg: Springer.

Johnson, W. L., & Lester, J. C. (2018). Pedagogical agents: Back to the future. *AI Magazine*, 39(2), 33–44.

Kavcic, A. (2004). Fuzzy user modeling for adaptation in educational hypermedia. *IEEE Transactions on Systems, Man, and Cybernetics*, 34(4), 439–449.

Kinnebrew, J., Loretz, K., & Biswas, G. (2013). A contextualized, differential sequence mining method to derive students' learning behavior patterns. *Journal of Educational Data Mining*, 5(1), 190–219.

Kinnebrew, J., Segedy, J., & Biswas, G. (2017). Integrating model-driven and data-driven techniques for analyzing learning behaviors in open-ended learning environments. *IEEE Transactions on Learning & Technology*, 10(2), 140–153.

Kline, R. B. (2015). *Principles and Practice of Structural Equation Modeling*. Guilford Publications.

Kulik, C. L. C., & Kulik, J. A. (1982). Effects of ability grouping on secondary school students: A meta-analysis of evaluation findings. *American Educational Research Journal*, 19(3), 415–428.

Kumar, G., Banchs, R. E., & D'Haro, L. F. (2015). Revup: Automatic gap-fill question generation from educational texts. In *Tenth Workshop on Innovative Use of NLP for Building Educational Applications* (pp. 154–161).

Kumpulainen, K., & Wray, D. (Eds.). (2003). *Classroom Interaction and Social Learning: Frome Theory to Practice*. Routledge.

Lane, H. C., Cahill, C., Foutz, S., Auerbach, D., Noren, D., Lussenhop, C., & Swartout, W. (2013). The effects of a pedagogical agent for informal science education on learner behaviors and self-efficacy. In K. Yacef, H. C. Lane, & J. P. Mostow (Eds.), *Proceedings of the 16th International Conference on Artificial Intelligence in Education (AIED2013)* (Vol. 6738, pp. 309–318). Springer. https://doi.org/10.1007/978-3-642-39112-5_32.

Lane, H. C., & Schroeder, N. L. (2022). Pedagogical agents. In B. Lugrin, C. Pelachaud, & D. Traum (Eds.), *The Handbook on Socially Interactive Agents: 20 Years of Research on Embodied Conversational Agents, Intelligent Virtual Agents, and Social Robotics* (Vol. 2). ACM Press.

Leelawong, K., & Biswas, G. (2008). Designing learning by teaching agents: The Betty's brain system. *International Journal of Artificial Intelligence in Education*, 18(3), 181–208.

Leinhardt, G., Crowley, K., & Knutson, K. (2003). *Learning Conversations in Museums*. Taylor & Francis.

Liu, H., Ma, W., Yang, Y., & Carbonell, J. (2016). Learning concept graphs from online educational data. *Journal of Artificial Intelligence Research*, 55, 1059–1090.

Ma, W., Adesope, O. O., Nesbit, J. C., & Liu, Q. (2014). Intelligent tutoring systems and learning outcomes: A meta-analysis. *Journal of Educational Psychology*, 106(4), 901.

MacLeod, L., Suruliraj, B., Gall, D., Bessenyei, K., Hamm, S., Romkey, I., Bagnell, A., Mattheisen, M., Muthukumaraswamy, V., Orji, R., & Meier, S. (2021). A mobile sensing app to monitor youth mental health: Observational pilot study. *JMIR mHealth and uHealth*, 9(10), e20638.

McClure, E. R., Guernsey, L., Clements, D. H., Bales, S. N., Nichols, J., Kendall-Taylor, N., & Levine, M. H. (2017). STEM starts early: Grounding science, technology, engineering, and math education in early childhood. In *The Joan Ganz Cooney Center at Sesame Workshop*.

McElhaney, K. W., Zhang, N., Basu, S., McBride, E., Biswas, G., & Chiu, J. L. (2020). Using computational modeling to integrate science and engineering curricular activities. In *Proceedings of the International Conference of the Learning Sciences (ICLS)* (Vol. 3, pp. 1357–1364). Nashville, TN, USA.

McLaren, B. M., DeLeeuw, K. E., & Mayer, R. E. (2011). Polite web-based intelligent tutors: Can they improve learning in classrooms? *Computers & Education*, 56(3), 574–584.

McReynolds, A. A., Naderzad, S. P., Goswami, M., & Mostow, J. (2020). Toward learning at scale in developing countries: Lessons from the global learning XPRIZE field study. In *Proceedings of L@S '20: Seventh ACM Conference on Learning @Scale*, August 12–14, 2020, Virtual Event, USA.

Melis, E., Andres, E., Büdenbender, J., Frischauf, A., Goguadze, G., Libbrecht, P., & Ullrich, C. (2001). ActiveMath: A generic and adaptive web-based learning environment. *International Journal of Artificial Intelligence in Education*, 12(4), 385–407.

Mizoguchi, R. (2020). A proposal for a new framework of learner modeling: From modeling "understanding" to "not understanding". *The Journal of Information and Systems in Education*, 19(1), 9–14.

Mizoguchi, R., & Bourdeau, J. (2016). Using ontological engineering to overcome AI-ED problems: Contribution, impact, and perspectives. *International Journal of Artificial Intelligence in Education*, 26(1), 91–106.

Moreno, K. N., Person, N. K., Adcock, A. B., Eck, R., Jackson, G. T., & Marineau, J. C. (2002). Etiquette and efficacy in animated pedagogical agents: The role of stereotypes. In *AAAI Symposium on Personalized Agents*, Cape Cod, MA.

Moreno, R., Mayer, R., & Lester, J. (2000). Life-like pedagogical agents in constructivist multimedia environments: Cognitive consequences of their interaction. In *World Conference on Educational Multimedia, Hypermedia and Telecommunications*.

Mostow, J. (2019). RoboTutor. www.robotutor.org.

Munshi, A., Rajendran, R., Ocumpaugh, J., Biswas, G., Baker, R. S., & Paquette, L. (2018). Modeling learners cognitive and affective states to scaffold SRL in open ended learning environments. In *Proceedings of the International Conference on User Modelling, Adaptation and Personalization (UMAP)* (pp. 131–138).

Nkambou, R., Mizoguchi, R., & Bourdeau, J. (2010). *Advances in Intelligent Tutoring Systems*. Springer-Verlag.

NSF INCLUDES Coordination Hub. (2020). Broadening participation in STEM: Evidence-based strategies for improving equity and inclusion of individuals in underrepresented racial and ethnic groups. (Research Brief No. 1).

Nye, B. D. (2014, June). Barriers to ITS adoption: A systematic mapping study. In *International Conference on Intelligent Tutoring Systems* (pp. 583–590). Cham: Springer.

Nye, B. D. (2015). Intelligent tutoring systems by and for the developing world: A review of trends and approaches for educational technology in a global context. *International Journal of Artificial Intelligence in Education*, 25(2), 177–203.

Ogan, A., Yarzebinski, E., Fernández, P., & Casas, I. (2015, June). Cognitive tutor use in Chile: Understanding classroom and lab culture. In *International Conference on Artificial Intelligence in Education* (pp. 318–327). Cham: Springer.

Orji, F. A., & Vassileva, J. (2021). Modelling and quantifying learner motivation for adaptive systems: Current insight and future perspectives. In *International Conference on Human-Computer Interaction* (pp. 79–92).

Orji, F. A., Vassileva, J., & Greer, J. (2021). Evaluating a persuasive intervention for engagement in a large university class. *IJAIED*, 27(4), 700–725. https://doi.org/10.1007/s40593-021-00260-4.

Ostrow, K., Heffernan, N., & Williams, J. J. (2017). Tomorrow's EdTech today: Establishing a learning platform as a collaborative research tool for sound science. *Teachers College Record*, 119(3), 1–36.

Oyibo, K., Orji, R., & Vassileva, J. (2017). The influence of culture in the effect of age and gender on social influence in persuasive technology. In *Adjunct Publication of the 25th Conference on User Modeling, Adaptation and Personalization* (pp. 47–52). https://dl.acm.org/doi/abs/10.1145/3099023 .3099071.

Panadero, E. (2017). A review of self-regulated learning: Six models and four directions for research. *Frontiers in Psychology*, 8, 422.

Pashler, H., McDaniel, M., Rohrer, D., & Bjork, R. (2008). Learning styles: Concepts and evidence. *Psychological Science in the Public Interest*, 9(3), 105–119.

Patikorn, T., & Heffernan, N. T. (2020, August). Effectiveness of crowd-sourcing on-demand assistance from teachers in online learning platforms. In *Proceedings of the Seventh ACM Conference on Learning@ Scale* (pp. 115–124).

Pearl, J., & Mackenzie, D. (2018). *The Book of Why: The New Science of Cause and Effect*. Basic Books.

Picard, W. R. (Eds.). (1997). *Affective Computing*. MIT Press.

Prihar, E., Patikorn, T., Botelho, A., Sales, A., & Heffernan, N. (2021, June). Toward personalizing students' education with crowdsourced tutoring. In *Proceedings of the Eighth ACM Conference on Learning@ Scale* (pp. 37–45).

Rajendran, R., Kumar, A., Carter, K. E., Levin, D. T., & Biswas, G. (2018). Predicting learning by analyzing eye-gaze data of reading behavior. *International Educational Data Mining Society* (pp. 455–461).

Razzaq, L. M., & Heffernan, N. T. (2009, June). To tutor or not to tutor: That is the question. In *Proceedings of the 2009 Conference on Artificial Intelligence in Education: Building Learning Systems That Care: From Knowledge Representation to Affective Modelling* (pp. 457–464). Amsterdam: IOS Press.

Razzaq, R., Ostrow, K. S., & Heffernan, N. T. (2020, July). Effect of immediate feedback on math achievement at the high school level. In *International Conference on Artificial Intelligence in Education* (pp. 263–267). Cham: Springer.

Reeves, B., & Nass, C. (1996). *The Media Equation: How People Treat Computers, Television, and New Media Like Real People and Places*. Cambridge University Press.

Renninger, K. A., Bachrach, J. E., & Hidi, S. E. (2019). Triggering and maintaining interest in early phases of interest development. *Learning, Culture and Social Interaction*, 23, 100260.

Renninger, K. A., & Hidi, S. (2016). *The Power of Interest for Motivation and Engagement*. Routledge.

RoboTutor LLC. (2019). RoboTutor_2019. https://github.com/RoboTutorLLC/RoboTutor_2019.

Rodrigo, M. M. T. (2021, July). Impediments to AIS adoption in the Philippines. In *International Conference on Human-Computer Interaction* (pp. 412–421). Cham: Springer.

Rodrigues, L., Palomino, P. T., Toda, A. M., Klock, A. C. T., Oliveira W., Avila-Santos, A. P., Gasparini, I., & Isotani, S. (2021). Personalization improves gamification: Evidence from a mixed-methods study. *Proceedings of the ACM Human-Computer Interaction*, 5(CHI PLAY), Article 287. https://dl .acm.org/doi/abs/10.1145/3474714.

Roschelle, J., Feng, M., Murphy, R. F., & Mason, C. A. (2016). Online mathematics homework increases student achievement. *AERA Open*, 2(4), 2332858416673968.

Savard, I., & Mizoguchi, R. (2019). Context or culture: What is the difference? *Research and Practice in Technology Enhanced Learning*, 14(1), 1–12.

Schroeder, N. L., & Adesope, O. O. (2014). A systematic review of pedagogical agents' persona, motivation, and cognitive load implications for learners. *Journal of Research on Technology in Education*, 46(3), 229–251.

Schroeder, N. L., & Adesope, O. O. (2015). Impacts of pedagogical agent gender in an accessible learning environment. *Journal of Educational Technology & Society*, 18(4), 401–411.

Schroeder, N. L., Adesope, O. O., & Gilbert, R. B. (2013). How effective are pedagogical agents for learning? A meta-analytic review. *Journal of Educational Computing Research*, 49(1), 1–39.

Segedy, J. R., Kinnebrew, J. S., & Biswas, G. (2015). Using coherence analysis to characterize self-regulated learning behaviors in open-ended learning environments. *Journal of Learning Analytics*, 2, 13–48.

Snyder, C., Hutchins, N., Biswas, G., Emara, M., Grover, S., & Conlin, L. (2019). Analyzing students' synergistic learning processes in physics and CT by collaborative discourse analysis. In *Proceedings of the International Conference on Computer Supported Collaborative Learning* (pp. 360–367). Lyon, France.

Sociology Group. (2022). What is culture: Basic elements of culture and features. https://www. sociologygroup.com/elements-of-culture-basic-elements-of-culture/.

Sosnovsky, S. (2014). Math-bridge: Closing gaps in European remedial mathematics with technology-enhanced learning. In *Mit werkzeugen mathematik Und stochastik lernen – Using Tools for Learning Mathematics and Statistics* (pp. 437–451). Springer Spektrum.

Sosnovsky, S., Hsiao, I. H., & Brusilovsky, P. (2012, September). Adaptation "in the wild": ontology-based personalization of open-corpus learning material. In *European Conference on Technology Enhanced Learning* (pp. 425–431). Berlin, Heidelberg: Springer.

Steenbergen-Hu, S., & Cooper, H. (2014). A meta-analysis of the effectiveness of intelligent tutoring systems on college students' academic learning. *Journal of Educational Psychology*, 106(2), 331.

Taub, M., Azevedo, R., Rajendran, R., Cloude, E. B., Biswas, G., & Price, M. J. (2021). How are students' emotions related to the accuracy of cognitive and metacognitive processes during learning with an intelligent tutoring system? *Learning and Instruction*, 72, 101200.

Thaker, K., Zhang, L., He, D., & Brusilovsky, P. (2020). Recommending remedial readings using student's knowledge state. In *13th International Conference on Educational Data Mining*, July 10–13, 2020, pp. 233–244.

UNESCO. (2021). Leading SDG 4 – Education 2030. UNESCO Website. https://en.unesco.org/themes/ education2030-sdg4.

Uy-Tioco, C. S. (2019). 'Good enough' access: Digital inclusion, social stratification, and the reinforcement of class in the Philippines. *Communication Research and Practice*, 5(2), 156–171.

VanLehn, K. (2011). The relative effectiveness of human tutoring, intelligent tutoring systems, and other tutoring systems. *Educational Psychologist*, 46(4), 197–221.

Veletsianos, G., & Shepherdson, P. (2016). A systematic analysis and synthesis of the empirical MOOC literature published in 2013–2015. *The International Review of Research in Open and Distributed Learning*, 17(2), 192–221.

Wang, S., Ororbia, A., Wu, Z., Williams, K., Liang, C., Pursel, B., & Giles, C. L. (2016). Using prerequisites to extract concept maps from textbooks. In *25th International Conference on Information and Knowledge Management* (pp. 317–326).

Weber, G., & Brusilovsky, P. (2001). ELM-ART: An adaptive versatile system for web-based instruction. *International Journal of Artificial Intelligence in Education*, 12(4), 351–384.

Winchell, A., Mozer, M., Lan, A., Grimaldi, P., & Pashler, H. (2018). Can textbook annotations serve as an early predictor of student learning? In *11th International Conference on Educational Data Mining*, Buffalo, USA, pp. 431–437.

XPRIZE. (2019). Empowering children to take control of their own learning. learning.xprize.org.

Yarbro, J. T., & Olney, A. M. (2021). Contextual definition generation. In *3rd Workshop on Intelligent Textbooks at 22nd International Conference on Artificial Intelligence in Education* (pp. 74–83). http://ceur-ws.org/Vol-2895/paper09.pdf.

Yin, C., Yamada, M., Oi, M., Shimada, A., Okubo, F., Kojima, K., & Ogata, H. (2019). Exploring the relationships between reading behavior patterns and learning outcomes based on log data from E-books: A human factor approach. *International Journal of Human–Computer Interaction*, 35 (4–5), 313–322.

Zhai, C., & Massung, S. (2016). *Text Data Management and Analysis: A Practical Introduction to Information Retrieval and Text Mining*. Morgan & Claypool.

Zhang, N., Biswas, G., Chiu, J. L., & McElhaney, K. W. (2019). Analyzing students' design solutions in an NGSS-aligned earth sciences curriculum. In *Proceedings of the 20th International Conference on Artificial Intelligence in Education (AIED)*, Chicago, pp. 532–543.

Zhang, N., Biswas, G., & Hutchins, N. M. (2021). Measuring and analyzing students' strategic learning behaviors in open-ended learning environments. *International Journal of Artificial Intelligence in Education*. Advance online publication. https://doi.org/10.1007/s40593-021-00275-x.

Index

Absolute Between-ROC Area
    (ABROCA) 356, 362
Abstract Syntax Trees (ASTs) 289, 291
academic behavior 83
academic emotions 73
Acceleration of Future Learning (AFL) 509
access
    equity to advanced technologies 580–81
    ethical AIED, equity of accessibility 581–3
accountability, learning analytics for
    teachers 345
accountable 104
accumulated advantage phenomenon 607
accuracy 507
    of data-driven feedback 297
achievement emotions 73
achievement goals 90
Acker, L. 19
ACM Digital Library 392
ACT* cognitive theory 14, 15
action control 71
action outcome 71
activation of emotions 73–4
ActiveMath 189
activity emotions 72
ACT-R theory 35
    of cognitive and learning 189
ACT-R tutors 233
Adams, D. M. 458
adaptation 374
    orchestration 311
Adaptive Coach for Exploration (ACE) 174
adaptive coaching 203, 205, 211
Adaptive CSP 116
adaptive hypermedia 616
adaptive instruction 127, 188, 490
adaptive learning 11, 309, 606
adaptive navigation support 615, 616
Adaptive Peer Tutoring Assistant (APTA) 203, 204
adaptive presentation 616
adaptive scripting 196, 428
    collaborative learning 427–8
adaptive textbooks 615, 616
adaptivity 187–8, 198
    in instructional approaches 209–11
Adaptivity Grid 187–8, 198, 205, 209, 210
Adesope, O. O. 612
administrators 122, 524, 525, 527, 528

Adult Temperament Questionnaire (ATQ) 540–41
advanced, analytic, and automated (AAA)
    approach 243
advanced machine-learning techniques 243
affect 68, 231–2, 506
affect detectors 509
Affective AutoTutor 490, 495
Affective class report card 324–5
affective experiences 68–71, 75, 81, 84, 93
affective neuroscience in education 77
affective regulation 88
affective visualization 241
AFL *see* Acceleration of Future
    Learning (AFL)
agent-based systems 252
agent-based tutors 278
agents
    conversational 209–10
    pedagogical 235–6, 278–9, 457
    SimStudent 145
    software 279
aggregate learner model 105, 106
aggregation bias 575
"AI-as-a-service" systems 560
AI-based adaptation games 199, 200, 443, 445
    AutoThinking 448–50
    ELEKTRA 450
    Gamified SQL Tutor 449, 450
    iSTART-2, 448, 450
    Maths Garden 448, 450
    MathSpring 446–7, 450
    Minerva 449, 450
    Policy World 446–8, 450
    Prime Climb 448–50
    SQL Tutor 449–50
AI-based assessment (AIBA) 8, 485, 486,
    497–8
    computational methods 491–6
    constructs 489–90
    data sources 490–91
    framework of 486–7
    goals 487–9
    procedures of 490
    visibility 496–7
AI-based character interaction 443, 457
    Betty's Brain 461–3
    Crystal Island 457–9, 464–5
    ELIA 462, 464

Squares Family 461–3
TLCTS 460–61
TurtleTalk 460–62
AI-based decision support games 199–201, 443, 451
  Decimal Point 450–54
  Gamified Lynnette 454, 457
  Keep Attention 456
  My Backpack 453, 455
  Physics Playground 453–5
  TALENT 454–6
  TLCTS 456–7
AI-based educational systems 274
  authoring tools for 273
  author of 274–5
AI-based educational technology 170
AI-based educational tools 524
AI-based instructional systems 38, 529
AI-based learning technologies 606
AI-based mastery learning system 526
AI-based mixed-reality game 472–3
AI-based orchestration system 318
AI-based planning techniques 17
AI-based tutors 527
AI bias 471, 571, 576
AI Character Interaction games 199, 201–2
AI developers 544, 545
AI dialogue systems 235–6
AIED community 71, 94, 199, 266, 318, 559
AIED domains, expanding range of 19–21
AIED Interface level 580
AIED systems 322
  decision policies for 317
  in developing countries 633–7
  digital learning games research in 442–5
  dynamics within 60–61
  elements within 106–7
  elements within learning system 108–9
  flows of individual learning data and learner model 108
  inferred data 108
  inherent complexity of 122
  intercultural and global dimensions of 245
  long-term individual learner model 108
  metacognition construct influenced area of 47–9
  metacognition research applied to 49
  metacognition role in future 58–9
  processed data 107–8
  processing steps 390
  raw data 107
AI EdTech educate participant
  case study with 539–43
  data analysis 542–4
  data sources identified and collected 541–2
  research literature about debate tutoring 540–41

AI-enabled learning 562
AI ethics *see* ethical AI
AI experts 474
AI–instructor co-orchestration 316
AI interfaces 229
  for education 243–5
Aikido movements 416
Ainsworth, S. 467–8
"AI-out-of-the-box" partnerships 561
"AI people" 554, 555
AI-powered technologies 609
AI Readiness 546–8
AI-supported interfaces 229
Ait-Khayi, Nisrine (2019) 262
Alard, Danielle 628
ALEKS *see* Assessment and LEarning in Knowledge Spaces (ALEKS)
Alelo 532, 534
Aleven, V. 6, 18, 50, 52, 120, 187–8, 201, 454, 465, 469
algebra tutor 14
algorithmic bias 574–6, 578
algorithmic discrimination 558–9
algorithmic fairness 586–7
allocative bias 577
Almiyad, M. A. 392, 401, 402
Alvi, S. 557
Amazon Mechanical Turk 265
Amira 531
AMOEBA system 426
analytics 6–7
  see also individual entries
Anderson, J. R. 14, 15, 18, 189
Anderson's ACT-R theory 233
  see also ACT-R theory
Andes' BN-based domain and student model 138–9, 492, 513
animated pedagogical agents 252
Anzai, Y. 34
application field 400
application-level data 353
Apprentice Learner Architecture 145–6
APTA *see* Adaptive Peer Tutoring Assistant (APTA)
aptitude–treatment interaction (ATI) 54, 510
Arasasingham, R. D. 150
AR interfaces *see* augmented reality (AR) interfaces
"arithmetic error" 31
Armour-Thomas, E. 312
Arnold, K. E. 350
Arroyo, I. 5, 93, 471, 472
artificial intelligence (AI) 11, 39, 41–2, 281, 390, 392, 441, 485, 553
  advanced assessment based on recent advances in 260–61

algorithmic bias and sources of bias in 574–6
and analytics techniques 423
applications 571
conversational ITSs, opportunities to improve
    257–65
co-orchestration with and without 314–17
in educational policy and governance 561–3
in education, global landscape for 548–50
ethics of 573–9
intelligent tutoring systems 40
orchestration systems without 313–14
as tool kit 40
artificial "learning companion" 20
Artificial Peer Learning environment using
    SimStudent (APLUS) 54
Artzt, A. F. 312
ASAT *see* Autotutor Script Authoring Tool
    (ASAT)
Asbell-Clarke, J. 176
ASPIRE 137, 138
assessment 528
    automated essay scoring 529–30
    formative assessment of language-based
        activities 530–32
    stealth assessment 528–9
Assessment and LEarning in Knowledge Spaces
    (ALEKS) 150, 189, 487, 527, 533
assessment systems 505
    evaluation of 506–7
asset-based approaches 614
assistance
    levels in instructional approaches 205–8
    levels of 186–7
    levels of instructional 185
ASSISTments 92, 154, 189, 529, 631–3
    platform 23
    project 324
    system 310, 356
ASTNN 291, 294, 295
ASTs *see* Abstract Syntax Trees (ASTs)
Atkinson's theory of motivation 83
ATQ *see* Adult Temperament
    Questionnaire (ATQ)
attentional deployment strategies 88
attitudes *vs.* emotions 76
attributional processes 84–5
attributions, types of 71
attrition 509
augmented reality (AR) 401
augmented reality (AR) interfaces 236–8
Ausin, M. S. 512
authoring 263
authoring environments and frameworks 18–19
Authoring Software Platform for Intelligent
    Resources in Education (ASPIRE) 277–8

authoring tools 273–4
    agent-based tutors 278
    for AI-based educational systems 273
    constraint-based tutors 277–8
    dialog-based tutors 279–80
    GIFT authoring system 280–81
    hierarchy of interaction granularity 274
    model-tracing tutors 276–7
    pedagogical agents 278–9
    possibilities 281–2
    software agents 279
    for types of ITSs 275–81
Autism Spectrum Conditions (ASCs) 462
autism spectrum disorder (ASD) 92
automated approach 140
automated essay scoring 529–30, 558
automated knowledge discovery 563
automated model discovery 142
automated writing evaluation (AWE) 485, 493
Autoscore 530
AutoThinking 199, 200, 470, 489
AutoTutor 5, 50–51, 236, 243, 252–4, 263, 279,
    487, 488, 490, 493, 494
Autotutor Script Authoring Tool (ASAT) 280
avatar 239, 278–80, 532
Avry, S. 429
awareness 68
    orchestration 311
awareness tools 208, 424
    group 428–9
    student 424
    teacher 192, 208, 424, 425, 429–30
Azevedo, R. 5, 21, 47, 52, 234

Baker, R. S. J. D. 128, 151, 202, 468, 586–8
Balacheff, N. 19
Ballweber, C. 465
Barab, S. 240
Barbaro, Nicole 7
Barnes, T. 6, 146
Barocas, S. 577, 578
baseline instruction 512
BASIC programming language 12
Baskin, A. B. 20, 23
Basu, S. 175
Battleship Numberline 468, 471
Bayer, V. 361
Bayesian knowledge tracing (BKT) 191, 194, 261,
    287, 292, 445, 492
Bayesian methods 492
Bayesian Networks (BN) 138–41, 433, 622
    algorithm 200, 449
    analysis 492
    exploration and self-explanation in 180
    for stealth assessment 129

Baylor, A. L. 612
Beanstalk 202, 468–70
behavioral interactions, within learning
    management systems 352
behavior-based data-driven student models, for
    OELEs 180
behavior data 491
behavior graphs 149
behaviors
    incorrect learning 147
    organizing mechanic of 79
    template-based 70
    of tutoring systems 189
behaviour discovery 109
Bell, M. 537
Bella 204
benchmark data 576
benchmark questions, user-centred definition of
    scrutability and control 112–17
Bernoulli Thompson sampling 632
best-performing decision tree model 144
Betty's Brain 5, 53, 146, 151, 152, 171, 172, 175,
    181, 203–4, 461–4, 470, 474n3, 488, 619,
    620, 622
between-subjects design 512, 514
bias
    algorithmic 574–6
    general forms of 573–4
    predictive modeling 359–61
    sources of 558, 574–6
big data 554, 571
"big five" theory 637
Bi-GRU Capsule Networks model 262
Bill and Melinda Gates Foundation 560
biometric data 491
BioWorld interface 233–4, 244
Bio-World system 19
BIP-II system 12
Birchfield, D. 238
Biswas, G. 53, 474n3
BKT *see* Bayesian knowledge tracing (BKT)
Blanchard, E. G. 627
blended learning 554
Blessing, Stephen 6
Blikstein, P. 584
Blockly 460
Bloom, B. S. 390, 583
Bodily, R. 427
Boland, R. J. 327
Bonar, Jeffrey 42n2
boundary object 275
brain assessment parameters and tools 639
Bransford, J. D. 509
Breazeal, C. 392, 402, 403
Brecht (Wasson), B. 18

Breuker, J. 18
Brinton, C. G. 177
broader EdTech domains 103
BROMP protocol 468
Brooks, C. 355
Brooks, Christopher 7
Brown, J. S. 12–13, 31
Brusilovsky, P.L. 18
bucketing values 577
Buffum, P. S. 472
Bull, S. 19, 106
Bunt, A. 195
Burton, R. R. 12

Cano, A. R. 469
CAPIT tutor 139
Carnegie Learning 532, 534, 550
Casadio, M. 402, 403
Casas-Ortiz, Albert 7
Cascade 20
case-based domain models 152
case-based knowledge 195
CASEL *see* Collaborative for Academic for
    Social and Emotional Learning (CASEL)
case study
    with AI EdTech educate participant 539–43
    to create psychomotor AIED systems 409–14
    DebateMate 543–6
    KSAS, psychomotor AIED systems 409–12
    KUMITRON, psychomotor AIED systems
        412–14
    Lime, data-driven supports evaluation
        298, 299
Catalyst/MCWeb system 150
CATO system 152
CATS *see* Culturally Aware Tutoring System
    (CATS)
causal map 171, 175, 203, 620
causal notion of fairness 587
CCK simulation *see* Circuit Construction Kit
    (CCK) simulation
Center for the Study of Adult Literacy
    (CSAL) 487
Centers for Disease Control and Prevention
    (CDC) 380
certification 16–17
Chan, T.-W. 20, 23
Chan Zuckerberg Initiative 560
Chase, C. C. 510
Chau, H. 149
Chen, X. 402
chess-playing computer program 39
Chi, M. T. H. 256
Chiang, M. 177
China

relationships between AI and education in 557
teaching mathematics in the USA *vs.* 582
Chinese AIED industry 557
Chua, Y. H. V. 432
CIRCSIM system 19
CIRCSIM-Tutor 18, 253
Circuit Construction Kit (CCK) simulation 171, 172, 178
Clancey, W.J. 17
Clark, D. B. 440
class-level models 317
classroom orchestration systems 311, 518
clickstream/trace data 352
"closing the analysis loop" 426
clustering analysis 145
coaching 187, 202, 205, 206
  adaptive 203, 205, 211
  more directive 205, 206
  more suggestive 205, 206
Cocea, M. 195
Cock, J. 176
Codes 433
code states 288
Code2Vec 291, 294, 295
coding 55, 80, 431, 433
  dual encoding 282
  emic 433
  schemes 431
cognitive, affective, metacognitive, and motivational (CAMM) processes 623
cognitive appraisal strategies 88
cognitive apprenticeship 20, 230–31, 233
cognitive conflicts 38
cognitive dissonance 608
cognitive load 509
cognitive load theory 192
Cognitive Mastery 191
cognitive modeling, in intelligent tutoring systems 354
cognitive/physical norm 571
cognitive processes 638
cognitive psychology 32, 36
cognitive psychology models 41
cognitive science 37
cognitive science theory 189
cognitive scientists 10
cognitive strategy 52
cognitive theory of emotion 468
Cognitive Tutor Authoring Tools (CTAT) 189, 276
cognitive tutoring systems 14–15
"Cognitive Tutor principles" 189
cognitive tutors 15, 50, 106, 132, 140, 488–90, 492, 496, 513
cognitivism 637

coherence analysis 622
Coh-metrix 428
Cohn, J. 279
collaboration 232
  researcher-led 357
  use of data gathered during students' 424
collaboration skills 134, 187, 609
Collaborative Evidence-Based Product Design 537
Collaborative for Academic for Social and Emotional Learning (CASEL) 89
collaborative learning 184, 196–8, 207–9, 422
  adaptive scripting 427–8
  awareness tools 424
  direct feedback 423–4
  direct formative feedback to learners 426–7
  group awareness tools 428–9
  group formation 425–6
  grouping students 423
  MUVEs support 239–41
  summative assessment 431–2
  supporting of 423–5
  teacher awareness tools 429–30
  trends and future challenges 433–4
  use of data gathered during students' collaboration 424
collaborative reflection, in MOOCs 376
collaborative VR environment 56
COLLER system 197
Collins, A.M. 12
commercial
  application 555
  games 497
  products 549
  sector 559, 565
  successes 195
commercialization 559–61
  small-scale 546–8
commercial systems 525, 527
common decimal misconception 201, 451
common source 282
comparative view scaffolds 334
competency-based progression 526
complex skill acquisition, computational theory of 34
composition 238, 239
compositional approaches, to assessing students' short responses 261
comprehensive student models 257–60, 266
computational-heavy models 294
"computational mathetics" 18
computational methods 486–7, 491
  Bayesian methods 492
  machine-learning methods 494–6
  NLP methods 491–4

computational theory, of complex skill
    acquisition 34
computational thinking (CT) 173, 200, 449, 469
Computational Thinking in Simulation and
    Modeling (CTSiM) 175
computer-assisted instruction (CAI) 4, 11, 12
Computer-Assisted Learning (CAL) 4
Computer Programming domain 7
computers 634
*Computers and Education: Artificial
    Intelligence* 555
computer simulations, for situating learning in
    authentic contexts 232
computer-supported collaborative learning
    (CSCL) 22, 24n8, 186, 196, 198, 275, 309,
    370–71, 373
computer-supported cooperative work
    (CSCW) 275
Conati, C. 5, 6, 20, 180, 195, 449, 469
concept maps 152
conceptual graphs 151, 152
conceptual learning 6, 10, 37, 250, 257
conceptual reasoning 250
condition-action rules 40
conditional knowledge 46, 59
connectivistMOOC (cMOOC) 375
conservation of matter 620
constraint-based modeling (CBM) 135, 137, 189
constraint-based tutoring approaches 14–15
constraint-based tutoring framework 23
constraint-based tutors 135, 137, 150, 154, 189,
    233, 277–8, 287
Constraint Satisfaction Problems applet (CSP
    applet) 178
"constructivist" approach 13
constructs 486, 489–90
contemporary metacognitive research 47
content model 616
contestable 104
context, methods that account for 262
contiguity hypothesis 33
control
    architecture of learning systems for 105–6
    user-centred definition of 112–17
control-dependent emotions 72
control-independent emotions 72
control interfaces
    metacognitive activities at 120–21
    standard scrutiny and 121
controllable 104
control-value theory (CVT) 71, 74
control value theory of emotions 232
conventional learner modeling methods 629
conventional technology-supported learning
    systems 628

conversational agents 209–10
conversational ITSs 251–2, 254, 266–7
    automating tutorial dialogue generation from
        textbooks 263
    effectiveness in improving learning 254–5
    opportunities to improve based on advances in
        AI 257–65
conversational tutors 261
conversation-based systems 254
Cook, R. 21
Cooper, A. 537
cooperative turn-taking activities 462
co-orchestration
    human–AI 315–17
    instructor–learner 315
    with and without AI 314–17
Corbi, A. 416
Co-reader project 204
corrective feedback 488
correct knowledge 137
correctness feedback 131
Course Insights 336, 343
    decision making and pedagogical
        action 340, 342
    drill-down recommendations 337, 338
    engagement comparison of the filtered *vs.*
        unfiltered distribution 338, 340
    filter recommendation interface 338, 339
    implications for practice 342
    insights 340
    learning process 338, 341
    manual filter builder panel 336–7
    sensemaking 338
Coursera MOOCs 375, 376
Course Signals 326, 350
course units (CUs) 382
Covarrubias, M. 402
COVID-19 pandemic 533
    stress impact on patterns of participation
        380–81
    student-mentor relationships during 379–80
Cowls, J. 572–3
Co-writer project 204
Cramer, H. 574, 577
creativity 276, 403, 496, 497, 609, 640
Cremonesi, P. 120
Criterion 494
critical issues, predictive modeling 356
    adoption, intervention, and theory 361–2
    bias and fairness 359–61
    cold start 358–9
    population sample 358
    replication, reproduction, generalization 356–7
    target outcome 357–8
    transparency and openness 359

critical perspectives 553
  algorithmic discrimination 558–9
  commercialization 559–61
  educational policy and governance 561–3
  ethical frameworks 563–5
  historical developments 554–5
  political economy 556–8
CrossLing 291
cross-stakeholder collaboration 544–6, 550
cross-validation 143–4
crowdsourcing 276–7
  way for personalized learning 630–33
crowdsourcing domain models 153
Cruz, W. M. 426
Crystal Island 178–80, 199, 201, 202, 458–9,
  464–5, 470
Crystal Island: EcoJourneys 239–40
CSCL *see* computer-supported collaborative
  learning (CSCL)
CS1 Java course 294
C2STEM 619
CTAT *see* Cognitive Tutor Authoring
  Tools (CTAT)
Cukurova, Mutlu 8
cultural bias 607, 608
culturally aware systems 629–30
Culturally Aware Tutoring System (CATS) 627
culturally congruent dialect 613
cultural modeling issues 627
cultural practices 231
culture
  Arabic and Iraqi 201
  Asian 627
  of collaboration 240
  language and 201, 460
  of learners 588
  learning-culture bias 583, 584
Cumming, G.D. 20
Curiosity Notebook 204
"curriculum information network" 12
CVT *see* control-value theory (CVT)
Czikszentmihalyi, M. 199, 441

Dacrema, M. F. 120
Dadu, A. 153
DALMOOC 376
Damasio, A. R. 76, 77
Danks, D. 574
dashboards 518
  learning analytics 241, 245, 322, 517–18
  teacher-facing 344
data
  behavior 491
  group interaction 642
  multimodal 491
  performance 490–91
data analysis 542–4

data bias 575
data cleaning 114
data collection 635–6
data-driven adaptive support 302
data-driven approaches 287
  OELES 176–9
data-driven feature detection (DDFD) algorithm
  289, 290, 296
data-driven features 289–90
data-driven feedback, accuracy of 297
data-driven methods 128
data-driven student modeling 175
  for game-based OELEs 178–9
data-driven supports, evaluation of 295–6
  data-driven feedback, accuracy 297
  effectiveness 297–8
  fallibility 298–301
  future research 302–3
  Lime (case study) 298, 299
  multi-criterion evaluation mechanism 296
data-driven techniques 157
"data-hungry" 294, 295
data-intensive techniques 422
data mining approaches 350, 426
data processing techniques 429
data sources 486, 490–91, 498
  identified and collected 541–2
data-storytelling, integrating elements of 336
Davies, Huw 8
Davis, D. 177
Dawson, S. 350
DBN *see* Dynamic Bayesian Network (DBN)
DBSCAN *see* Density-Based Spatial Clustering
  of Applications with Noise (DBSCAN)
DC-Trains 254
DebateMate 540–42
  case study 543–6
  collaboration between AI developers,
    researchers and educators 544–6
debate tutoring, research literature about 540–41
debuggable 104
Decimal Point 200–202, 450–54, 470–72
decision-making process 540, 541
  Course Insights 340, 342
  LearnerFlow 335
  teachers 327–8
  ZoomSense 331
decision shapes 289
decision support tools 7
Decision Tree Based Thompson Sampling 632–3
declarative knowledge 46, 59, 151
deep knowledge, pedagogical approaches to
  acquiring 251
deep knowledge tracing (DKT) 287, 354
deep-learning algorithms 622
deep learning applications 147
deep learning methods

application of 354
  usage of 294
deep learning models 292, 325
  use for source code analysis 291
deep neural networks 129
DeepTutor 254, 262
default mode (DM), of brain 78
defensive pessimism 90
de Jong, T. 19
Deloitte 549
del Soldato, T. 18
demographic data 353
denigration 578
Density-Based Spatial Clustering of Applications
  with Noise (DBSCAN) 145
deployment bias 577
deployment, ITS 21
Derry, S.J. 19
descriptive capabilities 334
descriptive learning analytics 323–5
  in LearnerFlow 332–6
  in ZoomSense 329–31
design-loop adaptivity 190, 210
Desmarais, M. C. 128, 151
detection task 51
developers, evaluation systems 517–19
developing countries 633–7
diagnosis 15–16
diagnostic capabilities 334
diagnostic learning analytics 323–5
  in Course Insights 336–42
  in LearnerFlow 332–6
diagnostic view scaffolds 334
dialog-based tutoring systems 235, 252, 254,
  279–80
digital divide 580, 581
digital gameplay 440
digital games 440
digital governance 564
digital learning, next generation of 640–43
digital learning games 199, 200, 202, 210, 440
  AI-based adaptation 445–50
  AI-based character interaction 457–64
  AI-based decision support 450–57
  definition of 442
  foundations of 441–2
  LA and/or EDM use for game analysis and
    improvement 464–9
  learned from research with AIED 469–70
  research in AIED 442–6
digital regulation 565
digital text-based learning 153
digital traces 422, 641
digital transformation 561
Dillahunt, T. 377
Dillenbourg, P. 20, 309–11, 425
direct data 107

direct formative feedback, to learners 426–7
discarding data 577
discovery learning 244
"discovery process" 16
discrimination task 51
discriminatory design 558
distance-learning institution in the UK 360
diversity-aware intelligent mentoring
  systems 641
diversity-aware social interaction spaces 642
Diziol, D. 428
DKT *see* Deep Knowledge Tracing (DKT)
D'Mello, S. K. 243
domain knowledge 16–17, 132, 134, 135, 150,
  174, 187, 492, 497
domain modeling paradigms 132, 642
  for AIED systems *see* domain modeling
    paradigms
  Bayesian Networks 138–41
  constraints 135–8
  create domain models using machine learning
    147–8
  examples and generalized examples 149–50
  for intelligent textbooks 148–9
  knowledge spaces 150–51
  machine learning 141–2
  new trends in 153
  reinforcement learning 146–7
  rules 132–4
  strengths and weaknesses of 154, 155
  supervised learning 142–5
  unsupervised learning 145–6
domain models
  of AIED system 128–9
  assessing student knowledge 129
  assessing student work 129
  creation using machine learning 147–8
  designing new learning content 132
  formative feedback to students 131
  functions of 129, 130
  recognizing student errors 131
  selecting individualized learning content 131
  solve problems to provide next-step hints 131
  vs. student model 128
  types of 151–3
  use in AIED systems 154, 155
domain ontologies 151
domains, of evaluation 541
domain-specific modeling languages (DSMLs)
  619–21
domain-value bias 583, 584
Domitrovich, C.E. 93
Dong, Y. 292
Doroudi, S. 361, 580, 581, 584
Dowel, N. 428
Downtown: A Subway Adventure 469
Dreams 282–3

drill-and-practice mastery learning-focused
   pedagogies 572
dropout 177, 325, 326, 375, 376
DSMLs *see* domain-specific modeling languages
   (DSMLs)
dual encoding 282
du Boulay, B. 2, 18, 184, 187
Duckworth, Angela 86
Duffy, M. C. 52
Duolingo 189, 608
Durlach, P. J. 488
Dweck, C. 85, 86
dynamic Bayesian network (DBN) 140, 174–5
Dynamic Decision Network 468
dynamic geometry environments 194

EarthShake 195
EBT *see* effort-based tutoring (EBT)
Eccles, J. S. 83
Echeverria, Jon 7
Echeverria, V. 432
ECHOES AIED system 582–3
ECHOES project 582
ecology 343, 589
economic processes 553
ecosystem
   educational AI 545
   learning 259, 306, 352
   socio-technological 585
   UK EdTech 550, 551
Edelson, D. J. 554
"edge AI" 624
EdTech industry 584
Educate Accelerator 538, 544, 546
Educate Golden Triangle 538, 539, 546
Educate Research Acceleration process 550
EDUCATE research accelerator programme
   549, 550
education
   control-value theory of emotion in 71
   emotion-focused research in 70–71
   emotion regulation theories related to 88–9
   motivational theories related to 82–4
   motivation regulation theories related to
      89–90
   neuroscience of emotion in 76–7
educational AI ecosystem 545
educational AI systems 117
educational assessment 487–8
educational data mining (EDM) 22, 200, 202,
   422, 464, 555
   Battleship Numberline 468
   Beanstalk 468–70
   Downtown: A Subway Adventure 469
   Heroes of Math Island 468

Physics Playground 468
Prime Climb 468
Reasoning Mind 468
Refraction 465–6
research 106, 129
ST Math 468
TC3Sim 468
use of 443
Zombie Division 465–8
Zoombinis 468–9
Educational Data Mining and Learning
   Analytic 370
educational experiences 525, 527, 559
educational games, of learning systems 611
educational outcomes 69, 88, 360, 581
educational policy 561–3
educational technologists 470, 474
educational technology (Edtech), products and
   services 538–9
Educational Testing Service (ETS) 252
"education domain" 10
education research 238
educators 31, 37, 48, 86, 322, 334, 376, 426, 428,
   498, 538–46, 550, 630–31, 641
edX platform 375, 376, 378
EER-Tutor 135, 496
effective modeling, student success 288, 292
   semi-supervised learning 295
   semi-supervised modeling for limited data
      size 294–5
   temporal modeling 292–4
effect size 513, 516
efficacy management 90
effort-based tutoring (EBT) 446
Ekman's Theory of Emotion 71
electrical power 634
electroencephalogram (EEG) 244, 639
ELEKTRA 450
ELEs *see* exploratory learning
   environments (ELEs)
ELIA 462, 464
Elle 204
Elliot, Scott 85
ELM-ART 189
ELM system 16
Elo, A. 449
Elo scoring model 449
Elsom-Cook, M. T. 16, 194
embodied cognition, psychomotor AIED systems
   415–16
embodiment 238
emotion 68, 70
   AIED research 80–81
   vs. attitudes and preferences 76
   control-value theory 71

distinguishing features of 75–6
distinguishing from other affective categories 74–5
early theories 71
in education, neuroscience of 76–7
emotional thought 77–8
implications for pedagogy 74
introspective *vs.* extrospective processes 78–9
key questions for emotion-focused research in education 70–71
learning assessment, importance of 637–8
vs. moods 76
social brain 79–80
subjective control and value 71–2
three-dimensional taxonomy of 72–4
visualization 92
emotional group awareness 429
emotional regulation 90–91, 232
Emotion API 462
emotion-focused research, in education 70–71
EMT dialogue *see* expectation and misconception tailored (EMT) dialogue
Engage 471, 472
engagement, theoretical foundations 374–5
Enhanced Entity-Relationship model (EER) 135
enjoyment 72
Enskill 254, 532
Environmental Detectives 237
environments
    Artificial Peer Learning environment using SimStudent 54
    authoring 18–19
    collaborative VR 56
    dynamic geometry 194
    exploratory learning 193–5
    game-based digital learning 86–7
    immersive virtual 236–7
    MUVEs 239–41
    OELEs *see* open-ended learning environments (OELEs)
    PIXIE 18
    SAFARI 18
    simulation-based learning 19
    virtual 234–7
epistemic emotions 73
epistemic network analysis 433
equity 471, 606–8
    of accessibility 581–3
    of access to advanced technologies 580–81
    of AIED's pedagogies 583–4
e-rater 529
error-directed feedback 191
errors during instruction 508
error-specific feedback 131, 156, 190, 207
eSpark 533

ESpark system 527
ethical AI 571–3
    algorithmic bias and sources of bias 574–6
    fairness 578–9
    general forms of bias 573–4
    harms 577–8
ethical AIED 572–3, 600
    algorithmic fairness in 586–7
    considerations and questions for AIED designers and users 590–99
    equity of accessibility of 581–3
    equity of access to advanced technologies in 580–81
    equity of AIED's pedagogies 583–4
    ethics of datasets, algorithms and methods in 586
    interaction between human and machine autonomy 584–5
    methodological considerations for 587–8
    strawman draft framework of 589–90
ethical frameworks 563–5
ethical implications 563, 571, 600
ethics, learning analytics 345
ethics washing 565
ETS *see* Educational Testing Service (ETS)
Eurohelp 21
European Regional Development Fund 538
European Union 101
evaluation, ITS 21
evaluation, of predictive models 355
evaluation bias 576–7
event-based trace data 352
Evidence-Centered Design (ECD) framework 173–4
evidence-informed EdTech 538
example-based approaches 156
example-based learning 206, 207
example-fading procedure 193
examples, domain modeling paradigms 149–50
example studying 191–3, 209, 210
example-tracing algorithm 149–50
example-tracing tutors 149, 150, 154, 189
ex-nomination 578
expectancy of success 83
expectancy-value theory 5, 83
expectation and misconception tailored (EMT) dialogue 493
Expectation-Maximization (EM) method 294–5
Experience API (xAPI) 352
experiential knowledge 37
expert-engineered approaches 140
expertise 231
expertise reversal 192–3
expert knowledge 175
explain 148, 179, 188, 192, 193, 209

explainability 7, 129, 148, 345, 580, 588
Explainable AI (XAI) 102, 117
explainable model 129
explanation-based tutor 19
explanatory models 148
Explicit Semantic Analysis (ESA) 261
exploratory learning 184, 193–6, 207–11
exploratory learning environments (ELEs) 193–5
exploratory visual analytics approach 336
Exponentially Weighted Moving Averages
    (EWMA) algorithm 411
expository text 373
eXpresser 195
eXtended MOOCs (xMOOCs) 375–6
externalizations 56, 422
extrinsic affective regulation 88
extrinsic motivation 83–4
extrinsic values of activities and outcomes 71
eye fixations/gaze 509
eye-tracking devices 622
eye-tracking systems 639
Eynon, Rebecca 8

face-to-face 422, 423, 425, 434, 540, 609
face-tracking devices 622
facial expression 71, 93, 94, 244, 325, 462, 491,
    495, 547
facial recognition algorithms 430
FACT orchestration system 316
fading 20, 150, 191, 210
fair, accountable, transparent and ethical (FATE)
    system 5, 101, 117
    scrutability in 102–4
fairness 559, 578–9
    definitions of 579
    learning analytics, for teachers 345
    predictive modeling 359–61
fairness through unawareness 587
Family Education Rights and Privacy Act
    (FERPA) 101
Fang, Ying 8
far transfer tests 508
FATE frameworks 559
FAtiMA 463
favor standardization 525
feature-based methods 288, 289, 292, 293, 296
feature-based student modeling 302
feature state vector 289
feedback 38, 487
    corrective 488
    formative 488
    summative 488
Feng, W. 177
FERPA *see* Family Education Rights and Privacy
    Act (FERPA)

Festinger, Leon 38
field, of AIED 157, 189
finalists' apps 636
Fincher, Sally 2
Finkelstein, S. 582, 613
Fischer, F. 311
Fitbits 92
FITS system 18
FlexiTrainer 279
Floridi, L. 572–3
formal theories, artificial intelligence 39–40
formative assessments 529
    of language-based activities 530–32
formative evaluation 513–14
formative feedback 186, 187, 190–91, 198, 202,
    206–8, 427, 488
    to students 131
FractionsLab 195
framework for ethical AIED 589–90
Framework for User Modeling and Adaptation
    (FUMA) 109, 177–9
    Behaviour Discovery phase 110
    User Classification phase 110, 112
Frasson, C. 18, 19, 22
Frederiksen, J. R. 16
Friedler, S. A. 579
FUMA *see* Framework for User Modeling and
    Adaptation (FUMA)
future learning
    acceleration of 509
    preparation for 509

gain score 508
game-based adaptivity 202
game-based digital learning environments 86–7
game-based learning 173, 184, 198–202,
    206, 207
game-based systems 118
game designers 282, 470, 474
games
    AI-based adaptation games *see* AI-based
        adaptation games
    AI-based decision support games *see* AI-based
        decision support games
    AI-based mixed-reality game 472–3
    AI Character Interaction games 199, 201–2
    digital 440
    digital learning *see* digital learning games
    Mission Game 460
    TALENT 454–6
    TugLet 152
    Zoombinis learning game 176
game score 509
games for learning 208
gamification

of learning systems 611
techniques 417
gamified AIED learning technology 443
Gamified Lynnette 443, 454, 457
Gamified SQL Tutor 443, 449, 450
gaming detectors 468
gaming the system 87, 142, 208, 530
Gardner, J. 356
Gašević, D. 7, 343
Gates, Bill 560
Gauthier, Gilles 22
gaze 491, 498, 509, 533
gaze data 180
Gecsei, J. 18, 19
General Charisma Inventory (GCI) 541
General Data Protection Regulation (GDPR) 101
generalizability 302, 357, 373
generalization, predictive modeling 356–7
generalized examples, domain modeling
    paradigms 149–50
Generalized Intelligent Framework for Tutoring
    (GIFT) 14, 259, 280–81
General Problem Solver (GPS) 629
generative approach 276
"generative CAI" 11
Genesereth, M.R. 12
Geogebra 194
geometry tutor 14
gesture 86, 204, 210, 278, 280, 460, 611, 625
GhasemAghaei, R. 241
GIFT *see* Generalized Intelligent Framework for
    Tutoring (GIFT)
Gilbert, S. B. 275
Gilbert, Stephen B. 6
Glaser, R. 19
glass box approaches 580
global dimension, of AIED 245
Global Learning XPRIZE 633–7
    computers 634
    data collection 635–6
    electrical power 634
    internet 635
    sensors 636
    support 636
    WiFi 635
Global North 606
Global South 606–8
GLUE!-PS 314
GLUEPS-AR 314
goal-directed feedback 191
goal orientation, research on 85–6
goal-oriented activities 462
goal-oriented self-talk 90
goals
    of AIBA 486–9

in AIED systems 194
    motivation 85–6
Gobert, J. D. 143–5, 152
Goldberg, B. 392
Golden Triangle Framework 550
Golden Triangle philosophy 544–5
González-Villanueva, L. 391
Goodfellow, R. 19
Google Glass technology 92
Google Scholar 392
Gooru 527, 533
governance 561–3
G-Power 516, 517
GPS *see* General Problem Solver (GPS)
grades 509
Graesser, A. C. 6, 243, 250, 255, 371
Granularity BNs 140
Greene, J. A. 48
Greer, J. E. 16
Griffiths, T. L. 147
grit 86
Gross, J. J. 88–90, 232
grounded feedback 191
grounded skills 170
group awareness tools, collaborative learning
    428–9
group-based interactive systems 640
group fairness 579
group formation, collaborative learning 425–6
group interaction data 642
growth mindset, motivation 85–6
Guess and check strategy 622
guided discovery 194
guiding tools 313
GUIDON system 17, 19
Gulson, K. N. 562
GuruTutor 254
Guthrie, E. R. 33
Guttag, J. V. 558, 575, 588

Habgood, M. P. J. 467
Hadwin, A. F. 46, 51
"hard science" domains 19
Harley, J. M. 89, 90, 232, 237
harms 577–8
harms of allocation 577–8
harms of representation 578
Harpstead, E. 465, 469
Harrari, Y. 585
Harter, S. 84
Hawn, A. 586–8
HCI-based computer-supported cooperative work
    community 22
Helping Other with Augmentation and Reasoning
    Dashboard (HOWARD) platform 241, 242

Help-Seeking Support Environment (HSSE) 50
help-seeking tutor 5, 50
Help Tutor 50
Henderlong Corpus, J. 83
Heraz, A. 639
Hernández-Leo, D. 316
Heroes of Math Island 468
heuristics 465
Hidden Markov Models (HMMs) 178–9, 400, 401
higher-level observational data 107
high-performing students 622
high-prior-knowledge (HPK) 606
high-quality interactions 377
historical theories 33–4
historic bias 575
history
    developments 554–5
    of ITSs with natural language interaction 252–4
    of online learning technologies 370–72
HMMs *see* Hidden Markov Models (HMMs)
Ho, A. 362
Hodaie, Z. 392
Holmes, Wayne 8
Holstein, K. 5, 7, 118, 361, 580, 581, 584
Holt, P. 16
homeostasis 78
Hooper, K. 229
HOWARD platform *see* Helping Other with Augmentation and Reasoning Dashboard (HOWARD) platform
Howe, Jim 2
HPK *see* high-prior-knowledge (HPK)
HSSE *see* Help-Seeking Support Environment (HSSE)
Huang, Yun 6
human–AI co-orchestration 309, 315–17
human-centred design 335
human-centred learning analytics 344–5
human–computer interaction (HCI) 58, 102, 104, 238, 531
    research in 344
human-in-the-loop 7
human labellers 577
human learning 10, 11, 34, 39, 54, 70, 77, 87, 563, 580, 588, 609, 611
human movement computing techniques 409
"Hunt the Wumpus" 12
hybrid approaches, OELES 174–6
hypermedia-based OELEs 171

IEA *see* Intelligent Essay Assessor (IEA)
IEEE Xplore 392
iFLYTEK 549

IJAIED *see* International Journal of Artificial Intelligence in Education (IJAIED)
IJMMS 24n3
Ikeda, M. 18
ill-defined domain 19
illustrative studies, learning analytics 329
    descriptive analytics in ZoomSense 329–31
    descriptive and diagnostic analytics in LearnerFlow 332–6
    diagnostic and prescriptive analytics in Course Insights 336–42
ImageNet 259
immediate feedback strategy 15, 290
immersive virtual environments 236–7
Immordino-Yang, M.H. 76, 77
IMS Caliper 352
inclusion
    criteria, psychomotor AIED systems 394–5
    designing virtual characters in STEM 611–14
    roadmap for leveraging pedagogical agents for STEM 613
inclusiveness 471
incomplete data, design for 119
incorrect knowledge 137
incorrect learning behaviors 147
independence, fairness 586
Independence BNs 140
individual fairness 579, 587
individual learner model 105, 106
    flows of 108
individual learning 127, 309
individual learning data, flows of 108
individual researcher replications 357
inequality 359, 360, 510, 559
inferred data 108, 114
influential design principle 38
informal learning 371, 613, 624, 640, 642
information, sources of 537
information overload 608–11
information visualization (InfoViz) 344
Inq-ITS system 143, 195, 211, 529, 534
inquiry learning 193, 206, 237, 315
    collaborative 56, 239
inquiry skills 143, 148, 152, 171, 174, 175, 195
inspectable 103
institutional data-sharing agreements 357
instruction
    adaptivity in instructional approaches 209–11
    AI-based instructional systems 38, 529
    baseline 512
    computer-assisted instruction 4, 11, 12
    errors during 508
    knowledge of domain of 127
    traditional teacher-led 525
instructional approaches 184, 185, 211–12

adaptivity in 209–11
collaborative learning 196–8
exploratory learning 193–6
game-based learning 198–202
learning-by-teaching 202–5
learning from examples 192–3
learning from problem solving 188–92
levels of assistance in 205–8
instructional design models 41
instructional design principles 37, 38
instructional design theories 36–9
instructional goals 184, 206, 211
"instructional planning" 17
instructional support 316
instructional systems 505, 506
    common variables 508–10
    comparing multiple versions of system
        512–15
    comparisons to baseline instruction 513–15
    evaluation of 507–8
    G-Power 516, 517
    outcome variables and moderators 510–11
    single condition studies 511–12
instructor–AI regulation 317
instructor assessment system 518
instructor–learner–AI co-orchestration 317
instructor–learner co-orchestration 315
instructor regulation 317
instructors 312
    sharing responsibility between learners
        and 315
    systems without AI 313–14
    understanding instructors' orchestration
        312–13
instructors, evaluation systems 517–19
Integration-Kid system 20
intelligence
    crafting textbooks augmented with 616
    enriching textbooks with 616
    extracting from textbook interaction data 618
intelligent CAI (ICAI) systems 11, 12
Intelligent Essay Assessor (IEA) 493, 529
intelligent interfaces 243
intelligent mentoring systems 640
    changing learning landscape 640
    diversity-aware intelligent mentoring
        systems 641
    mentoring 640–41
    M:1 mentoring 642
    M:M mentoring 642
    1:1 mentoring 641
    1:M mentoring 641
    research directions 642–3
intelligent nudges 642
"intelligent support for learning" 13

"intelligent support to learning in groups"
    (ISLG) 422
intelligent systems 392, 393, 497
Intelligent Teaching Assistant for
    Programming 277
Intelligent Team Tutoring Systems (ITTSs)
    280–81
intelligent textbooks 148–9
    adaptive textbook, with InterBook 614, 615
    crafting textbooks augmented with
        intelligence 616
    enriching textbooks with intelligence 616
    extracting intelligence from textbook content
        616–18
    extracting intelligence from textbook
        interaction data 618
intelligent tutoring systems (ITSs) 3, 14, 40, 42,
    127, 170, 188, 233–4, 250, 273, 392, 422, 427,
    485, 606
    cognitive modeling in 354
intelligent visual interfaces 241–3
IntelliMetric scoring system 494, 495
interaction 353
interaction granularity, hierarchy of 274
Interactive, Constructive, Active, and Passive
    (ICAP) framework 185, 255
interactive learning simulations 171
Interactive Strategy Training for Active Reading
    and Thinking (iSTART) 53–4, 490, 491, 495, 497
intercultural dimension, of AIED 245
interest 83, 90, 264, 317
    in capturing collaborative traces 433
    in digital games 440
    within educational research 355
    feature of 579
    fields of 392
    in leveraging reinforcement learning 146
    long-term interest development in STEM 613
    in professional learning 20
interface design 119, 120, 189, 229, 230, 232–4,
    240, 244, 245, 329
interfaces
    augmented reality 236–8
    BioWorld 233–4, 244
    control interface, metacognitive activities at
        120–21
    control interfaces, standard scrutiny and 121
    intelligent visual 241–3
    mixed-reality 236, 238–9
    Open Learner Model 113
    scrutiny *see* scrutiny interfaces
    teaching 230–32
    theory-driven *see* theory-driven interfaces
    virtual reality 236, 237
"intermediate correctness" 276

International Alliance to Advance Learning in
the Digital Era (IAALDE) 22
International Artificial Intelligence in Education
Society website 309
International Conference on Computers in
Education (ICCE) 22
*International Journal of Artificial Intelligence in
Education (IJAIED)* 49, 554, 559
International Journal of Man-Machine Studies 13
internet 635
interpretable/explanation-based semantic
similarity approaches 262–3
interpretable model 128–9
interpretable Semantic Textual Similarity task
(iSTS) 262, 263
interpretation process, of data
representations 328
intervene-on-failure model 532
interventions, predictive modeling 361–2
intractable student modelling 16
intrinsic affective regulation 88
intrinsic motivation 83–4, 199
intrinsic values of activities and outcomes 71
introspective *vs.* extrospective processes 78–9
IRT *see* Item Response Theory (IRT)
iSnap programming 288, 293
Isotani, S. 426
IAALDE *see* International Alliance to Advance
Learning in the Digital Era (IAALDE)
issue-based approach 152, 156
iStart 5
iSTART *see* Interactive Strategy Training for
Active Reading and Thinking (iSTART)
iStart-2, 200, 443
iSTART-2, 450
iSTART-ME 54
item response theory (IRT) 261, 445
ITS *see* intelligent tutoring systems (ITSs)
ITSPOKE 254

Jameson, A. 16
Jannach, D. 120
J48 decision tree algorithm 144
Jermann, P. 310
J-LATTE 496
Johnson, Lewis 474
JOLs *see* judgments-of-learning (JOLs)
Jones, M. 18
judgments 507
judgments-of-learning (JOLs) 60–61
justice 578

Kaendler, C. 312, 423
Karumbaiah, S. 356
Käser, T. 145
Kay, J. 5, 16, 18, 20, 21, 180

Keep Attention game 456
Kelly, K. 585
Khan Academy 154, 189
Khosravi, Hassan 7, 336
Kidaptive 527, 533
Kim, J. H. 392, 402–4
Kim, Y. 612
King, A. 196
Kinnebrew, J. S. 146
Kizilcec, R. F. 355, 361, 586, 587
Klopfer, E. 237
k-means clustering 426
knowledge 489, 506
of domain of instruction 127
of learning 563
subject-based assessment of 585
types of 37, 46
knowledge acquisition, natural language role in
251–2
knowledge assessment 179, 180
knowledge-based approaches, for student
modeling 173–4
knowledge-based tutors 18
Knowledge Checks 527
knowledge components (KCs) 260–61, 288, 289,
506, 518–19, 526
models 128, 131, 132
knowledge engineering approach 276
Knowledge-Learning-Instruction (KLI)
framework 185, 189
knowledge-poor approaches 264
knowledge representation, natural language role
in 251–2
knowledge-rich approaches 264–5
knowledge spaces 150–51
knowledge spaces theory 150
knowledge tracing 15
Knox, J. 8, 557
Koedinger, K. R. 8, 133, 150
Kollar, I. 311
Kovanović, Vitomir 7
KSAS 391, 405–8
psychomotor AIED systems, case study
409–12
K-12 schools 524
Kubrick, Stanley 253
Kuhn, Thomas 38
KUMITRON 109, 391, 396–9, 405–8, 417
psychomotor AIED systems, case study
412–14
Kummerfeld, Bob 5
Kurzweil, R. 585

LA dashboard *see* learning analytics (LA)
dashboard
Lajoie, Susanne P 6, 19, 175, 232, 244

Lallé, Sébastien 6
LAMS 197
Lane, H. C. 278
language 491
    BASIC programming language 12
    and culture 201, 460
    domain-specific modeling languages
        619–21
    Logo 13
language-based activities, formative assessment
    of 530–32
language learning 19
language skills 460, 497, 512, 609
Language Technologies 373
Lantern project 313
large-scale data collection 351
large-scale experimental replications 357
LARGO system 152
Latent AI readiness 548
Latent Dirichlet Allocation (LDA) 261, 380
Latent Semantic Analysis (LSA) 253, 493, 495
Laurillard, D. 19
LBITS system 277
"Lean" 539
LearnerFlow 332
    decision making and pedagogical action 335
    Filter panel 332, 333
    implications for practice 335–6
    initial evaluation 335
    insights 335
    modules 334
    sensemaking 334–5
learner/group sensing 642
learner metacognitive knowledge 54
learner modeling issues 629
learner modeling systems 506
LearnerNet 259
learner record store (LRS) 352
learners 17, 24n2
    assets and broaden adaptivity of PAs 613–14
    in authentic learning contexts 10
    communicate with 11
    comprehensible and opportunities for 23
    direct formative feedback to 426–7
    engaging in age of information overload
        608–11
    needs of 642
    sharing responsibility between instructors
        and 315
    to understand uncertainty 121
learnersourcing 153
learner states 490
learner–system interaction 54
learning
    in ACT-R theory 35
    collaborative *see* collaborative learning

    of complex cognitive skills 34–5
    from discourse 35–6
    from examples *see* learning from examples
    exploratory *see* exploratory learning
    game-based *see* game-based learning
    mechanisms of 34, 35
    positive emotions to 74
    from problem solving *see* learning from
        problem solving
    process of 58
    scrutability integrated into 120
    self-regulation of 317
    by teaching *see* learning by teaching
    of theories 34
    theories influence design of 230–32
learning analytics (LA) 200, 202, 322, 422, 464,
    498, 555
    Battleship Numberline 468
    Beanstalk 468–70
    Downtown: A Subway Adventure 469
    Heroes of Math Island 468
    Physics Playground 468
    Prime Climb 468
    Reasoning Mind 468
    Refraction 465–6
    ST Math 468
    TC3Sim 468
    use of 443
    Zombie Division 465–8
    Zoombinis 468–9
learning analytics and knowledge (LAK) 22
learning analytics (LA) dashboard 241, 245, 322,
    517–18
    applying theory and design practices 343–4
    effectiveness of 323
learning analytics (LA), for teachers 323,
    345–6
    applying theory and design practices 343–4
    descriptive and diagnostic learning analytics
        324–5
    fairness, accountability, transparency and
        ethics 345
    human-centred learning analytics 344–5
    illustrative studies *see* illustrative studies,
        learning analytics
    predictive learning analytics 325–6
    predictive modelling 343
    prescriptive learning analytics 326–7
    sensemaking and pedagogical actions 327–9
    specific/heterogeneous learning designs 342–3
    typology 323–4
learning analytics interfaces 330, 331, 335
Learning and Teaching Reimagined
    Initiative 560
learning assessment
    brain assessment parameters and tools 639

contribution of neurosciences 638–9
importance of emotions 637–8
traditional assessment 637
learning behaviours 572
learning bias 575–6
learning-by-teaching 53, 184, 202–5, 207, 208, 210
learning communities 251, 371, 375, 383
learning-culture bias 583, 584
learning curve analysis 465, 468
learning curves 508–9
learning data 101, 105, 107–9, 114, 117, 119, 127, 157, 258
learning ecosystem 259, 306, 309, 352
learning environment
    AI-empowered open-ended learning environments 618–24
    exploratory learning environments 193–5
    game-based digital learning environments 86–7
    OELEs *see* open-ended learning environments (OELEs)
    simulation-based learning environments 19
Learning Factors Analysis (LFA) 142, 287
learning from examples 184, 192–3
learning from problem solving 184, 188–92
learning gains 21, 35, 48, 57, 146, 197, 201, 204, 239, 254, 255, 293, 303, 431, 451, 458, 464, 509, 516, 518, 606, 630–32, 634
learning games
    digital *see* digital learning games
    Zoombinis 176
Learning Management Systems (LMS) 326, 350
    behavioral interactions within 352
learning outcomes 14, 35, 41, 60, 142, 150, 175, 260, 324, 325, 360, 361, 428, 450, 453–4, 456–8, 464, 467, 468
learning programming, computer gamified environments for 460
learning scenarios 71
learning sciences 70, 71, 74, 312
    conference 22
learning scientists 56, 230, 245, 373, 470, 474, 553
learning strategy 509
learning system reasoning, scrutability of 110, 112
learning systems
    elements within 108–9
    for scrutability and control, architecture of 105–6
learning technologies 86–7, 94
    to train teachers 93
learning theory 233, 345, 391
LearnSphere/Datashop project 259

Lee, B. 336
Lee, D. H. 392, 402–4
Lee, H. 361, 586, 587
Leemans, S. J. 337
legal bias 574
Lego blocks 609
Leonardo system 278
Lepper, M.R. 83, 84
Lesgold, A. 197
level behavioral traces, application 352–3
levels of assistance 186–7
    in instructional approaches 205–8
levels of instructional assistance 185
LFA *see* Learning Factors Analysis (LFA)
Li, S. 244
Li, Shan 6
Li, W. 360
Liao, T.T. 18
Lieberman, J. 392, 402, 403
LightSIDE 531
linguistic features e-rater extracts 494
LISP 136
LISP tutor 14
LiveLab 532–3
LMS *see* Learning Management Systems (LMS)
Lobo, J. L. 426
location-based AR app 237, 238
LOCO-Analyst 324
log data measures 510
Logistic Regression (LR) models 292
LOGO 2
Logo language 13
London, A. J. 574
Long, Y. 120, 201, 454
long short-term memory (LSTM) neural network 411
long-term goals, passion for 86
long-term individual learner model 108
long-term student model 137
loop 324
low-level observational data 107
low-prior-knowledge (LPK) learners 606
LP-ITS Tutor 495
LPK learners *see* low-prior-knowledge (LPK) learners
LSA *see* Latent Semantic Analysis (LSA)
LSTM 292
LSTM-based approach 262
Luckin, Rosemary 8
Lumilo 316, 324, 533

Ma, W. 606
Macfadyen, L. P. 350
Macgilchrist, F. 564

machine learning (ML) 141–2, 156, 290–92, 392, 494–6, 610
   advanced assessment based on recent advances in 260–61
   domain models creation using 147–8
machine-learning pipeline 574–5
machine-learning theories 260
Macmillan, S.A. 17
macro-adaptation 527
MACSYMA symbolic algebra system 12
MADE framework *see* Multimodal Affect for Design and Evaluation (MADE) framework
Mager, R. F. 395
Mager's educational objectives 415
   condition component of 401
   criterion of success component of 401–2
   performance component for 401
Magoulas, G. D. 195
Maharjan, Nabin 263
Makel, M. C. 357
malleable 510
Malmberg, J. 434
Malone, T. W. 441
management, orchestration 311
management-oriented tasks 316
Manathunga, K. 314, 316
mannequin-based simulators 239
Mao, Ye 6, 291, 293–5
Markov decision process (MDP) 146
martial arts 390, 409–12, 414, 417
Martin, J. D. 16
Martinez-Maldonado, R. 7, 241, 313
Marwan, S. 6, 290, 296, 297, 302
massive open online courses (MOOCs) 22, 105, 170, 171, 176, 177, 327, 350, 355, 370, 371, 375, 606, 607
   collaborative reflection in 376
   mentor support at Western Governors University 378–83
   social support impact in xMOOCs 375–6
   team-based MOOCs 376–8
mastery approach goals 85
mastery avoidance goals 85
mastery-based teaching system 109
mastery goals 85
mastery learning 190, 525–6
Math-Bridge system 617
MATHia 527, 532–4
Maths Garden 448
MathSpring 81, 154, 189, 200, 443, 446–7, 450, 457, 471
Matthew Effect 607
Mavrikis, M. 6, 195
Mayer, R. E. 230, 446
McArthur, D. 555

McCalla, G. I. 4, 17, 23
McLaren, B. M. 6, 7, 440
McNamara, Danielle S. 8
measurement bias 575
medical schools 37
Meier, A. 429
MEMOLAB system 20
memory
   LSTM neural network 411
   memory-augmented neural networks 55–6
memory-augmented neural networks 55–6
MENO-II system 12, 16
mental model 106, 112, 118, 250, 251, 256, 373, 377
mental processes 87, 422
mental workload 638
mentoring 640–41
mentors 374, 378–83, 641–3
Merten, C. 180, 278
meta-affect 68
meta-analysis 513
metacognition 46–7
   automatic detection of 55
   construct influenced area of AIED systems 47–9
   research applied to AIED systems 49
   review of existing AIED systems supporting 49–55
   role in future AIED systems 58–9
metacognition pedagogy 59–60
   applied to future AIED systems 55–7
metacognitive factors 179–80
metacognitive feelings 88
metacognitive knowledge 47, 49, 54
metacognitive processing-fostering AIED systems 57–8
metacognitive skills 50, 56, 57, 151, 170, 180, 584
meta-cognitive tools 313
meta-emotion 87–93
MetaHistoReasoning 175
meta-motivation theories 87–93
meta sequence-to-sequence learning 56
meta-skills 609
MetaTutor 5, 47, 49, 51–3, 171, 234–5, 244, 490, 495
Micarelli, Alessandro 3
Michalenko, J. J. 153
micro-adaptation 527
microphones 622
Mikolov, T. 261
Min Chi 6
Minerva 449, 450
Mirchi, N. 401, 402, 404
Mirrlees, T. 557

mirroring 186, 206, 208
mirroring tools 313
misconception 12, 14, 33, 41, 105, 106, 145, 494
    common decimal 201, 451
    potential 250, 253
    student 11, 33, 138, 141, 275, 300, 325
misleading data, design for 119
Mislevy, R. J. 173
Mission Game 460
Mission Rehearsal 254
Mitrovic, Antonija (Tanja) 2, 3, 6, 15, 136, 277
mixed approach 140
mixed-initiative conversational dialog 175
mixed-reality (MR) interfaces 236, 238–9
Mizoguchi, R. 18
ML-based domain models 147, 148, 157
M:1 mentoring 642
M:M mentoring 642
"model-based" AI research 23
modeled key SRL processes 51
modeling group interactions 422
models of inquiry processes 152
model tracing 14–15, 428
model-tracing algorithm 149
model-tracing tutors 18, 132–4, 154, 156, 276–7
moderators 510
MOOCs *see* massive open online courses
    (MOOCs)
moods *vs.* emotions 76
moral bias 574
moral dilemmas 434
more directive coaching 205, 206
more suggestive coaching 205, 206
motivation 68, 81–2
    AIED research 86–7
    attributional processes 84–5
    defined as 83
    early theories 83
    expectancy-value theory 83
    goals and growth mindset 85–6
    intrinsic and extrinsic motivation 83–4
    passion for long-term goals 86
    theories related to education 82–6
motivation regulation 90–91
motor skills 390, 391, 403, 414–17
MR interfaces *see* mixed-reality (MR) interfaces
MTDashboard system 313, 325
Muldner, Kasia 5
multi-agent formation algorithms 426
multichannel data integration 336
multi-criterion evaluation mechanism 296
Multimodal Affect for Design and Evaluation
    (MADE) framework 241, 243
multimodal analysis frameworks 622
multimodal analytics 208, 540, 623–4

multimodal data 491, 498
multimodal feedback 409
multimodality 238–9
multi-modal learning analytics 198
multinomial logistic regression 543
multi-stakeholder collaboration 545
multi-user virtual environments (MUVEs)
    239–41
multivariate time series data 293
Murray, T. 18
museum-/library-based learning scenarios 314
My Access! 494
My Backpack 201, 453, 455
MYCIN medical diagnosis expert system 17
My-Science-Tutor 254

Narayanan, A. 579
Narcissus 427
National Education Policy 2020 framework 562
National STEM Game Design Competition 440
NATO program 18
NATO-sponsored workshop, on "foreign
    language learning" 19
natural language-based knowledge
    representations 257
natural language interactions 250
    history of ITSs with 252–4
    theoretical foundations *see* theoretical
        foundations, natural language interactions
natural language processing (NLP) 40, 55, 201,
    235, 371, 457, 471, 491–4, 616, 618, 622
    advanced assessment based on recent
        advances in 260–61
    techniques 291
Navigo 200
Neagu, L. M. 392
near transfer tests 508
NEAT *see* Neuroevolution of Augmented
    Topologies (NEAT)
negative emotions 70, 73, 91, 441
negotiable 104
Nemorin, Selena 8
Neural Networks 392
NeurIPS Education Challenge 120
neurobiological brain processes 77
Neuroevolution of Augmented Topologies
    (NEAT) 400
neuroscience
    contribution in learning assessment 638–9
    of emotion in education 76–7
    research in 73
NeuroVR simulator 401
Nguyen, Huy A. 6, 7
Nguyen, Quan 7
Nichols, D.M. 20

NLP-based ITS systems 253, 254
noisy data, design for 119
non-learning academic data 353
non-null effect 516
non-player characters (NPCs) 199, 201, 202, 457–8, 460, 464
non-process-oriented metacognitive measures 48
norm 582
normalized gain score 508
Norman, D. A. 229
Norvig, P. 395
"not understanding" LM of 629, 630
NSF-funded Learner Data Institute 258, 259
nudges 641–2
NumberNet 314
Nwana, H.S. 18
Nye, B. D. 255

object focus of emotions 72–3
observational data 107
observation rubrics 510
OCC Theory of Emotion 71
Ocumpaugh, J. 356
OECD 561, 562
OELES *see* open-ended learning environments (OELES)
Ogan, A. 471, 606
Ohlsson, Stellan 5, 15, 19, 136, 233, 277
Ohlsson's Theory of Learning from Performance Errors 135
OLMs *see* Open Learner Models (OLMs)
OLM-supporting scrutiny, of learning data sources 110, 111
Olney, A. M. 6, 371
Olsen, J. K. 6, 7, 118, 316, 427, 432
OMNIBUS ontology 630
1:1 mentoring 641
1:M mentoring 641
one-on-one interactive instructional sessions 256
one-on-one learning 11
one-on-one tutoring 40
online learning technologies 370
  social analytics within history of 370–72
online support groups 374
online universities 372
ontological modeling issues 628
ontology engineering 630
open-ended domains 19, 156
open-ended learning environments (OELEs) 6, 53, 146, 170–73, 179–81, 618–19
  AI representations to support STEM learning 619–21
  analyzing students' learning behaviors 621–3
  data-driven approaches 176–9
  hybrid approaches 174–6

knowledge-based approaches for student modeling in 173–4
  self-regulated learning 623–4
Open Learner Models (OLMs) 106, 113, 116, 190, 208, 456–7, 580, 588
  interface 113
openness, predictive modeling 359
OpenSMILE 543
orchestration 310, 318
  definition of 309–11
Oriental iFly 549
O'Rourke, E. 465, 466
O'Shea, Tim 2, 12
outcome emotions 72
outcome fairness 579
outcome variable 510
overlay student model 616
overscripting 433

Papert, S. 13
Pardo, A. 363n1
Pardos, Z. A. 153, 529
Pareto, L. 463–4
Parong, J. 440
Partial Order Knowledge Structures (POKS) 151
participatory design 338, 344, 580, 588
Particle Swarm Optimization (PSO) 400
Path Analysis 622
pattern-based approaches 293
pattern coherence 622
pattern matcher 40
pattern matching 40
pattern support 622
Pavlik, P.I. 151
PCA *see* principal component analysis (PCA)
Peachey, D. 17, 23
pedagogical actions
  Course Insights 340, 342
  LearnerFlow 335
  teachers 327–9
  ZoomSense 331
pedagogical agents (PAs) 235–6, 278–9, 457
  animated 252
  critical influences of appearance and social interaction 612–13
  designing virtual characters for inclusion and diversity in STEM 611–14
  entry points to STEM and support for interest development 613
  identify learner assets and broaden adaptivity of 613–14
  roadmap for leveraging pedagogical agents for STEM inclusion 613
  support for social and emotional learning 613
pedagogical model 127, 131, 138, 146, 460

pedagogical strategies 17–18
pedagogy 184
    emotional thought 78
    expectancy-value theory 83
    goals and growth mindset 86
    implications for 74
    introspective *vs.* extrospective processes 79
    meta-emotion and meta-motivation theories 89
    students regulate emotions and motivation 91
Peddycord-Liu, Z. 468
peer-tutoring systems 203
Pekrun, Reinhard 71, 73, 232
Pelánek, R. 128
Pelletier, R. 18
perceived control 72
performance approach goals 85
performance avoidance goals 85
performance data 490–91
performance goals 85
Perie, M. 362
Perrotta, C. 563
personalized learning experience 562
personalization 524–5
    of activities and curricular content 527–8
    of content 528
    of student progression within curriculum
        525–7
personalized learning 562, 563
Personis-based systems, user-control perspective
    of 104
Personis model 114
persuasive technology 611
pervasive AI learning technologies 624–7
Petrushin, V.A. 16
PFL *see* Preparation for Future Learning (PFL)
"phantom village" errors 635
PhET simulations 194
Phiri, L. 314
Physical User Modelling (PhyUM) 109
Physics Playground (PP) 201, 202, 453, 455, 468,
    489, 497
physiological data 468, 624
physiological measures 509
Piaget, Jean 38
PIGEON algorithm 400, 402
Pinkwart, N. 152, 245, 556
PISA *see* Programme for International Student
    Assessment (PISA)
Pistilli, M. D. 350
PIXIE environment 18
planning, orchestration 311
Plants *vs.* Zombies 2, 497
PLATO 11
playing 12, 170, 199, 390, 440, 441, 458, 461–4,
    468–9, 472–3

Plucker, J. A. 357
PMER *see* Process Model of Emotion Regulation
    (PMER)
Poitras, E. G. 175
POKS *see* Partial Order Knowledge Structures
    (POKS)
policy-influencing organizations 561–2
Policy World 200, 446–8, 450
political economy 556–8
Porayska-Pomsta, K. 5, 8
positive emotions 73, 231–2
    to learning 74
positive feedback 137, 191
post-problem reflection 191
post-test score 508
posture 244, 432, 434, 491, 495, 509
potential misconception 250, 253
Pozdniakov, Stanislav 7
practice
    of AIED 157
    vs. theory 31–2
practice-oriented study of orchestration 312
pragmatic scrutability 118
prediction accuracy 351
predictive learning analytics 323, 325–6
predictive modelling
    adoption 361–2
    common data sources 351–3
    critical issues 356–62
    developments in 353–6
    in education matured 350
    evaluation of models 355
    population choices 355–6
    and teacher-facing analytics 343
    technical reporting 354–5
predictive value 579
preferences *vs.* emotions 76
Preparation for Future Learning (PFL) 509
pre-processing and labelling software 577
Prerequisite BNs 140
prescriptive learning analytics 323, 326–7
    in Course Insights 336–42
Pressey, S.L. 10, 11
pre-test score 508
Price, M. J. 91
Price, Thomas 6
Prieto, L. P. 311, 312
Prime Climb 200, 202, 448–50, 468, 492
principal component analysis (PCA) 146, 542
privacy 105, 107, 115, 243, 245, 258, 259, 363n1,
    528, 565, 600, 626
problem solving 208–10
problem-solving domains 13
problem-solving tutors 189, 279
procedural knowledge 46, 59, 151, 233

process data 186
processed data 107–8
process fairness 579
process model 232
Process Model of Emotion Regulation
   (PMER) 88
Process Tab 326
production rules 12–14, 46, 47, 51, 56, 132, 135,
   137, 145
professional community 250
professional learning models 640
Programme for International Student Assessment
   (PISA) 252
"programmer's apprentice" 12
programming
   iSnap 293
   Python 287
   skill discovery *see* skill discovery, for
      programming
programming-by-demonstration method 276
progress feedback 290
Project LISTEN 531
propensity score matching 514–15
prospective outcomes 72
protégé effect 203, 511
PROUST system 15–16
PSO *see* Particle Swarm Optimization (PSO)
psychological theories 32–3, 41
   historical theories 33–4
   learning complex cognitive skills 34–5
   learning from discourse 35–6
psychomotor AIED systems
   affective issues 416
   analysis of 395–403
   analysis of information flow in 403–9
   case studies to create 409–14
   categories of Simpson's psychomotor
      taxonomy 402–3
   condition component 401
   considerations for further research 415
   criterion of success component 401–2
   design of the feedback 404
   embodied cognition 415–16
   filtering process 392, 394
   first systematic review 391
   gamification techniques 417
   guidelines for standardization 415
   inclusion and exclusion criteria 394–5
   KSAS study 409–12
   KUMITRON system 412–14
   model the movement 404
   online psychomotor learning and learning at
      home 416
   performance component 401
   psychomotor intelligent systems 392, 393

psychomotor learning in open space 417
psychomotor learning in pairs 417
second systematic review 392
sense the movements 404
SR-2018 391–4
SR-2019 392–4
SR-2021 392–5
psychomotor intelligent systems 392, 393
psychomotor learning 390
   nature of field 391
   online and at home 416
   in open space 417
   in pairs 416–17
   research on 391
psychomotor skills 390
PubMed 392
Pyrenees probability tutoring system 293
Python programming 147, 150, 287

QA *see* Quest Atlantis (QA)
Q-matrix learning 287
qualitative
   assessments 318
   cognitive task analysis 157
   dimensions of AIED 581
   interactions 632, 633
   interpretations in context 75
   reasoning mechanism 620
qualitative models 151, 152
quantitative
   dimensions of AIED 581
   feedback 485
Quantitative Ethnography (QE) 433
Quest Atlantis (QA) 240
question-answering system 39
questionnaire measures 509–10

R 147
Rafferty, A. N. 147
Rajeswaran, P. 401, 402, 416
Ramachandran, S. 279
Ramineni, Chaitanya (2018) 530
RAND Corporation 555
Randomized Controlled Trials (RCTs)
   515–16
RapidMiner 147
raw data 107, 112–14, 117–19, 121
ReadingMirror 618, 619
Reading Tutor 531
RealSkill 549
real-time management 309, 310
reasoning
   conceptual 250
   scrutability of learning system 110, 112, 113
Reasoning Mind 468

receiver operating characteristic (ROC) curve 362
Recent Temporal Pattern Mining (RTP) 293, 294
reciprocal learning system 20
recognition 578
Recurrent Neural Network (RNN) 292
Recursive Neural Network (RNN) 261
Refraction 465–6, 471
refutational text 38
Regian, J.W. 18
regression discontinuity design 514, 515
regulation 68
    modeling of 93
regulative loops 186, 188
Reigeluth, C. M. 38
reinforcement learning 146–7
reinforcement learning algorithms 633
relevance condition, constraints 136
reliability 506, 507
"repair theory" 13
replication, predictive modeling 356–7
representational bias 575
reproduction, predictive modeling 356–7
Research Accelerator 551
researcher-led collaborations 357
research methods
    for emotions 94
    for motivation 94
response modulation strategies 88
responsibility, sharing between instructors and
    learners 315
RETE algorithm 40
retention tests 509
retrospective outcomes 72
Revision Assistant 531, 534
Rich, C. 12
Rickel, J. W. 18
Riggs, Meredith 7
Ritter, F. 35
Ritter, S. 6, 8, 279
Rivers, K. 150
RNN-based models 292
roadmap 612
    for leveraging pedagogical agents for STEM
        inclusion 613
Robins, Anthony 2
RoboTutor 634–7
roles
    metacognition in future, AIED systems 58–9
    of natural language in knowledge acquisition
        and representation 251–2
role sharing 314
role splitting 314
Roll, I. 50
Roscoe, Rod D. 8
Rosé, Carolyn 7, 431
Rowe, E. 458, 469

Rowe, Jonathan 6
RTP *see* Recent Temporal Pattern Mining (RTP)
Ruiz, S. 92
rule-based cognitive modeling 189
rule-based computational model 20
rule-based domain models 132–4
Rummel, N. 6, 197, 424
Rus, V. 6, 254, 255, 260, 262, 263, 371
Russell, S. J. 395, 585

SAFARI environment 18
SAIL Smart Space (S3) 316, 317
SAL *see* Sensitive Artificial Listener (SAL)
Saleh, A. 239, 240
Sankey Diagram 335
Santos, O. C. 7, 391, 416
satisfaction condition, constraints 136
Savard, I. 627
Sawyer, R. 458
scaffolding, types of 54–5, 60
scale
    large-scale data collection 351
    large-scale experimental replications 357
    small-scale commercialization 546–8
SCENT programming advisor 21
Schank, R. C. 20, 22, 554
Schmidt, Eric 560
Schmidt Futures 560
Schnaubert, L. 429
SCHOLAR system 11, 12, 253
school-based subject-domain teaching 572
Schroder, M. 236
Schroeder, N. L. 235, 612
Schwartz, D. L. 145, 509
science-based collaborative inquiry learning 56
ScienceDirect 392
Science Projects Integrating Computing and
    Engineering (SPICE) 619–21
scientific theories 37
Scopus 392
Scratch 460
scripts 427
    adaptable 428
    adaptive 428
scrutability 101, 102
    architecture of learning systems for 105–6
    of data-driven models 180
    of data elements 119
    discussion and research agenda 118–21
    distinctive nature in AIED 117–18
    driving simplicity 120
    in FATE landscape 102–4
    integrated into learning 120
    user-centred definition of 112–17
scrutability design mindset 119
scrutable 21, 101, 103, 113, 118, 180

scrutable systems 101, 103
  as partners 120
scrutable teaching system 116
scrutiny interfaces 110
  of learning system reasoning 110, 112, 113
  metacognitive activities at 120–21
  OLM-supporting scrutiny, of learning data
    sources 110, 111
SEL *see* social and emotional learning (SEL)
Self, J. A. 13, 16, 18, 20, 23, 445
Self-Assessment Tutor 50
self-consequating 90
self/co-regulation 186, 202
self-determination theory 199
self-directed exploration 170
self-directed learning 170
self-efficacy 506, 509
Self-Explanation Reading Training (SERT) 54
self-explanations approach 251
"Self-improving Quadratic Tutor" 2
self-regulated learning (SRL) 46, 48, 51, 60, 315,
  623–4
  component of 51–2
  phases of 46–7
  virtual environments support 234–5
self-regulation 171, 186, 231
  of learning 317
self-regulatory skills 59, 187
self-report 48, 51, 52, 80–81
Sellar, S. 562
Selwyn, N. 563
semantic analysis 493
semantic evaluation approaches 253
semantic model degeneracy 148
Semantic Web technologies 616
SemEval 263
semi-automatic approaches 265
semi-supervised learning 7, 142, 149, 288, 292,
  294, 295, 302, 303
semi-supervised modeling, for limited data size
  294–5
sensemaking
  Course Insights 338
  LearnerFlow 334–5
  teachers 327–9
  ZoomSense 330
Sensing-Modeling-Designing-Delivering
  (SMDD) framework 391, 403, 409
  architecture of KSAS system 410, 411
  architecture of KUMITRON system 412, 413
Sensitive Artificial Listener (SAL) 236, 244
sensors 636
separation, fairness 586
sequencing 38
SERT *see* Self-Explanation Reading
  Training (SERT)

7 Step EThICAL AI Readiness 547–8
Shabaninejad, S. 337
Shabrina, Preya 6
shareability 583
SHARE-IT project 582
Sharples, M. 21, 311
Sherlock system 17, 21
Shi, Y. 6, 145, 291, 294, 295
Shire, K. A. 402
Shirzad, N. 402
Shneiderman, Ben 344
short-term student model 137
short textual semantic similarity (STS) approach 262
Shute, V. J. 18, 19, 453, 468
Si, M. 279
Siemens, G. 363n1
Sime, J.-A. 16
similarity-based approaches 587
similarity-based fairness 587
Simon, H. A. 34, 37
Simpson, E. J. 395
Simpson's psychomotor taxonomy 395, 400, 414
SimStudent 5, 54–5, 204
  teachable agent 145
simulated students 145
simulation-based learning environments 19
simulations
  Circuit Construction Kit 171, 172, 178
  computer 232
  interactive learning 171
  PhET 194
  simulation-based learning 19
  Teleos 174
Singh, Shaveen 7
singular value decomposition (SVD) 493
Sinitsa, K.M. 16
SIS *see* student information system (SIS)
situated learning 230
  in authentic contexts, computer simulations
    for 232
Situated Multimedia Arts Learning Lab
  (SMALLab) 238
Situated Pedagogical Authoring System
  (SitPed) 278
situational feedback 204, 205, 208, 210
situation modification strategies 88–90
situation outcome 71
situation-related emotion regulation strategies 89
situation selection strategies 88, 90
Sjödén, B. 463
"skill acquisition" 14
Skill Builder 460
skill discovery, for programming 287–8
  data-driven features 289–90
  feature-based methods 288, 289
  machine-learning methods 290–92

skills 489, 609
    domain knowledge and 497
    organizing mechanic of 79
Skinner, A. 392
Skinner, B. F. 10, 11, 83
SKIVE 258
Sleeman, D.H. 12, 13, 17, 18
SlideTutor system 151
SMALLab *see* Situated Multimedia Arts
    Learning Lab (SMALLab)
small-scale commercialization 546–8
SMARTIES authoring system 630
SMDD framework *see* Sensing-Modeling-
    Designing-Delivering (SMDD) framework
SMISLE project 19
Smithtown 195
    inquiry environment 19
social agency theory 235
social analytics
    in AI education field 370
    challenges 373
    defined as 372
    within history of online instruction 370–72
    successes 373–4
    technical foundations 372–4
social and emotional learning (SEL) 89
    support for 613
social brain 79–80
social emotions 73
social implications 362
social support 371
    effect on outcomes 381–3
    impact in xMOOCs 375–6
    mentor support at WGU 378–83
    in online communities 383
    theoretical foundations 374–5
Society for Learning Analytics 354
socio-constructivist approach 251
socio-cultural bias 573
socio-technical level 580
socio-technological ecosystem 585
Socratic tutoring strategies 12
software agents 279
Soller, A. 186, 313, 431
Soloway, E. M. 12
Solution BNs 140
SOPHIE electronic troubleshooting
    environment 12
Sosnovsky, S. 151
Spain, R. D. 488
speech recognition technology 512
speech-/text-based discourse 432
SPICE *see* Science Projects Integrating
    Computing and Engineering (SPICE)
spoken language instruction 531–2

sports 400, 401, 625
SPRING 178, 179
Springer 392
SQL-Guide 151
SQL Select statement 136
SQL-Tutor 135, 136, 151, 449–50, 496
Squares Family 461, 463–4, 471, 474
Squiral assignment 289, 290
Squiral problem 288, 289
Squire, K. 237
Squirrel AI 550
SR-2018 391–3
    filtering process 392, 394
    inclusion and exclusion criteria 394–5
    outcomes of 395
SR-2019 392, 393
    filtering process 392, 394
    inclusion and exclusion criteria 394–5
    outcomes of 395
SR-2021 392, 393, 395
    filtering process 392, 394
    inclusion and exclusion criteria 394–5
    outcomes of 395
SRL *see* self-regulated learning (SRL)
stakeholders 56, 107, 122, 258, 275, 315, 318,
    322, 326, 344, 361, 430, 553, 559, 565, 581,
    583, 590
Stamper, J. 146
standard intelligent tutoring system
    architecture 14
standardization
    favor 525
    guidelines for 415
standardized tests (SAT) 351–2, 363n3
standard scrutiny 121
state-based data 352
statistical bias 574
statistical fairness 559, 586
stealth assessment 454, 496, 528–9, 534
STEAMER system 16–17, 19, 21
Stein, G. 402
STEM
    asset-based approaches 614
    equity and diversity to 612
    long-term interest development in 613
    roadmap for leveraging pedagogical agents for
        inclusion 613
STEM domains 14
    AI-empowered open-ended learning
        environments in 618–24
Stephens, Elizabeth J. 73
step-loop adaptivity 190–91, 209, 210
stereotyping 578
Stevens, A.L. 12
ST Math 468

strategies 490
  attentional deployment 88
  cognitive 52
  cognitive appraisal 88
  Guess and check 622
  immediate feedback 290
  "immediate feedback" 15
  learning 509
  pedagogical 17–18
  response modulation 88
  situation modification 88–90
  situation-related emotion regulation 89
  situation selection 88, 90
  Socratic tutoring 12
  tutoring 35
stratified assignment 512
structural equation modeling (SEM) 382, 468
Structural Topic Model package (STM) 380
Structured Query Language (SQL) 135
student information system (SIS) 351–2
student-mentor relationships, during pandemic
    379–80
student misconception 11, 33, 138, 141, 275,
    300, 325
student model 128
  constraint-based tutors 137
student modelling 15–16, 20, 287, 506
  effective modeling to predict student success
    292–5
  knowledge-based approaches for 173–4
  skill discovery, for programming 288–92
students
  assessing knowledge 129
  assessing work 129
  formative feedback to 131
  in high-rapport dyads 203
  natural language interactions 250
  recognizing errors 131
student success outcomes 351
STyLE-OLM system 151
subjective control 71
subjective task value 83
subjective value 71
sufficiency, fairness 586–7
suggestive coaching approaches 207
summative assessment, collaborative learning 431–2
summative evaluation 513–15
summative feedback 488
Sun, K. 363n1
supervised learning 142–5
Suppes, P. 11
support collaborative learning 239–41
Support Vector Machine (SVM) 294, 295
Support Vector Machine (SVM) algorithm
    400, 401

Suresh, H. 558, 575, 588
Sutherland, R. 19
SVD *see* singular value decomposition (SVD)
S/vL framework 186, 187, 189, 193, 198–200,
    202, 207, 208
Swiecki, Zachari 7
syntactic analysis 492–3

Tactical Language and Cultural Training System
    (TLCTS) 201, 237, 456–7, 460–61, 469, 470, 473
Tactical Language Training System 278, 279
TALENT game 454–6
task
  detection 51
  discrimination 51
  interpretable Semantic Textual Similarity task
    262, 263
  management-oriented 316
task domain 128, 132, 133, 138, 142, 152, 170,
    173, 176, 187, 189, 203
task-loop adaptivity 191, 210
task-related interactions 429
Tasso, C. 19
Taub, M. 53, 511
Tchounikine, P. 311, 427
TC3Sim 468
teacher and developer aids 506
TeacherASSIST 632, 633
Teacher Assistance tools 196
teacher awareness tools, collaborative learning
    429–30
teacher-facing dashboards 344
teacher-facing learning analytics 322, 323
  predictive modelling and 343
  to specific/heterogeneous learning designs
    342–3
teachers
  accountability, learning analytics for 345
  awareness tools 192, 208, 424, 425, 429–30
  collaborative learning 429–30
  decision-making process 327–8
  fairness, learning analytics for 345
  learning analytics *see* learning analytics (LA),
    for teachers
  pedagogical actions 327–9
  sensemaking 327–9
  transparency, learning analytics for 345
teacher support 532–3
teacher tools 208
teaching, learning by *see* learning by teaching
teaching assistants 560, 626
teaching interfaces, theories influence design of
    230–32
"teaching machines" 10
team-based learning 377

team-based MOOCs 376–8
technical reporting 354–5
technium concept 585
technologies 642
    AI-based educational technology 170
    AI-based learning technologies 606
    AI-powered technologies 609
    conventional technology-supported learning
        systems 628
    Edtech products and services 538–9
    gamified AIED learning technology 443
    Google Glass technology 92
    Language Technologies 373
    learning technologies 86–7, 94
    linguistic and cultural accessibility of 581
    online learning technologies 370–72
    persuasive technology 611
    pervasive AI learning technologies 624–7
    Semantic Web technologies 616
    speech recognition technology 512
technology-based educational systems, lifecycle
    of 403–4
technology-enhanced learning 185
telecommunication companies 606
Teleos simulation 174
template-based behaviors 70
temporal information 294, 304
temporal modeling 292–4
temporal patterns 293
temporal sequence 33
TERC 473–4
test-driven development (TDD) 115
tetralogues 252
textbook
    adaptive textbooks 615, 616
    conversational ITSs, automating tutorial
        dialogue generation from 263
    domain modeling paradigms for intelligent
        textbooks 148–9
    intelligent *see* intelligent textbooks
text mining techniques 153
theoretical foundations, natural language
    interactions
    animated pedagogical agents 252
    deep, conceptual knowledge 250–51
    pedagogical approaches to acquiring deep
        knowledge 251
    role in knowledge representation and
        acquisition 251–2
theoretical knowledge 37
theories of deliberate practice 189
theories of limited scope 36
theories of scaffolding 189
theory
    instructional design 36–9
    vs. practice 31–2

predictive modeling 361–2
    psychological 32–6
theory-based dual eye-tracking innovations 434
theory-driven design 5, 229
    interfaces 232–43
    interfaces for education 243–5
    of learning and teaching interfaces 230–32
theory-driven interfaces 232
    augmented reality interfaces 237–8
    computer simulations for situating learning in
        authentic contexts 232
    immersive virtual environments 236–7
    intelligent tutoring systems 233–4
    intelligent visual interfaces 241–3
    mixed-reality interfaces 238–9
    MUVEs support collaborative learning
        239–41
    pedagogical agents and AI dialogue systems
        235–6
    virtual environments support self-regulated
        learning 234–5
    virtual reality interfaces 237
theory of flow 199
*The Third International Conference on Artificial
    Intelligence and Education* 42n2
three-dimensional taxonomy of emotions 72
    activation of emotions 73–4
    object focus of emotions 72–3
    valence of emotions 73
TICCIT 11
Time-aware LSTM (T-LSTM) 293, 294
timing 47, 50, 58, 60, 256, 266, 310, 316,
    531, 583
TLCTS *see* Tactical Language and Cultural
    Training System (TLCTS)
toggling 79
The Tools for Rapid Automated Development of
    Expert Models (TRADEM) 278
topic emotions 73
TORMES 416
trace data 49, 50, 55, 59–61, 336, 350, 352,
    353, 360
tracking 5, 12, 16, 58, 92, 107, 634
TRADEM *see* The Tools for Rapid Automated
    Development of Expert Models (TRADEM)
traditional apprenticeships 230, 231
traditional teacher-led instruction 525
traditional textbooks 614
traditional xMOOCs 375
traffic light approach 148
training
    iSTART 53–4, 490, 491, 495, 497
    SERT 54
    TLCTS 201, 456–7, 460–61, 469, 473
Trait Emotional Intelligence Questionnaire
    (TEIQue) 541

traits 86, 170, 318, 351, 486, 493, 543, 630–32
    personality 58, 178, 485, 507, 540, 542, 637
transactive conversational behaviors 377
transactivity 377, 431
transfer test score 508
transparency 102–4, 148, 588
    learning analytics, for teachers 345
    predictive modeling 359
Treviranus, J. 582
trialogue 252
trustworthiness 571
Tsai, Y.-S. 363n1
TugLet game 145, 152
TurnItIn's Revision Assistant 531
"turtle" 13
TurtleTalk 460–62
tutored problem solving 189–91, 195, 196, 206, 207
tutorial dialogues 252
tutoring, research on 35
tutoring strategies 35
tutors 189
    ACT-R 233
    AI-based Tutors 527
    algebra 14
    CAPIT 139
    CIRCSIM-Tutor 18, 253
    cognitive 15, 50, 106, 132, 140, 488–90, 492, 496, 513
    conversational 261
    DeepTutor 254, 262
    dialog-based 279–80
    EER-Tutor 135, 496
    example-tracing 149, 150, 154, 189
    explanation-based 19
    Gamified SQL Tutor 443, 449, 450
    geometry 14
    GuruTutor 254
    help-seeking 5, 50
    knowledge-based 18
    LISP 14
    LP-ITS Tutor 495
    MetaTutor 5, 47, 49, 51–3, 171, 234–5, 244, 490, 495
    model-tracing 18, 132–4, 154, 156, 276–7
    My-Science-Tutor 254
    problem-solving 189, 279
    Reading Tutor 531
    RoboTutor 634–7
    Self-Assessment Tutor 50
    SQL-Tutor 135, 136, 151, 449–50, 496
    Updated Help Tutor 50
    Why-AutoTutor 254
    Why2/AutoTutor 489
tutor–student interaction 255
2001: A Space Odyssey (film) 253

two-loop framework 254
    effectiveness improvement 255–6
    effectiveness of conversational ITSs in improving learning 254–5
    length and density of interactive, intense learning sessions 256–7
2-sigma effect 21, 572, 583
two-tailed *t*-test 516

ubiquitous-AIED 624
    assumptions of 624–5
    design and policy implications for 626–7
    opportunities 625–6
UK EdTech ecosystem 550, 551
um-toolkit 18
uncertain data, design for 119
under-representation 578
under-resourced classrooms 606
United Nations Sustainable Development Goal 606
Unity-CT 173, 178
UNIZIN 357
unLOCKE project 581
unstructured activities 170
unsupervised learning 145–6
Updated Help Tutor 50
user classification 109
user modeling 235
user modelling, adaptation and personalization (UMAP) research area 23
users' comments 518
user studies 116
Use Your Brainz 497
US Next-Generation Science Standards 529

valence of emotions 73
valence of focus 72
validity 506
valuable scrutability 118
Van der Loos, H. F. M. 402
van Leeuwen, A. 7, 325
VanLehn, K. 8, 13, 16, 20, 31, 139, 186–9, 254, 255, 274, 276
Vantage Learning 494
Vassileva, J. 3, 17–18
ventromedial prefrontal cortex (vmPF) 77
Verbert, K. 427
Verdejo, M.F. 20
Villano, M. 16
virtual environments
    immersive 236–7
    support self-regulated learning 234–5
virtual human 56, 59
virtual reality (VR) 401
virtual reality (VR) interfaces 236, 237
visibility 486, 487, 496–7

visualization 92
visualization mantra 344
visual metaphors 335
Vivet, M. 18, 19
voice-based emotion features 543
Völkel, S. T. 245
VR interfaces *see* virtual reality (VR) interfaces
Vygotsky, L. S. 251, 425, 637

Walker, E. 197
Wang, L. 291, 292
Washington, P. 92
Wayang Outpost 446, 489, 492
Webb, P. T. 562
Web-Enabled Tutoring Authoring System
    (WETAS) 277, 278
Weber, G. 16
Web of Science 392
Wegner, Etienne 3
Wei, W. 402, 416
Weiner, Bernard 84
WEIRD populations 355
Weka 147
well-defined domains 3
Wenger, E. 18, 129
Western, educated, industrialized, rich and
    democratic (WEIRD) countries 606, 633–7
Western Governors University (WGU) 372
    COVID stress impact on patterns of
        participation 380–81
    mentor support at 378–9
    social support effect on outcomes 381–3
    student-mentor relationships during pandemic
        379–80
WEST system 12
Whack-A-Gopher 451
wheel-spinning 507
White, B.Y. 16
Why2 254
Why-Atlas 254
Why2-Atlas 513
Why-AutoTutor 254

Why2/AutoTutor 489
WHY system 12
Wiedbusch, Megan 5, 21
WiFi 635
Wigfield, A. 83
Wikipedia 153
Williamson, David (2018) 530
Williamson, B. 3, 8, 19, 600
Winkels, R. 18
Winne, P. H. 18, 46, 51
within-subjects design 512
Wolters, C. 90
Woolf, Bev 3
word2vec representation 261
Writing-Pal 254, 488
Wu, X. 575
Wu, Y. 426
Wylie, R. 256

XAI *see* Explainable AI (XAI)
XGBoost 294, 295
xMOOCs *see* eXtended MOOCs (xMOOCs)

Yacef, Kalina 3–4
Yamagiwa, S. 391
Yannier, N. 472
Yu, R. 361

Zhang, X. 575
Zheng, G. 529
Zhi, R. 289
Zhou, X. 468
Zombie Division 465–8, 470
zone of proximal development 463
Zoombinis 176, 181, 468–70, 473
ZoomSense 343
    decision making and pedagogical action 331
    implications for practice 331
    insights 331
    sensemaking 330
Zuckerberg, Mark 560